JUDICIAL REVIEW

COMPARATIVE CONSTITUTIONAL LAW ESSAYS, LECTURES AND COURSES (1985–2011)

Allan R. BREWER–CARÍAS

Professor of Law, Central University of Venezuela
Fellow, Trinity College, and Simón Bolívar Professor, University of Cambridge, UK (1985–1986).
Professeur Associé, Université de Paris II (1989–1990)
Adjunct Professor of Law, Columbia University, New York, (2006–2008).
Vice President, International Academy of Comparative Law (1982–2010).

JUDICIAL REVIEW

COMPARATIVE CONSTITUTIONAL LAW ESSAYS, LECTURES AND COURSES (1985–2011)

Fundación de Derecho Público
Editorial Jurídica Venezolana

Caracas

2 0 1 4

Hecho el Depósito de Ley
Depósito Legal: lf54020133402765
ISBN: 978-980-365-212-8

Edited by: Editorial Jurídica Venezolana
Avda. Francisco Solano López, Torre Oasis, P.B., Local 4, Sabana Grande,
Apartado 17.598 - Caracas, 1015, Venezuela
Teléfono 762-25-53 / 762-38-42/ Fax. 763-52-39
Email: fejv@cantv.net
http://www.editorialjuridicavenezolana.com.ve

Printed by: Lightning Source, an INGRAM Content company
Distributed by: Editorial Jurídica Venezolana International Inc.
Panamá, República de Panamá.
Email: editorialjuridicainternational@gmail.com

Formatting, Composition and Editing by: Francis Gil,
Letter: Times New Roman, 10.5. Line Spacing: 11.
Dimension text: 19 x 12.5. Dimension book: 22.9 x 15.2

CONTENT

II

THE JUDICIAL ACTION FOR "AMPARO" OR PROTECTION OF FUNDAMENTAL RIGHTS IN LATIN AMERICA (2006–2007)

III

CONSTITUTIONAL COURTS AS POSITIVE LEGISLATORS IN COMPARATIVE LAW (2010)

V

JUDICIAL REVIEW AND AMPARO PROCEEDING IN VENEZUELA (2006- 2011)

VI

THE QUESTION OF LEGITIMACY: HOW TO CHOOSE THE JUDGES OF THE SUPREME COURTS (2005)

AUTHOR'S NOTE

Judicial Review, as the power of judges to control the constitutionality of State acts, particularly of Legislation, not only is the most important subject of contemporary constitutional law, but also the most distinctive feature of all democratic constitutional systems.

That is why, all over the world, in all democratic States, independently of being subjected to a legal system based on the common law or on the civil law principles, the courts –special constitutional courts, supreme courts or ordinary courts– have the power to decide and declare the unconstitutionality of legislation when a particular statute violates the text of the Constitution or of its constitutional principles.

This power of the courts is the consequence of the consolidation in contemporary constitutionalism of three fundamental principles of law: first, the existence of a written constitution or of a fundamental law, conceived as a superior law with clear supremacy over all other statutes; second, the "rigid" character of such constitution or fundamental law, which implies that the amendments or reforms that may be introduced can only be put into practice by means of a particular and special constituent or legislative process, preventing the ordinary legislator from doing so; and third, the establishment in that same written and rigid constitution or fundamental law, of the judicial means for guaranteeing its supremacy, over all other state acts, including legislative acts.

Accordingly, in democratic systems subjected to such principles, the courts have the power to refuse to enforce a statute it consider to be contrary to the Constitution, considering it null or void, through what is known as the diffuse system of judicial review; and in many cases, they even have the power to declare the annulment of the said unconstitutional law, through what is known as the concentrated system of judicial review.

This latter system, that is the concentrated system of judicial review has been adopted in constitutional systems in which the judicial power of judicial review has been assigned to only one supreme court or to one special constitutional courts, as is the case, for example, of many countries in Europe and in Latin America.

The diffuse system of judicial review, on the other hand, is the system created more that two hundred years ago by the Supreme Court of the United States, and that so deeply characterizes the North American Constitutional system.

In contrast, the concentrated system of judicial review, although established in many Latin American countries since the 19th century, it was only effectively developed in the world particularly after World War II.

In Democratic States, in addition, the courts have the specific power to protect and guaranty the constitutional and fundamental rights of citizens, independently of it being declared in the text of the Constitutions or in International Treaties on Human Rights that in many countries even have constitutional rank and value. The fact is that in all countries, some sort of specific judicial review means of protection have been developed in order to immediately guarantee constitutional rights, being them specific injunctions, or special actions like the well known amparo action established in almost all Latin American countries as well as in Spain or Germany. These injunctions or protection actions are also part of the judicial review system of many countries.

This book precisely deals with this subject of Judicial Review, considered from a constitutional comparative law perspective, a matter that I have been studying for the past decades, and on which I have extensively published in books and articles, basically in Spanish.

In addition, I have also written many works in English (which, I must say, is not my first language), in particular for the preparation of Courses and Lectures that I have been asked to give or to deliver, many of which have not been published. Among them are the following texts now included in this book: first, the original version of the Course of Lectures I gave on "Judicial Review in Comparative Law," in the LL.M. Course at the Faculty of Law, University of Cambridge, UK., in 1985–1986; second, also the original version of the Lectures I gave on "Judicial Protection of Human Rights in Latin America. A Comparative Constitutional Law Study on the Latin American Injunction for the protection of Constitutional Rights ("Amparo proceeding")," in a Seminar at Columbia Law School in the City of New York during the academic Semesters of 2007–2008; third, the original text of the General Report I wrote on "Constitutional Courts as Positive legislators," for the XVIII International Congress of Comparative Law, Washington 2010; fourth, the original texts written in 2008 for the preparation of Lectures delivered in Fordham University School of Law, on "Judicial Review in Latin America," and on "Judicial Review and Amparo proceeding for the protection of human rights in Latin America and Philippines," that was due to be delivered in Manila, Philippines also in 2008, in an event organized by the Supreme Court of the Philippines; fifth, the texts of the Papers written for the Seminars on "Judicial Review in the Americas ... and Beyond" and on "Constitutional Litigations: Procedural Protections of Constitutional Guarantees in the Americas...and Beyond," organized by Professor Robert S. Barker, Duquesne University School of Law in Pittsburgh, November 2006, and November 2010; and sixth, the text of the presentation on "A question of Legitimacy: How to choose the Judges of Supreme Courts," that I made in a Round Table organized by the International Association of Constitutional Law at the University of Berlin in November 2005

Reviewing now all these materials, it was impossible for me not to remember the exact moment and circumstances of the writing of these texts, always fortunately accompanied by Beatriz, my wife, during our stay in Cambridge UK., almost thirty years ago, and in New York, where we began to have our residence almost ten years ago. Thanks to her love, help and support I was able to complete my work being able to devote to it all the hours, days, weeks and months needed.

In order to assure that these materials won't be lost, I have decided to publish them all together, in their original versions, sure that the research they contain on constitutional comparative law could be useful for all those who have interest in these matters.

In any case, the texts are just what they are: the written work of a law professor made as a consequence of his research for the preparation of his lectures, not pretending to be anything else.

New York, January 2014

I

JUDICIAL REVIEW IN COMPARATIVE LAW (1985–1986)

This Part on *Judicial Review in Comparative Law*, is the text of the original notes written during my tenure as *Simon Bolivar Professor* of the University of Cambridge, UK, and as *Fellow of Trinity College,* during the academic year 1985–1986. They were written for the preparation of the Course of Lectures I gave on *Judicial Review in Comparative Law*, in the *LL.M. Course* at the Faculty of Law, University of Cambridge, UK. This original text of the Course of Lectures was published in my book: *Études de droit public compare*, Académie Internationale de Droit Comparé, Éditions Bruylant, Bruxelles 2001, pp. 525–934. An abridged and revised version of this Course of Lectures was published as: *Judicial Review in Comparative Law* (Foreword by J.A. Jolowicz), Cambridge Studies in International and Comparative Law, Cambridge University Press, Cambridge 1989, 406 pp.

INTRODUCTION

Judicial Review, in its original North American sense, is the power of courts to decide upon the constitutionality of legislative acts, in other words, the judicial control of the constitutionality of legislation.

It has been said that judicial review is the most distinctive feature of the North American constitutional system[1] and we must add that, in fact, it is the most distinctive feature of almost all the constitutional systems in the world today. All over the world, with or without similarities to the North–American system of judicial review, the courts –special constitutional courts or ordinary courts– have the power to declare a law unconstitutional. Accordingly, they have the power to refuse to enforce

1 E.S. CORWIN, "Judicial Review," *Encyclopaedia of the Social Sciences*, Vol. VII–VIII, p. 457.

it, because it is considered null or void, and in some cases, they have the power to declare the annulment of the said unconstitutional law.

As we all know, the system of the United Kingdom is quite different and we could even say that the main feature that also distinguishes the British constitutional system is precisely the lack of judicial review of legislation. Perhaps that is why Professor D.G.T. Williams of this Faculty said:

> Most British judges and the vast majority of British lawyers must have had little or no contact with the problems and workings of judicial review.[2]

This substantial difference between the constitutional systems of the United Kingdom and, in general, the other constitutional systems in the world derives from a few but very important principles, unique to the British constitution, and influencing all of them. It is the principle of the sovereignty of Parliament, called by Dicey the "secret source of strength of the British constitution" or "element of power which has been the true source of its life and growth."[3]

This principle, with all its importance in constitutional law in Great Britain, is, at the same time, the most powerful obstacle to judicial review of the constitutionality of legislation. It implies that even if it is true that the courts in this country are the ultimate guarantors the rule of law, they are bound to apply an Act of Parliament whatever view the judges take of its morality or justice, or of its effects on important individual liberties or human right.[4] And this is because of the absence of a written constitution in the modern constitutional form, with its entrenched declaration of fundamental rights and liberties.

It will suffice at this point to quote the words of Lord Wilberforce in the House of Lords case of *Pickin* v. *British Railways Board* in 1974, in a conclusive way with regard to the consequences of parliamentary sovereignty and also concerning the absence of judicial review of legislation. In that particular case, it was stated:

> The idea.... that an Act of Parliament, public or private, or a provision in an Act of Parliament, could be declared invalid or ineffective in the courts on account of some irregularity in Parliamentary procedure, or on the ground that Parliament in passing it was misled, or on the ground that it was obtained by deception or fraud, has been decisively repudiated by authorities of the highest standing from 1842 onwards. The remedy for a Parliamentary wrong, if one has been committed, must be sought from Parliament, and cannot be gained from courts.[5]

---

2 D.G.T. WILLIAMS, "The Constitution of the United Kingdom", *Cambridge Law Journal*, 31, (1) 1972–B, p. 277.

3 A.V. DICEY, *England's Case Against Home Rule* (3rd. ed. 1887), p. 168 quoted by D.G.T. WILLIAMS, *loc. cit.*, p. 277.

4 T.R.S. ALLAN, "Legislative Supremacy and the Rule of Law: Democracy and Constitutionalism", *Cambridge Law Journal*, 44, 1, 1985, p. 116.

5 A.C. 765 (1974)– See the text also in O. HOOD PHILLIPS, *Leading Cases in Constitutional and Administrative Law*, London 1979, pp. 1–6. See the comments in P. ALLOTT, "The Court and Parliament: Who whom?", *Cambridge Law Journal*, 38, 1, 1979, pp. 80–81.

Therefore, this course on *Judicial Review in Comparative Law* naturally will not be related to the British constitutional system and could not be written from a British lawyer's point of view. Rather, it will be, and ought to be, a course on comparative foreign law on the subject in which we will study the most important systems of judicial means and actions that could be brought before the courts by individuals to obtain control of the legislation by the courts.

Because they are means which can also lead to judicial control of the constitutionality of legislation we will also study the most important actions that could be brought before the courts by individuals for the defense and protection of their fundamental freedoms and rights established in the constitution.

In this respect, the course will be divided into six parts. In the first part, we will study the concept of what is called in continental and Latin–American law, l'*État de droit*, *Estado de Derecho*, *Stato di diritto* or *Rechtstaat*; terms that do not have an exact equivalent in English. The expressions *legal state*, state *according to law* or *rule of law* have been used for the same purpose, though we think there is no real equivalent.

In this first part, we will study the main features of the modern *État de droit*, and in particular, the consequences of the limitation and distribution of state powers; the principle of legality, as a basic concept more related to the idea of the English concept of the rule of law; and the establishment of entrenched fundamental liberties and rights. All these features are related to the process of the constitutionalization of the *État de droit*, which we will refer to in the second part with particular historical references to the process of constitutionalization or constitutionalism in North America, France and Latin America in the late eighteenth and early nineteenth centuries. This concept of the state according to the law, old and new, is the one that leads us, in the non British contemporary constitutional systems, to the possibility of a judicial review of all the acts of the state, including, the judicial control of the constitutionality of legislative acts.

In the other four parts of the course, we will study in particular the judicial review of the constitutionality of legislation, which can be considered as we mentioned, one of the main consequences of the constitutionalization of the modern *État de droit*.

This judicial review of the constitutionality of legislation, in other words, of laws and other legislative acts, requires at least three conditions for it to function in a given constitutional system. In the first place, it requires the existence of a written constitution, conceived as a superior and fundamental law with clear supremacy over all other laws. Secondly, such a constitution must be of a "rigid" character, which implies that the amendments or reforms that may be introduced can only be put into practice by means of a particular and special process, preventing the ordinary legislator from doing so. And thirdly, the establishment in that same written and rigid constitution, of the judicial means for guaranteeing the supremacy of the constitution, over all other state acts, including legislative acts.

Judicial review of legislation as the power of courts to decide upon the constitutionality of legislation has been considered one of the main contributions of the

North American constitutional system to the political and constitutional sciences.[6] However, the so–called "American system" of judicial review is not the only one that exists in present constitutional law. There is also the so called "Austrian system" of judicial review, originally established in the 1920 Austrian constitution and the mixed systems, mainly in Latin America, that have adopted the main feature of both the American and Austrian systems.

The main distinction between both systems of judicial review of legislation, the American and the Austrian systems is based on the judicial organs that can exercise this power of constitutional control: The "American system" entrusts that power of control to all the courts of a given country. It is for this reason that the system is considered to be a decentralized or diffused one. On the contrary, the "Austrian system" entrusts the power of control of the constitutionality of laws either to one existing court or to a special court, and it is therefore considered a centralised or concentrated control system.

In the course, we will study the most important systems of each of those two types of judicial review. Within the "American system", we will analyse not only the North American system, but also a few of those systems that have been influenced by it including various Latin–American systems, such as the Mexican, and Argentinean systems. We will study also others that have developed in many of Britain's former colonies such as Canada, Australia and India, and those that over a certain period were influenced by the North American system such as the Japanese constitutional system in 1947.

Within the so–called "Austrian system" we will examine the most important continental European systems of constitutional courts or tribunals, such as the Austrian, the German, the Italian and the Spanish. We will also consider, although it is an incomplete centralized system, the French constitutional council system and its very important recent developments.

However, there are also mixed systems of control of the constitutionality of legislation. They combine the decentralized systems, characterized by the assignment of power of control to all judges with the features of the centralized system that empower the Supreme Court to declare the annulment of any particular law by means of a "popular action" that can be brought before the Supreme Court by any individual. The Colombian and Venezuelan systems offer good examples of this and also in an incomplete form, does the Swiss system. We will analyze individually and comparatively the most important of all those systems of judicial review or control of the constitutionality of legislation.

Finally, we will also study particular aspects of the control of constitutionality, related to fundamental liberties and rights. As we have already mentioned, one of the main features of the process of constitutionalization of the *État de droit* has been the formal establishment of an entrenched declaration of fundamental liberties and human rights in written constitutions with adequate guarantees. Within such guaran-

---

6 J.A.C. GRANT, "El control jurisdiccional de la constitucionalidad de las leyes: una contribución de las Américas a la Ciencia Política", *Revista de la Facultad de Derecho de México*, 45, 1962, pp. 417–437.

tees, there are judicial means for the protection of such liberties and rights, in particular special judicial actions, claims or writs established for that purpose by a given legal order.

Apart from the classic "writ of habeas corpus", there are the special "action for protection" (*amparo*) of fundamental rights developed since the last century in most Latin American countries, including the broadly known *juicio de amparo* –literally "judgment of protection"– of Mexico, and the recently developed equivalent recourse for protection in continental Europe, particularly in Germany and Spain. We will refer to all those institutions as a means for judicial review of legislation.

Therefore, this course will refer to judicial review of the constitutionality of legislative acts in comparative law in legal systems other than the system of Great Britain, where the control of the constitutionality of acts of Parliament by the courts is inconceivable and the protection of fundamental rights is ensured by the courts by means of ordinary remedies of common law and equity and not by special judicial means.

PART I
THE MODERN STATE SUBMITTED TO THE RULE OF LAW (ÉTAT DE DROIT)

I. THE MODERN ÉTAT DE DROIT

The subject of judicial review or judicial control over the exercise of power is, undoubtedly, one of the basic and most characteristic elements of all contemporary states. Due to the submission of the state to the rule of law, one can say that at present time, all states have some system of judicial control or review over activities resulting from the exercise of public powers. In this respect we can also say that the concept of judicial review over the exercise of power is essentially related to the classical but current concept of what in English terminology is known, as we have already mentioned, as the state according to law or the state according to the rule of law, equivalent to the German *Rechtstaat*, the French *État de droit*, the Spanish *Estado de Derecho* and the Italian *Stato di Diritto*. This concept of the state according to law is based on the principle that not only must all the power of the public bodies forming the state stem from the law, or be established by law, but also that those powers are limited by law.

According to this concept, the law becomes, as far as the state is concerned, not only the instrument whereby attributions of its bodies and officials are established, but also the instrument limiting the exercise of those functions. Consequently, the *État de droit*, or state according to the rule of law, is essentially a state with limited powers and subject to some form of judicial control. This obviously, has numerous connotations in the evolution of the modern state and also presents features peculiar to each of the major contemporary legal systems.

That is why we have considered it necessary, before studying the systems of judicial review in comparative law, to begin by detailing some of the characteristic elements of the *État de droit* in the modern world and reviewing briefly its historical evolution.

In the continental legal systems, in the course of the historical evolution of the modern state, as opposed to the Absolute state and the economic doctrine of mercantilism that sustained it, the *État de droit* emerged together with liberalism, which also sustained it. The historical event which marked the transition from one political –economic system to another was the French Revolution (1789). However, the change took place following a theoretical preparation that lasted for several decades prior to the Revolution.

Naturally, we do not intend to enter into a historical analysis of the evolution of the *État de droit* as one of the phases of the modern state. we believe, however, that it is essential to refer to certain aspects of that evolution so as to explain the basis of judicial control of the exercise of power in the modern world.

The *État de droit is*, as we have said, a state according to law, or to put it in a better way, a state whose power and activity are regulated and controlled by legal rules. Basically, therefore, the *État de droit* consists of the rule of law; law understood, in this context, to mean the normative acts which make up the legal order of the state.

Seen from this standpoint, the *État de droit* as a state with powers regulated and limited by the law and other legal instruments is the opposite of any form of absolute or Totalitarian state. That is to say, it is the opposite of any type of state possessing unlimited power, in the sense of power not subjected to legal control, or at least, insufficiently regulated and subject to law.

Therefore, the ideas of judicial control of state activity and limitation of state power by subjection to the law emerge as the central concepts involved in the *État de droit* always related to the fundamental rights and liberties.

In line with the foregoing, it can be said that the *État de droit* is characterised by the following fundamental principles:

In the first place, there is the principle of limitation of state power by the classical division into the legislative, executive and judiciary, to guarantee liberty and to curb possible abuse of one power in relation to another; and the consecration of the necessary autonomy of the Judiciary, even to control the submission of the state to the law.

The second principle that characterizes the *État de droit* is that of the rule of law, that is to say, the subjection of the state to the law, not only to formal law, but also to all the sources of the legal order of a given state. This implies, therefore, that all state bodies are subject to the law of that same state, and particularly to the law as enacted by Parliament. This has especially given rise to the principle of legality applied to government or administrative actions, according to which, the administration must act in accordance with the law and can be judicially controlled to that end. Consequently, a series of procedures has been established for the purpose of controlling administrative action in particular, but also to control the constitutionality of laws, as protection against despotism on the part of the legislative power.

These principles have led to others inherent in the *État de droit*: On the one hand, that of the primacy of the legislation regulating all state activity, both of the executive and of the judiciary, the law being understood in this context, basically, to mean the formal law, that is to say, laws drawn up by the legislative bodies of the state (Parliament); and on the other hand, the establishment of a hierarchical system of the legal order and consequently of the various rules comprised therein. This system classifies the different rules in various ranks, according to their respective sphere of validity, usually in relation to a supreme or higher law, which is the constitution.

The third principle that identifies the *État de droit* is the recognition and establishment of fundamental rights and liberties, as a formal guarantee contained in constitutional texts and providing for their effective enjoyment as well as political and judicial means of control to ensure such enjoyment.

These are all principles or expressions of a common objective essential to the *État de droit*: The limitation of power, which emerged in contrast to the unlimited power of the Absolute monarch in what has been considered the first historical form of the continental modern state, namely the absolute state.

Indeed, it can be said that the modern state came into being when the feudal regime was dissolved as a result, among other factors, of a process of centralization of power, giving rise to the European continental monarchies, in which political power was concentrated in a Sovereign, as a superior political unit in contrast with the territorial dispersal of power characteristic of feudalism. Thus the modern state came into being as an absolute state, a concept in which the idea of concentration of power was added to that of the absolute and perpetual sovereignty of the monarch, constituting supreme, absolute and perpetual power over the citizens of a republic.

Thus, Bodino[7] or Bodin, in his *Six Books of a Commonwealth* published in 1576, translated into English in 1606 and once used as a text book in Cambridge,[8] referred to Sovereignty as a condition for the existence of a state (a Commonwealth) by including it in his definition. He said:

> A Commonwealth may be defined as the rightly ordered Government of a number of families, and of those things which are their common concern, by a sovereign power.
>
> Sovereignty is that absolute and perpetual power vested in a commonwealth which in Latin is termed *majestas*...[9]

The modern state, represented in this sovereign monarchy, was what Hobbes termed the Leviathan (1651) the unitary personification of a multitude of men.

---

7 I. BODIN, *The Six Books of a Commonwealth*, London 1606 (ed. by Kenneth Douglas MC RAE), Cambridge, Mass 1962, Book I, Clap. VIII, p. 84.

8 P. ALLOTT, "The Courts and Parliament: Who whom?, *Cambridge Law Journal*, 38, (1) 1979, p. 104.

9 Quoted by P. ALLOTT, *loc. cit*, p. 104 from trans. Tooley (1960), Chaps. I and VIII of Book I.

In Hobbes own words:

> A multitude of men, are made one person, when they are by one man, or one person, represented: so that it be done with the consent of every one of that multitude in particular. For it is the unity of the representer, not the unity of the represented that make the person one. And it is the representer that bears the person and but one person; and unity, cannot otherwise be understood in multitude.[10]

This *Leviathan*, is no doubt, the Modern state.[11]

During the seventeenth and eighteenth centuries, this modern state was identified as we said with the absolute monarchies of the continent, in which all power was concentrated in one person, "the king", who exercised it in an unrestricted manner. Moreover, sovereignty was a personal attribute of the Monarch, and for this reason he was totally exempt from control in the exercise of his power, in view of his divine origin.[12] The monarch had only one duty, namely that of ensuring public order and the happiness of his subjects in the interest of the state, which is the reason for the existence not only of the recourse to *Raison d'État*,[13] but also of the exercise of the full powers characteristic of absolutism, in which the monarch was exempt from responsibility.

This exemption from responsibility is reflected in the classical expression "The crown can do no wrong" or *le roi ne peut mal faire*.

In systems such as the English one, this did not change until 1947, when, following the *Crown Proceeding Act,* it became possible to hold the Crown responsible before the Courts.[14] In any case, in the absolute state, the subject had no rights vis–à–vis the monarch; his only duty was to obey.

By contrast with the continental systems, the British experience is special. As Jennings stated, absolutism never developed in English history, except for a brief period under the Commonwealth, (1653) and even then, only moderately.[15]

Since the beginning of the thirteenth century, the king's authority in England was limited by his barons and that struggle is clear in the Magna Carta of 1215, consid-

---

10 T. HOBBES, Leviathan (ed. John Plamenatz), London 1962, Chap. XVI, p. 171. *Cf.* M. M. GOLDSMIDT, *Hobbes' Science of Politics*, NY 1966, p. 138.

11 A. PASSERIN D'ENTRÈVES, *The Notion of the State. An Introduction to Political Theory*, Oxford 1967, p. 11.

12 *Idem* p. 44–202.

13 *Idem* p. 44.

14 J.A. JOLOWICZ, "Torts", *International Encyclopaedia of Comparative Law*, Vol. XI, Chap. 13, (Procedural Questions), p. 13–41; H.W.R. WADE, *Administrative Law*, Oxford 1971, p. 17.

15 I. JENNINGS, *The Law and the Constitution*, London 1972, p. 46. "No King of England has ever been regarded by his contemporaries as an Absolute Monarch. The very concept is unknown in English Law", I. JENNINGS, *Magna Carta*, London 1965, p. 13. King Charles I in the trial opened in Westminster Hall 20–1–1649 refused to plead, as he would not recognize the jurisdiction of the Court or indeed of any court. He said, "The King cannot be tried by any superior jurisdiction on earth." On 21–1–1649 he was sentenced to dead. See M. ASHLEY, *England in the Seventeenth Century,* 1972, p. 89.

ered the origin and source of English constitutional law.[16] This Great Charter, as is well known, did not legislate for Englishmen generally, but really attempted to safeguard the rights of different classes according to their different needs, and therefore, churchmen, lords, tenants, and merchants were separately provided for.[17] Even though the Magna Carta with its clauses placing limitations upon arbitrary power, has been considered the first attempt to express in precise legal terms some of the leading ideas of constitutional government in England, its interpretation by lawyers, historians and politicians and mainly by the courts, has subsequently led to the consideration of the document as a mean of safeguarding people's liberties even if the *liberi homines* were originally excluded from its clauses.[18]

Subsequently, kings had to fight against the landowners and they did not always win. When the feudal lords disappeared, there was already a Parliament strong enough to limit royal authority, take over part of the king's power, discuss its limits and even, at times, to destroy a king whose ideas and actions transcended the limits considered reasonable by Parliament.[19]

In this context, the Revolution of 1642 was not really a social revolution, like the French, aimed at destroying a despotic system of government and the society on which it was based. Fundamentally, it was the result of a political struggle between king and Parliament.

The result of the Civil War that developed in England from the year 1642 and lasted 18 years was to make personalized monarchies impossible in future as well as to impede Parliament from attempting to perpetuate itself in defiance of public opinion. Thus, when the monarchy was restored after the Civil War, the whole position both of the monarchy and of Parliament had been altered.

Particularly after that Revolution, Parliament attained a position in the state which it had never possessed before, in the sense that it became as permanent a part of the government as the king himself, no longer a body to be called occasionally to assist king's government by sanctioning new legislation.[20]

It must be stated also that if it is true that as a result of that Revolution the authoritative position of Parliament had been secured, so had the supremacy of the law and mainly because of the increased national desire to see the law really supreme after the nation's experience under the Protectorate which had constantly found itself needing to violate the law.

That is why Sir William Holdsworth in his book *A History of English Law* said that the alteration of the relationship between king, Parliament and the courts and consequently of the executive, legislative and judicial powers led them to begin to

---

16 W. HOLDSWORTH, *A History of English Law*, Vol. II, Fourth Ed., London 1936, Reprinted 1971, p. 209.

17 *Idem* p. 211.

18 *Idem* p. 211.

19 I. JENNINGS, *The Law and the Constitution*, *cit.* p. 46–47.

20 W. HOLDSWORTH, *op. cit.*, Vol. VI, p. 161–162.

assume the legal position which they hold in modern law.[21] That was undoubtedly facilitated because of the enactment of the *Instrument of Government* or 1653, considered to be the first written constitution in the modern world[22] in the sense of a higher law not to be modified by Parliament.

However, the political developments in England up to the Restoration led eventually to the final victory of Parliament in 1689 regarding the other powers of the state.

With this Parliamentary supremacy, it can be said that the rule of law system, in the liberal sense, has existed in England, and it was, as a matter of fact, an Englishman, John Locke, theoretician of the English Revolution, who laid the basis for the doctrine of the Liberal state, which had so much influence on continental law, and on the notion of the modern *État de droit*.

As we have previously said the modern *État de droit* is characterized by a few but very important features that have been developed over the last two centuries, and we think it is worthwhile studying, for our purpose of further analysis, judicial review or protection of the constitution.

We want to analyse the main features or characteristics of the *État de droit* classifying them into three different parts: firstly the limitation of state power as a guarantee of freedoms; secondly, the submission of the state to the rule of law, that is to say in continental law terms, to the principle of legality; and thirdly, the establishment of fundamental rights and liberties in a constitution.

II. LIMITATION OF POWER AS A GUARANTEE OF LIBERTY

The first feature of the state according to law is the existence of a system of division or separation of powers. This means that Parliament or the legislative power draws up the legal rules, and the administrative and judicial bodies are responsible for enforcing them. This system of separation of powers, or rationalization of power, is also established as a guarantee to citizens of their respective rights, considering as legislators, in the strictly formal sense, only those elected bodies aimed at representing the people. Consequently, the executive body, despite the normative faculties with which it is endowed, cannot be considered as legislator, in the sense of drawing up rules which might, for example, limit individual rights and guarantees.

Furthermore, this system of separation of powers contains a fundamental component, namely the autonomy and independence of judges, which also serves to guarantee individual rights. Consequently, neither person holding legislative office, nor the executive can be considered as judges.

However, in the *État de droit* regime, the system of separation of powers is not absolute and rigid, since there are numerous interrelations between the various state bodies, which must exercise mutual control and limitation, through the so called system of weight and counterweight, or checks and balances, which, in fact, balances the system of state power. This system is characterized by several factors one of

21 *Idem* p. 163.

22 P. ALLOT, *loc. cit.*, p. 97.

which is the supremacy of the legislative power, as creator of the law vis–à–vis the executive and the judiciary, who are responsible for enforcing that law. But this primacy of the legislator is not necessarily tantamount to sovereignty, and to avoid absolutism on the part of the legislator, or what has been called "elected dictatorship",[23] the legislative power is necessarily subjected to the constitution. Thus, since the Legislator is limited by the constitution, a system must be set up to control the constitutionality of his acts, either by ordinary courts or by special courts, to guarantee the constitutionality of the laws.

But in this system of separation of powers, as we have already pointed out, the independence of the judiciary vis–à–vis the legislator and the executive is a fundamental element of the *État de droit* to such an extent that one can say that the genuine state according to the law is the one in which judges are autonomous and independent and, naturally, the one in which procedural guarantees exist, to avoid abuse of authority on the part of the judges.

Now, this principle of the separation of powers is at the very origin of the *État de droit*, as conceived by the theoreticians of absolutism, particularly Locke, Montesquieu and Rousseau.

1. Theoretical Backgrounds

In effect, John Locke, in his *Two Treatises of Government* (1690), became the first ideologist of the reaction against absolutism when he advocated the limitation of the monarch's political power. He based his proposal on the consideration of man's natural condition and the social contract of the society, which gave birth to the state. In Locke's opinion, the reason why men enter into a social contract is to preserve their lives, liberties and possessions, the three basic assets that he regards, in general, as "property." And it is this "property" that gives men political status. In Locke's own words:

> For liberty is to be free from restraint and violence from others which cannot be, where there is no Law: But freedom is not, as we are told, a liberty to dispose, and order, as he wishes his person, action, possessions, and his whole Property.[24]

Naturally, this social contract as conceived by Locke, changed man's natural condition, and could not give rise to the formation of a government under which men would be placed in a worse situation than they had previously been in. Consequently, an absolute government could not even be considered legitimate as a civil government was. If the state emerged as a protector of "natural rights" which did not

---

23 HAILSHAIN, *Elective Dictatorship*, 1976, quoted by P. ALLOTT, "The Courts and Parliament: Who whom? *Cambridge Law Journal*", Vol. 38, 1, 1979, p. 115. Hogg also has said that Parliament lead become "virtually an elective dictatorship. The party system makes the supremacy of a government like, the present, automatic and almost unquestioned." Quoted by M. ZANDERS, *A Bill of Rights*?, London 1980, p. 5.

24 J. LOCKE, *Two Treatises of Government* (ed. Peter Laslett), Cambridge 1967, paragraph 57, p. 324.

disappear with the social contract, their actual disappearance due to the action of an absolute state would justify resistance to the abuse of power.[25]

Now within the measures designed to rationalize and limit power, Locke developed his classical distribution of state functions, some of which he regarded as powers. In paragraph 131 of his book *Two Treatises of Government*, Locke said the following:

> And so whoever has the legislative or supreme power of any Common–wealth, is bound to govern by established standing Laws, promulgated and known to the people and not by Extemporary Decrees; by indifferent and upright Judges, who are to decide Controversies by those Laws; and to employ the force of the Community at home, only in the Execution of such Laws, or abroad to prevent or redress Foreign Injuries, and secure the Community from Inroads and Invasions.[26]

So, Locke distinguished four state functions, that of legislating, of judging, of employing forces internally in the execution of the laws and of employing those forces abroad, in defence of the community. He gave the name of *legislative power* to the first function, that of making the laws "to which the other powers are, and must be subordinated"[27] as he said. The third function he called the *executive power*, which involved "the execution of the municipal laws of the society within the latter and above its parts"[28] or components. The fourth function he called the federative power, which includes "the power of war and peace, leagues and alliances, transactions with all persons or communities outside the state."[29]

Of all the functions he assigned to any sovereign state, the only one which he did not regard as a "power" was the *function of judging*, with respect to which Peter Laslett, in his introduction to Locke's book, indicates that "it was not a separate power, but a general attribution of the state."[30]

In this effort to rationalize state functions, the novelty of Locke's thesis lies in the distinction between the faculty of legislating and that of employing the forces in the execution of the laws. In this context, it was not necessary to individualize the power of judging, which, particularly in England, was a traditional state function.

In any case, it is important to note that Locke confined himself to rationalizing and systematizing the functions of the sovereign state, but did not actually formulate a theory on the division of powers, much less their separation. What is more, no thesis can be inferred from Locke's work to the effect that the power of the state had to be placed in different hands to preserve liberty or guarantee individual rights, whilst

---

25 *Idem*, p. 211.

26 *Idem*, p. 371.

27 *Idem* paragraphs 134, 149, 150, p. 384, 385. Peter LASLETT commentaries, "Introduction", p. 117.

28 *Idem*, p. 117.

29 *Idem*, p. 383. In relation to the name given by LOCKE to this power he said: "if any one pleases. So the thing be understood, we are indifferent as to the name." *Idem*, p. 383.

30 P. LASLETT, "Introduction", *loc. cit.*, p. 118.

allowing for the parts to coincide.[31] He did however admit that if the powers were placed in different hands, a balance could be achieved; as he stated in his book: "balancing the Power of Government, by placing several parts of it in different hands.[32]

Perhaps then, Locke's fundamental contribution to the principle of the division of power lay in his criteria, according to which the executive and federative power must necessarily be in the same hands.[33] Also, his criteria of the *supremacy of the legislative power* over the others, to the extent that both the executive function and that of judging had to be performed in execution of, and in accordance with the laws adopted and duly published.[34] For Locke, this supremacy of the legislative power was precisely the consequence of the supremacy of Parliament over the monarch, resulting from the 1689 Revolution which, *supremacy*. We have mentioned, is the most characteristic feature of English public law, compared to continental systems.

This theory of the division of power, that had such a great influence on modern constitutionalism, mainly because of its conversion from the "division of power" to the "separation of power" both in the French Revolution and in the American and Latin–American Revolutions, had its fundamental formulation in Montesquieu's equally well known work.

According to Montesquieu, political liberty only existed in those states in which the power of the state, together with all corresponding functions, was not in the hands of the same person or the same body of magistrates.[35] That is why, in his famous work *De 1'Esprit des Lois*, he insisted that "it is an eternal experience that any man who is given power tends to abuse it; he does so until he encounters limits... In order to avoid the abuse of power, steps must be taken for power to limit power."[36]

From his comparative study of the various states existing at the time (174 8), Montesquieu reached the conclusion that England was the only state, the direct aim of which was political liberty. That is why, in the well–known Chapter VI of Volume XI of his book, he undertook to study the "constitution of England", and from that study he formulated his theory of the division of power into three categories:

> Legislative power, power to execute things which depend on international law, and power to execute things which depend on civil lawn the first case, the prince or magistrate makes laws for a period of time or for ever. In the second case, he makes peace or war, sends or receives ambassadors, establishes security, takes measures against invasion. In the third case, he

---

31 *Idem*, p. 117–118.

32 *Idem*, p. 107, 350.

33 *Idem*, p. 118.

34 M.J.C. VILE, *Constitutionalism and the Separation of Powers*, Oxford 1967, p. 36. (LOCKE: "There can be one supreme power, which is the legislative, to which all the rest are and must be subordinated", "for what can give laws to another, must need be superior to him", Chap. XIII, p. 149–150).

35 A PASSERIN D'ENTRÈVES, *The Notion of the State. An introduction to Political Theory*, Oxford 1967, p. 120.

36 MONTESQUIEU, *De l'Esprit des Lois* (ed. G. Truc), Paris 1949, Vol. I, Book XI, Chap. IV, p. 162–163.

> punishes crimes, or settles disputes between individuals. The latter we shall call the power to judge, and the other simply the executive power of the state.[37]

Following Locke's example, Montesquieu defined various state functions or faculties, rather than division of power: the function of making laws, that of judging and that of executing laws, the latter encompassing what Locke called executive and federative power.

However, the novelty of Montesquieu's division of power, and what distinguishes it from Locke's approach, is, on the one hand, his proposal that to guarantee liberty, the three functions must not be in the same hands. On the other hand, that in the division of power, they were to *be* on an equal footing, otherwise power could not curb power. In the same Chapter VI of Volume XI of De 1'Esprit des Lois, Montesquieu expressed the following opinion:

> When legislative power and executive power are in the hands of the same person or the same magistrate's body, there is no liberty... Neither is there any liberty if the power to judge is not separate from the legislative and executive powers... All would be lost if the same man, or the same body of princes, or noblemen or people exercised these three powers: that of making the laws, that of executing public resolutions and that of judging the wishes or disputes of individuals.[38]

As a result of all this, Montesquieu stated:

> Those princes who wanted to become despots, always began by taking possession of all the magistracies.[39]

Underlying this whole conception, there was also, of course, the concept of liberty, seen from the same standpoint as Locke. Montesquieu even said, in terms very similar to those used by Locke:

> It is true that in democracies the people seem to do what they want; but political liberty does not consist of doing what one wants. In a state, that is to say, in a society in which laws exist, liberty can only consist of being able to do what one should want to do, and not being obliged to do what one should not want to do.[40]

But in contrast to what existed according to the English constitution which he *was then* analysing, Montesquieu's concept involved no proposal whatsoever that any particular public authority should have priority over another. It is true that by defining the legislative authority as the "general will of the state" and the executive authority as the "execution of that general will",[41] it could be inferred that the latter, as far as the execution itself was concerned, was to submit to the will of the former,

---

37 *Idem*, Vol. I, pp. 163–164.

38 *Idem*, Vol. I, p. 164. In the same Chap. VI, Book XI MONTESQUIEU added that "Were (the judiciary power) joined with the legislative, the life and liberty of the subject would be exposed to arbitrary control; for the judge would, be then the legislator. Were it joined to the executive power, the judge might behave with violence and oppression." *Cf.* Ch. H. MCILWAIN, *The High Court of Parliament and its Supremacy*, Yale 1910, pp. 322–323.

39 *Idem*, Vol. I, p. 165.

40 *Idem*, Vol. I, Book XI, Chap. III, p. 162.

41 *Idem*, Vol. I, p. 166.

but not, of course, in the sense of political subordination. On the contrary, he conceived the three authorities as being so equal that they could act as a mutual restraint, as the only possible form of co–operation for the maintenance of political liberty. That is why Montesquieu concluded with his famous proposal: "these three powers should constitute a rest, or inaction. But since, as all things, they must necessarily move, they will be forced to move in concert."[42]

It is clear, in any case, that Montesquieu's concept like Locke's theory was devised for Absolutism. Both were theoreticians of absolutism. That is why their concepts of the division of the sovereign's power were a legal doctrine rather than a political postulate. In other words, the theory does not answer the question about who is to exercise sovereignty, but how power should be organized to achieve certain objectives.[43]

But in addition to Locke's and Montesquieu's contributions to the definition of the limitation of power, in the political theory, which led to continental reaction against the Absolute state, and the appearance of the *État de droit*, Rousseau's concept of law occupies a place of paramount importance. This concept subsequently led to the postulate of the submission of the state to the Law, which is of its own making. That is to say, it gave rise to the principle of legality and consolidation of the *État de droit* itself.

In effect, as Rousseau himself said, the social pact or contract is the solution to the problem of finding a form of association: "which defends and protects, with the whole common force, the person and goods of each member of the association, and in which each person, united with all, nevertheless obeys only himself and remains as free as before."[44]

Thus he said, "the transition is made from the natural to the civil state."[45] But, as Rousseau himself pointed out, "through the social pact we have given birth to the political body; we must now endow it with movement and a will, through legislation."[46]

Thus, –and this was the novelty of his proposal– it is the law, as a manifestation of the sovereign state resulting from the social pact, which sets the state in motion and provides it with the necessary will, since it is a question of "acts resulting from the general will and dealing with a general issue." Thus Rousseau not only built up the theory of the law as an "act of the general will", to which the conduct of the state itself and that of private individuals must be subjected, but he also established the principle of the generality of the law, which was to subsequently lead to the reaction against privileges, which is another basic element of the *État de droit*.[47]

---

42 *Idem*, Vol. I, p. 172.

43 A. PASSERIN D'ENTREVES, *op. cit.*, p. 121.

44 J.J. ROUSSEAU, *Du Contract Social* (ed. Ronald Grimsley), Oxford 1972, Book I, Chap. IV, p. 114.

45 *Idem*, Book I, Chap. VIII, p. 119.

46 *Idem*, Book II, Chap V, p. 134

47 *Idem*, Book II, Chap, V, p. 136.

However, Rousseau limited state functions to two: the making of laws and their execution, to which he applied the same terminology as Montesquieu: legislative power and executive power.[48] Nevertheless, it is not a question here either of a doctrine of separation of powers, but, along the same lines as Locke and Montesquieu, a doctrine of the division of one single power that of the sovereign, resulting from the social pact or from the integration of the general will.[49]

Neither was Rousseau in favor of placing the two functions of power –the expression of the general will by means of laws and the execution of those laws– in the same hands. So, adopting the same approach as Montesquieu, he also recommended that different bodies exercise them, although, unlike Montesquieu, he insisted on the need for the subordination of the body executing the law to the body making it. This, in Locke's approach and in the English system, was to ensure the subsequent supremacy of the legislation and the law, developed later in Europe. Furthermore, the supremacy of the law was to be the corner stone of public law within the framework of the *État de droit* in Europe, allowing the development of the principle of legality, particularly with regard to government.

In this respect Rousseau agreed with Montesquieu. Rousseau in fact stated: "Therefore, we understand a Republic to be any state which is governed by laws."[50] Montesquieu, for his part defined the "state" as "a Society in which laws exist."[51] Which is also a declaration of the fact that the existence of laws was a fundamental requisite for the existence of the state.

2. The American and French Revolutions

It can generally be said that the writings of Locke, Montesquieu and Rousseau made up the whole theoretical and political arsenal for the reaction against the absolute state and its replacement by the state according to law based on the separation of powers, as a guarantee of liberty. That reaction was to occur in Continental Europe, with the French Revolution (1789), and in North America, with the Independence (1776), based on the exaltation of individualism and liberty.

In effect, all the political theories previously y mentioned were based on the analysis of man's natural situation and the achievement of the social pact or contract which established a sovereign as a mechanism for the protection of liberty. This was the basis for the subsequent exaltation of individualism and the political consecration of rights, not only of the citizens of a particular state, but also those of man, with the consequent construction of political and economic liberalism.

It was also considered necessary for the power of the state, as a product of the social pact, to be divided and rationalized, to prevent its abuse by the sovereign. To that end, state functions were systemized and power was divided, thereby paving the

48 *Idem*, Book III, Chap, I, p. 153.

49 R. GRIMSLEY, "Introduction", in ROUSSEAU, *op. cit*, p. 35.

50 *Idem*, Book III, Chap. VI.

51 MONTESQUIEU, *op. cit.*, Book XI, Chap. III, p. 162.

way for the adoption of a different and more radical formula: that of the "separation of powers", as a *guarantee* of liberty.

As Madison pointed out at the beginning of American constitutionalism:

> The accumulation of all powers, legislative, executive, and judiciary in the same hands, whether of one, a few, or many, and whether hereditary, self–appointed or elective, may justly be pronounced the very definition of Tyranny.[52]

That is why the principle of the separation of powers was one of the essential elements of the American constitution. For example, the constitution of Massachusetts (1780) contained categorical expressions:

> In the government of this Commonwealth, the legislative department shall not exercise the executive and judicial powers, or either one of them: The executive shall never exercise the legislative and judicial powers, or either one of them: The judicial shall never exercise the legislative and executive powers, or either one of them: to the end it may be a government of laws not of men.[53]

Moreover, the sovereign's power was considered to be updated by the production of laws, which were believed to be not only indispensable for the existence of the state itself, but also a guarantee of civil and political liberty. And the legislative function occupied a superior position to that of the other executive functions.

Consequently, in this concept arising out of the French Revolution, all acts, both of the Sovereign and of private individuals, were subjected to the law, understood to be an act of the general will. This gave rise to the principle of legality.

The *État de droit* and liberalism are, therefore, based on the concepts of liberty, separation of powers, supremacy of the law and the principle of legality. As a result, the essence of the *État de droit* from the beginning, in contrast to the absolute state, lies in the principle of the submission of the state and its administration to legality, which is to say, the necessary regulation of the state by the law, which must set limits on power.

However, such submission was not always guaranteed definitively in European countries and in all those, which adopted the *État de droit* model. At the beginning, for example, the separation of powers in France presented the non–interference of one power with another in such a fashion that the judicial power could not guarantee individuals that government would be submitted to legality. Proof of this was the famous Law of Judiciary Organisation of 16–24th of August 1790, which specified:

---

52 J. MADISON, *The Federalist* (ed. B.F. Wright), Cambridge, Mass 1961, N° 47, p. 336.

53 Art. XXX. *Massachusetts General Law Annotated*, St. Paul, Minn. Vol. 1–A, p. 582. In 1776, the constitution of Virginia, also had a declaration on separation of powers, considered as "The most precise statement of the doctrine which had at that time appeared." M.J.C. VILE, *Constitutionalism and the Separation of Powers*, *cit*., p. 118. Article III of that constitution stated: "The Legislative, Executive and Judiciary departments, shall be separate and distinct, so that neither exercise the potters properly belonging to the others; nor shall any person exercise the powers of more than one of them at the same time, except that the Justice of the County Courts shall be eligible to either House of Assembly."

> Judiciary functions are, and shall always be separate from administrative functions. Any interference by judges in the activities of the administrative bodies, or any summons issued to the administrators by the said judges, for reasons relating to their functions, shall constitute a breach of duty.[54]

Subsequently, the Law of 16 *Fructidor* of the year III (1795) ratified that:

> The Courts are forbidden, under penalty of law, to take cognisance of administrative acts, whatever their nature.[55]

As a result, the evolution of administrative jurisdiction in France, as jurisdiction separate from the judicial order for judging the government itself, constituted an extreme form of separation of powers. If the government or administrators were to be judged, a special jurisdiction, different and separate from the judicial power, had to be set up and that developed through a lengthy process which led, eventually, to the establishment of the *Conseil d'Etat*.

On the other hand, in the concept of Parliament and the law resulting from the French Revolution, any kind of control over the constitutionality of the laws in continental Europe was inconceivable, and this continued to be the case up to the beginning of the present century. As we will see, there is still no system of direct control over the constitutionality of the laws in France, and it was only in the post–war periods the twenties, and later in the forties, that a system of this kind was developed in other European countries, but which is still inconceivable in the British legal system.

In any case, throughout the last century and during the present one, the evolution of the principle of the separation of powers and the primacy of the legislator has shown a growing tendency both towards the submission of the state and all its bodies to the law and to legality, and towards the establishment of judicial controls to that end, either by means of special tribunals separate from judicial power, or by the use of the courts of the judiciary itself. This submission and controlled, *inter alia*, to the very birth of administrative law in Europe and even in England, as an autonomous branch of the legal sciences as at the end of the last century.

The struggle for the submission of government to legality is an irreversible victory of the *État de droit* and has been implanted throughout the world nowadays.

The characteristics of the separation of powers naturally vary from one country to another and its original justification as a guarantee of liberty has been forgotten. In many cases it has been used for purposes never originally envisaged. In England for example, the separation of powers was maintained, but for the purposes of the supremacy of Parliament over the various state bodies, that is to say, to subject the courts and tribunals to Parliament, and even to allow the courts the possibility of controlling the administrative authorities. The same doctrine also prevailed in the United states of North America, but for the purpose of clearly separating the executive and legislative functions, and enabling the Supreme Court to even declare acts of Congress invalid, whereas in France, the principle was used to make the legisla-

---

54 J. RIVERO, *Droit Administratif*, Paris 1973, p. 129; J.M. Auby et R. DRAGO, *Traité de contentieux administratif*, Paris 1984, Vol. I, p. 379.

55 J. RIVERO, *op. cit.*, p. 129.

tive power supreme, but taking the separation to the extreme of preventing ordinary courts from controlling the legality of administrative acts, and eliminating any possibility of controlling the constitutionality of the legislator's acts.[56]

The North American constitution can indeed be considered a classical example of the division of powers, although it contains no precept specially designed for that division. The principle is, however, patent in several rules stipulating, for example, that all legislative powers are entrusted to Congress; that executive power is granted to the president; and that the judicial power of the United states is in the hands of the Supreme Court.[57] The rigidity of the division of powers is also evident from the fact that the Cabinet is absolutely independent from Congress, with which it has no formal communication.[58]

The principle has, however, undergone several changes, due to the constitution itself, to judicial interpretation, and to constitutional practice. In the first place there is, together with the principle of the separation of powers, a system of checks and balances, whereby the Executive has some participation in legislative power by veto and the annual address to Congress and in judicial power through the prerogative to pardon. Regarding the executive's right to appoint offices and ratify treaties, this requires the consent of the legislator, who also performs judicial functions in cases of impeachment, and is responsible, within the limits of the constitution, for the organization of judicial power. Finally, the courts are authorized to establish their rules of procedure, which is undoubtedly a legislative function, and they have also developed the power even to control the actions of Congress itself.[59]

3. The Sovereignty of Parliament

But in the concept of the separation of powers as a system of distributing power in such way that power curbs power, the English system was at variance.

Despite Montesquieu and all the literature produced in the eighteenth century with reference to England, as a living example of the separation of powers, the fact is that such separation has never been a reality and the situation at that time was, and has always been, that of the *heureux melange* –the successful mixture– to which Voltaire referred.[60]

Be that as it may, British constitutional history shows a series of groups and institutions contending the domination and participation in state power. This has brought about the phenomenon of a balance of powers, which has constantly given rise to a system of restriction and counter–restriction, although in the United Kingdom one power has always prevailed over the others. In general, the predominant

---

56 I. JENNINGS, *The Law and the Constitution*, London 1972, p. 25–28.

57 Arts. 1,1; 2,1 and 3,1.

58 M. GARCÍA–PELAYO, *Derecho constitucional comparado*, Madrid 1957, p. 350.

59 *Idem*, p. 350 and 351. In general, A and S. TUNC, *Le système constitutionnel des Etats Unies d'Amerique*, 2 vols. Paris 1954.

60 Quoted by M. GARCÍA–PELAYO, *op. cit.*, p. 283. *Cf.* G. MARSHALL, *Constitutional Theory*, Oxford 1971, p. 97.

power has been that of Parliament, but it fact the predominant power has been considered to be that of the government, due to its control over the House of Commons and to the practice of delegated legislation.

In this sense, Philip Allott in an article published a few years ago in the Cambridge Law Journal stated:

> The Executive has acquired an overall position of dominance, extending its authority in all three of the functional branches of Government –legislative, executive and judicial–. Above all, it has acquired a practical control over the House of Commons in Parliament, from which it has virtually excluded the House of Lords as a countervailing power.[61]

This fact has been pointed out by almost all the constitutional lawyers of the United Kingdom[62] and that is why Wade and Phillips in their book on constitutional and Administrative Law pointed out that "In absence of a written constitution, there is no formal separation of power in the United Kingdom."[63] and particularly between the legislative and the executive power; that the practical needs of the parliamentary government have obliged Parliament to trust governmental policy and accept the cabinet's wishes as far as the legislative programme is concerned, but retaining the right to amend, criticise, question and ultimately to annul, and also that practical needs have demanded considerable delegation to the executive of the power of rule regulation.[64]

But in spite of these facts, it is certainly clear that in the United Kingdom legal system, the idea of parliamentary sovereignty has been traditional, breaking with the continental and American principle of separate powers, which mutually curb each other.

This principle of parliamentary sovereignty is characterized *inter alia,* by the following elements:

In the first place, because of the absence of any formal distinction between constitutional and ordinary laws, which implies that in the absence of a written constitution, Parliament can, at any time, institute, by the ordinary method of law–making, reforms of a constitutional nature. Therefore, "the authority of Parliament to change the law is unlimited" and "since the sovereignty of Parliament is recognised by law,

---

61 P. ALLOTT, *loc. cit.*, p. 115.

62 For example, T.R.S. ALLAN has noted out that "the political consequence of the legal arrangement (that perceive the constitution as a legal order subject to, and dominated by, an unrestrained and all–powerful sovereign: the Parliament) is the overwhelming authority of a government with a majority of seats in the House of Commons", and that "It is this concentration of power which is seen as a threat to fundamental rights and liberties constitutional restraints are therefore needed to protect such rights from irresponsible legislative encroachment; the need is to counteract the "helplessness of the law in face of the legislative sovereignty of Parliament" (Sir Leslie Scarman), in "Legislative Supremacy and the rule of Law: Democracy and constitutionalism", the *Cambridge Law Journal*, Vol. 44, (1), 1985, pp. 111–112.

63 E.C.S. WADE and G. GODFREY PHILLIPS, *Constitutional and Administrative Law*, (9th ed. by A.W. BRADLEY), London 1985, p. 53.

64 *Idem*, p. 49, 564.

–said T.R.S. Allan, in an article published in the last issue of *The Cambridge Law Journal*,– it would be contrary to the rule of law to deny full force to enactments which change existing law."[65]

The second element that characterizes the principle of sovereignty of Parliament is the absence of any possibility of control over parliamentary activity. This implies that there is no court competent to decide upon the constitutionality of laws or acts of Parliament. Consequently, any act of Parliament, whatever it's content, must be applied by the courts of justice, and in no case can those courts fail to apply the said rules.

As Dicey said at the very beginning of his *An Introduction to the Study of the Law of the Constitution*,

> The principle of Parliamentary sovereignty means neither more nor less than this, namely, that Parliament... has, under the English constitution, the right to make or unmake any law whatever; and, further, that no person or body is recognised by the law of England as having a right to override or set aside the Legislation of Parliament.[66]

And regarding the courts, in the case of R. v. Jordan in 1967, a Divisional Court stated clearly that as Parliament was supreme, "there was no power in the courts to question the validity of an Act of Parliament."[67]

We have also mentioned the very important decision of the House of Lords, made in 1974 in the case of the *British Railways Board* v. *Pickin* in which Lord Reid stated that:

> The idea that a court is entitled to disregard a provision in an Act of Parliament on any ground must seem strange and startling to anyone with any knowledge of the history and law of our constitution", adding, "no court of justice can inquire into the manner in which (an Act) was introduced into Parliament, what was done previously to its being introduced, or what passed in Parliament during the various stages of its progress through both Houses of Parliament,

and concluding precisely that:

> The function of the Court is to co construe and apply the enactments of Parliament. The court has no concern with the manner in which Parliament or its officers carrying out its Standing Orders perform these functions;[68]

The third point that emerges from the principle of the supremacy of Parliament is that the law created by Parliament, that is to say, *the statutes*, have primacy over common law and over any form of legal creation. As stated by the Chancery Division in the case of *Cheney* v. *Conn (Inspector of Taxes)* in 1968:

---

65 T.R.S. ALLAN, *loc. cit*., p. 122.

66 A.V. DICEY, *An Introduction to the Study of the Law of the Constitution*, (Introduction by E.C.S. WADE), 10th Ed. 1973, p. 39–40.

67 O. HOOD PHILLIPS, *Leading Cases in Constitutional and Administrative Law*, London 1979, p. 1.

68 *Idem*, p. 2–5.

> What Statute says and provides is itself the law, and the highest form of law that is known to this country. It is the law which prevails over every other form of law, and it is not for the Court to say that a parliamentary enactment, the highest law in the country, is illegal.[69]

The fourth principle derived from the sovereignty of Parliament is that of the power of Parliament to prevail over judicial decisions themselves, since a bill could even be approved for the purpose of legalizing an illegal act, or exempting somebody from the legal consequences of a committed act. This is why it is said that "the legal authority of Parliament is absolute, not limited."[70]

For instance, Parliament's term of office, according to one of the conventions, is five years, but this period might be extended. Parliament can also regulate succession to the Throne, exclude persons who are not members of a particular religion, limit royal prerogatives, change the state religion, in short, make any decision with no limitation whatsoever. The principle implies that any act of Parliament can always be revised and changed by a subsequent act, either expressly or, in the case of conflict, implicitly. Consequently, important acts of Parliament such as the Habeas Corpus Act 1679, the Bill of Rights 1689, the Act of Settlement 1700, the Statute of Westminster 1931 and even the European Economic Communities Act 1972 can very well be revised by Parliament. No special majority is needed for this.[71]

Parliamentary sovereignty, in this form, is without doubt, one of the most important features of the constitutional system of the United Kingdom.

One of the consequences of parliamentary sovereignty, as pointed out by Prof. H.W.R. Wade, is that there are no constitutional guarantees, in the United Kingdom neither is there anything similar to what happens with written and rigid constitutions, which can only be changed by special procedures. This is undoubtedly an exception in the modern world, since most countries, even in the English speaking world have a written constitution represented by a formal document, protected, as a fundamental law, against any attempt by simple majorities to introduce reforms.[72]

However, not only are constitutional guarantees non existent in the United Kingdom, nor does it seem possible to create them, as Prof. H.W.R. Wade said, since, if an ordinary act of Parliament can reform any law, then it is impossible for Parliament itself to declare a law or statute to be non reformable, or only reformable subject to certain conditions. In other words, Parliament cannot modify or destroy its own "continuing sovereignty" for the courts will always obey its commands.[73]

In any case, parliamentary sovereignty in the United Kingdom as it exists today, has a profound effect on the position of judges. They are not guardians of a constitu-

---

69 *Idem*, p. 28. That is why, we think, George Winterton said that "the rule of law comes to mean rule of law as enacted by Parliament, and not the rule of the ancient common law ", in "'the British Grundnorm: Parliamentary Supremacy re–examined", *The Law Quarterly Review*, Vol. 92, 1976, p. 596.

70 T.R.S. ALLAN, *loc. cit.* p. 129. Also see E.C. WADE and G. GODFREY PHILLIPS, *op. cit.*, pp. 61–62.

71 H.W.R. WADE, *Administrative Law*, 5th ed. Oxford 1984, p. 27.

72 *Idem*, p. 28.

73 *Idem*, p. 28. See also G. WINTERTON, *loc. cit.*, p. 597.

tion or of constitutional rights, with, for example, power to declare certain legislative acts unconstitutional, as is the case with the Supreme Court of the United states.

That is why, no entrenched Bill of Rights can be adopted in this country. The adoption of it would, of course, involve the exercise of judicial review by the courts, that is to say, the power of domestic courts to protect certain fundamental freedoms even against the legislature itself,[74] and that would be against the principle of the sovereignty of Parliament.

Sir Ivor Jennings summarized the consequences of this main principle of the constitution of this country saying that parliamentary sovereignty essentially means two things. In the first place, it means that Parliament can legally pass legislation dealing with any matter: in Ivor Jennings words,

> Parliament may remodel the British constitution, prolong its own life, legislate ex–post facto, legalise illegalities, provide for individual cases, interfere with contracts and authorize the seizure of property, give dictatorial powers to the Government, dissolve the United Kingdom or the British Commonwealth, introduce communism or socialism, or individualism or fascism, entirely without legal restriction.[75]

That is to say that as there is no written or rigid constitution in the United Kingdom, Parliament is not limited by any text or superior fundamental rule. So, there is no possibility of exercising any kind of judicial control over the conformity of Parliamentary acts with a higher law, which means in our perspective that the principle of the rule of law is not applicable to Parliament.

4. The Distribution of Power

The idea of the state according to law with or without parliamentary sovereignty is based on the concept of the limitation and distribution of power, which may be observed in three aspects.

In the first place, it can be observed in a distribution of power between the state itself, on the one hand, and individuals or citizens on the other, in the sense that a sphere of liberty is established for individuals and citizens, even as a fact existing prior to the state. This implies limitations to state powers, in the sense that the faculty of the state to invade the sphere of fundamental rights is, in principle, limited.

This is true, in a certain way even in the United Kingdom with Parliamentary supremacy, the absence of an entrenched Bill of Rights and the unthinkable judicial review of legislation. As Winterton pointed out:

> For centuries, and certainly at the time of the 1688 Revolution, the concept of practically "inalienable" personal liberties has been a very strong feature of the British constitution: it is implicit in the British concept of the Rule of Law, and has led to the doctrine of natural justice in administrative law, as well as the rules for interpreting statutes so as not to threaten individual liberty.[76]

---

74 D.G.T. WILLIAMS, "The constitution of the United Kingdom", *The Cambridge Law Journal*, 31, (1), 1972–B, p. 279.

75 I. JENNINGS, *The Law and the Constitution, cit.*, p. 147.

76 G. WINTERTON, *loc. cit.*, p. 599.

The second aspect of the distribution of power in the *État de droit* relates to its organization by means of a principle of distribution of power between constituent and constituted power. Constituent power belongs and corresponds to the people who are sovereign and is reflected in a constitution, so that constituent act can only be taken by the latter, in accordance with the provisions of the constitution itself. Thus the bodies of the constituted power cannot invade the activities which correspond to the constituent power established in the constitution, and that is why all invasions of those activities invalidate acts taken in such a way.

Third and last, this principle of the distribution of power in the *État de droit* also refers to the organization of state power itself in the sphere of constituted power, by means of a system of division of power consisting of a series of attributions to the different state bodies.

This principle of organization or distribution of power has two connotations: in the first place, the classical horizontal division or separation of powers, that distinguish the various branches of public power in a nation, between the legislative, the executive (government and administration) and the judicial bodies. The aim of this division and distinction is to establish reciprocal restrictions and controls between the various state powers, and they are normally established in the constitution.

In addition to this, there is a second, vertical connotation that seeks a distribution of state power among its different territorial levels, resulting, for example, in the Federal state or politically decentralized forms of state. In these, the different territorial levels (national, federate states or Regions and Municipalities) exercise part of the public power, also within a system of distribution of jurisdictions established by the constitution.

These three forms of distribution and limitation of state powers bring in constitutional matters, and necessarily lead, when adopted by a state, to a system of judicial review to control the illegitimate invasions or interferences of one of such powers in the sphere reserved to the other. That exists, more or less in the constitutional system of the Western World today, because these countries have written and rigid constitutions with a formal declaration of fundamental rights and have either a federal organization or other systems of political decentralization.

In the constitutional system of the United Kingdom there is, on the contrary, no entrenched Bill of Rights, though the judicial protection of fundamental rights cannot imply the invalidation of acts of Parliament. No distinction is made between constituent and constituted powers due to the absence of a written constitution and the principle of sovereignty and supremacy of Parliament, though there is no control over the constitutionality of Parliamentary acts. Finally, the constitutional system is a unitarian one, with no power distributed in territorial units that could restrain the powers of Parliament, though there is no control of constitutionality of the vertical distribution of power.

III. SUBMISSION OF THE STATE TO THE LAW

The second main feature of the concept of the *État de droit* is the submission of the state to the law, which implies that all the actions of the public bodies of a given state and its authorities and officials must be carried out subject to the law and within the limits set by the law. Hence, there is the expression state according to the rule of law or in the Continental sense *État de droit*.

This principle is, perhaps, one of the main features of legal system today, although there are certainly as many interpretations as there are legal systems and even authors. It is also referred to by various expressions: For instance as we said, in the Continental and Latin–American legal systems, this principle of the submission of the state to the law is commonly identified with the "principle of legality"; in the American system, with the whole idea of constitutionalism or government under the law; and in the British constitutional system by the classical expression "rule of law."

All these expressions ultimately mean that state bodies should be subject to the law, although it is certain that these assertions do not always have the same meaning and scope in every system.

For instance, Sir Ivor Jennings said that the rule of law or government according to law, means "that all power came from the law and that no man, be he King or Minister or private person, is above the law."[77]

But, we may ask what about the sovereign, and in the case of the British constitution, what about Parliament? Jennings referred to "the Government according to law", and we could ask: does he include Parliament in that expression?, can we say that the whole principle of the state according to the law or submitted to the law, that is to say, that all power of state bodies came from the law, is also applicable to the British constitutional system? Or is it true that in general terms, the rule of law in the British legal system is rather a principle related to government, in the sense that the executive must be enforced by the courts, and is not a principle related to Parliament?

1. The Sovereign and the Law

We think we can start our approach to the analysis of this principle of the submission of the state to the law, as one of the main features of modern constitutionalism, by following the statement made by Prof. H.L.A. Hart in his book, *The Concept of Law*, when he said:

> Whenever there is law, there is a sovereign incapable of legal limitation.[78]

Consequently, in all modern legal systems, we can distinguish two powers: that of the constituent, that is to say, the sovereign body, and that of the constituted, formed by all the state organs. This is, as we have seen, one of the main consequences of the principle of limitation of state power: the division in a given society between the constituent and the constituted power, bearing in mind that the constituent power is in the hands of the sovereign, who exercises it with no legal limitation

---

77 I. JENNINGS, *Magna Carta*, London 1965, p. 9.

78 H.L.A. HART, *The Concept of Law*, Oxford 1961, p. 70. On p. 65 asserts: "in every society where there is law there is a Sovereign" ... "everywhere the existence of law implies the existence of such a. sovereign."

whatsoever, and that all the constituted powers are, on the contrary, limited above all by the rules laid down by the sovereign or constituent body. That is why this sovereign said Hart, "makes law for his subjects and makes it from, a position outside any law." Therefore, "there are, and can be, no legal limits on his law–creating powers." He concluded by saying "the legally unlimited power of the sovereign is his definition."[79]

In similar terms, C.M. McIlwain, speaking on the sovereign said: "it is the highest body legally able to make rules for the subject, and itself free of the law."[80]

If we therefore accept this theory, and the principle that in all legal order there is a sovereign not submitted to the law or legal limitations, how can we talk about the *État de droit* or the state submitted to the law?

This question, leads us again to the problem of sovereignty and the sovereign and in particular, to the task of identifying within the bodies and organs of the state, which one is the sovereign and therefore, not subjected to the law.

In a democracy, as Austin stated and this is in the essence of the *État de droit* it is not the elected representatives who constitute or form part of the sovereign body but the electors. Hence in England, Austin said, "speaking accurately, the members of the House of Commons are merely trustees for the body by which they are elected and appointed: and consequently the sovereignty always resides in the king's peers and the electoral body of the Commons." Similarly, he held the opinion that in the United States, sovereignty of each state of the Federal Union, "resides in the state's government as forming one aggregate body, meaning by a state's government not its ordinary legislature but the body of citizens which appoints its ordinary legislature."[81]

With regard to this distinction in a democracy, between the sovereign itself, the people, and the organs of the state, the Germans have made a useful distinction between what they choose to call the sovereign and the sovereign organ. (*Trager der Staatgewalt* or *Staatorgan*).[82] The sovereign that is to say the electoral body, has no legal limitations as a constituent power, but the sovereign organs not only have limitations imposed on them by the constituent power in the constitution, but are also subject to various types of control, even the political one by the same people who set them up, throughout for instance, by referendum.

In this perspective, we must again consider the concept of parliamentary sovereignty. In this respect, Hart points out the following alternative:

> There could only be legal limits on legislative power if the legislator were under the orders of another legislator whom he habitually obeyed; and in that case he

79 *Idem*, p. 64–5.

80 C.M. MCILWAIN, *Constitutionalism and the Changing World*, Cambridge 1939, p. 31.

81 J. AUSTIN, *The Province of Jurisprudence Determined* (ed. H.L.A. HART), London 1954 Lec. VI, p. 230, 231, 251, quoted by H.L.A. HART, *op. cit*., p. 72.

82 C.M. MCILWAIN, *op. cit*., p. 31.

would no longer be sovereign. If he is sovereign he does not obey any other legislator and hence there can be no legal limits on his legislative power.[83]

And that is, precisely, the main question. Is the legislative organ legally bound to observe constitutional restriction imposed by a constituent power, that is to say, by the people as sovereign? In that case, the legislative body would not then be the sovereign but only the sovereign organ, Conversely is the legislative body in a state, free of the Law and therefore with no constitutional or legal limits to its power because it is the only body that established the law of a country, without legal restriction? In this case it would be the sovereign itself.

We must generally accept that in the modern world, almost all legal systems establish legal limitations on the exercise of legislative organ power, normally incorporated in a written and rigid constitution, and do not identify the sovereign with that legally limited legislator or Parliament but rather with the people as an electoral body.

"Austin himself did not identify the sovereign with the legislature even in England" Hart said. This was his view although the queen in Parliament is, according to normally accepted doctrine, free from legal limitations on its legislative power, and so is often cited as a paradigm of what is meant by "a sovereign legislature" in contrast with Congress or other legislatures limited by a 'rigid' constitution."[84]

But in spite of this general principle of the sovereignty of Parliament in the British constitution in the legal state perspective as state subjected or submitted to law, even in the United Kingdom as a democracy, we must admit that the sovereign is in fact not really Parliament but the people of this country, as an electoral body. And that the real difference between the British constitution and the other constitutional systems in the world, is that of the degree of delegation of sovereign power given by the people to the legislative organ, in other words, "the manner in which the sovereign electorate chooses to exercise its sovereign power."[85]

Professor Hart pointed out the distinction in the following passages from his book:

> In England, ... the only direct exercise made by the electorate of their share in the sovereignty consists in their election of representatives to sit in Parliament and the delegation to them of their sovereign power. This delegation is, in a sense, absolute since, though a trust is reposed in them not to abuse the powers thus delegated to them, this trust in such cases is a matter only for moral sanctions, and the courts are not concerned with it, as they are with legal limitations on legislative power.[86]

By contrast, Hart added:

> In the United States, as in every democracy where the ordinary legislative is legally limited, the electoral body has not confined its exercise of sovereign power to the election of delegates, but has subjected them to legal restrictions. Here the electorate may be considered an

83 H.L.A. HART, *op. cit.*, p. 65.

84 *Ibid*, p. 72.

85 *Ibid*, p. 72.

86 *Ibid*, p. 73.

> "extraordinary and ulterior legislature" superior to the ordinary legislative which is legally "bound" to observe the constitutional restrictions and, in cases of conflict, the courts will declare the acts of the ordinary legislature invalid. Here then, in the electorate, is the sovereign free from all legal limitations which the theory requires.[87]

Then we can conclude by saying that this principle of the *État de droit* or of the state according to the law, implies that the sovereign body which has no legal limitations, can only be the people as electorate, and therefore that all state organs or bodies are subject to the law.[88] And law here means not only what we call in the continental systems "formal law", that is to say, a statute or act of Parliament, but also all the rules that constitute the legal order, in its hierarchical frame work with the constitution as the supreme norm or *grundnorm*.

In the constitutional systems with written constitutions, therefore when we referred to the state according to or subject to the law, in the word law, we must include all the sources of the legal order: the constitution itself and all the other norms deriving there from. On the contrary, the sense of the term "law" in the expression "rule of law" in the constitutional systems with non–written constitutions, basically means, "rule of law as enacted by Parliament,"[89] which in principle, with its sovereignty delegated by the sovereign has no legal limits on its activity.

And we say in principle, because in spite of everything that is said about the unlimited, absolute, omnipotent, all–powerful or unrestrained powers of Parliament that we find in almost all written works about constitutional law in Britain, it must be admitted that Parliament has in fact lot of limitations, precisely those that have kept the British constitution more or less unaltered since the end of the Glorious Revolution and the Declaration of Rights in 1689.

Lolme's famous statement that "Parliament can do everything but make a woman a man and a man a woman",[90] although not entirely impossible nowadays, is no more than an exaggeration tending to mean that Parliament has no legally entrenched limits upon its actions, because of the absence of a written and rigid constitution. But it does not mean that there could be arbitrariness in the exercise of Parliamentary Powers, and that in certain aspects, in political practice, there are absolutely no limits over Parliaments.

Firstly, there are some Acts of Parliament that can be considered at least from the perspective of constitutional law, as "constituent documents" limiting parliamentary action. In this respect, J.D.B. Mitchell qualified as "constituent documents" the Acts of Union of 1707 and the Ireland Act of 1800, even though the limitations imposed by them upon Parliament –he said–, are established "in such a way that any infringement of them is improbable."[91] He also mentions as limits upon Parliament, those established by convention, that is to say, habits of thought which are the prod-

---

87 *Ibid*, p. 73.

88 J.D.B. MITCHELL, *Constitutional Law*, Edinburgh 1968, p. 62.

89 G. WINTERTON, "The British Grundnorm: Parliamentary Supremacy re–examined", *The Law Quarterly Review*, 92, 1976, p. 596.

90 I. JENNINGS, *Parliaments*, Cambridge 1961, p. 2.

91 J.D.B. MITCHELL, *op. cit.*, p. 69–75.

uct of Parliamentary life. Like that related to the "doctrine of mandate" which states that a government which has lost general support in the country should not force major legislation through Parliament shortly before an election, even though such legislation may have been in its electoral programme.[92]

There are, moreover, limits in political practice, imposed y Parliament itself, that undoubtedly bind other Parliaments, in such a way that Parliament cannot reverse what a previous Parliament had done. For instance, one cannot imagine that Parliament could reverse the Statute of Westminster 1931, which limits the power of Parliament to legislate over a dominion without its consent;[93] nor can one imagine that Parliament could reverse the acts granting independence to the dominions or territories overseas and thus try to take away their independence.[94]

In the same context, discussions have taken place concerning the primacy of European community law in relation to domestic statutes, both before and after the European Communities Act 1972 was passed. In accordance with that Act, Community law must have primacy over domestic law, and therefore, Parliament must not enact future acts that conflict with Community Law, unless it amends the European Community Act itself. While the United Kingdom remains a member of the Community, in would be difficult in practice, for Parliament to exercise its legislative power through acts contradicting the application of Community Law.[95]

On the other hand, we can also say that limitations upon arbitrary powers have been fixed in the national tradition of this country, and perhaps it has been because of the absences of real threats against the constitution that the need to establish entrenched limits to the power of Parliament has not arisen.

As J.M. Snee pointed out in a Conference held in Harvard Law School on the occasion of the Bicentennial of John Marshall, in 1955:

---

92 *Ibid*, p. 56, 66, 67.

93 Section 4 of the Statute of Westminster, provides: "No Act of Parliament of the United Kingdom passed after the commencement of this Act shall extend, or be deemed to extend, to a Dominion as part of the law of that Dominion, unless it is expressly declared in that Act that that Dominion has requested, and consented to, the enactment thereof." *Cf.* C. TURPIN, *British Government and the Constitution*, London 1985, p. 27. In a contrary sense, Ilamish R. GRAY said that "The general tendency of constitutional lawyers is to reject the interpretation of section 4 which requires Parliament as a matter of law to act in a particular way for any particular purpose", in "The Sovereignty of the Imperial Parliament", *The Modern Law Review*, 23 (6), 1960, p. 647.

94 For example, The Zimbabwe Act, 1979, Section I (2) provides: "On and after Independence Day Her Majesty's Government in the United Kingdom shall have no responsibility for the government of Zimbabwe; and no Act of the Parliament of the United Kingdom passed on or after that day shall extend, or be deemed to extend to Zimbabwe as part of its law'. *Cf.* C. TURPIN, *op. cit.*, p. 27.

95 *Cf.* F.A. TRINDADE, "Parliamentary Sovereignty and the Primacy of European Community Law", *The Modern Law Review*, 35 (4), 1972, p. 375–402; S.A. DE SMITH, "The Constitution and the Common Market: a tentative appraisal", *The Modern Law Review*, 34 (6), 1971, p. 597–614; H.W.R. WADE, "Sovereignty and the European Communities", *The Law Quarterly Review*, 88, 1972, p. 1–5.

No British Parliament today would dare to put into practice the statement made by Lord Chancellor Northington in 1766 during the debate on the repeal of the Stamp Act:

Every Government can arbitrarily impose laws on all its subjects; there must be a supreme dominion in every state: whether monarchical, aristocratic, democratic, or mixed. And all the subjects of each state are bound by the laws made by government.

Nonetheless, the absolute supremacy of Parliament remains the orthodox doctrine of English constitutionalism, as expressed by Sir Hartly Shawcross in a speech reported in *The Times* 13 May 1946:

Parliament is sovereign; it can make any laws. It could ordain that all blue–eyed babies shall be destroyed at birth; but it has been recognised that it is no good passing laws unless you can be reasonably sure that, in the eventualities which they contemplate, these laws will be supported and can be enforced.

The English, of course, with an irritating but sublime confidence in their institutions are sure that no Parliament would so act.[96]

This confidence is largely justified in the United Kingdom even though there is no judicial review or control of the constitutionality of acts of Parliament, mainly because of the continuity of constitutional rule in the last three hundred years. Also because in spite of the absence of judicial review of Statutes as Professor A. Goodhart pointed out twenty years ago,

Judges, however, usually manage to get their own way: The House of Lords has been able to attain some of the same results which in the United states, are achieved by the first ten amendments. By a convenient fiction it assumes that Parliament always intends that its statutes will accord with natural justice; no statute will therefore be constructed to be retrospective or to deprive a person of a fair hearing or to prevent freedom of speech unless Parliament has so provided in the most specific terms.[97]

Accordingly, one can agree that some kind of limitation upon parliamentary power to enact legislation, in the United Kingdom has been developed by means of judicial interpretation, based on presumptions. So, as Prof. J. D. B. Mitchell said:

A statute is presumed, in the absence of clear words to the contrary, not to take away property without compensation, not to exclude the jurisdiction of the court, not to be retrospective, not to impose taxation.[98]

It has also been considered that precisely through such presumptions, effective protection can be given to fundamental rights and liberties, and therefore, arguments had arisen in the sense that with this presumptions of interpretation it is uncertain that the enactment of a formal Bill of Rights as part of English law would achieve better protection of traditional liberties. On the contrary, T.R.S. Allan said,

A common law presumption which commands the loyalty of the judges is as powerful an instrument for interpreting legislation so as to safeguard individual liberties as an enacted Bill of Rights.[99]

---

96 J.M. SNEE, S.J. "Leviathan at the Bar of Justice", in A.E. SUTHERLAND (ed.), *Government under Law*, Cambridge, Mass 1956, p. 106–107.

97 A.L. GOODHART, "Legal Procedure and Democracy", *The Cambridge Law Journal*, 22,1, April 1964, p. 52. *Cf.* J.D.B. MITCHELL, *op. cit.*, p. 13.

98 J.D.B. MITCHELL, *op. cit.*, p. 66.

However, in most other countries, the people or the electorate sovereign do not unluckily always have the confidence English people have in their own legislative organ or in presumptions of interpretation. On the contrary, experience abroad has shown that it has been precisely because of the actions of Parliaments, dominated by circumstantial majorities, that the worst attacks against human rights have been committed. On the other hand, in other countries the sovereign does not unluckily fear fictions or presumptions, duly applied, as a means of judicial protection of human rights. Whereas the majority of other countries today[100] feels the need to establish a written and rigid constitution, with an entrenched declaration of fundamental rights and liberties, precise dispositions for the limitation and distribution of state powers, mainly of the legislator and of the executive, and giving judges substantial power of control over the submission of all state organs to the constitution and to the law. From there comes the concept of the legal state.

2. The Law and the Legal Order

As we said at the beginning, in this expression, *État de droit* or state according to the law, or simply "the rule of law" mainly in legal systems with written constitutions the world "law" must be understood, not only in the sense of acts of Parliaments, Congress or legislative bodies, that is to say, Statutes in English terminology, but in the broader sense of legal order, comprising all the norms that regulate a given society according to its political constitution. In the same broader sense the expression "principle of legality" used in continental law, as equivalent to the rule of law, must be understood.

Therefore, "legality", in contemporary constitutional law is not only the submission to "formal law" as an act passed by the legislator, as it used to be in the last century in relation to administrative actions and as a consequence of the principle of the supremacy of the law, but means today submission to law as the legal order, including, the constitution and other deriving sources of law. Furthermore, in the contemporary world, the rule of law or the principle of legality not only refers to the submission of the executive to law controlled by the courts, but also the submission of all the state organs to the laws that regulate its functioning. In this sense, the principle of legality or the rule of law applicable to Parliament or to the legislative body, in systems with written constitution, are the rules contained in that constitution.

However, as we said from the historical point of view, the principle of legality in continental Europe was understood in the restricted sense. It was considered that, if the state was to be subject to the law, "law" in this expression was understood in its formal sense to mean an act issued by the legislator, considered to be the body representing the people, and as the expression of the general will.

---

99 T.R.S. ALLAN, "Legislative Supremacy and the Rule of Law: Democracy and Constitutionalism", *The Cambridge Law Journal*, 44, (1), 1985, p. 135.

100 With the exemption of the United Kingdom, New Zealand and Israel, all other countries of the world have written constitutions. *Cf.* O. HOOD PHILLIPS, *Reform of the Constitution*, London 1970, p. 4; F.M. AUBURN, "Trends in Comparative Constitutional Law", *The Modern Law Review* 35 (2), 1972, p. 129.

In this sense, the law as an act of the legislative body, was what Locke used to define the liberty of man under the law: He said:

> The liberty of man in society is to be under no other legislative power but the established, by consent, in the commonwealth; nor under the dominion of any will or restraint or any law, but what that legislative shall enact according to the trust put in it.[101]

Also, law, as the expression of the general will, in Rousseau's terminology was that enacted by the legislator.[102]

In this sense, the French Declaration of the Rights of Man and Citizen of 1789 was drafted and in which article 6 states the following:

> The Law is the expression of the general will; all citizens have the right to participate personally, or through their representatives, in its formation.[103]

Undoubtedly, in France during the last century (19th century) and throughout the present one (20th century), in general this restricted sense has generally been the one of the term "law" referred to the principle of legality

For instance, Raymond Carré de Malberg, one of the most important and classical constitutional writers of the beginning of this century, wrote the following, about the formal criteria for the definition of law:

> The parliamentary act of legislation resembles the work of an organ enjoying, in regard to the formulation of the laws, an exclusive special power, and in this sense it constitutes an act of the state power.

And he added,

> In the assembly of the deputies representing the Nation, the citizens themselves, all the citizens, in their capacity as constituent members of the nation are represented and thus participate in making laws.[104]

In this tradition, the law, as an expression of the general wills enacted by Parliament, was the fundamental guarantee of liberty. Moreover, the laws proposed for the limitation of power at the time of the beginning of the *État de droit* and after the French Revolution, were not as far as their contents were concerned, the statutes or laws usually approved by today's Parliaments, but "laws of liberties"[105] that is to say, laws designed to enable the members of the social body to evolve freely mainly because of the fact that the state had, as its main function, to enable the exercise of

---

101 J. LOCKE, *Two Treatises of Government* (ed. Peter Laslett), Cambridge 1967, Chapter 4.

102 J.J. ROUSSEAU, *Du Contrat Social* (ed. Ronald Grimsley), Oxford 1972, Book II, Chap V, p. 136–; Book III, Chap IV, p. 163.

103 See in W. LAQUEUR and B. RUBIN, *The Human Rights Reader*, 1979, p. 119. *Cf.* G. DE RUGGEIRO, *The History of the European Liberalism*, Boston 1967, p. 67.

104 Carré DE MALBERG, *La loi, expression de la volonté générale*, 1931, quoted by M. LETOURNEUR and R. DRAGO, "The Rule of Law as Understood in France", *American Journal of Comparative Law*, 7, 1958, p. 148.

105 E. GARCÍA DE ENTERRÍA, *Revolución francesa y administración contemporánea*, Madrid 1972, p. 16.

liberties by the citizens. That was the essence of liberalism in its political perspective, and in this regard, the Declaration of the Rights of Man and the Citizen stated:

> The aim of every political association is the preservation of the natural and inalienable rights of Man; these rights are liberty, property, security and the resistance to oppression.
>
> Liberty consists of the power to do whatever is non injurious to others; thus, the enjoyment of natural rights of every man has for its limit, only those that assure other members of society the enjoyment of those same rights; such limits may be determined by the law.[106]

This restricted meaning of the term law, as a formal law, in the definition of the principle of legality has been followed in contemporary times by French administrative writers[107] even though some followed the broader sense of the law, as "legal order", in the definition of the principle of legality[108] or of what Hauriou once called the *bloc legal* or *bloc de la legalite*[109].

In any event, the reason for this narrow sense of the law regarding the principle of legality in France, even in modern times and in spite of the written constitutions adopted by that country since 1791, is that it has normally been formulated in relation with the control of the executive or administration, due to the traditional concept in France of the supremacy of the law, and also to the traditional absence of any protection given to the people against legislative actions contrary to the constitution[110] with the exception of the recent development of the control of the constitutionality of laws by the constitutional Council.

In effect, with the development of the judicial control of the constitutionality of laws in France, thanks to the functioning of the constitutional Council and its recent decisions, and with the spreading of the American and Austrian models of judicial review of the constitutionality of legislative acts in legal systems with written constitutions, the difference between the constitution, as constituent rule and the law, meaning act of Congress or of the legislative power, subordinate to the former, is now accepted, and with it, the expansion of the principle of legality or rule of law.

In this perspective, the acts of the legislative body are *per se* derivative norms of the constitution and therefore subordinate to it. Consequently, the rule of law or the principle of legality in the contemporary *État de droit* also comprises the "rule of the constitution" or the "principle of constitutionality", and therefore those acts issued in direct execution of the constitution are submitted to it and can be controlled; hence the judicial control of the constitutionality of laws.

Now, two things we must pick up from what we have said:

---

106 Arts. 2 and 4. See in W. LAQUEUR and B. RUBIN, *op. cit.*, pp. 118–119.

107 Ch. EISENMANN, "Le droit administratif et le principe de legalité", *Etudes et documents*, Conseil d'Etat, N° 11, Paris 1957, p. 25–40; N. LETOURNEUR and R. DRAGO, *loc. cit.*, p. 149.

108 A. DE LAUBADERE, *Traité elémentaire de droit administratif*, Paris, N° 369; G. VEDEL, *La summission de l'administration a la loi* (extrait de la *Revue Al Ouanoun Wal Igtisad*, 22e année, Le Caire) no. 26, 31, 47, 58, 94, 165, 166, quoted by Ch. EISENMANN, *lot.cit.*, pp. 26–27.

109 Ch. EISENMANN, *loc. cit.*, p. 26.

110 A. TUNC, "Government under Law: a Civilian View" in Arthur E. SUTHERLAND (ed.), *Government under Law*, Cambridge, Mass 1956, p. 43.

First, that the principle of legality or rule of law in our context is referred to the state, namely to all state organs and powers, and not only to one mainly the executive or administrative power. As a result in a state with a written constitution, the legislative body is also bound by the principle of legality or the rule of law, in the sense that its activities are legally limited and, therefore, it can also be judicially controlled in most countries as is the administration.

Second, we must also stress that in the expression principle of legality or rule of law, the term "law" must be understood in the broader sense of legal order and not in the formal sense of act of Parliament or statute, thus comprising the constitution itself, the formal laws, and all the norms established in a legal system deriving from the constitution.

This approach leads us to the need to identify the basic trends of a legal system to determine which norms are applicable to each organ of the state, in other words, to establish the confines of the legality to which the various organs of the state are submitted.

In this sense, we must say above all that in all legal systems[111] in general, a distinction between those rules which form the constitution itself, as a higher positive law, and on the other hand, those provisions or rules of law which may be made by an authority delegated by the constitution exists and must exist. In other words, a distinction must be established between constituent law and ordinary legislation.

As McIlwain pointed out when referring to Bodin's thoughts on the matter:

> There is and there must be, in a every free state, a marked difference between those laws which a government makes and may therefore change, and the one which make the Government itself. The Government... is "free of the law" (said Bodin)... but by this he meant free only of the ordinary laws which the government itself has made or may make. He does not include among these laws, the fundamental principle of the constitution under which the government itself comes into being, which defines and sets bounds to the supreme organ in the government so created... The... supreme authority established and defined by a fundamental law is bound absolutely by that law, though he is free of all other laws.[112]

This distinction between constitutional rules of law and ordinary legislation, we stress, is of a fundamental character in modern constitutionalism, mainly of course, in written constitutional systems. If, as we have said, the principle of legality is that of the conformity or of the submission of all state acts to the law, in other words, the principle according to which all the activities of a state must conform to the Law, it is undoubtedly necessary to determine which is the rule of law which each act of the state must conform to. For this purpose, the rules of law that comprise a legal system, are deliberately or spontaneously, usually organized in a hierarchical way, so that there are norms of superior level that prevail over norms of inferior level.

---

111 G. MACCORMACK, "Law and Legal System", *The Modern Law Review*, 42 (3), 1979, p. 285–290: "Legal system" understood as a collection of rules of law that have in common their interrelation in a particular order, mainly hierarchical.

112 Ch. H. MCLLWAIN, *Constitutionalism and the Changing World*, Cambridge 1939, p. 73.

3. Hierarchical or Graduated Legal System and the Confines of the Principle of Legality

Kelsen's theory of a legal system as a hierarchy of norms is without doubt, a useful method for identifying the hierarchical relation between the rules of law composing a legal system. In this sense, each norm belonging to the system usually has its derivation in another norm, ending the chain of derivation in a *Grundnorm* or constitution, which is the ultimate reason for the existence of all the norms of the whole system.

When sneaking of "derivation" Kelsen referred to the mode of creation of norms, in the sense that a norm is always created according to a power established by another norm.[113]

Kelsen said:

> A plurality of norms or of rules of law constitute a unity, a system or an order when their validity depends on, in the final analysis, a unique rule or norm. This fundamental norm is the common source of validity of all the rules or norms that belong to the same order and form its unity. A rule of law thus belongs to a given order only when the possibility exists of making its validity depend on the fundamental norm that is on the foundation of this order.[114]

This theory of the graduated systemisation of the legal order in a hierarchical way, with the constitution at the apex was developed by Adolf Merkl, from the same so–called "school of Vienna" to which Hans Kelsen also belonged, mainly on the grounds of administrative law.[115] We refer to it, because it give us a good method of logical order for constructing a legal system containing the various normative levels involved in a legal order of any state at a particular point in time. It also provides us with a logical explanation for the formal validity of each of those normative levels. It also gives us the formal confines of the "legality" of each act of the state organs, related to the leveled position of each norm that is created in that legal system.

In effect, the positive law of any state, at a given point in time, consists not only of the laws as formal acts of Parliament, but also of other normative bodies, such as delegate legislation, regulations, customs, the general principles of law and a whole series of other rules, including case law, certain specific and individualized ones such as contracts, court judgments and various types of administrative acts and provisions. All these precepts that make up the legal order in force at a given time not only have different origins but also different ranks, and it is not a question of considering them as co–coordinated rules in juxtaposition.[116] On the contrary, every

---

113 H. KELSEN, *General Theory of Law and State*, trans. Wedberg, rep. 1901, p. 110 et seq., quoted by G. MacCormack, *loc. cit.*, p. 286.

114 H. KELSEN, *Pure Theory of Law*, Chap. IX; *Teoría pura del derecho*, Buenos Aires 1981, p. 135.

115 It was Adolf MERKL, from the same 'School of Vienna' who developed the legal system as a hierarchy of norms in the grounds of administrative law. See A. MERKL, *Teoría general del derecho administrativo*, Madrid 1935, p. 7–2. See also H. KELSEN, "La garantie juridictionnelle de la constitution (La Justice constitutionnelle)", *Revue du droit public et de la science politique en France et a l'ètranger,* Paris 1928, pp. 197–257.

116 H. KELSEN, *Teoría pura... cit.*, p. 147.

legal order has a hierarchical structure, with its rules distributed in various strata, more or less one above the other. But within this hierarchy, there must necessarily be a formal connection between the rules, because they are linked organically, despite their different origins and characteristics.

Consequently, the legal order cannot be interpreted as a mere inorganic and disorderly aggregate of components, or simply as a chance juxtaposition of rules. On the contrary, to fully understand the legal order of a state, all such components must be arranged in hierarchical order, so that they form a legal system, with various types of norms unified and related. That is to say, they must follow a systematic order, with relations of co–ordination and dependence between the different parts.

Now, as we have said, the principle, which establishes the relationship between all those legal rules of such varied origin, rank and scope, shaping them into a system, is the existence of a common basis of validity, in the form of a fundamental or superior rule. Thus, a set of rules of law constitutes a relatively independent legal system when the justification or validity of them all has its derivation in a single rule, on which they are all formally based. And this single rule is referred to, in relation to all the others, as the fundamental rule or the constitution.

This method of the construction of the legal order in force by means of a graduated system of rules is based on the fact that the creation of a legal rule is always founded on another legal rule. One can, therefore, speak of a superior rule and of an inferior one. For example, the establishment of ordinary laws or acts of Parliament is regulated by the constitution; the decision as to who is to enact delegate legislation and how it is to be enacted, is regulated by certain formal laws. Then judicial decisions and their procedural rules are subject to previous legal rules established in formal law and delegate legislation. Likewise, the validity rules of administrative acts are established in ordinary laws, delegate legislation and other general regulations, and so on.

Thus, the principle of the internal connection of a legal system consists of basing the validity of certain rules on the validity of others. According to this method, it can be said that each category of rules is based on others of higher ranking, and at the same time, serves as the basis for others of lower ranking. Consequently, the whole legal order in force constitutes a system, which is graduated in hierarchical structures, and in which each link depends on others while supporting others.

In accordance with this method, the validity of all the rules of a given legal order, ultimately, stems from the constitution, the latter being understood to mean the rule which regulates the whole structure of the legal system, which is at the apex of the legal order and on which, finally, the latter is based.

This method referring to the forms of submission of state organs and activities to the rule of law is not only applicable to legal orders with written constitutions, but also applies to those systems with unwritten constitutions. In the former, the application of the theory of the graduated or hierarchical system of rules is evidently clear, precisely because a formal constitutional document established as a supreme constituent rule exists. Whereas in other legal systems without written constitutions the process of systemization of the legal order is much more complicated, and that is why the legal system here consists of an amalgam of heterogeneous rules, established in statutes and common law,[117] which are applied by courts as rules of law, also including ancient laws enacted centuries ago, conventions, delegate legislation and so on.

In either case, the formal systemization of a legal order is nevertheless indispensable to the determination of the scope of application of the law to state bodies, because in both cases, situations very often arise in which two provisions, antagonistic in their content, apparently claim to be in force. In such cases it will always be necessary to find out which of the two is in force, to determine which one ranks higher or lower in the event of conflicts between two or more rules of law, which appear to be in force, and which state body is competent to decide which one is in force and which one is not.

In short, to solve the issue of the formal validity of the precepts applied to state bodies, it is necessary to formally systematize the whole set of rules of law in a unified structure, from the logical point of view. And that is precisely the reason why the method of the graduated system of rules of law provides an appropriate tool.

With this method, in the overall analysis of the legal order, it is possible to distinguish between those acts of state whose execution is immediately related to the constitution, that is to say, which are issued directly on the basis of constitutional powers, and those, whose execution is not directly related to the constitution and which are actually issued on the basis of powers that establish rules of law inferior to the constitution.

Among the acts immediately related to the constitution are, primarily, the "formal laws", that is to say, acts of Parliament issued in accordance with the provisions of the constitution, as well as formal acts of a legislative nature, drawn up by the politically decentralized territorial entities. For example, in a Federal state, there are the laws issued by the legislative bodies of the member states of the Federation; or the formal acts, also of a legislative nature, of the local and municipal authorities, when the latter have political autonomy.

In all such cases, the laws as formal acts of the legislative bodies constitute a direct exercise by them of a competence contained in the constitution of the state itself. Therefore, they are produced on the basis of a competence established in the constitution and exercised in direct execution of the constitution.

That is why we have said that in relation to acts of Parliaments, for instance, the rule of law that establishes limitations on its activities is the "rule of the constitution", in the sense that in a written constitutional system, the legislative body finds its confines of legality in the norms of the constitution. The principle of legality in relation to the legislative body, therefore, implies submission to the constitution, and judicial control over its acts can only be of a constitutional character.

---

117 "The law is today an amalgam of common law and statute law of such an interdependent kind that it is often difficult to say whether a particular result is determined by the statute or by ordinary case Law." P.S. ATIYAH, "Common Law and Statute Law", *The Modern Law Review*, 48, (1), 1985, p. 5.

In legal systems with written constitutions not only are the formal laws acts of direct execution of the constitution, but there are also acts of Parliament which are issued on the basis of attributions provided for directly in the constitution, and which are not defined as "formal laws" because they are not instruments regulating the conduct and activities of individuals, as is the case of normative parliamentary acts that regulate the organization and procedures of the legislature internally. They are what are called *interna corporis*, that is to say, acts that regulate the functioning of the Houses.

Parliament can also pass other acts, which are not "formal laws" nor acts with internal effects, and which are also issued on the basis of the direct execution of constitutional attributions. In many written constitutions, in effect, and because of the check and balance system of the separation of powers, a multitude of legislative interventions in executive activities has been established in a way that certain executive acts require, as a condition of validity, the approval of Congress or of the Legislative Assembly. That happens, for instance, in the appointment of some high ranking state officials in domestic administration or in the diplomatic corps; in contracting foreign loans or in the approval of various budget modifications. In many countries, the executive requires the approval, or the authorization of Congress, before taking any such actions.

All these acts of Parliament, even though they are not formal laws, enjoy the same formal hierarchy as the formal Law, in the sense that they are only submitted to the constitution, which regulates them. They are, therefore, subject to the principle of legality but in the sense of subjection to the constitution, and can also be judicially reviewed to enforce the constitutional rule to which they must be in accordance.

In these constitutional systems of written constitutions, this fundamental document also attributes in some cases direct powers to the head of state to exercise certain activities, which are not subject to regulation by the ordinary legislator. In such cases, there is the question of powers attributed by the constitution to the head of state, or of government, who exercises them, precisely, on the basis of those constitutional attributions, which can neither be regulated nor limited by the legislator through acts of Parliament.

Here it is a question of acts which normally concern the "government" in the political sense, and which are reserved for the head of state or of government. It is what is termed in European continental law "acts of government" or "political acts", more or less equivalent to the North American notion of "political questions", which, being acts of direct execution of the constitution, are not submitted to regulation by formal law, and are exercised by the head of state, based on the direct provisions of the constitution. Consequently, these acts of government also rank equal to formal laws, and they are only subject to what is established by the constitution, which determines its confines of legality.

Because of the traditional absence of judicial control of the constitutionality of state acts, and because of the limited power conferred upon the administrative judicial courts or tribunals in France and in other continental European countries, the doctrine of the *actes de gouvernement* or "political acts" as an exception to the principle of legality was developed during this century in the sense that they were not subject to judicial control by the administrative judicial courts.

In France, the decisions of the *Conseil d'État* declaring its incompetence to control such acts, led to the development of that doctrine, establishing a distinction between administrative action, which should be subject to judicial control, and governmental action, which was not subject to such control. This governmental action was progressively reduced to basically two fields: the acts of the head of state or of government in relation to the legislative body, for instance the power of the executive to submit bills to the legislature, and acts concerned with international relations, for example, the process of making or denouncing a treaty.[118] On the contrary, in a legal system with judicial review of the constitutionality of state acts, these "acts of government" if it is true that they would escape judicial review of the administrative judicial court because they are not subject to "formal law" and they are not administrative acts, they would nevertheless be subject to judicial control of the constitutionality. Here, again those acts of the head of state or of government are undoubtedly subject to the principle of legality, but here also legality means constitutionality (submission to the rule of the constitution). Therefore, if there were no system of judicial review of constitutionality, ordinary courts for administrative judicial control acts would declare their incompetence to control these on the grounds of unconstitutionality and not because they would have been an exception to the rule of law. Here again, in relation to each state act, the question is of the definition of the confines of what legality means to them, so as to establish its validity conditions.

In addition to the so called "acts of government" within the acts of the head of state or of government, in direct execution of the constitution, we can also add the so–called "decree laws", which rank equal to the "formal law" and which are produced in those cases in which the constitution attributes certain legislative powers to the executive power, that is to say, to the head of state. In such cases it is not simply a matter of delegating legislation but it is a question of acts with the force of "formal law", as far as their rank and content are concerned, and not issued by the ordinary legislator or by Parliament, but by the head of state or of government.

By virtue of their legislative content, these are normative acts of government which are also issued in direct execution of the constitution, on the basis of power established directly by the constitution, or on some occasions, delegated by Parliament in accordance with the provisions of the constitution. In such cases, the Decree–laws have the same hierarchy as ordinary formal Laws; although, by virtue of their content, ordinary formal law enacted by Parliament could replace them.

In all these cases, acts issued by constitutional bodies are acts in direct execution of the constitution and are, therefore, submitted only to the constitution. The principle of legality of the *État de droit*, that is to say, the necessary submission of state bodies to the law, as far as these constitutional bodies and acts issued in execution of the constitution are concerned, is tantamount to submission to the constitution. As we have already said, in these cases, "legality" is equivalent to "constitutionality" for Parliament and for the head of state, or government, in other words, submission

118 A. TUNC, "Government under Law: a Civilian View", *loc. cit.*, pp. 46–47.

to the constitution, or action in conformity with the rules established by the constitution and within constitutional limits.

Nevertheless, in the formal systematisation of the legal order, within this graduated system of production of rules and their execution, apart from all those acts issued in direct execution of the constitution, the rest of the state bodies, particularly in the administrative and judicial field, exercises its powers not in direct execution of constitutional rules, but rather in direct execution of the "legislation", that is to say of the formal laws or acts of parliament and even acts of government or decree–laws issued by the appropriate constitutional bodies, in turn, in direct execution of the constitution.

Thus, all administrative activities are ultimately acts in immediate execution of the "legislation", and mediate execution of the constitution, that is to say, in direct execution of the "legislation" and indirect execution of the constitution.

Consequently, the extent of the administration's submission to legality in the *État de droit* is greater than that of the submission to the rule of law of the supreme state bodies. Congress or Parliament is submitted to the constitution and also when the head of state or of government issues an act of government, he is only restricted by the constitution; whereas the administrative bodies and authorities are involved in a much more extensive area of legality, since they are submitted to the "legislation" and execute it. That is why in this field the principle of legality has taken on the meaning it normally has in relation to administrative action in the contemporary state.

This approach to the graduated system of legal order for the analysis of legal systems, as we have said, has enormous implications in the area of judicial control of the activities and actions of the state.

In effect, it would be no use formulating the principle of legality in the *État de droit,* in the sense of submission of the state to the rule of law, if some mechanism were not set up, whereby individuals could control the effective submission of state bodies to the law, by court action. This obviously leads us to the two major aspects of judicial review in the modern world, which are, of course, conditioned by the degree of execution of the acts of state vis–à–vis the constitution.

In effect, in those systems in which a written constitution exists, the maximum demonstration of the principle of legality is reflected in the establishment of two major systems of judicial control over the exercise of power: the control of constitutionality and the control of legality in the strictest sense of the term.

In the case of state acts issued in direct execution of the constitution, that is to say, acts of Parliament, such as statutes or *interna corporis*; or acts of the head of state or of government, such as acts of government, issued on the basis of powers granted directly and exclusively by the constitution, these must be subject to some system of judicial control of constitutionality for it, to be a *État de droit* in the fullest sense of the term.

It is to this end, for example, that constitutional tribunals have been set up in the European continental states, as constitutional bodies, with the basic aim of controlling the constitutionality of state acts issued in direct execution of the constitution.

The constitutionality of laws and acts as pertaining to the internal regulations of Parliament has been especially controlled, as well as that of acts of government and decree–laws.

It is not by chance that the countries in Europe in which the first constitutional tribunals were set up were precisely those in which the organization of the constitutional system was directly influenced by Kelsen's theory of a legal system as a hierarchy of norms. The precise purpose of these tribunals was to judge cases of unconstitutionality of state acts issued in direct execution of the constitution. That was the situation in Austria and Czechoslovakia in 1920, where the constitutions and legal systems of those countries were directly influenced by the doctrine of the Viennese School. But it was not until the nineteen–forties that constitutional tribunals were established in continental Europe, to judge the constitutionality of laws and acts of government, particularly those having the force of law.

On the other hand, we must stress that precisely because of the absence of a constitutional body entrusted with the control of the constitutionality of state acts in direct execution of the constitution, together with the expansion of the principle of legality in relation to administrative acts, this led, in many cases, to a distortion of the situation of the *État de droit*. Such distortion can be seen in the development of the previously mentioned doctrine of the "act of government" or "political act", aimed at excluding the judgment of the legality of certain state acts issued by the head of state from the competence of the administrative judicial courts. Thus, the famous doctrine of the "acts of government" in French law, or "political acts" in Italian or Spanish law, which was developed long before constitutional tribunals were established in those countries. As we have said, according to that doctrine, it was supposed that there were certain executive acts that, although improperly considered as administrative acts, were not, however, submitted to the control of legality by the administrative judicial courts. This was because they were considered to have been formulated initially for political reasons, or later, when the day of that doctrine was coming to an end, because it was considered that they referred to issues stipulated directly in the constitutions with reference to the relations between the different state powers or constitutional bodies, or to other states in the international order.

As we said, such acts were actually exempt from submission to administrative judicial control or from control of administrative legality, not because they were administrative acts issued for political reasons but because, contrary to what was asserted, they were not really administrative acts. In effect, they were acts of government issued in direct execution of the constitution, and the only control to which they could be submitted was the control of constitutionality, that means submission to the rule which was executed by their issuance, namely, the constitution itself. Since there was no control of the constitutionality of state acts in those countries, there could be no judicial control over such acts, which contributed to the distortion of the doctrine of the "act of government." In countries such as Spain and Italy, the subsequent establishment of control over the constitutionality of laws and executive acts with the force of laws resulted in the reduction or disappearance of the doctrine of the judicial immunity of political acts. They now come under the control of the constitutional tribunals.

In France, since there is no genuine control of the constitutionality of acts in execution of the constitution yet, the doctrine of the exemption of "acts of government" from judicial control still exists, giving rise to an area which is immune to the control of legality typical of the *État de droit*.

Now, in the United Kingdom legal system, in the absence of a written constitution, in the sense of a formal document of the nature of a fundamental law governing the basic principles of the actions of state bodies and establishing a set of entrenched rights and constitutional guarantees, there can be, of course, no judicial control over the constitutionality of certain acts. Consequently, when there is no written constitution, in a graduated legal system, there is nothing in the nature of a fundamental rule or constitution to serve as a source of validity of lower–ranking laws.

In the absence of any such formal constitution serving as a fundamental law, as we have seen the sovereign act in the British system is precisely the act of Parliament; hence the principle of parliamentary sovereignty which implies that as Parliament is not submitted to any superior rule, it produces the superior rules itself. In this sense, an act of Parliament is not submitted to any other rule, and its constitutionality could not, therefore, be controlled with respect to any formal document.

Consequently, in the British legal system, a control of the constitutionality of acts of Parliament is inconceivable in the terms provided for in continental, European or American legal systems. Hence, the establishment of a precise hierarchy in the production of rules of law is also very difficult, since there is no such written constitution and finally the supreme rule is the rule of Parliament. Besides, there are no degrees of validity among statutes.[119]

Nevertheless, in relation to the legal order below the acts of Parliament we think a system of a graduated or hierarchical legal order can, in fact, be developed and that it is possible to establish a systematization more or less of the entire legal order, based, naturally, on the concept of the superiority of acts of Parliament.

In any case, apart from acts issued in direct execution of the constitution in graduated legal systems which have given rise to the systems of judicial control of constitutionality, it is evident that the principle of legality plays a more important role at the second level of execution of the legal order, that is to say, those state acts issued in direct execution of the "legislation, or in indirect execution of the constitution. Here the principle of legality has developed in the fullest sense of the term, particularly in connection with the administration, both in the continental European and in the United Kingdom legal systems, giving rise to the judicial control of the legality of administrative acts or action, and therefore, to administrative law itself.

But this principle of legality, mainly in legal systems with written constitutions implies, of course, not only that the executive or administrative power is subject to the rule of law, but that the other organs of the state, including the legislative organs, are also subject to the rule of law. Therefore, what the rule of law is all about, in

119 *Halsbury's Laws of England*, 4th Ed. London 1974, Vol. 8, p. 531.

relation to which each state organ is submitted, varies and has a different confine or ambit, depending on the position that each norm or state act has in the hierarchical legal system. That is why, for the legislator, legality means constitutionality or submission to the constitution; as for the head of the state, with regard to acts of government, legality also means subjection to the constitution. In such cases, they are adopted in direct execution of the constitution, without the interference of acts of Parliament, so that they are submitted only to the constitution.

4. Principle of Legality and the Executive

As far as executive and judicial powers are concerned, the principle of legality or the rule of law has a wider sense. It includes not only the constitution itself, but also all state acts with a general and normative character, and especially those of "legislative" level that include not only acts of Parliament, but also all other state acts with the same legal force, as are those acts of the head of state issued within its constitutional powers. In the principle of legality related to the executive all the other sources of legal rules that bind administrative action are also included as well as the general principles of law, or principles of natural justice that are to be observed by public administration.

In this respect, it is obvious, in the contemporary public legal systems, that the principle of legality in relation to the executive and to administrative of action, is in fact, of more importance.

However, in the evolution of the contemporary state, the principle of legality was traditionally referred to the submission of the administration to the law, in the sense of "formal law", that is to say, acts issued by Parliament, it being understood by this that public administration always had to act on the basis of a pre–existent rule of law.

But, in continental legal systems, this principle of legality originally confined to submission to the formal law has been expanded to the extent that the term "legality" has become synonymous to legal order, in the sense that in a graduated legal system, the administration must be submitted to all the superior rules governing its activities. In this context, therefore, law is not just law in the formal sense, but it also includes international treaties signed by the respective states, delegate legislation and other resolutions of a general nature, as well as decree–laws and any other normative sources of law applied to the administration, including, the general principles of law.

Naturally, this principle of legality referring to public administration has been particularly implemented by the establishment of a system of control of the administration through the courts, either the ordinary courts or special administrative judicial courts, and by the establishment of the principle of the responsibility of the state, particularly for damage caused to individuals by state actions.

In short, the principle of legality in relation to the executive implies the establishment of a system of judicial review of administrative actions; that is to say, it demands the establishment of a system of administrative justice to control the submission of public administration, precisely, to legality.

In this sense, in the *État de droit*, unlike the situation in absolutist regimes, the activities of the administration are subject to complete judicial supervision through the judicial mechanisms provided for in ordinary law, or established in a particular administrative law system, and implemented through actions granted to individuals, to control any legal infractions which may be committed by the administration itself.

Occasionally, the theory of discretionary powers opened a void in the principle of legality, but, little by little, the progressive judicial control of these discretionary acts has been allowed with the result that, despite the liberty granted to the administration to make decisions, such acts are also submitted to a judicial control of legality. They are no longer considered in any country as an exemption to the principle of legality as was originally thought mainly under French administrative law.

When granting discretionary powers, the law lives the administration certain amount of freedom to take the most convenient action or decision according to its own interpretation. But it has been accepted and established through the judicial control of administrative action, that discretionary power has limits, and cannot transform itself into arbitrariness. Therefore, various limits to the exercise of discretionary power have been identified in continental European administrative law, derived from the principles of proportionality, rationality, non–discrimination, equity and justice.

It has also been accepted that the use of discretionary powers by the administration cannot lead to the violation of the general principles of administrative procedure, in particular, those connected to the right to a fair due process of law, granting the general right to citizens to look for their own defence. A demonstration of this is the right to a hearing before an administrative action could be taken, so that the individual who may be affected by that such a decision could have the opportunity to express his position regarding the administrative action and argue his rights.

All these principles leading to limiting discretionary power, even though originated in case law, have frequently been formally established in various countries in formal laws relating to administrative procedures. Venezuela can serve as an example of this process of formalization of the limits to discretionary power. Its Administrative Procedures Act of 1981[120] for instance, states in article 12:

> *Art. 12*. When a norm of a Statute or of a general regulation issued by the Executive, leaves an administrative measure or decision to be made by the competent authority on his own understanding such a measure or decision must maintain due proportionality and adequacy with the facts and aims established in the norm, and follow all the procedural rules and formalities needed for its validity and effectiveness.

That is to say, when an administrative authority has been granted by an act of Congress or by a general executive regulation, enough liberty to take any measure or make any decision based on its own understanding of the circumstances and timing of the given action, it must, first, respect the principle of proportionality of the administrative action; second, it must seek the aims for which the discretionary powers

120 A.R. BREWER–CARÍAS, *El derecho administrativo y la Ley orgánica de procedimientos administrativos*, Caracas 1982, p. 379–414.

were granted; third, it must observe the due fitness of the facts within such rules established in the norm; and fourth, it must always respect the procedural steps required for the validity and effectiveness of the administrative action.

Thus, the first limit of the discretionary power in that law is the duty imposed by it on all administrative authorities to respect due proportionality between the facts that motivated the administrative actions, and the consequences established in the latter. In that respect, if the norm authorises the administrative organ, for example, to apply a fine or penalty measured against two extremes, in accordance with its appreciation of the gravity of the offence, the action, that is to say, the fine or penalty imposed must have some proportion with the actual facts which occurred and which causes the administrative action deriving from rationality justice and equity.

This principle of proportionality as a limit to discretionary power leads to another, the principle of equality and non discrimination, in the sense that if in relation to a given fact a measure has been taken or a decision has been made against an individual, the same measure or decision must be made against other individuals, if the facts coincide. Of course, this also implies that the principle of impartiality as a general principle of administrative action, is also a limit on discretionary power.

But the norm of the Venezuelan Administrative Procedures Act that we are referring to as an example, also establishes as a limit on discretionary power, the need for a administrative authority to try to attain when taking a measure or making a decision, the aims established in the norm when granting power to public administration. Any deviation in obtaining or pursuing those aims can lead to judicial control of the administrative action by means of illegality, though the so called *détournement de pouvoir* in French administrative law.

Moreover, that same article of the Venezuelan Administrative Procedure Act established, also as a limit upon discretionary powers, the due fitness of the actual facts that motivated an administrative action with the ones established in the particular norm. That means that public authority must first determine the fact that had occurred; second, it must prove them, through the usual or technical means required; and third, it must qualify them appropriately, and finally, the facts must coincide with the ones established in the norm authorising the action. All these steps must be taken in accordance with the already mentioned principles of equality, impartiality and justice, so that any violation thereof leads to illegality.

Finally, the norm states that in the use of discretionary powers by public administration the administrative organ must always respect the procedural steps normally required for the validity and effectiveness of the administrative action. Within these procedural rules, we must underline the right to defend oneself that must be guaranteed in all administrative actions and which derives from the constitution itself. This right of every citizen to look for his own defence leads in the Administrative Procedures Act of Venezuela, to the formal establishment of a few other and derivative rights of the individual vis–à–vis public administration. For instance, the right to be heard always before a decision can be made that affects his rights and interests; the right to participate in administrative procedures that could affect those rights and interests; the right to be formally and personally notified of every decision that may affect him; the right to have access to all official documents filed in the dossier concerned and the right to copy those documents; the right to present evidence before the public administration in one's own defense; and the right to be notified of the means of appeal or other actions that the individual can use for his defense whether administrative or judicial.[121]

Therefore, as we can deduce from this example of a formal establishment of limits on discretionary powers by statute and not only by means of case law, the principle of legality related mainly to administrative action, has expanded considerably. All such limits on the discretionary powers of the executive, although now established, as we have seen from the Venezuelan example in particular laws or statues, have undoubtedly been developed through judicial decisions, (case law), even in civil law legal systems.

Of course, in common law legal systems, these limits have also been established in case law, particularly through the principles of natural justice.[122]

All these systems have in common the exclusion of the consideration of discretionary power as an exemption of the principle of legality or the rule of law, as well as the acceptance that even in its discretionary power granted by law, administrative action is entirely submitted to the rule of law.

But in relation to this exemption to the principle of legality as it was treated in continental European legal systems, a few decades ago, the same can be said of so–called government or political acts.

As we have said, in continental Europe, certain acts of the executive, such as political acts, were traditionally seen as being exempt from submission to legality. Nevertheless, even though such acts cannot be considered as administrative acts, not only has the Legal state made an effort to gradually reduce the number of such political acts exempt from control, but with the establishment in continental Europe of constitutional tribunals, it has been possible, in some countries to control the constitutionality of such acts of government, as acts in direct execution of the constitution.

In short, all the activities of the executive must be submitted to the principle of legality and must, therefore, be submitted to judicial review. Because of this, it is possible to demand that the administration be held responsible for damages caused by its actions. Of course, when we say that all activities of the executive must be submitted to the law, this naturally also includes all the normative activities of the executive itself, such as, regulations and different forms of delegated legislation, which are also submitted to review by independent judicial bodies.

5. The Rule of Law and Dicey's Concepts

As we said at the beginning, in the United Kingdom legal system, what the continental European legal systems call the principle of legality is included under the general term of "rule of law." It is true that this "rule of law" generally means the same as the *État de droit* for continental states, that is to say, it is the laws that govern, not men.

---

121 *Ibid*, p. 112–118.

122 See in general, P. JACKSON, *Natural Justice*, London 1979, p. 224.

However, there is perhaps a radical historical difference between the two systems: whereas the *État de droit* came into being on the continent as a rational system substituting the *Ancien Régime*, the "rule of law", since monarchical absolutism was unknown in England, is directly linked to the medieval doctrine of the *Reign of Law* in the sense that law, whether it be attributed to supernatural or human sources, ought to rule the world.[123]

Therefore, as Professor E.C.S. Wade said, Dicey did not invent the notion of the rule of law[124] but was the first writer to systematize and analyse the principle. That is why we think it is impossible to refer to the rule of law in the United Kingdom, without referring in one way or another to Dicey's approach, which has tended to govern modern discussion, on the subject.[125]

According to Dicey's classical definition, the rule of law means three things: the absolute predominance of the law; equality before the law; and the concept according to which the constitution is the result of the recognition of individual rights by judges.

With regard to the first meaning, Dicey stated that by rule of law,

> We mean... that no man is punishable or can be lawfully made to suffer in body or goods except for a distinct breach of law established in the ordinary legal manner before the ordinary courts of the land. In this sense, the rule of law is contrasted with every system of government based on the exercise by persons in authority of wide, arbitrary, or discretionary powers of constraint.[126]

As Dicey himself stated, in this sense, the rule of law means:

> The absolute supremacy or predominance of regular law as opposed to the influence of the arbitrary power, and excludes the existence of arbitrariness of prerogative, or even wide discretionary authority on the part of the Government. Englishmen are ruled by the law, and by the law alone; a man may with us be punished for a breach of law, but he can be punished for nothing else.[127]

In relation to this first meaning of the rule of law, we must observe that, as we have said, discretionary powers granted to government by the law is not necessarily equivalent to arbitrariness, on the contrary the government itself has limits in its exercise.

We must also observe when considering this first meaning of Dicey's rule of law, that whilst it is true that the government lacks arbitrary power, it is clear, however, that that power lies on Parliament, since, unlike the legislative bodies of other countries, Parliament's powers are not limited by a constitution. Consequently, the British

---

123 W. HOLDSWORTH, *A History of English Law*, Vol. II, London 1972, p. 121. *Cf.* E.C.S. WADE, "Introduction" to A.V. DICEY, *An Introduction to the Study of the Law of the Constitution*, London 1973, p. xcii.

124 E.C.S, WADE, "Introduction", *loc. cit.*, p. xcii.

125 J.D.B. MITCHELL, *op. cit.*, p. 53.

126 A.V. DICEY, *op. cit.*, p. 188.

127 *Ibid,* p. 202. In this concept, regular law is understood to mean statute law and common law, but the former has supremacy over the latter.

Parliament, by virtue of its sovereignty, possesses, in principle, unlimited–powers, not only to establish general rules, but also individual rules with any content.

Arbitrary regulation is not, therefore, constitutionally excluded, although, in principle, it must take the form of an act of Parliament or be authorized by such an act. But bearing in mind government's factual supremacy over Parliament, because of the fact that the latter's decisions are determined by the former owing to the party system, the result is that the decision on measures is actually made, in the last resort, by the government, which may request action from Parliament, even after having taken such measures. Thus, for example, it has been said Parliament ratified and legalized in 1931 a series of illegal acts issued by the Cabinet with reference to the abolition of the gold standard. In this case, the arbitrary power of Parliament served to sanction illegal acts.[128]

According to Dicey, the rule of law also means legal equality. In this sense, Dicey wrote:

> We mean in the second place, when we speak of the rule of law as a characteristic of our country, not only that with us no man is above the law, but (what is a different thing), that here every man, whatever be his rank or condition, is subject to the ordinary law of the realm and amenable to the jurisdiction of the ordinary tribunals.[129]

However, in explaining this second meaning, he went further, also applying the concept to government officials. He said:

> It means, again, equality before the law, or the equal subjection of all classes to the ordinary law of the land administered by the ordinary law courts. The rule of law in this sense excludes the idea of any exemption of officials or other from the duty of obedience to the law which governs other citizens or from the jurisdiction of the ordinary tribunals.[130]

In this sense, Dicey's concept of the rule of law, excludes the idea of any exemption in favor of public officials or other individuals, and naturally also excludes any idea of administrative judicial special courts in the French manner.

As a consequence of this statement, is his famous mistaken approach to "administrative law", which concludes that "there can be with us nothing really corresponding to the "administrative law", *droit administratif* "or the "administrative tribunals" (*tribunaux administratives*) of France.[131]

Dicey really denounced what he understood French administrative law to be. He said that the *droit administratif* rested at bottom on various "leading ideas alien to the conceptions of modern Englishmen", and within which he referred to the idea:

> That in France, the government and every servant of the Government, possesses, as representative of the nation, a whole body of special rights, privileges, or prerogatives as against private citizens, and that the extent of these rights, privileges or prerogatives is to be deter-

128 I. JENNINGS, *The Law and the Constitution, cit.* p. 57–58

129 A.V. DICEY, *op. cit.*, p. 193.

130 *Ibid.* p. 202–203.

131 *Ibid.* p. 203.

mined on principles different from the consideration which fix the legal rights and duties of one citizen towards another.[132]

All these privileges and prerogatives referred to by Dicey lead to what he considered to be the main one in the French system: the existence of special administrative courts to judge public bodies and officials ranked in a separate system of judicature different to the judicial power, having at its apex not the *Court de Cassation* but the *Conseil d'État*.

It has long been realized in Great Britain that Dicey's picture of administrative law was wrong[133] and that legal equality does not mean that the state bodies would be submitted to the same laws applicable to ordinary citizens. As Professor J.D.B. Mitchell stated:

> While the subjection of officials to law is desirable, it does not follow that this should in all cases, or generally, be a subjection to the law which is applicable to the ordinary citizen" (because)... it is clear that the powers of government cannot be those of an ordinary citizen... and that as far as rights are concerned public bodies and public officials cannot be governed by the ordinary law.[134]

Therefore, if it is desirable that the executive must in principle be subject to the same law as that governing the citizens, this does not, of course, exclude the possible need for the government, in view of its very nature, to have special prerogatives and powers. What the principle of the rule of law actually requires is that the government be granted no unnecessary privileges or exemptions in relation to ordinary laws. In this respect, for example, the fact that the crown could not be taken to court on the grounds of responsibility constituted an unnecessary privilege, which was eliminated in 1947 by the Crown Proceeding Act.[135]

In any event, in relation to this second meaning of the rules of law as developed by Dicey, we can conclude by saying that it really implies that government bodies should be subject to the law. In this same sense, we can say based on the principle of the sovereignty of Parliament, that is to say, that Parliament, in its capacity as the legislature, is sovereign and exempt from any legal control, that the principle of the rule of law means, that all government actions must be carried out in accordance with the law. In particular, when applied to administrative or governmental authorities, it implies that all of such authorities, when issuing any act, must do so by means of an authorization granted in a law that, in general, must be understood to be an act of Parliament. In other words, the rule of law implies that any government act, which may affect some individual rights or liberties, must be carried out strictly under the authority of an act of Parliament.

---

132 *Ibid.* p. 336–337. "An individual in his dealing with the state does not, according to French ideas, stand on anything like the same footing as that on which he stands in dealing with his neighbor", p. 337.

133 H.W.R. WADE, *Administrative Law*, Oxford 1984, p. 25.

134 J.D.B. MITCHELL, *op. cit.*, p. 58.

135 H.W.R. WADE, *op. cit.*, p. 24.

But the principle of the rule of law does not consist solely of submission to formal law. It also implies, as we have seen, the need for the administrative authority to submit to the principles and rules which limit any discretionary power granted to the said authority by an act of Parliament. That is the reason why it has been said that the principle of the rule of law was developed in relation to the administration, on the basis of judicial limitations upon the powers which may have been granted to the administrative authorities by acts of Parliament.[136] The object of all this is to prevent and avoid abuse in the exercise of discretionary powers.

In addition to the foregoing, the principle of the rule of law, as a specific manifestation of the *État de droit* and of the principle of legality in the United Kingdom legal system, implies that claims brought by individuals against administrative and government acts and officials must be judged by the judicial authority, that is to say, by judges completely independent of the executive bodies. Naturally, the principle of legality does not necessarily require that these judicial bodies that control administrative actions be separate from the ordinary judicial bodies. What legality and the state according to law demand is that control be exercised by judicial bodies, and in the countries with common law systems particularly in the United States and the United Kingdom, disputes between the administration and individuals are settled by the ordinary law courts.[137]

Thus, contrary to the practice in the French system, in which disputes relating to the control of the legality of administrative action are brought before administrative courts organized separately from the judicial hierarchy, but independent of the government, in the British system, the right to have the public administration appear before ordinary courts and independent judges, in matters of control of legality, is one of the most important elements of the concept of the rule of law.

The third meaning of the rule of law according to Dicey is that the constitution was the result of the recognition of individual rights by judges, and therefore, that these rights were not the result of a written constitution.

Dicey explained this third meaning of the rule of law as follows:

> We may say that the constitution is pervaded by the rule of law on the grounds that the general principles of the constitution (as for example the right to personal liberty, or the right of public meeting) are with us the result of judicial decisions determining the rights of private persons in particular cases brought before the courts; whereas under many foreign constitutions the security (such as it is) given to the rights of individuals results, or appears to result, from the general principles of the constitution.[138]

In other words, he described this third meaning of his conception of the rule of law by saying that this expression

---

136 L.L. JAFFE and E.G. HENDERSON, "Judicial Review and the Rule of Law: Historical Origins", *The Law Quarterly Review*, 72, 1956, pp. 345–364. See in general, B. SCHWARTZ and H.W.R. WADE, *Legal Control of Government*, Oxford 1978, p. 350.

137 J.M. EVANS, *de Smith's Judicial Review of Administrative Action*, Fourth Ed., London 1980, p. 11.

138 A.V. DICEY, *op. cit.*, p. 195.

> May be used as a formula for expressing the fact that with us the law of the constitution, the rules which in foreign countries naturally form part of a constitutional code, are not the source but the consequence of the rights of individuals, as defined and enforced by the courts.[139]

We do not think that this third meaning can be sustained firmly nowadays. The rights of individuals that a state have to ensure and protect today are not only personal liberties such as free speech which Dicey was concerned with but rather, rights such as the protection of physical well–being, having a proper home, being educated, having social security, a proper environment, etc., that cannot be the creation of judge–made law, on the contrary it requires complex legislation.[140] That is to say, "the common law does not assure the citizens economic or social well being."[141]

Therefore, if it is true that ordinary courts continue to play a fundamental role in the protection of individual rights, it is also true that statutory regulations are required for the enforcement of such rights. Thus, they cannot only be the result of the courts enforcement but also undoubtedly of their establishment in acts of Parliament. Also, we have to bear in mind the primacy of statutory law over common law, thus the latter can always be modified by Parliament, and the most fundamental liberties may be removed by statute.

Thus, Dicey's faith in the common law as the primary legal means for the protection of citizen's liberties against the state has been superseded and the experience of many western countries with entrenched declarations of human rights imposing legal limits upon the legislature to infringe it, has proved to be of value.

Anyway, despite the well known expansion of Dicey's concepts, particularly in regard to his distrust of administrative law, this discipline widely developed in this country during the present century (20th century), and within its own rules, new concepts arose regarding the rule of law, always related to governmental action and more closely to the principle of legality developed in continental Europe.

In order to understand this change, it will suffice to recall here two of the new and recent approaches to the matter.

The first is the concept developed by Professor H.W.R. Wade in his well–known book on *Administrative Law*, in which he identified five different although related meanings of the rule of law. First, that all governmental action must be taken according to the law, in the sense that all administrative acts that infringe individual rights must be authorized by law. Second, that government should be conducted within a framework of recognized rules and principles that restrict discretionary power, in the sense that an essential part of the rule of law is that of a system of rules for preventing the abuse of such discretionary power. Third, that disputes as to the legality of acts of government are to be decided upon by courts that are wholly independent of the executive, which in this country are the ordinary courts of law.

---

139 *Ibid*, p. 203.

140 J.D.B. MITCHELL, *op. cit.*, p. 54–55.

141 E.C.S. WADE and G. GODFREY PHILLIPS, *Constitutional and Administrative Law*, London 1982, p. 89.

Fourth, that the law should be even–handed between government and citizen, in the sense that even though it cannot be the same for both, the government should not enjoy unnecessary privileges or exemptions from ordinary law. And fifth, outside the sphere of public administration, the rule of law means that no–one should be punished except for legally defined crimes, a principle that applies, however, to administrative action in the sphere of administrative sanctions.[142]

In another more descriptive perspective, Joseph Raz enumerated a few principles, which can be derived from the basic idea of the rule of law, which undoubtedly complement the previously mentioned view of Professor Wade. Those principles are as follows: All laws should be prospective, open and clear; laws should be relatively stable; the making of particular laws should be guided by open, stable, clear and general rules; the independence of the judiciary must be guaranteed; the principles of natural justice must be observed; the courts should have review powers over the implementation of those principles; the courts should be easily accessible; and the discretion of the crime prevention agencies should not be allowed to hinder the law.[143]

All these meanings or principles related to the concept of the rule of law, in the British constitutional system and since Dicey's conception, are, of course, mainly related to the activities of the executive or government, and mainly to administrative action. Parliament, because of its sovereignty, is not included in the principle.

Therefore, because of the absence of a written constitution and the already mentioned principle of parliamentary sovereignty, Parliament, has in fact no entrenched law to which it must be kept submitted. Thus, it has no legal limits upon its activities, and its acts cannot be judicially reviewed because no court has the power to control their constitutionality. Here lies the real difference, nowadays, between the concept of the rule of law in the British constitutional system and the principle of legality in the legal states of continental Europe and America.

In continental Europe and America, the concept of the principle of legality also includes the legislative in the sense that Congresses, General Assemblies or Parliaments are , in general, submitted to and limited by the constitution, established as a written and rigid higher law, and that submission is judicially controlled by ordinary or special courts with sufficient power in some cases, even to annul unconstitutional laws.

Up to now, we have referred to two principles of the *État de droit* in the contemporary world, that of the distribution and limitation of state powers, and that of the submission of all state bodies to the principle of legality or the rule of law.

Now we whish to refer to the third of the main features of the *État de droit* that of the establishment of an entrenched bill of rights normally in a written constitution, that historically has always been essential to the notion of the *État de droit* and, of course, to liberalism.

---

142 H.W.R. WADE, *op. cit.,* p. 22, 24.

143 J. RAZ, "The Rule of Law and its Virtue", *The Law Quarterly Review*, 93, 1977, p. 198–202.

IV. THE DECLARATION OF FUNDAMENTAL RIGHTS AND LIBERTIES

In effect, as we said, the third characteristic of the *État de droit* is the establishment of a set of fundamental rights and liberties, normally enumerated in a formal declaration of constitutional rank or in a written constitution, in an entrenched way and with the necessary guarantees and legal security to prevent its violation by the state itself.

In this sense, the first characteristic of this formal establishment of fundamental rights is that it is one of the main consequences of the already mentioned principle of the distribution of powers essential to the state according to law.

We have said that the distribution of power finally reveals itself in three ways: first, in a distribution of power between the citizen and the state; secondly, in a distribution of power between constituent and constituted powers; and thirdly, in a distribution of power within the constituted power in a horizontal or vertical way, giving rise to the classical separation of state powers or to a politically decentralised form of the state.

The first form of distribution of powers, between citizens and the state is, precisely, the one related to the establishment of fundamental rights and liberties: the *État de droit* or state according to law always implies that there is a sphere of liberties granted to citizens out of reach of the state, and that the state also has powers and prerogatives to ensure its functions, ruled by particular rules different to those applied to individuals. This distribution of power between citizens and state, implying the formal establishment of fundamental rights and liberties for the former, must be, of course, of an entrenched form, resulting from a constituent power, and, therefore, not subject to amendment by ordinary legislation.[144]

In any case, the constitutional establishment of fundamental rights appears as a central element of liberalism, as a result of the distinction between state and society and of course of the *État de droit*. In the latter, its aims are considered as being the protection, guarantee and fulfillment of human rights and fundamental liberties, contrary to those of the absolute or totalitarian state, where these rights do not exist.

That is why at its origin, the distribution of power between a citizen's sphere of liberties and state powers lead to the concept in which, in principle, individual liberty was unlimited, whereas the powers of the state were limited, precisely because the state was set up for the protection of the former.

1. Theoretical Backgrounds and Historical Antecedents

This conception lies beneath the whole construction of the *État de droit* from the very beginning of its philosophical background, and again, we must recall Locke's concepts in his *Two Treatises of Government* (1690), without doubt, the great classic of the most liberal tradition, and the book that most influenced the birth of the *État de droit*.

---

144 AS O. HOOD PHILLIPS said: "The provision that cannot be amended by ordinary legislative procedure are said to be "entrenched." *Reform of the Constitution*, London 1970, p. 3.

In effect, the establishment of a political or civil society according to Locke, as opposed to absolute monarchy, implies an agreement between men,

> To join and unite into a community for their comfortable, safe, and peaceful living one among the other, in a secure enjoyment of their properties and a greater security against any that are not of it.[145]

Thereof, the power granted to the commonwealth, and in particular to the legislative, –he said–,

> Is not, nor can possibly be absolutely arbitrary over the lives and fortunes of the people, for it being but the joint power of every member of the society given up to that person or assembly which is legislator, it can be no more than those persons had in a state of nature before they entered into society and gave up to the community; for nobody can transfer to another more power than he has in himself, and nobody has an absolute arbitrary power over himself, or over any other, to destroy his own life, or take away the life or property of another. A man, as has been proved, cannot subject himself to the arbitrary power of another; and having in the state of nature no arbitrary power over the life, liberty, or possession of another, but only so much as the law of nature gave him for the preservation of himself and the rest of mankind, this is all he does or can give up to the commonwealth, and by it to the legislative power, so that the legislative can have no more than this. Their power, in the utmost bounds of it, is limited to the public good of the society. It is a power that has no other end but preservation, and therefore can never have a right to destroy enslave, or designedly to impoverish the subject.[146]

On this basis, Locke defined the "end of government" as "the good of mankind", and stated that "all the power government has is only for the good of the society." Therefore, opposed to civil society was the absolute arbitrary power or government without settled standing laws. Those, he said,

> Can neither of them consist with the end of society and government which men would not quit the freedom of the state of nature and tie themselves up under, were it not to preserve their lives, liberties, and fortune, and by stated rules of right and property to secure their peace and quiet. It cannot be supposed that they should intend, had they a power so to do, to give to any one, or more, an absolute arbitrary power over their persons and estates, and put a force into the magistrates hand to execute his unlimited will arbitrarily upon them. This –he ended– were to put themselves into a worse condition than the state of nature, wherein they had a liberty to defend their right against the injuries of others, and were upon equal terms of force to maintain it, whether invaded by a single man or many in combination.[147]

The conclusion of all this conception regarding to fundamental rights, or "property", as Locke identified them, was that,

> The supreme power cannot take from any man part of his property without his own consent; for the preservation of property being the end of government and that for which men enter into society, it necessarily supposes and requires, that the people should have property.[148]

---

145 J. LOCKE, *Two Treatises of Government*, quoted in W. LAQUER and B. RUBIN ed., *The Human Rights Reader*, New York 1979 p. 64.

146 *Idem*, p. 65.

147 *Ibid*, p. 66.

148 *Ibid*, p. 67

In this perspective, as we have seen, all the construction of the *État de droit* apparatus as opposed to that of the absolute state was based on the idea of the existence of man's liberties, that were inalienable and which cannot be renounced, and that the state was to be set up for the protection and maintenance of such liberties.

In this same sense, the other two theoreticians of the state, whose ideas helped the setting up of the liberal state, are clear and eloquent. Rousseau when referring to the nature of the rights of citizens, said:

> To renounce one's liberty is to renounce one's quality as a man, the rights and also the duties of humanity... such a renunciation is incompatible with man's nature, for to take away all freedom from his will is to take away all morality from his actions. In short, a convention which stipulates absolute authority on the one side and unlimited obedience on the other is vain and contradictory.[149]

Montesquieu, for his part, argued, as we have seen, that "political liberty" was to be found only in "moderate governments", that is to say, those where "there is no abuse of power",[150] and those only exist in systems –he thought–, like the English, where power checked power. Thus there is his theory of the distribution of power as a pre–requisite for political liberty.

In this context, England again had a long tradition, and even though the idea of "natural rights" has been said to be "strictly an (English) commodity for export, particularly to France, and to the American colonies",[151] the truth is that it had a tremendous influence both on English tradition of liberty and abroad.

The *Magna Carta* of 1215 is often referred to as the first declaration of fundamental rights. But in reality this Charter was the result of the struggle between the centripetal and centrifugal feudal forces, that is to say, on the one hand the king's forces, particularly as a result of the tyranny of King John, and the established central institution which administered a common law; and on the other hand, the forces of the barons of the kingdom, which sought disintegration which would mean independence and power, as well as the combined forces of landowners, ecclesiastics and traders.[152]

As a result of that struggle, the Great Charter was a formal charter in the feudal sense, that is to say, a free grant by the king. In fact, however, it resulted in a code for reforming laws passed by the whole body of barons and bishops, and thrust upon a reluctant king.[153] That is why it opened a new chapter in English history and has been seen as the origin and source of English constitutional law.[154]

---

149 J.J. ROUSSEAU, *The Social Contract*, quoted in W. LAQUER and B. RUBIN (ed.), *op. cit.*, p. 70.

150 MONTESQUIEU, *The Spirit of Laws*, quoted in W. LAQUER and B. RUBIN (ed.), *op. cit.*, p. 68–69.

151 K. MINOGUE, "The History of the Idea of Human Rights", in W. LAQUER and B. RUBIN (ed.), *op. cit.*, p. 6.

152 W. HOLDSWORTH, *A History of English Law*, Vol. II, London 1971, p. 207–208. *Cf.* F.W. MAITLAND, *The Constitutional History of England*, Cambridge 1968, p. 67.

153 F.W. MAITLAND, *op. cit.*, p. 67.

154 W. HOLDSWORTH, *op. cit.*, Vol. II, p. 209.

But, as we mentioned, the Great Charter is one of many formal examples of stipulations between the king and the feudal knights; in that sense, it was a *stabilimentum* or an enactment formulated by the king, church, barons and merchants as partners in the legislative powers of the nascent state, contained in a probatory document called a Charter. Thus, the Charter set forth a series of rights of a heterogeneous nature, all relating to the different classes participating in its enactment. Its clauses were classified into five groups; those granting the liberty of the church; those dealing with what is called feudal grievances; those relating to trade; those relating to central government; and those that placed limitation upon arbitrary power.[155]

In reality, therefore, the Great Charter contained nothing resembling a general declaration of fundamental rights of the English people. The freemen whose rights the document refers to were not all but just a fraction of Englishmen, particularly the barons, and if it is true that in some clauses the Magna Carta mentioned all *liberi homines* in a sense that could include the villain, as Sir William Holdsworth said,

> It is fairly clear that they were thus protected, not because it was intended to confer any rights upon them, but because they were the property of their lords, and excessive amercements would diminish their value.[156]

Thus, if it is true that the Magna Carta guaranteed all freemen certain rights of protection against the abuse of royal power, this is something quite different from a modern declaration of the rights of man and the citizen. In those days, only the Barons were *liberi homines*; they alone were *liberi* and they alone were considered as *homines*. Thus, historically speaking, the Magna Carta was an agreement between a feudal aristocracy and its king, to whom it renewed its homage in exchange for guaranteed rights. In that context the Magna Carta's 63 chapters contained limitations on the judiciary for example, the affirmation that no freeman could be imprisoned or arrested, except by a legal court, composed of people of his own class, or in accordance with the law of the land; limitations upon taxation power, and above all, the establishment of a resistance committee in the event of failure to maintain these prescriptions.

Thus, there is no reference in the Magna Carta to the people as a whole, and this could not be otherwise, since such a reality had not yet made its appearance in history. Naturally, those historical facts do not detract from its crucial importance in British constitutional history, due basically to the symbolic association attached to it.

What is true, is that the modern concept of fundamental rights, related originally to the idea of natural rights, only appears in more modern times after the medieval age finished in the course of the sixteenth century, and when the idea of duty gave way to the idea of rights[157] and due, as we have seen, in political theory to the theoreticians of the absolute state. Thus, the first formal expression of this new concept

---

155 *Idem*, p. 212.

156 *Idem*, p. 212.

157 "A common and useful way of describing the change from the medieval to the modern world is to say that the idea of *duty* gave way to the idea of right." K. MINOGUE, *loc. cit.*, p. 5.

can be found in the writ of *Habeas Corpus* developed by English courts, precisely because of the influence and interpretation of the Magna Carta. As Sir William Holdsworth pointed out:

> Whether or not the famous clause of Magna Carta, which enacted that 'no free man shall be taken or imprisoned or diseased or exiled or in any way destroyed except by the lawful judgment of his peers or by the law of the land', was intended to safeguard the principle that no man should be imprisoned without due process of law, it soon came to be interpreted as safeguarding it. Because it was interpreted in this way, it has exercised a vast influence, both upon the manner in which the judges have developed the writs which could be used to safeguard this liberty, and upon the manner in which the Legislature has assisted that development.[158]

And precisely, the Habeas Corpus Act of 1679 is perhaps the first formal law in modern times related to a fundamental right, that of personal liberty, although it was applied only to detention for 'any criminal or supposed criminal matters'. It was passed to secure that persons detained on criminal charges were brought speedily to trial and to ensure that the power to detain persons on criminal charges was not abused.[159]

The first formal act that refers to fundamental liberties in a wider sense in modern time is undoubtedly the *Bill of Rights* of 1689, enacted at the end which of the English Revolution of 1688–1689, and which marks the ultimate triumph of Parliament in its struggle against the crown.

This act of Parliament, adopted by the new true Parliament which resulted from the Convention Parliament in 1689, gave undoubted legal authority to all the provisions contained in the Declaration of Rights presented in February 1689 to Prince William and Princess Mary of Orange when the convention offered them the crown of England, and which contained all the major resolutions of the convention. Therefore, its contents, more than just a statement of rights, have been considered as a political document containing 'the rights of the nation'[160] as had previously been established by legislation.[161]

Regarding rights, however, the Bill of Rights gave legal effect to those rights mentioned in the Declaration by means of a provision stating that:

> All and singular the rights and liberties asserted and claimed in the said declaration, are the true, ancient, and indubitable rights and liberties of the people of this Kingdom, and so shall be esteemed, allowed, adjudged, deemed, and so taken to be.[162]

---

158 W. HOLDSWORTH, *op. cit.* Vol. IX, London 1966, p. 104.

159 E.C.S. WADE and G. GODFREY PHILLIPS, *Constitutional and Administrative Law*, ninth edition by A.W. BRADLEY, London 1980, p. 456.

160 L.G. SCHWOERER, *The Declaration of Rights, 1689,* 1981, p. 19, 291.

161 That is why W. HOLDSWORTH considered that in the Bill of Rights there is no "statement of constitutional principles", *op. cit.*, Vol. VI, London 1971, p. 241.

162 Quoted by P. ALLOT, "'The Courts and Parliament: Who Whom?, *The Cambridge Law Journal*, 38 (1), 1979, p. 98.

But in fact, the Declaration of Rights cannot only be thought of as a document tending only to restore the old and acknowledged rights of Englishmen which had been grievously violated by King James II. It must also be regarded, like the Bill of Rights, as a radical reforming document in the sense that it resolved long–standing disputes in ways favorable to Parliament and the individual, and according to the libertarian political principles that the Revolution embodied.

As L.G. Schwoerer stated in his study of the Declaration of Rights 1689, that Declaration and the Bill of Rights:

> Dealt with royal prerogatives that lie at the very heart of sovereignty; royal power respecting law, military authority, and taxation. They sought also to strengthen the role of Parliament, by claiming the rights of free election, free speech, free debate, free proceedings, and frequent meetings. And they guaranteed rights to the individual – to petition the King without fear of reprisal, to bear arms (under certain restrictions)' and to be protected against certain judicial procedures (excessive bail, excessive fines, cruel and unusual punishments, and the granting and promising of fines and forfeitures before conviction).[163]

In so doing, this document must be thought of as the necessary ingredient of the Revolution 1688–1689 so as not to be seen as a simple *coup d'Etat*. On the contrary, the Revolution has been thought of as real, not only because it destroyed the essential elements of the *ancien regime*, but also because it also restored certain rights which had been assaulted by the Stuarts and, in resolving certain long–term controversies, it created a new kingship. Thus in the new political system which was born, the principles of divine–right monarchy, the idea of direct hereditary succession, the prerogatives of the king over law, the military, taxation and judicial procedures which were to the detriment of the individual, all underwent radical changes; and Parliament definitively gained supremacy in its struggle against the king.

This revolution has been considered by Schowerer as

> The greatest, in the sense of being the most effective, of the revolutions that occurred in early modern European history. And its legacy was ongoing in the revolution (and the document accompanying it) that occurred at the end of the eighteenth century in the American colonies.[164]

The importance of the Bill of Rights 1689, therefore, lies in two principal aspects: first, because it paved the way for the transition from the ancient system of class rights towards modern individual rights in the sense that the Bill of Rights declared individual rights not of some privileged classes but of English people as a whole; and second, because of its influence in the first declarations of fundamental rights in modern times, those of the English colonies of North America.

2. The American and French Declarations and Their Influence

In fact, it has been considered that the first of the formal declarations of individual rights in the modern constitutional sense are the bills of the American colonies. They differed from the English precedents, mainly because in establishing those

---

163 L.G. SCHWOERER, *op. cit.*, p. 283.

164 *Idem*, p. 291.

rights, they did not refer to rights based on the common law and tradition, but rather to the rights derived from human nature and ratio. Thus the rights declared in the Bill of Rights of those colonies were natural rights which "do pertain to...(the people) and their posterity, as the basis and foundation of government" as the Virginia Declaration of Rights, 12–6–1776 stated.[165]

In the brief preamble to that Declaration, the relation between natural rights and government was clearly established, and thus the direct influence of Locke's theories in the sense that political society forms itself upon those rights as the basis and foundation of government.

The first three sections of the Declaration clearly followed these ideas:

> *Section 1*: That all men are by nature equally free and independent and have certain inherent rights, of which, when they enter into a state of society, they cannot by any compact, deprive or divest their posterity; namely, the enjoyment of life and liberty, with the means of acquiring and possessing property, and pursuing and obtaining happiness and safety.
>
> *Section 2*: That all power is vested in, and consequently derived from, the people; that magistrates are their trustees and servants and at all times amenable to them.
>
> *Section 3*: That government is, or ought to be, instituted for the common benefit, protection, and security of the people, nation, or community; of all the various modes and forms of government, that is best which is capable of producing the greatest degree of happiness and safety, and is most effectually secured against the danger of maladministration; and that, when any government shall be found inadequate or contrary to these purposes, a majority of the community hath an indubitable, inalienable, and indefensible right to reform, alter, or abolish it, in such manner as shall be judged most conducive to the public weal.[166]

In addition, Section 4 established the prohibition of privileges and Section 5 prescribed the separation of powers and the temporal condition of public offices.

From these sections in the Declaration, the theory of the social contract or pact, based on the existence of inherent and inalienable rights of man is clear; and the democratic basis of government also as its best and must just form, thus the theory of democratic representation through free elections (Section 7); and the right of resistance, a product itself of the social pact.

The other eleven sections are devoted to regulating a few fundamental rights, among which are the right to a speedy trial, with due guarantees; the right not to be condemned to excessive fines or to cruel and unusual punishment, and the freedom of the press.

The same fundamental liberal principles of the Virginia Declaration can also be found in the Declaration of Independence of the United States of America, approved less than one month later (4–7–1776). It stated:

> We hold these truths to be self–evident. that all men are created equal; that they are endowed by their Creator with certain unalienable rights; that among these are life, liberty, and the pursuit of happiness; that, to secure these rights, government is instituted among men, de-

165 See the text in J. HERVADA and J.M. ZUMAQUERO, *Textos internacionales de derechos humanos*, Pamplona 1978, p. 25.

166 *Idem*, p. 27–29.

> riving their just powers from the consent of the governed; that, whenever any form of government becomes destructive of these ends, it is the right of the people to alter or to abolish it and to institute new government, laying its foundation on such principles/and organizing its powers in such form, as to them shall seem most likely to effect their safety and happiness'.[167]

These declarations, undoubtedly, marked the beginning of the democratic and liberal era of the modern state according to law although the 1787 constitution of the United states did not contain a declaration of fundamental rights, it nevertheless constituted one of the main characteristics of American constitutionalism, that influenced modern constitutional law.[168] The 1787 constitution was criticized for the fact that it did not include a statement of fundamental rights, but that lack was resolved two years later when ten amendments to the constitution were drafted by the first Congress and approved on 25 September 1789 just one month after the French Declaration of the Rights of Man and Citizen.[169]

In effect, on 27 August 1789 the representatives of the French People, organized in the National Assembly, approved a Declaration of the Rights of Man and the Citizen, where all the fundamental rights of man were recognized and proclaimed in seventeen articles. The undoubted influence upon it of the American Declarations was decisive, particularly in the principle itself of the need of a formal declaration of rights, and in its contents. The mutual influences between the two continents at the time are well known: the French philosophers, including Montesquieu and Rousseau were studied in North America; French participation in the War of Independence was important; Lafayette was a member of the drafting committee of the Constituent Assembly which produced the French Declaration and who submitted his own draft based on the Declaration of Independence and the Virginia Bill of Rights; the *repporteur* of the constitutional Commission proposed "transplanting to France the noble idea conceived in North America"; and Jefferson himself was present in Paris in 1789, having succeeded Benjamin Franklin as American Minister to France.[170]

Anyway, the main objectives in both declarations were the same: to protect the citizen against arbitrary power and to establish the rule of law.

However, it is certain that the French Declaration was, of course, more directly influenced by the thoughts of Rousseau and Montesquieu. The drafters of the Declaration took from Rousseau the principles of considering the role of society as being related to the natural liberty of man, and the idea that the law, as the expression of the general will passed by the representatives of the nation, cannot be an instrument for oppression. They also took from Montesquieu his fundamental distrust of power, and therefore, the principle of separation of powers.[171] Of course, the rights proclaimed in the Declaration were natural rights of man, thus inalienable and univer-

---

167 *Idem*, p. 37.

168 Ch. H. McIlwain, *Contitutionalism and the Changing World*, Cambridge 1939, p. 66.

169 See the text in W. Laqueur and B. Rubin, *op. cit.*, p. 106–118. *Cf.* A.H. Robertson, *Human Rights in the World*, Manchester 1982, p. 7.

170 J. Rivero, *Les libertes publiques*, Paris 1973, Vol. I, p. 45; A.H. Robertson, *op. cit.*, p. 7.

171 J. Rivero, *op. cit*, p. 41–42.

sal. These were not rights that political society granted, but rights belonging to nature inherent in human beings.

This conception is clear in the text of the Declaration issued by the representatives of the French people, by "considering that the ignorance, forgetfulness or contempt of the rights of man are the sole causes of public misfortunes and of the corruption of government." The Declaration was, then, a perpetual reminder of the "natural inalienable and sacred rights of man."[172]

The first articles of the Declaration that recognized and proclaimed the rights of man and citizen, were, undoubtedly, a sort of compilation of all the liberal principles based on the ideas of Locke, Montesquieu and Rousseau, and concretised in the American Revolution. They were:

1. Men are born and remain free and equal in rights; social distinctions may be based only upon general usefulness.
2. The aim of every political association is the preservation of the natural and inalienable rights of man; these rights are liberty, property, security, and resistance to oppression.
3. The source of all sovereignty resides essentially in the nation; no group, no individual may exercise authority not emanating expressly therefrom.
4. Liberty consists of the power to coo whatever is not injurious to others; thus the enjoyment of the natural rights of every man has as its limits only those that assure to other members of society the enjoyment of those same rights; such limits may be determined only by law.
5. The Law has the right to forbid only actions which acre injurious to society. Whatever is not forbidden by law may not be prevented, and no one may be constrained to do what it does not prescribe.
6. Law is the expression of the general will all citizens have the right Lo concur personally, or through their representatives in its formation; it must be the same for all, whether it protects or punishes...

16. Every society in which the guarantee of rights is not assured or the separation of powers not determined, has no constitution at all.[173]

The rest of the Declaration concerned with individual rights, for instance, the principle *nullum crimen nulla poena sine legge*; the presumption of innocence until a declaration of guilt; the right of free expression and to free communication of ideas and opinions, considered in the Declaration as "one of the most precious of the rights of man"; and the right to property considered "sacred and inviolable."

We could say that the whole process of the development of the *État de droit* on the basis of this third, general feature, of the establishment of a declaration of rights, took its lead from these two formal declarations, the American and the French, subsequently incorporated into written constitutions.[174] They first had an impact in Latin America, long before in other European countries.

---

172 See the text in J. HERVADA and J.M. ZUMAQUERO, *op. cit.*, p. 39–40; W. LAQUEUR and B. RUBIN, *op. cit.*, p. 118.

173 *Idem*, pp. 41–49 and pp. 118–119.

174 The French declaration was incorporated in the preamble to the constitution of 1791.

In this sense, what can be considered as the third formal declaration of rights by an independent state in constitutional history was the Declaration of Rights of the People adopted by the Supreme Congress of Venezuela in 1811 four days before the formal Independence Act of the 5th July 1811 was issued.[175] The content of that Declaration followed the French one but in much more detail in its enumeration of rights, including new ones in relation to the previous American and French Declarations, such as the right to industrial and commercial freedom and the freedom to work; the right to consider ones home as inviolable, and the right to petition before authority without limitation. The Declaration was also incorporated as a final Chapter of the first of all Latin–American constitutions, the Venezuelan one of 21st December 1811 in 59 articles.[176]

Afterwards, the declarations of fundamental rights by all the newly the independent states of Latin America at the beginning of last century spread as a basic constitutional feature of our countries.

In any case, it must be said that in general, the American –North American and Latin–American– and the French declarations of rights were different in their content and meaning.

In the French Declaration, it was not a case of establishing a new state but of the continuation of a national state already in existence. Therefore, the concept of the citizen was taken for granted whereas in the American Declarations, new states were being built upon a new basis. In consequence the purpose of the French Declaration, as stated in its introduction, was to solemnly remind all members of the community of their rights and duties. Hence the new principle of individual liberty appeared only as an important modification within the context of a political unity already in existence.

Whereas in the North American and Latin–American declarations, the enforcement of rights was an important factor in the independence process, and thus of the building of the new states upon a new basis, particularly the principle of the sovereignty of the people with all its democratic content. Therefore, on the American Continent, the solemn Declaration of Fundamental Rights signified the establishment of principles on which the political unity of the nations was based, and the validity of which was recognized as the most important supposition in the emergence and formation of that unity.

In any case, after this process developed during the first decades of the last century (19th century), we can say that the general declaration of fundamental rights and liberties became normal practice all over the world. Therefore, it is difficult to find in the last and present centuries (19th and 20th century) written constitutions without a declaration or an enumeration of fundamental rights including not only the traditional liberties of men, but also the new social and economic rights developed during this century (20th century) within the framework of the welfare state.

---

175 See the text in A. R. BREWER–CARÍAS, *Las Constituciones de Venezuela*, Madrid 1985, pp. 175–177.

176 *Idem*, p. 196–200.

The general situation today is that declarations of fundamental rights have existed and exist in almost all countries, particularly as a part of their written constitutions. Moreover, after the horrors that were seen during the World War II, those declarations have even been internationalized not only as simple declarations without the means to enforce them, like the Universal Declaration of Human Rights and the American Declaration of Rights and Duties of Man, both of 1948, but also as formal international conventions and treatises, like the International Pacts of Civil and Political Rights and on Economic, Social and Cultural Rights 1966; the European Convention for the Protection of Human Rights and Fundamental Freedoms 1950; and the American Convention on Human Rights 1969, texts that in most of the countries that ratified them, are considered as formal laws and as part of the law of the land.[177]

In any case, what can be considered as a particular feature of the declarations of rights in the Legal state is that in general they were and are normally incorporated in written constitutions. Besides, those written constitutions had been and are also rigid, therefore the declarations of fundamental rights are normally entrenched declarations in the sense that the ordinary legislator cannot eliminate or modify their contents.

Of course, not all the rights contained in those declarations as fundamental ones are formally established in the same manner. Some of them, particularly traditional individual rights, like the right to live, are established in an absolute way in the sense that no legislation can be passed limiting its enjoyment. On the contrary, other rights are established in a way that the constitution itself allows for the possibility of the Legislator to regulate or limit those rights but only within the limits established in the constitution. However, in some cases, the constitutional authorization for the legislative power to regulate certain rights is established in a way that legislation must be passed for its effective enjoyment. That happens in some countries, where for instance, the right to strike in public services can only be exercised in cases expressly established in a law.

In any case, the establishment of an entrenched declaration of fundamental rights and freedoms, in a written and rigid constitution, implies that the first and most important guarantee of those rights is the principle of a "legal reserve" in favour of the legislative power for their regulation and limits according to what is determined in the constitution. That means, in all cases in which the constitution allows possible further regulation and limits to the enjoyment of rights, that those regulations and limits can only be established through formal laws or acts of Parliament. Therefore, the executive itself cannot set any limit whatsoever on constitutional rights. Only exceptionally, in the constitutional systems that allow the possibility for Parliament to delegate legislative powers to the executive, can it be possible, within the limits of the delegation, for the executive through delegate legislation or decree–Law, to establish regulations in relation to some rights.

---

177 See the text in M. TORRELLI and R. BAUDOUIN, *Les droits de l'homme et les libertes publiques par les textes*, Montreal, 1972, p. 388; J. HERVADA and J.M. ZUMAQUERO, *Textos internacionales de derechos humanos*, *cit*., p. 994.

Thus, within the concept of the state submitted to law, the principle relating to individual rights and liberties, which stipulates that an *État de droit* is one in which the state can only intervene in the sphere of individual liberties on the basis of a formal law, has a special meaning. A state according to law is, therefore, one in which intervention in individual liberties is only possible through formal law, and in which the administration cannot, therefore, invade this reserve granted to formal law.

This concept of the *État de droit* is evidently built against the administration, bearing in mind that only a state in which all administrative actions are subject to the law is really an *État de droit*. That is why the principle of legality related to the administration has been so characteristic of this concept of the state, together with the consequent establishment of a series of guarantees against abuse of power by the administration.

Naturally, in this concept of the *État de droit*, in which the law has supremacy over the administration and in which individual rights can only be regulated by the law, there is another fundamental characteristic, namely that of judicial independence, which is the only instrument capable of guaranteeing adequate judicial control over the exercise of power by the administration. Hence the definition of the *État de droit* as one in which judicial control of the administration exists, also referred to as a "state of Justice."

Therefore, in the constitutional *État de droit* or state according to the rule of law, the establishment and regulation of constitutional rights with or without possible further regulation by the legislator, implies the need of a system of guarantees of such rights: on the one hand, as already explained, guarantees of regulation and limitation through the so–called "legal reserve", and on the other guarantees against abuse of public powers in relation to those rights, through judicial mechanisms ensuring their implementation, either by means of the ordinary judicial remedies or through special ones, like the writ of *habeas corpus*, concerning individual liberty, or through special "actions of protection" to protect all constitutional rights or, in general, the means for the judicial control of the constitutionality of laws which may violate those rights.

3. The Situation of Fundamental Rights in the British Constitutional System

England has rightly been called the land of liberalism: Locke was English, Montesquieu's system is based on his interpretation of the English constitution; and from the point of view of positive law, the declarations of rights have their antecedents in English constitutional history. Because of those antecedents, in general, liberal democratic constitutions nowadays normally contain a declaration of rights. However, in the United Kingdom, in the absence of a written constitution, and apart from references to historical statutes, there is no declaration or special code relating to fundamental rights; therefore. as Sir Ivor Jennings has said, "there are no fundamental rights" and "there is no special protection for "fundamental rights."[178]

---

178 I. JENNINGS, *The Law and the Constitution*, London 1972, p. 40, 259.

Consequently, the rights of the British people equivalent, of course, to those established elsewhere in entrenched declarations, are based on two assumptions: in the first place, that citizens can do or say anything, provided it is not an infringement of a law or of other citizens' rights; and in the second place, that the authorities can only do what is permitted by statutory or common law.[179] Consequently, in the United Kingdom legal system, rights are expressed, in principle, not positively, but negatively. Hence, strictly speaking, rather than rights they are liberties.

That is why, as E.C.S. Wade and G. Godfrey Phillips pointed out "the approach of the law in Britain to the citizen's liberty has often been to treat it as a residual concept: The citizen may go where he pleases, and do or say what he pleases provided he does not commit a criminal offence or infringe the rights of others."[180] Accordingly, we can say that in the system of this country, the principle is that "anything is lawful which is not unlawful", in other words, "it is lawful to do anything which is not unlawful or which cannot be prohibited by public authorities."[181] Therefore, the essence of the provisions related to fundamental rights regulation in Britain is founded upon whom can establish unlawful actions or prohibit them. Naturally, these limits must be found primarily in legislation, that is to say, in Acts of Parliament.[182]

It was precisely this negative approach to fundamental rights in England that led Dicey to establish a contrast between the continental and the English constitutions, as we have seen, saying that on the continent, individual rights result, or appear to result, from the general principles of the constitution," whereas in England, "the general principles of the constitution (as for example the right to personal liberty, or the right of public meeting) are... the result of judicial decisions determining the rights of private persons in particular cases brought before the courts." As a result of which, –Dicey concluded– "the rules which in foreign countries naturally form part of a constitutional code, are not the source but the consequence of the rights of individuals, as defined and enforced by the courts."[183]

Dicey's views in relation to the situation of this country were expressed exactly one hundred years ago. The first edition of *An Introduction to the Study of the Law of the Constitution* was published in 1885. At that time, the role of Parliament and the Courts was quite different from today, and moreover, we have to consider the impact upon fundamental rights of the Welfare state or the Social *État de droit* as it is called in Continental Europe.

---

179 M. GARCÍA PELAYO, *Derecho constitucional comparado*, Madrid 1957, p. 278.

180 E.C.S. WADE and G. GODFREY PHILLIPS, *Constitutional and Administrative Law*, ninth edition by A.W. BRADLEY, London 1982, p. 441.

181 I. JENNINGS, *op. cit.*, p. 41, 262. "It asserts the principle of legality, that everything is legal that is not illegal."

182 Delegated Legislation in relation to fundamental rights, in principle, is only Possible in cases of state of emergency in accordance with the Emergency Powers Act 1920. E.C.S. WADE and G. GODFREY PHILLIPS, *op. cit.*, p. 567.

183 A.V. DICEY, *An Introduction to the Study of the Law of the Constitution*, with an "Introduction" by E.C.S. WADE, 1973, p. 195, 196, 203. See also WADE comments, p. CXVIII.

As makers of law Professor J.D.B. Mitchell said, "the courts have declined in importance. In part this is the obvious result of the development of Parliament, in part it is the result of changes in ideas about the functions of a state."

Moreover, he added,

> The development of the Welfare state has meant that rights with which individuals are increasingly concerned, protections or hedges against poverty, ill health, and the like, cannot be the creation of judge–made law as could be the –rights of speech, etc., with which Dicey was concerned. These newer rights can only be the result of complex legislation.[184]

And it has been so, even though the role of ordinary courts continues to be important as the ultimate guardians of fundamental rights, and not as their creators.

Nevertheless, despite all the British tradition, discussions have been held in the United Kingdom particularly during the last two decades, on the need and possibility of the enactment of an entrenched Bill of Rights.

The principal argument for a Bill of Rights is to restrain excess or abuse of power by public authorities, and it has been thought that with a Bill of Rights, the power to bring legal actions against the state and agencies of government will improve, in other words, it has been thought that a Bill of Rights is potentially a more fruitful source of remedies.[185]

This arguments in favor of the enactment of a Bill of Rights has been summarized by P.S. Atiyah, as follows:

> That there ought to be, and are, certain basic human rights which ought not to be at the mercy of a government and legislature; that –governments and legislatures derive their power from the people, and that the people cannot be assumed to have granted away unlimited and despotic powers just because they have elected a Parliament (by a process set by Parliament itself); that a majority of the people is no doubt entitled to elect a majority government and parliament to represent their views, but this does not give, and ought not to give, that government and parliament unlimited power to oppress the minority or minorities; and that at the very least, the basic structure of the democratic process– which alone gives legitimacy to the power of governments and parliaments ought to be entrenched so as to be unalterable by Parliament.[186]

Evidently, these arguments in favour of the enactment of a Bill of Rights in Britain, that follow the most orthodox liberal tradition, must take into account the well known principle of Parliamentary sovereignty. An entrenched Bill of Rights would limit the powers of the ordinary legislator to modify it, which is contrary to the main principle of the British constitution. On the other hand, a Bill of Rights formally entrenched in the constitution would mean that judges would become the ultimate arbiters of the powers of Parliament, and that, –it has been said– would be disastrous unless judges could be persuaded to alter their traditional methods of interpretation. "For traditional and crabbed methods of interpretation –P.S. Atiyah said–, could often lead to the invalidation of legislation which is absolutely necessary to keep

---

184 J.D.B. MITCHELL, *Constitutional Law*, Edinburgh 1968, p. 55.

185 M. ZANDER, *A Bill of Rights?*, London 1985, p. 27.

186 P.S. ATIYAH, *Law and Modern Society*, Oxford 1983, p. 109.

pace with changing values or conditions; huge tensions would then build up in the legal and political system, and general discredit could be thrown on the law."[187]

The main arguments against the enactment of a Bill of Rights have been exposed, clearly summarized and critiqued by Michel Zander in his pamphlet entitled *A Bill of Rights*?,[188] originally published ten years ago (1975). Among those arguments we may point out the following:

In the first place, it has been said that a Bill of Rights is an "un–British way of doing things,"[189] based on the well known apprehensiveness to written constitutions or constitutional documents, that in constitutional law derives from Dicey's concepts. To say that a Bill of Rights is "un–British" says M. Zanders, "is to show an ignorance of history."[190] In fact, as we have seen, this country invented the in Bill of Rights with the Magna Carta in 1215 and the Bill of Rights in 1689; it influenced the Declaration of Rights in the American Colonies 1776 and the content of the first ten amendments of the North–American constitution (1789); and in more recent times, the United Kingdom has been the main exporter of the ideas of fundamental rights and freedoms established in an entrenched way, to the Commonwealth countries on a scale without parallel in the rest of the world.[191] All the countries of the Commonwealth, except New Zealand, have written constitutions and a formal declaration of fundamental rights.

The second argument against the enactment of a Bill of Rights is that it is not needed because human rights are adequately protected in Britain. This has also been the main argument used to justify[192] why the European Convention on Human Rights has not been transformed into domestic law in the United Kingdom. "At the time of ratification, –Drzemczewski said– the government of the day assumed that domestic law was in full conformity with the Conventions provisions, and successive governments have since that time expressed the opinion that the rights and freedoms enumerated are in all cases already secured in domestic law."[193] In relation to this argument, Professor Zander, bearing in mind that in Britain a system of remedies rather than of rights exists, said that "the existing ways of getting remedies all

187 *Idem*, p. 111.

188 London 1985, p. 106.

189 *Idem*, p. 43.

190 *Ibidem*, p. 44.

191 A. LESTER, "Fundamental Rights: The United Kingdom Isolated?" *Public Law*, spring 1984, p. 56, 57; M. ZANDERS, *op. cit*, p. 28–30. To realize the extent of this contribution, we only have to mention the amendments adopted by the British Parliament in 1982, in regard to the British. North American Act 1867, renamed in 1982 the constitution Act 1867, in which the Canadian Charter of Rights and Freedom was included at the same time in which the last vestige of the colonial relationship with regard to constitutional amendments in Canada disappeared.

192 M. ZANDERS, *op. cit*., p. 45.

193 Q.Z. DRZEMCZEWSKI, *European Human Rights Convention in Domestic Law. A Comparative Study*, Oxford 1985, p. 178.

leave much to be desired",[194] and in fact, as Anthony Lester pointed out in his recent article about the isolation of the United Kingdom concerning fundamental rights and the European Convention, "no other country which belongs to the convention systems has been faced with so many cases" of importance, adding:

It is not the sheer volume of cases which is so telling, but the proportion of cases declared admissible by the commission and of cases decided against the United Kingdom.[195]

The third argument against the enactment of a Bill of Rights is based on the principle of sovereignty of Parliament, as we have seen. A Bill of Rights needs to be entrenched, and that would restrict Parliament's freedom to legislate in the future. As professor O. Hood Phillips said:

> The primary characteristic of our constitution is the legislative supremacy of Parliament. This means that Parliament can pass a law on any subject matter, even. of a fundamental constitutional nature, and can do so by the ordinary procedure of an Act of Parliament... this legally unlimited power of Parliament to make laws on any subject matter is a corollary of the absence of "entrenched" provisions and of the flexible nature of the British constitution. It also follows that we have no strictly fundamental rights.[196]

Along the same line of thought, Professor H.W.R. Wade says:

> ...The one inherent limit on (Parliamentary omnipotence, which is the consequence of that omnipotence itself, is that the Parliament of today cannot fetter the Parliament of tomorrow with any sort of permanent restraint, so that entrenched provisions are impossible.[197]

But in practice even this substantive formal argument is not really an obstacle to an entrenched Bill of Rights. Anthony Lester said in his article:

> Normally only the very young have fantasies of omnipotence. Growing up involves accepting the necessity for laws, rules and limits. A mature Parliament would not insist upon the continuous assertion of its fanatical absolute powers at the expense of individual justice. A, mature Parliament would use its sovereign law–making powers to confine those powers within proper constitutional limits.[198]
>
> In any case, the fact is that even if a Bill of Rights were adopted in an entrenched way, that would only imply that the provisions of the Bill of Rights would prevail unless subsequent enactment explicitly stated otherwise, which would not prevent the express will of Parliament from prevailing in the end. It would mean, however, "that the courts could strike down a statute as being contrary to the Bill of Rights unless it contained an express provision modifying the Bill of Rights to that extent.[199]

This leads us to a final argument against the enactment of an entrenched Bill of Rights in this country, related to the powers of courts to review acts of Parliament. As Professor D.G.T. Williams pointed out:

---

194 M. ZANDERS, *op. cit.*, p. 45.

195 A. LESTER, *loc. cit.*, p. 65.

196 O. HOOD Phillips, *Reform of the Constitution, cit*, p. 11, 12.

197 H.W.R. WADE, *Constitutional Fundamentals*, London 1980, p. 25.

198 A. LESTER, *loc. cit.*, p. 71.

199 M. ZANDERS, *op. cit.*, p. 70.

> An entrenched Bill of Rights would, of course, involve the exercise of judicial review by English and other courts of the United Kingdom, in the sense that would entrust domestic courts of a blank check to protect certain fundamental freedoms even against the legislature itself.[200]

Therefore, the real problem of a Bill of Rights, adopted in the ordinary, constitutional way of impeding its modification by ordinary legislation, in a constitutional system like the British one, is that it could imply the powers of courts to review the conformity of acts of Parliament with that Bill which could not be acceptable in the British constitutional system, unless greater modification of the constitution itself took place.

All these arguments could be overcome if the United Kingdom limited its search for establishing a positive code of rights and freedoms, by granting domestic status to the European Convention on Human Rights and therefore, allowing the courts to apply and interpret the Convention and to secure speedy and effective domestic remedies for the citizens of this country against the violation of their fundamental human rights.[201] This, it seems, is the best alternative to the matter today,[202] although it involves a number of questions regarding relations between international law and English law and the interpretation of the Convention in English law.[203]

In any case, if it is true that because of the absence of a declaration of rights protected by a constitutional supra–legality in the United Kingdom, there are in general no legal guarantees whatsoever for the existence of those rights faced with the will of Parliament, and this fact can lead both, to an expansion of the field of forbidden activities and to the granting of ample powers to authorities, the discussion in some respects is definitely a theoretical one.

The validity of rights in this country, at least from the point of view of a foreign lawyer, is inseparable from the total structure of the British constitution. Consequently, abolishing freedom and liberties would be tantamount to abolishing the entire British constitution, which makes no sense.

In any event, what we wanted to point out is that in the modern *État de droit*, further to the limitation of powers and the submission of all state organs to the rule of law, its third main feature is the existence of a formal declaration of fundamental rights and liberties, normally of an entrenched character and embodied in a written constitution. This is the general trend in today's constitutional law, with the exception, on this last point, and at least formally, of the United Kingdom constitutional systems, because of the absence of a Bill of Rights.

We have to refer now to the three main features or characteristics of the *État de droit* or state according to law at the present time, and to its development.

---

200 D.G.T. WILLIAMS, "The Constitution of the United Kingdom", *The Cambridge Law Journal*, 31, (1), 1972, p. 277.

201 A. LESTER, *loc. cit.*, p. 66.

202 M. ZANDERS, *op. cit.*, p. 83–89.

203 J. JACONELLI, *Enacting a Bill of Rights. The Legal Problems*, Oxford 1980, p. 270–277.

We have analysed the principle of limitation of powers, from its original conception as a division of powers to its final constitutional consecration as separation of powers. We also mentioned the various interpretations of this separation that each country can make, and finally we stressed the three meanings of the principle in the contemporary *État de droit*: the division of powers between state powers and the rights and liberties of citizens; the division between constituent and constituted powers; and within the latter, the division or separation of powers, in the horizontal way between legislative, executive and judiciary, and in the vertical way, between the different levels of political decentralization when it exists.

We have also seen the main consequences of the second leading feature of the *État de droit*: namely the submission of state organs to the rule of law, which led us not only to the analysis of the legal system as a hierarchical legal order with a written constitution at its apex, as generally exists in almost all countries to the world today, but also to establish the contrast with the British constitutional system, where the principle of the sovereignty of Parliament prevails over any other rule. In any case, we have seen how the submission of the state to the rule of law, in systems with or without written constitutions, has brought about the development of the principle of legality, and the reduction of its former exceptions, particularly on the sphere of discretionary powers.

Finally, we have also considered the third feature of the *État de droit*, namely the adoption of an entrenched declaration of fundamental rights and freedoms, and its historical development, and expansion all over the world, and the particular problems it poses for the British constitutional system.

Now, the development and adoption of these three elements of the Modern *État de droit* with all the diversities peculiar to each legal system, have been followed, in one way or another, by a process of constitutionalization, generally reflected by its incorporation in a written and often rigid constitution, as a fundamental and basic norm of the legal system. That is why the process of constitutionalization of the *État de droit* has been considered another of its basic aspects.

We now want to refer to that process of constitutionalization, particularly from a historical point of view, and its direct consequence namely, judicial review.

PART II

PROCESS OF CONSTITUTIONALIZATION OF THE ÉTAT DE DROIT

I. THE WRITTEN CONSTITUTIONAL PROCESS

The consolidation and further development of the *État de droit* from the beginning of the last century is, undoubtedly, closely related to the process of constitutionalization of the state. This process was characterized by the establishment of a system of norms of a higher level in a given legal order, containing in a global way, the basic rules related to the fundamental functions of the state, its different organs and powers and its interrelations, and related to the fundamental rights and liberties of the citizens.

Thus, the constitutionalization of the state according to law, started two hundred years ago with the introduction of written constitutions in the practice of politics. These written constitutions were conceived as formal documents containing the will of the people considered as sovereign in regard to the political organization of a nation. As a consequence of this process, the organs of the state, including kings and parliament, were converted, precisely, into such organs of the state, and sovereignty was in general depersonalised and attributed to the people represented by those organs.

During the last two centuries, after the approval of the first of the written constitutions of modern times, the Constitution of the United States of America in 1787, the practice of written constitutions had spread and written constitutions exist in almost every country in the world today, with very few exceptions, among which is that of the United Kingdom. Of course, the fact that in this country and in a few others such as Israel or New Zealand there is no written constitution, does not mean that there is no constitution at all. On the contrary, in these countries a collection of rules exists, partially written, partially unwritten, which establishes, regulates and governs its government.[204] Thus the constitutionalization of the state according to law has also taken place in constitutional systems with no written constitutions.

In any case, this process of constitutionalization of the *État de droit*, reflected in a constitution, has produced a system of guarantees of individual liberties, which are specified in the recognition of fundamental rights; the establishment of the division of powers; provision for the people's participation in legislative power by means of popular representation; and submission of the state to the rule of law. Most important of all in the context of modern constitutions, it has produced a system that responds to a political decision of society, adopted by the people, as a constituent power through a particular constituent assembly.

In particular, the principle of separation of powers, with its distinction between legislative, governmental and administrative bodies and courts of justice, has been considered a necessary content of any constitution since the eighteenth century, except in socialist countries, because it is thought, in itself, to be the organic guarantee against abuse of power on the part of the state. We have only to remember the article 16 of the 1789 French Declaration of the Rights of Man and the Citizen, which reads as follows:

> Every society in which the guarantee of rights is not assured or the separation of powers not determined has no Constitution at all.[205]

As we have said, the first written constitution in modern times was the American Constitution of 1787, the United States being the first common law country to have parliamentary sovereignty replaced by the paramount law of a constitution given by

---

204 M.C. WHEARE, *Modern Constitutions*, Oxford 1966, p. 1, 2.

205 See in W. LAQUEUR and B. RUBIN, *The Human Rights Reader*, 1979, P. 120.

the people, and its enforceable fundamental rights.[206] Indeed, the idea of a higher and fundamental law established as a social contract had also English origins and antecedents in the process of colonization.

The higher law background of the American Constitution,[207] can be traced back to the medieval doctrine of the supremacy of law, drawn from the pages of the works on the laws of England, by the greatest English medieval lawyer, Bracton (1569) mainly interpreted by Sir Edward Coke. This principle led to a reaction against the doctrine of the divine right of kings, based on the doctrine of divine origin of law upon which the basis of civil society is built, and on the principle that law is supreme above king and people equally.[208]

1. Historical Origins

Written constitutions of modern times, one can say, do not have their formal historical origins in the medieval charters, but particularly in the *Instrument of Government* (1653), considered to be the first written constitution in constitutional history.

Nevertheless, the remote antecedents of written constitutions can be found in the medieval formal pacts made between a prince and his vassals, or a prince and popular representation, which was subsequently taken as the expression of the will of the people.

Certainly, in the Middle Ages, these written agreements, which were called charters, were established between the Princes and their barons. The most famous of them is the *Magna Carta* of 1215. However, these documents were not constitutions in the modern sense of the word, although their legal nature has been interpreted in various ways. They have been termed laws, because they were issued by the king and took the form of royal concessions, and as such, they have even been described as public law contracts. They have also been present throughout British history, acting either as a factor of real integration, or as the ideological content of competition between parties, or as a symbol of the parliamentary party. And as of the eighteenth century, they even symbolized the spirit of the constitution in its entirety.

Actually, the Magna Carta was the result of a resistance movement by the privileged barons against the crown policy during the reign of King John (1199–1216).[209] It was just one of the many general charters established between the prince and his barons, guaranteeing them privileges in exchange for certain commitments on their part, which were created in feudal times.

Consequently, none of the distinctions belonging to modern constitutional law can be applied to medieval relations. The Magna Carta was a *stabilimentum*, that is to say, an agreement or stipulation lacking any precise sense of political law. The

---

206 A. LESTER, "Fundamental Rights: The United Kingdom Isolated", *Public Law,* 1984, p. 58.

207 See in general, F. CORWIN, "*The Higher Law" Background of American Constitutional Law*, New York 1955

208 T.F.T. PLUCKNETT, *A Concise History of the Common Law*, London 1956, p. 49.

209 See in general, I. JENNINGS, *Magna Carta*, London 1965, p. 9.

fact that it was in writing is no argument in favour of a constitution, and its very name, Magna Carta, is not explained historically by the fact that it contained a fundamental law in the sense of modern constitutions; it was a popular description to distinguish it from the *Carta Foresta* or Chart of the Forest of 1217 relating to hunting rights.[210]

The original name of the Magna Carta was *Cartam Libertatis* or *Carta Baronum*. It was only centuries later, during the Revolution, with Parliament's struggle against the absolutism of the Stuarts, that the modern sense was attributed to it, making it the origin of a Liberal constitution. But as Carl Smith has pointed out, it would be a historical error to see, even if only by approximation, anything in it analogous to a modern liberal or democratic constitution.[211] Nevertheless, in medieval times, it was considered to be an unalterable, fundamental and perpetual[212] part of the enacted law, and was confirmed by different kings more than thirty times thus being an important part of the progress of common laws.[213]

In the same English context, the first example of a modern written constitution is undoubtedly the *Instrument of Government* 1653, which was the result of the only real break that had occurred in English constitutional history and its political continuity.[214]

In effect, the Great Civil War, which started in 1642 and divided the country into Parliamentarians and Royalists, can be thought of as the final step in the long struggle between the parliament and the king. With its religious, economic and political causes and mutual accusations of breaking and subverting the fundamental law,[215] it brought about the execution of King Charles I, the destruction of the whole system of central government and the assumption of the government of the country by the Long Parliament (1649–1660).

Charles I went on trial and was executed in January 1649, and soon afterwards the monarchy and the House of Lords were abolished and England was named a Commonwealth or free state, under the control of the Army and of Oliver Cromwell.[216] Parliament carried out the wishes of the army, except when setting a limit on its own powers and its own existence. After long and futile negotiations, Cromwell finally dissolved Parliament by force in 1653. To take its place, he invited a number of proven Puritans to form an Assembly of Saints that shortly afterwards resigned their powers, and gave back their authority to Cromwell. Then the Council of army officers produced a written constitution for the government, known as the Instru-

---

210 W. HOLDSWORTH, *A History of English Law*, Vol. II, 1971, p. 207, 219.

211 C. SCHMIDT, *'Teoría de la Constitución* (Spanish ed), México 1961, p. 52–53.

212 Ch. H. MCILWAIN, *The High Court of Parliament and its Supremacy*, Yale 1910, p. 64–65.

213 W. HOLDSWORTH, *op. cit.*, Vol. II, p. 219.

214 M.C. WHEARE, *Modern Constitutions*, Oxford 1966, p. 9. *Cf.* J.D.B. MITCHELL, *Constitutional Law*, Edinburgh 1968, p. 27.

215 M. ASHLEY, *England in the Seventeenth Century*, London 1967, p. 76, 79, 80, 82.

216 *Cf.* W. HOLDSWORTH, *op. cit.*, Vol. VI, p. 146; M. ASHLEY, *op. cit.*, p. 91–92.

ment of Government 1653,[217] which shows all the features of a constitution as we understand it today.

The Instrument of Government made Oliver Cromwell "Lord Protector" of the Commonwealth of England, Scotland and Ireland, which he had united under one government. It conferred executive powers upon the Protector assisted by a Council of State containing both civilian and military members conceived as a body independent of both Protector and Parliament, that was to be elected including representatives of Scotland, Ireland and England.[218] However, when the Parliament met, not all its members accepted the "fundamentals" of the Protectorate Government and refused to accept the constitution under which it was assembled. Eventually it was dissolved mainly because it attempted to deprive Cromwell of sole control over the army; and Cromwell again found himself obliged to rule by means of the army.[219] This happened again and again until his death in 1658. As Sir William Holdsworth said of Cromwell: "He was the only man who could control the army, and consequently, the only man who could have any chance of establishing civil, as opposed to, military government."[220] Therefore, King Charles II was restored soon afterwards by a new Parliament under the terms of the Declaration of Breda 1660, which contained four principles or conditions: a general amnesty, liberty of conscience, security of property and payments of arrears to the army.[221] This Declaration was, indeed, not a constitution in the sense of the Instrument of Government, because in fact the Restoration meant a return to the old form of government, and no constitution was needed to that end. As K.C. Wheare said:

> Those who speak of an unbroken line of development in the history of English government... have a good deal of truth on their side. There was a break and an attempt to make a fresh start with a Constitution, but it failed, and the former order was restored.[222]

As we have said, the Instrument of Government (1653) and its modifications mainly through the Humble Petition and Advice[223] has been unanimously considered as the first written constitution in constitutional history of modern times. The immediate purpose of it was to establish a permanent and inviolable rule vis–à–vis the changing majority resolutions of Parliament. In all governments, Cromwell said, something fundamental is required, something like a Great Charter which is permanent and invariable, or if you wish, absolutely invulnerable. For example, the stipulation that Parliament can never declare itself to be a permanent corporation was, in Cromwell's opinion, one such fundamental principle.[224]

---

217 W. HOLDSWORTH, *op. cit.*, p. 146; M. ASHLEY, *op. cit*, p. 106.

218 W. HOLDSWORTH, *op. cit.*, p. 154–155.

219 W. HOLDSWORTH, *op. cit.*, p. 147; M. ASHLEY, *op. cit.*, p. 102.

220 W. HOLDSWORTH, *op. cit.*, p. 148.

221 *Ibid*, p. 165.

222 K.C. WHEARE, *op. cit.*, p. 10.

223 W. HOLDSWORTH, *op. cit.*, p. 157.

224 Quoted by C. SCHMIDT, *op. cit.*, p. 45.

Thus, historically speaking, one can say that the idea of a constitution arose out of the need to formally determine the composition or fundamental functions of the instruments of government. It is generally a sign of order, following institutional chaos created by a great political or social revolution, when a nation is liberated from a foreign conqueror, or when a nation is formed by the merging of small political units. It is on such occasions of historical and political decisions to reorganize or create a state that constitutions have come into being.

As Jennings has pointed out, that need arose in England in 1653, when the Parliament, having created an army to destroy the king, was destroyed by its own creation.[225] In this sense, the *Instrument of Government, which* made Cromwell *Lord Protector* and established a new legislature, was the first and only example of a written constitution in England. It only remained in force for a few years, and almost survived Cromwell himself.

However, this constitution anticipated many of the constitutional developments of the nineteenth and twentieth centuries. As Sir William Holdsworth pointed out, this Instrument of Government and its immediate modifications:

> Were the first attempt that Englishmen had made to construct a written constitution, and therefore they raised for the first time all the problems connected with its construction. Thus we get the idea of a separation of powers as a safeguard against the tyranny both of a single person and a representative assembly; the idea of stating certain fundamental rights of the subject; and the idea of rendering these rights permanent, by denying validity to any legislation which attempted to affect them..[226]

In any case, with that sole exception, England has never had a written constitution, which, I insist, does not mean that it has no constitution. The institutions required for the performance of various functions of the modern legal state have been set up in the United Kingdom, in keeping with political needs and following a permanent process of invention, reform and transformation. Hence Jennings' statement:

> If a Constitution consists of institutions and not of the paper that describes them, the British Constitution has not been made, but has grown, and there is no paper.[227]

2. The American Constitution (1787)

The modern practice of written constitutions actually began in the United States of America when the colonies separated from England, declaring themselves independent States (1776) and formulating their constitutions in writing. A Continental Congress in 1776 even invited all the colonies of the Union to draw up their own constitutions, as a political decision of the people.[228]

The movement towards independence from England began in the United States long before independence was finally declared in 1776, and the independent spirit

---

225 I. JENNINGS, *The Law and the Constitution*, London 1972, p. 7.

226 W. HOLDSWORTH, *op. cit.*, p. 157.

227 I. JENNINGS, *op. cit.*, p. 8.

228 A.C. MCLAUGHLIN, *A Constitutional History of the United States*, New York 1936, p. 106–109.

developed through the colonial assemblies, which had grown in power and influence during the first half of the eighteenth century, by resolving many of the colonists' problems at local level.[229] This assembly spirit was undoubtedly one of the main factors in the independent process. That is why the Declaration and Resolves of the First Continental Congress, 14 October 1774, bearing in mind that "assemblies have been frequently dissolved, contrary to the rights of the people, when they attempted to deliberate on grievances, resolved that 'the inhabitants of the English colonies in North America, by the immutable laws of nature, the principles of the English constitution, and the several charters or compacts", had their own rights, among which was:

> A right peaceably to assemble, to consider their grievances, and petition the king; and that all prosecutions, prohibitory proclamations, and commitments for the same, are illegal.[230]

Therefore, the process of separation of the English colonies in America from the mother country took place on the basis of two fundamental elements: the process towards independence of each one of the colonies, through their own representative governments; and the process towards the unity of the colonies, through the continental congresses. According to what was said by one of its principal protagonists, John Adams, "The Revolution and the Union developed gradually from 1770 to 1776."[231]

During that period, it was initially a process of intercolonial agreements designed to establish economic boycotts in resistance to the tax pretensions of England. In this context, the first joint meeting of historical and constitutional significance between these colonies was the New York Congress of 1765, which met to demonstrate the colonies' rejection of the Stamp Act passed by the English Parliament on 22 March 1765. This Act placed stamp duties on all legal documents, newspaper pamphlets, college degrees, almanacs, liquor licences and playing cards, and aroused hostility that spread in the colonies.

Besides the social and economic causes of this rejection, the political reaction was based on the cry "no taxation without representation." Thus the 3rd, 4th and 5th rights declared in the Resolutions of the Stamp Act Congress 19 October 1765 stated:

> 3rd That it is inseparably essential to the freedom of a people, and the undoubted rights of Englishmen, that no taxes should be imposed on them, but with their own consent, given personally, or by their representatives.
>
> 4th. That the people of these colonies are not, and from their local circumstances, cannot be represented in the House of Commons in Great Britain.

---

229 R.L. PERRY, (ed.), *Sources of our Liberties. Documentary Origin of Individual Liberties in the United States Constitution and Rights*, 1952, p. 261

230 *Idem*, p. 287, 288.

231 Quoted by M. GARCÍA–PELAYO, *Derecho constitucional comparado*, Madrid 1957, p. 325.

> 5th. That the only representatives of the people of these colonies, are persons chosen therein by themselves; and that no taxes ever have been, or can be constitutionally imposed on them, by their respective legislatures.[232]

In this Congress although a "due subordination to that august body, the Parliament of Great Britain", was declared, its representative character was questioned on the grounds that the taxes established in the Stamp Act had not been approved by the Colonial Assemblies. England annulled the Stamp Act, but imposed a series of customs duties on colonial products.

By 1774, it had become clear that the problems of individual colonies were really the problems of them all, and that brought about the need of united action by the Colonies, with the result that Virginia proposed that an annual Congress be held to discuss the joint interests of America. Thus, in 1774 the First Continental Congress met in Philadelphia with representatives from all the colonies, except Georgia.

The main political element discussed in the congress was the authority the colonies should concede to the Parliament, and on what grounds: either the law of nature, the British Constitution or the American charters.[233] It was decided that the law of nature should be recognized as one of the foundations of the rights of the colonies, and therefore not only the common law. Thus the Congress declared, as a Right of the inhabitants of the English Colonies in North America, in the same sense of the Resolutions of the Stamp Act Congress:

> That the foundation of English Liberty, and of all free government, is a right in the people to participate in their legislative council; and as the English colonists are not represented, and from their local and other circumstances, cannot properly be represented in the British Parliament, they are entitled to a free and exclusive power of legislation in their several provincial legislatures, where their rights of representation can alone be preserved in all cases of taxation and internal polity, subject only to the negative of their sovereign, in such manner as has been heretofore used and accustomed...[234]

Thus, in these resolutions, loyalty to the king was maintained, but the parliament was denied competence to impose taxes on the colonies.

As a result of this Congress, economic war was declared with the suspension of imports and exports to England. The economic war rapidly became a military one and the Congress met again in Philadelphia and adopted the "Declaration of the Causes and Necessity of Taking up Arms" of 6 July 1775, as a reaction against the "enormous", and "unlimited power" of the Parliament of Great Britain. Therefore, the American Revolution can be considered a revolution against the sovereignty of the English Parliament.

One year later, the second continental Congress, in its session of 2 July 1776, adopted a proposition whereby the colonies declared themselves free and independent:

---

232 R.L. PERRY (ed.), *op. cit.*, p. 270.

233 Ch. F. ADAMS (ed.) *The Works of John Adams*, Boston 1850, II, p. 374 quoted by R.L. PERRY, *op. cit.*, p. 275.

234 R.L. PERRY (ed.), *op. cit.*, p. 287.

> That these United Colonies are, and of right, ought to be, Free and Independent States; that they are absolved from all allegiance to the British Crown, and that all political connexion between them, and the state of Great Britain, is, and ought to be, totally dissolved.[235]

The Congress agreed to draw up a declaration proclaiming to the world the reasons for the separation from its mother country, and on the 4th July, the Declaration of Independence was adopted, in formal ratification of the act already executed.

This document is of universal historical interest, for it was the first time that juridical–political–rationalist legitimacy had made its appearance openly in history. There was no longer the recourse to common law, nor to the rights of Englishmen, but exclusively to God and to the laws of nature. There was no longer the recourse to the Bill of Rights, but to self–evident truths, namely:

> That all men are created equal; that they are endowed, by the Creator, with certain unalienable rights; that among these are life, liberty, and the pursuit of happiness. That to secure these rights, Governments are instituted among men, deriving their just powers from the consent of the governed; that whenever any form of government becomes destructive of these ends, it is the right of the people to alter or to abolish it, and to institute a new government, laying its foundation on such principles and organizing the powers in such form, as to them shall most likely effect their safety and happiness.[236]

Consequently, anything, which was not rationally adapted to the objectives established, was unjustified and illegitimate, and, the state was also organized in the most adequate way to achieve the said objectives.

Apart from the importance of this document for the United States, it is undoubtedly also of universal significance: its basic premise, as a syllogism, is constituted by all those acts of the crown which, according to Locke, define tyranny, and the conclusion of the syllogism is obvious: by violating the pact uniting him to his American subjects, the king had lost all claim to their loyalty, and consequently, the colonies became independent states.

Obviously, once the colonies had acquired their independence, they had to regulate their own political organization. Moreover, after the king's proclamation of rebellion on 23 August 1775, the Congress just before the Declaration of Independence urged all colonies to form separate governments for the exercise of all authority. It resolved:

> That it be recommended to the respective assemblies and conventions of the United Colonies, where no government sufficient to the exigencies of their affairs has been hitherto established, to adopt such government as mall, in the opinion of the representatives of the people, best conduce to the happiness and safety of their constituents in particular and America in general.[237]

Thus, the Bill of Rights and the Constitution or Form of Government of Virginia were adopted on 12 June 1776, and the other Constitutions of the States were adopted after the Declaration of Independence until 1787.

---

235 *Idem*, p. 317.

236 *Idem*, p. 319.

237 *Idem*, p. 318. A.C. McLaughlin, *op. cit.*, p. 107–108.

These colonial constitutions were of fundamental importance both for constitutional history in general and for the history of the United States itself, since they undoubtedly represented the triumph of the rational normative concept of the constitution, which could already be glimpsed in the Declaration of Independence. Furthermore, there were written systematic and coded constitutions, many of which were preceded by a table of rights inherent in human beings. In accordance with that table of rights the organic part of the constitution was set, adopting, naturally, as a fundamental principle the division of powers, which also made its entry for the first time in constitutional history with the principle of the sovereignty of the law.

Therefore, the rational normative concept of the constitution, with its table of rights, its division of powers, its sovereignty of the law, its distinction between constituent and constituted power, and its division of the constitution into a dogmatic and organic part, comes from America and its colonial constitutions, from where it proceeded to Europe, to the French Declaration of 1789, and through it, to modern constitutional law.

The idea of a Confederation or Union of Colonies was also formulated at the same time as the Declaration of Independence, thereby satisfying the need for a political union mainly derived out of the conduct of the war. Hence the adoption by the Congress, on 15th November 1777, of the "Articles of Confederation " is considered to be the First constitution.[238] It established a confederation and perpetual union between the States, the aim of which was the "common defence, the security of their Liberties and their mutual and general welfare"[239] in a system in which each state retained "its sovereignty, freedom and independence"[240] and any power, jurisdiction and right not expressly delegated to the United States in Congress.

The result was that the sole body of the Confederation was the Congress, in which each state had a vote. Consequently, the Confederation lacked direct taxation power, depended economically on the contributions of the States, had no executive body and only an embryonic form of judicial organization. Despite its weakness, the Confederation succeeded in carrying on the war for 7 years until it won. Following the victory, the precariousness of the Confederation made it necessary to establish a greater power to achieve national integration and a Federal Convention was called to meet, "for the sole and express purpose of revising the articles of Confederation."[241]

This led in 1787 to the adoption by the Congress of the Constitution of the United States that was the result of a series of general compromises[242] between the political and social components of the independent colonies, of which the following are the most outstanding:

---

238 R.B. MORRIS, "Creating and Ratifying the Constitution", *National Forum. Towards the Bicentennial of the Constitution*, fall 1984, p. 9.

239 A.C. MCLAUGHLIN, *op. cit.*, p. 131.

240 *Idem*, p. 137; R.L. PERRY, (ed.), *op. cit.*, p. 399.

241 R.L. PERRY (ed.), *op. cit.*, p. 401.

242 M. GARCÍA–PELAYO, *op. cit.*, p. 336–337.

In the first place, the compromise between Federalists and Antifederalists, which provided the Union the necessary competences for its existence, while maintaining the autonomy of the Federate States. From this compromise emerged the form of the Federal state,[243] which appeared for the first time in constitutional history as a political organization of States, through a system of political decentralization or vertical separation of powers. This compromise was one of the main contributions of the North American Constitution to modern constitutional law.

The second great compromise reflected in the constitution was, as a result of a long brewing confrontation, the compromise between large and small States of the Union regarding representation. That is to say, between a Congress in which the States would be represented in proportion to their population and a Congress with a confederate type of representation. The result was a bicameral system in which the House of Representatives was to be made up of a number of deputies proportional to the population of each state, whereas the Senate would comprise two representatives per state, regardless of its size, thus providing equality among the states.[244]

In relation to the latter, the third compromise of the Constitution was that between the North and the South, that is to say, the compromise between free states and pro–slavery states, according to which the slave population was estimated at three fifths in relation to the white population for the purposes of determining the population of each state, both for the appointment of representatives and for tax purposes.

The great slavery issue was also to produce a fourth compromise concerning the question of import and export duties and, therefore, on the import of slaves or its abolition. The middle ground solution led to the adoption of a clause impeding the Congress from making any decision prohibiting slave importation for twenty years, until the year 1808.[245]

The fifth compromise that we can identify in the American Constitution is that between democracy and the interests of the ruling classes, to avoid despotism when voting. Thus, limited mechanisms for voting were established, based on private property, as well as a mechanism for direct election of representatives to the House of Representatives as established by each state, and indirect election to the Senate.

The last and final compromise reflected in the constitution was the establishments of a system of separation of powers at federal level, thus, a check and balance system. Therefore, in addition to the legislative body, a strong presidency was provided for, to be occupied by a President elected for four years, by means of a system of indirect suffrage; and a Supreme Court was created, made up of judges elected for life by the two bodies furthest from the masses, the president and the Senate, being granted power to declare the unconstitutionality of acts issued by the other powers

243 R.B. MORRIS, *loc. cit.*, p. 12, 13; M. GARCÍA–PELAYO, *op. cit.*, p. 336; A.C. MCLAUGHLIN, *op. cit.*, p. 163.

244 M. GARCÍA–PELAYO, *op. cit.*, p. 336; R.B. MORRIS, *loc. cit.*, p. 10; A.C. MCLAUGHLIN, *op. cit.*, p. 179.

245 R.B. MORRIS, *loc. cit.*, p. 11; A.C. MCLAUGHLIN, *op. cit.*, p. 185.

against the constitution. Separation of powers and judicial review of the constitutionality of legislative acts are another two main contributions of the American constitution to modern constitutional law.

In addition to these compromises of the constitution of the United States, we must turn our attention to another two main contributions of America to constitutional law: First, constitutionalism itself, in the sense of the adoption of all those compromises of forms of government in a written constitution as fundamental law, and second republicanism, as an ideology of the people against monarchy and hereditary aristocracies,[246] based on political representation.

Eighteenth century Americans decided upon revolution to repudiate royal authority and to erect a republic in its place. Thus, Republicanism and to become republican was what the American Revolution had been about. That is why "the people" who then became the sovereign in constitutional history gave the constitution.

The constitution adopted in 1787, however, was conceived basically as an organic document, regulating the separation of powers within the organs of the new state, both horizontally and vertically among the legislative, the executive and judicial powers and between the states and the United States in accordance with the federal System.

In spite of the colonial antecedents, and of the proposals made in the Convention, it did not contain a Bill of Rights, except the right to representative government. The protests of the opponents of the new Federal system, led particularly by the antifederalits, during the ratification process brought about the adoption of the First Ten Amendments to the Constitution, on the 15th December 1791, containing the American Bill of Rights.[247]

3. The French Constitution (1791)

After the American Revolution, the constitutionalization of the Legal state was followed by the French Revolution 1789 and the adoption of the third constitution in the world, the French one dated 3 September 1791, the Polish Constitution promulgated on the 3rd May of the same year, 1791, being the second.[248]

Two years after the approval of the American Constitution and thirteen years after the Declaration of Independence of the United States, the French Revolution (1789) developed into a social revolution aimed at liquidating the *Ancient Regime*, represented by an absolute and personal monarchy.[249] The problem here, was not how to find a common denominator between thirteen independent states and build a new state from the remains of the English colonies as was the case in the American

---

246 G.S. WOOD, "The Intelectual Origins of the American Constitution", *National Forum, cit.*, Fall 1984, p. 5.

247 See the text in R.L. PERRY (ed.), *op. cit.*, pp. 432–433.

248 A.P. BLAUSTEIN, "The United States Constitution. A Model in Nation Building", *National Forum, cit.*, p. 15.

249 A. DE TOCQUEVILLE, *The Old Regime and the Revolution* (L'Ancien Régime et la Revolution)

constitutional process, but rather, how to transform an over–centralized state constructed around the old French monarchy, where the state was the monarch (*L'État c'est Moi*), into a new form of state in which the people, through the concept of the nation, were to participate. A revolution was needed and its first result was the weakening of the monarchy itself.

After 14th July 1789, two main decisions were made by the French National Assembly: the abolition of seigniorial rights on 4th August and the Declaration of the Rights of Man and of the Citizen on 26th August, both in 1789. Two years later, the First French Constitution of 3rd September 1791 was adopted, which even though still a monarchical constitution, it conceived the king as a delegate of the nation and subject to the sovereignty of the Law. The fact was that from that process onwards, the state was no longer the king, as an absolute monarch, but the organized people in a Nation subject to a constitution.

The Constitution of 1791 adopted a structure which later proved to be classical for the development of modern constitutional law, and which has been witnessed in some of the American States' constitutions. This structure established a clear distinction between a dogmatic part, containing individual rights and the limits and obligations of the state power, and an organic part, establishing the structure, attributions and relations between the various state bodies.[250]

The Constitution began with the Declaration of the Rights of Man and of the Citizen, already adopted by the Assembly on 26th August and approved by the king on the 5th October 1789. This text was inspired by the Declarations of the American States recently emancipated from England, mainly the Virginia Bill of Rights (1776). However, this does not mean that the Declaration was not basically a French one, a pure work of rationalism, inspired directly by the thoughts of Rousseau and Montesquieu.[251]

This Declaration of Rights that preceded the constitution can be characterized by the following major features: In the first place, its content constituted a formal adhesion to the principles of natural law and to the "natural" rights with which Man is born, so that the Law simply recognizes or declares them, but does not establish them. Thus the declaration had a universal character. It was not a declaration of Frenchmen's rights but the acknowledgement by the revolutionaries, of the existence of the fundamental rights of man, for all time and for all States. That was why De Tocqueville compared the political revolution of 1789 with a religious revolution, by saying that in the fashion of great religions, the political revolution established general rules, and adopted a message that spread abroad. This important aspect of the Declaration is related to the fact that the rights declared were natural rights.[252]

---

250 M. GARCÍA–PELAYO, *op. cit.*, p. 463.

251 J. RIVERO, *Les Libertes Publiques*, Vol. I, Paris 1973, p. 38–42.

252 A. DE TOCQUEVILLE, *op. cit.*, quoted by Y. MADIOT, *Droits de l'Homme et Libertes Publiques*, Paris 1976, p. 46.

Secondly, under Rousseau's influence, the Declaration was based on man's natural bounty, which implicitly rejected the idea of original sin, for as it stated:

> Ignorance, forgetfulness and contempt of the rights of Man are the sole causes of public misfortunes and of the corruption of governments.

Thirdly –and this is fundamental– from the legal and political point of view, the powers of the state were limited, inasmuch as it had to act within the limits imposed on it by such rights and consequently, under the sovereignty of the law, a principle which is established in the constitution.

Moreover, both the Declaration of Rights and the constitution itself were based on the affirmation of national sovereignty, introducing a concept which has been fundamental in French constitutional law, as it marked the beginning of a new basis for the legitimization of state power, as opposed to the monarchical legitimacy of the past, as well as a new assumption for the reorganisation of state bodies.

In the French Constitution, the idea of the nation emerged for the purpose of depriving the king of his sovereignty; but as sovereignty existed only in a person who exercised it, the concept of the nation emerged, as a personification of the people. To use Berthelémy's words:

> There was a sovereign person who was the King. Another sovereign person had to be found to oppose him. The men of the Revolution have found that sovereign person in a moral person: the Nation. They have taken the Crown away from the King and have placed it on the head of the Nation.[253]

But the nation in revolutionary theory was identified with what Sièyes called the "Third Estate." The Third Estate in the revolutionary States–General, compared to the other two "estates" (the nobility and the clergy), was the lower state or the nation as a whole. *Quest–ce que le Tièrs?* Was the question posed by Sièyes in his book, and the answer he gave was "all", "all the nation."[254] The privileged strata was excluded from the concept of the nation, confined then to the bourgeoisie.

The bourgeoisie, as stated by Sièyes, sought the "modest intention of having in the States General or Assembly an influence equal to that of the privileged",[255] but the real situation, and particularly because of its economic power and the reaction against privileges, led the bourgeoisie to obtain power, through the French Revolution, with popular support.[256] The French a Revolution, therefore has been considered a Revolution of the bourgeoisie, for the bourgeoisie and by the bourgeoisie,[257] and was basically an instrument against privileges and discrimination and for seek-

---

253 BERTHELEMY–DUEZ, *Traité elémentaire de droit constitutionnel*, Paris 1933, p. 74, quoted by M. GARCIA–PELAYO, *op. cit.*, p. 461.

254 E. SIEYES, "*Quést–ce que le tièrs Etat?*" (Ed. R. ZAPPETI), Genève 1970, p. 121.

255 *Idem*, p. 135.

256 "The people –the not privileged– of course where the ones that supported the Third State, that is to say, the bourgeoisie, because they did not have other alternative, in the sense that they could not support the nobility or the clergy, who represented the privileges." G. DE RUGGIERO *The History of the European Liberalism*, Boston 1967, p. 74.

257 G. DE RUGGIERO, *op. cit.*, p. 75, 77.

ing equality of all men in the enjoyment of their rights. Thus the Declaration of Rights of Man and of Citizen was qualified as being "the ideological expression of the triumph of the bourgeoisie."[258]

Anyway, sovereignty was in the Nation, as the Declaration of Rights expressly established:

> The source of all sovereignty is essentially in the nation; no body, no individual can exercise authority that does not proceed from it in plain terms.[259]

Therefore, after the Revolution, the basis of public authority in France ceased to be the divine right of the personal monarch, and started to be the sovereignty of the nation (*souveraineté nationale*), that was not to be exercised directly by the nation, but through its representatives.[260]

Thus, the French constitution was also a representative constitution, since the nation exercised its power through representatives, and it is precisely in the structure of representation that the social significance of the Revolution was specifically reflected, because, in accordance with the system of suffrage which was established, a large number of citizens was excluded from electoral activity.[261]

Moreover, the French constitution established another principle of modern public law, which is particularly developed in France and which is summarized in the following statements: "There is no authority in France superior to that of the law"[262] and the law was considered to be "the expression of the general will."

This is an affirmation of the legal state and of the idea that it is not men who command, but laws. Hence the state bodies could demand obedience only insofar as they are an expression of the law, to the extent, said the constitution, that the king himself "only reigns by law, and it is only in the name of the law that he can demand obedience."[263]

The first constitution of France of 1791, despite of the Revolution, continued to establish a monarchical government: the exercise of the executive power and a share, though very limited, of the legislative power was conferred upon the king. But he was nothing more than the chief public functionary; he was considered a

---

258 J.L. ARANGUREN, *Ética y política*, Madrid 1963, p. 293, 297, quoted by E. DÍAZ, *Estado de derecho y sociedad democrática*, Madrid 1966, p. 80.

259 Art. 3.

260 Although ROUSSEAU considered representative regime incompatible with the principle of national sovereignty: "Sovereignty consists in the general will and the general will cannot be represented; deputies of the people are only commissioners; they can decide nothing definitely." *Contract Social*, 3, 15, quoted by J. BRISSAUD, *A History of French Public Law*, London 1915, p. 546.

261 Under the influence of Sièyes, the Constitution established two categories of citizens: active citizens and passive citizens. G. LEPOINTE, *Histoire des institutions du droit public français au XIX Siècle.1789–1914*, Paris 1953, p. 44.

262 "Il n'y a point en France d'autorite superieur a celle de la loi." M. GARCÍA–PELAYO, *op, cit.*, p. 465–466.

263 Art. 4, Chap II, Sec. 1.

delegate of the nation, subject to the sovereignty of the law. Consequently, the monarch became a state body for the first time, and the ancient institution of divine right became a body of positive law. The king became king of the French people instead of king of France.[264]

Finally, the constitution also established a system of strict separation of powers, in accordance with what was stated in the Declaration of Rights of Man and the Citizen, in the sense that:

> Any society in which the separation of power is not determined has no constitution at all.[265]

However, in the French system of separation of powers a clear predominance of the legislative power was shown. Thus, the king neither convened, nor suspended, or dissolved the assembly; he had the power of veto, but only for suspension, and could not take any initiative, although he could invite the legislative body to take something into account.

The assembly, for its part, had no control over the executive, since the king's person was sacred and inviolable; ministers were only subject to penal responsibility. However, the assembly had important executive attributions such as the appointment of principal officials, the surveillance of departmental administration, the declaration of war, the ratification of treaties, etc.[266]

In Europe, therefore, since the French Revolution in 1789 and the 1791 constitution, constitutions during last century were generally the result of Revolutions, establishing the fundamental scheme of the *État de droit* with fundamental rights and division of powers, and with an additional characteristic, namely that the state was organized from a negative standpoint vis–à–vis its own powers, that means keeping in mind the protection of the citizens against the abuse of state power. Consequently, the ways and means of control over the state were even more organized than the state itself.

In this process of constitutionalization of the *État de droit*, the principle of constitutional rigidity was also established, in the sense that the constitution was really fundamental. It was a fundamental law, which could not be modified by ordinary legislation, requiring special procedures for its amendment. This gave rise to the development of the theory of constituent power. In the French example, this presupposed that the people were an existential political entity. As a result of the Revolution, the people became the subject of constituent power, became aware of their political capacity of action and provided themselves with a constitution, based on the assumption, clearly stated, of their political unity and capacity of action.

The constitution was then the fundamental law of the state, and was not to be modified easily. Thus, the distinction between the constituent power of the people and the legislative power was developed, and consequently the distinction between

264 G. LEPOINTE, *op. cit.*, p. 44.

265 Art. 16.

266 G. LEPOINTE, *op. cit.*, p. 45, 49.

constitutional acts (*lois constitutionelles*) and ordinary laws. The Nation always retained the right to change its constitution, but this could only be done following the means, which had been prescribed in the constitution itself. Nevertheless this did not prevent changes in the constitution and because of the revolutionary struggles, four constitutions were adopted in the eleven years between 1789 and 1800: that of 3–14 September 1791; 24th June 1793; 5 *Fructidor*, year III (1795); and that of 22nd *Frimaire*, year VIII (1800).

Any way, the significance of the French Revolution lies in the fact that it led to the establishment of an *État de droit*, in the sense that it produced a constitution which limited and controlled the exercise of state power, thereby endowing the modern state with a new political character. In this system, the nation, as subject of the constituent power, confronted the absolute monarch, eliminated his absolutism and completely took his place, which actually led to an increase in the power of the state itself.

Naturally, the American model exerted considerable influence in this respect: the Declaration of Independence of 1776 and the American Constitution of 1787 itself, were also the result of the decision adopted by the people of the United States, although, in the case of the United States, it was not a matter of transforming a state already in existence, as was the case in France, but rather a question of the constitution of a new political formation, the act of providing a constitution to accompany the political foundation of a new state.

4. The Inspiration of France and America and the Latin American Constitutionalism

After the American and French revolutions aimed at creating a republican federal state in the American case or to transform an absolute monarchical state into a republican state in the French case, the constitutionalization of the legal state in their respective constitutions at the end of the eighteenth century was followed all over the world, mainly in Latin America and Europe during the nineteenth century.

In Europe, the French constitution of 1795 particularly inspired the Spanish constitution of Cadiz 1812 and the Norwegian constitution of 1814,[267] but in Latin American countries, being colonies of Spain and Portugal, the influence of the American and French revolutions and constitutionalism was immediate and definitive. We will refer only to one of the Latin American countries, Venezuela, not only because it is our own country, but also because it was the first Latin American country to gain independence from Spain, the third country in the world whose Declaration of Rights of the People was approved by an elected Congress, and where the first of the Latin American constitutions was sanctioned in 1811.

In effect, one of the first reactions against the Spanish monarchy inspired by the French Revolution, was the so–called *San Blas* conspiracy in Madrid, intended to take place on the 3rd February 1796. It ended before it began; the conspirators were detained the day before, went on trial and a few of them deported to the colonies for

267 J.A. HAWGOOD, *Modern Constitutions since 1787*, London 1939, p. 51.

life imprisonment. The principal conspirators, including Juan Bautista Picornell, were sent to Venezuela, where they managed to get in touch with local conspirators, and in 1797 they developed what has been called the conspiracy of Gual y España, named after the two main participants: Manuel Gual and Jose María España.

Even though the conspiracy failed, it remained as the most serious attempt at liberation in all Latin America, and also produced one of the most important documents that inspired the subsequent constitutionalization process in our countries.

The conspirators published a booklet entitled Rights of Man and Citizens, in 1797 with an "address to the Americans", that in fact was a translation of the French Declaration of Rights of Man and the Citizen contained in the 1795 French Constitution.[268]

The importance of this document was that it inspired the Declaration of Rights of the People, approved by the first Venezuelan Congress four days before the Declaration of Independence was proclaimed on 5th July 1811, which at the same time was inspired by the American Declaration of Independence.

Therefore, Latin America received the direct influence of both revolutions, the American and the French and altogether at the beginning of its constitutionalization process, of the French Declaration of Rights of Man and Citizens and of the American Declaration of Independence. Subsequently, the first of the Latin–American Constitutions, the Federal Constitution of the States of Venezuela of 21st December 1811, followed not only all the general trends of the constitutionalization process of the *État de droit* existing at the time[269] but also the fundamental ideas of Hobbes, Bodin, Locke, Montesquieu and Rousseau, all reflected in the articles of the constitution.

In effect, the constitution firstly followed the formal shape of the French, containing 228 articles, much more than the few articles in the American constitution. It was also conceived in the way constitutions were afterwards developed, with both a dogmatic and an organic part. The dogmatic part contained a declaration of "The Rights of lean that are recognized and that are to be respected in the state" in 58 articles much more than the French model. The organic part established the fundamental framework of the state and its organs, in 140 articles.

Secondly, the constitution was adopted by the "people of the States of Venezuela, using our sovereignty", following the general trend of the American and French process in relation to the concept of national sovereignty and representation. The article 144 of the constitution, in this respect established:

> 144. The sovereignty of a country or supreme power to govern or direct community interests equitably essentially and originally lays in the general mass of its inhabitants, and is exercised by means of agents or representatives appointed and established in accordance with the Constitution.

---

268 P. GRASES (ed.), *Derechos del hombre y del ciudadano*, Caracas 1959, p. 105–121.

269 See the texts in A.R. BREWER–CARÍAS, *Las Constituciones de Venezuela*, Madrid 1985.

Thus, continued article 145 and 146:

> 145. No individual, no family or portion or group of citizens, no particular corporation, no village, city or county can confer upon itself national sovereignty, which is inalienable and indivisible, in essence and origin. Neither may any individual exercise governmental public functions unless it has been obtained by the Constitution.
>
> 147. Magistrates and officials of Government, invested with any kind of authority whether in the Legislative, Executive or Judicial Departments, consequently are simple agents and representatives of the people in their functions and are always responsible to the inhabitants for their public conduct through legal and constitutional means.

Thirdly, the constitution was conceived as a manifestation of the social contract according to Locke's and Rousseau's concepts, to protect the rights of the people once renounced to the natural condition of man. In this sense, the articles 141 and 142 stated:

> 141. Once men have set themselves up in a Society, they renounce that unlimited and licentious liberty in which their passions easily led them to indulge, passions characteristic only of the wild state. The establishment of a society presupposes the renouncement of those ill–fated rights, the acquisition of other sweeter and more pacific rights and subjection to certain mutual duties.
>
> 142. The social pact assures each individual the enjoyment and possession of his goods, without prejudice to the right of others to have theirs.

The articles 151 and 152 also stated:

> 151. The aim of society is the common happiness, and governments have been instituted to make man secure, protecting his physical and mental faculties, improving the sphere of his enjoyment and to produce the honest and equitable exercise of his rights.
>
> 152. These rights are liberty, equality, property and security.

Fourthly, the supremacy of law was formally declared in accordance with Rousseau's concept as the expression of the general will, and secured by sanctioning illegal acts as tyrannical. In this respect, the articles 149 and 150 stated:

> 149. The law is the free expression of the general will or of the majority of the citizens, indicated by the body of its representatives legally constituted. The law is founded on justice and on the common needs and must protect public and individual liberty against any oppression or violence.
>
> 150. Those acts committed against any person which do not fall within the cases and forms determined by the law, are iniquitous, and when they involve the usurpation of constitutional authority or the liberty of the people, they shall be considered to be tyrannical.

Fifthly, the constitution adopted the principle of separation of powers in accordance with Montesquieu's thoughts.

In the preamble to the constitution, when establishing the basis of the federal pact, it was stated:

> The various functions of the authority entrusted to the Confederation shall never be performed together. The Sovereign Power must be divided into Legislative, Executive and Judicial power, and entrusted to different bodies, independent both reciprocally and in their respective faculties.

Furthermore, article 189 stressed that:

> The three essential government departments, namely the Legislature, the Executive and the Judiciary must be as separate and mutually independent as is required by the nature of a free government or as is in keeping with the links which bind together the system of the Constitution in indissoluble friendship and unity.

Finally, the Venezuelan Constitution of 1811 adopted the federal form of the state following the American model, as a mean to unite several former colonial provinces that were highly decentralized in the Spanish system of colonial government. The federal scheme adopted in the United States was then the ideal system to be adopted in the now independent state, in which the provinces, kept their "sovereignty, liberty and independence" in all matters not assigned by the Federal Pact to the general authority of the Confederation.

But in fact, the federal form adopted in the organisation, establishing a weakened power in the federal government, undoubtedly provoked the crisis of the First Republic and the beginning of a ten–year war of independence. The crisis was also provoked by the absence of a unipersonal executive, because originally our country had a collective triunviral executive.

Simon Bolivar, in whose honour the Simon Bolivar Chair of this University is named, criticised the adoption of the federal form of the state in the first constitution and attributed the absence of political stability and continuity, mainly facing the counter offensive of the Spanish Empire, to the weakened and powerless republic that resulted from it. In 1815, in effect, he said:

> In the same way that Venezuela has been the American Republic that has made most progress in its political institutions, it has also been the clearest example of the inefficiency of the federal–democratic form for our nascent states.[270]

Four years later, in 1819, on the same matter, he insisted:

> The more I admire the excellencies of the Federal Constitution of Venezuela, the more I am persuaded of the impossibility of its application to our state and from my point of view it is a prodigy that whose model in the North part of America be still in force, so prosperily...[271]

Bolívar qualified the North American federal constitution as the most perfect at the time, but blamed the 1811 Venezuelan legislators for being:

> Seduced by the dazzling shine of happiness of the American people, thinking that the blessings they enjoy are the exclusive result of its form of government and not of the character and customs of its citizens. And in effect, the example of the United States because its prosperity, was too flattering so as not to be followed.[272]

He finished his argument against the federal form of the state, arguing that at the beginning of the republic, we were not yet prepared for a highly decentralized form of vertical division of power, and for adopting weak central government. He ex-

270 S. BOLÍVAR, "Carta de Jamaica" (1815), in *Escritos Fundamentales*, Caracas 1982, p. 97.

271 S. BOLÍVAR, "Discurso de Angostura" (1819), in *Escritos Fundamentales*, *cit*, p. 120.

272 *Idem*.

pressed conclusively, in relation to the copying of the North American federal system,

> I think that it would be better for America to adopt the Koran, than the government of the United States even if it is the best in the world.[273]

But in spite of Bolivar's recommendations, federalism in particular, spread throughout Latin America. Venezuela has always had a federal system of government and it is still a Federal state. In the same way, all the other large states in Latin America have a federal form of government, as is the case of Argentina, Brazil and Mexico.

Anyway, American and French constitutionalism inspired the process, both of independence and constitution framing all the Latin American States during the first half of the last century, which adopted the general trends of the constitutionalization of the *État de Droit*. The same influence happened to develop in most European countries.

The constitutionalization process of North America and France soon brought about the development of constitutional an political studies, and perhaps the first of the constitutional thinkers of modern times was Alexis de Tocqueville. Tocqueville was a Frenchman who visited the United States in the 1830's to study the penitentiary system and finished by publishing one hundred and fifty years ago, one of the most important books in the history of constitutional law: *Democracy in America* (1835), followed a few years later by another very important book of his own, this time related to the French Revolution and its constitutionalization process: The *Ancient Regime and the Revolution* (1856).

These two books have undoubtedly influenced the process of constitutionalization and democracy all over the world since their publication. Their influence upon the conception of the *État de droit* was definitive.

We want to stress the impact of the American process of constitutionalization in modern constitutional law, but we want to do so through De Tocqueville's prism as a continental European constitutional and political thinker when he discovered for Europe the principles of democracy and constitutionalism that had occurred on the other side of the Atlantic. It is also a way of celebrating the one hundred and fiftieth anniversary of the publication of his *Democracy in America* in 1835.

II. GENERAL TRENDS OF CONTEMPORARY CONSTITUTIONALISM

In effect, one can say that the fundamental principles and institutions of modern constitutional law had their factual origin in the American Revolution. This event and the whole process of independence and constitutionalism in the United States radically transformed the constitutional trends of the time, and established the basis of contemporary constitutional law.

An exceptional witness to those processes was Alexis De Tocqueville, perhaps the first modern constitutional thinker of the last century, whose studies regarding

273 S. BOLÍVAR (letter to D.F. O'LEARY), in *Escritos Fundamentales*, *cit.*, p. 200, 201.

the American and French Revolutions and their constitutional consequences were considered as masterpieces by his contemporaries in France and other European countries. Today, these books are still essential works for understanding the fundamental changes and trends that took place after the American and French Revolutions, as well as the causes of those processes.

Our intention, as we said, is to stress the fundamental contributions of the American Revolution to constitutional theory and Law, through De Tocqueville's prism, which we consider a fundamental one, since it was a European continental approach to the North American constitutional process, still unknown in this part of the world in the 1830's .[274]

De Tocqueville, for instance, stressed among the points of departure of the Anglo–Americans and its importance for the future, the situation of the English colonies in the seventeenth century and particularly that of New England.

He stated:

> All the general principles on which modern constitutions rest, principles which most Europeans in the seventeenth century scarcely understood and whose dominance in Great Britain was then far from complete, are recognised and given authority by the laws of New England; the participation of the people in public affairs, the free voting of taxes, the responsibility of governments officials, individual freedom, and trial by jury – all these things were established without question and with practical effect.[275]

Those "general principles on which modern constitutions rest", as De Tocqueville called them, today and after the American independence, are the following:

First, the notion of constitution itself, as a written document, of permanent value, containing a fundamental or higher law, which form the basis of the constitutionalization process.

Second, the notion of democracy itself, the democratic regime or state, and the concept of sovereignty belonging to the people and not to state organs.

Third, the political centralization or decentralization of the state, as a basic element for its organization, and its reflections on the Federal form of the state and upon the development of local government.

Fourth, the principle of separation of powers, and the different forms of government, particularly presidential or parliamentary governments.

Fifth, the role of the Judicial power, the Supreme Court of Justice and the judicial control of the constitutionality of legislation, and in the sixth place, the establishing of an entrenched declaration of fundamental rights and liberties.

All these six principles were, and still are, general principles on which modern and contemporary constitutions rested and still rest, and that identifies the modern *État de droit.* All those principles were analysed by De Tocqueville in relation to the

---

274 J.P. MAYER, "Foreword", A. DE TOCQUEVILLE, *Democracy in America* (edited by J.P. Mayer and M. Lerner), London 1968, p. XIII–XXXIII.

275 A. DE TOCQUEVILLE, *op. cit.*, p. 50.

American systems to which he dedicated his book even though in its Introduction of his book he said that he was:

> Very far from believing that they (the Americans) have found the only form possible for democratic government,[276]

and that he did

> Not think that American Institutions are the only ones, or the best, that a democratic nation might adopt.[277]

Any way, he studied all of them and made fundamental and still valid reflections on them, which we want to comment upon.

1. Constitutionalism

The first of the principles of present constitutional law is constitutionalism, that is to say, the trust which men place in the power of words formally written down to keep a government in order.[278]

As we have said, written constitutions in the modern world, with the exception of Cromwell's *Instrument of Government* 1653, can be considered a North American political invention based on three elementary notions: that of a greater and higher law placed above government and individuals; that of fundamental rights of individuals, which must be guaranteed in regard to the state, and that of a charter, where the submission of the state to the law, limiting its powers, and individual rights were to be expressly written, with some sense of permanence.

This practice of written constitutions was initiated in the English colonies in America when they became independent states in 1776, giving rise to the rational–normative concept of the constitution, as a written and systematic document, referring to the political organization of society, establishing the powers of the different state bodies and generally preceded by a list of rights inherent in man. Thus, the general division of the contents of modern constitutions into an organic and a dogmatic part, the former comprising the concept of separation of power and supremacy of the law, and the latter the declaration of fundamental rights. As we have seen, subsequent to the Declaration of Rights and the Constitution of Virginia in 1776, the practice of written constitutions spread to Europe and Latin America.

The basic element in the process of constitutionalization or of constitutionalism, is, of course, the concept that the constitution is a supreme and fundamental law, placed above all state powers and individuals. In this respect De Tocqueville when comparing the constitutions of France, England and the United States, pointed out:

> In France, the Constitution is, or is supposed to be, immutable. No authority can change anything in it; that is the accepted theory.

---

276 *Idem*, p. 17.

277 *Ibid*, p. 285.

278 W.H. HAMILTON, "Constitutionalism", *Encyclopaedia of the Social Sciences*, Vol. III, IV, p. 255.

> In England, Parliament has the right to modify the Constitution. In England, therefore, the Constitution can change constantly, or rather it does not exist at all. Parliament being the legislative body, is also the constituent one.
>
> American political theories are simpler and more rational –he said–.
>
> The American Constitution is not immutable, as in France; it cannot be changed by the ordinary authority of society as in England. It is a thing apart; it represents the will of the whole people and binds the legislators as well as plain citizens but it can be changed by the will of the people, in accordance with established forms ...[279]

And he concluded:

> In America, the Constitution rules both legislators and simple citizens. It is therefore the primary law and cannot be modified by a law. Hence it is right that the courts should obey the Constitution rather than all the laws.[280]

From this came as a consequence, the concepts not only of written constitutions, but also of rigid ones, and above all, the notion of the supremacy of the constitution that by the time De Tocqueville visited the United States, had been developed by Chief Justice Marshall in the famous *Marbury v. Madison* case 1803 decided by the Supreme Court. In relation to this principle of Constitutional Supremacy, in that case it was stated:

> It is a proposition too plain to be contested, that the Constitution controls any legislative act repugnant to it; or, that the legislature may alter the Constitution by an ordinary act.
>
> Between these alternatives there is no middle ground. The constitution is either a superior paramount law, unchangeable by ordinary means, or it is on a level with ordinary legislative acts, and, like other acts, is alterable when the legislature shall please to alter it.[281]

In the same case, Marshall then concluded with his formidable proposition related to written constitutions:

> Certainly all those who have framed written constitutions contemplate them as forming the fundamental and paramount law of the nation, and consequently, the theory of every such government must be, that an act of the legislature, repugnant to the constitution, is void.
>
> This theory is essentially attached to written constitutions, and is, consequently, to be considered by this court as one of the fundamental principles of our society.[282]

Constitutionalism through written, rigid and supreme constitutions is a principle developed as a general trend in modern and contemporary constitutional law, and is followed in almost all countries in the world, except in the United Kingdom and a very few other countries. In any case, it has been the common trend in Latin–American constitutionalism ever since 1811.

---

279 A. DE TOCQUEVILLE, *op. cit.*, p. 123.

280 *Idem*, p. 124.

281 *Marbury v. Madison*, 5 U.S. (1 Cranch) 137, 2L, Ed. 60 (1803). See text in R.A. ROSSUM and G. Alan TARR, *American Constitutional Law. Cases and Interpretation*, New York 1983, p. 70.

282 *Idem*, p. 70.

2. Democracy and the People's Sovereignty

The second of the principles developed in constitutional and political practice in the modern world, influenced by American constitutionalism is that of democracy as republicanism based on the concept of people's sovereignty. With the American Revolution, the traditional monarchical legitimacy of government was definitively substituted. The sovereign was no longer the monarch, but the people, and therefore the practice of democratic government was initiated in the modern world.

This was a fundamental concept in De Tocqueville's work, forming the very title to his book *Democracy in America*, in which he said:

> Any discussion of the political laws of the United States must always begin with the dogma of the sovereignty of the people.[283]

A principle that De Tocqueville considered to be "over the whole political system of the Anglo–Americans."[284]

He added:

> If there is one country in the world where one can hope to appreciate the true value of the dogma of the sovereignty of the people, study its application to the business of society, and judge both its dangers and its advantages: that country is America.[285]

To that end he devoted his book, precisely to study democracy in America.

Of course, democracy developed in America long before independence, and De Tocqueville located its exercise "in the provincial assemblies, especially that of the township" where it "spread secretly"[286] during colonial rule. But once the American Revolution broke out:

> The dogma of the sovereignty of the people came out from the township and took possession of the government; every class enlisted in its cause; the war was fought and victory obtained in its name; it became the law of laws.[287]

In accordance with this dogma of the sovereignty of the people, when it prevails in a nation, –he said–, "each individual forms an equal part of that sovereignty and shares equally the government of the state."[288] Thus he asserted that "America is the land of democracy."[289]

The title of the chapter one of the second part of his book said: "Why it can strictly be said that the people govern in the United States," and in its first paragraph De Tocqueville said:

> In America the people appoint both those who make the laws and those who execute them; the people form the jury which punishes breaches of the law. The institutions are de-

283 A. DE TOCQUEVILLE, *op. cit.*, Vol. 1, p. 68.

284 *Ibid*, p. 78.

285 *Ibid*, p. 68.

286 *Ibid*, p. 69.

287 *Ibid*, p. 69.

288 *Ibid*, p. 78–79.

289 *Ibid*, p. 216.

mocratic not only in principle but also in all their developments; thus the people *directly* nominate their representatives and generally choose them annually so as to hold them more completely dependent. So direction really comes from the people, and though the form of governments is representative, it is clear that the opinions prejudices, interests, and even passions of the people can find no lasting obstacles preventing them from being manifest in the daily conduct of society.[290]

But one of the main aspects to which De Tocqueville referred in relation to democracy, was "the main causes tending to maintain a democratic republic in the United States."[291] He said:

> Three factors seem to contribute more than all others to the maintenance of a democratic republic in the New World.
>
> The first is the federal form adopted by the Americans, which allows the Union to enjoy the power of a greater republic and the security of a small one.
>
> The second are communal institutions which moderate the despotism of the majority and give the people both a taste fox freedom and the skill to be free.
>
> The third is the way judicial power is organized. I have shown –he said– how the courts correct the aberrations of democracy and how, though they can never stop the movements of the majority, they do succeed in checking and directing them.[292]

Thus, he established the relation between democracy and decentralization, and he stated that the problems of the "omnipotence of the majority" and even the "tyranny of the majority"[293] was tempered by the almost non–existence of administrative centralization in North America,[294] and by the influence of the American legal profession.[295]

Democracy as a form of government, always attained or maintained, is the second general trend in modern and contemporary constitutionalism, inspired by the American constitutional process. All the constitutions in the world established it as a basic component of their political systems, and is the sign of our times, even though its maintenance has not always been secured.

3. The vertical distribution of State Powers: Federal State, Decentralisation and Local Government

In his study of the American constitution, one of the aspects to which De Tocqueville devoted much of his attention due to its importance to democracy, was that of political decentralisation or the vertical distribution of state powers among different political territorial units; the third main feature of modern constitutionalism.

---

290 *Ibid*, p. 213.

291 Title of Charter IX of 2nd part, *op. cit.*, p. 342.

292 *Idem*, p. 354.

293 *Idem*, p. 304, 309.

294 *Idem*, p. 323.

295 *Idem*, p. 324.

He observed:

> In no country in the world are the pronouncements of the law more categorical than in America, and in no other country is the right to enforce it divided among so many hands.[296]

He stressed that "nothing strikes a European traveller in the United States more than the absence of what we call government or administration .... Functions (are) multiplied... (and) by sharing authority in this way its power becomes, it is true, both less irresistible and less dangerous, but it is far from being destroyed.[297]

He concluded his observation:

> There is nothing centralized or hierarchical, in the constitution of American administrative power, and that is the reason why one is not at all conscious of it. The authority exists but one does not know where to find its representative.[298]

De Tocqueville observed that the distribution of powers in the vertical sense, in North America, was not produced by a process of decentralization but rather of centralization, in the sense that the township, the country and the States, first existed so that "The federal government was the last to take shape in the United States."[299]

In his own words:

> In most European nations political existence started in the higher ranks of society and has been gradually but always incompletely, communicated to the various members of the body social.
>
> Contrariwise, in America one may say that the local community was organized before the county, the county before the States; and the state before the Union.[300]

Referring to New England, he stated that the local communities there had taken complete and definite shape as early as 1650, and he stressed:

> Inside the locality there was a real active life which was completely democratic and republican. The colonies still recognised the mother country's supremacy; legally the state was a monarchy, but each locality was already a lively republic.[301]

Thus, from this historical approach, the importance that De Tocqueville assigned to local government as the source of democracy is classical. His famous words concerning local government are well known and always valid:

> The strength of free peoples resides in the local community. Local institutions are to liberty what primary schools are to society; they put it within the people's reach; they teach people to appreciate its peaceful enjoyment and accustoms them to make use of it.[302]

And he added: 'In the townships, ... the people are the source of power, but nowhere else do they exercise their power so directly';[303] that is why, he insisted, local

---

296 *Ibid*, p. 87.
297 *Ibid*, p. 86.
298 *Ibid*, p. 87.
299 *Ibid*, p. 72.
300 *Ibid*, p. 51.
301 *Ibid*, p. 51.
302 *Ibid*, p. 74.

institutions "exercise immense influence over the whole of society",[304] and concluded by saying that "political life was born in the very heart of the townships."[305]

Regarding the federal form of the state, a product of the process of political centralization in a highly decentralized society, De Tocqueville said:

> This constitution, which at first sight one is tempted to confuse with previous federal constitutions, in fact rests on an entirely new theory, a theory that should be hailed as one of the great discoveries of political science in our age.[306]

And in fact, one can say that the federal state came into being in history with the American constitution 1789, and even though the word "federal" or "federation" is not used in the constitution, it was in the United States that this form of political organisation was born.[307]

It did not respond to a previous scheme, but to practical need: the purpose was to seek a formula that made the existence of independent states compatible with a central power with enough attributions to act by itself at federal level.

This new institution, De Tocqueville said, cannot be compared to the confederations that existed in Europe well before the American constitution, mainly because the central power in the American constitution as he observed, "acts without intermediary on the governed, administering and judging them, as do national governments," adding:

> Clearly here we have not a federal government but an incomplete national government. Hence a form of government has been found which is neither precisely national nor federal; but things have halted there, and the new word to express this new thing does not yet exist.[308]

This "new thing" is precisely what in constitutional law is known as federal state, and although De Tocqueville admired its novelty, he also pointed out its defects, and clearly observed that it was not a product for export.

He said,

> The Constitution of the United States is like one of those beautiful creations of human diligence which give their inventors glory and riches but remains sterile in other hands.[309]

In this sense, in his book De Tocqueville referred to the case of Mexico in the 1830's with its imported federal system but his remarks can be applied to all Latin America. Tries Federal organization of the state was, precisely, one of the main features of American constitutionalism that was immediately followed by almost all large Latin–American countries.

---

303 *Ibid*, p. 75.

304 *Ibid*, p. 75.

305 *Ibid*, p. 79.

306 *Ibid*, p. 192.

307 *Cf.* M. García Pelayo, *Derecho constitucional comparado*, Madrid 1957, p. 215, 341.

308 A. De Tocqueville, *op. cit.*, p. 194.

309 *Ibid*, p. 203.

In contrast to the centralized states of Europe, and the national concentration of political power, De Tocqueville pointed out that "the most fatal of all defects which I regard as inherent in the federal system is the comparative weakness of the government of the Union", adding that "a divided sovereignty must always be weaker than a complete one."[310]

As we have said, this weakness referred to the federal form of the state, once adopted in the Venezuelan constitution 1811, 6 months after the Declaration of Independence, and which was precisely one of the main causes of the failure of the First Republic the following year. Thus, of Simon Bolivar definitively asserted in a letter to the governor of one of the Venezuelan provinces, (Barinas), on 12 August 1813:

> Never the division of power had established and perpetuated governments; only its concentration had infused respect for a nation.[311]

We mentioned before that Bolivar expressed all his life bitter criticism regarding the federal form of the state and its adoption in Venezuela, and always advocated a concentrated form of state power. In addition, for example, in his famous Manifesto of *Cartagena* of 1812, written the year following the sanctioning of the Constitution and after the failure of the First Republic, he expressed:

> What make the government of Venezuela more weaken was the federal form it adopted, following the exaggerated expression of the rights of man that by allowing them to self–government, braked the social pacts, and leads nations to anarchy. That is the real situation of the Confederation. Each Province had an independent government; and in accordance with its example, each Township wanted equal powers and adopted the theory that Man and towns the prerogative of establishing, as they liked the government that best suited them... The federal system, if it is true that is the most perfect and oriented to provide human happiness in society, is nevertheless, the most opposed to the interests of our new–born States.[312]

Later, in his address to the Angostura Congress, in 1819, he persisted in the same idea:

> The Venezuelans –he said– were not to get the magnificent federal system suddenly after the independence. We were not prepared for so much welfare; the good as well as the evil can kill when it is sudden and excessive.[313]

Finally, one year before his death, in a letter to his former aide–de–camp, Daniel Florencio O'Leary, he definitively qualified the federal system as a

> Regularized anarchy, or better still, the law that establishes the implicit duty of disassociation and destruction of the state with all its individuals.[314]

But in spite of Bolivar's remarks and criticism of Federations, in Venezuela's case, since those days of independence and after the 1830 constitution, the form of

310 *Ibid*, p. 204.

311 S. BOLÍVAR, *Escritos Fundamentales*, Ed. 1982, p. 63.

312 *Idem*, p. 61–62.

313 *Idem*, p. 140.

314 *Idem*, p. 200, 201.

our state has always been federal, and in the name of federation we had our bloodiest civil war and social revolution in the middle of last century: the Federal War of 1858–1863.

On the other hand, all the largest states of Latin America and of the world today have a federal form, to an extent that the federal system of government covers more than a half of the earths surface.

Anyway, although De Tocqueville was also a critic of the federal form of state, he conversely praised the beneficial effects of political decentralization and local government. He said:

> The partisans of centralization in Europe maintain that the government administers localities better than they can themselves; that may be true when the central government is enlightened and the local authorities are not, when it is active and they lethargic, when it is accustomed to command and they to obey...

But when people are enlightened, awake to their own interests, and used to thinking for themselves, as he had seen in America, he said that he was:

> Persuaded that in that case the collective force of the citizens will always be better able to achieve social prosperity than the authority of the government.[315]

He finally declared that:

> The political advantages derived by the Americans from a system of decentralization would make me prefer that to the opposite system.[316]

4. Separation of Powers and Presidential System of Government

In the constitution of the United States of 1787, and previously, in the various constitutions of the former colonies, the fourth principle of modern constitutionalism, the principle of separation of power within the more orthodox doctrine at the time, was formally expressed for the first time.

For instance, the first of those constitutions, the one of Virginia in 1776, stated (Art. III):

> The Legislative, Executive and Judiciary departments, shall be separate and distinct, so that neither exercise the powers properly belonging to the other; nor shall any person exercise the powers of more than one of them at the same time...

The American constitution has no similar norm within its articles, but its main objective was precisely to organize the form of government, within the principles of the separation of powers, but allowing various interferences between them in a check and balance system. Particularly, regulating the powers of the executive in what was a new way, giving rise to presidentialism as opposed to parliamentarism, and to a particular shape of the judiciary, never previously known in constitutional practice.

De Tocqueville referred, in his book, to these two aspects of the principle.

---

315 A. DE TOCQUEVILLE, *Democracy in America, cit.*, p. 110.

316 *Idem*, p. 113, 115.

Regarding the executive power, he immediately pointed out that in the United States, "maintenance of the republican form of government required that the representative of executive power should be subject to the national will"; thus, "the president is an elective magistrate... the one and only representative of the executive power of the nation."[317] But, he noted, "in exercising that power he is not completely independent."[318]

That was one of the particular consequences of the check and balance system of separation of powers adopted in the United States, but without making the executive dependent on parliament, as in parliamentary systems of government. That is why when comparing the European parliamentary system with the presidential system of the United States, De Tocqueville referred to the important part that the executive power played in America in contrast with the situation of a constitutional king in Europe.

A constitutional king, he observed, "cannot govern when opinion in the legislative chambers is not in accord with his."[319] In the presidential system, he said, conversely, the sincere aid of Congress to the president "is no doubt useful, but it is not necessary in order that the government should function."[320]

The separation of powers and the presidential system of government was followed very closely, sooner or later, in all Latin American republics after Independence or after the monarchical experience that a few countries had.

Thus, one can say that presidentialism is the sign of our constitutional system of government, and to such an extent, that parliamentarism has never developed in Latin America. This is rather a European form of government that Europe never managed to export to Latin America.

5. The role of the judiciary

But among the American born constitutional institutions, the one that perhaps has the most distinguished originality is the role assigned to the judicial power in the system of separation of powers. This is true even at the present time, and was so when De Tocqueville visited North America. He devoted a separate chapter of his book to the powers of judges and to its great political importance, beginning with this assertion:

> Confederations have existed in other countries besides America, and there are republics elsewhere than on the shores of the New World; the representative system of government has been adopted in several European States; but so far, I do not think that any other nation in the world has organized judicial power in the same way as the Americans.[321]

Three aspects of the organization and functioning of judicial power can be considered as a fundamental American contribution to constitutional law: the political

317 *Idem*, p. 148.

318 *Idem*, p. 149.

319 *Ibid*, p. 155.

320 *Ibid*, p. 156.

321 *Ibid*, p. 120.

role of judges; the institution of a Supreme Court; and judicial review of legislation. De Tocqueville noticed all three aspects.

The first thing he observed in the American institutions was the "immense political power"[322] attributed to judges, which he considered "the most important political power in the United States."[323] The reason for this immense power, said De Tocqueville:

> Lies in this one fact: the Americans have given their judges the right to base their decisions on the Constitution rather than on the laws. In other words, they allow them not to apply laws which they consider unconstitutional.[324]

Therefore, "there is hardly a political question in the United States which does not sooner or later turn into a judicial one";[325] thus the fundamental changes in political and social life in the United States that have been led by the Supreme Court decisions in all American history.

The second fundamental aspect of the Judiciary in American institutions, De Tocqueville stressed, was the high standing of the Supreme Court among the great authorities in the state. De Tocqueville observed:

> The Supreme Court has been given higher standing than any known tribunal, both by the nature of its rights and by the categories subject to its jurisdiction... a mightier judicial authority has never been constituted in any land.[326]

De Tocqueville explained these powers of the Supreme Court, in which he said, "the peace, prosperity, and very existence of the Union rest continually", by saying the following:

> Without (the judges of the Supreme Court)... the Constitution would be a dead letter; it is to them that the executive appeals to resist the encroachments of the legislative body, the legislature to defend itself against the assaults of the executive, the union to make the states obey it, the states to rebuff the exaggerated pretensions of the Union, public interest against private interest, the spirit of conservation against democratic instability.[327]

Thus, the whole system of check and balance in the separation of powers, in the United States relied and still relies on the Supreme Court, and on the power of judges to control the constitutionality of legislation, precisely, the third main feature of the judiciary in North America.

In effect, in relation to the supremacy of the constitution, De Tocqueville observed that it "touches the very essence of judicial power; it is in a way the natural right of a judge to choose among legal provisions that which binds him most strictly."[328] This led to the control of the constitutionality of law, a creation of

322 *Ibid*, p. 122, 124.

323 *Ibid*, p. 120.

324 *Ibid*, p. 122.

325 *Ibid*, p. 184.

326 *Ibid*, p. 184.

327 *Ibid*, p. 185.

328 *Ibid*, p. 123.

American constitutionalism, referred to by De Tocqueville with these simple and logical words:

> If anyone invokes in an American court a law which the judge considers contrary to the Constitution, he can refuse to apply it. That is the only power peculiar to an American judge, but great political influence derives from it.[329]

This was termed as being the "very essence of judicial duty" by John Marshall in the famous *Marbury v. Madison case* (1803), when referring to written constitutions and their fundamental and superior character, in relation to the other laws of society. This duty of the courts to consider acts of the legislature repugnant to the constitution void, was described in that famous case with the following logical arguments:

> If an act of the legislature, repugnant to the Constitution, is void, does it, notwithstanding its invalidity, bind the courts, and oblige them to give it effect? Or, in other words, though it be not law, does it constitute a rule as operative as if it was a law? This would be to overthrow in fact what was established in theory, and would seem, at first view, an absurdity too gross to be insisted on. It shall, however, receive a more attentive consideration.

Then concluding:

> It is emphatically the province and duty of the judicial department to say what the law is. Those who apply the rule to particular cases must, of necessity, expound and interpret that rule. If two laws conflict with each other, the courts must decide on the operation of each.
>
> So, if a law be in opposition to the Constitution; if both the law and the Constitution apply to a particular case, so that the court must either decide that case conformably to the law, disregarding the Constitution; or conformably to the Constitution, disregarding the law; the court must determine which of these conflicting rules governs the case. This is the very essence of judicial duty.[330]

This judicial duty, discovered by the North Americans, is another of the major contributions of American constitutionalism to contemporary constitutional law, and has been followed and developed all over the world judicial constitutional control, however, is essentially related to the federal form of the state as a mean to control unauthorized invasions and interferences between the decentralized powers of the state. That is why in all the Latin American countries with federal organizations, judicial review of legislation was immediately established under the American influence, a few decades before the first continental ever European experiences in the matter.

Today and ever since the last century, judicial review or control of constitutionality of laws is a general trend of Latin American legal systems, but in a much more original way than the North American system. Various Latin American countries, for instance, as is the case of Venezuela and Colombia since the last century, combine the North American system of judicial review that allows all courts to decide upon the applications of laws on constitutional grounds, with the power of the Supreme Court of Justice to declare a law void with general effects, when considered unconstitutional by means of a popular action granted to all citizens even without

329 *Ibid*, p. 124.

330 *Marbury v. Madison*, S.U.S. (1 Cranch), 137; 2 L. Ed. 60 (1803).

particular interest in the matter. This second control is an original Latin American mean of judicial review, developed only with approximate similarities after the twenties and in the forties in some continental European countries.

6. The entrenched Declaration of Fundamental Rights and Liberties

The sixth major contribution of North American constitutionalism to modern constitutional law has been the practice of establishing formal and entrenched declarations of fundamental rights and liberties. As we have said, the first modern declaration of this kind was adopted in the American colonies the same year of the Declaration of Independence, and in this sense the Declaration of Rights of Virginia 1776 is famous.

These declarations of the rights of man were new in history mainly because they were not based on common law or tradition, as the 1689 English Bill of Rights was, but on human nature. They were natural rights of people, declared politically by the new constituent powers of the colonies as a limit on state powers.

However, as we have also said, the American constitution, 1787, did not include a bill of rights in its articles, which aroused several objections during the convention. This led to the approval, two years later, of the first ten amendments that the American Bill of Rights contained.

Alexander Hamilton, justifying the absence of a Bill of Rights in the Constitution, said:

> That bills of rights, in the sense and to the extent in which they are contended for, are not only unnecessary in the proposed Constitution, but would even be dangerous. They would contain various exceptions to powers not granted; and, on this very account, would afford a colourable pretext to claim more than were granted.

He finished his argument by asking:

> For why declare that things shall not be done which there is no power to do?.[331]

This concept of rights as limitations of state powers was followed in the first ten amendments of the constitution but adding to it the concept of rights as natural rights of man established in the Declaration of Independence 1776. They both influenced all the formal and entrenched declarations of human rights that were adopted later, particularly the French Declaration of Rights of Man and the Citizen, (1789), and through the latter, the Latin American declarations, up to the present, where those declarations have been internationalised.

However, De Tocqueville did not devote particular comments in his book to the declaration of rights, undoubtedly, because by the time he visited America, the French Declaration of 1789 was already famous and unique. Nevertheless, he referred to specific rights, particularly important in North America like equality, freedom of press and political association,[332] and not always with complete acceptance. For instance, referring to freedom of press, he said:

---

331 A. HAMILTON in *The Federalist* (ed. B.F. Wright), Cambridge, Mass 1961, N° 84, p. 535.

332 A. DE TOCQUEVILLE, *op. cit.*, Vol. 1, p. 222, 232.

> I admit that I do not feel toward freedom of the press that complete and instantaneous love which one accords to things by their nature supremely good. I love it more from considering the evils it prevents than on account of the good it does.[333]

North American Independence (1776) and the North American constitution (1787) were the immediate results of a great revolution that gave birth to a new state; but at the same time they brought about an authentic revolution in the area of political and constitutional institutions in the world, giving rise to new forms of government and political acts. After the American Revolution, written constitutions, republicanism and sovereignty of the people, federal states, separation of powers in a system of check and balance, presidentialism and judicial review, were all new institutions that spread throughout the world. In the first place, they influenced definitively the shape of Latin American constitutionalism that began to develop twenty years afterwards.

Alexis De Tocqueville was the first European raised in the European continental system of law to study the importance and impact of the American Revolution one hundred and fifty years ago and led the way to major transformations of constitutional institutions in Europe. That is why we consider that we can still say today the same as John Stuart Mill wrote in 1840 about De Tocqueville's Democracy in America, in the sense that it was not only "the first philosophical book ever written on democracy as it manifests itself in modern society", but it was also a book that marked "the beginning of a new era in the scientific study of politics."[334]

Its influence all over the world, therefore, has been outstanding not only because of the book itself, but also because its aim was to study the American institutions that contributed the most to the shaping of modern constitutionalism.[335]

III. THE *ÉTAT DE DROIT* AND JUDICIAL REVIEW

The *État de droit* or the state according to the rule of law, as we have seen, can be characterized by three main trends:

First, as a state in which powers are limited, as a guarantee of liberty, and that limitation is established through a system of distribution and separation of powers.

The *État de droit*, in this perspective, is the contrary of the absolute state, and this limitation of powers is expressed in three sorts of state power distribution: in the *first place*, by a distinction between the powers of the state themselves and an area of liberties, freedoms and rights of citizens that are beyond the sphere of state action. In the *second place*, by a distinction in the state between constituent power, attributed to the people as sovereign electorate, which demonstrate its activity normally through a written constitution and the constituted powers, represented by the

---

333 *Idem*, p. 222.

334 J.S. MILL, *The Edinburgh Review*, October 1840, N° CXLV, p. 3, quoted by J.P. MAYER, "Tocqueville's Democracy in America: Reception and Reputation", in A. DE TOCQUEVILLE, *op. cit.*, Vol. I, p. XIX.

335 See for example, the references to the influence of DE TOCQUEVILLE book regarding judicial review in México, in R.D. BAKER, *Judicial Review in México. A Study of the Amparo Suit*, Austin 1971, p. 15.

organs of the state, comprising the legislature, all submitted to the constituent powers will. Finally, in the *third place*, by a separation of powers within the constituted organs, in a vertical and horizontal way. In the vertical way, the separation of powers leads to a system of political decentralization throughout state organs at various territorial levels, including the federal form of the state. In the horizontal way, the separation of powers leads to the classical division between the legislative, executive and judicial organs, with their respective powers in a check and balance system with established mutual interference and restraint.

The second main feature of the *État de droit* besides the distribution and separation of powers, is that the state is submitted to the rule of law, in the sense that all state organs are submitted to limits imposed by the law. Therefore, the only body not submitted to legal limitations is the sovereign, identified in most States with the electoral body. This is, as we have said, the constituent power whose actions are normally reflected in a written constitution.

In relation to the state organs, however, the rule of law or the principle of legality implies their necessary submission to the law, varying the scope or ambit of legality, in relation to the level that the particular acts of those state organs have in the graduated or hierarchical system of rules of law that, in general, can be established in all legal systems. In this context, we have said that legality in relation to state organs, means" legal order" and not just an act of the legislative organ. Therefore it could just mean "constitutionality", or submission to the constitution, if a particular act is issued in direct execution of the constitution; or "legality" in a broader sense, as submission to the legal order, if a state act is issued in indirect execution of the constitution. Regarding the administration, this is the traditional meaning of legality.

Finally, apart from the principles of distribution of powers and of the submission of the state to the rule of law, we have also referred to the third main feature of the modern *État de droit*, that of the establishment of an entrenched Bill of Rights, as a guarantee to individuals against state organs, normally in a written constitution.

These three main characteristics of the *État de droit*, in contemporary constitutional law, have been constitutionalized, in the sense that they have been formally established in a written and rigid constitution. Therefore, the *État de droit* implies that the principles of distribution and separation of powers, the subjection of the state organs to the rule of law, and the declaration of rights and liberties must all be embodied in a written constitution formulated in an entrenched way so as to be protected from changes introduced by the ordinary legislator.

However, all these principles of the *État de droit* and their establishment in a written and rigid constitution require some means of protection to guarantee the existence of the limits imposed on the state organs and on the enjoyment of individual rights. In this respect the argument of John Marshall in the famous *Marbury v. Madison case* decided by the United States Supreme Court was precise:

> To what purpose are powers limited, and to what purpose is that limitation committed to writing, if these limits may, at any time, be passed by those intended to be restrained? The distinction between a government with limited and unlimited powers is abolished, if those

limits do not confine the persons upon whom they are imposed, and if acts prohibited and acts allowed are of equal obligation.[336]

Moreover, along the same line of argument we can ask to what purpose are state powers limited, to what purpose is the principle of legality established, to what purpose are fundamental rights and liberties formally declared, and to what purpose are all those principles committed to writing in a constitution considered as fundamental law, if there is no mean of guaranteeing the existence and permanence of said limits, of the state organs submission to legality and of the effective enjoyment of the citizens, rights and liberties?

Therefore, the *État de droit* with all its characteristics, only exists if these means of protection of the Constitution and of legality are established, and if the judiciary is in charge of making those means of protection of the constitution effective.[337] Consequently, the courts in the *État de droit* must ensure the effectiveness of the limits imposed on the state organs, their submission to the rule of the constitution and to the principle of legality, and the enjoyment of the fundamental rights and liberties of individuals.

Thus, there is no *État de droit*, if there is no power granted to the courts of the state to control the submission of the state organs to the rule of law.

Therefore, we can say that the basic element of the *État de droit* or state submitted to the rule of law or to the principle of legality is the existence of a system of judicial review, aimed at controlling that submission to the rule of law of all the state acts, particularly, of legislative, administrative and even judicial acts. The two fundamental objectives of this system of judicial review are obviously: one to ensure that all those acts of the state are adopted or issued in accordance to the law of the said state; two, to ensure that state acts respect the fundamental rights and liberties of citizens.

Thus, we can distinguish two main judicial review systems in the contemporary *État de droit*: On the one hand, a system which seeks to control the conformity of all state acts to the law; and on the other hand, a system which seeks to guarantee the fundamental rights and liberties of individuals; both giving individuals, precisely, a fundamental right to accede to justice by means of judicial actions aimed at obtaining such control.

1. Judicial control of the conformity of State acts with the rule of law

As we said, the first of these systems of judicial review or control, has the purpose of ensuring the effective submission of state acts to the rule of law or to the principle of legality. However, as we have seen, the sphere or confines of "legality" are certainly not the same for all state acts. In other words, "legality" does not mean

336 *Marbury v. Madison*, 5.U.S. (1 Cranch) 137; (1803); 2 L, Ed 60 (1803). See the text in R.A. ROSSUM and G. A. TARR, *American Constitutional Law. Cases and Interpretation*, New York 1983, p. 70.

337 See in general, H. KELSEN, "La garantie juridictionnelle de la Constitution (La justice constitutionnelle)", *Revue du droit public et de la science politique en France et à l'étranger*, T. XLV, Paris 1928, p. 197–257.

the same for all acts of the state. Its meaning or the confines of legality for each of these acts, depends on the rank the specific act holds in the legal order, particularly in relation to the constitution or to the supreme law of the land.

So, one distinction above all can be traced in legal systems with written constitutions, namely that between state acts that are issued in direct execution of the constitution, and acts that are issued in indirect execution of the constitution. This distinction between state acts, leads, of course, to a distinction between the systems of judicial review or control that are laid down.

In effect, as we have studied, there are some state acts that are adopted in direct execution of the constitution, in the sense that they are acts that have their origin in powers granted directly in the constitution and itself to the state organ that produces them, and to which they must be submitted. In relation to these acts, the system of judicial review has and can only have the purpose of ensuring that the said acts are issued or adopted in accordance to the constitution itself. In this case, as Hans Kelsen pointed out in 1928:

> The guarantee of the constitution means guarantees of the regularity of the constitution's immediate subordinated rules, that is to say, essentially, guarantee of the constitutionality of laws.[338]

Therefore, with regard to those acts of the state, "legality" as we already know, is equivalent to "constitutionality", and judicial review or control of legality is also equivalent to judicial control or review of the constitutionality of such acts.

Of course, this distinction between acts issued in direct execution of the constitution and acts issued in indirect execution of the constitution, and consequently, the distinction between judicial control of constitutionality and the judicial control of legality only exists in the strictest sense of the term, in those legal systems possessing a written constitution as a fundamental law constituting the superior source of the whole legal order. Therefore, in systems without a written constitution, and where acts of Parliament are the supreme law, the distinction cannot be made and a system of judicial review of constitutionality cannot exist.

On the contrary, this control of constitutionality in legal systems with written constitutions has been developed particularly in relation to legislative acts, that is to say, to normative acts of Parliament. Hence, one usually speaks of judicial control of the constitutionality of legislation or simply of "judicial review of the constitutionality of legislation."[339]

In effect, if Parliament, Congress or the National Assembly as a representative of the sovereign people, is and must be the supreme interpreter of the law, and through the law, of the general will, it always does so in execution of constitutional rules, particularly in those cases where a written and rigid constitution exists, which cannot, therefore, be changed by the ordinary legislator. Consequently, the law as an act of Parliament is always submitted to the constitution, and when it exceeds the limits established by that constitution, the act of Parliament is unconstitutional and, there-

---

338 H. KELSEN, *loc.cit.*, p. 201.

339 M. CAPPELLETTI, *Judicial Review in the Contemporary World*, Indianapolis 1971, p. VII.

fore, liable to be annulled. As stated in the *Marbury* v. *Madison case* by the United States Supreme Court in 1803:

> Certainly all those who have framed written constitutions contemplated them as forming the fundamental and paramount law of the nation, and consequently, the theory of every such government must be, that an act of the legislature, repugnant to the Constitution, is void.[340]

Judicial control or review of constitutionality, therefore, affords the courts the possibility of determining the unconstitutionality of the laws, deciding not to apply them giving preference to what is stated in the constitution, and, in some cases, allowing some special courts to declare with general effect the nullity of the law considered unconstitutional.

But in legal systems with judicial review of constitutionality, all other acts of the legislature other than formal laws, which are also issued by Parliament in direct execution of the constitution, can also be submitted to judicial control of constitutionality likewise. This is the case, for example, of internal regulations for the functioning of legislative bodies, and of parliamentary acts of specific effect, issued for the purpose of authorising or approving some executive acts, like the appointment of some officials, or the adoption of some budget changes. All these acts, in written constitutional legal systems, are subject to and must be adopted according to the constitution, and therefore, can be judicially controlled to ensure their submission to the fundamental rules of the constitution.

Moreover, not only the acts of legislative bodies are subject to judicial control of constitutionality. In general, all acts of state bodies and organs issued in direct and immediate execution of the constitution are also subject to such control.

In particular, acts of government with or without the same force of formal law, issued by the head of state or by the government in direct execution of powers provided for directly in the constitution, and which due to the distribution of powers, cannot be regulated by Parliament, are also subject to judicial control of constitutionality.

In short, it is through this system of judicial review of the constitutionality of state acts that the effective submission of state organs to the constitution can be ensured when they execute it directly. Therefore, this is possible only in legal systems with written constitutions, where the courts have such powers of judicial review.

Consequently, when there is no written constitution, or when although this fundamental law exists, the courts do not have the power to control the constitutionality of legislative acts, the legal situation is very similar.

As Professor J.D.B. Mitchell pointed out:

> The mere fact of there being a written Constitution does not by itself necessarily mean that courts play any greater role in protecting individual rights or policing the Constitution.
>
> Where there is such a Constitution but courts do not possess the power to declare legislation unconstitutional, the only means by which the courts can protect the basic principles of that constitution from encroachment of erosions is by the restrictive interpretation of legisla-

340 *Marbury v. Madison*, 5.U.S. (1 Cranch), 137; (1803); 2 L, Ed. 60, (1803).

> tion. In such circumstances the position of the courts and the protection for fundamental constitutional principles do not differ materially from those which exist when there is no written Constitution.[341]

Therefore, the real difference between a legal system with a written constitution and one without a written constitution really lies in the powers granted to the courts to control the constitutionality of state acts. Professor Mitchell also mentioned this in relation to the British constitutional system:

> The real contrast with our own system is afforded by a system under which there is not only a written constitution but also a recognised power in the courts to declare legislation invalid as being unconstitutional.[342]

In any case, the control of the constitutionality of formal laws, or of any other state act issued in direct execution of the constitution, is only possible in those constitutional systems possessing a written constitution and , furthermore, where the constitution is rigid, that is to say, it cannot be changed through the channel of ordinary legislation.

The rules established in this type of constitution are, of course, applied directly, and the constitution itself occupies a pre–eminent rank in the hierarchy of the legal order. In this respect, it is precisely in the countries where the courts have been granted the power to control the constitutionality of the laws that the juridical–normative nature of the constitutions, that is to say, their obligatory nature, is clearest. Likewise, it is in those countries that the principle of the hierarchical pre–eminence of the constitution in relation to the ordinary laws has its origin.

This first system of judicial review of constitutionality, particularly of legislation is generally organized in two ways: by assigning the power to decide upon the unconstitutionality of laws to all the courts of the particular judicial order of a state, or by reserving that power to one judicial organ only, the Supreme Judicial Court of the country or to a special constitutional court or tribunal, giving rise to the distinction between the diffuse and concentrated systems of judicial review of constitutionality to whose study this book is devoted.

Apart from state acts adopted in direct execution of constitutional powers granted to state organs, in particular, legislative acts and acts of government, there are other state acts adopted in direct execution of the "legislation", that is to say, the first level of constitutional execution, whose legality not only means submission to the constitution but also to all the other rules of law comprised in the legal order. Therefore, in relation to those acts, particularly administrative and judicial acts, "legality" means submission to the legal order considered as a whole, and the *État de droit* must provide the means for judicial control or review to ensure the effective submission of the state organs to the rule of law when issuing such acts. This has led to the establishment of systems of judicial review of administrative actions and of judicial review of judicial decisions themselves in the modern *État de droit*.

---

341 J.D.B. MITCHELL, *Constitutional Law*, Edinburgh 1968, p. 13.

342 *Idem*, p. 13.

Regarding the judicial review of administrative action, or judicial control of administration, one can say that it is more developed in modern constitutional and administrative law, particularly as a result of the submission of administration to the principle of legality. So important has this system of judicial review been, that one can even say that judicial review of administrative action has given rise to the development of administrative law itself, not only in continental European countries but also in common law countries. It is through the exercise by the courts of their inherent power to control the legality of administrative action, that the fundamental principles of administrative law have been developed, particularly during the present century.

Therefore, judicial review of administrative action is the power of the courts to decide upon the legality of the activities undertaken by the administrative organs of the state, in other words, to decide in relation to the submission of the activities of the executive organs of the state to the law or rather to the principle of legality. Law, understood in this context, means legal order, that is to say, not only the formal law, but also all the norms and rules that are comprised in the legal order, including, of course, the constitution itself.

There is a substantial difference with regard to the organization of judicial review of administrative action, between the legal systems influenced by the European continental countries, mainly France, and the systems influenced by the Anglo–American common law countries. Judicial review in the Latin and German tradition is the power of special courts to decide on the legality of administrative action, when demanded through special judicial means, or actions granted to individuals with the necessary standing to bring an action to declare a particular administrative act void. This led to the development *of* the *contentieux administrative* recourses in continental Europe that are to be decided by special judicial–administrative courts. In some cases, these special courts were established completely separated from the ordinary courts, as is the case in France of the *jurisdiction contentieux administrative*. In other cases, the special judicial administrative courts are established within the ordinary judicial order, in the same manner as there are special courts in labour law, civil law or commercial law. In all these cases, not only are the remedies for judicial review special ones, but the courts that are to exercise the review power, are also special.

By contrast with this situation, the common law tradition on judicial review generally implies that the ordinary courts of justice are the ones that exercise the power of judicial review of administrative action through the ordinary remedies established in common law and also used in private law, although it is certain that in more recent times special remedies of public law have been developed.

Any way, all over the world, the most traditional and popular judicial control of the submission of the state to the rule of law has been the judicial review of administrative action.

However, the term *État de droit* does not only imply the need for systems of judicial review of the constitutionality of legislation and acts of government, and the judicial review of administrative action, in other words, the judicial control of legislative and administrative action to ensure its conformity with the rule of law, but also the need for establishing a system of judicial control of judicial decisions themselves.

The courts are, in effect, typical "executive" bodies of the state. Consequently all their activities in the application of the law must be submitted to the whole legal order, comprising the constitution, the formal laws and delegate legislation, and the regulations and other normative acts of the state organs. Consequently, in the *État de droit*, court decisions must be also subject to judicial control, which is normally implemented through two mechanisms.

On the one hand, the ordinary appeal systems that allow for control of the decisions of the inferior courts by the superior courts, within the hierarchy of the judicial system; and on the other, the system of control of the legality of judicial decisions through extraordinary remedies, as happens in continental law, for example with the *recours de cassation*, developed in the systems influenced by continental European procedural law.

By these means of control, Supreme Courts have the power to verify the legality of decisions made by inferior courts, and deciding upon them, taking into account the merits of the decision under appeal, or just controlling the legal aspects of the decision in the recourse of cassation. In this case, it is also a matter of control of the legality of state acts.

All these three systems of control of the submission of the state organs and acts to the rule of law, the control of the constitutionality of legislation, the judicial review of administrative action, and the judicial control of courts decisions, are basically a question of formal control, which seeks to determine the conformity of state decisions with the superior rules contained in the legal order, applicable to the concrete act. Of all three, the first one related to the control of the constitutionality of legislation, the protection of the constitution being its fundamental objective when its norms are executed directly by state organs, will be the subject in the subsequent parts of this course.

2. Judicial guarantees of Fundamental Rights

Apart from these judicial systems of control of state acts to ensure their submission to the principle of legality or to the rule of law, there is another system of control of state actions aimed specially at the protection of fundamental rights and liberties generally established in the constitution and which is normally established in the constitution as a guarantee for the effective fulfilment of such rights and liberties.

We have seen, in effect, that the principle of distribution of powers in the legal state, expresses itself in various ways, among them, in a system of distribution of powers between on the one hand, the sphere of the citizens and individuals which are granted by the constitution with various fundamental rights and liberties, that cannot be eliminated or restricted unless by the means established in the constitution; and on the other hand, the powers of the state organs. This distribution of powers is normally established in a written constitution or in an entrenched Bill of Rights, so that invasions of the sphere of fundamental rights and liberties by the state or even by other individuals, are subject to judicial control or protection.

This judicial protection of fundamental rights, in the end, is also a protection of the constitution itself because such rights and liberties are established in the constitution, and therefore, all violations or infringements upon such rights and liberties are at the same time, violations of the constitution.

The *État de droit* has developed mechanisms to assure the protection of these fundamental rights and liberties and to avoid their violation mainly by public bodies, either by actions brought before the ordinary courts through ordinary actions or remedies, or by special actions of protection brought before ordinary courts or before a special constitutional court.

As this course mainly deals with judicial review of the constitutionality of legislation, we will also refer to the judicial protection of these fundamental rights, particularly through special actions, when in order to protect them, the courts must also exercise their powers of judicial review of legislation.

As we can see, the concept of the *État de droit* is closely related to the judicial control of legality in a way that there is no state according to law if there is no judicial control of legality of state acts. Also, effective judicial control of legality of state acts cannot exist except within the frame of the *État de droit*.

The *État de droit*, as we have seen, implies the submission of all state organs and acts to the legal order, which the constitution has at its apex. This is the supreme law, to which all state acts must be submitted. Therefore, the control of the submission of state acts to the constitution, when exercised by the courts, is an essential aspect of the *État de droit* and is the one we are going to analyse in the four subsequent parts of this course, in which we will study the judicial control of constitutionality, mainly of legislation.

PART III

THE FOUNDATION OF JUDICIAL REVIEW OF THE CONSTITUTIONALITY OF LEGISLATION

I. THE LIMITED STATE ORGANS AND JUDICIAL REVIEW

Judicial review of constitutionality is the power of the courts to control the conformity with the constitution of acts of state, particularly of legislative acts, issued in direct execution of the constitution.

Therefore, in principle, judicial review can only exist in legal systems in which there is a written constitution, imposing limits on the state organs' activities and within such organs, on Parliament in particular. As a result, the power of the courts to control the constitutionality of state acts is not necessarily a consequence of the sole judicial power, but of the legal limitations imposed on state organs, particularly on Parliament and on the government, in a constitution established as a supreme law.

In this sense, judicial review of the constitutionality of state acts is the ultimate consequence of the consolidation of the *État de Droit* where the state organs are not sovereign, are subject to limits imposed by a constitution having the force of a superior law, and in particular, when the legislator is limited in his legislative action and there is judicial control over the "legality of laws."

Professor Paul Duez stressed the argument a few decades ago in an article published in the *Mélanges Hariou* when he wrote:

> Modern Public Law establishes as an axiom that Governments are not sovereign and that in particular, the Parliament is limited in its legislative action by superior legal rules, that it could not infringe; Acts of Parliament are submitted to the law, and no Act of Parliament can be contrary to the law.[343]

This is the principle accepted today in France but certainly not the one accepted in that country sixty years ago when Professor Duez wrote his essay and when the principle of the sovereignty of the National Assembly was still in force. That is why this article is of historical importance in France. In effect, Professor Duez, by establishing the principle of the limitation of all state organs by a constitution as a superior rule, added:

> But it is not sufficient to proclaim such a principle: it must be organized, and practical and effective measures, must be adopted to ensure it.[344]

Subsequently, he referred to the very important French system of judicial control related to public administration and to administrative action, through the *recours pour excès de pouvoir*; nevertheless, he said:

> The spirit of legality requires that a similar control be established in relation to legislative action,[345]

And concluded by saying that,

> There is not a real organized democracy, and a Legal state (*État de Droit*), except only where this control of legality of laws (Acts of Parliament) exists and functions.[346]

The logic of Professor Duez's statement in our perspective is certainly impeccable: No organ of the and state can be considered sovereign; and all state organs, particularly, the legislator in its actions are submitted to limit established in superior rules, embodied in a constitution.

Therefore, acts of Parliament must always be submitted to the law, and cannot be contrary to the law. Consequently, the spirit of legality imposes the existence and functioning not only of a control of legality of administrative acts, but also of a control of the legality of laws, as acts of Parliament. Only in countries where this control exists, are there truly organized democracies and *État de Droit*.

---

343 P. DUEZ, "Le contrôle juridictionnel de la constitutionalité des lois en France", *Mélanges Hauriou*, Paris 1929, p. 214.

344 *Idem*, p. 214.

345 *Idem*, p. 215.

346 *Ibid*. p. 215.

Therefore, this judicial control of the "legality of laws" is, precisely, the judicial control of the constitutionality of legislation and of other state acts issued in direct execution of the constitution, in relation to which legality means "constitutionality." Thus, there is the existence of judicial review of constitutionality that we are now going to study.

This judicial review of constitutionality is normally possible, of course, not only in those legal systems that have a *written* constitution as a supreme rule embodying the fundamental values of society, but when that superior rule is established in a rigid or entrenched way, in the sense that it cannot be modified by ordinary legislation. In principle, it is in a system of this kind that all the organs of the state are limited by and subject to the constitution and must therefore pursue their activities according to this supreme law.

This implies therefore, that not only are the traditional state organs for executing the law –the administration and the judges– subject to the law (Constitution and "legislation"), but that the organs which create the "legislation", particularly the legislative bodies, are also subject to the constitution.

Of course, a written and rigid constitution, situated at the apex of a legal system, not only demands that all the acts issued by state organs in direct execution thereof should not violate the constitution, but must also provide a guarantee to prevent or sanction such violations.[347] Thus, the judicial review of constitutionality as the power of the judiciary to control the submission of state organs to the superior rule of the country.

1. Execution of the Constitution and Control

Anyway, we have said a hierarchy of rules exists in all legal systems with written and rigid Constitutions.

Evidently, not all state acts have, therefore, the same level of derivation in creating legal rules. There are acts that directly and immediately execute the constitution, and that are subject to this superior rule alone; there are also state acts which execute the constitution in an indirect way, being at the same time acts issued in direct and immediate execution of "legislation", thus directly subject to it. Among the former are, basically, the formal laws and other acts of Parliament and acts of government issued in accordance with their constitutionally attributed powers; and among the latter, there are the administrative and the judicial acts.

In a *État de Droit* then, the guarantee of the rule of law must be established at the two mentioned levels of creation or derivation of legal rules by way of three judicial systems of control: first, the judicial review of constitutionality, established to control state acts issued in direct execution of the constitution; second, the judicial control of administrative action basically established regarding administrative acts; and

---

347 *Cf.* H. KELSEN, "La garantie juridictionnelle de la Constitution (La Justice constitutionnelle)" *Revue du droit public et de la science politique en France et à l'étranger*, T. XLV, 1928, p.197–257.

concerning judicial acts issued by courts, the judicial control system is thirdly established by systems of appeal or cassation.

Moreover, in the *État de droit,* which implies that in the constitution fundamental rights and liberties are established, judicial mechanisms of control must also be provided to protect and guarantee such rights against any act by the state that may violate them, and even against acts by individuals which may so affect them.

Our objective, in the subsequent parts of this course is to analyze the first of these systems of judicial control previously mentioned, judicial review of constitutionality, which, we insist, fundamentally refers to the acts of the state constitutional organs, in which the rule of law becomes the "rule of the constitution"; since they are acts that execute the constitution itself, directly and immediately.

2. State Acts Submitted to Control

Therefore, one of the acts subject to judicial review of constitutionality are formal laws or acts of Parliament, and it is precisely because of this that judicial review of constitutionality is often identified with the judicial review of the constitutionality of legislation.[348] However, laws are not the only state acts issued in direct execution of the constitution, and as an expression of constitutional powers. So too are other acts of Parliament, such as internal parliamentary rules of procedure and even other parliamentary acts that do not have the form of law and that are not normative, such as those established in the constitution regarding the relations between the Congress or Assembly and the other constitutional organs of the state. All these acts adopted by Parliament are subject to the constitution because they are issued by virtue of powers attributed directly in that fundamental text. Thus, in a *État de droit* they must also be liable to judicial review of constitutionality.[349]

Apart from these acts of Parliament, however, the government, in a *État de droit*, also issues acts that directly execute the constitution, which have the same status as laws in the hierarchical legal system, and which, in some cases, even have the same force as formal law.

In fact, in contemporary constitutional law, the government issues acts with the same force as the formal laws in a variety of forms, either as delegate legislation or because of powers established in the constitution itself. In these cases, they are executive acts with legislative content, and with the same ranking, force and power of derogation as the formal law established in acts of Parliament. For this reason, such executive acts issued in direct execution of the constitution are not administrative acts, but acts of government with normative and legislative content. Thus, they are also liable to judicial review of constitutionality.[350]

But we have seen that the government also has powers established in the constitution to produce certain acts without any legislative interference, for instance when

---

348 See, for example, M. CAPPELLETTI, *Judicial Review in Contemporary World*, Indianapolis 1971, p. VII.

349 *Cf.* H. KELSEN, *loc. cit.*, p. 228.

350 *Idem*, p. 229.

declaring a state of siege or the restriction of constitutional guarantees; when directing international relations or when vetoing an act of Parliament. All these acts, shaped by the continental European doctrine of administrative law, as "acts of government", are also subject to judicial review of constitutionality. It is true that in the traditional criteria of administrative law, such "acts of government" were developed to exclude them from judicial administrative control either because of their political content or motives or because they were issued by the government in its relations with other constitutional bodies, particularly with Parliament.[351] Nevertheless, as we have seen, these acts are also subject to the constitution, and they are also liable to be submitted to judicial review of constitutionality.[352]

Moreover, in contemporary legal systems and leaving aside problems arising from monist and dualist conceptions, international treaties and agreements are also subject to judicial review of constitutionality in the *État de droit*[353] whether this be directly, or by review of the acts of Parliament or government that introduce them into domestic law, also by virtue of constitutional powers granted to those state organs.

Therefore, all state acts issued in direct execution of the constitution in legal systems with written constitutions are subject to judicial review of constitutionality.

3. The Variety of Judicial Review

It is evident, however, that in comparative law no single system for judicial review of constitutionality exists, but rather a very varied range of systems in which not even all the state acts mentioned can be subject to judicial review.

In fact, different criteria can be adopted for classifying the various systems of constitutional justice or judicial review of the constitutionality of state acts, particularly of legislation,[354] but all are related to a basic criteria referring to the state organs that can carry out constitutional justice functions.

In effect, judicial review of constitutionality can be exercised by all the courts of a given country or only by the Supreme Court of the country or by a court specially created for that purpose.

In the first case, all the courts of a given country are empowered to judge the constitutionality of laws. This is the case in the United States of America, thus this system has been identified as the 'American system', because it was first adopted in the United States particularly after the famous *Marbury* v. *Madison* case decided by the Supreme Court in 1803. This system is followed in many countries with or without a common law tradition. This is the case, for example, in Argentina, Mexico, Greece, Australia, Canada, India, Japan, Sweden, Norway and Denmark. This sys-

351 See the classical work of P. DUEZ, *Les actes de gouvernement*, Paris 1953.

352 *Cf.* H. KELSEN, *loc. cit.*, p. 230.

353 *Idem*, p. 231.

354 See in general M. CAPPELLETTI, *op .cit.*, p. 45 and M. CAPPELLETI and J.C. ADAMS, "Judicial Review of Legislation: European Antecedents and Adaptations", *Harvard Law Review*, 79, 6, April 1966, p. 1207.

tem is also qualified as a diffuse system of judicial review of constitutionality,[355] because judicial control belongs to all the courts from the lowest level up to the Supreme Court of the country.

By contrast, there is the concentrated system of judicial review, in which the power to control the constitutionality of legislation and other state organs issued in direct execution of the constitution is assigned to a single organ of the state, whether to its Supreme Court or to a special court created for that particular purpose. In the latter case, it is also called the Austrian system because it was first established in Austria, in 1920. This system also called the "European model" is followed, for instance, in Germany, Italy, and Spain. It is called a concentrated system of judicial review, as opposed to the diffuse system, because the power of control over the constitutionality of state acts is given only to one single constitutional body that can be the Supreme Court of a given country or as in the Austrian or European model, to a specially created constitutional court 'or tribunal, that even though it exercised judicial functions, in general, it is created by the constitution outside ordinary judicial power, as a constitutional organ different to the Supreme Court of the country.

In regard to the judicial organs that can exercise the power of controlling the constitutionality of laws, other countries have adopted a mixture of the above mentioned diffuse and concentrate systems, in the sense that allow for both types of control at the same time. Such is the case in Colombia and Venezuela where all courts are entitled to judge the constitutionality of laws and therefore decide autonomously upon their inapplicability in a given process, and the Supreme Court has the power to declare the unconstitutionality of laws in an objective process. One can say that these countries have a diffuse and concentrated parallel system of judicial review at one and the same time, perhaps the most complete in comparative law.

But regarding the so–called concentrated systems of judicial review, in which the power of control is given to the Supreme Court or to a constitutional court, other distinctions can be observed.

In the first place, in relation to the moment at which control of the constitutionality of laws is performed, it may be prior to the formal enactment of the particular law, as is the case in France, or the judicial control of the constitutionality of laws which can be exercised by the court after the law has come into effect, as is the case in Germany and Italy.

In this respect, other countries have established both possibilities as is the case Spain, Portugal and Venezuela. In the latter, a law sanctioned by Congress prior to its enactment, can be placed by the president of the republic before the Supreme Court to obtain a decision regarding its constitutionality, and also the Supreme Court can judge the constitutionality of the law after it has been published and has come into legal effect.

Moreover, in relation to the concentrated systems of judicial review, two other types of control can be distinguished regarding the manner in which review is re-

355 M. CAPPELLETTI, "El control judicial de la constitucionalidad de las leyes en el derecho comparado", *Revista de la Facultad de Derecho de México*, 61, 1966, p. 28.

quired either incidentally or through an objective action. In the first place, the constitutional question is not considered justiciable unless it is closely and directly related to a particular process, in which the constitutionality of the concrete law is not normally necessary to the unique issue in the process. In this case, judicial control is incidental, and the Supreme Court or constitutional tribunal can only decide when it is required to do so by the ordinary court that has to decide the case. In this circumstance, it is basically the function of the ordinary courts, upon hearing a concrete case, to place the constitutional issue before the constitutional court.

Of course, the incidental nature of judicial review is essential to diffused control systems and, therefore, to all legal systems that follows the American model.

But in the field of the concentrated system of judicial review, the control granted to the constitutional court can also be exercised through direct action where the constitutionality of the particular law is the only issue in the process, without reference or relation to a particular process.

In this latter case, another distinction can be made, in relation to the *locus standing* to exercise the direct action of unconstitutionality: in most countries with a concentrated system of judicial review, only other organs of the state can place the direct action of constitutionality before the constitutional court, for instance, the head of government, or a number of representatives in Parliament.

Other systems of concentrated judicial review grant the action of constitutionality to individuals, whether requiring that the particular law affects a fundamental right of the individual, or by means of a popular action, in which any citizen can request the constitutional court or Supreme Court to decide upon his claim concerning the constitutionality of a given law, without particular requirement regarding his standing.

As we have seen, the basic division we can establish regarding the various systems of judicial review, depends in our opinion, upon the concentrated or centralized or diffuse or decentralized character of judicial control of constitutionality, that is to say, when the power of control is given to all the courts of a given country or to one special constitutional court or to the Supreme Court of that country. We have also said that some countries have even adopted both systems of judicial review that developed in parallel. Related to this main classification, as we said, other criteria can be adopted to identify the various systems of judicial control of the constitutionality of laws: the incidental and the principal or objective action systems.

But in relation to the main distinction between the diffuse and concentrated systems of judicial review, we can also distinguish other criteria for classifying the various systems, according to the legal effects given to the particular judicial decision of review.

Within this scope, we can distinguish decisions with *in casu et inter partes* or *erga omnes* effects, that is to say, when the judicial decision has effects only within the parties in a concrete process, or when it has general effects applicable to everyone.

For instance, in the diffused systems of judicial review, according to the American system, the decision of the courts in principle, only has effect relating to the parties of the process; effects that are closely related to the incidental character of judicial review.

Whereas in the concentrated system of judicial review, following the Austrian model, when the judicial decision is a consequence of the exercise of a objective action, the effects of such a decision are general, with *erga omnes* validity.

Thus, in the diffused systems of judicial review a law declared unconstitutional with *inter partes* effects, in principal is considered null and void, with no effect whatsoever. Therefore, in this case the decision in principle is retroactive in the sense that has *ex tunc*, or *pro pretaerito* consequences; that is to say, the law declared unconstitutional is considered never to have existed or never to have been valid. Thus, this decision, in principle, has "declarative" effects, in the sense that it declares the pre–existing nullity of the unconstitutional law.

In the concentrated systems of judicial review, on the contrary, a law declared unconstitutional, with *erga omnes* effect, in principle is considered annullable. Therefore, in this case, the decision is prospective, in the sense that has *ex nunc*, *pro futuro* consequences, that is to say, the law declared unconstitutional is considered as having produced its effect until its annulation by the court, or until the moment determined by the court subsequent to the decision. In this case, therefore the decision has "constitutive" effects, in the sense that the law will become unconstitutional only after the decision has been made.

Nevertheless, this distinction related to the effects of the judicial decision regarding the unconstitutionality of a law is not absolute. On the one hand, if it is true that in the diffuse systems of judicial review, the decision has *inter partes* effects, when the decision is adopted by the Supreme Court, as a consequence of the *stare decisis* doctrine, the practical effects of the decision, in fact, are general, in the sense that it binds all the lower courts of the country. Therefore, as soon as the Supreme Court has declared a law unconstitutional, no other court can apply it.

On the other hand, in concentrated systems of judicial review, when a judicial decision is adopted on an incidental issue of constitutionality, some constitutional systems have established that the effects of that decision are only related in principle, to the particular process in which the constitutionality question was raised, and between the parties of that process, even though this is not the general rule.

In relation to the declarative or constitutive effects of the decision, or its retroactive or prospective effects, the absolute parallelism with the diffuse and concentrated systems has also disappeared.

In the diffuse systems of judicial review, even though the effects of the declarative decisions of unconstitutionality of the law, are *ex tunc*, *pro pretaerito*, in practice exceptions have been made in civil cases to allow for the invalidity of the law not to be retroactive: In the same manner, in the concentrated systems of judicial review, even though the effects of the constitutive judicial decisions of unconstitutionality of the law, are *ex nunc*, *pro futuro*, in practice exceptions were needed to be made in criminal cases to allow for the invalidity of the law to be retroactive, and benefit the accused.

Our purpose in the subsequent parts of the course is to study all these systems of judicial review of constitutionality of state acts, and particularly of legislation in comparative law. To that end we will analyze the most important legal systems in contemporary constitutional law, classifying them in accordance with the main distinctions we have made between the diffuse and the concentrated systems of judicial review.

Before doing so, however, we consider it necessary to examine the juridical foundations of the judicial review of constitutionality, in which we will recall various aspects previously mentioned but particularly, relating them to the judicial review of constitutionality in the *État de droit* bearing in mind that if it is true that judicial review appeared with the *État de droit* at the beginning of the last century in the American Constitution, it has been the most recent trend it adopted in contemporary legal systems.

In analyzing those foundations of the judicial review of constitutionality in comparative law, we will refer to what has been called the legitimacy of judicial review, which was one of the main subjects of the 1984 Colloquium of the International Association of Legal Sciences, held in Uppsala.[356]

4. The Controlled and Limited Legislator

Judicial Review, it has been said, is "the culmination of the building of the *État droit*[357] and is the direct consequence of its constitutionalization process, that is to say, of the adoption of a constitution as a higher law, in which the organization of state powers and their limits are established and to which the fundamental rights of individuals are declared and guaranteed.

In this sense, judicial review as the power of the courts –ordinary or special constitutional courts– to control the constitutionality of legislation is, without doubt, the ultimate triumph of the individual against the absolute power of state organs, and particularly, against the supremacy and sovereignty of Parliaments.

Even in its origin, in the same manner as American constitutionalism emerged as a reaction against the sovereignty of the English Parliament, judicial review in its original American conception, was also a reaction against the legislative body and its powers.[358] The Congress, like all state organs, was to be submitted to the Constitution and therefore, all the laws of Congress sanctioned in violation of the Constitution were to be considered null and void. On the contrary, the Constitution would be a dead letter, or as Alexander Hamilton said: "would amount to nothing."[359]

356 L. FAVOREU and J.A. JOLOWICZ (ed.), *Le contrôle juridictionnel des lois. Légitimité, effectivité et developments récents*, Paris 1986, p. 316.

357 P. Lucas MURILLO DE LA CUEVA "El examen de la constitucionalidad de las leyes y la soberanía parlamentaria", *Revista de estudios politicos*, 7, Madrid 1979, p. 200.

358 E.S. CORWIN, *"The 'Higher Law' Background of American Constitutional law"*, NY 1955, p. 53 (Reprinted from *Harvard Law Review*, Vol. XLII, 1928–1929 (p. 149–185 and 365–409).

359 Alexander HAMILTON, *The Federalist* (ed. by B. F. Wright), Cambridge, Mass 1961, p. 491.

This conception is in the logic of the *État de droit*, and in this sense, Professor Jean Rivero, in his synthesis Report to the 2nd Colloquium held in Aix–en–Provence in 1981 on the subject "Cours Constitutionelles Européennes et Droits Fondamentaux" pointed out:

> The logic of the *Rechstaat* places the Constitution at the summit of the pyramid of norms, from which all other norms draw their validity. But we must recognize that over a long century this logic was stopped... because of the myth of the supremacy of the law, and therefore, to attain the last stage of the building of the Legal state, the one in which the legislator itself is subject to a superior norm, (the concept of the law) ought then to be transformed.[360]

Therefore, judicial review is the direct consequence of the culmination of the building of the *État de droit*, as a state whose organs are limited in their actions by a Constitution, which additionally establishes the fundamental rights of individuals and its means of protection against those state organs, and particularly, against the legislator. This led Professor Rivero to affirm that:

> The evolution of the *État de Droit* produced of course in relation to the French constitutional system, what Professor Rivero considered the extraordinary phenomenon of the acceptance of a superior authority to the legislator itself, in charge of imposing the respect of the Constitution on the legislator, possible.[361]

The constitutionalization of the *État de droit* therefore, is essentially linked to the idea of judicial review, and this is why Professor Mauro Cappelletti in one of his reports to the same Colloquium in Aix–en–Provence said that,

> Constitutionalism, in its most advanced state, has needed a state organ or a group of state organs, sufficiently independent of "political powers –the legislative and the executive– in order to protect a superior and relatively permanent rule of law, against the inherent temptations of power.[362]

These independent organs are the courts, considered as being the politically "less dangerous" or the "weakest" of the three state powers in charge of controlling the submission of the Legislative and Executive powers to the Constitution.

Therefore, the subject of judicial review of constitutionality, is essentially related to all the fundamental aspects of the contemporary state as a *État de droit* and particularly those relating to constitutionalism; to the separation of powers and to the role of Parliament; to the form of the state and particularly, to Federalism and political decentralization; to the system of Government, and to the fundamental rights of the individual. All these elements of the *État de droit* have undoubtedly served as a means to justify the need to establish a system of judicial review of the constitutionality of legislation and other state acts and of its legitimacy. They have also served to justify arguments in some cases, against the emergence of such control. In study-

360 J. RIVERO, "Rapport de Synthèse", in L. FAVOREU (ed.), *Cours constitutionnelles européennes et droit fondamentaux*, Aix–en–Provence 1982, p. 519.

361 *Idem*. p. 519.

362 M. CAPPELLETTI, "Necessité et légitimité de la justice constitutionnelle" in L. FAVOREU (ed.) *Cours constitutionnelles européennes et droit fondamentaux*, *cit*, p. 483. Also reproduced in *Revue internationale de droit compare*, 1981, (2), p. 647.

ing the foundations of judicial review of constitutionality I will then consider some of their main arguments for and against, as have been developed in contemporary constitutional law.

Anyway, we must admit that the possibility of a judicial control of the constitutionality of legislation and other state organs, only has its full juridical sense in a *État de droit* where the following principles derive from the submission of state organs to the rule of law: first, the principle of the organization of state powers in such a way as to eliminate all possibility of the unlimited exercise of power; secondly, the principle of a legal guarantee established against arbitrariness in the functioning of the state organs; thirdly, the establishment of the fundamental rights of individuals, as a limit upon the state itself; and fourthly, the formal expression of the afford mentioned principles in a fundamental law or Constitution, as a basic legal rule of state action.

II. THE CONSTITUTION AND ITS SUPREMACY

The *État de droit* is obviously closely related to the idea of a constitution as a fundamental norm and to the theory of a graduated or hierarchical system of the legal order, as Professor Manuel García Pelayo, former President of the Spanish Constitutional Tribunal said, it implies:

> That the constitution as a fundamental positive norm, links all the public powers, including Parliament, and thus, consequently, the law cannot be contrary to constitutional precepts, to those principles which arise or are to be inferred from them, and to the values which it aspires to put into practice. This, –he concluded–, is the essence of the *Estado de Derecho.*[363]

Therefore, the fundamental rule in the *État de droit*, as we have seen, is the primacy of the rule of law in the sense that all state organs are subject to the rule of law. This fundamental rule shows itself, above all, in two ways: first, in the primacy of the constitution over acts of Parliament and over all other state acts, particularly those issued in direct execution of the constitution; and second, in the primacy of acts of Parliament over all other state acts regulated by it, and to which they must be submitted.

However, when we say that the first consequence of the constitutionalization process in the *État de droit* is the primacy of the constitution this does not mean, of course, that the only constitutional norms that have primacy are the sole formal written articles of the constitution, but also the entirely of the fundamental values that are the pillar of the constitution itself and that, at the same time, are to be inferred from its norms. The role of the judiciary in this aspect, as we will see, has been and is essential.

1. The Constitution as a Higher and Effective Law

The whole possibility of judicial review of constitutionality is not only the ultimate result of the consolidation of the *État de droit*, but also in particular, of the

363 M. GARCÍA PELAYO, "El Status del Tribunal Constitucional", *Revista española de derecho constitucional*, 1, Madrid 1981, p. 18.

notion of the constitution as a higher and fundamental positive law itself with the characteristics of an effective law. That is to say, the constitution conceived "not as a mere guideline of a political, moral, or philosophical nature, but as a real law, itself a positive and binding law, although of a superior, more permanent nature than ordinary positive legislation."[364]

Therefore, one of the fundamental trends in modern constitutionalism is the concept of a constitution as a normative reality and not as an occasional political compromise of political groups, changeable at any moment when the equilibrium between them is modified. In this sense in the contemporary world, constitutions are effective juridical norms, which overrule the whole political process, the social and economic life of the country, and which give validity to the whole legal order.[365] In this sense, constitution, as a supreme real and effective norm, must contain rules applicable directly to state organs and to individuals.

In relation to the state, constitution today has the same fundamental character that it had in the origins of constitutionalism in North America, and that were later changed in Europe during the course of the last century.

The constitution was originally a fundamental law limiting state organs, and it declared the fundamental rights of individuals, as a political consensus given by the people themselves and, therefore, directly applicable for the courts. The adoption of this concept in continental Europe with the French Revolution was later modified by the monarchical principle, which turned the concept of the constitution into a formal and abstract code of the political system, given by the monarch, and not to be applied by the courts. The constitution in this context had no norm directly applicable to individuals who were only ruled by the formal laws, and even though it contained an organic part, the absence of means of judicial review brought about the loss of its normative character.

Nevertheless, in the European continental legal systems, the concept of the constitution has changed and is again closer to its original conception as a higher law with norms applicable to state organs and to individuals, judged by the courts. In this sense, we can consider as valid the terms of the American Supreme Court decision in *Trop.* v. *Dulles*, 1958, in which the following was stated in relation to the normative character of the constitution:

> The provisions of the constitution are not time–worn adages ox hollow shibboleths. They are vital, living principles that authorise and limit governmental powers in our nation. They are rules of government. When the constitutionality of an act of Congress is challenged in this

---

364 M. CAPPELLETTI, *Judicial Review of Legislation and its Legitimacy. Recent Development. General Report. International Association of Legal Sciences*, Uppsala 1984, (mineo), p. 20; also published as the "Rapport Général" in L. FAVOREU and J.A. JOLOWICZ (ed.). *Le contrôle juridictionnel des lois. Légitimité, effectivité et développement récents*, Paris 1986, pp. 285–300.

365 E. GARCÍA DE ENTERRÍA, *La Constitución como norma y el Tribunal Constitucional*, Madrid 1985, pp. 33, 39, 66, 71, 177, 187.

> Court, we must apply those rules. If we do not, the words of the constitution become little more than good advise.[366]

Therefore, in contemporary legal systems, constitutions are not those simple pieces of "good advise" or "time–worn adages"; on the contrary, their contents are of a normative character, which rule both governments and individuals. This is in true even in France, where in the traditional constitutional system after the 1875 Constitutional Laws, due to the exclusion of the declaration of rights from the text of the constitution,[367] its provisions were considered not to be directly applicable to individuals.

However, after recent decisions of the Constitutional Council adopted in the seventies, the *bloc de la constitutionalité*[368] has been enlarged to include the Declaration of Rights of Man and Citizens of 1789, the Preambles of the 1946 and 1958 Constitutions, and the fundamental principles recognised by the laws of the Republic.[369] This has led Professor Jean Rivero to say with regard to the creation of the law by the constitutional judge, that with the decisions of the Constitutional Council, based on "the constitution and particularly on its Preamble", a revolution has taken place. He wrote:

> In a single blow, the 1789 Declaration, the 1946 Preamble, the fundamental principles recognised by the laws of the Republic, have been integrated into the French constitution, even if the Constituent did not want it. The French constitution, has doubled its volume through the single will of the Constitutional Council.[370]

This normative character of the constitution, relating to state organs and to individuals, and its enforcement by the Courts, has also brought about a change in the so–called "programmatic norms" of the constitution, which have been considered as norms directly applicable only to the legislator.[371]

In effect, it is current to find in modern constitutions, even in the context of social and economic rights, norms that are, in fact, formulated as a political guideline directed to the legislator. This has led to the consideration that those constitutional norms were not directly applicable to individuals until the legislator itself had adopted formal laws in accordance with the "programme" established in the consti-

---

366 356 US 86 (1958).

367 J. RIVERO, *Les libertes publiques*, Vol. 1, Paris 1973, p. 70.

368 L. FAVOREU, "Le principe de constitutionalité. Essai de definition d'après la jurisprudence du Consel constitutionnel", in *Recueil d'etudes en 1'honneur de Charles Eisenmann*, Paris 1977, p. 33.

369 L. FAVOREU, *Le contrôle juridictionnel des lois et sa légitimité. Développements récents en Europe Occidentale*, Association Internationale des Sciences Juridiques, Colloque d'Uppsala 1984, (mineo), p. 8; also published in L. FAVOREU and J.A. JOLOWICZ, *op. cit.*, pp. 17–68.

370 J. RIVERO, "Rapport de Synthèse" in L. FAVOREU (ed.), *Cours constitutionnelles europeenes et droit fondamentar,* Aix–en–Provence 1982, p. 520.

371 E. GARCIA DE ENTERRIA, *op. cit.*, p. 37, 69. *Cf.* P. BISCARETTI DI RUFFIA and S. ROZMARYN, *La Constitution comme loi fondamentale dans les Etats de l'Europe occidentale et dans les Etats socialistes*, Torino 1966, p. 39.

tution. Therefore, only laws, issued for its legal development were to be applied by the courts.

The normative character of the constitution on the contrary, as a fundamental trend of contemporary constitutionalism, tends to overcome this programmatic character attributed to certain constitutional norms, and seek its enforcement by the courts as norms directly applicable to individuals, so as not to consider them as those pieces of "good advise" referred by Chief Justice Warren to in the *Trop v. Dulles case* (US. 1958). Therefore, those "programmatic norms" or provisions of state aims must be also enforceable by the courts as principles that must orientated the actions of the state.

Nevertheless, in contemporary constitutional law and in relation to judicial review, this judicial control of the constitution is essentially possible not only when a constitution exists as a real norm enforceable by the courts, but also when it has supremacy over the whole legal order, in the sense that it has primacy over all the rules of law contained in a given legal system. This supremacy of the constitution over the other rules of law, and particularly over acts of Parliament implies that the constitution is the supreme norm which establishes the supreme values of a legal order. From this position of supremacy, it can be taken as the parameter for the validity of the remaining legal rules of such a system.

2. English Background of the Constitutional Supremacy and the American Constitutionalism

This concept of the constitution as a higher law is, undoubtedly, the great creation of American constitutionalism, and a contribution to the universal history of law, and it is the basis of the very notion of judicial review.

This concept, particularly in North America, as developed by Edward S. Corwin in his well known work *The 'Higher Law' background of American Constitutional Law*,[372] incorporates the tradition of natural law in the version of Locke and Coke as the "law of laws", the "immutable law", that is to say, *lex legum*, *lex aeterna* and *lex immutabile.* That law was given concrete form in the pacts and charters of the American colonies, and later formalised as a fundamental law in a solemn document, precisely that document which was to become known by the term "constitution."

The concept of the constitution as a supreme or fundamental law, derived in North America from the technique of judicial review, which developed that constitutional supremacy stemmed, in fact, from English *common law*, considered as a fundamental law.

Prior to the seventeenth century, in the English system, *common law* as non legislated law, prevailed over statutes, considered as singular or exceptionally created norms in relation to the previously established common law.[373] This technique of the predominance of common law over statutes, or as Chief Justice Edward Coke stated,

372 E.S. CORWIN, *The 'Higher Law' Background of American Constitutional Law*, NY 1955; Reprinted from *Harvard Law Review*, Vol. XLII, 1928–1929, p. 149–185 and 365–409.

373 M. CAPPELLETTI, *Judicial Review in the. Contemporary World,* Indianapolis 1971, p. 36–37.

"the traditional supremacy of the common law over the authority of Parliament"[374] led to the famous *Bonham's case* 1610, in which Coke stated, that:

> It appears in our books, that in many cases, the common law will control acts of Parliament, and sometimes adjudge them to be utterly void: for when an act of Parliament is against common right and reason, or repugnant, or impossible to be performed, the common law will control it and adjudge such act to be void.[375]

That "common right and reason" was, undoubtedly, something fundamental, something permanent; in short, a higher law, binding on Parliament and on ordinary courts.

One of these fundamental laws, according to Coke, was precisely the *Magna Carta* of which he said was called

> Magna Charta, not for the length or largeness of it... but... in respect of the great weightiness and weighty, greatness of the matter contained in it; in a few words, being the fountain of all the fundamental laws of the realm.[376]

The Magna Charta was, therefore, considered a fundamental law and it is in this sense that it must be considered as the remote antecedent of modern constitutions.

But, with regard to the concept of a higher law binding acts of Parliament, Corwin referred to another case *Day* v. *Savadge* 1614, where Chief Justice Hobart, even though without direct reference to Bonham's case, stated:

> Even an act of Parliament, made against Natural Equity, as to make a Man Judge in his own cause, is void in itself; for *jura naturae sunt immutabilia* and they are *leges legum.*[377]

After the 1688–1689 Revolution, the principle of the supremacy of Parliament took place in English law and, therefore, the principle of general submission to legislative power. Even though, twelve years after the Revolution, Chief Justice Holt commented on Dr. *Bonham's* Case in the case City of *London v. Wood*, 1701 stating:

And what my Lord Coke says in Dr. Bonham's Case... is far from any extravagancy, for it is very reasonable and true saying, that if an act of Parliament should ordain that the same person should be party and judge, or which is the same thing, judge in his own cause, it would be a void act of Parliament; for it is impossible that one should be judge and party, for the judge is to determine between party and party.[378]

Nevertheless, Holt accepted the principle that,

---

374 Quoted by E.S. CONWIN, *op. cit.*, p. 38. Regarding the inconsistance of Coke's views see W. HOLDSWORTH, *A History of English Law*, Vol. V, London 1966, p. 475.

375 See the quotation and its comments in Ch. H. MCILWAIN, *The High Court of Parliament and its Supremacy*, Yale 1910, p. 286–301. See the criticisms on Lord Coke's concepts in L.B. BOUDIN, *Government by Judiciary*, NY 1932, Vol. I, p. 485–517.

376 E.S. CORWIN, *op. cit.* p. 54–55

377 *Idem*, p. 52.

378 *Idem*, p. 52.

> An act of Parliament can do no wrong" thus the supremacy of Parliament was already accepted, even though he considered that if it was against the principles of natural law –today's natural justice– it would only look pretty odd.[379]

It must be said that this supremacy of Parliament had a paradoxical direct effect on the development of judicial review in North America in the sense that before the Declaration of Independence, laws passed by the colonial legislatures were in several cases, pronounced invalid as contrary to the laws of England or to the colonial charters.[380] Therefore, as Mauro Cappelletti has said,

> Though the Glorious Revolution of 1688 marked the triumph of Legislative supremacy in England, the American colonies had nonetheless inherited both Coke's ideas regarding the subordination of Crown and Parliament to higher law and a judiciary accustomed to interpreting and at times ignoring legislative acts violating higher principles... Paradoxically the Glorious Revolution not only did not hinder, but rather it spurred the development of the new doctrine of judicial review.[381]

In his same book about *Judicial Review in the Contemporary World*, Cappelletti insisted on the same idea:

> The principle of parliamentary supremacy – and hence the supremacy of positive law which was introduced in England following the Glorious Revolution of 1688, produced quite different results in America than in England. In England the result was to remove every control over the validity of legislation from the judges, despite the early successes of Lord Coke's doctrine. In America, on the contrary, the result was to empower the colonial judges to disregard local legislation not in conformity with the English law. Thus the apparent paradox has been explained: how the English principle of the uncontrolled supremacy of the legislature helped, rather than hindered, the formation in America of an opposite system.[382]

In this way, if it is true that the dictum in *Dr. Bonham's case* after the final triumph of Parliament over the Crown had no place of importance in judicial decisions in England, it passed to America. As Professor E.S. Corwin said,

> To join there the arsenal of weapons being accumulated against Parliament's claims to sovereignty.[383]

Thus, the North American colonist linked up directly with the tradition of Coke, regarding the subordination of Crown and Parliament to a higher law embodied to a great extent in a particular document, that were after the Declaration of Independence the constitutions adopted by the new states. That is why in a few states, particularly in Pennsylvania and Vermont, after 1776, the idea that state laws could not be repugnant to their basic laws was emphasised; and the courts of New Jersey started to put the idea of judicial review into practice in 1780.[384]

---

379 Ch. H. McIlwain, *op. cit.*, p. 307

380 C.P. Patterson, "The Development and Evaluation of Judicial Review", *Washington Law Review*, 13, 1938, p. 75, 171, 353.

381 M. Cappelletti, *Judicial Review in the Contemporary World*, *cit.*, p.–38–39.

382 *Idem*, p. 40.

383 E.S. Corwin, *op. cit.*, p. 53.

384 W.J. Wagner, *The Federal States and their Judiciary*, The Hague 1959, p. 87–88.

During the Constitutional Convention of 1787 the problem of judicial review was only considered incidentally, and the discussions on the matter were related more to the supremacy of the constitution over the states legislation. Thus the principle that the constitution is the supreme law of the land which should be applied by judges, notwithstanding any disposition to the contrary in the constitutions or laws of the member states appears incorporated in the 1787 constitution. It is what is known as the "Supremacy Clause."[385]

We must additionally stress that in Article I, Section 9, some limitations where imposed on Congress in the constitution[386] and in 1789 the first amendment of the constitution, with the other nine aimed at establishing a Bill of Rights, was conceived as a limit on Legislative Power, stating that

> Congress shall make no law respecting an establishment of religion, or prohibiting the free exercise thereof; or abridging the freedom of speech or of the press; or the right of the people peaceable to assemble, and to petition the Government for a redress of grievances.

The "supremacy clause", the constitutional limitations imposed on Congress by the constitution and the authority given to the Supreme Court to "extend to all causes, in law and equity, arising under this constitution" (Article III, section 2), together with the "higher law" background of the constitutional system, led to the formal adoption of the doctrine of constitutional supremacy and therefrom of judicial review.

The supremacy of the constitution, considered as a higher and fundamental law was first developed in 1788 by Alexander Hamilton in *The Federalist*. When referring to the role of the courts as interpreters of the law; he stated:

> A constitution is, in fact, and must be regarded by the judges, as a fundamental law. It therefore, belongs to them to ascertain its meaning, as well as the meaning of any particular act proceeding from the legislative body. If there should happen to be an irreconcilable variance between the two, that which has the superior obligation and validity ought, of course, to be preferred; or, in other words, the constitution ought to be preferred to the Statute, the intention of the people to the intention of their agents.

He added in response to the assertion that "the rights of the courts to pronounce legislative acts void, because contrary to the constitution" would "imply a superiority of the judiciary to the legislative powers", the following:

> Nor does this conclusion –that the Courts must prefer the constitution over statutes– by any means supposes a superiority of the judicial to the legislative body. It only supposes that the power of the people is superior to both; and that where the will of the legislature, declared in its Statutes stands in opposition to that of the people declared in the constitution, the judges

---

385 Article VI, paragraph 2nd of the constitution state: "This constitution, and the Laws of the United States which shall be made in pursance thereof; and all Treaties made, or which shall be made, under the Authority of the United States, shall be the Supreme Law of the Land; and the Judges in every State shall be bound thereby, anything in the constitution or Laws of any State to the contrary notwithstanding."

386 For instance: "The privilege of the Writ of Habeas Corpus shall not be suspended, unless when in cases of Rebellion or Invasion the public Safety may require it. No Bill of Attainder–or ex post facto law shall be passed."

> ought to be governed by the latter rather than the former. They ought to regulate their decisions by the fundamental laws, rather than by those which are not fundamental.

Thus, his conclusive assertion that:

> No legislative act, therefore, contrary to the constitution, can be valid. To deny this, would be to affirm, that the deputy is greater than his principal; that the servant is above his master; that the representative of the people are superior to the peoples themselves; that men acting by virtue of powers, may do not only what their powers do not authorise, but what they forbid.

Thus, in *The Federalist*, Hamilton not only developed the doctrine of the supremacy of the constitution, but more importantly the doctrine of "the judges as guardians of the constitution", as the title of letter N° 78 reads, where Hamilton said, considering the constitution as a limit to state powers and particularly to the Legislative authority, that,

> Limitations of this kind can be preserved in practice no other way than through the medium of courts of justice, whose duty it must be, to declare all acts contrary to the manifest tenor of the constitution, void. Without this, all the reservations of particular rights or privileges would amount to nothing.[387]

The First Congress, in the first judiciary act of 1789 contemplated the possibility of invalidating statutes "repugnant to the constitution, treaties or laws of the United States" by the courts. This led the Federal Circuit Court in 1795 (*Vanhorne's Lessee v. Dorrance*) and in 1800 (*Cooper v. Telfair*) to declare state laws void on the grounds that they were repugnant to the states and to the federal constitutions.[388]

In fact, the principle of the supremacy of the constitution was first developed in relation to the legislation of the Federal states, in *Vanhorne's Lessee v. Dorrance* (1795), a federal circuit court case in which Justice William Paterson declared a Pennsylvania Statute invalid. In his charge to the jury, comparing the system of England and America, he said:

> Some of the judges in England, have had the boldness to assert, that an act of Parliament made against natural equity, is void; but this opinion contravenes the general position that the validity of an act of Parliament cannot be drawn into question by the judicial department; It cannot be disputed, and must be obeyed. The power of parliament is absolute and transcendent; it is omnipotent in the scale of political existence. Besides, in England there is no written constitution, no fundamental law, nothing visible, nothing real, nothing certain, by which a Statute can be tested. In America, the case is widely different: Every state in the Union has its constitution reduced to written exactitude and precision.

And he asked:

> What is a constitution? It is the form of government, delineated by the mighty hand of the people, in which certain First principles of fundamental laws are established. The constitution is certain and fixed; it contains the permanent will of the people, and is the supreme law of the land; it is paramount to the power of the legislation, and can be revoked or altered only by the authority that made it.

---

387 *The Federalist* (ed. by B.F. Wright), Cambridge, Mass 1961, p. 491 –493

388 W.J. WAGNER, *op. cit.*, p. 90–91.

Along the same line of thought, he also referred to legislation, by asking:

> What are legislatures? Creatures of the constitution; they owe their existence to the constitution; they derive their powers from the constitution; it is their commission; and, therefore, all their acts must be conformable to it, or else they will be void. The constitution is the work or will of the people themselves, in their original, sovereign, and unlimited capacity. Law is the work or will of the legislature in their derivative and subordinate capacity. The one is the work of the Creator, and the other of the creature. The constitution fixes limits to the exercise of legislative authority and prescribes the orbit within which it must move.

Justice Paterson concluded his statement delivered in 1795 by saying to the jury

> In short, gentlemen, the constitution is the sum of the political system, around which all legislature, executive and judicial bodies must revolve. Whatever may be the case in other countries, yet in this, there can be no doubt, that every act of the legislature, repugnant to the constitution, is absolutely void....[389]

Following these trends, and despite the Framers of the constitution intending that judicial review be one of the fundamental principles of the American constitutional system or not, it was first established in relation to federal laws in the Case celebrated *Marbury v. Madison* Case 1803.[390] In it the principle of supremacy of the constitution was the basic argument for the exercise of that power of judicial review by the Supreme Court.

In effect, Chief Justice Marshall aiming to determine whether the Supreme Court in accordance with the constitution, could exercise the authority given it by the Judiciary act 1789 to issue writs of mandamus to public officers, and considering that it "appears not to be warranted by the constitution", decided to "inquire whether a jurisdiction so conferred can be exercised", and to that end he developed the doctrine of the supremacy of the constitution based on the question "whether an act repugnant to the constitution can or can not become the law of the land."

To answer this question, he followed a logical approach, establishing first the principle of the supremacy of the constitution. He started his argument by accepting the idea of an "original right" of the people to establish the principles regulating "their future government", as "the basis on which the whole American fabric had been erected." This original right to adopt those "fundamental" and "permanent" principles, he considered, was a very great exertion, so was not to be "frequently repeated."

This "original and supreme will", he said, "organises the government... assigns to different departments their respective powers... (and) establishes certain limits not to be transcended by those departments." He considered that the government of the United States was of that kind, in which "the powers of the legislature are defined and limited", and it was precisely for the purpose "that those limits may not be mis-

---

389 2. Dallas 304 (1795). See the text in S.I. KUTLER (ed.), *The Supreme Court and the Constitution. Readings in American Constitutional History*, NY 1964 , p. 7–13.

390 5.U.S. (1 Cranch), 137; 2 L. Ed 60 (1803). In relation to this case see in general E.S. CORWIN, *The Doctrine of Judicial Review. Its Legal and Historical Basis and other Essays*, Princeton 1914, p. 1–78.

taken, or forgotten", that a written constitution containing those fundamental and permanent principles was adopted.

He then asked:

> To what purpose are powers limited, and to what purpose is that limitation committed to writing, if these limits may, at any time, be passed by those intended to be restrained? The distinction between a government with limited and unlimited powers is abolished if those limits do not confine the person on whom they are imposed, and if acts prohibited and acts allowed are of equal obligation.

Thus, he stressed the alternative as:

> A proposition too plain to be contested that the constitution controls any legislative act repugnant to it; or, that the legislative may alter the constitution by an ordinary act;

in relation to which, he stated:

> Between these alternatives there is no middle ground. The constitution is either a superior paramount law, unchangeable by ordinary means, or it is on a level with ordinary legislative acts, and, like other acts, is alterable when the legislature shall please to alter it.
>
> If the former part of the alternative be true, then a legislative act contrary to the constitution is not law; if the latter part be true then written constitutions are absurd attempts on the part of the people to limit a power in its own nature illimitable.

Of course, his conclusion was that the constitution was the "fundamental and paramount law of the nation", a principle that he considered "as one of the fundamental principles of our society." Therefore, he accepted the principle that "an act of the legislature repugnant to the constitution is void", considering "the very essence of judicial duty" to determine the rules that govern the case when a law is in opposition to the constitution. In such cases, he concluded, "the constitution is superior to any ordinary act of the legislature, the constitution and not such ordinary acts, must govern the case to which they both apply." The contrary, –he stated–, would mean to give "to the legislature a practical and real omnipotence... would be the same as prescribing limits and declaring that those limits may be passed at pleasure all of which, –he concluded–, would "subvert the very foundation of all written constitutions."

After this case, the principle of the supremacy of the constitution in the sense that it overrides any other law inconsistent with it, became one of the main features of modern Constitutionalism, and of course, of the possibility itself, of judicial review of legislation.

Nevertheless, the supremacy of the constitution in modern times is not only a matter of implication according to the logic of the *Marbury v. Madison* case, but is a consequence, in many cases, of express declarations in that sense in the constitution itself, as was the classic case of the 1920 Czechoslovakian constitution, which stated in article I, 1:

> All the laws contrary to the Constitutional Charter, to its parts and also to the Laws that modify or complement it, are invalid.

This sort of express declaration, considered by Hans Kelsen as one of the "objective guarantees" of the constitution,[391] can be as a common trend in contemporary constitutionalism, particularly, in the constitutions of Latin America[392] and Africa.[393] In the latter, as B.O. Nwabueze said:

> When a court declares a statute invalid for unconstitutionality it is merely acting as a mouthpiece, an instrumentality, of the constitution.[394]

However, the concept of Constitutional supremacy, the constitution considered as a fundamental and higher law built up by American Constitutionalism, was not followed in Europe in the last century, and was only adopted in the 20th century. This European immunity regarding the supremacy of the constitution and judicial review, taking into account the historical process developed after the French Revolution, is explained by the development of the monarchical principle, as a consequence of the restoration of the monarchical idea that made the monarch a preconstitutional source of power, all reducing the constitution to a simple formal code given by the monarch regarding the relation of the organs of the state, without any other outcome and in particular, without a dogmatic part related to fundamental rights and applicable to the citizen.[395] Additionally, both the principle of parliamentary sovereignty and the extreme interpretation of the separation of powers, the doctrine that gave the legislator immunity from the judicial power also contributed to the non–adoption of the principle of the supremacy of the constitution.

In Europe, the reception of the doctrine of supremacy of the constitution and of judicial review took place only after the First World War, mainly through the constitutional system designed by Hans Kelsen for his own country, Austria, and reflected in the 1920 Austrian constitution. It was also reflected in the constitution of Czechoslovakia in the same year.

Years later, after the Second World War, the Austrian system of constitutional supremacy and judicial review was adopted in Germany and Italy and through their influence, in other European constitutional systems.

As Professor Louis Favoreu recently pointed out, it has only been over the last decades that Europe has "rediscovered" the constitution as a superior law which establishes certain fundamental values of society out of reach of temporary or passing majorities, transferring the traditional sacred character of acts of Parliament to the constitution. Therefore, the constitution has been "rejuridicised" in the sense of now

---

391 H. KELSEN, "La guarantie juridictionnelle de la constitution. La Justice constitutionnelle", *Revue du droit public et de la science politique en France et à l'étranger*, Paris 1928, p. 214.

392 The Venezuelan constitution 1961 for example in article 46 establishes: "Every act of the Public Power which violates or impairs the rights guaranteed by this constitution is void...."

393 Constitution of Uganda (Art. 1), Kenya (Art. 3), Nigeria (Art. 1), Swaziland (Art. 2). *Cf.* B.C. NWABUEZE, *Judicial Control of Legislative Action and its Legitimacy. Recent Development* (African Regional Report), International Association of Legal Science. Uppsala Colloquium 1984 (mineo), p. 2.

394 *Idem*, p. 2.

395 E. GARCÍA DE ENTERRÍA, *op. cit.*, p. 55–56

being considered as a fundamental law directly enforceable by the judges and applicable to individuals.[396]

3. Supremacy and Rigidity of the Constitution

We have said that judicial review of constitutionality, particularly of the constitutionality of legislation, translated into a judicial control of legislative action, firstly requires the existence of a written constitution, a product of a constituent sovereign power, the people, conceived as a fundamental and enforceable real law with direct effects on both state organs and individuals. We have also said that for the existence of judicial review, the constitution is also required to have a hierarchical pre–eminence, superiority or supremacy over all the constituted powers established by the constitution itself.

This supremacy of the constitution is, of course, closely related to its rigid character, which means that the norms of the constitution are immune to the powers of the ordinary legislator. This characteristic of the constitution is the general trend in constitutional law all over the world, with the exception of systems like those of the United Kingdom, New Zealand and Israel, which have unwritten constitutions, therefore flexible ones.[397]

In principle, judicial review is essentially related to rigid constitutions,[398] although not all the countries with this kind of constitution have a system of judicial review, and it has also been accepted that even in systems with flexible constitutions some kind of judicial review is possible. Nevertheless, as we have said, the judicial control of the constitutionality of legislation finds its complete sense and meaning, in constitutional systems, with written and rigid constitutions, in which the fundamental law is adopted in an entrenched way, implying that its amendments and reforms can only take place through special procedures and not through ordinary legislative processes.

In this sense, for instance, Professor Maurice Duverger considered conclusively that "the existence of a judicial control of the constitutionality of laws needs the constitution to be a rigid constitution and not a flexible constitution."[399] And in fact, it is in the framework of rigid constitutions that one may distinguish between constitutional and ordinary norms, and where the principle of constitutional supremacy is definitively accepted.

In rigid constitutional systems the principle of *lex superior derogat legi inferiori* is the one to be applied when judging the constitutionality of laws; whereas in flexible constitutional systems, in which the constitution does not have the character of

---

396 L. FAVOREU, *Le contrôle juridictionnel des lois et sa légitimité. Développements récents en Europe occidentale*, *doc. cit.*, p. 23.

397 J. BRYCE, *Flexible Constitutions and Rigid Constitutions*, Spanish edition: *Constituciones flexibles y constituciones rígidas*, Madrid 1962, p. 19.

398 See in contrary, G. TRUJILLO FERNÁNDEZ, *Dos Estudios sobre la constitucionalidad de las leyes*, La Laguna 1970, p. 11, 17.

399 M. DUVERGER, *Institutions politiques et droit constitutionnel*, Paris 1965, p. 222.

supreme law, the conflict between legal norms is not that expressed by Chief Justice Marshall in the *Marbury v Madison* case, but between norms of equal rank. Therefore, in such cases, the traditional principles of interpretation: *lex posterior derogat legi priori* and *lex specialis derogat legi generali*[400] are in fact normally applicable. Consequently, judicial review is closely related to rigid constitutions, even though as we have said, not all the countries that have rigid constitutions, have a system of judicial review.

Nevertheless, if it is true that in flexible constitutional systems the absence of an entrenched constitutional text allows the ordinary legislator to reform or amend the constitution, and, therefore, prevent the development of an effective system of judicial review, it has been correctly pointed out that some distinction can be established between constitutional norms and ordinary legislative norms, not with regard to their formal aspects but in relation to their content. In rigid constitutions, the difference between these norms is especially a formal one, in the sense that constitutional norms are only amendable through special procedures, but the distinction also exists in flexible constitutions even though not in a formal sense, but in relation to the content of such norms.[401]

Thus if it is true that in flexible constitutions, judicial review in the formal sense cannot exist, it is not impossible in the substantive sense regarding the content of the norms.[402]

In this respect we can also say that in systems with flexible constitutions, certain conditions over reforming some acts of Parliament, allowing the formal control of the "constitutionality" of legislation can be established. In some respects, it is Israel's case that we must stress, a country that we said, has a non–written constitution.

In effect, in the 1948 Declaration of the Establishment of the State of Israel adopted on the eve of the termination of the British Mandate over Palestine, some fundamental principles were proclaimed by the People's Council, among which it was stated that a constitution was "to be drawn up by the Constituent Assembly not later than the 1st of October, 1945."[403] The constitution was never drafted and instead the Knesset passed what is called the *Harari* Resolution, in which "the Constitutional Legislative and Judicial Committee" was charged "with the duty to prepare a draft constitution for the state", following these guidelines:

> The constitution shall be composed of individual chapters in such a manner that each of them shall constitute a basic law in itself. The chapters shall be brought before the Knesset to

---

400 P. DE VEGA GARCÍA, "Jurisdicción constitucional y crisis de la Constitución", *Revista de estudios políticos*, 7, Madrid 1979 p. 94.

401 G. TRUJILLO FERNÁNDEZ, *op. cit.*, p. 17, 18.

402 P. Lucas MURILLO DE LA CUEVA, "El examen de la constitucionalidad de la leyes y la soberanía parlamentaria", *Revista de estudios políticos*, 7, Madrid 1979, p. 206.

403 A. SHAPIRA, *The Constitution and its Defense in Israel: Fundamentals, Guarantees Emergency Powers and Reform*, Internacional Congress on the constitution and its Defense, U.N.A.M. México 1982, (mimeo), p. 2–5. See also A. SHAPIRA, "Judicial Review without a Constitution: The Israeli Paradox", *Temple Law Quarterly*, 56, 1983, p. 405.

the extent at which the Committee will terminate its work and all chapters together will form the state constitution.[404]

It has been considered that with this Resolution, the constituent powers inherent in the first Knesset have passed on to all successive Knessets, and in its "continuing constituent authority" the Knesset has approved various "basic laws" related to the Knesset itself, to Israeli lands, to the president of the state, to the government, to the state economy, to the Army, and to Jerusalem Capital of Israel.[405] Some of these "basic laws" have been passed in an entrenched way, in the sense that their repeal or amendments can be adopted only by "a majority of the members of the Knesset." Among these "basic laws" is the "Basic law: The Knesset" passed in 1958, in which the Knesset limited its own parliamentary supremacy.

In 1969, the problem of the reviewability of ordinary legislation that is inconsistent with the basic laws was placed before the Supreme Court and was decided upon in the case *Bergman v Minister of Finance*.[406] The facts were the following: the Knesset passed a law providing for the financing of the political parties' election costs, out of public funds, and the funds were to be distributed in proportion to the party's representation in the outgoing Knesset and not in strictly equal terms. Dr. Bergman, a Tel–Aviv lawyer, challenged this statute as being inconsistent with the "Basic law–The Knesset", which provided not for proportional participation in the election but "for general, national... equal... elections", and he challenged the Statute considering that it was passed by the Knesset by less than the required absolute majority of its total membership for its amendment. The Supreme Court, although it did not expressly decide upon the constitutional questions, by stating that it was "far from purporting to affect whosoever the sovereignty of the Knesset as the legislative authority", in fact opened the way to judicial review of legislation inconsistent with the Basic Laws.[407] The decision, in fact, offered the Knesset two possible courses of action: it could either re–enact the Financing law, tainted with inequality as it was, by the absolute majority needed under the Basic law: the Knesset; or it could rectify the legislative scheme of financing so as to remove there from the unacceptable element of inequality.

Reacting to the *Bergman* case, the Knesset took two steps to rectify its mistakes: first, it adopted an amendment to the Financing law which cured its original defect of inequality; second, the Knesset passed, by an absolute majority, the Election law, 1969, which provided that:

---

404 A. SHAPIRA, *The Constitution ..., cit.*, p. 8.

405 *Idem*, p. 9.

406 23. P.D. (1) 693 (1969). See the references in J.D. WHYTE, *Judicial Review of Legislation and its Legitimacy: Developments in the Common Law World*, International Association of Legal Sciences, Uppsala Colloquium 1984, p. 57; A. SHAPIRA,*The Constitution... op. cit.*, p. 9–13.

407 J.D. WHYTE, *op. cit.*, p. 58.

> For the purpose of removing doubt it is hereby laid down that the provisions contained in the Knesset Election law are from the date of their coming into effect valid for ever legal proceeding and for every matter and purpose.[408]

The *Bergman* decision is without doubt of particular importance and as Professor Amos Shapira has pointed out, it can lead the way to judicial review of constitutionality in a country like Israel, with an unwritten and flexible constitution. Of course the Supreme Court did not invalidate the challenge law, but did not hesitate to investigate its validity by looking at the legislative journals to see if the Financial law had or had not been passed by an absolute majority. Furthermore, it did not declare the defective Financing law as unconstitutional and void, but ordered the Minister of Finance not to give effect to the law; it recognised the sovereignty of the Knesset or Parliament, but acknowledged the constituent power of the Knesset to bind itself and its successors through an entrenched clause of its Basic law. Finally, it was careful not to establish a precedent but really it revolutionised the Israeli legal system "by introducing *de facto* judicial supervision of the constitutionality of primary legislation."[409]

In conclusion, a principle of differentiation between higher law (Basic Laws) and ordinary law (regular Knesset legislation) can almost be established in Israel, even if it does not have a written constitution and the constitution is flexible; and after the *Bergman* decision a principle of judicial review can also be distinguished, even though it seems, it is only the beginning of a long ongoing process.

Of course, this special situation is exceptional and evidently not resolved definitively. What is admitted is that the supremacy of the constitution and judicial review of legislation is normally found in legal systems with written and rigid constitutions.

4. The Supremacy and the unwritten constitutional principles

Nevertheless, this assertion leads us to another problem related to written constitutions and to the possibility of judicial review. The problem concerning the scope of judicial review powers regarding the formal text of written constitutional rules and the admissibility of judicial review of legislation based on the unwritten principles and values of the written constitution. In other words, the question to determine is whether judicial control of the constitutionality of legislation must only be exercised in relation to norms contained in written articles of the constitution, or whether it can be exercised in relation to non written norms that result from deduction from the constitution and its spirit.[410]

The problem regarding the active role of the supreme Court has been widely discussed in North America particularly over the protection of fundamental rights, and

408 A. SHAPIRA, *The Constitution..., cit.*, p. 10.

409 *Idem*, p. 11.

410 L. FAVOREU "Rapport général introductif" in L. FAVOREU (ed.), *Cours constitutionnelles... cit.*, p. 45

has produced two antagonistic alternatives concerning the role of judges in judicial review: the interpretative and the non–interpretative role.[411]

According to the interpretative method, constitutional judges are limited to the application of the concrete norms established in the written constitution itself or clearly implicit therein; this was the model originally followed by Hamilton and Chief Justice Marshall and according to which legislation can only be invalidated by a deduction, whose fundamental premise is clearly found in the constitution.

At the other extreme, the non–interpretative model wants judges to go beyond the literal references of the constitution and to execute the norms that are not to be found within the boundaries of the written document, but that form the permanent and fundamental values of a given society and its political system.

In Thomas Grey's opinion, the purest form of the non interpretative model, which he considered almost dead in North America, recognises the general principles of republican government and natural justice of human rights, establish limitations on legislative authority, the actual words of the written text of the constitution or even its existence not being important.[412] This non interpretative model was followed by the Warren Court in the decisions concerning the discrimination issues and the protection of minorities,[413] bearing in mind that the 1789 constitution and the 1791 amendments did not establish the principle of equality and that the XIV Amendment (1868) only established an equal protection clause.[414]

The question regarding the choice between the interpretative model and the non–interpretative model, has been, and almost certainly will continue to be, one of the most important issues of the role of constitutional justice and of judicial review of legislation. The adoption of one model or the other depends, in fact, on the content of the constitution itself and on the way the articles of the constitutional text are written, and when they were written. The fact is that when a constitution is two centuries old, like the American one, it is impossible to solidify the known intentions of the framers who lived in a patriarchal society, which vanished long ago, particularly

411 J.H. ELY, *Democracy and Distrust. A Theory of Judicial Review*, 1980, p. 1–2; T. GREYZ, "Do We Have an Unwritten Constitution", *Stanford Law Review*, 27 1975, p. 703; T. GREY "Origins of the Unwritten Constitution: Fundamental Law in American Revolutionary thought", *Stanford Law Review*, 30, 1978, p. 843–847; E. GARCÍA DE ENTERRÍA, *op. cit*, p. 210–221; M. CAPPELLETTI, "El formidable problema del control judicial y 1a contribución del análisis comparado", *Revista de estudios políticos*, 13, Madrid 1980, p. 68–69 ("The Mighty Problem" of Judicial Review and the Contribution of Comparative Analysis, in *Southern California Law Review*, 1980, p. 409); B. CAINE, "Judicial Review: Democracy Versus Constitutionality", *Temple Law Quarterly*, 56, (2), 1973, p. 298.

412 T. GREY, "Origins...", *loc. cit.*, p. 844.

413 See particularly *Brown v. Board of Education of Topeka*, 347 U.S. 483 (1954). See the text in S.I. KUTLER (ed.) *op. cit.*, p. 548–552.

414 *Cf.* J.H. ELY, *op. cit*, p. 79–90; E. GARCÍA DE ENTERRÍA, *op. cit.*, p. 216–217. See also R. BERGER, *Government by Judiciary. The Transformation of the Fourteen Amendment*, 1977.

in relation to the so–called open–ended or open clauses of the constitution.[415] Those must be determined and that is the role of the courts.

Of course, the situation is different in constitutional systems with modern and detailed constitutional codes, where the non–interpretative model is difficult to develop, and in any case, the adoption of one model or the other depends on the juridical tradition of the particular country.

For instance, in the sphere of fundamental rights, the Swiss federal tribunal has largely developed the non–interpretative model for the protection of fundamental rights. In effect, important fundamental rights like personal liberty, freedom of opinion, the right to a previous hearing are not in the text of the federal constitution, but are recognised by the federal tribunal as non–written constitutional rights. In this respect, it has been said, the tribunal does not interpret the constitution but rather perfects it, because it considers it its duty as a constitutional judge to do so, and justifies this attitude by the fact that its function is precisely to guarantee the foundations of the democratic, and federal state submitted to the law.[416]

But on the contrary, as Professor Theo Ohlinger pointed out, the Austrian constitutional court does not follow a similar method of law making, and considers itself bound to the constitutional text even though it has to be interpreted. Nevertheless, this interpretation is considered as being of great importance in Austria because the most important norms of the constitution related to fundamental rights were written in the last century and have a formalistic and lapidarian style.

But even in those cases, the positivist orientation of the constitutional court is determinant and shows itself in a careful application of interpretative methods. Thus, when the constitutional court considers that the absence of a constitutional norm in a particular context is wrongful its role is to ask the constitutional legislator to fill the gap, considering itself incompetent to do so.[417]

In the sphere of the protection of fundamental rights, the role of the French Constitutional Council during the last decade as an example of the non–interpretative model must be stressed. It has been considered that the constitutional judges in France have not only surpassed the pure interpretative model, but have also reached the purest form of the non interpretative judicial control model, when they have decided to control the conformity of executive legislation to "general principles" or undefined, vague and non written "republican traditions", which have been "found" by the judges and defined as having a superior law rank.[418]

In this sense, the attitude of the French Constitutional Council radically changed in the 70's.After the important decision adopted on 16th July 1971[419] concerning the

---

415 J.H. ELY, *op. cit*, p. 13; E. GARCÍA DE ENTERRÍA, *op. cit*, p. 211.

416 T. OHLINGER, "Object et portée de la protection des droits fondamentaux Cours constitutionnelle antrichienne", in L. FAVOREU (ed.), *Cours constitutionnelles ...*, p. 335–336.

417 *Idem*, p. 346.

418 M. CAPPELLETTI, "El formidable problema..., *loc. cit.*, note 20, p. 69.

419 See in L. FAVOREU and L. PHILIP, *Les grandes décisions du Conseil Constitutionnel*", Paris 1984, p. 222–237.

liberty of association, the following contrasting position resulted: in 1958, when the constitution was drafted, in the Consultative Constitutional Committee it was considered that the role of the Constitutional Council was not to ensure the respect of the provisions of the preamble to the constitution; on the contrary, in 1971, the Constitutional Council accepted the positive law value of the preamble to the 1958 constitution with all its consequences[420] regarding what Professor Favoreu called the *bloc de constitutionnalité.*[421]

In effect, the preamble to the 1958 French constitution says:

> The French people, solemnly proclaim their subjection to the rights of Man and to the national sovereignty principles as have been defined by the Declaration of 1789, confirmed and completed by the Preamble to the constitution of 1946.

This preamble to the constitution was considered by the Constitutional Council itself, up to the 70's only as a principle for the orientation of constitutional interpretation, its competence being "strictly limited" by the constitutional text.[422]

Nevertheless this attitude changed after the Constitutional Council decision of 16th July 1971, when it was decided that a proposed law establishing a procedure to set up preliminary judicial controls for the acquisition of legal capacity by association was against the constitution. The proposed law was an amendment bill to a 1901 law relating to non–profit making associations submitted by the government to the National Assembly in 1970, which the Council considered unconstitutional,[423] using the following argument:

The 1958 constitution through the preamble to the 1946 constitution referred to the "fundamental principles recognised by the laws of the Republic" among which the principle of liberty of association must be listed.

In accordance with this principle, associations were to be constituted freely and could publicly develop their activities, the only condition being to make a previous declaration, – whose validity was not to be submitted to a previous intervention by either administrative or judicial authorities.

---

420 L. FAVOREU, "Rapport général introductif", *loc. cit.*, p. 45–46.

421 L. FAVOREU, "Le principe de Constitutionalité. Essai de definition d'apres la jurisprudence du Conseil Constitutionnel", *Recueil d'etude en Hommaqe a Charles Eisenman*, Paris 1977, p. 34.

422 L. HAMON, "Contrôle de Constitutionalité et protection des droits individuels. Apropos de trois decisions récents du Conseil Constitutionnel", *Recueil Dalloz Sirey 1974*, Chronique XVI, p. 85.

423 See the Constitutional Council decision in L. FAVOREU and J. PHILIP, *Les grandes décisions du Conseil Constitutionnel, cit.*, p. 222. See the comments of the 16 July 1971 decisions in J. RIVERO, "Note", *L'Actualité Juridique. Droit Administratif*, 1971, p. 537; J. RIVERO, "Principes fondamentaux reconnus par les lois de la Republique; une nouvelle categorie constitutionnelle?", *Dalloz 1974*, Chroniques, p. 265; and J.E. BARDSLEY, "The Constitutional Council and Constitutional Liberties in France", *The American Journal of Comparative Law*, 20, (3), 1972, p. 43; B. NICHOLAS, "Fundamental Rights and Judicial Review in France", *Public Law*, 1978, p. 83.

Thus, the Constitutional Council decided that the limits imposed on associations by the proposed bill establishing a prior judicial control of the said declaration were unconstitutional. In this way, Professor Rivero said,

> The liberty of association, which is not expressly established either in the Declaration or by the particularly needed principles of our times, but which is only recognised by a Statute of 1 July 1901, has been recognised by the Constitutional Council decision, as having a constitutional character, not only as a principle, but in ′relation to the modalities of its exercise.[424]

The significance of this decision was summarised by Professor Barry Nicholas, in an article published in the *Public Law Journal* in 1978, by saying:

> It made an unambiguous breach with the constitutional tradition of the supremacy of *loi*. It declared beyond any question that even within the area set aside for legislation by article 34 of the constitution there were fundamental principles, which Parliament could not alter or contravene. And above all, it declared that those fundamental principles were to be found not only in the constitution proper but also in its Preamble and via that Preamble, in the Preamble of 1946 (and presumably also in the Declaration of 1789).[425]

The decision of 16th July 1971 on the liberty of association is an example of the creative will of fundamental rights by the Constitutional Council, even though for that purpose it has based its decision on the preamble to the constitution, and through it, in what the preamble to the 1946 constitution considered the "fundamental principles recognised by the laws of the Republic." In general, therefore, to establish a fundamental right or liberty as such a "fundamental principle", the Constitutional Council has based itself on a particular existing statute, as happened with the liberty of association which was recognised by the Statute of 1 July 1901.

But in other cases,[426] as has happened with the right to self defence, the Constitutional Council has not based itself in a particular Statute for deducing a liberty based on "the fundamental principles recognised by the laws of the Republic." In effect, in a decision dated 19th–20th January 1981[427] the Constitutional Council radically changed the previous situation regarding the right to one's own defence, which was considered by the *Conseil d'État* simply as a general principle of law.[428] Conversely, after the 1981 decision, the Constitutional Council recognised it as part of the "principles and rules of constitutional value", an expression used by the Constitutional Council,

---

424 J. RIVERO, "Les garanties constitutionnelles des droits de l'homme en droit français", *IX Journees Juridiques Franco–Latino Americaines*, Bayonne 21–23 mai 1976, (mimeo), p. 11.

425 B. NICHOLAS, *loc. cit*., p. 89.

426 Decisions of 8 Nov 1976; 2 Dec 1976; 20 July 77, 19 January 1981; 20 January 1981, *Cf.* the quotations in F. LUCHAIRE, "Procedures et techniques de protection des droits fondamentaux. Conceil Constitutional français", in L. FAVOREU (ed.), *Cours constitutionnelles europeenes ..., cit*., p. 69, 70, 83.

427 L. FAVOREU et L. PHILIP., *Les grandes décisions..., cit*., pp. 490, 517.

428 *Cf.* D.G. LAVROFF, "El Consejo Constitutional francés y la garantía de las libertades públicas", *Revista española de derecho constitucional*, 1 (3), 1981, pp. 54–55; L. FAVOREU et L. PHILIP, *Les grandes décisions..., cit*., p. 213.

To designate in a generic manner all the norms that, without being contained in the text of the constitution itself, have Constitutional rank.[429]

Therefore, in France, "conformity with the constitution" as a consequence of the principle of constitutionality, is not understood today strictly as conformity with an express disposition of the constitution. On the contrary, since the 1970's, the notion of constitutional norms that could serve as reference norms to control the constitutionality of legislation is progressively understood in a wider sense, comprising dispositions or principles outside the constitutional text, and in particular, the Declaration of 1789, the preambles to the 1946 and 1958 constitutions, the fundamental principles recognised by the laws of the Republic, and the general principles of constitutional value.[430] All these sources of the principle of constitutionality enjoy the same supremacy character as the written articles of the constitution.

Anyway, the discussion concerning the need of a written or unwritten norm of reference to allow for the judicial control of the constitutionality of legislation is a permanent one, with different solutions in the various systems of judicial review,[431] even though a clear tendency to allow the non–interpretative method of judicial review and the active role of the constitutional judge can be observed.

5. The adaptation of the Constitution and its interpretation

Nevertheless, it is obvious that the normal and customary type of judicial control of constitutionality that has developed in all constitutional systems, where the principle of the supremacy of the constitution is established, is based on the existence of written rules in the constitution, to which all state organs, particularly the legislator, must conform. In this case, of course, the basic problem regarding judicial review of constitutionality, based on the interpretative model, refers to the degree of clarity of the particular constitutional text and, consequently, to the possibility of judicial review of legislation in relation to vague, imprecise or undetermined notions contained in constitutional articles and to the need for the constitutional judge to adapt the text of the constitution to ensure its effectiveness and supremacy.

As mentioned, the situation varies depending on the modernity or antiquity of the constitution, on the numerous or few provisions or regulations of the constitutional text, and on the preciseness or vagueness of the articles of the constitution.

But even modern constitutions, particularly concerning fundamental rights are written down in a synthetic, vague and elusive way, and their norms are generally expressed in ambiguous terms, full of worthy characteristics, like liberty, democra-

429 L. FAVOREU "Les décisions du Conseil Constitutiornel dans l'affaire des nationalisations", *Revue du droit public et de la science politique en France et à l'étranger*, T. XCVIII, N° 2, Paris 1982, p. 401.

430 L. FAVOREU, "L'application directe et l'effect indirect des normes constitutionnelles", *French Report to the XI International Congress of Comparative Law*, Caracas 1982, (mineo), p. 4

431 See E. SMITH, "Contrôle juridictionnel de la législation et sa légitimite. Dévelopment récents dans les cinq pays scandinaves", *Rapport au Symposium de l'Association Internationale des Sciences Juridique*, Uppsala 1984, (mimeo), p. 61. Also published in L. FAVOREU and J.A. JOLOWICZ (ed.), *Le contrôle juridictionnel des lois..., cit.*, pp. 225–282.

cy, justice, dignity, equality, social function, public interests,[432] all of which lead to the need for an active role by judges, when interpreting what have been called, the "precious ambiguities",[433] in which constitutions are written down.

Anyway, these vague and ambiguous phrases of constitutions, always express certain concepts or values related to the general foundations of the given society and its political system, and it is in relation to these that the constitutional judge must play his creative role determining the exact meaning of the concept.

They are what in the continental European legal systems are called the "undetermined legal concepts" or "imprecise juridical notions"[434] that are of course, also included in the constitution, more than anything because of its general character. The constitutional judge must fill in these concepts, pinpoint and determine their boundaries through an interpretative process, bearing in mind basically, the superior values followed by the constitution, and generally established in the preamble or in its first articles.

The position of the judge facing the constitution, therefore, is not different from the position he normally has facing all other laws, which must be interpreted, and if it is true that the judges must not substitute the legislator in deducing concepts which could be against what is written in the law, neither must they interpret the constitution in a way so as to arrive at concepts that could be contrary to the constitutional text and its fundamental values.[435]

But the constitutional judge always has an additional duty compared to the ordinary judge: he must defend the constitution and particularly, the values that are at its foundation at a given time. That is why the constitutional judge in his interpretative process must adapt the constitution to the current values of society, and of the political system, in order precisely, "to keep the constitution alive."[436] To that end, undoubtedly, the constitutional judge must develop a creative activity so as to allow the current and effective application of constitutions written, for instance, in the 19th century, to control the constitutionality of legislation.

In this respect, the constitution cannot be seen as a static document. On the contrary, it must be adapted to the evolution of social needs and institutions. The role of the constitutional judge in this process of adaptation of the constitution has been

---

432 M. CAPPELLETTI, "Necessité et légitimité de la justice constitutionelle" in L. FAVOREU (ed.), *Cours constitutionelle européenes et droit fundamentaux*, Paris 1982, p. 474

433 "If it is true that precision have a place of honor in the writting of a governmental decision, it is mortal when it refers to a constitution which wants to be a lively body." S.M. HUFSTEDLES, "In the Name of Justice", *Stanford Lawyers*, 14, (1), 1979, p. 3–4 quoted by M. CAPPELLETTI, "Nécessité et légitimité ...", *loc. cit*, p. 474. See the references in E. GARCIA DE ENTERRIA, *op, cit*, p. 229; L. FAVOREU, *Le contrôle juridictionnel des lois et sa légitimité..., cit.*, p. 32.

434 F. SAINZ MORENO, *Conceptos jurídicos, interpretación y discrecionalidad administrativa*, Madrid 1976; E. GARCÍA DE ENTERRÍA, *La lucha contra las inmunidades de poder en el derecho administrativo*, Madrid 1980, p. 32.

435 F. LUCHAIRE, "Procedures et techniques ...", *loc. cit.*, p. 83.

436 M. CAPPELLETTI, "El formidable problema ...", *loc. cit.*, p. 78.

crucial, as the role of the North American Supreme Court has demonstrated. In this respect, it suffices to recall the important decisions of the Supreme Court in the matter of discrimination in the educational system.

When referring to the XIV Amendment, for example, Chief Justice Warren said in *Brown v. Board of Education of Topeka* in 1954:

> In approaching this problem we cannot turn the clock back to 1868 when the Amendment was adopted, or even to 1896 when *Plessy v. Ferguson* was written. We must consider public education in the light of its full development and its present place in American life throughout the Nation. Only in this way can it be determined if segregation in public schools deprives these plaintiffs of the equal protection of the laws.

This assertion led Chief Justice Warren to conclude then,

> That in the field of public education the doctrine of "separate but equal" has no place. Separate educational facilities are inherently unequal. Therefore, we hold that the plaintiffs, and others similarly situated from whom the actions have been brought are by reason of the segregation complained of, deprived of the equal protection of the laws guaranteed by the Fourteenth Amendment.[437]

In the same sense, this adaptation of the constitution by the constitutional judge has recently been demonstrated in France by the Constitutional Council in the well known Nationalisation case in 1982 in which the article concerning the right of property in the Declaration of the Rights of Man and Citizen of 1789 was applied, and the right to property itself was then declared as having constitutional force. In its decision of 16 January 1982,[438] even though the article of the Declaration concerning property rights was considered obsolete and that its interpretation could not be given other than in a completely different sense to that which applied in 1789,[439] the Constitutional Council stated that:

> Taking into account that if it is true that after 1789 and up to the present, the aims and conditions of the exercise of the right to property have undergone an evolution characterised both, by a notable extension of its application to new individual fields and by limits imposed by general interests, the principles themselves expressed in the Declaration of Rights of Man have complete constitutional value, particularly regarding the fundamental character of the right to property, the conservation of which constitutes one of the aims of political society, and located on the same rank as liberty, security and resistance to oppression, and also regarding the guarantees given to the holders of that right and the prerogatives of public power.[440]

In this way, the Constitutional Council not only created constitutional right by giving the 1789 Declaration constitutional rank and value, but also adapted the "sacred" right to property established two hundred years ago, to the limitable right of our times, although its conservation led to the declaration by the Constitutional Council of certain articles in the Nationalisation act, as unconstitutional.

---

437 347 U.S. 483 (1954). See the text in S.I. KUTLER (ed.) *op.cit.*, p. 550.

438 See in L. FAVOREU et L. PHILIP, *Les grandes décisions ..., cit.*, p. 525–562.

439 L. FAVOREU, *Le contrôle juridictionnel des lois et sa légitimité..., cit.*, p. 32.

440 L. FAVOREU et L. PHILIP, *Les grandes décisions...*, p. 526. *Cf.* L. FAVOREU, "Les décisions du Conseil Constitutionnel dans l'affaire des nationalisations", *loc. cit.*, p. 406.

Anyway, what is certain today is that in all constitutional systems with written constitutions, the principle of constitutional supremacy exists so that constitutions are supreme laws, whose norms prevail over all others in a given legal order; and as we have said, this principle of the supremacy of the constitution applies not only to its written articles, but also to non written norms that can be deduced from the constitution by constitutional judges, as forming the superior values that lay at the foundation of a given society and of its political system.

Of course, the principle of the supremacy of the constitution would be a dead letter if the constitutional system did not provide for a whole set of constitutional guarantees to give effectiveness to the said constitutional supremacy. One of these guarantees is precisely, judicial review, that is to say, the powers given to judges – ordinary judges or special constitutional courts– to control the constitutionality of legislation and of all other state acts.

III. THE JUDICIAL GUARANTEE OF THE CONSTITUTION

One of the basic elements of the state submitted to law in systems with written constitutions is the principle of the supremacy of the constitution over all other norms in the legal order and over all state acts. Therefore, the supremacy of the constitution itself, being the foundation of the state and the basis of the whole legal order, implies that acts of Parliament and of the other organs of the state, cannot be contrary to the rules embodied in the constitution.

However, this supremacy also implies not only submission to the procedural and organic rules established in the constitution, but also the respect of the fundamental rights of individuals contained therein. As we have seen, modern constitutions contain both an organic and a dogmatic part. The former refers to the organisation of the state, the distribution and separation of powers and the procedural rules for its functioning. The latter refers to the fundamental rights of individuals and to the limits imposed on state organs regarding such rights. This implies, for instance, in relation to the legislative organ, not only the need to respect the rules of distribution of power, so as not to invade the powers assigned to the executive or judicial organs, but also to act in accordance with the procedural rules established in the constitution for the sanctioning of statutes. But it also implies that the legislator, when approving any statute, cannot in any way violate the fundamental rights guaranteed in the constitution.

Therefore, regarding its supremacy, the constitution must not only be seen as an organic and procedural rule, but also as a substantive rule. Therefore, for instance, a statute could be unconstitutional not only because procedural irregularities have taken place during its formation, but also when its contents are contrary to the principles established in the constitution regarding the rights of individuals. Then unconstitutionality could be not only formal, but also substantive.[441]

---

441 H. KELSEN, "La garantie juridictionelle de la constitution (La Justice constitutionnelle)", *Revue du droit public et de la science polotique an France et à l'étranger*, J. XLV, Paris 1928, p. 206.

But the supremacy of the constitution in itself would be juridically imperfect if there were no specially established guarantees to protect the constitution against unconstitutional acts of the state or against any breach in the constitutional order. Constitutional supremacy would mean nothing if there were no particular means of protection of the constitution, established namely in the organic and procedural rules contained in its norms and in the fundamental rights enumerated in its dogmatic part.

1. Judicial Review and the End of Parliamentary Absolutism

Two types of guarantees of the supremacy of the constitution can be distinguished: the political and the judicial guarantee. In general, the political guarantee of the constitution is exercised by the supreme representative political organ of the state, and is commonly adopted in legal systems where an extreme interpretation of the principle of the separation of powers or at the other extreme the principle of the unity of state powers prevails. This was the traditional solution in France up to the establishment of the Constitutional Council in the 1958 constitution, where the National Assembly was the only state power that could control the constitutionality of legislation; and it is the solution in almost all socialist countries, where the supreme representative political organ is the only one that can control the constitutionality of legislation.

Obviously, this system identifies the controlled organs with the organs of control,[442] and has been criticised in the socialist world, as being an inconvenient system for the protection of the constitution, or at least a system with an "insufficient suitability."[443]

As we mentioned, the argument in favour of this kind of means for the protection of the constitution is based on the principle of the unity of state power and on the rejection of the principle of separation of powers that characterises the public law system in socialist countries, which implies the supremacy power of the representative political organ of the state. Therefore, the logical consequence of this supremacy is the exclusion of the possibility of giving the power to control the constitutionality of laws to any other organ, and to consider any control that could be exercised by any other organ of the state different to the representative supreme one, illegitimate including the judicial organ.[444]

Nevertheless, three of the socialist countries, Yugoslavia, Czechoslovakia and Poland, have established a judicial guarantee of the constitution, assigning the power of control of the constitutionality of legislation to special constitutional courts, based

---

442 P. BISCARETTI DI RUFFIA, "Les Constitutions européenes: notions introductives" in P. Biscaretti di Ruffia and S. ROZMARYN, *La constitution comme loi fondamentale dans les Etats de l'Europe occidentale et dans les Etats socialistes*, Torino 1966, p. 70.

443 P. NIKOLIC, *Le contrôle juridictionnel des lois et sa légitimité. (Developnements récents dans les pays socialistes)*, Rapport, Association Internationale des Sciences Juridiques, Uppsala 1984 (mineo), p. 14. Also published in L. FAVOREU and J.A. JOLOWICZ (ed.), *Le contrôle juridictionnel des lois. Légitimité, effectivité et développements récents*, Paris 1986, p. 71–115.

444 *Idem.*, p. 17.

on the principle of the supremacy of the constitution and accepting, undoubtedly, a principle of separation of state powers.[445]

On the other hand, in systems with an extreme interpretation of the separation of powers or where the principle of the supremacy of Parliament still prevails, no system of judicial control of the constitutionality of legislation can, of course, be accepted. As we mentioned before, that was the situation in continental Europe, after the French Revolution and up to recent years, and is still the situation in the United Kingdom. In Europe, the monarchical regime and the principle of representation developed through the elected legislator, led to the adoption of the principle of the supremacy of Parliament over other state powers and, consequently, to the principle of the primacy of laws or acts of Parliament over other legal rules.

During the last century, in effect, it was inconceivable to the concept of liberalism, that there could be any deviation from the principle of the supremacy of the law as the expression of the general will; and this principle made it simply unthinkable, that Parliament could ever commit an error with respect to the constitution. The enemy of the constitution, in the liberal framework of the last century, was really the executive –the monarch– who was tempted to put his individual will before that of the people, as expressed in Parliament. Thus, the possibility that Parliament could be in error or act mistakenly was not conceivable.

This myth of the assembly as the absolute expression of the general will of the people, in which the certain and infallible collective spirit reposes, was without doubt, a historical product of French Jacobinism.

In effect it was Jacobinism, based on the absolute representative principle of the general will, which led to the dogma of parliamentary sovereignty in France. According to this principle, all power over the Assembly was resolutely proscribed and, of course, the judiciary power was a simple executive instrument of the laws passed by the Assembly, with absolutely no liberty even to interpret the laws. Thus, the well known figure of the *référé législatif* according to which judges were obliged to consult the National Assembly when they had doubts about the interpretation of a Statute.[446]

This limitation was based on the purest tradition of the thoughts of Montesquieu, who considered the national judges, "... as no more than the mouth that pronounces the words of the law, mere passive beings, incapable of moderating either its force

---

445 P. NIKOLIC said in its Raport to the Uppsala Coloquium that the introduction of this judicial control of the constitutionality of legislation in some socialist countries does not mean the introduction of important elements of the separation of powers in the assambly's government system (*doc. cit*., p. 19), but in explaining the suitables of that judicial control he said that it is exercise by an authority known and recognised *separately* and *different* from the legislative power, because it is precisely its legislative activity the one that it must control and evaluate (*doc.cit*., p. 21).

446 E. GARCÍA DE ENTERRÍA, *La Constitución como norma y el Tribunal Constitucional*, Madrid 1981, p. 164.

or rigor";[447] and was expressly established in the well known Statute of 16–24 August 1790 referred to the judiciary organisation. Article 10 of this law regulated the separation between Legislative and judicial power, by saying that, "the courts could not take part directly or indirectly in the exercise of legislative power, neither prevent nor suspend the execution of acts of the legislative body..." adding in article 12 that the Courts "could not make regulations, but they must always address themselves to the legislative body when they think it necessary to interpret a Statute or to make a new one."[448] The *référé législatif* then was the instrument of the legislative body for interpreting the laws, which could not even be done by the judges.

Therefore, it was precisely this Jacobin principle of the assembly, a product of the French Revolution, which maintained the negation of the legitimacy of the courts to be able to annul the normative products of the assembly for a long time; and in the United Kingdom it is precisely the same principle of the sovereignty of Parliament a product of the glorious Revolution of 1688, which actually prevents the courts from controlling the constitutionality of legislation. The judges, in accordance with this principle must apply laws and of course, interpret them, but they are not to control them because acts of the legislative body are the expression of the sovereign will of the people.

In this traditional framework of the separation of powers, a system of judicial review of the constitutionality of laws was considered a violation of the principle of parliamentary sovereignty, based on the pre–eminence of the legislative power over other state powers. This was because Parliament was constituted by the representatives of the people who, as such, in the representative democratic state represented the sovereign. Through this approach, any intervention by a constitutional body to limit the autonomy of the supreme representative organ of the state was considered inadmissible, and therefore, legislation could only be controlled by that supreme representative organ.

In any case, it is clear that this principle of popular sovereignty expressed in modern constitutions today as the basic dogma of the democratic *État de droit* is a political principle which refers to the constituent power of the state, represented in all the constituted bodies of the state, and not to the power of one or other of the constituted bodies which exercise public power. It thus cannot lead to a discussion about the relative sovereignty of the constituted state bodies, since all the bodies of the state are the product of the sovereign, and are its representatives. Thus, it makes no sense today to preach the sovereignty of Parliament, to reject a mechanism, which guarantees the constitution to which Parliament is also subject.

To reinforce the argument in another way, it should not be forgotten that in presidential and Parliamentary democratic systems, the president of the republic or the head of government are designated by popular election, and are thus also a product of the sovereignty of the people, just as Parliament is. From the moment the constitution attributes sovereignty to the people, it is definitely clear that this quality can-

447 Quoted by Ch. H. McIlwain, *The High Court of Parliament and its Supremacy*, Yale 1910, p. 323

448 Quoted by E. García de Enterría, *op. cit.*, p. 164, note 88.

not be affirmed in one body of the state with respect to another; therefore all the powers of state and all the bodies which carry them out find their legitimacy in the people. Thus, no constitutional body is or can be really sovereign, not even the Chambers of Parliament,[449] and all of them must be submitted to the constitution.

Furthermore, it should not be forgotten that in contemporary democracies, political and social forces produce a greater relativity in the constitutional functions of the state bodies, converting Parliament into a forum for the political parties and subjecting the government to necessary negotiations with them and with trade unions and pressure groups. On many occasions, this primacy of the parties has erased the principle of the separation of powers and has conversely led to its factual concentration in the hands of the government and or those of the parties themselves. Thus there can be no doubt about the need to adopt measures which serve to guide the activities of state bodies and those of the parties themselves, within constitutional channels.[450]

In any case, exception being made of the United Kingdom, this very myth of parliamentary sovereignty was broken in Europe. Review of constitutionality really appeared in Europe after the great crisis brought about by the First World War and by the tragedies that political irrationality caused throughout Europe. This led both to the transformation of the constitution into a normative code that could be directly applicable and enforceable, and to the establishment of a constitutional body for constitutional justice, which would ensure the supremacy of the constitution not only over the executive power which, apart from this, was controlled by another type of tribunal –but basically over Parliament; that is to say, over legislative acts, and particularly, the laws. Consequently, the sovereignty of Parliament ceased to be above justice, and judicial review of constitutionality was to become the instrument governing the subjection of Parliament to the constitution when, as a result of occasional majorities, the balance was upset among state powers, or in the rationality of political and social relations themselves. In fact, the terrible lessons learnt from the abuses of the Nazi and Fascist regimes in Europe, doubtlessly brought about a complete change in the existing myths and theories in Europe regarding the infallibility of the law. Thus, as Professor Favoreu pointed out, the Rousseaunian myth of the infallibility of the law and, thus, of Parliament which expresses the general will, began to collapse, and the celebrated formula, according to which the legislator could do no wrong, began to be re–examined.[451]

This European experience generated a skeptical wisdom regarding Parliaments and representativeness, and as Professor Mauro Cappelletti said, “it was realised that

---

449 P. Lucas MURILLO DE LA CUEVA, “El examen de la constitucionalidad de las leyes y la soberanía parlamentaria”, *Revista de estudios políticos*, 7, Madrid 1979, p. 212.

450 *Idem*, p. 212.

451 L. FAVOREU, *Le contrôle juridictionnel des lois et sa légitimité. Développements récents en Europe occidentale*. Association Internationale des Sciences Juridiques. Colloque d'Uppsala 1984 (mineo), p. 22. Published as “Actualité et légitimité du contrôle juridictionnel des lois en Europe Occidentale”, in *Revue du droit public et de la science politique en France et à l'étranger*, Paris 1984 (5), p. 1147 and 1201. Also published in L. FAVOREU and J.A. JOLOWICZ (ed.), *Le contrôle juridictionel des lois. Légitimité, effectivité et developments récents*, Paris 1986, p. 17–68.

there was too much illusion in the Liberal democratic theory" in the sense that most often the reality was far from the myth of the supremacy of the peoples will and that "Parliaments and their legislation, too, would become instruments of despotic regimes; and that majorities could themselves be brutally oppressive."[452] In fact, the legislators of Weimar Germany and Mussolini's Italy failed as guarantors of freedom. On the contrary, they became the instruments of circumstantial majorities for consolidating totalitarian regimes. Consequently, these two countries learnt from experience and in their new post–war constitutions they not only established entrenched fundamental values, freedoms and rights out of the reach of Parliament, but adopted the principle of the judicial review of constitutionality of laws, as it was previously established in the Austrian system in the 1920's.

In this way, the awareness that it was necessary to protect liberties not only from the executive, but also from the legislative grew. As Professor Jean Rivero described,

> The old idea that marked the liberal 19th century, that of the protection of liberty *by the law*, tended to be substituted by the experimental idea of the need of protection of liberties *against the law*. This evolution made the extraordinary phenomenon of the acceptance of a superior authority to the Legislator itself, of an authority in charge to impose upon the Legislator the respect of the constitution possible.[453]

Thus, European continental countries adopted the review of the constitutionality of laws following a different path from that of the North–American system, adopting the principle of judicial review for other reasons. According to what Professor Louis Favoreu said, the European phenomenon was less in response to a problem of legal logic –that is, in the *Marbury v. Madison* tradition, that a law contrary to the constitution could not be applied– than to a political logic. It was the fear of oppression by a parliamentary majority, which was decisive in the change in the position of the continental European countries regarding the review of the constitutionality of laws.[454]

This political logic of judicial review can also be found in the fact that the myth of representativeness of the general will as expressed by those elected, has broken down in many countries, particularly because the legislative body is frequently made up of men chosen by the political parties, and who definitely represent these parties, not being really, in fact, representatives of the general will.

Anyway, the idea that certain number of fundamental values should be established beyond the reach of a circumstantial or temporary majority, is what led, in– one way or another, to the transfer of the traditional sacredness of the law to the constitution.

---

452 M. CAPPELLETTI, *Judicial Review of Legislation and its Legitimacy. Recent Developments*, General Report. International Association of Legal Science Colloquium, Uppsala 1982, (mimeo), p. 19. Also published in L. FAVOREU and J.A. JOLOWICZ (ed.), *Le contrôle juridictionnel des lois... cit.*, p. 285–300.

453 J. RIVERO, "Rapport de Synthese" in L. FAVOREU (ed.), *Cours constitutionnelles europèenes et droit fondamentaux*, Aix–en–Provence 1982, p. 519.

454 L. FAVOREU, *Le contrôle juridictionnel…, doc. cit.*, p. 22.

Thus it was, after the Second World War, that the European continental countries "rediscovered the constitution as a text of juridical character"[455] or rather, when they discovered the true fundamental nature of the constitution as a higher and supreme law, applicable to all state organs and enforceable by the courts. In the words of Professor Mauro Cappelletti, what is really new in modern constitutionalism

> Is the serious attempt to conceive the constitution not as a mere guideline of a political, moral, or philosophical nature, but as a real law, itself a positive and binding law although of a superior, more permanent nature than ordinary positive legislation.[456]

And of course, this positive and superior law was to be applied to the legislator as well as to all the state organs. The Constitutional Council in France expressly declared that in the well–known Nationalisation decision of 16 January 1982, which stated that:

> Considering that if article 34 of the constitution places "the nationalisation of companies and its transfer from .the public to the private sector", in the sphere of the statute, that disposition as well as the one that assigns the role of determining the fundamental principles of the right to property, to the statute, does not excuse the legislator, when exercising its powers, from the respect of the principles and rules of constitutional value that are imposed upon all state organs.[457]

Professor Louis Favoreu, when referring to this decision of the Constitutional Council qualified it as a "fundamental affirmation of the complete realisation of the *État de droit* in France" comparing it to the previous situation in which the legislator "in fact escaped, if not legally, from the submission to a superior rule."[458]

Therefore, the supremacy of the constitution over Parliament marked the end of Parliamentary absolutism,[459] transformed the old concept of parliamentary sovereignty and led the way to constitutional review in France through the Constitutional Council, even though in a limited way and previously in a more complete way in other countries in continental Europe like Austria, Germany and Italy.

Another factor that contributed to the appearance of mechanisms for judicial review of the constitutionality of laws was the transformation of the very notion of "law" in the sense of an act of Parliament or statute. In fact, statutes –the work of the legislator, once the expression of the general will in the tradition of the XIX century– came to be seen, with the evolution of parliamentary systems, as acts adopted by both the parliamentary majority and the government, through a system of connecting vessels, through the political parties. In this form, the statutes are not necessarily the expression of the general will, approved by a solid and mythical majority, but as

---

455 L. FAVOREU, *Le contrôle juridictionnel..., doc.cit.*, p. 23.

456 M. CAPPELLETTI, *doc. cit.*, p. 20.

457 See in L. FAVOREU and L. PHILIP, *Les grandes décisions du Conseil Constitutionnel*, Paris 1984, p. 527. See also L. FAVOREU, "Les decision du Conceil Constitutionnel dans l'affaire des nationalisations", *Revue du droit public et de la science politique en France et à l'étranger*, 1962, p. 400.

458 L. FAVOREU, "Les decisions du Conceil Constitutionnel...", *doc. cit.*, p. 400.

459 J. RIVERO "Fin d'un absolutism", *Pouvoirs*, 13, Paris.1980, pp. 5–15.

Professor Jean Rivero said, they are "no more than the expression of the governmental will approved by a solidarian majority."[460] Moreover, with the evolution of the tasks of the state, the law has tended to become a more technical product, whose content as a result, frequently even escapes the effective control of Parliament, since it is the technocrats within the administration, who draw it up and settle its real content, without effective participation of members of Parliament. Therefore, judicial review is an effective tool to control the constitutionality of such acts of Parliament or statutes that are the expression of governmental will, rather than the expression of the general will.

Anyway, the supremacy of the constitution and its enforceable character over the legislative body has led to the adoption of judicial rather than political guarantees of the constitution, the latter being proven ineffective as the French example of the Conservative Senates (*Sénat Conservateur*) of the 1799 and 1852 constitution showed. Constitutions commonly established a distribution of state powers among the various state organs, and basically, assigned fundamental powers to the legislative body, which used to be considered unable to do wrong, as the expression of the general will. Therefore, politically speaking, its self control is really an illusion. But constitutions also establish fundamental rights of individuals and minorities even against majoritarian will; hence, as Professor Cappelletti correctly said, "no effective system of review can be entrusted to the electorate or to persons and organs dependent on and strictly accountable to, the majority's will"[461] that is to say to the representative legislator itself.

Therefore, contrary to the political systems of review of the constitutionality of legislation, the common trend of contemporary constitutionalism in constitutional systems with written constitutions is the existence of judicial means of protection of the constitution, through the assignment of effective powers of judicial control of the constitutionality of legislation to the courts, either ordinary or special constitutional courts.

2. Judicial review and its legitimacy

Thus one of the traditional powers of the state, the judicial power, considered the "least dangerous" of all state powers[462] and in fact, being the politically less dangerous of the state organs, has been given the power to defend the constitution and to control the constitutionality of legislation. This has, of course, led to the endless discussion of what Professor Cappelletti called "the mighty problem of judicial review", that is to say, the discussion related to the legitimate or illegitimate power given to state organs that are not responsible to the people, to control the acts of those who, on the contrary,

460 J. RIVERO "Rapport de synthesè", *doc. cit*, p. 519.

461 M. CAPPELLETTI, *doc. cit*, p. 23.

462 A. BICKEL, *The Least Dangerous Branch. The Supreme Court at the Bar of Politics*, Indianapolis 1962.

are politically responsible,[463] or from another angle, the democratic or non–democratic character of judicial review.[464]

Of course, the discussions have been developed either to justify the absence of judicial review in systems in which the sovereignty of Parliament prevails, or to criticised judicial review when judges have shown an outstanding activism in the adaptation of the constitution, in creating non–written constitutional rules or in attributing constitutional character to certain rules. In this context, judicial review has been considered illegitimate because it is believed that non–elected bodies must not control elected bodies of the state, and that non–elected state bodies must not determine which norm of the state is law, that is to say, which is constitutional or unconstitutional.

We think that this really is an abstract and Byzantine discussion, and that it will remain endless, mainly because it is orientated as if there were a problem of abstract legitimacy of judicial review that could be resolved in an abstract way, identifying democracy with sole representativeness. The problems of judicial review or of the powers assigned to judges to control the constitutionality of legislation cannot be explained or criticised on the grounds of legitimacy or illegitimacy considering the democratic principle as sole representativeness. Democracy does not exhaust itself in representativeness because it is as well, above all, a way of living, in which individual liberty and fundamental human rights are to be respected to a point that we can say that no effective judicial review of constitutionality is possible in undemocratic regimes,[465] particularly because in such regimes there cannot be effective independence of judges; and "it is clear that judicial review cannot be practised efficiently where the Judiciary has no guarantee of its independence."[466]

That is also why in most European countries it has been noted that after periods of dictatorship, systems of judicial review of constitutionality have been established, as was the case of Germany, Italy, Spain and Portugal.[467]

---

463 M. CAPPELLETTI, "El formidable problema del control judicial y la contribución del análisis comparado", *Revista de estudios políticos*, 13, Madrid 1980, p. 61–103 ('The Mighty Problem' of Judicial Review and the contribution of comparative analysis", *Southern California Law Review*, 1980, p. 409).

464 M. CAPPELLETTI, *Judicial Review of Legislation and its Legitimacy..., doc. cit*, pp. 24–32.

465 "An efficient system of judicial review is totally incompatible with any antilibertarian, absolute, dictatorial regime, as is ample proven by historical experience and comparative study" M. CAPPELLETTI, *Judicial Review of Legislation and its legitimacy..., loc. cit.*, p. 11.

466 J. CARPIZO and H. FIX–ZAMUDIO, *The Necessity for and the Legitimacy of the Judicial Review of the Constitutionality of the Laws in Latin America, Recent Development,* International Association of Legal Sciences. Uppsala Colloquium 1984 (mimeo), p. 22. Published in spanish "La necesidad y la legitimidad de la revisión judicial en América Latina. Desarrollo reciente", *Boletín mexicano de derecho comparado*, 52, 1985, pp. 31–64. Also published in L. FAVOREU and J.A. JOLOWICZ (ed.), *Le contrôle juridictionnel des lois..., cit.*, pp. 119–151.

467 L. FAVOREU, *Le contrôle juridictionnel des lois et sa légitimité..., doc. cit.*, p. 24. *Cf.* P. DE VEGA GARCÍA, "Jurisdicción Constitucional y Crisis de la Constitución", *Revista de estudios políticos*, 7, Madrid 1979, p. 108.

Therefore, in a representative and democratic regime, the power attributed to judges to control the deviations of the legislative body and the infringements by the representative body of fundamental rights is absolutely democratic and legitimate.[468] As Professor Jean Rivero stated in his final report to the 1981 International Colloquium of Aix–en–Provence on the protection of fundamental rights by constitutional courts in Europe:

> I think that the (judicial constitutional) control marks progress, in the sense that democracy is not only a way of attribution of power, but also a way of exercising it. And I think that all that reinforces the fundamental liberties of citizens goes along with the democratic sense.[469]

Along this same line of thought, Professor Eduardo García de Enterría referring to constitutional liberties and fundamental rights as limits imposed on state powers, stated:

> If the constitution established them, it is obvious that an occasional parliamentary majority who ignore or infringe them, is very far from being legitimate to do so based on the majoritarian argument, and is rather revealing its abuse of power and its possible attempts at exclusion of minorities. The protective function of the Constitutional Tribunal confronting that abuse, annulling the legislative acts which make an attempt on the liberty of a few or all citizens, is the only effective instrument against infringement; there is no other possible alternative if one prefers to have an effective guarantee of liberty, that could make it more than simply rhetoric in a constitutional document.[470]

This was also the main argument put forward by Hans Kelsen in his very important article published in the French *Revue du Droit Public et de la Science Politique en France et a l'étrangèr* in 1928, when arguing against the majoritarian argument. He said:

> If one sees the essence of democracy, not in the all powerful majority, but in the constant compromises between the groups represented in Parliament by the majority and the minority, and consequently in the social peace, constitutional justice appears as a means particularly proper for the achievement of this idea. The simple threat of an action to be brought before the Constitutional Court can be an adequate instrument in the hands of the minorities for preventing unconstitutional violations of juridically protected interests by the majority, and consequently being able to oppose the majority dictatorship, which is not less dangerous to social peace than the minority one.[471]

But democratic legitimacy of judicial review does not arise only through judicial protection of fundamental rights, but also through the protection of the organic part of the constitution, that is to say, through the control of the systems of distribution of powers adopted in the constitution.

---

468 E.V. ROSTOW "The Democratic Character of Judicial Review", *Harvard Law Review*, 193, 1952.

469 J. RIVERO "Rapport de Synthese", *loc. cit.*, p. 525–526. *Cf.* M. CAPPELLETTI, *Judicial Review of Legislation and its Legitimacy...*, *doc. cit*, p. 32.

470 E. GARCÍA DE ENTERRÍA, *op. cit.*, p. 190.

471 H. KELSEN, *loc. cit.*, p. 253.

In this respect, we must point out that the problem of legitimacy has never been posed regarding the vertical distribution of state powers in the politically decentralised or federal systems; on the contrary, judicial review is essentially and closely related to federalism.[472]

That is why the form of the state, and particularly federalism, as a vertical form of distribution of power, is among the most important political principles that have led to the establishment of judicial review of legislation and upheld its justification in contemporary constitutional law.

Federalism requires the affirmation of certain degree of supremacy for federal laws with regard to local, regional or state laws; and similarly with regard to the sphere of powers attributed to them, according to the system adopted for the vertical distribution of power. Thus it is not by chance that those countries with federal form of state and with politically decentralised state organisation were among the first to establish judicial review of the constitutionality of legislation. This happened in the United States of America and in all the federal states of Latin America in the last century. It also happened in Europe, in Germany, which has a federal form of state, and in the decentralised forms of the Italian regional state and the Spanish Autonomous Communities state.

In all these cases, it is evident that the need for judicial review or the establishment of a constitutional court is justified by the demand for a constitutional body, which could settle conflicts of powers between the national and regional bodies. One of the fundamental tasks of the constitutional courts in Austria, Germany, Italy and Spain, for example, is precisely the resolution of conflicts between the levels of the national state and the member states of the Federation, or the political regions, or the Autonomous Communities, according to the country, and similarly, conflicts that may arise between the regions or states themselves, or between them and the national level. Thus, it is political decentralisation, both in the federal states and in the so–called regional state that has encouraged the appearance and consolidation of constitutional tribunals responsible precisely for the function of constitutional review of legislation to guarantee the constitutional balance of the state and the territorial bodies. That is why, in federal states, or in politically decentralised states there are no doubts about the legitimacy of judicial review of constitutionality, and no debate has arisen on the matter, except to justify its existence and necessity.[473]

Therefore, the problems of legitimacy of judicial review of constitutionality are not referred to the guarantee of the constitution concerning federalism or political decentralisation or to the guarantee of the fundamental rights of the individual. The-

---

472 W.J. WAGNER, *The Federal States and their Judiciary*, The Hague 1959, p. 85.

473 In this sense, Hans KELSEN said in 1928 that "it is in Federal States where the constitutional justice aquiered the most considerable importance. It is not excesive to affirm that the political idea of the Federal State is not entirily realized without the institution of a constitutional Tribunal", *loc. cit.*, p. 24. *Cf.* L. FAVOREU, *Le contrôle juridistionnel des lois et sa légitimité...*, *doc. cit.*, p. 35.

se constitute limitations on legislative power in reference to which judicial control is exercised without discussion.[474]

Nevertheless, the same can not be said about the horizontal distribution or separation of powers. Even though it also imposes limitations on the legislative power, the acceptance of judicial review of the constitutionality of legislation has here prompted discussions over its legitimacy, based, particularly, on the notion of supremacy of Parliament over the other state powers. But on the other hand, it has given fundamental arguments in favour of judicial review, precisely, as the counter–weight's essential element, which should be established among the various state powers to guarantee the constitution.

In effect, the separation of powers as a consequence of the horizontal distribution of state powers among the state organs essentially requires an independent mechanism to guarantee the organic part of the constitution. This system of control is essential to the distribution of power particularly between the legislative and the executive power. Between them it is necessary to establish a third counterweight system so as to maintain the equilibrium that the constitution lays down. Thus, the powers granted to the judicial organs to control the constitutionality and legality of administrative actions, accepted without debate has been essentially related to the *État de droit*, as well as to control the constitutionality of legislation.

However, the tradition of the principles of Parliamentary supremacy on the one hand, and of separation of powers on the other, have been so powerful in Europe, that these have led to impeding ordinary judicial bodies from any possibility of judging the constitutionality of legislation, even though judicial review of legislation has been developed, but assigned to new constitutional organs. In this manner, the need for judicial review of legislation as a guarantee of the constitution has been adjusted to the principle of separation of powers that has traditionally considered any attempt to control the constitutionality of legislation an inadmissible intrusion by the judicial body in the sphere of the legislator.

It has been this confrontation between the need for constitutional judicial review as a guarantee or means of protection of the constitution and the principle of separation of powers that in continental Europe led to the creation of special constitutional bodies with the particular and special jurisdictional task of controlling the constitutionality of legislation, although not being part of the traditional structure of the Judiciary. Therefore the solution to said confrontation has been resolved by creating new constitutional bodies above the traditional horizontal separation of powers, – equally above the legislator, the executive and the courts– to ensure the supremacy of the constitution with respect to them all.

The "Austrian System" of judicial review or the "European model" as it has also been qualified[475] is characterised by the fact that constitutional justice has been at-

---

474 *Cf.* B.O. NWABUEZE, *Judicial Control of Legislative Action and its Legitimacy–Recent Developments*. African Regional Report. International Association of Legal Sciences. Uppsala Colloquium, 1984, (mimeo) p. 23. Also published in L. FAVOREU and J.A. JOLOWICZ (ed.), *Le contrôle juridictionnel des lois..., cit.*, p. 193–222.

tributed to a constitutional body organised outside ordinary judicial organisation, that is to say, outside the ordinary courts, and thus not integrated within the general structure of the Judiciary. The members of the constitutional tribunal, court or council do not become so by way of a judicial career, but rather are appointed, basically by political bodies, and in particular, by the Parliament and the executive. This system has given rise to a special constitutional organ, which, despite it's not being integrated within the Judiciary, resolves legal controversies according to the law, and thus pursues a proper jurisdictional activity.

These constitutional courts, councils or tribunals have been considered the "supreme interpreters of the constitution" as the Spanish Constitutional Tribunal Organic law qualified it[476]or as the "custodian of the constitution."[477] Professor Eduardo García de Enterría, currently (1985) judge in the European Court of Human Rights, referring to the Spanish Constitutional Tribunal, qualified it as a "commissioner of the Constituent power to sustain the constitution and to maintain all the constitutional organ in their strict quality of constituted powers,"[478] and the former president of the same Spanish Constitutional Tribunal Professor Manuel García Pelayo considered it "as a constitutional organ, established and structured directly in the constitution", and that:

> As regulator of the constitutionality, of the state action, it is the one called upon to give full existence to the *Estado de derecho* and to ensure the validity of the distribution of powers established in the constitution, both essential components in our times of the true Constitutional state.[479]

In this sense, and established as constitutional organs separately regarding the traditional legislative, executive and judicial organs, the European constitutional courts are conceived as being the supreme guarantor of the distribution of power in its various senses we have referred to.[480]

First of all, there is the distribution of the sphere of state power and the sphere of society; that is to say, between the powers of the state and the rights and liberties of individuals and groups. This principle of distribution of powers, expressly established in constitutions when they guarantee the rights and liberties of citizens must, moreover, be jurisdictionally guaranteed. This power of guaranteeing fundamental rights is frequently a power given to ordinary tribunals as well as to constitutional courts by means of "writs for protection" (*amparo*). In such cases, the courts are the

---

475 M. CAPPELLETTI, *Judicial Review of Legislation and its Legitimacy...*, p. 26; L. FAVOREU, "Actualité et légitimité du contrôle juridictionnel des lois en Europe occidental", *loc. cit.*, p. 1149.

476 Art. 1. Ley Orgánica del Tribunal Constitucional, Oct. 1979, *Boletín Oficial del Estado*, N° 239.

477 G. LEIBHOLZ, *Problemas fundamentales de la democracia*, Madrid 1971, p. 148.

478 E. GARCÍA DE ENTERRÍA, *op. cit.*, p. 198.

479 E. GARCÍA PELAYO, "El Status del Tribunal Constitucional", in *Revista española de derecho constitucional*, 1, Madrid 1981, p. 15.

480 *Cf.* M. GARCÍA PELAYO, *loc. cit*, p. 20.

guardians of the limits on the power of the state imposed by the constitution in relation to the respect for fundamental individual rights and liberties.

In the second place, there is the distinction between the constituent power and the constituted power. The effectiveness of this division is not limited to the moment only when the constitution is adopted, but should be demonstrated throughout its validity, as a result of its very existence. The function of constitutional justice is precisely that of guaranteeing that the constituted powers act within limits established by the constituent power, as set down in the constitution. It is thus the aim of the constitutional court to be the custodian of the primacy of the constituent power over the constituted power. Thus, even in cases of preventive review of constitutionality, when a collision arises between a norm and the constitution, either the norm is not to be sanctioned, or a constitutional reform must take place.

The third system of distribution of power is the horizontal division, that is to say, its distribution among constitutional bodies of the same constitutional rank. This division is also guaranteed by the constitutional courts, both at the level of the central powers of the state, and at other territorial levels. In this respect, at the level of the constitutional bodies of the state, for example, it is the constitutional court that is called upon to resolve conflicts of powers between, for example, the Government and Congress, or between the Chamber of Deputies and the Senate, or between other bodies of constitutional rank. In the horizontal distribution of power at lower territorial levels, the constitutional tribunal must also resolve conflicts that arise between the authorities at those levels.

The fourth aspect of the division of power is the vertical division, which consists in the distribution of powers among the various political decentralised levels of the state: the powers of the national state; those at intermediate level, whether these be federal member states or autonomous regions or communities of the regional states; and thirdly, those at the municipal or local level. In these cases, the state structured by a system of vertical distribution of powers must ensure that the various legislative provisions at the different levels do not invade the sphere of power of other levels. For example, there should be no invasion of the powers of the communities or regions by the national level or of those of the member states of a federation, and vice–versa. The same holds good for the municipal level: the constitutional court is precisely the body that must ensure that the municipal powers that are normally guaranteed in the constitutions or by acts issued at national or intermediate levels are not to be invaded.

Thus, the fundamental reason for justifying the establishment of constitutional court in continental Europe relates to the solution of conflicts between state bodies, since within the constitutional organisation, the constitutional court is the body in a position to prevent the invasion of the powers of others by one constitutional power, and objectively to ensure the maintenance of the balance that the constitution has established in the separation of powers.

In this way, the sharing of power among the national powers –for example, between Parliament and Government– and also the system of the distribution of powers among the powers in a vertical sense by the process of political decentralisation –whether this be federalism, or regionalism or purely and simply, any system of local political decentralisation– all these demand that there be a body to maintain a balance between these various powers, and this, without doubt, should be either a constitutional court or the supreme court of a given country.

But in the case of constitutional courts even though created as constitutional organs, independent and separate from the traditional legislative, executive and judicial organs of the state, and particularly, not within the organisation of the Judiciary, they always decide upon constitutional conflict by means of a jurisdictional action. Therefore, constitutional courts, as is the case of ordinary courts on the American judicial the review model or the supreme judicial court on the Latin American model, exercise constitutional justice and have a jurisdictional function.

Therefore, constitutional courts cannot be considered the "negative legislator" as Hans Kelsen considered,[481] but rather as constitutional organs with a jurisdictional function.

In effect, in order to refute the objection to constitutional justice based on the principle of separation of power, Hans Kelsen argued that the constitutional tribunal when annulling an act of Parliament, did not exercise jurisdictional activity but a negative legislative activity. He said:

> To annul a Statute, is to establish a general norm, because the annulment of a Statute has the same general character of its adoption, being, we can say, the same adoption but with a negative sign, and consequently in itself, a legislative function.[482]

In reality, the constitutional court when annulling a statute does not repeal it, and the annulment it can pronounce is not made based on discretionary powers but on legal criteria, applying a superior rule, the constitution, thus in no way does it exercise a legislative function.[483]

Its function is jurisdictional as is that assigned to the ordinary court[484] but characterised as being a guarantee of the constitution. And, if it is true that constitutional judges in many cases decide political issues when considering the constitutionality of legislative acts, they do so by legal methods and criteria, in a process initiated by a party with the required standing. And even in cases in which constitutional justice allows the possibility of exercising a popular action[485] to obtain a decision upon the unconstitutionality of a law by the Supreme Court, as is the case in Venezuela and Colombia, the judicial activity is developed by a process in which the Supreme Court decides a judicial controversy, although there are no proper parties in the traditional procedural law sense.

Nevertheless, the court must only act on the formal instance of or at the request of a person whose rights or interests are infringed by the particular law, and cannot

---

481 H. KELSEN, *loc. cit.*, p. 226.

482 *Idem,* p. 224.

483 A. PÉREZ GORDO, *El Tribunal Constitucional y sus funciones*, Barcelona 1982, p. 41.

484 H. KELSEN, eventually, accepted this view, *loc. cit.*, p. 226.

485 *Cf.* the argument in a contrary sense of B.O. NWABUEZE, *Judicial Control of Legislative Action ..., loc. cit.*, p. 3.

decide on its own initiative. Therefore, the role of a constitutional judge can in no way be considered a legislative function, but rather jurisdictional.

Anyway, as we have said, judicial review of constitutionality both on the American or European models, is conceived as being a constitutional guarantee of the distribution and limitation of state powers established in the constitution, exercised by independent bodies either the ordinary or special constitutional judges. Furthermore, constitutional judges are also the guarantee of the functioning of the particular system of government resulting from the way state powers are distributed, and of democracy itself. Its legitimacy lies in there.

In effect, judicial review can be considered one of the tools for ensuring the solution of political and social conflict, and therefore, for contributing to the peaceful development of democratic political activity, in resolving conflicts of a political nature. In Professor E. García de Enterría's words, judicial review is a "formidable instrument of political and social integration of society"[486] and this has proven to be so in resolving political conflicts between government and minorities, which the electorate cannot assist in resolving. As Professor L. Favoreu pointed out:

> When the majority and the opposition conflict on important issues without having recourse to an electoral decision, it is evident that recourse to a constitutional judge to decide upon the law adopted by the majority, has the virtue of calming the debate and transforming it more serenely. In many cases, when the decision of the constitutional judge has been adopted, the controversy is extinguished.[487]

In this respect, and as an illustration of this legitimacy of judicial review, Professor Favoreu in his comparative analysis of recent development of judicial review in continental Europe stressed the political conflict that arose from the sanctioning of laws in referring to abortion. The controversy raged in every country, both in Parliament and in public, but once decisions were made on the issue by the constitutional judge, the conflict died down.[488] The same happened in France over the most important aspects of the socialist government's programme once executed in the early eighties, particularly in relation to nationalisation and to decentralisation processes and which subsequently died down after the Constitutional Council adopted its corresponding decisions in 1982.[489]

The same happened, for example, in Spain, with the law for the Harmonisation of the Autonomous Communities. Once the constitutional tribunal resolved the conflict over the powers of the state and the Autonomous Communities in 1983, the debate declined in its intensity.[490]

---

486 E. GARCÍA DE ENTERRÍA, *op. cit.*, p. 192.

487 L. FAVOREU, *Le contrôle juridictionnel des lois et sa légitimité*, *cit.*, p. 6.

488 *Idem*, p. 36.

489 L. FAVOREU, "Les decisions du Consel Constitutionnel dans l'affaire des nationalisations", *loc. cit.*, p. 377; "Décentralisation et constitution", *Revue du droit public et de la science politique en France et à l'étranger*, Paris 1982, p. 1259–1295; and L. FAVOREU (ed.), *Nationalisations et constitution*, 1982.

490 P. BON, F. MODERNE and Y. RODRIGUEZ, *La justice constitutionnelle en Espagne*, 1984, p. 168.

Judicial review has also been a guarantee of the constitution when working as an instrument for the maintenance of political stability and continuity in democratic societies and, particularly, in parliamentary systems of government.

In fact, parliamentary systems of government are generally linked with judicial review, and in continental Europe, we can observe that in all the countries with a system of judicial review of constitutionality of legislation, a parliamentary or quasi–parliamentary regime exists. In the case of Germany, Italy and Spain in the classical way and also in the cases of France, Austria and Portugal where even though a government responsible to Parliament exists, a president elected by the people also exists. Anyway, the counter–weight of the opposition to a strong government supported by a parliamentary majority is judicial review. As Professor Favoreu said:

> There is a certain institutional logic in the political functioning of parliamentary systems of government, to encourage the development of mechanisms of judicial review of constitutionality as a reaction against the great power of the government block.[491]

Judicial review as a guarantee of political stability and continuity in parliamentary regimes has a shown itself to be a very important instrument when lessening the effects of political changes resulting from the alternation in power, particularly when a change in the majority in Parliament and in the government happens after a few years of leadership of one political force or party. This alternation of contrasting policies has occurred in almost all countries in continental Europe over recent decades, and was of particular importance in France in the early eighties.

In a recent article concerning "The Constitutional Council and the alternance", Professor Louis Favoreu demonstrated how the French Constituional Council, instead of being a restraint upon or an obstacle to political alternance, has been "the guarantor of the alternance":

> The Constitutional Council has first of all, permitted the alternance through the canalisation of the stream of change, ensuring its regulation; and furthermore with its decisions has given a regularised authentic certification to the measures taken by the new majority. In the end, the legislation of the new majority has passed through some kind of filter, but once the dispositions have been filtered and sifted, its promulgation gave a definitive juridical force to the dispositions, and it is no longer possible to attack them (at least on the grounds of its conformity with the constitution.[492]

This happened in France for example, with the laws concerning nationalisation, decentralisation, university teaching and municipal officials, between 1982 and 1984.[493] It also happened in Spain in the early eighties, and the example of the laws

---

491 L. FAVOREU, *Le contrôle juridictionnel des lois et sa légitimité, doc. cit.*, p. 25.

492 L. FAVOREU, "Le Conseil Constitutionnel et l'alternance", *Revue française de science politique (La constitution de la Cinquienne Republique*, 34, (4–5), Paris 1984, pp. 1005–1114.

493 L. FAVOREU, "Libertes locales et libertes universitaires. Les décisions du Conseil Constitutionnel du 20 janvier 1984", *Revue du droit public et de la science politique en France et à l'étranger*, 1984, pp. 687–730.

concerning the decentralisation process through the harmonisation of the Autonomous Communities, the *Rumasa* nationalisation and university teaching is clear.[494]

In such situations, the existence of constitutional review of legislation has had precisely the effect of avoiding any rapid breakdown in the constitutional balance, since the laws and reforms approved by the new majority were submitted to review by the constitutional judges, to determine which could be enacted according to the constitution, and which laws and reforms require constitutional review. Of course, as Professor Favoreu pointed out, in these cases, constitutional review may mean a restraint on the possibilities for action open to the majority with respect to the proposed reforms. On the other hand, if these reforms are brought into question before a constitutional Judge, and his verdict declares them to be in accordance with the constitution, in a certain way it authenticates them and they enjoy a supplementary authority.[495]

However, the defence of the constitution is not only an essential role of constitutional justice in order to guarantee the various systems of distribution of powers between the constituted organs of the state, and to ensure political stability and continuity, even in situations of political alternance of majorities, but also, as we mentioned, to guarantee the fundamental rights and liberties of individuals. This is, as we said, an essential part of the *État de droit* and one of the basic arguments used to defend the legitimacy of judicial review.

In effect, constitutional justice and judicial review of the constitutionality of legislation are bound up with the effective establishment of fundamental rights. Therefore, the need for the establishment of a system of judicial review also arises when there are entrenched declarations of fundamental rights and liberties linked with the constitutional values of a given society.

Nevertheless, even though the idea of fundamental rights established in a constitution, as a superior and effective rule of law in an entrenched way, has historical antecedents, it did not appear in Europe until after the Second World War. Therefore, the problem of establishing a system of judicial review, exception made to the Austrian and Czechoslovakian systems in the 1920's only arose in Europe after the Second World War, as a mean for defending the rights of man, precisely because these suffered the greatest violations in Europe. Here, once again, it is not by chance that it was in Italy and Germany when, for the first time in their constitutional texts, the validity of the rights of man and the need to organise mechanisms for their defence was affirmed, and among which, was the review of constitutionality of legislation.

At the other extreme, the absence of entrenched fundamental rights of individuals with constitutional rank, as a limit upon the legislator, is one of the main reasons for the absence of a system of judicial review of constitutionality, as happened in the United Kingdom. That is why Professor D.G.T. Williams correctly pointed out:

494 P. BON, F. MODERNE and Y. RODRIGUEZ, *op. cit.*, p. 168, 217.

495 L. FAVOREU, *Le contrôle juridictionnel des lois et sa légitimité*, *doc. cit.*, p. 37.

> The underlying problem either of an entrenched bill of Rights or of an entrenched federal structure for the United Kingdom is judicial review", because "the adoption of a Bill of Rights would, of course, involve the exercise of judicial review by the English Courts" that is to say, the power of domestic courts, "to protect certain fundamental freedoms even against the legislative itself.[496]

Anyway, what is definitely true in constitutional systems with written constitutions is that if the constitution pretends to be a supreme, obligatory and enforceable law, the constitutional system must establish means for its defence and guarantee. On the contrary, as Hans Kelsen used to say:

> A constitution without guarantees against unconstitutional acts, is not completely obligatory in its technical sense... A constitution in which unconstitutional acts and particularly, unconstitutional laws, remains valid because its unconstitutionality cannot lead to its annulment, is more or less, equivalent from a juridical point of view, to a desire without obligatory force.[497]

The judicial guarantees of the constitution, that is to say, the power given to judges –ordinary judges or special constitutional courts– to declare the unconstitutionality of state acts issued in violation of the constitution, or to annul those acts with general effects is, therefore, an essential part of the *État de droit.* It is a power to ensure precisely, that all state organs are submitted to the rule of law and, therefore, that they will respect the limits imposed upon them by the constitution, according to the system[498] of distribution of state powers adopted and that they will also respect the fundamental rights and liberties declared in the constitution itself.

Of course, there is no unique and uniform system of constitutional justice to guarantee and defend the constitution, nor is there one ideal system, which can be applicable to all countries. In contemporary constitutional law each country has developed its own system and precisely, it is to study their fundamental trends in comparative law that we will devote the following three parts, in which we will analyse separately the diffuse system of judicial review, the concentrated system of judicial review, and the mixed system of judicial review, which correspond, in broad terms, to three different models: the American, the European and the Latin American.

---

496 D.G.T. WILLIAMS, "The Constitution of the United Kingdom", *Cambridge Law Journal*, 31, 1972, pp. 278–279.

497 H. KELSEN, *doc. cit.*, p. 250.

498 As M. HIDEN said, "probably there are as many methods of securing the constitutionality of laws and regulations as there are countries with a written constitution", in "Constitutional Rights in the Legislative Process: the Finnish System of Advance Control of Legislation", in *Scandinavian Studies in Law* , 17, Stockholm 1973, p. 97.

PART IV
THE DIFFUSE SYSTEM OF JUDICIAL REVIEW

I. GENERAL FEATURES

The diffuse system of judicial review empowers all the judges and courts of a given country to act as a constitutional judge, in the sense that when applying the law, they are allowed to judge its constitutionality and therefore, not to apply a law in the concrete process when they consider it unconstitutional and void, giving priority to the constitution.

1. The Logic of the System

From a logical and rational point of view, this general power of all judges and courts to act as constitutional judges is the obvious consequence of the principle of the supremacy of the constitution. If the constitution is the supreme law of the land, in cases of conflict between a law and the constitution, the latter must prevail and it is the duty of the judiciary to say which law is applicable in a particular case. As Justice William Paterson stated in *Vanhorne's Lessee* v. *Dorrance* (1795) almost two hundred years ago:

> If a legislative act oppugns a constitutional principle the former must give way, and be rejected on the score of repugnance. I hold it to a position equally clear and sound, that, in such case, it will be the duty of the court to adhere to the constitution, and to declare the act null and void.[499]

Or as it was definitively stated by Chief Justice Marshall in *Marbury* v. *Madison* (1803):

> Those who apply the rule to particular cases, must of necessity expound and interpret that rule... so, if a law be in opposition to the constitution... the court must determine which of these conflicting rules governs the case: This is the very essence of judicial duty. If then, the courts are to regard the constitution, and the constitution is superior to any ordinary act of the legislature, the constitution, and not such ordinary act, must govern the case to which they both apply.[500]

Thus, supremacy of the constitution and judicial review as the power of all judges to defend the constitution and to control the constitutionality of legislation are essentially linked. That is why regarding the constitutions and laws of the federal states it was expressly established in the well known "supremacy clause" of Article VI, Section 2, of the American constitution, which states:

---

499 *Vanhorne's Lessec v. Dorrance*, 2 Dallas 304 (1795). See the text in S.I. KUTLER (ed.), *The Supreme Court and the Constitution. Readings in American Constitutional History*, NY 1984, p. 8.

500 *Marbury* v. *Madison*, 1 Cranch 137 (1803). See the text in S.I. KUTLER (ed.), *op. cit.*, p. 29.

> This constitution, and the laws of the United states which shall be made in Pursuance thereof; and all Treaties made, or which shall be made, under the Authority of the United States, shall be the supreme law of the land; and the Judges in every state shall be bound thereby, anything in the constitution or laws of the state to the contrary notwithstanding.

This supremacy clause was extended to federal laws in *Marbury* v. *Madison* through a logical and rational interpretation and application of the principle of the supremacy of the constitution, and has been expressly established in a general sense, as a positive rule in other countries.

In this sense, for instance, since 1910 Article 215 of the Colombian constitution established:

> In all cases of incompatibility between the constitution and the law, the constitutional dispositions will preferably be applied.[501]

In a similar sense, since 1897 the Venezuelan Civil Procedural Cod has also established in Article 20 that:

> When a law in force whose application is required, collides with any constitutional disposition, the courts will preferably apply the latter.[502]

2. The Compatibility of the System with all Legal Systems

Therefore, the diffuse system of judicial review of constitutionality of legislation is not a system peculiar to the common law system of law, incompatible with the civil or Roman law tradition, at all. On the contrary, it has existed since the last century in most Latin American countries, all of them being part of the Roman law family of legal systems.

This is the case of Mexico, Argentina and Brazil, which followed the American model and is also the case of Colombia and Venezuela, in which a mixed system of judicial review is followed.

It has also existed in Europe in countries with a Civil law tradition, like Switzerland and Greece. In Switzerland, the diffuse system of judicial review was first established in the 1874 constitution, even though in a limited way. Also in a limited manner, the Swiss system currently allows the courts to decide on constitutional grounds, upon the applicability of legislative acts of the cantons but not of federal laws.[503] In Greece, where a mixed system is also adopted, the 1975 constitution entrusts all courts with the power to apply no legal dispositions whose contents they consider to be contrary to the constitution.[504] In particular, Article 95 establishes:

---

501 See in J. ORTEGA TORRES (ed.), *Constitución Política de Colombia*, Bogotá 1985, p. 130. The origin of this norm can be traced up to the Legislative act, Nº 3, Art. 40, 1910.

502 The text is the one of the 1985 Civil Procedural Code. With similar words it was adopted in article 10 of the 1897 and 1904 Codes, and article 7 of the 1916 Code.

503 H. FIX–ZAMUDIO, *Los tribunales constitucionales y los derechos humanos,* México 1980, pp. 17, 84; A. JIMÉNEZ BLANCO, "El Tribunal Federal suizo", *Boletín de Jurisprudencia Constitucional*, Cortes Generales, 6 Madrid 1981, p. 477.

504 Art. 93, H. FIX–ZAMUDIO, *op. cit.*, p. 162; L. FAVOREU, *Le contrôle juridictionnel des lois et sa légitimité, Développements récents en Europe occidentale.* Association Internationale des

Art. 95. The courts shall be bound not to apply laws, the contents of which are contrary to the constitution.

Therefore, the diffuse system of judicial review exists and has functioned in legal systems with a common law tradition as well as those with a Roman law tradition. Thus, we do not agree with what Professors Mauro Cappelletti and John Clarke Adams said, in the sense that a fundamental incompatibility exists between the diffuse system of judicial review and the legal systems based on Roman law[505] or as Professor Cappelletti said elsewhere, when referring to the sole experience of Italy and West Germany prior to the creation of constitutional court, in the sense that those countries "fully revealed the unsuitability of the decentralised method for civil law countries."[506]

In our opinion the arguments in favour of the concentrated system of judicial review cannot be settled on the grounds of unsuitability or suitability with a particular system of law, but with the particular constitutional system adopted regarding the supremacy of the constitution. If the principle of constitutional supremacy is adopted, the logical and necessary consequence is the powers of the courts to decide which norm is to be applied when a contradiction exists between a particular law and the constitution, being obliged to give priority to the constitution as their very duty, regardless of the particular common law or Roman law system of the given country.

Another question relates to the practical legal effects of the adoption of a diffuse system of judicial review. In the absence of any kind of judicial review system in Europe before the 1920's and with the traditional framework of separation of power based on the sovereignty of the legislator and of the law, and the distrust of the courts to control legislative action, the criticisms of the diffuse systems of judicial review from the European side of the Atlantic are as old as the existence of the European model itself. For example, Hans Kelsen, the creator of the Austrian model in Europe referred to the problems raised by the diffuse system for justifying the "centralisation of the power to examine the regularity of general norms", stressing "the absence of unity in the solutions" and "the legal uncertainty " that results when a "court abstains from applying a regulation and even a law as irregular, while another court does the contrary."[507] In this same sense, Professors Mauro Cappelletti and John Clarke Adams stressed that the diffuse systems of judicial review "can lead to

---

Sciences Juridiques, Colloque d'Uppsala, 1984 (mimeo), p. 14. Also published in L. FAVOREU and J.A. JOLOWICZ (ed.), *Le contrôle juridictionnel des lois. Légitimité, effectivité et développements récents*, Paris 1986, pp. 17–68.

505 M. CAPPELLETTI and J.C. ADAMS, "Judicial Review of Legislation: European Antecedents and Adaptations", *Harvard Law Review*, 79 (6), 1966, p. 1215.

506 M. CAPPELLETTI, *Judicial Review in the Contemporary World*, Indiannapolis 1971, p. 59. In similar sense M. FROMONT considered that it is "difficult to admit" the diffuse system of judicial revue in countries with a roman law tradition. See "Preface" in J.C. BEGUIN, *Le contrôle de la constitutionalité des lois en Republique Federale d'Allemagne*, Paris 1982, p. 218.

507 H. KELSEN, "La guarantie juridictionnelle de la constitution (La Justice constitutionnelle)", *Revue du droit public et de la science politique en France et à l'étranger*, 1928, p. 218.

grave uncertainty and confusion, as one court may decide to enforce a Statute that another court will find invalid."[508]

But these problems exist in both common law and Roman law systems that followed the diffuse system of judicial review, and are not essentially peculiar to the countries with Roman law systems that have adopted it, as Professors Cappelletti and Adams seemed to demonstrate, basing their arguments on the corrective effects that regarding those problems have the doctrine of *stare decisis*, peculiar to the common law systems of law and alien to the Roman law systems. Their argument is as follows:

> Under the Anglo–American doctrine of *stare decisis*, a decision by the highest court in any jurisdiction is binding on all lower courts in the same jurisdiction, and thus as soon as the court has declared a law unconstitutional, no other court can apply it. The court does not need a specific grant of the power to declare a law invalid, nor must it decide anything beyond the applicability of the law in question to the concrete case; *stare decisis* does the rest by requiring other courts to follow the precedent in all succeeding cases. Thus, although the unconstitutional statute may remain on the book, it is a dead law.

Thus they finished their argument by saying that:

> *Stare decisis*, however, is not normally part of the Roman law systems, and thus in these systems, the courts are not generally bound even by the decisions of the highest court.[509]

Professor Cappelletti later developed the argument in his book *Judicial Review in the contemporary world*, when he said:

> Since the principle of *stare decisis* is foreign to civil law judges, a system which allowed each judge to decide on the constitutionality of statues could result in a law being disregarded as unconstitutional by some judges, while being held constitutional and applied by others. Furthermore the same judicial organ, which had one day disregarded a given law, might uphold it the next day, having changed its mind about the law's constitutional legitimacy. Differences could arise between judicial bodies of a different type or degree, for example, between ordinary courts and administrative tribunals or between the younger, more radical judges of the inferior courts and the older, more tradition conscious judges of the higher courts... The extremely dangerous results could be a serious conflict between the judicial organs and grave uncertainty as to the law.[510]

We insist that those problems deriving from the very principle of supremacy of the constitution exist in countries with both Common and Roman law systems of law, and if it is true that the doctrine of *stare decisis* is a correction of the problems, it is not absolute, because, as we know, not all cases in which constitutional matters are decided upon by lower courts can go before the United States Supreme Court which is the one that decides in a discretional way, which cases are to be considered by it.[511]

508 *Loc. cit.*, p. 1215.

509 *Idem*, p. 1215.

510 M. CAPPELLETTI, *op. cit.*, p. 58.

511 28 U.S. Code, Secc. 1254, 1255, 1256, 1257. See also Rule Nº 17 of the Supreme Court.

On the other hand, and even though the doctrine of *stare decisis* as known in Common law countries does not apply in those with a Roman law tradition, those who have adopted a diffuse system of judicial review have normally developed, in parallel, their own corrections to the problems posed with similar effect. For instance, in the Mexican system of *amparo*, the constitution established the principle that the particular law of *amparo* should establish the cases in which the *jurisprudencia* namely, the precedents derived from previous decisions of the federal courts, were to be considered obligatory.[512] Thus, the *Amparo law* has established the cases in which the supreme court and also other collegial circuit court decisions are to be considered as obligatory precedents, which happens only after five consecutive decisions to the same effect, uninterrupted by any incompatible ruling, have been rendered. The effects of the *jurisprudencia* even partially, have been considered equivalent to those resulting from the rule of *stare decisis*.

Furthermore, in the Mexican system of *Amparo*, the so called "*amparo* against laws" has also been developed as an extraordinary action of unconstitutionality of self–executing laws which could directly affect the rights of an individual, and that can be brought before the federal courts, allowing these courts to judge the unconstitutionality of a law without any relation to a particular process.[513]

Along the same line of facts, in Argentina and Brazil, countries that also closely followed the American model in the sense of the power granted to all the courts to decide upon the inapplicability of a law based on constitutional considerations, an institution called the "extraordinary recourse of unconstitutionality" has been developed, which can be brought before the supreme court against judicial decisions adopted at the last instance, when a federal law is considered as unconstitutional and inapplicable by a court.[514] In these cases, the decision adopted by the Supreme Court has *in casu et inter partes* effects, but being adopted by the highest court has factual binding effects upon the inferior court.[515] In the same sense, in some European countries with a Roman law tradition which have adopted the diffuse system of judicial review, special judicial mechanisms have been established to overcome the problems deriving from contradictory decisions of different courts on constitutional issues. It is the case in Greece in which the 1975 constitution regulates a special highest court with powers to decide upon the unconstitutionality of laws, when contradictory decisions on the matter have been adopted by the state Council, the court

---

512 Art. 107, Section XIII, paragraph 1 of the Constitution (ammendment of 1950–1951).

513 R.D. BAKER, *Judicial Review in México. A Study of the Amparo Suit*, Austin 1971, pp. 164, 250–251, 256, 259.

514 H. FIX–ZAMUDIO, *Veinticinco años de evolución de la justicia constitucional 1940–1965*, México 1968, pp. 26, 36; J. CARPIZO and H. FIX–ZAMUDIO, "La necesidad y la legitimidad de la revisión judicial en América latina. Desarrollo reciente", *Boletín mexicano de derecho comparado*, 52, 1985, p. 33. Also published in L. FAVOREU and J.A. JOLOWICZ (ed.), *Le contrôle juridictionnel des lois. Légitimité, effectivité et développements récents*, Paris 1986, pp. 119–151.

515 J.R. VANOSSI and P.E. UBERTONE, *Instituciones de defensa de la Constitución en la Argentina*, UNAM, Congreso Internacional sobre Ia Constitución y su Defensa, México 1982 (mimeo), p. 32.

of cassation or the auditory court. In such cases, the decisions of the special highest court have absolute and general effect regarding the constitutionality of laws.[516]

Finally, in the other mentioned countries with a Roman law tradition where the diffuse system of judicial review has been adopted, the correction to the problems of uncertainty and conflictiveness have been established by adopting a mixed model of judicial review, that is to say, by having the diffuse and concentrated systems operate in parallel. In Latin America it is the case in Guatemala,[517] Colombia and Venezuela. Particularly in the last two in parallel with the diffuse systems of judicial review legally established in positive law, the concentrated system of judicial review also exists; and through it, the supreme court is empowered to formally annul a law on the grounds of unconstitutionality with *erga omnes* effects, as required through a *popular action* that can be brought before the Supreme Court by any inhabitant of the country whosoever.

Therefore, in parallel with the powers of every court to decide the inapplicability of a law considered unconstitutional in a concrete case, the Supreme Court has the power to annul with general effect the laws contested as being unconstitutional.[518]

In the same sense, other European countries with a Roman law tradition which have adopted the diffuse system of judicial review, have also adopted the features of the concentrated systems in parallel giving the supreme court of the country the power to annul unconstitutional laws. It is the case in Switzerland where even though no constitutional judicial control is allowed regarding federal laws, the federal court has the power to declare the unconstitutionality of canton laws, with *erga omnes* effects when required by a special public law recourse in cases of violations of fundamental rights.[519]

Therefore, in the same sense of the development of the doctrine of *stare decisis* in the common law system countries, to resolve the problems of uncertainty and the possible conflictive character of judicial decisions made by different courts upon the unconstitutionality of laws which the diffuse system of judicial review could bring about, the countries with a Roman law tradition that have adopted the same diffuse system of judicial review have also developed various particular legal mechanisms to prevent the evil effect of those problems, either by giving obligatory character to precedents or by granting the necessary powers to declare the unconstitutionality of statutes to the supreme court of the country in some cases even with general and binding effects.

The eventual problems posed by the diffuse control of constitutionality of legislation, therefore, are common to countries with either common or Roman law sys-

---

516 E. SPILIOPOULOS, "Judicial Review of Legislative Acts in Greece", *Temple Law Quarterly*, 56, (2), Philadelphia 1983, pp. 496–500.

517 J.M. GARCÍA LAGUARDIA, *La defensa de la Constitución*, México 1983, p. 52.

518 A. R. BREWER–CARÍAS, *El control de la constitucionalidad de los actos estatales*, Caracas 1977; L.C. SACHICA, *El control de la constitucionalidad y sus mecanismos*, Bogotá 1980.

519 E. ZELLWEGER, "El Tribunal Federal suizo en calidad de Tribunal Constitucional", *Revista de la Comisión Internacional de Juristas*, Vol. VII (1), 1966, p. 119; H. FIX–ZAMUDIO, *Los Tribunales constitucionales ..., cit.*, p. 84.

tems of law, and cannot lead by themselves to consider the diffuse system of judicial review "incompatible" with the civil or Roman law system of law of a given country by the fact that in the latter the rule of *stare decisis* does not exist.

As we said, the only fact of compatibility that is absolute in this respect is that when the principle of the supremacy of the constitution exists, the logical consequence is the power of all judges, which are charged with applying the law, to decide upon the inapplicability of legislation when it contradicts the constitution, giving preference to the constitution itself. This was the original system of judicial review after the triumph of the constitution over the legislator.

Nevertheless in the European countries with a Roman law system of law, the traditional distrust of judicial power has led the way to the establishment of the concentrated system of judicial review, which has brought about the rediscovery of constitutional supremacy by other means. But this cannot lead us to consider the diffuse control of the constitutionality of legislation as being incompatible with civil or Roman law legal systems.

3. The Rationality of the System

As we have said, the essence of the diffuse system of judicial review is the very notion of constitutional supremacy: if the constitution is the supreme law of the land prevailing over all other laws, no state act contrary to the constitution can be an effective law, on the contrary, it must be considered as null and void. In the words of Chief Justice Marshall, if the constitution is "the fundamental and paramount law of the nation... an act of the legislature, repugnant to the constitution, is void."[520] In this respect, the effective guarantee of the supremacy of the constitution is that acts repugnant to it are in fact null and void, and as such have to be considered by the courts that are the state organs called upon to apply the laws.

A. *The Nullity of the Unconstitutional State Act*

The first aspect that shows the rationality of the diffuse system is the principle of the nullity of state acts and particularly of legislation repugnant to the constitution.

In principle, the nullity of a state act means that an act that pretends to be a juridical state act, objectively is not, because it is irregular in the sense that it does not correspond to the conditions established for its enactment by a norm of a superior rank. This was what Hans Kelsen called an "objective guarantee" of the constitution,[521] and it means that a state act that is null and void cannot produce any effect, and does not need another state act to be produced to withdraw its usurped quality of state act. On the contrary, if such another state act were needed, then the guarantee would not be the nullity of the state act, but its annullability.

Thus, in strict logic, the supremacy of the constitution means that all state acts that violate the constitution are null and void; and therefore, theoretically, all public

---

520 *Marbury v Madison* 5 US (1 Cranch), 137. (1803). See the text in S.I. KUTLER (ed.), *op. cit.*, p. 29.

521 H. KELSEN, *loc. cit.*, p. 214.

authorities and even individuals could be entitled to inspect its irregularity, to declared its existence and to consider the act neither valid nor obligatory. Of course, this could lead to juridical anarchy and, therefore, positive law normally establishes limits upon this power to examine the regularity of state acts, and reserves this power to the judges. Therefore, a state act that violates the constitution and is, therefore, null and void can only be examined by the courts and only the courts have the power to consider it as null and void.

However, even though the limits imposed by positive law on the examination power of the nullity of state acts exists, this fact does not mean that the guarantee of the constitution ceases to be the nullity of the state act and is converted into annullability. On the contrary, the nullity of the unconstitutional state act persists, but with the limitation deriving from the legal reserve granted to the judges to declare, in exclusivity, its nullity.

Thus, up to that moment, the irregular state act must be considered by other public authorities, particularly administrative authorities and by individuals, as being effective and obligatory; but once a judge declares it unconstitutional in relation to a particular process, then the act becomes null and void regarding that process.

In conclusion, in the diffuse systems of judicial review, the duty of all judges and courts is to examine the constitutionality of laws, and to declare, when necessary, that a particular law or statute should not be applicable to a particular process which the judge or the court is considering, because it is unconstitutional and therefore must be considered null and void.

B. *The Power of All Courts*

This leads us to the second aspect of the rationality of the diffuse system of judicial review, which is that the power to declare the unconstitutionality of legislation is assigned to all the judges in a given country.

In effect, if the constitution is the supreme law of the land, and the principle of supremacy is accepted, then the constitution overrides any other law inconsistent with it, whether this is expressly established in the written text of the constitution or is an implicit consequence of its supremacy. Consequently, the laws that violate the constitution or in any way are contrary to its norms, principles and values are, as we have said, null and void, and cannot be applied by the courts, which must give preference to the constitution.

Then all courts must decide the concrete cases they are considering, as Chief Justice Marshall said, "conformably to the constitution, disregarding the unconstitutional law" this being "of the very essence of judicial duty."[522] Therefore, this role in the diffuse system of judicial review must correspond to all courts and not only to one particular court or tribunal, and must not be seen only in terms of power con-

522 *Marbury v. Madison*, 5 US (1 Cranch), 137, (1803).

ferred upon the courts, but of the courts duty[523] to decide in conformity with the rule of the constitution, disregarding the laws contrary to its norms.

C. *The Incidental Character of the system*

This duty of all courts to give preference to the constitution and, therefore, not to apply laws which they consider unconstitutional and consequently null and void, leads us to the third aspect that shows the rationality of the diffuse system of judicial review of the constitutionality of legislation, which is that this duty of the courts can only be accomplished *incidenter tantum*, through a particular process that has been brought before them, and where the unconstitutionality of a particular law is neither "the issue" nor the principal issue in the process.

Therefore, a process must be initiated before a court on any matter or subject whatsoever, the diffuse system of judicial review of constitutionality being, consequently, always an incidental system of review. In it, the question of the unconstitutionality of a law and of its inapplicability is raised in a concrete case or process whatever its nature and in which the applicability or not of the concrete law is considered by the judge relevant to the decision of the case.

Hence, in the diffuse system of judicial review the main purpose of the process and of the court decision is not the abstract constitutionality or unconstitutionality of a law, or its applicability or inapplicability but rather the resolution of the concrete civil, criminal, administrative, commercial, or labour case.

The question of constitutionality thus is only an incidental aspect of a process, which must be considered by the judge only to resolve the applicability or not of a law to the decision of the concrete case, when there are questions concerning its unconstitutionality.

D. *The Initiative Power of the Courts*

Now, if it is a duty of the judges to apply the constitution in a concrete decision and not to apply a law considered unconstitutional to the resolution of the case, it must be said that in principle the fourth aspect of the rationality of the diffuse system must allow the judge to consider the constitutional question even on his own initiative, and therefore, even when none of the parties in the particular process have raised the question of the constitutionality of the law before the judge.

In fact, this is the direct consequence of the guarantee of the constitution, established as an objective guarantee which means the nullity of laws contrary to its norms, and is also the consequence of the reserve granted to the judges to declare the nullity and, consequently, the inapplicability of the unconstitutional law in a particular case.

---

523 Confront B.C. NWABUEZE, *Judicial Control of Legislative Action and its Legitimacy. Recent Development*. African regional report. International Association of Legal Sciences. Uppsala Colloquium, 1984 (mimeo), pp. 2–3. Also published in L. FAVOREU and J.A. JOLOWICZ (ed.), *Le contrôle juridictionnel des lois. Légitimité, effectivité et développements récents*, Paris 1986, p. 193–222.

Within this framework, the unconstitutionality of a law in relation to a particular process, cannot be left to the sole instance of one of the parties, and on the contrary, even if the parties do not raise the question of unconstitutionality before the judge, he has the duty of considering it and on his own initiative decide upon the unconstitutionality of a law.

Even though this aspect of the rationality of the diffuse system of judicial review is followed in many countries as in the case of Venezuela and Greece,[524] we must admit that, in general, procedural rules in most countries forbid courts to consider any questions on their own initiative, even questions of the constitutionality of laws, when deciding concrete cases.[525]

In any case, the common trend in this aspect of the rationality of this system of judicial review, is that the question of constitutionality can only be incidental through a particular process, always of course initiated by a party.

E. *The* inter partes *effects of the Court decision*

The fifth and final aspect of the rationality of the diffuse system of judicial review concerns the effects of the decision adopted by the court in regard to the constitutionality or applicability of the law in the concrete process; and this aspect of the effect of the judicial decision refers to two questions: first, who does the decision affect? And second when do the effects of the decision begin?

In relation to the first question, the rationality of the diffuse system of judicial review is that the decision adopted by the court only has effects regarding the concrete parties, in the concrete process in which the decision is adopted. That is to say, in the diffuse system of control of the constitutionality of legislation, the decision adopted upon the unconstitutionality and inapplicability of a law in a case only has *in casu et inter partes* effects related to the concrete case and exclusively to the parties who have participated in the process, and therefore, it cannot be applied to other individuals. This is a direct consequence of the aspect previously mentioned regarding the incidental character of the diffuse system of review as raised in a concrete process.

In effect, if the courts decision upon the constitutionality and applicability of a law on the grounds of constitutionality can only be adopted in a particular process developed between concrete parties, the logic of the system is that the decision only applies to that particular process and to those concrete parties and, hence, can neither benefit nor prejudice any other individual or any other process.

---

524 L. SPILIOTOPOULOS, "Judicial Review of Legislative Acts in Greece", *loc. cit.*, p. 479.

525 As B.C. NWABUEZE has said: "The fact that the duty is, and can only be performed at the instance of a person aggrieved by a violation of the law of the constitution by government reinforce the legitimacy of the function. What this means is that, given a justiciable violation of the constitution by the legislature, however flaGRANT, the court cannot, on its own initiative, intervene. It must wait until moved by someone", *doc. cit.*, p. 3. See the discussion on the matter, and the opinion in contrary sense in J.R. VANOSSI and P.E. UBERTONE, *op. cit.*, p. 24; in G. BIDART CAMPOS, *El derecho constitucional del poder*, Vol. II, Chap. XXIX; and in J.R. VANOSSI, *Teoría constitucional*, Vol. II, Buenos Aires 1976, pp. 318–319.

Thus, if a law is considered unconstitutional in a judicial case decision, this does not mean that the law has been invalidated and that it is not enforceable and applicable elsewhere. It only means that concerning the particular process and parties in which the inapplicability of the law has been decided by the court, the law must be considered unconstitutional, null and void, with no effect regarding other cases, other judges or other individuals.

Nevertheless, to avoid the uncertainty of the legal order and of contradictions in relation to the value of the laws, corrections have been made to these *inter partes* effects through the *stare decisis* doctrine or through positive law, when the decision is adopted by the Supreme Court of a given country.

F. *The Declarative Effects of the Court Decision*

These *inter partes* effects of the judicial decision in the diffuse system of judicial review are closely related to the other question concerning the effects of the decision in time, namely to when the declaration of unconstitutionality is to be effective, and also, of course, to the already mentioned aspect of the nullity as a guarantee of the constitution.

In effect, we have said that the first and foremost fundamental aspect of the rationality of the diffuse system of judicial review is that of the supremacy of the constitution over all state acts that leads to the consideration that laws contrary to the constitution are null and void, the most important guarantee of the constitution. Consequently, when a court decides upon the constitutionality of a law and declares it unconstitutional and inapplicable in a concrete case, it is because it considers the law null and void, as if it had never existed.

Therefore, the decision has *declarative* effects: it declares that a law is unconstitutional and consequently, that it has been unconstitutional ever since its enactment. Thus, the law whose inapplicability is decided upon, is considered by the court as never having been valid and as always having been null and void. That is why it is said that the decision of the court, as it is a declarative one, has *ex tunc*, *pro–pretaerito* or retroactive effects in the sense that they go back to the moment of the enactment of the statute considered unconstitutional preventing it from having any effect, of course, only concerning the concrete case decided by the court and regarding the intervening parties. The legislative act declared unconstitutional by a court in the diffuse system of judicial review, as a result, is considered as being null and void *ab initio*, and consequently is not annulled by the court who only declare its pre–existing nullity.

4. Conclusion

In conclusion, we can say that as a matter of fact, the principle the rationality of the diffuse system of judicial review works as follows:

The constitution has a supreme character over the whole legal order; thus, acts contrary to the constitution cannot have any effects, and are considered null and void.

All Courts have the power and duty of applying the constitution and the laws and, therefore, to give preference to the constitution over statutes, which violate it, and to declare them unconstitutional and inapplicable to the concrete process developed before the court.

The power and duty of the courts to consider a statute unconstitutional giving preference to the constitution can only be exercised in a particular process initiated by a party, where the constitutional question is only an incidental matter, and when its consideration is necessary to resolve the case.

This court judgment regarding the unconstitutionality and inapplicability of a statute in a particular process can be taken by the judge on his own initiative, because it is his duty to apply and respect the supremacy of the constitution.

The decision adopted by the court concerning the unconstitutionality and inapplicability of a law only has *inter partes* effects regarding the concrete case in which it is made; and it is of a declarative effect in the sense that it only declares the *ab initio* nullity of the statute. Thus, when declaring the statute unconstitutional and inapplicable, in fact, the decision has *ex–tunc*, and *pro pretaerito* effects in the sense that they are retroactive to the moment of the enactment of the statute, considered as not having produced any effect regarding the concrete process and parties.

Of course, this logic of the diffuse system of judicial review is not always absolute, and each legal system has developed corrections to the possible deviation that each one of the aspects of the rationality of the system may produce, concerning the nullity or annulability of the unconstitutional act; the power assigned to all or a limited number of courts to review constitutionality; the incidental character of the system; the initiative of judges or the need of a party requirement of the constitutional question; the *inter partes* or *erga omnes* effect of the decision and its declarative or constitutive character.

In analysing the most important diffuse systems of judicial review of the constitutionality of legislation we will refer to all those aspects of the rationality of the system and its special modifications.

II. THE AMERICAN SYSTEM OF JUDICIAL REVIEW

The most important example of the diffuse system of judicial review is, without doubt, the one developed in the United States of America since the beginning of the last century. The diffuse system of judicial review, therefore, can be considered as a North American constitutional product in origin. That is why this system of judicial review is also known in comparative law, as the "American system" [526]1), particularly, when opposed to one of the types of the concentrated system of judicial review, known as the "Austrian system" also because its origins are in the 1920 Austrian constitution. Judicial review is, consequently, not only the most distinctive feature of the American Constitutional system, but also one of the main contributions of American Constitutionalism to the theory and practice of constitutional law.

526 M. CAPPELLETTI, *Judicial Review in the Contemporary World*, Indianapolis 1971, p. 46.

1. Judicial review and judicial supremacy

When Alexis De Tocqueville visited America more than a hundred and fifty years ago, and described the political system of the United States, he stressed, in particular, the way Americans had organised their judicial power, which he considered unique in the world.[527] His observations about the powers of the courts, which he believed, "the most important power" of the country,[528] were directly referred to the powers for judicial review, whose basic trends can still be elaborated from them. He specifically pointed out that "that immense political power"[529] of the American courts, "lies in this one fact" –he said –:

> The Americans have given their judges the right to base their decisions on the constitution rather than on the laws. In other words, they allow them not to apply laws which they consider unconstitutional.[530]

Following the same idea, he said:

> If anyone invokes in an American Court a law which the judge considers contrary to the constitution, he can refuse to apply it.[531]

This power of American judges, De Tocqueville stressed, was "the only power peculiar to an American judge";[532] today, it must be said, it is the power common to all judges in legal systems with a diffuse system of judicial review.

Nevertheless, what was peculiar to the American system was that the power of all courts to "pass upon the constitutionality of legislative acts which fall within their normal jurisdiction to enforce and.... to refuse to enforce such as they find to be unconstitutional and hence void",[533] was not expressly established in the constitution. It was deduced from the whole constitutional system by the Supreme Court, particularly by Chief Justice John Marshall in the famous *Marbury* v. *Madison* case 1803,[534] based on two main arguments, first, the supremacy of the constitution, as a fundamental law, to which all other laws must be submitted; and second, the power and duty of the courts to interpret the laws, and not to apply laws repugnant to the constitution, which ought to be considered null and void.[535]

---

527 Alexis DE TOCQUEVILLE, *Democracy in America* (ed. by J.P. MAYER and M. LERNER), The Fontana Library, London 1968, Vol. 1, p. 120.

528 *Idem*, p. 122

529 *Ibid*, pp. 122, 124.

530 *Ibid*, p. 122.

531 *Ibid*, p. 124.

532 *Ibid*, p. 124.

533 E.S. CORWIN, "Judicial Review" *Encyclopedia of the Social Sciences*, Vols. VII–VIII, p. 457.

534 "... the responsability for introducing the practice (of judicial review of legislative acts) as a rule for the federal courts is placed primarily on the great chief justice." Ch. G. HAINES, *The American Doctrine of judicial supremacy*, Berkeley 1932, p. 122.

535 E.S. CORWIN, "*Marbury v. Madison* and the Doctrine of Judicial Review", *Michigan Law Review*, 12, 1914, p. 538.

This fundamental duty of the American courts has been clearly summarised by the Supreme Court in the United *States* v. *Butler* case in 1936, with the following words:

> The constitution is the supreme law of the land ordained and established by the people. All legislation must conform to the principles it lays down. When an act of Congress is appropriately challenged in the Courts as not conforming to the constitutional mandate the judicial branch of the Government has only one duty, –to lay the article of the constitution which is invoked beside the Statute which is challenged and to decide whether the latter squares with the former.
>
> All the Court does, or can do, is to announce its considered judgment upon the question. The only power it has, if such it may be called, is the power of judgment. This Court neither approves nor condemns any legislative policy. Its delicate and difficult office is to ascertain and declare whether the legislation is in accordance with, or in contravention of, the provisions of the constitution; and, having done that, its duty ends.[536]

According to this doctrine, the courts in the American system of judicial review are considered the special custodians or guardians of the terms of the written constitution,[537] not only of the "national" constitution but also of the constitutions of the various states.

According to the federal system, three branches of judicial review have been distinguished in the United States: a "national" judicial review, referring to the power of all courts to pass judgment upon the validity of acts of Congress under the United States Constitution; a "federal" judicial review, referring to the power and duty of all courts to prefer the United States Constitution over all conflicting state constitution provisions and statutes; and a "state" judicial review, referring to the power of state courts to pass judgment upon the validity of acts of the state legislatures under the respective state Constitutions.[538]

The "national" judicial review branch was the only one not expressly established in the constitution, and was deduced from the constitutional system by the Supreme Court. Whereas the "federal" judicial review branch was expressly established in what has been considered to be the "supremacy clause" of the constitution;[539] and the "state" judicial review branch is generally regulated in the constitutions of the states. Due to its importance, we will refer our comments on the general trends of the diffuse American system of judicial review, mainly to the "national" judicial review branch and the role of the Supreme Court.

However, before doing so, it must be pointed out that the power of judicial review in the American system derived from the concept of judicial supremacy can be exercised over all state acts, and not only over legislative acts. Therefore, all acts of Congress, constitutions and statuses of the states, all acts of the government and administration and even judicial acts are submitted to judicial review of constitution-

---

536 297 US. (1936).

537 Ch. G. HAINES, *op. cit.*, pp. 23, 221, 222.

538 E.S. CORWIN, "Judicial Review", *loc. cit.*, p. 457

539 Article VI, 2. See the comments of R. BERGER, *Congress v. The Supreme Court*, Cambridge, Mass 1969, pp. 223–284.

ality[540] and even though no treaty has ever been held to be unconstitutional by the courts,[541] in the leading *Missouri* v. *Holland* case (1920) it was clearly expressed that the constitutional validity of treaties and legislation resting on treaties may appropriately be the subject of judicial inquiry.[542]

Anyway, because of the importance of the subject to comparative analysis, we will basically refer to judicial review of legislative acts.

2. Judicial Review as a Power of All Courts

First of all, it must be said that judicial review as the power to control the constitutionality of legislation is a faculty conferred upon all courts and judges in the United States. Therefore, in the United States there is no special judicial body empowered to decide upon the constitutionality of state acts, particularly of legislation. Thus, all the courts, state courts, federal courts and the Supreme Court have the power of judicial review of constitutionality, and none of them have their jurisdiction limited in any special way at all, over the decision of constitutional questions.

Consequently, courts always decide upon constitutional matters or issues when they arise in the course of a concrete case and are necessary to the decision of the case brought before the court within its ordinary jurisdiction.

In general, and restricting our comments to the federal judicial system, courts, organised in the pyramidal format usual in contemporary legal systems, have either original or appellate jurisdiction. General original jurisdiction in the federal judicial system in the United States is vested in the "district courts" which are a large number of tribunals of territorial competence located throughout the country, generally coinciding with the territories of the states. The jurisdiction of these "district courts" extends to numerous types of controversies, particularly, civil and criminal cases arising out of the laws of the United States, controversies between citizens of different states, cases in which the United States is a plaintiff or defendant, *habeas corpus* proceedings, and cases arising out of federal civil rights litigation originating from violations by state officers of the constitutional rights of the plaintiff seeking damages or other relief.[543] It is in the course of these controversies that constitutional issues may be raised.

Over district courts, in the federal judicial system, there are the United States "courts of appeal." Federal judicial districts are organised into larger judicial units known as "circuits" and in each of these there is one court of appeal. These courts of

540 *Cf.* A. TUNC and S. TUNC, *Le système constitutionnel des Etats Unis d'Amerique*, Paris 1954, Vol. II, p. 272

541 P.G. KAUPER, "Judicial Review of Constitutional Issues in the United States" in H. MOSLER (ed.), Max–Planck–Institut für Ausländisches öffentliches recht und Völkerrecht, *Verfassungsgerichtsbarkeit in der Gegenwart* (Constitutional Review in the World Today) Internationalen Kolloquium, Heildelberg 1961), Köln–Berlin, 1962, p. 628.

542 *Missouri v. Holland*, 252 US 346 (1920) where the Court found that a "treaty in question does not contravene any prohibitory words to be found in the constitution" concluding that "we are of opinion that the treaty and statute must be upheld..."

543 28 US Code sec. 1331, 1332, 1345, 1346, 2241, 1343.

appeal in the American system do not have original jurisdiction and are strictly appellate tribunals, with very extensive jurisdiction derived from the fact that all the final decisions of the district courts may be appealed against, at them. The work of these courts of appeals in the federal judicial system is very important due to the fact that they perform the function of ultimate appellate courts, bearing in mind that only the most important cases can be taken from a court of appeal to the Supreme Court.

Additionally, it must be pointed out that if it is true that in general the jurisdiction of the courts of appeal is directed to the review of the decisions of a federal district court, by statute they have been given appellate jurisdiction to review the decisions of some important federal administrative agencies (e.g. National Labour Relations Board, Federal Power Commission), and special federal courts, like tax courts, in which constitutional issues frequently arise.

In other federal matters, there are specialised courts with original and appellate jurisdiction separate from the general system of the district and circuit courts, as in the case of the Court of Customs and Patent Appeals, the Court of Military Appeals and the Court of Claims.[544]

At the apex of the federal judicial system is the United States Supreme Court, which has not only an appellate jurisdiction, but also an original jurisdiction established in the constitution that cannot be enlarged upon by Congress.[545] The original jurisdiction refers to "cases affecting ambassadors, other public ministers and Consuls, and those in which a state shall be party"[546] and it is classified by the United States Code, in Sec. 1251, title 28, as exclusive and non–exclusive jurisdiction. It states as follows: The original and exclusive jurisdiction refers to all controversies between two or more states; and the original but not exclusive jurisdiction refers to all actions or proceedings brought by ambassadors or other public ministers of foreign states or to which consuls or vice consuls of foreign states are parties; all controversies between the United States and a state; and all actions or proceedings by a state against the citizen of another state or against aliens.

To summarise, the original jurisdiction of the Supreme Court refers to cases that may be brought directly before the court, which includes cases to which a state is a party and cases involving ambassadors. Disputes between two states commonly referring to conflicts regarding boundaries, water or mineral rights can be heard only by the Supreme Court, but other cases under the original non exclusive jurisdiction of the court can be heard alternatively by a district court.[547]

Consequently, because of the limited and less important nature of the original jurisdiction of the Supreme Court, it is evident that its most important activity as interpreter of the constitution and the laws and treaties of the United States is developed through its appellate jurisdiction, in which it operates as the court of last resort.

---

544 *Cf.* L. BAUM, *The Supreme Court*, Washington 1981, p. 10.

545 *Cf. Marbury v. Madison*, 5 US (1Cranch) 137 (1803); *Muskrat v. United States*, 219 US, 346, (1911).

546 Art. III, section 2 of the constitution.

547 *Cf.* L. BAUM, *op. cit.* p. 11.

In this respect, particularly in the field of constitutional matters, the Supreme Court appears as "the most important tribunal in the American system"[548] with a very broad appellate jurisdiction regulated by Congress, to ensure a final, authoritative, and uniform interpretation of the constitution and the laws and treaties of the United States.

Thus, the Supreme Court is authorised to review all decisions of the United States Courts of Appeal,[549] which, as we have seen, have the power to review the decisions of all the district courts so that in general the appellate jurisdiction of the Supreme Court can be extended to all cases originating in the federal court system.

In addition, the Supreme Court has appellate jurisdiction to review the decisions of the highest court of the various states, in all cases of federal laws, that is to say, cases that draw into question the validity of a federal statute or treaty or the validity o a state statute or where otherwise a claim of right under the constitution, treaties or laws of the United States is involved.[550] Finally, the Supreme Court also has appellate jurisdiction to review the decisions of specialised federal Courts, like the Court of Claims, the Court of Customs and Patent Appeals and the Court of Military Appeals.[551]

However, apart from the appellate jurisdiction following the hierarchical pattern of the judicial system, there are also cases in which the Supreme Court can act as an appellate court of last resort to review decisions of the federal district courts brought directly to the Supreme Court by means of an appeal. In this respect, the US Code establishes a right to appeal to the Supreme Court from the decision of any federal court, including federal district courts, "holding an act of Congress unconstitutional in any civil action, suit, or proceeding to which the United States or any of its agencies, or any officer or employee thereof, as such officer or employee, is a party."[552] Likewise the United States may appeal directly to the Supreme Court against any decision of a federal district court dismissing a criminal proceeding or setting aside a criminal conviction on the grounds of unconstitutionality of the federal criminal statute.[553] Finally, the US Code also allows any party to appeal directly "to the Supreme Court from an order granting or denying, after notice and hearing, an interlocutory or permanent injunction in any civil action, suit or proceeding required by any act of Congress to be heard and determined by a district court of three judges",[554] which is needed when either a federal or state statute is questioned on the grounds of its constitutionality.

548 B. SCHWARTZ, *American Constitutional Law*, Cambridge 1955, p. 129.

549 28, US Code 1254 which referes to the methods through which cases in the court of appeals may be reviewed by the Supreme Court.

550 28. US Code, 1257.

551 28. US Code, 1255, 1256.

552 28. US Code, 1252.

553 18. US Code, 3731.

554 28. US Code 1253, 2281, 2282, 2284.

3. The Mandatory or Discretionary Power of the Supreme Court for Judicial Review

As we can realise, the appellate jurisdiction of the Supreme Court is enormous so that the right to appeal to the highest tribunal has been restricted. Moreover, the Supreme Court has been progressively made the judge as to whether or not it would receive an appeal to it, being allowed to refuse to hear a case when it feels that the question involved is not one of sufficient importance.

The appellate jurisdiction of the Supreme Court, therefore, is twofold: mandatory and discretionary, the latter being the most important in the number of cases reviewed.

The main reform in this respect was taken by the 1925 Judiciary act[555] through which the discretionary appellate jurisdiction was widened, bearing in mind the public interest. This discretionary power to determine the cases to be heard by the court has changed the character of the Supreme Court as an ultimate appellate tribunal or an ordinary judicial body. As Professor B. Schwartz pointed out, it has resulted that today, the Supreme Court:

> Is a Court of Special Resort for the settlement only of such question as it deems to involve a substantial public concern, rather than the concerns only of private persons as such.[556]

The distinction between the mandatory and the discretionary appellate jurisdiction of the Supreme Court depends on the methods established in the US Code through which three cases may be reviewed by the Supreme Court. These three methods are the appeals, the petitions for writ of certiorari and the certifications.

A. *Right to Appeal and Mandatory Appellate Jurisdiction.*

Obligatory or mandatory appellate jurisdiction exists when a right of appeal is granted to a party to bring a case before the Supreme Court, and this is restricted to the following cases, all related to constitutional justice:

a. Cases in which a federal court, even district courts, has held an act of Congress to be unconstitutional, if the federal government is a party.[557]

b. Cases in which a federal court of appeal has held a state statute to be invalid as repugnant to the constitution, treaties or laws of the United States.[558]

c. Cases in which a state supreme court has drawn into question the validity of a treaty or statute of the United States (act of Congress) and the decision is against its validity.[559]

---

555 See TAFT, "The Jurisdiction of the Supreme Court under the Act of February 13, 1925", *Yale Law Review*, 35, 1925, p. 2.

556 B. SCHWARTZ, *op. cit.*, p. 139.

557 28 US Code, 1252.

558 28 US Code, 1254, 2.

559 28 US Code, 1257, 1 (Cases in which a State Supreme Court has ruled an act of Congress unconstitutional).

d. Cases in which a state supreme court has drawn into question the validity of a statute of any state on the grounds of its being repugnant to the constitution treaties or laws of the United States, and the decision is in favour of its validity.[560]

e. Cases decided by special three–judge federal district courts, bearing in mind that a special three judge federal court must be set up through the enlargement of the federal district court where normally only one judge sits to hear the case when a proceeding is initiated to enjoin either a federal or state statute on the grounds of its constitutionality.[561]

As can generally be seen, the right to appeal and the mandatory appellate jurisdiction of the Supreme Court are established when important constitutional issues are in question, and particularly, when an act of Congress is considered to be unconstitutional by a federal court or a state supreme court, or when a state statute has been considered to be unconstitutional by a federal court of appeal, or its constitutionality has been questioned before a state supreme court.

B. *The Discretionary Appellate Jurisdiction and the Writ of Certiorari*

In all other cases, whether or not they involve constitutional issues, the United States Supreme Court is authorised to review all the decisions of the federal courts of appeals, and of the specialised federal courts, and all the decisions of the supreme courts of the states involving issues of federal law, but on a discretionary basis, when considering a petition for a writ of certiorari.

In effect, in all such cases in which there is no right of appeal established and where the mandatory appellate jurisdiction of the Supreme Court is not established, they can reach the Supreme Court as petitions for certiorari, where a litigant who has lost in a lower court, petitions the Supreme Court to review the case, setting out the reasons why review should be granted.[562] This method of seeking review by the Supreme Court is expressly established in the following cases:

a. Cases decided by the federal court of appeals, granted upon the petition of any party to any civil or criminal case, before or after rendition of judgment or decree.[563]

b. Cases decided in the Court of Claim granted on petition of the United States or the claimant.[564]

c. Cases decided in the Court of Customs and Patent Appeals.[565]

d. Cases decided by the supreme courts of the states where the validity of a treaty or statute of the United States is drawn into question or where the validity of a

560 28 US Code 1257, 2 (Cases in which a State Supreme Court has upheld a State law against a claim that it conflicts with the constitution or a federal law).

561 28 US Code 1253, 2281, 2282, 2284.

562 L. BAUM, *op. cit.*, p. 81.

563 28 US Code, 1254, 1.

564 28 US Code, 1255, 1.

565 28 US Code, 1256.

state statute is drawn into question on the grounds of its being repugnant to the constitution, treaties or laws of the United States, or where any title, right, privilege or immunity is specially set up or claimed under the constitution, treaties or statues of, or commission held or authority exercised under the United States.[566]

In all these cases, as the Supreme Court's Rule N° 17 establishes when referring to the "considerations governing review on certiorari":

> A review on writ of certiorari is not a matter of right, but of judicial discretion, and will be granted only when there are special and important reasons therefore.[567]

The same Rule N° 17 adopted by the Supreme Court, listed the factors that might prompt the court to grant certiorari even though without "controlling nor fully measuring the court's discretion", as follows:

> a. When a federal court of appeal has rendered a decision in conflict with the decision of another federal court of appeal on the same matter; or has decided a federal question in a way in conflict with a state court of last resort; or has so far departed from the accepted and usual course of judicial proceedings, ox has so far sanctioned such a departure by a lower court, as to call for an exercise of this Court's power of supervision;
>
> b. When a state court of last resort has decided a federal question in a way in conflict with the decision of another state court of last resort or of federal court of appeal;
>
> c. When a state court or a federal court of appeal has decided an important question of federal law which has not been, but should be, settled by this Court, or has decided a federal question in a way in conflict with applicable decisions of this Court.[568]

According to this Rule, consequently, in order to promote uniformity and consistency in federal law, the following factors might prompt the Supreme Court to grant certiorari: 1. Important questions of federal law on which the court has not previously ruled; 2. Conflicting interpretations of federal law by lower courts; 3. Lower courts decisions that conflict with previous Supreme Court decisions; and 4. Lower court departures from the accepted and usual course of judicial proceedings.[569]

Of course, review may be granted on the basis of other factors, or denied even if one or more of the above mentioned factors is present. The discretion of the Supreme Court is not limited, and it is the importance of the issue and the public interest viewed by the Court in a particular case, which leads the Court to grant certiorari and to review some cases.

C. *The Jurisdiction of the Supreme Court in Cases of Certification*

Apart from the appeals and the petition for writ of certiorari, the appellate jurisdiction of the Supreme Court can be exercised through the request of certification by

---

566 28 US Code, 1257, 3.

567 Section 1. see in L. BAUM, *op. cit.*, p. 86.

568 *Idem.*

569 *Cf.* R.A. ROSSUM and G.A. TARR, *American Constitutional Law*, New York 1983, p. 28.

a federal court of appeal or by the Court of Claims, although it is very rarely employed.

In effect, the US Code establishes in section 1254, as one of the methods through which the decisions of the courts of appeals may be reviewed by the Supreme Court, the following:

> By certification at any time by a court of appeal of any question of law in any civil or criminal case as to which instructions are desired, and upon such certification the Supreme Court may give instructions or require the entire record to be sent up for decision of the entire matter in controversy.[570]

As a result, certification is the procedure whereby a lower federal court requests instruction from the Supreme Court on a point of law, relevant to the case under consideration. In these cases of certified questions, the Supreme Court is obliged to consider and answer the questions put to it.[571] In this situation, the Supreme Court does not normally deal with the whole case, but sends its instructions back to the court of appeal, even though the Court is authorised to require the entire case to be brought before it.

4. The Incidental Character of Judicial Review

A. *Cases and Controversies*

Judicial review of legislation, whether exercised by lower courts or by the Supreme Court in its original or appellate jurisdiction, is always a power that can only be exercised by the courts within the context of a concrete adversary litigation, when the constitutional issue becomes relevant and necessary to be resolved in the decision of the case.

In this respect, as we said, there is no special type of proceeding required for raising constitutional issues in the courts. As Professor Paul G. Kauper pointed out in his study on judicial review of constitutional issues in the United States:

> The constitutional question, if relevant to the disposition of the case and if asserted by a proper party in interest in an adversary proceeding, may be raised regardless of the nature of the proceeding. Thus it may be raised in the course of a civil proceeding between private parties where damages or other relief are sought; as a defence in a criminal proceeding under the criminal laws of the United States, as the basis for an injunction sought by a party in a proceeding directed either against public authorities or private persons to restrain the enforcement of a statute or an administrative order or other administrative action, in a mandamus proceeding to compel the performance of a public duty, in a damage action brought against the United States to collect taxes or to enforce a federal administrative order or in a declaratory judgment proceeding designed to obtain a judicial declaration of rights between opposing parties.[572]

---

570 28 US Code, 1254, 3.

571 P.G. KAUPER, p. 579, 608.

572 P.G. KAUPER, *loc. cit.*, pp. 586–587. *Cf.* J.A.C. GRANT "El control jurisdiccional de la constitucionalidad de las leyes: una contribución de las Américas a la ciencia política", *Revista de la Facultad de Derecho de México*, 45, México 1962, pp. 425–429.

Thus, the incidental character of judicial review, essential to the diffuse system, is the main trend of the American system, and has been developed by the Supreme Court by interpreting the expressions "cases" and "controversies" used in Article III, Section 2 of the constitution.

Therefore, no abstract judicial review of the validity of legislation is authorised in the United States[573] and judicial review by the courts can only be exercised within the limits of a concrete case or controversy, at the request of a party. In this respect, Justice Sutherland in *Frothinaham* v. *Mellon* (1923) was definitively conclusive:

> We have no power per se to review and annul acts of Congress on the grounds that they are unconstitutional. The question may be considered only when the justification for some direct injury suffered or threatened, presenting a justiciable issue, is made to rest upon such an act. Then, the power exercises is that of ascertaining and declaring the law applicable to the controversy.[574]

And in this same respect, it was stated in *Muskrat* v. *United States* (1911),

> By cases and controversies are intended the claims of litigants brought before the courts for determination by such regular proceedings as are established by law or customs for the protection or enforcement of rights, or the prevention, redress, or punishment of wrongs. Whenever the claim of a party under the constitution, laws, or treaties of the United States takes such a form that the judicial power is capable of acting upon it, then it has become a case. The term implies the existence of present or possible adverse parties whose contentions are submitted to the court for adjudication.[575]

Therefore, judicial review of constitutionality has only an incidental character in the United States, as an issue brought before the court in a concrete case or controversy. That is why Justice Brandeis in his concurring opinion to *Ashwander* v. *Tennessee Valley Authority* (1936), said that:

> The Court will not pass upon the constitutionality of legislation in a friendly, non–adversary, proceeding, declining because to decide such questions is legitimate only in the last resort, and as a necessity in the determination of real, earnest and vital controversy between individuals.[576]

---

573 In words of Chief Justice Stone, the Court has "considered practice not to decide abstract, hypothetical or contingent questions" *Alabama Federation of labor v. Mc. Adory*, 325 US, 450 (1945), p. 461.

574 *Frothingham v. Mellon*, 262, US 447 (1923).

575 *Muskrat v. United States*, 219 US, 346, (1911) In this case Justice Day, comenting *Marbury v. Madison* (1803), said: "In that case, Chief Justice MARSHALL, who spoke for the Court, was careful to point out that the right to declare an act of Congress unconstitutional could only be exercised when a proper case between opposing parties was submitted for judicial determination; that there was no general veto power in the Court upon the legislation of Congress; and that the authority to declare an act unconstitutional sprung from the requirement that the courts in administering the law and pronouncing judgement between parties to a case, and choosing between the requirements of the fundamental law established by the people and embodied in the constitution and an act of the agents of the people, acting under authority of the constitution should enforce the constitution as the Supreme Law of the land."

576 *Ashwander v. Tennessy Valley Authority* 297 US 288 (1936), p.345.

Consequently, the courts must not decide constitutional questions when they are convinced that the parties are acting in accord. "It never was thought –added Justice Brandeis in his concurrent opinion already mentioned– that, by means of a friendly suit, a party beaten in the legislature could transfer to the courts an. inquiry as to the constitutionality of the legislative act."[577]

Nevertheless, the need for cases or controversies to seek judicial review of the constitutionality of legislation does not prevent the possible questions of constitutionality from being raised in a declaratory judgment.

Even though discussed by the courts in applying state legislation, after the 1934 Federal Declaratory Judgment Act, it has been definitively accepted that, provided all other jurisdictional requirements are satisfied, federal courts are authorised to declare the rights of the parties in a case before them, although a specific form of remedy, such as a judgment for damages or an equitable decree, is not sought by the petitioner.[578]

In any case, it has been pointed out that even though of declaratory character, these judgments are not mere advisory opinions, in the sense that to be accepted a genuinely adversary proceeding between parties asserting appropriate interests must exist.[579] Thus, declaratory judgments are considered cases or controversies, and can be used to obtain a judicial decision upon constitutional issues.[580]

On the other hand, we must point out that judicial review being a power conferred on all courts to review the constitutionality of legislation in cases and controversies, the United States is not always necessarily a party in the proceedings, because, as we have seen, the constitutional question can be raised in any type of proceeding even when is it developed between private parties. Nevertheless, in all cases when the United States or any agency officer or employee thereof is not a party, and wherein the constitutionality of any act of Congress affecting the public interest is drawn into question, the court shall certify such facts to the attorney general, and shall permit the United States to intervene for presentation of evidence and for argument on the question of constitutionality. In such cases, the United States shall have all the rights of a party.[581]

Even if the consideration of constitutional issues must be confined to cases or controversies, the invalidity of the legislation must be raised by a party with sufficient standing and its resolution being necessary and indispensable for the decision of the case. In this respect, the Supreme Court has developed a few rules that have been considered as "self–restraint"[582] over its judicial review powers, particularly in

577 *Idem.*

578 28. US Code, secc 2201.

579 *Maryland Casualty Co. v. Pacific Coal and Oil Co.*, 312, US. 270 (1941).

580 *Nashville, C. and St. L. Ry. Co v. Wallace*, 288 US, 249 1933.

581 28 US Code, secc 2403.

582 See H.J. ABRAHAM, *The Judicial Process*, NY 1980, p. 373. These self–restrain has been summarized by Justice Rutledge as followed: "... Constitutional issues affecting legislation will not be determined in friendly, nonadversary proceedings; in advance of the necessity of deciding then; in broader terms than required by the precise facts to which the ruling is to be

three aspects specifically related to the incidental character of judicial review. The standing requirement and the evident and indispensable character of the constitutional question.

B. *The Personal Interest and the Constitutional Question.*

First of all, within a case or controversy, the court has developed the principle of the need of the constitutional issue to be alleged by a party and particularly, by a party that must show that it is the proper party with personal interest. As we have mentioned in *Frothinqham* v. *Mellon* (1923) the court expressly established that the constitutional questions:

> May be considered only when the justification for some direct injury suffered or threatened, presenting a justiciable suit is made to rest upon such an act...[583]

Along the same lines of thought Justice Brandeis said in the case *Ashwander* v. *Tennessee Valley Authority*, "the Court will not pass upon the validity of a statute upon complaint of one who fails to show that he is injured by its operation."[584] Therefore, to raise an issue of validity of a statute, the necessary standing to sue is required and to have such standing the party involving the invalidity of a statute must show, as was stated in *Frothingham* v. *Mellon* (1923):

> Not only that the statute is invalid, but that he has sustained or is immediately in danger of sustaining some direct injury as the result of its enforcement, and not merely that he suffers in some indefinite way in common with people generally.[585]

In this respect, and when considering the due standing of taxpayers to question the budget decisions of Congress[586] Chief Justice Burger in *United States* v. *Richardson* (1974), refereed to the always valid:

> Basic principle that to invoke judicial power the claimant must have a "personal stake in the outcome"... or a "particular concrete injury"..."that he has sustained... a direct injury"... in short, something more than generalised grievances.[587]

Therefore, not only is a case or a controversy needed for judicial review, but also that the constitutional issue should be alleged by a party with the necessary standing, that is to say, based on "his own legal rights and interests" affected by the act whose validity is questioned."[588] Moreover, even in cases in which the Supreme Court al-

---

applied; if the record presents some other ground upon which the case may be disposed of; at the instance of one who fails to show that he is injured by the statute's operation, or who has availed himself of its benefits; or if a construction of the statute is fairly possible by which the question may be avoided", *Rescue Army v. Municipal Court of Los Angeles*, 331 US 549, (1947) p. 569.

583 *Frothingham v. Mellon*, 262 US 447 (1923).

584 *Ashwander v. Tennessy Valley Authority*, 297 US 288 (1936), p. 346.

585 *Frothingham v. Mellon*, 262 US 447, (1923), p. 488.

586 See *Flast v. Cohen* 392 US. 83 (1968).

587 *United States v. Richardson*, 418, US. 966 (1974). *Cf. De Funis v. Odegaard*, 416, US 312 (1974).

588 *Warth v. Seldin*, 422 US 490 (1975).

lows persons or organisations or public authorities not party to a case before it, to file a brief as *amicus curae*, this only happens when they have a special interest in the matter, have applied for it to the Court or acted with the consent of the parties, their briefs being intended to support or supplement the arguments of the parties.[589]

Anyway, without the limitations imposed on the parties regarding standing to raise constitutional questions as stated by Justice Powell in *Wart* v. *Seldin* (1975) it would mean that:

> The courts would be called upon to decide abstract questions of wide public significance even though other governmental institutions may be more competent to address the questions and even though judicial intervention may be unnecessary to protect individual rights...[590]

The action to review the constitutionality of a law in the federal courts, therefore, is clearly not the *actio popularis* that exists in some concentrated and mixed systems of judicial review. On the contrary, in the United States, as Professor B. Schwartz pointed out:

> Citizens cannot bring it in the interest of the community as a whole, to see that the rule of law is respected by the legislative and executive branches. Unless the action is brought by one who has a direct personal interest, he does not have the standing required to bring the suit.[591]

But the requirement of standing to sue and to raise the constitutional question is not sufficient to be considered by the court; the party that alleges the invalidity of a statute must demonstrate its invalidity. The Supreme Court has, in this sense, established that there is a presumption of constitutionality and validity in the statutes approved by Congress, unless the opposite is clearly demonstrated.[592]

C. *The Evident and Indispensable Unconstitutionality*

This presumption of validity and constitutionality of the statutes lead us to the second of the self–restraints developed by the Supreme Court regarding its powers of judicial review. It is that the Court should declare an act of Congress unconstitutional, only when its invalidity is clear and undoubtedly established and demonstrated. The principle was established by Chief Justice Marshall in *Fletcher* v. *Peck* (1810), saying:

> The question whether a law be void for its repugnance to the constitution, is, at all times, a question of much delicacy, which ought seldom, if ever, to be decided in the affirmative, in a doubtful case... But it is not on slight implication and vague conjecture that the legislature is to be pronounced to have transcended its powers, and its acts to be considered as void. The

589 *Cf.* L. BAUM, *op. cit.*, pp. 74, 80, 91.

590 *Warth v. Seldin*, 422 US 490 (1975).

591 B. SCHWARTZ, *op. cit.*, p. 151.

592 *Ogden v. Saunders*, 12 Wheaton, 213 (1827) Justice Washington said: 'It is but a decent respect due to the wisdom, integrity and patriotism of the legislative body, by which any law is passed, to presume in favour of its validity' . Also in *Cooper v. Telfair*, 4 Dallas (4.US) 14 (1800) Justice Washington said: 'The presumption indeed, must always be in favour of the validity of laws, if the contrary is not clearly demostrated'.

opposition between the constitution and the law should be such that the judge feels a clear and strong conviction of their incompatibility with each other.[593]

Therefore, even though adopted by a majority of votes, the decision of the Supreme Court upon the unconstitutionality of an act of Congress must be based on clear, evident and conclusive reasons for its invalidity.

The third self–restraint developed by the Supreme Court upon its judicial review powers, also closely related to the need for a case or controversy where the constitutional issue is to be raised, is that the invalidity of a statute must only be resolved by the court when the decision upon the constitutionality or unconstitutionality of an act of congress is "absolutely necessary to the decision of the case."[594] Consequently, the courts must not decide upon the unconstitutionality of a statute, when it would not necessarily change its definitive decision over the rights of the parties; for example, when the question has insufficient relation with the controversy or when there are other ways of satisfying the claim of a party, without referring to the constitutional issue raised.

Chief Justice Marshall in *Ex parte Randolph* (1833) enunciated the rule, when saying:

> No questions can be brought before a judicial tribunal of greater delicacy than those which involve the constitutionality of a legislative act. If they become indispensably necessary to the case, the Court must meet and decide them; but if the case may be determined on other points, a just respect for the legislative requires that the obligation of its laws should not be unnecessarily and wantonly assailed.[595]

In this respect, Justice Brandeis, in his concurring opinion to *Ashwander* v. *Tennessee Valley Authority* (1936) insisted on one of the rules under which the Supreme Court has avoided passing upon a large part of the entire constitutional question by stating:

> The Court will not pass upon a constitutional question, although properly presented by the record, if there is also some other ground upon which the case may be disposed of.... thus, if a case can be decided on either of two grounds, one involving a constitutional question, the other a question of statutory construction or general law, the court will decide only the latter.[596]

Along the same lines, in *Crowell* v. *Benson* (1932), it was stated:

> When the validity of an act of the Congress is drawn in question, and even if a serious doubt of constitutionality is raised, it is a cardinal principle that this Court will first ascertain whether a construction of the statute is fairly possible by which the question may be avoided.[597]

---

593 *Fletcher v. Peck*, 6 Cranch 87 (1810).

594 *Burton v. United States*, 196, US. 283, 295 quoted in *Ashwander v. Tennessy Valley Authority*, 297 US 288 (1936).

595 *Ex parte Randolph*, 20 Fed. Cas. 242 (1833) quoted by W.J. WAGNER, *The Federal States and their Judiciary*, The Hague 1959, p. 97.

596 *Ashwander v. Tennessy Valley Authority*, 297, US. 288 (1936).

597 *Crowell v. Benson*, 285 US 22 (1932), quoted in *Ashwander v. Tennessy Valley Authority*, 297, US. 288 (1936).

Therefore, the decision upon the validity or invalidity of a statute must be indispensable and unavoidable in the resolution of the case; thus, if there are other ways of resolving the controversy avoiding the constitutional question, the court must follow that path. This leads to the criteria developed by the Supreme Court in the sense that statutes must be constructed, and interpreted, if possible, so as to avoid constitutional issues, and that the courts must draw interpretations in order to achieve this result.[598]

D. *The Exception: Political Questions*

Even when a constitutional issue is raised in a case or controversy by a party with the required standing, and the resolution of the invalidity of a statute being indispensable for the resolution of the case, the Court has considered as non justifiable certain "political questions" mainly related to the "separation of powers" and particularly with "the relationship between the judiciary and the co–ordinate branches of the Federal Government."[599]

The main source of questions considered as political and thus non justiciable by the Supreme Court are related to foreign affairs which involves as the Supreme Court stated in *Ware* v. *Hylton* (1796) "considerations of policy, considerations of extreme magnitude, and certainly entirely incompetent to the examination and decision of a Court of Justice."[600] Decisions concerning foreign relation therefore, as stated by Justice Jackson in *Chicago and Southern Air Lines* v. *Waterman Steamship Co.* (1948):

> Are wholly confined by our constitution to the political departments of the government. … They are decisions of a kind for which the Judiciary has neither aptitude, facilities nor responsibility and which has long been held to belong in the domain of political power not subject to judicial intrusion or inquiry.[601]

Even though developed mainly in the foreign affairs sphere, the Supreme Court has also considered certain matters relating to the government of internal affairs, a political question, and thus non justiciable; like the decision as to whether a state must have a republican form of government, which in *Luther* v. *Borden* (1849) was considered a "decision binding on every other department of the government, and could not be questioned in a judicial tribunal."[602]

Any way and even though that through the decisions of the Supreme Court, a list of "political questions" that the Court has considered as non–justifiable can be elaborated, the ultimate responsibility in determining them corresponds to the Supreme Court.

As the Court said in *Baker* v. *Carr* (1962):

---

598 *United States v. Congress of Industrial Organization* 335 US 106 (1948).

599 *Baker v. Carr*, 369 US 186 (1962).

600 *Ware v. Hylton*, 3 Dallas, 199 (1796)

601 *Chicago and Southern Air Lines v. Waterman Steamship Co.*, 333 US 103 (1948) p. 111.

602 *Luther v. Borden*, 48 US (7 Howard), 1 (1849).

> Deciding whether a matter has in any measure been committed by the constitution to another branch of government, or whether the action of that branch exceeds whatever authority has been committed, –said the Court– is itself a delicate exercise in constitutional interpretation, and is a responsibility of this Court as ultimate interpreter of the constitution...[603]

5. The Decision Upon the Constitutionality of the Statutes

Setting apart the problems related to political questions, considered by Professor Schwartz as a possible and undesirable exception to the principle of legality,[604] once a judicial decision is adopted by the courts on a constitutional issue, the classic problem of the effects of the judicial decision must be resolved.

The general "principle", in this matter, is that a judicial decision in matters of control of constitutionality in a diffuse system of judicial review, has *in casu et, inter partes* and *ex tunc* retroactive effects, that is to say, as a consequence of the decision the act considered unconstitutional must be understood for the parties in the case, to be null and void and as never having existed. This principle, however, has been tempered in its concrete application due to the requirements of legal reliability and justice.

A. *The* inter partes *effect and the* stare decisis *doctrine*

In effect, the decision adopted by an American court concerning a constitutional question in principle has relevancy only for the parties to the case. Thus the decision has no *per se* general effects and these effects do not apply *erga omnes*. The statute declared unconstitutional is not annulled by the court nor repealed by it, the legislature which enacted a statute being the only one who has the power to do so. Consequently, the statute declared null and void by a court continues on the books notwithstanding the adverse decision on its validity.

Nevertheless, when the decision upon the unconstitutionality of a statute is adopted by the Supreme Court, as far as the inferior courts are concerned the rule *stare decisis et non quieta movere* (let the decision stand) applies and the inferior courts are bound by the decision of the Supreme Court. In practice, the statute may be considered as no longer enforceable since it may be supposed that after the Supreme Court decision, if any other proceedings are brought under the same statute, they too will result in dismissal, because it may be anticipated that the Supreme Court which held the statute to be unenforceable in one case will find it equally unenforceable in the next case arising under it.[605]

On the other hand, it must be borne in mind that the Supreme Court, when ruling upon the constitutionality of a statute, interprets the constitution declaring at the same time which is the supreme law of the land. This declaration has binding effects on all state bodies though, including, as we said, the judiciary. This was expressly resolved by the Supreme Court in the *Cooper* v. *Aaron* case (1958) in which the

---

603 *Baker v. Carr*, 369 US 186 (1962).

604 B. SCHWARTZ, *op. cit.*, p. 157

605 *Cf.* P.G. KAUPER, *loc. cit.*, p. 611.

Court reaffirmed the binding effects of its previous decision in the *Brown* v. *Board of Education of Topeka* case (1954)[606] on segregation practices in education over all state bodies whether executive, legislative or judiciary.

In *Cooper* v. *Aaron,* the Court said:

> Article VI of the constitution makes the constitution the Supreme law of the land. In 1803, chief Justice Marshall, speaking for a unanimous Court, referring to the constitution as the fundamental and paramount law of the nation, declared in the notable *Marbury v. Madison* case... that "It is emphatically the province and duty of the judicial department to say what the law is." This decision declared the basic principle that the federal judiciary is supreme in the exposition of the laws of the constitution, and that principle has ever since been respected by this Court and the Country as a permanent and indispensable feature of our constitutional system. It follows that the interpretation of the Fourteenth Amendment enunciated by this Court in the Brown case is the supreme law of the land, and Art. VI of the constitution makes it of binding effect on the states anything in the constitution or laws of any state to the contrary notwithstanding...[607]

Therefore, we can say that the principle of *stare decisis* applies in the United States regarding the binding effects of the decisions of the Supreme Court over inferior courts, contributing to the uniformity of the interpretation of the constitution and tending to avoid contradictory decisions on constitutional issues by the Courts.

However, the *stare decisis* rule is not absolute, and in the United States it has less rigidity than in the British legal system,[608] particularly regarding the Supreme Court itself. As Justice Brandeis said in *Burnet* v. *Coronado Oil and Gas Co. (1972) stare decisis:*

> Is usually the wise policy, because in most matters it is more important that the applicable rule of law be settled than that it be settled right ... But in cases involving the Federal constitution, where corrections, through legislative action are practically impossible, this Court has often overruled its earlier decisions. The Court bows to the lessons of experience and the force of better reasoning, recognising that the process of trial and error, so fruitful in the physical sciences, is appropriate also in the judicial function.[609]
>
> "If adherence to precedent were the only judicial virtue –said Professor Bernard Schwartz–, it could hardly be gain said that the Supreme Court since 1937 has been among the least virtuous of modern judicial tribunals."[610]

In fact, over the last fifty years, one of the outstanding features of the Supreme Court of the United States has been the frequency with which it has repudiated its earlier attitude toward questions of constitutionality, not following decisions handed down by its predecessors and overruling many of its earlier decisions, "some of which

---

606 347 US 483 (1954).

607 *Cooper v. Aaron*, 358 US 1 (1958).

608 *Cf.* A. TUNC and S. TUNC, *Le droit des Etats Unies d'Amérique. Sources et techniques*, Paris 1955, p. 174; B. SCHWARTZ, *op. cit.*, p. 159.

609 *Burnet v. Coronado Oil and Gas Co.* 285 US 393 (1932), p. 406.

610 B. SCHWARTZ, *The Supreme Court. Constitutional Revolution in Retrospect*, New York 1957, p. 345.

had been regarded as settled in American law for the better part of a century."[611] This attitude of the Supreme Court has been explained by Justice Reed delivering the opinion of the Court in *Smith* v. *Allwright* (1944), in which a previous constitutional interpretation was overruled, with the following words:

> In reaching this conclusion we are not unmindful of the desirability of continuity of decisions in constitutional questions. However, when convinced of former error, this Court has never felt constrained to follow precedent. In constitutional questions, where corrections depend upon amendments and not upon legislative action, this Court throughout its history has freely exercised its power to re–examine the basis of its constitutional decisions. This has long been accepted practice, and this practice has continued to this day. This is particularly true when the decision believed erroneous is the application of a constitutional principle rather than an interpretation of the constitution to extract the principle itself.[612]

Nevertheless, even in its application to the lower courts, the *stare decisis* principle concerning Supreme Court decisions has different scope depending on the contents of the decision. For instance, in some situations a statute may be held to be invalid, only in its application to the situation before the court and not invalid on its face, in which case the statute may continue to have validity in its application to other situations.[613] The binding effect of a Supreme Court decision, therefore, will depend upon the nature of the attack on the statute, whether on its validity or only on its application to the party by reference to facts peculiar to it.

B. *The Nullity of Unconstitutional Acts and the Retroactive Effects of the Courts Decisions*

As far as the effects of the judicial decision on constitutional issues is concern, additional to the problems posed by the *inter partes* effect and the *stare decisis* doctrine concerning Supreme Court decisions, in a diffuse system of judicial review like the American one, the courts do not annul the statute considered unconstitutional, but only declare its nullity and invalidity, considering the unconstitutional act void and null *ab initio*. This was the general principle applied to the American system during the last century, which implied that the decisions of the Court on matters of constitutionality had *ex–tunc* and retroactive effects. This was the doctrine defined in the circuit Court *Vanhorne's Lessee* v. *Dorrance* case (1795) in which it was considered that a void act

> Never had constitutional existence; it is a dead letter, and of no more virtue or avail, than if it never had. been made... [614]

A hundred years later, (in *United States* v. *Realty* (1895) the Supreme Court expressed the same principle in more conclusive way, by saying that an:

> Unconstitutional act of Congress is the same as if there were no act.[615]

611 B. SCHWARTZ, *American Constitutional Law*, *cit.*, p. 159.

612 *Smith v. Allwright*, 321 US 649 (1944).

613 *Cf.* P.G. KAUPER, *loc. cit.*, pp. 611, 617.

614 *Venhorn's Lessee v. Dorrance*, 2 Dallas, 304 (1795).

615 *United States v. Realty Co.*, 163 US 427 (1895), p. 439.

Previously, in *Norton* v. *Selby County* (1886) the court had also said, that an

> Unconstitutional act is not a law; it confers no rights; it imposes no duties; it affords no protection; it creates no office; it is, in legal contemplation, as inoperative as though it had never been passed.[616]

Thus, the traditional principle of the nullity of the unconstitutional act, and therefore, the declarative effects of the judicial decision that considers a statute void and null, as if "it had never been passed" or if it "never had been made" was also applied in the United States. Consequently, judicial decisions on constitutional questions were considered to have *ex tunc* effects, thus, having retroactive effects.

Nevertheless, the rigidity of this doctrine led to a change in its application, and to establishing whether or not the retroactive effects of the decisions regarding each case in particular would apply, particularly because of the negative or unjust effects that could be produced by the possible decisions of the court regarding the effects already factualy produced by the statute considered invalid, and because of the binding effect of the Supreme Court decisions upon the lower court,. This was expressly stated by Justice Clark in *Linkletter* v. *Walker* (1965), in which the Supreme Court applied new constitutional rules to cases finalised before the promulgation of other rulers. The Court said:

> Petitioner contends that our method of resolving those prior cases demonstrates that an absolute rule of retroaction prevails in the area of constitutional adjudication. However, we believe that the constitution neither prohibits nor requires retrospective effect. As Justice Cardozo said, we think the federal constitution has no voice upon the subject. Once the premise is accepted that we –are neither required to apply, nor prohibited from applying a decision retrospectively, we must then weigh the merits and demerits in each case by looking to the prior history of the rule in question, its purpose and effect, and whether retrospective operation will further or retard its operation...[617]

Therefore, considering that "the past cannot always be erased by a new judicial decision",[618] the retroactive effects of the Supreme Court decisions in constitutional issues has been applied in a relative way. "The questions –said the Supreme Court in *Chicot County Drainage District* v. *Baxter State Bank* (1940)–, are among the most difficult of those that have engaged the attention of courts, state and federal, and it is manifest from numerous decisions that an all–inclusive statement of a principle of absolute retroactive invalidity cannot be justified."[619]

In this sense, Professor J.A.C. Grant said in his classical study on "The legal Effects of a Ruling that a Statute is Unconstitutional", contrary to what the Supreme Court said in *Norton* v. *Selby County* in 1886, "An unconstitutional act may give rise to rights. It may impose duties. It may afford protection. It may even create an office. In short, it may not be as inoperative as though it had never been passed."[620]

---

616 *Norton v. Selby County*, 118 US 425 (1886), p. 442.

617 *Linkletter v. Walker*, 381 US 618 (1965).

618 *Chicot County Drainage District v. Baxter State Bank*, 308 US 371 (1940), p. 374.

619 *Idem*.

620 J.A.C. GRANT, "The Legal Effect of a Ruling that a Statute is Unconstitutional', *Detroit College of Law Review*, 1978, (2), p. 207.

Therefore, the Supreme Court has recognised its authority to give or to deny retroactive effects to its ruling on constitutional issues, and the Supreme Courts of the states have done the same during recent decades.

For instance, in criminal matters, the Courts has given full retroactive effects to its rules when they benefit the prosecuted. In particular it has given retroactive effects to decisions in the field of criminal liability, permitting prisoners on application for *habeas corpus* to secure their release on the grounds that they are being held under authority of a statute which subsequent to their conviction was held to be unconstitutional.[621] The Court has also given retroactive effects to its decisions on constitutional matters, as referred to by Professor J.A.C. Grant, when it considers the rules essential to safeguard against convicting innocent persons, such as the requirement that counsel be furnished at the trial (*Gideon* v. *Wainwright*, 327 US, 335, 1963), or when the accused is asked to plead (*Arsenault* v. *Massachusetts*, 393 US 5, 1968), or when it is sought to revoke the probation status of a convicted criminal because of his subsequent conduct (*McConnell* v. *Rhay*, 393, US, 2, 1968), as well as the rule requiring proof beyond a reasonable doubt (*Ivan* v. *City of New York*, 407 US, 203, 1972). Its ruling concerning the death penalty has also been made fully retroactive (*Witherspoon* v. *Illinois*, 391, US, 510, 1968).[622]

In other criminal cases, the position of the Court has been to give no retroactive effects to its rulings on constitutional issues when it also benefits the prosecuted. As Professor Grant says, in 1977 the Supreme Court held that any change in the interpretation of the constitution that has the effect of punishing acts which were not penalized under the earlier interpretation cannot be applied retroactively, since as it stated in *Marks* v. *United States* (1977), "the notion that persons have a right to fair warning of that conduct which will give rise to criminal penalties, is fundamental to our concept of constitutional liberty."[623]

Therefore, the rule of retroactiveness on prospectiveness of the effects of the Courts decisions in criminal cases is not absolute, and has been applied by the Court considering the justice of its application in each case. Consequently, when the decision has not for instance affected the "fairness of a trial" but only the rights to privacy of a person, the Court has denied the retroactive effects of its ruling. Such was the case in *Linkletter* v. *Walker*, (1965) where Justice Clarke delivering the opinion of the Court stated:

> In ... the ... areas in which we have applied our rule retrospectively the principle that we applied went to the fairness of the trial, the very integrity of the fact finding process. Here ... the fairness of the trial is not under attack. All that petitioner attacks is the admissibility of evidence (illegally seized), the reliability and relevancy of which is not questioned, and which may well have had no effect on the outcome...[624]

---

621 *Ex parte Siebold*, 100 US 371, (1880).

622 J.A.C. GRANT, *loc.cit.*, p. 237.

623 *Marks v. United States*, 430 US 188 (1977), p. 191; J.A.C. GRANT, *loc.cit.*, 238.

624 *Linkletter v Walker*, 381, US, 618 (1965).

Therefore, as Professor Grant reported, when the purpose is merely to protect the privacy of the individual or to improve police standards, as in the case of new rules as to searches through electronic surveillance (*Desist* v. *United States*, 394, US, 244, 1969), or in connection with a lawful arrest (*Hill* v. *California*, 401, US, 797, 1971), police questioning, leading to confessions (*McMann* v. *Richardson*, 397, US, 759, 1970) or the use of incriminating reports filed by the accused (*Mackey* v. *United States*, 401 US, 667, 1971), the doctrine of non retroactiveness adopted in *Stovall* v. *Denno*[625] has been applied.[626]

It must also be mentioned that even in cases of rules related to the idea of the type of trial necessary to guard against convicting the innocent, the rules established by the Supreme Court have been made wholly prospective when to give them retroactive effect would impose what the Court considers unreasonable burdens upon the government brought about at least in part by its reliance upon previous rulings of the Supreme Court. This happened in *De Stefano* v. *Woods* (1968), which established that state criminal trials must be by jury[627] and in *Adam* v. *Illinois* (1972), established the right to counsel at the preliminary hearing whose retroactivity the Court said, "could seriously disrupt the administration of our criminal laws."[628]

On the other hand, in civil cases, it has been considered that the new rule established in a court decision on constitutional matters, cannot disturb property rights or contracts previously made. In this respect, the Supreme Court in *Gelpcke* v. *Dubuque* (1864) considered that a decision of the Supreme Court of Iowa, was to be given prospective effect only, by stating:

> The sound and true rule is, that if the contract, when made, was valid by the laws of the state as then expounded... and administered in its courts of justice, its validity and. obligation cannot be impaired by any subsequent action of legislation, or decision of its courts altering the construction of the law.[629]

This doctrine of prospectiveness was also developed and applied by state supreme courts regarding liability for acts of dependants. For instance the Supreme Court of Illinois in 1958 considered "unjust, unsupported by any valid reason, and (without) ... rightful place in modern day society" the rule previously established by the same Court (1898), that held that a school district cannot be held liable for the careless acts of the drivers of its school buses. In principle, the overruling of the 1898 decision could have led to its application retroactively; nevertheless bearing in mind that its full retroactivity might endanger the fiscal integrity of many small school districts, the Court stated:

> Retrospective application of our decision may result in great hardship to school districts, which have relied on prior decisions upholding the doctrine of tort immunity of school districts. For this reason we feel justice best be served by holding that, except as to the plaintiff

625 *Stovall v. Denno*, 388, US, 293, (1967).

626 J.A.C. GRANT, *loc.cit.*, 237.

627 *De Stefano v. Woods*, 392, US, 631 (1968).

628 *Adams v. Illinois*, 405, US, 278 (1972).

629 68 US (1 Wall) 175 (1864).

in the instant case, the rule herein established shall apply only to cases arising out of future occurrence.[630]

Finally it must also be stated that in administrative cages, the doctrine of *de facto* officers has lead to the adoption of the prospective rule effects of the decisions on judicial review. In this respect, in *State* v. *Carroll* (1871) the Supreme Court of Connecticut stated that a statute "... which creates an office and provides an officer to perform its duties, must have the force of law until set aside as unconstitutional by the courts",[631] thus the invalidity of the office could not affected the acts accomplished by the *de facto* officer.

C. *The Practical Effects of the Decision on Judicial Review*

As we have said, there are no special types of proceeding required for the raising of constitutional issues in the courts; therefore, the constitutional question car be raised incidentally in any type of proceeding. Nevertheless, in the United States, particular types of proceedings and remedies that are usually used for raising constitutional issues have been traditionally identified. These are apart from the declaratory judgment proceeding, the request for an injunction, for a writ of mandamus or for a writ of habeas corpus[632] which result in having concrete and particular effects, referred to constitutional justice.

For instance, the injunction against enforcement of a statute by a prosecutor or by public agencies is the most drastic remedy available in a case raising constitutional issues. It is equity proceeding of preventive and negative effects. It consists in the prohibition established regarding a subject to enforce certain acts that could be prejudicial to other subjects. Therefore, it is a preventive and protective proceeding, and its effects would depend on whether the decision holding a statute invalid considered the statute void in its face or invalid only in its application to factual circumstances peculiar to the person raising the issue. In this respect, Professor P.G. Kauper said, if an injunction is sought against the enforcement of a statute on the grounds that it is void on its face as an impairment of constitutional rights, the court's decree may be broad enough to prevent further enforcement of the statute against any other person, with the practical effect of making the statute completely unenforceable.[633]

Another remedy commonly used for controlling the constitutionality of statutes is the request for a writ of *mandamus*, which consists in a judicial order directed to a public officer, commanding him to perform certain acts regarding the petitioner which he is obliged to perform.[634]

---

630 *Molitor v. Kaneland Community Unit Dist. Nº 302*, 18 III. 2d at 25, 162 N.E. 2d at 96. quoted by J.A.C. GRANT, *loc. cit.*, p. 220.

631 *State v. Canoll*, 38 Conn. 449, (1871), quoted by J.A.C. GRANT, *loc. cit.*, p. 232.

632 G.H. JAFFIN, "Les modes d'introduction du contrôle judiciaire de la constitutionalité des lois aux Etats–Unis", in *Introduction a l'etude du droit comparé, Recueil d'etudes en l'honneur d'Eduard Lambert*, Paris 1938, Vol. II, p. 256.

633 P.G. KAUPER, *loc. cit.*, p. 620.

634 28 US Code 1361.

Finally, another remedy that is also used to test the constitutionality of a statute is the request for a writ of *habeas corpus* through which a person, who is being held in custody on a charge of violating a criminal statute, alleges its invalidity. If the claim in this proceeding is sustained, the court orders the release of the petitioner from official custody.

III. THE DIFFUSE SYSTEM OF JUDICIAL REVIEW IN LATIN AMERICA

In the middle of the 19th century, the American system of judicial review influenced most of the Latin–American systems, which we can say, generally adopted in one way or another, the diffuse system of judicial review. Alexis De Tocqueville's influential book, *Democracy in America*,[635] has been considered as having played a fundamental role in the adoption of the system, particularly regarding the Latin American countries with a federal form of state all of whom adopted a form of constitutional justice, as was the case in Argentina (1860), Mexico (1857), Venezuela (1858) and Brazil (1890). The system was also adopted in other countries like Colombia (1850) which had a brief federal experience, and even without connection with the federal form of state, in the Dominican Republic (1844) where it is still in force.[636]

Most of the Latin American systems of judicial review moved from the original diffuse system towards a mixed system, by adding concentrated aspects of judicial review, or adopting the mixed system from the beginning, but the Argentinean system remained the most similar to the American model,[637] though with its own natural characteristics. The Mexican system also remained as a diffuse system but with the peculiarities of the *juicio de amparo* (trial for constitutional protection), which has produced a unique and complex institution.

That is why when considering the diffuse system of judicial review in Latin America, we will now refer to the Argentinean and Mexican systems, leaving the

---

635 The first edition in Spanish of the book was issued in 1836, one year after the French and English edition. On the influence of the DE TOCQUEVILLE book on the matter, see J. CARPIZO and H. FIX–ZAMUDIO, "La necesidad y la legitimidad de la revisión judicial en América Latina. Desarrollo reciente", in *Boletín Mexicano de Derecho Comparado*, 52, 1985, p. 33; R.D. BAKER, *Judicial Review in México. A Study of the Amparo Suit*, Austin 1971, pp. 15, 33.

636 The 1844 constitution, as well as the 1966 constitution (Art. 46) established that 'are null and void all Laws, Decrees, Resolutions, Regulations or Acts contrary to the constitution'. Consequently all the Courts can declare an act unconstitutional and not applicable to the concrete case. *Cf.* M BERGES CHUPANI, "Report" in *Memoria de la Reunión de Cortes Superiores de Justicia de Ibero–America, El Caribe, España y Portugal*, Caracas 1983, p. 380.

637 A. E. GHIGLIANI, *Del control jurisdiccional de constitucionalidad*, Buenos Aires 1952, who speaks about "Northamerican filiation" of the judicial control of constitutionality in Argentinian law, p. 6, 55, 115. *Cf.* R. BIELSA, *La protección constitucional y el recurso extraordinario. Jurisdicción de la Corte Suprema*, Buenos Aires 1958, p. 116; J.A.C. GRANT, "El control jurisdiccional de la constitucionalidad de las Leyes: una contribución de las Américas a la ciencia política", *Revista de la Facultad de Derecho de México*, UNAM, T. XII, 45, 1962, p. 652; C.J. FRIEDRICH, *The Impact of American Constitutionalism Abroad*, Boston 1967, p. 83.

analysis of the Brazilian, Colombian and Venezuelan systems to when we study the mixed systems of judicial review.

1. The Argentinean System

A. *Judicial Control of the Constitutionality as a Power of All Courts*

The constitution of the Republic of Argentina of 1860 established in articles 31 and 100, in terms very similar to those of the American constitution, the principles of constitutional supremacy and the role of the judiciary.

Article 31, in similar terms to the "supremacy clause" of the American constitution, established:

> This constitution, the laws of the Nation that the Congress consequently approves and the treaties with foreign powers, are the supreme law of the Nation, and the authorities of each Province are obliged to conform to it, notwithstanding any contrary disposition which the provincial laws or Constitutions might contain.

On the other hand, article 100 referring to judicial power, established:

> The Supreme Court and the inferior Court of the Nation, are competent to try and decide all cases related to aspects ruled by the constitution, by the laws of the Nation and by the Treaties with foreign nations.

Therefore, in similar terms to the American constitution, the 1860 Argentinean constitution established no norm expressly conferring no judicial review power upon the Supreme Court or the other courts. Thus, in a similar way to the American process, judicial review in Argentina was also a creation of the Supreme Court, based on the principles of supremacy of the constitution and judicial duty when applying the law; and the first case in which it was exercised regarding a federal statute was the *Sojo* case, (1887), also concerning the unconstitutionality of a law that tried to enlarge the original jurisdiction of the Supreme Court[638] as was the *Marbury* v. *Madison* case.

Nevertheless, the question of the powers of the judiciary to control the constitutionality of legislation was a matter of discussion in the Panama Constitutional Convention in 1857–1858, where the predominant opinion on the subject was: first, the character of the constitution as a supreme law and the power of the courts to maintain that supremacy over the laws which infringed upon it; second, the limits imposed over the constituted powers by popular sovereignty, so that laws contrary to the principles embodied in the constitution, could not be binding on the courts; and

---

638 *Cf.* A.E. GHIGLIANI, *op. cit.,* p. 5; R. BIELSA, *op. cit.* p. 41, 43, 179 who speaks about a "pretorian creation" of judicial review by the Supreme Court, *op. cit.,* p. 179. *Cf.* J.R. VANOSSI and P.F. UBERTONE, *Instituciones de defensa de la Constitución en la Argentina*, UNAM, Congreso Internacional sobre la Constitución y su defensa, México 1982, (mimeo), p. 4; H. QUIROGA LAVIE, *Derecho constitucional*, Buenos Aires 1978, p. 481. Previously in 1863 the firsts Supreme Court decisions where adopted in constitutional matters but refered to provincial and executive acts. *Cf.* A.E. GHIGLIANI, *op. cit.*, p. 58.

third, that the judiciary was precisely the branch of the state organs which ought to have enough power to interpret the constitution regarding the other state powers.[639]

Therefore, through the work of the courts, the Argentinean system of judicial review has been developed over the last century as a diffuse system[640] in which all the courts have the power to declare the unconstitutionality of legislative acts, treaties,[641] executive and administrative acts and judicial decisions, whether at national or provincial levels.[642] This power of judicial review is, of course, reserved to the courts and the executive cannot decide not to apply a statute on unconstitutional grounds.

Therefore, in Argentina, the power to control the constitutionality of state acts is not reserved to one single judicial body or a group of them; it concerns all courts, of course, within the scope of the jurisdiction that each of them has.

In Argentina, being a federal state, the organisation of the judiciary led to two court systems established from their origin following the American model:[643] National and provincial courts. The provincial courts have jurisdiction over all matters of "ordinary law," (*derecho común*) like civil, commercial, criminal, labour, social security, and mining law and public provincial law (constitutional and administrative provincial law). In each Province there are courts of first and second instances, and at their apex a Superior Provincial Court.

At the national level, the national courts have jurisdiction over all matters regulated by "federal law"; particularly concerning constitutional and administrative law cases and in all cases in which the nation is a party or foreign diplomatic agents are involved. The organisation of the national courts is as follows: National courts with territorial jurisdiction in the first instance; national chambers of appeals, in the second instance, and at the apex the Supreme Court of Justice, that also acts as a third instance.[644]

The Supreme Court of Justice, the only judicial body created in the constitution and considering itself "final interpreter of the constitution" or as the defendant of the constitution",[645] has two sorts of jurisdiction: original and appellate. The original jurisdiction is established in the constitution and, therefore, is not enlargeable by

639 *Cf.* A.E. GHIGLIANI, *op. cit.*, p. 58.

640 N.P. SAGÜES, *Recurso Extraordinario*, Buenos Aires 1984, Vol. I, p. 91. J.R. VANOSSI and P.F. UBERTONE, *op. cit.* p. 2, 14. See also J.R. VANOSSI, *Teoría constitucional*, Buenos Aires, Vol. II, *Supremacía y control de constitucionalidad*, Buenos Aires 1976, p. 155.

641 In particular, regarding the unconstitutionality of Treaties and the posibility of the Courts to control them, A.G. GHIGLIANI, *op. cit.*, p. 62; J.R. VANOSSI, *Aspectos del recurso extraordinario de inconstitucionalidad*, Buenos Aires 1966, p. 91, and *Teoría constitucional*, *op. cit.*, Vol. II, p. 277.

642 *Cf.* R. BIELSA, *op. cit.*, pp. 120–148. J.R. VANOSSI and P.F. UBERTONE, *doc. cit.*, p. 6.

643 *Cf.* R. BIELSA, *op. cit.*, p. 57; A.E. GHIGLIANI, *op. cit.*, p. 55.

644 *Cf.* J.R. VANOSSI and P.F. UBERTONE, *doc. cit.*, p. 14–18; A.E. GHIGLIANI, *op. cit.*, p. 76.

645 R. BIELSA, *op. cit.*, p. 270; J.R. VANOSSI and P.F. UBERTONE, *doc. cit.*, p. 18.

statute, and concerns all matters related to ambassadors, ministers and foreign consuls and to which the Provinces are party.[646]

In its appellate jurisdiction, the Supreme Court has jurisdiction through two sorts of appeals: ordinary and extraordinary. In its appellate jurisdiction through ordinary appeals, the Supreme Court has the power of reviewing the decisions of the national chambers of appeal in the following cases:

1. Cases in which the nation is a party according to an amount fixed periodically;
2. Cases concerning extradition of criminals sought by foreign countries.
3. Cases concerning the seizure of ships in time of war and other cases concerning maritime law.[647]

In these cases of appellate jurisdiction through ordinary appeal, the Supreme Court acts as a court of third instance and last resort reviewing the whole case decided by the national chambers of appeals.

However, as we have said, the appellate jurisdiction of the Supreme Court of Justice can also be exercised through what has been called an "extraordinary appeal" that is in fact an "extraordinary recourse" that the party in a case decided by the national chambers of appeals and by the Superior Courts of the Provinces can bring before the supreme Court, in particular cases related to constitutional issues and with special conditions. This is, undoubtedly, the mean through which the Supreme Court normally decides upon the final interpretation of the constitution when reviewing the constitutionality of state acts, and consequently it is the most important mean for judicial review.

Before studying this "extraordinary recourse" we will refer to the general trends of the incidental character of the Argentinean diffuse system and its consequences.

B. *The Incidental Character of Judicial Review*

In effect, as a diffuse system of judicial review, the Argentinean system is essentially an incidental one, in which the question of constitutionality is not the principal object of a process; thus the constitutional issue can be at any moment and at any stage of any proceeding. This incidental character has led to considering the Argentinean System of judicial review, as an "indirect" control system,[648] because the constitutional issue can only be raised in a judicial controversy, case or process, normally through an exception, at any moment before the decision is adopted by the court, and therefore not necessarily in the *litis contestatio* of the proceeding.[649]

The principal condition for raising constitutional questions is that they can only be raised in a "judicial case" or litigation between parties;[650] therefore, they cannot

646 Art. 101.

647 *Cf.* R. BIELSA, *op. cit.*, p. 60–61; J.R. VANOSSI and P.F. UBERTONE, *doc. cit.*, p. 19.

648 A.E. GHIGLIANI, *op. cit.*, p. 75.

649 A.E. GHIGLIANI, *op. cit.*, p. 76.

650 Art. 100 of the constitution; *Cf.* R. BIELSA, *op. cit.*, p. 213, 214; A.E. GHIGLIANI, *op. cit.*, p. 75; J.R. VANOSSI and P.F. UBERTONE, *doc. cit.*, p. 23.

be raised as an abstract question before a court, and the courts cannot render declarative decisions upon unconstitutional matters.[651]

Nevertheless, the existence of a case or controversy in which the constitutional question could be raised is not only necessary, it is also indispensable that the question be raised by a party in the process with due interest in the matter, that is to say, which alleges a particular injury in his own right caused by the statute considered invalid.[652]

Consequently, the court on its own cannot raise constitutional issues in the Argentinean system. Thus, even if the court is convinced of the unconstitutionality of a statute, if a party has not raised the question, the Court is bound to apply the Statute to the decision of the case.[653] In this respect, it must be stressed that even though this has been the judicial doctrine invariably applied by courts, some authors have considered that the constitutional questions can be decided by courts without being raised by a party, based on the principle of constitutional supremacy and the notion of "public order."[654]

Nevertheless, an exemption to the need for party intervention when raising the constitutional issue has been established by the Supreme Court, allowing that the court can consider constitutional questions on its own, only in matters concerning the jurisdiction of the courts themselves and their functional autonomy. Consequently, the Supreme Court decided upon the unconstitutionality of a statute that enlarged its original jurisdiction of the supreme Court of Justice established in the constitution, although not being raised by a party.[655]

Furthermore and related to the incidental or indirect character of judicial review in the Argentinean system, the constitutional question raised in a case particularly due to the presumption of constitutionality of all statutes,[656] must be of an unavoiding character, in the sense that its decision must be essential to the resolution of the case which depends on it.[657] Moreover, the constitutional question must be clear and undoubted. Therefore, the declaration of unconstitutionality being considered an act of extreme gravity and the last ratio of the legal order, the court must abstain its consideration when there are doubts about the issue.[658] Thus when an interpretation of the statute

651 *Cf.* R. BIELSA, *op. cit.*, p. 213, 214; A.E. GHIGLIANI, *op. cit.*, p. 80; S.M. LOZADA, *Derecho Constitucional Argentino*, Buenos Aires 1972, Vol. I, p. 342.

652 S.M. LOZADA, *op. cit.*, p. 342; A.E. GHIGLIANI, *op.cit.*, p. 82; J.R. VANOSSI and P.E. UBERTONE, *doc. cit.*, p.23.

653 R. BIELSA, *op. cit.*, p. 198, 214; H. QUIROGA LAVIE, *op. cit.*, p. 479.

654 G. BIDART CAMPOS, *El derecho constitucional del poder*, Vol. II, Chap. XXIX; J.R. VANOSSI, *Teoría constitucional*, *op. cit.*, Vol. II, p. 318, 319.

655 *Cf.* J.R. VANOSSI and P.E. UBERTONE, *doc. cit.*, 25; .R. BIELSA, *op. cit.*, 255; H. QUIROGA LAVIE, *op. cit.*, p. 479.

656 A.E. GHIGLIANI, *op. cit.*, p. 89, 90.

657 A.E. GHIGLIANI, *op. cit.*, p. 89; S.M. LOSADA, *op. cit*, p. 341.

658 H. QUIROGA LAVIE, *op. cit.*, p. 480.

avoiding the consideration of the constitutional question is possible the court must follow this path.[659]

Finally, it must be said that in the Argentinean system, the Supreme Court of Justice has developed the same exception to judicial review established in the American system, concerning political questions, even though the constitution does not expressly establish anything on the matter.[660] These political questions are related to the "acts of government" of "political acts" doctrine developed in continental European law, and within which we can mention the following: the declaration of state of siege; the declaration of federal intervention in the provinces; the declaration of "public use" for means of expropriation; the declaration of war; the declaration of emergency to approve certain direct tax contributions; acts concerning foreign relations; the recognition of new foreign states or new foreign state governments; the expulsion of aliens, etc., In general, within these political questions there are acts exercised by the political powers of the state in accordance with powers exclusively and directly attributed to them in the constitution,[661] which can be considered the key element for their identification.

C. *The "Extraordinary Recourse" before the Supreme Court of Justice and Judicial Review*

We have said that the Supreme Court of Justice is vested in the Argentinean system, like it is in the United States, with two sorts of jurisdiction: original and appellate jurisdiction, and in the latter two other sorts can be distinguished: ordinary appellate jurisdiction and "extraordinary appellate jurisdiction" that can be exercised by the Supreme Court through the so called "extraordinary recourse", which accomplishes a similar result to the request for writ of *certiorari* in the United States Supreme Court activities.

But of course, the "extraordinary recourse" is quite different to the American request for writ of *certiorari*, in the sense that the Supreme Court of Justice does not have discretionary powers in accepting extraordinary recourses. Thus, in the Argentinean system, all the appellate jurisdiction of the Supreme Court, whether ordinary or extraordinary, is a mandatory jurisdiction, exercised as a consequence of a right the parties have, whether to appeal or to introduce the extraordinary recourse.

Nevertheless, the difference between the ordinary appeal and the extraordinary recourse is that although called "extraordinary appeal" this recourse is not properly an appeal: it is rather an autonomous recourse. When it is exercised, the Supreme Court does not act as a mere third instance court,[662] particularly because the Court does not review the motives of the judicial decision under consideration, regarding the facts; its power of review being concentrated only in aspects of law regarding

---

659 A.E. GHIGLIANI, *op. cit.*, p. 91.

660 J.R. VANOSSI and P.E. UBERTONE, *doc. cit.*, p. 11.

661 *Cf.* A.E. GHIGLIANI, *op. cit.*, p. 85; H. QUIROGA LAVIE, *op. cit.*, p. 482; S.M. LOSADA, *op. cit.*, p. 343; J.R. VANOSSI and P.E. UBERTONE, *doc. cit.*, p. 11, 12.

662 *Cf.* N. P. SAGÜES, *op. cit.*, p. 270; pp. 185, 221, 228, 275.

constitutional questions. That is why it has been said that the Supreme Court as a consequence of an extraordinary recourse, "does not act *jure litigatoris*" but *jure constitutionis*, does not judge a *questio facti*, but a *questio juris*."[663]

This substantive difference between the function of the Supreme Court as a consequence of the exercise of an appeal or an extraordinary recourse is followed by another formal difference, particularly, that contrary to the appeal, the extraordinary recourse must be motivated and founded on constitutional reasons.[664]

Even though it is called "extraordinary" it must be said that the ordinary appeal being reduced to the review of very few decisions of the National Chambers of Appeals, the "extraordinary recourse" is the judicial means through which the parties can most commonly reach the Supreme Court of Justice in order to obtain judicial review of constitutionality of state acts.[665] Particularly because, as we have mentioned, not only the definitive decisions of the National Chambers of Appeals can be the object of an extraordinary recourse but also the definitive decisions of the Superior Courts of the Provinces where the generality of ordinary law cases reach.

Now, the exercise of this extraordinary recourse is submitted to various particular rules, which must be stressed:

First of all, the extraordinary recourse can only be exercised in connection with constitutional matters, thus its importance regarding judicial review. In this respect, the extraordinary recourse can be exercised in three cases:

a. When in a case the question of validity of a treaty, an act of Congress or of another authority exercised in the Nation's name has been raised, and the judicial decision has been against the validity of the particular act;

b. When the validity of an act or decree of the Provincial authorities has been questioned on the grounds of its repugnance to the constitution, treaties or acts of Congress, and the judicial decision has been in favour of the validity of the particular act.

c. When the interpretation of a clause of the constitution, of a treaty or of an act of Congress or other national act has been questioned, and the judicial decision has been against the validity of a title, right, privilege or exemption founded in the said clause which has been a matter of the case.[666]

As a creation of the Supreme Court of Justice doctrine, the extraordinary recourse against "arbitrary judicial decisions" has also been accepted, being considered arbitrary judicial decisions those in which the right to defend one self in a proceeding is said to have been violated. It has also been accepted in cases of so called "institutional gravity", when the Supreme Court can be reached even though the

663 R. BIELSA, *op. cit.*, p. 222

664 *Cf.* R. BIELSA, *op. cit.*, pp. 245, 252.

665 *Cf.* J.R. VANOSSI and P.E. UBERTONE, *doc. cit.*, p. 19.

666 Statute 48, Art. 14. *Cf.* J.R. VANOSSI and P.E. UBERTONE, *cit.* p. 20; R. BIELSA, *op. cit.*, p. 210, 211; N.P. SAGÜES, *op. cit.*, p. 272.

extraordinary recourse would be normally inadmissible; and in cases when an "effective deprivation of justice" has been committed.[667]

The second rule referred to the admissibility of the extraordinary recourse states that the constitutional question must have been discussed in the proceeding in the lower courts, and considered in its decision, before it can be brought before the Supreme Court through the extraordinary recourse.[668] Therefore, the Supreme Court has rejected the recourse when the constitutional issue has not been discussed in the lower courts and has not been considered in the decision.[669] Furthermore, the constitutional issue must have been maintained in the various judicial instances in the lower courts and not abandoned by the interested party. On the contrary, the Supreme Court would reject the extraordinary. Recourse.[670]

In the third place, all the other aspects of the incidental character of judicial review already mentioned apply, of course, to the admissibility of the extraordinary recourse, and particularly the fact that it must be exercised by a party with direct interests in the matter, whose rights are affected by the decision regarding the invalidity of a statute, and that the solution of the constitutional question must be unavoidable and indispensable for the decision of the case. Regarding standing, it must be pointed out that in the Argentinean system, it is expressly accepted that public bodies whose acts have been questioned on the grounds of unconstitutionality and also the Public Prosecutor, have the quality of party regarding the exercise of the extraordinary recourse.[671]

D. *The Effects of the Decision on Judicial Review*

Finally, in the Argentinean system of judicial review, as a pure diffuse system, we must refer to the effects of the decision adopted by the courts when exercising their powers of judicial review of constitutionality.

First of all, it must be said that judicial decisions adopted on matters of constitutionality, whether adopted by inferior courts or by the Supreme Court when they consider a law to be unconstitutional, simply do not apply the invalid statute by giving preference to the constitution, but do not annul it. The courts in Argentina do not have the power to annul or repeal a law. That power is reserved to the legislator, and the only thing they can do is to refuse its application to the concrete case when they consider it unconstitutional.[672] The statute, therefore, when considered unconstitutional and non–applicable by the judge, is considered null and void, with no effect whatsoever[673] in the particular case. This leads to the consideration of the retroactive effect of the decision, bearing in mind its declarative character, thus *ex tunc, pro*

---

667 *Cf.* J.R. VANOSSI and P.E. UBERTONE, *doc. cit.*, p. 20.

668 *Cf.* R. BIELSA, *op. cit.*, pp. 190, 202, 203, 205, 209.

669 *Cf.* R. BIELSA, *op. cit.*, p. 204.

670 *Cf.* R. BIELSA, *op. cit.*, p. 260.

671 *Cf.* R. BIELSA, *op. cit.,* pp. 237, 238.

672 *Cf.* R. BIELSA, *op. cit.*, pp. 197, 198, 345; N.P. SAGÜES, *op. cit.,* p. 156.

673 *Cf.* A.E. GHIGLIANI, *op. cit.*, p. 95.

praeterito. We insist, however, that the statute remains valid and generally applicable and even the same court can change its criteria about its unconstitutionality and apply it in the future.[674]

That is why these effects of the judicial decision on constitutional matters, in the Argentinean system are strictly *inter partes* effect, a consequence of the diffuse character of the system. Thus the decision considering the nullity of a statute has effect only in connection with the particular process where the question has been raised and between the parties which have intervened in it and, therefore, has no *erga omnes* effects at all.[675]

On the other hand, in the Argentinean system, the decision on judicial review, even the decisions of the Supreme Court on constitutional issues are not obligatory for the other courts or the inferior courts.[676] Moreover, even though in the 1949 constitutional reform it was expressly established that the interpretation adopted by the Supreme Court of Justice upon the articles of the constitution would be considered binding on the national and provincial courts,[677] this article of the constitution was later repealed and the situation today is the absolute power of all courts to render their judgment autonomously with their own constitutional interpretation.

Nevertheless, it is certain that the Supreme Court of Justice being the highest court in the country with wide appellate jurisdiction, particularly through the extraordinary recourse, its decisions have a definitive influence upon all the inferior courts particularly when a doctrine has been clearly and reiteratedly established by the Court.[678]

E. *The recourse for* amparo *and judicial review*

Finally, regarding the Argentinean system, discussions have arisen concerning the possibility of the exercise of the diffuse system of judicial review, by the courts, when deciding recourse for *amparo* (constitutional protection) brought before them for the protection of fundamental rights. These recourses for constitutional protection can also be considered a creation of the courts,[679] particularly of the Supreme Court, beginning with the well known *Angel Siri* case decision of 27 December 1957,[680] in which the competence of ordinary courts to protect the fundamental rights of citizens, against violation from public authorities actions or from individu-

---

674 *Cf.* R. BIELSA, *op. cit.*, p. 196; A.E. GHIGLIANI, *op. cit.*, p. 92, 97; N. P. SAGÜES, *op. cit.*, p. 177.

675 *Cf.* H. QUIROGA LAVIE, *op. cit.*, p. 479.

676 *Cf.* R. BIELSA, *op. cit.*, pp. 49, 198, 267; A.E. GHIGLIANI, *op. cit.*, pp. 97, 98.

677 Art. 95 of the 1949 Constitution. *Cf.* C.A. AYANAGARAY, *Efectos de la declaración de inconstitucionalidad*, Buenos Aires 1955, p. 11; R. BIELSA, *op. cit.*, p. 268.

678 *Cf.* J.R. VANOSSI and P.E. UBERTONE, *doc. cit.*, p. 32.

679 *Cf.* G. R. CARRIO, *Algunos aspectos del recurso de amparo,* Buenos Aires 1959, p. 9; J. R. VANOSSI, *Teoría constitucional*, *cit.*, Vol. II, p.277.

680 See G. R. CARRIO, *op. cit.*, p.10.

als was definitively accepted,[681] through a special judicial means known as the *recurso de amparo*.

Now since its acceptance and despite the diffuse system of judicial review followed in Argentina, the Supreme Court established the criteria of the incompetence of the *amparo* judge to review the constitutionality of legislation, reducing the powers of the judge of *amparo* to decide only on acts or facts that could violate fundamental rights. Thus it was established that the *amparo* could not be granted when the complaint contained the allegation of unconstitutionality of a law on which the said acts or facts were based. Thus, the Supreme Court considered that the judicial decision in cases of recourse for *amparo* could not have declarative effects regarding the unconstitutionality of laws, due to the summarised nature of its proceeding.[682] This doctrine was followed later by law 16.986 of 18 October 1966 about the recourse for *amparo*, in which it was expressly established that the "action for constitutional protection (*amparo*) will not be admissible when the decision upon the invalidity of the act will require.... the declaration of the unconstitutionality of laws, decrees or ordinances."[683]

Nevertheless, and more recently in 1967, the Supreme Court, without declaring the unconstitutionality of the above mentioned disposition of law 16.986 in the *Outon* case,[684] in an implicit way, decided its inapplicability and accepted the criteria that when considering *amparo* cases, the courts have the power to review the unconstitutionality of legislation, which has been supported by the leading constitutional law authors of the country.[685]

Anyway, the acceptance of this means of judicial review of legislation, through the action for protection (*amparo*), could lead to a direct action of unconstitutionality, although of a diffuse character, which differs from the incidental normal character of the constitutional review system, which is commonly exercised as a consequence of an exception raised by a party in a concrete process, whose main objective is not the constitutional question.

On the contrary, in the action of *amparo* when founded on reasons of unconstitutionality of a law on which the concrete act that violates the fundamental right that the petitioners seek to be protected is based the unconstitutionality of the laws becomes a direct issue of the action itself. That is why it has been said that by accept-

---

681 See the Samuel Kot Ltd. case of 5 September, 1958, S.V. LINARES QUINTANA, *Acción de amparo*, Buenos Aires 1960, p. 25.

682 See the *Aserradero Clipper SRL* case 1961), J. R. VANOSSI, *Teoría constitucional, cit.*, Vol. II, p. 286.

683 Art. 2,d.

684 Outon case of 29 March 1967. J. R. VANOSSI, *Teoría constitucional, cit.*, Vol. II, p. 288.

685 G. J. BIDART CAMPOS, *Régimen legal del amparo,* 1969; G. J. BIDART CAMPOS, "El control de constitucionalidad en el juicio de amparo y la arbitrariedad o ilegalidad del acto lesivo", *Jurisprudencia argentina*, 23–4–1969; N. P. SAGÜES, "El juicio de amparo y el planteo de inconstitucionalidad", *Jurisprudencia argentina*, 20–7–1973; J. R. VANOSSI, *Teoría constitucional, cit.*, Vol. II, pp.288–292.

ing this feature of the action for protection, the Supreme Court has opened the way to a new direct means of judicial review of constitutionality of legislation.[686]

2. The mexican system of judicial review of the constitutionality of legislation

Also under the influence of the North American system of judicial review, as described by Alexis De Tocqueville,[687] a diffuse system of judicial review was adopted in the Mexican 1847 constitution,[688] by assigning to the federal courts the duty to "protect" the rights and freedoms established in the constitution, against any attack from the Legislative and Executive powers either of the Federation or of the states.

Article 25 of the Acts of Reforms of 1847, established:

> The courts of the federation will protect (*ampararán*) any inhabitant of the Republic in the exercise and conservation of the rights granted to him in the constitution and the constitutional laws, against any attack by the Legislative or Executive powers, whether of the Federation or of the states; the said courts being limited to give protection in the particular case to which the process refers, without making any general declaration regarding the statute or the act which brings it about.[689]

A similar article was definitively adopted later in the 1857 constitution, which produced, through a very important and special process, a unique jurisdictional institution, known as the *juicio de amparo*, ("trial for protection"), based today on the provisions of the constitutional text published in 1982, following the lines established in the 1917 constitution.

This "trial for protection" although it is the only judicial means which can be used for judicial review of the constitutionality of legislation, does not only have that purpose being a very complex institution which comprises at least five different judicial actions and proceedings which are generally differentiated between in countries with a civil law tradition. That is why before referring to the so called *amparo* against laws, a modality of the trial for protection which could be considered as a particular means of judicial review of the constitutionality of legislation, we will refer to the various aspects comprised in the trial for protection (*amparo*) and its relation to judicial review.

---

686 J. R. VANOSSI, *Teoría constitucional*, *cit.*, Vol. II, p.291.

687 *Cf.* R.D. BAKER, *Judicial Review in México. A Study of the Amparo Suit*, Texas 1971, p. 15, 33.

688 The Constitution of Yucatan of 1841 adopted the institution of *amparo* only in relation to that State. *Cf.* R.D. BAKER, *op. cit.*, p. 17.

689 See the text in J. CARPIZO, *La Constitución Mexicana de 1917*, México 1979, p. 271; R.D. BAKER, *op. cit.*, p. 23; and H. FIX–ZAMUDIO, "Algunos aspectos comparativos del derecho de amparo en México y Venezuela", *Libro Homenaje a la Memoria de Lorenzo Herrera Mendoza*, Caracas 1970, Vol. II, p. 336. See also H. FIX–ZAMUDIO "A Brief Introduction to the Mexican Writ of Amparo", *California Western International Law Journal*, San Diego 1977, p. 313.

A. *The trial of* amparo *and the diffuse system of judicial review*

The present bases of the trial for *amparo* are established directly in the constitution, which first of all, reserves the proceeding to the jurisdiction of the federal courts. In this respect, article 103 of the constitution states:

> Art. 103. The federal courts shall decide all controversies that arise:
>
> i. Out of law or acts of the authorities that violate individual guarantees;
>
> ii. Because of laws or acts of the federal authority restricting or encroaching on the sovereignty of the states;
>
> iii. Because of laws or acts of State authorities that invade the sphere of federal authority.

Therefore, only the federal courts have the power of judicial review and the trial for *amparo* can only be brought before them.[690]

The basic constitutional provisions related to this trial for *amparo* are established at the beginning of article 107 of the constitution:

> A trial for *amparo* shall always be held at the instance of the injured party.
>
> II. The judgment shall always be such that it affects only private individuals being limited to affording them shelter (*ampararlos*) and protection in the special cases to which the complaint refers, without making any general declaration as to the law or act on which the complaint is based.

In accordance with the entire provisions of this article 107 of the constitution, and of the regulations of the *Amparo* Law, the trial for *amparo* originally sought as a proceeding for the protection of constitutional rights and freedoms, today comprises five different aspects which in most civil law countries correspond to five different judicial proceedings. These five different aspects of the trial for *amparo*, have been systematised by Professor Héctor Fix–Zamudio,[691] as follows:

The first aspect of the trial for *amparo* is the so called *amparo de la libertad* (protection of liberty) in which the *amparo* proceeding functions as a judicial means for the protection of fundamental rights established in the constitution. In this respect the trial for *amparo* could be equivalent to the request for a writ of *habeas corpus* when it seeks the protection of personal liberty, but can also serve as the protection of all other fundamental rights established in articles 1 to 29 when violated by an act of an authority.[692]

---

690 *Cf.* R.D. BAKER, *op. cit.*, p. 91; J.A.C. GRANT, "El control jurisdiccional de la constitucionalidad de las leyes: una contribución de las Americas a la ciencia politica", *Revista de la Facultad de Derecho de México*, Vol. XII, 45, 1962, p. 657.

691 H. FIX–ZAMUDIO, *El juicio de amparo*, México 1964, p. 243, 377; H. FIX–ZAMUDIO, "Reflexiones sobre la naturaleza procesal del amparo", *Revista de la Facultad de Derecho de México*, 56, 1964, p. 980. H. FIX–ZAMUDIO, "Algunos aspectos comparativos del derecho de amparo en México y Venezuela", *loc. cit.*, p. 345; H. FIX–ZAMUDIO, "Lineamientos fundamentales del proceso social agrario en el derecho mexicano" in *Atti della Seconda Assemblea. Istituto di Dirito Agrario Internazionale a Comparato*, Vol I, Milán 1964, p. 402.

692 *Cf.* R.D. BAKER, *op. cit.*, p. 92.

The second aspect of the trial of *amparo* is that it also proceeds against judicial decisions[693] when it is alleged that they have incorrectly applied legal provisions, which results in the so called *amparo judicial* or *amparo casación*, that is to say, in a judicial recourse very similar to the recourse of cassation that exists in civil and criminal procedural law in the civil law countries, to control the legality of judicial decisions.

The third aspect of the trial for *amparo* is the so–called *amparo administrativo* through which it is possible to impugn administrative acts that violate the constitution or the statutes.[694] This aspect of the trial for *amparo* results in a means for judicial review of administrative action, equivalent to the French born *contentieux administratif* extended to almost all civil law countries.

The fourth aspect of the trial for *amparo* is the so called *amparo agrario* which is set up for the protection of peasants against acts of the agrarian authorities which could affect their agrarian rights, regulated by the agrarian reform provisions particularly referred to collective rural property.[695]

Finally, the fifth aspect of the trial for *amparo*, is the so called *amparo contra leyes* (*amparo* against laws), which can be used to impugn statutes that violate the constitution, which results in a means of judicial review of the constitutionality of legislation, exercised in a direct way in the absence of any administrative act of enforcement or judicial act of application of the statute considered unconstitutional. This aspect of the trial for *amparo* has been considered as the most specific in constitutional justice aspects.[696]

In all these five aspects of the trial for *amparo*, this particular means of constitutional judicial protection can be used as a means of judicial review of the constitutionality of legislative acts, in which cases they have the common trends of the diffuse system of judicial review, the fifth aspect of the *amparo* against laws, having additional peculiarities.

In effect, all the four first mentioned aspects of the trial for *amparo* can be used as a means for judicial review of legislation when a constitutional question, having been raised in a particular proceeding, the courts decide the case, based on a statute considered to be unconstitutional. In such cases, the party which alleges being injured in its private rights or interests by the decision, can exercise a recourse of *amparo* against the judicial decision, seeking judicial review of legislation.[697] In these cases, the recourse of *amparo*, being a review of a judicial decision, must be

---

693 Art. 107, III, V.

694 Art. 107, IV.

695 Art. 107, II.

696 H. FIX–ZAMUDIO, "Algunos problemas que plantea el amparo contra leyes", *Boletín del Instituto de Derecho Comparado de México*, UNAM, 37, 1960, 15, 20.

697 H. FIX–ZAMUDIO, "Aspectos comparativos del derecho de amparo..." *loc. cit.* p. 358, 359; "Algunos problemas que plantea el amparo...", *loc. cit.*, p. 22, 23.

brought before a Collegiate Circuit Court or the Supreme Court of Justice, according to their respective jurisdictions.[698]

In cases of this direct *amparo* brought before the Collegiate Circuit Courts, the constitution confers the power of reviewing them, only when constitutional issues are involved, to the Supreme Court. In particular, the constitution states:

> Decisions, in direct *amparo* rendered by a Collegiate Circuit Court are not revisable unless the decision involves the unconstitutionality of a law or establishes a direct interpretation of a provision of the constitution, in which case it may be taken to the Supreme Court of Justice, limited exclusively to the decision of actual constitutional questions.[699]

Nevertheless, the same constitutional provision states, the Collegiate Circuit Courts decisions in direct *amparo* are not revisable if they are based "on a precedent established by the Supreme Court of Justice as to the constitutionality of a law or the direct interpretation of a provision of the constitution."

Anyway, in all these cases of *amparo*, judicial review of legislation has an incidental character regarding a concrete judicial proceeding in which the constitutional question is raised and which brings about the use of the "recourse" of *amparo*, against the judicial decision which applied the unconstitutional statute.

Judicial review of legislation through the trial for *amparo*, therefore, has the general trends of the diffuse systems of judicial review according to the North American model,[700] even though with a few very important particular features which result from this unique judicial proceeding.

First of all, as we mentioned, the jurisdiction for a trial for *amparo* being reserved to the federal courts, judicial review of the constitutionality of legislation in Mexico is not a power of all courts but attributed only to the federal courts.

Secondly, the *amparo* trial being initiated either through a recourse of *amparo* in its first four aspects or through an action in the fifth aspect of the *amparo* against laws, is always developed against a "public authority", whether it be the judge who has dictated the judicial decision or the administrative authority that has produced the administrative act which are both the object of the recourse of *amparo*; or the legislative authorities that have approved the statute which is the object of the *amparo* against laws action. This aspect reveals another substantial difference between the Mexican system and the general diffuse system, in which the parties in the process in which a constitutional question is raised, continue to be the same.[701]

As we have said, in the first four aspects of the trial for *amparo,* the proceedings are initiated through a recourse of *amparo* normally exercised against a judicial decision, the situation being different in the fifth aspect of the trial for *amparo,* so called *amparo* against laws, in which judicial review of constitutionality of legislation is sought through an "action of unconstitutionality", rather than through a re-

698 Art. 107, V,VI. *Cf.* H. FIX–ZAMUDIO, "Algunos problemas que plantea el amparo...", *loc. cit.*, p. 22

699 Art. 107, IX.

700 J.A.C. GRANT, *loc. cit.*, p. 657.

701 *Idem*, p. 657–661.

course, which action is exercised against the legislative bodies that approved the challenged statute.

B. *The* amparo *against Laws*

In effect, as we have said, one of the five aspects of the trial for *amparo* is the so called "*amparo* against laws", whose peculiarity regarding the other aspects of the trial for *amparo* consists in the fact that in this case, it is a proceeding initiated through a direct action brought before a federal district court[702] by a plaintiff, against a particular statute, the defendants, being the supreme organs of "the state" which intervened in the process of formation of the statute, namely, the Congress of the Union, or the state Legislatures which produced it; the President of the Republic or the Governors of the states which enacted it, and the Secretaries of state which countersigned it and ordered its publication.[703] In these cases, the federal district courts decisions are revisable by the Supreme Court of Justice.[704]

The *amparo* against laws, therefore, is a direct action against a statute, the existence of a concrete administrative act or judicial decision for its enactment or its application not being necessary to its exercise.[705] Nevertheless, the constitutional question involved in this action is not an abstract one, and that is why only the statutes that inflict a direct injury on the plaintiff, without the necessity of any other intermediate or subsequent state act, can be the object of this action.[706] Therefore, the object of this action is self–executing statutes, that is to say, statutes that with their sole enactment, cause personal and direct prejudice to the plaintiff. That is why, in principle, the action seeking the *amparo* against laws must be brought before the court within 30 days after their enactment. Nevertheless, the action can also be brought before the Court within 15 days after the first act of enactment of the said statute so as to protect the plaintiff's rights to sue.[707]

C. *The effects of the decision on judicial review*

Regarding the effects of the judicial decision on any of the aspects of the trial for *amparo*, in which judicial review of constitutionality is sought whether in a pure incidental way or through the action to request an "*amparo* against laws", since the institution of the trial for *amparo* in the middle of the last century, the constitution has expressly established that the courts cannot "make any general declaration as to the law or act on which the complaint is based", the judgment affecting "only private individuals" and limited to affording them shelter and protection in a special

702 Art. 107, XII.

703 H. Fix–Zamudio, "Algunos problemas que plantea el amparo...", *loc. cit*., p. 21.

704 Art. 107, VIII,a.

705 *Cf.* R.D. Baker, *op. cit*., p. 164.

706 Self–executed Statutes (auto–aplicativas). *Cf.* R.D. Baker, *op. cit.* p. 167; H. Fix–Zamudio, "Algunos problemas que plantea el amparo...", *loc. cit.* p. 24.

707 Art. 21. Amparo Law. *Cf.* H. Fix–Zamudio, "Algunos problemas que plantea el amparo...", *loc. cit*., p. 32. *Cf.* R.D. Baker, *op. cit.* p. 171.

case to which the complaint refers."[708] Therefore, a decision in a "trial for *amparo*" in which judicial review of legislation is accomplished, can only have *inter partes* effects, and can never consist of general declarations with *erga omnes* effects.

Therefore, the courts in their decisions regarding the unconstitutionality of a statute do not annul or repeal it; therefore, the statute remains in the books and can be applied by the courts, the only effect of the declaration of its unconstitutionality being directed to the parties in a concrete process.

On the other hand, it must be said that the decisions of the trials for *amparo*, whether or not referred to judicial review, do not have general binding effects even regarding other courts, and are only obligatory to other courts in cases of established *jurisprudencia,* that is to say, of obligatory precedent. The constitution does not expressly establish when an obligatory precedent exists and refers to the special Organic law of the Constitutional Trial to specify "the terms and cases in which the *jurisprudencia* of the courts of the federal judicial power is binding, as well as the requirements for modifying it."[709] According to that Organic law *jurisprudencia* is established by the Supreme Court of Justice or by the Collegiate Circuit Courts when five consecutive decisions to the same effect, uninterrupted by any incompatible rulings are rendered,[710] but it can be modified when the respective Court pronounces a contradictory judgment with a qualified majority of votes of its members.[711]

Nevertheless, as *jurisprudencia* can be established by the federal Collegiate Circuit Courts and by the Supreme Court, contradictory interpretations of the constitution can exist, having binding effects upon the lower courts. In order to resolve these conflicts, the constitution establishes the power of the Supreme Court or of the Collegiate Circuit Court to resolve the conflict, when the contradiction is denounced by the Chambers of the Supreme Court or another Collegiate Circuit Court; by the Attorney General or by any of the parties to the cases in which the *jurisprudencia* was established.[712] Anyway the resolution of the contradiction between judicial doctrines, has the sole purpose of determining one single *jurisprudencia* on the matter, and does not affect concrete juridical situations, derived from the contradictory judicial decisions adopted in the respective trials.[713]

Finally, regarding the practical effects of the trial for *amparo*, it must be stressed that the constitution establishes a particular preliminary remedy during the trial for *amparo*, which consists of the possible suspension of the application of the contested state act, which in certain aspects is similar to the injunction in the North Ameri-

708 Art. 107, II, The principle is named the "Otero formula" due to its inclusion in the 1857 constitution under the influence of Mariano Otero. *Cf.* H, FIX–ZAMUDIO, "Algunos aspectos comparativos del derecho de amparo..." *loc. cit,.* p. 360; and H. FIX–ZAMUDIO, "Algunos problemas que plantea el amparo...", *loc. cit.*, p. 33, 37.

709 Art. 107, XIII, 1.

710 Art. 192, 193. See the quotations in R.D. BAKER, *op. cit.*, pp. 256, 257.

711 Art. 194. See the quotations in R.D. BAKER, *op. cit.* p. 263.

712 Art. 107, XIII. See the comments, in R.D. BAKER, *op. cit.,* p. 264.

713 Art. 107, XIII. See the comments in J.A.C. GRANT, *loc. cit.* p. 662.

can system but reduced to an *injunction pendente litis*.[714] In this respect, article 107 of the constitution established that:

> Contested acts may be subject to suspension in those cases and under conditions and guarantees specified by law, with respect to which account shall be taken of the nature of the alleged violation, the difficulty or remedying the damages that might be incurred by the aggrieved party by its performance, and the damages that the suspension might cause to third parties and the public interest.[715]

As we can see, although having peculiarities that can not be reproduced in any other legal system, the trial for *amparo* remains within its own particular trends, a means for judicial review that follows the features of the diffuse system of judicial review.

IV. THE DIFFUSE SYSTEM OF JUDICIAL REVIEW IN EUROPE AND IN OTHER CIVIL LAW COUNTRIES

The diffuse system of judicial review, apart from the Latin American experiences, has also been followed in other civil law countries, particularly in Europe (in Greece and in some Scandinavian countries) and in Japan. Other European countries with a civil law tradition have also adopted the diffuse system of judicial review, but mixing its features with elements of the concentrated systems, as is the case of Portugal and Switzerland, which we will analyse when studying the mixed systems of judicial review.

1. The Diffuse System of Judicial Review in Greece

In effect, after its establishment in the United States, and additional to the Latin American experiences, the diffuse system of judicial review was also followed in Greece, whose system has been considered to be "very similar to the United States' system of judicial review."[716]

A. *General Trends*

Based on the principle of the supremacy of the constitution, and on the rigid character of the 1844 and 1864 constitutions, the notion of judicial review was originally formulated by the Supreme Court of Greece in 1847, with limited scope, as the power of all courts to examine in a concrete litigation between parties, whether legislative act "bears all the forms that are necessary, according to the constitution, for the establishment of a legislative decision",[717] thus reduced to the formal constitutionality of statutes. In the same decision, the Court excluded the courts' judicial review power to examine the substantive constitutionality of statutes by stating that its jurisdiction did not include the examination of "the contents of the legislative

714 J.A.C. GRANT, *loc. cit.*, p. 652, note 33.

715 Art. 107, X.

716 E. SPILIOTOPOULOS, "Judicial Review of Legislative Acts in Greece", *Temple Law Quarterly*, 56 (2), Philadelphia 1983, p. 57.

717 Judgment N° 198 (1847), quoted in E. SPILIOTOPOULOS, *loc. cit.*, p. 471.

decision, because it cannot be assumed that the Power, which represents the sovereignty of the state, is acting unlawfully."[718] Later, in 1871 and 1879, the Supreme Court reversed its opinion regarding the limited scope of judicial review and considered that judicial review could refer to a statute when it "is in evident contradiction with a superior provision of the constitution" in which case "the court has the power not to apply it in the case that the court is hearing."[719]

The first constitution which expressly established judicial review powers of all courts was the 1927 constitution, in which article 5 was amended to include an interpretative clause, which in the Greek constitutional system has the same legal force as constitutional provisions, in which it was stated that "the true sense" of the provision which declares that the "judicial Power is vested in independent courts subject only to the law."[720]

> Is that the courts have the duty not to apply statutes, the contents of which are contrary to the constitution.[721]

This express constitutional norm concerning judicial review, even though eliminated from the constitution after 1935, and in accordance with the previous judge–made principle continued to be applied by the Supreme Court and the Council of state as a matter of "supplementary custom" of the constitution.[722] As Professor Epaminondas Spiliotopoulos said:

> On the basis of this judge–made law, and in the absence of the express constitutional provisions that had previously existed in the 1927 constitution, scholars of public law supported the theory that the power of the courts to review the constitutionality of statutes and to deny applications of those statutory provisions they considered unconstitutional derived from a supplementary custom of the constitution.[723]

The constitution of 29 September 1968, published by the military dictatorship, and even though without real enforcement particularly on the grounds of judicial review, re–established its constitutional basis by stating in article 118, that

> The courts have the duty not to apply provisions of statutes, legislative decrees and rules, which have been enacted in breach of the constitution or are contrary to its contents.[724]

This principle was also established later in the present 1975 constitution, in which it is stated that "The courts shall be bound not to apply laws, the contents of which are contrary to the constitution."[725] Along the same line of principles, article 87 of the constitution states:

---

718 *Idem*, p. 471.

719 Judgments N° 18 (1871) and N° 23 (1897), quoted by E. SPILIOTOPOULOS, *loc. cit.*, p. 472.

720 Art. 5.

721 See in E. SPILIOTOPOULOS, *loc. cit.*, p. 472, note 43.

722 *Cf. Idem*, 470, note 30 and p. 474.

723 *Idem*, p. 475.

724 See in *Información Jurídica*, 300, Madrid 1969, p. 103.

725 Art. 93, 4.

> Judges shall in the discharge of their duties be subject only to the constitution and the laws; in no case whatsoever shall they be obliged to comply with provisions enacted in abolition of the constitution.[726]

Thus, judicial review of legislation in the Greek constitutional system is an express constitutional duty and power of all judges, that can be exercised as in all the diffuse systems of judicial review, only when the courts decide upon a concrete case in which the challenged statute applies.

Nevertheless, contrary to the general rule in the common law countries, in which the constitutional question must always be raised by a party in the proceeding, in the Greek system, judicial review is a real duty and the courts can on their own and without party requirements, review the constitutionality of legislation. In this respect, as we have seen, the Greek system of judicial review follows the strict logic of the diffuse system, as is the case in Venezuela, but not the general pattern of the common law world.[727] Therefore, in Greece, the courts can proceed with the review *ex officio*, without a specific request being submitted by the litigants challenging the constitutionality of a statute. Of course, if such a request is presented, and this can only be by a party with personal interests in the matter, the court must examine the constitutional issue. But Professor Spiliotopoulos has said,

> In the absence of a specific request, the court may itself raise the questions when a doubt regarding the constitutionality of such a statute or provision arises during the adjudication of the case.[728]

Finally it must be said that in accordance with the general trends of the diffuse system of judicial review, the contents of the decisions of the courts according to the constitution is not to apply the unconstitutional statue, which is considered as null and void, hence, with no effect whatsoever regarding the concrete case. That is why, for instance, if the act held unconstitutional had abrogated or amended a previous statutory provisions, the Council of state has considered that the abrogation or amendment never took place, and has applied the previous provision as if it were effective and unammended.[729]

Therefore, the unconstitutional statute is not annulled by the courts, but only declared null and void, the decision having only *inter partes* effects. Furthermore, the courts' decisions upon constitutional questions are not binding regarding the same or another court in other cases where the same statutory provision may be challenged. Thus the *stare decisis* doctrine does not apply in the Greek system, and if the decisions of the Supreme Court or of the Council of state are followed by the inferior

---

726 Art. 87, 3.

727 *Cf.* B.O. NWABUEZE, *Judicial Control of Legislative Action and its Legitimacy. Recent Developments*. IALS, Uppsala Colloquium, 1984, (mimeo), p. 3; also published in L. FAVOREU and J.A. JOLOWICZ, *Le contrôle juridictionnel des lois. Légitimité, effectivité et développements récents*, Paris 1986, pp. 193–222.

728 E. SPILIOTOPOULOS, *loc. cit*, p. 479.

729 See judgment N° 2241 (1953), quoted by E. SPILIOTOPOULOS, *loc. cit.*, pp. 485, 123.

courts of the judiciary, it is due to practical reasons derived from the factual influence of the Supreme courts.[730]

B. *Constitutional Justice and Conflicting Judicial Review Adjudications: the Special Highest Court*

The diffuse system of judicial review in Greece, though very similar to the one developed in the United States of America, has a substantial differential element within it, derived from the particular organisation of the Greek judiciary.

In effect, the basic judicial bodies in Greece are organised in two fundamental and separate branches, with some similarities to the French model: a civil and criminal judiciary with a Supreme Court at its apex, and an administrative judiciary with a council of state at its apex.[731] Therefore there are two supreme judicial bodies with final appellate jurisdiction in the ordinary civil and criminal jurisdiction or in the administrative jurisdiction. Additionally the constitution establishes a third separate branch of the judicial power attributed to the Comptrollers Council, mainly concerned with public audit and financial matters.[732]

All the courts of the three branches of the judicial powers have the power of judicial review, and therefore, it can happen that the Supreme Court, in civil or criminal case, the Council of state, in administrative cases, or the Comptrollers Council, in audit matters, may render contradictory and conflicting judgments on constitutional issues, which could produce legal uncertainty.

To resolve possible conflicting decisions on constitutional matters between these judicial organisations, the 1968 constitution established a Constitutional Court,[733] which the 1975 constitution transformed into a Special Highest Court. The jurisdiction of this Special Highest Court has approximated the Greek system of judicial review to the mixed systems[734] but owing to its peculiar character due to the existence of three separate judicial organisations, its functions are rather a corrective effort regarding the inconsistencies that the diffuse system may cause in the three branches of the judiciary.

This Special Highest Court, according to article 100, has jurisdiction not only over constitutional aspects, bur also over electoral matters and the settlement of controversies related to the designation of rules on international law.[735] Furthermore, it

---

730 *Cf.* E. SPILIOTOPOULOS, *loc. cit.*, p. 486.

731 Art. 93–97, 1975 constitution. *Cf.* E. SPILIOTOPOULOS, *loc. cit.*, pp. 475–477, The Council of State although originally created in 1835, it initiated its functioning in 1929. *Cf.* E. SPILIOTOPOULOS, *loc. cit.*, p. 472, note 45.

732 Art. 98–99.

733 Art. 106. See in *Información Jurídica, cit.* p. 99–100. *Cf.* the comments regarding this Tribunal in H. FIX–ZAMUDIO, *Los Tribunales constitucionales y los derechos humanos*, UNAM, México 1980, pp. 160–161.

734 *Cf.* H. FIX–ZAMUDIO, *op. cit.*, p. 162.

735 Art. 100, 1, a,b,c,f.

acts as a jurisdictional conflict court like the French Tribunal of Conflicts;[736] but basically it acts as the final resort court for the settlement of controversies on constitutional matters between the supreme courts of the Judicial Power. In this respect, the constitution gives jurisdiction to this Special Highest Court, for the

> Settlement of controversies on whether a law enacted by Parliament is fundamentally unconstitutional, or on the interpretation of provisions of such law when conflicting judgments have been pronounced by the Council of State, the Supreme Court of the Comptrollers Council.[737]

This Special Highest Court is composed of the president of the Council of state, the president of the Supreme Court and the President of the Comptrollers Council, four Councilors of state and four members of the Supreme Court and when acting in the settlement of controversy on constitutional matters, its composition shall be expanded to include two ordinary law professors of the law schools of the country.[738]

According to the special law or statute no. 345 of 1978, which regulates the procedure to be followed by the Special Highest Court to settle controversies, a "controversy" arises when one of the supreme courts, when examining the constitutionality of a statute involved in the case, forms an opinion contrary to an opinion already expressed by another supreme court covering the same statute.[739] In that case, the controversy may be submitted to the Special Highest Court, in two ways incidental or principal.

The first means of an incidental character allows the supreme court whose opinion created the controversy to refer a preliminary judgment concerning the question of constitutionality, directly to the Special Highest Court, the final adjudication of the case being postponed. The second means of a principal character can be exercised when the Supreme Court concerned does not postpone its final adjudication and renders it, and the question can be brought before the Special Highest Court through a petition by the Minister of Justice, the Public Prosecutor of the Supreme Court, the state Commissioner to the Comptroller's Council, and the state Commissioner to the Administrative Justice; and also, by any person who has a legally protected interest including the party who has lost the case.[740]

The Special Highest Court examines only the question of constitutionality referred or submitted to it, and the decision rendered on the matter has *erga omnes* effects.[741] According to Article 100, of the constitution, "provisions of law declared unconstitutional shall be invalid as of the date of publication of the respective judgment, or as of the date specified by the ruling." Therefore, the decision of the Special Highest Court in principle, annuls the unconstitutional act, with *ex nunc*, pro-

---

736 Art. 100,1,d.

737 Art. 100,1,e.

738 Art. 100,2.

739 Art. 48, 2 quoted in E. SPILIOTOPOULOS, *loc. cit.*, p. 497.

740 *Cf.* E. SPILIOTOPOULOS, *loc. cit.*, p. 497.

741 Art. 51, Statute 345. quoted in E. SPILIOTOPOULOS, *loc. cit.*, p. 498, note 199.

spective effects, but the Special Highest Court can give its decision retroactive effects.[742]

Consequently, if after the Special Highest Court decision, a lower court renders a decision with respect to the constitutionality of a statute contrary to the opinion of the Special Highest Court, the litigants have the right to make an appeal, and if the said decision is adopted by one of the Supreme Courts, the parties have the right to submit a petition for a new hearing.[743]

However concerning the case in which the constitutional question was raised, the immediate effects of the Special Highest Court decision are different regarding the incidental or principal characters of the proceeding. If the proceeding was an incidental one and the final adjudication was postponed in a supreme court, after the judgment of the Special Highest Court is pronounced, the Supreme Court must continue its proceeding consistent with the Special Highest Court ruling.

But if the proceeding before the Special Highest Court was a principal one, and the supreme court concerned pronounced a final judgment prior to the Special Highest Court decision, instead of postponing it, that decision does not automatically have effect upon the Supreme Court final adjudication. Its results are that the litigants have the right within ninety days from the date on which the judgment of the Special Highest Court is pronounced to submit a special petition and demand a new hearing of the case by the Supreme Court, which then must apply the Special Highest Court ruling.[744]

Thus, in spite of the existence of this Special Highest Court to settle conflicting decisions on constitutional issues, and of the effects of its decision, it can be, considered that the general trends of the diffuse system of judicial review continue to prevail in the Greek system.

2. Judicial review in some of the Scandinavian Countries.

The other European countries with a diffuse system of judicial review are some of the Nordic or Scandinavian Countries, all of which have a parliamentary system of government and a unitarian form of the state. In particular in Sweden, Norway, Denmark and Iceland, a diffuse system of judicial review of legislation can be identified,[745] with the general trends of the North American model.[746]

In Finland, even though the general legal opinion is that no judicial review of legislation is accepted, and that there are no cases in which a court has questioned the constitutionality of an act of Parliament, the constitutional basis for judicial re-

---

742 E. SPILIOTOPOULOS, *loc. cit.*, p. 500.

743 Art. 51, statute 345. quoted in E. SPILIOTOPOULOS, *loc. cit.*, p. 499.

744 *Idem.*

745 *Cf.* E. SMITH, *Contrôle juridictionnel de la législation et sa légitimité. Développements récents dans les cinq pays scandinaves*, AISJ, Colloque Uppsala, 1984, (mimeo), pp. 2, 3, 4, 7, 50, 74. Also published in L. FAVOREU and J.A. JOLOWICZ, (ed.), *Le contrôle juridictionnel des lois..., cit.*, pp. 225–282.

746 *Idem, doc. cit.*, p. 12.

view is established although not regarding acts of Parliament, but inferior regulations.

According to Art. 92 of the Finnish constitution act of 1919, "if a provision in a decree is contrary to a constitutional or other law, it shall not be applied by a judge or other official."[747] Commenting on this article, Mikael Hiden, said: "any official or authority is empowered, and is duty bound, not to apply any legal provision below the level of acts of Parliament if he or it deems the provision to be contrary to the constitution or any act of Parliament."[748] Nevertheless, Hiden said, according to predominant legal opinion and due to the absence of courts decisions, it can be accepted that "the Finnish system does not recognise the judicial review of legislation in the most significant meaning of that expression, i.e. as exercised by courts in applying the law in a litigation";[749] instead, a system of control of legislation only exists prior to its enactment, during the legislative process, in which judicial bodies can intervene. In effect, the President of the Republic can request opinion on a bill before presenting it to Parliament, either from the Supreme Court or the Supreme Administrative Court or from both.[750] In fact, this is a form of "pre Parliamentary" control, and the decision of the courts in these cases is merely an "advisory opinion." Nevertheless, this form of preventive control of the constitutionality of legislation, added to the political control developed over bills in Parliament, seems to occupy an important place in the system.[751]

It must also be stressed that in Sweden there is also a preventive system of judicial review of bills. In this respect Article 8:18 of the constitution creates a "Council of the Laws" which is formed by members of the two highest courts of the Country (Supreme Court and Supreme Administrative Court), which is in charge of giving advice, among other things, on the relations between a bill and the Constitutional text, at the request of the Government and of Parliament.[752] This control, it must be said, only refers to bills drafted by the Government, and consequently cannot be exercised regarding the laws finally adopted by Parliament, and in no case is the advisory opinion of the Council obligatory either fox the Government or for Parliament.[753] That is why it has not been considered in the strictest sense as a judicial review control.[754]

Now, excluding Finland, in the other Scandinavian countries, as we have said, a system of judicial control of the constitutionality of legislation is accepted, even

747 See in M. HIDEN, "Constitutional Rights in the Legislative Process: the Finnish System of Advance Control of Legislation" *Scandinavian Studies in Law*, 17, Stockholm 1973, p. 97.

748 *Idem*, p. 97, 98.

749 *Ibidem*, p. 98. *Cf.* E. SMITH, *doc.cit.*, p. 12.

750 M. HIDEN, *loc. cit.*, p. 106.

751 E. SMITH, *doc. cit.*, p. 12.

752 See in E. SMITH, *op. cit.*, pp. 12, 20.

753 E. SMITH, *doc. cit.*, p. 20.

754 *Idem*, p. 20.

though with a very different longevity, beginning with Norway from 1890; and finishing with Sweden from 1960.[755]

The common fundamental trends of the judicial control of the constitutionality of legislation in the four Nordic countries, following the general features of the North American system of judicial review, have been summarised by Professor Eivind Smith, as follows:

First, the power of judicial review is attributed to all judges. Thus, there are not specialised judicial organs in charge of this control.

Second, constitutional questions must be raised in cases or controversies in ordinary civil criminal or administrative litigation, by a party having personal interests to do so.

Third, the constitutional issue raised in a particular process must only be decided upon if it is unavoidable for the resolution of the concrete case, and the judge has a certain criteria concerning the unconstitutionality of the act, which would depend on the degree of precision of the constitution.

Fourth, because constitutional questions must be considered in accordance with the normal procedural rules, the effects of the judicial decision on the matter, only applies to the parties in the process. The judges do not annul the laws but only limit their decisions to not applying the unconstitutional act to the concrete case, without *erga omes* effects.[756]

It has been in Sweden where the power of the courts to control the constitutionality of legislation, has been more recently recognised in the 1974 constitution.

In article 11:14 it states:

> When a (judicial or administrative) court finds a (legislative or executive) disposition contrary to the constitution or to other superior rules, or when it finds that the proceeding rules have not been observed in an essential point during the process of elaboration of the above mentioned disposition, it will be inapplicable.[757]

Even though this article, as written down could lead to the admissibility of *ex officio* powers of the courts to declare an unconstitutional statute inapplicable, in practice, the incidental character of the system where only a party can raise the constitutional issue in a particular process, is accepted.[758]

Anyway, although article 11:14 establishes a very broad system for judicial review, it must be stressed that the same article establishes a substantial restriction to the power conferred upon the judges to control the unconstitutionality of Acts of Parliament, when establishing that when the disposition whose unconstitutionality has been raised is adopted by Parliament or by the Government, the inapplicability can only be pronounced when the on record error is a "manifest" one.[759] Thus the

755 *Idem*, pp. 7–8.

756 *Idem*, p. 10–12, 62, 67, 74.

757 See in E. SMITH, *doc. cit*., p. 16.

758 E. SMITH, *doc.cit*., p. 18.

759 See in E. SMITH, *doc.cit*., pp. 17, 22.

determination of the manifest errors by the courts is an important restraint upon their control power vis–à–vis the political organs of the state.

Finally, we must also say that in Norway, where Professor Cappelletti and Adams found "at least in theory the most comprehensive power of judicial review found anywhere",[760] additional to the power of all courts to declare incidentally on the settlement of a specific case, the invalidity of statutes contrary to the constitution, the Supreme Court of the country can also be requested by Parliament to give advisory opinions on the constitutionality of Statutes.

3. The Diffuse System of Judicial Review in Japan

But outside the European and Latin American continents, a diffuse system of judicial review can also be identified in the Japanese Constitutional system. In effect, contrary to the tradition of the legal system of the country,[761] the 1946 constitution of Japan, drafted under overwhelming American influence,[762] established the basis of the diffuse system of judicial review in the country, regulated in only one Constitutional article, which states the following:

> Art. 81: The Supreme Court is the court of last resort with power to determine the constitutionality of any law, order, regulation or official act.[763]

In spite of the ambiguity of the text, and of the absence of any statutory regulation regarding its content[764] the Supreme Court has considered that the courts review power provided for in the constitution, "has been developed through interpretation of the American constitution."[765] Thus the system has developed as a diffuse judicial review system, in which no direct or abstract action can be brought before the Supreme Court to challenge a statute. This was expressly resolved by the Supreme Court in a 1952 decision involving an action brought directly before the Court by the Chairman of one of the main political parties for the declaration of unconstitutionality of a National Police Force. The Court dismissed the action and held that the judicial review power is part of the ordinary judicial power and its exercise is condi-

760 M. CAPPELLETTI and J.C. ADAMS, "Judicial Review of Legislation: European Antecedents and Adaptations", *Harvard Law Review*, 79, (6), 1966, p. 1217

761 *Cf.* Y. TANIGUCHI, *Judicial Control of Legislation and its Legitimacy in Japan*, IALS, Uppsala Colloquium 1984 (mimeo), p. 2. Also published in L. FAVOREU and J.A. JOLOWICZ (ed.), *Le contrôle juridictionnel des lois..., cit.*, pp. 175–190.

762 *Cf.* Y TANIGUCHI, *doc. cit.*, p. 7,3; Y. HIGUCHI, "Evolution récente du contrôle de la constituionnalité sous la Constitution japonaise de 1946", *Revue internationale de droit comparé*, 31, (1), Paris 1979, p. 22; T. FUKASE and Y. HIGUCHI, *Le constitutionnalisme et ses problèmes ou Japon. Une approche comparative*, Paris 1984, p. 28; J.D. WHYTE, *Judicial Review of Legislation and its Legitimacy: Developments in the Common Law* World, IALS, Uppsala Colloquium 1984 (mimeo), p. 61. Also published in L. FAVOREU and J.A. JOLOWICZ, *Le contrôle juridictionnel des lois..., cit.*, pp. 155–174.

763 See in Y. TANIGUCHI, *doc.cit.*, p. 2; J.D. WHYTE, *doc. cit.*, p. 62.

764 T. FUKASE and Y. HIGUCHI, *op.cit.*, p. 298.

765 Grand Bench, July 8, 1948: Keishu 2–8–801 quoted by Y. TANIGUCHI, *doc.cit.*, p. 2, note 3.

tioned by the existence of a concrete case of litigation that must be started in an appropriate lower court.[766]

Therefore, the Japanese judicial review system follows the theory of the diffuse system of judicial review as developed in the United States of America. Hence, judicial review is a power of all courts exercised within their own jurisdiction, the Supreme Court being at the apex of the judiciary.

The constitutional questions therefore, can only be raised in a particular case or controversy between actual parties, in which the challenged state act directly affects the legal relationship between those parties.[767] The object of control can be "any law, order, regulation or official act", which includes of course, any normative state act. Discussions have been held regarding the reviewability of international treaties and although there has not been any decision by the Supreme Court considering the unconstitutionality of a treaty, the court has not excluded, in principle, its power to declare its unconstitutionality. In the *Sunagawa* case (1959), when dealing with the Japan–US Security Treaty it is understood that the Court took the position that Treaties are also subject to judicial review, although the Court abstained from deciding upon the unconstitutionality of that Treaty, on the grounds of considering the issue "highly political" and in which "the unconstitutionality did not reveal itself in a clear and evident way."[768]

This position of the Courts lead not only to the "political questions" doctrine/ but to the rule of the presumption of constitutionality of Statutes, which means that a Constitutional issue must only be decided when unavoidable for the resolution of the case, and when there is no other way of interpreting the Statute to avoid its unconstitutionality.[769]

Regarding the effects of the decisions adopted in judicial review, the principle of the nullity of unconstitutional state acts is accepted. Consequently, the Courts decisions do not annul the unconstitutional act, only declare its inapplicability to the concrete case, and with *inter partes* effects.[770] Discussions have taken place regarding the retroactive effects of the decision,[771] but bearing in mind the wide acceptance by the Supreme Court of deciding upon the unconstitutionality of statutory provisions no longer in force,[772] the retroactive effects of the decision, in principle, are evident.

The role of the Supreme Court of Japan regarding judicial review, contrary to the American Supreme Court, has been considered as passive, in the sense that in the 40 years of enforcement of the constitution, the Supreme Court has only held statutes

---

766 Y. TANIGUCHI, *doc. cit.*, p. 3.

767 J.D. WHYTE, *doc.cit.*, p. 64

768 T. FUKASE and Y. HIGUCHI, *op. cit.*, p. 299; Y. TANIGUCHI, *doc. cit.*, p. 9.

769 Y. TANIGUCHI, *doc. cit.*, p. 14; T. FUKASE and Y. HIGUCHI, *op. cit.*, p. 299.

770 Y. TANIGUCHI, *doc. cit.*, p. 16; T. FUKASE and Y. HIGUCHI, *op. cit.*, p. 299.

771 Y. TANIGUCHI, *doc. cit.*, pp. 16–17.

772 Y. TANIGUCHI, *doc. cit.*, p. 11.

unconstitutional in three cases, decided between 1933 and 1976.[773] Before 1973, the active character of judicial review referred mainly to statutory provisions no longer in force [774] or to the affirmation of the constitutionality of challenged statutes,[775] and it was only after 1973 that the Supreme Court declared the unconstitutionality of a few statutory provisions. First, of an article of the Penal code concerning parricide which prescribed a more severe penalty for murder of a close relative than for ordinary homicide as violating the equality under the law clause.[776] Later, in 1975, the Supreme Court declared the unconstitutionality of a provision of the pharmaceutical affairs act which prescribed that a newly opened pharmacy had to be not less than a certain distance from an existing one, as violating the freedom to choose one's occupation.[777] Finally, in 1976, the Supreme Court declared unconstitutional a provision of the Public Office Election Law fixing the electorate for each election district, as violating the equality under the law clause as a consequence of the inequalities derived from the movement of population into the cities.[778]

After this judicial activism of the Supreme Court, developed between 1973 and 1976, over recent years there have been no new decisions by the Court declaring the unconstitutionality of Statues. This has been interpreted as a return to the previous doctrine of the "interpretation of laws according with the constitution" developed in the sixties.[779]

Finally it must be said that the doctrine of *stare decisis* is not accepted in Japan.[780] Thus the inferior courts are not legally bound by the decisions of higher courts, particularly by the decisions of the Supreme Court which refers only to the concrete case in which they are pronounced. Nevertheless, the authority of the Supreme Court produces de facto binding effects of its decisions upon the inferior courts.[781]

---

773 *Cf.* Y. HIGUCHI, *loc. cit.*, pp. 22, 31; T. FUKASE and Y. HIGUCHI, *op. cit.*, pp. 300, 307; Y. TANIGUCHI, *doc. cit.*, p. 17; J.D. WHITE, *doc. cit.*, p. 64.

774 Y. TANIGUCHI, *doc. cit.*, p. 11.

775 Y. TANIGUCHI, *doc. cit.*, p. 14; T. FUKASE and Y. HIGUCHI, *doc. cit.*, p. 301

776 *Aizawa v. Japan* 27 Sai–han Keishu 256 (1973); Grand Bench, April 4, 1973, Keishu 27–3–265 quoted in J.D. WHYTE, *doc. cit.*, p. 64; Y. TANIGUCHI, *doc. cit.*, p. 10, note 16; Y. HIGUCHI, *loc. cit.*, p. 31.32; T. FUKASE and Y. HIGUCHI, *op. cit.*, p. 308.

777 *K.K. Sumiyoshi v. Governor of Hiroshima Prefecture*, 665 Saibansho Jiho 1 (1975); Grand Bench, April 30, 1975 Minshu 29–4–572 quoted in J.D. WHYTE, *doc. cit.*, p. 65; Y. TANIGUCHI, *doc. cit.*, p. 10, note 17; Y. HIGUCHI, *loc. cit.*, p. 32; T. FUKASE and Y. HIGUCHI, *op. cit.*, pp. 308–309.

778 *Kurokawa v. Chiba Prefecture Election Commission*, 30, Sai–han Minshu 223 (1976), Grand Bench, April 14, 1976, Minshu 30–3–223, quoted in J.D. WHYTE, *doc. cit.*, p. 65; Y. TANIGUCHI, *doc. cit*, p. 11 note 19; Y. HIGUCHI, *loc. cit.*, pp. 32–33; T. FUKASE and Y. HIGUCHI, *op. cit.*, pp. 309–310.

779 Y. HIGUCHI, *loc. cit.*, p. 33; T. FUKASE and Y. HIGUCHI, *op. cit.*, p. 310.

780 J.D. WHYTEP, *doc. cit.* p. 63.

781 T. FUKASE and Y. HIGUCHI, *op. cit.*, 299.

On the other hand, the Supreme Court is not bound bay its own decisions, and has the power to override its previous decisions even on constitutional matters. This happened precisely in the Patricide case (1933) in which the Court overrode a previous 1950 decision in which it considered the constitutionality of Article 200 of the Penal Code which established the aggravation of the penalty for the parricide.[782]

V. SOME ASPECTS OF THE DIFFUSE SYSTEM OF JUDICIAL REVIEW IN COMMONWEALTH COUNTRIES.

Even though followed in various civil law countries as we have seen, the diffuse system of judicial review of the constitutionality of legislation can nevertheless be considered a common trend in common law countries with written constitutions, which are the overwhelming majority. As we have seen, in civil law countries, the diffuse system of judicial review, in its classical features, is a rare institution to be found only in a few countries in Latin America and in Europe, and in other civil law countries like Japan. In most of the civil law countries, which have adopted the diffuse system of judicial review, in fact, it has not remained in its pure and classical form, but has normally been mixed with trends of the concentrated system of judicial review. Therefore, it is in the common law world in which the diffuse system of judicial review has expanded.

In particular, and contrary to the situation of the United Kingdom constitutional system, the diffuse system of judicial review, is a common constitutional trend in almost all the commonwealth countries, formerly part of the British Empire. Thus, the majority of these countries have adopted a radically different principle for their constitutional system to the one, which prevails in the United Kingdom, where no judicial review of legislation is accepted.

In the establishment of this different constitutional system in the commonwealth countries, although due to various factors, the United Kingdom has nevertheless played, paradoxically, an important role.

In effect, it must firstly be said that all the commonwealth countries, with the single exception of New Zealand[783] have written constitutions and, in general, entrenched declarations of fundamental rights. Particularly during the processes of independence of the commonwealth countries developed during this century, or in the process of reshaping its constitutional system, as was the case of Canada in 1982, it is evident that the Westminster Parliament played a fundamental role in the drafting or establishing of the respective constitutional rules of the countries and in promoting the formal and entrenched declarations of fundamental rights.[784] Thus,

---

782 Y. HIGUCHI, *loc. cit.*, pp. 31–32.

783 *Cf.* J.D. WHYTE, *Judicial Review of Legislation and its Legitimacy: Developments in the Common Law World*, International Association of Legal Sciences, Uppsala Colloquium 1984, (mimeo), p. 89; Also published in L. FAVOREU and J.A. JOLOWICZ (ed.), *Le contrôle juridictionnel des lois. Légitimité, effectivité et developments récents*, Paris 1986, pp. 155–174. M. ZANDER, *A Bill of Rights?*, London 1985, p. 30.

784 A. LESTER, "Fundamental Rights: the United Kingdom Isolated?," *Public Law*, 1984, pp. 56–57; J.D. WHYTE, *doc. cit.*, pp. 96–97.

written constitutions, considered as the supreme law of the land in each of the commonwealth countries, with entrenched declarations of fundamental rights, presupposed the establishment of limits upon state powers, and particularly, upon legislative power.

Consequently, the principle of the sovereignty of Parliament, considered as a constitutional law "curiosity"[785] peculiar to the British constitutional systems, is not followed in most commonwealth countries,[786] in which Parliament is submitted to constitutional restraint as are all other state powers. The constitution, therefore, is considered the supreme law of the land, and consequently, any state act contrary to its dispositions, is considered null and void. For instance, this is expressly stated in the constitutions of the West Indian countries,[787] and of Nigeria in which it is declared that "if any law is inconsistent with the provisions of this constitution, this constitution shall prevail and that other law shall, to the extent of the inconsistency be Void."[788] Also, concerning fundamental rights, the Indian constitution states that "the state shall not make any law which takes away or abridges the rights conferred by this Part (Part III, Fundamental Rights) and any law made in contravention of this clause shall, to the extent of the contravention, be void."[789] Thus the doctrine of parliamentary sovereignty has been substituted in the commonwealth countries by the principle of constitutional supremacy, even though discussions have arisen in some countries regarding the British model. For instance, S.N. Ray, said of the Indian constitutional system,

> The framers of the Indian constitution were inclined in favour of the British principle of Parliamentary supremacy, but although they adopted the English model of Parliamentary government and made Parliament the focus of political power in the county and the dominant machinery to realise the goal of social revolution, they did not make it a sovereign legislature in the same sense and to the same extent as the British Parliament was sovereign. They placed as much supremacy in the hands of the legislature as was possible within the bounds of a written constitution with a federal distribution of powers and a bill of rights. In its turn, the judiciary has been assigned a superior position in relation to the legislature but only in certain respects. The constitution endows the judiciary with the power of declaring a law as unconstitutional if that is beyond the competence of the legislature according to the distribution of powers provided by the constitution, or if that is in contravention of the Fundamental Rights guaranteed by the constitution.[790]

---

785 S.O. GYANDOH Jr., "Interaction of the Judicial and Legislative Process in Ghana since Independence", *Temple Law Quaterly*, 56, 2, Philadelphia 1983, p. 354.

786 *Cf.* A.R. CARNEGIE, "Judicial Review of Legislation in the West Indian Constitutions", *Public Law*, London 1971, p. 276; Ch. OKPALUBA, "Challenging the Constitutionality of Legislative Enactment in Nigeria: the Factor of Locus Standi", *Public Law*, London 1982, p. 110; S.A. GYANDOH, Jr., *loc. cit.*, 351; E. MCWHINNEY, *Judicial Review*, Toronto 1969, p. 7.

787 A.R. CARNEGIE, *loc. cit.*, p. 276; J.D. WHYTE, *doc. cit.*, p. 32

788 Ch. OKPALUBA, *loc .cit.*, p. 110.

789 See in S.N. RAY, *Judicial Review and Fundamental Rights*, Calcuta 1974, p. 270.

790 *Idem*, pp. 69–70.

This Indian dilemma between Parliamentary Supremacy and judicial review was explained in an adequate way in the well known *A.K. Goplan v. State of Madras* case (1950) in which it was stated:

> In India the position of the judiciary is somewhere in between the Courts in England and the United States. While in the main leaving our Parliament and the state Legislatures supreme in their respective legislative fields, our constitution has, by some of the articles put upon the Legislature certain specified limitations.... in so far as there is any limitation on the legislative power, the Court must on a complaint being made to it, scrutinise and a ascertain whether such limitation has been transgressed and if there has been any transgression the Court will courageously declare the law unconstitutional, for the Court is bound by its oath to uphold the constitution.... Our constitution, unlike the English constitution, recognises the Courts supremacy over the legislative authority ... confined to the field where the legislative power is circumscribed by limitations put upon it by the constitution itself... But our constitution, unlike the American constitution, does not recognise the absolute supremacy of the Court over the legislative authority in all respects, for outside the restricted field of constitutional limitations our Parliament and the state Legislatures are supreme in their respective legislative fields and in that wider field there is no scope for the Court in India to play the role of the Supreme Court of the United States.[791]

Anyway, what is definitive in the Commonwealth Countries is that written Constitutions impose certain limits upon the legislature, particularly in relation to fundamental rights and to the vertical distribution of state powers, especially through the federal form of state which has contributed to the adoption of judicial review.[792]

However, even within the principle of parliamentary supremacy in the constitutional system of the United Kingdom, it must be also noted that the practice of judicial review regarding the former colonies and some commonwealth countries has also been a legacy of the United Kingdom constitutional system, because of the role played by the Privy Council as the final appellate Tribunal for the overseas Empire, particularly when exercising judicial review of the Constitutions of the self governing members of the Commonwealth and the concomitant power to strike down as invalid, those laws passed by the Parliament, of those countries contrary to the rules of the Imperial Parliament.[793] As Edward McWhinney pointed out:

> The Privy Council was the highest appellate tribunal of the old British Colonial Empire, and it exercised the right to scrutinise colonial legislation and ordinances and the administration thereof to ensure their conformance to the provisions of the Imperially granted constitution or charter of the colony concerned and ultimately to ensure their conformance to the principles of Imperial constitutional law as a whole.[794]

---

791 AIR 1950 SC 27; 1950 SCR 88 at 286–87, 288–90, quoted in S.N. RAY, *op. cit.*, p. 72–73. See the comments in pp. 259–268.

792 See particularly in relation to federalism and judicial review Ch. OKPALUBA, *loc. cit.* p. 111; E. MCWHINNEY, *op. cit.*, p. 14; and in relation to fundamental rights and judicial review, J.D. WHYTE, *doc. cit.*, p. 38.

793 E. MCWHINNEY, *op. cit.*, p. 49, 57; S.O. GYANDOH Jr., *loc. cit.*, p. 355

794 E. MCWHINNEY, "Constitutional Review in the Commonwealth", in H. MOSLER (ed.), Max–Planck–Institut für Ansländisches öffentliches recht and Völkerrecht, *Ve*

It must be said that this jurisdiction of the Privy Council remained in force until as late as 1949, when it was generally swept away by legislation of the individual commonwealth countries with a few exceptions (i.e. Australia, Trinidad and Tobago and New Zealand), in favour of the jurisdiction of the Supreme Courts of those countries. Thus, the Supreme Courts of the Commonwealth countries can be seen as the "lineal successors to the Privy Council",[795] and that is why it has been said regarding Canada that "after the abolition of the appeal to the Privy Council, the Canadian Supreme Court, for example, continues to exercise the power of judicial review in relation to legislation passed by the Canadian Parliament."[796] In a similar way, the High Court of Australia assumed the power to invalidate, on the grounds of unconstitutionality, legislation passed by the Australian Parliament on certain matters established on the Australian constitution, and in respect to which, therefore, "any appeal to the Privy Council was prohibited by the constitution."[797]

Apart from all those British antecedents, it is also accepted that judicial review of the Constitutionality of legislation, even though not always expressly established in the Constitutions of the commonwealth countries, was also widely developed in these countries under the influence of the American system of judicial review whose fundamental trends were received particularly during recent decades.[798] That is why, it can be said that in general terms, the system of judicial review in the commonwealth countries, follows the general trends of the diffuse system of judicial review, but with the particular feature that in all matters related to general law and of course, constitutional questions, the Supreme Courts of the Commonwealth Countries, following the British pattern have the final appeal jurisdiction.[799]

On the other hand some Commonwealth Countries have expressly established in their constitution, the jurisdiction of the Courts to judge upon constitutional questions regarding legislation, and in particular, they have established the jurisdiction of the Supreme Court on the matter.

For instance, the constitution of the Republic of Ireland provides that the jurisdiction of the High. Court, and, on appeal, of the Supreme Court, shall extend "to the question of the validity of any law having regard to the provisions of the constitution."[800]

A similar system exists in Trinidad and Tobago. The High Court of Justice has wide ranging jurisdiction, including interpretation of the constitution. The Appellate Division of the Supreme Court is vested in the Court of Appeal, and there is an ap-

---

Verfassungsgerichtsbarkeit, in der Gegenwart, Internationalen Kolloquium, Heidelberg 1961, Köln Berlin 1962, pp. 77–78.

795 E. MC WHINNEY, "Constitutional review ...", *loc. cit.*, p. 78.

796 E. MC WHINNEY, *Judicial Review, cit.*, pp. 58–59.

797 *Idem.*

798 *Cf.* E. MC WHINNEY, *Judicial Review, cit.*, pp. 236, 237; E. MC WHINNEY, "Constitutional Review", *loc. cit.*, pp. 79, 83, 87. Regarding India, *Cf.* S.N. RAY, *op. cit.*, p. 4, 72.

799 *Cf.* J.D. WHYTE, *doc. cit.*, p. 11; E. MC WHINNEY, "Constitutional review..." *loc. cit.*, p. 83.

800 *Cf.* B. CHUBB, *The Constitution of Ireland*, Dublin 1966, p. 31; *Cf.* K.C. WHEARE, *Modern Constitutions*, Oxford 1966, p. 101; J.D. WHYTE, *doc. cit.*, 72

peal as of right to it from decisions of the High Court on constitutional questions and fundamental rights. The peculiar regulation concerning Trinidad and Tobago, is that when the question is one of interpretation of the constitution from the Court of Appeal, there is an appeal to the Judicial Committee of the Privy Council.[801] Nevertheless, as Chief Justice C.A. Kelsick said:

> The Supreme Court of Trinidad and Tobago) as guardian of the constitution has the power to declare null and void Acts of Parliament which violate the provisions of chapter 1 or other entrenched provisions of the constitution where the act is not passed in the prescribed manner with the requisite majority for an alteration of those provisions.[802]

The constitution of India distinguishes between an original and appellate jurisdiction of the Supreme Court. The original and exclusive jurisdiction of the Supreme Court extends to:

> Any dispute between the Government of India and one car more states; or between the Government of India and any state or states on one side and one or more other states on the other; or between two or more states, if and in so far as the dispute involves any question on which the existence or extend of a legal right depends.[803]

The appellate jurisdiction of the Supreme Court in appeals from High Court an constitutional matters, is established as follows:

> An appeal shall lie to the Supreme Court from any judgment, decree or final order of a High Court in the territory of India, whether in a civil, criminal or other proceeding, if the High Court certifies that the case involves a substantial question of law as to the interpretation of this constitution.[804]

Nevertheless, the constitution states that the Supreme Court may grant special leave to appeal when "the High Court has refused to give such a certificate" and "it is satisfied that the case involves a substantial question of law as to the interpretation of this constitution."[805]

Other Commonwealth countries have established an exclusive jurisdiction of the Supreme Court on Constitutional issues, which leads to the adoption of a concentrated system of judicial review although it has been considered as being generally "intolerant" with the common law legal systems.[806] As we will see, such is the case in Papua New Guinea whose constitution gives the Supreme Court exclusive jurisdiction over questions of interpretation and application of Constitutional law, subject to the constitution. Consequently, when such a question arises in any Court or tribunal it shall be referred to the Supreme Court.[807] Special jurisdiction is also given to

---

801 C.A. KELSICK, "Report", in *Memoria de la reunión de Presidentes de Cortes Supremas de Justicia de Iberoamérica, el Caribe, España y Portugal*, Caracas 1983, p. 419.

802 *Idem*, p. 686

803 Art. 131. See in S.N. RAY, *op. cit.*, p. 290

804 Art. 132,1.

805 Art. 132,2

806 E. MC WHINNEY, "Constitutional Review ...", *loc.cit.*, p. 80

807 Art. 18, 19. See in J.D. WHYTE, *doc. cit.*, p. 25. *Cf.* in relation to Uganda, T.M. FRANCK, *Comparative Constitutional Process*, London 1968, p. 75.

the Supreme Court to enforce the fundamental Rights provisions of the constitution as well as to the National Court.[808]

As we mentioned, in general terms, the judicial review system followed in the commonwealth countries, is the diffuse system of judicial review, in accordance with the American model. Thus, it is traditional in these countries that courts *per se* and in an abstract way do not initiate actions, and that constitutional issues must be raised in a case or controversies, by a litigant with personal interest in the matter.[809] Nevertheless, a few exceptions to this principle could be found in the Commonwealth Countries Constitutional systems.

For instance, the constitution of Canada establishes the power of the Supreme Court to deliver "advisory opinions" ruling on an abstract constitutional issue referred to it by the federal government.[810] In a similar way, the constitution of India empowers the president to refer questions of laws or fact of particular nature or importance, to the Supreme Court to obtain opinion upon them–and the Court may, after such hearing as it thinks fit, report to the President its opinion there on.[811]

It must also be stressed that the constitution of the Republic of Ireland gives the President of the Republic the power to refer bills to the Supreme Court for an opinion as to whether the bill or any of its provisions is repugnant to the constitution.[812]

Finally, it must be said that due to the influence of the functioning of the British judicial organisation,[813] the *stare decisis* principle generally applies in the Commonwealth Countries, thus the decisions on Constitutional questions adopted by the Supreme Court even though of *inter partes* effects, have binding effects on the inferior courts. That is expressly stated in the constitution of India, where article 141 establishes that "the law declared by the Supreme Court shall be binding on all courts within the territory of India."[814] Nevertheless, regarding the Supreme Courts own decisions, the principle has been interpreted in a flexible way. The *stare decisis* doctrine, the Supreme Court has pointed out, is not an inflexible rule of law and cannot be allowed to perpetuate errors of the Supreme Court to the detriment of the general welfare of the people.[815]

---

808 Art. 57, 1. See in J.D. WHYTE, *doc. cit.*, p. 25.

809 *Cf.* S.N. RAY, *op. cit.*, pp. 77–89; Ch. OKPALUBA, *loc. cit.*, p. 112; E. MC WHINNEY, "Constitutional Review...", *loc.cit.*, pp. 83, 84

810 E. MC WHINNEY, "Constitutional Review ", *loc. cit.*, p. 83.

811 Art. 143. See in S.N.RAY, *op. cit.*, p. 294.

812 B. CHUBB, *op. cit.*, p. 22, 31; J.D. WHYTE, *doc. cit.*, p. 72.

813 J.D. WHYTE, *doc. cit.*, p. 11; E. MCWHINNEY, Judicial Review, *op. cit.*, p. 17.

814 See in S.N. RAY, *op. cit.*, p. 293

815 *Bengal Immunity v. State of Bihar*, AIR 1955 SC 661; (1955), 2 SCR 603, quoted by S.N. RAY, *op. cit.*, p. 85. *Cf.* P. TRIKAMDAS, "El Tribunal Supremo de la India", *Revista de la Comisión Internacional de Juristas*, Vol. VIII, Nº 1, 1967, p. 106.

PART V
CONCENTRATED SYSTEMS OF JUDICIAL REVIEW

I. GENERAL FEATURES

The concentrated system of judicial review, contrary to the diffuse system, is basically characterised by the fact that the constitutional system empowers one single state organ of a given country to act as a constitutional judge, in the sense of being the only state organ to decide upon constitutional matters regarding legislative acts and other state acts with similar rank or value, in a jurisdictional way.

This state body with the monopoly of acting as a constitutional judge, can either be the Supreme Court of Justice of the country, in its character as the highest court in the judicial hierarchy or it can also be a special Constitutional Court, Council or Tribunal, specially created by the Constitution to act as the only constitutional judge, and organised outside the ordinary judicial hierarchy. In both cases, the common trend regarding the activity of those bodies is that as constitutional judges they exercise a jurisdictional activity.

Therefore, the concentrated system of judicial review of the constitutionality of legislation, even though generally identified with the "European model" of special constitutional courts,[816] does not necessarily imply the existence of a special Constitutional Court, constitutionally organised separate from the ordinary judiciary. It only implies the assignment to a single state organ, which exercises jurisdictional activity, of the duty and power to act as a constitutional judge. This is the essence of the concentrated character of the system, contrasted with the diffuse system, whether the organ with constitutional justice power is the highest court of the judiciary or is a special constitutional body created outside the ordinary judicial organisation, not being essential to the distinction.

1. Logic of the System

From a logical and rational point of view, it can also be said that this power assigned to one state organ with jurisdictional activity to act as constitutional judge, is a consequence of the principle of the supremacy of the Constitution. In these systems of concentrated constitutional justice, the Constitution being the supreme law of the land, in cases of conflict between a state act and the Constitution, it is obvious that the latter must also prevail. But the constitutional system, in these cases, does not always empower all courts to act as constitutional judges, and in certain cases, it reserves the power to act as a constitutional judge to the Supreme Court of Justice or to a special constitutional court particularly regarding certain acts of the state, which

816 M. CAPPELLETTI, *Judicial Review in the Contemporary World*, Indianapolis 1971, pp. 50–53.

in cases of contradicting the Constitution, only the supreme court or the constitutional court has the power to annul it.

Therefore, it can be said that, in general terms, the logic of the system is also the supremacy of the constitution and the duty of the courts to say which law is applicable in a particular case,[817] but with a concrete limitation: the power to judge the unconstitutionality of legislative acts and other state acts of similar rank or value is reserved to the Supreme Court of Justice or to a Constitutional Court or Tribunal. Thus, in the concentrated system of judicial review, all courts only have the power to act as a constitutional judge and to decide upon the constitutionality of the other norms applicable to the case, other than statutes or acts adopted in direct execution of the Constitution.[818]

Consequently, the concentrated system of judicial review, based on the same principle of the supremacy of the Constitution, when reserving constitutional justice functions regarding certain state acts, to the Supreme Court or to a special Constitutional Court, cannot be developed by deduction through the work of the Supreme Court decisions, like it happened in the diffuse system of judicial review, as was the case for example, of the United States of America, the Republic of Argentina and some Commonwealth countries.

On the contrary, of course, due to the limits that the system imposes on the duty and power of all judges to say which law is applicable in the cases they are to decide, only when prescribed *expressis verbis* through constitutional regulations is it possible to establish the concentrated system of judicial review. It is the constitution, as the supreme law of the land, the only text that can establish limits upon the general power and duty of all courts to say which is the law applicable in a particular case, and assign that power and duty in certain cases regarding certain state acts, to a specific constitutional body, whether it be the Supreme Court of Justice or a constitutional court or tribunal.

Therefore, the concentrated system of judicial review can only be a jurisdictional system established and regulated expressly in the constitution, and the state organs to which the constitution reserves the power to act as constitutional judges regarding certain state acts, are always constitutional bodies, that is to say, state organs expressly created and regulated in the constitution whether they be the Supreme Court of Justice of a given country or a specially created constitutional court, tribunal or council.

---

817 *Cf.* W.K. GECK "Judicial Review of Statutes: A Comparative Survey of present Institutions and Practices", *Cornell Law Quarterly*, 51, 1966, p. 278.

818 *Cf.* M. GARCÍA PELAYO, "E1 'Status' del Tribunal Constitucional", *Revista española de derecho constitucional*, 1, Madrid 1981, p. 19; E. GARCÍA DE ENTERRÍA, *La Constitución como norma y el Tribunal Constitucional*, Madrid 1981, p. 65. In particular, in concentrated system of judicial review, the tribunals or courts empowered with administrative justice functions have always the power of acting as constitutional judge regarding administrative acts. See C. FRANK, *Les functions juridictionnelles du Conseil d'État dans l'ordre constitutionnel*, Paris 1974.

2. Compatibility of the System with all Legal Systems

Consequently, the concentrated system of judicial review of the constitutionality of legislation is not a system that can be considered peculiar to the civil law system of law, and incompatible with the common law tradition. It is only a system that must be expressly established and regulated in a written Constitution and it can therefore indifferently exist in systems with a common law tradition or with a civil law basis, though it is most commonly followed in civil law countries.

For instance, in Papua New Guinea, a country that gained its independence from Australia in 1975 and, therefore, with a common law tradition, the Constitution gives the Supreme Court exclusive jurisdiction over questions of interpretation and application of constitutional law, subject to the Constitution. Therefore, when such a question arises in any court or tribunal, it shall be referred to the Supreme Court.[819] In a similar sense, the 1966 Constitution of Uganda also established an exclusive jurisdiction of the High Court on constitutional matters. In this respect, article 95 stated that:

> Where any question as to the interpretation of this Constitution arises in any proceedings in any court of law, other than a court–martial, and the court is of the opinion that the question involves a substantial question of law, the court may, and shall if any party to the proceedings so request, refer the question to the High Court consisting of a bench of no less than three judges of the High Court.

The same article added:

> Where any question is referred to the High Court in pursuance of this article, the High Court shall give its decision upon the question and the court in which the question arose, shall dispose of the case in accordance with that decision.[820]

We must also refer to the system established in Ghana in the 1960, 1969 and 1979 Constitutions, which vested the Supreme Court with original and exclusive jurisdiction to exercise the power of judicial review. In effect, article 42 of the 1960 Constitution and article 106 of the 1969 Constitution stated:

> The Supreme Court shall have original jurisdiction in all matters where a question arises whether an enactment was made in excess of the powers conferred on Parliament by or under the Constitution, and if any such question arises in the High Court or an inferior court, the hearing shall be adjourned and the question referred to the Supreme Court for decision.[821]

Additionally, article 2 of the 1969 Constitution established a direct action that could be brought before the Supreme Court to seek judicial review, as follows:

> A person who alleges that an enactment or anything contained in or done under the authority of that or any other enactment is inconsistent with, or in contravention of, any provi-

---

819 Art. 18 and 19 of the Constitution. See in J.D. WHYTE, *Judicial Review of Legislation and its Legitimacy:Developments in the Common Law World*, IALS, Uppsala, Colloquium 1984, (mimeo), p. 25.

820 See in T.M. FRANCK, *Comparative Constitutional Process. Cases and Materials*, London 1968, pp. 75–76.

821 See in S.O. GYANDOH Jr., "Interaction of the Judicial and Legislative Processes in Ghana since Independence", *Temple Law Quarterly*, 56, 2, Philadelphia 1983, pp. 365–366, 370.

sion of this Constitution, may bring an action in the Supreme Court for a declaration to that effect.[822]

For the purpose of that declaration, added the Constitution, the Supreme Court shall "make such orders and give such directions as it may consider appropriate for giving effect to or enabling effect to be given to the declarations so made."[823] Those provisions regarding judicial review were also adopted in the 1979 Constitution,[824] but since 1971, they were interpreted by the Supreme Court to reduce the referral of proceeding cases to the Supreme Court, and to avoid referrals of frivolous submissions.[825]

Anyway, even though it is certain that the system of judicial review has not always functioned in some Commonwealth countries because of democratic instability,[826] what is certain is that the concentrated system of judicial review exists and has functioned in legal systems, with a common law tradition. Thus, there is the expression of Professor Edward McWhinney in the sense that common law "practice has always been intolerant of the notion of specialised, expert, tribunals on the continental model" [827] must be understood as referring to the specialised constitutional court, tribunal or council European system, but not, as he said, to a system "where jurisdiction is determined and limited in terms of subject matters,"[828] which refers to the very concept of the concentrated system of judicial review, when, for instance, assigned to a Supreme Court of Justice of a given country and not to a special non–judicial constitutional organ.

The concentrated system of judicial review cannot be reduced to the constitutional systems in which a constitutional court, tribunal or council exists; having produced a distortion of the approach to the system the misleading identification of the concentrated system with the European model of specialised constitutional courts, council or tribunal.

In effect, though the concentrated system of judicial review is also known as the "Austrian system"[829] or as the "European model",[830] based on the existence of a

---

822 *Idem*, p. 370.

823 Art. 2, *Idem*, p. 370.

824 *Idem*, p. 384.

825 *Republic v. Maikankan* (1971) 2 G.L.R., 473 quoted by S.O. GYANDOH Jr., *loc. cit.*, p. 386.

826 See in relation to Ghana the comments of S.O. GYANDOH Jr., *loc. cit.*, p. 395.

827 E. MCWHINNEY, "Constitutional Review in the Commonwealth", in H. MOSLER (ed.), Max–Plank–Institut für Ausländisches öffentliches recht and völkerrecht, *Verfassungs gerichtsbarkeit in der Gegenwart*, Internationales Kolloquium, Heidelberg, 1961, Köln–Berlin 1962, p. 80

828 *Idem*, p. 80.

829 M. CAPPELLETTI, *op. cit.*, p. 50; J. CARPIZO and H. FIX–ZAMUDIO, "La necesidad y la legitimidad de la revisión judicial en América latina. Desarrollo reciente", *Boletín Mexicano de Derecho Comparado*, 52, 1985, p. 36.

830 L. FAVOREU, "Actualité et légitimité du contrôl juridictionnel des lois en Europe occidentale", *Revue du droit public et de la science politique en France et à l'étranger*, Paris 1985

specialised constitutional court, tribunal or council created, in the constitution, with the power to act as a constitutional judge although organised outside the ordinary judiciary, we must insist that the feature that characterises the system is not the existence of such a special constitutional court, tribunal or council at all, but the exclusive attribution to a single constitutional state body of the power to act as a constitutional judge regarding certain state acts, whether that body be the existing Supreme Court of Justice of the country or a specially created constitutional court, council or tribunal.

The adoption of the system is always a constitutional option and decision according to the concrete circumstances of each country, but it does not necessarily imply the creation of special constitutional courts or bodies to ensure constitutional justice. In Europe, for instance, the flourishing of constitutional courts, tribunals or councils for the exercise of the concentrated system of judicial review, can only be seen as a concrete consequence of a peculiar constitutional tradition regarding the principles of the supremacy of the law, the separation of powers and the traditional fear of the judges to control legislative acts[831] and cannot lead to considering that "the" model of the concentrated system of judicial review consists in the creation of a constitutional body outside the ordinary judiciary to act as constitutional judge. Well before the European "discovery" of constitutional justice by creating those special constitutional courts or tribunals after the First World War, ever since the middle of the last century (19th century), other countries with a civil law tradition have developed concentrated systems of judicial review by attributing the original and exclusive jurisdiction to annul statutes and other state acts with similar rank and effects to their Supreme Courts of Justice when contrary to the constitution. This has been the common trend of the Latin American constitutional system, even though mixing the concentrated with the diffuse system of judicial review.

Therefore, from what we have said, three conclusions can be drawn: First, the concentrated system of judicial review can only exist when it is established *expressis verbis* in the constitution, therefore, it cannot be developed by interpretation of the principle of the supremacy of the constitution. Second, the concentrated system of judicial review characterised by the granting to one single constitutional body of the functions of constitutional justice, is compatible to any legal system, whether common law or roman law legal systems, even though it has widely developed in the civil law countries. Third, the concentrated system of judicial review does not only imply the attribution of the functions of constitutional justice to a special constitutional court, tribunal or council created separate to the ordinary judicial organisation. It also exists when constitutional justice functions are attributed to the existing Supreme Court of Justice of the country, even though in the latter case the sys-

---

(5), p. 1149. Also published in L. FAVOREU and J.A. JOLOWICZ (ed.), *Le contrôle juridictionnel des lois, Légitimité, effectivité et développments récents*, Paris 1986, pp. 17–68.

831 *Cf.* M. CAPPELLETTI, *op. cit.*, p. 54; M. CAPPELLETTI and J.C. ADAMS, "Judicial Review of Legislation: European Antecedents and Adaptation", *Harvard Law Review*, Vol 79, (6), 1966, p. 1211.

tem generally tends to mix its trends with elements of the diffuse system of judicial review.

3. Rationality of the System

As we have said, in a similar way as in the diffuse system of judicial review, the essence of the concentrated system of judicial review is also the very notion of the supremacy of the constitution: if the constitution is the supreme law of the land prevailing over all other laws, no state act contrary to it can be an effective law; on the contrary, it must be considered as null and void. Thus the main element that leads to the differentiation between both systems of judicial review is not, of course, a possible different notion of the constitution and its supremacy, but the type of guarantee adopted in the constitutional system to maintain that supremacy. As Hans Kelsen pointed out in 1928, these "objective guarantees" are the nullity or the annulability of the unconstitutional act. Nullity means –as he explained– the unconstitutional state act cannot be considered objectively as a juridical act, therefore in principle it is not necessary to take away its quality of usurped juridical act, by means of another juridical act. In this case, theoretically, everybody, public authorities or individuals would have the right to examine the regularity of the acts considered null and void, to declare the irregularity and to consider such acts as non valid and non obligatory. On the contrary, if another juridical act is necessary to establish the nullity of the unconstitutional act, the guarantee of the constitution would not be of nullity but of annulability.[832]

As we have seen, the nullity of unconstitutional state acts is the guarantee of the constitution that leads to the diffuse system of judicial review, even though as Kelsen pointed out, positive law normally restricts this power that anybody has of considering irregular acts as null and void,[833] and tends to attribute it exclusively to the courts, which is the general situation today due to the need for legal reliability.

On the other hand, it is precisely the other guarantee of the constitution, the annulability of the unconstitutional state acts, which leads to the concentrated system of judicial review.

A. *Annulability of Certain Unconstitutional State Acts*

In effect, the first aspect that shows the rationality of the concentrated system of judicial review is the principle of the annulability of certain state acts, particularly statutes and other acts issued in direct execution of the Constitution, when they are considered to be contrary to the constitution.

This annulability of a state acts as an objective guarantee of the constitution, and contrary to the situation concerning the nullity of such acts, means that a state act, even if it is irregular or unconstitutional, once issued by a public body it must be considered as such a state act, and therefore, valid and effective, until it is repealed

---

832 H. KELSEN, "La guarantie juridictionelle de la Constitution. La Justice constitutionnelle", *Revue du droit public et de la science politique en France et à l'étranger*, Paris 1928, p. 214.

833 *Idem*, p. 215.

by the same organ which produced it or until it is annulled by another state organ with constitutional powers to do so. It is precisely in the concentrated systems of judicial review, in which the constitution assigns the power to annul certain state acts when considered unconstitutional, to only one state organ, whether it be to the existing supreme court of justice or to a special constitutional body created separate from the ordinary judiciary, but with jurisdictional functions to act as a constitutional judge.

In fact, we must bear in mind that in the concentrated systems of judicial review, the annulability of state acts is not really the only guarantee of the constitution, and is always accompanied by the nullity. In a certain way it is a restriction to the nullity rule resulting from the violation of the constitution.

We have said, in effect, that in the case of the nullity of unconstitutional state acts that exist in the diffuse system of judicial review, in order to avoid juridical anarchy, positive law limits the theoretical general power that public authorities and individuals have to declare the inexistence of an unconstitutional state act and to consider it invalid, and reserves this power to the judges. This means that in fact, the unconstitutional state act can only be examined by the courts and only the courts have the power to consider it null and void, which means that up to that moment, the irregular act must be considered by other public authorities and individuals as being effective and obligatory. In the diffuse system of judicial review, once the court declares the invalidity of the unconstitutional act in relation to a particular process, then the act becomes null and void regarding that process.

It can be said that, in principle, this same situation exists even in constitutional systems with a concentrated system of judicial review regarding all other state acts different to those which can only be annulled by the Constitutional or the Supreme Courts. In effect, as we have said, regarding state acts of lower levels in the hierarchy of norms, for instance, administrative acts with normative effects, all judges in a concentrated system of judicial review normally have the power to consider them null and void when unconstitutional, with respect to the particular process in which they are questioned. In such cases, the guarantee of the constitution is the nullity of the unconstitutional state act, even though only the courts can assume it.

Therefore, what is peculiar to the concentrated system of judicial review is that constitutional positive law establishes an additional limitation concerning the effects of the unconstitutionality of state acts, in the sense that concerning certain acts, the power to declare their unconstitutionality and invalidity and therefore, to consider them to be without effect, has been exclusively reserved to one constitutional organ: the existing supreme court of justice or a special constitutional court, tribunal or council. In those cases, and regarding such certain acts, normally being legislative acts and other state acts of similar rank or effect in the sense of being issued in direct execution of the constitution, the guarantee of the constitution has been reduced to the annulability of the state act considered unconstitutional.

In conclusion, in constitutional systems with a concentrated system of judicial review, the duty of all judges and courts is also to examine the constitutionality of statutes and other state acts. Nevertheless when the state act questioned on the grounds of unconstitutionality is a statute or other state act issued in direct execution of the constitution, the ordinary courts cannot judge its unconstitutionality, That power is reserved to a special constitutional court or to the supreme court of a given country, which can annul the act. In this case the guarantee of the constitution is the annulability, in which case, the act is annulled with general effects, and not only considered or declared null and void in a particular case.

Leaving aside this particular reserve –which is the feature of the concentrated system of judicial review– all other courts, regarding the normative state acts not included in the reserve, have the power to examine their unconstitutionality. Moreover, when necessary the courts have the power to establish their inapplicability to a particular process that the court is considering, because it is unconstitutional and therefore must be considered null and void. In those other cases, the guarantee of the constitution certainly is the nullity.

B. *Power of a Special Constitutional Body Regarding the Annulment of Certain State Acts on the Grounds of Unconstitutionality*

This leads to the second aspect of the rationality of the concentrated system of judicial review, which is that the power to declare the nullity of legislation is assigned to one single constitutional organ with jurisdictional functions, whether it be the existing supreme court of a country or a specially created constitutional court, tribunal or council. Therefore, the concentrated system has a double particularity: first that the power to annul unconstitutional acts is assigned to a single constitutional organ with jurisdictional functions. Second, that the reserve assigned to that constitutional body to judge the unconstitutionality and declare the nullity of state acts concerns not all state acts, but rather a limited number of them normally identified with statutes (legislation) and other acts of Parliament or of the government issued in direct execution of the constitution, thus being subject to the sole rule of the constitution.

We have said that the concentrated system of judicial review does not necessarily imply the assignment of the power to annul statutes to a specially created constitutional court, tribunal or council in the European fashion, and that power can be assigned to the existing Supreme Court of Justice of a given country, as happened well before the constitutional court fashion developed after the 1920's in continental Europe.

In effect, since the middle of the last century (19th century), many Latin American countries have adopted a concentrated system of judicial review by assigning the supreme court of the country with the power to declare the nullity of legislation. This was the case in Colombia and Venezuela in which an authentic concentrated system of judicial review has existed since 1850 and in which the supreme courts have the monopoly of annulling statutes. It is true that normally the concentrated systems of judicial review in Latin America developed in the last hundred and thirty years have moved towards a mixed system of judicial review in which the diffuse and the concentrated systems of judicial review coexist. That is the system that currently exists, for instance in Colombia, Venezuela and Guatemala, which we will analyse further on in our course. Yet, some Latin American systems have remained concentrated ones, as is the case in Uruguay and Paraguay, in which countries the

Supreme Court of Justice has exclusive and original jurisdiction to declare the unconstitutionality of statutes.[834]

Of course, the modality of the concentrated system of judicial review that consists in establishing a special constitutional body, whether court, tribunal or council to act as a constitutional judge vested with original and exclusive power to annul statutes and other similar acts in rank or effects, because of its novelty, has marked the development of constitutional, justice during the recent decades, since the first constitutional courts were established in Austria and Czechoslovakia in 1920. The system was later adopted in Germany and Italy, after the Second World War, and more recently in Spain and Portugal. It has also been adopted in some socialist countries (Yugoslavia, Czechoslovakia and Poland) and has been developed with particular trends, in France. Under the influence of the European model, but in an incomplete way the system was adopted in the early seventies in Chile, where a Constitutional Tribunal was established, and more recently in Ecuador and Peru, where Constitutional Guarantees Tribunals have been created.

We will refer to all these experiences, but firstly we will concentrate our comments on the European model and in particular, on the analysis of the various Constitutional Courts experiences.

As we have said, even though constitutionalism developed in the theory and practice of constitutional law since the beginning of the last century (19th century), mainly as a contribution of the North American experience, it must be admitted that continental European constitutionalism remained on the fringes of the American conceptions, and a system of constitutional justice was not accepted in Europe until after the First World War, and took place through two paths. One concluded in the *Weimar* Constitution (1919), whereby Germany established a Tribunal entrusted with jurisdiction to settle disputes between the state constitutional powers, and more specifically, between the different territorial powers, vertically distributed as a result of the federal organisation of the state. The second was the Austrian system, the personal masterpiece of Professor Hans Kelsen, who conceived a system first expressed in the 1920 Austrian constitution and perfected by the 1929 constitutional reform.

In any case, it can be considered that the incorporation of a system of constitutional justice in Europe was due to the influence of Hans Kelsen's pure theory of law. This theory, as we have mentioned, conceived the constitutional norm as the grounds for the validity of all the norms of a given legal order, with a fundamental corollary: the need for a state body to guarantee the constitution, that is to say, to settle disputes over the consistency of all legal norms, both specific and general, with the superior hierarchy on which they are based, and in the last instance, with the constitution.[835]

---

834 H. GROS ESPIELL, *La Constitución y su Defensa*. Uruguay, UNAM, Congreso Internacional sobre la Constitución y su defensa México, 1982, (mimeo) p. 7; J.P. GATTO DE SOUZA, "El control constitucional de los actos del poder público", *Memoria de la reunión de Presidentes de Cortes Supremas de Justicia de Iberoamérica, el Caribe, España y Portugal*, Caracas 1983, p. 661; L.M. ANGAÑA, "Ponencia" (Paraguay), *idem*, p. 551.

835 H. KELSEN, *loc. cit*., pp. 201–223.

Kelsen himself established quite clearly that constitutional justice was in itself a special case of a more general issue, which consisted of the guarantee of the consistency of an inferior norm to a superior norm from whence it arose and its contents were determined. In the end constitutional justice was a guarantee of the constitution resulting from the "juridical pyramid" of the legal order whereby the unity and hierarchy of its different norms were established.

However, it should be noted that in addition to Austria, and also under the influence of Kelsen, Czechoslovakia was the first European country to adopt a system of constitutional control in the constitution of 29 February 1920.[836] The grounds for the establishment of the Czechoslovakian concentrated system of constitutional control are to be found, to be sure, in the existence of a constitutional norm, which explicitly sets forth the supremacy of the constitution over the rest of the legal order, by stating that, "All laws contrary to the Constitutional Charter and any part thereof, as well as laws that modify and complement it, are considered null and void";[837] and by explicitly prohibiting the courts from the possibility of exercising diffuse control over the constitutionality of laws.[838] In addition, the constitution established the obligation for all courts to consult with the Constitutional Tribunal, in cases of the enforcement of a law deemed to be in violation of the constitution. Those elements led to the concentration of constitutional jurisdiction to judge the constitutionality of laws in a single body, the Constitutional Tribunal, which continued to exist until 1938.[839]

Kelsen's conception of the concentrated system of judicial review, contrary to the diffuse system which, as we have seen, implies that all judges are entitled to abstain from enforcing laws they deem contrary to the Constitution, therefore results in the attribution of the exclusive power to declare the unconstitutionality of a law, and annul it, to a single state body, the constitutional tribunal, to which all courts must refer when they are in the situation of having to enforce a law of doubtful constitutionality. Consequently, in this system, ordinary courts lack the power to refrain from enforcing unconstitutional laws on their own.

In its original theoretical conception, this concentrated system of judicial control of constitutionality attributed to a special court, was not conceived by Kelsen as being the exercise of a jurisdictional function but rather as "a system of negative legis-

---

836 Art. I.1. See in P. CRUZ VILLALON, "Dos modos de regulación del control de constitucionalidad: Checoslovaquia (1920–1938) y España (1931–1936)", *Revista española de derecho constitucional*, 5, Madrid 1982, p. 119.

837 Art. I.1., *idem.*

838 Art. 102 established "The courts can verify the validity of executive regulations, when deciding upon a specific question of laws; concerning statutes they can only verify if they have been correctly published", see in P. CRUZ VILLALON, *loc. cit.*, p. 135.

839 It also should be noted that the Rumanian constitutional regime also established a system of judicial review of laws, in Article 103 of the Fundamental Charter of 29 March 1923. However, it was conferred only on the Court of Cassation, and later on it was eliminated by the People's Republic, under Soviet influence, from the terms of the Fundamental Law of 1948.

lation."[840] In fact, a constitutional court does not specifically decide upon the unconstitutionality of statutes on any assumption of a single fact; this is reserved for the *a quo* court raising the question of constitutionality. Its competence is normally limited to the purely abstract issue of the logical compatibility, which must exist between the statute and the constitution. Therefore, in this purely logical judgement, as there is no real enforcement of the law in any specific case, it was considered that it was not the case of jurisdictional activity which implied a concrete decision. This led Kelsen to maintain that when the constitutional tribunal declares a statute unconstitutional, the decision having *erga omnes* effects was a typical legislative action, hence the common assumption that the constitutional tribunal's decision has the force of law. That is also why it is considered that until that decision is adopted, the statute is valid and that explains why judges of ordinary courts are obliged to enforce it.[841]

Kelsen developed this conception as an answer to the possible objections that the jurisdictional control of legislative action could produce, based on the concept of the supremacy of Parliament so embodied in European constitutional law. Thus, by forbidding ordinary judges to abstain from enforcing the laws and granting the power to declare a statute unconstitutional with *erga omnes* effect to the constitutional court, the judiciary was subject to the laws adopted by parliament. At the same time, the primacy of the constitution over Parliament could be maintained. In this way, it was considered that the constitutional tribunal instead of competing with parliament became its logical complement. Its function was reduced to judging the validity of a statute with simple and rational logic, completely separate from the need to settle disputes in specific cases, and acting as a negative legislator, albeit a legislator which does not act spontaneously but at the request of the parties involved. In this way, legislative power was for Kelsen divided into two bodies: the first, parliament, the holder of political initiative, the positive legislator; and the second, the constitutional tribunal, entrusted with the power to annul laws which violate the constitution.[842]

Under this conception, of course, the constitutional court needed to be a constitutional body separate from all traditional state powers: thus it was not a judicial body.[843]

Anyway, today, even though the jurisdictional character –non legislative– of the activity developed by these special constitutional bodies rejecting its supposed negative legislator character[844] is accepted without discussion, the conception of attributing constitutional justice functions to a specially created constitutional body (constitutional court, tribunal or council) generally not located within the judiciary organi-

840 H. KELSEN, *loc. cit.*, pp. 224–226. See the comments of E. GARCÍA DE ENTERRÍA, *op. cit.*, pp. 57–132.

841 H. KELSEN, *loc. cit*, pp. 224–225.

842 See the comments on KELSEN's thought in E. GARCÍA DE ENTERRÍA, *op. cit.*, pp. 57, 58, 59, 131, and 132–133.

843 H. KELSEN, *loc. cit.*, p. 223.

844 M. CAPPELLETTI and J.C. ADAMS, *loc. cit.*, pp. 1218–1219.

sation has prevailed in continental Europe, and has given way to the "European model" of judicial review. This model developed in a certain way as the result of a compromise between the need of a system of constitutional justice derived from the notion of constitutional supremacy, and the traditional European conception of the separation of powers which denied the power to invalidate statutes to all judicial organs.[845]

Nevertheless, as we have said, it is improper to identify the concentrated system of judicial review with this "European model", because it is also a concentrated system, one in which the exclusive and original jurisdiction to annul statutes and other state acts is conferred upon the existing Supreme Court of Justice of a given country, and located at the apex of the judiciary organisation. Thus, the second aspect which shows the rationality of the concentrated system of judicial review is the assignment of the role of constitutional judge to annul statutes with *erga omnes* effects, to one single constitutional organ whether it be the supreme court of justice of a given country or a specially created constitutional court, tribunal or council.

C. *Principal and incidental character of the system*

Contrary to the diffuse system of judicial review, which is always of an incidental character, the concentrated system of judicial review can have either a principal or incidental character, in the sense that constitutional questions regarding statutes may reach the supreme court or the constitutional court, by virtue of a direct action or request brought before the court or by reference of the question to the court, from a lower court, where the constitutional question has been raised in a concrete proceeding, either *ex–officio* or through the initiative of a party.

Therefore, the third aspect that shows the rationality of the concentrated system of judicial review of the constitutionality of legislation, in which the power to annul statutes is attributed to a single court, is that the constitutional question can either reach the supreme court or the constitutional court, in a direct or principal form, through the exercise before the court of an action against the statute; or in an incidental form, when the constitutional issue is raised in a particular process in a lower court in which case the judge must refer his decision to the supreme court or the constitutional court, in order to subsequently render his final resolution of the case in accordance with the Supreme Court or Constitutional Court adjudication.

In both cases, the control of the constitutionality of legislation is a concentrated one, because one single organ is authorised to pass judgement upon the constitutionality of a statute, but this essential feature does not imply that the constitutional question must only be raised either in a principal or in an incidental way. It can be either one form or the other, or through both in parallel, depending on the concrete positive law regulations. Therefore, in our opinion, there is no evidence in comparative law, to identify the concentrated system of judicial review with the principal character of the method of reviewing the constitutional question, in which such a question is entirely disassociated from a concrete case. If this was true in the original

845 M. CAPPELLETTI, *op. cit.*, p. 67.

Austrian system established in 1920, it is no longer true in contemporary constitutional law,[846] where the concentrated system of judicial review can result from both methods, principal or incidental. In the principal method, the constitutional issue regarding a statute is the only and principal question of the process initiated through the exercise of a direct action that can be brought before the supreme court or the constitutional court, either by someone through an *actio popularis* or within some *locus standing* rules or by specific public officials and authorities. In the incidental method the constitutional issue is raised before an ordinary court as an incidental question aspect of a process, or the court can raise it *ex–officio*. This court is the one which must refer the constitutional question to the decision by the supreme court or by the constitutional court, the suspension of the decision of the concrete case being necessary until the constitutional issue is resolved by the supreme court or the constitutional court.

D. *Initiative Power on Judicial Review*

The constitutional question relating to the validity of a statute, as we have seen, is normally raised in the supreme court or in the constitutional court through an action or through reference by a lower court and in both cases, the constitutional judge must decide the issue on the basis of the law and without considering the facts.

In both cases, as we said, the constitutional question must be raised before the Supreme Court or the constitutional court, which does not have self initiative to act as a constitutional judge.[847] Thus the principle *nemo iudex sine actore* applies. But once a constitutional question has reached the court as a result of an action or of a lower court referral, the principle *ne iudex iudicet ultra petitum partis* does not apply. That is to say, the constitutional court as constitutional judge, once required by a party or through incidental means, has *ex–officio* powers to consider other questions of constitutionality, other than those already submitted.

However, if it is true that the supreme court or the constitutional court does not have its own initiative to initiate the constitutional justice proceeding regarding legislation, on the other hand it must be said that in the incidental method of concentrated judicial review, the lower courts that must refer the decision of the constitutional issue to the constitutional judge, can have the initiative in raising the issue for referral to the supreme court or to the constitutional court. That is to say, the ordinary courts when raising constitutional issues in the incidental method are not always bound by the requirements of the parties or of the public prosecutor, and when considering the particular case, they can raise the constitutional question *ex–officio* and refer it to the Supreme Court or the constitutional court for decision.

This is the consequence of the principle of the supremacy of the constitution and of the duty of all judges to apply the law. Moreover, if it is true that in the concen-

---

846 *Cf.* M. CAPPELLETTI, *op. cit*, pp. 69–72.

847 Exceptionally, the Federal Constitutional Tribunal of Yugoslavia has *ex officio* powers to initiate a proceeding of judicial review of legislation. See Art. 4, Law of the Constitutional Court of Yugoslavia. 31–12–1963, in B.T. BLAGOJEVIC (ed.), *Constitutional Judicature*, Beograd 1965, p. 16.

trated system of judicial review, the constitution has forbidden the ordinary courts to act as constitutional judges, this could not mean that if they consider a statute applicable to the decision of a concrete case unconstitutional, they do not have the power to raise the constitutional question and cannot refer it to the constitutional judge. The contrary would mean a break in the principle of constitutional supremacy and in the role of the judiciary when applying the law.

E. Erga omnes *effects of the Court decision*

The fifth and final aspect of the rationality of the concentrated system of judicial review as in the diffuse system, also concerns the effects of the decisions adopted by the supreme court or the constitutional court in regard to the constitutionality of the statute, according to the constitutional question posed in the action or in the lower court referral. This aspect of the effects of the judicial decision also refers in such cases, to two questions: first, whom the decision affects; and second, when do the effects of the decision begin.

In relation to the first question, the rationality of the concentrated system of judicial review is that the decision adopted by the constitutional court or the supreme court acting as a constitutional judge, has general effects, thus it applies *erga omnes*. This is particularly exact when judicial review is sought by a direct action brought before the constitutional court or the supreme court, in which there is no concrete case between parties whatsoever and in which proceeding there are no real parties in the strictest sense. When a direct action is brought before the constitutional judge, the process relation is not between a plaintiff and a defendant but basically between a petitioner and a statute whose constitutionality is challenged. In this case, the process is considered an objective process; consequently, the object of the decision upon the unconstitutionality of the statute being its annulment, its effects necessarily must be *erga omnes* and cannot be *inter partes* basically because of the absence of the said proper parties.

Nevertheless, in the concentrated system of judicial review even when sought by incidental methods, when a constitutional issue regarding a statute is raised in a concrete proceeding and the lower court refers it to decision by the supreme court or the constitutional court, its decision being concentrated on aspects regarding law only and not facts, also has *erga omnes* effects, that is to say, they are not limited to the concrete process and parties in which the constitutional question was originally raised.

In effect, in both cases of concentrated systems of judicial review, sought by principal or incidental methods, the supreme court or the constitutional court decides in abstract a question of constitutionality of a statute, without any reference to facts or to the concrete process in which the constitutional issue may be raised, if it be so. Therefore, the constitutional judge in the concentrated system is not deciding a constitutional issue only to decide a concrete case between parties. The constitutional judge, as we said, in these cases does not decide a concrete case, but only a question of constitutionality of a statute, therefore, the logic of the system is that the decision must apply in general, to everybody and to all state organs, thus the *erga omnes* effects.

Thus if a law is considered unconstitutional by the Constitutional Court or by the supreme court acting as constitutional judge, this means that the law thereof is annulled and cannot be enforceable and applicable not only to the resolution of a particular case, but elsewhere.

F. *Constitutive effects of the Supreme Court or Constitutional Court decision*

These *erga omnes* effects of the judicial decision in the concentrated system of judicial review are closely related to the other question concerning the effects of the decision in time, namely as to when the declaration of unconstitutionality is to be effective, and of course, as to the already mentioned aspect of the annulability of certain state acts, as a guarantee of the constitution.

In effect, we have said that the first and foremost fundamental aspect of the rationality of the concentrated system of judicial review, as it is in the diffuse system, is that of the supremacy of the constitution over all state acts which leads to the consideration that the laws contrary to the constitution must be null and void. We have also said that, even if the guarantee of the constitution in the concentrated systems of judicial review in principle is also the nullity of the unconstitutional state acts, regarding certain state acts, like the legislative ones, the constitution has restricted its own guarantee by reserving the appreciation and declaration of its nullity to only one single constitutional organ: the supreme court or a specially created constitutional court, tribunal or council, to which the exclusive power of declaring the nullity of the said state acts has been granted.

Consequently, when a constitutional judge decides upon the unconstitutionality of a law and establishes it, the decision has a *constitutive* effect: it declares the nullity of a law because it is unconstitutional, the law having produced effects up to the moment in which its nullity is established. Thus the law, whose nullity is declared and established, is considered in principle by the court as having been valid up to that moment.

That is why it is said that the decision of the court, as it is a constitutive one, has *ex–nunc*, *pro futuro* or prospective effects, in the sense that, in principle, they do not go back to the moment of the enactment of the statute considered thereon unconstitutional, the effects produced by the annulled statute until that annulment being considered valid.

The legislative act declared unconstitutional by a constitutional judge in the concentrated system of judicial review, therefore, is considered as a valid act until its annulment by the court, having produced complete effects until the moment, when the court annuls it.

Nevertheless, this element of the logic of the concentrated system of judicial review is normally tempered by the constitutional system itself, when a distinction is established between the unconstitutionality errors, or defects that can affect statutes, whether they produce its absolute or relative nullity. Therefore, in cases when constitutional errors that may affect a statute produce an absolute nullity, when the annulment of the statute is decided upon by the constitutional judge, it evidently produces as an outcome *ex–tunc* effects of the decision, because a statute considered null and void in an absolute form is not capable of producing any effect. Thus in those cases, the annulment of the statute has *pro–pretaerito* or retroactive effects, being considered null and void *ab initio*. On the contrary, if the constitutional errors or defects of the statute, which lead to its annulment by the constitutional judge, are not so grave as to produce its absolute nullity but only its relative nullity, the effects of the annulment of the statute are only *ex–nunc*, *pro futuro*.

4. Conclusion

In conclusion we can say that as a matter of principle, the rationality of the diffuse system of judicial review works as follows:

The Constitution has a supreme character over the whole legal order; thus, acts contrary to the Constitution cannot have any effects, and are considered null and void.

In principle, and concerning state acts of a lower rank in the legal order, all courts have the power and the duty to apply the constitution and the laws, and therefore, to give preference to the constitution and statutes over those state acts which violate them, and to declare them unconstitutional and inapplicable to the concrete process developed before the courts. Nevertheless, regarding certain state acts, normally statutes (laws) and other acts issued in direct execution of the constitution, this fundamental text expressly reserves the power to examine and declare the unconstitutionality of such acts, and to annul them to one single constitutional organ, whether it be the supreme court of a given country or a specially created constitutional court, tribunal or council.

This power of the particular constitutional judge to declare the nullity of certain state acts, can only be exercised when required whether by means of a direct action brought before it against the unconstitutional statute, to be examined in an abstract way, or when a lower court refers a constitutional question that has been raised in a concrete process to the constitutional judge. In the latter case, the incidental character of the issue has suspensive effects, and the case before the ordinary court will only be decided after the constitutional judge has rendered his decision on the constitutionality of the statute, also in an abstract way without referring to the facts of the concrete process.

The judgement of the Constitutional Court must then be taken when required through a principal or incidental method, regarding the constitutionality of legislation, it not being possible to raise the constitutional question *motu proprio* or *ex–officio* by the constitutional judge. Nevertheless, when the constitutional question is brought before the constitutional judge it has *ex–officio* power to consider other constitutional issues; and in cases of incidental means the lower court that raised the issue has *ex–officio* powers to do so, and is not limited to the parties' initiative.

The decision adopted by the court concerning the unconstitutionality of a law, has *erga omnes* effects regarding all state organs and individuals; and it is of a constitutive effect in the sense that it pronounces the nullity of the statute, thus, it annuls it. When declaring the nullity of the statute, therefore, the decision has *ex–nunc*, and *pro futuro* effects in the sense that they are not retroactive. In that case the annulled act must be considered as having produced its effects as a valid act prior to its annulment, unless when it is considered that it is affected by an absolute nullity.

Of course, in the concentrated systems of judicial review, this logic is not always absolute, and each legal system has also developed corrections to the possible deviation that each one of the aspects of the rationality of the system may produce concerning the nullity or annulability of the unconstitutional act; the initiative of the court; the *inter partes* or *erga omnes* effects of the decision and its declarative or constitutive character.

In analysing the most important concentrated systems of judicial review of the constitutionality of legislation particularly to those that follow the European model, we will refer to all the aspects of the rationality of the system and its special modifications.

II. ORIGIN OF THE "EUROPEAN MODEL" OF JUDICIAL REVIEW AND THE AUSTRIAN SYSTEM OF THE CONSTITUTIONAL TRIBUNAL

1. European Antecedents

The concentrated system of judicial review based on the assignment of the exclusive power to control the constitutionality of legislation to a single constitutional state body, specially created outside the normal organisation of the judicial power, is basically a European institution: it was originated in Europe, where it was developed particularly after the two World Wars, and has remained in Europe[848] giving rise to the so called "European model" of judicial review[849] also qualified as the "Austrian system."[850] It is not, of course, the only expression of the concentrated system of judicial review, because as we have mentioned, its essence is not the existence of a constitutional court or tribunal established separate from the ordinary judicial power, but the concentration of powers of judicial review of the constitutionality of legislation in one single organ, that can perfectly be the existing supreme court of a country situated at the apex of judicial power.[851] Therefore, the concentrated system of

848 Exceptionally and without doubt, under the European influence, some Latin American Countries have established Constitutional Tribunals. Is the case of Chile, Guatemala, Ecuador and Peru, with various and different control power that except in the case of Guatemala (J.M. GARCÍA LAGUARDIA, *La Defensa de la Constitución*, UNAM, México, 1983, p. 52) lead to the conclusion that the similarities with the European model are more a matter of names or denominations, than of power of control. See in general, H. FIX–ZAMUDIO, *Los tribunales constitucionales y los derechos humanos*, UNAM, México, 1980; H. FIX–ZAMUDIO, Veinticinco años de evolución de la justicia constitucional 1940–1965, UNAM, México, 1968.

849 L. FAVOREU, "Actualité et légitimité en contrôle juridictionnel des lois en Europe occidental", *Revue du droit public et de la science politique en France et à l'étranger*, Paris 1984 (5), p. 1149. Also published in L. FAVOREU and J.A. JOLOWICZ (ed.), *Le contrôle juridictionnel des lois. Légitimité, effectivité et développments récents*, Paris 1986, pp. 17–68.

850 M. CAPPELLETTI, *Judicial Review in the Contemporary World*, Indianapolis 1975, p. 46.

851 In the system followed, for instance in Uruguay, Panama, and Paraguay, and in the Latin American Countries that follows a mixed system (Venezuela and Colombia i.e.)

judicial review is not equivalent to the "European model", which is only one of its expressions, although the most notable one.

The "Austrian system" was originated in Europe after the First World War under the influence of the ideas and direct work of Hans Kelsen, particularly regarding the concept of the supremacy of the constitution and the need for a jurisdictional guarantee of that supremacy;[852] but it was also a direct result of the absence of a diffuse system of judicial review of the constitutionality of legislation whose exclusion was expressly or indirectly established in the Constitution.

In this respect, the Austrian Constitution has traditionally established a prohibition directed towards ordinary judges, to "examine the validity of laws, decrees or international treaties duly enacted";[853] and the Czechoslovakian Constitution of 1920 indirectly led to the same principle when reducing the powers of ordinary judges regarding laws, to only "verify if they have been correctly published."[854]

Therefore, if the diffuse system of judicial review was prohibited, and reticence regarding judges to control legislation was still a main pillar of the doctrine of separation of power, the only means through which the supremacy of the constitution could be guaranteed was by creating a constitutional organ, not being part of the Judicial power, and originally even without jurisdictional powers, in charge of controlling the constitutionality of legislation, but as a "negative legislator."[855]

According to these fundamental conditioning ideas, the first constitutional tribunals were established in Czechoslovakia and Austria, in their respective Constitutions of the 29 February and 1st October 1920. The Czechoslovakian Tribunal during its existence did not develop an effective control of constitutionality, it disappeared in 1938[856] and was only re–established under the socialist system in 1968.[857] Nevertheless, its original regulations can be considered as the first antecedents of the European model of judicial review.

The general trends of that Czechoslovakian system, were the following:

The Constitution expressly established the principle of its supremacy, considering "invalid" statutes contrary to its regulations and to the constitutional laws,[858] but,

---

852 H. KELSEN, "La garantie juridictionnelle de la Constitution (La Justice constitutionnelle), *Revue du droit public et de la science politique en France et à l'étranger*, Paris 1928, pp. 197–257.

853 Art. 89.1 See. E. ALONSO GARCÍA, "El Tribunal Constitucional austriaco" in *El Tribunal Constitucional*, Instituto de Estudios Fiscales, Madrid 1981, Vol I, p. 414; M. CAPPELLETTI, *op. cit*., p. 72.

854 Art. 102. See P. CRUZ VILLALON, "Dos modos de regulación del control de constitucionalidad: Checoslovaquia (1920–1938) y España (1931–1936), *Revista española de derecho constitucional*, 5, 1982, p. 135.

855 H. KELSEN, *loc. cit*, pp. 223, 224 and 226.

856 P. CRUZ VILLALON, *loc. cit*., pp. 129–139.

857 P. NIKOLIC, *Le contrôle juridictionnel du lois et sa légitimité*, IALS, Uppsala Colloquium 1984, (mimeo), p. 46. Also published in L. FAVOREU and J.A. JOLOWICZ (ed.) in *Le contrôle juridictionnel des lois... cit*., pp. 72–112.

858 Art. I, 1 of the Introductory Law to the Constitution.

as we said, reduced the role of the courts regarding the statutes, to only "verify if they have been correctly published."[859] Thus the monopoly for the appreciation of the unconstitutionality of statutes whether of the national Parliament or of the legislatures of the autonomous territorial units, was attributed to a Constitutional Tribunal created in the Constitution [860] and regulated by a special law enacted immediately after the enactment of the Constitution.[861] This constitutional body had only constitutional justice power with no other kind of attribution.[862]

The question of the unconstitutionality or invalidity of statutes could only be brought before the Constitutional Tribunal in an abstract way through a "recourse of unconstitutionality of statutes",[863] without any relation to a particular case. Thus the method for seeking judicial review was a direct one through a direct action exercised only by some legislative and judicial state organs: the Chambers of the National Assembly, the Supreme Court, the Supreme Administrative Court and the Electoral Tribunal.[864]

The Constitutional Tribunal did not have *ex–officio* powers on constitutional issues [865] 18) and the action could only be brought before the Tribunal within a period of 3 years following the publication of the statute.[866]

Finally, the effects of the decision of the Constitutional Tribunal were *erga omnes* and *ex–nunc*, *pro–futuro*, from the day of the publication of the decision.[867]

Due to its permanence and its reestablishment in 1945 the Austrian Constitutional Tribunal, created in the 1920 Constitution, was to be the leading institution of the "European" concentrated system of judicial review. Hans Kelsen, a member himself of the Constitutional Tribunal until 1929, formulated the original general trends of the institution, very similar to the Czechoslovakian one. They were reviewed by the constitutional amendments of 1925 and 1929, the latter being a fundamental one which gave the Tribunal its actual shape embodied in the 1945 Constitutional Law which has also been amended many times.[868]

---

859 Art. 102.

860 Art. III, 2 of the Introductory Law to the Constitution

861 Law of the Constitutional Tribunal of 9 March 1920.

862 *Cf.* P. CRUZ VILLALON, *loc. cit*., p. 135.

863 Art. 121, a) of the Constitution.

864 Art. 9, Law of the Constitutional Tribunal.

865 *Cf.* P. CRUZ VILLALON, *loc. cit*., p. 138.

866 Art. 12. Law of the Constitutional Tribunal.

867 Art. 20. Law of the Constitutional Tribunal.

868 *Cf.* E.A. GARCIA, *loc. cit*., p. 413; M. CAPPELLETTI, *op. cit*., p. 71; F. ERMACORA, "Procédures et techniques de protection des droits fundamentaux. Cour Constitutionnelle autrichienne", in L. FAVOREU (ed.) *Cours constitutionnelles européennes et droit fundamentaux*, 1982, p. 189.

2. The Austrian Constitutional Tribunal

The Austrian Constitutional Tribunal is regulated in the 1945 Constitution[869] as a constitutional organ established separate from the Judicial Power. Its basic regulations are established in the special Federal Law of the Constitutional Tribunal of 1953 modified on various occasions[870] and in the Interior Rules of the Tribunal enacted by itself[871] in accordance with its auto–regulatory power, which confirms its independence in the political system.

It is conceived as a constitutional organ independent of the other organs of the state, although its members are appointed by the executive power with participation of the legislative power.[872] In accordance with article 147 of the Constitution, the Tribunal is composed of a President, a Vice–President, twelve members and six alternate members. The President, the Vice–President, six members and three alternate members are appointed by the President of the Republic following a proposal from the Federal Government, and they must be chosen from among magistrates, public officers and University Law professors. The other six members and the other three alternate members are appointed by the President of the Republic following a proposal formulated by the National Council and the Federal Council, which are the legislative organs.

Consequently, the appointment of the members of the Tribunal follows the normal political rules of the country and the normal influence of the political parties,[873] which was clearly envisaged by Kelsen in 1928, when referring to the danger of political influence over the activities of the Tribunal. He said:

> If this danger is particularly important, it is preferable to accept the legitimate participation of the political parties in the formation of the Tribunal, rather than its hidden and uncontrollable influence...[874]

Nevertheless, the constitution has established various restrictions to secure the impartiality of the Tribunal members establishing a marked participation of the legal profession,[875] and forbidding the members of the government or of the legislative organs or the principal leaders of the political parties to be members of the Tribunal. In particular, concerning the President and Vice–President of the Tribunal, they

869 Arts.137–148, Constitution of I May 1945. See a Spanish version of the Constitution in I. MÉNDEZ DE VIGO, "El Verfassungsgerichthof (Tribunal Constitucional Austríaco)", *Boletín de Jurisprudencia Constitucional*, Cortes Generales, 7, Madrid 1981, pp. 555–560.

870 Law N° 85, 1953. See in T. OHLINGER, *Legge sulla Corte Costituzionale Austriaca*, Firenze, 1982.

871 Art. 148 of the Constitution. The Internal Regulation of the Tribunal of 1946, can be seen in T. OHLINGER, *op. cit*, p. 137.

872 See the general considerations made in this respect by H. KELSEN, *loc. cit.*, pp. 226–227.

873 F. ERMACORA, *loc. cit.*, pp. 190–191.

874 H. KELSEN, *loc. cit.*, p. 227.

875 Art. 147.3. *Cf.* H. KELSEN, *loc. cit.*, p. 227.

must not have occupied a political position for at least four years previous to their appointment.[876]

In a different way to the Czechoslovakian antecedent in which the Constitutional Tribunal was conceived exclusively as a constitutional judge, the Austrian Constitutional Tribunal combines its functions of judicial review, with other powers related to political and organic matters. These other attributions are the following:

In the first place, a series of jurisdictional powers to settle controversies in which the political bodies of the Federal state are involved. Some of these controversies are derived from the Federal system and the vertical distribution of state power, and are as follows:

First, the Constitutional Tribunal has jurisdiction regarding patrimonial actions against the Federation, the States, (*Lander*) the districts, the municipalities or associations of municipalities, when they could not be resolved in an ordinary judicial procedure or by administrative resolution.[877] Therefore, these actions are exceptional and suppletory and are referred to patrimonial relations regulated by public law.[878]

Second, the Constitutional Tribunal has jurisdiction to resolve all conflicts between constitutional organs, and particularly, conflicts of jurisdiction between administrative and judicial authorities; conflicts of jurisdiction between courts, and in particular, the conflict over the distribution of state powers in the vertical way, between the Federation, and the *Lander*, or between the *Lander.*[879] It must also be said that regarding conflicts between the Federation and member states, article 138, paragraph 2 of the Constitution attributes the Constitutional Tribunal specific powers concerning the interpretation of the Constitution to determine when hearing a request of the Federal or States government before a concrete conflict has arisen, whether the regulation of a specific matter is constitutionally assigned to the Federal legislator or to the States legislatures. In this case, the decision prevents disputes over the powers attributed in the vertical distribution of state power, because it is adopted before any state act is issued, and by adopting it the constitutional tribunal is empowered to interpret the constitution on those matters.[880]

Finally, regarding the federal conflicts of powers, the third attribution of the Constitutional Tribunal is to interpret agreements adopted between the different levels of the Federal state, particularly between the Federation and the *Lander* or between the *Lander*, all as a result of the cooperative federalism system followed in Austria.[881]

---

876 Art. 147.4.

877 Art. 137.

878 *Cf.* E. ALONSO GARCÍA, *loc. cit.*, pp. 421–422.

879 Art. 138.

880 *Cf.* F. ERMACORA, *loc. cit.*, p. 191. In this case it is considered that the Constitutional Tribunal exercises a "previous judicial review of status": W.K. GECK, "Judicial Review of Statutes: a Comparative Survey of Present Institution and Practices", *Cornell Law Quarterly*, 51, 1966, p. 266.

881 Art. 138.a. and 15,a.

In the second place, the Constitutional Tribunal has another series of jurisdictional powers regarding elections and referenda. First the Tribunal is empowered to decide upon actions that could be brought before it against the election of the President of the Federation, of the representatives to the Assemblies, of the representatives of the organs of the Professional Associations, and against the elections of government officials to the *Lander* and at municipal level. It also has jurisdiction to resolve the loss of the respective mandate of elected representatives.[882] On the other hand, the Tribunal also has jurisdiction to decide upon any claim against the result of a referendum directed to approve certain laws.[883]

In the third place, the Constitutional Court also has jurisdiction to decide upon accusations brought before it, against the supreme organs of the Federation or of the *Lander*, based on constitutional liability derived from illegalities,[884] the decision of which could produce the loss of office and even the temporal loss of political rights.[885]

Finally, in the fourth place, the Constitutional Tribunal is empowered to act as a constitutional judge controlling the constitutionality of laws, executive regulations and Treaties, and also granting constitutional protection against the violation of fundamental rights. These final attributions are directly related to judicial review.

3. The Constitutional Tribunal and Judicial Review

In effect, among the various jurisdictional powers of the Constitutional Tribunal in the Austrian system, the Constitution assigns it the role of constitutional judge, with power to review the constitutionality of statutes, treaties and executive regulations, in a concentrated way, which can be sought by two methods: principal and incidental.

The first aspect to be noticed in the Austrian system is that the exclusive power to review the constitutionality of state acts assigned to the Constitutional Tribunal, not only includes legislative acts, but also treaties and executive regulations.

Regarding legislative acts, judicial review refers to federal and *Lander* statutes[886] and concerning international treaties, the Constitutional Tribunal has had the power to decide upon their "illicity" or unconstitutionality only since 1964.[887] In both cases, the state acts object of judicial review can be considered acts issued in direct execution of the constitution, regarding which the control of constitutionality is the consequence of the hierarchical expression of the legal order.[888] In accordance with that scheme, judicial review of executive regulations, normally subordinated to the

---

882 Art. 141.

883 Art. 141,3.

884 Art. 142.

885 Art. 142.4.

886 Art. 140,1.

887 Art. 140.a.*Cf.* H. KELSEN, *loc. cit.*, p. 232.

888 *Cf.* H. KELSEN, *loc. cit.*, pp. 228–231.

legislation, is generally attributed in Europe to the administrative jurisdiction and not to the Constitutional Courts.

But in spite of such general trends according to H. Kelsen's thought on the matter, judicial review of executive regulations in Austria is also attributed to the Constitutional Tribunal. In this respect, Professor Kelsen said:

> Without doubt these executive regulations are not acts immediately subordinate to the Constitution; their irregularity immediately consists of their illegality and only in a mediate way, their constitutionality. If, in spite of that, we propose to extend the attributions of the constitutional jurisdiction to them, it is not due to the mentioned relativity of the opposition between direct and indirect constitutionality, but taking into consideration the natural boundary between general and particular juridical acts.[889]

Consequently, according to Kelsen, only the particular acts of state (administrative or judicial) were to be excluded from constitutional jurisdiction.[890] Thus, executive regulations, or administrative acts with general effects, were also submitted to the jurisdiction of the Constitutional Tribunal. And this happened in Austria, where the Constitution assigns power to the Tribunal to decide upon the "illegality" of the decrees of the federal or *Lander* authorities and even of the ordinances at local level and the general regulations of professional associations.[891]

4. Methods of Control and the Ex–Officio Powers of the Constitutional Tribunal

According to the Constitution, there are two basic methods for seeking the jurisdiction of the Constitutional Tribunal, through a direct petition or action and in an incidental way, although in its original 1920 feature, the only established method was the principal one, exercised through a petition reserved only to certain political organs of the state.[892] The 1929 and 1975 constitutional reforms enlarged the standing requirements to interpose the direct petition, and in 1929 the incidental method of judicial review was also established. Additionally, the Constitutional Tribunal has been empowered by the constitution to raise constitutional issues *ex–officio*. It is also possible to distinguish another method of seeking judicial review, this time, indirect, as a consequence of the exercise of the constitutional protection actions or complaints regarding fundamental rights. Thus, five different methods seeking judicial review can be distinguished in the Austrian system.

A. *Direct Petition for Unconstitutionality*

The first method is the direct petition for unconstitutionality of statutes that can be brought before the Constitutional Tribunal, as follows: regarding federal statutes, at the request of the government of the *Lander* or of one third of the members of the National Council (Parliament); and regarding the *Lander* statutes, at the request of

---

889 *Idem*, p. 230.

890 *Idem*, p. 233.

891 Art. 139, 1. *Cf.* E. ALONSO GARCÍA, *loc. cit.*, p. 434.

892 *Cf.* M. CAPPELLETTI, *op. cit.*, pp. 72– 73.

the Federal government, the Constitutions of the Lander being authorised by the Federal Constitution to give the right to petition to one third of the members of their legislatures.[893] It must be noted that by granting standing to interpose the direct petition to one third of the representatives in the legislative bodies, the 1975 constitutional reform has given the opposition a means for controlling the laws adopted by the majority,[894] following the trends developed in other European countries.

Regarding executive regulations, the direct petition of illegality can be brought before the Constitutional Tribunal, by the governments of the *Lander* if the object of judicial review is a federal decree; and if it is a decree of the Lander executive authorities, by the Federal Government and also by the municipalities regarding executive acts of local government control.[895]

Regarding international treaties, the Constitution disposes the analogous application of the previous mentioned rules, differentiating between Treaties approved by the National Council and those enacted by executive means.[896]

B. *Direct action of unconstitutionality*

Nevertheless, in the Austrian system the direct request for unconstitutionality is not only reserved to political organs. Since the 1975 constitutional reform, a direct action or recourse has also been granted to individuals who can bring it directly before the Constitutional Court, but only when they deem their rights directly violated by a statute or an executive regulation. It is necessary that the norm in question be directly applicable to them, without any other further judicial decision or individual administrative act.[897] In this case, the claimant must express in his action, how the statute, without any further judicial decision or administrative act, can really affect his rights directly. Therefore, this action or constitutional complaint, is not an *actio popularis*, which was not recommended by Kelsen for the purpose of judicial review,[898] on the contrary, it is an action submitted to specific requirement for standing.

On the other hand, the action cannot be brought directly before the Constitutional Tribunal against a statute, if there have been judicial decisions or administrative acts enforced in application of the said statute. Therefore, if any possibility of an administrative or judicial decision to be produced in a reasonable degree still exists, recourse must first be interposed against those decisions before the Administrative Court, or other Court of Justice or even the Constitutional Court itself. In those cases, the constitutional issue could be raised in an incidental way or *ex–officio* by the Constitutional Court.[899]

893 Art. 140, 1.

894 Art. 139, 1.

895 *Cf.* L. FAVOREU, *loc. cit.*, p. 1152.

896 Art. 140, a.

897 Art. 140, 1

898 H. KELSEN, *loc. cit.*, p. 245.

899 *Cf.* L. FAVOREU, *loc. cit.*, p. 1153.

C. *Incidental method for judicial review*

The constitutional question concerning state acts cannot only be brought before the Constitutional Tribunal through a direct petition or action. Since the 1929 constitutional reform an incidental method for judicial review has been established in Austria, enlarged later, in 1975.

According to the constitution, the constitutional question regarding statutes, could reach the Constitutional Tribunal by a referral formulated by the administrative court, the supreme court of justice or any court of appeal when they must apply the law in a concrete proceeding.[900] Regarding executive regulation, the constitutional question through the incidental means for its annulation, could be brought before the constitutional tribunal by any court.[901]

In such cases, the incidental referral formulated before the Constitutional Tribunal has suspensive effects regarding the concrete proceeding in which the constitutional question has been raised, which could only be continued after the constitutional tribunal's judgment has been adopted.[902]

Even though the supreme courts and the courts of appeal do not have judicial review power in the Austrian system, which is concentrated, this incidental means for judicial review gives them in a certain way, as Professor Cappelletti pointed out, not only the power but the duty "not to apply laws whose constitutionality is in doubt, without having first heard the binding judgment of the Constitutional Court,"[903] which means that those courts have the power to appreciate the unconstitutionality of legislation, though not to annul laws.

D. Ex–Officio *powers for constitutional review*

Apart from the two principals and from the incidental methods of judicial review, the Constitution empowers the Constitutional Tribunal to raise on its own initiative, any constitutional question regarding statutes and executive regulations, in cases developed before the Tribunal, in which a statute or an executive regulation must be applied for resolution.[904] This could be considered as a fourth method of judicial review in the Austrian system also envisaged by Hans Kelsen[905] although it is not unlimited. The Constitution establishes that even though the Tribunal could have the conviction that a statute is unconstitutional because it was enacted in an unconstitutional way, if the complete annulment of the statute could mean a manifest prejudice against the juridical interests of the individual claimant in a direct ac-

---

900 Art. 140.1.

901 Art. 139.1.

902 Art. 57 Law of the Constitutional Tribunal.

903 M. CAPPELLETTI, *op. cit.*, p. 74.

904 Art. 139, 1 and 140.1, 3.

905 H. KELSEN, *loc. cit.*, p. 247.

tion, or of the plaintiff in the proceeding in which an incidental question was brought before the Tribunal, it must not annul the statute.[906]

E. *Indirect means for judicial review and the Protection of Fundamental Rights*

Finally, in the Austrian system a fifth method of judicial review can be distinguished through which the Constitutional Tribunal could be called upon to decide upon the unconstitutionality of statutes, in an indirect way, as a consequence of the exercise of a direct recourse or complaint for constitutional protection of fundamental rights.

In effect, the Constitution established the right of individuals to bring before the Constitutional Tribunal recourses or complaints against administrative acts when the claimant alleges that they infringe a right guaranteed in a constitutional law.[907] This is the basic rule that has contributed to the development of a special judicial means of protection of fundamental rights in Europe, although in a concentrated way which establishes the difference with the recourse for protection developed in Latin American countries.

However, the relation between this recourse for protection of fundamental rights against administrative acts of particular effect and judicial review of constitutionality, is that it could also be based on the allegation that the administrative act prejudiced the claimant because it has applied an illegal decree, an unconstitutional law or an international treaty contrary to the rule of law,[908] in which cases the Constitutional Tribunal must decide upon the constitutional issue.

5. Effects of Judicial Review

In all these five methods of judicial review of legislation the decision of the Constitutional Tribunal upon the constitutionality of statutes and decrees, when declaring the unconstitutionality of state acts, has *erga omnes* effects, thus binding on all the courts and administrative authorities.[909] The decision has also *constitutive* effects in the sense that it annuls the statute or the decree, *pro–futuro, ex–nunc*.

Nevertheless, the Tribunal has powers to annul statutes or decrees already repealed, thus without formal validity,[910] which, in principle, supposes the retroactive effects of the judicial review, this being an exception to the *ex–nunc* effects.

Anyway, according to the general rule of prospectiveness, proposed as a matter of principle by Hans Kelsen,[911] the factual situations or the situations verified before

---

906 Art. 140, 3.

907 Art. 144.

908 Art. 144.

909 Art. 139, 6; 140, 7.

910 Art. 139, 4; 140, 4. *Cf.* H. KELSEN, *loc. cit.*, p. 234.

911 H. KELSEN, *loc. cit.*, p. 242. For instance, regarding the Austrian system, L. Adamouch stated in 1954: "To the decision of the Constitutional Tribunal which declares that the unconstitutionality of a statute, one cannot assigne a simple declarative value; it do not establishes that a concrete statute has been null from its origin, whose effects are to be nul *ex–tunc*, that is to

the annulment of the statute or decree, will continue to be submitted to its regulation, except in the case considered in the decision, unless the Tribunal decides otherwise.[912] Thus, the Tribunal in its own decision can temper the possible negative consequences of the *ex–nunc* rule.

But in general the effects of the Tribunal decision only begin the day of the publication of the consequent repeal of the annulled act, by the executive authority concerned, unless the Tribunal establishes a delay for the expiration of the effects of the annulled act[913] not in excess of one year. In such cases, and on a purely discretionary basis, the Tribunal can postpone the beginning of the ex–nunc effects due to the annulment of the statute.

On the other hand, concerning statutes, their annulment could bring about a situation in which other statutes previously repealed by the annulled one, will restart their validity beginning the day in which the annulment is effective, unless the Tribunal decides otherwise,[914] which confirms the *ex–nunc* effects.

Finally, regarding treaties, the Constitutional Court has no power to annul them directly when unconstitutional, but must only declare their unconstitutionality which implies, first that the treaty could not be applicable from the day in which the decision is made public by the state organ which is due to execute it, unless the tribunal fixes a delay in which the treaty could continue to be applied;[915] and second, that if the treaty is due to be applied by laws or decrees, any of these will cease to have effects.[916]

III. JUDICIAL REVIEW IN THE FEDERAL REPUBLIC OF GERMANY: THE FEDERAL CONSTITUTIONAL TRIBUNAL

1. The Weimar Antecedents

Also after the Second World War, and under the federal Constitution of *Weimar* of 11 August 1919, the basic elements for the development of a constitutional system of judicial review were established in Germany, although dispersed among a set of courts and tribunals. In particular, a limited system of concentrated judicial review can be found within the powers attributed to the Tribunal of the Empire (*Reichsgericht*), the highest court in the ordinary judiciary, which had powers to resolve the compatibility of laws passed by member states of the Federation (the

say, as it were an act without any juridical value from its origin; on the contrary, the decision of the Constitutional Tribunal only annules the unconstitutional statute, that is to say, destroys *ex nunc* its juridical existence, exactly as it would have been abolished by a successive legislative act, and as that this act would have ended its juridical existence." in "Esperienza della Corte Constituzionale della Republica Austriaca", *Revista italiana per la scienze giuridiche*, Milan 1954.

912 Art. 139, 6; 140, 7.

913 Art. 139, 5; 140, 5.

914 Art. 140, 6.

915 Art. 140 a, 1.

916 Art. 140 a, 2.

Lander) with Imperial legislation.[917] Another special court, the Tribunal of state Justice (*Staatsgerichthof*), had the special task of resolving constitutional litigation arising within a *Lander* which lacked special courts to do so; also, public law conflicts arising between different *Lander* or between the Empire and one *Lander*, when these cases fell outside the jurisdiction of any other court of justice of the Empire.[918] This Tribunal of state Justice was also empowered to try accusations against the President, the Chancellor and the Imperial Ministers, for infractions of the Constitution.[919]

But during the *Weimar* Republic, discussions were developed regarding the powers of all courts to control the constitutionality of laws when deciding cases submitted for their decision, and the Tribunal of the Empire adopted particular judicial decisions in this respect.

The decision of the *Reichsgericht* of 4 November 1925 is famous. In it, the Tribunal in accordance with article 102 of the Constitution which established the submission of the judges to the laws, stated:

> The submission of the judge to the law does not exclude the power of the judge to question the validity of statutes of the Empire or of certain of its dispositions when they are in opposition to other pre–eminent dispositions that must be observed by the judge. This is the case when a statute is in opposition to a juridical principle established in the Imperial Constitution...[920]

And the Imperial Tribunal concluded in a way which can be considered as the general admission of the diffuse system of judicial review in Germany by stating in a very similar way to what was stated in the *Marbury* v. *Madison* case:[921]

> The Imperial Constitution, not containing any disposition in accordance to which the decision upon the constitutionality of a statute of the Empire would have been taken away from the judges and transferred to another specific organ, the power and the duty of the judge to examine the constitutionality of statutes of the Empire must be recognised.[922]

Anyway the situation of the system up to 1933 was not completely clear, and judicial review of federal laws by all courts, particularly lower courts whose decisions

917 Art. 13 of the Constitution. *Cf.* the text in F. RUBIO LLORENTE, "El Tribunal Constitucional alemán", *Revista de la Facultad de Derecho*, UCV, 18, Caracas 1959, p. 116; J.C. BÉGUIN, *Le contrôle de la constitutionnalité des lois en Republique Fédérale d'Allemagne*, Paris 1982, p. 19; F. SAINZ MORENO, "Tribunal Constitucional federal alemán", *Boletín de Jurisprudencia Constitucional*, Cortes Generales, 8, Madrid 1981, p. 603; G. MÜLLER, "El Tribunal Constitucional federal de la República Federal de Alemania", *Revista de la Comisión Internacional de Juristas*, Vol VI, Ginebra 1965, p. 222.

918 Art. 19 of the Constitution.

919 Art. 59.

920 See the quotations in C.J. FRIEDRICH, "The Issue of Judicial Review in Germany", *Political Science Quarterly*, 43, 1928, p. 188; H.G. RUPP, "Judicial Review in the Federal Republic of Germany", *The American Journal of Comparative Law*, 9, 1960, p. 31; J.C. BÉGUIN, *op. cit.*, p. 15.

921 H.G. RUPP, *loc. cit.*, p. 31.

922 See note 4, supra.

were unable to be reviewed through appeals by the Supreme Court, was not always accepted and was frequently criticised.[923] This led to an important change in the establishment of a system of constitutional justice in West Germany, in the Constitution of the Federal Republic of Germany of 23 May 1949.

2. Concentrated System of Judicial Review in West Germany and its Coexistence with a Limited Diffuse System of Review

In effect, the Constitution of 1949 created a Federal Constitutional Tribunal which, although being part of the Judicial Power as are all other federal and *Lander* courts[924] is considered the "supreme guardian of the Constitution"[925] having "the last word on the construction of the Federal Constitution."[926] Thus it is the state organ in which all constitutional jurisdictional questions have been concentrated.

To accomplish this role of constitutional judge, the Federal Constitutional Tribunal was organised in the federal law referred to in the Constitution[927] as a constitutional organ of the Federation, "autonomous and independent regarding all other constitutional organs,"[928] even with self–regulatory powers.[929]

The status of the Federal Constitutional Court, as a constitutional organ, is also reflected in its composition. According to the Constitution, its members are elected by the fundamental politico–representative organs of the Federation: the *Bundestag* (National Council) and the *Bundesrat* (Federal Council), in equal numbers in each case, but the elected members may not be members of both Councils or of the Federal government nor of any of the corresponding organs of a Land.[930] All the members of the Tribunal are considered to be federal judges, although only a proportion of them must be elected from active federal judges.[931]

Based on all these constitutional provisions regarding the organisation, composition and powers of the Federal Constitutional Court it has been considered by one of its former Presidents, a "neutral power" within the state. It has a constitutional pre–

---

923 *Cf.* J.C. BÉGUIN, *op. cit.*, p. 13–21; H.G. RUPP, *loc. cit.*, p. 32; M. CAPPELLETTI, *Judicial Review in Contemporary World*, Indianapolis 1971, pp. 50–51–59,64.

924 Art. 92.

925 G. MÜLLER, *loc. cit.*, p. 216; F. SAINZ MORENO, *loc. cit.*, p. 606.

926 H.G. RUPP, "The Federal Constitutional Court and the Constitution of the Federal Republic of Germany", *Saint Louis University Law Journal*, Vol XVI, 1971–1972, p. 359.

927 Art. 94,2. The Law on the Organization and Procedure of the Federal Constitutional Tribunal (FCT. Law) was published the 12 March 1951. See the whole text in F. RUBIO LLORENTE, *loc. cit.*, pp. 125–167. The Law has been modified in various opportunities: 1956, 1959, 1963 and 1970. The present text up to date is of 3 February 1971, modified in 1974 and 1976. *Cf.* F. SAINZ MORENO, *loc. cit.*, p. 604.

928 Art. 1,1 FCT Law.

929 Art. 30, 2 FCT Law, The Interior regulation of the Tribunal was published in 1975 and reformed in 1978.

930 Art. 94, 1. Constitution.

931 The Tribunal is divided in two Chambers (*Senaten*), each one with 8 judges, three of them elected from active federal judges. Arts. 4, 5. FCT Law.

eminence over all other state organs, particularly because of the various powers that the Constitution assigns it related to constitutional justice and judicial review powers, and which has also been considered, as "not having been conferred to any other constitutional tribunal, or supreme court" in any other country.[932]

The Federal Constitutional Tribunal, therefore, is the expression of a concentrated system of judicial review, particularly of federal and *Lander* statutes, established to "protect the legislator against the ordinary judicial power",[933] but its establishment did not eliminate completely the diffuse system of judicial review in West Germany, which in a limited way is exercised by all courts. In other words, according to the general trend in all concentrated systems of judicial review, the concentration of the powers of constitutional justice in one single organ, is only established regarding certain state acts, with the result that in relation to all other state acts not specified in the concentrated powers, the supremacy of the constitution allows all the other courts to control their constitutionality in a diffuse way. This general trend is followed in the West German system.

In effect, according to article 93, section 2 of the Federal Constitution, in matters of judicial review of legislation, the Federal Constitutional Tribunal has the exclusive power to review the constitutionality of federal laws and laws of the *Lander*, but considering as such, the laws that have been passed by the legislators established in the 1949 Constitution. Therefore, statutes adopted before 1949, can be the object of judicial review in a diffuse system by all courts, as well as executive regulations or normative decrees, whose constitutional judicial review is not reserved to the Federal Constitutional Tribunal.[934] Nevertheless, pre–constitutional legislation can be constitutionally reviewed by the Federal Constitutional Tribunal but only by means of the direct action which leads to the abstract control of norms [935]

Therefore, the West German constitutional system has established a concentrated system of judicial review by attributing exclusive powers to control the constitutionality of state acts, and particularly of legislation to the Federal Constitutional Tribunal. It has also established so by allowing the ordinary courts the power of review in a diffuse system regarding pre–constitutional legislation and executive regulations.

On the other hand, it must also be stressed that as a consequence of the federal system, the Federal Constitution has not reserved the absolute monopoly of the concentrated system of judicial review to the Federal Constitutional Court. In general, each *Lander* has its own constitutional court empowered to control the violations of the *Lander* constitutions and to settle constitutional litigations within each *Lander.*[936]

932 G. MÜLLER, *loc. cit.*, pp. 216–221.

933 J.C. BEGUIN, *op. cit.*, p. 93.

934 *Cf.* G. MÜLLER, *loc. cit.*, p. 233; J.C. BEGUIN, *op. cit.*, p. 69, 94.

935 *Cf.* G. MÜLLER, *loc. cit.*, p. 234.

936 *Cf.* J.C. BEGUIN, *op. cit.*, p. 27, 43–46.

3. Federal Constitutional Tribunal as a Constitutional Jurisdiction

But at the federal level, the Federal Constitutional Tribunal as the supreme guardian of the Constitution, has the monopoly of its defence derived from a very wide range of powers attributed to it in the Constitution, and in accordance with which, in the federal law which regulates its functioning and organisation.[937] These powers, all of a jurisdictional nature, can be classified into six groups of attributions through which the tribunal guarantees the protection of the politico–constitutional order; the distribution of state powers; the electoral representative character of the political system; the protection of fundamental rights; the interpretation of the Constitution, and control of the constitutionality of all normative state acts.

The first group of jurisdictional powers of the Federal Constitutional Tribunal relates to what may be called the protection of the politico–constitutional order embodied in the Constitution, or in other words, the protection of the state against actions taken by political parties, individuals or public officials. In relation to political parties, which in the constitutional system of the Federal Republic are the main means by which "the political will of the people"[938] is formed, the Constitutional Tribunal is empowered to declare them unconstitutional, when

> By reason of their aims or the behaviour of their adherents (they) seek to impair or destroy the free democratic basic order or to endanger the existence of the Federal Republic of Germany.[939]

The protection of the state against individuals is regulated in the Constitution particularly as a consequence of the abuse of the exercise of certain freedoms and liberties, which could endanger the constitutional order. In this respect, the Federal Constitutional Tribunal is empowered[940] to decide upon the deprivation of the freedom of speech, especially the freedom of the press, the freedom of education, the freedom of assembly, the freedom of association, the secrecy of mail, post and telecommunications, property and the right of asylum, by those who abuse those rights by using them to fight against the fundamental and free democratic order, and who consequently make themselves unworthy of those freedoms.[941]

Finally, regarding state officials, the Constitutional Tribunal functions as protector of the state being empowered to take cognisance of accusations brought against the Federal President by the *Bundestag* or the *Bundesrat* for voluntary infraction of the Constitution or of other federal laws;[942] and of accusations brought against fed-

---

937 Art. 93, Constitution.

938 Art. 21, 1 Constitution.

939 Art. 21, 2. Constitution. In 1952 and 1956, the Tribunal declared unconstitutional a neo–nazi party (*sozialistischen Reichspartei*) and the communist party (*Kommunistische Partei Deutschlands*). *Cf.* he reference in F. SAINZ MORENO, *loc. cit.*, p. 622.

940 Art. 18 Constitution.

941 Art. 36–42 FCT Law.

942 Art. 61 Constitution.

eral judges who undermine the principles of the Constitution, or the constitutional order of a Land.[943]

The second group of constitutional jurisdictional powers of the Federal Constitutional Tribunal relates to the institutional functioning of the state and empowers the tribunal to resolve constitutional conflicts and litigations regarding the vertical and horizontal distribution of state powers.

In this respect, regarding the federal form of the state, the Tribunal has jurisdiction in cases of "difference of opinion over the rights and duties of the Federation and the *Lander*, particularly in the execution of federal law by the Lander and in the exercise of federal supervision;"[944]28) and "on other disputes involving public law, between the Federation and the *Lander*, between different *Lander* or within a *Lander*, unless recourse to another court exists."[945]

But also in relation to the vertical distribution of powers, the Constitutional Tribunal has jurisdiction to resolve conflicts between the Federal and *Lander* powers and the municipalities, in the sense that it shall decide "on the complaints of unconstitutionality, entered by municipalities or association of municipalities on the grounds that their right to self–government... has been violated by a law other than a Land law open to complaint to the respective Land Constitutional Court."[946] This competence leads directly to one of the means of judicial review of legislation.

On the other hand, regarding the horizontal distribution of state power, that is to say, the resolution of conflicts between the constitutional organs of the Federation, the Federal Constitutional Tribunal shall decide upon the interpretation of the Constitution, "in the event of disputes concerning the extent of the rights and duties of a highest federal organ or of other parties concerned who have been vested with rights of their own by the Constitution or by a regulation of a highest federal organ."[947]

These "highest federal organs" whose conflicts must be decided upon by the Tribunal, are the *Bundestag*, the *Bundesrat*, the President of the Federation, the Federal Government and the Permanent Commission of the *Bundestag*. The political parties have also been considered as having quality to allege violations to their rights as participants in constitutional life.[948]

The third group of constitutional jurisdictional powers attributed to the Federal Constitutional Tribunal concerns the electoral–representative basis of the political system, in relation to which the Tribunal must resolve "the claims against the decisions of the *Bundestag* over the validity of an election or the acquisition or loss of the condition of representative to the *Bundestag*";[949] and also, the recourses against

943 Art. 98, 2 Constitution.

944 Art. 93, (1), 3 Constitution.

945 Art. 93, (1), 4 Constitution.

946 Art. 93, (1), 4 Constitution.

947 Art. 93, (1), 1 Constitution.

948 J.C. BÉGUIN, *op. cit.*, p. 40.

949 Art. 41, 2 Constitution; Art. 13, 3 FCT Law.

referenda when a new division of the federal territory is adopted as a result of the modification of the boundaries of the *Lander*.[950]

The fourth group of constitutional jurisdictional powers assigned to the Constitutional Tribunal concerns the protection of fundamental rights and freedoms against the state. Specifically the Federal Constitution empowers the Tribunal to decide "on complaints of unconstitutionality", which may be entered by any person who claims that one of his basic constitutional rights has been violated by public authority.[951] This power of the Constitutional Tribunal established in the 1951 Statute of the Tribunal and only regulated in the 1969 amendment to the Constitution, has given rise to a very important recourse for the protection of fundamental rights against public authorities, as is the "trial for *amparo*" developed in Latin America called the "constitutional complaint" which has contributed to the consideration of fundamental rights and freedoms as a limit upon the powers of the state.

The fifth group of constitutional jurisdictional powers of the Federal Constitutional Court related to constitutional justice, concerns the interpretation and application of the Constitution and of federal legislation. Two attributions of the Constitutional Tribunal can be distinguished regarding the interpretation of the Constitution. First, the power of the Tribunal to decide cases in which a constitutional court of a *Lander*, when interpreting the Federal Constitution, intends to deviate from a decision previously made by the Federal Constitutional Tribunal or by the constitutional court of another *Lander*.[952] Second, the power of the Tribunal to resolve upon the continuity of the validity of a pre–constitutional law as federal law.[953]

Regarding the application of federal law, a third attribution of the Constitutional Tribunal may be distinguished regarding international law which in accordance with the Constitution forms part of the federal law.[954] In this respect, if in the course of a litigation before a court, doubt exists as to whether a rule of public international law is an integral part of federal law and whether such a rule directly creates rights and duties for the individual, the court shall obtain a decision from the Federal Constitutional Court.[955]

Finally, the sixth group of constitutional jurisdictional powers attributed to the Federal Constitutional Tribunal, as a constitutional judge, are the powers to control the constitutionality of normative state acts, comprising legislative acts. It is precisely this function of verifying the constitutionality of normative state acts, in which the character of the Tribunal reveals itself in full, as the constitutional organ laid down in the Constitution for the purpose of judicial review of legislation.

For the accomplishment of these functions, the constitutional questions regarding normative acts of the state can reach the Constitutional Tribunal by three methods: a

---

950 Art. 29 Constitution. *Cf.* G. MÜLLER, *loc. cit.*, p. 229.

951 Art. 93, (1), 4,a). Constitution.

952 Art. 100, 3 Constitution.

953 Art. 126 Constitution.

954 Art. 2,2 Constitution.

955 Art. 100, 2 Constitution.

direct request or complaint brought before the Tribunal; an incidental referral placed before the Tribunal by a lower court; or through an indirect way when the Constitutional Tribunal must decide upon the unconstitutionality of a state act, for the resolution of another of the constitutional jurisdictional proceedings different to the abstract or concrete control of normative acts of the state.

4. Constitutional Control of Normative State Acts Through Direct Requests or Complaints

The first method established in the Federal Constitution for the purpose of judicial review of state normative acts is through the exercise of a direct request, action or complaint brought before the Federal Constitutional Tribunal with the purpose of seeking its decision exclusively upon the unconstitutionality of a statute or other normative act of the state.

This direct means for judicial review, according to the constitution, can be exercised through two specific actions: first, by a request formulated by some state organs, called the abstract control of norms; and second, by the exercise of a constitutional complaint brought by any person who claims that one of his fundamental rights has been violated by the specific statute or act, or by a Municipality who claims that its right to self–government has been violated by a federal law.

A. *Request for the Abstract Control of Norms*

The request for the abstract control of norms (*Die abstrakte Normenkontrolle*), that is to say, the exercise of judicial review powers by the Constitutional Tribunal without reference to a particular case or process, is established in article 93, section 1, N° 2 of the Constitution, when it states that the Constitutional Tribunal shall decide:

> In case of differences of opinion or doubts on the formal and material compatibility of federal law or *Lander* law with this Basic Law, or on the compatibility of *Lander* law with other federal laws, at the request of the Federal Government, of a *Lander* Government or of one third of the *Bundestag* members.[956]

This power attributed to the Constitutional Tribunal has led to the development of what may be called an "objective" judicial review proceeding because it has as its only purpose the ensuring of the maintenance of the hierarchy system of norms, in an abstract way.[957]

As we said, the Constitution gives the right to formulate the request only to the Federal Government, the Government of a *Lander* and to one third of the *Bundestag* members,[958] allowing in the latter case the parliamentary minorities to have access to the Tribunal, and challenge the statutes approved by the majority. It also establishes that the representatives of the interested constitutional organs that have par-

956 Also see Art., *76–88* FCT Law.

957 *Cf.* J.C. BÉGUIN, *op. cit.*, p. *60;* H.G. RUPP, "Judicial Review...", *loc. cit.*, p. *35;* G. MÜLLER, *loc. cit.*, p. 231.

958 Art. 76 FCT Law.

ticipated in the formation of the challenged normative act must be heard[959] by the Tribunal. Nevertheless, it must be said that in the proceeding there are no proper parties.[960]

The request, in fact, is formulated against a state act, not against a state organ, and the Constitutional Tribunal must decide the constitutional question in an abstract way, being allowed, moreover, to raise other constitutional questions *ex–officio* regarding the challenged act, or other of its articles.[961]

The objective character of the proceeding and the powers of the Constitutional Tribunal as a guardian of the Constitution are, furthermore, confirmed by the fact that even when a request is withdrawn by the state organ, the Tribunal can continue the proceeding when it is justified as being in the general interest.[962]

On the other hand, it must be said that this objective proceeding for the abstract control of the norms, refers to all normative state acts. Thus, it is not a proceeding for this sole purpose of judicial review of legislative acts in its formal sense, but can be referred to any other normative act of the state, including pre–constitutional statutes, executive normative decrees and international treaties and even, constitutional amendments.[963] In particular, all the statutes through which international treaties are approved, are subject to judicial review, and it has been applied, for example, in relation to state acts concerning the laws of the European Community.[964] But even though the general trend of judicial review of legislation in West Germany is its *a posteriori* character regarding treaties an exception to this principle is established, in the sense that the Constitutional Tribunal decision upon the constitutionality of its approving statute, must be adopted after its sanction but before the treaty begins its effects.[965]

B. *Constitutional Complaint Against Statutes*

But the abstract control of norms, additional to the request formulated by state political organs, can also be exercised by the Federal Constitutional Tribunal as a result of a constitutional complaint that any person can bring before the Tribunal when he claims that one of his basic or fundamental rights has been directly violated by a normative state act. This "constitutional complaint", only constitutionalised in 1969 was originally established in the 1951 Federal Statute of the Constitutional Tribunal,[966] and is conceived as a special judicial means for the protection of fun-

959 Art. 77 FCT Law.

960 *Cf.* J.C. BEGUIN, *op. cit.*, p. 61*;* G. MÜLLER, *loc. cit.*, p. 231.

961 Art. 78 FCT Law. *Cf.* J.C. BÉGUIN, *op. cit.*, p. 61*;* F. SAINZ MORENO, *loc. cit.*, p. 613.

962 *Cf.* J.C. BÉGUIN, *op. cit.*, p. 61; F. SAINZ MORENO, *loc. cit.*, p. 613.

963 *Cf.* J.C. BEGUIN, *op. cit.*, p. 63.

964 L. CONTASTINESCO, "L´introduction et le contrôle de la constitutionnalité des traités et en particulier des traites européens en droit allemand", *Revue belge de droit international*, 2, 1969, pp. 425–459.

965 *Cf.* F. SAINZ MORENO, *loc. cit.*, p. 613.

966 Art. 90. FCT Law.

damental rights and freedoms against any action of the state organs which violates them. Therefore, it is not a specific action only directed to obtain judicial review of legislation, but it can be used for that purpose, when exercised against a statute.

The constitutional complaint after the 1969 constitutional amendment is expressly established in article 93, section 1, N° 4a of the Constitution when attributing the Federal Constitutional Tribunal power to decide:

> On complaints of unconstitutionality, which may be entered by any person who claims that one of his basic rights or one of his rights under paragraph (4) of article 20, under articles 33, 38, 101, 103, or 104 has been violated by public authority.[967]

Therefore, the constitutional complaint can be brought before the Tribunal against any state act, whether legislative, executive or judicial, but in all cases, it can only be exercised once the ordinary judicial means for the protection of the fundamental rights that have been violated, are all exhausted.[968] Consequently, the constitutional complaint is a subsidiary mean of judicial protection of fundamental rights,[969] and if there are other judicial recourses or actions that can serve the purpose of protecting fundamental rights, the constitutional complaint is not admissible, except when the Constitutional Tribunal considers the matter as being of general importance or when it considers that the claimant is threatened by a grave and irremediable prejudice if it is sent to the ordinary judicial means for protection.[970]

As we said, the constitutional complaint can be exercised directly against a statute or any other normative state act on the grounds that it directly impairs the fundamental rights of the claimant. In that case, it leads directly to the exercise of a judicial review of normative state acts function by the Constitutional Tribunal. As a result of this constitutional complaint, the statute when unconstitutional must be declared null. [971]

The basic condition for the admissibility of constitutional complaints against laws is, of course, the fact that the challenged statute or normative state act, must personally affect the claimant's fundamental rights, in a direct and current way, without the need for any further administrative application of the norm. On the contrary, if this further administrative application is needed, he must wait for the administrative execution of the statute and complain against it. This direct prejudice caused by the normative act on the rights of the claimant, as a basic element for the admissibility of the complain, justifies the delay of one year after its publication established for the introduction of the action before the Tribunal.[972] It also explains the power of the Constitutional Tribunal to adopt provisional protective measures

967 See also Arts. 90–96 FCT Law.

968 Art. 90, 2 FCT Law.

969 Art. 19.4 of the Constitution establishes in general that "Should any person's rights be violated by public authority resource to the courts shall be open to him. If jurisdiction is not specified, recourse shall be to the ordinary courts."

970 Art. 90, *2* FCT Law.

971 Art. 95, 3, B FCT Law.

972 Art. 93, 1, B FCT Law.

regarding the challenged statute, *pendente litis*, in the sense that the Tribunal can even theoretically, suspend the application of the challenged law.[973]

Finally, regarding this constitutional complaint, article 93, section 1, N° 4b of the Constitution, also empowers the constitutional tribunal to decide:

> On complaints of unconstitutionality, entered by communes (municipalities) or association of communes (municipalities) on the ground that their right to self–government under article 28 has been violated by a law other than a *Lander* Law open to complaint to the respective land constitutional court.

Hence, the direct constitutional complaint against laws is not only attributed to individuals for the protection of their fundamental rights, but also to the local government entities, for the protection of their autonomy and right to self–government guaranteed in the Constitution, against federal statutes that could violate them. In these cases, it also results in a direct means of judicial review of statutes of legislation.

5. Incidental Method of Judicial Review

The second method established in the Federal Constitution for the purpose of judicial review of statutes, is the incidental method, called the concrete control of norms (*Konkrete Normenkontrolle*) established in article 100 of the Constitution, as follows:

> If a court considers unconstitutional a law the validity of which is relevant to its decision, the proceeding shall be stayed, and a decision shall be obtained from the *Lander* court competent for constitutional disputes if the Constitution of a Land is held to be violated, or from the Federal Constitutional Court if this Basic Law is held to be violated. This shall also apply if this Basic Law is held to be violated by *Land* Law or if a *Land* Law is held to be incompatible with a federal law.[974]

According to this constitutional provision, the concentrated system of judicial review of legislation in the West German constitutional system is, of course, confirmed. It is so mainly because of the implicit prohibition for the courts to control the constitutionality of statutes, although as we have seen, they retain power to control the constitutionality of pre–constitutional legislation and of executive normative acts of the state in a diffuse manner.

Therefore, contrary to the abstract control of norms, in which the petition can refer to any normative state act, the concrete control of norms only refers to statutes in its formal sense.[975]

In this incidental method of judicial review, the constitutional question of a statute always reaches the Constitutional Tribunal through the referral made by any court[976] before the Tribunal, when in a concrete proceeding being developed before

---

973 Art. 32 FCT Law. *Cf.* J.C. BÉGUIN, *op. cit.*, p. *158–163;* F. SAINZ MORENO, *loc. cit.*, p. 626.

974 See also Arts. 80–82 FCT Law.

975 *Cf.* G. MÜLLER, *loc. cit.*, p. 233*;* F. SAINZ MORENO, *loc. cit.*, p. 614.

976 *Cf.* G. MÜLLER, *loc. cit.*, p. 232; F. SAINZ MORENO, *loc. cit.*, p. 614; H.G. RUPP, "Judicial Review ..." *loc. cit.*, p. 32.

it the court considers a law unconstitutional, the validity of which is relevant to its decision in the case. Therefore, the constitutional question in this case, is always of an incidental character, related to the decision of a concrete case by a court; thus it must be related to a case and be determinant to its resolution.

In this case, if it is true that the courts do not have the power to declare statutes null, and do not have *ex–officio* power to decide not to apply them, conversely they have the power to appreciate the unconstitutionality of the statutes,[977] 61) by formulating a referral of a constitutional question before the Constitutional Tribunal.

Furthermore, the judge must be convinced of the unconstitutionality of the statute, that is why he must lay the foundations of his referral to the Tribunal, by explaining in which way his decision depends on the validity of the statute, and which constitutional disposition it is incompatible with.[978]

On the other hand, the referral of constitutional questions of statutes to the Federal Constitutional Tribunal is a power attributed to the courts, which can be exercised *ex–officio*, and whose exercise is not submitted to the will of the parties. Consequently, the referral the courts may send to the Constitutional Tribunal is independent from the parties allegations concerning the unconstitutionality of a statute provision,[979] thus the incidental method of judicial review that it may bring about is not necessarily motivated by an exception alleged by a party.

Anyway and although being of an incidental character, the powers of the Constitutional Tribunal are limited to the consideration of the constitutional question raised in the referral. Thus the Constitutional Tribunal does not review the case on its merits and only decides the question of whether or not the statute which a lower court considers unconstitutional, is repugnant to the Constitution.[980] That is why this proceeding for judicial review, in the concrete control of norms, like the abstract control of norms, is also considered an objective proceeding.[981] Thus, once the Constitutional Tribunal decides upon the constitutional question referred to it by a lower court, the latter must resume the proceedings and render its judgment in accordance with the Constitutional Tribunal decision which has general binding effects.[982]

6. Indirect method of judicial review

As we have seen, the basic means for the concentrated system of judicial review in the Federal Republic of Germany are petitions for the abstract control of norms and constitutional complaints against laws that can be brought before the Constitutional Tribunal, in a direct way, on the one hand. On the other hand, there are the referrals made by any court before the Constitutional Tribunal through the incidental method, to seek a concrete control of statutes. Additional to these means for review,

---

977 *Cf.* J.C. BEGUIN, *op. cit.*, p. 92.

978 Art. 80,2 FCT Law.

979 Art. 80, 3 FCT Law.

980 Art. 81 FCT Law.

981 *Cf.* J.C. BEGUIN, *op. cit*, P. 93.

982 Art. 31, 1 FCT Law.

in the West German constitutional system one can distinguish a third method of judicial review of legislation, which can be considered an indirect one, due to the fact that the powers of review of the Constitutional Tribunal are not exercised as a consequence of a direct request or of a constitutional complaint against a statute or of a incidental referral made to it by a lower court, but as an indirect question that can be raised in a proceeding that is developed before the Constitutional Court, conceived as having another direct or immediate purpose, different to the sole constitutional review of a statute.

This indirect method for judicial review of the unconstitutionality of statutes, can be developed in the following principal situations:

In the first place, as a consequence of a constitutional complaint for the protection of a fundamental right when exercised, not directly against a statute, but against a judicial decision which is considered to have violated the rights and freedoms of a person because it applied a statute which is alleged to have been unconstitutional.[983] In this case, the Constitutional Tribunal must decide upon the unconstitutionality of the statute indirectly challenged before it.

In the second place, the Constitutional Tribunal can also exercise its powers of judicial review of legislation in an indirect way, when deciding upon conflicts between constitutional organs of the Federation,[984] that is to say, disputes concerning the extent of the rights and duties of the highest federal organs established in the Constitution. In cases of conflict, for instance, between the President and the *Bundestag*, the proceeding has a subjective character, thus it is developed in a contradictory way between parties, and can lead to an indirect control of the constitutionality of statutes, only when the act that causes prejudices to the rights and duties of a state organ is a statute, particularly those directed to regulate the functioning of public powers. In this case, however, it is considered that the court does not have annulatory powers regarding the statute unless the abstract control of norms method is accumulated.[985]

7. Effects of the decisions of the Federal Constitutional Tribunal on judicial review and its ex–officio powers

Now, regarding the effects of the federal constitutional tribunal decisions when exercising its powers of judicial review of the constitutionality of normative state acts, particularly of legislation, the general rule is that the tribunal declares the nullity of the unconstitutional provision of the statute or normative act. In this respect, article 78 of the Federal Law of the Constitutional Tribunal established that:

> If the Constitutional Tribunal reach the conviction that the federal law is incompatible with the Constitution, or that the law of a *Lander* is incompatible with the Constitution or with another norm of federal law, it declares its nullity in its decision.[986]

983 Art. 93, 1, 4,a) FCT Law.

984 Art. 93, 1, 1 Constitution.

985 *Cf.* J.C. BÉGUIN, *op. cit.*, pp. 78–81; F. SAINZ MORENO, *loc. cit.*, p. 612.

986 See also Art. 95, 2 FCT Law.

This decision can be in accordance with the contents of the petition, the constitutional complaint or the court referral, according to the method used for obtaining judicial review, but in adopting it the Constitutional Tribunal is not bound by their respective contents, in the sense that it has *ex–officio* powers to raise another constitutional question and thus, to decide, *ultra petita*. That is why the same article 78 of the Federal Law of the Constitutional Tribunal established that:

> If other dispositions of the same statute are incompatible with the Constitution, or another norm of federal law, the Constitutional Tribunal can declare them null at the same time.

The decisions of the Constitutional Tribunal are always obligatory for all constitutional organs of the Federation and of the *Lander*, as well as for all the authorities, the courts[987] and, of course, for the individual. Thus, courts decisions, including those adopted in a judicial review proceeding, have *erga omnes* effects. In particular, in cases of abstract or concrete control of norms, exercised through a petition of a state organ or through a referral by a lower court in which the Constitutional Tribunal declares the nullity of a statute, the decision has the same force as a statute[988]) in the sense of its obligatory *erga omnes* character, including the Constitutional Court itself.[989]

However, contrary to Hans Kelsen's conception of the effects of the decision of the constitutional judge in a concentrated system of judicial review when declaring the nullity of a statute,[990] and to the Austrian model, in accordance with the German constitutional tradition [991] in cases of abstract and concrete control of norms and when deciding upon a constitutional complaint against a statute, when a statute is declared null, it is understood that it is declared null and void *ab initio*, that is to say, the decision of the Tribunal has *ex–tunc*, retroactive effects.[992] This traditional doctrine is confirmed by the fact that the legislator in the Federal Law of the Constitutional Tribunal has expressly limited its scope by establishing that after a statute has been declared null because of its unconstitutionality, only criminal proceedings can be reviewed in cases in which the final judicial decision would have been based on the said statute declared null.[993] All other final and non–reviewable judgments and administrative acts resting on the statute declared null, will stand unchangeable, but their enforceability, if not yet made, would be illicit.[994]

---

987 Art. 31, 1 FCT Law.

988 Art. 31, 2 FCT Law.

989 R. Bocanegra Sierra "Cosa Juzgada, vinculación, fuerza de ley en las decisiones del Tribunal Constitucional alemán", *Revista Española de Derecho Constitucional*, N° 1, 1981, p. 269.

990 H. Kelsen, "La garantie juridictionnelle de la Constitution (La Justice constitutionnelle), *Revue du droit public et de la science politique en France et à l'étranger*, Paris 1928, p. 243.

991 J.C. Beguin, *op. cit.*, pp. 209–228.

992 *Cf.* F. Sainz Moreno, *loc. cit.*, p. 624; H.G. Rupp, "Judicial Review...", *loc. cit.*, p. 37; R. Bocanegra Sierra, *loc. cit.*, p. 268.

993 Art. 79, 1 FCT Law.

994 Art. 79, 2 FCT Law.

Finally, it must be stressed that in the West German system of judicial review, the criterion of the presumption of constitutionality of statutes[995] also exists as a matter of principle, according to which the Constitutional Tribunal has tended not to declare statutes null on the grounds of unconstitutionality, if it is possible to interpret them as consistent with the Constitution. In this sense, the Constitutional Tribunal, in many cases, has followed the method of "interpretation according to the Constitution" through which avoiding the declaration of the nullity of a statute, which would be unconstitutional if interpreted in a certain manner, it has nevertheless considered it valid within the ambit of another interpretation established by the Tribunal "according to the Constitution."[996]

In other cases, even though the Constitutional Tribunal has considered a statute unconstitutional, in order to avoid a possible vacuum in the legal order that could be produced by the nullity of the state act, the declaration of nullity is not adopted. Instead, the court only declares its "simple unconstitutionality" and in some cases has referred the matter to the Legislator to rectify the unconstitutional disposition.[997] Finally, in other cases, the Constitutional Tribunal, although considering a statute consistent with the Constitution, has, nevertheless, referred the matter to the legislator with indications for the rectification of the statute, so as to convert it into being "absolutely constitutional" and, therefore, avoiding any possible future declaration upon its unconstitutionality.[998]

IV. JUDICIAL REVIEW IN ITALY: THE CONSTITUTIONAL COURT

1. Constitutional compromise and the Constitutional Court as its guarantor

Immediately after the Second World War, and even before the creation of the Federal Constitutional Tribunal in the Federal Republic of Germany, the Constitution of the Italian Republic of 1st January 1948 also created a Constitutional Court, charged with controlling the constitutionality of statutes and other state acts with the same force, as the basic element of a concentrated system of judicial review of constitutionality. Nevertheless, the system only started to function in 1956 when the Constitutional Court initiated its activities. Up to that year, the pre 1948 Constitution system of judicial review persisted, being on the contrary a diffuse system of judicial review according to which, all ordinary courts had the power not to apply statutes they considered unconstitutional, when resolving concrete cases to which the said statutes applied.[999]

---

995 H.G. RUPP, "Judicial Review…", *loc. cit.*, p. 38; J.C. BÉGUIN, *op. cit.*, p. 185.

996 *Cf.* J.C. BÉGUIN, *op. cit.*, pp. 184–207; F. SAINZ MORENO, *loc. cit.*, p. 625.

997 Art. 32,2 and 79 FCT Law. *Cf.* J.C. BÉGUIN, *op. cit.*, p. 232–266; F. SAINZ MORENO, *loc. cit.*, p. 624.

998 *Cf.* C. BÉGUIN, *op. cit.*, p. 266–293; F. SAINZ MORENO, *loc. cit.*, p. 624–625.

999 M. CAPPELLETTI, "La justicia constitucional en Italia", *Boletín del Instituto de Derecho Comparado de México*, 30, 1960, p. 41; M. CAPPELLETTI, *Judicial Review in the Contemporary World*, Indianapolis 1971, p. 50.

The radical change in the system can be attributed to various factors, but above all, to the new rigid character attributed to the 1948 Constitution contrasting with the flexible one of the monarchical Fundamental Law (*Statuti Albertini*) of 1848,[1000] thus the need to protect the Constitution against the legislative power particularly after the totalitarian experiment of fascism, and the need to protect and defend fundamental rights and freedoms regarding state powers,[1001] give way to a concentrated system of judicial review. The constitutional court, therefore, was conceived as the organ in charge of the guarantee of the "constitutional compromise" embodied in the Constitution to establish a democratic regime in which the powers of the state organs were limited.[1002] As Professor Giovanni Cassandro, former member of the Constitutional Court said:

> The Court is the constitutional organ which secures the balance among the various powers of the state, preventing any one of them from trespassing the limits imposed by the Constitution, and thus ensures an orderly development of public life and the observance of the Constitutional rights of citizens.[1003]

Therefore, the Constitutional Court in Italy, as the guarantor of the Constitution,[1004] was also established as a "constitutional organ",[1005] independent from all other state organs, although not in an express positive law way as was the case of the Federal Constitutional Tribunal in West Germany[1006] or of the Constitutional Tribunal in Spain.[1007] Nevertheless, the position of the Constitutional Court as an independent and paritarian constitutional organ has been recognised without discussion, and is reflected in various aspects concerning the status of its members, its adminis-

1000 *Cf.* A. PIZZORUSSO, "Procedures et techniques de protection des droits fondamentaux. Cour Constitutionnelle italienne", in L. FAVOREU (ed.), *Cours constitutionnelles europeeures et droit fondamentaux*, Paris 1982, p. 195; J. RODRIGUEZ–ZAPATA y PEREZ, "La Corte Constitucional Italiana: ¿Modelo o advertencia?, in *El Tribunal Constitucional*, Instituto de Estudios Fiscales, Madrid 1981, Vol. III, p. 2416.

1001 *Cf.* G. CASSANDRO, "The Constitutional Court of Italy", *American Journal of Comparative Law*, 8, 1959, p. 3.

1002 *Cf.* F. RUBIO LLORENTE, *La Corte Constitucional italiana*, Caracas 1966, pp. 2–4.

1003 G. CASSANDRO, *loc. cit.*, p. 12; *Cf.* J. RODRÍGUEZ–ZAPATA y PÉREZ, *loc. cit.*, p. 2417.

1004 The Constitutional Court in its decision N° 13 of 1960 the Court defined its functions, as essentialy "the exercise of a function of constitutional control, of the supreme guarantee of the observance of the Constitution ... by the Constitutional organs of the state and of the Regions" (quoted by F. RUBIO LLORENTE, *loc. cit.*, p. 10, note 27); and in his decision N° 15 of 1969 has defined itself as the "highest organ for the guarantee of the republican order, to which exclusively corresponds ensure the rule of the Constitution over all the other constitutional agents." Quoted by J. RODRÍGUEZ–ZAPATA y PÉREZ, *loc. cit.*, p. 2420.

1005 A. SANDULLI, "Sulla posizione della Corte Costituzionale nel sistema degli organi supremi dello Stato", *Rivista trimestrale di diritto pubblico*, 1960, p. 705.

1006 Art. 1,1, Federal Law of the Federal Constitutional Tribunal (1951).

1007 Art. 1,1, Organic Law of the Constitutional Tribunal (1978).

trative and budgetary autonomy, the absence of any external control that could be exercised over it,[1008] and its auto–regulatory powers.[1009]

Furthermore, the independence of the Constitutional Court regarding the traditional organs of the state guaranteed by Constitutional Law N° 1 of February 1948, also results from the paritarian form established for the appointment of its members, which is attributed not only to the politico–representative organs of the state as is the case in West Germany, but to the three traditional powers of the state: the President of the Republic, the Parliament and the Judicial Power. In effect, in accordance with the Constitution[1010] and Statute N° 87 (1953) concerning the Court,[1011] the Constitutional Court is composed of fifteen members, appointed in the following manner: five are appointed by the ordinary and administrative judicial order, as follows: three by the Court of Cassation, one by the Council of state and one by the Court of Accounts, chosen from among members of the judiciary, even retired members.

The second five members are elected by Parliament, both chambers sitting in joint session, by a majority of three fifths of the members of the assembly, chosen from among judges, ordinary professors of law in universities, or lawyers having practised twenty years or more before the supreme judicial organs of the Republic; and the last five members are appointed by the President of the Republic.

As we said, the Constitutional Court is conceived in the Italian constitutional system, as a constitutional organ independent from the other state organs, in charge of maintaining the power balance among them. For that purpose it was created separate from the traditional state powers, and particularly from the Judicial Power, regarding which the Constitutional Court itself established differences.[1012]

But although not being a judicial organ, discussions were developed at the beginning of the functioning of the Constitutional Court regarding the nature of the powers it exercised. In this respect, its judicial character was rejected, and the idea of the negative legislator was initially accepted[1013] under the influence of Hans Kelsen. But eventually, the jurisdictional character of the functions of the Court is today the predominant thesis initially due to the work of Professor Mauro Cappelletti.[1014] Thus, like the other European Constitutional Courts particularly the Austrian and

---

1008 A. SANDULLI, *loc. cit.*, p. 718: *Cf.* J. ROGRÍGUEZ–ZAPATA y PÉREZ, *loc. cit.*, p. 2428–2441; G. CASSANDRO, *loc. cit.*, pp. 13–14.

1009 Art. 14 Statute N° 87 of 11 March 1953, Norms on the Constitution and Functioning of the Constitutional Court. See the text in F. RUBIO LLORENTE, *op. cit.*, pp. 48–55.

1010 Art. 135.

1011 Statute N° 87 (1953), Arts. 1–4.

1012 Decision N° 13, 23 March 1960. Quoted by F. RUBIO LLORENTE, *loc. cit.*, p. 10.

1013 P. CALAMANDREI, *La illegittimitá costituzionale delle leggi nel processo civile*, Padova, 1950, p. 57; H. FIX–ZAMUDIO, "La aportación de Piero CALAMANDREI al derecho procesal constitucional", *Revista de la Facultad de Derecho de México*, 24, 1956, p. 191.

1014 M. CAPPELLETTI, *La giurisdizione costituzionale dele libertá* (Primo studio sul ricorso costituzionale con particolare riguardo agli ordinamenti tedesco, suizzero a austriaco), Milano 1955, p. 112; M. CAPPELLETTI, "La justicia constitucional ...", *loc. cit.*, p. 52; F. RUBIO LLORENTE, *loc. cit.*, pp. 10–13.

Spanish Tribunals, the Constitutional Court in Italy is conceived as an independent constitutional body separate from the Judiciary, which exercises jurisdictional functions when resolving and deciding upon conflicts regarding the constitutionality of state acts and the submission of all the activities of the state organs to the Constitution. Therefore, as happened in the Austrian and German experiences, the Constitutional Court in Italy not only has powers of judicial review of legislation. It can also settle other constitutional disputes particularly deriving from the vertical and horizontal systems of distribution of state powers adopted in the Constitution, although not in the wider sense of the West German system.

2. Jurisdiction of the Constitutional Court

In effect, three main sets of competences of the Constitutional Court can be identified in accordance with the Constitution.

The first general attribution of the Constitutional Court is related to the settlement of "conflict of attribution", which may arise among the powers of the state. These conflicts of attributions or powers can derive from the vertical distribution of state powers, particularly regarding the Regions, and the horizontal distribution of state powers among the constitutional organs.

In effect, the Italian Republic has been constitutionally organised as a "Regional State", which is a form of political decentralization very close to the federal form of state, but with its own peculiarities. Nevertheless, what both forms of political decentralization have in common is a basic distribution of state powers in the vertical sense, over territorial autonomous units, called "Regions" in the Regional State. Therefore, similar to the functions of the Federal Constitutional Tribunal in West Germany, which must settle controversies between the Federation and the *Lander*, in the Italian Republic the Constitutional Court has the power to resolve and settle conflicts of attributions that may arise between state and Regions, if the state invades the sphere of Regional authority or if a Region exceeds its own sphere[1015] invading the National state powers or between the regions themselves, if they invade the attributions of other Regions.

The conflict, in such cases, arises as a consequence of administrative acts, and when deciding it, the Constitutional Court not only decides to which level of state powers the challenged attribution belongs, but has the power to annul the administrative act that brought it about,[1016] also to suspend *pendente litis* its effects, when serious reasons to do so exist.[1017]

It must be said that these are the only cases in which the Italian Constitutional Court can declare the nullity of an administrative act, having no other jurisdiction to judge the unconstitutionality of administrative acts.[1018]

1015 Art. 134 Constitution; Art. 39 Statute N° 87.

1016 Art. 38 Statute N° 87.

1017 Art. 40 Statute N° 87.

1018 F. RUBIO LLORENTE, *op. cit.*, p. 16.

However, the conflicts of attributions between the state and the Regions can also have their origin in legislative acts of the state. In that case their resolution by the Constitutional Court is made through a direct means for judicial review of legislation exercised by the Regions and to which we will refer later on.

But as we said, in the Italian constitutional system the conflict of attributions may not only arise between the vertically distributed state powers, but also between the powers constitutionally assigned to the various national constitutional organs.

In this respect, the Constitutional Court also has jurisdiction to resolve these conflicts "for the delimitation of the sphere of attributions determined for the various powers by constitutional norms",[1019] for instance, between the Chamber of Deputies and the Senate, or between the President of the Republic and Parliament. But it is obvious that the conflict of attributions between the state powers in the horizontal distribution of the state power in the Italian constitutional system, is not only possible between the traditional three powers of the state, but can also arise regarding other state organs, not subordinated to them, for instance, the Superior Council of the Judicature, the Court of Accounts, and the National Economic Council. In this respect, Professor Aldo Saudulli, also a former Constitutional Court judge, has said that the expression "state powers" must be understood to comprise "all the bodies of the state organisation which, in accordance with the constitutional order, are in such a situation that its activities are not subject to any kind of external control by any other state organ (even constitutional state organs)."[1020]

Anyway, in all these cases of conflicts of attributions between constitutional organs of the state, the Constitutional Court must resolve the sphere of attributions conferred upon the various state powers by constitutional norms, [1021] and must declare to which state organ the challenged power belongs, and when an act has been produced inflicted with incompetence, the Court must also annul it.[1022]

The second general competence of the Constitutional Court, in a similar way to the Austrian and West German systems, refers to cases of accusations against or of impeachment of the President of the Republic for crimes of undermining the Constitution and high treason, and against the President of the Council of Ministers and the Ministers for crimes committed by them in the exercise of their functions.[1023] The accusation in these cases can only be brought before the Court by Parliament, which must vote on it in a joint session of its two chambers.

The third jurisdictional power of the Constitutional Court refers to referenda and the Constitution empowers the Court to judge upon the admissibility of derogatory

---

1019 Art. 37 Statute N° 87.

1020 A. SANDULLI, "Die Verfassungsgerichtsbarkeit in Italia", in E. MOSLER (ed.), *Verfassungsgerichsbarkeit in der Gegenwart* (Constitutional Review in the World Today), Max–Plank–Institut Internationalen Kolloquium, Heidelberg, 1961, Köln–Berlin 1962, p. 310; quoted by F. RUBIO LLORENTE, *op. cit.*, p. 36.

1021 Art. 37, Statute N° 87.

1022 Art. 38, Statute N° 87.

1023 Arts 90, 134 Constitution. Statute N° 20, of 25 January 1962. See the text in F. RUBIO LLORENTE, *op.cit.*, p. 55–61.

referenda that can be presented for the abrogation of ordinary laws, exception being made of taxation and budget laws, laws granting amnesty and pardon, and laws authorising the ratification of international treaties.[1024] Nevertheless, the statute referred to in article 75 of the Constitution, which must regulate the above mentioned admissibility conditions and modalities for the derogatory referenda, has not yet been approved.

Finally, the fourth set of jurisdictional powers of the Constitutional Court of Italy refers to judicial review of the constitutionality of legislation, that is to say, to laws (statutes) and other state acts with the same force to which we will refer next.

Thus, the Italian Court does not have jurisdiction over electoral matters and political parties[1025] as the West German Federal Constitutional Tribunal has, and more important to notice, the Italian Constitutional Court does not have powers to act as a direct guarantor of fundamental rights and freedoms, not having attributions to decide upon constitutional complaints or recourses for constitutional protection as they exist in the West German, Austrian and Spanish systems of constitutional justice,[1026] particularly, when exercised against laws. Nevertheless, the need for a direct action before the Constitutional Court was a matter of discussion during the drafting of the Constitution. Moreover, in one of the first drafts of the text, the main form of judicial review of legislation was established through a direct recourse of unconstitutionality that could be brought before the Constitutional Court, as an *actio popularis*, accessible to all citizens without the need of an injury to be done to their subjective rights, an action that needed to be exercised during a one year period after the publication of the statute.[1027] This proposal for a popular action of unconstitutionality was later rejected, mainly due to political reasons,[1028] the means for judicial review of legislation being reduced basically to an incidental system of judicial review concentrated in the Constitutional Court, combined with a limited principal means of review and a preventive system established only regarding certain state acts.

3. Scope of judicial review in the Italian system

Therefore, the Italian system of judicial review of constitutionality is a concentrated system according to which the Constitutional Court is the only state body to have exclusive jurisdiction to determine the conformity of legislation with the Constitution, comprising in the term "legislation", as established in the Constitution, the

---

1024 Art. 74, 75 Constitution; Art. 2 Constitutional Statute N° 1, 11 March 1953. See the text in F. RUBIO LLORENTE, *op. cit.*, pp. 46–47.

1025 Regarding political parties Professor RUBIO LLORENTE says that the Constitutional Court can only decide upon the constitutionality or unconstitutionality of them, only by indirect means when a question of constitutionality is referred to the Court concerning a statute sanctioned based on article 18 (prohibition of secret on paramilitary societies), 49 (freedom of association in political parties), or on the Transitory Disposition XII (prohibition of any form of reorganization of the fascist party) through which a party or a political organization could be dissolved. F. RUBIO LLORENTE, *op. cit.*, p. 16.

1026 *Cf.* A. PIZZARUSSO, *loc. cit.*, p. 168.

1027 F. RUBIO LLORENTE, *op. cit.*, pp. 4–5.

1028 *Idem*, pp. 5–6.

laws (statutes) and other state acts with the force of law,[1029] either of the National state or of the Regions. As a result, formal laws are subject to constitutional control. Also the decree–laws, enacted by the executive by virtue of parliamentary delegation,[1030] or in cases of urgency,[1031] those considered as being "acts with force of law." On the other hand, the *interna corporis* of Parliament, issued in direct execution of the Constitution, are also subject to constitutional control by the Constitutional Court[1032] taking into account their similar rank to statutes, in the hierarchy of the legal order.

Other points should be stressed with respect to these "legislative" acts, which are subject to control. The first is the admissibility of control of constitutionality in the case of laws contrary to the Constitution but passed before their enactment and which, in principle, could be considered to have been tacitly repealed by it. The Constitutional Court has accepted exercising control upon these pre–constitutional laws but only through the incidental method when the issue of constitutionality is raised before an ordinary judge in a concrete case and he refers the question for examination by the Constitutional Court.[1033]

The second aspect refers to the actual enforcement of the laws submitted to control; and specifically as to whether it is possible to raise the issue of constitutionality with respect to repealed laws, which have already lost their force. The Italian Constitutional Court has repeatedly declared its competence to hear disputes concerning the constitutionality of these repealed laws, thus no longer in force, considering that they could have created situations, the persistence of which after their repeal, could have justified constitutional control.[1034]

The third aspect has to do with the objective of this control, which is not only a substantive control in the sense of determining if the statute is consistent with the constitution in its normative contents or not, but also a formal control over acts submitted to constitutional review, regarding the procedures followed for its sanctioning.[1035]

On the other hand, the jurisdictional powers of the Constitutional Court to review the constitutionality of legislation, refer not only to the confrontation of legislative acts with the constitution itself, but also to "constitutional laws" that can be enacted in accordance with article 138 of the Constitution to amend it. The *bloc* of constitutionality, therefore, is particularly composed, other than the principles, which could be deduced from the constitutional text, of the Constitution and the "constitutional

---

1029 Art. 1. Constitutional Statute N° 1, 9 February 1948.

1030 Art. 75 Constitution.

1031 Art. 77 Constitution. These Decree–Laws issued in emergency situations must be submitted to Parliament the following day of its enactment and only when they are convalidated by Parliament, they can be questioned on constitutional grounds.

1032 *Cf.* F. RUBIO LLORENTE, *op. cit.*, p. 23.

1033 Decision N° 1, 1956. Quoted by F. RUBIO LLORENTE, *op. cit.*, p. 35; *Cf.* G. CASSANDRO, *loc. cit.*, p. 5.

1034 Decision N° 4, 1959. Quoted by F. RUBIO LLORENTE, *op. cit.*, p. 22.

1035 *Cf.* G. CASSANDRO, *loc. cit.*, p. 4.

laws" to which all other norms must conform. But the "constitutional laws" being regulated for their enactment by the Constitution, which establishes their scope and possible contents, can also be submitted to constitutional review by the Constitutional Court.[1036]

Finally, regarding the scope of judicial review exercised by the Constitutional Court, one must stress the discussions that have arisen as a consequence of the terms used in article 134 of the Italian Constitution, in the sense that the Constitutional Court has jurisdiction to settle disputes dealing with "constitutional legitimacy" of laws and state acts with force of law,[1037] which could lead to the conclusion as happened in the administrative justice field regarding the control of administrative acts, that the Court could control the merits of legislative activities.

In principle, this power attributed to the Constitutional Court deals only with matters of abstract repugnancy of state acts with the Constitution in the sense that the Court must control the submission of the legislator to the constitution and the limits to its activities established in it, the Court not being authorised to judge upon the motives and merits the legislator could have had when enacting a statute. In this respect, the 1953 Statute N° 87 of the Constitutional Court expressly states:

> Art 28. The Constitutional Court control over the legitimacy of laws or an act with force of law, excludes any value judgement of policy nature and any judgement upon the use Parliament makes of its discretionary power. But even with a text of this clarity, the Constitutional Court, always within the ambit of this norm, since 1960, has controlled the "arbitrariness" or "non arbitrariness" of the legislator concerning the legislation enacted in relation to the principle of equality and non discrimination, and the "rationality" of the distinctions established in legislation.[1038]

4. Incidental method of judicial review

As we have said, the basic means for raising questions of constitutionality of legislation before the Constitutional Court and undoubtedly, the most important means for keeping statutes and legislative acts within the framework of the Constitution in the Italian system, is the incidental method expressly regulated in the 1948 Constitutional Statute N° 1, which contained the norms related to the trials of constitutional illegitimacy and to the independence guarantees of the Constitutional Court. Article 1 of that Constitutional Statute, states:

> The question on the constitutional illegitimacy of a law (statute) or of an act of the Republic with force of law, raised *ex officio* or alleged by one of the parties in the course of a trial, and not evidently considered unfounded by the judge, must be referred to the Constitutional Court for its consideration.

1036 G. CASSANDRO, *loc. cit.*, pp. 3–4. *Cf.* F. RUBIO LLORENTE, *op. cit.*, p. 20.

1037 The term is also used in article 1, Constitutional Statute N° 1, 9 February 1948; and in arts 23–36 Statute N° 87, 1953.

1038 *Cf.* The Court Decisions and the opposite doctrine on this matter in F. RUBIO LLORENTE, *op. cit.*, pp. 17–19; and G. ZAGREBELSKI, "Object et portée de la protection des droits fondamentaux. Cour Constitutionnelle italienne", in L. FAVOREU (ed.), *Cours constitutionnelles europées et droits fondamentaux*, Paris 1982, p. 330.

This incidental method of judicial review has been regulated in the 1953 Statute N° 87 in which its fundamental provisions are to be found, which reinforce the concentrated incidental character of the Italian system of judicial review.[1039]

In accordance with this 1953 Statute N° 87, in the course of a process developed before a court, either party or the Public Prosecutor may raise the question of constitutional legitimacy in the form of a petition, indicating, firstly the provisions of the law or the act with force of law of the state or of the Region, containing defects of "constitutional illegitimacy"; and secondly, the provisions of the Constitution or of the "constitutional laws" which have allegedly been violated.

Once the issue of constitutionality is raised before the ordinary judge, he must made a decision referring the issue to the Constitutional Court, when it is a "prejudicial" question, that is to say, if the case does not allow him to take a decision avoiding the issue of "constitutional legitimacy", and also when the judge considers that the issue raised before him is not evidently unfounded.[1040] In other words, if the judge considers that the issue of constitutionality has sufficient basis and its resolution is essential for the decision of the process, then he must decide upon the existence of both conditions and therefore refer the question to the Constitutional Court, sending with the referral the statement made by the parties or by the Public Prosecutor and the whole file of the case, whose proceeding must be suspended.

The judge, in a motivated decision, can reject the constitutional question alleged by the parties or by the Public Prosecutor when he considers that it has no relevance to the case or has no due foundation. However, this rejection does not prevent the parties from later raising the question in any stage of the proceeding.[1041]

But as the 1948 Constitutional Statute N° 1 and the 1953 Statute N° 87 state, the issue of constitutional legitimacy may also be raised *ex–officio* by the judge hearing the case. In that event, he must also make a decision in which he must include the precise indication of the provisions of the law or of the acts with the force of law considered unconstitutional, as well as the norms of the Constitution or of the constitutional laws deemed to have been violated by the challenged statute. The judge must also justify in his decision the "prejudicial" character of the question and the reasons for considering the statute unconstitutional.

Anyway, when raising the constitutional question concerning the constitutional illegitimacy of a statute or of a state act with force of law, the judge is not bound by the will of the parties: he can reject their allegations upon constitutional issues and can raise them *ex–officio*. In all such cases, it is the judge who must decide upon the unconstitutionality of the statutes, although he has no power to annul them and his powers are limited to referring the question to the Constitutional Court.

Furthermore, neither is the Constitutional Court when considering the constitutional question referred to it, bound by the parties of the original process in which the constitutional issue was raised; therefore, even if those parties of the *a quo* proc-

---

1039 M. CAPPELLETTI, "La justicia constitucional…", *loc. cit.*, pp. 44, 45.

1040 Art. 23, Statute N° 87, 1953.

1041 Art. 24, Statute N° 87, 1953.

ess must be called upon and heard, as well as the executive authority concerned (President of the Council of Ministers or of the Regional Board),[1042] the proceeding developed before the Court, is not an adversary one developed *inter partes*, rather it is of a non adversary and objective nature, developed independent of the will of the parties and even in cases of abandonment of action or when a voluntary dismissal of the case has taken place.[1043]

As we have said, in the Italian system of judicial review, this incidental method is the most important mean for seeking constitutional review of legislation and, therefore, it has been considered as having limited scope, particularly regarding statutes that could directly affect individual rights. As Professor Cappelletti said:

> The inconvenience of this system results from the fact that certain statutes, particularly those called by the Mexican constitutional doctrine auto–applicable (auto effective or auto–executive), could immediately infringe the juridical sphere of certain individuals, without the need of being "concretised" by an executive or applicative act; thus, at least regarding these laws, the sole incidental control of constitutional legitimacy, could appear as insufficient.[1044]

5. Direct method of judicial review and its regional scope

But in spite of its predominant incidental concentrated character, the Italian system of judicial review also allows a direct method of judicial review, although limited, and in a certain way very closely related to the powers of the Court to resolve conflicts of attributions between state and Regions.

In effect, article 2 of Constitutional Statute N° 1 of 9, February 1948 attributes the resolution of questions of constitutional illegitimacy to the Constitutional Court brought before it through a direct action that can only be exercised by a Region against national legislation or statutes of other Regions. This article states the following:

> Art 2. When a Region deems that a statute or an act with force of law of the Republic invades the sphere of competences attributed to it in the Constitution, it can present before the Court, upon deliberation of the Regional Board, the question of constitutional illegitimacy within thirty days of the publication of the statute or of the act with force of law.[1045]

Therefore, the first recourse or direct action of unconstitutionality accepted in the Italian constitutional system is the one that the Regions could bring before the Constitutional Court against legislative acts of the Republic, which in fact, results in a conflict of attributions between national and regional levels,[1046] not based on an administrative act, but rather on a statute or other national act with force of law, particularly decree–laws. Nevertheless, this action or recourse cannot be brought before

---

1042 Art. 25, Statute N° 87, 1953. The parties or the public official may not appeal before the Court, Art. 26. *Idem*.

1043 Art. 22, Complementary Norms of the Court. *Cf.* F. RUBIO LLORENTE, *op. cit.*, p. 24; G. CASSANDRO, *loc. cit.*, p. 6; A. PIZZORUSSO, *loc. cit.*, p. 176.

1044 M. CAPPELLETTI, "Judicial Review...", *loc. cit.*, p. 45.

1045 See also Art. 32 Statute N° 87, 1953.

1046 *Cf.* F. RUBIO LLORENTE, *op. cit.*, p. 25.

the Court the other way round, that is to say, by the Republic against the Regional statutes, in which cases the question must be treated as a conflict of attributions in the sense already mentioned.[1047]

On the other hand, the direct action or recourse of unconstitutionality in accordance with the 1948 Constitutional Statute N° 1 can also be brought before the Constitutional Court by a Region against a statute or another act with and force of law of another Region and considered constitutionally illegitimate, when it deems its competences have been violated by it.[1048]

The proceedings in such cases of direct action are considered in a sense as adversary, because contrary to the situation in the incidental method, in the principal one the will of the parties carries weight in the sense that the "waiver of the action, if accepted by all parties, extinguishes the proceeding."[1049]

6. Preventive method of judicial review of regional legislation

Finally, the Constitution also establishes a preventive means of judicial review but limited only to controlling the constitutionality of regional legislation[1050] by the Constitutional Court, by attributing to the Council of Ministers the power to bring a direct action or recourse against regional statutes, before their enactment, before the Court, within fifteen days following the formal information that the President of the Regional Board must send when a regional bill is approved in a second vote by the Regional Council.[1051]

In these cases, when the preventive judicial review request is brought before the Court, the enactment of the challenged regional statute must be suspended until a decision is adopted[1052] in which case, if it is of unconstitutionality, its promulgation would be impossible.

7. Effects of the Constitutional Court decisions

In all cases of judicial review of the constitutionality of legislation, the Constitutional Court must decide, "within the limits" of the action or referral,[1053] which are the norms considered "illegitimate", that is to say, unconstitutional. Thus, in accordance with the terms of Statute N° 87, it has been considered that the Constitutional Court does not have *ex–officio* powers to consider other constitutional issues different to those submitted to it by the referral in the incidental method or in the action or recourse in the direct or principal method of judicial review. In this respect, the Court has powers only to declare "which other legislative dispositions whose ille-

---

1047 Art. 39 Statute N° 67, 1953.

1048 Art. 2; See also Art. 33 Statute N° 87, 1953.

1049 Art. 25, Complementary Norms of the Court. *Cf.* G. CASSANDRO, *loc. cit.*, p. 8.

1050 Art. 127 Constitution.

1051 Art. 31 Statute N° 87, 1953.

1052 Art. 128 Constitution.

1053 Art. 27 Statute N° 87, 1953.

gitimacy is a consequence of the decision adopted",[1054] but cannot declare the unconstitutionality of legislative dispositions other than those indicated in the referral by the ordinary judge or in the direct action.

On the other hand, the Constitutional Court decision in which the unconstitutionality of a statute is declared, has *erga omnes* effects and therefore, the act "cannot be applied onwards from the day following the publication of the decision."[1055] Therefore, it must be considered that the decision has a constitutive character[1056] in the sense that it annuls the unconstitutional statute, its effect being *ex–nunc*, *pro futuro*. This rule, has been widely discussed[1057] and the Constitutional Court has interpreted the constitutional norm (art 136) which states that the act declared unconstitutional cannot be applied onwards from the day after the publication of the Court decision, in the sense that:

> The decision upon the unconstitutionality, if it is true that it leaves out all the effects irrevocably produced by the norm declared unconstitutional, on the contrary it produces effects upon the juridical situations not yet exhausted, when they are still susceptible to being regulated in a different manner as a consequence of the decision. Thus the declaration of unconstitutionality of a statute produces its inapplicability to all the relations judicially controverted as and when they are still not the object of a decision with *res judicata* force, with the consequence that in all stages of the trial, the judge even *ex–officio* must take into account the said decision of constitutional illegitimacy when deciding the concrete juridical relation of a case, in the same way and to the same extent as if it were a *ius superveniens*.[1058]

This criterion of the Constitutional Court, in fact, confirms the constitutive character of the effects of the decisions declaring the unconstitutionality of statutes, whose exceptions are established in the 1953 Statute N° 87, in which the retroactive effects of the decision are only applicable in criminal cases, when a judicial condemnation has been pronounced based on a statute declared unconstitutional, in which case its execution and its criminal effects must cease.[1059]Another indirect exception of the *ex–nunc* effects of the decision results from the already mentioned possibility of annulment of statutes already repealed.[1060]

Another issue, which has been raised regarding the effects of the Constitutional Court decision on issues of constitutional illegitimacy, is that of the effects of the decision, which reject the question of unconstitutionality for lack of foundation. Initially Professor Calamandrei maintained that these decisions were to be considered authentic interpretations of the Constitution, that should prevent future challenges and therefore had *erga omnes* effects.[1061] Discussions have taken place regarding the matter, and today it can be said that the same Constitutional Court has limited the

---

1054 Art. 27 *Idem*.

1055 Art. 136 Constitution; Art. 30, Statute N° 87, 1953.

1056 *Cf.* G. CASSANDRO, *loc. cit.*, p. 6.

1057 *Cf.* F. RUBIO LLORENTE, *op. cit.*, p. 12 and 29–33.

1058 Decision N° 3491, 1957. Quoted in F. RUBIO LLORENTE, *op. cit.*, p. 30.

1059 Art. 30 Statute N° 87, 1953.

1060 See note N° 1034.

1061 P. CALAMANDREI, *op. cit.*, p. 71.

effects of its decisions declaring the lack of foundations of the unconstitutionality issue, to the principal process in which the issue was first raised; therefore, that decision has a binding efficacy on the concrete case, with the full authority of *res judicata.*[1062] To reach this conclusion, it has been considered that because the general norm of the Italian legal system is to limit the effects of judicial decisions to the case in dispute, the norm of Article 136 of the Constitution, which attributes *erga omnes* effects to declarations of unconstitutionality has an exceptional character, which cannot be the object of extensive interpretation. The result is that this *erga omnes* character cannot be applied to decisions that dismiss or reject issues of unconstitutionality.[1063]

Another criterion that have been exposed are that of the preclusive effect of the Court decision, in the sense that the incidental question of constitutionality cannot be raised twice in the same process in its original form. Nevertheless, this does not preclude the possibility of it being raised in another process, or even, that the parties could raise new issues of unconstitutionality judged negatively by the Court on a previous occasion.[1064]

V. JUDICIAL REVIEW IN SPAIN: THE CONSTITUTIONAL TRIBUNAL

1. Second Spanish Republic antecedents: Constitutional Guarantees Tribunal

The third European experience in establishing a concentrated system of judicial review, after the 1920 Czechoslovakian and Austrian constitutional justice regulations, was developed in the Second Spanish Republic, in accordance with the Constitution of 9 December 1931, which created a Tribunal of Constitutional Guarantees. The system established was a concentrated system of judicial review, in which the direct influence of the Austrian experience and the thoughts of Hans Kelsen, can be found,[1065] although with its own peculiarities and also with its own historical antecedents in the projects of the First Republic in 1873.[1066]

In effect, the 1931 judicial review system was conceived as a concentrated one, in which the Tribunal of Constitutional Guarantees had exclusive powers to judge upon the constitutionality of statutes, through two methods: an incidental and a principal one. Additionally, the Constitution regulated recourse of constitutional protection (*recurso de amparo*) also to be exercised before the Tribunal for the protection of fundamental rights.

1062 *Cf.* F. RUBIO LLORENTE, *op. cit.*, pp. 32–33.

1063 M. CAPPELLETTI, "La justicia constitucional… ", *loc. cit.*, pp. 56–57.

1064 *Idem*, p. 57.

1065 J.L. MELIÁN GIL, *El Tribunal de Garantías Constitucionales de la Segunda República Española*, Madrid 1971, pp. 16–17, 53; P. CRUZ VILLALON, "Dos modos de regulación del control de constitucionalidad: Checoslovaquia (1920–1938) y España (1931–1936), *Revista española de derecho constitucional*, 5, 1982, p. 118.

1066 J.L. MELIÁN GIL, *op. cit.*, p. 9; N. GONZÁLEZ–DELEITO DOMINGO, *Tribunales constitucionales. Organización y funcionamiento*, Madrid 1980, p. 21.

The incidental mean for judicial review was established in article 100 of the Constitution, which stated:

> When a court of justice would have to apply a law (statute) which it deems to be contrary to the Constitution, it must suspend the proceeding and send a consultative request to the Tribunal of Constitutional Guarantees.

Additionally, the Constitution assigned competence to the Tribunal of Constitutional Guarantees to take cognisance of the "recourse of unconstitutionality of laws"[1067] conceived as an autonomous action, which could be exercised before the Tribunal by the Public Prosecutor, the Government of the Republic, the Regions and by "any individual or collective person, even if it was not directly injured",[1068] which in fact converted it into a popular action.

Nevertheless, this concentrated system of judicial review so broadly established in the 1931 Constitution was reduced in the Organic Law of the Tribunal enacted in 1933. In it, the "recourse of unconstitutionality of laws" was conceived only as an incidental mean of judicial review, sought *ex–officio* by a court or as a consequence of an exception raised in a concrete proceeding by the party whose rights could result in being affected by the application of the challenged statute, or by the Public Prosecutor.[1069] In this way, the system, exclusively incidental, was distanced from the Austrian model and followed trends of the diffuse system of judicial review regarding the effects of the Tribunal decisions declaring the unconstitutionality of state acts, in the sense that they were not *erga omnes* but were reduced only regarding "the concrete case of the recourse or the consultation."[1070] Thus, the statutes were not annulled by the Tribunal but only considered inapplicable to the concrete case.[1071] The Organic Law of the Constitutional Guarantees Tribunal was broadly criticised for this restriction regarding constitutional dispositions, and was the first to be the object of a recourse of unconstitutionality.[1072] Anyway, less than five years after the promulgation of the Constitution, it was repealed in 1936 and with it, the system of judicial control of constitutionality was eliminated. It has only been with the publication of the new democratic Constitution of 27 December 1978 that a new system of judicial review has been established in Spain, with the creation of the Constitutional Tribunal later regulated in the "Organic Law of the Constitutional Tribunal" of 3 October 1979.[1073]

1067 Art. 121. See the text in J.L. MELIÁN GIL, *op. cit.*, p. 11; N. GONZÁLEZ–DELEITO DOMINGO, *loc. cit.*, p. 22.

1068 Art. 123. *Idem.*

1069 Art. 30–33. Organic Law 1933. See in J.L. MELIÁN GIL, *op. cit.*, pp. 14, 29.

1070 Art. 42, *Idem*, p. 30.

1071 J.L. MELIÁN GIL, *op. cit.*, p. 30.

1072 *Idem*, p. 45; N. GONZÁLEZ–DELEITO DOMINGO, *op. cit.*, p. 23.

1073 Organic Law 2/1979. See the text in *Boletín Oficial del Estado*, N° 239, 5 October, 1979.

2. Constitutional Tribunal as a European model

Having been established after the consolidation of the main continental European experiences of constitutional justice, the Spanish judicial review system adopted the most important features of the European model, being influenced by the West German, Italian and French regulations. That is why, up to the creation of the Constitutional Tribunal in Spain, it was said that the Federal Constitutional Tribunal of West Germany had the widest jurisdiction on constitutional matters compared to any other tribunal or supreme court in the world.[1074] After 1978, this assertion was no longer true, and the Constitutional Tribunal of Spain was the one generally considered as the constitutional organ with the most complete jurisdiction in constitutional matters.[1075] But today, at least on the grounds of judicial review and constitutional justice, this can be said in Europe, of the Constitutional Tribunal of Portugal established in the 1982 Constitutional revision, in which a mixed system of judicial review of legislation has been established.

Nevertheless, the Spanish system can be considered as an illustrative example of the concentrated European model of judicial review[1076] which has proved its workability over recent years.

Of course, not all the normative acts of the state are subject to exclusive constitutional review by the tribunal, and as in other European countries it is admitted that the preconstitutional legislation even though reviewable by the tribunal, can be reviewed in a diffuse way by all courts.[1077]

Anyway, in accordance with the Constitution, the Constitutional Tribunal is conceived as a constitutional organ, thus independent and separate from the Judicial Power, but with jurisdictional functions as the guarantor of the constitutionality of state action.[1078] In this respect, article 1 of the Organic Law 2/1979 concerning the Tribunal, expressly establishes that:

1074 G. MÜLLER, "El Tribunal Constitucional Federal de la República Federal de Alemania", *Revista de la Comisión Internacional de Juristas*, Vol VI, (2), 1 5, p. 221.

1075 *Cf.* E. GARCIA DE ENTERRIA, *La Constitución como norma y el Tribunal Constitucional*, Madrid 1981, p. 137; P. BON, F. MODERNE and Y. RODRIGUEZ, *La justice constitutionnelle en Espagne*, Paris 1982, p. 41; L. FAVOREU, "Actualité et légitimité du Contrôle juridictionnel des lois en Europe occidentale." *Revue du droit public et de la science politique en France et à l'étranger*, Paris 1984 (5), p. 1154.

1076 P. BON, F. MODERNE and Y. RODRÍGUEZ, *op. cit.*, p. 41.

1077 J. SALAS, "El Tribunal Constitucional Español y su competencia desde la perspectiva de la forma de Gobierno: sus relaciones con los poderes Legislativo, Ejecutivo y Judicial", *Revista española de derecho constitucional*, 6, 1982, p. 165.

1078 M. GARCÍA PELAYO, "El Status del Tribunal Constitucional", *Revista española de derecho constitucional*, 1, 1981, pp. 11–34; F. RUBIO LLORENTE, "Sobre la relación entre Tribunal Constitucional y poder judicial en el ejercicio de la jurisdicción constitucional", *Revista española de derecho constitucional*, 4, 1982, pp. 35–67, As an independent organ it also has autoregulatory powers: Art. 2,2 Organic Law 2/1979.

> The Constitutional Tribunal, as the supreme interpreter of the Constitution, is independent from the other constitutional organs and it is only submitted to the Constitution and to this Organic Law.

According to article 159 of the Constitution, the tribunal is composed of 12 members appointed from among magistrates and public prosecutors, university professors, public officials and qualified lawyers with over 15 years practice. The members of the tribunal are appointed by the king, in the following manner: four are appointed on the proposal of a three fifths majority of the members of Congress; four on the proposal of the same majority of the Senate; two on the Government's proposal; and two on the proposal of the General Council of the Judicial Power. Thus, as happens in the Italian system, all the three traditional powers of the state intervene in the appointment of the members of the Tribunal. As also happens in the other European systems, so as to avoid the politicalisation of the Tribunal, the Constitution is quite explicit as to the incompatibilities with respect to its members. It stipulates that the status of being a member of the Constitutional Court is incompatible with any representative mandate, with political and administrative posts, with directive functions in a political party or trade union, or employment by them, with a judicial or public prosecutor career and with any other professional or commercial activity. It is also stipulated that the members of the Constitutional Tribunal have the same incompatibility as the members of the Judiciary.

The competences of the Tribunal can be classified into three main groups: the resolution of constitutional conflicts between state powers; the decision of the recourses of constitutional protection (*recursos de amparo*) of fundamental rights; and the control of the constitutionality of legislation.

The first major group of powers assigned to the Constitutional Tribunal refers to the resolution of constitutional conflicts between state organs, in accordance with the vertical and horizontal systems of distribution of state powers adopted by the Constitution. In Spain, the Constitution has organised the form of the state, as a "State of Autonomous Communities", in a similar way to the Regional state formula of the Italian Constitution; therefore, a particular system of political decentralization has been adopted, in which the Autonomous Communities are the most important pillars of the territorial organisation of the state.[1079] Therefore, the Constitutional Tribunal is empowered to resolve "the conflicts of attributions between the state and the Autonomous Communities and conflicts between the latter."[1080]

But within this same sort of jurisdiction, the Constitutional Tribunal has been empowered by the Organic Law that regulates it to resolve conflicts of competences or attributions between the constitutional organs of the National state, that is to say, those conflicts that confront "the Government with the Congress of Deputies, the Senate or the General Council of the Judicial Power; or any of those constitutional organs between themselves."[1081] The justification of the competence of the Constitutional Tribunal in conflicts between constitutional bodies, as in all the other Euro-

1079 Art. 2, 137, 143 Constitution.

1080 Art. 161, 1,c Constitution; Art. 60–72 Organic Law 2/1979.

1081 Art. 59, 3; 73–5 Organic Law 2/1979.

pean constitutional justice systems, seems evident. Any conflict between political entities is, in itself, a constitutional conflict, which questions the organic system established by the Constitution itself. Consequently, the Constitutional Tribunal is the only adequate body for the settlement of such conflicts, which affect the very essence of the Constitution, the distribution of powers, which it establishes, and the competences distributed by it.

The judgments pronounced in settlement of conflicts of competence have *inter partes* effects because the content of these judgments basically consists of a declaration on the entitlement of the constitutional bodies, for example, Congress, the Senate or the General Council of the Judiciary, to the competence in dispute.[1082]

However, when the declaration on entitlement implies the declaration of the nullity[1083] of the normative provision issued by the body declared to be incompetent, the judgment must be published for it to have *erga omnes* effects.[1084]

The second major block of attributions of the Constitutional Tribunal relates to the decision of the *recursos de amparo* (recourse for constitutional protection). It can be directly brought by individuals before the Constitutional Tribunal, when they deem their constitutional rights and liberties violated by dispositions, juridical acts or simple factual actions of the public powers of the state, the Autonomous Communities and other public territorial entities or by their officials.[1085] This recourse for the protection of fundamental rights cannot be exercised directly against statutes, which violate fundamental rights in a direct way,[1086] as in the West German system. Therefore, it can only be exercised against administrative or judicial acts and acts without force of law produced by the legislative authorities,[1087] and only when the ordinary judicial means for the protection of fundamental rights have been exhausted.[1088] Consequently, the recourse for *amparo* in general results in a direct action against judicial acts[1089] and can only indirectly lead to judicial review of legislation when the particular state act challenged by it is based on a statute considered unconstitutional.[1090]

Finally, the third group of attributions of the Constitutional Tribunal refers to judicial review of legislation, which can be exercised through a direct or principal recourse or in an incidental way. The Constitutional Court can also exercise the power of judicial review in an indirect way and regarding certain state acts, in a preventive way. Therefore, four different means of judicial review of legislation can be distinguished in the Spanish system.

1082 Art. 75, 2 Organic Law 2/1979.

1083 *Idem.*

1084 Art. 164, 1 Constitution.

1085 Art. 161, 1, b) Constitution; Art. 41, 2 Organic Law 2/1979.

1086 *Cf.* . GARCÍA DE ENTERRÍA, *op. cit.*, p. 151.

1087 Art. 42 Organic Law 2/1979.

1088 Art. 43, 1 Organic Law 2/1979.

1089 *Cf.* FAVOREU, *loc. cit.*, pp. 1155–1156.

1090 Art. 55,2 Organic Law 2/1979.

3. Direct control of the constitutionality of legislation

The first of the means through which judicial review powers can be exercised by the Constitutional Tribunal, and upon which it is empowered to decide, is through the "recourse of unconstitutionality against laws and normative acts with force of law",[1091] through which "the Constitutional Tribunal guarantees the primacy of the Constitution and judges the conformity or inconformity" of the laws and normative acts with force of law with it.[1092]

In a very similar way to the Italian formula, the state acts that can be the object of this direct recourse of unconstitutionality are the laws (statutes) and other state acts with the same force of laws, which include the "Statutes of Autonomy" approved by Parliament for the Autonomous Communities, and also the organic laws and the ordinary laws approved by Parliament;[1093] international treaties;[1094] the *interna corporis* regulations of the Chambers and Parliament; [1095] the other normative acts of the National state with force of law, including the decree–laws enacted by the Government,[1096] either through delegate legislation[1097] or in cases of urgent and extraordinary necessity;[1098] and finally, the normative regulations of the legislative assemblies of the Autonomous Communities. [1099]

It must also be noted that pre–constitutional laws can also be controlled on the ground of their constitutionality by the Constitutional Tribunal even though, as we said, they can be declared inapplicable by any judge when considered unconstitutional,[1100] particularly because the Constitution expressly states in its Derogatory Disposition, N° 3, that "all dispositions repugnant to what is established in this Constitution are repealed."

This recourse of unconstitutionality can be brought before the Constitutional Tribunal by the President of the Government, the "Peoples Defendant", fifty Deputies or fifty Senators;[1101] and also by the Collegiate executive organ and the Legislative Assemblies of the Autonomous Communities when the challenged acts are laws or other state acts with similar force of law which affect their respective autonomy am-

1091 Art. 161,1,a Constitution.

1092 Art. 27,1 Organic Law 2/1979.

1093 Art. 27,2, a,b) *Idem.*

1094 Art. 27,2,c) *Idem.*

1095 Art. 27,2,d) *Idem.*

1096 Art. 27,2 ,b) *Idem.*

1097 Art. 82 Constitution.

1098 Art. 86 Constitution.

1099 Art. 27,2,f) Constitution.

1100 Art. 27,2,f) Constitution.

1101 This has been expressly admitted by the Constitutional Tribunal. *Cf.* J. SALAS, *loc. cit.*, pp. 165–166.

bit.[1102] In any case, the recourse can only be brought before the Tribunal within a delay of three months following the publication of the challenged act.[1103]

The radical difference between the direct action or recourse of unconstitutionality established in Spain, and the Italian model in which, for instance, the standing of the Government is limited to challenging only the regional laws, must be stressed. On the contrary, in the Spanish system, the standing attributed to the various political organs, including the President of Government, implies their right to challenge any law or state act with force of law on the grounds of unconstitutionality.[1104]

But regarding the dispositions and decisions of the organs of the Autonomous Communities that can be challenged by the Government, what the Constitution establishes is the suspensive character of the recourse in relation to the challenged acts.[1105]

Just as in the West German system, the aim of this direct action on the ground of unconstitutionality is to exercise an abstract control over normative state acts, without reference to a particular conflict in which it would be necessary to elucidate the constitutional issue. Thus, in these cases it is simply a question of an abstract discrepancy over the interpretation of the Constitution in relation to a particular law.[1106] On the other hand, and although the state organs whose normative acts must be called upon and could be heard[1107] the proceeding for the decision of this recourse of unconstitutionality can be considered an objective one in which the political organs which initiated it and the representatives [1108] of the state organs whose statutes and acts are challenged, do not have the strict procedural position of parties[1109] the abandonment of the recourse not being conceivable.[1110]

4. Incidental method of judicial review of legislation

The second method of judicial review in the Spanish system is the incidental one, established in article 163 of the Constitution as follows:

> When a judicial organ considers in a process, that a norm with rank of law applicable to the case and on whose validity its decision depends, could be contrary to the Constitution, it must refer the question to the Constitutional Tribunal in the manner and with the effects established in the law, which in any case will be of a suspensive character.[1111]

1102 Art. 162,1,a) Constitution; Art. 32,1 Organic Law 2/1979.

1103 Art. 33 Organic Law 2/1979.

1104 S. GALEOTTI and B. ROSSI, "El Tribunal Constitucional en la nueva Constitución española: Medios de impugnación y legitimados para actuar", *Revista de estudios políticos*, 7, Madrid 1979, p. 125.

1105 Art. 30 Organic Law

1106 E. GARCÍA DE ENTERRÍA, *op. cit.*, p. 140.

1107 Art. 34 Organic Law 2/1979.

1108 Art. 82,1 *Idem*.

1109 J. GONZÁLEZ PÉREZ, *Derecho procesal constitucional*, Madrid 1980, p. 101.

1110 *Idem*, p. 197.

1111 See also Art. 35,1 Organic Law 2/1979.

The first aspect that must be stressed regarding this incidental means of judicial review is that in the Spanish system, the judges are the only organs authorised to raise the constitutional question, although they can act either *ex–officio* or on the instance of a party.[1112] Therefore, the parties can raise the constitutional question, at any stage in the concrete process, but it is the judge who must appreciate it in a non appealable decision,[1113] and only when he considers the specific norm contrary to the Constitution, must he refer the question to the Tribunal.

In accordance with the Organic Law that regulates the Tribunal, this constitutional question can be raised by the Judge only once the proceeding in the concrete case has concluded and within the delay to decide the case, that is why the issue does not have suspensive effects, in the sense that the proceeding must continue up to the stage of possibility of the adoption of the final decision.[1114]

The referral must express the statute or norm with force of law whose constitutionality is questioned, the constitutional norm that is supposed to be infringed and the judge must specify and justify to what extent the decision in the concrete proceeding depends on the validity of the norm in question, that is to say, he must justify the pre–judiciary character of the constitutionality of the statute or normative act regarding the concrete process.

Anyway, before adopting his own decision on the matter, the judge must hear the Public Prosecutor and the parties regarding the constitutional issue.[1115] But once the issue of unconstitutionality has been raised before the Constitutional Tribunal, the parties of the *a quo* proceeding have no right to intervene in the constitutional process, the Constitutional Tribunal only being obliged to notify the question to the representatives of the organs whose acts have been challenged, in order to allow them to argue before the Tribunal on the matter.[1116]

Regarding this incidental mean for constitutional review, different regulations that exist in the Spanish system in relation to the German model must be stressed: in the latter, the incidental constitutional question can only be raised by a court before the Constitutional Tribunal when the judge is convinced of the unconstitutionality of the particular statute; whereas in the Spanish system it is sufficient for the judge to consider that the applicable norm "could be contrary to the Constitution" though, more similar to the Italian system in which the judge must raise the constitutional question only when he considers that it is not evidently unfounded.[1117]

1112 Art. 35,2 *Idem.*

1113 *Idem*

1114 See J.M. RODRÍGUEZ OLIVER, "Sobre los efectos no suspensivos de la cuestión de inconstitucionalidad y la Ley Orgánica 2/79 de 3 de Octubre" *Revista española de derecho administrativo*, 25, Madrid 1980, pp. 207–222.

1115 Art. 35,2 Organic Law 2/1979.

1116 Art. 37,2 *Idem.*

1117 *Cf.* S. GALEOTTI and B. ROSSI, *loc. cit.*, p. 134.

5. Indirect means of judicial review of legislation

Apart from the direct and incidental methods of judicial review, in the Spanish system a third method for seeking before the Constitutional Tribunal judicial review of legislation in an indirect way can be distinguished, when the constitutional question is raised in other constitutional processes developed before the Tribunal, whose objectives are not the direct review of legislation. This can happen in cases of conflicts of attributions between constitutional organs and in cases of recourses for constitutional protection (*amparo*) of fundamental rights.

The first case refers to constitutional conflicts regarding competences or attributions directly assigned by the Constitution, the statutes of autonomy and the Organic or ordinary Laws, intended to delimit the ambit of their competences. These conflicts may oppose the state and the autonomous communities, two or more of which, and the Government with the Congress of Deputies and the Senate or the General Council of the Judicial Power.[1118] In such cases, the Constitutional Tribunal has admitted for instance, that if the conflict arises from an executive regulation which is additionally considered to be based on an unconstitutional statute, in those cases the constitutionality of the latter must be reviewed by the Tribunal.[1119]

Anyway, the Constitution establishes that if the controverted attribution would have been assigned by a statute or a norm with rank of law, the conflict of competence must be carried out from the beginning or from when the issue of unconstitutionality is raised, in the same procedural manner established for the recourse of unconstitutionality.[1120]

The other indirect means of judicial review of legislation can be found as a consequence of the exercise of a recourse for the protection (*recurso de amparo*) of fundamental rights that can be brought before the Tribunal by any person with direct interest in the matter, against state acts of a non legislative character.[1121] However, if the recourse for protection is based on the fact that the challenged state act is based on a statute that at the same time infringes fundamental rights or freedoms, the Tribunal must proceed to review its constitutionality through the procedural rules established for the direct action or recourse of unconstitutionality.[1122]

Regarding this indirect method of judicial review of legislation, the Constitutional Tribunal has considered that the interpretation of the Organic Law concerning its functioning, particularly its article 52,2,

> Compels one to understand that the unconstitutionality of a statute that violates fundamental rights and liberties could be alleged by the claimant, from which it can be deduced that a direct claim of unconstitutionality by individuals is admissible, although limited to the laws which violate or prejudice the rights and liberties established in the Constitution and to cases

---

1118 Art. 59 Organic Law 2/1979.

1119 Decision N° 39/1982. Quoted in J. SALAS, *loc. cit.*, p. 148, note 23.

1120 Art. 67 Organic Law 2/1979.

1121 Art. 161,1,b) Constitution; Art. 41,2 Organic Law 2/1979.

1122 Art. 52,2 Organic Law 2/1979.

in which the claimant has suffered a concrete and actual injury in his own rights and always that constitutional protection is irrescindable from the unconstitutionality of the statute.[1123]

6. Preventive judicial review system of legislation

Apart from the systems of direct and incidental control of the constitutionality of legislation, and from the indirect means of judicial review, which can be referred to laws and other acts with force of law, including, international treaties, Organic Laws and Statutes of Autonomies of the Autonomous Communities, these state acts can also be the object of a preventive system of judicial review, which can be considered, in the Spanish system, as being an important innovation compared the German and Italian models, and more along the lines of the French system.[1124]

In particular, the Spanish Constitution expressly establishes that the signing of international treaties, which contain dispositions contrary to the Constitution, imposes a previous constitutional review. Therefore, the Government, or either of the Chambers of Parliament, can request the Constitutional Tribunal to decide whether a contradiction between an International Treaty to be signed and the Constitution[1125] exists or not. In this case, it is evident that the constitutional review system adopted is a preventive one and regarding international treaties, it coexists with the direct, incidental and indirect means for judicial review of constitutionality that can also be exercised regarding them. All these means of review can be used not only indifferently, but also even successively.[1126] Anyway, when the preventive mean of control is requested, the Court must hear the representative of the state organs concerned.[1127]

However, although the preventive system of control is only established in the Constitution regarding international treaties, due to the fact that it authorises the legislator to assign any other competences to the Constitutional Tribunal,[1128] the Organic Law 2/1979 has extended preventive control of constitutionality to the statutes of autonomy and to organic laws, regarding that it is possible to exercise "a recourse of unconstitutionality, with previous character", by the same political organs that can exercise the direct recourse of constitutionality against them.[1129] This preventive mean of control is specifically important regarding the Statutes of Autonomy of the Autonomous Communities which must be approved by referendum.[1130] Although a direct recourse could be exercised against them, it is obvious that a preventive control as established in the Organic Law, could avoid political difficulties deriving from the possible annulment of a statute after its approval by referendum.

1123 Decisions 55/57/1981. Quoted in J. SALAS, *loc. cit.*, p. 148, note 23.

1124 E. GARCÍA DE ENTERRÍA, *op. cit.*, p. 156.

1125 Art. 95 Constitution.

1126 M. ARAGÓN, "El control de constitucionalidad en la Constitución Española de 1978", *Revista de estudios políticos*, 7, Madrid 1979, p. 183.

1127 Art. 78,2 Organic Law 2/1979.

1128 Art. 161 ,1,d) Constitution.

1129 Art. 79 Organic Law.

1130 Art. 152,2 Constitution.

It must also be noted that regarding Organic Laws, when it is an Organic Law directed for the approval of an international treaty,[1131] its preventive constitutional control produces in addition, another means of controlling the constitutionality of international treaties, this time an indirect–preventive mean of control, due to the close link between the approval law and the treaty.[1132]

In such cases of preventive control of constitutionality the effects vary regarding the act subject to control: if it is an international treaty not definitively consented to by the state yet, and the tribunal declares that it contradicts the Constitution, its definitive enactment could only be possible through a reform of the Constitution;[1133] regarding statutes of autonomy or organic laws, the declaration of the unconstitutionality of their dispositions has binding effects and, therefore, it implies that the procedure for their definitive adoption cannot continue unless they were suppressed by the respective state organ.[1134] Anyway, in this latter case, the decision of the tribunal rejecting or declaring the unconstitutionality of dispositions of a statute of autonomy or of an organic law, does not prejudge the future decision that could be taken if direct recourses of unconstitutionality are exercised against them, after their enactment.[1135]

7. Effects of the decision of the Constitutional Tribunal on Judicial Review

Now, regarding the effects of the decisions of the Constitutional Court in matters of judicial review of the constitutionality of legislation, the Spanish constitutional and legal system provides a few dispositions in which the different situations that can result are regulated.

The first aspect resolved in positive law refers to the power of the Constitutional Tribunal as a constitutional judge, and as supreme interpreter of the Constitution, in the sense that a question of unconstitutionality of a statute cannot be raised *ex–officio* by the Tribunal. However, once the issue has been brought before it, the Tribunal has *ex–officio* powers to raise other unconstitutionality questions regarding the particular challenged norm, and can "found the declaration of unconstitutionality in the violation of any other constitutional disposition, being invoked or not in the course of the process."[1136] Moreover, it can also extend the declaration of unconstitutionality to other dispositions of the statute, when a partial challenge has been made, in cases of correction or as a consequence of the declaration of the challenged dispositions.[1137]

The second aspect established in the Constitution relates to the force attributed to Constitutional Court decisions, as supreme interpreter of the Constitution, in the sense that they "have the value of *res judicata* from the day following its publica-

---

1131 Art. 93 Constitution.

1132 P. BON, F. MODERNE and Y. RODRÍGUEZ, *op. cit.*, p. 260.

1133 Art. 95,1 Constitution.

1134 Art. 79,4,b) Organic Law 2/1979.

1135 Art. 79,5 *Idem.*

1136 Art. 39,2 Organic Law 2/1979.

1137 Art. 39,1 *Idem.*

tion", and of course, as in all the European constitutional courts, against such decisions it is not possible to exercise any recourse.[1138] Thus the decisions adopted by the Constitutional Court in any proceeding of judicial review, are "obligatory regarding all public powers and have general effects from the date of their publication in the Official Journal of the state."[1139]

The third aspect expressly regulated in the Constitution and the Organic Law of the Tribunal concerns the effects of the decision regarding to whom they apply, and when they begin, and an important distinction is made between the decision that declares the unconstitutionality of a norm and those decisions that reject the alleged unconstitutionality.

Regarding the decisions that declare the unconstitutionality of a statute or other norms with force of law through any of the means for judicial review, either when the Constitutional Court decides upon a recourse of unconstitutionality, or when it decides upon a question of constitutionality raised incidentally, or when it declares the unconstitutionality of a statute through an indirect way, in all such cases the Constitution establishes its *erga omnes* effects, in the sense that they "have full effects regarding everybody."[1140] Additionally, in cases of incidental means of judicial review, the Constitutional Court must immediately inform the respective court that must decide the process, which in its turn must notify the parties to it. In this case, the Organic Law of the Tribunal states that "the judge or court would be subject to the decision from when it learns about it, and the parties from when they are notified."[1141]

On the other hand, according to the provisions of the Constitution, the "declaration of unconstitutionality" or "declaration of nullity" of a statute means its annulment, the guarantee of the Constitution being the annulability of the unconstitutional state acts rather than their nullity. Consequently, the statute declared unconstitutional is annulled, having the declaration *ex–nunc, pro futuro* effects.[1142] That is why the Constitution expressly establishes that "the decisions already adopted in judicial proceedings will not lose their *res judicata* value",[1143] and the Organic Law of the Tribunal also establishes that:

> The decisions which declare the unconstitutionality of statutes, dispositions or acts with force of law; will not allow the review of judicial proceedings ended by decisions with *res judicata* force in which the unconstitutional act would have been applied.[1144]

However, as is the general trend in the concentrated system of judicial review in Europe, the exception to the *ex–nunc* effects is established regarding criminal cases,

---

1138 Art. 164,1 Constitution.

1139 Art. 38,1; and Art. 87,1 Organic Law 2/1979.

1140 Art. 164,1 Constitution; 38,1 Organic Law 2/1979.

1141 Art. 38,3 Organic Law 2/1979.

1142 *Cf.* J. AROSEMENA SIERRA, "El recurso de inconstitucionalidad", in *El Tribunal Constitucional*, Instituto de Estudios Fiscales, Madrid 1981, Vol. I, p. 171.

1143 Art. 161,1,a) Constitution.

1144 Art. 40,1 Organic Law 2/1979.

in which a limited retroactive effect is permitted, extended to administrative justice decisions in cases of administrative sanction cases. Article 40, 2 of the Organic Law of the Tribunal in this respect establishes the possibility of reviewal of judicial processes, in cases of:

> Criminal or administrative justice processes concerning sanctioning proceedings in which, as a consequence of the nullity of the applied norm, a reduction of the penalty or sanction results, or an exclusion, exemption or limitation of liability also results.

Constitutional review of legislation by the Constitutional Tribunal, apart from the direct recourse or the incidental means, can also be exercised as a consequence of an indirect question that can be raised in a proceeding of a recourse for protection (*amparo*) of fundamental rights, or in cases of conflict of attributions between constitutional organs or between the state and the Autonomous Communities. In the first case, the declaration of unconstitutionality of a statute considered unconstitutional applied in a particular act that affects the fundamental rights of an individual is possible, and its effects are the same as already mentioned.[1145] In cases of conflict of attributions, the Organic Law of the Tribunal authorises it to annul the acts that originate the conflicts or were adopted invading competences of other organs, and to decide what might be necessary regarding the situations created based on the annulled act as produced by it.[1146]

On the other hand, the Organic Law of the Constitutional Tribunal expressly regulates the effects of the decisions in cases of rejection of the question raised before it as well, and two solutions have been given depending on the nature of the rejection. In effect, if it is a rejection based on the constitutional question in its substantive aspect, in the sense that the Tribunal considers the unconstitutional allegations are invalid, the rejection decision will prevent any other future allegation of the constitutional question "through the same means", founded in the violation of the same constitutional norm.[1147] Thus, if the constitutional question was raised through a recourse or direct action of unconstitutionality, the rejection of the action does not prevent the possibility of the question being raised through an incidental means of review.

But also in cases of recourses of unconstitutionality against statutes, dispositions or acts with force of law, if the rejection was based on formal reasons, the decision will not prevent the same statute, disposition or act being the object of a constitutional question raised when applied in other processes,[1148] and of course of another recourse in which the formal questions would have been corrected.

1145 Art. 55,2 *Idem.*

1146 Arts 66; 75,1 *Idem.*

1147 Art. 38,2 *Idem.*

1148 Art. 29,2 *Idem.*

VI. CONSTITUTIONAL JUSTICE IN THE SOCIALIST EUROPEAN COUNTRIES

The European model of judicial review, based on the attribution of the powers to control the constitutionality of statutes and other legislative acts to one constitutional organ of the state has, additional to the experiences of Western Europe, also been followed in some socialist countries, in a way that can be considered dissident insofar as the traditional socialist concept of the organisation of the state is concerned.

In effect, one of the basic principles of the constitutional systems of the socialist countries mainly derived from the influence of Soviet constitutionalism is the principle of the unity of state powers based on the assignment of all legislative and executive powers of state to its representative democratic body. Thus, this representative political organ of the state is conceived as the supreme organ of state power, and as the only one able to create the law and control the activities of all other state organs.[1149] This concept, of course, implies the rejection of any form of separation of state powers,[1150] at least theoretically, and in a certain way, regarding the legislative body, of the difference between the constituent and the constituted bodies of the state. The Constitutions of the socialist countries in general have a pre–eminent character over the whole legal order[1151] but at the same time, the organ that can control the submission to the constitutional rule is the supreme organ of the state, which is the one that can also modify the Constitution. Consequently, an essential incompatibility exists between the principle of the unity of state power and the supremacy and sovereignty of parliament which represents the popular will, with any sort of judicial control of the constitutionality of statutes adopted by parliament, exercised by an extra parliamentary organ.[1152]

Nevertheless, three socialist countries, Yugoslavia, Czechoslovakia and Poland have developed advanced systems of constitutional justice. That must be seen as a sign of departure from the principle of the unity of state power even though it is commonly rejected by socialist authors, who see those experiences more as a departure from the Soviet interpretation of the principle, than from the principle itself. For instance, referring to the Yugoslav theory and system, Vladimir Krivic, a former President of the Constitutional Court of the Socialist Republic of Slovenia, said that it:

1149 S. ROZMARYN, "La Constitution, loi fondamental de l'État socialist" in P. BISCARETTI DI RUFFIA and S. ROZMARYN, *La Constitution comme loi fondamentale dans les Etats de l'Europe occidentale et dans les Etats socialistes*, Turin 1966, p. 108.

1150 P. NIKOLIC, *Le contrôle juridictionnel des lois et sa legalité. Développements récents dans les pays socialistes*, IALS, Uppsala, Colloquium, 1984, mimeo) p. 15. Also published in L. FAVOREU and J.A. JOLOWICZ ed.) *Le contôle juridictionnel des lois. Légitimité, effectivité et développements récents*, Paris 1986, pp. 71–115. P. KASTARI, "Le caracter normatif et la préeminence hierarchique des Constitutions", *Revue International de Droit Comparé*; Paris 1966, p. 843.

1151 S. ROZMARYN, *loc. cit.*, p. 99; P. NIKOLIC, *op. cit.*, p. 7; P. KASTARI, *loc. cit.*, p. 841.

1152 H. ROUSSILLON, "Le problème du contrôle de la constitutionnalité des lois dans les pays socialistes", *Revue du droit public et de la science politique en France et à l'étranger*, 1977, p. 76; S. ROZMARYN, *loc. cit.*, p. 108. *Cf.* P. NIKOLIC, *op. cit.*, p. 17.

> Represents no departure from the principle of the unity of powers, but a departure from the rigid, formalistic, strictly dogmatic, bureaucratic Stalinist conception of the unity of authority with its wrong ideas about the function of legality and the status of the judicature under the socialist order.[1153]

Nevertheless, being considered a departure or not from the principle of the unity of power, the adoption of concentrated systems of judicial review in some socialist countries is generally based on a principle of vertical distribution of state powers, normally with a federal form which, as V. Krivic said, "calls, *ipso facto*, for an agency whose independent and authoritative status the republics and the Federal authority";[1154] and it is also based on the limitations imposed upon the politic representative organ of the state in the Constitution, regarding other state bodies. Additionally, the declaration of fundamental and self–government rights, has justified the establishment of an extra parliamentary and independent state organ for controlling the constitutionality of statutes and other normative acts of the state organs.[1155]

The first socialist country to establish a Constitutional Court was Yugoslavia in 1963, and, more recently, Czechoslovakia followed the example in 1968. In Poland, the 1982 Constitution has established a limited jurisdictional control of constitutionality of statutes. It means that the created Constitutional Court does not decide definitively upon their unconstitutionality, but must only refer its appreciation to the decision of the legislative organ in its character as the supreme organ of power.[1156] Thus, only in the Yugoslav and Czech systems, is it possible to distinguish a jurisdictional organ with powers to annul legislative acts.

1. Judicial Review in Yugoslavia: the Constitutional Court

The Constitution of Yugoslavia and the Constitutions of its Federated Socialist Republics, promulgated in April 1963 and reformed in 1975, in effect, established what can be considered an advanced concentrated system of judicial review. The main idea is "to prevent violations of the system laid down by the Constitution and usurpation of rights to the prejudice of citizens or self–governing bodies, as well as to enforce respect for law and the Constitution by all, the highest social organisms and state officials included."[1157] The system brought about the establishment of a Constitutional Court of Yugoslavia, regulated by a special statute promulgated the same year 1963, as well as the establishment of Constitutional Courts in the six Republics of the Federation.[1158]

1153 *V.* Krivic, "Foreword", in B.T. Blagojevic ed.), *Constitutional judicature*, Beograd 1965, p. 6.

1154 *V.* Krivic, *loc. cit.*, p. 4.

1155 P. Nikolic, *op. cit.*, p. 21.

1156 P. Nikolic, *op. cit.*, p. 52.

1157 *V.* Krivic, *loc. cit.*, p. 5.

1158 Law of the Constitutional Court of Yugoslavia CCY), 31 December 1963. See the text in B.T. Blagojevic (ed.), *op, cit.*, pp. 15–36; *V.* Krivic, *loc. cit.*, p. 3.

A. *Jurisdiction of the Constitutional Court*

The Constitutional Court is conceived as an "independent Federal organ" whose main function is to "ensure protection of constitutionality and legality on the basis of the Constitution acting within its rights and duties as laid down by the Constitution",[1159] which it accomplishes through three basic sets of attributions concerning the settling of disputes between the socio political communities, the protection of fundamental rights and liberties, and judicial review of constitutionality.

The first set of attributions confers the Constitutional Court powers to "settle disputes involving rights and duties between the federal authority and a Republic, between the Republics, and between other socio political communities from the territory of different Republics."[1160] This power of the Court is, undoubtedly, one direct consequence of the establishment in the Federative Socialist Republic of Yugoslavia, of a series of autonomous solutions to its fundamental political, economic and social aims, which separate it from the Soviet model. In accordance to which V. Krivic said, "the autonomy of numerous organisms, including in the first place the self–governing working organisations and communes, and their extensive powers in the making of bye–laws made it imperative to set up a social agency which would ban bureaucratic interference with the competencies of the "inferior" self–governing bodies on the part of the superior ones, and which would perform the same function "horizontally" between the various self–governing organisations and bodies."[1161]

When resolving these conflicts or disputes of competencies, the Court has the power to fix a particular obligation for a socio–political community and to order the elimination of the consequences brought about by the act or action which caused the violation or interference of attributions.[1162]

It must also be said that besides conflicts between socio–political organs of the state, the Constitutional Court has also competence to settle all "conflicts of jurisdiction that may arise between courts of law and federal authorities, and also between courts of law and other state authorities from the territory of different Republics."[1163]

The second set of attributions of the Constitutional Court relates to the protection of self governing rights and other fundamental rights and liberties granted by the Constitution, in cases where said rights and liberties are violated by a particular act or action on the part of federal or central authorities whose activities in the exercise of public powers extend to the whole territory of Yugoslavia.[1164] This power of the Court is exercised when a proposal for protection is presented only when the ordi-

1159 Art. 1, Law CCY, 1963. The Court is also authorized to "independently adopt its Rules of Procedures and other general acts affecting its organization and operation." Art. 16 Law CCY.

1160 Art. 43, Law CCY, 1963.

1161 *V.* KRIVIC, *loc. cit.*, p. 4.

1162 Art. 44, Law CCY, 1963.

1163 Art. 46, *Idem.*

1164 Art. 36,1 *Idem.*

nary recourse for the protection of such rights and liberties have already been exhausted,[1165] and is presented "by any one who had his right of self–government or other fundamental rights or liberties as granted by the Constitution, violated", as well as by a socio–political organisation on behalf of their members.[1166]

This "proposal for protection", as we said, can only be presented before the Constitutional Court against a "particular act or action of an authority or organisation."[1167] Thus it is not possible against normative acts; and the ruling of the Court must consist, subject to the circumstances of the case, of the abolition of the act and of the elimination of the consequences brought about by such an act.[1168]

Finally, the third set of attributions relates to the area of judicial review, the Constitutional Court is empowered to review "the constitutionality and legality of prescriptions and other general acts" with binding authority,[1169] and this attribution is conceived, basically, as a power of the Court that can be exercised *ex–officio*, or when hearing a request for constitutional review presented by state organs or by individuals. This power of judicial review exercised by the Constitutional Court, allows it to make rulings concerning the compatibility of laws with the Constitution; the compatibility of a republican law with federal law; and the compatibility of other dispositions and general acts made by authorities and organisations with the Constitution, with Federal Law and with other Federal dispositions.[1170]

B. Ex–Officio *Powers of the Constitutional Court*

The Constitutional Court is empowered by the law that regulates its functioning to "initiate the procedure for judging the constitutionality and legality of a disposition or other general acts on its own initiative", in which case any member of the Court may request such a procedure to be initiated and a decision to be taken thereupon.[1171]

The Court can also on its own initiative give its opinion concerning "the compatibility of the Constitution of a republic with the Constitution of Yugoslavia" to the Federal Assembly,[1172] and it is also authorised to "offer opinions and proposals to the Federal Assembly for the enactment and amendment of laws, for the provision of authentic interpretation and for taking measures to ensure constitutionality and legality and protect the self–governing rights and the other rights and liberties of citizens and organisations"[1173]

1165 Art. 36,3 *Idem.*
1166 Art. 37 *Idem.*
1167 Arts 36, 39 *Idem.*
1168 Art. 39 *Idem.*
1169 Art. 2 *Idem.*
1170 Art. 17 *Idem.*
1171 Art. 4 *Idem.*
1172 Art. 18 *Idem.*
1173 Art. 3 *Idem.*

These *ex–officio* powers of the Yugoslav Constitutional Court to initiate, in a general way, judicial review of legislation, and to give its opinion on constitutional matters without formal request to the Federal Assembly are, perhaps, the most distinguishable features of the Yugoslav system, which are not to be found in any other legal system.

C. *Request for Judicial Review and Popular Action*

The Constitutional Court of Yugoslavia can also exercise the powers of judicial review, when a request is presented before the Court by some state organs, or by any person through a popular action. In the first case, when the request is presented by "authorities of organisations specified under the Constitution" or by an assembly of a commune, a district or an autonomous province, or by Federal Secretaries or Republican Secretaries, or by authorities of a socio–political community,[1174] the Court is obliged to initiate the procedure "for considering the constitutionality" of legislation.[1175] In the second case, when a popular action is exercised by individuals, the Court shall itself decide whether to initiate the procedure or not.[1176]

It is important to notice that this popular action established in the Yugoslavian system which authorises "anyone" to request the Constitutional Court to initiate a procedure for judicial review of legislation[1177] is also exceptional in European countries, even though in such cases the Court is not obliged to initiate it, which confirms its own powers on the matter. Moreover, in cases of judicial review proceedings, when a request has been made, it must also be mentioned that the Constitutional Court is not bound by the points raised in the proposal concerned but may also examine the constitutionality of other dispositions or acts not challenged by the proponent as unconstitutional.[1178]

D. *Decision of the Constitutional Court on Judicial Review*

Finally, concerning the decisions of the Constitutional Court on judicial review of constitutionality of statutes, it must be noticed that contrary to the situation in other European countries, the decision of the Yugoslavian Court upon the unconstitutionality of a norm does not cause the immediate annulment of the normative act, and in fact, three different stages can be distinguished in the proceeding.

First of all, prior to making a decision, the Constitutional Court, having regard to the circumstances brought out within the preliminary procedure, may give an opportunity to the representative body or other authority or organisation concerned to eliminate the incompatibility of a disposition or other general act with the Constitution and/or Federal Law.[1179] In this way, the Court avoids declaring an act unconsti-

1174 Art. 19 *Idem.*

1175 Arts 4, 19 *Idem.*

1176 Art. 4 *Idem.*

1177 Art. 4 *Idem.*

1178 Art. 23 *Idem.*

1179 Art. 24 *Idem.*

tutional, allowing the state organ to make the necessary corrections to it. In this stage and concerning the challenge of republican law when incompatible with the Constitution or with federal law or in cases of incompatibility between republican law with federal laws which the Court finds contrary to the Constitution, the Court can rule that the dispositions of the republican law or of the federal law are not to be applicable pending the issue of its final decision.[1180]

Secondly, in cases of incompatibility between federal law and the Constitution, or between republican law and the Constitution or federal law, the Constitutional Court does not annul the act immediately. However, it must announce its ruling to the parties concerned and notify the Federal or the republican Assemblies concerned, allowing them to bring the challenged act into conformity with the Constitution or the Federal Law.

In the third place, the Law of the Court establishes that if the public authority does not correct the unconstitutional act within six months from the date when the Constitutional Court announced its decision, then "the Court shall issue a ruling establishing that the law involved has ceased to have effect",[1181] or in cases of incompatibility between the republican law and the Constitution or with federal law, the Court may "abolish such republican law if it involves a manifest violation of the prerogative of the federal authorities."[1182] These decisions, of course, have binding authority [1183] and have *erga omnes* effects.

Even though the Law of the Court uses two expressions for the qualification of its decisions, upon unconstitutionality of normative acts, abrogation or abolishment of the unconstitutional challenged act, particularly when referring to statutes at federal or republican level or in relation to other normative acts different to statutes,[1184] in both cases, the general effect of the decision in time is equivalent to the annulment of the act, thus, *ex–nunc*, *pro futuro*. Therefore, the annulled act "shall not be applicable as from the date of publication of the Courts' ruling in the official gazette of the Federation",[1185] and neither the dispositions or other general acts serving for the enforcement of the unconstitutional statute; shall be applicable if the ruling of the Court implies that such acts are contrary to the Constitution.[1186] Additionally, regarding the future, the Court can give its opinion as to which legal rules are to be applicable pending the issue of a new statute conforming to the Constitution to replace the one invalidated. [1187]

Now, regarding the particular relations originated by the statute declared unconstitutional, even when they have begun before the date of publication of the Court's

1180 Art. 25 *Idem.*

1181 Art. 25 *Idem.*

1182 Art. 25 *Idem.*

1183 Arts 2,2; 72 *Idem.*

1184 Art. 26 *Idem.*

1185 Art. 29 *Idem.*

1186 Art. 30 *Idem.*

1187 Art. 34 *Idem.*

decision, the unconstitutional act shall not be applicable to them if a valid settlement of the relations is still pending on that date.[1188]

Regarding final and valid acts issued in particular cases in application of the unconstitutional law, the law of the tribunal establishes a general difference according to the abrogation or the abolition of the unconstitutional act. When the normative act has been abolished the law of the tribunal in a general exception to the *ex–nunc* effects, it assigns to anyone who may have had a right of his violated by a valid particular act issued in application of the unconstitutional normative act to seek review of such act by the Court of Law or other authority that issued it; and they must do so within a delay of six months after the publication of the Court decision.[1189]

Additionally, the Court can also rule that a court of law or other competent authority concerned is to be bound to review all acts or certain categories of particular acts produced based on the unconstitutional statute on the demand of citizens or organisations whose rights were violated.[1190]

In relation to all other Court decisions on constitutional review matters, the Law of the Court establishes a few exceptions to the *ex–nunc* effects, and allows for the retroactive applicability of the annulment, particularly in criminal cases and violations of self–governing rights.[1191] In particular, in criminal cases, the Law of the Constitutional Court gives the right to whoever had criminal sanctions imposed upon him, to seek the review of such act by the Court of Law or other competent authority that imposed the sanction.[1192]

Finally, it must be stressed that the powers of the Constitutional Court are also very significant in the interpretation of the Constitution in cases in which the Court does not find a law or other normative act incompatible with the Constitution, but considers that in practical application such a law has been constructed in a manner contrary to the Constitution. In such cases, the Court may lay down, through a decision, the significance thereof corresponding to the Constitution to be observed when enforcing such law or other normative act.[1193]

2. Control of Constitutionality in Czechoslovakia: the Federal Constitutional Court

As we have said, Czechoslovakia was the first European country to have a concentrated judicial review system established in its Constitution of 1920, which created a Constitutional Court that existed until 1938.[1194] After the Second World War,

1188 Art. 29 *Idem.*

1189 Art. 32 *Idem.*

1190 Art. 31,4 *Idem.*

1191 Art. 31,1,2 *Idem.*

1192 Art. 31,1 *Idem.*

1193 Art. 28 *Idem.*

1194 *Cf.* P. CRUZ VILLALON, "Dos modos de regulación del control de constitucionalidad: Checoslovaquia 1920–1938) y España 1931–1936), *Revista española de derecho constitucional*, 5, 1982, p. 115.

the Constitution of 1948 followed the Soviet model, thus without any form of judicial review of constitutionality, and it has been in the Constitution of 27 October 1968 in which not only a definitive federal form of state was adopted, but also a concentrated system of judicial review was established, following the Yugoslav model.[1195] Thus, there is a Federal Constitutional Court and two Constitutional Courts in each of the Republics of the Czech federation.

Judicial review power of the Federal Constitutional Court relates to all laws enacted by the Federal Assembly and by the Czech National Councils, as well as to all the general provisions of the administrative bodies, both of the Federation and of the Federated Republics.[1196]

As happens with decisions of unconstitutionality adopted by the Yugoslav Constitutional Federal Court, the decisions of the Czech Court do not imply the immediate cessation of the effects of the challenged act, but rather, imply only the obligation, following the publication of the decision, for the bodies that passed the provisions contrary to the Fundamental Charter, or as the case may be, contrary to the Federal Law, to redraft them and make them consistent with the Constitution. They have six months to carry out this task. The challenged dispositions only cease to be effective when this time period has elapsed.[1197]

The Czech Federal Constitutional Court is also empowered to settle disputes of competences between the bodies of the Federal Republic and those of one or other of the two Federated Republics, or between the internal organs of the latter.[1198]

Lastly, among the most important attributions of the Constitutional Federal Court of Czechoslovakia is that of the protection of the rights and freedoms established in the Constitution against their violation by provisions or acts of the Federal Authorities, when the ordinary law does not establish any other jurisdictional safeguards.[1199]

VII. CONCENTRATED SYSTEMS OF JUDICIAL REVIEW IN LATIN AMERICA

Judicial review has a long tradition in Latin America, and over the course of more than a century it has been adopted in one way or another in all Latin American countries. As we have seen, some have adopted the diffuse system of judicial review, as is the case in Argentina and Mexico. In most countries, a mixed system is followed, in which the diffuse system functions in parallel with the concentrated system of judicial review assigned to the Supreme Court or to a specially created Constitutional Court.

Nevertheless, examples can also be found of a pure concentrated system in which the powers of judicial review of constitutionality of legislation have been exclusively attributed to the Supreme Court of Justice of the country or to a specially cre-

---

1195 *Cf.* H. FIX–ZAMUDIO, *Los tribunales constitucionales y los derechos humanos*, México 1980, p. 129; P. NIKOLIC, *op. cit.*, p. 46.

1196 Art. 86, 1; Art. 87 Constitutional Law. See in P. NIKOLIC, *op. cit.*, p. 48.

1197 Art. 93, 90 Constitutional Law. See in P. NIKOLIC, *op. cit.*, p. 49.

1198 Art. 92 Constitutional Law. See in H. FIX–ZAMUDIO, *op. cit.*, p. 131.

1199 Art. 92 Constitutional Law. See in H. FIX–ZAMUDIO, *op. cit.*, p. 132.

ated Constitutional Court, or in some cases, to both in parallel. This are the systems we will now refer to, leaving for the last part of this book the study of the concentrated systems of judicial review exercised by a supreme court or a constitutional court mixed with the diffuse system of judicial review.

1. Supreme Court of Justice as a Concentrated Organ for Judicial Review: Panama, Uruguay, and Paraguay

As we said, some Latin American countries have established a concentrated system of judicial review by assigning the exclusive power to control the constitutionality of legislation to their Supreme Court of Justice, as the judicial organ situated at the apex of the judiciary. As an example of this modality, the constitutional systems of Panama, Uruguay and Paraguay can be mentioned.

In this respect the Constitution of Panama established the exclusive power of the Supreme Court of Justice to "guard the integrity of the Constitution,[1200] and to control the constitutionality of legislation, through two means: a direct action or an incidental referral sent by a lower court.

The direct action is conceived as a popular action that could be brought before the Supreme Court by "any person", denouncing the unconstitutionality of laws, decrees, decisions, or acts whether on a substantive or formal basis. In this case, the decision must be adopted by the Court after hearing the Solicitor General of the Nation.[1201]

But the Constitution also establishes that when in an ordinary judicial process, the judge, *ex–officio* or at the request of any of the parties, notices that the legal or executive normative act applicable to the case is unconstitutional, he must submit the question of unconstitutionality to the Supreme Court, while being allowed to continue the proceeding of the case until the decision stage.[1202]

In both cases, the decision of the Supreme Court is obligatory,[1203] and non revisable.[1204]

In the Uruguayan system, the Constitution [1205] attributes exclusive and original jurisdiction to declare the unconstitutionality of statutes and other state acts with force of law to the Supreme Court of Justice, whether based on substantive or formal reasons.[1206] In accordance with the Constitution, the declaration of unconstitutionality of a statute and the inapplicability of the disposition encumbered by it, could be

1200 Article 188, 1. Constitution.

1201 Article 188, 1.

1202 Article 188, 2.

1203 Art. 188, *in fine*.

1204 Art. 189.

1205 The system was originaly established in 1934 and 1951.See H. GROSS ESPIELL, *La Constitución y su Defensa, Uruguay*, Congreso La Constitución y su defensa, UNAM, 1982 (mimeo), p. 7, 11. The system was maintained in the 1966 Constitution, in the Institutional Act N° 8 of 1977 and in the Institutional Act N° 12 of 1981. *Idem,* pp. 16–20.

1206 Art. 256.

requested from the Supreme Court by all who deem their direct, personal and legitimate interests have been injured.[1207] Thus a requirement of standing, very similar to the one established regarding judicial review of administrative action, is established.

The competence of the Supreme Court on judicial review, can be sought through two means: first, through a direct action, when there is no judicial proceeding pending of decision; second, through an incidental means, through a referral made before the Supreme Court by any court.

This second mean can be exercised *ex–officio* by the lower court, or as a consequence of an exception raised by any party.[1208] In this case, the judge must refer a briefing of the question to the Supreme Court and should continue with the proceeding up to the stage of deciding upon the case. After the Supreme Court has adopted its decision, the court must make its own decision in the case in conformity with the latter.[1209]

In both cases, in the Uruguayan system, the effects of the Supreme Court decisions are exclusively referred to the concrete case, having effects only regarding the proceedings in which they were adopted.[1210] Of course this disposition is clear regarding the incidental means of judicial review but, not in cases in which the constitutional question has been raised through a direct action. In such cases Statute N° 13747 of 1969[1211] concerning the constitutional justice process establishes that the decision has efficacy to prevent the applicability of the norms declared unconstitutional regarding who has exercised the action and obtained the decision, being allowed to use it as an exception in any judicial proceeding, including the judicial review of administrative action.[1212]

Following the Uruguayan model, we must also mention the system of Paraguay in which the Constitution empowers the Supreme Court to decide upon actions and exceptions in order to declare the unconstitutionality and inapplicability of dispositions contrary to the Constitution."[1213] As we said, the proceeding can be initiated through an action or an exception, and in the latter case, the proceeding in the concrete case must continue until the decision stage. In any case, the decision of the Supreme Court only has effects regarding the concrete case or the petitioner.[1214]

1207 Art. 258. *Cf.* H. GROSS ESPIELL, *op. cit.*, pp. 27, 28; J.P. GATTO DE SOUZA, "Control de la constitucionalidad de los actos del poder público en Uruguay", *Memoria de la Reunión de Presidentes de Cortes Supremas de Justicia de Iberoamérica, El Caribe, España y Portugal*, Caracas 1982, pp. 661–662.

1208 Art. 258.

1209 Arts 258, 259.

1210 Art. 259.

1211 See in H. GROSS ESPIELL, *op. cit.*, p. 29.

1212 *Idem.*

1213 Arts 200, 207.

1214 L.M. ARGAÑA, "Control de la constitucionalidad de las leyes en Paraguay", en *Memoria de la Reunión de Presidentes de Cortes Supremas de Justicia de Iberoamérica, El Caribe, España y Portugal*, Caracas 1983, pp. 550–551; 669–671.

2. Parallel Concentrated System of Judicial Review Attributed to a Supreme Court and the Constitutional Tribunal: Chile and Ecuador

Among the Latin American Countries, we must refer to the cases of Chile and Ecuador, whose constitutional systems have established a concentrated system of judicial review, but attributing it to two separate constitutional organs: the Supreme Court of Justice, through incidental means, and a Constitutional Tribunal, through direct means.

A. *The Chilean Experience*

(a) *Supreme Court of Justice and the Incidental Method of Judicial Review*

Since the 1925 constitutional reform in Chile, the second paragraph of article 86 authorises the Supreme Court of Justice to declare the inapplicability of a law in force, on the grounds of unconstitutionality. This reform substantially modified the previously existing situation, in which the unanimous opinion was that the Courts could not declare the inapplicability of an unconstitutional law, since there was no constitutional provision granting them that power. Consequently, the 1925 reform represented an important step towards the control of the constitutionality of law.[1215]

This norm of the Constitution still in force states as follows:

> The Supreme Court, in the concrete cases which it is conducting or in cases which were raised before it through recourses originated in proceedings developed before other courts, can declare any legal disposition contrary to the Constitution inapplicable to that case. This recourse can be exercised in any stage of the proceeding, without its suspension.

Consequently, the Constitution establishes a concentrated system of judicial review of incidental character before the Supreme Court of Justice, through the institution called the "recourse of inapplicability of statutes."[1216]

However, this system of judicial review did not, of course, resolve constitutional conflicts between state organs, many of which were originated in questions of unconstitutionality of statutes and other norms of equal force. The continuous conflict between those organs which was one particularity of political life in Chile, was one of the main factors that contributed to the establishment of a constitutional organ, other than the Supreme Court, to settle that type of conflict.[1217] Thus, the constitutional reform of 21 January 1970 created a Constitutional Tribunal with a variety of functions of judicial review and relating to the settlement of conflicts of attributions between the state organs. The Tribunal was dissolved in 1973 as a result of a military coup that dissolved the Congress. Since the main function of the Constitutional Court was to settle conflicts between the executive and the legislature, and since the latter could not appear before the Court, due to the fact that the National Congress had been dissolved, the existence of the Court was no longer justified. Thus the

1215 *Cf.* O. TOVAR TAMAYO, *La jurisdicción constitucional*, Caracas 1983, p. 103.

1216 See the text in H. FIX–ZAMUDIO, *Los tribunales constitucionales y los derechos humanos*, México 1980, p. 143, note 251.

1217 E. SILVA CIMMA, *El Tribunal Constitucional de Chile (1917–1973)*, Caracas 1977, p. 12–20.

Court ceased to function.[1218] The Constitutional court was later re–established by articles 81 and 83 of the political Constitution approved by referendum on 11 September 1980, and drawn up by the Military Junta, in the exercise of its constituent power. The Court was assigned attributions similar to those established by the Fundamental Charter of 1970, and its functioning is regulated in the Organic Constitutional Law of 12 May 1981 passed by the Government Junta.[1219]

(b) The Constitutional Tribunal and its Powers

In accordance with these recent regulations, the attributions of the tribunal are the following:[1220]

In the first place, it is competent to judge upon the constitutionality of organic laws, prior to their promulgation, or of those, which interpret a particular precept of the Fundamental Charter.

It is also authorised by means of a request to exercise preventive control over any issues, which may arise during the processing of ordinary project of law, or constitutional amendments, as well as international treaties submitted for the approval of Congress.

It is also competent to resolve issues of constitutionality concerning executive decrees with force of law; claims against the President of the Republic when he fails to promulgate a law, when he should have done so, or when he promulgates a different text, or issues unconstitutional decrees or regulates subjects reserved to formal law.

The Court also decides upon conflicts arising regarding decrees or resolutions issued by the President of the Republic, when the Office of the General Comptroller, on the grounds of unconstitutionality, has denied the registration of which.

In the second place, the Court is authorised to settle other issues, other than the control of constitutionality, particularly the constitutionality of the calling of plebiscites, as well as questions relating to an individual's constitutional or legal eligibility for appointment to the office of Minister of state.

These powers of the Constitutional Court were originally established in 1970, and the 1980 Constitution additionally grants it attributions not included in the 1970 Constitution, particularly the competence to judge the unconstitutionality of organisations and political parties or movements, as well as the responsibility of persons who transgress, or have transgressed the constitutional order of the Republic,[1221] more in consonance with the military regime.

1218 E. SILVA CIMMA, *op. cit.*, p. 219; H. FIX–ZAMUDIO, *op. cit.*, p. 150.

1219 H. FIX–ZAMUDIO, "Dos leyes orgánicas de tribunales constitucionales latinoamericanos: Chile y Perú", *Boletín mexicano de derecho comparado*, 51, 1984, p. 943.

1220 Art. 82, Constitution 1980.

1221 H. FIX–ZAMUDIO, "Dos leyes orgánicas…", *loc. cit.*, p. 947.

Now, in the area of judicial review the Chilean Constitutional Tribunal has been empowered to review the constitutionality of legislation through two specific ways: a preventive control and a limited *a posteriori* control.

(c) Preventive Control of Constitutionality of Legislation

In the first place, the Constitution establishes the power of the Tribunal to resolve constitutional questions that could arise during discussions of Organic Constitutional Laws, of statutes intended to interpret a constitutional disposition of any bill or project of constitutional amendment and of international treaties submitted to Congress for approval.[1222]

In all such cases, following the French model, the control exercised by the Constitutional Tribunal is a preventive one, and can be obligatory or exercised through a petition. In the case of Organic Constitutional Laws and of statutes that interpret a constitutional disposition, the preventive control of the Tribunal is obligatory, in the sense that the President of the corresponding Chamber of Congress must always send such texts to the Tribunal within five days after being sanctioned. Thus, this preventive control is not only obligatory but is also exercised *ex–officio* by the tribunal, and that is why in this case, the proceeding is not adversary. If in its decision the Tribunal considers one or more of the text dispositions unconstitutional, it must send it back to the corresponding Chamber, where its President in his turn must send it to the President of the Republic for promulgation, but without the dispositions considered unconstitutional

In the case of other bills, projects of constitutional amendments or international treaties, the exercise of the preventive control by the Constitutional Tribunal is only possible when a petition is formulated before the promulgation of the text, and during the discussion of the project, by the President of the Republic or by any of the Congress Chambers or by one fourth of their members. That is why the petition does not have suspensive effects over the legislative procedure and the proceeding before the Tribunal is an adversary one: the Tribunal must notify the interested constitutional organs and hear their arguments. The decision of the Tribunal considering unconstitutional dispositions of a project of a statute or a treaty, prevents its promulgation.[1223]

(d) Judicial Review Powers of the Constitutional Tribunal through Direct Means

Additional to the preventive control of legislation, the Constitutional Tribunal has also powers of judicial review of an *a posteriori* character, but only exercised regarding decrees with force of law, that is to say, those issued by the President of the Republic, by virtue of powers delegated by Congress, and also regarding presidential powers when promulgating statutes. Thus substantive judicial review of con-

1222 Art. 82 Constitution 1980, Art. 26–37 Organic Law 1981. See the comments in H. FIX–ZAMUDIO, "Dos leyes orgánicas ...", *loc. cit.*, p. 948.

1223 *Idem*, p. 949.

stitutionality of legislation by the Constitutional Tribunal does not proceed against statutes once in force, but only against executive decrees with force of law.

In the first case; regarding the unconstitutionality of decree laws, the powers of the Tribunal on matters of unconstitutionality are exercised when a request is brought before it after a decision has been adopted by the General Comptrollers Office regarding the registration or not of the decree. In effect, in Chile, one of the traditional functions of the General Comptrollers Office has been the control of executive decrees, which results in their registration, or rejection of it. As a consequence, controversies traditionally arise as regards the constitutionality or legality of the executive decrees, when the Office of the General Comptroller raises objections concerning there in compatibility with the Constitution.

Prior to the existence of the Court, these controversies were settled by one of the parties, that is to say, by the executive, which could insist on the registration of the decree, which, in the Comptroller's opinion, might be unconstitutional, with the backing of the signatures of all the Ministers.[1224]

This situation was changed after the 1970 constitutional reform, according to which if the General Comptrollers Office rejects a decree law, the President of the Republic can no longer insist on it being registered. Instead, within a time limit of 30 days after the rejection, the President can raise the question before the Constitutional Court, which has the last word on the matter of unconstitutionality. Likewise, if, on the contrary, the General Comptroller registers a decree law, either of the Chambers of Congress, or more than one third of their active members, is authorised to raise the issue of unconstitutionality of the decree law before the Tribunal, also within a time limit of 30 days from the publication of the decree.

The procedure in such cases is of an adversary character, and the Tribunal can declare the unconstitutionality of the decree law, with binding effects, in which case it cannot be enforced. But, if the Tribunal declares that the disposition of the decree law is constitutional, the decision has also binding effects and particularly the Supreme Court of Justice cannot declare it inapplicable when exercising its concentrated diffuse powers of judicial review.[1225]

In the second place, the *a posteriori* judicial review powers of the Constitutional Tribunal can also be exercised regarding statutes but only in relation to the formalities of their promulgation by the President of the Republic. In effect, the Constitution attributes the Tribunal competence to resolve claims that can only be exercised by the Chambers of Congress, in cases in which the President of the Republic does not promulgate a statute when he should, or when he promulgates a text other than the one that proceeds constitutionally.[1226] In such cases, the constitutional review control does not in fact refer to the substantive aspects of the statutes, but only to the

---

1224 H. FIX–ZAMUDIO, *op. cit.*, p. 148, 149; O. Tovar Tamayo, *op. cit.*, pp. 132–133.

1225 H. FIX–ZAMUDIO, "Dos leyes orgánicas ", *loc. cit.*, pp. 949–950; O. TOVAR TAMAYO, *op. cit.*, p. 137.

1226 Art. 82. See H. FIX–ZAMUDIO, "Dos leyes orgánicas…", *op. cit.*, p. 949.

way the President of the Republic exercises his power when promulgating statutes, the decision of the Tribunal being directed to the correction of the promulgation.

B. *Parallel–Concentrated System of Judicial Review in Ecuador and the Tribunal of Constitutional Guarantees*

Among the Latin American countries that have adopted a double concentrated system of judicial review attributed to two different constitutional organs, the case of Ecuador must also be mentioned, in which the Supreme Court of Justice has exclusive power to judge the constitutionality of legislation through a diffuse system, and the Tribunal of Constitutional Guarantees is empowered to exercise judicial review of legislation in a concentrated way. Both systems of judicial review are based on the principle of supremacy of the Constitution expressly established as follows:

> The Constitution is the supreme law of the state. The secondary norms and all others of inferior hierarchy must maintain their conformity with the constitutional dispositions. The laws (statutes), decrees, ordinances, dispositions, international treaties or accords which, in any way, would be in contradiction with the Constitution or alter its disposition, will have no value. [1227]

In accordance with this proclaimed constitutional supremacy, the constitution of 1909, reformed in 1983, assigns the power to exercise judicial review power in a diffuse way, to the Chambers of the Supreme Court of Justice, to the Tax Tribunal and to the Administrative Justice Tribunal by, attributing them competences to declare in concrete cases taken over from a lower court, the inapplicability of any legal norm contrary to the Constitution."[1228] This decision according to the express provision of the Constitution, "does not have obligatory force but only in the concrete case in which it is pronounced", thus its effects are *inter partes*.

However, the same 1978 Constitution also established an institution called the Tribunal of Constitutional Guarantees, with a wide composition of its members in charge of watching out for the execution of the Constitution, by requesting actions from authorities and public officials.[1229] The Tribunal was originally empowered to formulate observations regarding decrees, accords, regulations or resolutions dictated in violation of the Constitution or the Statutes, once hearing the authorities, which dictated them. If its observations were not followed, the Tribunal was authorized to publish them in the press and notify the National Chamber of Representatives, for them to take a resolution.[1230]

1227 Art. 137. Constitution of 15 January 1978.

1228 Art. 138. Constitution.

1229 Art. 141, 1 Constitution. The Tribunal is composed by 3 members elected by the National Chamber of Representatives; the President of the Supreme Court of Justice; the Attorney General; the President of the Supreme Electoral Tribunal; one representative of the President of the Republic; one representative of Workers; one representative of the Association of employers; and two representatives of the people, elected by electoral bodies composed by the Mayors of Cantons and by the rovincial authorities Art. 140. Constitution.

1230 Art. 141, 2 Constitution.

This Tribunal of Constitutional Guarantees was also empowered to take cognisance of complaints that any citizen could bring before it when the Constitution had been violated. In such cases, the Tribunal could prepare the accusation against the public official involved, and was to send it to the National Chamber of Representatives, for their prosecution.[1231]

But in accordance with the constitutional reform approved in 1983, in force since 1984[1232] the Tribunal of Constitutional Guarantees has also been attributed the exclusive power to suspend the effects of unconstitutional legislative acts, in what can be considered a concentrated system of judicial review. This power, up to the constitutional reform of 1983 had been attributed to the Supreme Court of Justice.

In effect, since 1984, the Tribunal of Constitutional Guarantees has had the exclusive power to "suspend totally or partially, at any moment, *ex officio* or following a party's petition, the effects of laws (statutes), ordinances or decrees that were unconstitutional whether in substance ox in form."[1233] This "suspension" of the effects of legislation is, undoubtedly, an important judicial review remedy regarding unconstitutional acts, although the Tribunal must submit its decision for the National Chamber of Representatives resolution. In accordance with the Constitution neither the decision of the Tribunal nor the resolution of the National Chamber of Representatives has "retroactive effects,[1234] although they have *erga omnes* effects.

This can be deduced, particularly regarding the Tribunal "suspensive" decision, from what is established in the Constitution regarding the inapplicability of legislation by the Chambers of the Supreme Court, the Tax Court or the Administrative Justice Court with *inter partes* effects in processes developed before them.

In these latter cases, it must be stressed that these courts must notify their decisions to the Supreme Court, which if it accepts the criterion must inform the Tribunal of Constitutional Guarantees which could exercise its competences to suspend the effects of the challenged act.[1235]

VIII. PREVENTIVE JUDICIAL REVIEW SYSTEM IN FRANCE: THE CONSTITUTIONAL COUNCIL

All the concentrated systems of judicial review that follow the European model can be characterised by the establishment of various means of judicial control of the constitutionality of legislation once in force, that is to say, once enacted and after its juridical normative effects have begun. Only in an exceptional way do some European concentrated systems allow for a preventive means of control regarding certain

1231 Art. 141, 3 Constitution.

1232 G. ZAMBRANO PALACIOS, "Control de la constitucionalidad de los actos del poder público", *Memoria de la Reunión de Presidentes de Cortes Supremas de Justicia de Iberoamérica, El Caribe, España y Portugal*, Caracas 1983, pp. 677, 678.

1233 Art.138. Constitution 1978.

1234 Art. 138. Constitution 1978.

1235 Art. 138 Constitution 1978.

state acts, as happens in Italy with regional legislation and in Spain with organic laws and international treaties.

The basis for the existence of an *a posteriori* judicial review system has been the overcoming of the dogma of the sovereignty of parliament and of the law, and of the rigidities of the principle of separation of powers. As we have seen, judicial review implies the existence of a written and rigid constitution with normative character directly applicable to individuals, through which limits are imposed upon all constitutional organs, even the legislator, whose activities must conform to its text and therefore can be subject to jurisdictional review.

Those principles overcome by the European countries that followed the concentrated system of judicial review, have been of particular importance in the development of the French constitutional system, and if it is true that the contemporary trends of constitutionalism have also affected its traditional basis, it has been only for the establishment of a preventive system of judicial review, which undoubtedly is an incomplete system for the review of legislation deemed unconstitutional.

Of course, the adoption of a preventive system of judicial review in France and the activity developed by the Constitutional Council have been considered of revolutionary character[1236] because they mean the acceptance of the principle of constitutionality and the submission of the legislator to constitutional limits,[1237] but if it is compared with the system of judicial review adopted in the other European countries, we must conclude by considering that the French judicial review system is a limited one,[1238] the statutes once in force not being submitted to constitutional justice control.

1. Historical Background

The French preventive system of judicial review of legislation was definitively established in the Constitution of 5 October 1958, in which the Constitutional Council was regulated[1239] as a constitutional organ of the state in charge of the preventive review of legislation, that is to say, of the role of establishing its "conformity with the Constitution... before its promulgation."[1240] As we have said, this institutional innovation is the result of a reaction against at least two of the traditional bases of

---

1236 J. RIVERO, *Le Conseil Constitutionnel et les libertés*, Paris–Aix–en–Provence 1984, p. 168.

1237 L. FAVOREU, "Le principe de constitutionnalité. Essai de definition d'après la jurisprudence du Conseil Constitutionnel", *Recueil d'etudes en Hommage a Charles Eisenmann*, Paris 1977, pp. 33–48.

1238 See the comments concerning the legitimacy of the *a priori* French systems of control in a comparative perspective in L. FAVOREU "Actualité et légitimité du contrôle juridictionnel del lois en Europe occidentale", *Revue du droit public et de la science politique en France etàa l'étranger*, Paris 1984 (5), p. 1183–1187. Also published in L. FAVOREU and J.A. JOLOWICZ (ed.), *Le contrôle juridictionnel des lois. Légitimité, effectivité et développements récents*, Paris 1986, pp. 17–68.

1239 Arts 56–63 Constitution 1958.

1240 Art. 61.

the French constitutional system: the absolutism of the law and the rejection of any judicial interference regarding other state powers, particularly parliament.

In effect, one of the most important political dogmas resulting from the French Revolution was the deep mistrust of the revolutionary legislator regarding judges, which denying them any possibility of controlling the other state powers, particularly the legislator and the executive. This antijudicial reaction had its political grounds in the role played by the pre–revolutionary *Parlements*, as Higher Courts, when examining the laws and decrees submitted to them to ensure that they did not contain "anything contrary to the fundamental laws of the Kingdom" which gave them an important conservative political power.[1241]

This distrust of the judicial power led to an extreme revolutionary interpretation of the principle of separation of powers. It resulted in prohibiting all judges not only from reviewing legislative and administrative acts, which explains why, in its origin, the Court of Cassation was a legislative organ and why the Council of state was an executive organ, but even from interpreting the laws, which power was also reserved to the legislator exercised by decree enacted at the request of the judges through the so–called *reféré législatif*, when there were any doubt about the text of a law.[1242] Therefore, as Montesquieu regarded them, the judges were *la bouche de la loi*, that is to say, "the mouth that pronounces the words of the law, mere passive beings, incapable of moderating either its force or rigour."[1243]

This extreme interpretation of the separation of powers, the supremacy of the law and the role of judiciary had up to this century (20th century) a tremendous influence on the shaping of continental constitutional law. That is why, as we have seen, it has only been during recent decades that a change has been introduced in Europe, particularly through the adoption of systems of judicial review of legislation, even though not by the ordinary judges or by the Supreme Courts of the countries, but by a specially created constitutional tribunal as a constitutional organ but with jurisdictional power.

The same lines were followed in the establishment of the Constitutional Council in France, but perhaps with a more political than jurisdictional character at least in its origin in which direct antecedents can be found in French constitutional history.

In effect, the French tradition before the creation of the Constitutional Council in 1958 was the attribution of the function of guaranteeing the Constitution to a special political body. This happened with the Conservative Senate of the Constitution of the year VIII of the 22 *Frimaire*, and with the attributions of the Senate in the Constitutional Charter of 1852.[1244] It was repeated in the 1946 Constitution, which attributed the undertaking of the preventive control of the constitutionality of the laws

1241 M. CAPPELLETTI, *Judicial Review in the Contemporary World*, Indianapolis 1971, pp. 33–35; F. Luchaire, *Le Conseil Constitutionnel*, Paris 1980, pp. 5–6.

1242 *Idem*

1243 MONTESQUIEU, *De l'Espirit of Laws*, Book XI, Ch VI, quoted by Ch. H. MCILWAIN, *The High Court of Parliament and its Supremacy*, Yale, 1910, p. 323.

1244 C. FRANCK, *Les functions juridictionnelles du Conseil Constitutionnel et du Conseil d'État dans l'ordre constitutionnel*, Paris 1974, pp.44–46; F. LUCHAIRE, *op. cit*., pp. 10–11.

sanctioned by the National Assembly to a political body called the *Comite Constitutionnel*, to determine if their promulgation required a previous amendment of the organic part of the Constitution. Consequently, it was a very limited system of constitutional control. As a result, if the Committee deemed that the law was in fact contrary to the Constitution, it was returned to the Assembly for reconsideration, and if the Assembly confirmed its first decision, then it was necessary to proceed to reform the Constitution just as if it were a revision explicitly requested. However, the law could not be enacted until the reform had been concluded.[1245]

2. The Constitutional Council and its Jurisdiction

Based on the background of the French tradition and of the 1946 Constitutional Committee, the 1958 Constitution created the Constitutional Council,[1246] which in accordance with Maurice Duverger's ideas was a kind of "supreme political jurisdiction" entrusted with power to control the constitutionality of the law and the regularity of presidential and parliamentary elections. The term "political jurisdiction" used by Duverger to describe this body expresses the rather atypical[1247] and ambiguous[1248] nature of the institution: it is assigned the role of a judge, but must exercise its activities in the political arena, and more important, with political motivations. Its members enjoy the independence of all Magistrates and judges, but are politically recruited and appointed.

Therefore discussions have traditionally arisen in France regarding the jurisdictional character of the Constitutional Council,[1249] which today are definitively admitted even giving rise to a distinction between the "judicial power" and a more broad "jurisdictional power", the latter being constructed to comprise other than ordinary judiciary and administrative justice functions, the constitutional justice attributions of the Constitutional Council.[1250]

In accordance with the Constitution, the composition of the Constitutional Council, other than by *ex–officio* members who are the former Presidents of the Republic, is composed of nine members appointed in a paritarian way, three by the President

---

1245 F. LUCHAIRE, *op. cit.*, p. 13.

1246 The Constitutional Council is ruled by Title VII, article 53 to 63 of the 1958 Constitution, (*Journal Official* du 5–10–1958) and by the Organic Law N° 58–1067 of 7th November, 1958. (*Journal Officiel* du 9–11–1958). Article 61, 2 of the Constitution was modified on 21st October, 1974 by a Constitutional Reform; and the Organic Law of the Tribunal was modified by the Organic Law N° 59–223 of 4th February 1959 (*Journal Officiel* du 7–2–1959) and by the Organic Law of 26–12–1974 that followed the Constitutional ammendment.

1247 W.K. GECK, "Judicial Review of Statutes: a Comparative Survey of Present Institutions and Practices", *Cornell Law Quarterly*, 51, 1966, pp. 256–259.

1248 A. HAURIOU, *Institutions politiques et droit constitutionnel*, Paris.

1249 F. LUCHAIRE, "Le Conseil Constitutionnel. Est–il une juridiction", *Revue du droit public et de la science politique en France et à l'étranger*, 1979; F. Luchaire, *op. cit.*, pp. 33–56.

1250 T. RENOUX, *Le Conseil Constitutionnel et l'autorité judiciaire. L'elaboration d'un droit constitutionnel juridictionnel*, Paris 1984, p. 19.

of the Republic, three by the President of the National Assembly and three by the President of the Senate.[1251]

The functions of the Council members are incompatible with those of members of Government, of Parliament and of the Economic and Social Council.[1252] Council members cannot be appointed to any public office[1253] during their term, nor are they allowed to take political stands on issues which have been or could be susceptible to a decision by the Council.[1254] They are also prohibited from accepting positions of responsibility or administrative posts in any political party or group, nor can they mention their post in any document which could lend itself to publication on any public or private activity.[1255]

The Constitutional Council, in addition to its consultative attributions, in the area of judicial review is also the judge of the constitutionality of legislation and of electoral and referendum disputes. Therefore, three types of competences can be distinguished for the Constitutional Council: to act as a consultative body, to exercise electoral jurisdiction and to control the constitutionality of legislation.

The first of the competences attributed to the Constitutional Council refers to the exercise of a series of functions of a consultative nature, and indeed, of political importance. These consultative functions refer to determining when the President of the Republic is unable to perform his functions,[1256] and to give its opinion regarding the situations and measures to be taken in cases of extraordinary circumstances.[1257]

In the first case, the consultative functions of the Council are directed towards preventing the President of the Republic from exercising his functions, in which it wields genuine decision–making power, when requested by the government when it considers the President of the Republic unfit to carry out his functions.

We should stress that the Constitution does not define the notion of being "unfit to perform" (*empêchement*) insofar as it does not specify if it means a physical disability or unfitness resulting from sickness or an accident. Thus the power of appreciation of the Constitutional Council is practically unlimited. If the Constitutional Council declares the unfitness or disability of the President to be of a definitive nature, it must call new elections between twenty and fifty days following its decision. Nevertheless, the Constitutional Council can confirm the existence of a *force majeure* preventing it from calling the election, in which case, as would occur in the event of temporary incapacity, the President of the Republic would be replaced by the President of the Senate, who is empowered to exercise all of the former attribu-

1251 Art. 56 Constitution; Art. 1, Organic Law 58–1067.

1252 Art. 57 Constitution; Art. 4, Organic Law 58–1067.

1253 Art. 5 Organic Law 58–1067.

1254 Art. 7 Organic Law 58–1067.

1255 Art. 2, Decret 13–1–1959. See in F. LUCHAIRE, *op. cit.*, p. 71.

1256 Art. 7. Constitution.

1257 Art. 16. Constitution.

tions, with the exception of the right to dissolve the Assembly, or to call a referendum.[1258]

The second consultative function of the Constitutional Council concerns the opinion it must give when consulted by the President of the Republic regarding the situation and the measures that must be taken when a serious and immediate threat against the institutions of the Republic, the independence of the Nation, the integrity of its territory or the execution of international accords exists, or when the regular functioning of the constitutional public powers is interrupted. In order to adopt the necessary measures in the circumstances, the President as well as the Prime Minister and the President of the Assemblies must consult the Constitutional Council, which must refer to the conditions established in the Constitution for the exercise of extraordinary powers in which case the opinion must be published.[1259]

Additionally, the Constitutional Council must be consulted on all measures that the President of the Republic intends to take under Article 16 of the Constitution, in which case, the opinion of the Constitutional Council would not be published.[1260]

The second group of competences of the Constitutional Council deals with its role as Supreme Electoral Tribunal, not only for parliamentary elections, but also for presidential elections and referenda.[1261] Regarding parliamentary elections, the Constitutional Council has constitutional powers to decide upon the regularity of elections of Deputies and Senators[1262] and as a result the Council can annul any election or can amend its reported results and is even empowered to declare another candidate as having been regularly elected.[1263] To this end, every parliamentary election can be challenged before the Tribunal, within a ten day period, by any elector of the respective electoral circumscription, following a contradictory procedure in which the contested parliamentary assembly and the candidate whose election is under question are entitled to make observations.[1264]

Regarding the control of presidential elections[1265] the powers of the Constitutional Council are not restricted to the settlement of disputes, that is to say, they are not reduced to reviewing the regularity of an election if contested, but to watch out for the regularity of the elections. To this effect, the Constitutional Council, in the case of a challenged presidential election, is entrusted with the task of adopting and proclaiming the final results of the electoral process.[1266] Moreover, the Constitutional Council *ex–officio*, when it has evidence of serious irregularities which could

1258 Arts 7, 11, 12. Constitution. Art. 31 Organic Law 58–1067.

1259 Art. 16. Constitution. Arts 52, 53 Organic Law 58–1067.

1260 Art. 54 Organic Law 58–1067.

1261 Art. 58–60. Constitution.

1262 Art. 59. Constitution.

1263 Art. 41 Organic Law 58–1067.

1264 Art. 39,40 *Idem.*

1265 Art. 30 *Idem.*

1266 Art. 27 Organic Law 58–1064 7–11–58 concerning the election of the President of the Republic. *Journal Officiel* du 9–11–58.

prevent the sincerity of the election and affect its overall result, can pronounce the nullity of the election, in which case the government must fix a new date for a new election.[1267]

On the other hand, the Constitutional Council also participates in the electoral process when the government deems it necessary to replace the normal vote counting procedure, carried out at the level of the heads of Departments, and of the territories, by a centralized vote count taken in Paris. In accordance with the Organic Law on the Presidential Election the decree establishing this measure must have the favourable opinion of the Constitutional Council,[1268] thus granting this body the real decision–making power in the matter.

Anyway, regarding disputes over presidential elections, only the Prefects or Heads of the respective territories may exercise a recourse before the Constitutional Council within the 48 hours following the closure of the ballot count,[1269] but electors have no right to exercise such a recourse. Nevertheless, this restriction of standing is balanced when considering the already questioned *ex–officio* powers of the Council to annul an election.

The third competence regarding electoral disputes of the Constitutional Council relates to the control of referenda. In this respect the Council must be first consulted on the organisation of the operations of the referendum,[1270] that is to say, its technical application. Second, it must supervise both the operations and the final vote count, and then proclaim the results.[1271]Third, in the case of disputes relating to the referendum, the Constitutional Council also examines and decides on every claim raised before it.[1272] The Organic Law of the Constitutional Council does not clearly establish who is entitled to make such claims, but, in view of the nature of a referendum, that is to say, a popular consultation via direct votes, it could be considered that every elector has the right to request a decision from the Constitutional Council.[1273] Anyway, if the Council confirmed irregularities, it must decide then, in a sovereign manner, whether to maintain the operation of the referendum or to change it, making a statement on its partial annulment.[1274]

The third group of competencies of the Constitutional Council is the control of constitutionality of legislation, of a preventive character, which is conceived in the Constitution basically as a mean of preventing encroachment of competencies between the constitutional organs of the state, and particularly to keep parliament within its constitutional boundaries. Thus, in its origin, the Constitutional Council was established as the guarantor of the organic part of the Constitution and only af-

---

1267 Art. 22 Organic Law 58–1064.

1268 Art. 23 *Idem.*

1269 Art. 19 *Idem.*

1270 Art. 46 Organic Law 58–1067.

1271 Art. 60 Constitution. Art. 51 Organic Law 58–1067.

1272 Art. 50 Organic Law 56–1067.

1273 *Cf.* F. LUCHAIRE, *op. cit.*, p. 277.

1274 Art. 50 Organic Law 58–1067.

ter 1971, has it also been considered, although indirectly, as the guarantor of the fundamental rights of the citizen against the laws.[1275]

This control of the constitutionality of legislation, as we said, is conceived in France as a preventive or *a priori* control in the sense that it is exercised over acts not yet enforced, because they have not been enacted. Regarding laws, the control only proceeds against statutes sanctioned by the Assemblies but not yet promulgated by the President of the Republic, and it is precisely this aspect, which brings about the great difference between the French system of judicial review and the other European systems, in which the main control of constitutionality is jurisdictionally exercised against acts that have been promulgated and that are in force.

In accordance with the French Constitution, the judicial review powers of the Constitutional Council can be classified into two groups: the preventive control of the constitutionality of non promulgated legislation; and the preventive control over the distribution of normative powers between the law and the executive regulations.

3. Preventive Control of the Constitutionality of non Promulgated Legislation

The preventive control of the constitutionality of non promulgated legislation, is exercised by the Constitutional Council in two ways: in a compulsory way regarding parliamentary regulations, and organic laws, and in a facultative way regarding ordinary laws and international treaties.

A. *Obligatory Control of the Constitutionality of Organic Laws and Parliamentary Regulations*

In accordance with article 61 of the Constitution, organic laws and the internal regulations of parliamentary assemblies before they are promulgated, must be submitted to the Constitutional Council for its decision as to whether they are consistent with the Constitution.

In the case of Organic Laws, the Prime Minister who must state, when appropriate, if the decision is urgent, must submit them to the Constitutional Council. In the case of parliamentary regulations or modifications to the regulations adopted by one of the Assemblies, they must be submitted to the Constitutional Council by the President of the Assembly.[1276]

B. *Facultative Control of the Constitutionality of Ordinary Laws and of International Treaties*

In addition to organic laws and parliamentary regulations, the President of the Republic, the Prime Minister or the President of one of the Assemblies can also submit ordinary laws before their enactment to the Constitutional Council. Moreover, the 1974 Constitutional reform adds a new option: 60 representatives or senators may submit the question of constitutionality regarding ordinary laws to the

1275 J. RIVERO, *op. cit.*, pp. 13–14.

1276 Art. 61 Constitution. Art. 17 Organic Law 58–1067.

Constitutional Council,[1277] thereby giving minorities the means to challenge majority decisions.

This facultative control of constitutionality also applies to international treaties and in this case, the Constitutional Council must decide whether an international treaty contains clauses contrary to the Constitution, when requested by the President of the Republic, the Prime Minister or the President of one of the Assemblies, in which case the authorisation for its signing or for its approval could only be possible after a constitutional reform takes place.[1278]

The proceeding in this case is contradictory and the authority that submits an international treaty or a law to the Constitutional Council for constitutional control, must immediately notify such action to the other authorities entitled to require a decision of the Constitutional Council.[1279]

C. *Suspensive Effects of the Recourses and the Decision of the Council*

In any case in which the Constitutional Council is requested for control of constitutionality before the enactment of organic laws, parliamentary regulations, ordinary laws and international treaties, as soon as the Council hears the request, it has suspensive effects and the promulgation of the normative text under challenge is suspended.[1280] The Council has a month to make a decision, although in an urgent case, the government may request that this term be reduced to eight days.[1281]

The decision of the Council that must be motivated and published in the *Journal official*[1282] can be to declare that the challenged statute is not contrary to the Constitution, in which case the suspensive delay of its promulgation ends.[1283] But the decision of the Constitutional Council may be to declare the normative text unconstitutional, in which case the non promulgated normative text cannot be promulgated nor enforced.[1284]

In relation to international treaties, as we have said, if the Constitutional Council decides that an international treaty contains a clause contrary to the Constitution, the authorisation to ratify or approve it must be postponed until the Constitution has been amended.[1285]

The declaration of unconstitutionality by the Constitutional Council always takes two forms regarding the text of the challenged act: if the Constitutional Council deems that an unconstitutional provision of a statute is inseparable from the rest of

---

1277 Art. 61. Constitution.

1278 Art. 54. Constitution.

1279 Art. 54, 61. Constitution. Art. 18 Organic Law 58–1067.

1280 Art. 61. Constitution.

1281 Art. 61. Constitution.

1282 Art. 20 Organic Law.

1283 Art. 21 Organic Law 58–1067.

1284 Art. 62. Constitution.

1285 Art. 54. Constitution.

the text, the full text of the law therefore cannot be promulgated;[1286] on the contrary, if the Council deems that the unconstitutional provisions can be separated from the text, the President of the Republic can either enact the incomplete text, or call for a second discussion by the Chambers.[1287]

In any case, the decision of the Constitutional Council is not revisable and has binding effects on all public powers and administrative and jurisdictional authorities.[1288]

4. Preventive Control of the Distribution of Normative Competences

Concerning preventive judicial review, another fundamental competence of the Constitutional Council is intended to protect the distribution of normative competences between the law and the executive regulations. In effect, the 1958 French constitution, deviating from the parliamentary tradition of modern states and as a result of an obvious antiparliamentary reaction, established a system for the distribution of competences between parliament and government, based on assigning parliament exclusive power over matters expressly enumerated in the Constitution, which resulted in an extreme restriction of parliamentary powers.

In effect, in accordance with Article 34 of the Constitution, a list of subjects whose regulation is attributed to the competence of parliament is enumerated covering the statutes it can dictate and Article 37 lays down that in all other matters, outside those that form the domain of the law (statute), the regulatory powers upon them are attributed to the executive, thus reducing the power of parliament to a series of clearly enumerated subjects and leaving the remainder of the normative competences to the executive power.

This system of distributing normative state powers, of course, causes innumerable disputes between the law and the executive regulations, thus between parliament and the executive power, which the Constitutional Council must settle. Therefore, to resolve conflicts, the Council must intervene to ensure the compliance of constitutional provisions, but without examining the definitive normative text. Here the Constitutional Council really intervenes at the time of drafting the respective texts, to authorise or to prohibit their continuation until the final version of the text is ready. Of course, this competence of the Council is exercised in two aspects with regard to statutes and to the exercise of the regulatory executive powers.

A. *Preventive Control of Bills*

In the first aspect, the intervention of the Council concerns the procedure for the drafting of statutes and their reforms. In effect, the Government may be opposed to the continuation of the discussion of a bill by the Assembly, when it considers that it includes matters which are not under the domain reserved to the law in Article 34 of

1286 Art. 22 Organic Law 58–1067.

1287 Art. 23. *Idem.*

1288 Art. 62. Constitution.

the Constitution, and in the organic laws adopted for their enforcement, and when it deems it contrary to the powers of normative character assigned to Government.[1289]

In this case, the President of the Assembly involved can come to an agreement with the government opposition whereby neither the proposal nor the reform is discussed. If, however, it disagrees with the government, the Constitutional Council is called upon to settle the conflict by any of the interested organs and must adopt the decision within an 8–day period. In that case, the discussion of the law or of the legislative amendment to which the government is opposed is immediately suspended.[1290] In addition, the authority that requests the intervention of the Constitutional Council in the conflict, must notify all other authorities with the same competence to request a decision from the Constitutional Tribunal.[1291]

B. *Constitutional Control of Statutes Regarding Executive Regulations*

The second intervention of the Constitutional Council in the distribution of competences between the law and executive regulations, concerns the exercise of regulatory power by the government, when it attempts to modify statutes that can occur in two different cases. Firstly, when the statute in question has been adopted before the delimitation of the legislative domain in the 1958 Constitution but the matters concerned enter within the executive normative powers. Secondly, when the statutes have been adopted after the 1958 delimitation, invading the executive normative powers but were not submitted to the control of the Constitutional Council before enactment.

Under the first hypothesis, the government is free to modify the existing pre–constitutional statutes, which refer to matters of the domain reserved to it by the Constitution. In such cases, the Government is only obliged to adopt the corresponding decree, after it has requested and obtained a consultative opinion from the Council of state.[1292]

The second hypothesis deals with the exercise of executive regulatory power to modify statutes adopted by Parliament after the 1958 Constitution, in areas that fall under the executive normative domain. In such cases, the government is empowered to pass the respective regulatory decree only when the Constitutional Council has declared the executive regulatory nature of the matter.[1293] In this way, if a government, through neglect or by deliberate political will does not submit a non promulgated statute which falls outside the domain reserved for the legislative power to the Constitutional Council before its enactment, successive governments are not bound by this decision and can submit the statute in question to the Constitutional Council,

---

1289 Art. 41. Constitution.

1290 Art. 27 Organic Law 58–1067.

1291 *Idem.*

1292 Art. 37. Constitution.

1293 Art. 37. Constitution.

and if it declares its executive regulatory subject character, the government can modify it quite simply by decree.[1294]

Therefore, in the field of the delimitation of normative competences between executive regulatory power and statutes, the control of the Constitutional Council does not really apply to executive regulations themselves, only to the statutes. Executive regulations and the possible encroachment they might make upon the domain reserved to the legislator by Article 34 of the Constitution are subject to control by the Council of State which could lead to the divergences of criterion between the latter and the Constitutional Council.[1295]

5. Substantive Control of Constitutionality of Legislation and the Principle of Constitutionality

As we have seen, the fundamental role attributed to the Constitutional Council in France, in accordance with the 1958 Constitution, relates to controlling the conformity of legislation with the Constitution in a preventive way. But the 1958 Constitution being basically an organic constitution, that is to say, one in which the distribution of powers between the different state organs is its main objective, in the first decade of its functioning, the Constitutional Council acted as the guardian of the maintenance of that distribution particularly regarding the relation between parliament and government, in other words the relations between the law (Statutes) and the executive regulatory powers.

The French Constitution, as we have seen, does not have an express declaration or enumeration of constitutional rights, which led to it being interpreted as a text not directly applicable to individuals, the only declaration of the Constitution concerning fundamental rights of individuals being its Preamble in which it is stated that

> The French people solemnly proclaim their adherence to the Rights of Man and to the principles of national sovereignty as have been defined in the Declaration of 1789, confirmed and completed by the Preamble of the 1946 Constitution.

A similar Preamble was established in the 1946 Constitution, which the then Constitutional Committee considered as not being directly enforceable.[1296] Nevertheless, no special provision in this respect was established in the 1958 Constitution.

This normative reality led the Constitutional Council to enlarge its own judicial review powers in what has been considered its *Marbury v. Madison* decision[1297] the one adopted on the 16 July 1971 concerning the freedom of associations [1298]63); in which to declare a statute sanctioned by parliament unconstitutional, the Council based itself on the Preamble and through it on the "fundamental principles recog-

---

1294 See also Arts 24–26 Organic Law 58–1067.

1295 C. FRANCK, *op. cit.*, p. 167.

1296 Art. 34. Constitution 1946. *Cf.* J. RIVERO, *op. cit.*, p. 11; L. FAVOREU, "Le principe ...", *loc. cit.*, p. 34.

1297 J. RIVERO, *op. cit.*, p. 140.

1298 See in L. FAVOREU and L. PHILIP, *Les grandes decisions du Conseil Constitutionnel*, Paris 1984, pp. 222–237.

nised by the laws of the Republic and the Declaration of the Rights of Man and the Citizen of 1789." Within these principles and rights, the Council assigned constitutional rank to the freedom of associations and declared the unconstitutionality of a statute it deemed contrary to it, thus, to the Constitution.[1299] Consequently, not only was the "bloc of constitutionality" enlarged by the Constitutional Council, which, since then, has comprised, other than the formal text of the Constitution, the fundamental principles recognised by the laws of the Republic and the Declaration of the Rights of Man and the Citizen of 1789,[1300] but the Council has also become the guardian of freedoms.[1301]

Therefore, the Constitutional council has claimed for itself the power and duty to control the conformity of non promulgated statutes, not only according to Articles 34 and 37 of the Constitution, which govern the distribution of competences between parliament and the executive normative powers, but also according to the Constitution in full, which includes the general principles of a constitutional character as they arise from the Universal Declaration and from the Preamble, and the fundamental rights of individuals. Of course, in pursuing this task, the recourse opening the way for parliamentary minorities to seek judicial review through the 1974 constitutional amendment, has been of fundamental importance, as it has shown in other basic decisions of the Council, like the one adopted on the 16 January and 11 February 1982 in the *nationalisation* case,[1302] in which the "bloc of constitutionality" was again enlarged, to comprise the "principles and rules of constitutional value"[1303] to which the Legislator is also submitted.

Finally, it must be mentioned that in addition to these transformations pressured by the Constitutional Council decisions regarding submission of all state organs to the Constitution and its principles, including the legislator, the control of constitutionality of legislation has also been enlarged through the work of the other main jurisdictional organs in France, the Council of State and the Court of Cassation.

In particular, the Council of State since its decision *Sindicat General des Ingenieurs–Counceils* of 26 June 1959[1304] has exercised constitutional control over

---

1299 *Cf.* other comment upon the decision in B. NICHOLAS, "Fundamental Rights and Judicial Review in France", *Public Law* 1978, pp. 82–92; J. E. BEARDSLEY, "The Constitutional Council and Constitutional Liberties in France", *The American Journal of Comparative Law*, 20, 1972, p. 431–452; C. FRANCK, *op. cit.*, p. 208.

1300 *Cf.* F. LUCHAIRE, "Procédures et techniques de protection des droits fondamentaux. Conseil Constitutionnel Francais", in L. FAVOREU ed.), *Cours constitutionnelles européenes et droits fondamentaux*, Paris 1982, pp. 64–73.

1301 M. CAPPELLETTI, "El formidable problema del control judicial y la contribucion del análisis comparado", *Revista de estudios políticos*, 13, Madrid 1980, p. 71.

1302 See in L. FAVOREU and L. PHILIP, *op. cit.*, pp. 524–562. See the comments in L. FAVOREU (ed.) *Nationalisations et Constitution*, Aix–en–Provence, 1982; J. RIVERO, *op. cit.*, pp. 109–125.

1303 L. FAVOREU, "Les decisions du Conseil Constitutionnel dons l'affaire des nationalisations", *Revue du droit public et de la science politique en France et à l'étranger*, 1982, p, 401.

1304 See in *Recueil Sirey* Jurisprudence, 1959, p. 392 (note Drago). See the comments on C. FRANK, *op. cit.*, p. 200; M. CAPPELLETTI, "El formidable problema... ", *loc. cit.*, p. 70.

executive normative acts (decree laws) adopted in accordance with the powers attributed to the executive in Article 37 of the Constitution, not regarding the possible submission of executive regulations to the statutes sanctioned by Parliament because of the equally distributed powers of both constitutional organs, but regarding the Constitution, and moreover, "the general principles of law which result basically from the Preamble of the Constitution" which "are imposed on the regulatory executive authority, even in the absence of a legislative disposition."[1305]

On the other hand, the Court of Cassation in a very important decision of 24 May 1975, *Administration des Douanes v Société Cafés Jacques Varbre S.A.*, [1306] led the way to the exercise of a diffuse system of judicial review in France, by establishing the power of courts to refuse to apply statutes promulgated after the treaties of the European Economic Community, contrary to those treaties which in the French constitutional system (as are all international treaties) have "authority superior to statutes."[1307] This possibility of a diffuse system of judicial review of course, could lead to its general admissibility, in particular regarding statutes contrary to the fundamental rights of individuals, not only because the European Convention of Human Rights ratified by France is part of the French legislation,[1308] but also because of the express acceptance by the Constitutional Council of the constitutional rank, value and character of the fundamental rights contained in the 1789 Declaration. Of course, to that end, the reluctance of the courts to control the constitutionality of statutes so traditional in France, must be overcome, and that is a fundamental task they have in the future, to which achievement the three principal jurisdictional organs of the state have led the way.

IX. LIMITED CONCENTRATED SYSTEM OF JUDICIAL REVIEW IN BELGIUM: THE ARBITRATION COURT

Finally, regarding the concentrated systems of judicial review in Europe, a limited version can be identified in Belgium. In effect, due to the establishment of a decentralised political form of the state in Belgium, first programmed in the 1970 constitutional reform and later executed in the 1980 constitutional reform,[1309] in a similar way to the "Regional state" organisation formula adopted in Italy and Spain, the need for the establishment of an independent constitutional organ to resolve con-

1305 See in C. FRANCK, *op. cit.*, p. 200.

1306 See in *Dalloz* (Jurisprudence), 1975, p. 497. See the comments in M. CAPPELLETTI and W. COHEN, *Comparative Constitutional Law*, Indianapolis 1979, pp. 156–168; M. CAPPELLETTI, "El formidable problema...", *loc. cit.*, p. 72.

1307 Art. 55. Constitution.

1308 *Cf.* A.Z. DRZEMCZEWSKI, *European Human Rights Convention in Domestic Law. A Comparative Study*, Oxford, p. 71.

1309 F. PERIN, *La nouvelle subdivision du Royaume: les Communautes et les Regions*, XI Congrès International du Droit Comparé, Caracas 1982, (mimeo), p. 10. See the text in *La Constitution belge et ses lois d'application*, Cabay, Louvain–La–Neuve, 1985.

flicts between the various political entities, brought about the creation of an Arbitration Court for that purpose in the same 1980 amendment to the Constitution.[1310]

In effect, in accordance with that constitutional reform, the Kingdom of Belgium was divided into Regions and Communities, as political decentralised units in which organisation and functioning the linguistic and ethnic divisions of the country play a fundamental role. Thus, conflicts between national power and those attributions assigned to the Regions and Communities need to be resolved. Hence, the creation of the Court of Arbitration composed of 12 members: six French speaking members, who form the French language part of the Court, and six Flemish speaking members who represent Flemish speaking communities. The members of the Court are appointed by the king for life, from a list with twice the number submitted by the Senate, adopted by a two thirds majority of its members present. The candidates who must be over 40 years of age, must either have held posts for five years as judicial or administrative magistrates, or be professors of law, or they must have been members of the Senate or of the Chamber of Deputies for at least eight years. Both linguistic groups must share an equal distribution of the two above–mentioned categories.[1311]

The Court of Arbitration has been conferred a limited competence to judge the conformity of laws and decrees only with respect to the rules established in or based on the Constitution to determine the respective competences of the state, of the communities and of the regions."[1312] Therefore, the judicial review powers of the Court are referred exclusively to certain disputes of competences between state bodies, in a similar way to the powers attributed to the constitutional tribunals on the European model.

The powers of the Arbitration Court can be exercised through direct or incidental means. In effect, the first method of seeking judicial review regarding conflicts of attributions is through a direct recourse brought before the Court by the Council of Ministers or by the executive body of the communities or the regions, requesting the annulment of any legislative act on the grounds that it infringes the vertical distribution of powers established in the Constitution. The right of the Presidents of the legislative assemblies to bring before the Court this direct action at the request of two thirds of their members is also foreseen. In any case, the recourse must be presented before the Court within the period of one year following the publication of the challenged act,[1313] and the Court can decide, when demanded by a party, to suspend the

---

1310 Art. 107 Constitution (29–7–1980) See also "Loi portant l'organisation, la competence et le fonctionnement de la Cour d'arbitrage" (L.C.A.) 28–6–83, in *La Constituttion belge..., cit.*, p. 105. *Cf.* L. FAVOREU, *Le contrôle juridictionnel des lois et sa légitimité. Dévelopments récents en Europe occidentale*, AILS, Uppsala Colloquium 1984, (mimeo), p. 15. Also published as "Actualité et Légitimité du contrôle juridictionnel des lois en Europe occidentale", *Revue du droit public et de la science politique en France et à l'étranger*, 1984 (5), p. 1166; and also in L. FAVOREU and J.A. JOLOWICZ (ed.), in *Le contrôle juridictionnel des lois.Légitimité, effectivité et développments récents*, Paris 1986, pp. 17–68.

1311 Arts. 21, 22, L.C.A.

1312 Art. 1, 1 L.C.A.

1313 Art. 2, 1 L.C.A.

application of the challenged statute or decree, in which case it must decide the recourse within a delay of three months.[1314]

The final Court decisions on the matter can declare the nullity of the unconstitutional act, "having absolute *res judicata* authority from its publication in the *Moniteur Belge*",[1315] which means that they have *erga omnes* effects. Additionally, it has been considered that such decisions have retroactive effects,[1316] thus, *ex–tunc, pro praeterito*.

The second method through which a constitutional question can reach the Court of Arbitration is the incidental one, when the issue is referred to the Court by any ordinary court before which, in a concrete case, the question of conformity of a statute or a decree with the constitution, on matters of vertical distribution of state powers, has been raised.[1317] The ordinary courts do not have *ex–officio* powers to refer constitutional questions before the Court, but have an important appreciation power when considering the issue raised by a party in the case.[1318]

Anyway, the decision of the Court of Arbitration in these incidental judicial review cases, has binding effects, not only upon the ordinary court that has referred the question, but also upon all other courts that must intervene in the same case.[1319]

PART VI
THE MIXED SYSTEMS OF JUDICIAL REVIEW

As we have seen, the systems of judicial review followed in comparative constitutional law can be classified into two main groups: the diffuse systems of judicial review, in which all courts have the power and duty to judge the constitutionality of legislation and to decide not to apply statutes when they deem them unconstitutional; and the concentrated systems of judicial review, in which the power to declare the unconstitutionality of statutes and to annul them is attributed to a single constitutional organ, either the Supreme Court of the country or a specially created Constitutional Court. In general, with their own particular trends, and as a consequence of the principle of the supremacy of the constitution, all the countries in the world with written and rigid constitutions have adopted one or other system.

Nevertheless, in accordance with their general trends, and having their common basis in the principle of the supremacy of the Constitution, those systems of judicial review of the constitutionality of legislation are not only compatible with all legal systems thus existing and functioning, either in countries with a common or Roman

1314 Art. 8, L.C.A.

1315 Art. 7, L.C.A.

1316 L. Favoreu, *loc. cit.*, p. 1168.

1317 Art. 15, 2 L.C.A.

1318 L. Favoreu, *loc. cit.*, p. 1168.

1319 Art. 17, L.C.A.

law tradition. Moreover, they can coexist in a particular country, giving rise to what we have called the mixed system of judicial review in which the maximum protection of the Constitution is established, at least formally in the Fundamental Charter. In Europe, a mixed system of judicial review exists in Portugal and in a more limited way in Switzerland, and many of the countries in Latin America follow this mixed pattern, as are the cases of Colombia, Venezuela, Guatemala and Brazil.

I. CONTROL OF CONSTITUTIONALITY IN THE PORTUGUESE REPUBLIC

The Constitution of the Republic of Portugal approved by a Constituent Assembly in April 1976 established the basis of a mixed system of judicial review of the constitutionality of legislation, in which the Council of the Revolution, its Constitutional Commission and the ordinary courts played a very important role,[1320] giving birth to the most complete system of judicial review in Europe, in which the basic elements of the European model and of the French system were adopted in parallel with elements of the diffuse system of judicial review. That mixed system of judicial review was maintained in the First Revision of the Constitution approved by the Constitutional Law N° 1/82 of 30th September 1982,[1321] in which it is regulated as we said, by what can still be considered today, the most complete system of judicial review in Europe.

1. The principle of Constitutional Supremacy and its Consequences

The 1982 Constitution is not only a written and rigid Constitution,[1322] but is expressly conceived as the supreme law of the *Lander*, to which all other state acts must be submitted. In this respect, Article 3 of the Constitution states:

> The state shall be subject to the Constitution and based on democratic legality.
>
> The validity of the laws and other state acts of the autonomous regions and local authorities shall depend on their being in accordance with the Constitution.

The consequence of this supremacy clause is also expressly established in the text of the Constitution, in which article 277 states:

> Provisions of law that infringe a provision of the Constitution or the principles laid down therein are unconstitutional.

Therefore, the supremacy of the Constitution and of the principles laid down in its provisions implies that laws and state acts contrary to them are unconstitutional and thus, invalid. Of course, the consequence of this assertion is the establishment of a complex system of judicial review of the constitutionality of state acts, in which a

---

1320 See in general J. CAMPINOS, *La Constitution portugaise de 1976 et sa garantie*, UNAM, Congreso sobre La Constitución y su Defensa, (mimeo), México, Agosto 1982; M. GONZALO, "Portugal; El Consejo de la Revolución, su Comisión Constitucional y los Tribunales ordinarios como órganos de control de la constitucionalidad", *Boletín de jurisprudencia constitucional*, Cortes Generales, 8, Madrid 1981, pp. 630, 640.

1321 Published in the *Diario da Republica*, 1st series, N° 227.

1322 Article 290 establishes material limits to constitutional revision.

diffuse system exists in parallel with a concentrated system attributed to a Constitutional Court.

The Constitutional Court" was created by the Constitution, within the judicial power,[1323] as a constitutional organ "competent to judge whether acts are unconstitutional and illegal" in accordance with its provisions"[1324] and also competent to judge questions related to the exercise of its functions by the President of the Republic and to electoral matters.[1325] The Constitutional Court is composed of thirteen judges, ten being named by the Assembly of the Republic and three co–opted.[1326]

2. Diffuse system of judicial review and the direct appeal before the Constitutional Court

In accordance with article 207 of the Constitution

> The Courts shall not apply unconstitutional provisions or principles to matters brought before them.

This constitutional provision authorises all the courts of the country not to apply unconstitutional provisions or principles, which comprise not only statutes, but also decree–laws, executive regulations, regional acts or any other normative state acts, including international treaties. Therefore, the Constitution establishes the power of all courts not to apply norms they deem unconstitutional in the concrete case, and also a real duty to do so. Thus, it is a power that can be exercised *ex–officio* by any court although any party in the concrete case or the Public Prosecutor can raise the constitutional question.

The control of the constitutionality of legislation, therefore, is a diffuse control attributed to all courts regarding the concrete cases in which the issue is raised, and which the courts must resolve when deciding the case. Thus, when they consider a norm unconstitutional, the norm is considered invalid regarding the concrete case, that is to say, with *inter partes* effects as well as *ex–tunc*, *pro praeterito* effects, in the sense that regarding the case and the concrete parties, the normative act is considered as never having been valid.

However, in the Portuguese constitutional systems, the most interesting feature of this diffuse system of judicial review, is the direct appeal established before the Constitutional Court against judicial decisions in which constitutional questions are decided, in a similar way to the extraordinary recourse of unconstitutionality, in the Argentinean and Brazilian systems or to the direct appeals before the Supreme Court in the United States.

In effect, in what is called the "concrete scrutiny for the constitutionality" following West German terminology, but in a very different way to the "concrete control of norms" developed by the West German Federal Constitutional Tribunal, arti-

1323 Art. 212.

1324 Art. 213,1.

1325 Art. 213,2.

1326 Art. 284.

cle 280 of the Portuguese Constitution establishes the right to appeal before the Constitutional Tribunal against any court decisions when they firstly, refuse to apply any provision of law on the grounds that it is unconstitutional: or secondly, when they apply a provision of a law the unconstitutionality of which has been raised during the proceedings.[1327]

This appeal must be compulsory exercised by the Department of the Public Prosecutor in cases in which a court of justice refuses to apply any provision of an international convention, a legislative act or a regulative decree on the grounds that it is unconstitutional.[1328] But in cases in which a court applies a provision of law the unconstitutionality of which has been raised by a party during the proceeding, then only that party has the right to appeal before the Constitutional Court.[1329]

But the powers of the Constitutional Court to hear appeals against lower court decisions in Portugal are not limited to constitutional control, but to diffuse control of legality, in the following cases:

First, when the courts refuse to apply a provision of a regional instrument on the grounds that it is illegal since it violates the statute of the autonomous regions or general law of the Republic; second, when the courts refuse to apply a provision of an instrument emanating from an organ of supreme authority on the grounds that it is illegal since it violates the statutes of an autonomous region; and thirdly, when the court applies a provision the illegality of which has been raised during the proceedings on the grounds of violating regional autonomies. In this latter case, only the interested party which raised the question has the right of appeal.[1330]

On the other hand, the Public Prosecutor is obliged to appeal against court decisions in which a provision of law previously judged unconstitutional or illegal by the Constitutional Tribunal itself is applied.[1331]

In any of these cases of appeals before the Constitutional Court, they shall be restricted to the question of unconstitutionality or illegality depending on the case.[1332] Therefore, the Tribunal does not review the case on its facts, its judicial review powers being limited to the constitutional question.

The Constitutional Tribunal decisions in these cases of constitutional review through appeals have effects only regarding the concrete case, thus they are *inter partes*, and only when the Constitutional Court has judged any provision of law unconstitutional in three concrete cases, can it judge and rule with generally binding validity on the unconstitutionality of the law.[1333]

1327 Art. 280,1,a,b.

1328 Art. 280,2.

1329 Art. 280,4.

1330 Art. 280, 3,a,b,c; 280,4.

1331 Art. 280,5.

1332 Art. 280,6.

1333 Art. 281,2.

3. Concentrated system of judicial review and the powers of the Constitutional Tribunal

In parallel with the diffuse system of judicial review, the Constitution of the Portuguese Republic has also established a concentrated system of judicial review of legislation, not only of promulgated state acts, thus *a posteriori* to their efficacy, but also in a preventive way, following the French model.

A. *Preventive Control of Constitutionality*

In effect, a preventive control of constitutionality is established regarding international treaties and agreements, formal laws and decree–laws, when the Constitutional Tribunal is requested by the President of the Republic; and regarding regional legislative decrees or executive normative acts, when requested by the Ministers of the Republic.

In the first case, article 278 of the Constitution establishes:

> The President of the Republic may request the Constitutional Court to judge preventively the constitutionality of any provision of an international treaty that has been submitted to him for ratification, and acts sent to him for promulgation as a law or decree–law or an international agreement the act of approval of which has been sent to him for signature.[1334]

Nevertheless, as we said, regional legislative acts and other executive normative acts can also be submitted to the Constitutional Tribunal for preventive constitutional review by the Minister of the Republic regarding "any provision of a regional legislative decree or a decree implementing a general law of the Republic that has been sent to them for signature."[1335]

In such cases of preventive judicial review, if the Constitutional Court rules that a provision of any act or international agreement is unconstitutional, the act must be vetoed by the President of the Republic or by the Minister concerned, and must be sent back to the organ that approved it.[1336] In principle, the act must not be promulgated or signed unless the organ that approved it expurgates the provision judged unconstitutional[1337] the possibility of requesting another preventive control of constitutionality of the reformulated act being expressly authorised.[1338]

But in cases of Treaties or laws, one can say that the Tribunals' decisions are not absolutely imperative and can be enacted in spite of their unconstitutional defect, if the Assembly of the Republic adopts a decision maintaining the provisions judged unconstitutional.

In effect, in cases in which the Assembly does not expurgate the unconstitutional provision of an international treaty found to be unconstitutional by the Tribunal, it could be ratified if the Assembly approves it by a two third majority of the members

1334 Art. 278,1.

1335 Art. 278,2.

1336 Art. 279,9.

1337 Art. 279,2.

1338 Art. 279,3

present.[1339] In a similar way in cases of formal law, even when their unconstitutionality has been declared by the Tribunal through a preventive means of control, the Assembly of the Republic can confirm them by a two thirds majority of the members present.[1340] In such cases, in spite of the constitutional objection the acts can be enforced, the majority required for its confirmation or ratification not being the same required for constitutional revision.[1341]

B. *Abstract Control of Constitutionality*

The constitutionality of legislation can also be the object of an "abstract scrutiny" by the Constitutional Tribunal, exercised through a direct mean or action.

In effect, the unconstitutionality of any provision of law can be the object of a request that can be formulated before the Constitutional Court by the President of the Republic, the President of the Assembly of the Republic, the Prime Minister, the Ombudsman, the Attorney–General, or one tenth of the members of the Assembly of the Republic.[1342] Additionally, the regional assemblies or the chairmen of the regional governments can also exercise the direct request of unconstitutionality against laws, on the grounds that the rights of the autonomous regions have been violated.[1343] The Constitution also regulates this direct request or action on the grounds of their illegality, against regional acts on the basis that the statute of the region or general law of the Republic has been violated, in which case, additional to the public bodies mentioned above, the Minister of the Republic in the autonomous region is entitled to formulate it.[1344]

The effects of the Constitutional Tribunal decisions in these cases of abstract control of norms are also expressly regulated in the Constitution. In effect, it stated that its decisions in cases of direct request of unconstitutionality has generally binding effects, thus *erga omnes*, "as from the entry into force of the provision ruled unconstitutional or illegal and shall determine the restoration with retroactive effects, of the provisions that it may have revoked."[1345] Regarding pre–constitutional legislation, that is to say, if the unconstitutionality of a norm is due to infringement of a later constitutional provision, the ruling of the Court shall produce effects only as from the entry into force of the new constitutional provision.[1346]

These two express dispositions of the Constitution lead to the consideration that the general rule existing in the Portuguese system of judicial review is that decisions declaring the unconstitutionality of a state act, have *ex–tunc*, *pro praeterito* effects,

1339 Art. 279,4.

1340 Art. 279,2.

1341 Art. 288,1.

1342 Art. 281,1,a.

1343 Art. 281,1,a. The archipelagos of the Azores and Madeira have been organized within the state, as Autonomous Regions. Art. 227.

1344 Art. 281,1,b. See also Art. 281,1,c.

1345 Art. 282,1.

1346 Art. 282,2.

except in "cases already judged", which, in principle, "shall be safeguarded, except if the Constitutional Court decides otherwise when the provision concerns penal or disciplinary matters or illegal acts in violation of mere social rules and is less favourable to the accused."[1347]

Anyway, the powers of the Tribunal in this respect are very wide, and the Constitution expressly establishes that "when required by legal security, reasons of equity or public *interest* of exceptional importance, which shall be justified, the Constitutional Tribunal may fix the effects of unconstitutionality or illegality in a more restrictive way",[1348] thus, being possible to correct the inconvenient effects that could be produced by the rigidity of the retroactive general effects of the decisions.

4. Unconstitutionality by Omission

Finally, in the Portuguese constitutional system, additional to the preventive and *a posteriori* means of judicial review, the Constitution assigns the Constitutional Court powers to exercise another means of control of the constitutionality of state action, in what is called the "unconstitutionality by omission", which is not to be found in any other Western European country and follows in a certain way, the powers attributed to the Constitutional Tribunal of Yugoslavia.

In effect, the Constitution establishes that

> At the request of the President of the Republic, the Ombudsman or, on the grounds that the rights of the autonomous regions have been violated, the President of the regional assemblies, the Constitutional Tribunal shall judge and verify failure to comply with the Constitution by omission on the part of the legislative acts necessary to implement the provisions of the Constitution.
>
> When the Constitutional Court verifies the existence of unconstitutionality by omission, it shall communicate the fact to the competent legislative organ.

This exceptional power attributed to the Constitutional Tribunal was originally established in the 1976 Constitution as the result of the negotiations carried out by the Council of the Revolution in 1975, on behalf of the Armed Forces Movement, and the Political Parties, with a view to establishing a certain number of principles which were to be compulsorily observed and maintained by the respective parliamentary groups in the Constituent Assembly.[1349]

Up to the sanctioning of the 1982 First Revision of the Constitution, in which this "constitutional control by omission" was definitively established, it was exercised on two occasions by the then Council of the Revolution. In 1977, it recommended the adoption of legislative measures to the Assembly of the Republic with a view to enforcing the norms of Article 46 of the 1976 Constitution, whereby, among other aspects, organisations with a fascist ideology were banned. The main contribution made by this Council decision lay in having spelt out the necessary conditions for the existence of "legislative omission." In the first place, it established that the

---

1347 Art. 282,3.

1348 Art. 282,4.

1349 J. CAMPINOS, *loc. cit.*, p. 35.

constitutional norm could not be self applicable and secondly, that the competent body to adopt the legislative measures must have violated its obligation to dictate norms, to a degree that it obstructed the observance of the constitutional norm by the very ones for whom the legal mandate was intended. Therefore, this condition was not verified if the legal order contained any prescriptions which made the constitutional norm applicable.[1350]

In a second case, in 1978, the Council of the Revolution recommended the competent legislative bodies to adopt legislative measures for guaranteeing the applicability of Article 53 of the Constitution to domestic servants, which conferred upon these workers the right to rest and recreation, by limiting the length of the working day, establishing the weekly rest period as well as periodic paid holidays. On this second occasion, the essential contribution of the decision lay in the extensive interpretation carried out by the Constitutional Commission regarding the initiative to request control by omission,[1351] which in the 1982 Constitution was reduced to the President of the Republic or the Ombudsman at the national level, and to the Presidents of the Regional Assemblies in cases of violation of the rights of the autonomous regions.

II. LIMITED MIXED SYSTEM OF CONSTITUTIONAL JUDICIAL REVIEW IN SWITZERLAND

The other European country that has adopted a mixed system of judicial review, although in a very limited way, is Switzerland, where judicial review is accepted regarding cantonal laws and federal executive regulations, but absolutely excluded regarding federal legislation.

1. The Absence of Judicial Review Over Federal Legislation

In effect, since the main constitutional reform of 1874 in which the judicial federal courts were organised, the Federal Tribunal was vested with the task of seeing that the Constitution and federal laws were observed[1352] and in particular, the following clause was inserted in article 113 of the Constitution:

> In all cases above mentioned the Federal Tribunal shall administer the laws passed by the Federal Assembly, and such ordinances of that Assembly as are of general application. It shall likewise act in accordance with treaties ratified by the Federal Assembly.[1353]

This norm, even though referred to what in Switzerland are called "cases of public law", that is to say, cases arising from conflicts between the confederation and the cantons or between cantons themselves, was soon interpreted by the Federal Tribunal as being applicable to all other cases, particularly to civil and criminal law cases, in the sense that in all judicial cases the Federal Tribunal was always bound to

---

1350 *Idem*, p. 42.

1351 *Idem*, p. 42.

1352 Art. 90. Constitution 1874. See the text in W.J. WAGNER, *The Federal States and their Judiciary*, The Hague 1959, p. 104.

1353 Art. 113. Constitution 1874.

apply the laws as enacted by the federal legislature, without having any power to review or control their constitutionality. On the other hand, this was a consequence of the principle of the supremacy of Parliament and its laws over all other state organs and acts, including the judiciary and it was also a consequence of the idea that democracy demanded the recognition of the absolute character of the will of the people's representatives, or of that expressed by the people themselves. Thus, the primacy of the Legislature was unquestioned as the supreme authority, the courts not being qualified to question and discuss the validity of applicability of federal legislation."[1354] That is why in a decision adopted in 1876, the Federal Tribunal stated:

> It must be recognised as a principle of ...the Swiss federal and cantonal constitutional law that the authority of the legislative powers is supreme, and the Courts are not empowered to deny the validity and applicability of a law or decree enacted by the legislative authorities on the grounds that their content is repugnant to the Constitution; it belongs to them only to check formally whether they really face a law enacted in a way conforming to the Constitution [1355]

It can be said that this doctrine is still the one prevailing in Switzerland, in spite of efforts to modify it,[1356] and a similar clause to that of article 113 was for instance inserted in the 1912 constitutional amendment, in which it was stated regarding administrative justice cases that "The administrative court shall apply federal legislation and treaties approved by the Federal Assembly." [1357]

Consequently, in the Swiss system, no judicial review is admitted either by the Federal Tribunal or by any other court in the country regarding federal laws and other acts of general effects of the federal legislature,[1358] and also regarding executive decrees with force of federal law adopted by the Federal Council executing extraordinary powers.[1359]

Therefore, judicial review is limited in Swiss constitutional system only to cantonal laws and to executive regulations at federal level, and it can be exercised, either in a diffuse or a concentrated way.

1354 E. ZELLWEGER, "El Tribunal Federal suizo en calidad de Tribunal Constitucional", *Revista de la Comisión Internacional de Juristas*, 7, 1966, p. 114.

1355 B. GER. 2, 98, 105 (1876). Quoted by W.J. WAGNER, *op. cit.*, p. 105; and E. ZELLWEGER, *loc. cit.*, p. 126.

1356 See for example, A. GRISEL, "Réflexious sur la juridiction Constitutionnelle et Administrative en Suisse", *Etudes et documents*, 28, Conseil d'Etat, Paris 1976, pp. 262–272.

1357 Art. 114 A. See the text in W.J. WAGNER, *op. cit.*, p. 106.

1358 The 1962 "Federal Law on Assembly procedures and on the form, publication and validity of legislative acts" defines them as follows: "Federal Laws are legislative acts of unlimited duration containing rules of law. Legislative acts containing rules of law are all general or abstract norms "which imposes obligations on, or grants rights to individuals and corporations, or regulates the organization, jurisdiction or functions of authorities, or establishes a procedure." Federal resolutions of general and binding effect are legislative acts of unlimited duration containing rules of law. See in E. ZELLWEGER, *loc. cit.*, p. 125.

1359 E. ZELLWEGER, *loc. cit.*, p. 127.

2. Limited Diffuse System of Judicial Review

In effect, regarding cantonal law, which, of course, due to the federal form of the state must conform to the Constitution, and also regarding federal executive regulations, not considered as "federal legislation", all the courts have the power in the Swiss system to control their constitutionality.

Indeed, as in any diffuse system of judicial review, this verification of the constitutionality of state acts, is only of an incidental and prejudicial character, motivated by the need to apply a particular cantonal norm in a concrete case. The provision that is considered to have violated the Constitution or federal law, is not annulled by the Judge, who only declares it not applicable to the resolution of the case.[1360]

On the other hand, even though, no judicial review is admitted regarding federal legislation, it has been recognised the power of all courts to verify whether a statute to be applied in a concrete case has or has not been duly published, thus, a diffuse system of judicial review is possible regarding federal legislation but only limited to formal aspects concerning its publication.[1361]

3. Limited Concentrated System of Judicial Review

In parallel with the limited diffuse system of judicial review, in the Swiss system a limited concentrated system of judicial review attributed to the Federal Tribunal has also been established, exercised by means of a direct action called the "recourse of public law."

In effect, this Federal Tribunal, as the supreme judicial organ of the country, is the supreme and last instance in all judicial cases, and particularly in criminal, civil and administrative cases, for which it is divided into various sections.

One of these sections is the Public law and administrative law section, through which the Federal Tribunal acts as the court of last resort in all administrative justice cases, and as a constitutional court.[1362]

In its character as constitutional judge, the Federal Tribunal through the "Public Law division" of its Public Law and Administrative Section is particularly empowered to resolve and settle conflicts of competences resulting from the distribution of state powers within the Federal system. It can also decide the public law recourses that can be brought before it on constitutional matters.

Regarding the first set of attributions of the Tribunal in the settlement of conflicts of attributions, its Public Law Division is in charge of resolving conflicts of attributions that may arise between federal and cantonal authorities, as well as those that may arise between cantons themselves in connection with the delimitation of the legal domain attributed to them.[1363]

1360 E. ZELLWEGER, *loc. cit.*, p. 127.

1361 W.J. WAGNER, *op. cit.*, p. 106; A. JIMÉNEZ BLANCO, "El Tribunal Federal suizo." *Boletín de jurisprudencia constitucional*, Cortes Generales, 6, Madrid 1981, p. 478.

1362 *Cf.* E. ZELLWEGER, *loc. cit.*, p. 119; A. JIMÉNEZ BLANCO, *loc. cit.*, p. 478.

1363 *Cf.* A. JIMÉNEZ BLANCO, *loc. cit.*, p. 479; E. ZELLWEGER, *loc. cit.*, p. 119.

However, where the constitutional justice powers of the Tribunal are more specifically related to judicial review matters are in the second of the competences attributed to it, concerning the resolution of public law recourses that can be brought before it on constitutional matters, against cantonal dispositions.

In the Swiss system, in effect, the recourse of public law is conceived as the means for controlling the conformity of cantonal acts[1364] particularly normative and other acts of the cantonal Legislature,[1365] with federal law, and can be exercised by any interested individual or corporation, for the following reasons: 1°) Violation of any of the citizens' constitutional rights; 2°) violation of "concordats", that is to say, public law agreements between cantons; 3°) violation of international treaties, except in cases of infringement of civil or criminal law provisions contained in some treaties by decision of the cantonal authorities; and 4°) violation of federal law dispositions relating to the delimitation of areas of competence of the authorities.[1366]

Also considered as public law recourses, are those concerning the citizens' right to vote, and those relating to cantonal elections and voting, regardless of the cantonal constitutional or federal law provisions applicable.[1367]

These Public law recourses before the Swiss Federal Tribunal are essentially of a subsidiary nature, that is to say, they are only admissible when the alleged violation of the right cannot be brought before any other judicial authority through other legal means established either under federal or cantonal law.[1368] Consequently, the action cannot be admitted unless all existing cantonal remedies have been exhausted. Nevertheless, this requisite of previous exhaustion of ordinary legal procedures does not apply to actions relating to the violation of freedom of establishment, the prohibition of double taxation in fiscal matters, the citizen's right to appear before his "natural" judge, and the right to legal aid,[1369] which can be brought before the Federal Tribunal in a principal way.

Citizens and "corporations" whose rights are violated by cantonal acts or provisions of general binding effect or who, even in the absence of any such violation, are personally affected by the said acts or provisions, are entitled to bring a public law recourse.[1370] The term "corporation" is understood by law to mean private law entities, which includes companies and professional associations.[1371]

1364 The conformity of administrative federal acts with federal law is also judge by the Federal Tribunal but through the recourse of administrative law. *Cf.* A. GRISEL, *loc. cit.*, p. 255.

1365 The control of the constitutionality of Cantonal Constitution have been excluded. *Cf.* E. ZELLWEGER, *loc. cit.*, p. 124.

1366 Art. 84 Law of Judiciary Organization. See the text in E. ZELLWEGER, *loc. cit.*, p. 120.

1367 Art. 85, a Law of Judiciary Organization.

1368 Art. 84,2 *Idem. Cf.* A. GRISEL, *loc. cit.*, p. 255; E. ZELLWEGER, *loc. cit.*, p. 122; W.J. WAGNER, *op. cit.*, p. 109.

1369 Art. 86,2 Law of Judiciary Organization.

1370 Art. 88 *Idem.*

1371 E. ZELLWEGER, *loc. cit.*, p. 123.

Exceptionally, a public law action could also be brought before the Tribunal by public law entities, to protect their sphere of autonomous action vis–à–vis administrative bodies of higher rank. In this respect, for example, a municipality can impugn acts of the canton of which it is a dependency, by means of a public law recourse brought, in this case, on the grounds of violation of municipal autonomy.[1372]

In general, the Tribunal does not have *ex–officio* powers to consider constitutional questions other than those denounced in the recourse by the claimant, and it has refused to consider facts not alleged in the ordinary judicial proceeding previously exhausted.[1373]

In any such case of the exercise of these constitutional justice powers, when the Federal Tribunal considers that a cantonal act is unconstitutional, it annuls the act with *erga omnes* effects,[1374] thus applicable to everybody and not only to the parties involved in the proceedings.

III. MIXED SYSTEM OF JUDICIAL REVIEW IN VENEZUELA

As we have seen, a complete mixed system of judicial review in Europe only exists in Portugal; and in Switzerland it also exists but in an incomplete form. The European countries have chosen to follow either the diffuse system, or more recently, the concentrated system of judicial review, attributed to a specially established constitutional court, tribunal or council. That is why the experiences of Austria, West Germany, Italy and Spain have given rise to what has been called the European model of judicial review.

We have also seen that in other parts of the world, particularly in Latin America, the two main systems of judicial review, the diffuse and the concentrated, have also been followed, but with a particular trend, namely, that of the important role generally attributed to the Supreme Court of Justice of the country. In those which follow the American model, the Supreme Court of Justice appears as the supreme interpreter of the Constitution, through the extraordinary recourses that can be brought before it; and in those which have adopted a concentrated system of judicial review, the power to declare the unconstitutionality of legislation and to annul laws is attributed exclusively to the Supreme Court of the country, the establishment of a Constitutional Court separate from the Supreme Court, being exceptional.

But in Latin America mixed systems of judicial review established since the middle of the last century, (19th century), it can also be distinguished in a few countries giving rise to what can be considered today as a Latin American model of judicial review. This mixed system has developed particularly in Brazil, Colombia, Guatemala and Venezuela, to which we will now refer to, beginning by analysing the Venezuelan system, perhaps the most complete mixed system together with that of Colombia.

1372 *Idem*, p. 123.

1373 A. GRISEL, *loc. cit.*, p. 255.

1374 W.J. WAGNER, *op. cit.*, p. 109.

1. Constitutional Supremacy and Judicial Review

The Venezuelan constitutional system is based on the principle of constitutional supremacy, the Constitution being considered as a normative charter not only organising the exercise of public power, but also establishing the fundamental rights of citizens. Thus, it is considered an embodiment of positive norms directly applicable to individuals, a characteristic that has developed from the very beginning of our constitutional process in 1811.[1375] This principle of the supremacy of the Constitution has inevitably led to the development of a system of judicial review of constitutionality of state acts, established more than a hundred years ago.[1376] The Supreme Court of Justice explained the system in 1962 when deciding a popular action brought before it against the Law of approval of the Extradition Treaty signed with the United States of America, as follows:

> The existence of a judicial control of the constitutionality of state acts exercised by the Highest Tribunal of the Republic, has been traditional in Venezuela, and is indispensable in any regime, which pretends to subsist as a state submitted to the rule of Law (*Estado de Derecho*). The unconstitutionality is always anti–juridical and contrary to the principle that compels the Public Power, in all of its branches, to subject itself to the constitutional and legal norms, which define its attributions. The unconstitutionality is an outrage against the citizen's rights and against the legal order in general, which have their supreme guarantees in the Fundamental Law of the state. In countries ruled freely, all private or governmental activities must necessarily be maintained within the limits established in the Fundamental Charter, which prescriptions, as the solemn expression of the popular will in the Public Law sphere, are norms of inescapable observance for those who govern and those who are governed, from the most humble of citizens up to the highest powers of the state. From the principles established in the Constitution, from the norms drawn up by it, whether in its organic or in its dogmatic parts, the laws and all dispositions enacted after must be simple developments; and as unconstitutional and thus, improper they would be considered if they exceed that character, as unconstitutional and also improper as would be any other act of the Public Powers which openly contravenes what is established in the fundamental Law.[1377]

As a consequence of this principle of constitutional supremacy, the 1961 Venezuelan Constitution, following a constitutional tradition that can be traced back to the 1858 Constitution[1378] established in article 215 the competence of the Supreme Court of Justice to review the constitutionality of laws and other normative acts of the national, state or municipal deliberative bodies, of executive regulations and acts

1375 See Allan R. BREWER–CARÍAS, *Instituciones políticas y constitucionales*, Caracas 1985, Vol. I, p. 342.

1376 See the comments regarding the mixed system of judicial review of constitutionality as a consequence of the principle of the supremacy of the Constitution, in R. FEO, *Estudios sobre el Código de procedimiento civil venezolano*, Caracas 1904, Vol. I, pp. 26–35; R. MARCANO RODRÍGUEZ, *Apuntaciones Analíticas sobre las materias fundamentales y generales del Código de procedimiento civil venezolano*, Caracas, Vol. I, pp. 36–38; BORJAS, *Comentarios al Código de procedimiento civil*, Caracas Vol. I, pp. 33–35.

1377 Supreme Court of Justice in Plenary Session, 15–3–62. See in *Gaceta Oficial* Nº 760 Extra., 22–3–62, pp. 3–7.

1378 See J. G. ANDUEZA, *La jurisdicción constitucional en el derecho venezolano*, Caracas 1955 p. 46.

of government adopted by the President of the Republic. That is to say, it provides for judicial review of the constitutionality of all state acts; judicial and administrative acts also being subjected to special means for reviewing their legality and constitutionality through the recourses of cassation and appeals, and through special administrative judicial actions.

In particular, judicial review of constitutionality of state acts at the national level is referred to laws and other acts with the same rank or force of law (other acts of parliament without the form of law, and Decree Laws and other government acts), and to executive regulations adopted by the national executive. At the member state level of our Federation, judicial review refers to laws issued by the Legislative Assemblies; and, at the municipal level, to Municipal Ordinances adopted by the Municipal Councils. This review power of the constitutionality of state acts allows the Supreme Court of Justice to declare them null and void when they violate the Constitution. It thus constitutes a concentrated system of control of the constitutionality of laws and other state acts.

Moreover, Article 20 of the Civil Proceedings Code allows all Courts and Tribunals of the Republic to declare all normative state acts inapplicable in a given case, when they consider them unconstitutional and, hence, to give preference to constitutional rules. Thus, the system here established is also a diffuse system of judicial review. Therefore, as now happens in the Portuguese system, it can be said of the Venezuelan system of judicial review of the constitutionality of laws and other state acts, that it is one of the most extensive in comparative law, since it mixes the diffuse system of judicial review of the constitutionality of laws with the concentrated systems.[1379]

With respect to this mixed character of the Venezuelan system, the Supreme Court has analysed the ambit of judicial review of the constitutionality of laws in our country, and has pointed out that this is the responsibility

> Not only of the Supreme Court of the Republic, but also of the judges in general, whatever their rank and standing may be. It is sufficient for an official to form part of the judiciary for him to be a custodian of the Constitution and, consequently, to apply it's ruling preferentially over those of ordinary laws... Nonetheless, the application of the fundamental rules by the judges, only has effects in the concrete case at issue and, for that very reason, only affects the interested parties to the conflict. In contrast, when constitutional illegitimacy in a law is declared by the Supreme Court when exercising its sovereign function, as the interpreter of the Constitution, and in response to the pertinent action, the effects of the decision extend *erga omnes* and have the force of law. In the first case, the review is incidental and special, and in the second, principal and general. When this happens –that is to say when the recourse is autonomous– the control is either formal or material, depending on whether the nullity has to do with an irregularity relating to the process of drafting the law, or whether –despite the

1379 See in general, Allan R. Brewer–Carías, *El control de la constitucionalidad de los actos estatales*, Caracas 1977; and also "Algunas consideraciones sobre el control jurisdiccional de la constitucionalidad de los actos estatales en el derecho venezolano", *Revista de Administración Pública*, 76, Madrid 1975, pp. 419–446.

legislation having been correct from the formalist point of view– the intrinsic content of the ruling suffers from substantial defects.[1380]

Consequently, the Venezuelan system of judicial review is a mixed one, in which the diffuse system functions in parallel with the concentrated system of judicial review assigned to the Supreme Court of Justice.

2. Diffuse System of Judicial Review

As we have said, the Venezuelan Civil Procedure Code since 1897 has established the following, in article 20:

> Art. 20. When the law whose application is demanded conflicts with any provision of the Constitution, the judges will give preference to the latter.[1381]

According to this norm, the diffuse system of judicial review allows any judge, from the lowest judicial rank to the Supreme Court of Justice, to decide not to apply a law in a concrete case that conflicts with any provision of the Constitution when the application of that law is demanded by a party to litigation. This is, no doubt, the basic consequence of the principle of the supremacy of the Constitution, as considered since the beginning of the present century by all the commentators of the Code.[1382]

According to this power attributed to all judges, the diffuse system of judicial review in Venezuela can be characterised by the following trends:

A. *Pre–eminence of the Constitution and the Nullity of Unconstitutional Acts*

Firstly as we have said, the power attributed to all judges to control the constitutionality of legislation is the natural consequence of the principle of the supremacy of the Constitution. The judges are bound by the Constitution and have the duty to apply it; therefore, if a law is unconstitutional, they cannot apply it and must give preference to the Constitution, because an unconstitutional law can have no value.

It must be said that this was the basic principle established ever since the beginning of our constitutionalism, in the 1811 Constitution in which it has been considered that an implicit diffuse judicial review system was adopted.[1383]

1380 See Federal Court (which in 1961 was substituted by the Supreme Court of Justice), 19–6–1953 *Gaceta Forense*, 1, 1953, pp. 77–78.

1381 The text of the norm in Spanish is as follows: "Cuando la ley vigente, cuya aplicación se pida, colidiere con alguna disposición constitucional, los jueces aplicarán ésta con preferencia." The text was originally adopted in the 1897 Code (Art. 10), followed by the 1904 Code (Art. 10) and the 1916 Code (Art. 7). In the 1985 Code the only change introduced in relation to the previous text, is the word "judges" which substituted the word "Tribunals." See the text of the 1897, 1904 and 1916 Codes in *Leyes y Decretos Reglamentarios de los Estados Unidos de Venezuela*, Caracas 1943, Vol. V.

1382 See note 2, Supra.

1383 H. J. LA ROCHE, *El control jurisdiccional de la constitucionalidad en Venezuela y Estados Unidos*, Maracaibo 1971, p. 24; T. "El recurso de inconstitucionalidad en la Constitución venezolana de 1811", in *El pensamiento constitucional de Latinoamérica* 1810–1830, Congreso de Academias e Institutos Históricos, Actas y Ponencias, Caracas 1962, Vol. 3, p. 208.

In effect, article 227 of the 1811 Constitution established:

> The present Constitution, the laws to be adopted in its execution and the Treaties to be subscribed under the authority of the Union Government will be the supreme law of the state in the whole Confederation, and the authorities and inhabitants of the provinces are bound to religiously obey and observe them without excuse or pretext; but the laws enacted against the text of the Constitution will have no value unless they fulfil all the required conditions for a just and legitimate revision and sanction.[1384]

According to this norm, in the same sense as the American model, unconstitutional laws were considered null and void, as they could have no effect whatsoever.

The guarantee of the Constitution in that case was the nullity of the unconstitutional act, and not its annulability. Thus the judges were not bound to apply unconstitutional laws and acts, the contrary, as established in the 1830 Constitution, all public officials had the duty not to "obey or execute orders evidently contrary to the Constitution or the laws."[1385]

Now concerning fundamental rights and freedoms, ever since the 1893 Constitution the *nullity* of the laws, which violated or harmed them, as their basic guarantee has been expressly established.[1386] That is why the present 1961 Constitution expressly establishes that

> Art.46: Every act of the Public Power which violates or impairs the rights guaranteed by this Constitution is void, and the public officials and employees who order or execute it shall be held criminally, civilly or administratively liable, as the case may be, and orders of superiors manifestly contrary to the Constitution and the laws may not serve as an excuse.

Consequently, it can be said that since the 1811 Constitution, the diffuse system of judicial review of legislation, based on the principle of the supremacy of the Constitution and the nullity and infectivity of unconstitutional acts, has existed in Venezuela following the implicit North American constitutional trends, particularly until 1897, when it was expressly established as a power of all judges in the Civil Procedure Code.

It must be mentioned also that in the 1901 Constitution, following the approval of the 1897 Civil Procedure Code, the power of all judges to control the constitutionality of laws was ratified. In that Constitution, competence to declare which disposition would prevail in a concrete case, when a lower judge *motu proprio* or at party instance, would have referred a constitutional question to the Supreme Court, was attributed to the Supreme Court. Nevertheless, it was expressly established that this referral did not have suspensive effects on the procedure, and that the lower judge was empowered to decide the constitutional question if through the opportunity of adopting his own decision, the Supreme Court opinion was not received by the lower court.[1387]

1384 See in Allan R. BREWER–CARÍAS, *Las Constituciones de Venezuela*, Madrid 1985, p. 203.

1385 Art. 186. See in Allan R. BREWER–CARÍAS, *Las Constituciones ..., cit.*, p. 353.

1386 Art. 17. See in Allan R. BREWER–CARÍAS, *Las Constituciones..., cit.*, p. 531.

1387 Art. 106, 8 in Allan R. BREWER–CARÍAS, *Las Constituciones ..., cit.*, pp. 579–580. See the comments regarding this norm in R. FEO, *op. cit.*, Vol. I, pp. 32–33.

Anyway, historically and in the present constitutional system, our country has always had, following the American model, a diffuse system of judicial review according to which all courts have the power to examine the constitutionality of laws and not to apply them when considering them to be unconstitutional, giving preference to the Constitution. Of course, the expression "laws" used in the Civil Procedure Code has always been interpreted in an extensive way, comprising not only formal laws approved by Congress, but also all normative state acts, including executive regulations.

B. *Incidental Character of the System and the* Ex–Officio *Powers of the Judges*

Following the general trends of all diffuse systems of judicial review, the Venezuelan system also has an incidental character, that is to say, the judge can only review the constitutionality of a law and decide not to apply it, when deciding a concrete case brought before him by a party, in which the constitutional question is not, of course, the principal issue submitted for his decision, but only an incidental question regarding the law which the judge must apply for the resolution of the case as required by a party.

Therefore, the power of judges to control the constitutionality of legislation can only be exercised within a concrete adversary litigation, regarding the law whose application is demanded by a party, and when the constitutional issue is relevant to the case and necessary to be resolved in their decision. But in the Venezuelan system, the constitutional issue itself can be raised *ex officio* by the judge when deciding the concrete case it not being required, as happens in the North American system, to be alleged by a party. Therefore, the Venezuelan diffuse system of judicial review although incidental, is not a control that it is exclusively exercised through an "exception of unconstitutionality"[1388] rose by a party. On the contrary, it can be exercised by the judge, *motu proprio* as stated in the 1901 Constitution.[1389]

C. *Effects of the judicial decision and absence of extraordinary means of appeals or recourses*

On the other hand, the nullity of unconstitutional laws, particularly those that violate fundamental rights; being the guarantee of the Constitution, the decision of the courts in the diffuse system of constitutional control has declarative effects. That is to say, the judge when deciding not to apply a law in a concrete case declares it unconstitutional and, therefore, considers it unconstitutional ever since its enactment (*ab initio*), thus as never having been valid and as always having been null and void. Consequently, the decision of the court in the concrete case evidently has *ex–tunc* and *pro pretaerito* or retroactive effects, preventing the unconstitutional and inapplicable law from having any effect in the case. Thus, the judge's decision is not a declaration "of nullity" of the law he considered unconstitutional, but rather a declaration that the law "is unconstitutional." In declaring the law inapplicable to the con-

1388 See a contrary opinion in H.J. La Roche, *op. cit.*, pp. 137, 140, 150, 162; and in J.G. Andueza, *op. cit.*, pp. 37–38.

1389 Art. 106, 8.

crete case, he plainly judges that the law could never have produced effects in the particular case; he judges it not to have existed and never to have done so. In other words, when he declares that the law is inapplicable to a particular case which was supposed to have been governed, in the past, by a law whose applicability is demanded by one of the parties to the case, the Judge is "ignoring" the –in his opinion– unconstitutional law, and thus considering it never having had effects on the particular case brought before him.

Of course, these declarative and *ex–tunc* effects of the decision, only refer to the concrete parties, in the concrete process in which the decision is adopted.

Thus, the decision only has *in casu et inter partes* effects,[1390] as a consequence of the incidental character (*incidenter tantum*) control. Therefore, if a law has been considered unconstitutional in a concrete judicial case decision, and the judge decided not to apply it to the case but gave preference to the Constitution, this does not mean that the law has been invalidated and is not enforceable and applicable elsewhere. According to the Civil Procedure Code, judges have no competence to make declarations of the nullity of the unconstitutional law, or to annul it, these attributions being exclusively assigned in the Constitution to the Supreme Court.[1391] Thus, in the diffuse system of review, the decision in which the judge decides not to apply a law in the concrete case only means that concerning that particular process and parties, the law must be considered unconstitutional, null and void, but with no effects regarding other cases, other judges or other individuals.

Therefore, the fact that a law is declared inapplicable by reason of unconstitutionality by a judge in a particular case does not affect its validity nor is it equivalent to a declaration of nullity. The law as such continues to be valid, and will only lose its general effects if repealed by another law [1392] or if annulled by the Supreme Court of Justice.[1393]

In any case, in the Venezuelan procedural system, the *stare decisis* doctrine has no application at all, the judges being sovereign in their decisions, only submitted to the constitution and the law. Therefore, decisions regarding the inapplicability of a law considered unconstitutional do not have binding effects, neither regarding the same judge who may change his legal opinion in other cases, nor regarding other judges or courts, even if the decision is made by a higher court. On the other hand, unlike the American or Argentinean systems, in the Venezuelan system of constitutional judicial control, there are no extraordinary means of appeal or recourses against judicial decisions in which constitutional questions are involved that could be brought before the Supreme Court.

On the contrary, judge's decisions are only subject to the ordinary means of appeal and to the recourse of cassation, following the general rules established in the Civil Procedural Code. It was only in the 1901 Constitution that the Federal Court

1390 See the Federal Court decision of 19–6–1953, in *Gaceta Forense* N° 1, 1953, pp. 77–78.

1391 *Cf.* R. MARCANO RODRÍGUEZ, *op. cit.*, Vol. I, p. 37.

1392 Art. 177, 1961 Constitution.

1393 Art. 215, 3, 4, 1961 Constitution.

was assigned the power to establish general criterion in constitutional matters referred to by lower courts, when a constitutional issue was raised in concrete judicial cases, which power was eliminated in the subsequent constitutional reform of 1904. In effect, article 106, 8 of the 1901 Constitution established as an attribution of the Federal Court, to

> Declare in the shortest possible delay which disposition must prevail in the special case which is referred to it *motu proprio* or at the instance of the interested party by the authority which is due to apply the law, in the delay established for adopting its decision, when the said authority considers that a collision exists between the Federal or state Laws with the Constitution of the Republic.[1394]

Notwithstanding this consultative power of the Federal Court, when a referral was made before it, it had no suspensive effect in the concrete process, which, said the 1901 Constitution, was not to be stopped and when the opportunity to decide it came without having received the Federal Court opinion, the lower court was to decide in accordance with the Civil Procedure Code, that is to say, reviewing by itself the constitutionality of legislation, in the concrete case.

Nevertheless, the possible contradictions that could arise between different court decisions, with the consequent uncertainty in the legal order, have been corrected ever since 1858 in Venezuelan constitutional system, through the establishment, in parallel with the diffuse system of judicial review, of a concentrated system of constitutional control assigned to the Supreme Court of Justice.

3. Concentrated system of judicial review

A. *Historical antecedents*

In effect, in parallel with the diffuse system of judicial review a concentrated system of judicial review has existed in Venezuela ever since the 1858 Constitution by attributing the power to annul laws and other normative state acts, with general effects, when declared unconstitutional, to the Supreme Court.

The 1858 Constitution in effect, attributed competence to the Supreme Court to

> Declare the nullity of legislative acts sanctioned by the Provincial Legislatures, when petitioned by any citizen, when they are contrary to the Constitution.[1395]

Thus, in 1858 a popular action was established to seek the control of the constitutionality of legislative acts adopted at provincial level. It was a limited concentrated judicial review system, which did not refer to the national legislative act, but it can be considered the direct antecedent of the current popular action established after 1893. It was originally intended to protect the invasions by the Provinces of the competences of the Central Power, and that is why in the 1864 Constitution that consolidated the Federal form of the state, the principle of protection was reverted

---

1394 Art. 106,8. See the text in Allan R. BREWER–CARÍAS, *Las Constituciones de Venezuela, cit.* p. 579.

1395 Art.113, 8. *Idem*, p. 392.

so as to sanction the invasions of the competences and rights of the Member States by the Federal level. In this sense, the 1864 Constitution expressly established that:

> Art. 92. Any act of Congress or of the National Executive which violates the rights of the Member States guaranteed by the Constitution or which harm its independence, must be declared null by the High Court, when the majority of the Legislatures demand it.[1396]

Thus, the 1864 Constitution eliminated the popular action and limited the standing to seek judicial review of legislation to the legislatures of the state members of the Federation. Nevertheless, that same Constitution attributed competence to the Federal High Court to declare which law was in force when collisions existed between the national laws, these and the member states legislation, and between the laws of the various member states[1397] which authorised some sort of judicial review regarding the legislation of the member states in relation to federal regulations.

This situation stood invariable until 1893, when the constitutional reform of that year extended the powers of judicial review of legislation of the Supreme Court to a point very similar to the present one.

The 1893 Constitution attributed competence to the Federal High Court to

> Declare which is the law, decree or resolution in force when a collision exists between the national acts, or those with one of the States, or between the acts of the States, and any of those acts with the Constitution.[1398]

In this way, the Supreme Court powers of judicial review of constitutionality were re–established, extended not only to laws, but also to decrees and resolutions, and maintaining the protective norm of the rights of the member states against the invasions of their competences by the federal or national power.[1399]

On the other hand, in the same 1893 Constitution, the guarantee of the fundamental rights of citizens was established for the first time in our constitutional history in an express form, by stating that:

> The rights recognised and established in the Constitution will not be harmed or damaged by the laws which regulate their exercise, and those which do so will be considered unconstitutional and will have no effects.[1400]

Finally, the same 1893 Constitution assigned the Federal High Court powers to declare the nullity of all state acts that could be dictated by a usurped authority or as a consequence of a direct or indirect request by force or by a subversive people's gathering,[1401] acts which were expressly declared null in the text of the Constitution.[1402]

1396 Art. 92. *Idem*, p. 422

1397 Art. 89, 9. *Idem*, p. 422

1398 Art. 110, 8. *Idem*, p. 540

1399 Art. 123. *Idem*, p. 541

1400 Art. 17. *Idem*, p. 531

1401 Art. 110, 9. *Idem*, p. 540.

1402 Arts. 118, 119, *Idem*, p. 541

Therefore, as a result of all these constitutional dispositions, we can say that it was in 1893 that a complete and effective concentrated system of judicial review was established in Venezuela, followed by the diffuse system of judicial review expressly established four years later in the Civil Procedural Code of 1897.

The system of the 1893 Constitution, with the only exception of a short period of three years between 1901 and 1904,[1403] has more or less been maintained in all subsequent constitutional texts and reforms but with a tendency to widen the means of control. In effect, in 1925 the possibility of also declaring the nullity of the Municipal ordinances that violated the Constitution was added to the powers of the Supreme Court,[1404] and in 1936, Executive Regulations were added to the list of acts submitted to constitutional judicial review.[1405] Anyway, it was in the 1936 Constitution adopted after the end of a 35 year dictatorship, that the concentrated system of judicial review was definitively established when the Constitution assigned the Supreme Court, then the Federal and Cassation Court, power to declare the nullity of all acts of the Public Powers which violated the Constitution.[1406]

Finally, it must be said that in parallel with the regulations of judicial review of the constitutionality of legislation (national, state and municipal legislation), after the 1925 Constitution[1407] the system of judicial review of administrative action was also expressly established giving way to the development of the judicial control of administrative acts through an administrative jurisdiction established within the Judiciary.[1408] Constitutional jurisdiction, therefore, was reserved to the Supreme Court and in general terms, is only concerned with legislative acts whether at national, state or municipal level, or national acts enacted in direct execution of the Constitution, like Decree–Laws and other acts of government.[1409]

In this respect, the 1961 Constitution in force today establishes as a competence of the Supreme Court of Justice the power to declare in the first place, the total or partial nullity of national laws and other acts of the legislative bodies that are in conflict with the Constitution. In the second place, it can declare the total or partial nullity of state laws, Municipal Ordinances and other acts of the deliberative bodies of the States and Municipalities that are in conflict with the Constitution; and third, the nullity of regulations and other acts of the National Executive when they violate the Constitution.[1410]

1403 The 1901 Constitution eliminated the atributions of the Supreme Court to control directly the constitutionality of legislation and only established and incidental diffuse control based in a referral of the constitutional question to the Supreme Courts by the lower courts. Art. 106, 8. See the text in Allan R. BREWER–CARÍAS, *Las Constituciones... cit.*, p. 579.

1404 Art. 34 and Art. 120,11. *Idem*, p. 705–706.

1405 Art. 34 and Art. 123, 11. *Idem*, p. 824

1406 Art. 123, 11. *Idem*, p. 824.

1407 Art. 120, 12. *Idem*, p. 715.

1408 Allan R. BREWER–CARÍAS, *El control de la constitucionalidad... cit.*, pp. 27–29.

1409 *Idem*, pp. 33–114

1410 Art. 215, ord. 3,4 and 6.

These attributions have been developed by the organic Law of the Supreme Court of Justice of 1976,[1411] in which it can be said, all state acts of a normative character (legislation of the three territorial levels and executive regulations) and all other state acts issued in direct execution of the Constitution are submitted to judicial review of constitutionality by means of a direct popular action.[1412] This action or recourse of unconstitutionality leads, indeed, to an *a posteriori* judicial review, exercised after the challenged acts have come into effect, which is the most important and most commonly exercised. But in the Venezuelan constitutional system, an *a priori* judicial review, particularly of national legislation, can also be distinguished, exercised by the Supreme Court at the request of the President of the Republic, before the promulgation of the laws. Therefore, the concentrated system of judicial review can be both preventive and *a posteriori*.

B. *Preventive control of constitutionality of laws*

In effect, since 1945, the Venezuelan Constitution has expressly established the possibility of a judicial preventive control of the constitutionality of national laws, including the special laws through which Congress approves international treaties, by the Supreme Court of Justice, at the request of the President of the Republic, and as a consequence of its powers of veto regarding legislation approved by Congress.[1413] The present 1961 Constitution in article 173 establishes, in effect, the procedure for the enactment of laws, and in particular the possibility of the Presidential veto to legislation, in the following way.

The President of the Republic shall promulgate the law within ten days after the date of receipt, but within that period, with the approval of the Council of Ministers, he may ask Congress for its reconsideration, giving an explanation with reasons, in order to amend certain provisions or withdraw its sanction of all or part of the law. The Chambers in joint session shall decide on the points raised by the President of the Republic and may write a new text for the provisions objected to and those connected therewith.

When a decision has been adopted by two thirds of those present, the President of the Republic shall proceed with the promulgation of the law within five days following its receipt, and he may not offer new objections. But when a simple majority has reached the decision, the President of the Republic may choose between promulgating the law or returning it again to Congress within the same five–day period for a new and final reconsideration. In this latter case the decision of the Chambers

---

1411 Art. 42, ord. 1,2,3,4,11,12 of the Organic Law of the Supreme Court of Justice (LOCSJ), 30–7–76, *Gaceta Oficial* N° 1893 Extra, 30–7–76.

1412 Nevertheless, the Supreme Court has established in a decision of the Plenary Session of 29–4–1965 that the Laws of approval of international treaties could not be submitted to judicial review. See the decision and critics in Allan R. BREWER–CARÍAS, *El control de la constitucionalidad... cit.*, pp. 48–52.

1413 Art. 91, Constitution 1945. See in Allan R. BREWER–CARÍAS, *Las Constituciones... cit.*, p. 850. In the same sense, Art. 90, Constitution 1953, *Idem*, p. 947.

in joint session is definitive, even by a simple majority, and promulgation of the law must be made within five days following its receipt.

In any case –adds article 173 of the Constitution– if the objection is based on unconstitutionality, the President of the Republic may, within the period fixed for the promulgation of a law, that is to say, within five days following the receipt of the law after Congress' reconsideration, have recourse to the Supreme Court of Justice, requesting its decision as to the alleged unconstitutionality.[1414] The Court shall decide within a period of ten days, counted from the date of receipt of the communication from the President of the Republic. Nevertheless, if the Court denies the complaint of unconstitutionality, or does not decide within the aforementioned period, the President of the Republic must promulgate the law within five days after the decision of the Court or the expiration of the period indicated.[1415]

On the contrary, if the Court accepts the alleged unconstitutionality it must decide the case and that will prevent the sanctioned law from being promulgated.[1416]

Although the Constitution does not establish the possibility and consequences of a delayed decision of the Court upon the unconstitutionality of a law at the request of the President, after the expiry of the delay of ten days established in the Fundamental text, it can be considered that the expiry of that delay and the subsequent compulsory promulgation of the law, do not prevent the Court from the possibility of declaring the nullity of the law once in effect, based on its concentrated powers of judicial review of promulgated legislation.

C. *Direct control of constitutionality*

Additionally to the diffuse and preventive systems of judicial review in the Venezuelan constitutional system, the control of the constitutionality of legislation – national, state and municipal legislation– and other state acts issued in direct execution of the Constitution, can also be exercised in a concentrated way by the Supreme Court of Justice at the request of any body, through a popular action, whose antecedents can be traced back to 1858.

(a) Popular action and the principal character of the process

In effect, the fundamental feature of the judicial review powers of the Supreme Court to control the constitutionality of legislation is that it has been set up as a consequence of a popular action, that is to say, of a recourse open to any inhabitant of the Republic in full possession of his rights.[1417]

1414 Art. 42,2 LOCSJ attributed powers to the Court to "decide upon the Unconstitutionality of laws requested by the President of the Republic before its promulgation."

1415 Art. 173. 1961 Constitution.

1416 Thus, in this case, Article 175 of the Constitution which confers the President and Vice–President of the Congress to promulgate laws not promulgated by the President of the Republic, within the prescribed delay, does not apply.

1417 See the decision of the Federal Court (CF) of 2–2–60 in *Gaceta Forense* N° 27, Caracas 1960, pp. 107–108; and the decision of the Supreme Court of Justice, in Politico–Administrative Chamber (CSJ–SPA) of 3–10–63, *Gaceta Forense* N° 42 Caracas 1963, pp.

Thus, the concentrated system of judicial review in Venezuela is always of a principal character, which can only be exercised by the Supreme Court when a popular action is brought before it. This popular action, as stated by the Supreme Court in 1971, is open to:

> Any member of the general public (hence its name) is intended to defend a public interest which is, at the same time, the simple interest of the petitioner who, for this reason alone, need not be vested with any other standing or judicial interest.

For this reason, the popular action in Venezuela is instituted, the Court has added:

> To contest the validity of an act by the Public Power, which by virtue of its normative and general character, acts *erga omnes* and thus its validity affects, and is of interest to all, equally.[1418]

From this stems one of the great differences between the popular action of unconstitutionality and actions seeking judicial review of administrative acts. The first requires no special standing: a "simple interest" in legality is sufficient. By contrast, if an administrative act with individual effects is contested in the administrative jurisdiction, it is required that the petitioner is entitled to some subjective right, or have a personal,– legitimate and direct interest in the legality of the act.[1419]

But regarding the popular action, it must be pointed out that its popularity, traditionally wider, has been restricted in some way since 1976 by the Organic Law of the Supreme Court of Justice, which requires that the challenged law must violate "the rights and interests of the petitioner" in some way.[1420]

In this way, the traditional, absolutely "popular" nature of the action of unconstitutionality has been legally restricted, but, without it ceasing to be a "popular action."

In effect, this restriction can be considered reasonable, and can only affect standing in extreme cases: for instance, if the challenged law is a law of a member state, at least it is required that the petitioner be resident of the said state or has some particular interest located in that state.[1421]

Anyway, doubts about the extent of the restriction to the popularity of the action have been clarified by the Supreme court, which has considered that the legal reference to the need that the challenged law affected "the rights and interests" of the petitioner does not mean that the popular action has been eliminated, and that a special standing requirement has been established to bring such action before the Court. The object of the popular action, the Court has said, is the "objective defence of the

---

16–20; of 6–4–64, *Gaceta Oficial* N° 27.373 of 21–2–64; of 30–5–63 *Gaceta Forense* N° 52, Caracas 1968, p. 109; and of 25–9–73, *Gaceta Oficial* N° 1643 Extra. 21–3–74.

1418 See CSJ–SPA, 18–2–71 in *Gaceta Oficial* N° 1472 Extra. 11–6–71. *Cf.* CSJ–SPA, 6–2–64 in *Gaceta Oficial* N° 27373, 21–2–64.

1419 See, for example, CSJ–SPA, 18–7–71 in *Gaceta Oficial* N° 1472 Extra. 11–6–71. See article 121 LOCSJ.

1420 Art. 112 LOCSJ.

1421 Allan R. BREWER–CARÍAS, *El control de la constitucionalidad... cit.*, p. 122.

majesty of the Constitution and its supremacy" and if it is true that the Organic Law of the Supreme Court requires that the petitioner is affected in his rights or interests, this expression must be interpreted in a "restrictive way." Thus the Court has concluded that when the popular action is exercised against legislative acts,

> A presumption exists that at least relatively, the challenged act of general effects, affects the rights or interests of the petitioner in his condition as a Venezuelan citizen in some way unless the contrary shows itself evident from the text of the complaint.[1422]

Anyway, from this popular character of the recourse of unconstitutionality another difference results regarding the recourses established for reviewing administrative action. As the action of unconstitutionality refers to legislative acts, thus with general effects or those with the same rank as laws, it is not subject to any expiry period; it is inextinguishable.[1423] However, judicial actions against administrative acts, when referred to acts with particular effects must be exercised within a delay of six months,[1424] after which they expire.

In relation to the popular nature of the action of unconstitutionality, it is also clear that, as it is open to any person whose rights and interests have been violated, the fact that deficiencies may exist in the petitioner's legal representation is no impediment to acceptance of the recourse, since the supposed legal representative could equally well bring the action in a personal capacity.[1425]

On the other hand, not only individuals and public corporations have standing to bring a popular action of unconstitutionality before the Supreme Court, but the Prosecutor General is also entitled to do so[1426] and, in general, any public officer. Thus, even the President of the Republic has been recognised by the Supreme Court as having standing to bring a popular action against legislative acts before the Court.[1427]

(b) *Objective character of the process*

The direct consequence of the popular character of the action for requesting judicial review of legislation by the Supreme Court in the Venezuelan system is the objective character of the process developed before the Court. The action is not presented against a state organ, for example, the Congress or the President of the Republic at all, but is only directed against a state act: the law. Thus, there are no parties to the process in the strictest sense. The petitioner is not a plaintiff and there is no defendant in the strict sense. The process is a judicial process against a state act,

---

1422 See decision of the Supreme Court of Justice in Plenary Session (CSJ–CP) of 30–6–82 in *Revista de Derecho Público* N° 11, Caracas 1982, pp. 135–138.

1423 See CSJ–SPA, 3–10–63 in *Gaceta Forense* N° 42, 1963, pp. 20–21.

1424 Art. 134 LOCSJ.

1425 See CF 12–6–52, *Gaceta Forense* N° 1, Caracas 1953, pp. 48–50; CF 22–2–60, *Gaceta Forense* N° 27, 1960, pp. 107–108; and CSJ–SPA, 25–9–73, in *Gaceta Oficial* N° 1643 Extra. 21–3–74.

1426 Art. 116 LOCSJ.

1427 See CSJ–SPA 3–10–63 in *Gaceta Forense* N° 42, 1963, pp. 19–20.

for instance a law, which can be initiated by any individual or corporation, or by any public official, even a member of the Supreme Court in his personal capacity. Thus, if it is true that the Court in itself does not have self initiating power to act as a constitutional judge, and an action must be brought before it for exercising its powers of judicial review,[1428] this popular action could personally be exercised by a member of the Court.

On the other hand, as there are no defendants in the process it is not required that any person be summoned;[1429] and only the head of the legislative body and the Prosecutor General are notified, the latter in cases in which he himself is not the petitioner.[1430] In any case, the Court must order the publishing of a notice requesting the intervention of any interested person in the process. Thus, in the same way that any citizen whose rights and interests have been prejudiced may exercise the action of unconstitutionality of laws and other state acts of legislative rank, so any citizen with the same simple interest has the right to present writs and briefs to the Court, against or in defence of the law or act being challenged.[1431]

In any case, the popular action of unconstitutionality must be brought before the Supreme Court by means of a petition for remedy in which the petitioner must clearly state the act which he is impugning[1432] and indicate precisely the breach of the Constitution denounced – that is to say, both the grounds for the petition and the constitutional rules that are said to have been violated.[1433] However, given that this is a popular action in which the validity of a law and the supremacy of the Constitution are at stake, in our opinion the Court is able to appraise by virtue of its function, whether the contested act is in breach of the Constitution, as a result of defects not alleged by the petitioner,[1434] and does not have to limit the hearing to the unconstitutionality denounced by it.[1435] Therefore if it is true that the popular action must be

1428 Art. 82 LOCSJ

1429 See Federal and Cassation Court in Politico–Administrative Chamber (CFC–SPA) 20–11–40, in *Memoria de la Corte Federal y de Casación*, 1941, pp. 264–268.

1430 Art. 116 LOCSJ.

1431 Art. 137 LOCSJ. Before the promulgation of the 1976 LOCSJ, see in contrary sense CSJ–CP, 12–6–68 in *Publicaciones del Senado*, 1968, p. 190; and CSJ–SPA, 27–5–70, *Gaceta Forense* N° 68, 1970, p. 111.

1432 Art. 113 LOCSJ. *Cf.* CSJ–SPA, 23–1–69 in *Gaceta Forense* N° 63, 1969, p. 95.

1433 Art. 113 LOCSJ. *Cf.* decision of the Federal and Cassation in Plenary Session (CFC–CP), 14–12–50 in *Gaceta Forense* N° 6, 1950, pp. 46–47; CSJ–SPA, 11–8–64, *Gaceta Forense* N° 45, 1964, pp. 185–186.

1434 In this respect, the Attorney General's Office has indicated that the constitutionality of legislative acts is a matter of prime public interest. Thus, in cases in which such matters are considered, the judges powers are not, nor can be, limited by what is alleged or proven in the complaint. See *Doctrina de la Procuraduría General de la República 1963*, Caracas 1964, pp. 23–24.

1435 As has been held by the Supreme Court. See CSJ–CP, 15–3–62. *Gaceta Oficial* N° 760 Extra, 22–3–62. In this respect, J.G. ANDUEZA holds that the decision of the Court may not contain *ultra petita*, *op. cit.*, p. 37.

brought before the Court by a petitioner[1436] the Supreme Court is not totally subject to his will, and if the petitioner for instance, abandons the action once undertaken, the Court is empowered to continue with the hearing.[1437]

(c) Grounds for the action

The only grounds that can be claimed for the action of unconstitutionality are violations or collisions with the Constitution; that is to say, grounds of unconstitutionality[1438] whether of a substantive or of a formal or adjective character.

The Supreme Court of Justice, however, has maintained that not all constitutional rules, when violated, provide grounds for the exercise of judicial review.

On the contrary, it has frequently been required that a directly operative rule is at issue, and the Court has not annulled a law when violations of a programmatic rule have been alleged.[1439] This does not mean, however, that judicial review of legislation cannot be exercised based on constitutional principles.

For instance, article 50 of the Constitution expressly establishes that:

> Art. 50. The enunciation of rights and guarantees contained in this Constitution must not be construed as a denial of others which, being inherent in the human person, are not expressly mentioned herein. The lack of a law regulating these rights does not impair the exercise thereof.

Thus, the Supreme Court of Justice could exercise judicial review control of legislation, on the grounds of violations of rights inherent in the human person, not enunciated expressly in the Constitution.

Anyway, the complaint of unconstitutionality must necessarily involve a "logical link –by way of a serious and necessary motivation– between the act contested and the rule which is said to have been broken by it."[1440] For this reason, the Court has considered complaints of infractions of constitutional rules to be formally insufficient when such a link does not appear in the petition.

In any case, it is clear that the act, which is challenged, may constitute a breach of the Constitution when it contradicts the spirit and purpose of a constitutional rule,[1441] and not only when there is a literal contradiction between the rules and the challenged act.

1436 Art. 82 LOCSJ

1437 Art. 87 LOCSJ, *Cf.* J.G. ANDUEZA, *op. cit.*, p. 37

1438 Reasons of illegality may not thus be alleged. See CSJ–SPA, 13–2–68, in *Gaceta Forense* N° 59, 1969, pp. 85–86.

1439 See CSJ–CP, 12–6–69, in *Gaceta Forense* N° 65, 1969, p. 10; CSJ–SPA, 27–4–69, in *Gaceta Forense* N° 64, 1969, p. 23; and CSJ–SPA, 13–2–68 in *Gaceta Forense* N° 59, pp. 85–86.

1440 See CSJ–SPA, 21–12–67, in *Gaceta Forense* N° 58, 1968, p. 68.

1441 See the decision of the Federal Court, 25–3–58, in *Gaceta Forense* N° 19, 1958, p. 58. To the contrary, the Attorney General's Office has maintained that an infraction of the "motives" of the Constitution cannot be the cause for the annulment of a legal text. See *Doctrina de la Procuraduría General de la República 1964*, Caracas 1965, p. 158. Elsewhere, how-

(d) Content of the Court's decision

According to the provisions of the Organic Law of the Supreme Court of Justice, in its final decision, the Court, once the grounds on which the action has been founded have been examined, shall declare the nullity of the challenged act or of its articles when accepted.[1442]

Accordingly, the Court is under an obligation to examine *all* the grounds on which the action founded, but the Organic Law does not limit this appraisal solely to those grounds alleged by the petitioner. In view of the issue of unconstitutionality involved in these popular actions, in my opinion as the procedure is in the nature of an inquiry, the Court is able to assess grounds for unconstitutionality, which are not alleged by the petitioner.

Regarding the contents of the decision, the Supreme Court pointed out in 1966 that:

> It is the function of the Court, when exercising its power to review the constitutionality of acts of the legislative bodies, to declare the nullity of the act which is challenged if it is in any way in conflict with the precepts of the Constitution, and as a consequence of that declaration, to proclaim the legal annulment or, alternatively, to sustain it in full force instead of the assumptions which were advanced.[1443]

In 1976, however, the Organic Law of the Supreme Court of Justice, in the provisions common to the popular action and to the recourses for judicial review of administrative action, includes an article which after insisting that "In its final decision, the Court shall declare whether or not the nullity of the act which is being contested is admitted, and shall determine the effects of its decision over time",[1444] it adds the following:

> Art. 131. ...Also, according to the terms of the corresponding petition, the Court may order the payment of sums of money and the restitution of damages, for whose origin the Administration has responsibility and may also make the necessary provisions for re–establishing the subjective legal situations prejudiced by the activity of the administration.

The placing of this rule might lead us to think that the Court's verdict when deciding upon a popular action may have a condemnatory content. However, the references the article makes to "the Administration" and to "administrative activity" would make it inapplicable to any supposed responsibility of the state for a legisla-

---

ever, the same Attorney General's Office has held that the Constitution is being violated when the law intends to achieve ends different to those proposed by the Constitution, and not only when there exists some literal contradiction between the rule in the Constitution and the legal rule. See *Doctrina de la Procuraduría General de la República 1969*, Caracas 1970, p. 111. In general, on the various grounds for unconstitutionality of laws, see *Doctrina de la Procuraduría General de la República 1966*, Caracas 1967, pp. 170–174.

1442 Articles 119 and 130.

1443 See CSJ–SPA, 20–1–66, in *Gaceta Forense* N° 51, p. 13. *Cf.* CFC–SPA, 2–12–41, in *Memoria de la Corte Federal y de Casación*, 1942, pp. 335–338, and 13–7–42, in *Memoria de la Corte Federal y de Casación,* 1943, pp. 174–175.

1444 Art. 131. Repeating what is expressed in article 119.

tive act. This shows the legislature's intention of confining the damages claimed only to cases of judicial review of administrative action.

Finally, it must be said that the decision of the Supreme Court can also be that of rejecting the action when without grounds, and in particular, if the Court considers that the action was rash and obviously unfounded, it can impose a fine on the petitioner,[1445] through which the possible inconveniences that can be produced by the popular character of the action, can be overcome.

D. *Effects of concentrated control decisions*

As we have seen, the Court decision in the concentrated system of judicial review can be that of accepting the petition and thus, declaring the nullity of the unconstitutional challenged law, or it can also be that of rejecting the action dismissing the alleged unconstitutionality of the law. The effects of those decisions, are, of course, different, as the Supreme Court has established.

(a) Effect of the dismissal decisions

In effect, in cases in which the Court decision is to declare the action unjustified, thus considering the reported unconstitutional defects to be without basis, the effects of the decision are *erga omnes* with respect to the constitutionality of the law, at least as far as it concerns the challenged articles and the defects reported.[1446] Moreover, in relation to these rejected defects, the decision has the force of *res judicata*, which, of course, does not extend to other similar legislative acts, which may be contested for the same defects. In this respect, the Civil Cassation Chamber of the Supreme Court of Justice has analysed this problem when considering the effects of a decision of the Politico–Administrative Chamber of the same Supreme Court in which a Municipal Ordinance was annulled on the grounds of unconstitutionality. The situation was as follows: the Politico Administrative Chamber of the Supreme Court in a previous decision had dismissed a popular action exercised on the grounds of unconstitutionality against a Municipal Ordinance of one Municipality of the Republic (in the case of the *Bocono* District); and in a civil and different procedure in which a Municipal Ordinance of another Municipality (in the case of the *Valera* District) –but similar to the former– had to be applied, a party alleged its constitutionality, bringing before the Cassation Chamber of the Supreme Court the previous decision of the Politico–Administrative Chamber.

In this respect the Cassation Chamber stated that:

> It is to be observed that, although said decision produces *res judicata erga omnes*, this is limited strictly to the matter itself which was decided on, that is, the constitutionality of the ordinance of the *Bocono* District, and there can be no question of extending it to that of the *Valera* District, nor to any other, despite the fact that they deal with the same matter and that their regulations are, by chance, similar.

1445 Art. 119.

1446 See CSJ–CPA, 20–1–66, in *Gaceta Forense* N° 51, 1966, p. 13.

> In this case, the question of the constitutionality of the *Valera* District Ordinance was raised, both as incidental and as an exception, and the lower courts which decided in this case were completely at liberty to consider and decide, under Article 7 of the Civil Procedures Code, whether or not the Ordinance brought before them was unconstitutional, without being bound to any *res judicata* whatever, because there was no such thing. They found that the Ordinance in question is not unconstitutional, and ordered that it be complied with.
>
> The same occurs with this Civil, Mercantile and Labour Cassation Chamber , which is not bound in the least by the *res judicata* pronounced in some different matter, in which a decision was reached on the constitutionality of an Ordinance, different from the one which is required to be complied with here. Had the decision of the Political and Administrative Chamber dealt with the *Valera* District ordinance, then for this Chamber –as for all– the constitutionality of that Ordinance would have been beyond discussion, as it would have been covered by *res judicata.*
>
> As it is not precisely that Ordinance which is at issue, but another different one, this Chamber has the full and absolute jurisdiction, liberty and discretion to decide, for the purposes of these proceedings, whether the Ordinance that is in question here is in conflict with the National Constitution or not, in terms of the infractions of which the challenged judicial decision is accused, as a result of the lower judge having complied with the provisions of that Ordinance which, according to the appellant, are unconstitutional.
>
> The criterion established by that Politico Administrative Chamber when setting out the grounds for its decision, merits the greatest respect and attention from this Civil Cassation Chamber when reaching verdicts on similar matters, but does not bind it –in the same way that its own criterion on matters decided previously does not bind it– if it finds sufficient reasons to modify it.[1447]

A few basic principles can be deduced from this Supreme Court decision of 1963:

First, the absolute powers of all judges to control the constitutionality of legislation through the diffuse system of judicial review.

Second, the power of the Supreme Court to control the constitutionality of legislation in a concentrated way, the decisions adopted in this case, having *erga omnes* effects.

Third, the *res judicata* effects of the decisions of the Supreme Court concerning the constitutionality of legislation, either when a legislative act is annulled or when a popular action of unconstitutionality is dismissed, only refers to the particular and specific law challenged before the Court, and cannot be extended to other legislative acts.

Therefore, the decision of the Supreme Court dismissing a popular action against a legislative act, and thus, admitting its constitutionality, has *erga omnes* and *res judicata* effects in the sense that the constitutionality of the act must be accepted by all courts who are bound to follow the criterion established by the Supreme Court. Hence, they cannot through their diffuse judicial review powers decide not to apply the law on the grounds of its constitutionality. Particularly in another decision of the Civil, Mercantile and Labour Cassation Chamber of the Supreme Court of Justice of

---

1447 See Civil, Commercial and Labor Cassation Chamber of the Supreme Court of Justice, (CSJ–SCCMT), 12–12–63, in *Gaceta Forense* Nº 42, 1963, pp. 667–672.

1971, the Court was even clearer. It established that a decision by the Politico Administrative Chamber of the Court in which it dismissed a popular action of unconstitutionality should necessarily be applied by the Cassation Chamber, as well as by all Courts, as it was a pronouncement with *erga omnes* force. By virtue of this, the Cassation Chamber allowed a remedy for cassation, sought with respect to a lower court decision which had not applied a Politico Administrative Chamber's decision which had considered a municipal act valid, disallowing a petition for its annulment.[1448]

(b) Effects of decisions declaring the nullity of the legislative act

The decision of the Court when declaring the challenges legislative act annulled –either totally or with respect to those of its articles against which action is lodged– it produces cessation of the effects of the act, and the Court being also authorized to declare null all other acts carried out on the basis of the act which is declared null.[1449]

In such cases, the effects of the Court's decision, as we said, are of general value that is to say *erga omnes* and the Supreme Court itself has always maintained this. For instance in 1938, the former Federal and Cassation Court sustained the following:

> The Federal and Cassation Court is the highest level in the judicial hierarchy; *res judicata* established by it, even supposing it were mistaken doctrinally, is the last word by the Judiciary, against which nothing and nobody can prevail in law, neither the Court itself, nor the other two Powers(of the state). As it is a federal institution with exclusive power to annul –*erga omnes*– the laws and acts of the Public Power, which are in violation of the Constitution, it thus constitutes the sovereign interpreter of the constitutional text and of ordinary laws, and the sole judge of acts by the Public Powers and high officials of state. Any official, however high–ranking he may be, or any of the other Public Powers which seek their own interpretation of the Law to prevail over the interpretation and application established by the Court

---

1448 See CSJ–SCCMT, 11–8–71, in *Gaceta Forense* N° 73, 1971, p. 477. In this respect, the Attorney General's Office has described the effects of a declaration denying a popular action of unconstitutionality, in the following terms: "The decision on constitutionality grounds like any other judicial decision, produces *res judicata*. That... obtained in objective jurisdiction, whether it be favourable or unfavourable, always produces effects *erga omnes*. Consequences of great interest, such as that of irrevocability, follow from this principle. When the Federal Court declares the action inadmissable because the state act which is challenged lacks the defects which are denounced against, this decision may not be reviewed as it enjoys all the characteristics of any decision which produces *res judicata*: it may not be discussed nor changed." "In a case in which the Federal Court has denied a popular action of unconstitutionality, and nonetheless, this is brought again, for the same reasons and supported by the same constitutional provisions, the Court must disallow the new action as this is already *res judicata*. In consequence, the Court should apply *ex–officio* the previous decision or decide the exception of *res judicata* filed by the Attorney General. (J.G. ANDUEZA, *La Jurisdicción Constitutional en el derecho venezolano*, Universidad Central de Venezuela, Facultad de Derecho, Vol. II, Caracas, p. 99)". See *Doctrina de la Procuraduría General de la República 1963*, Caracas 1964, p. 199.

1449 See CSJ–CP, 4–4–74, in *Gaceta Oficial* N° 1.657, Special, 7–6–74.

> when reaching decisions and verdicts on the same matter, usurps power and violates the Constitution and the laws of the Republic.[1450]

In this respect, the same former Federal and Cassation Court described its decisions in 1939 as "provisions complementary to the Constitution and Laws of the Republic, which produce *erga omnes* effects";[1451] and in a decision in 1949 it indicated that its decisions "come to form a special legislation, arising from the secondary Constitutive Power which this High Court exercises in these matters."[1452]

The former Federal Court that followed the latter as the constitutional body for judicial review of legislation agreed with this criterion, and in 1953, indicated that as its decisions have *erga omnes* effects, they "take on force of law."[1453]

More recently, the Civil, Mercantile and Labour Cassation Chamber of the Supreme Court of Justice was precise in this respect in a decision on 12 December, 1963:

> Absolute review of constitutionality is exercised firstly by the full–court session of the Supreme Court of Justice (*Pleno* Court) when it declares the nullity of a national law by reason of its unconstitutionality. This decision deprives the law, or that part of it which is annulled, of effect, and has the force of *res judicata, erga omnes*. This nullity is declared as a result of what is known as a popular action.
>
> A similar power is exercised by the Politico–Administrative Division of this Supreme Court, also by popular action –but only with respect to state laws and Municipal ordinances– and its verdict also produces *res judicata, erga omnes*.
>
> This is to say that the declaration of the constitutionality or unconstitutionality of a law by principal (popular) action is definitive and produces effects against everyone, since that supposed law ceases to be such from the moment it is declared unconstitutional. The same occurs with state Laws and Municipal Ordinances which are pronounced unconstitutional.[1454]

Consequently, according to the doctrine established by the Court, the verdict declaring the unconstitutionality of a law, and thereby annulling it, has *erga omnes* effects and an absolute character as *res judicata.*

E. *Question of the temporal effects of concentrated constitutional review*

In the context of the effects of Supreme Court decisions declaring nullity of laws by reason of unconstitutionality, the fundamental problem that doubtlessly arises in Venezuela is that of the moment in which these are produced. In other words: Is the law which is declared null considered to have produced effects until declared null by

---

1450 See CSJ–SPA, 17–11–38, in *Memoria de la Corte Federal y de Casación 1939*, pp. 330–334.

1451 See CFC–SPA, 21–3–39, in *Memoria de la Corte Federal y de Casación 1940*, p. 176.

1452 See CFC–SPA, 16–12–40, in *Memoria de la Corte Federal y de Casación* 1941, p. 311.

1453 See CF, 19–6–53, *Gaceta Forense* N° 1, 1953, pp. 77 and 78. The Supreme Court has also held in a decision of its Politico Administrative Chamber that "the effects of the decisions issued by the Court when exercising this power only extend to the time during which the constitutional precet on which they are based continues valid." See in *Gaceta Forense* N° 62, 1968, p. 106–113.

1454 See CSJ–SCCMT, 12–12–63, in *Gaceta Forense* N° 42, 1963, pp. 667 to 672.

the Court, or is it considered, on the contrary, never to have produced effects? From another point of view: Does the Court's decision have effect from the moment it is published, or are its effects retroactive to the moment the act that has been annulled was first published?

The Organic Law of the Supreme Court of Justice of 1976, as we have seen, does not resolve the question. It only establishes that in its decision, the Supreme Court must "determine the effects of its decision in time."[1455] Now, with, two systems of judicial review: the diffuse and the concentrated systems, existing in parallel in the Venezuelan constitutional system, the confusion about the judicial review decision effects in both cases, and the application of the doctrine of the nullity guarantee of the diffuse system to the concentrated system, ignoring the difference between them, has been frequent.

Of course, in order to define this problem accurately, it is necessary to distinguish clearly the effects of the diffuse system of judicial review of constitutionality of state acts totally different from the effects of the concentrated system of judicial review of constitutionality. As we have said, the confusion, which has existed between the effects of these two types of review, has lead to error even within the Supreme Court Chambers themselves.

(a) Principles referring to both systems of judicial review

We have said, in effect, that under the diffuse system of judicial review, any judge in a concrete case may appraise the constitutionality of a law, decide it is unconstitutional, and thus, not apply it to the resolution of the case in question, with *inter partes* effects. In this way, all judges of the Republic are constitutional judges. We have also pointed out that, in Venezuela, a concentrated system of judicial review assigned to the Supreme Court of Justice, also exists. In this role, it is considered the supreme interpreter[1456] and defender[1457] of the Constitution, responsible for being the balancing point in the application of the principle of the separation of powers, [1458] (84) when deciding whether the "juridical extinction" of legislative acts challenged through a popular action or when maintaining them in full force.[1459]

The effects of constitutional review differ in the two cases, and in the absence of a law specifically governing constitutional jurisdiction,[1460] solutions must be found in comparative law, which have frequently been utilized by the Supreme Court of

1455 Art. 119 and 131 LOCSJ

1456 This implies the irreversibility of its decisions. See Article 211 of the Constitution. The doctrine has, however, been established for many years by the Court itself. See, for example, CFC–SPA, 17–11–38, in *Memoria de la Corte Federal y de Casación 1939*, p. 330.

1457 See CFC–SPA, 4–3–41, in *Memoria de la Corte Federal y de Casación* 1942, p. 128–130.

1458 See CFC–SPA, 3–5–39, in *Memoria de la Corte Federal y de Casación 1940*, p. 217; and 17–4–41, in *Memoria de la Corte Federal y de Casación 1942*, p. 182.

1459 See CSJ–SPA, 20–1–66, in *Gaceta Forense* Nº 51, 1968, p. 13.

1460 See, for example the Draft Constitutional Jurisdiction Law in Comisión de Administración Pública, *Informe sobre la reforma de la administración pública nacional*, Caracas 1972, Vol II, p. 47 et seq. See the text also in Humberto J. LA ROCHE, *op. cit.*, pp. 215–238.

Justice when reaching its decisions. But, indeed, it is neither appropriate nor possible to apply the characteristics of constitutional review of laws in the American model, which is exclusively diffuse in nature, to constitutional review of laws as exercised by the Supreme Court of Justice of Venezuela, which is a concentrated one.

As we have said, in the diffuse system of judicial review of the constitutionality of law assigned in Venezuela to all Courts, the decision declaring the inapplicability of a law considered unconstitutional in a concrete case does not affect its validity. Thus it has only a declarative effect, extended only *inter partes*, and *pro pretaerito*. In the words of André and Susan Tunc in their masterful analysis of the North American constitutional system, with respect to decisions in the diffuse system of judicial review:

> The law is neither repealed nor annulled. It is purely and simply not recognized, as if it were not a law, but rather, it could be said, a simple appearance of law, and the rights of the parties are regulated as if it had never been approved... The Court is limited, purely and simply, to ignore the law ... From (which)... stems the retroactive effect of the declaration of unconstitutionality.[1461]

Consequently, the "retroactivity" of the declaration of inapplicability of a law only makes sense when we bear in mind that the judge considers it never to have produced effects, in which case the declaration of unconstitutionality operates *ex tunc*, as it is simply a decision declaring pre–existing unconstitutionality or nullity. In this respect, for instance, we have said that it is justified to deliberate on the constitutionality of a law, which, although already repealed, was applied while still in force to the particular case, which the judge is hearing. Although the law may already have been repealed at the time of the decision, the declaration that it is inapplicable is important to the proceedings.[1462]

However, as we already know, these effects of the diffuse system of judicial review are quite different to those of the concentrated system of judicial review, as have been clearly developed in comparative law. In the concentrated system of judicial review as exercised by the Supreme Court in the Venezuelan system, the Court "declares the nullity" of the law[1463] that is to say, annuls it. Up to the moment when the Court's decision is published, the law must be considered valid and effective, producing all its effects despite its unconstitutionality.

In fact, as Professor Cappelleti indicated, when emphasising the difference between the concentrated and diffuse methods of constitutional review:

> It can be said that, while the United States' system of judicial review of constitutionality of laws has a purely *declaratory character*, conversely, the Austrian system has the nature of

1461 See A. and S. TUNC, *Le système constitutionnel des Etats Unies d'Amerique*, Paris 1954, Vol. II, pp. 294 and 295.

1462 It has thus been said that, if the judicial verdict passed in constitutional review of laws has retroactive effects, as occurs with diffuse review, then clearly reapealed laws may be annulled, since this puts an end to the effects which the law may have produced while in force. See J.G. ANDUEZA, *op. cit.*, pp. 56–57.

1463 Art. 215, paragraphs 3 and 4. 1961 Constitution.

a *constitutive* control of invalidity, and consequent inefficacy of laws contrary to the Constitution. From this, it is quite coherent to conclude that while in the first system, the effects (purely declarative) operate *ex tunc* that is, retroactively –it is, in effect, a simple declaration of a pre–existing nullity–, in the Austrian system, on the contrary, the effects of the decision of unconstitutionality (which are constitutive, that is to say, of annulment, operate *ex nunc*, and thus *pro futuro*, which excludes retroactive effects of the annulations.[1464]

To this difference between the diffuse and concentrated constitutional judicial review systems of legislation, another fundamental one must be added – in the latter, the "general" nature of the annulment, which while lacking retroactive effects (since, as has been said, these are *ex nunc* or *pro futuro*), as we have seen do however operate *erga omnes.*[1465]

Anyway, what can definitively be said in comparative law is that in general the most important systems of concentrated constitutional judicial review of laws attribute general effects backwards to the past (that is, *ex tunc*, *pro praeterito*) to all decisions in which unconstitutionality and nullity of laws is declared.

Hence, those decisions are not merely declaratory, nor do they have retroactive effects, but are solely constitutive. In systems like those Italy and Germany, as we have seen, which do attribute certain effects backwards to the past to the Constitutional Courts decisions in which a law is annulled, in general, these are fundamentally restricted to criminal matters. The solution adopted by these legislations is logical. It would have monstrous repercussions on juridical stability to maintain that the effects of decisions declaring the nullity of a law considered unconstitutional are merely declaratory, and that acts, which took place before the law was declared null, are thus taken as never having been passed. It might, however, be equally unjust in criminal cases, if decisions passed under a law, which is subsequently annulled, were not affected by its annulment. This is why the Italian and German legal systems establish an exception, regarding criminal cases, to the principle that the effects of decisions declaring the nullity of laws deemed unconstitutional only produce effects towards the future.

Moreover, the situation of conflict that could arise between juridical stability and criminal decisions, as we have also mentioned, has lead the North American Supreme Court to establish the programmatic exceptions to the opposite principle. We have seen that constitutional review being diffuse in character in the United States,

---

1464 See Mauro CAPPELLETTI, "El control judicial de la constitucionalidad de las leyes en el derecho comparado" *Revista de la Facultad de Derecho de México*, 61, 1966, p. 58–59.

1465 See, for example, CFC–SPA, 17–11–38, in *Memoria de la Corte Federal y de Casación 1939*, pp. 330 334; CF. 19–6–53, in *Gaceta Forense* N° 1, 1953, p. 77; CSJ–CP, 29–4–65, published by the *Imprenta Nacional*, Caracas 1965, pp. 113–116. *Cf. Doctrina de la Procuraduría General de la República 1963*, Caracas 1964, pp. 199–201. In other words, as CAPPELLETTI points out, "once the decision of unconstitutionality is pronounced, the corresponding law is deprived of effects in a general manner, exactly as if it had been abrogated by a subsequent law, and vice versa, all the legislative provisions prior to the unconstitutional law regain their validity" (*loc. cit.*, p. 59). Thus, the effects of the concentrated constitutional review system are radically different from the particular, *inter partes* effects of the diffuse constitutional review system.

the effects of decisions declaring laws unconstitutional are merely declaratory and thus retroactive in nature. Despite this, however, case law has extended this retroactive nature only to criminal cases. On the contrary, it respects the effects produced in civil and administrative matters on the basis of a law, which is declared unconstitutional.[1466]

Now, as the constitutional judicial review power that the 1961 Venezuelan Constitution attributes to the Supreme Court of Justice[1467] is similar to that termed concentrated in comparative law, it is evident that, in the absence of any constitutional or legal positive rule, the effects of the declaration of nullity of a law on the grounds of its unconstitutionality can only be produced *erga omnes*, but towards the future. That is to say, in principle, Supreme Court decisions are constitutive, *pro futuro* with *ex nunc* effects, which cannot generally be extended backwards to the past, thus they cannot be retroactive. This criterion can be said, is followed not only by authors on constitutional law,[1468] but also by decisions of the Supreme Court of Justice, although the Court has not been consistent in the matter.

In effect, the Supreme Court of Justice in Venezuela is divided into three Chambers: the Politico–Administrative, the Civil Cassation and the Criminal Cassation Chambers, and can also act in *Pleno* or Plenary session. According to the Constitution, the concentrated system of judicial review is exercised only in *Pleno* and by the Politico–Administrative Chambers, which sustain the criterion of the constitutive effects of their decisions. This criterion has been contradicted by the Civil Cassation Chamber, which does not have powers of concentrated judicial review, when it has interpreted the effects of the decisions of the former.

(b). Criterion of the constitutional organs with powers to annul laws: The Supreme Court in Pleno and its Politico–Administrative Chamber

In effect, the Supreme Court has expressly maintained that:

> Laws are made to be executed, and should thus be accomplished even when, contingently, they may be declared constitutionally null, as the result of a sufficient action. They are only rendered invalid by the definitive decision declaring their nullity.[1469]

1466 *Cf.* M. CAPPELLETTI, *loc. cit.*, pp. 63–64.

1467 Article 215, Paragraphs 3 and 4.

1468 In his book on *La jurisdicción constitucional en el derecho venezolano*, (*cit.*), José Guillermo ANDUEZA has abundantly and finally demonstrated that the decision declaring nullity by reason of unconstitutionality which all acts by the Public Powers enjoy, means that these produce all their legal effects until such time as they are pronounced null by the Court. Consequently, the Court's decision should necessarily respect the effects which the state act produced while it was in force" (p. 93), since "it produces a change in the effects of a state act. That is to say, the sentence renders ineffective a previously valid act." (p. 94). According to ANDUEZA himself, and following the most orthodox doctrine, "what characterizes constitutive sentences is the absence of retroactive effects. These continue always *pro–futuro*, *ex nunc*; that is to say, that the decision produces its effects from the day of its publication", (p. 94). We do not then share the opinion of J. J. LA ROCHE, *El control jurisdiccional en Venezuela y Estados Unidos*, *cit.*, p. 153.

1469 CFC, 20–12–40, *cit.*, by J.G. ANDUEZA, *op. cit.*, p. 90.

In other words, in the corresponding decision by the Supreme Court, declaring the nullity of a law on the grounds of its unconstitutionality, it limits itself to "proclaiming the juridical annulment" of the law to which objection is made.[1470] That is to say, the Supreme Court has maintained that laws produce all their effects until they are annulled since, as it indicated in another decision, "acts which are annullable are valid and, once passed, fully produce all their effects until they are declared null."[1471] and, while the effects of decisions declaring nullity by reason of unconstitutionality are general and *erga omnes* in nature,[1472] it is clear that, when it declares a law to be null, the Supreme Court's decision comes to form part, *mutatis mutandis* –as the Supreme Court has said– of "a special legislation arising from the secondary Constitutive Power which this High Court exercises",[1473] since such decisions "are complementary provisions of the Constitution and laws of the Republic."[1474]

In other words, as the Supreme Court, it has stated the effects of these decisions "extend *erga omnes* and have the force of law."[1475]

Thus, if a law, declared null on the grounds of its unconstitutionality, is deprived of effect in a general manner by the respective decision, just as if it had been abrogated by a later law, it is clear then that just as the law cannot have retroactive effects, so neither can the decision declaring the law's nullity which is deemed to have "force of law" as the same Supreme Court has considered. This affirmation is so logical that, in some Latin American constitutional systems, the classic principle of the lack of retroactivity of laws[1476] has been expressly extended to decisions of the Supreme Court or of the Tribunal of Constitutional Guarantees as happens in Ecuador.[1477]

This principle that the effects of the Supreme Court's decisions declaring the nullity of laws considered unconstitutional are not retroactive, stems from the nature of the decisions, which are *constitutive* and not declaratory. It was expressly recognized by the Politico Administrative Chamber of the Supreme Court itself when, in 1965, it decided to declare the nullity of a Municipal Ordinance which created a tax contravening a prohibition contained in paragraph 4 of Article 18 of the Constitution,[1478] and rejected the petitioner's request "that the Municipality be ordered to repay the

1470 See CSJ–SPA, 20–1–66 in *Gaceta Forense* N° 51, 1966, p. 13.

1471 See CSJ–SPA, 15–2–67 in *Gaceta Forense* N° 55, 1967, p. 70.

1472 *Cf.* CFC–SPA, 17–11–38, *Memoria de la Corte Federal y de Casación 1939*, p. 330; 21–3–39, *Memoria de la Corte Federal y de Casación 1940*, p. 176; 16–12–40, *Memoria de la Corte Federal y de Casación 1941*, p. 311; and of the CF, 19–6–53, in *Gaceta Forense* N° 1, 1953, pp. 77 and 78.

1473 See CFC–SPA, 16–12–40, in *Memoria de la Corte Federal y de Casación 1941*, p. 311.

1474 See CFC–SPA, 21–3–39, in *Memoria de la Corte Federal y de Casación 1940*, p. 176.

1475 See CF, 19–6–53, in *Gaceta Forense* N° 1, 1953, pp. 77, 78.

1476 Article 44 of the Constitution.

1477 Art. 141,4. Constitution of Ecuador 1983. See the comments of J.G. ANDUEZA, *op. cit.*, p. 94.

1478 Art. 18,4. 1961 Constitution.

sums of money which it had received by collecting the contribution under discussion ..." as it was considered unfounded.[1479]

In this way, the Court acknowledged the nature of its decision to annul the ordinance, as being constitutive and having effects towards the future, since otherwise, had it had considered the effects of the decision to be merely declaratory, *ex tunc*, it would have proceeded to order the Municipality to repay as requested.

Later, in 1968, the Court emphasized the presumption of the constitutionality of laws when it pointed out that

> National legislative acts, once passed and published, keep their effectiveness and validity until such time as they are repealed by the body which passed them or are annulled by the Court and, meanwhile, their legitimacy also extends to actions taken by other authorities under powers which the laws attribute to them.[1480]

For this reason, once a law is declared null on the grounds of its being unconstitutional, if retroactive effects were granted to the decision, this would be equivalent to depriving all acts taken in compliance with the law of their effects, thus severely prejudicing juridical stability.

In the same year, 1968, the Supreme Court incidentally recognized that its decisions were constitutive and not declaratory, when it maintained that:

> The effects of the decisions passed by the Court when performing its function of judicial review of the constitutionality of laws, only extend for the duration of the validity of the constitutional rule on which... (the Court's decisions) are based. Consequently, it is possible that a legal provision which is annulled because it is unconstitutional– but which in fact has continued to form a part of some legal instrument which has not been so repealed recover legal force with the coming into effect of some other norm which repeals the constitutional rule on

---

1479 See CSJ–SPA, 18–11–65, *Gaceta Forense* N° 50, 1967, p. 111. This was also the criterion of the former Federal and Cassation Court in Cassation Chamber when, in a decision in 27 February, 1940, it expressly decided the following: "The decision which is appealed, to deny the action, is founded on the fact that the Municipal Ordinance which gave rise to the fine being placed to the plaintiff for an infraction of one of its Articles, was issued by a competent authority and produced all its effects until the day it was declared null by the Federal and Cassation Court, which was the Tribunal which was competent for this purpose. The effects of the verdict of cassation cannot be made retroactive to the date that Ordinance expired, but rather they are produced from the date of that decision. As, on the other hand, the plaintiff did not appeal against the fine, he agreed to the fiscal sanction that was imposed on him, and the decision appealed concludes that there was no undue payment. The damages claimed as a consequence of that payment are thus denied. This Court considers that the grounds stated, on which the lower court bases his decision are according to the legal principles which govern this matter. In our Administrative Law, Municipal Ordinances issued under the powers which the National Constitution grants the Municipalities "have the character of local laws, and as such, it follows to apply to them the rule of the non–retroactivity of their provisions. As these Ordinances are the work of an administrative authority, invested with a part of the Public Power, these acts retain all their legal validity even in the case in which they suffer from defects which would make them anulable, until such time as their nullity is declared by the competent Court." See CFC–SPA 27–2–40 in *Memoria de la Corte Federal y de Casación*, 1941, p. 20.

1480 See CSJ–SPA, 13–2–68, in *Gaceta Forense* N° 59, 1969, p. 85.

which the Court had founded its decision to declare the law null, or one which radically changes the previous legal system[1481]

If the situation described by the Court in its decision is possible, it is precisely because the effects produced by the law, before the decision to annul it, remain intact, as a result of its constitutive effect. Otherwise, the disturbance of the legal order would be unbearable, since if the decisions of the Court in which it exercises constitutional review of laws were retroactive, that is to say, merely declaratory, *ex tunc*, not only would those acts performed under the law declared null be rendered without effect, but if the unconstitutional law were non–existent, this would leave no room for the possible case in which it recovers its validity if the Constitution under which it was declared unconstitutional were modified, as pointed out by the Court. We thus insist that, in our opinion, the effects of decisions in which the Supreme Court declares laws null on the grounds of their being in breach of the Constitution are those proper to constitutive judgements, that is to say, they only produce effects towards the future.

This statement may also be inferred from other decisions of the Supreme Court of Justice itself in relation to petitions for the annulment of laws already repealed. In fact it can be said, as Professor Andueza indicated, "that the position adopted with respect to these petitions depends on the position taken with respect to the effects of the decision upon constitutionality."[1482] If retroactive effects are attributed to these clearly, laws, which have been repealed, may be annulled, thus putting an end to the effects, which the law may have produced during the time it was in force. If the decision is only binding *pro futuro*, however, it becomes then contradictory to annul a non–existent law, since by virtue of the principle of the presumption of constitutionality –which covers all acts of state– the effects produced while the law was in force cannot be destroyed.[1483]

On the basis of this alternative, we can say that ever since 1949, the Court has denied petitions for the annulment of laws, which have been repealed. In fact, although in 1940 the Supreme Court held that there was reason to demand the annulment of a law which had been repealed, since "the annulment works retroactively and suppresses all the effects which had been produced by the application of the voided law"[1484] this opinion changed radically as of 1949, not only in relation to the dismissal of actions of unconstitutionality of laws which had already been repealed, but also in relation to the solely constitutive effects of decisions in which the Court declared laws null on the grounds of their being in breach of the Constitution.

In effect, the Court held in 1949 that "this High Court's constitutional powers to review the constitutionality of laws refer only to laws in force", thus when a petition is made for it to annul a law which has already been repealed, "the Court lacks any matter on which to decide."[1485] In 1966, the Politico Administrative Chamber of the

1481 See CSJ–SPA, 19–12–68, in *Gaceta Forense* N° 62, 1969, p. 112.

1482 See J.G. ANDUEZA, *op. cit.*, pp. 56–57.

1483 *Idem.*

1484 See CFC–SPA, 13–1–41, in *Memoria de la Corte Federal y de Casación* 1941, p. 102.

1485 See CFC–CP, 21–12–49, in *Gaceta Forense* N° 1, 1949, p. 15.

Supreme Court of Justice upheld the same criterion when it specified that, among the decisive circumstances with respect to proceedings in actions of unconstitutionality, "the very existence of the act challenged as being in breach of the Constitution and which is to constitute precisely the matter or object of the process, is especially important", and that if the action applies to the annulment of an act whose validity has expired, it thus "lacks an object."[1486]

Now, according to this criterion, it is clear that in Venezuela, generally speaking, Supreme Court decisions declaring laws annulled on the grounds of unconstitutionality have general effects, *erga omnes*. However, these effects only extend towards the future in the sense that they annul a law that, while it produced effects up to the moment when the decision was published, it is legally suppressed as of that moment. The effects of the Court decision, in this respect, cannot be retroactive, which effects are reserved to merely declaratory decisions, but only *pro futuro* as is the case with constitutive judgements.[1487]

There is no doubt, in our opinion, that in Venezuela, the aims of the constitutional review powers exercised by the Supreme Court of Justice under paragraphs 3 and 4 of Article 215 of the Constitution, as a concentrated system of judicial review, are to annul laws (the Constitution says "declare the nullity", and not "declare the unconstitutionality"). This annulment is performed with *erga omnes* effects that extend *ex nunc* (*pro futuro*), by means of a decision termed "constitutive", in contrast to "declaratory",[1488] unless dealing with cases of absolute nullity under express constitutional provisions, as we shall see.

1486 See CFC–CP, 20–01–66, in *Gaceta Forense* N° 51, 1968, pp. 13 and 14.

1487 This, and none other, for example, was the opinion of the Court in the decision which declared the nullity of Article 20 of the law approving the Contract signed between the National Executive and the Banco de Venezuela, S.A., passed on 15 March, 1962 (See CSJ–CP in FC, in *Gaceta Oficial* N° 760 Extra, 22–03–62 and to realize this it is sufficient to take the opinion of the presiding judge in that verdict, SARMIENTO NUÑEZ, as expressed in his dissenting opinion from the Supreme Court of Justice decision which denied the petition for nullity by reason of unconstitutionality of paragraph 14 of Article II of the Law approving the Extradition Treaty signed between Venezuela and the United States of America on 29 April, 1965. In his dissenting opinion, the presiding Magistrate in the sentence declaring the nullity of Article 20 of the law approving the contract signed between the National Executive and the Banco de Venezuela, S.A., insisted on the distinction between diffuse and concentrated constitutional review systems of laws in Venezuela, and indicated that, in the former, as exercised by the Courts under Article 7 of the Civil Proceedings Code (now Art. 20), the decision is relative in nature, since it affects only the particular case in question, and does not bind future cases of this or other Courts." By contrast, decisions of the Supreme Court of Justice, (in concentrated review systems) are absolute in nature; the nullity of the law is proclaimed *erga omnes*, that is, with respect to all cases, and produces effects *ex nunc*, that is to say, as of the decision." See CSJ–SPA, 29–7–65, published by the *Imprenta Nacional*, 1965, p. 74).

1488 In this respect, it must be pointed out that this general principle which is universal in comparative law and accepted by Venezuelan case law and doctrine, was followed by these who drafted the Law of Constitutional Jurisdiction, when they established, in Article 19 of the draft that: "The laws which are declared unconstitutional may not be applied nor shall have any effect whatsoever, from the day following the publication in the Official Gazette or,

(c) *Contradicting criterion of the Civil Cassation Chamber of the Supreme Court*

However, this criterion that has been followed uncontested by the Supreme Court in *Pleno* Court and in its Politico–Administrative Chamber through which the Supreme Court exercises its competence to annul laws and other acts of state with general effects, has been contradicted by the Civil, Commercial and Labour Cassation Chamber of the same Supreme Court of Justice, in a decision passed on 10 August 1978, in which, while hearing a recourse of cassation, this Chamber broached the matter of deciding and determining the effects of *Pleno* Court decisions when declaring the annulment of laws.

In effect, the Cassation Chamber decision was adopted after a *Pleno* Court decision of 15 March 1962; it declared the nullity of an article of a Law approving a contract for the fulfilment of the National Treasury auxiliary service, signed between the Republic and a private bank.

The article in question exonerated the bank from paying municipal taxes, which was considered unconstitutional. Thus once annulled by the Supreme Court the Federal District Municipality brought a civil suit against the private bank for payment of taxes incurred during the ten years previous to the Court's decision –which is the expiry period for claims for municipal taxes–, interpreting the decision in which the annulment was declared, as producing *ex tunc* effects, that is, declaratory and retroactive. The bank alleged that these were constitutive in nature, and the Civil, Commercial and Labour Cassation Chamber of the Supreme Court, when it heard the case for the cassation of the decision made by a civil court which had ordered the bank to pay the taxes as required, applied what it called "its own doctrine" as follows:

> Laws are constitutional or unconstitutional. The former are so because they conform to the rules of the National Constitution. The latter are unconstitutional when they include violations or breaches, which would contradict the content of constitutional rules. Until such time as they are declared unconstitutional, they are rendered obligatory by a presumption of their legitimacy. If so declared however, –that presumption is removed by the declaration of nullity and everything they meant in the past is erased. That is to say that the decision declaring nullity is declaratory in nature, and its effects are, in principle, backwards to the past; retroactive, *ex tunc*. This conclusion follows freely from logical principles, since the declaration of nullity seeks to re–establish the legal order disturbed by an unconstitutional law. This Chamber does not hesitate to follow this doctrine, which is upheld by leading authorities, both national and foreign. Thus the decision which is being appealed against is correct in considering as declaratory the decision passed by the Supreme Court of Justice on 15 March, 1962, in which it annulled Article 23 of the Law approving the extension of the contract signed between the Federal Executive and the *Banco de Venezuela*, as being unconstitutional. As that Law was

---

failing such publication, as of ten days after it is signed. When a definitive criminal decision has been pronounced on the basis of these, and is being executed, it shall cease, as shall all other penal effects." (See Draft Law of Constitutional Jurisdiction drawn up by Profs. MARTÍN–RETORTILLO, RUBIO LLORENTE and Allan R. BREWER–CARÍAS in Comisión de Administración Pública, *Informe sobre la reforma de la administración pública nacional*, CAP, Caracas 1972, Vol. II, p. 551).

> contested by means of a principal and direct action of unconstitutionality, the annulment pronounced by the Supreme Court is without question absolutely declaratory in nature, and thus its effects extend both backwards to the past (*ex tunc*) and towards the future (*ex nunc*). Leading authorities indicate that "that law which is declared unconstitutional should be regarded, to all intents and purposes, as if it had never possessed legal force." This doctrine stems from precise constitutional texts, which endow the Supreme Court with power to "declare the total or partial nullity of national laws", without indicating therein what the nature or character of such nullity is. Within this doctrine, however, one must accept the possible existence of limiting cases, such as when considerations of higher justice or overriding public interest make it advisable to temper the rigour of its effects. Among the cases in which this occurs is the immutability of the *res judicata* arising from firm, final verdicts, which should, in principle, be maintained. In the case in question, however, this exceptional situation does not arise, since the interest at issue is eminently private by nature. Thus, as the decision of 15 March 1962– in which the Supreme Court of Justice declared the nullity on the grounds of unconstitutionality of Article 20 of the above law approving the contract signed between the National Executive and the *Banco de Venezuela*, is declaratory in nature, its *ex tunc* effects are correct and normal to this type of decision. The appellate decision thus did not violate the legal provisions mentioned in the petition when it ordered the bank to pay the taxes which had been demanded.[1489]

In this way, as a result of decisions by its component Chambers, the Supreme Court of Justice itself has established contradictory criteria. In *Pleno* Court, and in the Politico–Administrative Chamber, it has maintained the constitutive nature, *pro futuro* and *ex nunc* effects of its decisions to annul on the grounds of unconstitutionality, laws and other state acts with general effect, which may be contested by means of popular action. By contrast, the Civil, Commercial and Labour Cassation Chamber – which incidentally has no competence for declaring laws null on the grounds of unconstitutionality, but rather has a reduced competence for hearing recourses of cassation, attributed to the *Pleno* Court and the Politico–Administrative Chamber decision different effects from those accepted by themselves by deciding that those decisions declaring nullity on the grounds of unconstitutionality were declaratory in nature (not constitutive) with *pro praeterito* (not *pro futuro*) and *ex tunc* (not *ex nunc*), effects.

This is, without doubt, an inadmissible contradiction, since not only is the Civil, Commercial and Labour Cassation Chamber of the Supreme Court not competent to declare the nullity of laws, but also, in attributing *ex tunc* effects to the decisions of another Chamber and to those of the *Pleno* Court, contrary to their own criterion, it has done so erroneously. The Cassation Chamber has resorted to doctrinal criteria, which relate to the diffuse systems of judicial review, their application to the concentrated systems of judicial review, being absolutely inadmissible.

In any case, since 1976, Article 131 of the Organic Law of the Supreme Court of Justice has been central to both interpretations, because it endows both the *Pleno* Court and the Politico–Administrative Chamber with power to establish "the effects of their decisions with time." Thus, despite the fact that the effects of their decisions declaring the nullity of laws on the grounds of unconstitutionality should, in princi-

---

1489 See CSJ–SCCMT, 10–8–78 in *Gaceta Forense* N° 101, 1978, pp. 591–592.

ple, continue to be constitutive, *pro futuro ex nunc*,[1490] the Court may correct the unfavourable effects that may be produced by the rigidity of this principle, particularly in matters of constitutional rights and guarantees, and give its decision retroactive *pro praeterito*, *ex tunc* effects.

In our opinion, even in cases relating to constitutional rights and guarantees, the problem of the rigidity of the principle of the *ex tunc*, *pro futuro* effects of decisions annulling laws, which could mean that a law that violates a constitutional guarantee, despite its having been declared null, could have produced effects up to the time of that declaration, is resolved, since the Constitution itself guarantees against this situation. It declares the absolute nullity of "acts by the Public Power" –including laws– which prejudice constitutional rights and guarantees."[1491]

Thus, it is the absolute nullity of certain acts, as provided for in the Constitution, which allows certain decisions in which the Court declares the nullity of a law to have retroactive effects, backwards to the past, and for them to be considered declaratory and *ex tunc* in nature.

(d) Objective Guarantee of the Constitution: Absolute or Relative Nullity

In fact, in relation to the effects, with time, of Supreme Court decisions declaring the annulment of laws on the grounds of their unconstitutionality, what must be clarified in the Venezuelan constitutional system is the objective guarantee of the Constitution established in the Fundamental text, particularly regarding the concentrated system of judicial review. In other words, when the Supreme Court of Justice declares the nullity of a law, which violates the Constitution, does the Court adopt its decision based on the annulability or relative nullity of the unconstitutional law, or, does it annul the law based on the grounds of absolute nullity, because the Constitution provides for cases of absolute nullity? To resolve this dilemma it is necessary to determine whether all unconstitutional laws are "annullable acts" or whether, on the contrary, the possibility exists of unconstitutional acts with defects such that they are considered by the legal order, as "null and void acts."[1492]

As we have said, the general rule in Venezuela is that Supreme Court decisions declaring the nullity of laws are constitutive. Thus the unconstitutional laws are, in principle, state acts liable to relative annulment, that is to say, annullable acts, setting aside only two possible cases, and here we have the exceptions to the rule.

1490 Fox example, in a decision of the Politico Administrative Chamber of the Court on 23–2–84, declaring the nullity by reason of unconstitutionality of an act installing the Legislative Assembly of a state of the Federation, the Court provided expressly that "this decision shall have no retroactive effects whatsoever in relation to procedures carried out in the Legislative Assembly." (Consulted in original).

1491 Art. 46. 1961 Constitution.

1492 As pointed out by J.G. ANDUEZA, "the difference which exists between an act null and an anulable one should be seen in the nature of the judicial pronouncement. If the decision is solely declaratory, with retroactive effects, when the act is anulled *pro–praeterito*, we may affirm that we are in the presence of absolute nullity. By contrast, when the judge passes a constitutive judgement with effects *ex–nunc*, *pro futuro*, the defect produces only the anulability of the state act", *op.cit.*, pp. 92–93.

In fact, despite the power legally attributed to the Supreme Court to determine the effects with time of its decisions, the Venezuelan Constitution only allows the interpreter to infer that Supreme Court decisions that declare the nullity of a law, have *per se* the character of a declaratory judgement, producing full effects backwards to the past, in such cases in which the Constitution itself declares a law or state act as "null and void" or without effects. This possibility is provided for only in Articles 46 and 119 of the Constitution. In effect, article 46 of the Constitution establishes the following:

> Art. 46. All acts of the Public Power that violate or impair the rights guaranteed by this Constitution are null, and public officials and employees who order or execute them shall be held criminally, civilly and administratively liable, as the case may be, and orders from their superiors evidently contrary to the Constitution and the laws may not serve as an excuse.

According to this first express exception, a law, which, for example, establishes discrimination, based on "race, creed, sex or social status", expressly violates the right to equality guaranteed in Article 61 of the Constitution, and is "null" under the text of Article 46. The defect is such that the nullity is absolute, and the act can produce no legal effect and should not even be applied by any authority, the contrary originating responsibility. In such cases, the Court's decision declaring the nullity of the law on the grounds of its being unconstitutional can be no more than merely declaratory, by virtue of the express text of the Constitution. It is a question, in fact, of certifying a nullity already established in the Constitution, which extinguishes the law in the past and into the future, in the sense that, as the law is declared "null" by the Constitution itself, it is considered as never having been able to produce effects. In the possible cases in which rights guaranteed by the Constitution are at stake, and which are regulated by Article 46 of the Constitution, the Supreme Court decision declaring the nullity of the unconstitutional law cannot have constitutive effects, neither can it consequently leave the effects produced by an unconstitutional law which violates fundamental rights prior to its being declared null by the Court intact.

The second exception to the principle of the constitutive effect of the Supreme Court's decisions declaring the nullity of unconstitutional laws is expressly regulated by Article 119 of the Constitution, which establishes that:

> All usurped authority is without effect, and its acts are null.

By usurpation of authority should be understood "the defects accompanying all acts decreed by a person totally lacking authority",[1493] that is to say, "the usurper is he who exercises authority and puts it into effect without any type of investiture, either regular or established. The concept of usurpation, in this case, arises when a person who has no *auctoritas* acts as an authority",[1494] in the sense in which the Constitution employs the term "authority." Thus, as the Constitution states, usurped authority is without effects and its acts are null. This second case in which the express text of the Constitution declares an act of state "null" and without effect, a

1493 See Allan R. BREWER–CARÍAS, *Las instituciones fundamentales del derecho administrativo y la jurisprudencia venezolana*, Caracas 1964, p. 62.

1494 *Idem*. p. 59.

defect such that the nullity is absolute, that the Supreme Court decision declaring the nullity for example, "of a law of a government organised by force",[1495] can only have the effect of declaring a nullity already expressly established in the Constitution itself.

We must emphasize, however, that apart from these two express provisions of the Constitution by which the text of the Constitution itself declares a law absolutely null, with the consequence that the Supreme Court of Justice's decisions declaring the nullity of an unconstitutional law have merely declaratory effects, when in other cases the Supreme Court of Justice declares the nullity of an unconstitutional law it is considered, as a general rule, to be defective in such a way as to entail its relative annulment, and the only cases that are admissible as exceptions to this general principle adopted in our constitutional system, are those cases in which the Supreme Court itself expressly establishes absolute annulment in its decisions,[1496] which may be based on Article 131 of the Organic Law of the Supreme Court of Justice, in certain cases, for example, of the usurpation of functions, which is an entirely different constitutional concept from that of the usurpation of authority.[1497]

If, however, the Supreme Court omits to characterize the law whose nullity is declared defective to the point of absolute nullity, extending the effects of its: annulment backwards to the past, the general principle of relative nullity is taken to apply, and neither the ordinary courts nor even the Cassation Chambers of the Supreme Court may substitute the powers of the *Pleno* Court or the Politico–Administrative Chamber, and judge for themselves the effects of the latter's decisions.

In accordance with what has been said, thus it can be concluded, as the general principle in the Venezuelan constitutional system that any Supreme Court decision passed in *Pleno* Court, or in its Politico–Administrative Chamber[1498] in which it declares the nullity of a law considered unconstitutional has *erga omnes* effects, the decision being in nature (*ex–nunc*) and producing relative annulment, unless the text of the decision itself declares the law absolutely null, with *ex tunc* effects or the Court bases its pronouncement on the provisions of Articles 46 and 119 of the Constitution, in which case it is declaratory by nature.

However, even in these cases the retroactive character of the decision is not absolute, but rather entails that all the concrete situations arising from the application of the law declared null are susceptible to objection,[1499] and thus that in many possi-

1495 Article 250, 1961 Constitution.

1496 In certain isolated sentences in this respect, the Court has annulled a Municipal Ordenance as contrary to equality under tax, and indicated that the infractions invalidated all its provisions to the point of absolute nullity." See CFC–SPA, 28–3–41, in *Memoria de la Corte Federal y de Casación*, 1942, p. 158. *Cf.* J.G. ANDUEZA, *op. cit.*, p. 93.

1497 See Allan R. BREWER–CARÍAS, *Las instituciones fundamentales... cit.*, p. 60

1498 Under article 215, paragraphs 3 and 4. 1961 Constitution.

1499 This is the opinion, with which we agree, of the Office of the Attorney General of the Republic. We differ in that the Attorney General's Office considers that all sentences declaring the nullity of a law are declaratory in nature, and thus have effects towards the past. See the

ble instances it could be held that legal situations would continue intact, if they were not challenged by the interested parties.

Lastly, it should be pointed out that whatever the effects with time of a law being declared null on the grounds of its being unconstitutional are, it is evident that the effects towards the future continue for as long as the Constitution that gave rise to the annulment is in force. Thus, as the annulment is declared on the basis of the violation of a particular constitutional rule, if that rule were to lapse as the result of constitutional reform, it would cause the decision declaring unconstitutionality to lose its *erga omnes* effects, and the law declared unconstitutional would regain its validity. The Supreme Court has expressly accepted this possibility.[1500]

4. Judicial Review and the Fundamental Right to Constitutional Protection (*Derecho de Amparo*)

As we have said, the Venezuelan system of judicial review has been developed as a mixed system, in which the diffuse and concentrated systems of judicial review perform in parallel. But in addition to the constitutional and legal provisions specifically related to judicial review of the constitutionality of legislation that we have previously analysed, as far as judicial review is concerned we must also consider the right to constitutional protection (*derecho de amparo*) as a fundamental right estab-

---

opinion in *Doctrina de la Procuraduría General de la República*, 1968, Caracas 1969, p. 20, in particular p. 25.

1500 This has been expressly decided by the Supreme Court of Justice in a decision of 19 December, 1968, in the following terms: "It is as well to warn, moreover, that the effects of the decisions which the Court passes when exercising this power only extend for the time for which the constitutional precept on which they are based continues in force. In consequence, it is possible that a legal provision which is anulled because it is contrary to the Constitution –but which in fact has continued to form part of a legal instrument which has been revoked– recover its legal effect when a reform comes into effect repealing the Constitutional precept on which the Court rested in order to declare it null, or when the previously established regime changes radically.

Such was the situation created when –after the Federal and Cassation Court passed the verdict mentioned by the petitioner, on April, 1951– the constitutional order in force at that time was reformed by the Constitutions published respectively in 1953 and 1961. In 1951, the restrictions which provided the basis for the Federal and Cassation Court to declare null the rules which the plaintiff refers to in his petition still served as a basis for the federal and Cassation Court to deny municipal competence over the tax on industrial and trade permits, and subjected the power of local authorities to levy taxes. But when the Constitution was reformed in 1953, those restrictions were removed, and among the categories taxable by the Municipal Power it included those indicated in the current National Constitution, and in particular, the tax on industrial and trade permits. This being the case, the Municipal Council of the Federal District was not subject to the aforementioned constitutional limitations when, in the exercise of its autonomy and of the power granted to it in the Fundamental Charter, to levy taxes it sanctioned the current Ordinance on the Permit for Industry and Trade in 1958, and if the activity of that body could not be bound by provisions, which like those of the 1936 Constitution, had already been revoked, less could it be so bound by what was decided in a decision whose effects are limited to the duration in force of the legal provisions which served as its basis." See CSJ–SPA, 19–12–68, in *Gaceta Forense* N° 62, 1968, pp. 106 to 113. *Cf.* CSJ–SPA, 29–10–68, in *Gaceta Forense* N° 62, 1968, pp. 37–39.

lished in the Constitution, through which judicial review of legislation can also be obtained.

In effect, one of the most important democratic innovations in all Venezuelan constitutional history was the establishment of the right to protection (*Amparo*) in Article 49 of the 1961 Constitution. It not only extended the adjective system for the protection of fundamental rights and liberties set up in an incomplete form in previous constitutional texts[1501] that had culminated in the establishment in 1947 of the writ of *habeas corpus*[1502] as a protection for personal liberty, but led to the creation of a special institution. This right to protection (*amparo*) established in the 1961 Constitution as a legal protection, presents peculiarities that distinguish it from similar contemporary institutions for the protection of constitutional rights and guarantees established, both in Europe and in Latin America.[1503]

A. *Constitutional basis of the right to protection*

In effect, article 49 of the Constitution declares the following:

> Article 49. According to the law, the Courts will protect all inhabitants of the Republic in the enjoyment and exercise of the rights and guarantees established in the Constitution.
>
> The procedure will be brief and summary, and the competent judge will be empowered to immediately re–establish the infringed legal situation.

Despite this being, as said, an innovation in our constitutional tradition, the document explaining the motives of the constitutional project in 1960 limited its comments on the matter by saying in Section III on "Rights, Duties and Guarantees", that the right to protection "was sanctioned" and subsequently adding that "with respect to protection, only the general principles were established, which the law must regulate; but so as not to suspend its effects until the respective law is passed, the right of *habeas corpus* was sanctioned in the constitutional Temporary Provisions, thus regulating it provisionally." In this respect, the Fifth Temporary Provision of the Constitution established the rules of procedure for "the protection of personal liberty, until such time as the special law regulating it is passed, as stipulated in Article 49 of the Constitution."[1504]

Thus, according to these rules, the 1961 Venezuelan Constitution sanctioned the" right to protection as a fundamental right that can be exercised by recourse to a variety of legal means, aimed at protecting all constitutional rights and guarantees, including that of personal liberty, so as to ensure that they are enjoyed and exercised by all inhabitants of the Republic. The document explaining the motives of the Pro-

---

1501 See the historical analysis of these constitutional rules in E. AGUDO FREITES "Estado actual de la acción de *amparo* en Venezuela", *Estudios sobre la Constitución. Libro Homenaje a Rafael Caldera*, Universidad Central de Venezuela, Caracas 1979, Vol. II, pp. 659–773.

1502 Art. 32, Constitución 1947

1503 See in general H. FIX–ZAMUDIO, *La protección procesal de los derechos humanos ante las jurisdicciones nacionales*, Madrid 1982.

1504 See the "Exposition of Motives" of the Constitution, *Revista de la Facultad de Derecho*, Universidad Central de Venezuela, N° 21, pp. 371–420; particularly pp. 380–381.

ject of Constitution in 1960 thus described the "right of *habeas corpus*" as a specific means of the broader "right to protection."

According to the Constitution, the protection (*amparo*) has been consequently sanctioned *as a constitutional right* of the inhabitants of the country, to require of *all* the Courts within their own jurisdiction and according to the provisions of the law, that they protect and ensure the enjoyment and exercise of *all the rights and guarantees* established by the Constitution or inherent in the human person, against any distress, whether by public authorities or individuals, by means of proceedings that should be brief and summary, and that allow the judge to restore the infringed legal situation immediately.[1505]

Hence, the Constitution does not establish only "one" action or writ of protection as a particular means for legal protection, but rather a "right to protection" as a fundamental right which can, and in fact is exercised through a variety of legal actions and recourses, including a direct "action for protection" of a subsidiary nature.

Thus, article 49 of the Constitution does not establish a particular constitutional *adjective* "guarantee" of constitutional rank to protect constitutional rights, but moreover, what it has established is a true "constitutional right", the right of everyone to be protected by the courts in the enjoyment and exercise of their constitutional rights and guarantees. This character of the *amparo*, as a "constitutional right" is the basic element that identifies the Venezuelan institution[1506] and that leads to its consideration not as a single action or complaint, but as a right. This criterion was the one that in our opinion, led the Supreme Court in 1983, to change its criterion established in 1970, regarding the possibility of the exercise of the action for protection, even in the absence of the law regulating and developing the constitutional dispositions on the matter.[1507]

The question could be stated as follows: If the norm of article 49 were to establish an "action or recourse" for protection, then article 50 of the Constitution which lays down that the absence of laws regulating the exercise of "constitutional rights" would not impede their exercise, would not be applicable[1508] on the contrary, if article 49 of the Constitution was to establish a "fundamental right", as it is done, then article 50 of the Constitution would be applicable,[1509] and even without the law of the right of *amparo*, this right could be constitutionally exercised. The latter is the

1505 The right of protection (Art. 49 Constitution) is thus different to the broader right to access to justice specifically regulated in Article 68 of the Constitution.

1506 See Allan R. BREWER–CARÍAS, "El derecho de *amparo* y la acción de *amparo*", *Revista de derecho público,* Nº 22, Caracas 1985, pp. 51–61.

1507 See Supreme Court of Justice in Político–Administrative Chamber, 20–10–83, *Revista de Derecho Público,* Nº 16, Caracas 1983, p. 169.

1508 See the opinion stated by the Attorney's General Office in *Doctrina de la Procuraduría General de la República 1970*, Caracas 1971, p. 35.

1509 See J.R. QUINTERO "Recurso de *amparo*. La cuestión central en dos sentencias y un Voto Salvado" in *Revista de la Facultad de Derecho,* Nº 9, Universidad Católica Andrés Bello, Caracas 1969–1970, pp. 161–162–166. See the judicial decision and its dissident opinion in pp. 180–206. See the text also in O. MARÍN GÓMEZ, *Protección procesal de las garantías constitucionales de Venezuela. Amparo y Habeas Corpus*, Caracas 1983, pp. 229–250.

predominant criterion followed by the courts, and in our opinion is the most distinguishable feature of the *amparo* institution in Venezuela.

B. Amparo *as a Right to Judicial Means for Protection*

The consolidation of "constitutional protection" as a fundamental right to judicial means for protection, has as a direct consequence, namely that the *amparo* is neither exactly an "action" nor a "remedy", since the Constitution does not identify the right to protection with any specific legal means. Thus, as conceived in the Constitution, "protection" (*amparo*) may take the form of recourse in the strict sense of the review of judicial or administrative decisions, or it may take the form of an "autonomous action" which does not necessarily entail the review of a given state act. For this reason, the protection may consist equally of a "recourse" or of an "autonomous action." This depends on the legal regulations.

However, as conceived in article 49 of the Constitution, *amparo* is established not only as a right of the inhabitants of the Republic to be protected in the enjoyment and exercise of the rights and guarantees established by the Constitution, but it really also takes on the nature of "a duty" of the Courts to protect all inhabitants of the Republic in the enjoyment and exercise of such rights and guarantees. For this reason, article 49 begins by stating, "The Courts shall protect..." This is why we have indicated that *amparo*, as it appears in the text of the Constitution, is not conceived as a single judicial recourse or action, nor as a single autonomous action, necessarily independent of all other judicial remedies and actions contemplated for the defence of constitutional rights and guarantees. Rather, the Constitution is sufficiently broad and flexible to allow the legislator to organize a variety of legal means for the defence of civil rights and guarantees, whether these are by means of ordinary legal actions, or in cases where these do not allow adequate protection of rights, through the general and subsidiary means, "action for protection."

Thus, many legal means can, and indeed do exist that afford protection to individuals in the enjoyment and exercise of their constitutional rights, by means of brief and summary proceedings, in which the judge is empowered to immediately re–establish infringed legal situations. In all such cases, it is not that the ordinary means substitute the right of protection (or diminish it), but that they can serve as the judicial means for protection. For this purpose, in many cases they need to be perfected, which is the legislator's future task.

Despite the several means for the legal protection of constitutional rights and guarantees that ensure the "right to protection" contemplated in the Constitution, there is no doubt that, given the all inclusive nature of the protection which the Fundamental Text establishes "according to the Law", for the real effectiveness of that right to protection, it is evident that a subsidiary "action for protection" must be identified, and accepted, but only if those other ordinary legal means that can serve for the protection of constitutional rights and guarantees, formally established by law, are insufficient.

Thus, the "right to protection" can be ensured by a variety of existing legal means (actions and recourses), in which case, the "right to protection" is not identified with any specific legal action. But in the case of the "action for protection" –

which, as it has been said, is of a subsidiary nature in that it is admissible only when there is no other means of protection or relief formally provided for in the legal system, this subsidiary "action for protection" does appear as differentiated from other means for the legal protection of rights and guarantees, and for the defence of the Constitution itself.

Indeed, this leads us to point out the substantial difference that exists between the Venezuelan "right to protection"– and even the subsidiary "action for protection" contemplated in the Constitution, and the Mexican "trial for *amparo*", which is really a mixture, under one name, as we have seen, of five legal actions which in the Venezuelan legal system are completely distinct. These actions that in Mexico are covered by the heading *juicio de amparo* are: firstly, the protection of personal liberty, which is basically the remedy of *habeas corpus*; secondly, what is known as the "*amparo* against laws", which substitutes the direct action of unconstitutionality of laws; thirdly, the "*amparo* cassation", which is really the same as the recourse of cassation; fourthly, what is known as "administrative protection", which leads to judicial review of administrative acts; and fifthly, the Mexican system of protection also includes what is known as "agrarian *amparo*" for the protection of the rights of peasants.[1510]

By contrast with the Mexican situation, the right to protection contemplated in article 49 of the Venezuelan Constitution, as we have pointed out, firstly ensures the possibility of protection when fundamental rights are infringed by state acts by means of the action of unconstitutionality of laws (popular action), or through the decision of any judge not to apply a law in the diffuse system of judicial review of constitutionality; by means of the recourse of cassation with respect to judicial decisions; and by means of the administrative remedies against administrative actions. Additionally, it ensures the possibility of protection of fundamental rights against infringement by other individuals through ordinary judicial means. To ensure the effectiveness of all these ordinary judicial means to serve as means for protecting fundamental rights, the legislator must of course perfect them. For instance, in cases of popular action, when its grounds are the infringement of a constitutional right or guarantee, due to the absolute nullity implied, the Supreme Court might be empowered to suspend the effects of the impugned law while the case is being decided. In the procedure of the recourse of cassation, when the complaint against the impugned judicial decision is based on the violation of a fundamental right, the motives for the admissibility of the recourse could be widened, as well as the judicial decisions that could be impugned. In the proceeding of judicial review of administrative action, when the grounds of the actions are the violation of fundamental rights, the expiry delay for the actions to be exercised could be eliminated, due to the absolute nullity involved, and the judge must be allowed to use his powers more freely to declare the emergency situation of the process, shortening delays, and to suspend the effects of the challenged administrative act while the final decision of the case is produced.

1510 Héctor FIX–ZAMUDIO, "Algunos aspectos comparativos del derecho de *amparo* en México y Venezuela", *Libro Homenaje a la Memoria de Lorenzo Herrera Mendoza*, Universidad Central de Venezuela, Caracas 1970, Vol. II, pp. 344–356.

C. *"Action for Protection" as a Subsidiary Means*

However, as we have said, additional to all the ordinary means, the right to protection allows adequate protection to be achieved for constitutional rights and guarantees, by means of an "action for protection", as a subsidiary judicial means. It, of course, appears in the legal system as completely different from the popular action of unconstitutionality of laws, the recourse of cassation, and from actions for judicial review of administrative actions.

In this case, the "action for protection" appears as a much broader subsidiary action for protecting absolutely all constitutional rights and guarantees including the enjoyment and exercise of personal liberty.

Now, one of the features of this autonomous subsidiary legal action, called the "action for protection", is that it does not presuppose that other previous legal means have to be exhausted before it can be exercised. This differentiates the institution of the "action for protection" in Venezuela from the "recourse of protection" (*recurso de amparo*) or the "constitutional complaint" which has recently developed in Europe, particularly in Germany and in Spain. In these countries, the protective remedy is really an authentic "recourse" that is brought, in principle, against judicial decisions. In Germany, for example, to bring a constitutional complaint for the protection of constitutional rights before the Federal Constitutional Tribunal, the available ordinary judicial means need to be previously exhausted, which definitively entails a recourse against a judicial decision, even though, in exceptional cases, a direct complaint for protection may be allowed in certain specific cases and with respect to a very limited number of constitutional rights.[1511] In Spain, all legal recourses need to be exhausted in order to bring a *"recurso de amparo"* of constitutional rights before the Constitutional Tribunal, and, particularly when dealing with protection against administrative activities, the ordinary means for judicial review of administrative decisions must be definitively exhausted. For this reason, the recourse for protection in Spain is eventually a means for judicial review of decisions taken by the Administrative Judicial review courts.[1512]

On the contrary, the subsidiary "action for protection" in Venezuela is not conditional upon the previous exhausting of other legal means, and thus it does not result as recourse against judicial decisions either.

It is, as it has been pointed out, a subsidiary legal action in that it is only admissible when no other legal action in the legal system exists to seek the protection of fundamental rights and their immediate reestablishment by means of brief, summary proceedings.

1511 K. SCHLAICH, "Procedures et techniques de protection des droits fondamentaux. Tribunal Constitutionnel Fédéral allemand", in L. FAVOREU (ed.), *Cours constitutionnelles européenes et droits fondamentaux*, Paris 1982, pp. 105–164.

1512 See, J.L. GARCÍA RUÍZ, *Recurso de amparo en el derecho español*, Madrid 1980. F. CASTEDO ALVAREZ, "El recurso de *amparo* constitucional" en Instituto de Estudios Fiscales, *El Tribunal Constitucional*, Madrid 1981, Vol. I, pp. 179–208.

In this sense, in order to adequately understand the subsidiary character of the "action for protection", as an autonomous action, we must bear in mind what we have said about the protective character of other judicial means, among which are the actions for judicial review of administrative acts. It is not the case that the action for protection requires the previous exhausting of the actions for judicial review of administrative acts, when these violate fundamental rights, but that the action for judicial review can be itself considered in that case, as a means for protection of fundamental rights. Thus, only when no judicial means for protection exists, and in the case of administrative acts, when actions for their judicial review are not effective as a means for protection due to the particular circumstances of the case, the "action for protection" would be admissible.

On the other hand, it should be noted that according to the Constitution, the right to protection may be exercised according to the law, before "the Courts", and thus, as it has been said, the organization of the legal and procedural system does not provide for one single judicial action to guarantee the enjoyment and exercise of constitutional rights to be brought before one single Court.

The legal system may, and indeed does, regulate systems for the protection of constitutional rights and guarantees by means of ordinary actions, through brief and summary proceedings in which the judge has power to re–establish the infringed subjective legal situations immediately, which differentiates the system from those in Europe, particularly from the action for protection in Germany or in Spain which is one, single action, to be brought before one, single Court, and which serves as a mechanism for the protection of certain constitutional rights and guarantees.[1513]

On the contrary, the right to protection in Venezuela is expressed in several legal judicial means which may be brought before all the Courts, and which may serve as a protection by means of pre–existing actions and remedies, so long as provision is made for brief, summary proceedings with powers for the judge to restore the infringed subjective legal situations. For this reason, and given this all–inclusive characteristic, the "action for protection" as such is subsidiary in nature, which implies that it is not the only action or recourse admissible for protection but that, rather, it may also be obtained by other legal means regulated by the legal system.

D. *Protection of all Constitutional Rights and Guarantees*

However, whether by use of pre–established legal means or through subsidiary autonomous action, the right to protection as expressed in the Constitution is to protect all the rights and guarantees that the Constitution establishes. This protection constitutes a fundamental guarantee of human rights, which in turn entails certain implications. Above all, the objective of the right to protection, according to the Constitution, is to protect the enjoyment and exercise of constitutional rights and guarantees, and thus, it applies not only to individuals as holders of such rights, but also to cases in which these rights are exercised by companies or corporations. There can be no doubt that, given the scope with which article 49 of the Constitution

---

1513 *Cf.* H. FIX–ZAMUDIO, "El derecho de *amparo* en México y en España. Su influencia recíproca", *Revista de estudios políticos*, N° 7, Madrid 1979, pp. 254–255.

declares the "right to protection", the expression "all the inhabitants" cannot be understood to refer solely to individuals, rather that it also refers to all entities or organizations, since the rights established in the Constitution are moreover not only rights of individuals, but many of them are also rights of collective entities.

At the same time, however, the protection of the enjoyment and exercise of constitutional rights and guarantees is embodied in the Constitution not only regarding public actions, which may disrupt the enjoyment and exercise of such rights, but also regarding disruptions, which may originate from other private individuals. The Constitution makes no distinction in this respect, and thus an action for protection is perfectly admissible against actions by individuals, the action for protection has doubtlessly been conceived as a traditional means of protection against actions by the state and its authorities. However, despite this tradition of conceiving the action for protection as a means of protecting rights and guarantees against public actions, we consider that, in Venezuela, the scope with which this is regulated by article 49 allows the action for protection to be brought against individual actions, that is to say, when the disruption of the enjoyment and exercise of rights originates from private individuals or organizations.

This also differentiates the Venezuelan system from that which exists in other systems such as those in Mexico or Spain, in which the "action for protection" is solely conceived against public actions.[1514] For this reason, as we have said, in Spain the action for protection is expressed as a review of decisions by the administrative judicial court when reviewing administrative acts.[1515]

On the other hand, in the case of protection from disruption originating from public authorities, it should be affirmed, without doubt, that as regulated by article 49 of the Constitution, this protection is admissible against all public actions, that is to say, against all state acts as well as against any other action by public officials. The right to protection has, of course, been regulated, in many cases in this field, by judicial means already established in the legal system. For example, as far as unconstitutional laws, which affect constitutional rights and guarantees, are concerned, it is admissible to bring a popular action before the Supreme Court of Justice, which can be considered as a means for protection. Also, when a judge decides not to apply a law, under article 20 of the Civil Procedural Code, because he decides that it infringes a constitutional right, he also ensures protection of that right.[1516] The same occurs with actions brought before the administrative judicial Tribunals against administrative acts, which constitute a means for the protection of constitutional rights and guarantees when the basis for impugning the administrative act is the violation of the enjoyment and exercise of such rights and guarantees, and the judicial suspen-

---

1514 *Idem*, pp. 254–255. On the contrary in Argentina is accepted the recourse of "*amparo*" against individual actions. *Kot* case of 5.9.1958. See G.R. CARRIO, *Algunos aspectos del recurso de amparo*, Buenos Aires 1959, p. 13.

1515 *Cf.* J. GONZÁLEZ PÉREZ, *Derecho procesal constitucional*, Madrid 1980, p. 278.

1516 See Allan R. BREWER–CARÍAS, *El control de la constitucionalidad de los actos estatales*, Caracas 1978.

sion of the effects of the impugned act may be obtained immediately, and is admissible against any type of administrative act, both express and implied.[1517]

Additionally, it must be said that the subsidiary action for protection is admissible against any action by the administration, even when this does not constitute a formal administrative act and is thus not open to actions before the administrative jurisdiction. That is to say, it would be admissible, for example, against material acts by the administration; its *de facto* methods; its failure to act or to fulfil an obligation; in short, against any action or omission by the administration, and even, of course, against specific acts which may not be contested before the administrative judicial courts.

Indeed, the subsidiary action for protection may also be admissible against actions by the legislative body against which there are no legal means for objection, and may even be brought against judicial decisions against which no legal means of appeal exist or have been contemplated, or the recourse of cassation could not be exercised.

We have said, however, that the action for protection also constitutes a means for the protection of the enjoyment and exercise of *all* rights and guarantees established in the Constitution. To support this, it is sufficient to mention that article 49 is placed under Chapter I containing the "General Provisions" of Title III, which refers to "Constitutional duties, rights and guarantees", bearing in mind that the remaining five chapters separately regulate: duties; and individual, social, economic and political rights.

By virtue of its position in the Constitution, there is nothing to suggest that the right to protection in Venezuela constitutes a means for the protection of certain rights only but that rather, it relates, on the contrary, to all rights and guarantees established in the Constitution. This, of course, leads to the assertion that the right to protection and the subsidiary "action for protection" are means for protecting, not only those rights and guarantees listed in articles 43 to 116 of the Constitution, but also all the rights inherent in the human person, even when not specified in the Constitution, and in this respect, the full value of article 50 of the Constitution can be appreciated. This provides that:

> Article 50. The declaration of rights and guarantees contained in the Constitution is not to be taken to mean the negation of others, such which, as they are inherent in the human being, do not figure expressly therein. The lack of a law regulating these rights does not prejudice its exercise.

The action for protection also protects all those rights that are inherent in the human being, but which do not appear expressly in the Constitution, as it is not necessary to pass a law to guarantee their exercise. One result of the provisions of Article 50, is, of course, to give substantial importance to the series of human rights listed in the U.N. Universal Declaration of the Rights of Man, and in the Interna-

1517 Allan R. Brewer–Carías, "Tipos de acciones y recursos contencioso–administrativos y el tema de la legitimación", in *Conferencia sobre la reforma de la justicia administrativa en Costa Rica*, Corte Suprema de Justicia, Marzo, 1986.

tional Conventions that regulate human rights, such as those of the American Human Rights Convention, or the International Pacts on Civil and Political, and Economic and Social Rights, which are, moreover, laws of the Republic, because they have been approved in Congress by special laws.[1518] But, though limiting our comments to the rights described in the Constitution, however, we must stress the fact that what is termed *amparo* is the right to a legal means for protecting the enjoyment and exercise of absolutely all those constitutional rights, which means that a difference is established with respect to other *amparo* institutions particular to Latin America.

In fact, if the situation in Latin America is analysed comparatively, the following criteria can, in general, be identified. In the first place, the system that identifies *amparo* with judicial protection from arbitrary detention (*habeas corpus*) always entails a writ requiring that the person detained be shown. This was the legal tradition, for example, in Chile. Secondly, there is the system, that identifies *amparo* as a means for the protection of all rights, except that of personal liberty, which is granted a special means of protection, such as the remedy of *habeas corpus*. This system, in fact, distinguishes between the two types of action, the action for protection and the writ of *habeas corpus*, and is the tradition in the Argentinean, and Brazilian systems.

Thirdly, *amparo* is also seen as a means for the protection of all rights and guarantees enshrined in the Constitution, and it has been the tradition in Central America, particularly in Guatemala, Honduras and Nicaragua, in contrast to the situation in Europe, for example, in which the remedy is established for the protection of certain rights only.[1519] This happens, for example, in Spain, where the recourse of protection is reserved for the protection of a limited group of constitutional rights only, equivalent to what the Venezuelan Constitution has characterised as "individual rights."[1520]

We have pointed out that *amparo* is conceived in Venezuela as the right to a legal means (action or remedy) for the protection of all constitutional rights and guarantees absolutely, not only, of course, of individual rights, but also of the social, political and economic rights expressed in the Constitution. Also, as *amparo* is intended for the protection of all the rights and guarantees expressed in the Constitution, this implies that what is known as the right of *habeas corpus* is really a part of the right to protection, or if preferred, one manifestation of *amparo*. This is made clear by the regulation in the Fifth Temporary Provision of the Constitution, which lays down that "until such time as the special law is passed, according to Article 49, protection of the right to personal liberty shall proceed according to..." a series of procedural rules laid down therein, aimed at protecting individuals against the loss of or restriction to their liberty, in violation of their constitutional rights. When this Temporary Provision speaks of "protection for personal liberty" and refers to Article 49, it is simply affirming that the right to protection expressed in Article 49 is also

1518 See *Gaceta Oficial* N° 31.256 de 14–6–77 and N° 2.146 Extra. de 28–1–78.

1519 Allan R. Brewer–Carías, *Garantías constitucionales de los derechos del hombre*, Caracas 1976, p. 69.

1520 Art. 53, ord. 2. Spanish Constitution 1978.

intended to protect personal liberty, and that a special temporary procedure is established in this provision, but without really setting up the right of *habeas corpus* in Venezuela, as distinct from the general right to protection regulated by Article 49 of the Constitution.

E. *The Meaning of Violation of the Rights and Guarantees Protected by the Right to* Amparo

From the terms of Article 49 of the Constitution, it can be said that the objective protected by the right to protection is the enjoyment and exercise of constitutional rights and guarantees, and of course, protection for the enjoyment and exercise of such rights and guarantees is admissible, not only when some *direct* violation of a constitutional rule occurs, but also of course, when there is a violation of the legal rules that regulate the enjoyment and exercise of such rights. We consider that, there is no foundation whatsoever in Venezuela for wishing to restrict the exercise of the subsidiary action for protection only to cases in which a "direct violation" of the Constitution occurs.[1521]

In effect, we must bear in mind that the regulation of constitutional rights and guarantees in Venezuela is not uniform, and that the manner in which they are embodied in the Constitution gives rise to differing effects of such rights and guarantees.[1522] In fact, we may identify, in the first place, the "absolute rights", among which are the right to life, the right not to be held incommunicado, not to be subjected to torture or other procedures that cause moral or physical suffering, which is the same thing as the right to the integrity of the person, and the right not to be condemned to prison for life, or to punishments that are defamatory or that restrict personal liberty for more than thirty years.[1523] These rights are expressed in the Constitution in such a way that it can be said that they are rights that can neither be limited nor regulated even by the legislator, and that are, moreover, the only rights which may not be restricted or suspended by executive decision based on the powers attributed to the President of the Republic in cases of emergency or disturbances that may disrupt the peace of the Republic, or in serious circumstances which affect its economic or social life. With the exception of these absolute rights, all other rights and guarantees, by contrast, are liable to limitation or regulation by the Legislator, and may be subject to measures for their restriction or suspension.[1524]

A second type of constitutional right comprises those whose exercise may be restricted or suspended by the President of the Republic, even though, in principle, the

1521 See the decision of the Supreme Court in Politico–Administrative Chamber of 28–10–83 in *Revista de derecho público*, Nº 16, Caracas 1983, p. 169.
See the comments of René DE SOLA, "Vida y vicisitudes del recurso de *amparo* en Venezuela", *Revista del Instituto Venezolano de Derecho Social*, 47, Caracas 1985, p. 58, (also published in *Revista SIC*; 472, Caracas 1985, 74.

1522 Allan R. BREWER–CARÍAS, *Instituciones políticas y constitucionales*, Caracas 1985, Vol. II, p. 491.

1523 Art. 58; 60,3; 64,7.

1524 Art. 241 Constitution.

legislator may not limit them. This stems from the manner in which the Constitution expresses the rights, for example, to protection of honour, reputation and privacy; the right not to take an oath or to make self–incriminating statements; not to remain imprisoned once officially released from jail; not to be punished twice for the same crime; the right to equality and freedom from discrimination; the right to religious freedom and to freedom of thought; the right to petition and to receive timely response; the right to be judged by one's ordinary judges; the right to defence; the right of association; the right to health protection; the rights to education and to work; and the right to vote.[1525]

A third category of rights, stemming from the Constitution, is that composed of those rights which may be limited by the legislator, even though in a limited way. This category contains, for instance, the prisoner's right, before being sentenced, to be heard "as indicated by the law"; the right to inviolability of the home, except in cases of search "according to the law and the decision of the courts"; the right to inviolability of correspondence, except in cases of inspection or fiscal supervision of accounting documents "according to the law"; the right to take public office, with the only restrictions being conditions of aptitude "required by law."[1526]

The fourth category comprises a series of constitutional rights that can be regulated and limited by the legislator in a wider form. Among such rights would be the right not to be detained unless caught *in fraganti*; "in the cases and with the formalities established in the law"; the right not to be conscripted "but within the terms established by law"; the freedom of movement "with the condition established by law"; the right to follow a cult under the "supreme inspection of the National Executive according to the law"; the right to carry on economic activities with no other limitations than those established by law by reasons of security, health or other social interests; the right to property, submitted to the "contributions, restrictions and obligations established by law based on public or social interests"; the right to political association and to public demonstration "according to the formalities established by law."[1527] In all such cases, the exercise of rights is definitively subject to what the legislator stipulates, and within quite considerable margins.

The fifth and final category of constitutional rights and guarantees is formed by those established in such a manner that their exercise is definitively subject to legal regulation. Among such rights would be, for example, that of using the organs for the administration of justice "under the terms and conditions established by the law"; that of joining associations "according to the law"; the right to strike "under the conditions set by the law", and in the public services, "in those cases permitted by the law"[1528] all such cases, the manner in which the Constitution expresses the rights and guarantees requires that, they be regulated by the Law so as to be exercised at all. From this classification of rights and guarantees into five groups, ac-

---

1525 Arts. 59; 60,4; 60,6; 60,8; 61; 65; 66; 67; 68; 69; 71; 76; 78; 84; 111.

1526 Arts. 60,5; 62; 63; 112.

1527 Arts. 60,1; 60,2; 60,9; 64; 65; 96; 99; 114; 115.

1528 Arts. 68; 70; 92.

cording to the Constitution,[1529] it is evident that there is no sense in holding that the right to protection, and in particular, the subsidiary "action for protection", is admissible only when the Constitution is "directly violated", since many rights are not only embodied in the Constitution, but rather, by virtue of the Constitution itself, their exercise is subject to provisions and regulations established by the Legislator. The right to protection is thus also admissible against violations of laws, which regulate the enjoyment, and exercise of rights.

F. *Object of the Right to Protection: The Enjoyment and Exercise of Constitutional Rights and Guarantees*

We have pointed out that the right to protection, as regulated by the Constitution, has the definitive aim of ensuring the *enjoyment and exercise* of constitutional rights and guarantees. Precisely for this reason, the Constitution grants the power to immediately "re–establish the infringed juridical situation" to the competent judge, and precisely for this reason also provides that "the procedure should be brief and summary."

This aim of the remedy of ensuring the enjoyment and exercise of constitutional rights and guarantees entails that the judge, of course, has power to adopt preventive and cautionary measures, but bearing in mind that the legal means of protection, and even the subsidiary action for protection, are not necessarily exhausted thereby.

In other words, the protection for the enjoyment and exercise of constitutional rights and guarantees does not only entail, nor is it exhausted by the adoption of some immediate measure, by means of a brief and summary proceeding which re–establishes the infringed legal situation, but rather that the action or remedy for protection by means of legal proceedings –whether through subsidiary action for protection, or by means of the actions available under ordinary law– needs the judge in the case of *amparo* to decide on the substantive issue and give a verdict as to the legality and legitimacy of the "violation" of the right in question, without prejudice to the fact that, by means of brief and summary mechanisms, decisions may be adopted during the proceedings to immediately re–establish the infringed legal situation.

G. *Amparo as a Right and not as a Single "Recourse" or "Action", and its Consequences*

In our opinion, and after analysing the constitutional text, the following conclusions can be formed:

First, the Constitution consecrates a *right to protection*, and not any particular "action" or "remedy" before a particular Court. This right is established as a fundamental right of individuals and collective persons.

Second, the right to protection implies an *obligation* of all Courts to protect according to the law, against disturbances of the enjoyment and exercise of rights and guarantees. Thus, the development that the legislator may, and has done with this

---

1529 Allan R. BREWER–CARÍAS, *Instituciones políticas..., cit.*, Vol. II, pp. 492–490.

right to protection may take the form, as has happened, of pre–existing actions or remedies, or may consist of a subsidiary action for protection, which is admissible when actions and remedies for protection cannot be effective by means of a brief and summary procedure with powers for the judge to protect fundamental rights and immediately re–establish the infringed legal situation.

Third, the right to protection may thus be guaranteed by means of *actions and recourse* contemplated in the legal order, (the popular action of unconstitutionality; the power of all judges to decide not to apply a law considered unconstitutional; actions for judicial review of administrative actions; the provisional system of *habeas corpus*), or by means of the subsidiary and autonomous action for protection, whose development by the courts has recently begun[1530] and that can be brought before any court according to its subject of attributions.

Fourth, the right of protection is admissible to guarantee the enjoyment and exercise of *all* constitutional rights and guarantees. It may be put into effect with respect to disturbances of individual rights, as well as those of social, economic and political rights.

Fifth, the right to protection seeks to assure protection of constitutional rights and guarantees against *any disturbance* in their enjoyment and exercise, whether this is originated by *private* individuals or by *public* authorities. In the case of disturbance by public authorities, the right of protection is admissible against legislative, administrative and judicial acts, by means of the actions and recourses contemplated in the legal order (the action of unconstitutionality, the recourse of cassation, or actions for judicial review of administrative actions) when they allow a legal situation which has been infringed, to be re–established by means of a brief and summary procedure, or by means of the subsidiary autonomous action for protection. Moreover, this action for protection is admissible against material acts or courses of action of the administration, thus it is not then admissible against administrative acts only.

Sixth, by virtue of the different ways in the Constitution for regulating fundamental rights, the right to protection can be exercised to protect the enjoyment and exercise of constitutional rights and guarantees, *not only when there has been some direct violation of the Constitution*, but also when what has been violated are the legal developments which, by virtue of the Constitution, regulate, limit and even allow the exercise of such rights. Of course, protection must be exercised against an activity that directly violates a fundamental right established in the Constitution, whether it be regulated by law or not, and whether or not the violation is contrary to what the law developing the right establishes.

Seventh, the decision of the judge as a consequence of the exercise of this right to protection, whether this be by means of pre–existing actions or recourses means of the subsidiary and autonomous "action for protection", should not limit himself to precautionary or preventive measures, but should re–establish the infringed legal situation. To

---

1530 Allan R. BREWER–CARÍAS, "La reciente evolución jurisprudencial en relación a la admisibilidad del recurso de *amparo*", *Revista de derecho público*, N° 19, Caracas 1984, pp. 207–218.

this end he should make a pronouncement on the substantive issue brought before him, namely the legality and legitimacy or otherwise of the disturbance of the constitutional right or guarantee that has been reported as infringed.

Eighth, as we have seen, the Venezuelan system of judicial review, being a mixed one, in which the diffuse system of judicial review has been fully developed, that is to say, it can be exercised by all Courts in whatever kind of judicial proceeding, it is obvious that judicial review of legislation is a power that can be exercised by the Courts as a consequence of any action or recourse for protection of fundamental rights and of course, when deciding an autonomous "action for protection" of fundamental rights, when for instance, their violation is infringed by a public authority act based on a law deemed unconstitutional. In such cases, if the judge gives the protection requested through an order similar to the writs of mandamus or to the injunctions, he must previously declare the law based on which the challenged action was taken, inapplicable on the grounds of it being unconstitutional. Therefore, in such cases, judicial review of the constitutionality of legislation is also exercised when an action for protection of fundamental rights is exercised as a consequence of the diffuse system of judicial review.

IV. MIXED SYSTEM OF JUDICIAL REVIEW IN COLOMBIA

A mixed system of judicial review has also been established in Colombia since 1910. In it, the power attributed to all courts to declare the inapplicability of laws they deem contrary to the Constitution performs in parallel with a concentrated system of judicial review attributed to the Supreme Court, also through the exercise of a popular action.[1531] Although it has been qualified as non–systematic, disperse and incongruous,[1532] when this system is analysed in comparative law, it can be considered like the Venezuelan, as one of the most complete constitutionally established systems of judicial review in contemporary constitutionalism.

As we have said, the system as a mixed one, was originally established in the 1910 Constitutional Reform in which the principle of the supremacy of the Constitution was expressly adopted with the consequent jurisdictional control of the constitutionality of laws assigned to the Supreme Court of Justice.[1533] It was in the 1910 Constitution in which the role of "guardian of the integrity of the Constitution" that it is still today in the Fundamental text, was attributed to the Supreme Court of Justice for the first time[1534] and it was also in the same Constitution that the principle of the diffuse system of judicial review acquired constitutional rank, established today in article 215 of the Constitution, which states:

1531 Concerning the mixed character of the system see: J. VIDAL PERDOMO, *Derecho constitucional general*, Bogotá 1985, p. 42; D.R. SALAZAR, *Constitución Política de Colombia*, Bogotá 1982, p. 305; E. SARRIA, *Guarda de la Constitución*, Bogotá, p. 78.

1532 See L.C. SACHICA, *El control de constitucionalidad y sus mecanismos*, Bogotá 1980, p. 59, 66; L.C. SACHICA *La Constitución y su defensa*, Congreso Internacional sobre la Constitución y su Defensa, UNAM, México 1982, (mimeo), p. 38.

1533 *Cf.* L.C. SACHICA, *La Constitución ...* p. 38; L.C. SACHICA, *El control ...*, *cit.*, p. 73.

1534 *Cf.* D.R. SALAZAR, *op. cit.*, p. 304.

Art 215. In all cases of incompatibility between the Constitution and a law, the Constitution rule must be applied in preference.

Nevertheless, even before the constitutional reform of 1910, we can say that the basis of the diffuse system of judicial review according to the North American and Latin American models, during the 19th century had already been established with a legislative rank in article 5 of Law N° 57 of 1887. It prescribed in a very similar way to the present article 215 of the Constitution, that "when there was incompatibility between a constitutional provision and a legal one, the former will be preferred."[1535]

Anyway, since 1910, the Colombian constitutional system has mixed both the diffuse and the concentrated systems of judicial review, but with two other mechanisms of control: a preventive one, as a consequence of the veto powers of legislation given to the President of the Republic, and an obligatory one, concerning executive acts adopted in a state of emergency.

1. Diffuse System of Judicial Review Through the "Exception of Unconstitutionality"

As we said, article 215 of the present Colombian Constitution provides the basis of the diffuse system of judicial review, according to which all judges have the power to decide not to apply a law in a concrete process, when they deem it contrary to the Constitution. The system, as it has been developed, functions entirely according to the North American model, particularly, because it has been conceived as an "exception of unconstitutionality."

In effect, the text of the Constitution does not exclude the possible *ex officio* powers of all judges to decide themselves and without party requirement, not to apply a particular law to the resolution of the case when they deem it to be unconstitutional, as happened in Venezuela. However, the unanimity of the Colombian commentators understands that what is established in article 215 of the Constitution, is an "exception of unconstitutionality", in the sense that in all cases, the constitutional question must be raised in a process by one of the parties through an exception regarding the applicability of a law;[1536] a party that must show a personal and direct interest in the non–application of the law in the concrete case.[1537]

Of course, in these cases of diffuse constitutional control, the judges cannot annul the law or declare its unconstitutionality, nor can the effects of their decision be extended or generalized. On the contrary, as happens in all other diffuse judicial review systems, the court must limit itself to deciding not to apply the unconstitutional law to the concrete case, of course only when it is pertinent to the resolution of the case. That decision only has effects concerning the parties to the case. Therefore, as with similar systems elsewhere, the law whose application has been denied in a concrete case, continues to be in force and other judges can moreover continue

1535 See the text in J. VIDAL PERDOMO, *op. cit.*, p. 40; and in E. SARRIA, *op. cit.*, p. 77.

1536 *Cf.* J. VIDAL PERDOMO, *op. cit.*, pp. 47–48; L.C. SACHICA, *El control ... cit.*, p. 64; E. SARRIA, *op. cit.*, p. 77; D.R. SALAZAR, *op.cit.*, p. 307; A. COPETE LIZARRALDE, *Lecciones de derecho constitucional*, Bogotá, pp. 243–245.

1537 A. COPETE LIZARRALDE, *op. cit.*, p. 246.

to apply it. Even the judge who chose not to apply it in a concrete case, can change his mind in a subsequent process.[1538]

However, regarding the text of article 215 of the Constitution, in which the diffuse system of judicial review has its basis, we must mention the doubts that have arisen in Colombia concerning the scope of its regulations. In effect, some authors have considered that the power regulated in that norm, concerns not only judges but all public officials, an interpretation that has been rejected by others.[1539] We really think that this is an inadmissible discussion. In our opinion, it is logical and the only interpretation compatible with juridical certainty, the one that considers the text of such a norm, as conferring review powers only to the courts and judges. In a state submitted to the rule of law, only the judges can be judges of the constitutionality of legislation. On the contrary, the attribution of constitutional review powers to all public officials particularly of the executive power, with the task of applying the law, could lead to anarchy, and is inadmissible in a *État de droit*.

2. Direct Control of Constitutionality of Legislation through a Popular Action

In addition to the diffuse system of judicial review, the Colombian Constitution also provides for a concentrated system of judicial review attributed to the Supreme Court of Justice. In this respect, article 214 of the Constitution establishes under Title XX related to "Constitutional Jurisdiction", the following

> Art 214. The guarding of the integrity of the Constitution is assigned to the Supreme Court of Justice. Consequently, in addition to the attributions assigned to it in this Constitution and the laws, it shall have the following:...
>
> 2. To definitively decide the unconstitutionality (*inexequibilidad*) of all laws and Decrees enacted by the Government according to the attributions referred to in articles 76, paragraphs 11 and 12, and 80 of the Constitution (Decrees with the force of law), when denounced before it as unconstitutional by any citizen...[1540]

Thus, according to this article, a concentrated system of judicial review is attributed to the Supreme Court of Justice, which exercises it when required through an action that can be brought before it by any citizen. That is to say, through a popular action, that can be based on any grounds of unconstitutionality, whether substantive or formal.

1538 *Cf.* L.C. SACHICA, *El control...cit.*, p. 65.

1539 *Cf.* the various opinions in A. COPETE LIZARRALDE, *op. cit.*, p. 244; E. SARRIA, *op. cit.*, p. 78; J. VIDAL PERDOMO, *op. cit.*, p. 48; L.C. SACHICA, *La Constitución ... cit.*, p. 44.

1540 Through the Legislative Act N° 1 of 1979, this article was reformed, and it assigned the Supreme Court the rol not only to "guard the integrity of the Constitution", but its "supremacy." *Cf.* L.C. SACHICA, *El control... cit.*, p. 142. Nevertheless, that reform resulted ineffective 'because the Supreme Court in decision of 3–11–81 declared the unconstitutionality of that Legislative Act N°1 of 1979, based on defects of procedure. See the reference in J. VIDAL PERDOMO, *op. cit.*, p. 49. The power attributed to the supreme court as constitutional judge has been regulated by the Decree 432 of 1969. See the text in J. ORTEGA TORRES (ed.), *Constitución Política de Colombia*, Bogotá 1985, p. 148.

A. *Objective Character of the Process*

As a result of the "popular" character of the action of unconstitutionality, that is to say, that it can be exercised by any citizen without any particular requirement of standing, the subsequent process developed before the Supreme Court can be considered as an objective one. It is not the result of an action brought before the court against the state or any state organ, but against a law or a state act with the force of law, and that is why, in principle, any citizen can intervene in the procedure whether aiding the petitioner's position or as defender of the challenged law.[1541] Due to its popular character, in any case of action of unconstitutionality, the Attorney General of the Nation must also intervene as head of the Public Prosecutors Office.[1542]

The objective character of the process also results from the fact that the Supreme Court of Justice can consider any other defects of a constitutional nature to the one denounced by the petitioner or by the citizens, that have participated in the process, and can declare the unconstitutionality of the law submitted to control.[1543] Thus, the defects of unconstitutionality that were contained in the action do not limit the powers of the Court as guardian of the integrity of the Constitution, being authorised to examine *ex officio* the impugned act and to confront it with all the constitutional dispositions.[1544] On the other hand, also as a consequence of the role assigned to the Court, the withdrawal of the action by the petitioner has no effect, and the Court must continue its constitutional examination.[1545]

Finally, and also as a result of the "popular" character of the action, in principle there is no precise delay in which it must be exercised, thus, it is inextinguishable and that is why it has been considered a political right of the citizens.[1546] Nevertheless, the constitutional reform of 1979, later ineffective, sought to establish that when the grounds of the action were based on procedural or formal defects of the challenged law, the action could only be brought before the Court within a delay of one year after its enactment.[1547]

B. *Object of the Concentrated Judicial Review System*

As stated in article 215 of the Constitution, the object of the popular action as a means for judicial review of constitutionality, is "all the laws" and decrees with force of law, that is to say those issued by the executive as a consequence of the attribution of extraordinary powers or special legislative authorizations by Con-

1541 This was expressly established in the constitucional reform sanctioned by the Legislative Act N° 1 of 1979. *Cf.* L Carlos SACHICA, *El control...* p. 150. The present Constitution only establishes the free intervention of any citizen when the state Act impugned is a Decree of Emergency. See Art. 215,2 and Arts. 121 and 122 Constitution; and Art. 14 Decree 432 of 1969.

1542 Art. 215,2. Constitution.

1543 Art. 29. Decree 432 of 1969.

1544 L.C. SACHICA, *El control..., cit.*, p. 106.

1545 A. COPETE LIZARRALDE, *op. cit.*, p. 246.

1546 L.C. SACHICA, *La Constitución..., cit.*, p. 45

1547 *Cf.* L.C. SACHICA, *El control..., cit.*, pp. 73, 151.

gress,[1548] and also those issued by the executive on matters concerning the economic, social and public works plans when Congress fails to sanction them within a particular delay.[1549]

Thus, the judicial review powers of the Supreme Court refer to legislative acts and decrees with the force of law, executive regulations also being submitted to judicial review of constitutionality, but by the Council of State.[1550]

Nevertheless, in spite of the very wide constitutional review powers assigned to the Supreme Court concerning "all the laws" of the Nation, which for instance, comprise legislative acts containing constitutional reforms by formal defects,[1551] the Court itself has restricted the scope of its review powers and has excluded certain laws from being examined on the grounds of unconstitutionality. This is particularly true regarding laws of approval of other state acts, such as administrative contracts and international treaties. In these cases, the Supreme Court by case law has limited its judicial review powers and has abstained from exercising constitutional control over those laws.[1552] In particular, concerning international treaties and contrary to the general trend, for instance in continental Europe, the Colombian Supreme Court has considered that controlling the constitutionality of a law of approval of an International Treaty would mean the breaking of the international obligations of the state, additional to the criterion traditionally followed in Colombia, regarding the superior hierarchy of international treaties regarding internal public law.[1553]

C. *Compulsory Judicial Review of Executive Emergency Decrees*

Within the state acts submitted to judicial review through the exercise of a popular action, we must also mention decrees issued by the President of the Republic when a state of siege is declared as a consequence of an external war or of internal commotion or when the economic and social order of the country is gravely altered.[1554] In such cases, the Colombian Constitution establishes a compulsory judicial review proceeding according to which the day following their enactment, the President of the Republic must submit them to the Supreme Court, which must then "definitively decide upon their constitutionality."[1555] As we mentioned, in the proceeding, any citizen is allowed to participate whether in defence of or in the attack on the constitutionality of such Decrees.[1556] Once the Court has pronounced its deci-

1548 Art. 76, paragraphs 11 and 12. Constitution.

1549 Arts. 76 paragraph 4; 80 and 215, paragraph 2.

1550 Art. 216 Constitution.

1551 *Cf.* L.C.SACHICA, *El control... cit.*, p. 144; J. VIDAL PERDOMO, *op. cit.*, p. 49.

1552 *Cf.* L.C. SACHICA, *El control... cit.*, pp. 79–84

1553 *Cf.* L.C. SACHICA, *El Control... cit.*, p. 80

1554 Arts. 121, 122 Constitution.

1555 Arts. 121, 122 Constitution. Art. 13 Decree 432 of 1969.

1556 Art. 215 Constitution. Art. 14 Decree 432 of 1969

sion, it has *erga omnes* effects and the value of *res judicata*, thus no further action of unconstitutionality can be exercised against those acts.[1557]

D. *Role of the Constitutional Chamber of the Supreme Court*

As we have said, the powers to control the constitutionality of state acts are assigned in the Constitution of Colombia, following the general trend of the Latin–American systems, to the Supreme Court of Justice, which exercises it in Plenary session.[1558] Nevertheless, in the 60's and influenced by the European model of judicial review, attempts were made to create a Constitutional Court to substitute the Supreme Court in its role of Supreme Guardian of the Constitution.[1559] The project was rejected, and in the 1968 constitutional reform, within the Supreme Court of Justice, a Constitutional Chamber or Division was created instead, composed of four members of the Court specialising in public law,[1560] with the special task of studying cases of unconstitutionality previous to the decision of the Plenary session, and proposing projects of resolutions to it.[1561] Thus, the Constitutional Chamber has merely an advisory character and no power of decision on constitutional questions. It must be mentioned that the constitutional reform adopted by the Legislative Act N° 1 of 1979, tended to give the Constitutional Chamber self decision powers in almost all matters of unconstitutionality, except those regarding the unconstitutionality of constitutional reforms due to formal defects and that of executive decrees issued in cases of state of Siege or economic emergency.[1562] Nevertheless, Legislative Act N° 1 of 1979 was itself declared unconstitutional by the Supreme Court in 1981[1563] and consequently, the 1979 constitutional reform ceased to be effective.

E. *Effects of the Supreme Court decision on judicial review*

As happens in all concentrated systems of judicial review, the Supreme Court decisions, when declaring the unconstitutionality of a legislative act, have general and *erga omnes* effects.[1564] Additionally, the decision has *res judicata* value, and its contents are obligatory to everyone. In particular, the value of *res judicata* to the Supreme Courts decisions rejecting the action, and thus, declaring the constitutionality of the challenged law, has been recognized, in which cases, the courts through

1557 As was established in the constitutional reform sanctioned by the Legislative Act N° 1 of 1979, later annuled. See J.C. SACHICA, *El control... cit.*, pp. 148–149.

1558 Art. 215 Constitution. Art. 1, Decree 432 of 1969

1559 See the comments of H. FIX–ZAMUDIO, *Los tribunales constitucionales y los derechos humanos*, México, 1980, pp. 151–152.

1560 Art. 1. Decree 432 of 1969.

1561 Art. 3. Decree 432 of 1969.

1562 *Cf.* L.C. SACHICA, *El control... cit.*, p. 59.

1563 Décision of 1–11–81. See in *Revista Foro Colombiano,* N° 151–152, 1982. See the comments in J. VIDAL PERDOMO, *op. cit.*, p. 49.

1564 *Cf.* A. COPETE LIZARRALDE, *op. cit.*, p. 245; L.C. SACHICA, *El control..., cit.*, p. 68.

their diffuse control powers cannot declare the inapplicability of the law on the same grounds of unconstitutionality rejected by the Supreme Court.[1565]

On the other hand, regarding time, the endless discussions of the *ex tunc* or *ex nunc* effects of the Supreme Court decision on judicial review, has also taken place in Colombia, even though the majority of authors tends to assign them only *ex nunc, pro futuro* effects.[1566] Thus the laws declared unconstitutional by the Supreme Court due to their presumption of constitutionality, in principle are effective until their annulment is declared by the Court, the juridical situations originated by the law prior to its annulment being only submitted to review through ordinary judicial means.[1567]

Anyway, regarding legislative acts containing constitutional reforms, when declared unconstitutional, they become totally and definitively inapplicable after the declaration. However, the effects produced by the act declared unconstitutional are intangible. Consequently, in such cases, the decision has no retroactive effects; and the constitutional rules revoked or amended by the constitutional reform declared unconstitutional are revived,[1568] thereby returning to the constitutional system in force prior to the enactment of the annulled reform.

3. Preventive Judicial Review of Legislation

Finally, it must be mentioned that in addition to the *a posteriori* concentrated judicial review system, since 1886, the Colombian Constitution has established a preventive judicial review method of laws, as a consequence of the veto powers of legislation assigned to the President of the Republic.[1569]

When a law is vetoed based on substantive or procedural constitutional issues, if the legislative chambers insist on its promulgation, the President of the Republic must send the project of law to the Supreme Court, which must take its decision within a six day delay.

In the event of the Supreme Court declaring the bill unconstitutional, the project must be filed, but if the Supreme Court rejects the constitutional objections raised by the President, then he is obliged to promulgate it.[1570]

V. MIXED SYSTEM OF JUDICIAL REVIEW IN GUATEMALA

Also following the North American model based on the principle of the supremacy of the Constitution[1571] the 1921 Guatemalan Constitution established the power of the Court to declare in their decisions the inapplicability of any law or disposition

1565 *Cf.* A. COPETE LIZARRALDE, *op. cit.*, p. 246; L.C. SACHICA, *El control... cit.*, p. 172

1566 *Cf.* L.C. SACHICA, *El control... cit.*, p. 68; E. SARRIA, *op. cit.*, p. 83

1567 E. SARRIA, *op. cit.*, p. 83

1568 J. VIDAL PERDOMO, *op. cit.*, p. 46

1569 Arts. 90 and 215,1. Constitution. Art. 11, Decree 432 of 1969.

1570 Art. 90 Constitution.

1571 See the comments regarding the constitutional process of Guatemala during the 19th Century in J.M. GARCÍA LA GUARDIA, *La defensa de la Constitución*, México 1983, pp. 52–53.

of the other state powers when contrary to the norms contained in the Constitution of the Republic.[1572]

This power of the Courts, which can be termed a diffuse power of judicial review, was maintained in all constitutional texts up to the present Constitution of 1965 in which a concentrated system of review attributed to a specially created Constitutional Court was established in addition to the diffuse system. Thus, the Guatemalan system of judicial review can also be considered a mixed one.

1. Diffuse system of Judicial Review

In effect, the 1965 Constitution expressly establishes the principle of the supremacy of the Constitution and the subsequent nullity of all state acts contrary to it, prescribing the duty of the judges to give preference to the Constitution in cases of laws being in conflict with the Constitution.

In particular, article 77 establishes the general norm by stating that

> The laws, government dispositions, and any other order which regulates the exercise of the rights guaranteed in the Constitution shall be *ipso jure* null if they diminish, restrict or distort them.[1573]

Additionally, article 246 establishes:

> The Courts of Justice will always observe the principle that the Constitution must prevail over any law or international Treaty.

Consequently, according to these norms, the judicial review power attributed to all courts of justice, is conceived in the Constitution as a duty of the judges, which they can therefore exercise *ex officio*,[1574] in deciding a concrete case, that is to say, without the requirement of a party to the case. Nevertheless, when a party to the case raises a constitutional question regarding a law or a part of it, the judges must decide upon the question.[1575] Anyway, due to the purely incidental character of the review, article 246 of the Constitution states:

> If the unconstitutionality of a law is declared, the decision must limit itself to establishing that the legal disposition is inapplicable to the case and the question must be sent to Congress.[1576]

The party requirement regarding constitutional questions can be brought before the ordinary Court in the concrete case, either through the concrete claim or as an exception in the process. In any case, prior to the judge's decision of the case and thus, prior to the decision of the constitutional question, the judge must hear the parties and the Public Prosecutor.[1577]

1572 Article 93, c. Constitution 1921.

1573 See also Article 172 Constitution 15–9–1965.

1574 J.M. GARCÍA LA GUARDIA, *op. cit.*, pp. 56–57.

1575 Art. 246 Constitution.

1576 This norm has been developed in the legislative Decree N° 8, Articles 96–104. See J.M. GARCÍA LA GUARDIA, *op. cit.*, p. 58.

1577 J.M. GARCÍA LA GUARDIA, *op. cit.*, p. 58.

As in all diffuse systems of judicial review, judge's decision when declaring the inapplicability of a law on the grounds of unconstitutionality, has declarative effects, in the sense that it establishes a pre–existent nullity with retroactive or *ex tunc* effects, but exclusively related to the parties to the case[1578] (*in casu et inter partes*).

2. Concentrated System of Judicial Review and the Constitutional Court

However, the 1965 Constitution, following the European model and additional to the diffuse system of judicial review, also established a concentrated system, by assigning the exclusive power to declare the unconstitutionality of laws, and thus, to annul them with *erga omnes* effects, to a Constitutional Court.[1579]

This Constitutional Court, although created in the Constitution,[1580] is not conceived as a permanent organ, but as a temporal one that only functions when required to exercise judicial review. It has 12 members, appointed as follows: four by the Supreme Court of Justice, and the rest designated by the Supreme Court of Justice, by a draw from within the members of the Court of Appeals and the Administrative Justice Tribunal. The President of the Constitutional Court is the President of the Supreme Court of Justice.[1581]

The judicial review powers of the Constitutional Court are exercised when requested through a "recourse of unconstitutionality" conceived as a direct action[1582] that can be exercised against "laws and governmental dispositions of general effects when considered to be totally or partially unconstitutional."[1583]

The standing to bring the action before the Constitutional Court is a specific one, thus differing from the popular action that can be brought before the Supreme Courts of Venezuela and Colombia. In particular, this "recourse of unconstitutionality" can only be brought before the Court by the following: the Council of state, conceived in the Guatemalan constitutional system, as a consultative institution; the Public Prosecutor, when requested to do so by the President in a decision adopted in the Council of Ministers; and finally, by any individual or entity directly affected by the unconstitutionality of the law or the challenged governmental act, assisted by ten lawyers.[1584] Thus, the standing has been considered extremely limited.[1585]

In the proceeding of the recourse of unconstitutionality, if the Public Prosecutor does not bring the action before the Court, he must be notified and in principle, he

---

1578 *Idem*, p. 59.

1579 See H. FIX–ZAMUDIO, *Los tribunales constitucionales y los derechos humanos*, México 1980, p. 136

1580 Art. 262 Constitution. The Court and the recourse of unconstitutionality is regulated in the Law of *amparo*, *habeas corpus* and constitutionality of 3–5–1966. See the reference in H. FIX–ZAMUDIO, *op. cit.*, p. 137.

1581 Art. 266 Constitution, Art. 105 Law

1582 H. FIX–ZAMUDIO, *op. cit.*, p. 138.

1583 Art. 263 Constitution. Art. 106 Law.

1584 Art. 264 Constitution. Art. 107 Law.

1585 H. FIX–ZAMUDIO, *op. cit.*, p. 64.

must defend the constitutionality of the challenged act, even though he can express his conformity with the alleged unconstitutionality.[1586]

We must also mention, as an important feature of the proceeding before the Constitutional Court of Guatemala, that the Court can provisionally suspend the effects of the challenged law or executive act during the process, when the unconstitutionality is notorious and could produce irreparable damage.

This decision of suspension of the effects of the law or executive act of general contents has general effects and an *erga omnes* character and must be published in the official Journal.[1587]

The final decision of the Court if it is of declaring the unconstitutionality of the law, has also *erga omnes* effects, but as in all concentrated systems of judicial review, with *ex nunc* effects. Thus, the decision has a constitutive character, with *pro futuro* consequences, and without any effect back towards the past.[1588] Only when a temporal suspension of the effects of the law has been decided by the Court during the procedure the final decision declaring the unconstitutionality of the law can have *ex tunc* effects, but back to the date of the suspensive decision of the effects of the challenged law.[1589]

3. Judicial Review and the Constitutional Protection (*Amparo*)

Finally, it must also be mentioned that in Guatemala, a special judicial means for constitutional protection (*amparo*) of the fundamental rights established in the Constitution, following the Mexican model,[1590] has been established.

The main purpose of this *amparo* as all the institutions of this kind in Latin America is to seek "the maintenance of or the restitution to the aggrieved person of the enjoyment of the rights and guarantees established in the Constitution."[1591] Nevertheless, according to the Guatemalan Constitution the *amparo* is also admissible in order "to declare, in concrete cases that a law, an executive regulation or any other act of an authority is not obligatory for the petitioner, because it contravenes or it restricts any of the rights guaranteed in the Constitution."[1592] Thus, through the *amparo* action, the judge can exercise his powers of judicial review in an incidental way *incidenter tantum*, in accordance with the diffuse system, and declare a law deemed unconstitutional because of violation of fundamental rights inapplicable.

The concrete effect of the judge's decision granting *amparo* to the petitioner, is to suspend the application of the law or executive regulation regarding the petitioner, and restore when necessary, his juridical situation previously infringed.[1593]

1586 J.M. García La Guardia, *op. cit.*, p. 63

1587 Art. 263 Constitution. Art. 106 Law.

1588 Art. 108 Law.

1589 J.M. García La Guardia, *op. cit.*, p. 67; H. Fix–Zamudio, *op. cit.*, p. 140.

1590 H. Fix–Zamudio, *op. cit.*, p. 136

1591 Art. 80,1 Constitution

1592 Art. 80,2 Constitution

1593 J.M. Garcia La Guardia, *op. cit.*, p. 50; H. Fix–Zamudio, *op. cit.*, p. 136

VI. MIXED SYSTEM OF JUDICIAL REVIEW IN BRAZIL

The Brazilian system of judicial review, like the Argentinean, can be thought of as one of the Latin American systems that had followed the North American model more closely,[1594] although it can now be thought of as a mixed system, after the establishment in the 1934 Constitution, of a direct action of unconstitutionality that can be brought before the Supreme Court of Justice to impugned laws.

1. Historical Background

In effect, the Federal Constitution of 1891 clearly influenced by the North American constitutional system[1595] assigned the Supreme Federal Tribunal the power to review, through an extraordinary recourse, the decisions of the federal courts and of the courts of the Member States, in which the validity or the application of the treaties or Federal Laws was questioned, and the decisions were against; or in which the validity of laws or government acts of the states was questioned on the grounds of being contrary to the Constitution or to the federal laws, and the decisions considered the challenged laws or acts valid.[1596] As a consequence of this express constitutional attribution, the Federal Law 221 of 1894[1597] assigned the power to judge upon the validity of obviously unconstitutional laws and executive regulations, and to decide their inapplicability in concrete cases, to all federal judges. Thus, the diffuse system of judicial review of legislation was established in Brazil as from the end of the last century, and was perfected through the subsequent constitutional reforms of 1926, 1934, 1937, 1946 and 1967.[1598] Therefore, we can say that the main feature of the Brazilian system of judicial review is its diffuse character, with all its consequences according to the American model.

In addition to the diffuse system of judicial review, a concentrated system of review was established in the 1934 Constitution, by attributing power to the Supreme Federal Tribunal to declare the unconstitutionality of member state Constitution or laws (state laws) when required to do so by the Attorney General of the Republic.[1599] Thus, a direct action of unconstitutionality was established as from 1934, to defend federal constitutional principles, against Member state acts,[1600] later developed in subsequent Constitutions [1601] up to its extension after the 1965 Constitu-

1594 H. FIX–ZAMUDIO and J. CARPIZO, "Amerique latine" in L. FAVOREU and J.A. JOLOWICZ (ed.), *Le contrôle juridictionnel des lois*, Paris 1986, p. 121.

1595 O.A. BANDEIRA DE MELLO, *A teoria das Constituiçoes rigidas*, Sao Paulo 1980, p. 157; J. Alfonso DA SILVA, *Sistema de defensa da Constituiçao brasileira*, Congreso sobre la Constitución y su Defensa, UNAM, México 1982, p. 29. (mimeo).

1596 Art. 59, III, 1. 1981 Constitution.

1597 Art. 13,10. Law 221 of 20 November 1984

1598 O.A. BANDEIRA DE MELLO, *op. cit.*, pp. 158–237

1599 Art. 12,2. 1934 Constitution.

1600 J. Alfonso DA SILVA, *doc. cit.* p. 29

1601 Also in the Law N° 2271 of 22 July 1954.

tional Amendment, to control all normative acts of state, whether federal or of the Member States.[1602]

Consequently, the Brazilian system can be considered a mixed one in which the diffuse system of judicial review operates in combination with a concentrated system.[1603]

2. Diffuse system of judicial review

In the American Model and in the Argentinean experience the powers of the courts to control the constitutionality of legislation were derived from the principle of constitutional supremacy as applied by the Supreme Court. Contrary to that, the diffuse system of judicial review arose in Brazil from express provisions in the 1891 Constitution, and[1604] it is still based on constitutional norms. In this respect, the present Constitution establishes the competence of the Supreme Federal Tribunal to judge through extraordinary recourses, cases decided in the last resort by other courts or judges, when the challenged judicial decisions: first, were against any disposition of the Constitution or denied the enforcement of a Treaty or federal law; second, when they declared the unconstitutionality of a Treaty or of a federal law; and third, when they deemed a law or other local government act challenging the Constitution or a federal law valid.[1605]

According to this norm, not only is the diffuse system of judicial review established, but the power of the Supreme Tribunal to intervene in all processes in which constitutional questions have been resolved, is also established.

A. *Incidental character of the system and the exception of unconstitutionality*

As we mentioned, the diffuse system of judicial review in Brazil follows the general trends of the American model also developed in Argentina. Therefore, all the courts of first instance have the power not to apply laws (federal, state or Municipal laws) they deem unconstitutional, when a party to the process has raised the question of constitutionality. Thus, the judges have no *ex officio* power to judge the constitutionality of the laws, and can only exercise it when the question of constitutionality has been raised by the interested party as an exception or defence in the process.[1606] The constitutional question, once raised, has a preliminary character regarding the final decision of the case, which the judge must decide beforehand.

1602 *Cf.* J. Alfonso DA SILVA, *doc. cit.*, p. 31

1603 A. BUZAID, "La accion directa de inconstitucionalidad en el derecho brasileño", *Revista de la Facultad de Derecho*, UCAB, Nº 19–22, Caracas 1964, p. 55; O.A. BANDEIRA DE MELLO, *op. cit.*, p. 157.

1604 *Cf.* J. Alfonso DA SILVA, *doc. cit.*, pp. 32, 34; J. Alfonso DA SILVA, *Curso de direito constitucional positivo*, Sao Paulo 1984, p. 17.

1605 Art. 119, III b,c, Constitution. J. Alfonso DA SILVA, *Sistema... doc. cit.*, p. 43; O.A. BANDEIRA DE MELLO, *op. cit.*, p. 215.

1606 J. Alfonso DA SILVA, *Curso...* p. 18; J. Alfonso DA SILVA, *Sistema... doc. cit.*, pp. 33, 37, 58.

Of course, the decision of the courts on constitutional matters has only *in casu et inter partes* effects, and the unapplied law is considered null and void *ab initio*. Thus, the decision has *ex tunc*, retroactive effects.[1607]

The constitutional question can also be considered in a second instance, through the normal appeals process, in which case, when the court of second instance is a collegiate court, the decision upon matters of unconstitutionality of legislation must be adopted by a majority vote decision of its members.[1608]

B. *Extraordinary recourse before the Supreme Federal Tribunal*

The Brazilian Constitution, ever since the establishment of the constitutional review judicial system in 1891, has always expressly regulated the power of the Supreme Court to review lower courts decisions on matters of constitutionality, through an extraordinary recourse that can be brought before the Tribunal, by the party to the process who has lost the case.[1609]

This extraordinary recourse of unconstitutionality, as we mentioned, proceeds only when the Superior Courts of Appeal have made decisions that are considered contrary to the Constitution or that deny the validity of a treaty or federal law; when the decisions declare the unconstitutionality of a treaty or of a Federal Law; and when they deem a local government law or act that has been challenged as unconstitutional or contrary to a federal law valid.[1610]

It must be mentioned that due to the constitutional questions that are the object of the proceeding before the Supreme Federal Tribunal, the Attorney General can always intervene; and can also intervene in any process pending decision, to raise constitutional questions, which must be decided by the Tribunal.[1611]

Finally it must be said that when deciding constitutional questions, the Supreme Federal Tribunal must adopt its decision with the vote of the majority of its members.[1612] The decision, as the first instance one, when declaring the unconstitutionality of a law, has *inter partes* and *ex tunc* effects.[1613] In such cases, the Tribunal in fact recognises the *ab initio* unconstitutionality of the law, in a decision which has declarative effects, but does not annul or repeal the law, which continues in force and to be applicable.

In the Brazilian system, an additional feature can be distinguished: once adopted by the Tribunal the decision must be sent to the Federal Senate which has the power, according to the Constitution, to "suspend the execution of all or part of a law or decree, declared unconstitutional by the Supreme Federal Tribunal through a defini-

---

1607 J. Alfonso DA SILVA, *Sistema... doc. cit.*, pp. 41,64; A. BUZAID, *loc. cit.*, p. 91.

1608 This qualified vote was first established in the 1934 Constitution Art. 179), and is always required. See O.A. BANDEIRA DE MELLO, *op. cit.*, p. 159.

1609 J. Alfonso DA SILVA, *Sistema... doc. cit.*, p. 44

1610 Art. 199. III, b,c. Constitution.

1611 J. Alfonso DA SILVA, *Sistema... doc. cit.*, p. 44

1612 D.A. BANDEIRA DE MELLO, *op. cit.*, p. 218

1613 J. Alfonso DA SILVA, *Sistema... doc. cit.*, pp. 69, 71

tive decision,[1614] in which case the effects of the Senate decisions have, of course, *erga omnes* and *ex nunc* effects.[1615]

Anyway, it must be said that in Brazil, like in the North American system, a presumption of constitutionality also exists regarding laws and other state acts. Consequently, only when the unconstitutionality of a law appears to be without doubt, the Tribunal can declare its unconstitutionality. Thus, in case of doubt, it must reject the question and consider the law constitutional, and applicable in the concrete case.[1616]

3. Concentrated system of judicial review

Additional to the diffuse system of judicial review, as we have said, the Brazilian Constitution has since 1934 also adopted a concentrated system of review attributed to the Supreme Federal Tribunal, through a direct action that can be brought before the Tribunal only by the Attorney General of the Republic. This direct action of unconstitutionality can be of two types: the intervention direct action and the generic direct action.

The so–called "intervention direct action" was originally established in the 1934 Constitution as a means for the protection of the federal constitutional principles regarding States legislation.[1617] The Constitution in effect established the possibility for the Federal Government to intervene in the Member States, to secure the observance of the following principles: republican form of government; independence and harmony of powers; temporal character of electoral functions; non re–election of governors for the next term; municipal autonomy; submission of administrative accounts; and guarantees of the Judicial Power.[1618].

Now, when any of these principles are violated by a member state, the federal power can intervene in it. But previous to that intervention, the Attorney General must submit the question of unconstitutionality of the member state acts when contrary to those principles, for examination by the Supreme Federal Tribunal, through a direct action.[1619] If the final decision of the Tribunal is to declare the unconstitutionality of the challenged Member state law or act, it must be published and sent to the President of the Republic for it to suspend, by Decree, the execution of the challenged act, and if necessary, to order federal intervention in the Member state.[1620] Thus in this case, the effects of the Tribunal decision are considered to be declarative[1621] and with *erga omnes* effects.[1622]

1614 Art. 42, VII Federal Constitution

1615 J. Alfonso DA SILVA, *Sistema...*, *doc. cit.*, p. 73.

1616 *Cf.* T.B. CAVALCANTI, *Do controle de constitutionalidade*, Rio do Janeiro, 1966, p. 69.

1617 Art.7 Constitution 1934. O.A. BANDEIRA DE MELLO, *op. cit.*, p. 170; J. Alfonso DA SILVA, *Sistema... doc. cit.*, p. 31.

1618 Art. 10 Constitution. O.A. BANDEIRA DE MELLO, *op. cit.*, . 221.

1619 Art. 11,1 Constitution. Art. 1 Law N. 2271 of 22–7–1954 and Law N° 4337 of 1–6–1964. A BUZAID, *loc. cit.*, pp. 76–78.

1620 Art. 11,2 Constitution. Art. 9 Law N° 4337 of 1–6–1964. A. BUZAID, *loc. cit.*, p. 53

1621 See O.A. BANDEIRA DE MELLO, *op. cit.*, p. 212; A. BUZAID, *loc. cit.*, p. 95. In contrary sense see J. Alfonso DA SILVA, *Sistema... doc. cit.*, p. 76.

Only when the act is declared unconstitutional by the Tribunal, federal intervention can take place.[1623]

In the 1946 Constitution, in addition to the interventive direct action, what is called a generic direct action of unconstitutionality[1624] was established. This action differs from the one already mentioned by the fact that it is intended not to protect certain constitutional principles regarding member state laws and acts only, but any of the dispositions of the Constitution.

The Constitution, in effect, attributes competence to the Supreme Federal Tribunal at the request of the Attorney General of the Republic, to decide upon the unconstitutionality of any law or act of a normative character, either federal or of a Member state.[1625] In this case, if the Supreme Federal Tribunal declares the unconstitutionality of the federal or state law or normative act, a copy of the decision must be sent to the Federal Senate, which has the power to "suspend the execution of all or part of the law or decree declared unconstitutional by a definitive decision of the Supreme Federal Tribunal.[1626]

Discussions have taken place among Brazilian constitutional law authors regarding the effects of the Supreme Federal Tribunal decision declaring the unconstitutionality of a law, as a consequence of a generic direct action, particularly due to the fact that the Constitution assigns the aforementioned power to the Federal Senate. It has been considered, in effect, that the Supreme Federal Tribunal decisions in such cases of generic direct actions of unconstitutionality do not have, in themselves, *erga omnes* effects[1627] their contents being only to verify the existence or not of a defect of unconstitutionality in the challenged act.[1628] Thus, it has been thought to have declarative effects, thus, with *ex tunc* repercussions.[1629] Only the Senate decision of suspension of the execution of the law is considered to have *erga omnes* effects.[1630]

4. Indirect Means for Judicial Review of Legislation

Additional to the diffuse and concentrated systems of judicial review, an indirect means for judicial review, through the actions for protection of fundamental rights

1622 J. Alfonso DA SILVA, Sistema..., *doc. cit.*, p. 76. In contrary sense see A. BUZAID, *loc. cit.*, p. 96.

1623 A. BUZAID, *loc. cit.*, pp. 79, 97; O.A. BANDEIRA DE MELLO, *op. cit.*, p. 222.

1624 J. Alfonso DA SILVA, *Sistema... doc. cit.*, p. 31; A. BUZAID considers this action as the only one in Brazil whose principal object is the declaration of the unconstitutionality of a law, *loc. cit.*, p. 84.

1625 Art. 119, I, 1. Constitution; Law N. 4337 of 1–6–1964. J.A. Alfonso DA SILVA, *Curso... cit.*, p. 18.

1626 Art. 42, VII, Constitution.

1627 J. Alfonso DA SILVA, *Sistema... doc. cit.*, pp. 54,64,69; In contrary sense see O.A. BANDEIRA DE MELLO, *op. cit.*, pp. 201, 213.

1628 J. Alfonso DA SILVA, *Sistema.., doc. cit.*, p. 74

1629 O. BANDEIRA DE MELLO, *op. cit.*, p. 201; A. BUZAID, *loc. cit.*, p. 96.

1630 J. Alfonso DA SILVA, *Sistema... doc. cit.*, pp. 54,64,69,73; In contrary sense see A. BUZAID, *loc. cit.*, p. 95.

and liberties and through a popular action established to seek the protection of public assets, can also be identified in the Brazilian constitutional system.

A. *Mandado de segurança and habeas corpus actions and judicial review*

In effect, since 1934,[1631] the Constitution of Brazil has expressly established the *mandado de segurança* as a special means for the protection of fundamental rights, other than personal liberty, which is protected through the recourse for *habeas corpus*. Thus, in the Brazilian constitutional system there are two special actions for the constitutional protection of fundamental rights: the *mandado de segurança* and the *habeas corpus* actions.

In particular, the *mandado de segurança* is intended to protect actual individual rights not protected through *habeas corpus*, whoever the authority responsible for the illegality or abuse of powers may be.[1632] Nevertheless, it has been traditionally considered that the laws or any other normative act of state, cannot be the object of an action requesting either *habeas corpus* or a *mandado de segurança.*[1633]

In this respect, as happened with the Argentinean recourse for *amparo* until recent changes within the Supreme Court decisions, the abstract control of the constitutionality of laws is not possible through the exercise of the actions for a *mandado de segurança*, or *habeas corpus*. In other words, no direct action against laws can be exercised through the *mandado de segurança*, or *habeas corpus* actions, even if they are what the Mexican system calls auto–applicative or self executing laws.[1634] Nevertheless, such actions can serve as an indirect means of judicial review, according to the diffuse system, when they are exercised against an act of any authority when executed based on a law deemed unconstitutional. Thus, it is only the concrete situation that results from the execution or application of the law or normative act, the one that can be directly impugned by means of these actions for protection of fundamental rights, and only in an indirect way and in accordance with the diffuse method of review, that laws can be controlled by the courts on the grounds of their unconstitutionality.

B. *Popular Action for the Protection of Public Assets and Judicial Review*

Also, ever since the 1934 Constitution[1635] in the Brazilian constitutional system, a *popular action* as a special means devoted to invalidate illegal acts, which could

1631 Art. 113,33 Constitution 1934. A. RÍOS ESPINOZA, Presupuestos constitucionales del mandato de seguridad", *Boletín del Instituto de Derecho Comparado de México*, UNAM, 46, 1963, p. 71. (Also published in H. FIX–ZAMUDIO, A. RÍOS ESPINOSA and N. ALCALÁ ZAMORA, *Tres sstudios sobre el mandato de seguridad brasileño*, México 1963, pp. 71–96.

1632 153,21 Constitution

1633 *Cf.* A. Alfonso DA SILVA, "*Sistema... doc. cit.*, p. 47; H. FIX–ZAMUDIO, "Mandato de seguridad y juicio de *amparo*", *Boletín del Instituto de Derecho Comparado de México*, UNAM; 46, 1963, pp. 11, 17. Also published in H. FIX–ZAMUDIO, A. RÍOS ESPINOSA, N. ALCALÁ ZAMORA, *op. cit.*, pp. 3–69; A. RIOS ESPINOSA, *loc.cit.*, p. 88

1634 H. FIX–ZAMUDIO, *loc. cit.*, p. 16; A. Alfonso DA SILVA, *Sistema... doc. cit.*, pp. 46,47.

1635 O.A. BANDEIRA DE MELLO, *op. cit.*, p. 174

affect the assets of public entities, has been instituted.[1636] In particular, it is an action open to any citizen and principally directed to impugn administrative acts, which, therefore, cannot be brought before the courts to impugn, in a direct way, laws or normative acts on the grounds of being unconstitutional. Nevertheless, in this case, the popular action can be an indirect means of judicial review of legislation, if the concrete administrative act which causes damage to the assets of any public entity, is based on a law deemed unconstitutional. Nonetheless, it has been considered a direct means of judicial review of legislation, in cases in which damage to the assets of public entities is directly caused by the law or decree.[1637] In such cases, the powers of review of legislation exercised by the judges, of course, follow the general pattern of the diffuse system of review.

VII. THE TRIBUNAL OF CONSTITUTIONAL GUARANTEES AND THE MIXED SYSTEM OF PERU

Finally, a mixed system of judicial review can also by the distinguished in Peru, where the 1979 Constitution established the basis for a diffuse system of judicial review and additionally created a Tribunal of Constitutional Guarantees, with concentrated powers of judicial review, following the Spanish model.[1638]

In effect, the Constitution of Peru of 12 July 1979, in force since the 28th July 1980,[1639] following a long tradition, has established in article 23 the diffuse system of judicial review as follows:

> Art. 236. In case of incompatibility between a constitutional norm and an ordinary legal one, the judge must prefer the former. In similar way, he must prefer the legal norm above any other inferior norm.

According to this constitutional disposition, all judges can exercise their power of judicial review of legislation, deciding not to apply a law, which they deem unconstitutional. This must by done in an incidental way when required by a party to the case, and with *inter partes* effects.[1640] This power of judicial review, without doubt, can be considered a diffuse one, even though not commonly exercised by the courts.[1641]

Additionally to the diffuse system of judicial review, a concentrated system of judicial review has also been established in Peru since 1980. In effect, another example of a specially created constitutional organ for judicial review of constitutionality of legislation in Latin America, is the Tribunal of Constitutional Guarantees

---

1636 Art. 153, 31 Constitution.

1637 J. Alfonso DA SILVA, *Açao popular constitucional. Doutrina a proceso*, Sao Paulo 1968, p. 129; J. Alfonso DA SILVA, *Sistema... doc. cit.*, p. 49.

1638 See D. GARCÍA BELAUNDE, "La influencia española en la Constitución peruana (a propósito del Tribunal de Garantías Constitucionales)", *Revista de derecho político*, UNED, 16, Madrid 1982–1983, p. 201.

1639 See D. GARCÍA BELAUNDE, "La nueva Constitución peruana", *Boletín mexicano de derecho comparado*, 40, 1981.

1640 See D. GARCÍA BELAUNDE, "La influencia española...", *loc. cit.*, pp. 205–207.

1641 *Idem*, p. 205

created by the Peruvian Constitution of 1979 as a "control organ of the Constitution" made up of nine members appointed in a paritarian way (three each) by the Congress, the executive power and the Supreme Court of Justice.[1642] Its functioning has been regulated by the Organic Law of the Tribunal of Constitutional Guarantees of 19 May 1982.[1643]

This Tribunal of Constitutional Guarantees, with jurisdiction throughout the territory of the Republic, is competent in two basic aspects, relating to constitutional supremacy: first, it has jurisdictional power to control the constitutionality of legislation; and second, it is competent to decide, in the last resort, as a cassation court, recourses regarding lower courts decisions on *habeas corpus* and *amparo* recourses[1644]

As a jurisdictional organ for judicial review, the Tribunal of Constitutional Guarantees is competent

> To declare, on the petition of a party, the partial or total unconstitutionality of laws, legislative decrees, regional norms of a general character, and municipal ordinances which contravene the Constitution as a matter of form or substance.[1645]

The "parties" that are authorised to interpose an action of unconstitutionality are the President of the Republic, the Supreme Court of Justice, the Public Prosecutor of the Republic, sixty members of Parliament, twenty Senators, or fifty thousand petitioning citizens whose signatures must be certified by the National Electoral Board.

The power of the Tribunal on judicial review is not bound by the will of the parties contained in the action requests, and can exceed them, by declaring the unconstitutionality of dispositions other than the challenged ones, when the ruling is a consequence or is in connection with the action contents and also by declaring the unconstitutionality of the statute or norm based on the violation of any other constitutional disposition, even not invoked in the proceeding.[1646]

In the case of statutes, the effects of the ruling upon its unconstitutionality are not immediate regarding their validity. In effect, similar to the Yugoslavian solution, once the decision is adopted it must be communicated to the President of the Congress, so that the latter may pass a law repealing the provision contrary to the Constitution. When 45 days have elapsed with out the new derogatory rule having been promulgated, the unconstitutional provision is understood to have been nullified and the Tribunal must publish the decision in the Official Gazette.[1647]

On the other hand, when the ruling of unconstitutionality relates to other normative state acts, different to formal laws, the Tribunal must order the publication of

---

1642 Art. 296. Constitution 28–7–80.

1643 See the comments in H. FIX–ZAMUDIO, "Dos leyes orgánicas de Tribunales Constitucionales latinoamericanos: Chile y Perú", *Boletín mexicano de derecho comparado*, 51, México 1984, p. 943.

1644 Art. 298 Constitution.

1645 Art. 298,1 Constitution.

1646 Art. 40 Organic Law.

1647 Art. 301 Constitution.

the ruling in the Official Gazette, and it becomes effective the day following publication[1648]

In both cases, the Tribunal decision declaring the unconstitutionality of a statute or other normative state acts, once published, has *erga omnes* effects, and in accordance with an express provision of the Constitution, they "do not have retroactive effects"[1649] thus they are only *ex nunc*, *pro praeterito*. Therefore, the Organic Law of the Tribunal establishes that decisions declaring the unconstitutionality of a normative state act, cannot serve as support to review judicial processes already concluded in which the unconstitutional norms were applied. Nevertheless, in accordance with the general exception principle of the possible retroactivity of statutes in penal, labour or taxation cases,[1650] the Organic Law allows the retroactive applicability of the Tribunal decision in proceedings in which its effect could be favourable to the convicted person, the worker or the tax payer.[1651]

But additional to the concentrated means of judicial review that can be exercised before the Tribunal of Constitutional Guarantees, the 1980 Constitution also establishes the actions of *habeas corpus* and *amparo*, as special means for the protection of fundamental rights. The former directed to protect personal liberty and the latter, as a means for the protection of all other fundamental rights recognised in the Constitution.[1652] Through the exercise of these two actions the ordinary judge can also exercise judicial review powers when the alleged violation of the fundamental right is based on a norm incompatible with the Constitution. In such cases, the judge can declare the said norm inapplicable.[1653]

Thus, a limited principle of a diffuse system can also be distinguished in Peru, as a consequence of the exercise of the actions for protection of fundamental rights, and which performs in parallel with the concentrated system.

Anyway, the ordinary courts decisions on matters of constitutional protection (*habeas corpus* and *amparo*) are subject to ordinary appeals before the Superior Courts, and against the decisions of the latter, recourse based on reasons of nullity, which can be exercised before the Supreme Court. The decisions of the latter can additionally be the object of a recourse of cassation before the Tribunal of Constitutional Guarantees in order to examine whether or not the Supreme Court has violated or erroneously applied the law.[1654]

1648 Art. 302 Constitution.

1649 Art. 300 Constitution.

1650 Art. 187 Constituion.

1651 Art. 41 Organic Law.

1652 Arts 295, 298,2 and 305. Constitution 1980.

1653 See H. FIX–ZAMUDIO, "Ley peruana de *habeas corpus* y *amparo*", *Boletín mexicano de derecho comparado*, 50, 1984, p. 575.

1654 *Idem*, p. 579.

II

THE JUDICIAL ACTION FOR "AMPARO" OR PROTECTION OF FUNDAMENTAL RIGHTS IN LATIN AMERICAN (2006–2007)

This Part on "*The Judicial Action for Amparo or Protection of Fundamental Rights in Latin America,*" is the text of the original notes written during my tenure as *Adjunct Professor of Law* at Columbia Law School, Columbia University in the City of New York during the academic Semesters of 2007–2008. They were written for the preparation of the Lectures I gave in the Seminar on *Judicial Protection of Human Rights in Latin America. A Comparative Constitutional Law Study on the Latin American Injuction for the protection of Constitutional Rights ("Amparo proceeding"),* at Columbia Law School.[*]

INTRODUCTION

Latin American countries have a longstanding tradition on extensive constitutional declarations of human rights. Since the beginning of republican constitutionalism in 1811, Latin American constitutions have enshrined a Bill of Rights and the authority of courts to adjudicate on constitutional violation.

Particularly during the second half of the XX Century, these declarations have been progressively enlarged, adding economic, social, cultural, environmental and indigenous rights to the traditional list of civil rights and political liberties; and have entrenched, in many cases, not only such rights and liberties, but also principles relating to the social goals of the State and of the political system.

---

* The original text was published by the Columbia Law School for the exclusive use of the students (New York, 2006, 383 pp.). An abridge and revised version of this Course of Lectures was published in 2009: *Constitutional Protection of Human Rights in Latin America. A Comparative Study of Amparo Proceedings*, Cambridge University Press, New York 2009, 432 pp.

However, Latin American Countries have also had a long history of human rights violations and disdain. That is why, in an effort to ensure for its effective guaranty and enforcement, another main trend in Latin America has been to formally insert all human rights, *expressis verbis,* in the texts of the Constitutions.

Additionally to the enlargement of the constitutional declarations, a new tendency among these countries has been to constitutionalize the rights enumerated in the dully ratified international treaties and conventions on human rights, therefore expanding the constitutional declarations and provisions with the ratification of such international instruments.

Moreover, regarding statutes, other Constitutions have granted pre–emptive status to duly ratified international treaties or conventions on human rights, whenever the treaty provides for more favourable provisions in the exercise of a human right. Some Constitutions even go as far as granting this pre–emption with respect to other constitutional provisions.

Together with this expansive and protective process of human rights declarations, Latin American constitutions have incorporated into their constitutional text, specific judicial remedies for the protection of constitutional rights; which in some constitutions, has been incorporated itself as a civil right, and not merely as a procedural or adjective device to guarantee human rights.

Accordingly, and in addition to the writ of *habeas corpus*, and *habeas data*, the individual's constitutional right to be protected on their fundamental rights has prompted the development of a peculiar Latin American institution known as: suit, judgment or writ of "amparo". The "amparo" was initially established in Mexico in 1857 where it was developed as the "amparo suit" or judgment (*juicio de amparo*). Particularly during the last century (XX Century), the "amparo" spread all over Latin America but took a different shape to the Mexican "amparo".

The Mexican suit of "amparo" is a very complex institution –found exclusively in Mexico– developed with the purpose of both protecting human rights and as a mean for judicial review of the constitutionality and legality of statutes, administrative actions, judicial decisions, as well as peasant's rights protection. On the contrary, in the rest of the Latin American countries, the "amparo" action or recourse was established as a specific judicial remedy with the exclusive purpose of protecting human rights and freedoms, so that it can be said that many of the "amparo" actions or recourses in these later countries became more effective as a means of protection of human rights than the original Mexican institution [1].

This course is intended to examine the most recent trends in the constitutional and legal regulations in all Latin American countries regarding the "amparo" suit, action or recourse– including the old *habeas corpus* writ and the new *habeas data* actions or recourses. By means of a comparative constitutional law approach, also with reference to the United States civil rights injunctions, the course will analyze

---

1 See Joaquín BRAGUE CAMAZANO, *La Jurisdicción constitucional de la libertad. Teoría general, Argentina, México, Corte Interamericana de Derechos Humanos*, Editorial Porrúa, México 2005, p. 156.

this Latin American institution departing from the regulation of the "amparo" guarantee established in Article 25 of the 1969 American Convention of Human Rights which entered into force in 1978 after being ratified by all Latin American States.

The main purpose of this course is to study the character of this judicial remedy both from the perspective of the constitutional right and the action or procedural recourse for protection; to identify the courts with jurisdiction to grant the protection; to examine the general procedural rules to bring an "amparo"; to determine the kind of constitutional rights worthy of protection by means of an "amparo" (whether all constitutional rights or only some of them, namely "fundamental rights", should be covered); to analyze the individuals or legal entities that may be entitled to the protection of an "amparo", that is, the aggrieved, affected or injured party (the plaintiff); to study the standing requirements to file the action; to analyze the potential proper defendants in the judicial process, namely, the party perpetrator of the nuisance, whether a State body, a public officer, individuals or private entities; to analyze the particular types of public or private actions or omissions that can cause the violation of constitutional rights, with particular reference to the various State acts which can be the object of the "amparo" action or recourse: statutes, administrative acts or judicial decisions, as well as State bodies' omissions; and finally, to study the purpose of the protection that may be awarded and the available remedies for the re–establishment of the individual or collective rights infringed, as well as the means for the enforcement of the judicial adjudication[2].

One of the main aspects to be analyzed regarding the "amparo" suit in Latin America is the one referred to the special character of this judicial mean. This particularity comes from the fact that the "amparo" is not incorporated in the general judicial procedures law regulations, but specifically regulated in the Constitution, as a separate and specific mean for the protection of human rights. In this respect, it is also relevant to our analysis, the justification for such treatment, particularly when compared with other legal systems that also effectively protect human rights, but by means of the normal or common judicial actions, recourses or writs.

In other words, we will examine why Latin American countries have established a special judicial mean for human rights protection; considering that, in general terms, the most important duty of all the Judiciary as the Judicial Branch of Government, in any country, is to decide and resolve in specific cases, questions or controversies regarding individual rights and interests. That is, the reasons why the common and general judicial means established in the Civil Codes and Civil proce-

---

2 See in general Allar R. BREWER–CARÍAS, *El amparo a los derechos y libertades constitucionales. Una aproximación comparativa*, Cuadernos de la Cátedra Allan R. Brewer—Carías de Derecho Público, N° 1, Universidad Católica del Táchira, San Cristóbal 1993, 138 pp; also published by the Inter Americanl Institute on Human Rights, (Interdisciplinary Course), San José, Costa Rica, 1993, (mimeo), 120 pp. and in *La protección jurídica del ciudadano. Estudios en Homenaje al Profesor Jesús González Pérez*, Tomo 3, Editorial Civitas, Madrid 1993, pp. 2.695–2.74; and Allan R. BREWER–CARÍAS, *Mecanismos nacionales de protección de los derechos humanos (Garantías judiciales de los derechos humanos en el derecho constitucional comparado latinoamericano),* Instituto Interamericano de Derechos Humanos, San José 2005.

dures Codes of Latin America are not the only devoted to guaranteeing the effective protection of human rights.

CHAPTER I.
THE CONSTITUTIONAL DECLARATIONS OF HUMAN RIGHTS IN LATIN AMERICA

I. RIGHTS: CONSTITUTIONAL RIGHTS, HUMAN RIGHTS, CIVIL RIGHTS, FUNDAMENTAL RIGHTS

In general terms, the Judiciary is established in any country in order to decide cases and to make binding judgments which affect personal and proprietary rights. In this regard, the expression "rights" is used to describe that which is legally guaranteed and due to a person; or the power, privilege or immunity secured to a person by law. That is to say, rights are legal or constitutional situations that empower a person to act (freedom of expression) or not to act (conscience objection), usually being personal freedoms or liberties what oblige the State and other individuals not to interfere with or obstruct the exercise of rights of others.

But rights can also be considered as legal situations that entitle a person to request something or to receive goods or services form a public entity (right to health protection or right to education) in which case the State is obliged to furnish services or to accomplish certain activities. In both cases, the rights are recognized and protected, the violation of which is a wrong.

It can be said that in any society, from a legal point of view, all persons are in one way or another in one of two situations: either they are in a legal situation or condition of having power to do something or request something, or in a legal situation of having some duties or obligations to accomplish. In some cases, a person may have the right to act or not to act, or to make, to enjoy or to take advantage of something, or to dispose of determined possessions. In all these legal interpersonal relations, they are in a status or position of being empowered.

But in other cases, the same person can be in the legal situation of having a duty to accomplish; that is, they can be in a position of being obliged to respect, to refrain from, to abstain from or to render or give certain services or goods to others.

What is certain is that it is inconceivable that a society could exist without such personal interrelations of powers and duties. If one person for instance, has freedom of religion or speech as a constitutional right, that situation always implies that the State, the public officials and every other individual have the duty to respect, to abstain from embarrassing or to impede the freedom of others. In this case, the situation of the obliged person is a status of having the duty to abstain from interfering with the freedom of others.

In other cases, if the constitutional right is not conceived as a right to act or not to act, that is, as a freedom, but instead is conceived as a right to receive certain services or goods, for instance health care, education or cultural services, that situation implies that the State has the duty to render those services in the form of public utilities. In this situation, the status of the obliged person is to act or to provide something to others.

So rights are always attributed to persons, whether as freedoms to act or as rights to receive something; and in both situations, "persons" are not only human beings but also entities or corporations recognized by law as having rights and duties.

Now, among the "rights" attributed to a person, it is possible to distinguish those which are declared or recognized in the Constitution, that is to say, "constitutional rights". Those rights can not only be attributed to natural persons or human beings, but also to artificial persons like entities or corporations. This is the case, for instance, of property rights or the right to due process of law.

Other rights, conversely, such as the right to life or in general, the rights known as freedoms, like freedom of association, freedom of expression or freedom of speech are only attributed to human beings. Thus, the expression "human rights", in a strict sense, is referred to those attributed to human beings. Among these it is also possible to distinguish those called in North American law as "civil rights", or civil liberties, that is, the individual rights of personal liberty or freedom guaranteed in the Constitution, such as freedom of speech, press, assembly, or religion guaranteed by the First Amendment of the U.S. Constitution.

However, "civil rights" do not exhaust the list of constitutional rights, which nowadays also comprises social, economic, cultural and environmental rights. It may be true that civil rights were those first declared in the Constitutions, but at present time they are accompanied by a long list of other rights belonging to what has been called other "generations" of rights.

In other countries, mainly in Europe, as evidenced in the cases of Germany and Spain, the expression "fundamental rights" is also used in the Constitutions, in order to identify certain constitutional rights that can be protected by a special judicial mean of protection or "amparo", which in general terms are equivalent to the individual or civil rights. This expression of "fundamental rights" is also used in the Colombian Constitution, to identify a category of constitutional rights, mainly the individual rights, which are of immediate application and can be protected by the "acción de tutela".

These regulations, in particular, tend to distinguish among the constitutional rights, those that can be considered as "justiciable rights" particularly by means of the specific judicial action or recourse of "amparo", and constitutional rights not considered "fundamental rights". The latter group is left to be protected by means of the general or common judicial means. Constitutional rights can always be considered essentially justiciables, but their "justiciability" –as the quality or state of being appropriate or suitable for reviewing by a court–, will vary depending on the judicial means available in the legal system for such purpose. In some countries, all constitutional rights are justiciables by means of the general judicial means of protection, such as in the United States; in other countries all constitutional rights are justiciables by means of a specific judicial mean of protection like the *habeas corpus* or "amparo" action or recourse, such as in the case of Venezuela; and in other countries, the constitutional rights are protected by a special mean of protection if they are "fundamental rights", being the other constitutional rights justiciables through the common judicial means.

In the United States, regarding rights, the word "fundamental" is used when referring to civil rights that are protected in the Constitution, as "fundamental civil rights". As has been ruled by the Supreme Court in *United States v. Wong Kim Ark*, 169 U.S. 649; 18 S. Ct. 456; 42 L. Ed. 890; (1898) on March 28, 1898, referring to "**fundamental civil rights** for the security of which organized society was instituted, and which remain, with certain exceptions mentioned in the Federal Constitution…"

Thus, this expression "fundamental rights" is commonly used with various meanings: form a formal point of view, they can be considered as the rights embodied in the Constitution; from a substantive point of view, fundamental rights can also be considered as are the most important rights that according to their own principles and value are recognized in a society[3]; and from a judicial point of view, they are such when they can be judicially protected by special means as the "amparo".

Our intention is to analyze the process of constitutionalization of rights in modern constitutionalism, and for this purpose it is possible to consider all "constitutional rights" as "human rights", in spite of the fact that some of them are also attributed to artificial persons. This is why, for the purpose of this Course, the expressions "constitutional rights" and "human rights" are used in an equivalent sense.

II. THE CONSTITUTIONAL DECLARATIONS OF HUMAN RIGHTS

1. The North American and French Declarations

The declaration of rights in the text of the Constitutions began with constitutionalism itself, and with the very notion of Constitution as a superior law[4].

This happened with at the Convention of Virginia in 1776, at the beginning of the Independence process of the American Colonies, when the first Declaration of Rights in constitutional history was approved. Practice followed subsequently by the other Colonies.

This practice differed from the English precedents, mainly because in establishing entrenched rights, they did not refer to rights based on the common law and tradition, but rather to the rights derived from human nature and reason. Thus the rights declared in the Bill of Rights of those colonies were those natural rights which "do

---

3 See Alfonso GAIRAUD BRENES, "Los Mecanismos de interpretación de los derechos humanos: especial referencia a la jurisprudencia peruana" in José F. PALOMINO MANCHEGO, *El derecho procesal constitucional peruano. Estudios en Homenaje a Domingo García Belaunde*, Editorial Jurídica Grijley, Lima, 2005, Tomo I, p.124.

4 See in general Allan R. BREWER–CARÍAS, *Reflexiones sobre la Revolución Americana (1776) y la Revolución Francesa (1789) y sus aportes al constitucionalismo moderno,* Cuadernos de la Cátedra Allan R. Brewer–Carías de Derecho Administrativo, Universidad Católica Andrés Bello, N° 1, Editorial Jurídica Venezolana, Caracas, 1992.

pertain to ... [the people] and their posterity, as the basis and foundation of government" as the Virginia Declaration of Rights stated.

In the brief preamble to that Declaration (which precedes the text of the Constitution or Form of Government of Virginia of June 29, 1776), the relation between natural rights and government was clearly established. Also evident is the direct influence of Locke's theories in the sense that political society forms itself upon those rights as the basis and foundation of government. That is why the Declaration was based on the fact of the existence of "inherent rights" to all men, which by nature were declared "equally free and independent" (I); enumerating as individual rights the following: the "enjoyment of life and liberty"; the right to "acquiring and possessing property" (I) so that no property could be taken from any person for public usage without his consent (VI); "the freedom of the press" (XII); and the freedom of religion "according to the dictates of conscience" (XVI).

The due process of law rights were also declared, by stating the right of all men in criminal prosecutions "to demand the cause and nature of his accusation, to be confronted with the accusers and witnesses, to call for evidence in his favor, and to a speedy trial by an impartial jury of his vicinage, without whose unanimous consent he cannot be found guilty, nor can he be compelled to give evidence against himself"; and also "that no man be deprived of his liberty except by the law of the land or the judgment of his peers" (VIII); "that excessive bail ought not to be required, nor excessive fines imposed; nor cruel and unusual punishments inflicted" (IX); and that no "general warrants… may be commanded to search suspected places without evidence of a fact committed, or to seize any person or persons not named, or whose offence is not particularly described and supported by evidence" (X).

The Virginia Declaration also guaranteed, as a political right, the right of suffrage and to have free elections of representatives (VI).

Finally, a collective right was also declared, a right appertaining to "a majority of the community" and considered as "an indubitable, unalienable, and indefeasible right" to "reform, alter or abolish" any government founded "inadequate or contrary" to the purposes set forth in the Declaration (III).

The same fundamental liberal principles of the Virginia Declaration can also be found in the Declaration of Independence of the United States of America, approved less than one month later (July 4, 1776), holding as a self evident truths "That all men are created equal; that they are endowed by their Creator with certain unalienable rights; that among these are life, liberty, and the pursuit of happiness"; and that, "to secure these rights, government is instituted among men, deriving their just powers from the consent of the governed"; "that, whenever any form of government becomes destructive of these ends, it is the right of the people to alter or to abolish it and to institute new government, laying its foundation on such principles and organizing its powers in such form, as to them shall seem most likely to effect their safety and happiness".

These declarations, undoubtedly, marked the beginning of the democratic and liberal era of the modern rule of law constitutionalism.

Although the 1787 Constitution of the United States did not contain a declaration of fundamental rights, such Declarations nevertheless constituted one of the main characteristics of American constitutionalism, influencing modern constitutional law.

The 1787 Constitution was criticized for the fact that it did not include a Bill of Rights, but this deficiency was solved two years later when ten first Amendments to the Constitution were drafted by the first Congress and approved on September 29, 1789 just one month after the approval on August 26, 1789 of the French Declaration of the Rights of Man and of the Citizen.

The Bill of Rights entered in force in 1791 after the last ratifications were approved by Vermont and Virginia, where "certain rights" were enumerated, but with the express statement that said enumeration, "shall not be construed to deny or disparage other [rights] retained by the people" (IX), thus, reinforcing the "declarative" character of the constitutional declaration of rights.

The following "certain rights" were the ones declared: the freedom of religion and of the exercise of cult; freedom of speech, or of the press; the right to peaceably assemble, the right to petition the Government (I); the right to keep and bear arms (II); the right to not accept quarters of soldiers in any house in time of peace, without the consent of the owner (III); and the right of the people to be secure in their persons, houses, papers, and effects, against unreasonable searches and seizures (IV).

The due process of law rights were also declared as follows: only to be condemned by the Judiciary; not to be subject twice to prosecution for the same offence; not to be witness against himself, nor be deprived of life, liberty, or property, without due process of law; nor shall private property be taken for public use without just compensation (V). In criminal prosecutions, the right of the accused to a speedy and public trial, by an impartial jury of the State and district wherein the crime shall have been committed, which district shall have been previously ascertained by law; and the rights to be informed of the nature and cause of the accusation; to be confronted with the witnesses against him; to have compulsory process for obtaining witnesses in his favor, and to have the assistance of counsel for his defence (VI). Additionally, in suits at common law, the right of trial by jury; and the right not to have re–examined the fact tried by a jury except according to the rules of the common law (VII). Finally, the right people have not to be asked for excessive bail, nor to be imposed of excessive fines, nor to be subjected to cruel and unusual punishments (VIII).

The Bill of Rights contained in the first Ten Amendments was complemented with the declaration of other rights in subsequent Amendments. In 1865, the prohibition of slavery and involuntary servitude (XIII); in 1868, 1970 and 1920, the right to elect representatives, to vote and to be elected, as political rights (XIV,2,3; XV; XIX); and in 1868, the right to citizenship; the right of persons not to be deprived of life, liberty, or property by any State, without due process of law; and the right to have equal protection of laws (XIV,1).

The general trend to declare human rights in the Constitutions, as superior laws, seeking their entrenchment, was immediately followed by the French Revolution, first adopting the Declaration of the Rights of Man and of the Citizen by the National Assembly on August 26, 1789 and second by embodying it at the beginning of the 1791 First French Constitution[5].

In the drafting of the seventeen articles of the Declaration recognizing and proclaiming all the fundamental rights of man, the influence of the American Declarations was decisive, particularly in the principle itself of the need of a formal declaration of rights, and in its contents. The mutual influence that the continents had on each other at the time are well known: the French philosophers, including Montesquieu and Rousseau were studied in North America; French participation in the War of Independence was important; Lafayette was a member of the drafting committee of the Constituent Assembly which produced the French Declaration and submitted his own draft based on the Declaration of Independence and the Virginia Bill of Rights; the *repporteur* of the Constitutional Commission proposed "transplanting to France the noble idea conceived in North America"; and Jefferson himself was present in Paris in 1789, having succeeded Benjamin Franklin as American Minister to France[6].

The main objectives in both declarations were the same: to protect the citizen against arbitrary power and to establish the rule of law.

However, it is certain that the French Declaration was, of course, more directly influenced by the thoughts of Rousseau and Montesquieu. The drafters of the Declaration took from Rousseau the principles of considering the role of society as being related to the natural liberty of man, and the idea that the law, as the expression of the general will passed by the representatives of the nation, cannot be an instrument for oppression. They also took from Montesquieu his fundamental distrust of power, and therefore, the principle of separation of powers also embodied in the Virginia Declaration[7].

Of course, the rights proclaimed in the French Declaration were also natural rights of man, thus inalienable and universal; rights that was not granted by political society, but rights inherent to the nature of human beings.

This conception is clear in the justifying text of the Declaration issued "considering that the ignorance, forgetfulness or contempt of the rights of man is the sole causes of public misfortunes and of the corruption of government"; originating a perpetual reminder of the "natural inalienable and sacred rights of man."

The rights and freedoms were recognized and proclaimed forwarded by these declaration of principles: that "men are born and remain free and equal in rights"

5 See in general Allan R. BREWER–CARÍAS, *Reflexiones sobre la Revolución Americana (1776) y la Revolución Francesa (1789) y sus aportes al constitucionalismo moderno,* Cuadernos de la Cátedra Allan R. Brewer–Carías de Derecho Administrativo, Universidad Católica Andrés Bello, Nº 1, Editorial Jurídica Venezolana, Caracas 1992.

6 J. RIVERO, *Les libertés publiques*, Dalloz, Paris, 1973, Vol. I, p. 45.

7 J. RIVERO, *op. cit*, p. 41–42.

(1); that "liberty, property, security, and resistance to oppression" are "natural and inalienable rights of man" (2); that "liberty consists of the power to do whatever is not injurious to others; hence the enjoyment of the natural rights of every man has as its limits only those that assure to other members of society the enjoyment of those same rights; limits that can only be determined by law (4); that "nothing may be prevented which is not forbidden by law", and that "no one may be constrained to do what it is not provided for by law (5); that "all citizens have the right to concur personally, or through their representatives" in the formation of the law, as the "expression of the general will"; and that the law "must be the same for all, whether it protects or punishes" (6). There is express reference to the following civil rights: rights to free expression and to free communication of ideas and opinions, considered in the Declaration as "one of the most precious of the rights of man"; the right of every citizen to "speak, write, and print with freedom" (11); the right not to "be disquieted on account of his opinions, including his religious views" (10); and the right to property considered "sacred and inviolable", and the right to be "equitably indemnified" when someone is deprive of his property because of a legally determined public necessity, (17).

The rest of the Declaration refers to the due process of law rights: the right of all persons not to "be accused, arrested, or imprisoned except in the cases and according to the forms prescribed by law" (7); the right to be punished "only as are strictly and obviously necessary" and only when the punishment is "legally inflicted in virtue of a law passed and promulgated before the commission of the offence" (8); and the right of all persons to be "held innocent until they shall have been declared guilty" (9).

As for political rights, the Declarations recognized the right of all citizens to be "equally eligible to all dignities and to all public positions and occupations" (6); and the right to "require of every public agent an account of his administration" (15)

The whole process of the development of modern constitutionalism based on the rule of law or the *État de droit*, began with the products of the American and French revolutions and with the general principles they motivated: the idea of Constitution as a superior and fundamental law adopted by the people as sovereign; the democratic and republican principles, based on popular representation, the separation of powers, in the horizontal and the vertical systems; the role of the Judicial Branch, and the formal Declarations of Rights; principles that were subsequently incorporated into all written constitutions of the modern world.

2. The Influence in Latin America

These principles first had an immediate impact in Latin American constitutionalism, long before than in other European countries[8].

8 See in general Allan R. BREWER–CARÍAS, *Los derechos humanos en Venezuela: casi 200 años de historia*, Biblioteca de la Academia de Ciencias Políticas y Sociales, Serie Estudios, N° 38, Caracas 1990.

We must bear in mind that the process of independence of the Spanish Colonies in Latin America started in 1810, only twenty three years after the sanctioning of the American Constitution, and seven years after the Marbury v. Madison landmark judicial review case. This happens in a moment in which Spain was occupied by French troops after Napoleon had imposed to the invaded realm the Bayonne Constitution of 1808. Spain was fighting for independence from France, and the American Colonies, repudiating the French invasion, began to seek independence from Spain.

So the principles of modern constitutionalism were first adopted in Latin America, from 1811 on, before than in Spain. In Spain these principles were embodied with a monarchical framework a few months after –in the Cadiz 1812 Constitution– which remained in force only for two years, until the Monarchy was restored in 1814. The important aspect to be stressed out is that no Spanish constitutional influence can be found in the beginning of Latin American modern constitutionalism, which basically followed the North American trend.

It can be said that, in general, the American –North American and Latin–American– constitutional revolution process and its declarations of rights were very different to the French and even the Spanish ones.

In the French Revolution and Declaration, it was not a case of establishing a new state but of the continuation of a national state already in existence, within the monarchical principle. The same occurred in Spain. On the contrary, in the American Revolution and Declarations, new states were being built upon a new basis.

The purpose of the French Declaration, as stated in its introduction, was to solemnly remind all members of the community of their natural rights and duties. Hence the new principle of individual liberty appeared only as an important modification within the context of a political unity already in existence.

On the other hand, in the North American and Latin–American declarations, the enforcement of rights was an important factor in the independence process, and thus, in the building of the new states upon a new basis. Particularly relevant was the principle of the sovereignty of people with all its democratic content. Therefore, on the American Continent, the solemn Declaration of Fundamental Rights meant the establishment of principles on which the political unity of the nations was based, and the validity of which was recognized as the most important assumption in the emergence and formation of that unity.

Putting aside the Haiti Constitution of 1805, it can be said that the third formal declaration of rights by an independent state in constitutional history was the "Declaration of Rights of the People" adopted by the Supreme Congress of Venezuela in 1811 four days before the formal Venezuelan Independence Act of July 5th, 1811, was approved.

The content of that Declaration followed both the French and the American Declarations, but was much more detailed in the enumeration of rights, including new ones such as the right to industrial and commercial freedom and the freedom to work (20); and the right to consider peoples' home as an inviolable asylum (22). In the declaration of the rights of people, there is also a reference to a social right when it states that "instruction is necessary for all. The society must favor with all its power the progress of public reason to put instruction at the reach of all" (Ch. 4, 4).

The Declaration was also incorporated as a final Chapter of the first of all Latin–American constitutions, the Venezuelan Constitution of December 21, 1811[9], in 59 extensive articles, among which, as an example, articles 151 ff. can be pointed out. This set of articles follow what was established in the French and American declarations, stating that governments are established in order to guarantee the exercise of rights of man, namely "liberty, equality, property and security", defining such rights as follows:

> 153. Liberty (freedom) is the power to do whatever is not injurious to others or to society, which limits can only be establish by law.
>
> 154. Equality consists in that the law must be the same for all citizens, whether it punishes or protects.
>
> 155. Property is the right of everybody to enjoy and dispose goods acquired with its work and industry.
>
> 156. Security exists within the guaranty and protection that the society gives to each of its members regarding the preservation of their person, their rights and properties.

These two Venezuelan Declarations of Rights of 1811 mark the beginning of a very long tradition of almost 200 hundred years of continuous, extensive and always enlarging Latin American Declarations of Rights; a tradition very different from the European one.

3. The Situation in France

For instance, we must remember that in France, after the Declaration of 1789, no other Declaration of Rights was adopted. After the 1875 Constitutional Laws[10] even its contents were excluded from the text of the Constitution, considering that their provisions were not directly applicable to individuals. That is why the 1958 French Constitution only refers to human rights in an indirect way when it states in its Preamble that "The French people, solemnly proclaim their subjection to the rights of Man and to the national sovereignty principles as have been defined by the Declaration of 1789, confirmed and completed by the Preamble to the constitution of 1946".

Moreover, this Preamble to the Constitution was initially considered by the Constitutional Council itself, only as a principle for the orientation of constitutional interpretation[11]; criteria that began to change after the Constitutional Council decision

---

9 See in general Allan R. BREWER–CARÍAS, *Las Constituciones de Venezuela,* Universidad Católica del Táchira (Venezuela), Instituto de Estudios de Administración Local y del Centro de Estudios Constitucionales (España), Madrid 1985, 1.086 pp. A second edition was published by Academia de Ciencias Políticas y Sociales, Caracas, Biblioteca de la Academia de Ciencias Políticas y Sociales, Caracas 1997.

10 J. RIVERO, *Les libertés publiques*, Vol. 1, Paris, 1973, p. 70.

11 L. HAMON, "Contrôle de Constitutionalité et protection des droits individuels. A propos de trois décisions récents du Conseil Constitutionnel", *Recueil Dalloz Sirey 1974*, Chronique XVI, p. 85.

of July, 16, 1971 regarding the freedom of association, when it was decided that a proposed law establishing a particular judicial controls in order for an association acquiring legal capacity, was against the Constitution. The proposed statute was an amendment bill to a 1901 statute relating to non–profit associations, which the Council considered unconstitutional[12], using the following argument:

The 1958 Constitution through the Preamble to the 1946 Constitution referred to the "fundamental principles recognized by the laws of the Republic" among which the freedom of association must be listed.

In conformity with this principle, associations were to be constituted freely and could publicly develop their activities. The only condition to this association was making a previous declaration, the validity of which was not to be submitted to a previous intervention by either administrative or judicial authorities.

Thus, the Constitutional Council determined that the limits imposed on associations by the proposed bill establishing a prior judicial control of said declaration, were unconstitutional. This decision allowed Professor Jean Rivero to say,

> "The liberty of association, which is not expressly established either in the Declaration or by the particularly needed principles of our times, but which is only recognized by a Statute of July 1st., 1901, has been recognized by the Constitutional Council decision, as having a constitutional character, not only as a principle, but in relation to the modalities of its exercise"[13].

This decision of 1971 is an example of the creative tendency regarding fundamental rights of the Constitutional Council, even though for that purpose its decision was based on the Preamble to the Constitution, and through it, in what the Preamble to the 1946 Constitution considered the "fundamental principles recognized by the laws of the Republic." In general, therefore, to establish a fundamental right or liberty as a "fundamental principle", the Constitutional Council based itself on a particular existing statute, as happened with the liberty of association which was recognized by the Statute of July 1st, 1901.

But in other cases[14], as has happened with the right to self defense, the Constitutional Council has not based itself in a particular Statute for deducing a right based

12 See the Constitutional Council decision in L. FAVOREU, y J. PHILIP, *Les grandes décisions du Conseil Constitutionnel*, Paris 1984., p. 222. See the comments of the 16 July, 1971 decisions in J. RIVERO, "Note", *L'Actualité Juridique. Droit Administratif*, 1971, p. 537; J. Rivero, "Principes fondamentaux reconnus par les lois de la Republique; une nouvelle categorie constitutionnelle?", *Dalloz 1974*, Chroniques, p. 265; and J.E. BRADSLEY, "The Constitutional Council and Constitutional Liberties in France", *The American Journal of Comparative Law*, 20, (3), 1972, p. 43; B. NICHOLAS, "Fundamental Rights and Judicial Review in France", *Public Law*, 1978, p. 83.

13 J. RIVERO, "Les garanties constitutionnelles des droits de l'homme en droit français", *IX Journees Juridiques Franco–Latino Americaines*, Bayonne 21–23 mai 1976, (mimeo), p. 11.

14 Decisions of 8 Nov. 1976; 2 Dec. 1976; 20 July 77, 19 January 1981; 20 January 1981, *Cf.* the quotations in F. LUCHAIRE, "Procedures et techniques de protection des droits fondamentaux. Conseil Constitutionnel français", in L Favoreu (ed.), *Cours constitutionnelles européennes et droit fondamentaux*, Aix–en–Provence 1982, pp. 69, 70, 83.

on "the fundamental principles recognized by the laws of the Republic." In that decision dated January 19th–20th 1981[15], the Constitutional Council radically changed the previous approach regarding the right to one's own defense, which was considered by the *Conseil d'État* simply as a general principle of law[16]. Conversely, after the 1981 decision, the Constitutional Council recognized it as part of the "principles and rules of constitutional value", an expression used by the Constitutional Council to describe in a generic manner all the norms that, without being contained in the text of the constitution itself, have Constitutional status[17].

Therefore, in France, "conformity with the constitution" as a consequence of the principle of constitutionality, is not understood today strictly as conformity with an express disposition of the Constitution. Since the 1970's, the notion of constitutional norms that could serve as reference norms to control the constitutionality of legislation has been progressively understood in a wider sense, comprising dispositions or principles outside the constitutional text, and in particular, the Declaration of 1789, the Preambles to the 1946 and 1958 Constitutions, the fundamental principles recognized by the laws of the Republic, and the general principles of constitutional value[18]. All these sources of the principle of constitutionality enjoy the same authority as the written articles of the Constitution.

This process of adaptation of the Constitution by the constitutional judge was also confirmed in France in the decision of the Constitutional Council in the *Nationalizations* case of 1982. In this case, the Council applied the article concerning property rights of the 1789 Declaration, thus declaring such right as having constitutional status. In the decision dated January 16 1982[19], the Council considered that even though the relevant article of the 1789 Declaration was obsolete, and that it ought to be interpreted in a completely different way from the sense it had in 1789[20], it:

> Considering that, after 1789 and up to date, the purposes and conditions of the exercise of property rights have evolved because of the expansion of its range of application regarding new individual domains and because of the limitations imposed by the general interest, the principles contained in the Declarations of Man's Rights have full constitutional value, regarding both the fundamental character of the right to property, being its preservation one of the objectives of political society, located in the same level as liberty, security and resistance

---

15 L. FAVOREU and L. PHILIP, *Les grandes décisions..., cit.*, pp. 490, 517.

16 *Cf.* D.G. LAVROFF, "El Consejo Constitucional francés y la garantía de las libertades públicas", *Revista española de derecho constitucional*, 1 (3), 1981, pp. 54–55; L. FAVOREU and L. PHILIP, *Les grandes décisions..., cit.*, p. 213.

17 L. Favoreu, "Les décisions du Conseil Constitutionnel dans l'affaire des nationalisations", *Revue du droit public et de la science politique en France et à l'étranger*, T. XCVIII, N° 2, Paris, 1982, p. 401.

18 L. FAVOREU, "L'application directe et l'effect indirect des normes constitutionnelles", *French Report to the XI International Congres of Comparative Law*, Caracas, 1982, (mineo), p. 4

19 See L. FAVOREU y L. PHILIP, *Les grandes décisions..., cit.*, pp. 525–562

20 L. FAVOREU, *Le contrôle juridictionnel des lois et sa légitimité. Développements récents en Europe Occidentale*, Association Internationale des Sciences Juridiques, Colloque d'Uppsala 1984, (mineo), p. 32; also published in L. FAVOREU and J.A. JOLOWICZ, *Le contrôle juridictionnel des lois. Légitimité, effectivité et developments récents*, Paris 1986, pp. 17–68.

to oppression, as well as the guaranties given to the holders of such right and the public bodies prerogatives..."[21].

Consequently, the Constitutional Council in this case, not only "created" a fundamental constitutional right when giving constitutional rank and value to the 1789 Declaration, but "adapted" the former "sacred" and absolute property right set forth 200 hundred years ago creating the limited and limitable right of our times. Its preservation led the Council to declare some articles of the Nationalization Law as unconstitutional.

Since these decisions of the Constitutional Council adopted in the seventies, the *block of constitutionality*[22] was enlarged precisely to include the Declaration of Rights of Man and Citizens of 1789 and the Preamble of the 1946 Constitution, by means of interpretation of the 1958 Constitution Preambles, and of the fundamental principles recognized by the laws of the Republic[23]. This also led Professor Rivero to assert, with respect to the activism of the Constitutional Council, that with those decisions –based on "the constitution and particularly on its Preamble"–, a revolution has taken place, stating that "In a single blow, the 1789 Declaration, the 1946 Preamble, the fundamental principles recognized by the laws of the Republic, have been integrated into the French Constitution, even if the Constituent did not want to do it. The French Constitution has doubled its volume through the single will of the Constitutional Council"[24]. The author concludes by saying that "Through the single will of the Constitutional Council the French Constitution has doubled its volume"[25].

This process of expansion of constitutional declarations of rights can be considered as one of the main characteristics of the recent evolution of modern constitutionalism, in which various "generations" of rights can be distinguished.

III. THE EXPANSION OF THE CONSTITUTIONAL DECLARATIONS OF RIGHTS BEGINNING WITH THE INDIVIDUAL AND CIVIL RIGHTS

1. The Individual and Civil Rights

In effect, the initial human rights set forth in the Constitutions, as was the case of the North American Bill of Rights or the French Declaration of Citizens and Man's

21 L. FAVOREU y L. PHILIP, *Les grandes décisions..., cit.*, p. 526. *Cfr.* L. FAVOREU, "Les décisions du Conseil Constitutionnel dans l'affaire des nationalisations", *Revue du droit public et de la science politique en France et à l'étranger*, T. XCVIII, N° 2, Paris 1982, p. 406.

22 L. FAVOREU, "Le principe de constitutionalité. Essai de définition d'après la jurisprudence du Conseil constitutionnel", in *Recueil d'études en l'honneur de Charles Eisenmann*, Paris, 1977, p. 33.

23 L. FAVOREU, *Le contrôle juridictionnel des lois et sa légitimité. Développements récents en Europe Occidentale*, Association Internationale des Sciences Juridiques, Colloque d'Uppsala, 1984, (mineo), p. 8; also published in L. FAVOREU and J.A. JOLOWICZ, *op. cit.*, pp. 17–68.

24 J. RIVERO, "Rapport de Synthèse" in L. FAVOREU, (ed.), *Cours constitutionnelles europeenes et droit fondamentar,* Aix–en–Provence, 1982, p. 520.

25 *Idem*, p. 520.

Rights, or of the XIX Century Latin American constitutional declarations of human rights, have been considered the "First declaration" of human rights, containing those rights essential to human nature, or essential to the quality of the human being, and which are common to all human persons. These rights were precisely those referred to in the French declaration, when stating that "The aim of all political association is the preservation of the natural and imprescriptibly rights of man". At the end of the XVIII Century those rights were reduced to freedom, equality before the law, personal safety and safety of property. To these original human rights, the American Bill of Rights added the freedom of religion and cult, freedom of speech and of the press, the right to peaceably assemble, the right to petition, the due process of law guaranties, the right to move and the right to vote. During the XX Century the list of political rights was also enlarged, adding to the right to vote the right to public demonstration, the right to participate in political parties, the right to seek for asylum and in general terms, the right to participate in political life.

All those rights have configured what has been called the "First generation" of human rights[26], as civil or individual rights essential to all human beings, which were regulated in all of the XIX and XX Centuries' constitutions. This First generation of rights is still important, particularly regarding the justiciability of human rights. For instance, in the Spanish Constitution, they are equivalent to "fundamental rights" in order to be protected by means of the "amparo" recourse that can be brought before the Constitutional Tribunal.

In effect, Article 53,2 of the Spanish Constitution empowered any citizen to ask for the protection ("tutela") of the liberties and rights recognized in Article 14 and in the first Section of the Second Chapter of the Constitution. This protection is sought before the regular courts through a process based on the principles of preference and speed, and when appropriate, through the recourse of "amparo" before the Constitutional Court. This last recourse shall be applicable to objections of conscience recognized in Article 30. Accordingly, as mentioned before, the recourse of "amparo" is only reserved to protect certain constitutional rights equivalent in general contemporary terms to the First generation of Rights, called "fundamental rights", which are the following: The right to equality before the law, without any discrimination (Article 14); the right to life and to physical and moral integrity and not to be subjected to torture or inhuman or degrading punishment or treatment, and the right to the abolishment of death penalty (Article 15); the freedom of ideology, religion, and cult (Article 16); the right to personal liberty and security, particularly regarding detentions (Article 17); the right to honor, to personal and family privacy and to identity; the right to the inviolability of home; and the right to secrecy of communications (postal, telegraphic, and telephone communication) (Article 18); freedom to move (Article 19); the rights to freely express and disseminate thoughts, ideas and opinions through words, writing, or any other means of reproduction and the right to

26 The classification of human rights in "generations", only serves to more or less appreciate the chronological trends of the evolution process of their constitutionalization. See Antonio A. CANÇADO TRINDADE, "Derechos de solidaridad", in *Estudios Básicos de Derechos Humanos*, Vol. I, Instituto Interamericano de Derechos Humanos, San José, 1994, pp. 64 ff.

freely communicate or receive truthful information without any kind of censorship (Article 20); the right to peaceful and unarmed assembly and the right to demonstrate (Article 21); the right to association (article 22); the right to participate in public affairs, directly or through representatives freely elected in periodic elections and the right to accede, under conditions of equality, to public functions and positions (Article 23); the right to be effectively protected by judges and courts in the exercise of their rights; the right to self defense and the due process of law rights (no self–incrimination, the presumption of innocence) (Article 24); the *Nulla Poena Sine Lege* rights (Article 25); the right to personal and collective petition (Article 29); and the right oppose conscientious objection for exemption from compulsory military service (Article 30).

All these rights are the civil or political rights that for example, have also been declared in the United Nations International Covenant on Civil and Political Rights of 1966.

One recently enacted Constitution in which all these individual or civil rights are regulated in an extensive way is the 1999 Venezuelan Constitution. I want to highlight this example, not only because it is an illustration of contemporary tendency to constitutionalize human rights by means of very rich and progressive declarations, but also because it is an example that even with such impressive declarations, there is still an absence of an effective independent and autonomous Judiciary, that renders very difficult the justiciability of such rights.

In the Venezuelan Constitution above all one can find a group of very important regulations related to the constitutional guarantees of human rights, that is to say, to the instruments that allow the exercise of such rights.

In this regard, the following guarantees are largely regulated: general freedom in the sense of the right of every one to develop its own personality with only the limits connected to the other individuals rights and to the social and public interest (Article 20); the general principle of the non–retroactive effects of statutes (Article 24); the principle of the nullity of any State act that violates constitutional rights and the principle that all public officials that produced or executed them, are liable (Article 25); and the general principle of equality before the law forbidding any kind of discrimination (Article 21). The Constitution also regulates, following the Spanish Constitution provision, the right of any person to have access to the courts in order to demand enforcement of his rights and interests, including the collective or diffuse rights; the right to obtain effective protection of his rights and to obtain a promptly corresponding decision (Article 26).

The Constitution also regulates the persons' right to have the immediate guarantee or protection of his constitutional rights by means of effective actions or recourse such as the action of "amparo"; the action of protection of personal freedom or *habeas corpus*; and the action of *habeas data* devoted to protect personal data from public or private data bank institutions (Article 27).

On the other hand, the rights to due process of law are also expressly regulated, as well as the right to access to justice, which impose the duty to the Judiciary to only decide cases in accordance with the standards established in the Constitution and the law. The rights to the due process had been established in detail in Article 49, which requires that "due process be applied to all judicial and administrative actions", specifically regulating the following guarantees: the right to self defence; the presumption of innocence; the right to be heard; the right to be judged by the competent and pre–existing judge, that must be independent and impartial; the guarantees against self indictment; the principle of *nullum crimen nulla poena sine lege*; the principle of *non bis in idem* and the guarantee of the State's liability for errors or judicial delays.

Nevertheless, of all the constitutional guarantees of human rights, there can be no doubt that the most important is the guarantee of legality in the sense that only by means of statutes constitutional rights can be limited and restricted. Hence the reference in all constitutional articles on constitutional rights to the "law", is made to law in the sense of statutes (formal law), as acts emanating from the National Assembly acting as a legislative body (Article 202). Additionally, these are the only acts that can restrict or limit constitutional guarantees, as provided in Article 30 of the American Convention on Human Rights, pursuant to the interpretation of the Inter American Court for Human Rights (Advisory Opinion N° 6).

One aspect that we must mention is that even with these kind of constitutional guarantees, the same Constitution provides a formula for its bypassing and potential violation, when regulating the possibility for the Assembly to "delegate legislative powers" in the President of the Republic, by means of so–called "enabling laws" (Article 203), whereby he can dictate executive acts with the rank and value of statutes on any subject (Article 206, Ordinal 8). This provision contrasts with the previous 1961 Constitution which used to set forth that the President could only regulate, by means of enabling laws, matters related to the economy and finance (Article 190, Ordinal 8)[27].

The 1999 Constitution provision, instead, has unfortunately opened up a constitutional loophole that allows the National Assembly and the President, even with the impressive range of rights and guarantees embodied in the Constitution, to violate the guarantee of legality which, as stated above, is the most important guarantee for the effective enforcement and execution of human rights.

When referring to constitutional guarantees, it should finally be mentioned that under Article 29 of the Venezuelan Constitution, the State is expressly compelled to investigate and legally sanction any human rights violations committed by its authorities, and Article 30 establishes the State's obligation to wholly indemnify victims of human rights abuse attributable to the State, including the payment of damages. The State shall also protect victims of ordinary offences and endeavor to have the guilty parties repair the damage caused.

Title III, Chapter III of the Venezuelan Constitution is devoted to regulate civil or individual rights, beginning with the right to life, as inviolable thus banning the

27 See Pedro NIKKEN, "Constitución Venezolana de 1999: La habilitación para dictar decretos ejecutivos con fuerza de ley restrictivos de los derechos humanos y su contradicción con el derecho internacional", in *Revista de Derecho Público*, N° 83, Editorial Jurídica Vvenezolana, Caracas, 2000, p. 5 ff.

death penalty (Article 43). This right has also been reinforced by obliging the State to protect "the life of people when deprived of their freedom, rendering military or civil service, or in any other way are submitted to its authority".

The Constitution also expressly regulates the peoples right to a name (identification right) (Article 56); the right to the inviolability of personal freedom (Article. 44), establishing guarantees against arrest and detention, and the prohibition to be held incommunicado (Article 44), the prohibition of slavery or servitude (Article 54) and prohibition of forced disappearance of people.

It is also regulated in detail the right to personal safety (Article 46), with the following rights: the right to not be subjected to torture or degrading punishment; the right of those arrested to be treated with respect on their human dignity; the right to consent upon experiments or treatments; and the liability of public officials for infringements of such rights.

The text of the Constitution, in accordance with the tradition of previous texts, additionally enshrines the inviolability of the home (Article 47); the inviolability of private communications (Article 48); free passage or right to move (Article 50); the right to petition and to a timely response (Article 51); and the right of association (Article 52). This last right, however, has certain constitutional limitations first with respect to judges, who may not associate (Article 256); and second a very inconvenient one, referred to the intervention of the State in the internal elections of labor unions and professional associations, which must be organized by the National Electoral Council, as one of the five branches of government (Electoral Power) (Article 293, 6).

In relation to individual rights, the Constitution also guarantees the right to public or private unarmed assemble, without requiring any previous permits from authorities (Article 53); the right to the free expression of thought, ideas and opinion, by any means and without censorship (Article 57); and the right to "opportune, true and unbiased" information, as well as the right to response and correction when directly affected by incorrect or offensive information (Article 58). Express regulation also exists regarding the right to religious freedom and cult (Article 59); the right to protection of honor, privacy, self image, confidentiality and reputation (Article 60); the right to freedom of conscience (Article 61); and the right to be protected by the State (Article 55).

All these civil rights can be protected by means of the amparo and habeas corpus actions set fourth in article 27 of the Constitution.

2. The social, economic and cultural rights

But regarding the already mentioned "fundamental rights" listed in the Spanish Constitution in order to guaranty their protection by means of the "amparo" recourse –mainly referred to civil rights, it must be indicated that additionally to those civil and political rights, the Spanish Constitution has listed within the "fundamental rights", two social rights: the right to education, including the freedom to teach and to create educational institutions (Article 27); and the workers right to found unions and to strike in defense of their interest (Article 28). These rights are thus also protected by means of the recourse of "amparo".

These social rights can be considered as part of the so called Second Generation of human rights referred to the social, economic and cultural rights, which began to be incorporated in the constitutional declarations of Rights with the Mexican Constitution of 1917 and with the Weimar Constitution of Germany of 1919. All those rights were also the object of the United Nations International Covenant on Social, Economic and Cultural Rights of 1966.

But in fact, well before the adoption of the UN Covenant, after World War II, and due to the Welfare State model that spread all over the Occidental world, almost all Latin American Constitutions started to incorporate in their Declarations of rights, additionally to the civil and political rights, the social, economic, and cultural rights. In this sense, the right to education and the right to health care were constitutionalized, as well as the labor rights: the right to work, the right to membership of labor unions, the right to strike, the right to social security; and additionally, the right to equal treatment at work and the right to a salary. The rights to social benefits and to have stability at work and the right to bargain collectively for labor benefits.

Other rights that were progressively constitutionalized, were the right to have proper housing and the right to cultural heritage; as well as all the right to social protection or welfare, such as the right to have family, children protection, maternity and disabled persons protections.

Many of these social rights were incorporated in the Constitutions in order to set forth a constitutional duty or obligation for the State to provide social protection to the people or to render certain public services, as public utilities.

On the other hand, also as Second generation of rights, additionally to the property rights, the economic rights were also constitutionalized, particularly the economic freedom which implies the freedom of industry and trade and the freedom to work.

The 1999 Venezuelan Constitution can be mentioned not only regarding the regulation of these social, economic and cultural rights, but also as an example of extensive and complex policy declarations, regarding which is difficult to find the necessary relation between right and obligation[28]. On the other hand, the Constitution, in a highly paternalistic and State oriented trend, attributes innumerable social obligations to the State bodies, and in the compliance of which society's participation is expressly excluded. Thus, in the 1999 Constitution, the State is responsible for almost all social goals and welfare, a task impossible to be accomplished, even with the rich oil producing State that Venezuela is, where in the first six years of the enforcement of the Constitution (1999–2005), because the rising oil prices, State revenues rose to a level never dreamed before. The tragic result has been that in the same period of time, in parallel to the State populist distribution of money policy, poverty has risen.

---

28 See in general Allan R. BREWER–CARÍAS, *Derecho Constitucional Venezolano. La Constitución de 1999*, Editorial jurídica Venezolana, Caracas 2004, 2 vols.

Anyway, regarding constitutional regulations, the Constitution starts by regulating a group of social rights, referring to families (Article 75); maternity and paternity (Article 76); marriage "between a man and a woman" (Article 77); children and teenagers (Article 78); young people (Article 79); the elderly (Article 80); and to disabled (Article 81); with express regulation of the obligation of televised media to include subtitles and translation into sign language for people with hearing problems (Article 101).

The Constitution also expressly regulated, as a declaration, the people's right to a dwelling place, that must be "adequate, sure, comfortable, hygienic with the essential utilities, including an habitat that humanizes family, neighborhood and communal relations" (Article 82); and the right to health care (Article 83), imposing on the State the obligation to create, oversee and administer a "national public health system", that must be inter–sectorial, decentralized and participative, integrated with the social security system, governed by the principles of freeness, universality, integrity, fairness, social integration and solidarity (Article 84).

Hence, the health service is constitutionally conceived as being integrated with the social security system (as a sub–system), and also conceived as being free and universal, which bears no relationship whatsoever with the social security system established for the affiliates or the insured. It is also set forth with constitutional rank, that public health goods and services are considered as State ownership and shall not be privatized. Finally, it is set forth that the organized community shall have the right and duty to participate in decisions regarding the planning, execution and control of specific policies at the public health institutions (Article 84).

Article 85 of the Constitution establishes that the State shall be obliged to finance the public health system by means of tax income, the obligatory contributions to social security and any other source of financing determined by law. The State shall also guarantee a health budget that covers the objectives of the health policy. Finally, the above–mentioned Article 85 indicates that the State "shall regulate public and private health institutions"; this being the only ruling that names private health institutions, but merely as subjects to regulation.

In regard to the right to social security, Article 86 of the Constitution regulates it "as a non–lucrative public service that guarantees the health and assures protection in contingencies concerning maternity, paternity, sickness, invalidity, catastrophic illnesses, disability, special needs, labor risks, loss of employment, old–age, widowhood, orphanage, housing, costs derived from family life and any other circumstance of social welfare".

In the same Chapter relative to social and family rights, the 1999 Constitution, in a way similar to the 1961 Constitution, incorporated the group of labor rights into the text of the Constitution, but this time it broadened them and reinforced them even more, raising many rights to a constitutional rank. Thus, the right and duty to work was expressly regulated (Article 87); as well as the right to equality at work (Article 88); the State protection of work (Article 89); the workday and right to rest (Article 90); the right to a salary (Article 91); the right to social benefits (Article 92); the right to work stability (Article 93); responsibilities at the workplace (Article

94); the right to join a labor union (Article 95); the right to collective bargain (96); and the right to strike (Article 97).

In regard to the right to join labor unions, the very inconvenient State's influence over the unions' functions should be emphasized, by reason of Article 293.6 of the Constitution, which states that the National Electoral Council shall be the organ competent to "organize the elections of labor unions and professional associations". In Venezuela, therefore, the unions are not free to organize their own elections of their authorities and representatives, since such elections organization shall be carried out by the State.

On the other hand, Title III, Chapter VI of the Constitution enshrines a series of rights regarding culture, such as cultural freedom and creation, and intellectual property (Article 98); cultural values and the protection of cultural heritage (Article 99); the protection of popular culture (Article 100) and cultural information (Article 101), establishing that the State shall guarantee the broadcasting, reception and circulation of cultural information. To this end, the media is duty–bound to assist in the broadcasting of the values of popular tradition and the work of artists, composers, filmmakers, scientists and other such creators of culture.

With regards to education, Article 102 of the Constitution begins by establishing, in general terms, that "education is a human right and an essential social duty, democratic, free and obligatory". The consequence of this is the provision under Article 102 that imposes on the State the obligation to assume education as an "indeclinable function" and one of maximum interest at all its levels and types, and as an instrument of scientific, humanistic and technological knowledge at the service of society. Hence, constitutionally speaking, education is declared a public utility or service, emphasizing however that: "the State shall encourage and protect any private education that is rendered according to the principles provided in the Constitution and the Law".

The right to an integral education, the free nature of public education and the obligatory character of all levels of education from pre–school to diversified secondary level, are also regulated. Insofar as State school education is concerned, this shall be free up to pre–university level (Article 103). The teachers´ regime is also established (Article 104); as are the right to educate (Article 106), and the obligatory teaching of environmental and civic education; as well as the history and geography of Venezuela (Article 107). Article 108 also emphasizes that social communication media, both public and private, shall contribute to the citizens' education. Additionally, the 1999 Constitution formalizes the principle of the universities' autonomy (Article 109); regulates the regime of the liberal professions (Article 105); the regime of science and technology (Article 110); and the right to sporting activities (Article 111).

All these social rights imply State obligations and can also be enforced by means of the "amparo" action or recourse, as has been used mainly regarding social protection rights, like maternity rights, and right to education and health care.

The 1999 Constitution also incorporates in Chapter VII, with detail, the economic rights of people, as follows: on the one hand economic freedom (Article 112); and on the other the right to property and right to only be expropriated by means of due process and just compensation (Article 115). This form of regulation follows the orientation of Venezuelan constitutionalism, although certain variations with regard to its equivalent in the previous 1961 Constitution (Article 99), should be emphasized: *firstly*, it is not mentioned that private property shall perform a social function, as indicated in the 1961 Constitution; *secondly,* in the 1999 Constitution the attributes of the ownership of property (use, possession and disposal) are detailed, where such provision were previously a legal matter (dealt with under Article 545 of the Civil Code); and *thirdly*, in regard to expropriation, the new constitutional text provides that the payment of fair compensation be "timely". Thus the regulation guarantees more strongly the right to ownership of property. But in contrast to these guarantees, it can be said that never before the State has occupied more land without proper compensation as has occurred since the enactment of the Constitution in 2000, particularly in the country side.

The Constitution also forbids any kind of confiscation of goods, except in the cases allowed by the Constitution itself, by way of exception and due process, to the goods and property of national or foreign individuals or companies guilty of corruption crimes committed against public property, or those who have illicitly enriched themselves acting as public officials, or in cases of enrichment arising from commercial, financial or other activities associated with the illicit traffic of drugs and narcotics (Articles 116 and 271).

Additionally, Title VI of the 1999 Constitution is dedicated to the regulation of the socio–economic system. Amongst its regulations, Article 307 should be mentioned, since it declares the regime of large rural estates (*latifundio*) as being contrary to social interest, and encouraging the legislator to tax idle land and to establish the measures necessary to transform such land into productive economic units, also rescuing land being eminently agricultural land.

This same regulation establishes the right of peasants and other countryman to own land, pursuant to the methods and cases specified by the respective law. This implies the establishment of constitutional State obligations to protect and encourage associative and individual ownership mechanisms in order to guaranty farm production, and to control the sustainable organization of farm land in order to ensure food and agricultural potential.

The same article exceptionally provides that the legislator create taxlike contributions to facilitate the funding for the financing, research, technical assistance, technology transfer and other activities promoting productivity and competition in the agricultural sector.

3. The collective rights

More recently, in the past decades, a Third generation of rights has developed, related to collective rights, considered as human kind rights or solidarity rights, like the right to have a healthy environment; the right to development; the right to free competition; the consumer's rights to have products and services of quality; the right to have a certain standard of living; the right to human kind heritage, the rights of the indigenous communities and even the right to peace, as is set forth in the Colombian Constitution of 1991 (Article 22).

Many recent constitutions have incorporated such rights in their texts, as has happened with the right to have a healthy environment, to which Constitutions devote extensive articles. This is the case of the 1994 Argentinean Constitution, whose article 41 states that:

(1) All inhabitants are entitled to the right to a healthy and balanced environment fit for human development in order that productive activities shall meet present needs without endangering those of future generations; and shall have the duty to preserve it. As a first priority, environmental damage shall bring about the obligation to repair it according to law.

(2) The authorities shall provide for the protection of this right, the rational use of natural resources, the preservation of the natural and cultural heritage and of the biological diversity, and shall also provide for environmental information and education.

(3) The Nation shall regulate the minimum protection standards, and the provinces those necessary to reinforce them, without altering their local jurisdictions.

(4) The entry into the national territory of present or potential dangerous wastes, and of radioactive ones, is forbidden.

Before the Argentinean Constitution, the 1988 Constitution of Brazil initiated the constitutionalization process of the rights to healthy environment, with its article 255, in which it is also regulated the general policy of the State regarding environment, as follows:

"All persons are entitled to an ecologically balanced environment, which is an asset for the people's common use and is essential to healthy life, it being the duty of the Government and of the community to defend and preserve it for present and future generations.

(1) In order to ensure the effectiveness of this right, it is incumbent upon the Government to:

I. preserve and restore essential ecological processes and provide ecological handling of the species and ecosystems;

II. preserve the variety and integrity of Brazil's genetic wealth and supervise entities engaged in research and handling of genetic material;

III. determine, in all units of the Federation, territorial spaces and components which are to receive special protection, any alteration and suppression only being allowed by means of a law, and any use which adversely affects the integrity of the attributes which justify their protection being forbidden;

IV. demand, according to the law, for the installation of works or activities which may cause significant degradation of the environment, a prior environment impact study, which shall be made public;

V. control the production, marketing, and use of techniques, methods, and substances which represent a risk to life, to the quality of life, and to the environment;

VI. promote environmental education at all school levels and public awareness of the need to preserve the environment;

VII. protect the fauna and the flora, all practices which jeopardize their ecological function, cause the extinction of species or subject animals to cruelty being forbidden according to the law.

(2) Those who explore mineral resources shall be required to restore the degraded environment according to the technical solution required by the proper government agency, according to the law.

(3) Conduct and activities considered harmful to the environment shall subject the individual or corporate wrongdoers to penal and administrative sanctions, in addition to the obligation to repair the damages caused.

(4) The Brazilian Amazon Forest, the Atlantic Woodlands, the "Serra do Mar", the "Pantanal Mato Grossense" and the Coastline are part of the national wealth, and they shall be used, according to the law, under conditions which ensure preservation of the environment, including the use of natural resources.

(5) Vacant governmental lands or lands seized by the States through discriminatory actions, which are necessary to protect natural ecosystems, are inalienable.

(6) Power plants operated by nuclear reactor shall have their location defined in a federal law and may otherwise not be installed.

Following this general pattern, the right to the environment is also regulated in the Constitutions of Colombia (Article 79), Cuba (Article 27), Chile (Article 8), Ecuador (Articles 86–91); Guatemala (Articles 97–98), Mexico (Article 4), Panamá (Article 114), Paraguay (article 7), Perú (Article 22) and Venezuela (Articles 127–129).

In the 1999 Venezuelan Constitution, which we have been commenting as a Latin American example of contemporary constitutional declarations of rights, and as an innovation is the regulation of rights relative to the environment –establishing standards for the right and duty to enjoy and maintain a healthy environment (Article 127); the territorial land planning policy (Article 128); environmental impact studies and the toxic substances régime; and the obligatory inclusion of environmental clauses in public contracts (Article 129).

Another constitutional innovation regarding economic matters, but as collective rights, is regulated by Article 117, referred to the right of everybody to possess quality goods and services, as well as adequate and non–deceptive information of the products and services they consume; to freedom of choice; and to a fair and dignified treatment. In this case, in fact, the Constitution has established a collective right of the Third generation, as well as in Article 113 referred to the prohibition of monopoly and to the abuse of dominion position in trade competitions relations.

Also regarding collective rights, the rights of the indigenous peoples have been regulated in a very extensive way in many recent Constitutions of Latin America, as has happened in the Constitutions of Colombia (Articles 171, 246, 329, 330), Ecuador (Articles 83–85), Mexico (Article 2), Paraguay (Articles 62–67) and Venezuela (Articles 119–126).

In the latter, Chapter VIII contains a group of regulations of the rights of the indigenous people, in contrast with the previous Constitution of 1961 (Article 77) which contained only a brief protection regulation. In this regard, the 1999 Constitution recognizes "the existence of indigenous peoples and communities, their social, political and economic organization; their cultures, usages and customs, languages and religions; and their habitat and their original rights over their ancestral and traditional lands, necessary for developing and guaranteeing their life–styles" (Article

119). The Constitution sought to neutralize the danger that might arise from this regulation in regard to the national territory integrity, by stating that "since they represent cultures with ancestral roots, the indigenous people are part of the Nation, the State and the sole, sovereign and indivisible Venezuelan people", where the term "people" should not be interpreted in the sense provided under international law (Article 126).

Apart from this, the Constitution provided a set of regulations relative to the development of natural resources to be found in indigenous habitats (Article 120); to the indigenous cultural values (Article 121); to the right of the indigenous people to integral health care (Article 122); and to indigenous people's rights to the collective intellectual property of their knowledge, technologies and innovations (Article 124). Finally, Article 125 of the Constitution enshrines the indigenous people's right to political participation, with Article 126 of the Constitution guaranteeing "indigenous representation in the National Assembly and the consultant bodies of the federal and local entities that have indigenous populations, pursuant to the law."

In all these cases, the Constitutions regulates these rights not as individual rights, but as collective rights, which are also different to the individual rights that can be collectively claimed, like the labor rights.

Some of these rights have been the object of international regulations, as is the case of the right to development incorporated in article 1 of the United Nations Declarations on the Right of Development (1986), as follows:

> 1. The right to development is an inalienable human right by virtue of which every human person and all peoples are entitled to participate in, contribute to, and enjoy economic, social, cultural and political development, in which all human rights and fundamental freedoms can be fully realized.
>
> 2. The human right to development also implies the full realization of the right of peoples to self–determination, which includes, subject to the relevant provisions of both International Covenants on Human Rights, the exercise of their inalienable right to full sovereignty over all their natural wealth and resources.

Finally, it must be mentioned that beside these collective rights, in the contemporary world, a Fourth generation of human rights is beginning to appear, yet in the process to be constructed, such as the human right to the protection of the human genome and the genetic identity and also the rights to the informatics technology progress.

4. The problem of the relation between rights and obligation in the constitutional declarations

As mentioned before, when analyzing the subject of rights and freedoms, as constitutional rights, they essentially are legal situations of power that individuals hold within a society, by which they have the right to do or not to do, to make, to act or to be protected. Being situations of power, they must always have a direct relationship with other legal situations of duty that are held by the State or by other individuals in the same society, in the sense that if somebody has the power to act, some other person has the duty to refrain from or to impede that action; or if somebody has the right to be protected for instance on his health, the State is obliged to developed institutions in order to care for the health of individuals.

Hence a society cannot be conceived without these direct relations among the subjects that act therein, between those situations of power that are correlative to situations of duty. That is to say, a society cannot be imagined without this interrelation between subjects that, on the one hand, hold the legal power to do, enjoy, use or have, and other subjects that, on the other hand, are in a legal situation of duty, respect, abstention, rendering or giving. In other words, there is always a relationship between a right and an obligation or, in general, between a power and a duty.

From a legal viewpoint, human rights are legal situations of power that are consubstantial with human nature or with the quality of being human, in fact, with the quality of man, and which all men have in equal measure, but in whose regime and declaration, of course, the principle of relation or correlatively with duties has to be always present. Thus, if there is an active subject that has a right, there always has to be someone with an obligation (a passive subject) towards that right, that is, someone who is obliged to abstain from or to perform certain activities to satisfy the enjoyment of those determined rights; therefore there can be no right without a correlative obligation.

In this sense, for instance, there cannot be a human right "to not to get ill." This is a wish, a political declaration, a general purpose of society, but not a right, because correlatively to that dream there is no a particular subject with the duty of ensuring that peoples will not get ill.

In the case of the Venezuelan Constitution, for example, one of the problems that arise when facing the most ample and excellent listing of human rights contained in it, is the confusion that can be found in the constitutional text between good intentions, declarations of public policy and constitutional rights. In some cases, illusion or frustration can derive from the impossibility of satisfying certain aims that have been formulated as social rights, that, because of conceptual impossibility, cannot originate obligations or obligated parties.

This happens with several social rights and guarantees established in the Constitution that are simply impossible to satisfy literally. They are excellent declarations of principle and intent of an unquestionably teleological nature, but it is difficult to conceive them as "rights", since there cannot exist a subject with the obligation to satisfy them.

Such is the case, for example, of the "right to health", enshrined as an "essential social right and obligation of the State, that it shall guarantee as part of the right to life" (Article 83). The fact is that it is impossible for anybody to guarantee somebody else's health, and therefore that constitutionally the "right to health" be established. This would be like, as mentioned before, establishing in the Constitution the right to not become ill, which is impossible since nobody can guarantee to another person that they are not going to become ill.

Constitutional formulas in these matters, however, are quite similar over Latin America. In some cases health is declared public property, as provided in the Constitution of El Salvador: "... the health of the inhabitants of the Republic is considered public property" (Article 65). The Constitution of Guatemala (Article 95) regulates health in a similar sense, and for this reason, both Constitutions establish that the State and the people are under the obligation to ensure its conservation and reestablishment. In this sense it can be said that the right to health is more conceived as a collective right, rather than an individual right.

Yet apart from these general declarations of a constitutional nature, in the majority of the Constitutions of Latin America, the "right to health" is expressly established within the fundamental or constitutional rights of the people (Bolivia, Article 7.a; Brasil, Articles 6 and 196; Ecuador, Article 42; Nicaragua, Article 59; Venezuela, Article 84). This fundamental right corresponds "equally" to all people, as declared in the Constitution of Nicaragua (Article 59); and the Constitution of Guatemala reaffirms this, providing that "the enjoyment of good health is a fundamental right of every human person, and there shall be no discrimination whatsoever in this regard" (Article 93).

Therefore, this constitutional formula of the "right to health", as mentioned above, in fact constitutes a declaration of principles relative to the State's commitment and that of society as a whole to the human person, which would be very difficult to identify "literally" as a real "constitutional right", except from the collective point of view, since such description or declaration lacks the principle of reciprocity.

Nevertheless, it can be said that what the Constitutions seeks to establish with this formula, from the individual rights point of view, is in fact the right of all people to have their health protected by the State, whose corresponding obligation is to ensure the care and recuperation of the health of the people.

For this reason, other Latin American Constitutions declare, more exactly, as an individual right, "the right to the protection of health" (Honduras, Article 145); or they refer more precisely to the right of all people to the protection of their health" (Chile, Article 19,9; Mexico, Article 4; Peru, Article 7); or that "their health be cared for and protected" (Cuba, Article 50); or that "all people be guaranteed access to the promotion, protection and recuperation of health" (Colombia, Article 49). In Panama, Article 105 of the Constitution even provides that:

> "The individual, as part of society, is entitled to the promotion, protection, conservation, restitution and rehabilitation of his or her health and the obligation to maintain such health, this being understood to be complete physical, mental and social well–being".

In certain cases, as occurs in the above–mentioned Constitution of Venezuela, it could be said that both formulas are mixed together, when, for example, Article 83 provides that "health is an essential social right", moreover adding that "all people shall have the right to the protection of their health." A similar situation occurs in Article 68 of the Constitution of Paraguay, where, under the heading "right to health", it establishes that "the State shall protect and promote health as being a fundamental right of the individual and in the interest of society."

Another case that can be highlighted as an example of this relationship between constitutional declarations and the relation of rights with duties, is the right that the Venezuelan Constitution enshrines in favor of "all people to an adequate, safe, comfortable and healthy dwelling, with all the basic essential utilities and a habitat that humanizes family, neighborhood and community relationships" (Article 82). This "right", as written, is impossible to satisfy, and not even a rich State can be obliged to satisfy it. It is, rather, a declaration of principles or intent, beautifully structured, that cannot however lead to identifying a party that is obligated to satisfy it, and much less to the State. Here, good intentions and social declarations were confused with constitutional rights and obligations, which cause a different type of legal relationship that are even justifiable or entitled to constitutional protection. What in fact can and must be constructed from such "right to dwelling", in the obligation of the State to provide everyone with the means and conditions to have such a home.

IV. CHANGES IN THE OBLIGED PARTY REGARDING CONSTITUTIONAL RIGHTS AND FREEDOMS

In any case, according to the initial concept behind the formulation of the declaration of civil rights, the responsible party in the relation right/duty was the State. This means that the rights were originally formulated before the State, in order to be protected from State actions or intrusions, so the active subject was always man, a citizen, and the passive subject – the obligated party – was the State.

This initial concept of the formulation of constitutional rights, particularly regarding civil or individual rights, even led to their justiciability by means of the "amparo" action or recourse always conceived as a protection mechanisms against the State. So in its origin, the "amparo" action was not conceived to protect individuals from other individuals' offences.

This of course changed later on with the alteration of the way of conceiving the relationship between rights and duties (in the sense that the passive subject in the constitutional rights is not only the State). The latter continues to be so, but not exclusively, since the field of the passive subject has been progressively universalized, to the point where there now exist obligations –that is, situations of duty in the field of rights– that correspond, naturally, to individuals, to groups, to communities, and even to the international community. This is the case of the Third generation of rights like the right to development, a right which, moreover, is not only held by man as an individual but by peoples and communities and also the international community.

On the other hand, referring to the necessary relationship between situations of power and situations of duty, it can be found that the situations of duty, –those corresponding to the passive subject, are not always of the same nature.

Often the situations of duty are configured as situations of being obliged to provide or to give or render something, accomplishing a positive obligation, that is to say, as obligations to render, give or make. This is the common situation regarding social rights, such as the right to education or right to health care, in relation to which the State is obliged to carry out a positive activity, or to render a public service or utility, that the citizens have the right to received or enjoy, as the active subjects in the legal relation.

In other fields, constitutional rights instead of being rights to receive something as a service, are rather "freedoms", because the situation of the passive subject, for example of the State itself, does not correspond to any obligation to do or to give. In these cases, the obligation is basically an obligation to abstain from acting, to not disturb, to not harm, to not stop, to not deprive. Therefore, from the strictly legal viewpoint, these are more freedoms rather than rights. For example, the freedom of moving implies more a correlative situation of duty consisting in the obligation to restrict the free circulation of people; the freedom or the right to free expression of thoughts, to free speech or to free press implies the State's duty not to bother, not to censor, not to prevent or impede the exercise of such rights.

This relation between the various situations of power and duty leads to a clear distinction between freedoms and rights, when the situation of the obligated subject is not, in the case of freedoms, an obligation to give or to do, but rather not to do, to abstain. In contrast, in the rights as such, there is an obligation to render, as occurs, for example, in general, in public services and, particularly, in those of a social nature (health, education).

From this point of view, regarding the rights in strict sense, it can be said that in general, the obliged party is the State, that is the party with the duty to provide health care or education to the people; instead, regarding freedoms, not only the State is obliged not to restrict, or not to impede its exercise, but also other individuals have the duty to abstain or to refrain. That is why, in contemporary constitutional law, the action of "amparo" in many countries can also be exercised against individuals and not only against the State, as was the initial constitutional trend.

V. THE DECLARATIVE NATURE OF THE CONSTITUTIONAL DECLARATIONS OF RIGHTS AND THE OPEN CONSTITUTIONAL CLAUSES

From a legal point of view, and regarding all the "generations" of rights, it is important to note how the declarations are not "constitutive" of such rights, in the sense that they do not create such rights, but rather, as their name itself implies, are of a declaratory nature, that is, they only recognize the existence of rights. Therefore neither the Constitutions nor the International Conventions create or establish them, but rather admit them as being inherent to the human person, as natural rights.

From this angle, the most important aspect of the expansion process of the constitutional declarations of human rights in Latin America, has been the progressive and continuous incorporation in the Constitutions of the "open clauses" of a person's rights, which has also arisen through the influence of the United States IX (1791) in which it is stated that "the enumeration in the Constitution, of certain rights, shall not be constructed to deny or disparage others retained by the people".

The express enshrining of clauses of such sort in the Constitutions confirms that the list of constitutional rights does not end with those that are expressly listed in the constitutional declaration, but that all others rights which are inherent to the human person or those declared in international instruments are also considered as human rights.

In this respect it can even be said that all Latin American Constitutions, with only very few exceptions (Cuba, Chile, Mexico and Panamá), contain open clauses of the rights, according to which it is expressly indicated that the declaration and enunciation of the rights that is made in the Constitution shall not be understood to be a denial of others not listed therein, that are inherent to the human person or to human dignity. Clauses of this type are to be found, for example, in the Constitutions of Argentina (Article 33), Bolivia (Article 33), Colombia (Article 94), Costa Rica (Article 74), Ecuador (Article 19), Guatemala (Article 44), Honduras (Article 63), Nicaragua (Article 46), Paraguay (Article 45), Peru (Article 3), Uruguay (Article 72) and Venezuela (Article 22).

In the Dominican Republic, the Constitution is less expressive, only indicating that the constitutional list (Articles 8 and 9) "is not limitative, and therefore does not exclude other rights and duties of a similar nature" (Article 10).

Regarding the rights inherent to human persons referred to in many of the open clauses, the former Supreme Court of Justice of Venezuela in a decision of January 31, 1991 (Case: *Anselmo Natale*), stated:

> "The inherent rights of a human person are natural, universal rights which find their origin and are direct consequence of the relationships of solidarity among men, of the need for the individual development of mankind and for the protection of the environment."

Therefore the same Court concluded by stating that

> "...such rights are commonly enshrined in Universal declarations and in national and supranational texts, and their nature and content as human rights shall leave no room for doubt, since they are the very essence of a human person and shall therefore be necessarily respected and protected" [29].

Accordingly, Article 22 of the Constitution of Venezuela, following the tradition of previous Constitutions, expressly establishes that "the enunciation of the rights and guarantees contained in this Constitution and in the international instruments on human rights shall not be understood to be a denial of others that being inherent to the human person, are not expressly set forth in those texts"; adding that "the absence of the regulating statute of such rights do not impede its exercise" (Article 22).

This article, like Article 94 of the 1991 Colombian Constitution and Article 44 of the Guatemalan Constitution, refers to the "inherent rights of a human person", thus incorporating notions of a natural right, in the sense that human rights precede the State and the Constitutions themselves. The Constitution of Paraguay, in the same sense, refers to "rights inherent to human personality" (Article 45).

But in the case of Colombia and Venezuela, the open clause allows for the identification of rights inherent to human persons, not only regarding those listed in the Constitution, but also in international human rights instruments, thus considerably broadening their scope. On the other hand the clause has allowed national Courts to identify human rights inherent to human beings not expressly regulated in the Constitutions, but set forth in international instruments. It was the case during the nineties of the former Supreme Court of Justice of Venezuela, which annulled statutes

---

29 See the reference in Carlos AYALA CORAO, "La jerarquía de los instrumentos internacionales sobre derechos humanos", en *El nuevo derecho constitucional latinoamericano, IV Congreso venezolano de Derecho constitucional*, Vol. II, Caracas, 1996, and in *La jerarquía constitucional de los tratados sobre derechos humanos y sus consecuencias*, México, 2003.

basing its rulings in the violation of rights set forth in the American Convention which were considered as rights inherent to human beings according to open clause incorporated in article 50 of the 1961 Constitution.

In effect, in 1996, the Supreme Court of Justice, when deciding a judicial review action brought before the Court against the State of *Amazonas* legislation setting its territorial division, ruled that being the State mainly populated by indigenous people, the sanctioning of the statute without hearing the opinion of the indigenous communities, violated the constitutional right to political participation. Such right was not expressly regulated in the 1961 Constitution, so the Court founded its ruling in the open clause enshrined in Article 50 of the Constitution (equivalent to Article 22 of the 1999 Constitution), considering the right to political participation as inherent to human being, in particular, as a "general principle of constitutional rank in a democratic society", adding, regarding the case, that "because of being a minorities rights (indigenous peoples in the case), it must be judicially protected, according to Article 50 of the Constitution, to the great international treaties and conventions on human rights, and to the national and states legislation". In the December 5, 1996 ruling it was provided:

> In the case, there was no evidence of the accomplishment of the previsions regarding citizens participation, lacking the statute of its original legitimacy derived from the popular hearing. The defendants argued that the advice of public bodies such as the Ministry of the Environment and the Environment Autonomous Services of the Amazon States where asked, as well as the advice of some indigenous organization. The Court deems that such procedure does only constitute a timid and insignificant expression of the constitutional right to political participation in the process of elaborating statutes, which must be guarantied before and pending the legislative activity and not only when the legislation is promulgated... Regarding a statute referred to the political–territorial division of a State like the Amazonas State (mainly populated by indigenous communities), it is a statute that changes and modifies the economic and social conditions of the region, the vital environment of individuals, the municipal boundaries, the land ownership regime and the daily life of indigenous peoples. Thus their participation must be considered with special attention, due to the fact that indigenous peoples are one of the most exposed groups to human rights violations, due to their socio–economic and cultural conditions, in which habitat intervenes various interest some times contrary to the legitimate rights of autochthonous populations... It is in this context that the rights of indigenous peoples acquire more force, as it is expressly recognized by this Court[30].

According to the aforementioned, the Court's decision referred to the violation of constitutional rights of minorities set forth in the Constitution and in the international treaties and conventions on human rights, particularly the right to citizenship participation in the statute elaborating process, particularly because no public consultation was made in the case to the minority indigenous communities, as a consequence of which, the Court decided to annul the challenged statute.

The following year, in 1997, another important decision was issued by the former Supreme Court of Justice of Venezuela, this time annulling a national (federal) statute referred to wicked and crooked persons (Ley de vagos y maleantes) which

30 Caso: *Antonio Guzmán, Lucas Omashi y otros,* in *Revista de Derecho Público,* N° 67–68, Editorial Jurídica Venezolana, Caracas, 1996, pp. 176 ff.

was considered unconstitutional, based on the "constitutionalization of human rights process according to Article 50 of the Constitution", because such statute "violated *ipso jure* the international conventions and treaties on human rights which had acquired constitutional rank". In its November 6, 1997 ruling, the Supreme Court considered the challenged statute which allowed executive detentions without due process to persons considered wicked or crooks, as infamous, supporting its decision on Article 5 of the Universal Declaration on Human Rights, and in the American Convention on Human Rights "which has been incorporated on internal law as self applicable regulation reinforced by courts decisions that has given the Convention constitutional force, which implies the incorporation to our internal legal order of the regime set forth in the international conventions". The Court considered that the challenged statute was unconstitutional because it omitted the guaranties for a fair trail set forth in Articles 7 and 8 of the American Convention and Articles 9 and 14 of the International Covenant on Human Rights, and because it was discriminatory violating Article 24 of the same American Convention, transcribing in the ruling text the entire text of those articles. The Court also referred in its annulling ruling, to the existence of "reports of human rights organization which openly condemn the Venezuelan legislation on wicked and crook persons, particularly on the grounds of promoting the sanction of a statute on citizen's security protection"[31].

More recently, and regarding the challenging of the proposed call for a consultative referendum for the convening of a National Constituent Assembly by the elected President of the Republic in December 1998, which was not regulated in the 1961 Constitution as a mean for constitutional review or reform, the Supreme Court in January 1999, issued two rulings deciding interpretative recourses, allowing the convening of such Constituent Assembly by means of a referendum based on the peoples right to political participation also founded in the open clause on human rights set forth in Article 50 of the Constitution, considering it as an implicit, constitutionally not enumerated right inherent in the human person.

Considering the referendum as a right inherent to the human person, the Court specifically indicated that:

> This is applicable, not only from a methodological point of view, but ontologically as well, since if the right to a constitutional referendum were considered to depend on a reform of the current Constitution, it would be subordinate to the will of the constituted power, which in turn would be placed above the sovereign power. The absence of such a right in the Fundamental Charter must be interpreted as a gap in the Constitution, since it could not be sustained that the sovereign power had renounced, *ab inicio*, the exercise of a power that is the work of its own political decision.[32]

31 See in *Revista de Derecho Público* N° 71–72, Editorial Jurídica Venezolana, Caracas, 1997, pp. 177 ff.

32 See in *Revista de Derecho Público,* N° 77–80, Editorial Jurídica Venezolana, Caracas, 1999, p. 67

The conclusion of the Court's decision was that it was not necessary to previously reform the Constitution in order to recognize the referendum or popular consultation on whether to convene a Constituent Assembly as being a constitutional right[33].

Open clauses of human rights, of the same nature, which have served in Latin American countries to resolve important constitutional issues, are found in almost all their Constitutions, even with different contents. The Constitution of Ecuador, for instance, indicates that "the rights and guarantees provided in this Constitution and in international instruments do not exclude others derived from the nature of the human person and are necessary for his or her full moral and material development (Article 19). This provision is complemented by Article 18 in which it is stated that the rights and guaranties enshrined in the Constitution and in the international instruments, are directly and immediately applicable by and before any court or authority; and that the absence of regulatory statutes can not be alleged in order to justify the violation or the ignorance of the rights set forth in the Constitution, or to reject the action for its protection, or to deny the recognizance of such rights.

In Nicaragua, the Constitution is more detailed regarding the listing of international instruments and, as such, more limitative, when its Article 46 provides as follows:

> **Article 46**.– Every person in the land shall enjoy State protection and the recognition of the rights inherent to the human person, of the unrestricted respect, promotion and protection of human rights, and of the full enforcement of the rights consigned in the Universal Declaration of Human Rights; in the American Declaration of the Rights and Duties of Man; in the International Covenant on Economic, Social and Cultural Rights; in the United Nations' International Covenant on Civil and Political Rights; and in the American Convention on Human Rights of the Organization of American States.

In other cases, such as the Constitution of Brazil, the open clause, without referring to the inherent rights of human persons, indicates that the listing in the Constitution of right and guaranties, does not exclude others "derived form the regime and principles adopted by the Constitution or by international treaties to which the Federative Republic of Brazil is a party" (Article 5.2). However, pursuant to the majority of international instruments, the rights listed therein are considered human attributes, and therefore the effect when applying this enunciative clause is the same.

Other Latin American Constitutions also contain these open clauses allowing for the extension of the human rights listed in the text of the Constitution, even though perhaps with some lesser scope regarding the previous examples.

It is the case of the Constitution of Costa Rica when indicating that the enunciation of rights and benefits it contained does not exclude others "which derive from the Christian principle of social justice" (Article 74), expression that nonetheless must be interpreted in the sense of occidental notion of human dignity and social justice.

---

33 See the comments in Allan R. Brewer–Carias, "La configuración judicial del proceso constituyente o de cómo el guardián de la Constitución abrió el camino para su violación y para su propia extinción", in *Revista de Derecho Público,* N° 77–80, Editorial Jurídica Venezolana, Caracas, 1999, pp. 453 ff.

In other Constitutions, the open clauses on human rights refer to the sovereignty of the people and the republican form of government and therefore more emphasis is made on regarding political rights, than on the inherent rights of human persons, as occurs in Argentina, where Article 33 of the Constitution states that:

> "The declarations, rights and guaranties enumerated in the Constitution, can not be understood as to deny others rights and guaranties not enumerated, but that rose from the principle of the people's sovereignty and from the republican form of government".

An almost exact regulation is contained in article 35 of the Constitution of Bolivia. Also in similar way, other Constitutions make reference to the rights derived both from the republican form of government and from the representative nature of the government as well as from the dignity of man. This is the case of Uruguay where Article 72 of the Constitution states that "the enunciation of rights, duties and guaranties made by the Constitution does not exclude the others that are inherent to human personality or derive from the republican form of government". Also in Peru Article 3 of the Constitution refers to "others guaranteed by the Constitution, nor others of an analogous nature or that are based on the dignity of man, or on the sovereignty of the people, of the democratic rule of law and of the republican form of government".

Also in Honduras, Article 63 states that

> "The declarations, rights and guaranties enumerated in this Constitution, must not be understood as a denial of other unspecified declarations, rights and guarantees, rising from sovereignty, the republican, democratic and representative form of Government and from the dignity of man".

Naturally, in all these cases, the incorporation of open clauses in the Constitution regarding human rights, as mentioned before regarding the Venezuelan constitutional provision, implies that the absence of statutory regulation of such rights cannot be invoked to deny or undermine the exercise of these rights by the people, as is expressed in many Constitutions (Argentina, Bolivia, Paraguay, Venezuela, and Ecuador). This, of course responds to the principle of the direct applicability of the Constitution in human rights matters, which excludes the traditional concept of the so–called "programmatic clauses" which was constructed under the constitutionalism of some decades ago, particularly in the question of social rights, which impeded their being exercised until legally regulated, and also impeded their justiciability.

In this regard, as mentioned, the Constitution of Ecuador is careful to point out the following:

> *Article 18.* The rights and guarantees determined in this Constitution and in the international instruments in force, shall be directly and immediately enforceable by and before any judge, court or authority...
>
> ...The lack of statutes shall not be alleged in order to justify the violation or ignorance of the rights established in this Constitution; to dismiss actions by reason of these facts; or to deny the recognition of such rights.

VI. ABSOLUTE OR LIMITATIVE CHARACTER OF THE DECLARATIONS

It must also be noted, on the other hand, that the constitutional enunciation of rights, notwithstanding the increase of scope we have mentioned, and even including the enunciative character of their constitutional declarations, has been laid down in parallel with the establishment of a specific scope for the limitations to such rights.

It is true that there are absolute rights, as are all the rights considered and declared as inviolable and not limitable, such as the right to life, the right to not be tortured, and the right to not receive shameful sentences or the right self defense.

But beyond these, there exists the principle of the limitability of rights and freedoms, whose borderline is always marked by both the rights of others persons and public and social order, because, unquestionably, rights are exercised in society and they have many titleholders. This requires, therefore, the need to conciliate the exercising of rights by everyone, in order that it not bring about, in particular, the violation of other people's rights and, in general, of public and social general order.

Of course, this principle can lead to extreme dangerous situations such as the one which unfortunately still remains in the Constitutions of Cuba, which leaves open an "unlimited" possibility of limitations to human rights, founded on the conservation of principles that can only be determined by the established Power, thus rendering the rights futile. In this regard, Article 62 of the Cuban Constitution provides that: "None of the citizens' recognized freedoms may be exercised against the provisions of the Constitution and the laws, or against the existence and purposes of the socialist State, or against the Cuban people's decision to construct socialism and communism. Offences against such principle are punishable."

Generally speaking however, and leaving aside this fortunately isolated case, the limitation to rights allowed by the Constitutions are only linked to the demands for public and social general order and to the exercise of the same rights by others.

Legally speaking, this all leads to important matters that concern the exercise of rights. Firstly, that any limitation confronts a fundamental guarantee in the sense that is constitutionally required that they be imposed only by means of statutory regulations or by a formal law sanctioned by the elected legislative body.

In this regard and as we have mentioned before, in spite of the advances contained for instance in the 1999 Constitution, with its exhaustive list of rights and the constitutionalization of international treaties concerning human rights, a specific negative aspect of its regulations which signifies a serious and potential harm to the guarantee of the principle of legality, is the establishment of the broad legislative delegation in the President of the Republic (Article 302), that can lead to executive limitations of constitutional rights.

On the other hand, mention must be made of the progressive search for the balance that must exist between the different rights, which must be done in such a way that the exercise of one right does not imply the infringement of another. That is the reason for the principles of indivisibility and interdependence in the enjoyment and exercise of rights; a matter that cannot be completely resolved through the sole provision of the Constitution. It only can be achieved through the progressive application of such texts by an effective and efficient Judiciary, which is the only branch of government that can clarify when the exercise of one right shall outweigh that of another.

There have been many legal cases, for example in relation to freedom of speech, that have determined how far freedom of speech can signify, for instance, the infringement of a child's rights, or to what extent freedom of speech can affect the right to privacy. In these cases the judge is the one who has to decide which right shall prevail in a specific moment, or under what circumstances precedence shall be given to the rights of a child, for example, as has happened in court cases in Venezuela, in regard to the right to free expression of thought[34].

In this task of interpretation, the principles of progressiveness, interdependence, reasonableness, *favor libertatis* and the concept of the essential nucleus of rights, among others, are essential for guaranteeing for they exercise and enforceability.

CHAPTER II.
THE CONSTITUTIONALIZATION OF THE INTERNATIONALIZATION OF HUMAN RIGHTS

I. THE CONSTITUTIONAL AND INTERNATIONAL REGULATIONS

Human rights today are not solely a matter concerning constitutional law and constitutional regulations. Progressively, and particularly after the Second World War, they have been also a main and essential matter of international law. During the past decades both branches of law have mutually feedback one to the other in setting forth declarations and regulations regarding human rights.

Initially, and particularly until the Second World War, the human rights regulations were the process of a constitutionalization process, by mean of the expansion of the declarations of rights, freedoms and guarantees enshrined in the Constitutions. This was the case of the initial declarations of civil rights in the XVIII Century American and French Constitutions, and of the extensive subsequent chapter devoted to enumerate constitutional rights in all the Latin American Constitutions.

The first stage of the protection of human rights process was, then, a process of constitutionalization of the declarations of human rights.

That first stage was then followed by a second one, that of the internationalization of the constitutionalization of human rights, particularly after the Second World War, characterized not only by the general approval in the United States and in the Organization of American States in 1948 of general declarations on human rights, but also by the approval of multilateral treaties on the matter. It was, undoubtedly, the evil and most aberrant violations of human rights uncovered after the end of the

34 See for example, Allan R. Brewer–Carías *et a. Los derechos del niño vs. los abusos parlamentarios de la libertad de expresión*, Colección Opiniones y Alegatos Jurídicos, N° 4, Editorial Jurídica Venezolana, Caracas, 1994.

War that provoked such international reaction seeking for the protection of human right as a matter of international and supranational law, not being considered enough for the effective protection and enforcement of rights, their sole national constitutional provisions.

For this purpose, a re–arrangement of the concept of sovereignty was needed, in order for the States to accept the imposition of international law over national regulations. International law began to play an important role in the establishing of limits to constitutional law itself, as a result of the new international principles and commitments that came about after the War to guarantee peace.

Therefore it is not surprising that precisely following the end of the War began the process of internationalization of human rights, with the adoption in 1948 of both the American Declaration of the Rights and Duties of Man by the Organization of American States, and the Universal Declaration of Human Rights by the United Nations Organization. Those declarations were followed only two years latter by the first multilateral treaty on the matter, the 1950 European Convention on Human Rights, which entered into force in 1953.

Regarding the American Declaration adopted in 1948, its contents referred basically to civil, social and political rights, as follows: right to life, liberty and personal security (I); right to equality before the law (II); right to religious freedom and cult (III); right to freely search information, to opinion, and expression (IV); right to protection of honor, personal reputation and privacy (V); right to family and to its protection (VI); rights to maternity and children protections (VII); right to residence and move (VIII); right to the inviolability of the home (IX); right to the inviolability and transmission of correspondence (X); right to the preservation of health (XI); right to education (XII); right to culture (XIII); right to work and to fair remuneration (XIV); right to leisure time (XV); right to social security (XVI); right to the recognition of personality (XVII); right to fair trial (due process) (XVIII); right to nationality (XIX); right to vote and to political participation (XX); right to assembly (XXI); right to association (XXII); right to property (XXIII); right to petition (XXIV); right to personal liberty and to protection from arbitrary arrests (XXV); and right to presumption of innocence, to impartial hearing (XXVI), to seek for asylum (XXVII).

The process of internationalization of human rights was consolidated in 1966, with the adoption of the United Nations International Covenant on Civil and Political Rights, and the International Covenant on Economic, Social and Cultural Rights, both in effect since 1976; and, in 1969, with the adoption of the American Convention on Human Rights, which also entered into force in 1976.

The International Covenant on Civil and Political Rights declared the following rights: the right to life and restrictions on death penalty (6); the right not to be subjected to torture or to cruel, inhuman or degrading treatment or punishment, and without his free consent to medical or scientific experimentation (7); the prohibition of slavery, servitude and compulsory labor (8); the right to liberty, to personal security, not to be subjected to arbitrary arrest or detention, and only to be deprived of his liberty by means of due process of law (9); the right of detainees to be treated with humanity and with respect for the inherent dignity of the human person (10);

the right not to be imprisoned due to contractual obligations (11); the right to liberty of movement and freedom to choose residence (12); the right of aliens to be expelled only by means of due process (13); the rights and guaranties of due process of law, among them: to be equal before the courts; to have a fair and public hearing by a competent, independent and impartial tribunal established by law; to be presumed innocent; to be informed and to self defense; to not to be compelled to testify against himself or to confess guilt; to the reviewing of the convicting judicial decision; and the *non bis in idem* right (14); the *nulla pena sine lege* right (15); the right to be recognized as a person (16); the right to privacy, honor and reputation (17); the right to freedom of thought, conscience and religion (18); the right to hold opinions and to express them and the freedom to seek, receive and impart information and ideas (19), except in cases of propaganda for war and incitement to discrimination, hostility or violence (20); the right of peaceful assembly (21); right to freedom of association, including the right to form and join trade unions (22); the rights to protections of family, the right of men and women to marry and to found a family (23); the right of children to be protected, to have a name and a nationality (24); the citizens rights to take part in the conduct of public affairs, to vote and to be elected, and have access to public service (25); the right to be equal before the law and to the equal protection of the law 26); and the minority groups rights to enjoy their own culture, to profess and practice their own religion, or to use their own language (27).

Article 2 of the International Covenant expressly provides for the obligation of each State Party to respect and to ensure to all individuals within its territory and subject to its jurisdiction the rights recognized in the Covenant, without distinction of any kind, such as race, color, sex, language, religion, political or other opinion, national or social origin, property, birth or other status. Additionally, the State Parties are obliged to take the necessary steps, in accordance with its constitutional processes and with the provisions of the present Covenant, "to adopt such laws or other measures as may be necessary to give effect to the rights recognized in the present Covenant".

In particular, regarding the judicial guarantee for the protection of the rights declared in the Covenant, article 2,3 oblige each State Party:

> "(a) To ensure that any person whose rights or freedoms as herein recognized are violated shall have an effective remedy, notwithstanding that the violation has been committed by persons acting in an official capacity;
>
> (b) To ensure that any person claiming such a remedy shall have his right thereto determined by competent judicial, administrative or legislative authorities, or by any other competent authority provided for by the legal system of the State, and to develop the possibilities of judicial remedy;
>
> (c) To ensure that when granted, the competent authorities shall enforce such remedies".

Accordingly, the Covenant also establishes a general right of any person not only to have access to justice for the protections of their rights but to have at their disposition an effective remedy to seek protection to their rights not only against public official actions but also against individual actions.

Regarding the International Covenant on Economic, Social and Cultural Rights, it declares the following rights: the right to work (6); the right to the enjoyment of just and favorable conditions of work, in particular, remuneration with fair wages providing decent living; safe and healthy working conditions; equal opportunity, and rest, leisure and reasonable limitation of working hours (7); the right of everyone to form and join trade unions and the right of trade unions to function freely; and the right to strike (8); the right of everyone to social security, including social insurance (9); the right to family, marriage, maternity and children's protection (10); right of everyone to an adequate standard of living for himself and his family, including adequate food, clothing and housing, and to the continuous improvement of living conditions (11); the fundamental right of everyone to be free from hunger (12); the right of everyone to the enjoyment of the highest attainable standard of physical and mental health and to health care (13); the right of everyone to education, the liberty of parents to choose for their children schools, other than those established by the public authorities, and the liberty of individuals and bodies to establish and direct educational institutions (13) and the right of everyone to culture and to enjoy the benefits of scientific progress (14).

Article 2,2 of the Covenant obligated the States Parties to guarantee that the rights enunciated in it will be exercised without discrimination of any kind as to race, color, sex, language, religion, political or other opinion, national or social origin, property, birth or other status; and Article 3 obligated them to ensure the equal right of men and women to the enjoyment of all economic, social and cultural rights set forth in the Covenant. In Article 4 of the Covenant, the guarantee of legality concerning the social, economic and cultural rights was set forth by stating that the States Parties "recognize that, in the enjoyment of those rights provided by the State in conformity with the present Covenant, the State may subject such rights only to such limitations as are determined by law only in so far as this may be compatible with the nature of these rights and solely for the purpose of promoting the general welfare in a democratic society".

Nevertheless, in contrast with what was established in the International Covenant on Civil and Political Rights, in the International Covenant on Economic, Social and Cultural Rights, no justifiability rights for their enforcement were set forth.

II. THE AMERICAN INTERNATIONALIZATION OF HUMAN RIGHTS

The American Convention on Human Rights, as mentioned, was approved in the Organization of American States General Assembly in Costa Rica in 1969, and entered into force in 1979. It has been ratified by all Latin American Countries, all of which have recognized the jurisdiction of the Inter American Court on Human Rights. It must be noted that the only American country that has not signed the Convention is Canada, and the United States of America, even though has signed the Convention on June 1st, 1977 at the OAS General Secretariat, has not yet ratified it.

The American Convention has extreme importance in Latin America, being its content mainly referred to civil and political rights. Regarding economic and social rights, the Convention just limits its scope to declare that "the States Parties undertake to adopt measures, both internally and through international cooperation, especially those of an economic and technical nature, with a view to achieving progressively, by legislation or other appropriate means, the full realization of the rights implicit in the economic, social, educational, scientific, and cultural standards set forth in the Charter of the Organization of American States".

Now, regarding civil and political rights, the American Convention declares the following rights:

Article 3. Right to Juridical Personality:

Every person has the right to recognition as a person before the law.

Article 4. Right to Life:

1. Every person has the right to have his life respected. This right shall be protected by law and, in general, from the moment of conception. No one shall be arbitrarily deprived of his life.
2. In countries that have not abolished the death penalty, it may be imposed only for the most serious crimes and pursuant to a final judgment rendered by a competent court and in accordance with a law establishing such punishment, enacted prior to the commission of the crime. The application of such punishment shall not be extended to crimes to which it does not presently apply.
3. The death penalty shall not be reestablished in states that have abolished it.
4. In no case shall capital punishment be inflicted for political offenses or related common crimes.
5. Capital punishment shall not be imposed upon persons who, at the time the crime was committed, were under 18 years of age or over 70 years of age; nor shall it be applied to pregnant women.
6. Every person condemned to death shall have the right to apply for amnesty, pardon, or commutation of sentence, which may be granted in all cases. Capital punishment shall not be imposed while such a petition is pending decision by the competent authority.

Article 5. Right to Humane Treatment:

1. Every person has the right to have his physical, mental, and moral integrity respected.
2. No one shall be subjected to torture or to cruel, inhuman, or degrading punishment or treatment. All persons deprived of their liberty shall be treated with respect for the inherent dignity of the human person.
3. Punishment shall not be extended to any person other than the criminal.
4. Accused persons shall, save in exceptional circumstances, be segregated from convicted persons, and shall be subject to separate treatment appropriate to their status as unconvicted persons.
5. Minors while subject to criminal proceedings shall be separated from adults and brought before specialized tribunals, as speedily as possible, so that they may be treated in accordance with their status as minors.
6. Punishments consisting of deprivation of liberty shall have as an essential aim the reform and social readaptation of the prisoners.

Article 6. Freedom from Slavery

1. No one shall be subject to slavery or to involuntary servitude, which are prohibited in all their forms, as are the slave trade and traffic in women.
2. No one shall be required to perform forced or compulsory labor. This provision shall not be interpreted to mean that, in those countries in which the penalty established for certain crimes is deprivation of liberty at forced labor, the carrying out of such a sentence imposed by a competent court is prohibited. Forced labor shall not adversely affect the dignity or the physical or intellectual capacity of the prisoner.

3. For the purposes of this article, the following do not constitute forced or compulsory labor:
   a. work or service normally required of a person imprisoned in execution of a sentence or formal decision passed by the competent judicial authority. Such work or service shall be carried out under the supervision and control of public authorities, and any persons performing such work or service shall not be placed at the disposal of any private party, company, or juridical person;
   b. military service and, in countries in which conscientious objectors are recognized, national service that the law may provide for in lieu of military service;
   c. service exacted in time of danger or calamity that threatens the existence or the well–being of the community; or
   d. work or service that forms part of normal civic obligations.

Article 7. Right to Personal Liberty

1. Every person has the right to personal liberty and security.
2. No one shall be deprived of his physical liberty except for the reasons and under the conditions established beforehand by the constitution of the State Party concerned or by a law established pursuant thereto.
3. No one shall be subject to arbitrary arrest or imprisonment.
4. Anyone who is detained shall be informed of the reasons for his detention and shall be promptly notified of the charge or charges against him.
5. Any person detained shall be brought promptly before a judge or other officer authorized by law to exercise judicial power and shall be entitled to trial within a reasonable time or to be released without prejudice to the continuation of the proceedings. His release may be subject to guarantees to assure his appearance for trial.
6. Anyone who is deprived of his liberty shall be entitled to recourse to a competent court, in order that the court may decide without delay on the lawfulness of his arrest or detention and order his release if the arrest or detention is unlawful. In States Parties whose laws provide that anyone who believes himself to be threatened with deprivation of his liberty is entitled to recourse to a competent court in order that it may decide on the lawfulness of such threat, this remedy may not be restricted or abolished. The interested party or another person in his behalf is entitled to seek these remedies.
7. No one shall be detained for debt. This principle shall not limit the orders of a competent judicial authority issued for no fulfillment of duties of support.

Article 8. Right to a Fair Trial

1. Every person has the right to a hearing, with due guarantees and within a reasonable time, by a competent, independent, and impartial tribunal, previously established by law, in the substantiation of any accusation of a criminal nature made against him or for the determination of his rights and obligations of a civil, labor, fiscal, or any other nature.
2. Every person accused of a criminal offence has the right to be presumed innocent so long as his guilt has not been proven according to law. During the proceedings, every person is entitled, with full equality, to the following minimum guarantees:
   a. the right of the accused to be assisted without charge by a translator or interpreter, if he does not understand or does not speak the language of the tribunal or court;
   b. prior notification in detail to the accused of the charges against him;
   c. adequate time and means for the preparation of his defense;

d. the right of the accused to defend himself personally or to be assisted by legal counsel of his own choosing, and to communicate freely and privately with his counsel;
e. the inalienable right to be assisted by counsel provided by the state, paid or not as the domestic law provides, if the accused does not defend himself personally or engage his own counsel within the time period established by law;
f. the right of the defense to examine witnesses present in the court and to obtain the appearance, as witnesses, of experts or other persons who may throw light on the facts;
g. the right not to be compelled to be a witness against himself or to plead guilty; and
h. the right to appeal the judgment to a higher court.

3. A confession of guilt by the accused shall be valid only if it is made without coercion of any kind.
4. An accused person acquitted by a nonappealable judgment shall not be subjected to a new trial for the same cause.
5. Criminal proceedings shall be public, except insofar as may be necessary to protect the interests of justice.

Article 9. Freedom from Ex Post Facto Laws

No one shall be convicted of any act or omission that did not constitute a criminal offense, under the applicable law, at the time it was committed. A heavier penalty shall not be imposed than the one that was applicable at the time the criminal offence was committed. If subsequent to the commission of the offence the law provides for the imposition of a lighter punishment, the guilty **person shall benefit there from.**

Article 10. Right to Compensation

Every person has the right to be compensated in accordance with the law in the event he has been sentenced by a final judgment through a miscarriage of justice.

Article 11. Right to Privacy

1. Everyone has the right to have his honor respected and his dignity recognized.
2. No one may be the object of arbitrary or abusive interference with his private life, his family, his home, or his correspondence, or of unlawful attacks on his honor or reputation.
3. Everyone has the right to the protection of the law against such interference or attacks.

Article 12. Freedom of Conscience and Religion

1. Everyone has the right to freedom of conscience and of religion. This right includes freedom to maintain or to change one's religion or beliefs, and freedom to profess or disseminate one's religion or beliefs, either individually or together with others, in public or in private.
2. No one shall be subject to restrictions that might impair his freedom to maintain or to change his religion or beliefs.
3. Freedom to manifest one's religion and beliefs may be subject only to the limitations prescribed by law that are necessary to protect public safety, order, health, or morals, or the rights or freedoms of others.
4. Parents or guardians, as the case may be, have the right to provide for the religious and moral education of their children or wards that is in accord with their own convictions.

Article 13. Freedom of Thought and Expression

1. Everyone has the right to freedom of thought and expression. This right includes freedom to seek, receive, and impart information and ideas of all kinds, regardless of frontiers, either orally, in writing, in print, in the form of art, or through any other medium of one's choice.
2. The exercise of the right provided for in the foregoing paragraph shall not be subject to prior censorship but shall be subject to subsequent imposition of liability, which shall be expressly established by law to the extent necessary to ensure:
   a. respect for the rights or reputations of others; or
   b. the protection of national security, public order, or public health or morals.
3. The right of expression may not be restricted by indirect methods or means, such as the abuse of government or private controls over newsprint, radio broadcasting frequencies, or equipment used in the dissemination of information, or by any other means tending to impede the communication and circulation of ideas and opinions.
4. Notwithstanding the provisions of paragraph 2 above, public entertainments may be subject by law to prior censorship for the sole purpose of regulating access to them for the moral protection of childhood and adolescence.
5. Any propaganda for war and any advocacy of national, racial, or religious hatred that constitute incitements to lawless violence or to any other similar action against any person or group of persons on any grounds including those of race, color, religion, language, or national origin shall be considered as offenses punishable by law.

Article 14. Right of Reply

1. Anyone injured by inaccurate or offensive statements or ideas disseminated to the public in general by a legally regulated medium of communication has the right to reply or to make a correction using the same communications outlet, under such conditions as the law may establish.
2. The correction or reply shall not in any case remit other legal liabilities that may have been incurred.
3. For the effective protection of honor and reputation, every publisher, and every newspaper, motion picture, radio, and Television Company, shall have a person responsible who is not protected by immunities or special privileges.

Article 15. Right of Assembly

The right of peaceful assembly, without arms, is recognized. No restrictions may be placed on the exercise of this right other than those imposed in conformity with the law and necessary in a democratic society in the interest of national security, public safety or public order, or to protect public health or morals or the rights or freedom of others.

Article 16. Freedom of Association

1. Everyone has the right to associate freely for ideological, religious, political, economic, labor, social, cultural, sports, or other purposes.
2. The exercise of this right shall be subject only to such restrictions established by law as may be necessary in a democratic society, in the interest of national security, public safety or public order, or to protect public health or morals or the rights and freedoms of others.
3. The provisions of this article do not bar the imposition of legal restrictions, including even deprivation of the exercise of the right of association, on members of the armed forces and the police.

Article 17. Rights of the Family

1. The family is the natural and fundamental group unit of society and is entitled to protection by society and the state.
2. The right of men and women of marriageable age to marry and to raise a family shall be recognized, if they meet the conditions required by domestic laws, insofar as such conditions do not affect the principle of nondiscrimination established in this Convention.
3. No marriage shall be entered into without the free and full consent of the intending spouses.
4. The States Parties shall take appropriate steps to ensure the equality of rights and the adequate balancing of responsibilities of the spouses as to marriage, during marriage, and in the event of its dissolution. In case of dissolution, provision shall be made for the necessary protection of any children solely on the basis of their own best interests.
5. The law shall recognize equal rights for children born out of wedlock and those born in wedlock.

Article 18. Right to a Name

Every person has the right to a given name and to the surnames of his parents or that of one of them. The law shall regulate the manner in which this right shall be ensured for all, by the use of assumed names if necessary.

Article 19. Rights of the Child

Every minor child has the right to the measures of protection required by his condition as a minor on the part of his family, society, and the state.

Article 20. Right to Nationality

1. Every person has the right to a nationality.
2. Every person has the right to the nationality of the state in whose territory he was born if he does not have the right to any other nationality.
3. No one shall be arbitrarily deprived of his nationality or of the right to change it.

Article 21. Right to Property

1. Everyone has the right to the use and enjoyment of his property. The law may subordinate such use and enjoyment to the interest of society.
2. No one shall be deprived of his property except upon payment of just compensation, for reasons of public utility or social interest, and in the cases and according to the forms established by law.
3. Usury and any other form of exploitation of man by man shall be prohibited by law.

Article 22. Freedom of Movement and Residence

1. Every person lawfully in the territory of a State Party has the right to move about in it, and to reside in it subject to the provisions of the law.
2. Every person has the right lo leave any country freely, including his own.
3. The exercise of the foregoing rights may be restricted only pursuant to a law to the extent necessary in a democratic society to prevent crime or to protect national security, public safety, public order, public morals, public health, or the rights or freedoms of others.
4. The exercise of the rights recognized in paragraph 1 may also be restricted by law in designated zones for reasons of public interest.
5. No one can be expelled from the territory of the state of which he is a national or be deprived of the right to enter it.

6. An alien lawfully in the territory of a State Party to this Convention may be expelled from it only pursuant to a decision reached in accordance with law.
7. Every person has the right to seek and be granted asylum in a foreign territory, in accordance with the legislation of the state and international conventions, in the event he is being pursued for political offenses or related common crimes.
8. In no case may an alien be deported or returned to a country, regardless of whether or not it is his country of origin, if in that country his right to life or personal freedom is in danger of being violated because of his race, nationality, religion, social status, or political opinions.
9. The collective expulsion of aliens is prohibited.

Article 23. Right to Participate in Government

1. Every citizen shall enjoy the following rights and opportunities:
   a. to take part in the conduct of public affairs, directly or through freely chosen representatives;
   b. to vote and to be elected in genuine periodic elections, which shall be by universal and equal suffrage and by secret ballot that guarantees the free expression of the will of the voters; and
   c. to have access, under general conditions of equality, to the public service of his country.
2. The law may regulate the exercise of the rights and opportunities referred to in the preceding paragraph only on the basis of age, nationality, residence, language, education, civil and mental capacity, or sentencing by a competent court in criminal proceedings.

Article 24. Right to Equal Protection

All persons are equal before the law. Consequently, they are entitled, without discrimination, to equal protection of the law.

But additionally to all the previous rights, in these American Convention, and in a different way to what was established in the International Covenant on Civil and Political Rights, it was expressly set forth as the right of everyone to judicial protection of human rights, by means of the "amparo" action, recourse or suit, as follows:

Article 25. Right to Judicial Protection

1. Everyone has the right to simple and prompt recourse, or any other effective recourse, to a competent court or tribunal for protection ("*que la ampare*") against acts that violate his fundamental rights recognized by the constitution or laws of the state concerned or by this Convention, even though such violation may have been committed by persons acting in the course of their official duties.
2. The States Parties undertake:
   a. to ensure that any person claiming such remedy shall have his rights determined by the competent authority provided for by the legal system of the state;
   b. to develop the possibilities of judicial remedy; and
   c. to ensure that the competent authorities shall enforce such remedies when granted.

Finally, in order to ensure fulfillment of the commitments made by the States Parties to the Convention, the Inter–American Commission on Human Rights, and the Inter–American Court of Human Rights were created (33). For that purpose the Convention recognized the right of any person or group of persons, or any nongovernmental entity legally recognized in one or more member states of the Organization, to lodge petitions with the Commission containing denunciations or complaints of violation of the Convention by a State Party (44), as well as the power of the State Parties to allege before the Commission that another State Party has committed a violation of a human right set forth in the Convention (45). Following a very extensive regulated procedure, the Commission can bring before the Inter American Court on Human Rights cases of violation of the State Parties obligations and if the Court, following the procedure set forth in the Convention, finds that there has been a violation of a right or freedom protected by the Convention, the Court shall rule that the injured party be ensured the enjoyment of his right or freedom that was violated, and if appropriate, can also rule that the consequences of the measure or situation that constituted the breach of such right or freedom be remedied and that fair compensation be paid to the injured party (63).

The general rule of admissibility of the petition is that "the remedies under domestic law have been pursued and exhausted in accordance with generally recognized principles of international law"(Article 46,1,a); rule that has the following exceptions: when in the internal law of the State the due process for the protection for the violated rights is non existent; when the affected party has been impeded in his rights to access to the internal jurisdictional recourses, or when he has been impeded of exhausting them; or when a unjustified delay has occurred regarding such recourses (Article 77,2 of the Internal regulation of the Commission).

Even though the petition before the Inter–American Commission has been qualified as an "international amparo"[35], not being the Commission a jurisdictional body, the initial petition can not qualify as a judicial mean. Eventually, the Commission is the only body that can bring before the Inter American Court a request for protection on behalf individuals. On the contrary, in the European system, individuals can bring direct petitions against Member States before the European Tribunal on Human Rights regarding the protection of human rights.

Nevertheless, it must be mentioned that in some Latin American Constitutions, as is the case of the 1999 Venezuelan Constitution, the right to petition for the protection of human rights before international organizations has been regulated as an individual constitutional right. In this regard, Article 31 sets forth:

> **Article 31.** According to what is set forth in the treaties, covenants and conventions on human rights ratified by the Republic, everybody has the right to file petitions or complaints before the international organizations created for such purposes, in order to seek for the protection (amparo) of his human rights.

The Constitution also imposes the State the obligation, according to the procedures provided in the Constitution and the statutes, to adopt the necessary measures in order to comply with the decisions of the abovementioned international organizations.

Anyway, since the beginning of its activities in 1979, the Commission and the Court have been very active in the exercise of its functions, having decided in nu-

---

35 See Carlos AYALA CORAO, "Del amparo constitucional al amparo interamericano como institutos para la protección de los derechos humanos" in *Memoria del VI Congreso Iberoamericano de derecho constitucional*, Tomo I, Bogotá, 1998.

merous cases against State parties for violations of human rights. The Courts consultative opinions and rulings now constitute the basic doctrine on human rights in Latin America.

Finally, regarding international treaties, mention must also be made to the African Charter of Human Rights, adopted in 1981. The fact, in any case, is that since the establishment of the United Nations, many other declarations and treaties referring to human rights –more than 70– have been adopted, creating various international organizations on human rights, including two International Courts –the European and the Inter American Courts–as international judicial organs with the purpose of assuring the accomplishment of State obligations regarding human rights and to protect them.

From all these international regulations on human rights, it can be clearly appreciated that following the initial process of constitutionalization of human rights by means of the progressively enlarged national constitutional declarations, which took place up to the Second World War, a second stage was developed, marked by the internationalization of such constitutionalization process, by means of the international declarations of rights.

III. THE CONSTITUTIONALIZATION OF THE INTERNATIONALIZATION OF HUMAN RIGHTS

But in recent times, we have witnessed a third stage on the process of protecting human rights, which can be characterized as a process now again of constitutionalization but of the internationalization of human rights, that has developed precisely, by the incorporation in the constitutional internal regulations, of the international systems of protection.

This process can be characterized, first of all by the process of giving internal constitutional or statutory rank to the international instruments on human rights, that is to say, by setting forth expressly in the Constitutions, the value to be given to both the international declarations and treaties on human rights regarding the internal constitutional norms and statutes concerning human rights, even determining which shall prevail in the event of there being a conflict among them.

This is a matter that of course must be regulated in the Constitutions themselves, whether by mean of enshrining the regulatory rank of international treaties in the constitutional texts, or by means of setting forth in the Constitutions for the rules for constitutional interpretation of human rights and of the international instruments referring to them.

1. The supra constitutional rank of international instruments of human rights

In many Latin American Constitutions the question of the internal normative value and rank of the international human rights instruments has been expressly resolved in four different ways: by granting the international instruments supra–constitutional rank, constitutional rank, supra–legal rank or statutory rank[36].

Firstly, certain Constitutions have expressly set forth the supra–constitutional rank of human rights declared in international instruments. This has implied giving the international regulation a superior rank regarding the Constitution itself, therefore prevailing over their provisions.

Such is the case, for example, of the Constitution of Guatemala, whose Article 46 sets forth the general principle of pre–eminence of International law, by stating that in declaring that "in human rights matters, the treaties and conventions accepted and ratified by Guatemala shall have pre–eminence over internal law", in which it must be included other that the statutes, the Constitution itself. Based on this prevalence of international treaties, the Constitutional Court has decided cases applying the American Convention, as was the case of the decision issued on May 27, 1997 regarding freedom of expression and the rectification rights. In the case, by means of an "amparo" action, a person asks the constitutional protection of the Court regarding the news published in two news papers referring to his as forming part of a band of criminals, and asking before the Court to be respected in his right to seek for the rectification of the news by the news papers. Even tough the constitutional right to seek for rectification in cases of news published affecting the honor, reputation and privacy of any body is not expressly set forth in the Constitution, the Constitutional Court applied Articles 11, 13 and 14 of the American Convention which guarantee the right of any affected party by news papers information to "rectification and response that must be published in the same news paper", considering such provisions as forming part of the constitutional order of Guatemala[37].

Also in Honduras, Article 16 of the Constitution sets forth that the all treaties subscribed with other States (not only related to human rights), are part of internal law; and Article 18 establishes the pre–eminence of treaties over statutes in case of conflict between them. In addition, the Honduran Constitution admits the possibility of ratification of treaties contrary to what is set forth in the Constitution, in which case they must be approved according to the procedure set forth for constitutional

36 For a general comment regarding this classification, see Rodolfo E. PIZA R., *Derecho internacional de los derechos humanos: La Convención Americana*, San José, 1989; Carlos AYALA CORAO, "La jerarquía de los instrumentos internacionales sobre derechos humanos", in *El nuevo derecho constitucional latinoamericano*, IV Congreso venezolano *de Derecho constitucional*, Vol. II, Caracas, 1996 and *La jerarquía constitucional de los tratados sobre derechos humanos y sus consecuencias*, México, 2003; and Humberto HENDERSON, "Los tratados internacionales de derechos humanos en el orden interno: la importancia del principio pro homine", en *Revista IIDH*, Instituto Interamericano de Derechos Humanos, N° 39, San José, 2004, pp. 71 y ss. See also, Allan R. BREWER–CARÍAS, *Mecanismos nacionales de protección de los derechos humanos*, Instituto Internacional de Derechos Humanos, San José, 2004, pp.62 y ss.

37 See in *Iudicum et Vita, Jurisprudencia nacional de América Latina en Derechos Humanos*, N° 5, Instituto Interamericano de Derechos Humanos, San José, Costa Rica, Diciembre 1997, pp. 45 ff.

revision (Article 17). A similar regulation is established in Article 53 of the Peruvian Constitution.

In Colombia, the Constitution has also established a similar provision, with Article 93 providing that: "international treaties and conventions ratified by Congress, which recognize human rights and forbid their limitation in states of emergency, shall prevail over internal law". In this case, also, internal law must be understood to comprise not only statutes but the Constitution itself.

The Constitutional Court of Colombia in a decision N° T–447/95 of October 23, 1995, recognized the right of everybody to have an identity as a right inherent to human being, basing its ruling in what is set forth in the international treaties and covenants, for which it was recognized supra constitutional and supra legal rank. The Court began by referring to previous ruling of the former Supreme Court of Justice which had determined their supra–legal value, by arguing:

> Since 1928 the Supreme Court of Justice has given prevalent value to international treaties regarding legislative internal order; due to the fact that such international norms, by will of the Colombian state, enter to form part of the legal order with supra legal rank, setting forth the coactive force of provisions the signing State has the obligation to enforce. The supra legal value has been expressly established in article 93 of the Constitution of Colombia, as has been recognized by the Supreme Court of Justice, arguing that it must be added that such superiority has been sustained as an invariable doctrine that "is a public law principle, that the Constitution and the international treaties are the superior law of the land and their dispositions prevail over the legal norms contrary to their provisions even if they are posterior laws"[38].

In the same decision, the Constitutional Court referred to the "supra constitutional" rank of international treaties, which implies the State's obligation to guarantee the effective enforcement of human rights, basing the constitutional provision on Article 2,2 of the International Covenant on Human Rights and in Article 2 of the American Convention on Human Rights. The Court stated:

> The American Convention and the United Nations International Covenants set forth that the obligation of the States is not only to respect civil and political rights but also to guarantee, without discrimination, its free and complete enjoyment by any person subjected to its jurisdiction (Article 1, American Convention; Article 2,1 International Covenant on civil and political rights). For that purpose, these covenants that have been ratified by Colombia, and consequently prevail in the internal order (Article 93 Constitution), set forth that the Member States have the obligation according to the constitutional proceedings, to adopt "the legislative or other character measures in order to make human rights effective" (Article. 2, American Convention; Article 2,2, International Covenant on Civil and Political Rights). According to this authorized doctrine, the Constitutional Court considers that the judicial decisions and particularly this Court's rulings must be among the "other character" measures abovementioned, due to the fact that the Judiciary is one of the Branches of the Colombian State, which

---

38 See the text in *Derechos Fundamentales e interpretación Constitucional, (Ensayos–Jurisprudencia)*, Comisión Andina de Juristas, Lima, 1997; and in Carlos AYALA CORAO, "Recepción de la jurisprudencia internacional sobre derechos humanos por la jurisprudencia constitucional", *Revista del Tribunal Constitucional*, N° 6, Sucre, Bolivia, Nov. 2004, pp. 275 y ss.

> has the duty to adopt the necessary measures in order to make effective the persons' rights"...Consequently it is legitimate for the judges and particular for the Constitutional Court, when deciding cases, to consider within the legal order the rights recognized in the Constitution and in the Covenants"[39].

Based in the abovementioned, and considering that Article 29,C of the American Convention forbids the interpretation of its provisions that preclude other rights or guarantees that are inherent in the human personality and that give a very wide sense to the interpretation of such rights, the Court concluded that being "the right to have an identity implicitly set forth in all the international covenants and conventions, and thus, legally protected" it is possible to affirm such right "as being inherent to human person fully guaranteed due to the obligatory force of the international covenant" which also set forth the right to dignity and to the free development of own personality"[40].

To a certain point, the case of the 1999 Constitution of Venezuela could also be placed under this first system of supra–constitutional hierarchy of human rights contained in treaties, with its Article 23, which provides that:

> "Treaties, covenants and conventions referring to human rights, signed and ratified by Venezuela, shall have constitutional hierarchy and will prevail over internal legal order, when they contain regulations regarding their enjoyment and exercise, more favorable than those established in this Constitution and the statutes of the Republic. Those treaties and conventions shall be immediately and directly applicable by the courts and all other official authorities.

By declaring that human rights enshrined in international instruments shall prevail over internal legal order, when containing more favorable conditions of enjoyment and exercise such rights, it is referring not only to what is declared on statutes, but also in the Constitution. This undoubtedly grants supra–constitutional rank to such rights.

This article of the 1999 Constitution, without doubt, is one of the most important ones in matters of human rights[41], not only because it sets forth the supra–constitutional rank of human rights treaties, but because it prescribes the direct and immediate applicability of such treaties by all courts and authorities of the country. Its inclusion in the new Constitution was a significant advancement in the completion of the protection framework of human rights.

But unfortunately, this very clear constitutional provision has been interpreted by the Constitutional Chamber of the Supreme Court in a way openly contrary to what it states, and to what was the intention of the proponents and of the Constituent. In effect, in a decision N°1942 of July 7th, 2003 when resolving a judicial review action on the constitutionality of some Penal Code articles regarding the freedom of ex-

---

39 *Idem.*

40 *Idem.*

41 See the author's proposal of the draft of this article to the National Constituent Assembly, in Allan R. BREWER–CARÍAS, *Debate Constituyente, (Aportes a la Asamblea Nacional Constituyente)*, Fundación de Derecho Público, Caracas, 1999, pp. 88 y ss y 111 y ss.

pression that where challenged because they were contrary to international treaties, the Constitutional Chamber ruled as follows:

First, the Chamber stated that Article 23 of the Constitution contained two key elements: "1) It refers to human rights applicable to human beings; 2) It refers to norms setting forth rights and not to decisions or opinions of institutions, resolutions of bodies, etc, established in the treaties; thus it only refers to norms that created human rights".

The Constitutional Chamber was repetitive by stating that: "It is a matter of prevalence of norms which conform treaties, covenants or Agreements (synonym expressions) referred to human rights, but not to reports or opinions of international bodies which pretend to interpret the scope of international instruments". The Chamber concluded that it is clear that according to Article 23, "the constitutional hierarchy of treaties, covenants or conventions refers to its norms which once integrated into the Constitution, the only institution capable of interpreting them vis–à–vis Venezuelan law, is the constitutional judge according to Article 335 of the Constitution, only the Constitutional Chamber"; insisting in the same proposition by stating that:

> "Once the human rights substantive norms contained in Conventions, covenants and treaties have been incorporated to the constitutional hierarchy, the maximum and last interpreter of them, vis–à–vis internal law, is the Constitutional Chamber, which determines the content and scope of the constitutional norms and principles (Article 335), among them are the treaties, covenants and conventions on human rights, duly subscribed and ratified by Venezuela"

From this proposition, the Constitutional Chamber concluded that "is the Constitutional Chamber the only one that determines which norms on human rights contained in treaties, covenants and conventions, prevail in the internal legal order; as well as which human rights not incorporated in such international instruments have effects in Venezuela"; concluding that:

> "This power of the Constitutional Chamber on the matter, derived from the Constitution, cannot be diminished by adjective norms contained in the treaties or in other international texts on human rights subscribed by the country, allowing the States parties to ask international institutions for the interpretation of rights referred to in the Convention or covenant, as established in Article 64 of the Approbatory statute of the American Convention of Human Rights, San José Covenant, because otherwise, the situation would be of a constitutional amendment, without following the constitutional procedures, diminishing the powers of the Constitutional Chamber, transferring it to international or transnational bodies, with the power to dictate obligatory interpretations"[42].

The Constitutional Chamber based its decision on sovereignty principles, arguing that decisions adopted by international courts cannot be enforced in Venezuela, but only when they are in accordance with the Constitution. Thus, the supra constitutional rank of treaties when establishing more favorable regulations regarding human rights was suddenly eliminated by the Constitutional Chamber, assuming an

42 See the text in *Revista de Derecho Público,* N° 93–96, Editorial Jurídica Venezolana, Caracas, 2003, pp. 136 ff.

absolute monopoly of Constitution interpretation, which, according to the constitution, the Chamber does not have.

The main problem regarding this restrictive criterion on the interpretation of international instruments is that unfortunately the ruling was set forth as an obligatory interpretation of the Constitution limiting the general powers of any court to resolve by means of judicial review on the matter, directly applying and giving prevalence to the American Convention regarding constitutional provisions.

This restrictive interpretation was really issued in a ruling devoted to deny any constitutional value and rank to the recommendations of the Inter–American Commission on Human Rights, thus refusing to consider unconstitutional some articles of the Penal Code regarding restrictions to the freedom of expression when referring to public officials that were contrary to the recommendations of the Commission which was argued were obligatory for the country.

The Constitutional Chamber argued that according to the American Convention, the Commission may formulate "recommendations" to the governments in order for them to adopt progressive measures in favor of human rights within their internal laws and constitutional prescriptions, as well as provisions to promote the respect of such rights (Article 41.b), adding:

> If what is recommended by the Commission must be adapted to the Constitution and statutes of the States it means they do not have obligatory force, because the internal laws or the Constitution could be contrary to the recommendations. Thus, the articles of the Convention do not refer to the obligatory character of the recommendations, in contrast, they refer to the powers assigned to the other organ: the Court, which according to Article 62 of the Convention, can give obligatory interpretations of the Convention when requested by the States, which means that they accept the opinion,
>
> If the Court has such power, and the Commission does not, it is compulsory to conclude that the recommendations of the latter do not have the character of the opinions of the former, and consequently, the Chamber declares that the recommendations of the Inter American Commission of Human Rights are non obligatory regarding internal law.
>
> The Chamber considers that the recommendations must be weigh up by the Member States. They must adapt their legislation to the recommendations if they do not collide with the constitutional provisions, but for such adaptation there is no timing set, and until it is done, the statutes in effect which do not collide with the Constitution, or according to the Venezuelan courts with the human rights enshrined in the international conventions, will remain in force until declared unconstitutional of repealed by other states"[43].

Eventually, the Chamber concluded stating that the recommendations of the Commission regarding what has been called the "*leyes de desacato*" (statute protecting public officials from public criticism), are only the Commission's point of view without any imperative effect, and an alert directed to the States in order for them, in the future, to repeal or to reform them adapting them to international laws. Unfortunately, the Constitutional Chamber forgot that what the States are obliged to do regarding the recommendations, is to adopt the necessary measures in order to adapt

43 See the text in *Revista de Derecho Público,* N° 93–96, Editorial Jurídica Venezolana, Caracas, 2003, pp. 136 ff.

their internal law to the Convention, measures that do not exhaust themselves with only repealing or reforming statutes, being one of such measures, precisely, the judicial interpretation which could be adopted by the constitutional judge in accordance with the Commission's recommendations. Contrary to what was resolved by the Venezuelan Tribunal, in Argentina, once the Inter American Commission determined that the amnesty statutes (*Punto Final* and *Obediencia Debida*) and the pardon measures adopted regarding the crimes committed by the military dictatorship were contrary to the American Convention, some courts began to consider such statutes as unconstitutional because they were in violation of international law[44].

The Venezuelan Constitutional Chamber, in any case, concluded its restrictive interpretation by stating: that: "A different interpretation means giving the Commission a supranational character which weakened the Member State's sovereignty, something that is prohibited by the Constitution"[45]. Anyway, after the Constitutional Chamber's ruling, the Penal Code was reformed but not in the relevant parts regarding the crimes referred to as "*leyes de desacato*". This decision was contrary to what was decided in 1995 by the Argentinean Congress regarding the same matters, by repealing the articles related to the same crimes in compliance with the Inter American Commission recommendation on the matter[46]

The restrictive approach of the Venezuelan Constitutional Chamber regarding the importance on internal law of the Inter American Commission on Human Rights recommendations was previously stated in a decision dated May 5th, 2000. In this decision the Constitutional Chamber objected the quasi–jurisdictional powers of the Inter American Commission on Human Rights. The case was as follows: after a magazine (*Revista Exceso*) filed an "amparo" action before the national jurisdictions seeking constitutional protection of its right to free expression and information, the plaintiff went before the Inter American Commission on Human Rights denouncing the mal functioning of internal jurisdiction regarding the amparo action filed, and seeking international protection against the Venezuelan State for violation of its rights to freedom of expression and due process and against judicial harassment practices against one of its journalist and the director of the magazine. In the case, the Inter American Commission issued provisional protective measures.

---

44 Decision de 4–03–2001, Juzgado Federal N° 4, caso: *Pobrete Hlaczik. Cit*., por Kathryn Sikkink, "The transnacional dimension of judicialization of politics in latin America", in Rachel Sieder et al (ed), *The Judicalization of Politics In Latin America,* Palgrave Macmillan, New York, 2005, pp. 274, 290.

45 Decision N° 1942 of July, 15, 2003, in *Revista de Derecho Público,* N° 93–96, Editorial Jurídica Venezolana, Caracas, 2003, pp. 136 ff. i.

46 Case: *Verbistky, Report of the Comisión* N° 22/94 of September 20, 1994, case: *11.012* (Argentina). See the comments by Antonio CANÇADO TRINDADE, "Libertad de expresión y derecho a la información en los planos internacional y nacional", in *Iudicum et Vita, Jurisprudencia nacional de América Latina en Derechos Humanos*, N° 5, Instituto Interamericano de Derechos Humanos, San José, Costa Rica, Diciembre 1997, pp.194–195. See the "Informe sobre la compatibilidad entre las leyes de desacato y la Convención Americana sobre Derechos Humanos de 17 de febrero de 1995", in *Estudios Básicos de derechos Humanos*, Vol. X, Instituto Interamericano de Derechos Humanos, San José, 2000.

When the time arrived to decide the "amparo" action, the Constitutional Chamber considered that in the case, the plaintiff's due process rights had been effectively violated (independently of its right to freedom of expression), but regarding the provisional measures adopted by the Inter American Commission, qualifying it as "unacceptable", the Chamber stated that:

> [The Constitutional Chamber] also considers unacceptable the instance of the Inter American Commission on Human Rights of the Organization of American States in the sense that asking for the adoption of measures that imply a gross intrusion in the country's judicial organs, like the suspension of the judicial proceeding against the plaintiff, are measures that can only be adopted by the judges exercising their judicial attributions and independence, according to what is stated in the Constitution and the statutes of the Republic. Additionally, article 46,b of the American Convention on Human Rights set forth that the petition on denunciations or complaint for the violations of the Convention by a State, requires the presentation and exhaustion of the internal jurisdiction remedies according to the generally accepted principles of international law, which was allowed in this case, due to the fact that the judicial delay was not attributable to the Chamber" [47].

This unfortunate ruling can also be considered contrary to Article 31 of the Venezuelan Constitution which sets forth the individual rights of anybody to bring before the international organizations on human rights, as it is the Inter American Commission on Human Rights, petitions or complaints to seek protection (amparo) of their violated rights. How can this right be enforced if it is the same Constitutional Chamber the one that refuses to accept the jurisdiction of the Commission?

In contrast to this reaction of the Venezuelan Constitutional Chamber, the situation is different in other countries, as is the case of Costa Rica, in which the Constitutional Chamber of the Supreme Court, in its decision N° 2313–95, based the annulment of Article 22 of the Journalist College Organic Statute (imposing the obligatory membership of the Journalist College in order to exercise the profession), on what the Inter American Court decided in its Advisory Opinion N° OC–5 of 1985[48], stating that "if the Inter American Court on Human Rights is the natural organ for the interpretation of the American Convention on Human Rights, the force of its decision when interpreting the Convention and judging on the national statutes ac-

47 Case: *Faitha M.Nahmens L. y Ben Ami Fihman Z.* (*Revista Exceso*), Exp. N° 00–0216, decisión N° 386 de 17–5–2000. See in *cit.*, en Carlos AYALA CORAO, "Recepción de la jurisprudencia internacional sobre derechos humanos por la jurisprudencia constitucional" en *Revista del Tribunal Constitucional*, N° 6, Sucre, Bolivia, Nov. 2004, pp. 275 y ss.

48 Opinión Consultiva OC–5/85 de 13 de noviembre de 1985. *La colegiación obligatoria de periodistas (arts. 13 y 29 Convención Americana sobre Derechos Humanos). In such Opinion the Inter American Court considered that "the compulsory affiliation of journalists is incompatible with article 13 of the American Convention, because it impedes any other person to the full use of the Medias as a mean to express or transmit his information*"; and also "that the Costa Rican Organic Statute on Journalists (Ley n° 4420 of September 22, 1969), which is the subject of this Opinion, because it impedes certain persons to be affiliated to the Journalists Collage, and consequently, it is incompatible because it impedes the full use of the Media as a vehicle to express and transmit information".

cording to the Convention, have the value of an interpreted norm"[49]. Consequently, the Chamber concluded the case by arguing that because Costa Rica was the Member State which requested from the Inter American Court its Advisory Opinion:

> "When the Inter American Court on Human Rights, in its OC–O5–85 unanimously decided that the obligatory affiliation of journalists set forth in Statute N° 4420 is incompatible with article 13 of the American Convention on Human Rights because it impedes persons the access to the Media, [such Opinion] cannot but oblige the country that started the complex and costly procedure of the Inter American system of protection of human rights"

On the other hand, and according to the case law decisions of the Constitutional Chamber of Costa Rica, the constitutional system of this country can also be classified within the category of those that give supra constitutional rank to the international treaties on human rights when they contain more favorable provisions on the matter. Accordingly, in the abovementioned decision 2313–95, the Constitutional Chamber considered that:

> Being international instruments in force in the country, Article 7 of the Constitution does not apply, due to the fact that Article 48 of the same Constitution contains a special provision regarding treaties on human rights, giving them a normative force of constitutional level. To the point, as has been recognized by this Chamber's jurisprudence, the international instruments on human rights in force in Costa Rica, have not only a similar value to the Political Constitution, but they prevail over the Constitution when giving to persons more rights or guaranties (vid. decisions N° 3435–92 and N° 5759–93)[50].

Consequently, in the same 2313–95 decision, the Constitutional Chamber when considering its own powers of judicial review of constitutionality stated that:

> The Constitutional Chamber not only declares violations of constitutional rights, but of all the universe of fundamental rights set forth in the international instruments on human rights in force in the country. From this point of view, the Constitutional Chamber's recognition of the normative contents of the American Convention on Human Rights, as was interpreted by the Inter American Court on Human Rights in its Consultative Opinion OC–05–85, is natural and absolutely according with its wide powers. So, without needing to duplicate rulings, based on the same arguments of that Opinion, the Chamber considers that it is clear for Costa Rica that the norms of Statute N°40… are illegitimate and contrary to the right to information in the wide sense which is developed in Article 13 of the San José of Costa Rica Covenant, as well in Articles 28 and 29 of the Political Constitution.

Now, back to the Venezuelan situation, mention must be made to the fact that before the abovementioned restrictive interpretation was issued, many Venezuelan courts, when dealing with other matters, did apply the American Convention on

---

49 Decision N° 2312–05 of May, 9, 1995, in Rodolfo PIZA ESCALANTE, *La justicia constitucional en Costa Rica,* San José, 1995; and en Carlos Ayala Corao, "Recepción de la jurisprudencia internacional sobre derechos humanos por la jurisprudencia constitucional" en *Revista del Tribunal Constitucional*, N° 6, Sucre, Bolivia, Nov. 2004, pp. 275 y ss.

50 See also the text of the decisión in Alfonso GAIRAUD BRENES, "Los Mecanismos de interpretación de los derechos humanos: especial referencia a la jurisprudencia peruana" en José F. Palomino Manchego, *El derecho procesal constitucional peruano. Estudios en Homenaje a Domingo García Belaunde*, Editorial Jurídica Grijley, Lima, 2005, Tomo I, p. 133, note 21.

Human Rights, thus declaring its prevalence vis–à–vis the Constitution and statutory provisions.

This is the case of the constitutional right to appeal judicial decisions before a superior court. According to the 1976 general statute regulating the special jurisdiction for judicial review of administrative acts (*jurisdicción contencioso–administrativa*)[51], some administrative acts, such as those of independent Administrations, were to be challenged before the First Court on judicial review of administrative action, in a proceeding that had to be decided in a sole instance, without any appeal before the corresponding Chamber of the Supreme Court of Justice. The 1999 Constitution only set forth the right to appeal regarding criminal cases in which a person would be declared guilty (Article 49,1); thus, in other cases, like judicial review of administrative acts, no constitutional norm guarantees the right to appeal. In particular cases, the appeal was brought before the Administrative Review Chamber of the Supreme Court alleging the unconstitutionality of the statutorily limits to appeal, and a few judicial decisions were taken by means of judicial review (diffuse method), admitting the appeal, based on "the right to appeal the judgment to a higher court", that is set forth in Article 8,2,h of the American Convention on Human Rights, which was considered as forming part of internal constitutional law of the country.

The matter eventually also reached the Constitutional Chamber of the Supreme Tribunal of Justice, which in a decision N° 87 of March 13, 2000 stated:

> If this provision (Article 8,2,h of the American Convention) is compared to Article 49,1 of the Constitution in which the right to appeal only corresponds to those who have been declared guilty in criminal cases, including an authorization to set forth statutory exceptions, it must be interpreted that the norm of the Convention is more favorable to the exercise of such right, due to the fact that it guarantees the right of everybody to be heard not only regarding to criminal procedures, but also regarding rights and obligations in civil, labor, taxation or any other procedure, in which the right to appeal without any exception is established; assigning such right to the category of minimal guarantee of anybody, independently of its condition in the proceeding, and governed by the principle of equality".
>
> If this international provision of the American Convention is compared with the first paragraph of Article 185 of the Organic statute on the Supreme Court of Justice, it must be interpreted that the latter is incompatible with the former, because it denies in absolute terms, the right that the Convention guarantees" [52].

Based on the aforementioned, the Constitutional Chamber concluded its ruling by stating that it:

> "recognized and declared, based on what is set forth in Article 23 of the Constitution, that Article 8,1 and 2,h of the American Convention on Human Rights, is part of the Venezuelan constitutional order; that its dispositions regarding the right to appeal are more favorable re-

---

51 See the comments in Allan R. BREWER–CARÍAS y Josefina CALCAÑO DE TEMELTAS, *Ley Orgánica de la Corte Suprema de Justicia,* Editorial Jurídica Venezolana, Caracas, 1978.

52 Case: *C.A. Electricidad del Centro (Elecentro) y otra vs. Superintendencia para la Promoción y Protección de la Libre Competencia. (Procompetencia)* en *Revista de Derecho Público*, N° 81, Editorial Jurídica Venezolana, Caracas, 2000, pp. 157 y ss.

garding the exercise of such right in relation to what is set forth in Article 49,1 of the Constitution; and that such provisions are of direct and immediate application by courts and authorities"[53].

The Constitutional Chamber even resolved in its obligatory interpretation, to re–write the statute, stating:

> Consequently, and taking into account that last first paragraph of Article 185 of the Organic Statute of the Supreme Court of Justice sets forth that: "Against the First Court decisions in the matter listed in numbers 1 to 4 of such provision, no recourse or appeal will be heard"; that such provision is incompatible with the one set forth in Article 8,1 and 2,h of the American Convention of Human Rights which have constitutional hierarchy and are of prevalent application; that Article 334 of the Constitution sets forth that "In case of incompatibility between this Constitution and a statute or other legal norm, the constitutional provisions will apply, being attributed such power to decide to all courts in any case, even in an ex officio manner"; this (Constitutional) Chamber leaves without application the aforementioned disposition contained in the first paragraph of Article 185 of the Organic Statute, applying instead, in the case (File 99–22167), the provision of second paragraph of the same Article 185 of the Statute, which states: "Against definitive decisions of the same (First) Court…an appeal can be brought before the Supreme Court of Justice (rectius: Supreme Tribunal of Justice)". So is decided"[54].

2. The constitutional rank of international instruments of human rights

Secondly, other Constitutions also attributed in an express way the constitutional rank to international treaties on human rights, thus acquiring the same normative hierarchy as those set forth in the Constitution.

Two types of constitutional regimes can be distinguished in this group: Constitutions that confer constitutional rank on all international instruments of human rights, and Constitutions that only grant such rank to a group of instruments that are expressly listed in the Constitution.

In the *first group*, for example, is to be found Peru's 1979 Constitution, repealed in 1994, which in its Article 105 established that "the precepts contained in treaties on human rights, shall have constitutional hierarchy..." and therefore "...cannot be modified except by the procedure in force for reforming the Constitution."

Among the *second type* is to be found the 1994 Constitution of Argentina which grants to a group of treaties and declarations in force at the time, specifically listed in Article 75.22 of the Constitution, a hierarchy superior to the laws, that is, constitutional rank, listing only the following: the American Declaration of the Rights and Duties of Man; the Universal Declaration of Human Rights; the American Convention on Human Rights; the International Covenant on Economic, Social and Cultural Rights; the International Covenant on Civil and Political Rights and its Facultative Protocol; the Convention on the Prevention and Punishment of the Crime of Genocide; the International Convention on the Elimination of All Forms of Racial Discrimination; the Convention on the Elimination of All Forms of Discrimination

53 *Idem.*

54 *Idem.*

against Women; the Convention against Torture and Other Cruel, Inhuman or Degrading Treatment or Punishment; the Convention on the Rights of the Child.

These instruments as set forth in the Constitution, "pursuant to the conditions determining their validity, shall have constitutional hierarchy, shall not abrogate any article of the first part of this Constitution, and shall be understood to be complementary to the rights and guarantees recognized by such Constitution." Apart from this, "they may only be denounced, if such were the case, by the Executive, with prior approval of two thirds of the total members of each Chamber."

In regard to other human rights treaties different to those listed in Article 75,22, the Constitution established that they could enjoy such constitutional hierarchy, provided that they were approved by a qualified majority of 2/3 of the total members of the Senate and the Chamber of Deputies.

According with these constitutional provisions, the Supreme Court of the Nation of Argentina, has applied the American Convention on Human Rights, giving prevalence to its provisions regarding internal statutes, as has happened regarding the Criminal Procedural Code. In contrast to what is set forth in the American Convention, the Criminal Procedural Code excluded from the right to appeal, some judicial decisions according to the amount of the punishment. The Supreme Court of the Nation declared the invalidity on the grounds of its unconstitutionality of such limits, applying the American Convention which in Article 8, 1,h guarantees "the right to appeal the judgment to a higher court"[55].

Additionally, in Argentina, the courts have also considered the decisions of the Inter American Commission and of the Inter American Court as obligatory, even before the international treaties on human rights were constitutionalized. In a decision dated July 7, 1992 the Supreme Court applied the Inter American Court Advisory Opinion OC–7/86[56], stating that "the interpretation of the Covenant, additionally, must be oriented by the decisions of the Inter American Court on Human Rights, one of its purposes being the interpretation of the San José Covenant"[57].

---

55 Decision of April, 4, 1995, Giroldi, H.D. an others. See the references in Aida KEMELMAJER DE CARLUCCI and María Gabriela ABALOS DE MOSSO, "Grandes líneas directrices de la jurisprudencia argentina sobre material constitucional durante el año 1995", in *Anuario de Derecho Constitucional latinoamericano 1996*, Fundación Konrad Adenauer, Bogotá, 1996, pp. 517 ff.; and in Carlos AYALA CORAO, "Recepción de la jurisprudencia internacional sobre derechos humanos por la jurisprudencia constitucional" in *Revista del Tribunal Constitucional*, N° 6, Sucre, Bolivia, Nov. 2004, pp. 275 ff.

56 Advisory Opinion OC–7/86 August 29, 1986. *Exigibilidad del derecho de rectificación o respuesta (arts. 14.1, 1.1 y 2 de la Convención Americana sobre Derechos Humanos).*

57 Case *Miguel A. Ekmkdjiam, Gerardo Sofivic and others*, in Ariel E. DULITZKY, "La aplicación de los Tratados sobre Derechos Humanos por los tribunales locales: un estudio comparado" in *La aplicación de los tratados sobre derechos Humanos por los tribunales locales*, Centro de Estudios Legales y Sociales, Buenos Aires, 1997. See Carlos AYALA CORAO, "Recepción de la jurisprudencia internacional sobre derechos humanos por la jurisprudencia constitucional" en *Revista del Tribunal Constitucional*, N° 6, Sucre, Bolivia, Nov. 2004, pp. 275 ff.

In 1995, the same Supreme Court considered that due to the recognition by the Argentinean State of the Inter American Court jurisdiction to resolve on cases referred to the interpretation and application of the American Convention, its decisions "must serve as a guide for the interpretation of constitutional provisions"[58]. In other decisions the Supreme Court has repealed lower court decisions when considering that their interpretation was made in an incompatible way regarding the decision's doctrine of the Inter American Commission on Human Rights[59]

Reference should also be made to the case of Panama, where even though the Constitution has no express provision regarding the normative rank of treaties, from the jurisprudence of the Supreme Court such rank can be deducted, when considering that any violation of an international treaty is considered as a violation of Article 4 of the Constitution.

In effect, Article 4 of the Panamanian Constitution only sets forth that "The Republic of Panama respects the norms of international law". Thus, such norm has allowed the Supreme Court of Justice to consider as a constitutional violation any violation to norms of international treaties. In a decision of March 12, 1990, the Supreme Court declared the unconstitutionality of an Executive Decree which established general arbitrary conditions for the exercise of the rights to free expression and press, and stated that:

> Such act violates article 4 of the Constitution that oblige the national authorities to respect the international law norms. In the case under examination, as stated by the plaintiff, it is a matter of violation of the International Covenant on Human Rights and of the American Convention on Human Rights approved through statutes 14–1976 and 15–1977, which rejects any prior censorship regarding the exercise of the freedoms of expression and press, as fundamental human rights"[60].

One of the consequences of giving constitutional rank to international treaties, for instance, to the American Convention, is that the rights declared in it are out of the reach of the legislative body, which cannot legislate diminishing in any way the enforcement or scope of such rights.

It is the case, for instance, of the due process of law rights enshrined in the American Convention on Human Rights, like the right to a fair trial. According to Article 8,1 of the Convention "every person has the right to a hearing, with due guarantees and within a reasonable time, *by a competent, independent, and impartial*

---

58 Case H Giroldi/Cassation Recourse, April 7, 1995 in *Jurisprudencia Argentina*, Vol. 1995–III, p. 571. See Carlos AYALA CORAO, "Recepción de la jurisprudencia internacional sobre derechos humanos por la jurisprudencia constitucional" in *Revista del Tribunal Constitucional*, N° 6, Sucre, Bolivia, Nov. 2004, pp. 275 ff.

59 Case: *Bramajo*, September 12, 1996, in *Jurisprudencia Argentina*, Nov. 20, 1996. See Carlos AYALA CORAO, "Recepción de la jurisprudencia internacional sobre derechos humanos por la jurisprudencia constitucional" en *Revista del Tribunal Constitucional*, N° 6, Sucre, Bolivia, Nov. 2004, pp. 275 y ss.

60 *Véase* en *Iudicum et Vita, Jurisprudencia nacional de América Latina en Derechos Humanos*, N° 5, Instituto Interamericano de Derechos Humanos, San José, Costa Rica, Diciembre 1997 pp. 80–82

tribunal, previously established by law, in the substantiation of any accusation of a criminal nature made against him or for the determination of his rights and obligations of a civil, labor, fiscal, or any other nature". And regarding the right to personal liberty, Article 7,2 and 7,5 set forth the right of every person not to " be deprived of his physical liberty except for the *reasons and under the conditions established beforehand by the constitution* of the State Party concerned or by a law established pursuant thereto"; and the right of "any person detained *shall be brought promptly before a judge or other officer authorized by law to exercise judicial power* and shall be entitled to trial within a reasonable time or to be released without prejudice to the continuation of the proceedings".

These rights are also enshrined in the national Constitutions and due to their declaration in the Convention, have constitutional rank, therefore, they are protected by the amparo and habeas corpus recourses, the latter being regulated in Article 7,6 of the Convention which sets forth the right of anyone who is deprived of his liberty to "be entitled to recourse to a competent court, in order that the court may decide without delay on the lawfulness of his arrest or detention and order his release if the arrest or detention is unlawful"; right that cannot "be restricted or abolished".

These provisions prohibit, in Latin America, any possibility for the creation or special commissions to try any kind of offenses; and also prohibits for civilians to be tried by ordinary military courts and of course by military commissions. It also prohibits the creation of special courts to hear some criminal procedures after the offenses have been committed, in the sense that every person has the right to be heard only before courts existing prior to the offenses. For instance, in the Cantoral Benavides case, the Inter American Court on Human Rights decided that Peru violated Article 8,1 of the Convention because Mr. Cantoral Benavides had been prosecuted by a military judge, which was not the "competent independent and impartial judge" provided for in that provision. Consequently the Court considered that Peru had also violated Article 7.5 of the Convention because the victim had been brought before a criminal military court[61]. By ruling this way it can even be considered that the Court has ruled that not any judiciary body can examine the legality and reasonability of a detention, but only those that do not violate the principle of "natural judge"[62].

---

61 Case *Cantoral Benavides*, Augst 18, 2000. Paragraph 75: Also, the Court considers that the trial of Mr. Luis Alberto Cantoral–Benavides in the military criminal court violated Article 8(1) of the American Convention, which refers to the right to a fair trial before a competent, independent and impartial judge (*infra* para. 115). Consequently, the fact that Cantoral–Benavides was brought before a military criminal judge does not meet the requirements of Article 7(5) of the Convention. Also, the continuation of his detention by order of the military judges constituted arbitrary arrest, in violation of Article 7(3) of the Convention. Paragraph 76: The legal principle set forth in Article 7(5) of the Convention was not respected in this case until the accused was brought before a judge in the regular jurisdiction. In the file, there is no evidence of the date on which this occurred, but it can be reasonably concluded that it took place in early October 1993, since on October 8, 1993, the 43rd Criminal Court of Lima ordered that the investigation stage of a trial be opened against Cantoral–Benavides.

62 See Cecilia MEDINA QUIROGA, *La Convención Americana: Teoría y Jurisprudencia*, Universidad de Chile, Santiago 2003, p. 231

And this is in fact one of the cores of the due process of law rights according to the Convention, the right to be heard by a competent court set forth not only by statute but by a statute that must be sanctioned previously to the offense. This is a provision tending to proscribe ad hoc courts or commissions. The Inter American Court has referred to this due process of law right in the Ivcher Bronstein case. In such case, the Peruvian Executive Commission of the Judiciary, weeks before a Resolution depriving Mr. Bronstein of his Peruvian citizenship was issued, altered the composition of a Chamber of the Supreme Court and empowered such Chamber to create in a transitory way, specialized Superior chambers and Public Law specialized courts. The Supreme Court Chamber created one of such courts and appointed its judges, who heard the recourses filed by Mr. Bronstein. The Inter American Court ruled as follows:

> **114.** The Court considers that, by creating temporary public law chambers and courts and appointing judges to them at the time that the facts of the case sub judice occurred, the State did not guarantee to Mr. Ivcher Bronstein the right to be heard by judges or courts "previously established by law", as stipulated in Article 8(1) of the American Convention[63].

The Inter American Court also ruled on these matters in the Castillo Petruzzi and others Case, where it decided that:

> **129.** A basic principle of the independence of the judiciary is that every person has the right to be heard by regular courts, following procedures previously established by law. States are not to create "[t]ribunals that do not use the duly established procedures of the legal process [...] to displace the jurisdiction belonging to the ordinary courts or judicial tribu-nals"[64].

Particularly regarding the need of a competent court, and referring to the military courts, the Inter American Commission on Human Rights has considered that "to prosecute ordinary crimes as though they were military crimes simply because they had been committed by members of the military breached the guarantee of an independent and impartial tribunal"[65]; and the Inter American Court ruled in the Castillo Petruzzi et al. case that due process of law rights were violated when ordinary common offenses are transferred to the military jurisdiction; that judging civilians for treason in such courts imply to exclude their "natural judge" to hear those proceedings; and that because military jurisdiction is set forth for the purpose of maintaining order and discipline within the Armed Forces, civilians cannot incur in conducts contrary to such military duties. The Courts ruled as follows:

> **128.** The Court notes that several pieces of legislation give the military courts jurisdiction for the purpose of maintaining order and discipline within the ranks of the armed forces. Application of this functional jurisdiction is confined to military personnel who have committed some crime or were derelict in performing their duties, and then, only under certain circum-

---

63 Case *Ivcher Bronstein*, February 6, 2001. Paragraphs 113–114

64 Case *Castillo Petruzzi* el al., May 30, 1999, paragraph 129. The quotation correspond to *Basic Principles on the Independence of the Judiciary*, adopted by the Seventh United Nations Conference on the Prevention of Crime and Treatment of Offenders, held in Milan August 26 to September 6, 1985, and confirmed by the General Assembly in its resolutions 40/32 of 29 November 1985 and 40/146 of 13 December 1985.

65 Case *Genie Lacayo*, January 29, 1997. Paragraph 53.

stances. This was the definition in Peru's own law (Article 282 of the 1979 Constitution). Transferring jurisdiction from civilian courts to military courts, thus allowing military courts to try civilians accused of treason, means that the competent, independent and impartial tribunal previously established by law is precluded from hearing these cases. In effect, military tribunals are not the tribunals previously established by law for civilians. Having no military functions or duties, civilians cannot engage in behaviors that violate military duties. When a military court takes jurisdiction over a matter that regular courts should hear, the individual's right to a hearing by a competent, independent and impartial tribunal previously established by law and, a fortiori, his right to due process is violated. That right to due process, in turn, is intimately linked to the very right of access to the courts"[66]

Finally, in the Durand and *Ugarte Case*, the Inter American Court ruled that:

> **117.** In a democratic Government of Laws, the penal military jurisdiction shall have a restrictive and exceptional scope and shall lead to the protection of special juridical interests, related to the functions assigned by law to the military forces. Consequently, civilians must be excluded from the military jurisdiction scope and only the military shall be judged by commission of crime or offenses that by its own nature attempt against legally protected interests of military order[67].

This excludes not only the processing of civilians by military courts, but additionally the possibility to assign to military courts to hear cases of common felonies committed by military, even in the exercise of its functions. As was ruled by the same Inter American Court:

> **118.** In this case, the military in charge of subduing the riots that took place in El Frontón prison resorted to a disproportionate use of force, which surpassed the limits of their functions thus also causing a high number of inmate death toll. Thus, the actions which brought about this situation cannot be considered as military felonies, but common crimes, so investigation and punishment must be placed on the ordinary justice, apart from the fact that the alleged active parties had been military or not[68].

In contrast with the aforementioned, the absence of similar constitutional provisions in the United States allows those discussions to continue regarding the validity of military commissions set up by a military order of Nov. 13, 2001, to try non–citizens for "acts of international terrorism", after the September 11 terrorist attacks. This discussion was reported on March 26, 2006, in The New York Times[69] showing the struggle for supremacy between the courts and the Government, which can be briefed as follows:

According to the Detainee Treatment Act sanctioned on December 2005, the federal courts jurisdiction has been excluded over cases brought by detainees at the United States naval base at Guantánamo Bay, Cuba. In the case, *Hamdan v. Rumsfeld*, referred to a person held since 2002, the court must decide whether it retains the right to proceed with this case; a matter that has not being discussed since

66 Case *Castillo Petruzzi* et al, May 30, 1999, Paragraph 128 and 132

67 Case *Durand and Ugarte*, August 16, 2000, paragraph 117

68 *Idem*, Paragraph 118

69 See Linda GREENHOUSE "Detainee case Will Pose delicate Question for Courts. A White House Challenge to Jurisdiction", *The New York Times* March 27, 2006, p. A12.

the immediate aftermath of the Civil War, in which the Supreme Court permitted Congress to divest the Court of jurisdiction over a case it has already agreed to decide. In the Ex Parte McCardle case, after arguments had been heard in an appeal brought by William H. McCardle, a Mississippi newspaper editor who was taken into custody and charged by the military government with fomenting insurrection; Congress, fearing that a Supreme Court ruling in favor of the editor could result in invalidating military control of the former Confederate state, enacted a law to deprive the court of jurisdiction. The court then dismissed the appeal, rejecting the argument that with the new statute it was permitting Congress to usurp the judicial function.

In the new case Hamdan v. Rumpfel N° 05–184, the administration also filed a motion with the court in January 2006, just days after the Detainee Treatment Act was signed into law, urging immediate dismissal of Mr. Hamdan's appeal. On February 21, the court declined to act on the motion, announcing instead that it would take up the jurisdictional question as part of the argument on the merits of the case. Contrary to the McCardle case in which the Congress spoke clearly in the court–stripping amendment, the Detainee Treatment Act seems to be ambiguous on its application to pending, as opposed to future, cases.

According to the Detainee Treatment Act, Guantánamo detainees are tried by a military commission and will have only a circumscribed right to a subsequent appeal in federal court, in which they can not raise the basic challenge to the commission's operation that Mr. Hamdan is presenting in his Supreme Court case. Military commissions are not new in the United States; they were first used during the war with Mexico in the 1840's. But there have been none since the World War II era.

The main point to be resolved is if any Congressional enactment or inherent power authorized the administration to set up a special tribunal without the procedural protections offered by American military law and required by the Geneva Conventions; and if conspiracy, is or is not a war crime, and if it is or not subject to trial by military commissions. In the end, the question at hand is if the Geneva Conventions apply in the cases related to the Guantanamo detainees, and if their protections can or cannot be invoked by individual detainees[70].

The reference to the case is made in order to highlight what happens in cases such as the United States where there is no express constitutional rank with the right to be tried by judicial competent independent and impartial courts established before the offenses were committed, as set forth in the American Convention on Human Rights; and if the discussions regarding the struggle on the supremacy between the courts and the Government can still be developed as above mentioned; as well as the exclusion of any injunctive protection of rights in such cases. In Latin America, after so many cases and stories of ad hoc commissions or special courts to try people with no due process of law rights, the provisions of the American Convention and those set forth in the Constitutions, do not allow even the discussion to be sustained. The due process of law, with all its content, is a constitutional right, and its enforcement is out of the reach of Congress and no legislation can be passed to restrict the courts

70 *Idem*

jurisdiction. And being it a constitutional right, the amparo and habeas corpus protection can always be sought by the affected party, and eventually reach the American Court on Human Rights for the protection, as shown in the aforementioned cases.

3. The supra statutory rank of international treaties on human rights

Thirdly, other Latin American Constitutions have expressly established the supra–legal rank of international treaties and conventions in general, including those relative to human rights. In these systems, the treaties are subject to the Constitution, but prevail over the statutes.

This was the solution followed in the Constitutions of Germany (Article 25), Italy (Article 10) and France (Article 55), and in Latin America is the solution followed in the Constitution of Costa Rica, which provides that: "Public treaties, international agreements and covenants duly approved by the Legislative Assembly shall, as of their enactment or the day they themselves set forth, have superior authority to that of the laws" (Article 7). Nevertheless, as mentioned above, the jurisprudence of the Constitutional Chamber has given constitutional rank to international treaties on human rights, and even supra constitutional rank in cases in which they contain more favorable provisions regarding the exercise of such rights.

In this respect, the Constitutional Chamber has for instance, directly applied the American Convention on Human Rights, as prevailing regarding statutes, arguing that the legal "norms which contradict [a treaty] must be considered simply as repealed, by virtue precisely of the superior rank of the treaty (decision 282–90, case of violation of Article 8.2 of the American Convention on Human Rights by the repealed Article 472 of the Criminal Procedures Code). Thus, when considering that Article 8.2 of the American Convention "recognizes as a fundamental right of everybody who has been criminally indicted, to appeal the judicial decision"; the Chamber considered that Article 472 of the Criminal Procedure Code which limits the exercise of the cassation recourse, had to be considered as "not set forth" and understand "that the cassation recourse is a mean legally given to any condemned person regarding whatever sanction imposed in a criminal procedure". The Constitutional Chamber in a subsequent decision N° 719–90 accepted a judicial review action declaring the unconstitutionality of said Article 474 of the Criminal procedure Code, deciding its annulment and considering that the limits set forth in such article to the right to appeal in cassation in favor of any criminally condemned person, as "not being set forth".

It must be noted, that in another Constitutional Chamber decision (N° 1054–94), the challenging of Article 426 of the Criminal Procedures Code which denies appeal regarding decisions on other non criminal contraventions, was rejected according to the jurisprudence set by the Chamber, based on the fact that what the Chamber has clearly decided is that "what is established in the said American Convention is the fundamental right to appeal given to anybody condemned in a criminal procedures, and not indistinctively in other matters".

Now, regarding the supra legal rank of treaties and their prevalence over internal statutes in case of conflict, in a similar sense, Article 144 of the Constitution of El

Salvador provides the legal status of treaties and their prevalence with respect to the statutes in the event of conflict, when stating that: "International treaties executed by El Salvador with other States or with international organisms, shall constitute laws of the Republic upon entering into force, pursuant to the provisions of the treaty itself and of this Constitution," adding the regulation that: "The statute shall not modify or abrogate that which is agreed upon in the treaty for El Salvador" and that: "In the event of conflicts between the treaty and the statute, the treaty shall prevail".

In accordance with these provisions, the Constitutional Chamber of the Supreme Court of Justice of El Salvador has also applied International treaties on human rights, on deciding cases on which the international regulations are considered to prevail. It was the case of a November 17, 1994 decision issued regarding a provisional detention of a former commander of the irregular armed forces, ordered in a defamatory criminal trial brought against him. The Chamber stated that "For the adequate comprehension of the provisional detention institution in our system, we must additionally bear in mind –according to Article 144 of the Constitution, what is set forth in the international treaties ratified by El Salvador"[71]. So the Court analyzed Articles 11,1 of the Universal Declaration on Human Rights, and Article 9,3 of the International Covenant on Civil and Political Rights, which refers to the presumption of innocence and to the exceptional character of the preventive detention, which must not be considered as a general rule. The Court also analyzed Article XXVI of the American Declarations of Human Rights, referred as well to the presumption of innocence; and Articles 7,2 and 8,2 of the American Convention on Human Rights, which refer to the rights of persons regarding detentions, particularly the principle *nulla pena sine lege*. From the aforementioned the Court concluded by stating that "It is within this –constitutional and international– context where the analysis of the provisional detention must be framed, because such provisions, due to their superior place in the normative hierarchy, are obligatory"[72].

Consequently and based on the international regulations, regarding the preventive detention the Chamber concluded that "It must never be considered as a general rule in criminal proceedings –as expressly forbidden in Article 9,3 of the International Covenant on Civil and Political Rights–, so that it cannot be automatically decided", because it cannot be understood as an anticipated sanction. On the contrary, in order to be decided, it needs in each case the judge's evaluation of the circumstances regarding its need and convenience for the protection of fundamental public interest.

Based in the aforementioned, the Chamber concluded regarding the case, that "when the provisional detention was decided, the judge did not base its decision in any justification at all, thus being unconstitutional"[73].

---

71 See in *Iudicum et Vita, Jurisprudencia nacional de América Latina en Derechos Humanos*, Nº 5, Instituto Interamericano de Derechos Humanos, San José, Costa Rica, Diciembre 1997, p. 157

72 *Idem*, p. 157.

73 *Idem*, p. 158.

In another decision of the Constitutional Chamber of the Supreme Court of El Salvador issued on June 13, 1995, the Chamber declared the unconstitutionality of a local government regulation (*Ordenanza municipal*) setting forth restrictions to the exercise of the political rights to meeting and demonstration, basing its decision in Article 15 of the American Convention on Human Rights and in Article 21 of the International Covenant on Civil and Political Rights, according to which limitations to such rights can only be regulated by means of statutes. The Chamber argued as follows: "The international treaties in force in our country, having supremacy regarding secondary regulations, and among them, the Municipal Code, recognized the freedom of meeting and public demonstration and established that such rights can only be subjected to limitations or restrictions as are necessary in a democratic society and are provided in statutes", which "must be sanctions by the Legislative Assembly following the formalities set forth in the Constitution". The Chamber also ruled that such statute, according to Article XXVIII of the American Declaration on Human Rights, can only set forth limitations subjected to the "principle of reasonability", which means that they must be "intrinsically just, that is to say, that they must be in accordance to certain rules of enough value in order to give the sense to the substantive notion of justice enshrined in the Constitution". In this regard, the Chamber concluded its decision regarding the case, declaring the unconstitutionality of the challenged municipal regulation, stating:

> Non of these elements are found in the challenged instrument on grounds of unconstitutionality, that is to say, it is a typical case of authority abuse, not only because without any authorization it regulated a constitutional right, but because it usurped a function reserved to the Legislative body

The Constitution of Mexico, when referring to international treaties is the one among the Latin American countries which more closely resembles the North American constitutional provision, stating:

> **Article 133.** This Constitution, the laws (statutes) of Congress of the Union and all the treaties that have been made and shall be made in accordance therewith by the President with the approval of the Senate according to the Constitution, shall be the supreme law of the Union. The judges of each state shall conform to the Constitution, laws and treaties, in spite of any disposition in contrary to them that could be contained in the Constitutions and statutes of the States.

According to this traditional supremacy clause, treaties were also traditionally considered as having the same rank as statutes. This was decided by the Supreme Court of the Nation by the ruling C/92, June 30, 1992, in which it stated that because the statutes have the same rank that treaties have, "immediately below the Constitution in the hierarchy of norms of the Mexican legal order", and:

> "international treaties cannot be the criteria in order to determine the unconstitutionality of a statute, nor vice versa. Thus, the Commerce and Industrial Associations Statute cannot be considered unconstitutional because it is contrary to what is regulated in an international treaty"[74]

74 Tesis P. C/92, in *Gaceta del Semanario Judicial de la Federación*, N° 60, diciembre de 1992, p. 27.

But this criteria has been abandoned by the same Supreme Court in a ruling of revision of an amparo decision N° 1475/98, in which the Court, interpreting Article 133 of the Constitution according to the 1969 Vienna Convention on Treaties determined that because "the international compromises are assumed by the Mexican State as a whole and obliged all its authorities regarding international community", the international treaties are located in a second level immediately under the Constitution and above the federal and local statutes[75].

Among this group of countries that gives international treaties on human rights a superior rank regarding statutes, it can also be mentioned the case of Paraguay. The Constitution has a supremacy clause similar to the North American and Mexican one, with the following text:

> **Article 137.** On the supremacy of the Constitution. The supreme law of the Republic is the Constitution. The latter, the international treaties, covenants and agreements approved and ratified, the statutes sanctioned by Congress and the other legal hierarchical inferior regulations accordingly issued, integrate the positive national law in the enunciated preference order.

Nonetheless, this constitutional clause has a peculiarity regarding other similar clause, since it enunciates the order of preference given to the legal regulations; thus, the treaties being located under the Constitution but above the statutes. Additionally, the Article is complemented by Article 141 of the same Constitution which provides that "international treatises approved by the National Congress and which are duly ratified, are part of the internal legal order with the hierarchy established in Article 137"

According to these provisions, the Court of Appeal in criminal cases, First Chamber, in a decision dated June 10, 1996, revoked a judicial decision of an inferior court which had sentenced a person for a defamation offence regarding a public politician person. The argument of the Court was that in a "democratic society, the politicians are exposed to citizens criticism" and that in "no way individual interest can prevail over public interest", invoking for the revocation not only constitutional articles, but also Article 13 of the American Convention on Human Rights[76]

4. The statutory rank of international treaties on human rights

In *fourth* place, regarding the legal hierarchy of international instruments of human rights, it can be said that in general, constitutional systems have attributes to international treaties the same hierarchy as of statutes. It can be considered as the

75 *Véase* Guadalupe BARRENA y Carlos MONTEMAYOR "Incorporación del derecho internacional en la Constitución mexicana", *Derechos Humanos. Memoria del IV Congreso Nacional de Derecho Constitucional*, Vol. III, Instituto de Investigaciones Jurídicas, UNAM, México, 2001, *cit.*, por Humberto HENDERSON, "Los tratados internacionales de derechos humanos en el orden interno: la importancia del principio *pro homine*", en *Revista IIDH*, Instituto Interamericano de Derechos Humanos, N° 39, San José, 2004, p. 82, nota 15.

76 See in *Iudicum et Vita, Jurisprudencia nacional de América Latina en Derechos Humanos*, N° 5, Instituto Interamericano de Derechos Humanos, San José, Costa Rica, Diciembre 1997 pp. 82–86.

most widespread system in contemporary constitutional law, following the orientation begun by the Constitution of the United States of America, in which Article VI. 2, states:

> This Constitution, and the laws of the United States which shall be made in pursuance thereof; and all treaties made, or which shall be made, under the authority of the United States, shall be the supreme law of the land; and the judges in every state shall be bound thereby, anything in the Constitution or laws of any State to the contrary notwithstanding.

In such systems, therefore, "international law is part of the law of the land", the treaties having the same legal rank as the statutes. They are subject to the Constitution, and in their application regarding statutes, they are governed by the principles of subsequent law and special law in regard to the derogatory effects they may have.

Is the case of Uruguay, Article 6 of the Constitution only provides that in all treaties a clause must be incorporated regulating that "the differences between the parties must be decided by mean of arbitration or other peaceful means". In the article, no reference is made regarding the hierarchy of treaties in the legal order or human rights.

Nonetheless, for instance, the Supreme Court of Justice on a decision of October 23, 1996, directly applied international treaties in order to reject the question of unconstitutionality raised in the case by the Public Prosecutor regarding the Press Statute, whose regulations guarantied the right of the defendant to the be prosecuted while in freedom. The case referred to a press offence trial for critics to the President of Paraguay, in which the plaintiff was the Paraguayan Ambassador to Uruguay. In the case, the Public Prosecutor raised the question of unconstitutionality arguing that the Press Statute, when allowing only to certain persons to be tried while in freedom, violates the equality principle set forth in Article 7 of the American Declaration of Human Rights, and Article 24 of the American Convention on Human Rights. In order to decide the question, rejecting the Public prosecutor's argument, the Supreme Court carefully analyzed the human right of free expression, making reference to Article 19 of the International Covenant of Civil and Political Rights; to Article 13.1 of the American Convention on Human Rights; to the Consultative Opinion OC–O5 of the Inter American Court on Human Rights referred to the incompatibility of the freedom of expression with the obligatory affiliation of journalists to the Journalist's College in Costa Rica; and to the presumption of innocence right "expressly set forth in the international Declarations and Conventions to which the country has adhered or that in one way or another oblige it (Universal Declaration on Man's Rights, art. 11; International Covenant on Human Rights, art 14.4; and Inter American Convention on Human Rights, art. 8.2)", all allowing the defendant to be trial in freedom[77].

The Dominican Republic constitutional system can also be classified in this group of countries in which their Constitutions give treaties the same legal rank as statutes. Precisely due to that fact, being the Dominican Republic one of the very

---

77 See in *Iudicum et Vita, Jurisprudencia nacional de América Latina en Derechos Humanos*, N° 5, Instituto Interamericano de Derechos Humanos, San José, Costa Rica, Diciembre 1997 pp. 72–79.

few Latin American Countries that do not have in its Constitution expressly regulated the "amparo" action or recourse as a special judicial mean for the protection of human rights; the Supreme Court did apply the American Convention of Human Rights in order to admit the "amparo" recourse.

In effect, Article 3 of the Dominican Republic Constitutions states that "The Dominican Republic recognizes and applies international law regulations, general and American ones, when they have been approved by the State organs", and accordingly, in 1977 the Congress approved the American Convention on Human Rights, whose Article 8 and 25,1 as abovementioned, regulate the general due process of law rules and the "amparo" action or recourse for the judicial protections of human rights. Thus, according to these regulations, if it is true that the Constitution does not set forth the "amparo" action, it is regulated in the American Convention and then it can be exercised by anybody seeking protection of his human rights. But the problem was the absence of procedure rules, comprising the absence of formal attribution to specific courts of the power to decide upon "amparo" suits. That explains why actions or recourses of "amparo" were never brought before courts, until 1999, when a private company, the Avon enterprise, did so before the Supreme Court of Justice, against a judicial decision on labor matters, alleging violations of constitutional rights.

The Supreme Court, in a decision of February 24, 1999 admitted the "amparo" suit brought before the Court by *Productos Avon S.A.*, an enterprise, declared the "amparo" as a "public law institution" and prescribed in the decision the basic rules of procedure for such actions[78]. The case developed as follows:

1. The plaintiff company claimed that a judicial decision on labor matters, issued by a lower court, violated its rights to be judged by the competent court of justice, asking the Supreme Court: First: To declare in its ruling that the "amparo" recourse be considered as a Dominican is a public law institution; and second, that the Supreme Court, according to the provisions of the Organic Judicial statute which attributed to the Supreme Court the power to resolve on adjective matters when a specific procedure does not have a statutory regulation, to set forth the procedure to be followed regarding the "amparo" recourses. Additionally, the plaintiff asked the Court to issue a preliminary order suspending the effects of the challenged judicial labor decisions, pending the course of the trial.

2. The Supreme Court, in order to decide, fixed the criteria that the international treaties invoked by the plaintiff, particularly Articles 8 and 25,1 of the American Convention on Human Rights, as internal Dominican law, have the purpose to guarantee the judicial protection of fundamental rights recognized in the Constitution, the law and the said Convention, against acts which violate such rights, committed

78 See in *Iudicum et Vita, Jurisprudencia nacional de América Latina en Derechos Humanos*, N° 7, Tomo I, Instituto Interamericano de Derechos Humanos, San José, Costa Rica, Diciembre, 2000 p. 329 ff. See the comments regarding the decisión in Allan R. BREWER–CARÍAS, "La admisión jurisprudencial de la acción de amparo en ausencia de regulación constitucional o legal en la República Dominicana", *Idem*, pp. 334 ff.

by any person acting or not in their public functions thus also against individuals actions. In this regard, the Supreme Court decided that:

> "Contrary to what has been decided in the sense that the offending acts must be issued by judicial officials or persons acting in such functions, the "amparo" recourse, it is considered that as a protection mechanism of individual freedom in its various aspects, the "amparo" must not be excluded as a judicial remedy in order to resolve situations originated by persons accomplishing judicial functions. Article 25,1 of the Convention, provide that the "amparo" recourse is open in favor of anybody against acts which violate his fundamental rights "even when the violation is committed by individuals not acting exercise of public functions"; evidently including the judicial functions; ... as well as against any action or omission from individuals or public administration officials, including omissions or non jurisdictional administrative acts from the courts, if they affect a constitutional protected right"[79].

In this regard, the Dominican Republic Supreme Court decision is considered a very important ruling, clearly stating that the "amparo" recourse can be filed against individuals, following the broad conception of the "amparo" action initiated in Argentina, and followed in Uruguay, Chile, Perú, Bolivia and Venezuela. The narrow conception excluding the "amparo" recourse against individuals is followed in Mexico, Brazil, Panama, El Salvador and Nicaragua. The Dominican Supreme Court also followed the broad conception of "amparo" admitting the action against judicial decisions, as it is accepted in the American Convention, contrary to the tendency observed in other Latin American countries that excluded judicial decisions from the "amparo" recourse, as is the case of Argentina, Uruguay, Costa Rica, Panama, El Salvador, Honduras and Nicaragua.

In Colombia, the 1991 statute regulating the action of "tutela" also admitted the amparo against judicial rulings, but the Constitutional Court annulled the corresponding article, considering that it violated the right to *res judicata* effects of definitive judicial decisions[80]. Nonetheless, the "tutela" against judicial decisions has indirectly been admitted when arbitrariness is alleged against judicial decisions[81]

3. Regarding the Dominican Republic Supreme Court decision, it additionally decided that even in the absence of procedural rules for the "amparo" recourse, contrary to what happens regarding habeas corpus recourses (where there is a statute establishing the competent court and the procedure); and because the amparo recourse is a simple, speedy and effective judicial mean for the protection of all constitutional rights other than those protected by means of habeas corpus, no judge can refuse to admit it adducing the absence of statutory regulation. For that purpose, the Supreme Court invoked its power according to Article 29,2 of the Judicial organization Statute, to establish the procedural rules in order to avoid the confusion that can cause the absence of such rules. Consequently, the Supreme Court decided "to declare that the recourse set forth in Article 25,1 of the November 22, 1969 San José,

---

79 *Idem*. p. 332.

80 Decision C.543 of September 24, 1992. See in Manuel José CEPEDA ESPINOSA, *Derecho Constitucional Jurisprudencia*, Legis, Bogotá, 2001, p. 1009 ff.

81 Decision T–213 of May 13, 1994. See in Manuel José CEPEDA ESPINOSA, *Derecho Constitucional Jurisprudencia, Legis*, Bogotá, 2001, p. 1022 ff.

Costa Rica American Convention on Human Rights, is an institution of Dominican positive law, due to its approval by the National Congress through resolution N° 739 of December 1977, according to Article 3 of the Constitution".

On the other hand, the Supreme Court resolved the practical problems derived from the acceptance of the "amparo" suit, by setting forth the procedural rules, as follows: First, by determining that the competent courts to decide on the matter are the courts of first instance in the place in which the challenged act or omission has been produced; and second, by stating adjective rules of procedure, similar to those established in Articles 101 and following of the Statute N° 834 of 1978, adding references to the delay to bring the action before the court, to the hearing that has to take place, the delay for the decision and the delay for the appeal. The Supreme Court finally remembered, in order to avoid abuses in the use of the action, that the "amparo" recourse must not be understood as the introduction of a third instance in the judicial process[82].

This Dominican Republic Supreme Court 1999 decision, taken in absence of constitutional and statutory regulations regarding the "amparo" action, admitting this judicial means for protection of all human rights according to what is set forth in the American Convention on Human Rights, is without doubt a very important one, not only regarding the "amparo" recourse or action as a specific judicial means for human rights protection, but also regarding the enforcement within internal law of the American Convention on Human Rights.

IV. THE INTERPRETATIVE CONSTITUTIONAL RULES REGARDING THE INTERNATIONAL INSTRUMENTS ON HUMAN RIGHTS

Now, in absence of express constitutional regulations regarding the hierarchy of international treaties on human rights in the internal legal system, –whether constitutional, supra statutory or statutory rank–, such instruments can also acquire constitutional value and rank by means of different constitutional interpretation rules. In other words, the rights declared in international treaties can also be considered as constitutional rights, by means of other constitutional regulations or techniques: first, by referring the interpretation of constitutional rights to what is set forth in the international treaties; second, by enshrining in the Preambles or general declarations of the Constitutions references to the universal declarations on human rights.

In the first place, some Constitutions expressly set forth a guiding rule for interpreting human rights declared in their text, requiring that such interpretation must be made in accordance to what is set forth in the international treaties on human rights. This is the technique found in the Spanish Constitution, where article 10,2, states:

---

82 See the text *Iudicum et Vita, Jurisprudencia nacional de América Latina en Derechos Humanos*, N° 7, Tomo I, Instituto Interamericano de Derechos Humanos, San José, Costa Rica, Diciembre 2000 p. 329 y ss. See the comments in Allan R. BREWER–CARÍAS, "La admisión jurisprudencial de la acción de amparo en ausencia de regulación constitucional o legal en la República Dominicana", *Idem*, pp. 334 ff.

> The norms concerning fundamental rights or freedom recognized in the Constitution, must be interpreted in accordance to the Universal Declaration of Human Rights and the international treaties and conventions referred to the same matter ratified by Spain.

In similar way, the Portuguese Constitution also sets forth, that:

> **Article 16,2.** The provisions of the Constitution and laws relating to fundamental rights are to be read and interpreted in harmony with the Universal Declaration of Human Rights.

These two constitutional provisions, without doubt, influenced the drafting of the 1991 Colombian Constitution, where Article 93 establishes:

> **Article 93.** The rights and duties enshrined in this Charter shall be interpreted pursuant to the international treaties on human rights ratified by Colombia.

Following this constitutional provision, all State bodies, not just the courts, have to interpret the constitutional regulations regarding human rights pursuant to the provisions of the international treaties on the matter. The result of this constitutional principle of interpretation is the recognition of an equal rank and constitutional value for those constitutional rights declared in international treaties, which are the ones that will guide the interpretation of the rights enshrined in the Constitution.

This interpretative technique has been frequently used by the Constitutional Court in Colombia when interpreting the extent of constitutional rights, as was the case in a decision of February 22, 1996 issued when deciding a judicial review action filed on the grounds of unconstitutionality against the statute which regulates Television networks, considered by the plaintiff as being contrary to the constitutional right to inform.

The Constitutional Court began its decision by arguing that:

> "the internal validity of a statute is not only subjected to the conformity of its regulations to what is set forth in the Constitution, but also to what is prescribed in the international treaties approved by Congress and ratified by the President of the Republic".
>
> As clearly set forth in Article 93 of the Constitution, the conformity of the internal legislation to international treaties and obligations of the Colombian State regarding other States and supranational entities, is imposed more severely by the Constitution when the matter relates to the application and exercise of fundamental rights. According to such article of the Constitution, the international treaties and covenants approved by Congress and ratified by the Executive in which human rights are recognized and its limitations are prohibited in states of exception, prevail regarding the internal legal order.
>
> The constitutional article declares in a straightforward manner that the rights and duties enshrined in the Constitution must be interpreted in accordance to the international treaties on human rights ratified by Colombia"[83].

Based on the abovementioned, the Constitutional Chamber then referred in its decision to the constitutional right to freedom of expression of thoughts and of information, following what is set forth in Article 19,3 of the International Covenant on Human Rights and in Article 13,2 of the American Convention on Human

---

83 See in *Iudicum et Vita, Jurisprudencia nacional de América Latina en Derechos Humanos*, N° 5, Instituto Interamericano de Derechos Humanos, San José, Costa Rica, Diciembre 1997 pp. 34–35.

Rights, particularly regarding the universality of the exercise of such rights "without any considerations of frontiers"; concluding by ruling that:

> To forbid in the national territory the installation or functioning of land stations devoted to receive and later to diffuse, transmit or distribute television signals coming from satellites, whether national or international, is a flagrant violation of the right to be informed which everybody has pursuant to Article 20 of the Constitution[84].

The interpretative technique of human rights according to what is established in international instruments on the matter has also been established, for instance, in the Peruvian Constitutional Procedure Code, by article V that sets forth:

> **Article V.** *Interpretation of constitutional rights.* The content and the scope of constitutional rights protected by means of the constitutional process established in this Code (including habeas corpus and amparo) must be interpreted according to the Universal Declaration on Human Rights, the treaties on human rights, as well as to the decisions issued by the international courts on human rights established according to treaties in which Peru is a Party".

1. The constitutional general references to the universal declarations on human rights

The second interpretative technique through which international declarations on human rights acquired constitutional rank and value, results from the general declarations enshrined in the Preambles or the constitutional text precisely referring to those international declarations on human rights.

Regarding the Preambles of the Constitution, many of the Post War Constitutions contain general declarations regarding human rights, with particular reference to universal declarations. The classic example is the 1958 French Constitution in which, without containing in its text a Bill of Rights, the following general declaration is contained in its Preamble:

> The French people hereby solemnly proclaim their dedication to the Rights of Man and the principle of national sovereignty as defined by the Declaration of 1789, reaffirmed and complemented by the Preamble to the 1946 Constitution.

By means of this general declaration the Constitutional Council has enlarged the constitutionality block, attributing constitutional value and rank to all the fundamental rights contained in the 1789 Declaration of Rights of Citizens and Man[85].

In other Constitutions, the Preambles contain general declarations in order to define a general purpose of the Constitution and to give a general orientation to State and society actions seeking the respect and full enforcement of human rights. For instance, the Preamble of the 1999 Venezuelan Constitution declares that the Constitution itself was sanctioned in order to "assure the rights to life, to work, to cultural heritage, to education, to social justice and to equality without any kind of discrimination", promoting "the universal and indivisible guarantee of human rights".

---

84 *Idem*, p. 37.

85 See the references in Allan R. BREWER–CARÍAS, *Judicial Review in Comparative Law*, Cambridge, 1989.

The Constitution of Guatemala also expressly declares in its Preamble that its text shall "encourage full enforcement of human rights within a stable, permanent and popular institutional order, where governed and governors shall proceed in strict observance of the law".

Being in those cases the general purpose of the countries' Constitution to guarantee, promote and encourage the full enjoyment and enforcement of human rights referred to their universal context, the rights enshrined in the international declarations and treaties can be considered or interpreted as having the same value and rank to those expressly declared in the Constitution's texts themselves.

Other Constitutions contain similar general declarations, not in their Preambles, but within their texts, when regulating specific aspects of the State bodies functioning and setting forth, for instance, the need for the effective guaranty that must be given to anybody to enjoy and exercise constitutional rights. In these cases, upon constituting as a State obligation the respect of human rights or to assure that they are properly enforced, it has been interpreted that such rights generally acquire constitutional rank and value even if not expressly listed in the constitutional declarations.

Such is the case of the Constitution of Chile, whose 1989 reform included a declaration pursuant to which it was expressly recognized that the exercise of sovereignty is limited by "respect for the essential rights to be found in human nature", also prescribing as a "duty of State bodies to respect and promote such rights guaranteed by this Constitution, as well as by international treaties ratified by Chile and currently in force" (Art. 5,II). Hence, if it is the State's duty to respect and promote human rights that are guaranteed by international treaties, such rights acquire the same rank and value as the constitutional rights expressly listed in the constitutional text itself. Moreover, the reference to "essential rights to be found in human nature" permits and requires that not only those expressly listed in the Constitution be identified as such, but also those established in international treaties and, what is more, those not expressly declared but that are part of human nature itself.

The Constitution of Ecuador also prescribes the State's obligation "... to respect and have respected the human rights guaranteed by this Constitution" (Article 16); assuring to "all its citizens, with no discrimination whatsoever, the free and effective exercise and enjoyment of the human rights established in this Constitution and in the declarations, covenants, agreements and other current international instruments in force."

Therefore, in these cases, the State's obligation refers not only to its guaranteeing the exercise and enjoyment of the rights listed in the Constitution, but all those named in international instruments too, which therefore can be considered as acquiring the same rank and value of constitutional rights.

In this regard, special reference should be made to the Constitution of Nicaragua which establishes the general declaration that all people shall not only "enjoy State protection and the recognition of rights inherent to the human person and the unrestricted respect, promotion and protection of their human rights", but also the protection of the State for the "full enforcement of the rights enshrined in the Universal

Declaration of Human Rights; in the American Declaration of the Rights and Duties of Man; in the United Nations' International Covenant on Civil and Political Rights; and in the American Convention on Human Rights of the Organization of American States."

In this case, the Constitution's reference to certain international instruments, due to the international dynamic on these matters, can only be interpreted as a non–exhaustive statement, given the preceding declarations referred in general to human rights and to those inherent to the human person.

Based on Article 46 of the Nicaraguan Constitution, statutes have been challenged on the grounds of unconstitutionally because they violate rights declared in international treaties. It was the case of the judicial review process of the 1989 General statute on Medias (*Ley General sobre los medios de la Comunicación Social (Ley N° 57)*, in which the Supreme Court, in its decision of August 22, 1989, even if it rejected the "amparo of unconstitutionality" recourse filed against the statute, in order to decide, the Court extensively considered the denounced violations not only regarding Article 46 of the Constitution but, through it, also considered articles of the Human Rights Declaration, the International Covenant on Civil and Political Rights and the American Convention on Human Rights[86].

Finally, the Constitution of Brazil proclaims that the State in its international relations, is ruled by the principle of the prevalence of human rights (Article 4,III); and that being constituted as a democratic rule of law State, it has as one of its foundations the dignity of human person (Article I, III). Regarding in particular human rights, Article 5,2 of the Constitutions declares, that:

> The rights and guarantees set forth in the Constitution do not exclude others which can result from the regime and principles therein set forth or from the international treaties on which the Federative Republic of Brazil may be part.

This article has been interpreted as a mean for inserting the Constitution in the general trend of Latin American constitutionalism that gives a special treatment in internal law to the rights and guarantees internationally guarantied.

2. The enforcement of rights regardless of their statutory regulation

In addition to the abovementioned, regarding the process of constitutionalization of the internationalization of human rights, special reference must be made to constitutional clauses which prescribe the right to the enforcement of constitutional rights regardless of the existence or not of statutory regulations.

In these sense, for instance, the Venezuela Constitution since 1961 established that "The lack of statutory regulations of rights (inherent to human beings) does not impede their exercise" (Article 50), in the sense that there is no need for a statute to be enacted in order for the exercise of the constitutional rights. This is the same reg-

---

86 See the text in *Iudicum et Vita, Jurisprudencia nacional de América Latina en Derechos Humanos*, N° 5, Instituto Interamericano de Derechos Humanos, San José, Costa Rica, Diciembre 1997, pp. 128–140. See the comments of Antonio CANÇADO TRINDADE, "Libertad de expresión y derecho a la información en los planos internacional y nacional", *Idem*, p. 194.

ulation that can be found for instance in the Ecuadorian Constitution in which Article 18 states: "The absence of statute cannot be alleged in order to justify or ignore rights set forth in this Constitution, or to not admit actions for their protections, or to deny the acknowledgment of such rights".

Regarding the Venezuelan regulation, now enshrined in Article 22 of the Constitution, it must be indicated that it has serve for the acknowledgment and enforcement of very important constitutional rights, like precisely, the enforcement of the right to "amparo".

In effect, the right to "amparo" was originally set forth in the 1961 Constitution, as follows:

> **Article 49**. The courts shall protect ("ampararán") all inhabitants of the Republic in the exercise of their rights and guarantees set forth in the Constitution, according to the law (statute). The procedure shall be brief and speedy and the competent judge will have the power to immediately restore the infringed legal situation.

The wording of this article was interpreted by the courts in the sense that the acceptability of the amparo suit was conditioned to the previous enactment of the statute regulations on the matter, particularly because the same Constitution expressly regulated in a transitory way the procedure for the habeas corpus action, pending the sanctioning of such statute, "in order to not leave (its applicability) suspended". From this regulation the courts then understood that the intention of Article 49 was to condition the admissibility of the amparo action to the previous sanctioning of the statute on the matter, providing only in an exceptional way for the immediate acceptability of the habeas corpus action[87].

In this sense, the Supreme Court of Justice in 1970 regarding the amparo suit, considered Article 49 to be a "programmatic" one, thus not directly applicable, being necessary the previous enactment of the statute on the matter, in order to bring before a court an action of amparo. The Court said:

> The article is not a direct and immediately applicable stipulation by the courts, but only a programmatic one directed to Congress that is the competent body to regulate for constitutional guarantees; interpretation reinforced by the transitive constitutional regulation on habeas corpus[88].

This constitutional judicial approach regarding the acceptability of the amparo action began to change after the approval by Congress in 1977, of the 1969 American Convention on Human Rights and in 1978, of the International Covenant on Civil and Political Rights; treaties that regulated the specific need for a simple and speedy judicial mean for the protection of human rights. Consequently, contrary to

---

87 See Allan R. BREWER–CARÍAS, *Instituciones Políticas y Constitucionales*, Tomo V, *Derecho y Acción de Amparo*, Universidad Católica del Táchira, Editorial Jurídica Venezolana, Caracas, 1998, pp. 111 ff.

88 See in *Gaceta Forense*, N° 70, Caracas, 1970, pp. 179 y ss; and in Allan R. BREWER–CARÍAS, "La reciente evolución jurisprudencial en relación a la admisibilidad del recurso de amparo", in *Revista de Derecho Público,* N° 19, Editorial Jurídica Venezolana, Caracas, 1984, pp. 207 ff.

the Supreme Court initial interpretation –which at the time had no *stare decisis* effects– the lower courts began in 1982 to accept amparo suits, funding directly their rulings in the American Convention[89]; situation that finally lead the Supreme Court to change its criteria by applying the open clause on human rights inherent to persons, and particularly the provision that states that the absence of a regulatory statute regarding human rights cannot affect the exercise of the rights declared in the Constitution. In a decision of October 20, 1983 the Supreme Court thus admitted the possibility of the filling of the constitutional protective amparo action regarding any constitutional right. Notwithstanding the Court said in its ruling that:

> "By admitting the possibility of the exercise of the amparo recourse, the Court must draw the attention of the lower courts, to be prudent and rational when using the powers granted in the Constitution (for the immediate constitutional protection of human rights), in order to fill the gap produced by the absence of the regulatory statute"[90].

The Organic Amparo statute for the protection of constitutional rights and guarantees was finally sanctioned in 1988[91], giving way to the massive use of this judicial mean for protection of human rights, particularly because of the unsuitability of the common judicial mean for that purpose. Nonetheless, it was by mean of the application of the open clause regarding human rights that the amparo suit was previously accepted.

3. The principle of progressive interpretation of constitutional rights

Finally, mention must be made to the principle of progressive interpretation of human rights, which implies that as a matter of principle, no interpretation of statutes related to human rights can be admitted if the result is the diminishing of the effective enjoyment, exercise or guarantee of constitutional rights; and also that in case involving various provisions, the one that should prevail is the one that contains the more favorable regulation[92]. As stated by the former Supreme Court of Justice of Venezuela, the principle of progressiveness in human rights implies the need to preferably apply the most favorable provision to human rights, whether of constitutional law, international law or ordinary law"[93]. Consequently, the interpretation of statutes must always be guided by the principle of progressiveness, in the sense that it must always result in more protection regarding rights.

---

89 See the references in A. R. BREWER–CARÍAS, "La reciente evolución jurisprudencial en relación con la admisibilidad del recurso de amparo", *Revista de Derecho Público*, N° 19, Editorial Jurídica Venezolana, Caracas, 1984, pp. 211 ff.

90 See in *Revista de Derecho Público*, N° 11, Editorial Jurídica Venezolana, Caracas, 1983, pp. 167–170.

91 *Gaceta Oficial* N° 33.891 de 22–01–1988. See Allan R. BREWER–CARÍAS y Carlos AYALA CORAO, *Ley Orgánica de Amparo sobre derechos y garantías constitucionales*, Caracas, 1988.

92 See in general, Pedro NIKKEN, *La protección internacional de los derechos humanos. Su desarrollo progresivo*, Instituto Interamericano de Derechos Humanos, Ed. Civitas, Madrid, 1987.

93 Decision of July, 30, 1996, in *Revista de Derecho Público*, N° 67–68, Editorial Jurídica Venezolana, Caracas, 1996, p. 170.

The principle of progressiveness is expressly regulated, for example, in the 1999 Constitution of Venezuela, where Article 19 provides that the enjoyment and exercise of human rights shall be guaranteed to everybody by the State, "... pursuant to the principle of progressiveness and without any discrimination."

Other Constitutions also expressly establish it as a principle of interpretation, as may be seen in Article 18 of the Ecuadorian Constitution which provides that "... in matters of constitutional rights and guarantees, the interpretation that most favors its effective enforcement shall be the one upheld."

This principle of the progressive interpretation of human rights regulations is equivalent to the *pro homines* principle of interpretation, which has been defined as "the hermeneutical criteria that conditions all the human rights law, according to which the widest and most protective provision must be applied in the sense that one must always prefer the provision that is in favor of man (*pro homine*)"[94]. The principle has been incorporated in the Ecuadorian Constitution when specifying the method of interpretation that must be applied in matters of rights and guaranties established in the Constitution, in the sense that the interpretation must be done in the way "that most favors its effective enforcement" (article 18)[95]. It also has been deducted as incorporated in other Constitutions, as is the case of Chile and Peru, when they provide as one of the essential purposes of the State the protection of human rights. It was the case of the 1993 Peruvian Constitution which stated that "the defense of human beings and the respect of their dignity are society and State goal" (Article 1); and is the case of the Chilean Constitution when it provides that it is "the duty of the State to respect and promote human rights guaranteed in the Constitution, as well as in the international treaties in force ratified by Chile" (art. 5)[96]. In Peru, the Constitutional Tribunal, when choosing the most favorable interpretation for the protection of human rights, has defined "the *pro homine* principle as the one according to which a rule referred to human rights must be interpreted 'in the most favorable way for the person, that is, for the beneficiary of the interpretation' "[97]

94 See Mónica PINTO, "El principio *pro homine*. Criterio hermenéutico y pautas para la regulación de los derechos humanos", in *La aplicación de los tratados sobre derechos Humanos por los tribunales locales*, Centro de Estudios Legales y Sociales, Buenos Aires, 1997, p. 163. Also see, Humberto HENDERSON, "Los tratados internacionales de derechos humanos en el orden interno: la importancia del principio *pro homine*", in *Revista IIDH, Instituto Interamericano de Derechos Humanos*, N° 39, San José, 2004, p. 92.

95 See Hernán SALGADO PESANTES, *Manual de Justicia Constitucional Ecuatoriana*, Corporación Editora Nacional, Quito, 2004, p. 92.

96 See Iván BAZÁN CHACÓN, "Aplicación del derecho internacional en la judicialización de violaciones de derechos humanos" in *Para hacer justicia. Reflexiones en torno a la judicialización de casos de violaciones de derechos humanos*, Coordinadora Nacional de Derechos Humanos, Lima, 2004, p.27; Humberto HENDERSON, "Los tratados internacionales de derechos humanos en el orden interno: la importancia del principio *pro homine*", en *Revista IIDH, Instituto Interamericano de Derechos Humanos*, N° 39, San José, 2004, p.89, nota 27.

97 See decisión 1049–2003–AA/TC of January 30, 2004 in Alfonso GAIRAUD BRENES, "Los Mecanismos de interpretación de los derechos humanos: especial referencia a la jurisprudencia peruana" en José F. PALOMINO MANCHEGO, *El derecho procesal constitucional peruano.*

As it has been indicated by Henderson, the *pro homine* principle has various application forms: first, when various provisions on human rights can be applied in the case, the one to be chosen is the one with the best and must favorable provisions regarding the individual; second, in cases rulings succession, it must be understood that the last provision does not repeal the previous one if this has better and more favorable provisions which must be preserved; and third, when it is a matter of application of just one legal provision on human rights, the same must be interpreted in the way resulting more favorable to the protection of the person[98].

In a certain way this *pro homine* interpretation was the one that guided *Chief Justice Warren* of the United States Supreme Court in its 1954 opinion in *Brown vs Board of Education of Topeka, Kansas*, 347 U.S. 483 (1954). in which, when referring to the XIV Amendment, he said that:

> In approaching this problem, we cannot turn the clock back to 1868 when the Amendment was adopted, or even to 1896 when *Plessy v. Fersugon* was written. We must consider public education in the light of its full development and its present place in American life throughout the Nation. Only in this way can it be determined if segregation in public schools deprives these plaintiffs of the equal protection of the laws.

From this, he concluded saying:

> We conclude that in the field of public education the doctrine of "separate but equal" has no place. Separate educational facilities are inherently unequal. Therefore, we hold that the plaintiffs and others similarly situated for whom the actions have been brought are, by reason of the segregation complained of, deprived of the equal protection of the laws guaranteed by the Fourteenth Amendment. This disposition makes unnecessary any discussion whether such segregation also violates the Due Process Clause of the Fourteenth Amendment".

This principle of progressivism, regarding the interpretation of constitutional rights, has also been incorporated in the American Convention on Human Rights in which Article 29 provides the following rules regarding "restrictions regarding interpretation", in the sense that "no provision of this Convention shall be interpreted as":

a. permitting any State Party, group, or person to suppress the enjoyment or exercise of the rights and freedoms recognized in this Convention or to restrict them to a greater extent than is provided for herein;
b. restricting the enjoyment or exercise of any right or freedom recognized by virtue of the laws of any State Party or by virtue of another convention to which one of the said states is a party;
c. precluding other rights or guarantees that are inherent in the human personality or derived from representative democracy as a form of government; or
d. excluding or limiting the effect that the American Declaration of the Rights and Duties of Man and other international acts of the same nature may have.

Estudios en Homenaje a Domingo García Belaunde, Editorial Jurídica Grijley, Lima, 2005, Tomo I, p. 138.

98 See Humberto HENDERSON, "Los tratados internacionales de derechos humanos en el orden interno: la importancia del principio *pro homine*", in *Revista IIDH, Instituto Interamericano de Derechos Humanos*, no. 39, San José, 2004, pp. 92–96.

Regarding the specific principle of progressiveness set forth in the Venezuelan Constitution, it also has implied that if a constitutional right is regulated with different contexts in the Constitution and in international treaties, then the most favorable provision must prevail and be applicable to the interested party.

In an "amparo" decision issued by the former Supreme Court of Justice on December 3, 1990, the Court applied the principle regarding the rights of a pregnant public official not to be unjustifiably dismissed of her job during pregnancy. At that time, the Organic Statute on Labor did not regulate such right, and it was only set forth in the Covenant N° 103 of the Labor International Organization and in the Convention eliminating all forms of discrimination against women. Regarding the constitutional provisions, Article 74 only provided for the general right to maternity protection. Notwithstanding the Supreme Court in the concrete case, after analyzing the protection asked by the employee whose dismissal impede her to enjoy the pre and post natal rest, admitted the "amparo" and declared the requested protection. In its decision, the Supreme Court ruled as followed:

> "The right not to be dismissed when pregnancy and the right to enjoy a pre and post natal rest are rights inherent to human beings that are constitutionalized due to Article 50 of the Constitution which stated that "the enunciation of rights and guarantees contained in the Constitution must not be understood to deny others not expressly within regulated. The lack of regulatory statute regarding such rights does not impede its exercise…".
>
> Consequently, from all these supranational regulations and particularly due to the protection set forth in article 74 of the Constitution, which guaranties the protection of maternity and of the pregnant women, such protection being materialized through the right of the pregnant working women not to be dismissed and the right to enjoy the pre and post natal rest…
>
> Based in such clear and conclusive dispositions, this Court considers that any attempt from the employer to diminish the right of the pregnant women not to be dismissed without justification or disciplinary reasons, and the consequent effect of denying the right to pre and post natal rest, constitute an evident and flagrant violation of the constitutional principle set forth in Articles 74 and 93 of the Constitution…"[99]

CHAPTER III.
THE JUDICIAL MEANS FOR THE PROTECTION OF HUMAN RIGHTS

I. THE CONSTITUTIONAL GUARANTEES TO THE DECLARATIONS OF RIGHTS

Constitutional declarations of rights, in the Constitutions or in international treaties and covenants, would be of no use at all, unless supported by a set of constitutional guarantees of the exercise of such rights.

---

99 See in *Revista de Derecho Público*, N° 45, Editorial Jurídica Venezolana, Caracas, 1991, pp. 84–85. See the references in decisión sentenciaos July 30, 1996 in *Revista de Derecho Público,* N° 97–98, Editorial Jurídica Venezolana, Caracas, 1996, p. 170.

The first of all constitutional guaranties is the guaranty of the supremacy of the Constitution and of entrenched declarations of human rights therein contained; the second is the judicial guaranty, that is to say, the set of judicial means established in benefit of persons in order to assure the effective exercise of such rights, and the effective protection of them.

In other words, the insertion of Declarations of rights in the Constitutions would be of no use to the citizen unless there is a fundamental right that establishes their supremacy, which can be enforced in court.

In fact, the idea of Rule of Law is indissolubly bound to the idea of the Constitution as an essential and supreme rule, which shall prevail over any state rule or action. This was the great and principal contribution of the American Revolution to modern constitutionalism, and its progressive development has provided the basis for the constitutional systems of justice in the modern world, particularly those aimed at protecting and defending the rights and freedoms enshrined in the Constitutions.

It can be said that this idea of constitutional supremacy, that is, of the Constitution as a fundamental and supreme law, was first developed in America in 1788 by Alexander Hamilton in *The Federalist*[100] when referring to the role of judges as interpreters of the law, stating:

> "A constitution is, in fact, and must be regarded by the judges, as a fundamental law. It therefore, belongs to them to ascertain its meaning, as well as the meaning of any particular act proceeding from the legislative body. If there should happen to be an irreconcilable variance between the two, that which has the superior obligation and validity ought, of course, to be preferred; or, in other words, the constitution ought to be preferred to the Statute, the intention of the people to the intention of their agents".

He added in response to the assertion that "the rights of the courts to pronounce legislative acts void, because contrary to the constitution" would "imply a superiority of the judiciary to the legislative powers", the following:

> "Nor does this conclusion –that the Courts must prefer the constitution over statutes– by any means supposes a superiority of the judicial to the legislative body. It only supposes that the power of the people is superior to both; and that where the will of the legislature, declared in its Statutes stands in opposition to that of the people declared in the constitution, the judges ought to be governed by the latter rather than the former. They ought to regulate their decisions by the fundamental laws, rather than by those which are not fundamental".

Thus, his conclusive assertion that:

> "No legislative act, therefore, contrary to the constitution, can be valid. To deny this, would be to affirm, that the deputy is greater than his principal; that the servant is above his master; that the representative of the people are superior to the peoples themselves; that men acting by virtue of powers, may do not only what their powers do not authorize, but what they forbid'.

Thus, in *The Federalist*, Hamilton not only developed the doctrine of the supremacy of the constitution, but most importantly the doctrine of "the judges as

100 *The Federalist* (edited by B.F. Wright), Cambridge, Mass. 1961, pp. 491–493.

guardians of the constitution", as the title of letter N° 78 reads, where Hamilton said, considering the constitution as a limit to state powers and particularly to the Legislative authority, that,

> "Limitations of this kind can be preserved in practice no other way than through the medium of courts of justice, whose duty it must be, to declare all acts contrary to the manifest tenor of the constitution, void. Without this, all the reservations of particular rights or privileges would amount to nothing".[101]

But among Hamilton's proposals, I would like to place more emphasis on the idea itself that since the Constitution is the expression of the will of the people, the principal constitutional right the people can have, is the right to that supremacy, that is to say, the right to the respect for and preservation of their own will as expressed in the Constitution. The consequence of this principle is the other derived and fundamental principle, that the Judiciary shall have the power to declare null and void any state or federal law that is contrary to the Constitution[102]. It is clear, that nothing would be gained by stating that the Constitution, being the expression of the will of the people, shall prevail over that of the State entities and over individual actions, if the people do not have the right to demand the respect of the Constitution.

For this precise reason, one of the most recent Latin American Constitutions, that of Colombia (1991), expressly enshrines the principle of constitutional supremacy as follows:

> "**Article 4**. The Constitution is the rule of rules. Whenever a case of incompatibility between the Constitution and a statute or another legal norms, arises the constitutional provisions shall be applied ..."

The 1999 Constitution of Venezuela similarly establishes that: "... the Constitution is the supreme rule and basis of the legal system" (Article 7) and that "in case of incompatibility between this constitution and a statute or other legal norm, the constitutional provisions shall be applied, being the courts empowered to decide, even ex officio" (Article 334).

In both countries this implies that the custody of the basic constitutional right of the citizen to the protection of such supremacy, is assured by means of: first, the judicial review powers regarding statutes attributed to all court and judges (Article 4, Colombia; Article 334, Venezuela); second, the popular action that can be brought before the Constitutional Court (Colombia, Article 214) or Constitutional Chamber of the Supreme Tribunal (Venezuela, Article 336) in order to seek the concentrated judicial review of constitutionality of statutes; third, by means of the exercise of specific actions for protection of constitutional rights, as is the case of the actions of *habeas corpus*, of "amparo" or of habeas data (Articles 30 and 86, Colombia; Article 27, Venezuela).

---

101 *The Federalist* (ed. by B.F. Wright), Cambridge, Mass 1961, p. 491 –493.

102 See referentes to the cases *Vanhorne's Lessee v. Dorrance, 1776* and *Masbury v. Madison,* 1803 in Allan R. BREWER–CARÍAS in *Judicial Review in Comparative Law,* Cambridge University Press, Cambridge, 1989.

Therefore, modern constitutionalism is founded not only on the principle of constitutional supremacy, but also on the principle that the *citizens have a constitutional right to such supremacy*, that in fact, pursuant to the principle of separation of powers, becomes *a fundamental right to the judicial protection of such constitutional supremacy*, both regarding the organic part of the Constitution (separation of powers, territorial distribution of powers), as well as regarding the dogmatic part of the Constitution (human rights), for the preservation of which a set of guarantees are established.

Among these guarantees it can be mentioned, the "objective guarantee" which declares that any acts contrary to the Constitution shall be considered null and void. The principle, explained in the twenties by Hans Kelsen[103], has been incorporated in the Latin American Constitutions since the beginning of the XIX Century, as occurred with the Venezuelan Constitution of 1811.

This principle implies that any State body decision that is contrary to the fundamental rights established in the Constitution is null and void, as has been set fourth in the 1999 Venezuelan Constitution:

> "**Article 25**: Any State authority act that violates or lessens the rights guaranteed in this Constitution and the law, is null; and the public officials which orders or execute them shall be criminally, civil and administratively liable, without any possible excuses based on superior orders".

In the particular case of Peru, Article 31 lists the right of citizens to participate in public affairs through: a referendum; legislative initiative; removal or revocation of authorities and the demand for accounting; the right to be elected and freely choose their representatives; the right of the local population to participate in the municipal government of its jurisdiction; and the right to vote; adding that "any act that forbids or limits the citizen's exercise of his or her rights is null and punishable."

Other constitutional guaranty of the declarations of human rights, perhaps the most important, is the legislative privilege to set fourth restrictions or limitations to constitutional rights, which can only by established by statutes, that is to say, by the laws passed by the legislative body and not by executive regulations.

There is also, of course, the guarantee of liability, or the guarantee that the public officials or individuals responsible for the injury or nuisance are legally obligated or accountable under civil, criminal and administrative law.

Apart from all the above–mentioned guarantees, the other basic guarantee of constitutional rights is of course, precisely, the possibility of bringing claims before the courts in order to assure that such rights are protected, preventing its violation or restoring the aggrieved party in its exercise. Hence, the fundamental guarantee of constitutional rights is definitely the judicial guarantee.

---

103 See Hans KELSEN: «La garantie jurisdictionnelle de la Constitution (La justice constitutionnelle)», *Revue du droit public et de la science politique en France et à l'étranger*, Paris, 1928, p. 250.

II. THE JUDICIAL GUARANTEE OF CONSTITUTIONAL RIGHTS

1. The right to have access to justice and the protection of rights

In any country subjected to the rule of law, the judicial branch of government is established not only to guarantee the enforcement of the law, but in particular, to hear and decide cases or questions of rights affecting personal and proprietary interests, making the necessary binding judgments on them. Of course, among those rights to be protected and enforced by the Judiciary, are the constitutional rights.

In effect, in all constitutional judicial systems, the most classical of citizens' rights is to have access to justice. This is the right to obtain judicial protection and enforcement of one's rights and interests. This is the essential reason for the organization of the Judiciary, to assure the judicial guarantee of personal and proprietary rights.

However, the Judiciary not always accomplishes its fundamental duty, as has occurred in Latin America, where in spite of the constitutional declarations, many countries still are facing a rather dismal situation regarding the effectiveness of the Judiciary as a whole, as an efficient and just protector of fundamental rights.

In Venezuela, for example, the 1999 Constitution declares that the State is a "... democratic and social State of law *and justice*," emphasizing justice as being among the uppermost values of the legal system and of the State's actions (Article 2). To this end, it is expressly stated that "... the State shall guarantee free, accessible, impartial, ideal, transparent, autonomous, independent, liable, fair and timely justice, without undue delay, and without senseless formalities or reversals" (Article 26).

It is really very difficult to find in any Constitutions in the contemporary world, similar sort of magnificent declarations about justice and the Judiciary, to which, the Supreme Tribunal of Venezuela, has referred to very eloquently, by stating:

> Consequently, when the Constitution qualified the State as a State of law and justice and set fourth Justice and preeminence of fundamental rights as a superior value of the legal order, it is only stressing that all public entities –and specially the Judiciary– must inexorably privilege a notion of justice above formalities and technicalities that belongs to a formal legality which certainly has give way to a new State conception. And this notion of Justice has a special meaning in the fertile field of the judicial proceeding in which the right to self defense and the due process of law rights (article 49), the search for the truth as an consubstantial element of justice, in which the former must not be scarified due to the omission of non essential formalities (article 257); bearing in mind that access to justice is set forth in order to allow citizens to ask for the enforcement of their rights and could obtain their effective and expedite judicial protection, without undue delays and without useless formalities and procedural reviews (article 26); all of which conform a Cosmo vision of a Lawful State, of the parties as element of democracy, and of the inescapable duty of the Judiciary and judges to maintain processes and judgments within the constitutional values and principles[104].

---

104 See decision N° 949 Politico Administrative Chamber of the Suporeme Court of Justice (SPA–CSJ) of April 26, 2000, in *Revista de Derecho Público*, N° 82, (abril–junio), Editorial Jurídica Venezolana, Caracas, 2000, pp. 163 ff.

But in spite of these marvelous declarations, in order to achieve these aims of the State of Justice, the most elemental institutional condition needed, in any Country, is the existence of really autonomous and independent judges, empowered to interpret and apply the law, achieving justice in an impartial way; and that can effectively protect citizens, particularly when referring to the enforcement of rights against State actions.

For that purpose, an effective Judiciary has to be built upon the principle of separation of powers. On the contrary, if the Government controls the courts and judges, no effective guarantee exists regarding constitutional rights, particularly when the offender party is a governmental agency. In this case, and in spite of all constitutional declarations, it is impossible to speak of rule of law.

The braking news in the December 28, 2005 edition of *The New York Times* (front page left), was the title: "When Chinese Sue the State, cases are Often Smothered"; referring to the fact that if it is true that "the number of people wanting to sue the government is large and growing", the truth is that " the number of people who succeed in filing cases against the government is minuscule", concluding by stating that: "So you could say there is a gap between theory and practice". The article referred to the impossibility for peasants to even file complaints seeking compensation for the take over of farmed land converted for the construction of roads and commercial, noting that "the case would not even be registered and there would be no rejection notice, either", and adding: "They met Kafkaesque obstacles at every turn. The only party that used the courts successfully was the state–linked construction company. It won an injunction in March declaring peasants' protest illegal"; judicial decision that –in this case–, was massively published in the village and even "the party boss read the text of the decision over the village's loudspeakers". The "villagers said –points out the article– that they were outraged that the court acted so quickly after suppressing their own suit" adding that they "discovered that the law is what they say", "What they practice is power"[105]

This reportage sounds familiar when authoritarian governments take control of States, as has so frequently happened in Latin American history, and for instance, as it has been occurring since 1999 in Venezuela. There, the "gap between theory and practice" is abysmal; the "State of Justice" being in the hands of a government controlled Judiciary. Just one example can enlighten the situation:

Since 1976, and for 25 years, Special Courts for judicial review of administrative action, acting within a democratic regime, developed a very important jurisdiction in order to control the legality of Public Administration activities.

In July 17, the Venezuelan Federation of Doctors or Physicians, brought before the Judicial Review of Administrative Actions First Court in Caracas, a nullity claim against the Mayor of Caracas and the Ministry of Health act taken in conjunction with the Caracas metropolitan College of Doctors, by which these bodies, regulated the hiring of Cuban doctors for a health program called "*Barrio Adentro*" (Inside the Slums); which the Federation of doctors considered discriminatory against the rights

105 Article by Joseph Kahn, *The New York Times*, December 28, 2005, pp. A1 and A10.

of Venezuelan doctors to exercise medicine, allowing foreign doctors to exercise the profession without complying with the Medicine Profession Statute regulations for the exercise of such profession. So the Federation also filed an "amparo" action seeking the collective protection of the Venezuelan doctor's constitutional rights"[106].

In August 21, 2003, the Court issued a preliminary injunction considering that there were sufficient elements to consider the equality before the law right violated. The Court ordered the suspension of the Cuban doctor's hiring and ordered the Collage of Doctors to substitute the Cuban doctors already hired by Venezuelan or foreign doctors who had fulfilled the Statute regulations in order to exercise the medical profession.

The preliminary injunction could not be executed; was rejected and ignored by the Ministry of Health and by the Mayor, and even the President of the Republic in his weekly TV program said that the judicial decision would not be executed[107]. In the mean time, the offender parties, on September 5th, 2003 also brought an "amparo" action before the Constitutional Chamber of the Supreme Tribunal, demanding the Supreme Court to take over the case; which decided on September 25, 2003, based on jurisdictional arguments. The result was the Supreme Tribunal, assuming the case, annulling the lower Court decision and intervening its attributions to ensure the non execution of the preliminary injunctions initially issued. Three years latter, no other decision was taken on the case.

But in the meantime, other governmental decisions were taken: days after the Supreme Tribunal's decision, in September 2005, Secret Service officials seized the lower Court, after detaining a clerk on futile motives; the President of the Republic publicly called the President of the lower Court a bandit[108]"; and a few weeks later, the Special Commission of intervention of the Judiciary, dismissed all the five judges of the Lower Fist Court, basing its decision in a supposedly "inexcusable error" they had incurred in when deciding a case in 2002[109]. The decision was protected by the Bar Associations of all States[110] and also by the International Jurist Commission[111]; but in fact the lower First Court remained suspended and closed[112] for more

106 See Claudia NIKKEN, "El caso "Barrio Adentro": La Corte Primera de lo Contencioso Administrativo ante la Sala Constitucional del Tribunal Supremo de Justicia o el avocamiento como medio de amparo de derechos e intereses colectivos y difusos" in *Revista de Derecho Público*, N° 93–96, Editorial Jurídica Venezolana, Caracas, 2003, pp. 5 y ss.

107 "*Váyanse con su decisión no sé para donde, la cumplirán ustedes en su casa si quieren...*" (You can go with your decision, I don't know where; you Hill enforced in your house, if you want...) Talk in the TV programme *Aló Presidente*, N° 161, August 24, 2004

108 Public declaration, September 20, 2004.

109 See the information in *El Nacional*, Caracas, November 5, 2004, p. A2. In the same page, the dismissed President of the First Court said: "La justicia venezolana vive un momento tenebroso, pues el tribunal que constituye un último resquicio de esperanza ha sido clausurado" (Venezuenal Judiciary lives a tenebrous moment, due to the Fac. that the last resort of espoir Court has been shout down").

110 See the Communiqué of the Asociación Venezolana de Derecho Administrativo, in *El Nacional*, Caracas, October 12, 2003, A–5.

111 See in *El Nacional,* Caracas, November 18,–2004, p. A–6.

than ten months[113], during which no judicial review of administrative action could be sought. This was the governmental response to a judicial decision which affected a very sensitive governmental populist program; response which was expressed trough the government controlled Judiciary administration[114]. It must be borne in mind that the same Commission for the intervention of the Judiciary, has dismissed without due process almost all judges. As a result of these massive dismissals the Judiciary ended up being composed by the end of 2005 by more that 90% of provisionally appointed judges, thus dependent of the ruling power[115].

One of the main political critics to the party–democratic system that functioned in Venezuela from 1961 up to 1998, was the exclusively political appointment process of the Supreme Court Justices by the National Congress. That is why in the 1999 Constitution a parliamentary proceeding was set forth, in order to limit the discretionary power of the National Assembly, assigning to a Proposing Committee integrated exclusively by representatives of civic society, the task to choose and postulate before the Assembly the candidates to be appointed Justices. Unfortunately, the Statute sanctioned for that purpose turned the independent Committee into traditional parliamentary commission, politically controlled, which was challenged by the Peoples Defender before the Constitutional Chamber on grounds of unconstitutionality, but the suit was never decided. Additionally, in the case, the Constitutional Chamber resolved that the Constitution did not apply for the appointment of the same Justices by ratification.

Thus, since 2000, the result has been a more partisan governmental controlled Supreme Tribunal, with the aggravating circumstance of the power the Constitution vested in the National Assembly to dismiss the Supreme Tribunal Justices by vote of two thirds of its members, which the Statute concerning the Tribunal has unconstitutionally modified, adding a procedure for "the annulment of the appointment act" just by the absolute majority voting, which was used in 2004[116].

Thus, with Justices of the Supreme Tribunal politically appointed and politically dismissible, the independence and autonomy of the Judiciary in Venezuela is simply an illusion; and without such independence and autonomy, it is difficult to think on effective guarantees of constitutional rights.

Unfortunately, after more than 40 years of democratic ruling the time has come for Venezuela to have an authoritarian regime, showing that the historical pendulum movement between democracy and authoritarian regimes continues to be a general pattern in Latin America constitutional history, as has occurred in other countries and in other times.

---

112 See in *El Nacional*, Caracas, October 24, 2003, p. A–2.

113 See in en *El Nacional*, Caracas, July 16,2004, p. A–6.

114 See Allan R. Brewer–Carías, "La progresiva y sistemática demolición institucional de la autonomía e independencia del Poder Judicial en Venezuela 1999–2004", in *XXX Jornadas J.M Dominguez Escovar, Estado de derecho, Administración de justicia y derechos humanos*, Instituto de Estudios Jurídicos del Estado Lara, Barquisimeto, 2005, pp.33–174.

115 *Idem*.

116 *Idem*.

Anyway, the lesson to be learned is that judicial guarantee of constitutional rights requires an independent and autonomous Judiciary, conducted out of reach of the government.

Other question is that even in democratic regimes; some times the Judiciary appears to be incapable of guaranteeing the effective resolution of disputes, thus respecting individual rights and protecting constitutional rights. Justice has not always been swift and efficient; on the contrary, it has proved to be slow; and slowness in judicial matters leads to the opposite, that is, injustice.

Thus the first and main problem of the Rule of Law in Latin America, even in democratic regimes, is the functioning of the judicial systems; which has provoked that almost all Latin American countries have taken on the challenge of restructuring the Judiciary, seeking to make it truly independent and giving truth to the provision of all the Constitutions. This is the cornerstone of the Rule of Law, in the sense that judges shall act only pursuant to the law, without being influenced by outside the law factors, whether they are exercised by other public bodies or by political pressures.

But beyond their substantive independence, Judge must also be personally independent to act, which has to do with their appointment stability. In this regard, again, for example, the Venezuelan 1999 Constitution has established, in general terms, the regime for entering the judicial career and promotion only "through public competition that assures suitability and excellence," guaranteeing "citizen's participation in the procedure of selection and appointment of the judges." The consequence is that they may not be removed or suspended from their positions except through a legal proceeding before a disciplinary jurisdiction (Article 255). This, again, unfortunately is just a theoretical aim, because all contests for judge's appointment have been suspended since 2002. Almost all judges are being provisionally appointed without citizen participation, and there is no disciplinary jurisdiction for their dismissal. Furthermore, the suspension and dismissal of all judges corresponds to a Commission for the intervention of the Judiciary that is not regulated in the Constitution[117]

On the other hand, and beyond achieving independence, the other challenge in all our countries, is to assure the effective administration of justice, that is to say, that the judicial cases be decided surpassing the trend of slow and unjust administration of justice. This is why reforms such as the ones being carried out in many countries on matters of procedure are so essential, since many of the procedures were conceived in other times and now only serve to delay, obstruct, slow down and, finally, not resolve cases.

These reforms had even led many countries to seek other mechanisms for solving disputes and conflicts, like conciliation and arbitration systems. The "privatization of justice" –as it has been called– has been developed in order to guarantee the individual's right to recur to means of arbitration or conciliation without having to resort to the ordinary courts of justice. This approach is not new at all: in the 1824 Stature

117 *Idem.*

of the Regime of Administration of Justice of the Republic of Colombia (Colombia, Venezuela and Ecuador) it was stated that all citizens had the constitutional and fundamental right to be able to resolve their conflicts by means of arbitration, and even established the obligation to attempt to resolve disputes through arbitration or conciliation, before resorting to an ordinary legal procedure. In this regard, the 1999 Constitution of Venezuela also states that the law "... shall promote arbitration, conciliation, mediation and any other alternative means to resolve dispute" (Article 258).

Finally, regarding the administration of justice, another aspect that has to be mentioned is the matter of access to justice, which is another of the major problems surrounding the constitutional protection of constitutional rights in Latin America. The access to justice and the right to have effective judicial protection are enshrined in the Constitutions, as can be found in the 1999 Constitution of Venezuela in which it is expressly provided that "Everybody shall have the right of access to the institutions of administration of justice to assert their rights and interests, including collective and diffuse rights and interests; the right to the effective protection of such rights, and the right to obtain a prompt corresponding decision" (Article 26). For that purpose, adds the Constitution, that "the procedure is a fundamental instrument in achieving justice", and therefore "procedural laws shall establish the simplification, uniformity and effectiveness of the proceedings and shall adopt a brief, oral and public procedure" in order to ensure that "justice not be sacrificed because of the omission of non essential formalities" (Article 257).

The formula provided in Spain's 1978 Constitution is far more precise:

> **Article 24.1**. All persons have the right to obtain effective protection from the judges and the courts in the exercise of their rights and legitimate interests, and in no case may there be a lack of defense.

However, even when not expressly enshrined in the constitutional texts, this right to have access to justice for the protection of people's rights and interests – including the constitutional rights – is an essential element of all contemporary constitutional systems, and in many cases it is what guarantees the right to protection ("amparo") of constitutional rights and freedoms even when the legal system has not established specific procedural means or special courts that are designed to guarantee such protection.

Nonetheless, in practice, access to justice has not always been guaranteed to everybody, and huge portions of the population simply know nothing about judicial protection mechanisms, since they have no possibility of accessing to justice to resolve disputes because of the costs and complications involved. Moreover, the Latin American State has not been able to establish the appropriate legal assistance mechanisms that for decades have been recognized and have been developed in European countries, as judicial assistance, but which we have been unable to be established in our countries to offer everyone the possibility of access to the judicial institutions.

In any case, the deterioration of the Judiciary in our countries is not a recent event, it has been occurring over several decades, with many generations involved. That is why the Judiciary reform program, while being one of the most important elements in achieving effective internal protection of constitutional rights, is something that has to be carried out over a lengthy period. The systematic change of the Judiciary and of the way justice is administered is not even a task of one generation, but rather of several generations, provided there is a consciousness of the need to establish such mechanisms and to initiate reform.

Any way, as I have noted, the Judiciary and the judicial system is established in any country in order to protect peoples' rights, and to resolve controversies between parties.

2. Judicial means for the protection of constitutional rights

Legal or constitutional rights are both to be protected and enforced by the courts by means of the judicial proceedings set forth for that purpose in procedural law, without being necessary or indispensable the establishment of specific judicial means only devoted to assure that protection. But of course, this is not excluded, and its existence depends on how the Judiciary accomplished its protective role regarding human rights.

That is why, in contemporary world, especially regarding constitutional rights and freedoms (those embodied in the constitutional Declarations of Rights), their judicial protection and guarantee can be achieved in two ways: first, by means of the general established (ordinary or extraordinary) suits, actions, recourses or writs set fourth in procedural law in order to have a right or duty judicially enforced; or second, in addition to the general means, by means of specific judicial suits, actions or recourses seeking remedies particularly established in order to protect and enforce constitutional rights and freedoms and to prevent and redress wrongs regarding those rights.

That is, the judicial guarantee of constitutional rights can be achieved through the general procedural regulations in order to enforce any kind of personal or proprietary rights and interest, as is the general trend in the United States and in Europe. It can also be achieved by means of specific judicial proceeding established only and particularly for the protection of the rights declared in the Constitution, being the latter the general trend in Latin America, mainly because the general judicial means have been insufficient for granting effective protection to the latter.

Our purpose in this Course of Lectures is to analyze this specific judicial means for protection of human rights in Latin America, generally called the "amparo" suit, action or recourse, but bearing in mind that such protection can also be achieved by the general judicial means, including the procedures set forth in case of urgency. This is the situation in Europe and in the United States, to which I want to refer first.

3. The United States judicial means for the protection of rights (including constitutional rights)

In the United States, following the British procedural law tradition, the protection of human rights, civil rights or constitutional rights (those embodied in the Bill of Eights), has always been achieved through the general ordinary or extraordinary judicial means, and particularly, be means of the remedies established in Law or in Equity.

This distinction between Law and Equity in order to construct two judicial system of courts, traditionally inherent to the Anglo–American legal system, has also penetrated the civil law countries, where the judges can also decide cases based on "*equidad*", term also used in procedural law. For example, in the Venezuelan Civil Code, article 12 impose the judges the duty to decide cases in conformity with the rules of law (*normas de derecho*), unless a statute authorize them to decide accordingly to "*equidad*"; and article 13 the indicates that the courts will decide the merits of the case based on to "*equidad*" only when asked to do so by the agreed consent of the parties and the rights involved in the controversy are rights that can be renounced or transferred, such as property rights. Only regarding arbitration the Code distinguishes between "law arbiters" (*árbitros de derecho*) and arbitrators. The former must always decide according to the legal procedure and to the law; the latter will proceed with complete liberty, according to their most convenient view in the parties' interest, particularly according to "equidad" (article 618).

The Venezuelan Constitution, when referring to the State as rule of law and Justice, also uses the expression "*justicia equitativa*" (equitable justice), which has lead the Supreme Court to consider the possibility of the existence of two sorts of jurisdictions: law and equity jurisdiction, identifying within the latter, the "peace judges" (*jueces de paz*), which in the local neighborhoods must try to decide controversies by means of conciliation and when resulting impossible, according to equity except when a law solution is imposed by a statute (art. 3, Peace Justice Statute). Peace judges must also decide according to equity when expressly asked by the parties. Regarding this concept of "*equidad*", the Constitutional Chamber of the Supreme Court has indicated that the concept:

> Of difficult comprehension, refers to a value judgment, related to the idea of justice when applied to a concrete case, view that is not based on the law, but in the conscience, the moral, the natural reason and other values. Due to the personal and subjective character of these values, the treatment of decisions based upon them ought to be different to the decisions issued based on legal norms" [118].

But with exceptions (such as the "peace judges" jurisdictions), in general, it can be said that in civil law countries the law jurisdiction prevails, and no general distinction can be found between law and equity courts. In the United Stated, on the contrary, it is fundamental to distinguish between trial or causes at law and actions in equity; as well as legal remedies as opposed to equitable ones. The latter being the ones in which the judicial resolution "does not come from established principles but simply derives from common sense and socially acceptable notions of fair play"[119].

Both are used for the protection of rights, to the point that the most common definition of remedy is "the means by which rights are enforced or the violation of

118 Decision N° 1139 of October, 10, 2000 (Amparo case: *Héctor L. Quiroga*), in *Revista de Derecho Público*, N° 84, Editorial Jurídica Venezolana, Caracas, 2000, p. 351.

119 See William TABB and Elaine W. SHOBEN, *Remedies*, Thomson West, 2005, p. 13.

rights is prevented, redressed or compensated"[120]. Of course they are not judicial means only conceived for the protection of constitutional rights, because remedies can and are also commonly used for the protections of rights based upon statutes and also derived from common law.

The most important procedural rule regarding remedies is that equitable remedies are always subordinated to the legal ones, in the sense that they proceed when the remedy at law is inadequate; in other words, the legal remedies are preferred in any individual case if they are adequate. As it was stated in *In re Debs case*, 158 U.S. 564, 15 S.Ct 900, 39 L Ed. 1092 (1895): "As a rule, injunctions are denied to those who have adequate remedy at law. Where the choice is between the ordinary and the extraordinary process of law, and the former are sufficient, the rule will not permit the use of the latter"[121]

The most common legal remedies are the damage remedies, the restitution remedies and the declaratory remedies.

The damage or compensatory remedies allow the injured party or the plaintiffs to seek compensation for losses sustained in violations of his rights. It is the main instrument to resolve disputes in contract law and regarding torts cases. These compensatory remedies find their equivalent in the actions for damages and prejudices in civil law countries.

On the other hand, restitution remedies are intended to restore property to its rightful owner or to obtain from the plaintiff any illegal profits or unjust enrichment he obtained as a consequence of the wrong made to the plaintiff property. The judicial ordinary writ or order commanding the offender party to do or to refrain from doing something that can be issued in these cases of restitution remedies, are the writ of detinue, issued to recover personal property; the writ of ejectment, for the recovery of land; the writ of entry, which allows a person wrongfully dispossessed of real property to enter and retake the property; and the writ of possession, issued to recover the possession of a land. In civil law countries, the equivalent remedies are the property restitution action ("*acción reivindicatoria*") or the action for enrichment without cause. It can also be identified as an equivalent the actions to restore possession of land or to prevent its invasions ("*interdictos*").

The declaratory remedies are intended to obtain from a court a declaration of the rights or legal relations between parties, being commonly used in cases or controversy, to determine the constitutionality of a statute. It is also used to construct a private instrument between parties so that the interested party may obtain a resolution of the dispute. The latter is equivalent to the declaratory actions on civil law countries, and the former, to the petition to declare in a case or controversy, the non applicability of a statute on the grounds of its unconstitutionality, requesting the prevalent application of the Constitution. .

The equitable remedies they are the coercive ones, particularly injunctions, by means of which a court of equity can decide that the plaintiff or aggrieved party is

---

120 See William TABB and Elaine W. SHOBEN, *Remedies*, Thomson West, 2005, p. 1.

121 See in Owen M. FISS, *Injunctions*, The Foundation Press, 1984, p. 8.

entitled to an extraordinary relief consisting of an order issued by a court commanding the defendant or the offender party to do something or not to do something, that is to say, to refrain from doing specific acts. They are called coercive remedies because they are backed by the contempt power, that is to say, the power of the court to directly sanction the disobedient defendant.

Particularly regarding the protection of civil or constitutional rights, in the United States the coercive remedies that has been used, as extraordinary ones, are the following: first, the writ of injunction, in its four types: preventive, structural, restorative and prophylactic; and second, the writ of habeas corpus.

In civil law countries, where "equitable" courts do not exist, the most common equivalent legal action to all these extraordinary coercive or equitable remedies or writs, are precisely the actions of "amparo" and of habeas corpus, for the protection of constitutional rights.

Regarding injunctions, and following what William M. Tabb and Elaine W. Shoben had explained[122], the four mentioned types of injunctions can be characterized as follows:

The preventive injunction, –preventive in the sense of avoiding harm– is a court order designed to avoid future harm to a party by prohibiting or mandating certain behavior by another party. In other words, to prevent the defendant from inflicting future injury to the plaintiff. These preventive injunctions can be mandatory, prohibitory or quia–timed injunctions.

The mandatory injunction consists in orders issued to the defendant to do an affirmative act or to mandates a specific course of conduct. Regarding the violations of rights made by public authorities, within the mandatory injunction it must be mentioned the writ of mandamus, issued by a court to compel a government officer to perform certain duties or to execute actions which is obliged to do.

Regarding the prohibitory injunction, they are the ones issued in order to forbid or restrain an act. Among these prohibitory remedies it can be also mentioned the writ of prohibition, when used as an instrument to correct judicial actions by preventing lower judicial courts from acting in certain way.

It can also be distinguished the quia–timet injunction, consisting of an order granted to prevent an action that has been threatened but has not yet violated the plaintiff rights. All these injunctions can be permanent injunctions that affect the legal relationship of the parties until subsequently modified or dissolved

All the above mentioned preventive injunctions, are "preventive" in the sense that they tend to avoid harm, and therefore are not equivalent to the preliminary injunctions. This is important to be stressed in order to avoid wrongs, particularly when comparing with the civil law countries institutions. In Spanish language, the expression "preventive measures" is used to identify what would be "preliminary or interlocutory injunctions" and not preventive injunctions. Thus, regarding the interlocutory injunctions (preliminary injunctions and temporary restraining orders), the

---

122 See William M. TABB and Elaine W. SHOBEN, *Remedies*, Thomson West, 2005, pp.86 ff.

general equivalent procedural decision in the civil law counties would be what has been called the "unlisted preventive measures" ("*medidas cautelares innominadas*") that can be issued in order to preserve the status quo or to restore the factual situation during the specific trial development.

On the other hand, the structural injunction, were developed by the courts after the *Brown v. Board of Education* case (347 U.S. 483 (1954); 349 U.S. 294 (1955), in which the court declared the dual school system discriminatory, using injunction as an instrument of reform, by means of which the courts in certain cases, have undertaken the supervision over institutional State policies and practices where constitutional exists in those institutions. As described by Owen S. Fiss:

> "Brown gave the injunction a special prominence. School desegregation became one of prime litigative chores of courts in the period of 1954–1955, and in these cases the typical remedy was the injunction. School desegregation not only gave the injunction a greater currency, it also presented the injunction with new challenges, in terms of both the enormity and the kinds of tasks it was assigned. The injunction was to be used to restructure the educational systems throughout the nation.
>
> The impact of Brown on our remedial jurisprudence –giving primacy to the injunction– was not confined to schools desegregation. It also extended to civil rights cases in general, and beyond civil rights to litigation involving electoral reappointments, mental hospitals, prisons, trade practices, and the environment. Having desegregated the schools of Alabama, it was only natural to Judge Johnson to try to reform the mental hospitals and then the prisons of the state in name of human rights –the right to treatment or to be free from cruel and unusual punishment– and to attempt this Herculean feat through injunction. And he was not alone. The same logic was manifest in actions of other judges, North and South"[123].

Thus, structural injunctions can be considered a modern constitutional law instrument specifically developed for the protection of human rights, particularly in State institutions; instrument that has been considered to " become an implicit part of the Constitutional guarantee of protecting individual rights from inappropriate government action"[124].

In the third place, the restorative injunctions must be mentioned, also called reparative injunctions, devoted to correct a past wrong situation. In these cases, the court order is devoted to require the defendant to restore the plaintiff to the position it occupied before the defendant committed the wrong. In order to protect a constitutional right, as for instance the right to be elected, the court order can also consist in the repetition of the election process itself.

Among these restorative remedies, it can also be mentioned the writ of error, consisting in an order for the revision by reasons of unconstitutionality, of a judicial decision of a lower court.

Finally, there are also the so called prophylactic injunctions, issued also to safeguard the plaintiff's rights, preventing future harm, by ordering certain behaviors

---

123 See Owen M. FISS, *The Civil Rights Injunctions*, Indiana University Press, 1978 pp. 4–5; and in Owen M. FISS and Doug RENDELMAN, *Injunctions*, The Foundation Press, 1984, pp. 33–34.

124 See William M. TABB and Eliane W. SHOBEN, *Remedies*, pp. 87–88.

from the defendant, other than the direct prohibition of future actions. These prophylactic injunctions refer to behavior indirectly related to the prohibited conduct, for instance devoted to ask the defendant to develop positive actions in order to minimize the risk of the repetition of the wrong in the future.

But other than by means of injunctions in order to protect freedom as a constitutional right particularly against government actions, the other extraordinary remedy in the United States –following the long British tradition–, is the writ of habeas corpus, the oldest judicial mean for the protections of life and personal integrity. It has also been employed to bring a person before a court in order to proof or certify that he is alive and in good health, or to determine that his imprisonment is not illegal. It has also been used to obtain review of the regularity of the extradition or the deportation process, of the right to bail or its amount.

In conclusion, as seen in the brief analysis of the remedies in United States law, the protection of constitutional rights is assured by these general (ordinary or extraordinary) judicial means known as remedies, particularly the injunctions and the writs, most of which can also be used to protect legal (non constitutional) rights. So the Constitution in the United States does not provide for a specific judicial means for the protection of human rights, contrary to what happens in Latin America.

4. The protection of human rights in France and Italy through the general judicial means

The situation in Europe, in general terms, with the exception of Germany and Spain –where the Constitutions provide an "amparo" recourse, is similar to the one of the United States: the protection of human rights is assured by general judicial means, and in particular by the extraordinary preliminary and urgent proceedings devoted to prevent an irreparable injury from occurring, issued before or during a trail and before the court has the chance to decide the case, but also with the particular procedural development that in many cases, they have become permanent orders.

This is the case in France with the institution known as the *référé,* the case or Italy with the extraordinary urgent measures and the case of Spain with the precautionary measures (*"medidas cautelares"*).

In France, the Civil Procedural Code sets forth the distinction between proceedings regarding the decision of the substance and proceedings refers to decisions that must be taken before setting on legal grounds (*"avant dire droit"*); these are the writs of *référé*, which are judicial decisions issued in case of urgency, after a party request in order that the court adopt the necessary measures to immediately protect a right.

There are to types of *référés*[125]: first, the provisional one consisting in orders issued to prevent imminent damages or to order the cessation of an evidently illicit action. They are devoted to protect rights in a preliminary and interlocutory way

125 See R. LINDON, "Le juge des référés et la presse", *Dalloz 1985*, Chroniques, 61. See the comments by Enrique PAILLAS, *El recurso de protección ante el derecho comparado,* Santiago de Chile, 1990, pp. 19–26.

pending the trial, that is, pending the judicial decision of the merits. The *référé* can be issued (art. 809 CPC). This *référés* are equivalent to the preliminary injunctions in the North American system, both designated to preserve the status quo in order to prevent irreparable damages before the court decides the substantive merits of the dispute[126].

Second, the other *référérs* are the ones issues in cases of urgency, based in the existence of an evidently illicit conduct that affects an unquestionable right, for its protection. The defendant, of course, must furnish the appropriate proof of the existence of the rights and of the manifest illegality of the defendant actions. These *référés* can also consist in conservatory or restitution measures to prevent imminent damages or to stop illicit actions, and also, orders issued to the plaintiff to accomplish particular duties if the obligations is proved. In this case, the principal procedural element is the need for the court to summon the defendant in order to hear his argument in an oral hearing (art. 811 CPC). These *référé* are equivalent to the preventive or structural injunctions in the North American system, in the sense that they are not only devoted to protect constitutional or human rights but any legal right, and because their permanent injunctions. In France they are qualified as "provisional" judicial decisions but only in the sense that they do not produce substantive *res judicata* effects, that is, a definitive judicial decision regarding the merits which could prevent the principal lawsuit that can be brought before the courts. On the contrary, as it happened with the "amparo" decisions in almost all Latin American countries, the *référé* only produces formal *res judicata* effects in the sense that no other *référé* can be issued in the same matter, and between the same parties.

Thus, in the latter case, the *référé* is a judicial decision that is taken independently of the resolution of the controversy on the merits in the principal lawsuit that eventually can be brought before the courts. Consequently, the principal consequence of this "provisional" character of the decision is that if there is no principal lawsuit regarding the substantive merits of the case brought before the courts, the *référé* decisions becomes permanent.

As mentioned, and as it happened in the United States, the *référés* in France are a general procedural mean to seek judicial protection of any rights, and not only constitutional or human rights; but regarding the latter, they have been used successfully to protect them.

For instance, it has been used in controversies between individuals, for the protection of the constitutional right to privacy, and particularly to the individual right to each one's owns image. In 1980, the *Reader's Digest* magazine published in the front cover of one of its issues, the photo of a doctor showing him practicing medicine, in circumstance regarding which he did not give the magazine any consent for the publication. Consequently, he asked the Court of Great Instance of Paris the due protection, which on November 1980 decided on *référé* as follows: The Court took into account that in the cover of the issue N° 405 of the magazine, Dr. Antoine Chapman's photography was published in support of an article referring to Hospital patients rights regarding the medical treatment they can receive; that the photog-

126 See William M. TABB and Eliane W. SHOBEN, *Remedies*, Thomson West, 2005, p. 4.

raphy of Dr. Chapman that was published has no relation to his work and life as a physician; and that according to deontological rules of the medical profession, physicians can avoid any kind of advertisement. Then the Court concluded considering that Dr. Chapman has an individual right to his own image, before his own patients and his colleagues, and that consequently, that the publication of his photo, without his consent, in the cover of a non professional magazine of great diffusion, and in a moment in which he was exercising his medical profession produced an evidently illicit overturn. The consequence was the judicial order directed to the magazine to publish in the following issue, a notice indicating that D. Chapman never gave his consent for the publication of his photograph in the previous issue[127].

In a similar case in 1981, a photo of a practicing lawyer was published in the weekly magazine *Le Nouvel Observateur*, showing her acting with her gown in courts; the photograph was published in order to support an article regarding the legal practice by women and also was published without her consent. In order to grant the *référé* protection, the same argument of absence of consent of the lawyer to publish her photo in a non professional magazine prevail, considering the courts also, in the case, that the deontological rules of the legal profession allow to avoid any kind of advertisement. The court also considerer the right of the lawyer to give of her self the image she wanted to her clients and colleagues. The publication of the photo was also considered an illicit overture of her rights that had to be stopped. Thus the judicial order directed to the weekly magazine to publish in the following issue, the notice that the defendant never gave authorization for the publication[128].

The *référé* protection to constitutional rights has also been used to protect rights against public official actions. For instance, regarding the constitutional right to free enterprise, a case was decided in 1983, as follows: In the town Saint Cry–sur–Mer, Mr. Decurgis was the owner of a bar located near a public square, having next to the bar, a stand in which he used to sell fruits and legumes to the passing people. The Mayor of the town ordered the closing of the square passage, impeding the customers to have access to Mr. Decurigs stand, who could then not sell his merchandise. He asked judicial protection via *référé*, not for his supposedly property rights which he did not have, but for his right to develop economic and commercial activities, which has not been forbidden by any formal administrative act. The Court considered the right to develop commercial and industrial activities, as a fundamental public freedom of persons which cannot be limited by the *de facto* activities (*voi de fait*), expressed without any previous formal administrative act issue as a consequence of an administrative procedure, which was non existent in the case. Consequently the *référé* decision ordered the mayor to restore the situation Mr. Decurigs had before the arbitrary municipal action was taken[129].

127 See the references in Enrique PAILLAS, *El recurso de protección ante el derecho comparado,* Santiago de Chile 1990, pp. 22–23.

128 See in Enrique PAILLAS, *El recurso de protección ante el derecho comparado,* Santiago de Chile 1990, pp 23–24.

129 See in Enrique PAILLAS, *El recurso de protección ante el derecho comparado,* Santiago de Chile 1990, p. 26.

The *référé* has also been used in France for the protection of property rights, regarding industrial factories against illegal occupation of its premises by the workers. In such cases, the Courts, even though recognizing the workers constitutional right to strike, in protection of the property rights of the owners of the factory and their rights to have access to their property, considered illegal the *de facto* occupation of the premises by the workers (*voi de fait illegal*), contrary to the owners rights, that prevented the continuation of work and impede the free entrance to the buildings. The ruling was an order directed to the workers to leave the premises, and if the order was not to be voluntarily carried out then it authorized the use of the police to do so.

In similar situations, injunction has been issued in the United States, even brought before the courts by the Attorney General asking for the protection of property rights of the United States regarding mail, and the protection of freedom of interstate commerce and of transportation of the mail, against striking workers members of the American Railway Union who in 1894 had sit in the railroad premises paralyzing the traffic in Chicago. Without challenging the workers right to quit work and without interfering with the organization of labor, the court considered that the strike interfered with the operation of trains carrying mail and with interstate commerce, and ordered the end of the sit in. In the well known *In Re Debs* case 158 U.S. 564, 15 S.ct. 900,39 L. Ed. 1092 (1895), the Supreme Court set forth the basic principles of injunctions, particularly regarding the power the courts have to punish the disobedience of its injunctive rulings by imposing fines and ordering imprisonment for contempt[130].

In Italy, the judicial mean equivalent to the French *référé* is the proceeding in case of urgency set forth in the Civil Procedural Code within the precautionary measures. According to article 700 of such Code those who have fundamental motives to fear that during the period in an ordinary process to enforce its rights, they can be threatened by an imminent and irreparable prejudice, may go before the court asking for the necessary urgent decisions that, according to the circumstances, could be suitable in order to provisionally assure the effects of the decision on the merits. Even though it is a precautionary power that can be used to protect any right, it has been used for the protection of constitutional rights such as the right to protection of health, environmental rights, rights to have a name and right to one owns' image[131]

Mention has also to be made to the same institution of the in nominate precautionary judicial power established in the Latin American Procedural Code, which have also been used for the protection of human rights when asked for in ordinary procedures. In this regard, for instance, the reform of the Civil Procedure Code sanctioned in the eighties set forth in Articles 585 and 588, that when there is an evident risk that the execution of the decision be illusory and provided there is accompanying evidence which constitutes a serious presumption of such circumstance and of

130 See Owen M. FISS and Doug RENDELMAN, *Injunctions,* The Foundation Press, Mineola New York 1984, p. 13.

131 See Enrique PAILLAS, *El recurso de protección ante el derecho comparado,* Santiago de Chile, 1990, p. 46.

the right claimed, the court may adopt the precautionary decisions it considers appropriate, when there exists a well–founded fear that one of the parties may cause to the rights of the other party serious or difficult to repair harms. In these cases, to avoid the damage, the court may authorize or prohibit the execution of determined acts, and adopt the decisions that are intended to stop the damage from continuing. With a provision of this nature, the ordinary judge has very broad powers when protecting constitutional rights.

But in fact, these in nominated precautionary judicial powers have only been set forth in recent times in the Latin American civil procedure codes. Thus, in absence of those emergency judicial powers, including the injunction powers attributed to ordinary judges, and because the inefficiency of the general available judicial means in order to obtain an effective and quick protection of constitutional rights, the general trend in almost all of Latin America since the XIX Century has been the progressive regulation of special judicial means exclusively set forth for the protection of constitutional rights, as is the institution named the suit, action or recourse of "amparo", protection or tutelage.

III. THE SPECIFIC JUDICIAL MEANS FOR THE PROTECTION OF HUMAN RIGHTS

1. Origins of the Latin American "amparo" suit

The origin of this specific Latin American judicial mean for the protection of constitutional rights and guaranties can be found in Mexico. In what was called the Constitutional "Reforms Act" of 1848, a special provision devoted to guarantee the fundamental rights declared in the Constitution, was incorporated (article 5), setting forth that in order to assure the human rights recognized in the Constitution, a statute had to regulate the guaranties of freedom, security, property and equality of all inhabitants of the Republic, and also had to establish the means for its enforcement. No statute was sanctioned but this disposition has always been considered as the remote antecedent of the "amparo" trial or law suit.

The "*Acta de Reformas*" provision was followed by the so called "*formula Otero*", a draft proposal made by one of the members of the Constitutional Commission, embodied in Article 25 of the 1848 Constitution, with the following text:

> **Article 25**. The courts of the federation will protect (*ampararán*) any inhabitant of the Republic in the exercise and conservation of the rights granted to him in the constitution and the constitutional statutes, against any offensive action by the Legislative or Executive powers, whether of the Federation or of the states; the said courts being limited to give protection in the particular case to which the process refers, without making any general statement regarding the statute or the act provoking the decision.[132]

132 See the text in J. CARPIZO, *La Constitución Mexicana de 1917*, México 1979, p. 271; Robert D. BAKER, *Judicial Review in Mexico. A Study of the Amparo Suit*, Texas University Press, Austin, 1971, p. 23; and H. FIX–ZAMUDIO, "Algunos aspectos comparativos del derecho de amparo en México y Venezuela", *Libro Homenaje a la Memoria de Lorenzo Herrera Mendoza*, Caracas, 1970, Vol. II, p. 336. See also H. FIX–ZAMUDIO "A Brief Introduction to the

From this "formula" the main characteristics of the "amparo" suit have always been that it only precedes against public entities actions (Legislative or Executive) and that the judicial decision adopted cannot have general effects, but rather, only effects regarding the concrete controversy and the parties involved, following in the latter case, the general trends of the effects decision of judicial review ruling in the United States.

Based on this Article 25 of the Constitution and even without a regulatory statute, the first judicial judgment of amparo was issued on August 13, 1848, impeding the exile of a citizen without due process.

The 1857 Constitution developed further the amparo institution, setting forth that any controversy derived from a statute or any other authority act which violates the individual guaranties, or from statutes or acts of the Federation which violate or restrict the sovereignty of the States, will be resolved by the Federal courts as a result of the aggrieved party petition, by means of a judicial decision issued after following a formal proceeding; decision that cannot refer but only to the particular individuals, only in order to protect and "*ampararlos*" in the special case to which the process refers to, without making any general statement regarding the statute or the challenged act (arts. 101 and 102).

The unanimous opinion regarding the origin of the amparo suit in México in the XIX Century, before its subsequent development, coincides in affirming that its antecedents are to be found in the North American system of judicial review of the constitutionality of statutes, which was known in Mexico through the readings of the book by Alexis de Tocqueville, *Democracy in America* (1835), in which he refers to the role of the Judiciary on matters of judicial review once the *Marbury v. Madison* Supreme Court decision of 1803 was issued[133].

When Alexis De Tocqueville visited America almost two hundred years ago, and described the political system of the United States, he stressed, in particular, the way Americans had organized their judicial power, which he considered unique in the world.[134] His observations about the powers of the courts, which he believed, "the most important power" of the country,[135] were directly referred to the powers for judicial review, whose basic trends can still be elaborated from them. He specifically pointed out that "that immense political power"[136] of the American courts, "lies in this one fact" –he said– "The Americans have given their judges the right to base

Mexican Writ of Amparo", *California Western International Law Journal*, San Diego 1977, p. 313.

133 See Roberet D. BAKER, *Judicial Review in Mexico. A Study of the Amparo Suit*, University of Texas Press, Austin1971, pp. 15, 33; Eduardo FERRER MAC–GREGOR, *La acción constitucional de* amparo *en México y España, Estudio de Derecho Comparado*, 2nd Edition, Edit. Porrúa, México D.F. 2000; Héctor FIX–ZAMUDIO, *Ensayos sobre el derecho de amparo,* Universidad Nacional Autónoma de México, Editorial Porrúa, México 2003

134 Alexis DE TOCQUEVILLE, *Democracy in America* (ed. by J.P. Mayer and M. Lerner), The Fontana Library, London, 1968, Vol. 1, p. 120.

135 *Idem*, p. 122.

136 *Ibid*, pp. 122, 124.

their decisions on the constitution rather than on the laws. In other words, they allow them not to apply laws which they consider unconstitutional[137], adding that "If anyone invokes in an American Court a statute which the judge considers contrary to the constitution, he can refuse to apply it.[138] This power of American judges, De Tocqueville stressed, was "the only power peculiar to an American judge"[139], which at the time was correct. Today, it must be said, it is the power common to all judges in legal systems with a diffuse system of judicial review.

The influence of that American judicial review powers can be clearly appreciated regarding the original Mexican amparo regulation, particularly regarding the cases and controversy requirement, a basic element for judicial review and the amparo suit as well as the common exclusively the inter partes effects of the judicial decision.

But the original Mexican amparo institution devoted in the beginning to protect constitutional rights against authority acts, subsequently evolved into a unique and very complex judicial institution, that is not to be found in any other Latin American country, not only designed to guarantee judicial protection of constitutional rights against the State acts or actions, but as a multipurpose institution that additionally is used for the protection of personal freedom, equivalent to the habeas corpus writ (called "*amparo libertad*"); for judicial review of constitutionally of statutes (called "*amparo contra leyes*"), with trends similar to the North American diffuse system of judicial review; for judicial review of constitutionality and legality of judicial decisions (called "*amparo casación*") similar to the cassation recourse that existed in almost all civil law countries; for judicial review of administrative actions (called "*amparo administrativo*"), equivalent to the judicial review of administrative acts jurisdictions developed in almost all civil law countries, following the influence of the French contentieux– administrative jurisdiction; and for the protection of peasants rights derived from the agrarian reform process (called "*amparo agrario*") equivalent to the agrarian jurisdictions that can be found in almost all Latin American countries.

All those jurisdictions and judicial means in Mexico are all under the same "amparo" name and umbrella; which as mentioned, is a unique case in comparative law. No other country in the world follows the Mexican "amparo" omni comprehensive approach, by mean of which the original "amparo" judicial mean for the protection of constitutional rights was deformed in the sense that what in almost all civil law countries are separate actions, recourses or jurisdictions, with very different objectives, in Mexico all are called "amparo". On the other hand, this omni comprehensive trend of the Mexican amparo resulting form the effort to expand its protection, in the end paradoxically has provoke that the effective protection of constitutional rights in practice has been weakened[140]. Thus, it can be said that what really

137 *Ibid*, p. 122.

138 *Ibid*, p. 124.

139 *Ibid*, p. 124.

140 See the coments in this regard in Joaquín BRAGE CAMAZANO, *La Jurisdiccoión Constitucional de la Libertad (Teoría general, Argentina, México, Corte Interamericana de Derechos*

spread in almost all the other Lain American countries from the Mexican "amparo" institution, was only the name given to the special judicial means for the protection of constitutional rights (amparo), but not at all of its complex content, as mentioned, unique to the Mexican system.

In other Latin American countries, also since the beginning of the XIX Century antecedents of the "amparo" can be found. In Venezuela, for instance, in the 1811 Declaration of Rights of the people, it was specifically provided the right to petition in order to protect such rights, as follows: "The citizens freedom of petition before public authorities in order to ask for the protection of his rights, in any way can be impeded or limited" (Article 22). This declaration was followed by the 1830 Constitution declaration regarding the need to a special protective means of the constitutional rights, in which was stated that: "Every person must find a prompt and safe remedy according to the law, regarding the injuries and damages suffered in their persons, properties, honor and esteem" (Article 189).

And according to this constitutional provision, it was the Organic Statute on the Judiciary of 1950 that attributed to the Superior Courts powers: "To decide recourses of force, "amparo" and protection against written and oral orders or prescription, given by authorities of the Republic" (Article 9), using for the first time the word "amparo" to identify a judicial mean; as well as the person's right to ask for "amparo" to freedom rights (habeas corpus), as follows:

> **10**. In case in which any public official were forming criminal cause against any person or had issued a detention order, the interested party or anybody acting in his name, can bring before the Superior Court by means of "amparo" or protection; and the latter, ordering the suspension of the procedure, will ask the files and the presence of the party (en vida), and if it finds the petition according to justice, will level the oppressive order".

Nevertheless, and inspite of these provisions, in Venezuela the "amparo" action was only developed after the enactment of the Constitution of 1961. Yet, in the XIX Century, in the Venezuelan 1897 Civil Procedure Code, judicial review as a power of all judges to consider null and void legal provisions contrary to the Constitution –in the North American legal tradition– was formally inserted in positive law, allowing judicial protection of constitutional rights. Article 20 of such Code provides: "When the law whose application is requested is contrary to any provision of the Constitution, the judges will give preference to the latter[141].

In other Latin American countries the amparo action or recourse as well as the habeas corpus recourse were introduced in positive law since the XIX century, as

---

Humanos), Editorial Porrúa, Instituto Mexicano de Derecho Procesal Constitucional, México, 2005, p. 156.

141 The text of the norm in Spanish is as follows: "Cuando la ley vigente, cuya aplicación se pida, colidiere con alguna disposición constitucional, los jueces aplicarán ésta con preferencia." The text was originally adopted in the 1897 Code (Art. 10), followed by the 1904 Code (Art. 10) and the 1916 Code (Art. 7). In the 1985 Code the only change introduced in relation to the previous text, is the word "judges" which substituted the word "Tribunals." See the text of the 1897, 1904 and 1916 Codes in *Leyes y Decretos Reglamentarios de los Estados Unidos de Venezuela*, Caracas, 1943, Vol. V.

follows: regarding habeas corpus in Brasil (1830), El Salvador (1841), Argentina (1863) and Perú (1897), and regarding the amparo action or recourse in Guatemala (1879), El Salvador (1886), Honduras (1894), Nicaragua (1911), Brasil (*mandado de securança* 1934), Panama (1941), Costa Rica (1946), Venezuela (1961), Bolivia, Paraguay, Ecuador (1967), Panama (1972), Perú (1976), Chile (*recurso de protección* 1976) and Colombia (*acción de tutela* 1991). In Argentina, since 1957, the amparo action was admitted through court decisions and regulated in positive law in 1966; and in the Dominican Republic, since 2000 the Supreme Court has admitted the amparo action.

Currently (2006), in all Latin American countries, exception made of Cuba, the habeas corpus and amparo suits, actions or recourses ("*acción de protección*" in Chile and "*acción de tutela* in Colombia) it exists as a specific judicial means exclusively designed for the protection of constitutional rights; in all of them, exception made of the Dominican Republic, the provision for the action is embodied in the Constitutions and in all of them, exception made of Chile and Panamá, the ations of amparo have been expressly regulated in special statutes.

2. The judicial review methods as means for the protection of human rights

In the other hand, the regulation of the "amparo" actions in Latin America, must also be considered as a particular means for the protection of Constitution and of its supremacy regarding specifically the declarations of rights; a method of judicial review that complements the general systems of judicial review of the constitutionality of statutes developed in Latin America, also since the XIX century: the diffuse and the concentrated methods of judicial review.

According to the so called "American model", the diffuse method of judicial review empowers all the judges and courts of a given country to act as a constitutional judge, in the sense that when applying the law, they are allowed to judge its constitutionality and therefore, not to apply it in the concrete process when they consider it unconstitutional and void, giving priority to the Constitution[142]. This diffuse system of judicial review of constitutionality of legislation is not a system peculiar to the common law system of law and is perfectly compatible with the civil or Roman law tradition. It has existed since the XIX Century in most Latin American countries, as is the case of Dominican Republic (1844) [143], Mexico (1857), Colombia (1850), Argentina (1860), Brazil (1890) and Venezuela (1897). In Mexico, Argentina and Brazil, the method strictly follows the American model; and in Colombia, Venezuela and Perú, it exists in a mixed system with the concentrated method of judicial re-

142 See Allan R. BREWER CARÍAS, *Judicial Review in Comparative Law*, Cambridge University Press, Cambridge 1989.

143 The 1844 constitution, as well as the 1966 constitution (Art. 46) established that 'are null and void all Laws, Decrees, Resolutions, Regulations or Acts contrary to the constitution. Consequently all the Courts can declare an act unconstitutional and not applicable to the concrete case. *Cf.* M. BERGES CHUPANI, "Report" in *Memoria de la Reunión de Cortes Superiores de Justicia de Ibero–América, El Caribe, España y Portugal*, Caracas, 1983, p. 380.

view. The diffuse method is also applied in some European countries with a civil law tradition, like Switzerland, Greece and Portugal.

The duty of the courts on the diffuse model of judicial review can only be accomplished *incidenter tantum*, through a particular process (cases and controversies) that have been brought before them, and where the unconstitutionality of a particular statute is neither "the issue" nor the principal issue in the process. Therefore, a process must be initiated before a court on any matter or subject whatsoever, the diffuse system of judicial review of constitutionality being, consequently, always an incidental system of review. In these cases, the decision adopted by the Supreme Court has *in casu et inter partes* effects, that is, effects related to the concrete case and exclusively to the parties who have participated in the process, and therefore, it cannot be applied to other individuals. The judicial decision has also declarative effect in the sense that it only declares the *ab initio* nullity of the challenged statute. Thus, when declaring the statute unconstitutional and inapplicable, in fact, the decision has *ex–tunc*, and *pro pretaerito* effects in the sense that they are retroactive to the moment of the enactment of the statute, considered as not having produced any effect regarding the concrete process and parties.

Finally, it must be said that in order to avoid the uncertainty of the legal order and contradictions due to the multiple decisions that can refers to constitutional issues, corrections have been made to these *inter partes* effects through the *stare decisis* doctrine or through positive law, when the decision is adopted by the Supreme Court of a given country[144].

But Latin American countries have also followed the so called "Austrian" or European model of judicial review, established well before it was invented in Europe, as a concentrated method, by Hans Kelsen in 1920[145]. In Latin America, since the XIX century some countries have adopted it as the only method of judicial review and others, mixed with the diffuse method of judicial review.

The concentrated method of judicial review, contrary to the diffuse system, is basically characterized by the fact that the constitutional system empowers one single state organ of a given country to act as a constitutional judge, in the sense of being the only State organ called to decide upon constitutional matters regarding legislative acts and other State acts with similar rank or value, in a jurisdictional way.

This state body with the monopoly of acting as a constitutional judge can either be the Supreme Court of Justice of the country, in its character as the highest court in the judicial hierarchy or it can also be a special Constitutional Court, Council or Tribunal, specially created by the Constitution.

Therefore, the concentrated system of judicial review of the constitutionality of legislation, even though generally identified with the "European model" of special

---

144 *Idem.*

145 See H. KELSEN, "La garantie juridictionnelle de la Constitution (La Justice constitutionnelle), *Revue du droit public et de la science politique en France et à l'étranger*, Paris 1928, pp. 197–257; Allan R. BREWER CARÍAS, *Judicial Review in Comparative Law*, Cambridge University Press, Cambridge 1989.

constitutional courts,[146] does not necessarily imply its existence. It only implies the assignment to a single state organ, which exercises jurisdictional activity, of the duty and power to act as a constitutional judge, with powers to declare the nullity of state acts, which has to be established and regulated expressly in the Constitution.

Contrary to the diffuse system of judicial review, which is always of an incidental character, the concentrated system of judicial review can have either a principal or incidental character, in the sense that constitutional questions regarding statutes may reach the supreme court or the constitutional court, by virtue of a direct action, some times a popular action, or request brought before the court or by reference of the question to the court, from a lower court, where the constitutional question has been raised in a concrete proceeding, either *ex–officio* or through the initiative of a party.

The decision adopted by the constitutional court or the supreme court acting as a constitutional judge in the concentrated method, has general effects, thus it applies *erga omnes*. Additionally the decision has a *constitutive* effect in the sense that: it declares the nullity of a statute which produces effects up to the moment in which its nullity is established. That is why it is said that the decision of the court, as it is a constitutive one, has *ex–nunc*, *pro futuro* or prospective effects, in the sense that, in principle, they do not go back to the moment of the enactment of the statute considered thereon unconstitutional, the effects produced by the annulled statute until that annulment are still considered valid.

In Latin America, since the middle of the XIX Century many countries have adopted a concentrated method of judicial review by assigning the supreme court of the country with the power to declare the nullity of legislation. This was the case in Colombia and Venezuela in which an authentic concentrated method of judicial review has existed since 1850 and in which the supreme courts have the monopoly of annulling statutes. It is also the case of Panamá, Uruguay and Paraguay.

Subsequently, in many countries the system moved to a mixed one, in which the diffuse and the concentrated systems of judicial review coexist, as is the case of Brazil, Colombia, Peru, Venezuela, Peru and Guatemala.

Also, in Latin America, some countries have established Constitutional Courts or Tribunal in order to perform the concentrated method of judicial review, as is the case of Guatemala, Chile, Perú, Ecuador and Colombia.

Therefore, the judicial protection of constitutional rights in Latin America, additionally to the amparo actions or recourses, can be achieved by means of the diffuse and concentrated methods of judicial review.

3. The European "amparo" actions

Finally, we must mention that as a result of the regulation of the concentrated method of judicial review, in Austria, Germany and Spain, a specific judicial means for the protection of some constitutional rights was also established.

146 M. Cappelletti, *Judicial Review in the Contemporary World*, Indianapolis, 1971, pp. 50–53.

In effect, the "Austrian method" of judicial review was originated in Europe after the First World War under the influence of the ideas and direct work of Hans Kelsen, particularly regarding the concept of the supremacy of the constitution and the need for a jurisdictional guarantee of that supremacy;[147] but it was also a direct result of the absence of a diffuse system of judicial review of the constitutionality of legislation whose exclusion was expressly or indirectly established in the Constitution; and of the traditional European distrust regarding the judiciary to control the constitutionality or legislation. Thus, in order to accomplish such task it was necessary to establish an independent State body.

Accordingly, the first constitutional tribunals were established in Czechoslovakia and Austria, in their respective Constitutions of February 29 and October 1st 1920. Due to its permanence and its reestablishment in 1945, the Austrian Constitutional Tribunal, created in the 1920 Constitution, was to be the leading institution of the "European" concentrated system of judicial review. Hans Kelsen, a member himself of the Constitutional Tribunal until 1929, formulated the original general trends of the institution, very similar to the Czechoslovakian one, regulated in the 1945 Constitution[148] and in the Federal Law of the Constitutional Tribunal of 1953, modified on various occasions[149].

But in Austria, the Constitutional Tribunal not only has the power to act as a constitutional judge controlling the constitutionality of statutes, executive regulations and Treaties, but also to grant constitutional protection against the violation of fundamental rights. For this purpose, any individual has the right to bring before the Constitutional Tribunal, recourses or complaints against administrative acts when the claimant alleges that they infringe a right guaranteed in the constitution (art. 144).

This was the origin of the development of a special judicial means for the protection of fundamental rights in Europe, although in a concentrated way which establishes the difference with Latin American "amparo" recourses.

The Austrian model influenced the establishment of the a concentrated system of judicial review in the Second Spanish Republic, in accordance with the Constitution of December 9 1931, by which a Tribunal of Constitutional Guarantees was created[150]. The system was also conceived as a concentrated one, in which the Tribunal of

---

147 H. KELSEN, "La garantie juridictionnelle de la Constitution (La Justice constitutionnelle), *Revue du droit public et de la science politique en France et à l'étranger*, Paris, 1928, pp. 197–257.

148 Arts.137–148, Constitution of I May 1945. See a Spanish version of the Constitution in I. MÉNDEZ DE VIGO, "El Verfassungsgerichthof (Tribunal Constitucional Austríaco)", *Boletín de Jurisprudencia Constitucional*, Cortes Generales, 7, Madrid, 1981, pp. 555–560.

149 Law N° 85, 1953. See in T. OHLINGER, *Legge sulla Corte Costituzionale Austriaca*, Firenze, 1982.

150 J.L. MELIÁN GIL, *El Tribunal de Garantías Constitucionales de la Segunda República Española*, Madrid, 1971, pp. 16–17, 53; P. Cruz VILLALÓN, "Dos modos de regulación del control de constitucionalidad: Checoslovaquia (1920–1938) y España (1931–1936), *Revista española de derecho constitucional*, 5, 1982, p. 118.

Constitutional Guarantees had exclusive powers to judge upon the constitutionality of statutes, and additionally, the power to protect fundamental rights by means of a recourse of constitutional protection called "*recurso de amparo*", regarding which some authors have also found some influence of the Mexican "amparo"[151].

After the Second World War, also following the Austrian model, the 1949 Constitution of Germany created a Federal Constitutional Tribunal as the "supreme guardian of the Constitution"[152] having "the last word on the construction of the Federal Constitution."[153]. The Tribunal is empowered to decide in a concentrated way, upon petitions for the abstract control of norms and constitutional complaints against laws that can be brought before it in a direct way, or by the referrals made before it by any lower court to seek a concrete control of statutes. Additional to these means for judicial review, it was also established a constitutional complaint for the protection of a fundamental right that can be brought before the Federal Constitutional Tribunal against a judicial decision which is considered to have violated the rights and freedoms of a person because it applied a statute which is alleged to have been unconstitutional (Art. 93, 1, 4,a) FCT Law).

Finally, regarding an "amparo" action, we must mention the current Spanish regulations established in the 1978 Constitution with the creation of the Constitutional Tribunal, later regulated in the "Organic Law of the Constitutional Tribunal" of 3 October 1979[154], which had establish a concentrated method of judicial review, considered as an illustrative example of the concentrated European model[155]. In accordance with the Constitution, the Constitutional Tribunal is conceived as a constitutional organ, thus independent and separate from the Judicial Power, but with jurisdictional functions as the guarantor of the constitutionality of state action.[156]

Additionally to its functions to decide the "recourse of unconstitutionality against laws and normative acts with force of law" (art. 161, 1,1 Constitution), through which "the Constitutional Tribunal guarantees the primacy of the Constitution and judges the conformity or inconformity" of the laws and normative acts with force of law with it (art. 27, 1, Organic Law 2/79), the Constitutional Tribunal is empowered

---

151 See Eduardo FERRER MAC–GREGOR, *La acción constitucional de* amparo *en México y España, Estudio de Derecho Comparado*, 2nd Edition, Edit. Porrúa, México D.F. 2000

152 See G. MÜLLER, "El Tribunal Constitucional federal de la República Federal de Alemania", in *Revista de la Comisión Internacional de Juristas*, Vol VI, Ginebra 1965, p. 216; F. SAINZ MORENO, "Tribunal Constitucional federal alemán", *Boletín de Jurisprudencia Constitucional*, Cortes Generales, 8, Madrid 1981, p. 606

153 See H. G. RUPP, "The Federal Constitutional Court and the Constitution of the Federal Republic of Germany", *Saint Louis University Law Journal*, Vol XVI, 1971–1972, p. 359.

154 Organic Law 2/1979. See the text in *Boletín Oficial del Estado*, N° 239, 5 October, 1979.

155 See P. BON, F. MODERNE and Y. RODRÍGUEZ, *La justice constitutionnelle en Espagne*, Paris 1982, p. 41.

156 M. GARCÍA PELAYO, "E1 Status del Tribunal Constitucional", *Revista española de derecho constitucional*, 1, 1981, pp. 11–34; F. Rubio Llorente, "Sobre la relación entre Tribunal Constitucional y poder judicial en el ejercicio de la jurisdicción constitucional", *Revista española de derecho constitucional*, 4, 1982, pp. 35–67, As an independent organ it also has autoregulatory powers: Art. 2,2 Organic Law 2/1979.

to decide the *recursos de amparo* (recourse for constitutional protection), that can be directly brought by individuals before the Constitutional Tribunal, when they deem their constitutional rights and liberties violated by dispositions, juridical acts or simple factual actions of the public bodies, the Autonomous Communities and other public territorial entities or by their officials (Art. 161, 1, b) Constitution; Art. 41, 2 Organic Law 2/1979). This recourse for the protection of fundamental rights cannot be exercised directly against statutes, which violate fundamental rights in a direct way,[157] as in the West German system. Therefore, it can only be exercised against administrative or judicial acts and acts without force of law produced by the legislative authorities (Art. 42 Organic Law 2/1979), and only when the ordinary judicial means for the protection of fundamental rights have been exhausted (Art. 43, 1 Organic Law 2/1979.). Consequently, the recourse for *amparo* in general results in a direct action against judicial acts [158] and can only indirectly lead to judicial review of legislation when the particular state act challenged by it is based on a statute considered unconstitutional (Art. 55,2 Organic Law 2/1979).

The general trend of the European "amparo" recourse, in contrast to the Latin American institution, is that it is conceived as a concentrated judicial mean for the protection of fundamental rights against State actions, by assigning the power to decide them to a single Constitutional Tribunal; and only to protect certain constitutional rights listed in the Constitutions as "fundamental" rights, more or less equivalent to civil or individual rights. In contrast, in Latin American countries, the "amparo" action or recourse, exception made of Costa Rica and Panamá, can be exercised before all courts; exception made, at least formally, of Chile and Colombia, always for the protection of all constitutional rights, including social and economic ones; and in many countries can be exercised not only against State acts but also against individuals.

CHAPTER IV.

THE LATIN AMERICAN "AMPARO" ACTION OR RECOURSE AND THE AMERICAN CONVENTION ON HUMAN RIGHTS

I. THE "AMPARO" ACTION, RECOURSE OR SUIT: A LATIN AMERICAN CONSTITUTIONAL INSTITUTION

Section 9, clause 2 of the Constitution of the United States regulates –although in an indirect way– the writ of habeas corpus, when it states that "The Privilege of the Writ of Habeas Corpus shall not be suspended, unless when in Cases of Rebellion or Invasion the public Safety may require it".

157 *Cf.*, Eduardo García de Enterría, *La Constitución como norma y el Tribunal Constitucional*, Madrid 1985, p. 151.

158 *Cf.* Favoreu, "Actualité et légitimité du Contrôle juridictionnel des lois en Europe occidentale." *Revue du droit public et de la science politique en France et à l'étranger*, Paris 1984 (5), pp. 1155–1156.

In contrast, as has been mentioned before, since the XIX Century, additionally to the common and general judicial guarantees of constitutional and other rights –and sometimes in parallel to the habeas corpus recourse–, a group of specific judicial remedies for the guarantee of constitutional rights has been developed in Latin America, expressly intended to protect those constitutional rights. Those are the action, recourse or suit of "amparo", also known as action of "tutela" (Colombia), recourse for "protección" (Chile), or in Brazil, the "*mandado de segurança*"[159].

In all of its versions, it is always a specific judicial guarantee set forth in order to protect constitutional rights, and is generally enshrined in the Constitutions, although it has also been developed without express constitutional or statutory provisions, as is case of the "amparo" recourse in the Dominican Republic.[160]

At present, the "amparo" action or recourse is expressly regulated in the Constitutions of Argentina, Bolivia, Brasil, Chile, Colombia, Costa Rica, Ecuador, El Salvador, Guatemala, Honduras, México, Nicaragua, Panamá, Paraguay, Perú, and Venezuela. Sometimes the provision also includes the protection of personal liberty, although most countries have set forth a different recourse of habeas corpus for the specific protection of personal freedom and integrity and even an habeas data recourse, of more recent creation, for the protection of personal data.

My purpose now is to make a general and brief reference to the constitutional regulations on the amparo process, action or recourse in the Latin American Constitution, which I will referred according to the way they establishes the amparo action: together with the habeas corpus and habeas data; only together with the habeas corpus, or comprising the protection of personal freedom.

1. Constitutions establishing the three protective judicial means: amparo, habeas corpus and habeas data

A. *"Amparo", habeas corpus and habeas data in Argentina*

In effect, in Article 43 of the Constitution of Argentina, introduced in the reform of 1994, these three specific actions for human rights protection ("amparo", habeas data and habeas corpus actions), are expressly regulated. Regarding the "amparo" action, the Constitution provides[161]:

---

159 See, in general, Allan R. BREWER–CARÍAS, *El "amparo" a los derechos y garantías constitucionales (una aproximación comparativa),* Editorial Jurídica venezolana, Caracas, 1993.

160 As is the case of the Dominican Republic. See Juan DE LA ROSA, *El recurso de "amparo". Estudio Comparativo. Su aplicación en la República Dominicana*, Santo Domingo, 2001; Allan R. BREWER–CARÍAS, "La admisión jurisprudencial de la acción de "amparo", en ausencia de regulación constitucional o legal en la República Dominicana» in *Revista IIDH*, Instituto Interamericano de Derechos Humanos, N° 29, San José, January–June 1999, pp. 95–102; and in *Iudicium et vita, Jurisprudencia en Derechos Humanos*, N° 7, Edición Especial, Tomo I, Instituto Interamericano de Derechos Humanos, San José, 2000, pp. 334–341.

161 **Article 43.** Toda persona puede interponer acción expedita y rápida de "amparo", siempre que no exista otro medio judicial mas idóneo, contra todo acto u omisión de autoridades publicas o de particulares, que en forma actual o inminente lesione, restrinja, altere o amenace,

Artícle 43.– Any person shall file a prompt and summary proceeding regarding constitutional guarantees, provided there is no other legal remedy, against any act or omission of the public authorities or individuals which currently or imminently may damage, limit, modify or threaten rights and guarantees recognized by this Constitution, treaties or laws, with open arbitrariness or illegality. In such case, the judge may declare that the act or omission is based on an unconstitutional rule.

Therefore, the "amparo" action can only be brought before a court if there is no other more suitable judicial mean. It proceeds not only against public official acts or omissions, but also against private individuals acts or omissions, for the protection of all constitutional rights and guaranties, not only the ones set forth in the Constitutions but also in international treaties and in statutes. Thus, the "amparo" action directly proceeds for the protections of all rights declared in international treaties ratified by Argentina.

The Constitution also provides a collective action of "amparo" that can be filed by the affected party, the people's defendant and Associations that seek general purposes, in order to protect collective rights. The rights protected are particularly the environment, free competition, user and consumer rights as well as rights of general collective incidence.

Additionally to the "amparo" action, the Argentinean Constitution also sets forth what in Latin America has been called the action of habeas data. This Constitution provides that any person can file a suit in order to acquire knowledge about data with reference to himself, contained in public or private registry or data banks set for preparing reports and about the purpose of this data. In case of falsity or discrimination, the plaintiff can also seek for its suppression, rectification, confidentiality and actualization. Nonetheless, the Constitution provides that the filing of this action must not affect the secrecy of journalistic information sources.

The Constitution also regulates the habeas corpus action, stating that:

---

con arbitrariedad o ilegalidad manifiesta, derechos y garantías reconocidos por esta Constitución, un tratado o una ley. En el caso, el juez podrá declarar la inconstitucionalidad de la norma en que se funde el acto u omisión lesiva.

Podrán interponer esta acción contra cualquier forma de discriminación y en lo relativo a los derechos que protegen al ambiente, a la competencia, al usuario y al consumidor, así como a los derechos de incidencia colectiva en general, el afectado, el defensor del pueblo y las asociaciones que propendan a esos fines, registradas conforme a la ley, la que determinará los requisitos y formas de su organización.

Toda persona podrá interponer esta acción para tomar conocimiento de los datos a ella referidos y de su finalidad, que consten en registros o bancos de datos públicos, o privados destinados a proveer informes, y en caso de falsedad o discriminación, para exigir la supresión, rectificación, confidencialidad o actualización de aquellos. No podrá afectarse el secreto de las fuentes de información periodística.

Cuando el derecho lesionado, restringido, alterado o amenazado fuera la libertad física, o, en caso de agravamiento ilegitimo en la forma o condiciones de detención, o en el de desaparición forzada de personas, la acción de habeas corpus podrá ser interpuesta por el afectado o por cualquiera en su favor y el juez resolverá de inmediato, aun durante la vigencia del estado de sitio.

When the right affected, restrained, altered or threatened is that of physical freedom, or in case of an illegitimate worsening of procedure or conditions of detention, or in case of forced disappearance of persons, the action of habeas corpus can be filed by the affected party or by any other person on his behalf. In such cases, the judge will resolve immediately, even in state of siege

Therefore, in Argentina, by means of the three above mentioned specific remedies, any person can seek for the protection of all human rights declared in the Constitution, international treaties and statutes that could be violated by public officials and by individuals.

The three actions have been regulated in three separate statutes: the "amparo" Action Statute (*Ley de acción de "amparo", Ley 16986/ 1966*), the Habeas Corpus statute (*Ley 23098/1984*) and the Personal Data Protection Statute (*Ley 25366/2000*).

B. *"Mandado de segurança", "mandado de injunção", habeas corpus and habeas data in Brazil*

In Brazil, Article 5 of the Constitution, after enumerating all the constitutional rights and guarantees, provides the actions for protection (the habeas corpus, the *mandado de segurança* the *mandado de injunção* and the habeas–data), as follows[162]:

"The habeas corpus to anybody who suffers o there is a threaten to suffer violence or coactions on his moving freedom because of illegality or authority abuse;

---

162 **Article 5º**– Todos são iguais perante a lei, sem distinção de qualquer natureza, garantindo–se aos brasileiros e aos estrangeiros residentes no País a inviolabilidade do direito à vida, à liberdade, à igualdade, à segurança e a propriedade, nos termos seguintes:

–conceder–se–á habeas–corpus sempre que alguém sofrer ou se achar ameaçado de sofrer violência ou coação em sua liberdade de locomoção, por ilegalidade ou abuso de poder;

–conceder–se–á mandado de segurança para proteger direito líquido e certo, não amparado por habeas–corpus ou habeas–data, quando o responsável pela ilegalidade ou abuso de poder for autoridade pública ou agente de pessoa jurídica no exercício de atribuições do poder público;

–o mandado de segurança coletivo pode ser impetrado por:

partido político com representação no Congresso Nacional;

organização sindical, entidade de classe, ou associação legalmente constituída e em funcionamento há pelo menos um a no, em defesa dos interesses de seus membros ou associados;

–conceder–se–á mandado de injunção sempre que a falta de norma regulamentadora torne inviável o exercício dos direitos e liberdades constitucionais e das prerrogativas inerentes à nacionalidade, à soberania e à cidadania;

–conceder–se–á habeas–data:

para assegurar o conhecimento de informações relativas à pessoa do impetrante, constantes de registros ou bancos de dados de entidades governamentais ou de caráter público;

para a retificação de dados, quando não se prefira fazê–lo por processo sigiloso, judicial ou administrativo;

The *mandado de segurança* in order to protect any true and enforceable right not protected by means of habeas–corpus or habeas–data, when a public authority or an agent of a legal person acting exercising public functions is responsible for the illegality or the abuse.

It must be noted that the *mandado de segurança* is excluded regarding individual's acts or omissions; and that the Constitution also provides a *mandado de segurança coletivo* that can be excersised by political parties with Congressional representation, labor unions, class entities or associations legally established and with one year of activities in defense of their members or associates.

Additionally, the Constitution sets forth the *mandado de injunção* in cases that due to the absence of regulatory statutes, the exercise of constitutional rights and freedoms and the prerogatives inherent to nationality, sovereignty and citizenship, would become unviable".

The Constitution also regulates:

The habeas data in order to ensure the knowledge of information referred to the plaintiff, contained in registries or databanks of governmental or public bodies; or to rectify the data when the petitioner decides not to do so through a confidential process, either administrative or judicial.

The procedural rules regarding the mandado de segurança are set forth in Lei N° 1.533, of December 31,1951.

C. *"Amparo", habeas corpus and habeas data in Ecuador*

The Constitution of Ecuador also provides for the three fundamental means developed for the protection of human rights: the habeas corpus, habeas data and "amparo"; but not all as judicial remedies, contrary to the general trend of Latin America.

Article 95 of the Constitution[163] provides a detailed set of rules regarding the habeas corpus, as a right of "any person who thinks that he has been illegally deprived of his freedom"; but not as a right to a judicial remedy.

---

163 **Artículo 93.**– Toda persona que crea estar ilegalmente privada de su libertad, podrá acogerse al hábeas corpus. Ejercerá este derecho por sí o por interpuesta persona, sin necesidad de mandato escrito, ante el alcalde bajo cuya jurisdicción se encuentre, o ante quien haga sus veces. La autoridad municipal, en el plazo de veinticuatro horas contadas a partir de la recepción de la solicitud, ordenará que el recurrente sea conducido inmediatamente a su presencia, y se exhiba la orden de privación de libertad. Su mandato será obedecido sin observación ni excusa, por los encargados del centro de rehabilitación o del lugar de detención.

El alcalde dictará su resolución dentro de las veinticuatro horas siguientes. Dispondrá la inmediata libertad del reclamante si el detenido no fuere presentado, si no se exhibiere la orden, si ésta no cumpliere los requisitos legales, si se hubiere incurrido en vicios de procedimiento en la detención o, si se hubiere justificado el fundamento del recurso.

Si el alcalde no tramitare el recurso, será civil y penalmente responsable, de conformidad con la ley.

El funcionario o empleado que no acate la orden o la resolución será inmediatamente destituido de su cargo o empleo sin más trámite, por el alcalde, quien comunicará tal decisión a la Contraloría General del Estado y a la autoridad que deba nombrar su reemplazo.

In the Constitution such right to habeas corpus is conceived as an a administrative request, in the sense that it must be filed not before a judge, but only before the corresponding local government authority or mayor (alcalde), being possible that the request be filed directly by the affected person or through another person, even without the need of a written power of attorney. Within 24 hours from the filing of the request, the local government authority must order that the aggrieved person be immediately brought before him, and that the order of detention be shown. The administrative order, according to the Constitution, "must be obeyed without any comment or excuse by the persons in charge of the center of detention".

It is also the "alcalde" who must issue the decision of the case in a 24 hour delay, deciding the immediate freedom of the claimant if the detainee were not brought before it, or the detention order were not shown, or such order does not fulfill the legal conditions, if the detention was irregular, or if the claim was justified.

The public official who disobeys the order will be immediately dismissed of his position by the mayor, without any other proceeding; decision that must be informed to the General Comptroller's Office and to the authority that must appoint his substitute.

Regarding the habeas data, Article 94 of the Constitution also conceives it as a right that all persons have, to access to the documents, data bank of reports referring to the person, or his properties, that are in public or private entities, as well as to know what is their use and purpose.

The person can request before the respective official for the data to be actualized or rectified, removed or annulled, when erroneous or when it illegitimately affects the claimant's rights.

In the Ecuadorian Constitution only the "amparo" action is directly conceived as a judicial remedy, for which, Article 95[164] sets forth extensive regulations:

El funcionario o empleado destituido, luego de haber puesto en libertad al detenido, podrá reclamar por su destitución ante los órganos competentes de la Función Judicial, dentro de los ocho días siguientes a aquel en que fue notificado.

164 **Artículo 95.**– Cualquier persona, por sus propios derechos o como representante legitimado de una colectividad, podrá proponer una acción de "amparo" ante el órgano de la Función Judicial designado por la ley. Mediante esta acción, que se tramitará en forma preferente y sumaria, se requerirá la adopción de medidas urgentes destinadas a cesar, evitar la comisión o remediar inmediatamente las consecuencias de un acto u omisión ilegítimos de una autoridad pública, que viole o pueda violar cualquier derecho consagrado en la Constitución o en un tratado o convenio internacional vigente, y que, de modo inminente, amenace con causar un daño grave. También podrá interponerse la acción si el acto o la omisión hubieren sido realizados por personas que presten servicios públicos o actúen por delegación o concesión de una autoridad pública.

No serán susceptibles de acción de "amparo" las decisiones judiciales adoptadas en un proceso.

También se podrá presentar acción de "amparo" contra los particulares, cuando su conducta afecte grave y directamente un interés comunitario, colectivo o un derecho difuso.

Para la acción de "amparo" no habrá inhibición del juez que deba conocerla y todos los días serán hábiles.

Article 95. Any person, by his own rights or as representative of a collectivity, can file an action of "amparo" before the judicial organ indicated by statute. By means of this action that must be carried out in a preferred and summary way, it will be necessary to adopt urgent measures in order to stop, prevent or immediately remedy the consequences of an illegitimate act or omission of a public authority, which violates or could violate any right enshrined in the Constitution or in an international treaty or convention in force, and that in an imminent way threatens to cause a grave harm. The "amparo" action can also be filed if the act or the omission is executed by persons rendering public services or that act by delegation or concession from a public authority.

Judicial decisions issued in a procedure cannot be challenged by means of the "amparo" action.

The "amparo" action can also be filed against individuals, when its conduct affects grave and directly a communitarian or collective interest or a diffuse right.

In the "amparo" action there will be no inhibition from the judge that must decide it, and all days will be court day.

The judge must immediately convene the parties, to hear them within the next 24 hours in a public hearing, and in the same decision, if reasons exists, will order the suspension of any act which could signified a violation to a right. .

Within the next 48 hours, the judge must issue a decision, which must be immediately executed, even though such decision can be appealed before the Constitutional Tribunal for its confirmation or repeal.

The statute must determine the sanctions applicable to the authorities or persons who disobey the judicial resolutions and the judges who violated the "amparo" procedures. In order to assure the accomplishment of the "amparo" decisions, the judges can adopt any pertinent measures; even ask the police for help.

All procedural norms contrary to the "amparo" action will not be applicable, nor the dispositions that could delay its quick application.

The habeas corpus, habeas data and the "amparo" –the last two ones as judicial remedies, are regulated in the Constitutional Judicial Review Statute (*Ley de Control Constitucional*, Ley N° 000. RO/99) of July 2nd, 1997.

El juez convocará de inmediato a las partes, para oírlas en audiencia pública dentro de las veinticuatro horas subsiguientes y, en la misma providencia, de existir fundamento, ordenará la suspensión de cualquier acto que pueda traducirse en violación de un derecho.

Dentro de las cuarenta y ocho horas siguientes, el juez dictará la resolución, la cual se cumplirá de inmediato, sin perjuicio de que tal resolución pueda ser apelada para su confirmación o revocatoria, para ante el Tribunal Constitucional.

La ley determinará las sanciones aplicables a las autoridades o personas que incumplan las resoluciones dictadas por el juez; y a los jueces y magistrados que violen el procedimiento de "amparo", independientemente de las acciones legales a que hubiere lugar. Para asegurar el cumplimiento del "amparo", el juez podrá adoptar las medidas que considere pertinentes, e incluso acudir a la ayuda de la fuerza pública.

No serán aplicables las normas procesales que se opongan a la acción de "amparo", ni las disposiciones que tiendan a retardar su ágil despacho

D. *"Amparo", habeas corpus and habeas data in Paraguay*

Since the Constitution of Paraguay is a more recent one, not only has it regulated in a very extended way the "amparo" and habeas corpus recourses as constitutional guaranties regarding the rights declared in the Constitution (art. 131), but has also expressly regulated the habeas data recourse.

Regarding the habeas corpus, Article 133 of the Constitution[165] sets forth that this guaranty can be filed before any First Instance judge of the corresponding circuit, by he affected person or by someone on his behalf, without needing power of attorney, and distinguishes three types of habeas corpus: preventive, restorative and generic.

The preventive habeas corpus can be filed by any person in the situation of imminent deprivation of his physical freedom, in order to seek for the examination of the legitimacy of the circumstances that, according to the affected party, could threaten his freedom, as well as for an order to stop such restrictions.

The restorative habeas corpus can be filed by any person that is in the situation illegal deprivation of his freedom in order seek for the rectification of the circumstances of the case. In this case, the judge will order the appearance of the detainee within the following 24 hours, with a report from the public or private agent who detained him. When the summoned party doesn't accomplish the order, the judge must go to the site where the person is confined, and in such place make a judgment on the merits and arrange his immediate freedom, similarly as if the appearance of the detainee would have been accomplished, and the requested report filed. If there

---

165 **Artículo 133.– Del Habeas Corpus.** Esta garantía podrá ser interpuesto por el afectado, por sí o por interpósita persona, sin necesidad de poder por cualquier medio fehaciente, y ante cualquier Juez de Primera Instancia de la circunscripción judicial respectiva.

El Hábeas Corpus podrá ser:

Preventivo: en virtud del cual toda persona, en trance inminente de ser privada ilegalmente de su libertad física, podrá recabar el examen de la legitimidad de las circunstancias que, a criterio del afectado, amenacen su libertad, así como una orden de cesación de dichas restricciones.

Reparador: en virtud del cual toda persona que se hallase ilegalmente privada de su libertad puede recabar la rectificación de las circunstancias del caso. El magistrado ordenará la comparecencia del detenido, con un informe del agente público o privado que lo detuvo, dentro de las veinticuatro horas de radicada la petición. Si el requerido no lo hiciese así, el Juez se constituirá en el sitio en el que se halle recluida la persona, y en dicho lugar hará juicio de méritos y dispondrá su inmediata libertad, igual que si se hubiere cumplido con la presentación del detenido y se haya radicado el informe. Si no existiesen motivos legales que autoricen la privación de su libertad, la dispondrá de inmediato; si hubiese orden escrita de autoridad judicial, remitirá los antecedentes a quien dispuso la detención.

Genérico: en virtud del cual se podrán demandar rectificación de circunstancias que, no estando contempladas en los dos casos anteriores, restrinjan la libertad o amenacen la seguridad personal. Asimismo, esta garantía podrá interponerse en casos de violencia física, psíquica o moral que agraven las condiciones de personas legalmente privadas de su libertad.

La ley reglamentará las diversas modalidades del hábeas corpus, las cuales procederán incluso, durante el Estado de excepción. El procedimiento será breve, sumario y gratuito, pudiendo ser iniciado de oficio.

were no legal motives to authorize the deprivation of freedom, it will dispose the immediate release; and in case of existence of a written order from a judicial authority, will envoy the back grounds to whom ordered the detention.

Finally, the generic habeas corpus recourse is intended to seek rectification of circumstances that are not comprised in the two above mentioned cases, restrict freedom or threatened personal safety. Also, this guaranty could be filed in cases of physical, psychical or moral violence which aggravates the conditions of persons already legally deprived from freedom.

The Constitution refers to a statute for the regulation of the habeas corpus guaranty, by means of a procedure that must be brief, succinct and without cost; clarifying that it is admissible in states of emergency situations and that it can be initiated *ex officio*.

Regarding the "amparo" recourse, Article 134 of the Constitution[166] states that it can be filed before the competent judge by any person that considers himself gravely damaged in his rights of guaranties set forth in the Constitution or in statutes or in imminent danger of being, by means of an authority or individual obviously illegitimate act or an omission, provided that because of the urgency of the case, the situation cannot be resolved through the ordinary judicial means. The procedure will be brief, succinct and without cost, and a popular action will be accepted in the cases allowed by the statute.

The judge will have the power to safeguard the right or guaranty or to immediately restore the infringed legal situation.

In electoral matters or related to political organizations, the jurisdiction will correspond to the electoral judiciary.

The Constitution sets forth that the "amparo" will not be admissible in judicial proceedings, nor against judicial decisions, nor in the procedure of formation, sanction and promulgation of statutes.

---

166 **Artículo 134.– Del "amparo".** Toda persona que por un acto u omisión, manifestamente ilegítimo, de una autoridad o de un particular, se considere lesionada gravemente, o en peligro inminente de serlo en derechos o garantías consagradas en esta Constitución o en la ley, y que debido a la urgencia del caso no pudiera remediarse por la vía ordinaria, puede promover "amparo" ante el magistrado competente. El procedimiento será breve, sumario, gratuito, y de acción popular para los casos previstos en la ley.

El magistrado tendrá facultad para salvaguardar el derecho o garantía, o para restablecer inmediatamente la situación jurídica infringida.

Si se tratara de una cuestión electoral, o relativa a organizaciones políticas, será competente la justicia electoral.

El "amparo" no podrá promoverse en la tramitación de causas judiciales, ni contra actos de órganos judiciales, ni en el proceso de formación, sanción y promulgación de las leyes.

La ley reglamentará el respectivo procedimiento. Las sentencias recaídas en el "amparo" no causarán estado.

Finally, regarding the habeas data recourse, Article 135 of the Constitution[167], declares that any person may have access to the information and data referring to himself or to his properties that are in official or private public registries, and to know about the use and purpose of such information. The interested party can also ask from the competent judge, the update, the rectification or the destruction of the registries if they are erroneous or when they illegitimately affected his rights.

The statutory regulations regarding "amparo" are set forth in the "amparo" Statute (*Ley 341/71 reglamentaria del "amparo"*) de 1971.

E. *"Amparo", habeas corpus and habeas data in Perú*

The Constitution of Peru enumerates the constitutional guaranties in its Article 200, and among them, in particular, the actions of habeas corpus, "amparo" and habeas data[168].

The action of habeas corpus is admissible regarding any fact or omission of any authority, public official or person that harms or threatens the individual freedom or the related constitutional rights.

The action of "amparo" is admissible against any fact or omission of any authority, public official or person, which harms or threatens the other rights recognized in the Constitution. Nonetheless, according to the Constitution, the action of "amparo" is not admissible against legal norms or against judicial decisions adopted in a regular proceeding.

Regarding the habeas data action, the same Article 200 of the Constitution regulates its admissibility against the fact or omission of any authority, public official or person, which harms or threatens the following rights declared in Article 2, sections 5,6 and 7 of the Constitution:

First, the right to request without expressing motives, and to receive required information from any public entity, in the legal delay, with the due cost implied; ex-

---

167 **Artículo 135.– Del habeas data.** Toda persona puede acceder a la información y a los datos que sobre si misma, o sobre sus bienes, obren en registros oficiales o privados de carácter público, así como conocer el uso que se haga de los mismos y de su finalidad. Podrá solicitar ante el magistrado competente la actualización, la rectificación o la destrucción de aquellos, si fuesen erróneos o afectaran ilegítimamente sus derechos.

168 **Artículo 200.**– Son garantías constitucionales:

La Acción de *Hábeas Corpus*, que procede ante el hecho u omisión, por parte de cualquier autoridad, funcionario o persona, que vulnera o amenaza la libertad individual o los derechos constitucionales conexos.

La Acción de *"amparo"*, que procede contra e hecho u omisión, por parte de cualquier autoridad, funcionario o persona, que vulnera o amenaza los demás derechos reconocidos por la Constitución. No procede contra normas legales ni contra resoluciones judiciales, emanadas de procedimiento regular.

La Acción de *Hábeas Data*, que procede contra el hecho u omisión, por parte de cualquier autoridad, funcionario o persona, que vulnera o amenaza los derechos a que se refiere el artículo 2°, incisos 5, 6, y 7 de la Constitución....

ception is made regarding the information referred to the personal privacy and those expressly excluded by statute or because of national security reasons.

Second, to secure that the information services, computerized or not, public or private, do not provide information affecting the personal and familiar intimacy.

Third, to honor and good reputation, to personal and familiar intimacy and to one's own voice and image.

The Constitution expressly states that the habeas corpus and "amparo" actions would not be suspended during exception constitutional regimes (art. 137). In such cases, when these actions are filed regarding restricted or suspended rights, the competent court will examine the reasonability and proportionality of the restrictive act, but is not allowed to challenge the state of emergency or of site declaration.

All the constitutional guaranties, including the habeas corpus, "amparo" and habeas data actions have been regulated in the Constitutional Procedure Code (*Código Procesal Constitucional*) of 2005.

2. Constitutions establishing the two protective judicial means: amparo and habeas corpus

A. *"Amparo" and habeas corpus in Bolivia*

In Bolivia, the Constitution regulates both, the "amparo" and the habeas corpus recourses, as follows[169]:

---

169 **Artículo 18.**– Toda persona que creyere estar indebida o ilegalmente perseguida, detenida, procesada o presa podrá ocurrir, por sí o por cualquiera a su nombre, con poder notariado o sin él, ante la Corte Superior del Distrito o ante cualquier Juez de Partido, a elección suya, en demanda de que se guarden las formalidades legales. En los lugares donde no hubiere Juez de Partido la demanda podrá interponerse ante un Juez Instructor.

La autoridad judicial señalará de inmediato día y hora de audiencia pública, disponiendo que el actor sea conducido a su presencia. Con dicha orden se practicará citación personal o por cédula en la oficina de la autoridad demandada, orden que será obedecida sin observación ni excusa, tanto por aquella cuanto por los encargados de las cárceles o lugares de detención sin que éstos, una vez citados, puedan desobedecer arguyendo orden superior.

En ninguna caso podrá suspenderse la audiencia. Instruida de los antecedentes, la autoridad judicial dictará sentencia en la misma audiencia ordenando la libertad, haciendo que se reparen los defectos legales o poniendo al demandante a disposición del juez competente. El fallo deberá ejecutarse en el acto. La decisión que se pronuncie se elevará en revisión, de oficio, ante el fallo.

Si el demandado después de asistir a la audiencia la abandona antes de escuchar la sentencia, ésta será notificada validamente en estrados. Si no concurriere, la audiencia se llevará a efecto en su rebeldía y oída la exposición del actor o su representante, se dictará sentencia.

Artículo 19.– Fuera del recurso de "habeas corpus" a que se refiere el artículo anterior, se establece el recurso de "amparo" contra los actos ilegales o las omisiones indebidas de los funcionarios o particulares que restrinjan, supriman o amenacen restringir o suprimir los derechos y garantías de la persona reconocidos por esta Constitución y las leyes.

El recurso de "amparo" se interpondrá por la persona que se creyere agraviada o por otra a su nombre con poder suficiente de esta Constitución, ante las Cortes Superiores en las capitales

First, Article 18 refers to the habeas corpus recourse by stating that any person who thinks is being undue or illegally persecuted, detained, prosecuted or held, can, by himself or through any other person acting on his behalf, with or without power of attorney, file a suit before the District Superior Court or before any local judge, in order to ask for the respect of the legal formalities. In such cases, the judicial authority must immediately fix a day and hour for a public hearing ordering the appearance of the plaintiff before his presence; order which must be obeyed without excuse, not being a valid argument the obedience of superior orders. In no case the hearing can be suspended, and in it, once knowing about the antecedents, the judicial authority must decide ordering the freedom of the plaintiff, which must be sent before the competent judge, and must amend the legal wrongs.

Regarding the "amparo" recourse, Article 19 of the Constitution states as follows:

> **Article 19.**– Besides the recourse of habeas corpus, the recourse of "amparo" is set forth against the illegal acts or the undue omissions of public officials or of individuals, which restrict, suspend or threaten to restrict or to suspend the person's rights and guarantees recognized in the Constitution and in statutes.
>
> The recourse must be filed by the aggrieved person or by another on his behalf, before the Superior Courts of the Department's capitals or before the local judges of the provinces, and decided in a speedy procedure. The Public Prosecutor can also file the recourse on behalf of the affected person if he has not or could not file it.

Therefore, the "amparo" action is set forth for the protection of all constitutional rights declared in the Constitution and statutes. Additionally, about the Bolivian constitutional regulation, it must also be noted the possibility to file the "amparo" action against individuals, and not only against public officials; and the provision that the "amparo" judicial protection will only be issued "if there is no other mean or legal recourse for the immediate protection of the restricted, suspended or threatened rights or guarantees". Another important procedural regulation refers to the need to

---

de Departamento y ante los Jueces de Partido en las provincias, tramitándose en forma sumarísima. El Ministerio Público podrá también interponer de oficio este recurso cuando no lo hubiere o no pudiere hacerlo la persona afectada.

La autoridad o la persona demandada será citada en la forma prevista por el artículo anterior a objeto de que preste información y presente, en su caso, los actuados concernientes al hecho denunciado, en el plazo máximo de cuarenta y ocho horas. La resolución final se pronunciará en audiencia pública inmediatamente de recibida la información del denunciado y, a falta de ella, lo hará sobre la base de la prueba que ofrezca el recurrente.

La autoridad judicial examinará la competencia del funcionario o los actos del particular y, encontrando cierta y efectiva la denuncia, concederá el "amparo" solicitado siempre que no hubiere otro medio o recurso legal para la protección inmediata de los derechos y garantías restringidos, suprimidos o amenazados, elevando de oficio su resolución ante el Tribunal Constitucional para su revisión, en el plazo de veinticuatro horas.

Las determinaciones previas de la autoridad judicial y la decisión final que conceda el "amparo" serán ejecutadas inmediatamente y sin observación, aplicándose, en caso de resistencia, lo dispuesto en el artículo anterior.

send *ex officio* the judicial decision to the Constitutional Tribunal for its revision before this court.

The "amparo" and the habeas corpus actions are regulated in the Constitutional Tribunal Statute (*Ley Nº 1836 del Tribunal Constitucional*) enacted in 1998, even though the Constitutional Tribunal of Bolivia only has reviewing powers over judicial decisions on the matter.

B. *Recourse for "tutela" and habeas corpus in Colombia*

In Colombia, in addition to the habeas corpus recourse, the 1992 Constitution sets forth the "amparo" recourse but naming it "recurso de tutela", using a word that in Spanish has the same general meaning as "amparo" and as "protección".

In this regard, referring to the habeas corpus, Article 30 of the Constitution states[170]:

> **Article 30**.– Anyone who is deprived of his freedom, or who thinks has been illegally deprived of it, has the right to claim before any judicial authority for Habeas Corpus, personally of through any other person, which must be decided in 36 hours.

Regarding the action of "tutela" or "amparo", Article 86 of the Constitution provides[171] as follows:

> **Article 86.**– Everyone has the action of "tutela" in order to claim before the courts, by himself or by any other person acting on his behalf, at any moment and lieu, by means of a preferred and summary proceeding, the immediate protection of their constitutional fundamental rights, whenever they are violated of threatened by actions or omissions of any public authority.

---

170 **Artículo 30.**– Quien estuviere privado de su libertad, y creyere estarlo ilegalmente, tiene derecho a invocar ante cualquier autoridad judicial, en todo tiempo, por sí o por interpuesta persona, el Habeas Corpus, el cual debe resolverse en el término de treinta y seis horas.

171 **Artículo 86.**– Toda persona tendrá acción de tutela para reclamar ante los jueces, en todo momento y lugar, mediante un procedimiento preferente y sumario, por sí misma o por quien actúe en su nombre, la protección inmediata de sus derechos constitucionales fundamentales, cuando quiera que éstos resultaren vulnerados o amenazados por la acción o la omisión de cualquier autoridad pública.

La protección consistirá en una orden para que aquel respecto de quien se solicita tutela, actúe o se abstenga de hacerlo. El fallo, que será de inmediato cumplimiento, podrá impugnarse ante el juez competente y, en todo caso, éste lo remitirá a la Corte Constitucional para su eventual revisión.

Esta acción sólo procederá cuando el afectado no disponga de otro medio de defensa judicial, salvo que aquella se utilice como mecanismo transitorio para evitar un perjuicio irremediable.

En ningún caso podrán transcurrir más de diez días entre la solicitud de tutela y su resolución.

La ley establecerá los casos en los que la acción de tutela procede contra particulares encargados de la prestación de un servicio público o cuya conducta afectare grave y directamente el interés colectivo, o respecto de quienes el solicitante se halle en estado de subordinación o indefensión.

> The protection will consist in an order directed to who is sued in tutela, in order for him to act or to abstain from acting. The decision will be of immediate accomplishment, but it can be challenged before the competent judge, who in this case, must send the case to the Constitutional Court for its possible revision.
>
> This action can only be filed when the aggrieved party has no other means for its judicial defense, unless it is used as a transitory mechanism to prevent an irremediable prejudice.
>
> In no case more that 10 days can elapse from the request of tutela and its resolution.
>
> The statute will provide the cases in which the tutela will proceed against individuals that are in charge of providing public services or those whose conduct may affect collective interests in a grave and direct manner, or those to whom the claimant is in a situation of subordination or is defenseless.

Thus, the "tutela" action was constitutionally regulated to protect only certain constitutional rights, those listed in the Constitution as "fundamental" or considered as such because their conexity with the latter, in general, against public official violations, but also against only certain individual damaging actions. It must be said that notwithstanding the limitations regarding the protected rights, by means of judicial interpretation, the list of protected rights through the "tutela" has been progressively enlarged.

In Colombia, the incorporation of the tutela action in the 1991 Constitution with the additional creation of the Constitutional Court, triggered a very important and drastic change regarding the effective judicial protection of constitutional rights, allowing the access to justice to peoples that where previously excluded.

The tutela action has been regulated in the statute–decree N° 2591 of November 19th, 1991 which has been developed by decree N° 306 of February 19th 1992 and decree N° 382 of July 12, 2000.

C. *"Amparo" and habeas corpus in Costa Rica*

The Constitution of Costa Rica has expressly regulated the right of persons to file recourses of habeas corpus and "amparo" in order to seek for the protection of constitutional rights.

In this regard, Article 48 of the Constitution states that "every person has the right to the habeas corpus recourse in order to guarantee his personal freedom and integrity, and to the "amparo" recourse in order to maintain and reestablish the enjoyment of the rights enshrined in this Constitution, as well as those fundamental rights set forth in international instruments on human rights applicable in the republic"; assigning to the Constitutional Chamber of the Supreme Court the legal authority to decide them[172].

---

172 **Artículo 48.**– Toda persona tiene derecho al recurso de hábeas corpus para garantizar su libertad e integridad personales, y al recurso de "amparo" para mantener o restablecer el goce de los otros derechos consagrados en esta Constitución, así como de los de carácter fundamental establecidos en los instrumentos internacionales sobre derechos humanos, aplicables en la República. Ambos recursos serán de competencia de la Sala indicada en el artículo 10.

Since the creation of the IV Chamber (Constitutional Chamber) of the Supreme Court, Costa Rica has also experienced a very important change regarding the access to justice and the effective protection of human rights.

Both the habeas corpus and the "amparo" recourses are regulated in the Constitutional Judicial Review statute (*Ley de la Jurisdicción Constitucional, Ley Nº 7135*) of October 11th, 1989.

D. *Recourses for protection and of habeas corpus in Chile*

In Chile, Articles 20 and 21 of the Constitution regulate the recourse of protection (*recurso de protección*) but directing it only to a precise list of constitutional rights, and additionally, the habeas corpus recourse, as follows[173]:

> **Article 20.**– Anyone who, as a result of arbitrary or illegal acts or omissions suffers privation, perturbation or threat in the legitimate exercise of the rights and guaranties set forth in Article 19, numbers 1., 2., 3. clause fourth, 4., 5., 6., 9. final clause, 11., 12., 13., 15., 16., with respect to freedom to work and the right to freedom of contracting, and clause fourth, 19., 21., 22., 23., 24. and 25. by his own or anyone on his behalf, may file a complaint before the respective Appellate Courts, which shall immediately adopt the necessary measures in order to reestablish the rule of law and assure due protection to the affected party without prejudice to the other rights that it may allege before the respective authority or court.

---

173 **Artículo 20.**– El que por causa de actos u omisiones arbitrarios o ilegales, sufra privación, perturbación o amenaza en el legítimo ejercicio de los derechos y garantías establecidos en el artículo 19, números 1., 2., 3. inciso cuarto, 4., 5., 6., 9. inciso final, 11., 12., 13., 15., 16. en lo relativo a la libertad de trabajo y al derecho a su libre elección y libre contratación, y a lo establecido en el inciso cuarto, 19., 21., 22., 23., 24. y 25. podrá ocurrir por sí o por cualquiera a su nombre, a la Corte de Apelaciones respectiva, la que adoptará de inmediato las providencias que juzgue necesarias para restablecer el imperio del derecho y asegurar la debida protección del afectado, sin perjuicio de los demás derechos que pueda hacer valer ante la autoridad o los tribunales correspondientes.

Procederá también, el recurso de protección en el caso del Nº 8. del artículo 19, cuando el derecho a vivir en un medio ambiente libre de contaminación sea afectado por un acto arbitrario e ilegal imputable a una autoridad o persona determinada.

Artículo 21.– Todo individuo que se hallare arrestado, detenido o preso con infracción de lo dispuesto en la Constitución o en las leyes, podrá ocurrir por sí, o por cualquiera a su nombre, a la magistratura que señale la ley, a fin de que ésta ordene se guarden las formalidades legales y adopte de inmediato las providencias que juzgue necesarias para restablecer el imperio del derecho y asegurar la debida protección del afectado.

Esa magistratura podrá ordenar que el individuo sea traído a su presencia y su decreto será precisamente obedecido por todos los encargados de las cárceles o lugares de detención. Instruida de los antecedentes, decretará su libertad inmediata o hará que se reparen los defectos legales o pondrá al individuo a disposición del juez competente, procediendo en todo breve y sumariamente, y corrigiendo por sí esos defectos o dando cuenta a quien corresponda para que los corrija.

El mismo recurso, y en igual forma, podrá ser deducido en favor de toda persona que ilegalmente sufra cualquiera otra privación, perturbación o amenaza en su derecho a la libertad personal y seguridad individual. La respectiva magistratura dictará en tal caso las medidas indicadas en los incisos anteriores que estime conducentes para restablecer el imperio del derecho y asegurar la debida protección del afectado.

The recourse of protection will also be admitted in case of number 8 of Article 19, when the right to live in a pollution–free environment would be affected by an arbitrary or illegal act attributed to a public official or to an individual

The Chilean regulation, as the Colombian one, is exceptional in Latin America, because it limits the protected rights only to a list expressly set forth in the Constitution, mainly referred to civil rights. The consequence is that all other constitutional rights not enumerated as protected by the recourse of protection, must be enforced by means of the ordinary judicial procedures. In this regard, the Chilean and Colombian Constitutions followed the pattern set by the German and Spanish constitutional regulations regarding the "amparo" recourse.

In Chile, the Constitution also provides for the habeas corpus recourse, as follows:

> **Article 21.** Anybody being under arrest, detained or held–up in violation of what is set forth in the Constitution or in the statutes, can file before the court indicated by statute, by himself of by anyone on his behalf, a request for an order granting the protection of legal formalities, and the immediate adoption of the measures necessary in order to reestablish the rule of law and assure the due protection of the affected party.
>
> The court can order the person be brought before his presence and his orders must be precisely accomplished by all those in charge of prisons or detentions sites. Once the history of antecedents is known, the court will order the immediate release of the plaintiff, that the legal defects be repaired or to send the plaintiff before the competent judge. The court must always act by means of a brief and summary proceeding, correcting ex officio such defects or informing to whom it might concern in order for its correction.
>
> The same recourse can be filed in favor of any person that may illegally suffer any privation, perturbation or threatening of his personal freedom and individual safety. In such cases, the judge will order the measures previously indicated, in order to reestablish the rule of law and assure the due protection of the affected party.

The chilean "recurso de protección" has not yet been statutorily regulated, being only regulated in the constitution and by a supreme court regulation: *auto acordado de la corte suprema de justicia sobre tramitación del recurso de protección de garantías constitucionales, 1977.*

E. *"Amparo" and habeas corpus in El Salvador*

In El Salvador, Article 247 of the Constitution also sets forth two different specific judicial means for the protection of all constitutional right: the "amparo" action and the habeas corpus action, the latter for the protection of personal freedom[174].

---

174 **Art. 247.**– Toda persona puede pedir "amparo" ante la Sala de lo Constitucional de la Corte Suprema de Justicia por violación de los derechos que otorga la presente Constitución.

El habeas corpus puede pedirse ante la Sala de lo Constitucional de la Corte Suprema de Justicia o ante las Cámaras de Segunda Instancia que no residen en la capital. La resolución de la Cámara que denegare la libertad del favorecido podrá ser objeto de revisión, a solicitud del interesado por la Sala de lo Constitucional de la Corte Suprema de Justicia.

Regarding the violation of the rights granted in the Constitution, every person has the right to request "protection ("amparo") before the Constitutional Chamber of the Supreme Court of Justice.

Regarding the protection of personal freedom, the habeas corpus can be requested before the same Constitutional Chamber of the Supreme Court of Justice or before the Second Instance courts not located in the capital city. In the latter case, the decisions of such courts, when denying the freedom of the plaintiff, could be subjected to revision by the Constitutional Chamber of the Supreme Court of Justice., when requested by the interested party

The regulation of the "amparo" and habeas corpus action is set forth in the 1960 Statute on Constitutional proceedings (*Ley de Procedimientos Constitucionales*) of 1960, as amended in 1997.

F. *"Amparo" and habeas corpus in Honduras*

In the case of Honduras, the Constitution provides for two separate actions for the protection of human rights: "amparo" and habeas corpus[175].

Regarding habeas corpus, Article 182 of the Constitution states that

> "the State recognizes the guaranty of habeas corpus or personal exhibition"; thus, any aggrieved person or any other in his name has the right to file [the action], when illegally detained or in any way restrained in the enjoyment of his individual freedom; and when in his illegal detention or imprisonment; torments, tortures, abuses, illegal exaction and any repression, restriction or unnecessary annoyance regarding his individual safety or for the order of prison applied to the detainee".

The same article adds that the habeas corpus action may be filed without power of attorney or formality of any kind, orally or in writing, by means of any sort of communication, in any day and without costs. In no case shall the judges reject the

---

175 **Artículo 182.–** El Estado reconoce la garantía de habeas corpus o de exhibición personal. En consecuencia, toda persona agraviada o cualquiera otra en nombre de ésta tiene derecho a promoverla:

Cuando se encuentre ilegalmente presa, detenida o cohibida de cualquier modo en el goce de su libertad individual; y,

Cuando en su detención o prisión legal, se apliquen al detenido o preso, tormentos, torturas, vejámenes, exacción ilegal y toda coacción, restricción o molestia innecesaria para su seguridad individual o para el orden de la prisión.

La acción de habeas corpus se ejercerá sin necesidad de poder ni de formalidad alguna, verbalmente o por escrito, utilizando cualquier medio de comunicación, en horas o días hábiles o inhábiles y libres de costas.

Los jueces o magistrados no podrán desechar la acción de habeas corpus y tienen la obligación ineludible de proceder de inmediato para hacer cesar la violación a la libertad o a la seguridad personal.

Los tribunales que dejaren de admitir estas acciones incurrirán en responsabilidad penal y administrativa. Las autoridades que ordenaren y los agentes que ejecutaren el ocultamiento del detenido o que en cualquier forma quebranten esta garantía incurrirán en el delito de detención ilegal.

action of habeas corpus, and they shall have the ineludible duty to immediately proceed in order to put an end to the violations to personal freedom or safety.

The courts that fail to admit these actions will become criminally and administratively liable. The authority that orders or the agent that executes the concealing or that in any way harm this guaranty, will incur in the illegal detention offence.

Regarding the recourse of "amparo", Article 183 of the Constitution also states that "the State recognizes the guaranty of '"amparo"'[176], thus any aggrieved person or any other on his behalf has the right to file the recourse, in order to be maintained or to be restored in the enjoyment of the rights and guaranties set forth in the Constitution; and in order to have a declaration made that a statute or an authority resolution, act or fact does not oblige the plaintiff and is not applicable because it contravened, diminished or distorted any of the rights recognized in this Constitution"

The Constitution adds that the "amparo" recourse must be filed according to the statute; which in the particular case, is the Constitutional Judicial Review statute (*Ley sobre la Justicia Constitucional*) of 2004.

According to these regulations, the "amparo" action is conceived for the protection of all rights declared or recognized in the Constitution, against public authority actions or facts, and regarding individuals, is only admissible when they act with authority delegated powers.

G. *"Amparo" and habeas corpus in Nicaragua*

Regarding the "amparo" action, in Nicaragua[177], the Constitution only provides that "the persons whose constitutional rights have been violated or are in peril of being violated, can file according to the case the recourse of personal exhibition or [the recourse] of "amparo", in accordance with the "amparo" statute". No constitutional precision exists regarding the origin of the violation, so that if it is true that the recourse could then be brought against violations provoked by public officials and individuals, there are no provisions admitting it in the latter case

Thus, in the Constitution, for the protection of all constitutional rights, two specific judicial actions are regulated: personal exhibition (habeas corpus) and "amparo"; both regulated in the "amparo" statute (*Ley de "amparo"*) of 1988.

---

176 **Artículo 183.–** El Estado reconoce la garantía de "amparo". En consecuencia toda persona agraviada o cualquiera otra en nombre de ésta, tiene derecho a interponer recurso de "amparo":

Para que se le mantenga o restituya en el goce o disfrute de los derechos o garantías que la Constitución establece; y,

Para que se declare en casos concretos que una ley, resolución, acto o hecho de autoridad, no obliga al recurrente ni es aplicable por contravenir, disminuir o tergiversar cualesquiera de los derechos reconocidos por esta Constitución. el recurso de "amparo" se interpondrá de conformidad con la ley

177 **Artículo 45.–** Las personas cuyos derechos constitucionales hayan sido violados o estén en peligro de serlo, pueden interponer el recurso de exhibición personal o de "amparo", según el caso y de acuerdo con la Ley de "amparo".

H. *"Amparo" and habeas corpus in Panama*

Following the general trend of Latin American Constitution, the Constitution of Panama also distinguishes two specific judicial means for the protection of constitutional rights, habeas corpus and "amparo".

Regarding habeas corpus, according to Article 23 of the Constitution[178], "any individual detained in cases not prescribed in or without fulfilling the formalities prescribed in the Constitution and statutes, by means of the habeas corpus recourse will be freed at his request or at the request of other person. The recourse can be filed immediately after the detention and without consideration regarding the applicable punishment".

The habeas corpus recourse must be treated with prevalence to other pending cases, by means of a very brief procedure, which cannot be suspended because of the hours or non working days.

The Constitution of Panama, in its Article 50[179], also regulates the recourse of "amparo", setting forth the right of any person to have revoked any order to do or not to do, issue by any public servant which violates the rights and guaranties set forth in the Constitution. For that purpose, the recourse of "amparo" regarding constitutional guaranties can be filed before the competent court at his request of by any other person; being subject to a brief procedure.

Thus, the "amparo" is also conceived in Panamá for the protection of constitutional rights against authority actions, not being admitted against individual unconstitutional actions.

The statutory regulation regarding habeas corpus and "amparo" are set forth in the Judicial Code (*Código Judicial, Libro IV Instituciones de garantía*), Articles 2574–2614 (habeas corpus) and 2615–2632 (*"amparo" de garantía constitucionales*).

I. *Habeas corpus in Uruguay*

The Constitution of Uruguay, even if it is true that it does not provide expressly for the action or recourse of "amparo", it can be deducted from its Article 7 when it

---

178 **Artículo 23.**– todo individuo detenido fuera de los casos y a la forma que prescriben esta Constitución y la Ley, será puesto en libertad a petición suya o de otra persona, mediante el recurso de habeas corpus que podrá ser interpuesto inmediatamente después de la detención y sin consideración a la pena aplicable. El recurso se tramitará con prelación a otros casos pendientes mediante procedimiento sumarísimo, sin que el trámite pueda ser suspendido por razón de horas o días inhábiles.

179 **Artículo 50.**– Toda persona contra la cual se expida o se ejecute, por cualquier servidor público, una orden de hacer o no hacer, que viole los derechos y garantías que está constitución consagra, tendrá derecho a que la orden sea revocada a petición suya o de cualquiera persona.

El recurso de "amparo" de garantías constitucionales a que este artículo se refiere, se tramitará mediante procedimiento sumario y será de competencia de los tribunales judiciales.

declares the right of all inhabitants of the Republic "to be protected in the enjoyment of their life, honor, freedom, safety, work and property" [180].

Nonetheless, similarly to the Dominican Republic Constitution, the Uruguayan Constitution only regulated the action of habeas corpus, in Article 17[181], which states:

> **Article 17**.– In case of undue imprisonment, the interested party or any person can file before the competent judge the habeas corpus recourse in order to have the authority that has ordered the apprehension to immediately explain and justify its legal motive, being subjected to what the judge decides.

Notwithstanding, the "amparo" recourse has been regulated in the 1988 "Amparo" Law N° 16011 (*Ley de "amparo"*).

J. *Habeas corpus in Dominican Republic*

The Constitution of the Dominican Republic is one of the very few Latin American Constitution which does not expressly regulate the "amparo" action as a specific judicial mean for the protection of constitutional rights. Nonetheless, as mentioned above, this omission did not impede the Supreme Court of Justice from admitting and regulating the "amparo" action, applying for that purpose the Inter American Convention on Human Rights.

The basis procedure rules for amparo where established by the Supreme Court in its 1999 decision declaring the amparo recourse as a public positive law institution.

Regarding constitutional guaranties, the Constitution only sets forth the judicial guaranties for the protection of personal safety, by means of the action of habeas corpus. In this respect, Article 8 of the Constitution[182] provides that being "the effec-

---

180 **Artículo 7°.**–Los habitantes de la República tienen derecho a ser protegidos en el goce de su vida, honor, libertad, seguridad, trabajo y propiedad. Nadie puede ser privado de estos derechos sino conforme a las leyes que se establecen por razones de interés general.

181 **Artículo 17.**– En caso de prisión indebida el interesado o cualquier persona podrá interponer ante el Juez competente el recurso de "habeas corpus", a fin de que la autoridad aprehensora explique y justifique de inmediato el motivo legal de la aprehensión, estándose a lo que decida el Juez indicado.

182 **Artículo 8.**– Se reconoce como finalidad principal del Estado la protección efectiva de los derechos de la persona humana y el mantenimiento de los medios que le permitan perfeccionarse progresivamente dentro de un orden de libertad individual y de justicia social, compatible con el orden público, el bienestar general y los derechos de todos. Para garantizar la realización de esos fines se fijan las siguientes normas:

1. La inviolabilidad de la vida. En consecuencia no podrá establecerse, pronunciarse ni aplicarse en ningún caso la pena de muerte, ni las torturas, ni ninguna otra pena o procedimiento vejatorio o que implique la pérdida o la disminución de la integridad física o de la salud del individuo;
2. La seguridad individual. En consecuencia:
    a) No se establecerá al apremio corporal por deuda que no proviniere de infracción a las leyes penales;

tive protection of human rights the principal purpose of the State", the habeas Corpus statute will provide the way to proceed in a succinct way in order to secure, among others, with the compliance of the following individual safety rights: a. Not to be subject to corporal constraint because of debts not originated in violation of criminal statutes; b. Not to be imprisoned or to have restricted his freedom without motivated written judicial order, except in cases of flagrant crime; c. To be immediately freed at ones request or by any other person on one's behalf when deprived from one's freedom without due cause or without the legal formalities, on cases not set forth in the statutes; d. In case of detention, to be brought before a judicial authority within a 48 hour delay or to be freed; e. To be freed or to be subjected to prison within a delay of 48 hours after the detainee is brought before the judicial authority; f. Not to be transported from one prison to another without written and motivated judicial order.

The habeas was initially regulated by the 1978 Habeas Corpus statute (*Ley de habeas corpus*), and since 2002 it is regulated in the Procedural Criminal Code (Ley 76–02) (articles 381–392).

3. Constitutions Establishing the Amparo as the General Protective Judicial Means

A. *"Amparo" in Guatemala*

In the case of Guatemala, as is the case of México, the Constitution provides only one specific judicial mean for the protection of all constitutional rights, the "amparo" action, comprising the protection of personal freedom.

---

b) Nadie podrá ser reducido a prisión ni cohibido en su libertad sin orden motivada y escrita de funcionario judicial competente, salvo el caso de flagrante delito;

c) Toda persona privada de su libertad sin causa o sin las formalidades legales, o fuera de los casos previstos por las leyes, será puesta inmediatamente en libertad a requerimiento suyo o de cualquier persona;

d) Toda persona privada de su libertad será sometida a la autoridad judicial competente dentro de las cuarenta y ocho horas de su detención o puesta en libertad;

e) Todo arresto se dejará sin efecto o se elevará a prisión dentro de las cuarenta y ocho horas de haber sido sometido el arrestado a la autoridad judicial competente, debiendo notificarse al interesado dentro del mismo plazo, la providencia que al efecto se dictare;

f) Queda terminantemente prohibido el traslado de cualquier detenido de un establecimiento carcelario a otro lugar sin orden escrita y motivada de la autoridad judicial competente;

g) Toda persona que tenga bajo su guarda a un detenido estará obligada a presentarlo tan pronto como se lo requiera la autoridad competente. La Ley de Hábeas Corpus, determinará la manera de proceder sumariamente para el cumplimiento de las prescripciones contenidas en las letras a), b), c), d), e), f) y g) y establecerá las sanciones que proceda; ...

In this regard, Article 265 of the Constitution sets forth the "amparo"[183], with the purpose of protecting the people against the threats of violations to their rights to restore their effectiveness in case of violations. The Constitution emphatically states that "There is no scope that is not susceptible of "amparo", and that ["amparo"] "will proceed whenever the authority acts, resolutions, dispositions or statutes imply a threat, restriction or violation of the rights guaranteed by the Constitution and the statutes".

The constitutional provision only refers to authorities, but nonetheless, the amparo has been admitted for the protection of all rights declared in the Constitution and also in statutes, also against individual actions.

The regulation of the action of "amparo" is set forth in the 1986 "Amparo", Personal Exhibition and Constitutionality Statute (*Ley de "amparo", exhibición personal y de constitucionalidad*).

B. *Suit for "amparo" in México*

As was already mentioned, the specific judicial means for the protection of human rights, named "amparo" in Latin America, has its origin in Mexico, where it has been regulated in the Constitution since the XIX Century.

But from a remedy originally inspired in the North American injunctions, the Mexican institution of "amparo", was conceived as a suit, not only for the protection of constitutional rights and guaranties, but also to resolve what in other Countries is the object of different actions and procedures, in particular, judicial review of constitutionality of statutes, judicial review of administrative action and judicial review of judicial decisions (cassation).

But in particular, regarding the protection of constitutional rights and guaranties, in the Mexican Constitution the "amparo" is conceived as a general trail initiated be means of an action that can be brought before the courts for the protection of all individual guarantees declared in the Constitution, but only against actions of authorities such as statutes, judicial decisions or administrative acts, and not against private individual actions.

Article 107 of the Constitution regulates in a very extensive and detailed way the procedural rules for the exercise of the "amparo" action, as well as the competent courts. In its basic regulations[184], this article provides that all controversies that

183 **Artículo 265.**– Procedencia del "amparo". Se instituye el "amparo" con el fin de proteger a las personas contra las amenazas de violaciones a sus derechos o para restaurar el imperio de los mismos cuando la violación hubiere ocurrido. No hay ámbito que no sea susceptible de "amparo", y procederá siempre que los actos, resoluciones, disposiciones o leyes de autoridad lleven implícitos una amenaza, restricción o violación a los derechos que la Constitución y las leyes garantizan.

184 **Artículo 107.**– Todas las controversias de que habla el Artículo 103 se sujetaran a los procedimientos y formas del orden jurídico que determine la ley, de acuerdo a las bases siguientes:

I. El juicio de "amparo" se seguirá siempre a instancia de parte agraviada;

could arise "out of statutes or acts of the authorities that violate individual guarantees" (art. 103,I), as set forth in Article 107, shall be subject to the legal forms and procedure prescribed by the statute, on the following bases:

> I. The trial in "amparo" shall always be held at the instance of the injured party.
>
> II. The judgment shall always be such that it affects only private individuals and it is limited to the preserving (ampararlos) and protecting them in the special case to which the complaint refers, without making any general declaration as to the statute or act on which the complaint is based.

II. La sentencia será siempre tal, que solo se ocupe de individuos particulares, limitándose a ampararlos y protegerlos en el caso especial sobre el que verse la queja, sin hacer una declaración general respecto de la ley o acto que la motivare....

III. Cuando se reclamen actos de tribunales judiciales, administrativos o del trabajo, el "amparo" solo procederá en los casos siguientes:

a) Contra sentencias definitivas o laudos y resoluciones que pongan fin al juicio, respecto de las cuales no proceda ningún recurso ordinario por el que puedan ser modificados o reformados, ya sea que la violación se cometa en ellos o que, cometida durante el procedimiento, afecte a las defensas del quejoso, trascendiendo al resultado del fallo; siempre que en materia civil haya sido impugnada la violación en el curso del procedimiento mediante el recurso ordinario establecido por la ley e invocada como agravio en la segunda instancia, si se cometió en la primera. Estos requisitos no serán exigibles en el "amparo" contra sentencias dictadas en controversias sobre acciones del estado civil o que afecten al orden y a la estabilidad de la familia.

b) Contra actos en juicio cuya ejecución sea de imposible reparación, fuera del juicio o después de concluido, una vez agotados los recursos que en su caso procedan, y

c) Contra actos que afecten a personas extrañas al juicio;

IV. En materia administrativa el "amparo" procede, además, contra resoluciones que causen agravio no reparable mediante algún recurso, juicio o medio de defensa legal. No será necesario agotar estos cuando la ley que los establezca exija, para otorgar la suspensión del acto reclamado, mayores requisitos que los que la ley reglamentaria del juicio de "amparo" requiera como condición para decretar esa suspensión; ....

VIII. Contra las sentencias que pronuncien en "amparo" los jueces de distrito o los tribunales unitarios de circuito procede revisión. de ella conocerá la Suprema Corte de Justicia:

a) Cuando habiéndose impugnado en la demanda de "amparo", por estimarlos directamente violatorios de esta constitución, leyes federales o locales, tratados internacionales, reglamentos expedidos por el Presidente de la República de acuerdo con la Fracción I del Artículo 89 de esta constitución y reglamentos de leyes locales expedidos por los gobernadores de los estados o por el jefe del Distrito Federal, subsista en el recurso el problema de constitucionalidad;

b) Cuando se trate de los casos comprendidos en las fracciones II y III del Artículo 103 de esta constitución. La Suprema Corte de Justicia, de oficio o a petición fundada del correspondiente tribunal colegiado de circuito, o del procurador general de la República, podrá conocer de los "amparos" en revisión, que por su interés y trascendencia así lo ameriten. En los casos no previstos en los párrafos anteriores, conocerán de la revisión los tribunales colegiados de circuito y sus sentencias no admitirán recurso alguno;

In particular, in the case of "amparo" against judicial decisions on civil, criminal, or labor matters, the writ of *"amparo"* shall be granted only:

1. Against final judgments or awards against which no ordinary recourse is available by virtue of which these judgments can be modified or amended, whether the violation [of the individual guarantees] is committed in the judgments or awards, or whether, if committed during the course of the trial, the violation prejudices the petitioner's defense by going beyond the outcome of the judgment; provided that in civil or criminal judicial matters timely objection and protest were made against it by means of the ordinary appeal, or if it occurred in the first instance, were raised in the second instance. None of these conditions are required in cases of "amparo" against judicial decisions referring to controversies related to personal statute and that affect the family stability and order.
2. Against acts at the trial, the execution of which would be irreparable out of court, or at the conclusion of the trial, once all available recourses have been exhausted.
3. Against acts that affect persons who are strangers to the trial.

In administrative matters, *"amparo"* may be filed against decisions which cause an injury that cannot be remedied through any legal recourse, trial, or defense. It shall not be necessary to exhaust these remedies when the statute that established them, in order to allow the suspension of the contested act, demands greater requirements than the regulatory statute for trials in *"amparo"* as a condition for ordering such suspension.

All the judgments in *"amparo"* rendered by district courts when a statute is impugned as unconstitutional or in cases of violation of individual guaranties, are subject to review by the Supreme Court of Justice (107, VIII). The Supreme Court, ex officio or when asked by the lower court or by the public prosecutor, may resolve the revision of "amparo" whose revision have been sought, if it considers it of interest or importance (art. 107, VIII).

The "amparo" suit has been regulated in the "amparo" statute developing Articles 103 and 107 of the Constitution (*Ley de "amparo" reglamentaria de los artículos 103 y 107 de la Constitución Política)* of 1935, which has been amended many times.

C. *"Amparo" in Venezuela*

The Venezuelan Constitution since 1961 has regulated the "amparo" not as a specific judicial means for the protection of constitutional right, but as a constitutional right in itself, of all persons to be judicially protected in the enjoyment of all human rights. This tradition has been followed in the 1999 Constitution, which guaranties the right of every person to have access to the Judiciary in order to have enforced his rights and interest, including the collective or diffuse ones, and to have the effective protection of the same, and to obtain in a speedy way the corresponding decision. For such purpose, "the State must guarantee a free justice, accessible, impartial, suitable, transparent, autonomous, independent, responsible, equitable, expeditious, without delay, without formalisms and useless repositions" (art. 26).

But in particular, regarding "amparo", Article 27 of the Constitution[185] sets forth the right to legal protection as follows:

> **Article 27.** Everyone has the right to be protected by the courts in the enjoyment and exercise of constitutional rights and guarantees, including even those inherent to persons not expressly mentioned in this Constitution or in international instruments on human rights.
>
> Proceedings on the action of constitutional "amparo" shall be oral, public, brief, free of charge and unencumbered by formalities, and the competent judge shall have the power to immediately restore the infringed legal situation infringed or the closest possible equivalent thereto.
>
> All time shall be available for the holding of such proceedings, and the court shall give priority to constitutional claims over any other matter. The action of "amparo" regarding freedom or safety, may be exercised by any person and the detainee shall be immediately transferred to the court, without delay. The exercise of this right shall not be affected in any way by the declaration of a state of exception or restriction of constitutional guarantees.

From this regulation, the "amparo" in conceived in Venezuela, as a constitutional right that all individuals have, to be protected on their human rights, even on those not expressly declared in the Constitution or in international treaties, but that are inherent to human beings, against any harm or threat from public officials or individuals. The action of "amparo" is thus expressly regulated, comprising the protection of individual freedom and safety.

But additionally, the Venezuelan Constitution has also set forth the habeas data recourse, by stating in its Article 28[186]:

> **Article 28.** Anyone has the right of access to the information and data concerning him or his goods which are contained in official or private registries, with the exceptions that may be established by statute, as well as to know what use is being made of the same and the purpose thereof, and to petition the competent court for the updating, rectification or destruction of er-

---

185 **Artículo 27.**– Toda persona tiene derecho a ser amparada por los tribunales en el goce y ejercicio de los derechos y garantías constitucionales, aun de aquellos inherentes a la persona que no figuren expresamente en esta Constitución o en los instrumentos internacionales sobre derechos humanos.

El procedimiento de la acción de "amparo" constitucional será oral, público, breve, gratuito y no sujeto a formalidad, y la autoridad judicial competente tendrá potestad para restablecer inmediatamente la situación jurídica infringida o la situación que más se asemeje a ella.

Todo tiempo será hábil y el tribunal lo tramitará con preferencia a cualquier otro asunto. La acción de "amparo" a la libertad o seguridad podrá ser interpuesta por cualquier persona, y el detenido o detenida será puesto bajo la custodia del tribunal de manera inmediata, sin dilación alguna. El ejercicio de este derecho no puede ser afectado, en modo alguno, por la declaración del estado de excepción o de la restricción de garantías constitucionales.

186 **Artículo 28.**– Toda persona tiene derecho de acceder a la información y a los datos que sobre sí misma o sobre sus bienes consten en registros oficiales o privados, con las excepciones que establezca la ley, así como de conocer el uso que se haga de los mismos y su finalidad, y a solicitar ante el tribunal competente la actualización, la rectificación o la destrucción de aquellos, si fuesen erróneos o afectasen ilegítimamente sus derechos. Igualmente, podrá acceder a documentos de cualquier naturaleza que contengan información cuyo conocimiento sea de interés para comunidades o grupos de personas. Queda a salvo el secreto de las fuentes de información periodística y de otras profesiones que determine la ley.

roneous records and those that unlawfully affect the petitioner's right. The petitioner may also have access to documents of any nature containing information whose knowledge could be of interest to communities or groups of persons. The foregoing is without prejudice to the confidentiality of sources from which information is received by journalists, or secrecy in other professions as may be determined by statute.

According to these constitutional provisions, the "*amparo*" has been consequently regulated *as a constitutional right* of the people, to require the protection of courts to ensure the enjoyment and exercise of *all the rights and guarantees* established by the Constitution or being inherent to the human being, against any distress, whether by public authorities or individuals, by means of proceedings that should be brief and summary, and that allow the judge to immediately restore the infringed legal situation[187].

Hence, the Constitution does not establish only "one" action or writ of protection as a particular remedy, but rather a "right to protection" as a fundamental right which can, and in fact is, exercised through a variety of legal actions and recourses, including a direct "action for protection" of a subsidiary nature.

Thus, the Constitution does not establish just a particular constitutional *adjective* "guarantee" of constitutional rank to protect constitutional rights, but moreover, what it has established is a true "constitutional right", the right of everyone to be protected by the courts in the enjoyment and exercise of their constitutional rights and guarantees. This character of the *amparo*, as a "constitutional right" is the basic element that identifies the Venezuelan institution[188] and that leads to its consideration not as a single action or complaint, but as a right. This criterion was the one that in our opinion, as abovementioned, led the Supreme Court in 1983, to change its criterion established in 1970, regarding the possibility of the exercise of the action for protection, even in the absence of the law regulating and developing the constitutional dispositions on the matter.[189]

The question could be stated as follows: If the norm of Article 49 were to establish an "action or recourse" for protection, then Article 50 of the Constitution which lays down that the absence of laws regulating the exercise of "constitutional rights" would not impede their exercise, would not be applicable[190] on the contrary, if Article 49 of the Constitution was to establish a "fundamental right", as it is done, then Article 50 of the Constitution would be applicable,[191] and even without the law of

---

187 The right of protection (Art. 27 Constitution) is thus different to the broader right to access to justice specifically regulated in Articles 26 and 48 of the Constitution

188 See Allan R. BREWER–CARÍAS, "El derecho de *amparo* y la acción de *amparo*", in *Revista de derecho público,* N° 22, Editorial Jurídica Venezolana, Caracas, 1985, pp. 51–61.

189 See Supreme Court of Justice in Político–Administrative Chamber, October 20, 1983, in *Revista de derecho público,* N° 16, Editorial Jurídica Venezolana, Caracas, 1983, p. 169.

190 See the opinion stated by the Attorney's General Office in *Doctrina de la Procuraduría General de la República 1970*, Caracas, 1971, p. 35.

191 See J.R. QUINTERO "Recurso de *amparo*. La cuestión central en dos sentencias y un Voto Salvado" in *Revista de la Facultad de Derecho*, N° 9, Universidad Católica Andrés Bello, Caracas, 1969–1970, pp. 161–162–166. See the judicial decision and its dissident opinion in

the right of *amparo*, this right could be constitutionally exercised. The latter is the predominant criterion followed by the courts, and in our opinion is the most distinguishable feature of the *amparo* institution in Venezuela.

II. THE INTERNATIONALIZATION OF THE "AMPARO" IN THE LATIN AMERICA

As can be deducted from the constitutional regulations of the "amparo" right, action or recourse in all Latin American Countries, additional to the regulations of the habeas corpus and habeas data recourses, the existence of special judicial means for the protection of human rights can be considered as a general feature of Latin American constitutionalism; with Latin American origin and without real precedents in the historical European regimes.

That is why this characteristic institution of Latin American constitutionalism, was originally regulated in the American Declaration of the Rights and Duties of Man approved by the Ninth International Conference of American States, held in Bogotá, Colombia, in April 1948, in which Article 18 set forth:

> **Article XVIII.** Every person may resort to the courts to ensure respect for his legal rights. There should likewise be available to him a simple, brief procedure whereby the courts will protect him (*lo ampare*) from acts of authority that, to his prejudice, violate any fundamental constitutional rights[192].

> A similar regulation was later incorporated in Article 8 of the Universal Declaration of Human Rights adopted by United Nations in December the same year 1948. In the English version of the Declaration, Article 8 just states that: "Everyone has the right to an effective remedy by the competent national tribunals for acts violating the fundamental rights granted to him by the constitution or by law". Nonetheless, in the Spanish version, the wording is nearest to the American Declaration wording:

> **Article 8,** Toda persona tiene derecho a un recurso efectivo, ante los tribunales nacionales competentes, *que la ampare* contra actos que violen sus derechos fundamentales reconocidos por la constitución o por la ley.

A free English translation of this text will show not only a right to an effective remedy but a right to an effective remedy for the protection of human rights: "Every person has the right to an effective recourse before the national competent courts, for his protection (*que la ampare*) against acts that violate his fundamental rights recognized in the Constitution and in statutes".

After this first International Declarations, in 1950 the European Convention on Human Rights, which was the first international convention on human rights, also

---

pp. 180–206. See the text also in O. MARÍN GÓMEZ, *Protección procesal de las garantías constitucionales de Venezuela. Amparo y Habeas Corpus*, Caracas, 1983, pp. 229–250.

192 The Spanish vesion of article 18 is as follow: Derecho de justicia: Artículo XVIII: Toda persona puede ocurrir a los tribunales para hacer valer sus derechos. Asimismo debe disponer de un procedimiento sencillo y breve por el cual la justicia *lo ampare* contra actos de la autoridad que violen, en perjuicio suyo, alguno de los derechos fundamentales consagrados constitucionalmente.

regulated the right to effective recourses in cases of violations of human rights, as follows:

> **Article 13.** Everyone whose rights and freedoms as set forth in this Convention are violated shall have an effective remedy before a national authority notwithstanding that the violation has been committed by persons acting in an official capacity[193].

The 1966 International Covenant on Civil and Political Rights of the United Nations, Article 2,3 also regulated the right to an effective remedy in case of violations of human rights, as follows, by obligating the Stats parties to undertake:

> a) To ensure that any person whose rights or freedoms as herein recognized are violated shall have an effective remedy, notwithstanding that the violation has been committed by persons acting in an official capacity;
>
> b) To ensure that any person claiming such a remedy shall have his right thereto determined by competent judicial, administrative or legislative authorities, or by any other competent authority provided for by the legal system of the State, and to develop the possibilities of judicial remedy;
>
> c) To ensure that the competent authorities shall enforce such remedies when granted[194].

Finally, the 1969 American Convention on Human Rights declared the right to judicial protection, or more precisely, to the "amparo" recourse, as follows:

Article 25. Right to Judicial Protection

1. Everyone has the right to simple and prompt recourse, or any other effective recourse, to a competent court or tribunal for protection (que la ampare) against acts that violate his fundamental rights recognized by the constitution or laws of the state concerned or by this Convention, even though such violation may have been committed by persons acting in the course of their official duties.
2. The States Parties undertake:
   a. to ensure that any person claiming such remedy shall have his rights determined by the competent authority provided for by the legal system of the state;
   b. to develop the possibilities of judicial remedy; and
   c. to ensure that the competent authorities shall enforce such remedies when granted[195].

---

193 The Spanish version of article 13 is: **Artículo 13. Derecho a un recurso efectivo**. Toda persona cuyos derechos y libertades reconocidos en el presente Convenio hayan sido violados tiene derecho a la concesión de un recurso efectivo ante una instancia nacional, incluso cuando la violación haya sido cometida por personas que actúen en el ejercicio de sus funciones oficiales.

194 The Spanish version is: Article 2,3. Cada uno de los Estados Partes en el presente Pacto se compromete a garantizar que:

a) Toda persona cuyos derechos o libertades reconocidos en el presente Pacto hayan sido violados podrá interponer un recurso efectivo, aun cuando tal violación hubiera sido cometida por personas que actuaban en ejercicio de sus funciones oficiales;

b) La autoridad competente, judicial, administrativa o legislativa, o cualquiera otra autoridad competente prevista por el sistema legal del Esta do, decidirá sobre los derechos de toda persona que interponga tal recurso, y desarrollará las posibilidades de recurso judicial;

c) Las autoridades competentes cumplirán toda decisión en que se haya estimado procedente el recurso.

1. The "amparo" in the American Convention on Human Rights

This article of the American Convention regulates the "amparo" recourse for the protection of human rights, as their judicial guarantee *par excellence*, both those regulated in the Constitutions and other internal legal regulations of the Party States, as well as those listed in international declarations. That is why the Inter American Court on Human Rights has considered this Article 25 as a "general provision that gives expression to the procedural institution known as "amparo", which is a simple and prompt remedy designated for the protection of all of the rights recognized in the Constitution and laws of the States parties and by the Convention"; thus, that "can be applied to all rights" [196].

But the American Convention, in Article 7 regarding the right to personal liberty and security, also provides for the recourse of habeas corpus as follows:

> 6. Anyone who is deprived of his liberty shall be entitled to recourse to a competent court, in order that the court decides without delay on the lawfulness of his arrest or detention and order his release if the arrest or detention is unlawful. In States Parties whose laws provide that anyone who believes himself to be threatened with deprivation of his liberty is entitled to recourse to a competent court in order that it decides on the lawfulness of such threat, this remedy may not be restricted or abolished. The interested party or another person on his behalf is entitled to seek these remedies.

Examining the habeas corpus and the "amparo" together, it is possible to conclude, as asserted by the Inter American Court on Human Rights,

> "that ""amparo"" comprises a whole series of remedies and that habeas corpus is but one of its components. An examination of the essentials aspects of both guarantees, as embodied in the Convention and, in their different forms, in the legal systems of the States parties, indicates that in some instances habeas corpus functions are an independent remedy. Here its primary purpose is to protect the personal freedom of those who are being detained or who have

---

195 The Spanish version is as follows: **Artículo 25. Protección Judicial.** Toda persona tiene derecho a un recurso sencillo y rápido o a cualquier otro recurso efectivo ante los jueces o tribunales competentes, *que la ampare* contra actos que violen sus derechos fundamentales reconocidos por la Constitución, la ley o la presente Convención, aun cuando tal violación sea cometida por personas que actúen en ejercicio de sus funciones oficiales.

Los Estados partes se comprometen:

a) a garantizar que la autoridad competente prevista por el sistema legal del Estado decidirá sobre los derechos de toda persona que interponga tal recurso;

b) a desarrollar las posibilidades de recurso judicial, y

c) a garantizar el cumplimiento, por las autoridades competentes, de toda decisión en que se haya estimado procedente el recurso.

196 See Advisory Opinion OC–8/8 Habeas corpus in emergency situations), paragraph 32. (El artículo 25,1 de la Convención es una disposición de carácter general que recoge la institución procesal del "amparo", como procedimiento sencillo y breve que tiene por objeto la tutela de los derechos fundamentales").

been threatened with detention. In other circumstances, however, habeas corpus is viewed either as the "“amparo” of freedom" or as an integral part of "amparo"[197].

These regulations can be considered the culmination of the process of internationalization of the constitutionalization of human rights, in particular regarding the provision of specific judicial means for their protection. So, if it is true that since the XIX Century, the "amparo" and habeas corpus recourses or actions, were initially regulated in many Latin American Constitutions; since the seventies, they have now passed to be regulated in a general way in an International Convention that has been ratified by all Latin American Countries, where, in general terms –as has been previously analyzed, it has been recognized as having constitutional o supra statutorily rank. Regarding both guarantees the Inter American Court of Human Rigts, has considered "the writs of habeas corpus and of "amparo" among those judicial remedies that are essential for the protection of various rights whose derogation is prohibited by Article 27 (2) and that serve, moreover, to preserve legality in a democratic society"[198].

After its ratification, it has been the Convention the one that has pushed for the subsequent process of constitucionalization of the internationalization of the "amparo", being the inspiration for many of the new Latin America constitutionals reforms or regulations, sanctioned during the last two decades, particularly regarding the "amparo" recourse.

Nowadays, therefore, the right to a judicial guaranty of human rights ("amparo" and habeas corpus) set forth in the American Convention is also an international obligation imposed on the States Parties to guarantee their peoples these effective protective remedies of their human rights. This goes so far as to the point that lack of internal regulations and effective function, constitutes a breach of the Convention.

Referring in particular to the "amparo", from what it is set forth in Article 25 of the American Convention, as well as from the regulations of the other international instruments on human rights, the internationalization of the "amparo" recourse has concluded in the design of a specific remedy for the protection of human rights, considered by the Inter American Court on Human Rights, as "one of the basic pillars not only of the American Convention, but of the rule of Law in a democratic society"[199]; which can be characterized by the following elements:

First, in the American Convention the "amparo" is conceived as a specific judicial recourse or action, that is, as a judicial guaranty; but it is also conceived as a fundamental human right in itself, that is to say, the right of citizens to be protected by the Judiciary;

---

197 Advisory Opinion OC–8//87 of January 30, 1987 (Habeas Corpus in Emergency Situations), paragraph 34

198 Advisory Opinion OC–8/87 of January 30, 1987 (Habeas Corpus in Emergency Situation), paragraph 42; Advisory Opinion OC–9/87 of October 6, 1987 (Judicial Guarantees in Status of Emergency), paragraph 33.

199 See Case: *Castillo Páez,* p. 83; Caso: *Suárez Roseo,* p. 65 and caso: *Blake,* p. 102. See the referentes in Cecilia MEDINA QUIROGA, *La Convención Americana: teoría y jurisprudencia,* IIDH, San José, 2003, p. 358.

Second, the remedy is conceived to protect all human rights recognized in the Constitutions, in the statutes or in the international instruments;

Third, the recourse in order to seek the judicial protection must be simple, brief and effective;

Fourth, the recourse can be brought before the competent courts, which must be independent and autonomous according to the general terms of the international instruments;

Fifth, the protection refers to any kind of violations of human rights, thus produced by acts issued by private individuals as well as by public officials, even when acting in the course of their official duties;

Sixth, the effectiveness of the recourse is related to the effective repair of the offence by means of the enforcement of the judicial decision by the competent authorities.

The most important consequence of the internationalization of the "amparo", is that according to Article 1,1 of the Convention, the States Parties are obligated not only "*to respect*" the right to "amparo" recognized herein, but also "*to ensure* to all persons subject to their jurisdiction the free and full exercise" of such right, without any discrimination. This "implies the duty of States parties to organize the governmental apparatus and, in general, all the structures through which public power is exercised, so that they are capable of ensuring the free and full enjoyment of human rights"[200].

The actions of the State Parties in order to comply with this obligation are not only formal ones, in the sense that it "is not fulfilled by the existence of a legal system designed to make it possible to comply with this obligation, it also requires the government to conduct itself so as to effectively ensure the free and full exercise of human rights"[201]. On the contrary, as stressed by the Inter American Court on Human Rights, referring to the "amparo" as a judicial guaranty of human rights,

> "for such a remedy to exist, it is not sufficient that it be provided for by the Constitution or by law or that it be formally recognized, but rather it must be truly effective in establishing whether there has been a violation of human rights and in providing redress"[202].

2. The meaning of the regulation of the "amparo" in the American Convention

As mentioned before, Article 25 of the Convention provides that everyone has the right to simple and prompt recourse, or any other effective recourse, to a competent court or tribunal for protection (*que la ampare*) against acts that violate his fun-

200 Case: *Velásquez Rodríguez,* Judgement July, 29, 1988, Paragraph 166.

201 *Idem*, paragrapf 167

202 Advisory Opinión OC–9/87 of October 6, 1987 (Judicial Guarantees in Status of Emergency), paragraph 24. See in similar sense, Case: *Comunidad Mayagna (Sumo) Awas Tingni,* paragraph 113; Caso: *Ivcher Bronstein,* paragraph 136; Caso: *Cantoral benavides,* paragraph 164; caso: *Durand y Ugarte,* paragraph 102.

damental rights recognized by the Constitution or laws of the state concerned and by the American Convention itself.

From this precise provision derives the framework that this action for the protection of fundamental rights should have in internal law[203] and which demands constitutionalization strategies for different countries in which Constitutions establish what could be considered restrictions to the exercise of the right to "amparo".

3. The "amparo" as a Human Right

Firstly, the American Convention conceives the "amparo" as a human right in itself, when providing that everybody "has the right" to a recourse. This does not mean that people only have a specific adjective law instrument for the protection of other rights, but that everyone has a human right in itself to obtain constitutional protection or "amparo" regarding all human rights.

Thus, we are in fact in the presence of a human right of the people to have at their disposal an effective, simple and prompt judicial means for the protection of their rights; which additionally, is considered in the Convention as one of the "fundamental" rights that cannot be suspended or restricted in cases of state of emergency.

Article 27 of the Convention allows that in time of war, public danger, or other emergency that threatens the independence or security of a State Party, certain measures to be taken derogating its obligations under the Convention to the extent and for the period of time strictly required by the exigencies of the situation, provided that such measures are not inconsistent with its other obligations under international law and do not involve discrimination on the ground of race, color, sex, language, religion, or social origin. In paragraph 2 of the same article, it set forth that

> "The foregoing provision does not authorize any suspension of the following articles: Article 3 (Right to juridical personality), Article 4 (Right to life), Article 5 (Right to humane treatment), Article 6 (Freedom from slavery), Article 9 (Freedom from ex post facto laws), Article 12 (Freedom of conscience and religion), Article 17 (Rights of the family), Article 18 (Right to a name), Article 19 (Rights of the child), Article 20 (Right to nationality), and Article 23 (Right to participate in Government), or of the judicial guarantees essential for the protection of such rights".

The Inter American Court on Human Rights has issued two Advisory Opinions on the matter regarding the possibility of the suspension of the "amparo" and habeas corpus provisions, having concluded that "the suspension of the legal remedies of habeas corpus or of "amparo" in emergency situations cannot be deemed to be compatible with the international obligations imposed on these States by the Conven-

---

203 *Véase* Allan R. BREWER–CARÍAS, "El "*amparo"* en América Latina: La universalización del régimen de la Convención Americana sobre Derechos Humanos y la necesidad de superar las restricciones nacionales" in *Ética y Jurisprudencia*, 1/2003, Enero–Diciembre, Universidad Valle del Momboy, Facultad de Ciencias Jurídicas y Políticas, Centro de Estudios Jurídicos "Cristóbal Mendoza", Valera, Estado Trujillo, 2004, pp. 9–34.

tion"[204], being incompatible with "legality in a democratic society" which must be preserved[205].

But in spite of the American Convention provision considering the "amparo" as a human right, it is true that in the majority of internal legislation of Latin American Countries, the "amparo" has not been provided as a constitutional right in itself and it has taken the form of, rather, been regulated as an specific adjective action. In other words, the "amparo" has been regulated as a specific remedy or judicial means of protection, either a recourse of "amparo", "tutela" or protection, or as an action of *habeas corpus* or *habeas data*.

Instead, the American Convention sets forth the judicial protection of human rights, by mean of a prompt, simple and effective remedy that could be not only the specific action of "amparo" or habeas corpus, but another judicial mean, such as it occurs in countries where an "action of "amparo"" is not specifically regulated, as it is the case in the United States, England, France or Italy; but where although no legal means called "action of "amparo"" exist, there are nevertheless adequate mechanisms for the effective protection of human rights by means of ordinary judicial remedies. Nonetheless, it can be said that in some Latin American countries, following the orientation of the American Convention and, moreover, in advance of the adoption of such Convention, the "amparo" was conceived as a constitutional right in itself, and it has been developed with those characteristics, such as in the case of Mexico and Venezuela and also in the case of Colombia.

4. The "amparo" as a judicial guarantee

Secondly, the recourse of "amparo" enshrined in Article 25 of the Convention devoted to regulate the "Right to judicial protection", must of course always be a judicial mean of protection. This feature differentiates the provisions of the American Convention from those of the International Covenant on Civil and Political Rights (Article 2,3) and of the European Convention on Human Rights, which only provides for an effective recourse, without qualifying it as "judicial".

The judicial protection mechanisms referred to such article of the American Convention is undoubtedly inspired in the Latin American action of "amparo", but it can be said that its scope may be wider. It comprises of course the Colombian action of tutela and the Chilean action of protection, but it also comprises all other judicial remedies that in an effective, simple and prompt way can protect human rights. The Convention speaks of an effective, prompt and simple means that may be of any type. Therefore, in fact, it can be any effective judicial means, and not necessarily a single and unique action of "amparo". In other words, the Convention not necessarily refers to an only and single judicial remedy, but rather that there can and must be a collection also effective, of ordinary legal means for the protection of human rights. That is why, regarding "amparo", in general terms most of the Latin American legislations set forth that this specific means has a subordinate nature, in the

---

204 Advisory Opinion OC–8//87 of January 30, 1987 (Habeas Corpus in Emergency Situations), paragraph 43.

205 *Idem*, paragraph 42

sense that it proceeds only when there are no other effective judicial means that can protect human rights; in similar sense than the subordinate character the Anglo–American injunction has.

On the other hand, referring to the judicial character of the action or recourse, the Convention also set forth that they can be brought before the "competent courts", thus being the intention of the Convention to set forth an essential function of the Judiciary, as also happens, for instance, under the Anglo–American systems, where the "amparo" exists in the various writs of injunctions, but without being named as such. In these systems judges routinely issue *mandamus*, *injunction* and *prohibition* orders or decisions, equivalent to the ""amparos" in Latin America. However, this is part of the routine actions of the Judiciary, without it being a specific judicial mean.

On the other hand, when the American Convention refers to the "competent courts" in order to decide "amparo" remedies, it is not referring to only one specific court, but to all the Judiciary. That is why, pursuant to the Convention and Latin American tradition, competence in "amparo" matters are in general essentially belonging to the Judiciary, in the sense that such competence shall belong to "the tribunals" – to all of them and not just one of them–, which is in fact a characteristic of the European model, in particular that of Germany and Spain, where competence in "amparo" matters is held by one single Tribunal, the Constitutional Tribunal.

Unfortunately, however, this reduction of the judicial competence to constitutionally protect through an "amparo" has occurred in some Latin American countries, upon assigning it to one single tribunal, particularly the Supreme Court. This is the case of the Constitutional Chamber of the Supreme Courts of Costa Rica, El Salvador and Nicaragua, where such courts are the exclusively competent to hear the recourse of "amparo".

Whatever the case, and apart from the examples mentioned, in all other countries of Latin America, judicial competence in matters of "amparo" is diffused, in the sense that it is a power that is attributed, generally speaking, to the courts of first instance or circumscription courts, but it is not concentrated in one single institution. What the concentration of the hearing of the "amparo" in one single judicial institution finally does is to restrict access to justice for the effective protection of rights.

5. The "amparo" as a simple, prompt and effective judicial guarantee

Thirdly, in any case, the judicial recourse that the Convention guarantees, as set forth in Article 25 and as has been stressed by the Inter American Court on Human Rights, must be all together "simple, prompt and effective"[206].

Regarding the simplicity, it refers to a procedure that must lack the dilatory procedural formalities of ordinary judicial means, imposed by the need to grant a constitutional –not ordinary– protection; and regarding the prompt character of the recourse, the Inter American court has argued about the need for a reasonable delay

206 Case: *Suárez Romero,* Paragraph 66.

for the decision, not considering "prompt" recourses which were resolved after "a long time"[207].

The effective character of the recourse refers to the fact that it will be capable to produce the results for which it has been created[208]; in words of the Inter American Court on Human Rigths,

> "it must be truly effective in establishing whether there has been a violation of human rights and in providing redress. A remedy which proves illusory because of the general conditions prevailing in the country, or even in the particular circumstances of a given case, cannot be considered effective. That could be the case, for example, when practice has shown its ineffectiveness: when the Judicial Power lacks the necessary independence to render impartial decisions or the means to carry out its judgments; or in any other situation that constitutes a denial of justice, as there is an unjustified delay in the decision; or when, for any reason, the alleged victim is denied access to a judicial remedy"[209].

Thus, it is not enough for being effective that a recourse be regulated in internal law for the purpose of protecting human rights, being necessary the existence of basic conditions to function and be applied with the expected results. In this regard, for a judicial recourse to be effective, above all is necessary for the Judiciary to be really independent and autonomous, so for instance in the case Ivcher Bronstein, the Inter American Court decided that in Peru at the time, the conditions of independence and autonomy of the court were not satisfied in the national proceeding, so the recourses that the plaintiff had had not been effective"[210]. The Inter American Court has also considered that a recourse is not effective when impartiality lacks in the corresponding court[211].

6. The "amparo" as a judicial guarantee for the protection of everyone's rights and guarantees

Fourthly, it should be emphasized that the Convention regulates a right that is guaranteed to "everyone", that is to say, everybody in the very broadest sense, without distinction or discrimination of any kind: individuals, nationals, foreigners, legally able or not, corporations or entities of public or private law.

It is true that Article 1,2 of the Convention sets forth that "for the purposes of this Convention, "person" means every human being". Nonetheless, Article 25 when guaranteeing the judicial protection right refers to such rights as corresponding to everyone and not to every person, so that regarding internal national law, artificial persons or legal entities have the right to the "amparo" recourse for the protection of their rights, like for instance, the due process of law and non discrimination rights.

207 Case: *Ivcher Bronstein,* paragraph 140.

208 Inter American Court on Human Rights, case: *Velásquez Rodríguez,* paragraph 66.

209 Advisory Opinión OC–9/87 of October 6, 1987 (Judicial Guarantees in Status of Emergency), paragraph 24.

210 Case: *Ivcher Bronstein,* paragraph 139.

211 Case: *Tribunal Constitucional* paragraph 96

But setting forth the "amparo" as a judicial remedy for the protection of any person or entity, that is to say, as a personal remedy, its results in principle, benefit the plaintiff, so that the effects of the "amparo" do not extend to third parties.

This feature gives rise, firstly, to the problem of the protection of collective rights, an initiative attributed in some legislation to the Ombudsmen or Defenders of Human Rights. But the fact is that it has been progressively admitted in much internal statutes, the possibility for the communities to exercise the action of "amparo", when collective constitutional rights are being violated. Additionally, as a consequence of reforms tending to increase citizens access to justice, some statutes have set forth remedies for the protection of diffuse or widespread interests, particularly in regard to third generation rights, such as the protection of the environment or consumers rights.

In this sense, the standing to bring the action before the courts has being gradually constructed to allow interested parties to act in representation of diffuse or collective interests, when dealing with constitutional rights, the violation of which affects the community as a whole. In certain Constitutions, such as the Venezuelan Constitution of 1999, there is already no question regarding the possibility of exercising the recourse of "amparo" to protect collective and diffuse rights, already widely developed by case law. Some statutes have even expressly provided such protection, as occurs with the Organic statute for the Protection of the Child and the Teenagers, where a "recourse of protection" is regulated. This recourse may be brought before the Tribunal for the Protection of the Child and the Teenagers "against facts, acts or omissions of individuals, public and private entities and institutions that threaten or violate collective or diffuse (widespread) rights of the children and teenagers" (Article 177,5 and 318).

Another aspect related to the standing to file the action of "amparo", as previously mentioned, related to the assertion of the American Conventions that the right to "amparo" is held by everyone, is the question of whether the public entities can be plaintiff on matters of "amparo". Public entities also have constitutional rights, such as the right to non discrimination, right to due process or right to own defense. Therefore, public entities are perfectly entitled to bring actions, so that the action of "amparo" is not only conceived as actions against the State.

In some countries it may even be considered that there is a constitutional "amparo" set forth in benefit of political entities, as the States and Municipal government in a Federation, when the respective Constitution guarantees their autonomy. In these cases, the constitutional guarantee set forth in the constitutional texts with respect to territorial autonomy, can also be the object of an action for protection, as has been admitted in Mexico and Germany.

But in other countries, as has been the case in Venezuela, even if the constitutional guarantee of municipal autonomy has been judicially discussed at the Supreme Court, the Constitutional Chamber in a restrictive interpretation has rejected the admissibility of the "amparo" action for such purposes, adopting a restrictive scope rule confining "amparo" only to constitutional rights and not to constitutional territorial guaranties[212].

7. The "amparo" as a judicial guarantee for the protection of all constitutional rights and guarantees

Fifthly, pursuant to the Convention this right to an effective judicial means of protection before the courts, is established for the protection of all the constitutional rights contained in the Convention, the Constitution and statutes or those that are inherent to the human person. Therefore all rights established in international instruments are also entitled to protection. Thus the open clauses of the constitutional rights acquires here all their value, protecting them even when they are not listed in the texts, but which are subject to constitutional protection since they are inherent to the human person and human dignity.

Consequently, according to the American Convention, all rights can be protected by means of "amparo" actions. As mentioned, those declared in the texts of the Constitutions, of the statutes, of the American Convention, as well as those that are inherent to the human person. As has been stated by the Inter–American Court of Human Rights in its *Advisory Opinion* (OC–8/87) analyzing Article 25,1 of the Convention: "The above text is a general provision that gives expression to the procedural institution known as ""amparo"," which is a simple and prompt remedy designed for the protection *of all of the rights* recognized by the constitutions and laws of the States Parties and by the Convention."[213]

Therefore, pursuant to the Inter–American system, there is a complete and unlimited catalogue of the rights to be protected. However, in some cases, perhaps because of the influence of the European model of "amparo" recourse, particularly the one regulated by Germany and Spain, the rights protected by mean of "amparo" have been reduced to some of the rights listed in the constitutional text. Is the case, for example, of the German Constitution, which only admits the action of "amparo" for what it calls "fundamental rights," which constitutes only one species of the constitutional rights. In Spain too, the rights that may be protected by an "amparo" recourse are those expressly listed as "fundamental".

None of the above can be derived from the American Convention or from the majority of Latin American Constitutions, wherein all constitutional rights are subject to "amparo". Therefore it may be said that the Constitutions that establish a determined array of rights that are to be protected by means of a recourse to "amparo", are incompatible with the international obligations that are imposed on such States by the Convention. The American Convention does not allow the exclusion of constitutional protection by means of the "amparo" of determined constitutional rights, or in other words, it does not allow that the "amparo" be reduced to a protection only in respect of determined rights declared in a Constitution.

---

212 See Decision N° 1395 of November 11, 2000 (Case: *Gobernación del Estado Mérida y otros vs. Ministerio de Finanzas*), in *Revista de Derecho Público,* N° 84, Editorial Jurídica Venezolana, Caracas, 2000, pp. 317 ff.

213 Advisory Opinion OC–8/87 (Habeas Corpus in Emergency Situations), paragraph 32

Consequently, systems such as those regulated by the constitutional texts of Chile and Colombia may be considered to be incompatible with the American Convention. In fact, in the case of Chile, the Constitution lists the rights that may be the object of recourse to protection (Article 20), and in the case of Colombia, the Constitution also includes a list of the "fundamental rights" that may be the object of protection. However, the courts in Colombia have fortunately been gradually correcting this restriction through constitutional interpretation, in such a way that today, due to the interrelation, universality, indivisibility and interdependence of rights, there are almost no constitutional rights that can not be protected by means of the action of "tutela".

In contrast to such cases of restrictive constitutional provisions on constitutional rights that may be the object of protection by means of a recourse to "amparo", "tutela" or protection, there are other Constitutions that expressly set forth as being within the scope of protected rights not only all constitutional rights, but also those that are declared in the international system of protection of human rights. This is the case, for example, of the Constitution of Costa Rica, which lists among the rights subject to protection by recourse of "amparo" those rights "of a fundamental nature established in the international instruments on human rights, applicable to the Republic" (Article 48).

In an even broader sense, the 1999 Constitution of Venezuela expressly states that the right to "amparo" includes protection of "constitutional rights and guarantees, even those that are inherent to the human person and which do not expressly figure in this Constitution or in the international instruments of human rights" (Article 27), which must be interpreted to mean that not only the constitutional rights and guarantees and those listed in international instruments are subject to protection, but also all those inherent to the human person, even when they are not expressly listed in the Constitution itself or in international instruments.

8. The "amparo" as a judicial guarantee for the protection of all constitutional rights and guarantees, against any violation or harm from the State or individuals

Sixthly, the protection that the Convention regulates is against any act, omission, fact or action that violates human rights and, of course, which threatens to violate them too, because it is not necessary to wait for the violation before being able to have recourse to the means of protection. This implies that this means of protection has to be able to exist before the violation occurs, when there is a real threat of such violation and, of course, before any violation or threat of violation, no matter who is the author. This is to say that no action or omission that could imply a violation of rights, shall be excluded from the "amparo", whether it emanates from individuals or from the authorities under any guise whatsoever, be it a statute, an administrative act, a judicial decision, a *fait accompli*, an action or an omission, or just a fact.

All this implies that the recourse of "amparo" can be brought before the courts against any persons. It must be remembered that the recourse of "amparo" was always originally conceived as a judicial means of protection against the State, precisely because human rights were initially conceived regarding the State, and as a limit to the actions of public entities. However, the progressive universalization of human rights as inherent to the human person, independently of who must respect them, the scope of protection has been widening, to the point of admitting that the "amparo" can also be a recourse against private individuals. Thus, pursuant to the American Convention, which makes no distinction in this regard, the "amparo" proceeds not only against impairment of human rights originated by a public entity, but also by a private individual.

In this regard, it may be said that the action of "amparo" against individuals in Latin America is broadly admitted, following a trend that began in Latin America, more precisely in Argentina in the 50s, when the possibility of exercising a recourse of "amparo" against individuals was admitted. This situation is in sharp contrast with what occurs in Europe where the "amparo" is essentially only exercised against the public authorities.

Nevertheless, certain restriction of this principle of universality of "amparo" that is a characteristic of Latin America can be found in some Constitutions that set forth that "amparo" can only proceed regarding certain individuals, such as those who act as agents exercising public functions, or who exercise some kind of prerogative, or who are in a position of control, for example, when rendering public services, by mean of a concession. This is the case, for example, in Costa Rica, Guatemala and Colombia.

Other countries following the European model as is the case of Mexico, Brazil, Panama, El Salvador and Nicaragua simply excluded any possibility of filing a recourse of "amparo" against private individuals; a situation distant itself from the orientation of the American Convention.

But regarding the constitutional protection against actions of the State, another scope of reduction of "amparo" that contrasts with the universality deriving from the American Convention, refers to the acts of the authorities that may be challenged by means of a recourse of "amparo". Pursuant to the American Convention and the universal shaping of the recourse of "amparo", there cannot and must not exist a single State act that escapes its scope. If the "amparo" is a legal means for the protection of human rights, it is and has to be against any public action that violates them, and therefore it cannot be conceived that there can be certain acts of the State that are excluded from the possibility to be challenged by amparo.

Nevertheless, a tendency towards exclusions can be identified in Latin America in different aspects:

In some cases, the exclusion refers to actions of certain public authorities, such as the electoral authorities, whose actions, in some countries like Peru, Costa Rica and Uruguay, are expressly excluded from the recourse of "amparo".

In other cases, Peru also as an example, exclusion from the scope of constitutional protection of the "amparo" is provided with respect to the acts of the National Council of the Judiciary.

On the other hand, the exclusion from the scope of protection of the recourse of "amparo" can refer to certain State actions, as happened with regard to the statutes and judicial decisions. Some countries, for example, Colombia, Brazil and Uruguay, exclude the possibility of filing the recourse of "amparo" against statutes, that is, in general terms against regulations. In contrast, in other countries "amparo" against statutes is admitted as is the case of Mexico, where the "amparo" against statutes began, even if in certain cases this requires self–application of the statute. In Venezuela, even though according to the Organic Statute of "amparo" the recourse is widely admitted against statutes, the Supreme Court has also developed the need for the statute to be self–applicable, in order to admit the "amparo" remedy.

In other cases, the restriction of "amparo" refers to judicial decisions. In principle, when judges decide particular cases, they too can infringe constitutional rights; and no judge is empowered to violate a constitutional right in his decisions. Therefore the recourse of "amparo", must also be admitted against judicial decisions. Nonetheless, in some countries the recourse of "amparo" against judicial decisions is expressly excluded, as is the case of Argentina, Uruguay, Costa Rica, Panama, El Salvador and Nicaragua. Yet, in other countries, like Colombia, although it is expressly regulated the admission of "amparo" against judicial decisions, in 1992, an unfortunate decision considered its admissibility as contrary to the principle of *res judicata*, so the Constitutional Court annulled the respective article of the statute[214]. But in spite of the annulment, progressively, all the main courts and the Council of State have admitted the action of "amparo" against judicial decisions, on the grounds of their arbitrary content (judicial *voi de fait*)[215].

9. The "amparo" as a judicial guarantee that can be filed at any time, including in situations of emergency

Seventhly and finally, the "amparo" recourse as well as the habeas corpus, are judicial means of protection that can be filed by the interested party at any time, without exception. Particularly, the right cannot be limited because of exceptional situations or states of emergency.

In particular, it must be mentioned that Article 27,1 of the American Convention allows that in time of war, public danger, or other emergency that threatens the independence or security of a State Party, "it may take measures derogating from its obligations under the present Convention to the extent and for the period of time strictly required by the exigencies of the situation, provided that such measures are not inconsistent with its other obligations under international law and do not involve discrimination on the ground of race, color, sex, language, religion, or social origin".

Nonetheless, in Article 27,2 it is expressly provided that no suspension at all is allowed regarding the following rights: right to juridical personality (Article 3); right to life (Article 4); right to humane treatment (Article 5); freedom from slavery (Article 6); freedom from ex post facto laws (Article 9); freedom of conscience and reli-

---

214 See Decision C–543, September 24, 1992 in Manuel José CEPEDA, *Derecho Constitucional Jurisprudencial. Las grandes decisiones de la Corte Constitucional*, Legis, Bogotá, 2001, pp. 1009 ff.

215 See Decision T–231, May 13, 1994 in Manuel José CEPEDA, *Derecho Constitucional Jurisprudencial. Las grandes decisiones de la Corte Constitucional*, Legis, Bogotá, 2001, pp. 1022 ff.

gion (Article 12); rights of the family (Article 17); right to a name (Article 18); rights of the child (Article 19); right to nationality (Article 20): and right to participate in Government (Article 23), "or of the judicial guarantees essential for the protection of such rights". Thus, the right to judicial protection of all those rights by means of "amparo" and habeas corpus cannot be suspended in situations of emergency.

The Inter–American Court of Human Rights in its *Advisory Opinion* (OC–8/87) of January 30, 1987 (Habeas Corpus in Emergency Situations) has referred to the question of whether habeas corpus as a judicial remedy "may remain in effect as a means of ensuring individual liberty even during states of emergency, despite the fact that Article 7 is not listed among the provisions that may not be suspended in exceptional circumstances". The Court concluded that if the exercise of State powers even in states of emergency has limits, "it follows that writs of habeas corpus and of "amparo" are among those judicial remedies that are essential for the protection of various rights whose derogation is prohibited by Article 27(2) and that serve, moreover, to preserve legality in a democratic society". Therefore, the Court ruled that "the Constitutions and legal systems of the States Parties that authorize, expressly or by implication, the suspension of the legal remedies of habeas corpus or of "amparo" in emergency situations cannot be deemed to be compatible with the international obligations imposed on these States by the Convention"[216].

Afterwards, the Inter–American Court of Human Rights in its Advisory Opinion (OC–9/87) of October 6, 1987 (Judicial Guarantees in States of Emergency) emphasizes its ruling, holding that "the judicial guarantees essential for the protection of the human rights not subject to derogation, according to Article 27(2) of the Convention, are those to which the Convention expressly refers in Articles 7(6) and 25(1), considered within the framework and the principles of Article 8, and also those necessary to the preservation of the rule of law, even during the state of exception that results from the suspension of guarantees"[217]. Thus, the final Opinion of the Court was:

1. That the "essential" judicial guarantees which are not subject to derogation, according to Article 27(2) of the Convention, include habeas corpus (Art. 7(6)), "amparo", and any other effective remedy before judges or competent tribunals (Art. 25(1)), which is designed to guarantee the respect of the rights and freedoms whose suspension is not authorized by the Convention.
2. That the "essential" judicial guarantees which are not subject to suspension, include those judicial procedures, inherent to representative democracy as a form of government (Art. 29(c)), provided for in the laws of the States Parties as suitable for guaranteeing the full exercise of the rights referred to in Article 27(2) of the Convention and whose suppression or restriction entails the lack of protection of such rights.

---

216 Advisory Opinion oc–8/87 of January 30, 1987 (Habeas corpus in emergency situations), Paragraph 37, 42 and 43.

217 Advisory Opinion oc–9/87 of October 6, 1987 (Judicial Guarantees in States of Emergency), Paragraph 38.

3. That the above judicial guarantees should be exercised within the framework and the principles of due process of law, expressed in Article 8 of the Convention[218].

In general terms, the foregoing is the parameter that the American Convention establishes for the "amparo", and this is precisely what should prevail in the internal legal systems, where a huge effort has to be made from the constitutional perspective in order to adapt the internal regulations to such international system of protection of human rights.

CHAPTER V. THE AMPARO AS A CONSTITUTIONAL REMEDY WITHIN THE LATIN AMERICAN DIFFUSE AND CONCENTRATED SYSTEMS OF JUDICIAL REVIEW OF LEGISLATION

I. THE AMPARO AS A SPECIFIC JUDICIAL GUARANTEE FOR THE PROTECTION OF CONSTITUTIONAL RIGHTS AND FREEDOMS AND THE SYSTEMS OF JUDICIAL REVIEW OF LEGISLATION

In contrast to the Mexican and Venezuelan systems of amparo, which comprises the protection of personal freedom (habeas corpus), in the rest of Latin American countries, the amparo and the habeas corpus have been constitutionally regulated as judicial guarantees for the protection of constitutional rights and freedoms, by establishing in both cases a specific recourse or an action for such purpose. These specific means of judicial protection some times are only exercised before one single court; but in the majority of cases, they are exercised before the universe of courts of first instance.

Of course, such specific actions for the protection of constitutional rights and guarantees, are a substantial part of the judicial review systems of legislation that have been developed in Latin America since the XIX century, where it is possible to distinguish tree systems: the ones that apply the diffuse method ("American Model") of judicial review; and the ones that apply the concentrated method ("Austrian Model") of judicial review; and a last one, typically Latin American, that conforms a mixed system of judicial review in which the diffuse method of judicial review is combined with the concentrated one.

Judicial review of constitutionality[219] is the power of the courts to control the conformity of acts of the state with the Constitution, particularly of legislative acts, issued in direct application of the Constitution. Therefore, in principle, judicial review can only exist in legal systems in which there is a written Constitution, imposing limits on the state organs' activities and within such organs, on Parliament in particular. As a result, the power of the courts to control the constitutionality of state

218 *Idem*, paragraph 41.

219 See Allan R. BREWER–CARÍAS, *Judicial Review in Comparative Law,* Cambridge University Press, Cambridge, 1989.

acts is not necessarily a consequence of the sole judicial power, but of the legal limitations imposed on state organs, particularly on Parliament and on the government, in a constitution established as a supreme law.

In this sense, judicial review of the constitutionality of state acts is the ultimate consequence of the consolidation of the *rule of law (État de Droit)* where the state organs are not sovereign, are subject to limits imposed by a constitution having the force of a superior law, and in particular, when the legislator is limited in his legislative action and there is judicial control over the "legality of laws.".[220]

Therefore, acts of Parliament or Congress must always be submitted to the law, and cannot be contrary to the law. Consequently, the spirit of legality imposes the existence and functioning not only of a control of legality of administrative acts, but also of a control of the legality of laws as acts of Parliament. Only in countries where this control exists, are there truly organized democracies and *État de Droit*.

Therefore, this judicial control of the "legality of laws" is, precisely, the judicial control of the constitutionality of legislation and of other state acts issued in direct execution of the constitution, in relation to which legality means "constitutionality." Thus, there is the existence of judicial review of constitutionality that we are now going to study.

This judicial review of constitutionality is normally possible, of course, not only in those legal systems that have a *written* constitution as a supreme rule embodying the fundamental values of society, but when that superior rule is established in a rigid or entrenched way, in the sense that it cannot be modified by ordinary legislation. In principle, it is in a system of this kind that all the organs of the state are limited by and subject to the constitution and must therefore pursue their activities according to this supreme law.

This implies therefore, that not only are the traditional state organs for executing the law –the administration and the judges– subject to the law (Constitution and "legislation"), but that the organs which create the "legislation", particularly the legislative bodies, are also subject to the constitution.

Of course, a written and rigid constitution, situated at the apex of a legal system, not only demands that all the acts issued by state organs in direct execution thereof should not violate the constitution, but must also provide a guarantee to prevent or sanction such violations.[221] Thus, the judicial review of constitutionality as the power of the judiciary to control the submission of state organs to the superior rule of the country.

Different criteria can be adopted for classifying the various systems of constitutional justice or judicial review of the constitutionality of state acts, particularly of

220 *Ibid.* p. 215.

221 *Cf.* H. KELSEN, "La garantie juridictionnelle de la Constitution (La Justice constitutionnelle)" *Revue du droit public et de la science politique en France et à l'étranger*, T. XLV, 1928, p.197–257.

legislation.[222] However, all of them are related to a basic criteria referring to the state organs that can carry out constitutional justice functions.

In effect, judicial review of constitutionality can be exercised by all the courts of a given country or only by the Supreme Court of the country or by a court specially created for that purpose.

In the first case, all the courts of a given country are empowered to judge the constitutionality of laws. This is the case in the United States of America, thus this system has been identified as the "American model", because it was first adopted in the United States particularly after the famous *Marbury* v. *Madison* case decided by the Supreme Court in 1803. This system is followed in many countries with or without a common law tradition. This is the case, for example, in Argentina, Mexico, Greece, Australia, Canada, India, Japan, Sweden, Norway and Denmark. This system is also qualified as a diffuse system of judicial review of constitutionality,[223] because judicial control belongs to all the courts from the lowest level up to the Supreme Court of the country.

By contrast, there is the concentrated system of judicial review, in which the power to control the constitutionality of legislation and other state organs issued in direct execution of the Constitution is assigned to a single organ of the state, whether to its Supreme Court or to a special court created for that particular purpose. In the latter case, it is also called the Austrian system because it was first established in Austria, in 1920. This system is also called the "European model" and is followed, for instance, in Germany, Italy, and Spain. It is a concentrated system of judicial review, as opposed to the diffuse system, because the power of control over the constitutionality of state acts is given only to one single constitutional body that can be the Supreme Court of a given country or as in the Austrian or European model, to a specially created constitutional court or tribunal, that even though it exercises judicial functions, in general, it is created by the constitution outside ordinary judicial power, as a constitutional organ different to the Supreme Court of the country.

In regard to the judicial organs that can exercise the power of controlling the constitutionality of laws, other countries have adopted a mixture of the above mentioned diffuse and concentrate systems, in the sense that they allow for both types of control at the same time. Such is the case in Colombia and Venezuela where all courts are entitled to judge the constitutionality of laws and therefore decide autonomously upon their inapplicability in a given process, and the Supreme Court has the power to declare the unconstitutionality of laws in an objective process. One can say that these countries have a diffuse and concentrated parallel system of judicial review at one and the same time, perhaps the most complete in comparative law.

---

222 See in general M. CAPPELLETTI, *Judicial Review in the Contemporary World*, Indianapolis 1971, p. 45 and M. CAPPELLETI and J.C. ADAMS, "Judicial Review of Legislation: European Antecedents and Adaptations", *Harvard Law Review*, 79, 6, April 1966, p. 1207.

223 M. CAPPELLETTI, "El control judicial de la constitucionalidad de las leyes en el derecho comparado", *Revista de la Facultad de Derecho de México*, 61, 1966, p. 28.

But regarding the so–called concentrated systems of judicial review, in which the power of control is given to the Supreme Court or to a constitutional court, other distinctions can be observed.

In the first place, in relation to the moment at which control of the constitutionality of laws is performed, it may be prior to the formal enactment of the particular law, as is the case in France, or the judicial control of the constitutionality of laws which can be exercised by the court after the law has come into effect, as is the case in Germany and Italy.

In this respect, other countries have established both possibilities as is the case Spain, Portugal and Venezuela. In the latter, a law sanctioned by Congress prior to its enactment, can be placed by the President of the Republic before the Supreme Court to obtain a decision regarding its constitutionality, and the Supreme Court can also judge the constitutionality of the law after it has been published and has come into legal effect.

Moreover, in relation to the concentrated systems of judicial review, two other types of control can be distinguished regarding the manner in which review is required either incidentally or through an objective action. In the first place, the constitutional question is not considered justiciable unless it is closely and directly related to a particular process, in which the constitutionality of the concrete law is not normally necessary to the unique issue in the process. In this case, judicial control is incidental, and the Supreme Court or constitutional tribunal can only decide when it is required to do so by the ordinary court that has to decide the case. In this situation, it is basically the function of the ordinary courts, upon hearing a concrete case, to place the constitutional issue before the constitutional court.

Of course, the incidental nature of judicial review is essential to diffuse control systems and, therefore, to all legal systems that follow the American model.

But in the field of the concentrated system of judicial review, the control granted to the constitutional court can also be exercised through direct action where the constitutionality of the particular law is the only issue in the process, without reference or relation to a particular process.

In this latter case, another distinction can be made, in relation to the *locus standing* to exercise the direct action of unconstitutionality: in most countries with a concentrated system of judicial review, only other organs of the state can place the direct action of constitutionality before the constitutional court, for instance, the head of government, or a number of representatives in Parliament.

Other systems of concentrated judicial review grant the action of constitutionality to individuals, whether requiring that the particular law affect a fundamental right of the individual, or by means of a popular action, in which any citizen can request the constitutional court or Supreme Court to decide upon his claim concerning the constitutionality of a given law, without particular requirement regarding his standing.

As we have seen, the basic division we can establish regarding the various systems of judicial review, depends in our opinion, upon the concentrated or centralized or diffuse or decentralized character of judicial control of constitutionality, that is to say, when the power of control is given to all the courts of a given country or to one special constitutional court or to the Supreme Court of that country. We have also said that some countries have even adopted both systems of judicial review that developed in parallel. Related to this main classification, as we said, other criteria can be adopted to identify the various systems of judicial control of the constitutionality of laws: the incidental and the principal or objective action systems.

But in relation to the main distinction between the diffuse and concentrated systems of judicial review, we can also distinguish other criteria for classifying the various systems, according to the legal effects given to the particular judicial decision of review.

Within this scope, we can distinguish decisions with *in casu et inter partes* or *erga omnes* effects, that is to say, when the judicial decision has effects only within the parties in a concrete process, or when it has general effects applicable to everyone.

For instance, in the diffused systems of judicial review, according to the American system, the decision of the courts in principle, only has effect relating to the parties of the process; effects that are closely related to the incidental character of judicial review.

Whereas in the concentrated system of judicial review, following the Austrian model, when the judicial decision is a consequence of the exercise of an objective action, the effects of such a decision are general, with *erga omnes* validity.

Thus, in the diffuse systems of judicial review a law declared unconstitutional with *inter partes* effects, is in principle considered null and void, with no effect whatsoever. Therefore, in this case the decision in principle is retroactive in the sense that it has *ex tunc*, or *pro pretaerito* consequences; that is to say, the law declared unconstitutional is considered never to have existed or never to have been valid. Thus, this decision, in principle, has "declarative" effects, in the sense that it declares the pre–existing nullity of the unconstitutional law.

In the concentrated systems of judicial review, on the contrary, a law declared unconstitutional, with *erga omnes* effect, is in principle considered annullable. Therefore, in this case, the decision is prospective, in the sense that has *ex nunc*, *pro futuro* consequences, that is to say, the law declared unconstitutional is considered as having produced its effect until its annulment by the court, or until the moment determined by the court subsequent to the decision. In this case, therefore the decision has "constitutive" effects, in the sense that the law will become unconstitutional only after the decision has been made.

Nevertheless, this distinction related to the effects of the judicial decision regarding the unconstitutionality of a law is not absolute. On the one hand, if it is true that in the diffuse systems of judicial review, the decision has *inter partes* effects, when the decision is adopted by the Supreme Court, as a consequence of the *stare decisis* doctrine, the practical effects of the decision, in fact, are general, in the sense that it binds all the lower courts of the country. Therefore, as soon as the Supreme Court has declared a law unconstitutional, no other court can apply it.

On the other hand, in concentrated systems of judicial review, when a judicial decision is adopted on an incidental issue of constitutionality, some constitutional systems have established that the effects of that decision are only related in principle, to the particular process in which the constitutionality question was raised, and between the parties of that process, even though this is not the general rule.

In relation to the declarative or constitutive effects of the decision, or its retroactive or prospective effects, the absolute parallelism with the diffuse and concentrated systems has also disappeared.

In the diffuse systems of judicial review, even though the effects of the declarative decisions of unconstitutionality of the law, are *ex tunc*, *pro pretaerito*, in practice, exceptions have been made in civil cases to allow for the invalidity of the law not to be retroactive. In the same manner, in the concentrated systems of judicial review, even though the effects of the constitutive judicial decisions of unconstitutionality of the law are *ex nunc*, *pro futuro*, in practice, exceptions were needed to be made in criminal cases to allow for the invalidity of the law to be retroactive, and benefit the accused.

Our purpose in the following parts of the course is to study all these systems of judicial review of constitutionality of state acts, and particularly of legislation in comparative law. To that end we will analyze the most important legal systems in contemporary constitutional law, classifying them in accordance with the main distinctions we have made between the diffuse and the concentrated systems of judicial review.

Following the main distinction of methods of judicial review, and since also the specific actions for protection of constitutional rights and guaranties are means that can serve for judicial review of legislation, we will analyze the regulation of the amparo and habeas corpus actions or recourses in Latin America, classifying the Countries in accordance to the method of judicial review that exists in each of them, as follows:

a) The amparo action in countries with only a diffuse system of judicial review: the case of Argentina.

b) The amparo action in countries with only a concentrated system of judicial review: the case of Costa Rica, El Salvador, Bolivia, Chile, Honduras, Panama, Paraguay and Uruguay.

c) The amparo action in countries with mixed systems (diffuse and concentrated) of judicial review: in addition to Mexico and Venezuela, the case of Nicaragua, Brazil, Colombia, Dominican Republic, Ecuador, Guatemala and Peru.

II. THE AMPARO ACTION IN COUNTRIES WITH ONLY A DIFFUSE SYSTEM OF JUDICIAL REVIEW: THE CASE OF ARGENTINA

Argentina is the only Latin American country where the diffuse method of judicial review remains as the only one established to control the constitutionality of legislation. The other Latin American Countries that have the diffuse method of judicial review, have it mixed with the concentrated method, as is the case of Mexico and Venezuela, already studied, and of Brazil, Colombia, Dominican Republic, Ecuador, Guatemala and Peru.

Thus the amparo and habeas corpus actions in Argentina are essential adjective tools for judicial review, at present fully regulated by the Argentinean Constitution through the constitutional reform of 1994 (Article 43), following the guidelines of the American Convention on Human Rights, and having, moreover, developed the action of *habeas data*[224].

As above mentioned, the recourse of amparo was developed in Argentina as was the judicial review itself, as a result of a judicial doctrine[225] set forth by the Supreme Court in the Angel Siri Case of 27 December 1957,[226] in which the competence of ordinary courts to protect the fundamental rights of citizens, against violation from public authorities actions or from individuals was definitively accepted[227]. Prior to that date, in 1984, when interpreting Article 18 of the Constitution, which set forth the guarantee of all persons not to be arrested except by virtue of a written warrant of the competent authority, Congress, through Law 23.098, regulated the *habeas corpus* for the protection of physical and personal freedom against illegal or arbitrary detentions[228].

Insofar as other constitutional rights are concerned, they were protected through the ordinary judicial means, considering the courts that the habeas corpus could not be used for such purpose. Thus, in the absence of a legal provision, the Supreme Court of the Nation rejected the application of *habeas corpus* to obtain judicial protection to other constitutional rights. That is why in the Case *Bartolo* in 1959 the Supreme Court ruled that "nor in the text, or in the spirit, or in the constitutional tradition of the habeas corpus institution, can be found any basis for its application to the right of property, the freedom of commerce and industry …; against the abuses or infringements of individuals or public officers regarding rights, the statutes and court decisions set forth administrative and judicial remedies"[229].

This situation radically changed in 1957, as a result of the resolution of the case of *Angel* Siri, who was director of the Newspaper (Mercedes) in the Province of Buenos Aires. After the Government closure of the Newspaper, Mr Siri brought before a criminal court a petition requesting amparo of the freedom of press and his

---

224 See: Juan F. ARMAGNAGUE *et al.*, *Derecho a la información, hábeas data e Internet*, Ediciones La Roca, Buenos Aires 2002; Miguel Ángel EKMEKDJIAN *et al.*, *Hábeas Data. El derecho a la intimidad frente a la revolución informática*, Edic. Depalma, Buenos Aires, 1998; Osvaldo Alfredo GOZAÍNI, *Derecho Procesal Constitucional, Hábeas Data. Protección de datos personales. Ley 25.326 y reglamentación (decreto 1558/2001)*, Rubinzal–Culzoni Editores, Santa Fe, Argentina, 2002

225 *Cf.* G. R. CARRIO, *Algunos aspectos del recurso de amparo,* Buenos Aires, 1959, p. 9; J. R. Vanossi, *Teoría constitucional, cit.*, Vol. II, p. 277.

226 See G. R. CARRIO, *op. cit.*, p. 10.

227 See the Samuel KOT Ltd. case of 5 September, 1958, S.V. Linares Quintana, *Acción de amparo*, Buenos Aires, 1960, p. 25.

228 See: Néstor Pedro SAGÜES, *Derecho Procesal Constitucional. Hábeas Corpus*, Volumen 4, 2nd Edition, Editorial Astrea, Buenos Aires, 1988.

229 See the referente in Joaquín BRAGE CAMAZANO, *La jurisdicción constitucional de la libertad (Teoría general, Argentina, México, Corte Interamericana de Derechos Humanos*), Editorial Porrúa, Instituto Mexicano de Derecho Procesal Constitucional, México, 2005, p. 66.

right to work declared in the Constitution. The court rejected the claim arguing that the petition filed was a habeas corpus, which only protected physical and personal freedom. Once the judicial decision was confirmed by a superior court, an extraordinary recourse was filled against the decision before the Supreme Court, which in a decision of December 27, 1957 admitted the action of amparo. The argument of the Supreme Courts was that in the case, it was alleged the violation of the constitutional guarantee of freedom of press and the right to work; and that the arbitrary governmental decision violated those rights being proved, they have to be protected by the courts and so the absence of a statutory regulation on the amparo recourse is not a valid argument to reject the judicial protection,. In brief, the Supreme Court argued that the constitutional rights and guaranties of peoples, once embodied in the Constitution, must always be judicially protected regardless of the existence of a regulatory statute on the matter[230].

The second important decision of the Argentinean Supreme Court was issued the next year in the *Case Kot*, of October 5th, 1958. In this case, the action of amparo was brought before a court by Samuel Kot, the owner of a factory whose premises had been occupied by its workers on strike. Having been initially rejected, eventually the action of amparo was admitted by the Supreme Court ordering the restitution of the factory to his owner. The Court decided that in any case in which it appears clear and in a manifest way the illegitimacy of a restriction to any of the essential constitutional rights, and also the grave and irreparable damages that can be caused if the question is referred to be resolved by the judicial ordinary means; the courts must immediately re–establish the restricted right, applying the habeas corpus procedure, by means of the prompt amparo recourse.

Nonetheless, in the case, the Court warned the whole Judiciary that in these cases of constitutional protection, the judicial power had to be exercised in a prudent way in order to avoid the complete substitution of the ordinary judicial means; that is to say, that by means of the prompt amparo guarantee, all the ordinary controversies where contradictory rights must be discussed, resulted being resolved. The Supreme Court resolved in the case, precisely that it was not wise to compel the plaintiff, whose property was taken, to seek for its restitution by mean of the ordinary judicial proceedings.

The other very important issue decided by the Supreme Court in the *Kot Case*, was that the amparo not only protected against acts of authorities but also against private individuals illegitimate actions based on the principle that in spite of the existence of an ordinary procedure, it was nevertheless admissible if the processing of the latter could cause serious and irreparable harm[231].

---

230 See the reference in José Luis LAZZARINI, *El juicio de amparo*, La Ley, Buenos Aires, 1987, pp. 26 ff y 373 ff.; Alí Joaquín SALGADO, *Juicio de amparo y acción de inconstitucionalidad*, Ed. Astrea, Buenos Aires, 1987, pp. 5.

231 See the reference in José Luis LAZZARINI, *El juicio de amparo*, La Ley, Buenos Aires, 1987, pp. 243 ff; Alí Joaquín SALGADO, *Juicio de amparo y acción de inconstitucionalidad*, Ed. Astrea, Buenos Aires, 1987, pp. 6.; Susana ALBANESE, *Garantías Judiciales. Algunos requisitos del debido proceso legal en el derecho internacional de los derechos humanos*, Ediar

The judicial creation of the amparo lead to the approval of the 1966 Law 16.986[232] on the action of amparo, which nevertheless only regulates the action of amparo against acts of the State; so the amparo action against private parties is filed by means of the provisions of the Code of Civil and Commercial Procedure of the Nation (Article 32,1, Sub–sections 2 and 498)[233].

Thus, pursuant to Article 1st of Law 16.986, the action of amparo can be brought before a court against any act or omission of a public authority which in an overtly arbitrary or illegal manner, currently or imminently harms, restricts, alters or threatens, the rights or guarantees that are explicitly or implicitly recognized by the National Constitution, with the exception of individual freedom protected by *habeas corpus*.

Therefore, this is an action that can be brought before any judge of First Instance with jurisdiction over the place where the act takes place or where it has or could have effect, following the rules of jurisdiction attached to the concerned matter (Article 4, Amparo Law), for the protection of all constitutional rights and freedoms (even those implicitly recognized in the Constitution) against acts or omissions of the public authorities, except for those decisions or acts emanating from the Judiciary or against statutes. On the other hand, it is an action that is admissible only when no other judicial or administrative recourses or remedies exist to assure the protection. Thus, in order to bring the action of amparo, all judicial or administrative recourses or remedies that may assure the constitutional protection of the right or guarantee in question must be exhausted, since if they in fact exist, then the amparo is inadmissible, unless they are incapable of redressing the damage and their processing can lead to serious and irreparable harm. Thus the amparo is considered an exceptional proceeding.

The same regulatory trend is set forth in Article 321 of the Civil Procedure Code regarding the amparo against private damaging actions, in which it is also stressed that the action is only admissible in cases in which the urgent reparation of the damages or the immediate end of the challenged actions are needed, and always if the controversy, because of its nature, cannot be resolved by means of the ordinary judicial procedure.

On the other hand it must be stressed that even thought the actions of amparo are in general exercised before the judges of first instance, the cases can reach the Supreme Court of the Nation, by means of an extraordinary recourse when in the judicial decision a matter of judicial review of constitutionality is resolved[234].

S.A. Editora, Comercial, Industrial y Financiera, Buenos Aires, 2000; Augusto M. MORILLO *et al., El amparo. Régimen procesal*, 3rd Edition, Librería Editora Platense SRL, La Plata, 1998, 430 pp.; Néstor Pedro SAGÜES, *Derecho Procesal Constitucional. Acción de Amparo*, Volumen 3, 2nd Edition, Editorial Astrea, Buenos Aires, 1988.

232 See José Luis LAZZARINI, *El juicio de amparo,* Buenos Aires, 1987; Néstor Pedro SAGÜÉS, *Derecho Procesal Constitucional. Acción de Amparo,* Buenos Aires, 1988.

233 J. L. LAZZARINI, *op. cit*., p. 229.

234 See Elias GUASTAVINO, *Recurso extraordinario de inconstitucionalidad,* Ed. La Roca, Buenos Aires, Argentina, 1992

This leads us to make a few comments regarding the judicial review system in Argentina[235], which follows very closely the North American model, also founded in the supremacy clause of the 1860 Constitution which set forth:

> **Article 31.** This constitution, the laws of the Nation that the Congress consequently approves and the treaties with foreign powers, are the supreme law of the Nation, and the authorities of each Province are obliged to conform to it, notwithstanding any contrary disposition which the provincial laws or Constitutions might contain.

On the other hand, Article 100 referring to judicial power, set forth:

> The Supreme Court and the inferior Courts of the Nation, are competent to try and decide all cases related to aspects ruled by the constitution, by the laws of the Nation and by the Treaties with foreign nations.

Therefore, in terms similar to the American constitution, the Argentinean Constitution does not expressly confer any judicial review power upon the Supreme Court or the other courts; being also judicial review a creation of the Supreme Court, based on the principles of supremacy of the Constitution and judicial duty when applying the law.

The first case in which judicial review power was exercised regarding a federal statute was the *Sojo* case, (1887), also concerning the unconstitutionality of a law that tried to enlarge the original jurisdiction of the Supreme Court[236] as was the *Marbury* v. *Madison* case.

Nevertheless, the question of the powers of the judiciary to control the constitutionality of legislation was a matter of discussion in the Parana Constitutional Convention in 1857–1858, where the predominant opinion on the subject was: first, the character of the Constitution as a supreme law and the power of the courts to maintain its supremacy over the statutes which infringed it; second, the limits imposed over the constituted powers by popular sovereignty, so that statutes contrary to the principles embodied in the Constitution, could not be binding on the courts; and

---

235 See in general Néstor Pedro SAGÜÉS, *Derecho procesal Constitucional,* Tomo I, Cuarta edición, 2002; Ricardo HARO, *El control de constitucionalidad,* Editorial Zavalia, Buenos Aires, Argentina, 2003; Juan Carlos HITTERS, "La jurisdicción constitucional en Argentina" en Domingo GARCÍA BELAUNDE, y Francisco FERNÁNDEZ SEGADO, (Coordinadores), *La jurisdicción constitucional en Iberoamérica,* Ed. Dykinson, Madrid, España, 1997; Maximiliano Toricelli, *El sistema de control constitucional argentino,* Editorial Lexis Nexis Depalma, Buenos Aires, Argentina, 2002.

236 *Cf.* A.E. GHIGLIANI *Del control jurisdiccional de constitucionalidad,* Buenos Aires, 1952., p. 5; R. BIELSA, *La protección constitucional y el recurso extraordinario. Jurisdicción de la Corte Suprema,* Buenos Aires, 1958. p. 41, 43, 179 who speaks about a "pretorian creation" of judicial review by the Supreme Court, *op. cit.,* p. 179. *Cf.* J.R. Vanossi and P.F. Ubertone, *Instituciones de defensa de la Constitución en la Argentina,* UNAM, Congreso Internacional sobre la Constitución y su defensa, México, 1982, (mimeo), p. 4 (also Publisher as "Control jurisdiccional de constitucionalidad". en *Desafíos del control de constitucionalidad,* Ediciones Ciudad Argentina, Buenos Aires, Argentina, 1996), H. QUIROGA LAVIE, *Derecho constitucional,* Buenos Aires, 1978, p. 481. Previously in 1863 the firsts Supreme Court decisions where adopted in constitutional matters but refered to provincial and executive acts. *Cf.* A. E. GHIGLIANI, *op. cit.,* p. 58.

third, that the Judiciary was precisely the branch of government which ought to have enough power to interpret the Constitution regarding the other of the State.[237]

Therefore, through the work of the courts, the Argentinean system of judicial review was developed over more than a century ago as a diffuse system[238] in which all the courts have the power to declare the unconstitutionality of legislative acts, treaties,[239] executive and administrative acts and judicial decisions, whether at national or provincial levels.[240] This power of judicial review is, of course, reserved to the courts and the executive cannot decide not to apply a statute on unconstitutional grounds.

Therefore, in Argentina, the power to control the constitutionality of state acts is not reserved to one single judicial body or a group of them; it concerns all courts, of course, within the scope of the jurisdiction that each of them has.

Argentina, being a federal state, has two court systems established from their origin following the American model in the organization of the judiciary:[241] National and provincial courts. The provincial courts have jurisdiction over all matters of "ordinary law," (*derecho común*) like civil, commercial, criminal, labor, social security, and mining law and public provincial law (constitutional and administrative provincial law). In each Province there are courts of first and second instances, and at their apex a Superior Provincial Court.

At the national level, the national courts have jurisdiction over all matters regulated by "federal law"; particularly concerning constitutional and administrative law cases and in all cases in which the Nation is a party or foreign diplomatic agents are involved. The organization of the national courts is as follows: National courts with territorial jurisdiction in the first instance; national chambers of appeals, in the second instance, and at the apex the Supreme Court of Justice, that also acts as a third instance.[242]

The Supreme Court of Justice, the only judicial body created in the Constitution, considers itself "final interpreter of the Constitution" or "the defendant of the Constitution",[243] and has two sorts of jurisdiction: original and appellate. The original jurisdiction is established in the Constitution and, therefore, is not extendible by statute, and concerns all matters related to ambassadors, ministers and foreign consuls and to which the Provinces are party (art. 101).

---

237 *Cf.* A.E. GHIGLIANI, *op. cit.*, p. 58.

238 N.P. SAGÜES, *Recurso Extraordinario*, Buenos Aires, 1984, Vol. I, p. 91. J.R. Vanossi and P.F. UBERTONE, *op. cit.* p. 2, 14. See also J.R. VANOSSI, *Teoría constitucional*, Buenos Aires, Vol. II, *Supremacía y control de constitucionalidad*, Buenos Aires, 1976, p. 155.

239 In particular, regarding the unconstitutionality of Treaties and the posibility of the Courts to control them, A.G. GHIGLIANI, *op. cit.*, p. 62; J.R. VANOSSI, *Aspectos del recurso extraordinario de inconstitucionalidad*, Buenos Aires, 1966, p. 91, and *Teoría constitucional*, *op. cit.*, Vol. II, p. 277.

240 *Cf.* R. BIELSA, *op. cit.*, pp. 120–148. J.R. VANOSSI and P.F. UBERTONE, *doc. cit.*, p. 6.

241 *Cf.* R. BIELSA, *op. cit.*, p. 57; A.E. GHIGLIANI, *op. cit.*, p. 55.

242 *Cf.* J.R. VANOSSI and P.F. UBERTONE, *doc. cit.*, p. 14–18; A.E. GHIGLIANI, *op. cit.*, p. 76.

243 R. BIELSA, *op. cit.*, p. 270; J.R. VANOSSI and P.F. UBERTONE, *doc. cit.*, p. 18.

In its appellate jurisdiction, the Supreme Court has jurisdiction through two sorts of appeals: ordinary and extraordinary. In its appellate jurisdiction through ordinary appeals, the Supreme Court has the power of reviewing the decisions of the national chambers of appeal in the following cases: 1. Cases in which the Nation is a party according to an amount fixed periodically; 2. Cases concerning extradition of criminals sought by foreign countries; and 3. Cases concerning the seizure of ships in time of war and other cases concerning maritime law.[244]

In these cases of appellate jurisdiction through ordinary appeal, the Supreme Court acts as a court of third instance and last resort reviewing the whole case decided by the national chambers of appeals.

However, as we have said, the appellate jurisdiction of the Supreme Court of Justice can also be exercised through what has been called an "extraordinary recourse" that the party in a case decided by the national Chambers of appeals and by the Superior Courts of the Provinces can bring before the Supreme Court, in particular cases related to constitutional issues and with special conditions. This is, undoubtedly, the judicial mean through which the Supreme Court normally decides upon the final interpretation of the Constitution when reviewing the constitutionality of state acts, and consequently it is the most important mean for judicial review.

Before analyzing this "extraordinary recourse", reference has to be made to the general trends of the incidental character of the Argentinean diffuse system and its consequences.

In effect, as a diffuse system of judicial review, the Argentinean system is essentially an incidental one, in which the question of constitutionality is not the principal object of a process; thus the constitutional issue can be at any moment and at any stage of any proceeding. This incidental character has led to considering the Argentinean system of judicial review, as an "indirect" control system,[245] because the constitutional issue can only be raised in a judicial controversy, case or process, normally through an exception, at any moment before the decision is adopted by the court, and therefore not necessarily in the *litis contestatio* of the proceeding.[246]

The principal condition for raising constitutional questions is that they can only be raised in a "judicial case" or litigation between parties;[247] therefore, they cannot be raised as an abstract question before a court, and the courts cannot render declarative decisions upon unconstitutional matters.[248]

Nevertheless, the existence of a case or controversy in which the constitutional question could be raised is not only necessary, it is also indispensable that the question be raised by a party in the process with due interest in the matter, that is to say,

---

244 *Cf.* R. BIELSA, *op. cit.*, p. 60–61; J.R. VANOSSI and P.F. UBERTONE, *doc. cit.*, p. 19.

245 A.E. GHIGLIANI, *op. cit.*, p. 75.

246 A.E. GHIGLIANI, *op. cit.*, p. 76.

247 Art. 100 of the constitution; *Cf.* R. Bielsa, *op. cit.*, p. 213, 214; A.E. GHIGLIANI, *op. cit.*, p. 75; J.R. VANOSSI and P.F. UBERTONE, *doc. cit.*, p. 23.

248 *Cf.* R. BIELSA, *op. cit.*, p. 213, 214; A.E. GHIGLIANI, *op. cit.*, p. 80; S.M. LOZADA, *Derecho Constitucional Argentino*, Buenos Aires, 1972, Vol. I, p. 342.

which alleges a particular injury in his own right caused by the statute considered invalid.[249]

Consequently, the court on its own cannot raise constitutional issues in the Argentinean system. Thus, even if the court is convinced of the unconstitutionality of a statute, if a party has not raised the question, the Court is bound to apply the Statute to the decision of the case.[250] In this respect, it must be stressed that even though this has been the judicial doctrine invariably applied by courts, some authors have considered that the constitutional questions can be decided by courts without being raised by a party, based on the principle of constitutional supremacy and the notion of "public order."[251]

Nevertheless, an exemption to the need for party intervention when raising the constitutional issue has been established by the Supreme Court, allowing the court to consider constitutional questions on its own, only in matters concerning the jurisdiction of the courts themselves and their functional autonomy. Consequently, the Supreme Court decided upon the unconstitutionality of a statute that enlarged its original jurisdiction of the Supreme Court of Justice established in the Constitution, although not being raised by a party.[252]

Furthermore and related to the incidental or indirect character of judicial review in the Argentinean system, the constitutional question raised in a case particularly due to the presumption of constitutionality of all statutes,[253] must be of an un avoiding character, in the sense that its decision must be essential to the resolution of the case which depends on it.[254] Moreover, the constitutional question must be clear and undoubted. Therefore, the declaration of unconstitutionality being considered an act of extreme gravity and the last ratio of the legal order, the court must abstain its consideration when there are doubts about the issue.[255] Thus when an interpretation of the statute avoiding the consideration of the constitutional question is possible the court must follow this path.[256]

Finally, it must be said that in the Argentinean system, the Supreme Court of the Nation has developed the same exception to judicial review established in the North American system, concerning political questions, even though the Constitution does not expressly establish anything on the matter.[257] These political questions are relat-

---

249 S.M. LOZADA, *op. cit.*, p. 342; A.E. GHIGLIANI, *op.cit.,* p. 82; J.R. VANOSSI and P.E. UBERTONE, *doc. cit.*, p.23.

250 R. BIELSA, *op. cit.*, p. 198, 214; H. QUIROGA LAVIE, *op. cit.*, p. 479.

251 G. BIDART CAMPOS, *El derecho constitucional del poder*, Vol. II, Chap. XXIX; J.R. VANOSSI, *Teoría constitucional, op. cit.*, Vol. II, p. 318, 319.

252 *Cf.* J.R. VANOSSI and P.E. UBERTONE, *doc. cit.*, 25; .R. Bielsa, *op. cit.*, 255; H. QUIROGA LAVIE, *op. cit.*, p. 479.

253 A.E. GHIGLIANI, *op. cit.*, p. 89, 90.

254 A.E. GHIGLIANI, *op. cit.,* p. 89; S.M. LOSADA, *op. cit*, p. 341.

255 H. QUIROGA LAVIE, *op. cit.*, p. 480.

256 A.E. GHIGLIANI, *op. cit.*, p. 91.

257 J.R. VANOSSI and P.E. UBERTONE, *doc. cit.*, p. 11.

ed to the "acts of government" or "political acts" doctrine developed in continental European law, and within which we can mention the following: the declaration of state of siege; the declaration of federal intervention in the provinces; the declaration of "public use" for means of expropriation; the declaration of war; the declaration of emergency to approve certain direct tax contributions; acts concerning foreign relations; the recognition of new foreign states or new foreign state governments; the expulsion of aliens, etc., In general, within these political questions there are acts exercised by the political powers of the state in accordance with powers exclusively and directly attributed to them in the Constitution,[258] which can be considered the key element for their identification.

The Supreme Court of the Nation is vested in the Argentinean system, like it is in the United States, with two sorts of jurisdiction: original and appellate jurisdiction, and in the latter two other sorts can be distinguished: ordinary appellate jurisdiction and "extraordinary appellate jurisdiction" that can be exercised by the Supreme Court through the so called "extraordinary recourse", which accomplishes a similar result to the request for writ of *certiorari* in the United States Supreme Court.

But of course, the "extraordinary recourse" is quite different to the American request for writ of *certiorari*, in the sense that the Supreme Court of the Nation does not have discretionary powers in accepting extraordinary recourses. Thus, in the Argentinean system, the appellate jurisdiction of the Supreme Court, whether ordinary or extraordinary, is a mandatory jurisdiction, exercised as a consequence of a right the parties have, whether to appeal or to introduce the extraordinary recourse.

When the extraordinary recourse is filed, the Supreme Court does not act as a mere third instance court,[259] particularly because the Court does not review the motives of the judicial decision under consideration, regarding the facts; its power of review being concentrated only in aspects of law regarding constitutional questions. That is why it has been said that the Supreme Court, as a consequence of an extraordinary recourse, "does not act *jure litigatoris*" but *jure constitutionis*, does not judge a *questio facti*, but a *questio juris*."[260]

This substantive difference between the function of the Supreme Court as a consequence of the exercise of an appeal or an extraordinary recourse is followed by another formal difference, particularly, that contrary to the appeal, the extraordinary recourse must be motivated and founded on constitutional reasons.[261]

Even though it is called "extraordinary" it must be said that the ordinary appeal being reduced to the review of very few decisions of the National Chambers of Appeals, the "extraordinary recourse" is the judicial means through which the parties can most commonly reach the Supreme Court of Justice in order to obtain judicial

---

258 *Cf.* A.E. GHIGLIANI, *op. cit.*, p. 85; H. QUIROGA LAVIE, *op. cit.*, p. 482; S.M. LOSADA, *op. cit.*, p. 343; J.R. VANOSSI and P.E. UBERTONE, *doc. cit.*, p. 11, 12.

259 *Cf.* N. P. SAGÜES, *op. cit.*, p. 270; pp. 185, 221, 228, 275.

260 R. BIELSA, *op. cit.*, p. 222.

261 *Cf.* R. BIELSA, *op. cit.*, pp. 245, 252.

review of constitutionality of state acts.[262] Particularly because, as we have mentioned, not only the definitive decisions of the National Chambers of Appeals can be the object of an extraordinary recourse but also the definitive decisions of the Superior Courts of the Provinces where the generality of ordinary law cases reach.

Now, the exercise of this extraordinary recourse is submitted to various particular rules, which must be stressed:

First of all, the extraordinary recourse can only be exercised in connection with constitutional matters, thus its importance regarding judicial review. In this respect, the extraordinary recourse can be exercised in three cases:

a. When in a case the question of validity of a treaty, an act of Congress or of another authority exercised in the Nation's name has been raised, and the judicial decision has been against the validity of the particular act;

b. When the validity of an act or decree of the Provincial authorities has been questioned on the grounds of its repugnance to the Constitution, treaties or acts of Congress, and the judicial decision has been in favor of the validity of the particular act.

c. When the interpretation of a clause of the Constitution, of a treaty or of an act of Congress or another national act has been questioned, and the judicial decision has been against the validity of a title, right, privilege or exemption founded in said clause which has been a matter of the case.[263]

As a creation of the Supreme Court of the Nation doctrine, the extraordinary recourse against "arbitrary judicial decisions" has also been accepted. Arbitrary judicial decisions are considered those in which the right to defend one self in a proceeding is said to have been violated. It has also been accepted in cases of so called "institutional gravity", when the Supreme Court can be reached even though the extraordinary recourse would be normally inadmissible; and in cases when an "effective deprivation of justice" has been committed.[264]

The second rule referred to the admissibility of the extraordinary recourse states that the constitutional question must have been discussed in the proceeding in the lower courts, and considered in its decision, before it can be brought before the Supreme Court through the extraordinary recourse.[265] Therefore, the Supreme Court has rejected the recourse when the constitutional issue has not been discussed in the lower courts and has not been considered in the decision.[266] Furthermore, the constitutional issue must have been maintained in the various judicial instances in the lower courts and not abandoned by the interested party. On the contrary, the Supreme Court would reject the extraordinary recourse.[267]

---

262 *Cf.* J.R. VANOSSI and P.E. UBERTONE, *doc. cit.*, p. 19.

263 Statute 48, Art. 14. *Cf.* J.R. VANOSSI and P.E. UBERTONE, *cit.* p. 20; R. BIELSA, *op. cit.*, p. 210, 211; N.P. SAGÜES, *op. cit.*, p. 272.

264 *Cf.* J.R. VANOSSI and P.E. UBERTONE, *doc. cit.*, p. 20.

265 *Cf.* R. BIELSA, *op. cit.*, pp. 190, 202, 203, 205, 209.

266 *Cf.* R. BIELSA, *op. cit.*, p. 204.

267 *Cf.* R. BIELSA, *op. cit.*, p. 260.

In third place, all the other aspects of the incidental character of judicial review already mentioned apply, of course, to the admissibility of the extraordinary recourse, and particularly the fact that it must be exercised by a party with direct interests in the matter, whose rights are affected by the decision regarding the invalidity of a statute, and that the solution of the constitutional question must be unavoidable and indispensable for the decision of the case. Regarding standing, it must be pointed out that in the Argentinean system, it is expressly accepted that public bodies whose acts have been questioned on the grounds of unconstitutionality and also the Public Prosecutor, are considered party regarding the exercise of the extraordinary recourse.[268]

Finally, in the Argentinean system of judicial review, as a pure diffuse system, we must refer to the effects of the decision adopted by the courts when exercising their powers of judicial review of constitutionality.

First of all, it must be said that judicial decisions adopted on matters of constitutionality, when they consider a statute to be unconstitutional, whether adopted by inferior courts or by the Supreme Court, they simply do not apply the invalid statute by giving preference to the Constitution, but there is no annulment. The courts in Argentina do not have the power to annul or repeal a law. That power is reserved to the legislator, and the only thing they can do is to refuse its application in the concrete case when they consider it unconstitutional.[269] The statute, therefore, when considered unconstitutional and non–applicable by the judge, is considered null and void, with no effect whatsoever[270] in the particular case. This leads to the consideration of the retroactive effect of the decision, bearing in mind its declarative character, thus *ex tunc, pro praeterito.* We insist, however, that the statute remains valid and generally applicable and even the same court can change its criteria about its unconstitutionality and apply it in the future.[271]

That is why these effects of the judicial decision on constitutional matters, in the Argentinean system are strictly *inter partes* effect, a consequence of the diffuse character of the system. Thus the decision considering the nullity of a statute has effect only in connection with the particular process where the question has been raised and between the parties which have intervened in it and, therefore, has no *erga omnes* effects at all.[272]

On the other hand, in the Argentinean system, the decision on judicial review, even the decisions of the Supreme Court on constitutional issues are not obligatory for the other courts or the inferior courts.[273] Moreover, even though in the 1949 constitutional reform it was expressly established that the interpretation adopted by the

---

268 *Cf.* R. BIELSA, *op. cit.*, pp. 237, 238.

269 *Cf.* R. BIELSA, *op. cit.*, pp. 197, 198, 345; N.P. Sagües, *op. cit.,* p. 156.

270 *Cf.* A.E. GHIGLIANI, *op. cit.*, p. 95.

271 *Cf.* R. BIELSA, *op. cit.*, p. 196; A.E. Ghigliani, *op. cit.*, p. 92, 97; N. P. SAGÜES, *op. cit.,* p. 177.

272 *Cf.* H. QUIROGA LAVIE, *op. cit.*, p. 479.

273 *Cf.* R. BIELSA, *op. cit.*, pp. 49, 198, 267; A.E. GHIGLIANI, *op. cit.*, pp. 97, 98.

Supreme Court of Justice upon the articles of the Constitution would be considered binding on the national and provincial courts,[274] this article of the constitution was later repealed and the situation today is the absolute power of all courts to render their judgment autonomously with their own constitutional interpretation.

Nevertheless, it is certain that the Supreme Court of Justice, because it is the highest court in the country with wide appellate jurisdiction, particularly through the extraordinary recourse, its decisions have a definitive influence upon all the inferior courts particularly when a doctrine has been clearly and reiterated established by the Court.

Finally, regarding the Argentinean system, discussions have arisen concerning the possibility of the exercise of the diffuse system of judicial review, by the courts, when deciding recourse for *amparo* brought before them for the protection of fundamental rights.

Now since its acceptance and despite the diffuse system of judicial review followed in Argentina, the Supreme Court established the criteria of the incompetence of the *amparo* judge to review the constitutionality of legislation, reducing the powers of the judge of *amparo* to decide only on acts or facts that could violate fundamental rights. Thus it was established that the *amparo* could not be granted when the complaint contained the allegation of unconstitutionality of a law on which the relevant acts or facts were based. Thus, the Supreme Court considered that the judicial decision in cases of recourse for *amparo* could not have declarative effects regarding the unconstitutionality of statutes, due to the summary nature of its proceeding.[275] This doctrine was followed later by law 16.986 of 18 October 1966 about the recourse for *amparo*, in which it was expressly established that the "action for *amparo* will not be admissible when the decision upon the invalidity of the act will require.... the declaration of the unconstitutionality of statutes, decrees or ordinances."(art. 2,d).

Nevertheless, in 1967, the Supreme Court, without declaring the unconstitutionality of the above mentioned disposition of law 16.986 in the *Outon* case,[276] in an implicit way, decided its inapplicability and accepted the criteria that when considering *amparo* cases, the courts have the power to review the unconstitutionality of legislation, which has been supported by the leading constitutional law authors of the country.[277]

---

274 Art. 95 of the 1949 Constitution. *Cf.* C.A. Ayanagaray, *Efectos de la declaración de inconstitucionalidad*, Buenos Aires, 1955, p. 11; R. Bielsa, *op. cit.*, p. 268.

275 See the *Aserradero Clipper SRL* case (1961), J. R. VANOSSI *Teoría constitucional, cit.*, Vol. II, p. 286.

276 Outon case of 29 March 1967. J. R. VANOSSI, *Teoría constitucional, cit.*, Vol. II, p. 288.

277 G. J. BIDART CAMPOS, *Régimen legal del amparo,* 1969; G. J. BIDART CAMPOS, "El control de constitucionalidad en el juicio de amparo y la arbitrariedad o ilegalidad del acto lesivo", *Jurisprudencia argentina*, 23–4–1969; N. P. Sagües, "El juicio de amparo y el planteo de inconstitucionalidad", *Jurisprudencia argentina*, 20–7–1973; J. R. J. R. VANOSSI, *Teoría constitucional, cit.*, Vol. II, pp.288–292; José Luis LAZZARINI, *El juicio de amparo*, La Ley, Buenos Aires, 1987, pp. 80, 86; Alí Joaquín SALGADO, *Juicio de amparo y acción de inconstitu-*

Anyway, the acceptance of this means of judicial review of legislation, through the action for *amparo*, could lead to a direct action of unconstitutionality, although of a diffuse character, which differs from the incidental normal character of the constitutional review system, which is commonly exercised as a consequence of an exception raised by a party in a concrete process, whose main objective is not the constitutional question.

On the contrary, in the action of *amparo,* when founded on reasons of unconstitutionality of a statute on which the concrete act that violates the fundamental right that the petitioners seek to be protected is based, the unconstitutionality of the laws becomes a direct issue of the action itself. That is why it has been said that by accepting this feature of the action for protection, the Supreme Court has opened the way to a new direct means of judicial review of constitutionality of legislation.[278]

III. THE AMPARO ACTION IN COUNTRIES WITH ONLY A CONCENTRATED SYSTEM OF JUDICIAL REVIEW

Argentina is the only Latin American country that has kept the diffuse method of judicial review as the only one in order to control the constitutionality of legislation.

Others Latin American countries have also followed the trend of adopting only one system of judicial review, but on the opposite side, attached only to the concentrated method. It is the case of Bolivia, Chile, Costa Rica, El Salvador, Honduras, Panama, Paraguay and Uruguay, countries that have the concentrated method of judicial review as the only existing one in the country by reserving to the Supreme Court or to a Constitutional Tribunal the monopoly to control the constitutionality of legislation.

Notwithstanding, regarding the amparo and habeas corpus actions, the exclusive attribution of the Supreme Court or Constitutional Tribunal are not always empowered with judicial review, and on the contrary, in the majority of the countries with concentrated method of judicial review, the amparo jurisdiction corresponds to a universality of courts and judges.

Thus, regarding amparo in countries with concentrated method of judicial review, the systems can be classified distinguishing those where amparo is also attributed to the judicial review concentrated organ or is attributed to the whole judiciary.

1. The amparo action exercised before one single tribunal: the Constitutional Chamber of the Supreme Court in Costa Rica and El Salvador

Perhaps the most common trend of the amparo in Europe, existing only in countries with a concentrated system of judicial review as a means of judicial protection

---

cionalidad, Ed. Astrea, Buenos Aires, 1987, p. 58; Joaquín BRAGE CAMAZANO, *La jurisdicción constitucional de la libertad (Teoría general, Argentina, México, Corte Interamericana de Derechos Humanos)*, Editorial Porrúa, Instituto Mexicano de Derecho Procesal Constitucional, México, 2005, pp. 71, 117.

278 J. R. VANOSSI, *Teoría constitucional*, *cit.*, Vol. II, p. 291.

of constitutional rights and guarantees, is to consider it as a single action or recourse that can only be brought before one single Tribunal specialized in constitutional matters. This is the case of the actions or recourses of amparo established in Germany[279], Austria[280] and Spain[281].

This system is also followed in some Latin American countries with concentrated systems of judicial review, when setting forth a sole and exclusive court to hear the actions of amparo and habeas corpus, as is the case of the Constitutional Chamber of the Supreme Court of Costa Rica and El Salvador.

This is also the case of the Supreme Court of Justice of Nicaragua, but with the basic distinction that in this country there is a mixed system of judicial review.

A. *The recourse of amparo in Costa Rica*

In Costa Rica, as mentioned above, every person has a right the file the recourse of *habeas corpus* in order to guarantee his personal freedom and safety, and the recourse of amparo to maintain or reestablish the enjoyment of the other rights set forth in the Constitution, as well as the fundamental rights established in international instruments on human rights that are applicable to the Republic (Article 48, Constitution).

According to the 1989 Constitutional Jurisdiction Law, both recourses can only be brought before the Constitutional Chamber of the Supreme Court of Justice[282]. Articles 2,a and 4 of such statute provide the specific attribution of that Constitutional Chamber to "guarantee by means of the recourses of habeas corpus and amparo, the rights and freedoms set forth in the Constitution and the human rights recognized by international law applicable in Costa Rica".

Regarding the habeas corpus recourse, Article 15 of the Law set forth that its purpose is to guaranty personal freedom and integrity, against acts or omissions from an authority of any kind, including judicial, against that freedom's threats and against the unduly disturbance and restrictions to such freedom adopted by authorities, as well as against illegitimate restrictions regarding the right to move from one place to another within the Republic, or the right to stay, to leave and to come back to its territory (Art. 15).

---

279 See I. V. MUNCH. "El recurso de amparo constitucional como instrumento jurídico y político en la República Federal de Alemania", *Revista de Estudios Políticos,* N° 7, Madrid, 1979, pp. 269–289; Klaus SCHLAICH, "El Tribunal constitucional alemán", in L. Favoreu *et al.*, *Tribunales Constitucionales Europeos Derechos Fundamentales,* Madrid, 1984, pp. 133–232.

280 See F. ERMACORA, "El Tribunal Constitucional Austríaco" in the *Tribunal Constitucional,* Dirección General de lo Contencioso del Estado, Instituto de Estudios Fiscales, Madrid, 1981, Volumen I, pp. 409–459.

281 See Joan Oliver ARAUJO, *El recurso de amparo,* Palma de Mallorca, 1986; Antonio MOYA GARRIDO, *El recurso de amparo según la doctrina del Tribunal Constitucional,* Barcelona, 1983; José L. CASCAJO CASTRO and Vicente GIMENO SENDRA, *El recurso de amparo,* Madrid, 1985; Antonio CANO MATA, *El recurso de amparo,* Madrid, 1983.

282 See, in general, Rubén HERNÁNDEZ VALLE, *La tutela de los derechos fundamentales*, Editorial Juricentro, San José 1990.

Pursuant to this same Law, and regarding the recourse of amparo, it is stated that it proceeds against any provision, agreement or resolution and, in general, against any action, omission or simple material action that is not founded on an effective administrative act, of the services or public institutions that have violated, violate or threatens to violate any of such rights (Article 29). The amparo not only proceeds against arbitrary acts, but also against actions or omissions founded on norms which are arbitrarily interpreted or unduly applied.

However, the Law excludes the amparo action against statutes or other regulatory provisions, unless they are challenged together with the individual acts that apply them or when the contents of the norms are automatically applicable, in the sense that their provisions become immediately obligatory simply upon their passing. It also excludes the amparo against the judicial resolutions and actions of the Judiciary, against acts carried out by the authorities upon executing judicial decisions, and against the acts or provisions of the Supreme Tribunal of Elections in electoral matters (Article 30).

Costa Rica's Law also regulates the action of amparo against actions or omissions of those private law subjects, but in a way similar to the Colombian regulation, only when they act or should act in exercise of public functions or powers or are by law or by fact in a position of power against which ordinary judicial remedies are clearly insufficient and tardy in guaranteeing the fundamental rights and freedoms established in the Constitution and the human rights recognized by International Law in force in Costa Rica (Article 57).

In particular, the same Law of Constitutional Jurisdiction specifically regulates the recourse of amparo to guarantee the right of correction or response to any person affected by incorrect or harmful report issued against him or her by the mass media, in order that it be rectified or responded by the same broadcaster. The Law regulates a specific procedure for such purpose (Articles 66 *et seq.*).

The recourse of amparo of Costa Rica, therefore, is conceived as a judicial means of constitutional protection against actions of the Public Administration, against individual's actions when exercising Public Authority, and against self–applicable laws or regulatory acts, which is brought directly before the Constitutional Chamber of the Supreme Court of Justice against the agent or titleholder of the institution or representative of the entity that appears to be the author of the offence, without it being necessary to exercise any administrative recourse prior to bringing the action.

On the other hand, the Constitutional Chamber of the Supreme Court of Costa Rica before which are filed the amparo recourses, was created as a result of the constitutional reform of 1989, with additional powers to declare the unconstitutionality of statutes and other State acts, with annulatory effects (Art. 10). Accordingly, in Costa Rica and following a long legislative tradition of absence of diffuse method of judicial review, a concentrated system of judicial review was established attributing exclusively to the Constitutional Chamber by mean of different judicial instruments like the action of unconstitutionality and the judicial referrals[283].

Article 73 of the Constitutional Jurisdiction Law sets forth the action of unconstitutionality that can be brought before the Chamber against any statute or regulation, when in their drafting it violates any essential constitutional formality, when a constitutional amendment has been approved in violation of the constitutional procedure, when a statute is contrary to the Constitution because opposing an international treaty or agreement, when an international convention or agreement is signed, approved or ratified in a contrary way to the Constitution provisions or when an international convention or agreement in its contents and effects infringe the Constitution or a constitutional principle. The decisions of the Chamber when declaring the unconstitutionality of the challenged statute have annulatory and *erga omnes* effects. The decisions also have declarative and retroactive ex tunc effects, except regarding bona fide acquired rights or consolidated legal situations by means of prescription, caducity of a judicial decision (Article 92).

This action can be exercise in an incidental or principal way. The incidental way may be brought before the Constitutional Chamber by any party in a judicial procedure, even in cases of habeas corpus and amparo, and in administrative procedures before Public Administration in which case the constitutional question must be raised as a reasonable mean for the protection of the rights and interest of the affected parties (Article 75).

The principal unconstitutionality action can only be brought before the Constitutional Chamber by the General Comptroller, the Attorney General, the Public Prosecutor an the Peoples' Defendant (Article 75). Nonetheless, the action can also be brought before the Chamber in cases of absence of individual harm or in cases devoted to the defense of diffuse or collective interests, in which cases, the action is brought against regulation or auto applicable statutes which do not require additional State actions for its enforcement. In these cases, no individual interest must be raised being then the constitutional action similar to a popular action.[284]

In addition to the action of unconstitutionality, the other important mean for judicial review is the judicial referrals on constitutionality matters that the courts can raise before the Constitutional Chamber when there are doubts regarding the constitutionality of the regulation or the statute that they must apply for the resolution of the case (Article 120). In these cases, the court must prepare a resolution where it must raise the constitutional questions to be sent to the Constitutional Chamber. The judicial procedure must be suspended until the Chamber decision is taken, which has obligatory character and res judicata effects (articles 104 and 117).

---

283 *Véase* en general Rubén HERNÁNDEZ VALLE, *El Control de la Constitucionalidad de las Leyes*, San José, 1990.

284 See Rubén HERNÁNDEZ VALLE, *El Control de la Constitucionalidad de las Leyes*, San José, 1990.

B. *The recourse of amparo in El Salvador*

In a similar way to the Costa Rican regulations, also in El Salvador, the Constitutional Chamber of the Supreme Court of Justice is the judicial body with the exclusive power to decide recourses of amparo for the protection against all the violations of the rights granted by the Constitution (Article 247). Also, regarding the *habeas corpus* recourses to protect personal freedom, the power to decide them is likewise attributed to the Constitutional Chamber of the Supreme Court of Justice.

Nonetheless, when the aggressive action takes place outside the capital, the habeas corpus recourse can be filed before the Chambers of Second Instance (article 42). In such cases, the decision of the Chambers that denies the liberty of the aggrieved party may be subject to review, at the request of the interested party, by the Constitutional Chamber of the Supreme Court of Justice.

Both actions, amparo and habeas corpus, have been regulated in the 1960 Law N° 2996 of Constitutional Proceedings, amended in multiple occasions up to 1997, setting forth that the action of amparo proceeds against any kind of actions or omissions of any authority, public official or decentralized bodies or of the judicial definitive decisions issued by the Judicial review of administrative action Chambers which violate the rights guaranteed in the Constitution or impede its exercise. When the State is the aggrieved party, the Constitutional Chamber must order the suspension of the challenged act (Article 12).

The Law disposed that the action of amparo can only be filed when the act against which it is formulated, cannot be reparable within the procedure by means of other remedies.

In cases in which the amparo is funded in the illegal detention or undue restriction of personal freedom, the protection must be sought through the habeas corpus recourse. In this regard, Article 38 of the same Law set forth the right of everyone to dispose of himself, considering that such right is harmed, when the person is detained against his will, due to threats, to fear to injury, constraint or other material obstacles, in which cases it is understood that the person is reduced to prison and in custody of authority or of the private persons that made the detention (Art. 38).

In all these cases of non–legally authorized prison, confinement, custody or restriction, or which is exercised in a way not legally authorized, the aggrieved party has the right to be protected by writ of personal exhibition (article 40).

In El Salvador, also a concentrated system of judicial review has been set forth in the Constitution, resulting from the creation of the Constitutional Chamber of the Supreme Court by means of the constitutional reforms of 1991–1992. The Constitution attributed to the Chamber the general and exclusive power not only to resolve the amparo and habeas corpus recourses but to declare the unconstitutionality of statutes, decrees and regulations, also with *erga omnes* effects. The unconstitutionality action is conceived in the Constitutional Proceeding Law as a popular action that can be brought before the Chamber by any citizen (Articles 2 and 10).

2. The amparo action exercised before a universality of courts: the case of Bolivia, Chile, Honduras, Panama, Paraguay and Uruguay

With the exception of the tree abovementioned cases of Costa Rica, El Salvador and Nicaragua, where the judicial protection of constitutional rights is concentrated in the Supreme Court, in all the other Latin American countries the actions or recourses of amparo and habeas corpus, as a specific judicial guarantees of constitutional rights and freedoms, are regulated in a diffuse way in the sense that it can be filled before a wide universe of courts instead of being concentrated in one sole Tribunal. This is the case of all other Latin American countries. In addition to the Mexican and Venezuelan systems already analyzed of the amparo as a constitutional right and as a remedy, it is also the case of Argentina, Bolivia, Brazil, Colombia, Chile, Dominican Republic, Ecuador, Guatemala, Honduras, Panama, Paraguay, Peru and Uruguay.

But regarding the countries where a concentrated system of judicial review exists as the only method to control the constitutionality of legislation, like Bolivia, Chile, Honduras, panama, Paraguay and Uruguay, the jurisdiction to decide amparo and habeas corpus actions is attributed to multiple courts.

A. *The recourse of amparo in Bolivia*

According to the Constitution of Bolivia, the recourse of constitutional amparo can be brought before the High Courts in the Department capitals or before the District Judges in the Provinces, against any illegal act or unlawful omission of officials or private individuals that restrict, suppress or threaten to restrict or withhold personal rights and guarantees recognized by the Constitution and the statutes (Art. 19).

The recourse of amparo must be brought by the person who believes to have been wronged or by another sufficiently authorized person in his name, being extremely summarily processed. The Public Prosecutor may also bring, *ex officio*, this recourse when the affected party does not or is unable to do so. In these cases the amparo can only be conceded, provided there is no other means or legal recourse for the immediate protection of the restricted, suppressed and threatened rights and guarantees.

The Constitution also set forth the habeas corpus that can be filed by any person who believes to be illegitimately prosecuted, detained, or imprisoned or by another in his name, with or without power of attorney, Superior Courts of District or any Local judge, asking that the formalities be observed (Article. 18).

Regarding the recourse of habeas data it can also be brought before Superior Courts of District or any Local judge, by any person who believes himself to be illegitimately impeded from knowing, or to object or obtain the removal or rectification of data registered in any physical, electronic, magnetic or computerized in public or private files or data banks, that could affect his fundamental right to personal or familiar intimacy and privacy, self image, honor or reputation recognized in the Constitution (Article 23)

The tree recourses had been developed by Law 1.836 of 1998 on the Law of the Constitutional Tribunal, which states that the constitutional amparo shall be admitted "against any unlawful resolution, act or omission of an authority or official, provided there is no other procedure or recourse available to immediately protect the rights and guarantees, and also against any unlawful act or omission of a person or group of private individuals that restricts, suppresses or threatens the rights or guarantees recognized by the Political Constitution of the State and the Laws" (Article 94).

In Bolivia, according to the Constitution (Article 120,7), and the Law of the Constitutional Tribunal (Article 7,8), all the judicial decisions issued on amparo or habeas corpus must be sent to the Constitutional Tribunal in order to be reviewed. According to Articles 93 and 102,V of the Law on the Constitutional Tribunal, the decisions on amparo and habeas corpus must be sent ex officio to the Constitutional Tribunal in a 24 hours delay for their revision, without causing any suspension on its enforcement.

The revision, in the case of Bolivia, different to the Argentinean, Brazilian, Colombian and Venezuelan extraordinary recourses for revision, is not a recourse, but an obligatory revision that the Constitutional Tribunal must do, to which the decisions must be sent by the courts.

Even though the 1861 Constitution introduced in Bolivia the diffuse system of judicial review following the North American model, by means of the 1994 constitutional reform, the judicial review system in Bolivia was transformed into an exclusively concentrated one[285], corresponding to the Constitutional Tribunal, which began its functioning in 1999, the exclusive power to declare the nullity of statutes declared unconstitutional, with *erga omnes* effects[286].

Therefore, the Constitutional Tribunal has the attribution to control the constitutionality and to guaranty the supremacy of the Constitution, the respect and enforcement of fundamental rights and guarantees as well as the constitutionality of conventions and treaties (Art. 1 of the Law). Thus the courts, except by means of amparo, habeas corpus and habeas data, cannot rule on constitutional matters, and can only refer the control of constitutionality of statutes to the Constitutional Tribunal.

In such character of the Constitutional Tribunal as having the monopoly of judicial review, it also has the power to review the judicial decisions on amparo and

---

285 See in general José Antonio RIVERA SANTIVAÑEZ, "La jurisdicción constitucional en Bolivia. Cinco años en defensa del orden constitucional y democrático" en *Revista Iberoamericana de Derecho Procesal Constitucional* N° 1, enero, junio 2004, Ed. Porrúa, 2004; José Antonio RIVERA SANTIVAÑEZ, "El control constitucional en Bolivia" en *Anuario Iberoamericano de Justicia Constitucional*. Centro de Estudios Políticos y Constitucionales N° 3, 1999, pp. 205–237; José Antonio RIVERA SANTIVAÑEZ, "Los valores supremos y principios fundamentales en la jurisprudencia constitucional" in *La Justicia Constitucional en Bolivia 1998–2003*, Ed. Tribunal Constitucional–AECI, Bolivia, 2003. pp. 347 y ss.; Benjamín Miguel HARB, "La jurisdicción constitucional en Bolivia" en *La Jurisdicción Constitucional en Iberoamérica,* Ed. Dykinson, Madrid, España, 1997, pp. 337 y ss, p. 131.

286 Jorge ASBÚN ROJAS, "Control constitucional en Bolivia, evolución y perspectivas" en *Jurisdicción Constitucional,* Academia Boliviana de Estudios Constitucionales. Editora El País, Santa Cruz, Bolivia, 2000, p. 86.

habeas corpus, and consequently to seek for the uniform interpretation of the Constitution.

B. *The "recourse of protection" in Chile*

Chile's 1980 Constitution, with antecedents in Constitutional Act Nº 3 (Decree–Law 1.552) of 1976, sets forth the recourse of protection of certain constitutional rights and freedoms that may be brought before the competent Courts of Appeals to immediately adopt the rulings they consider appropriate for re–establishing the rule of law and assuring the due protection of the affected party, without prejudice to the other rights that may be enforced before the corresponding authority or tribunals (Article 20)[287].

According to the Constitution, as we have analyzed, this recourse of protection is only set forth to protect the specific rights enshrined in "Article 19, Numbers 1; 2; 3 Subsection 4; 4; 5; 6; 9 Final Subsection; 11; 12; 13; 15; 16 related to the freedom to work and the freedom of free choice and free contracting, and the terms established in Subsection 4; 19; 21; 22; 23; 24 and 25". The recourse of protection is also admitted in the case of Article 19, Number 8, when the right to live in an environment free of contamination is affected by an arbitrary and illegal act attributable to a determined authority or person.

Pursuant to Article 21 of the Constitution, also in matters of constitutional rights protection, specifically regarding to personal freedom and safety, any individual who is under arrest, detained or imprisoned with infringement of the provisions of the Constitution or the statutes, by himself or by any one in his name, may request from the competent court, to order that legal formalities be observed and to immediately adopt the necessary provisions for the re–establishment of the rule of law and to assure the due protection of the affected party.

The court may order that the person be brought before it and its decree shall be precisely obeyed by those in charge of the prisons or places of detention. Once instructed of the antecedents, it shall order the immediate release or the correction of any legal defects, or order that the person be placed at the disposal of the competent judge, proceeding summarily and promptly, and correcting itself such defects or instructing whoever it corresponds to correct them.

The same recourse, in likewise, may be brought in favor of any person who illegally suffers any other deprival, disturbance or threat to the right to personal freedom and individual safety. In such cases, the respective court shall pronounce the above–mentioned measures it deems appropriate for re–establishing the rule of law and ensuring due protection of the affected party.

---

287 See (in general): Pedro ABERASTURY *et al.*, *Acciones constitucionales de* amparo *y protección: realidad y prospectiva en Chile y América Latina*, Editorial Universidad de Talca, Talca 2000, Chile; Juan Manuel ERRAZURIZ GATICA *et al.*, *Aspectos procesales del recurso de protección,* Editorial Jurídica de Chile, Santiago de Chile, 1989; Sergio LIRA HERRERA, *El recurso de protección. Naturaleza Jurídica, Doctrina, Jurisprudencia, Derecho Comparado,* Editorial Jurídica de Chile, Santiago de Chile, 1990; Enrique PAILLAS, *El recurso de protección ante el derecho comparado,* Editorial Jurídica de Chile, Santiago de Chile, 1990.

It must be noted that Chile is one of the few Latin American countries where the recourse of amparo or protection has not been regulated by a special statute. This lack of special statute does not impede its exercise in an efficient way, not only against public authorities harmful's actions but against individuals too. Some cases decided during the eighties', reported by Paillas[288] may illustrate this fact.

For instance, in a case, a farmer brought before a court an action for protection against a neighbor that had demolished the fence dividing their land, and by rebuilding it in another place it affected the plaintiff property rights. The court ordered the re–establishing of the fence to its original place, considering that the arbitrary action of the defendant threatened the property rights of the plaintiff. The decision sought to maintain the existing legal factual situation, in the sense that the recourse of protection was not set forth to resolve property controversies and to establish the real land division, for which the ordinary judicial means are regulated.

In other case, protection was granted to a physician and Medicine professor whose incorporation to the National Health Service was banned, because violation of the non discrimination constitutional guaranty. In other case, a protection was granted against a factory, ordering to halt the production of human consuming products until a ventilation system was set in the premises, in order to expel the gases produced. In the case, the plaintiffs were the neighbors who alleged violation to their rights to a healthy environment. A recourse of protection was filed by the Universidad Austral because of the occupation of its buildings by students, in which case the protection was granted because a violation to the University's rights to teach and to use its own property was found. In all these cases, no decision was issued in order to resolve in a definitive way the legal controversy between parties regarding their respective rights. The decision of the recourse for protection was adopted just in order to resolve a factual problem and to preserve the situation affected by arbitrary actions, re–establishing the existing situation, in order for the interested parties to resolve their rights dispute by the ordinary judicial means.

Nevertheless, in other cases, the recourse for protection were brought before the courts in order to resolve controversies in a definitive way, for which no ordinary judicial mean were available for the resolution of the problem in a prompt an effective way. It is the case, for instance, of ignoring indubitable rights. It was the case of the owner of a land who sought protection to his property right against a railway Company authorized by the state to extract materials from the land for the building of a railway. The court granted the protection because the violation of property rights, not only by the Railway Company but also by the public body which authorized the seizure of the materials.

In all the cases, it can be said that the common denominator is always the urgency needed for the protection.

One aspect that must be highlighted is that in Chile, even though the judicial decisions regarding the recourses of protection are constitutional matters, when decid-

288 See in Enrique PAILLAS, *El recurso de protección ante el derecho comparado,* Santiago de Chile, 1990, pp. 80 ff

ing the case, the courts cannot adopt any decision on judicial review of legislation. Since 1970 a Constitutional Tribunal was created in Chile, in charge of exercising a concentrated judicial review of statutes[289]; but since the 2005 constitutional reform, all sort of decisions on judicial review of legislation, even in concrete cases, have been concentrated in the Tribunal. Thus, when deciding a recourse of protection, if the court considers that the applicable statute is unconstitutional, it cannot decide on the matter, but has to refer the case to the Constitutional Tribunal for its decision.

In this regard, Article 82, 6 of the Constitution assigns the Constitutional Tribunal the power to resolve the inapplicability of statutory provisions in any case before any ordinary or special court, when contrary to the Constitution. Thus, the Constitutional Tribunal has the monopoly of judicial review. In these cases, according to the same Article 82 of the Constitution, the question of unconstitutionality of a statute can be raised by any of the party to the case or by the court that is hearing the case. The Constitutional Tribunal through any of its Chambers may declare without any possibility to be challenged, the admissibility of the question as long as it verifies that a judicial action is pending before an ordinary or special court, that the application of the challenged statutory provision can be decisive to resolve the case and that the challenge is reasonably founded. The same Chamber can decide the suspension of the proceedings where the action of inapplicability on grounds of unconstitutionality has been raised.

When the Constitutional Tribunal has decided in a concrete case the inapplicability of a statutory provision, the decision has only *inter partes* effects. Following, by means of a public action, the question of the unconstitutionality of the provision can be brought before the same Constitutional Tribunal, seeking a ruling in order to annul the statute with general *erga omnes* effects (article 82,7).

C. *The action of amparo in Honduras*

Pursuant to Article 183 of its Constitution, in Honduras the State recognizes the guarantee of amparo; therefore, any offended party, or another in his or her name, shall be entitled to bring a recourse of amparo to uphold or reinstate the enjoyment or benefit of the rights or guarantees established by the Constitution; and in order that he or she declares in specific cases that a law, resolution, act or fact of authority does not apply to the petitioner, nor is it applicable, since it contravenes, diminishes or distorts one or other of the rights recognized by this Constitution. Also pursuant to Article 182 of the Constitution, the State recognizes the guarantee of *habeas corpus* (*exhibición personal*), consequently, any affected party or any other person in his or her name is entitled to bring such action when illegally imprisoned, detained

289 See in general Raúl BERTELSEN REPETTO, *Control de constitucionalidad de la ley,* Editorial Jurídica de Chile, Santiago, Chile, 1969; Francisco Zúñiga Urbina, *Jurisdicción constitucional en Chile,* Tomo II, Ed. Universidad Central de Chile, Santiago, 2002; Humberto NOGUEIRA ALCALÁ, "El Tribunal Constitucional chileno" en *Lecturas Constitucionales Andinas* N° 1, Ed. Comisión Andina de Juristas, Lima, Perú, 1991; Lautaro RÍOS ÁLVAREZ, "La Justicia Constitucional en Chile" en *La Revista de Derecho* N° 1, Ed. Facultad de Derecho, Universidad Central, Santiago, Chile, 1988; Teodoro RIVERA, "El Tribunal Constitucional" en *Revista Chilena de Derecho*, Volumen 11, N° 23, Santiago, Chile, 1984.

or in any way deprived of the individual's right to enjoy freedom; and when in the course of the legal detention or imprisonment, torment, torture, humiliation, illegal extortion and any unnecessary force, restriction or molestation is applied for his or her individual safety or by order of the jail.

These actions were regulated by the 1936 Act of Amparo, until it was repeal by the 2004 Law of Constitutional Justice, in which the follow regulations should be highlighted [290]:

Regarding the purpose of the action of amparo and pursuant to the orientation of the American Convention on Human Rights (Article 25), its exercise is admitted against facts, acts, omissions or threats by any State Authority, including decentralized and de–concentrated entities, municipal corporations and autonomous institutes; those maintained by public funds and those that act through delegation of a State entity by reason of a concession, contract or other valid resolution (Article 42).

The power to hear the action of amparo is attributed to all levels of courts as follows:

According to Article 9 of the Law on Constitutional Justice, all actions of habeas data and the amparo recourses in cases of violation of fundamental rights perpetrated by the President of the Republic, the Appellate Courts, the Accounting Superior Tribunal, the General Attorney of the Republic, the Electoral Supreme Tribunal and by other officials with national jurisdiction, must be brought before the Constitutional Chamber of the Supreme Court of Justice which was created in the 2000 constitutional reform.

The Courts of Appeals are the competent courts to hear the amparo in cases of violation of fundamental rights perpetrated by the Departmental courts and sectional, executor judges and justices of peace, as well as by all political, administrative or military department or section employees (Article 10).

Finally, in the lower level of the Judiciary, the ordinary courts (Jueces de Letras) are competent to hear the amparo recourses in any other cases of violations of fundamental rights and particularly those perpetrated by lower level public officials, by municipal corporations or its members, comprising the police judges and auxiliary mayors (Article 11).

On the other hand, all the above mentioned courts have the power to hear and decide the habeas corpus or personal appearance recourse for the rights of personal freedom and safety (Article 13).

In matters concerning amparo, the most important characteristics of the Law's regulations are as follows:

---

290 See Allan R. BREWER–CARÍAS, "La reforma del sistema de justicia constitucional en Honduras", en *Revista Iberoamericana de Derecho Procesal Constitucional. Proceso y Constitución* (Directores Eduardo FERRER MAC–GREGOR y Aníbal QUIROGA LEÓN), Nº 4, 2005, Editorial Porrúa, México, pp. 57–77; and "El sistema de justicia constitucional en Honduras" in *El sistema de Justicia Constitucional en Honduras (Comentarios a la Ley sobre Justicia Constitucional)*, Instituto Interamericano de Derechos Humanos, Corte Suprema de Justicia. República de Honduras, San José, 2004, pp. 1–148

The rights protected, pursuant to the guidelines of the American Convention, are those recognized in the Constitution and in the Treaties, covenants and other international instruments of human rights (Article 41,1).

Respecting the standing to sue, the action of amparo may be brought by any person without distinction, whether an individual or a legal entity, and it may also be brought by any person in representation of the aggrieved party (Article 44).

With respect to the defendant party, as has been said, the amparo shall be admitted against acts of any authority, such as norms, judicial decisions or administrative acts and also against omissions or threats of violation (Articles 13 and 41). The amparo shall also be admitted against private parties, although to a limited extent, in respect of institutions maintained by public funds and those acting by delegation of a State entity by virtue of a concession, contract or other valid resolution (Article 42).

The processing of the amparo, on the other hand, shall take preference over any other matter, except for cases of *habeas corpus* (Article 51).

A procedure of two instances is established in the Law and in all cases an obligatory consultation of the decisions is set forth. Regarding the decisions issued by the department courts, they must be sent in consultation before the Appellate Courts. The decision issued by these Appellate Courts can be subject to review by the Constitutional Chamber of the Supreme Court by means of the parties' request for study. In such cases the Constitutional Chamber has discretionary power to resolve the admissibility of the request (article 68). Regarding the decisions adopted in first instance by the Appeals Courts in questions of amparo, they must also be sent for consultation before the Constitutional Chamber of the Supreme Court (Article 69).

Thus, the Constitutional Chamber can always be the last resort to decide upon the matters of amparo. According to the Constitution, it can be said that the Honduran system of judicial review is conceived as a mixed one, combining the diffuse and the concentrated ones, the latter in the hands of the Constitutional Chamber. Regarding the diffuse method of judicial review of legislation, Article 320 of the Constitution set forth that "In cases of incompatibility between a constitutional norm and an ordinary statutory one, the courts must apply the former". A constitutional provision regarding the diffuse method of judicial review cannot be clearer[291]. Notwithstanding, and following the legislative practice of the past, the final version of the Law on Constitutional Justice of 2004, failed to regulate such method, setting forth a one and only concentrated method of judicial review of legislation by attributing to the Constitutional Chamber the power to annul statutes on the grounds of their unconstitutionality. Nevertheless, the diffuse method always persists by means of the amparo recourse, because in it, precisely, the court decision can be can be a judicial declaration that in the specific cases, a law is not to be enforced against the claimant nor is it applicable, since it contravenes, diminishes or distorts a right recognized by this Constitution" (183,2 Constitution).

291 See Allan R. BREWER–CARÍAS, "El sistema de justicia constitucional en Honduras" in *El sistema de Justicia Constitucional en Honduras (Comentarios a la Ley sobre Justicia Constitucional)*, Instituto Interamericano de Derechos Humanos, Corte Suprema de Justicia. República de Honduras, San José, 2004, pp. 27 ff.

Regarding the concentrated method of judicial review, the Constitution sets forth that "The statutes can be declared unconstitutional on grounds of form or in its contents" (Article 184), corresponding to the Constitutional Chamber of the Supreme Court the exclusive hearing and resolution on the matter (Article 315,5). The most important aspects of this concentrated method of judicial review are the followings:

Regarding the object of judicial review, the actions of unconstitutionality that can be brought before the Constitutional Chamber are about the statutes and general applicable norms, except regulations, that must be challenged before the administrative action judicial review courts; constitutional amendments approved contrary to the formalities set forth in the Constitution; approbatory statutes of international treaties sanctioned without following the constitutional formalities (Article 17); and against statutes that contravene the provisions of an international treaty or convention in force in Honduras (article 76).

The action of unconstitutionality can be brought before the Constitutional Chamber in a limited standing rule, set forth in the Law on Constitutional Justice following the Constitution, reduced to those persons having a personal, direct and legitimate interest (Article 77).

The concentrated method of judicial review can also be exercised in an incidental manner, as an exception of unconstitutionality of a statute that can be raised in any process (Article 82), or by the referral of the case that any court can make to the Constitutional Chamber of the Supreme Court before deciding the case (Article 87). In such cases, the proceeding must continue in the lower court up to the stage of deciding the case, in which it must be suspended waiting for the Constitutional Chambers decision on the constitutional question (Article 77).

In both cases, whether through the action of unconstitutionality or by means of the incidental constitutional question, the decision of the Constitutional Chamber has *erga omnes* effects, with repealing character (Article 94).

D. *The action of amparo in Panamá*

The amparo action of constitutional guaranties is set forth in Article 50 of Panama's 1972 Constitution, reformed in 1978, 1983 and 1994, for the benefit of any person against whom an order to do or not to do is issued or enforced by any public servant, which violates the rights and guarantees enshrined in this Constitution. In such cases the person has the right to have the order revoked at his request or that of any other person on his behalf." According to the same article, "the recourse of amparo of constitutional guarantees shall be brought by means of a summary procedure and shall be the competence of the judicial tribunals"[292].

Article 23 of the Constitution also sets forth the habeas corpus recourse in favor of any individual arrested in a manner or in cases other than those prescribed by the Constitution and the statute. In such cases, the person shall be released at his request or that of another person, by means of the recourse of *habeas corpus*, which may be

292 See: Lao SANTIZO P., *Acotaciones al* amparo *de garantías constitucionales panameño,* Editorial Jurídica Sanvas, San José, Costa Rica, 1987.

brought immediately following the arrest and irrespective of the applicable punishment.

The regulation related to the amparo action and to the habeas corpus recourse is set forth in the Judicial Code of Panama. Regarding the amparo of constitutional guaranties, according to Article 2615 of the Code, it can be brought against any kind of acts that harm or injure the fundamental rights and guaranties set forth in the Constitution, having the form of an order to do or not no do, when the seriousness and imminence of the damage they cause requires an immediate repeal. It can also be brought against judicial decisions when all the existing judicial means to impugn it have been exhausted; but cannot refer to judicial decisions adopted by the Electoral Tribunal, the Supreme Court of Justice or any of its Chambers.

Pursuant to Article 2.616 of the Legal Code, the following are the competent courts to hear claims of amparo:

1. The Supreme Court of Justice, for acts issued by authorities or officials with rule and jurisdiction in the whole Republic or in two or more provinces.
2. The District High Courts, for acts issued by public servants with rule and jurisdiction in one Province; and
3. The Circuit Judges for acts issued by public servants with rule and jurisdiction in one district or part of such district.

The distribution of the judicial power to resolve in matters of amparo and habeas corpus among all levels of the Judiciary contrast with the judicial review system of Panama, conceived as a concentrated one, by attributing to the Supreme Court of Justice the exclusive power to decide upon the constitutionality of legislation.

Article 203,1 of the Panamanian Constitution gives the Supreme Court the exclusive role to protect the integrity of the Constitution and to control the constitutionality of legislation by means of two different methods: a direct popular action or by mean of a question of constitutionality that can be raised as an incident before a lower court.

Regarding the action of unconstitutionality, in similar terms as the Colombian and Venezuelan regulations, it is conceived as a popular action that can be brought before the Supreme Court by anybody in order to denounce the unconstitutionality of statutes, decrees, decisions or acts, founded in substantive or formal questions (Article 2556).

On the other hand, the question of the unconstitutionality of legal or executive norms applicable to a case can be raised by the parties to the case or ex officio by the respective court, in which case the incidental question must be sent to the Supreme Court for its decision. The procedure must be suspended at the stage previous to the decision that can only be issued once the Supreme Court has adopted its decision on the constitutional matters (Article 2557 Judicial Code).

In both cases, the Supreme Court decision is final, definitive, obligatory and with non retroactive effects, and must be published in the Official Gazette (article 2573 Judicial Code).

E. *The petition for amparo in Paraguay*

The 1992 Constitution of Paraguay also expressly regulates as constitutional guarantees, the petition for amparo, the action of *habeas corpus* (Article 133)[293] and the action of *habeas data* (Article 135).

Regarding the petition for amparo, according to Article 134 of the Constitution, it can be filed by anyone who considers himself seriously affected by a clearly illegitimate act or omission, either by governmental authorities or individuals, or who may be in imminent danger that the rights and guarantees set forth in the Constitution or the statutes may be curtailed, and whom, in light of the urgency of the matter cannot seek remedy through regular legal means. In such case, the affected person may file a petition for amparo before a competent judge. Proceedings will be brief, summary, and free of charge, and of popular action in the cases set forth by legislation.

The judge is empowered to safeguard rights, guarantee, or immediately restore the legal situation that existed prior to the violation.

The amparo petition which has been regulated in the 1971 Law 341 of Amparo, is not admissible against judicial decisions and resolutions and when the matter refers to the individual freedom protected by the recourse of habeas corpus (Article 2).

According to Article 3 of the Law of Amparo, the petition for amparo can be filed before any first instance court with jurisdiction in the place where the act or omission could have effect. Nonetheless, the Constitution provides that, regarding electoral questions and matters related to political organization, the competent court will be that of the electoral jurisdiction (Article 134).

The recourses of habeas data and habeas corpus must also be filed before the judges of first instance (Article 133); and in some cases the habeas corpus recourse before the Supreme Court (Article 259,5).

Except for the resolutions of the amparo petition, habeas corpus recourse or habeas data action, which in general corresponds to all courts of first instance, all other constitutional matters dealing with judicial review of legislation are the exclusive attribution of the Constitutional Chamber of the Supreme Court of Justice. Therefore, in Paraguay, since the 1992 Constitution, a concentrated system of judicial review[294] has existed, by attributing the Supreme Court of Justice the power to decide actions and exceptions seeking to declare the unconstitutionality and inapplicability of statutes contrary to the Constitution. Article 260 of the Constitution, assigns the Constitutional Chamber created in 1995, the power to hear and resolve upon the unconstitutionality of statutes and other normative instruments, declaring in the con-

---

293 See: Evelio FERNÁNDEZ ARÉVALOS, *Habeas Corpus Régimen Constitucional y legal en el Paraguay*, Intercontinental Editora, Asunción, Paraguay 2000.

294 See in general, Norbert LÖSING, "La justicia constitucional en Paraguay y Uruguay" en *Anuario de Derecho Constitucional Latinoamericano 2002.* Ed. KAS, Montevideo, Uruguay, 2002; Luis LEZCANO CLAUDE, *El control de constitucionalidad en el Paraguay,* Ed. La Ley Paraguaya S.A. Asunción, Paraguay, 2000.

crete case, the inapplicability of their dispositions that are contrary to the Constitutions. The decision, thus, only has effects for the concrete case.[295]

The Constitutional Chamber also has the power to decide upon the unconstitutionality of judicial definitive or interlocutory decisions, declaring their nullity when contrary to the Constitution. In all these cases, the procedure can be initiated by means of an action before the Constitutional Chamber of the Supreme Court or through an exception raised in any instance, in which case the files must be sent to the Constitutional Chamber.

This is confirmed by Article 18,a) of the Civil Procedure Code which set forth that the when a judge hearing a concrete case considers the applicable statute contrary to the Constitution, even ex officio, he may send the files to the Supreme Court of Justice, in order for the Court to decide the question of unconstitutionality.

In particular, regarding actions of amparo, Article 582 of the same Civil Procedure Code (Law N° 600, 1995), set forth that when in order to decide an action for amparo, the competent court must determine the constitutionally or unconstitutionality of a statute, decree or regulation, the court must send the files to the Constitutional Chamber of the Supreme Court of Justice, who as soon as possible, must declare the unconstitutionality when evident.

F. *The action of amparo in Uruguay*

Notwithstanding the general declarations contained in Articles 7,72 and 332 of the 1966 Constitution, the action of amparo in Uruguay was expressly regulated by Law 16.011 of 1988, which establishes that any person, human or artificial, public or private, may bring an action of amparo against any act, omission or fact of the state or public sector authorities, as well as of private individuals that in a illegitimate evident way, currently or imminently impair, restrict, alter or threaten unlawfully any of the rights and freedoms expressly or implicitly recognized by the Constitution (Article 72), except in those cases where an action of *habeas corpus* is admitted.

This action of amparo for the protection of all constitutional rights and freedoms may be brought before the judges of First Instance in the matter corresponding to the act, fact or omission under dispute and of the place where they produce effect (Article 3)[296].

However, Law 16.011 excludes from action of amparo, all judicial acts issued in judicial controversies, no matter their nature and irrespective of the court that issues them; also acts of the Electoral Court, whatever their nature; as well as the statutes

295 L.M. ARGAÑA, "Control de la Constitucionalidad de las Leyes en Paraguay", *Memoria de la Reunión de Presidentes de Cortes Supremas de Justicia en Iberoamérica, el Caribe, España y Portugal*, Caracas, 1982, pp. 550, 551, 669, 671.

296 See (in general): Luis Alberto VIERA *et al.*, *Ley de Amparo. Comentarios, Texto Legal y Antecedentes legislativos a su sanción. Jurisprudencia sobre el* amparo, 2nd Edition, Ediciones IDEA, Montevideo, 1993; Miguel Ángel SEMINO, "Comentarios sobre la acción de amparo en el Derecha uruguayo", en *Boletín de la Comisión Andina de Jurista,* N° 27, Lima, 1986,

and decrees of departmental governments that have force of statute in their jurisdiction (Article 1).

This action of amparo in the Uruguayan system is only admitted when there are no other judicial or administrative means available for obtaining the same result of protection or amparo, or when, if they were to exist, are clearly ineffective for protecting the right Article 2).

In the process of amparo, constitutional questions may arise regarding the unconstitutionality of statutes, but the ordinary court cannot resolve them, and a referral to the Supreme Court must be made. This is the consequence of the concentrated method of judicial review of legislation that exists in Uruguay[297].

Article 256 of the Uruguayan Constitution, since 1934[298], assigns to the Supreme Court of Justice the exclusive and original power to declare the unconstitutionality of statutes and other State acts with force of statutes, whether founded on formal or substantive reasons.

This declaration of unconstitutionality of a statute and its inapplicability can be requested be means of an action of unconstitutionality that can be filed before the Supreme Court by all those who deem that their personal and legitimate interests have been harmed (Article 258)[299]. Thus, regarding standing, the Uruguayan regulation has similarities with the Honduran one.

The constitutional question can also be submitted to the Supreme Court in an incidental way by a referral made ex officio or as a consequence of an exception of unconstitutionality raised by a party to a concrete process, by an inferior court (art. 258). In such cases, the inferior court must send to the Supreme Court an abstract of the question, the case having to be suspended at the stage of deciding it. Once the Supreme Court has decided, the inferior court must then decide according to what the Supreme Court has ruled (Articles 258, 259).

In all cases, the decisions of the Supreme Court on matters of constitutionality only refer to the concrete case in which the question is raised (Article 259). This

---

297 See in general José KORSENIAK, "La Justicia constitucional en Uruguay" en *La Revista de Derecho*, año III, enero–junio 1989, Facultad de Derecho, Universidad Central, 1989; Héctor GROS ESPIELL, "La jurisdicción constitucional en el Uruguay" en *La Jurisdicción Constitucional en Iberoamérica*, Ed. Universidad Externado de Colombia, Bogotá, Colombia, 1984; Eduardo ESTEVA G. "La jurisdicción constitucional en Uruguay" en Domingo GARCÍA BELAUNDE, y Francisco FERNÁNDEZ SEGADO, (Coord.), *La Jurisdicción Constitucional en Iberoamérica*. Ed. Dykinson, Madrid, España, 1997; Norbert Lösing, "La justicia constitucional en Paraguay y Uruguay" en *Anuario de Derecho Constitucional Latinoamericano 2002*. Ed. KAS, Montevideo, Uruguay, 2002,

298 Originally, the system was established in 1934, and latter in 1951. See H. GROSS ESPIELL, *La Constitución y su Defensa*, Congreso, "*La Constitución y su Defensa*", UNAM, 1982 (policopiado), pp. 7,11. The siystem remained in the 1966 Constitution, in the "Acta Institucional N° 8 de 1977" and in the "Acta Institucional N° 12 de 1981". *Idem*, pp. 16, 20.

299 Artículo 258. See H. GROSS ESPIELL, *op. cit.*, pp. 28, 29; J.P. GATTO DE SOUZA, "Control de la Constitucionalidad de los Actos del Poder público en Uruguay", *Memoria de la Reunión de Presidentes de Cortes Supremas de Justicia en Iberoamérica, el Caribe, España y Portugal*, Caracas, 1982, pp. 661, 662.

principle is clear regarding the incidental mean of judicial review where the question of constitutionality is raised in a concrete case, but originates doubts regarding the action of unconstitutionality. According to the Law N° 13747 of 1969[300], which regulates the procedures in matters of judicial review, the decision of the Supreme Court impede the application of the challenged norms declared unconstitutional regarding the plaintiff, authorize its use as an exception in all other judicial proceedings, including the judicial review of Public administration activities[301].

CHAPTER VI.

THE AMPARO AS A CONSTITUTIONAL REMEDY WITHIN THE LATIN AMERICAN MIXED SYSTEMS (DIFFUSE AND CONCENTRATED) OF JUDICIAL REVIEW OF LEGISLATION

In the middle of the XIX Century, the North American system of judicial review influenced some Latin American countries which also adopted the diffuse system of judicial review. Alexis De Tocqueville's influential book, *Democracy in America,* [302] is considered to have played a fundamental role in this process, particularly regarding the Latin American countries with a federal form of state, all of whom adopted a form of constitutional justice, as was the case in Argentina (1860), Mexico (1857), Venezuela (1858) and Brazil (1890). The system was also adopted in other countries with a brief federal experience like Colombia (1850) and even without connection with the federal form of state in the Dominican Republic (1844), where it is still in force.

But all the Latin American diffuse systems of judicial review, except for Argentina which remained the most similar to the American model[303], moved from the original diffuse system towards a mixed system, by adding the concentrated method of judicial review, or by adopting the mixed system from the beginning with its own

300 See H. GROSS ESPIELL, *op. cit.*, p. 29.

301 *Idem.*

302 The first edition in Spanish of the book was issued in 1836, one year after the French and English edition. On the influence of the De Tocqueville book on the matter, see J. CARPIZO and H. FIX–ZAMUDIO, "La necesidad y la legitimidad de la revisión judicial en América Latina. Desarrollo reciente", in *Boletín Mexicano de Derecho Comparado*, 52, 1985, p. 33; R.D. Baker, *Judicial Review in México. A Study of the Amparo Suit*, Austin 1971, pp. 15, 33.

303 A. E. GHIGLIANI, *Del control jurisdiccional de constitucionalidad*, Buenos Aires 1952, who speaks about "Northamerican filiation" of the judicial control of constitutionality in Argentinian law, p. 6, 55, 115. *Cf.* R. BIELSA, *La protección constitucional y el recurso extraordinario. Jurisdicción de la Corte Suprema*, Buenos Aires 1958, p. 116; J.A.C. GRANT, "El control jurisdiccional de la constitucionalidad de las Leyes: una contribución de las Américas a la ciencia política", *Revista de la Facultad de Derecho de México*, UNAM, T. XII, 45, 1962, p. 652; C.J. FRIEDRICH, *The Impact of American Constitutionalism Abroad*, Boston 1967, p. 83.

natural characteristics. Even the Mexican system with the peculiarities of the *juicio de amparo* also moved from the original diffuse system to the current mixed system.

Due to the mixed character of the judicial review system, in all the countries that have adopted the mixed system of judicial review, except for Nicaragua, the amparo actions can be filed before a universe of courts, as happens in Brazil, Colombia, Dominican Republic, Ecuador, Guatemala, Peru, Mexico and Venezuela. In Nicaragua, on the contrary, only the Supreme Court can hear actions of amparo.

I. THE AMPARO ACTION OR RECOURSE IN MIXED SYSTEMS OF JUDICIAL REVIEW, EXERCISED BEFORE ONE SINGLE TRIBUNAL: THE CASE OF THE SUPREME COURT OF NICARAGUA

In Nicaragua, the Supreme Court of Justice is the one called to hear and decide the recourse of amparo (Art. 164,3), which –according to Article 45 of the Constitution, corresponds to those "whose constitutional rights have been violated or are in danger of violation". Only two other Latin American countries assign to their Supreme Court the monopoly to decide amparo actions, Costa Rica and El Salvador, but with the difference that there, the judicial review system followed is an exclusively concentrated one, exercised by a Constitutional Chamber of the Supreme Court.

The recourse of amparo in Nicaragua is set forth against any provision, act or resolution, and in general against any action or omission of any official, authority or agent that violates or attempts to violate the rights and guarantees enshrined in the Constitution; and the recourse of *habeas corpus* in regulated in favor of those whose freedom, physical integrity and safety have been violated or are in danger of being violated (Articles 188 and 189 of the Constitution). Both recourses are of the exclusive competence of the Supreme Court of Justice to hear them (Article 164,3).

According to the 1988 Law of Amparo, the recourse of amparo proceeds against any disposition, act or resolution and in general, against any action or omission of any public official, authority or agent which violates or threatens to violate the rights and guaranties declared in the Constitution (Article 3). Thus, no amparo recourse can be filled against private individual's actions or omissions.

On the other hand, regarding the recourse of personal exhibition (habeas corpus), it proceeds in favor of those persons whose freedom, physical integrity and security are violated or in danger of being violated by any public official, authority, entity or public institution, autonomous or not, and acts restrictive of personal freedom of any inhabitant of the Republic performed by individuals (Art. 4)

As mentioned, the Supreme Court of Justice is the only competent tribunal to finally decide the recourse of amparo. According to Article 25 of the Amparo Law, the amparo recourse must be brought before the Courts of Appeals or its Civil Chambers, where the first path of the proceeding must be accomplished, including the suspension of the challenged act. The files must then be sent for the accomplishment of the final path of the procedure to the Supreme Court of Justice until the final decision. Even in cases in which the Courts of Appeals reject to hear the recourse, the plaintiff can bring the case by mean of an action de amparo before the Supreme Court, against the illegitimate act of fact (*vía de hecho*).

In cases of illegal detentions made by any authority, the recourse of personal exhibition must be filed before the Courts of Appeals or their Criminal Chambers. In cases of acts restrictive of freedom made by individuals, the habeas corpus must be filed before the Criminal District courts (Art. 54).

In Nicaragua, even though the Supreme Court is the only competent court to decide the amparo and personal exhibition recourses, as well as a recourse of unconstitutionality of statutes, the judicial review system is not a concentrated one but a mixed one, because all courts, in accordance with the principle of constitutional supremacy (Article 182 of the Constitution), can be considered as having the general power to decide upon the unconstitutionality of statutes when deciding concrete cases, with only *inter partes* effects.

The recourse of unconstitutionality is conceived as a direct action that can be brought before the Supreme Court by any citizen against any statute, decree or regulation (Article 2 of the Amparo Law). The decision is thus conceived as a popular action, and the Supreme Court's decision when declaring the unconstitutionality of the impugned act, has also general and formal *res judiciata* effects. The statute declared in contravention with the Constitution cannot be applied after the Court's decision has been adopted (Articles 18 and 19).

It must be highlighted that the question of the unconstitutionality of a statute, decree or regulation can also be raised in a particular case before the Supreme Court by the corresponding party in the proceeding of a recourse of cassation or of a recourse of amparo, in which cases, if the Supreme Court in its decision, in addition to the cassation of the judicial decision and to the constitutional protection to be granted to the party, must declare the unconstitutionality of the statute, decree or regulation, with the same general effects. Nonetheless, the decision cannot affect third party rights acquired from those statutes or regulations (Articles 20 and 22).

The Amparo Law also provides that in any judicial case in which a decision that cannot be challenged by mean of a cassation recourse has been adopted, resolving the matter with express declaration of the unconstitutionality or a statute, decree or regulation, the respective court must send its decision to the Supreme Court. The latter can ratify the unconstitutionality of the statute, decree or regulation and declare its inapplicability. In such case the decision cannot affect third party rights acquired from those statutes or regulations (Articles 21 and 22)

As mentioned, with the only exception of Nicaragua, in all other Latin American countries that follow the mixed system of judicial review combining the diffuse and concentrated method of judicial review of the constitutionality of statutes, the amparo recourse proceedings follows the diffuse trends, and can be filed before a universality of courts and not before one single court. It is the case of the systems of Brazil, Colombia, Dominican Republic, Ecuador, Guatemala, Mexico, Perú and Venezuela.

II. THE AMPARO ACTION OR RECOURSE IN MIXED SYSTEMS OF JUDICIAL REVIEW EXERCISED BEFORE A UNIVERSALITY OF COURTS: THE CASE OF MEXICO, VENEZUELA, BRAZIL, COLOMBIA, DOMINICAN REPUBLIC, ECUADOR, GUATEMALA AND PERÚ

As has been mentioned before, the supremacy of the Constitution in a democratic society, as the product of the people's will expressed by means of the constituent power, implies that the Constitution cannot be modified except only by means of the constitutional revision process enshrined by the people in the same Constitution. The people as creator of the Constitution have a right to its preservation and to its supremacy.

The consequence of such right to he supremacy of the Constitution is the set of guaranties the Constitution set forth in order to protect it, by means of the judicial review power attributed to the Judiciary or by means of the actions for protection of the Constitution that can be filed before the courts.

In both cases, if people have a constitutional right to the supremacy of the Constitution and its contents, it also has a constitutional right to the protection of such supremacy, referred not only to the organic part of the Constitution (State organization and division and separation of powers) but also regarding its dogmatic side, that is, the constitutional rights and freedoms declared in the Constitution as pertaining to the people. Thus, everyone has rights guarantied in the Constitution, and everyone has the constitutional right to be effectively protected by the Judiciary in the enjoyment and exercise of such constitutional rights.

The consequence of such approach is that there is a fundamental right that can be distinguished, above all, and it is the right to the judicial control for the enforcement of the Constitution, in order to assure the submission of the State organs to the latter.

Concerning the organic part of the Constitution, this right implies: first, the right to judicial review of legislation (statutes), by means of direct actions of unconstitutionality brought before a constitutional court in a concentrated method of judicial review or by mean of the diffuse method of judicial review where the constitutionality of statutes can be challenge before any court; second, the right to judicial review of administrative action, generally by special administrative courts, on ground of constitutionality and legality; and third, the right to judicial review of judicial decisions through ordinary (appeals) or extraordinary (cassation) means of review.

Moreover, regarding the dogmatic part of the Constitution, this fundamental right to effective judicial protection of constitutional supremacy is also manifest in a right to judicial protection of the constitutional rights and freedoms of the people, either by ordinary judicial effective actions or recourses, or by means of specific actions or recourses of "amparo" or other judicial means of immediate protection of such rights. These provisions of constitutional guarantees to the constitutional rights and freedoms are an essential characteristic of contemporary democratic constitutionalism, the basis of which continues to be the unequivocal statement of Article 16 of the 1789 Declaration of the Rights of Man and the Citizen:

> Any society in which no provision is made for guaranteeing rights or for the separation of powers, has no Constitution.

The consequence of this fundamental right to constitutional supremacy and the right to its judicial protection undoubtedly implies the power/duty attributed to the courts for the purpose of guaranteeing constitutional supremacy, either by annulling State acts (statutes, administrative acts, judicial resolutions) that are contrary to the Constitution, or by re–establishing constitutional rights and freedoms impaired by illegitimate actions, both by State entities and by private individuals.

Such citizens' constitutional right, as all rights of the people guaranteed in the Constitution, can only be limited by the same Constitution. That is why statutory legal restrictions to this right to Constitutional supremacy and to "amparo" protection would be incompatible with their fundamental right character, whether manifested for instance in the exclusion of some State act to be challenged or of some constitutional rights whose violation cannot be immediately protected by the "amparo" action. Constitutional supremacy is an absolute notion that admits no exception, and therefore neither of the constitutional right could be excluded from the judicial protection guarantees, unless, of course, provided by the Constitution itself.

Anyway, as already mentioned, regarding the Latin American "amparo", the national constitutional and statutory regulations allow to distinguish two general systems according to whether the "amparo" of constitutional rights and freedoms is conceived to be *per se* a *constitutional right*, at the same time being a judicial guarantee in multiple ways; or as a specific judicial remedy for the protection of constitutional rights.

1. The "amparo" as a constitutional right

Firstly, the "amparo" of constitutional rights and freedoms may be conceived in the constitutional system as a constitutional right of the citizens, derived from the right to the supremacy of the Constitution and to obtain judicial protection from all courts regarding such rights and freedoms. Such means of judicial protection may be ordinary judicial means, or a specific judicial means of immediate protection.

In these cases, therefore, the amparo has been regulated as a constitutional right, hence originating not just one judicial guarantee (action or recourse) of "amparo", but multiple judicial proceedings, both ordinary and specific, for the protection of constitutional rights and freedoms. Such is the case of Mexico and Venezuela where, in addition, no distinction is made between an amparo action and an habeas corpus action, being the latter just an amparo directed to protect personal freedom and safety.

A. *The Mexican suit of "amparo"*

As has been mentioned before, under Article 25 of the 1847 Act of Constitutional Reforms, Mexico introduced *the right of all inhabitants of the Republic to be legally protected by the courts* of the Federation regarding the rights and guarantees granted to them by the Constitution, against any attack by the Executive or Legislative Authorities, thereby establishing that the federal courts had the duty to provide protection only in concrete cases, without making general declarations concerning the act in question. This is how it arose the figure of constitutional "amparo", as a constitutional right of all people to the protection of their constitutional rights and freedoms, the subsequent development of which, has shaped the so–called "judgment or trail of amparo".

This amparo suit, according to Article 1,1 of the Amparo Law, is set forth in order to resolve any controversy arisen from statutes and authorities' acts which violate individual guaranties. But also, according to the same article, it also has the purpose of resolving any controversy produced by federal statutes or authorities acts harming or restricting the States sovereignty or by States statutes of authorities' acts invading the sphere of federal authority.

In this case of amparo, the judicial protection is granted by means of a quick and efficient procedure, characterized by the absence of formalisms, the intermediary role the judge has between the parties, the inquisitorial character of the procedure which grants the judge with wide and inclusive *ex officio* powers to conduct and direct the process and the concentration of the procedure in only one hearing[304].

This "trial of amparo", if it is true that is the only judicial means that can be used for the judicial protection of constitutional rights and guarantees and also for judicial review of the constitutionality of statutes, does not only have that purpose, being a very complex procedural institution which comprises at least five different judicial actions and proceedings which are generally differentiated processes in the other countries with a civil law tradition.

These five different aspects of the trial for *amparo*, have been systematized by Professor Héctor Fix–Zamudio[305], as follows:

The first aspect of the trial for *amparo* is the so called "*amparo de la libertad*" (protection of freedom) in which the "*amparo*" proceeding functions as a judicial means for the protection of fundamental rights established in the Constitution. In this respect the trial for *amparo* could be equivalent to the request for a writ of *habeas corpus* when it seeks the protection of personal liberty, but can also serve as the protection of all other fundamental rights established in Articles 1 to 29 when violated by an act of an authority[306].

The second aspect of the trial of *amparo* is that it also proceeds against judicial decisions (Art. 107, III, V Constitution) when it is alleged that they have incorrectly

---

304 Héctor FIX–ZAMUDIO, *Ensayos sobre el derecho de amparo,* Universidad Nnacional Autónoma de México, Editorial Porrúa, México, 2003.

305 H. FIX–ZAMUDIO, *El juicio de amparo*, México 1964, p. 243, 377; H. FIX–ZAMUDIO, "Reflexiones sobre la naturaleza procesal del amparo", *Revista de la Facultad de Derecho de México*, 56, 1964, p. 980. H. FIX–ZAMUDIO, "Algunos aspectos comparativos del derecho de amparo en México y Venezuela", *loc. cit.*, p. 345; H. FIX–ZAMUDIO, "Lineamientos fundamentales del proceso social agrario en el derecho mexicano" in *Atti della Seconda Assemblea. Istituto di Dirito Agrario Internazionale a Comparato*, Vol I, Milán, 1964, p. 402; Eduardo FERRER MAC–GREGOR, *La acción constitucional de* amparo *en México y España, Estudio de Derecho Comparado*, 2nd Edition, Edit. Porrúa, México D.F., 2000; Ignacio BURGOA O., *El juicio de amparo*, Twenty–eighth Edition, Editorial Porrúa S.A., México, 1991.

306 *Cf.* R.D. BAKER, *Judicial Review in México. A Study of the Amparo Suit*, Texas, 1971, p. 92.

applied legal provisions, which results in the so called "*amparo judicial*" or "*amparo casación*", that is to say, in a judicial recourse very similar to the recourse of cassation that exists in civil and criminal procedural law in the civil law countries, to seek control of the legality or constitutionality of judicial decisions by the Supreme Courts of Justice. The institution is called *recurso de casación* following the French word *casation*, being in general the attribution of the Court on cassation or of the Supreme Court in their Civil, Labor and Criminal Cassation Chambers. It is an extraordinary judicial recourse which proceeds against definitive and final judicial decisions issued after the exhaustion of all ordinary appeals, and that can only be founded on violations of the Constitution and statutes or of the judicial procedural formalities. By this judicial mean, the Supreme Court assures the uniformity of legal interpretation and judicial application of law. As mentioned, in all Latin American countries it is a specific extraordinary judicial recourse, except in México, where it is one of the modalities of the amparo trail.

The third aspect of the trial for *amparo* is the so–called "*amparo administrativo*" through which it is possible to impugn administrative acts that violate the Constitution or the statutes (Art. 107, IV Constitution . This aspect of the trial for *amparo* results in a mean for judicial review of administrative action, equivalent to the French born *contentieux administratif* extended to almost all civil law countries.

It must be also stressed that in the majority of Latin American countries, in some way influenced by the French administrative law doctrine, some kind of special courts and recourses have been created in order to control the legality and constitutionality of Public Administration's actions and in particular, of administrative acts, seeking their annulment. Even in some countries, such as Colombia, a *Consejo de Estado* has been created following the *Conceil d'État* French model, as the head of a Judicial Review of Administrative Action separate Jurisdiction. In the other countries, the head of the Jurisdiction has been located in the Supreme Court, and the main purpose of it, as mentioned, is to challenge administrative acts seeking their annulment, when being considered unconstitutional or illegal. The important trend of such Jurisdiction is that it is not only devoted to protect human or constitutional rights, but in general, the legality of the administrative actions.

Again in this regard, the Mexican system is also an exception in the sense that for controlling the legality of administrative action and for the protection of individual constitutional rights and guaranties, the administrative amparo has been developed. Consequently, in similar way to the Anglo–American tradition, the ordinary courts are in charge of controlling the Public Administration, but in the case of México, by means of the amparo suit.

The fourth aspect of the trial for *amparo* is the so called *amparo agrario* which is set up for the protection of peasants against acts of the agrarian authorities which could affect their agrarian rights, regulated by the agrarian reform provisions particularly referred to collective rural property (Art. 107, II).

Finally, the fifth aspect of the trial for *amparo*, is the so called *amparo contra leyes* (*amparo* against laws), which can be used to challenge statutes that violate the Constitution, which results in a means of judicial review of the constitutionality of legislation, exercised in a direct way in the absence of any administrative act of enforcement or judicial act of application of the statute considered unconstitutional. This aspect of the trial for *amparo* has been considered as the most specific in constitutional justice aspects.[307]

In all these five aspects of the trial for *amparo*, this particular means of constitutional judicial protection can be used as a means of judicial review of the constitutionality of legislative acts, in which cases they have the common trends of the diffuse system of judicial review, the fifth aspect of the *amparo* against laws, but have additional peculiarities.

In effect, all the four first mentioned aspects of the trial for *amparo* can be used as a means for judicial review of legislation when a constitutional question, having been raised in a particular proceeding, the courts decide the case, based on a statute considered to be unconstitutional. In such cases, the party which alleges being injured in his rights or interests by the decision, can exercise a recourse of *amparo* against the judicial decision, seeking judicial review of legislation.[308] In these cases, the recourse of *amparo*, being a review of a judicial decision, must be brought before a Collegiate Circuit Court or the Supreme Court of Justice, according to their respective jurisdictions (Art. 107, V,VI).[309]

In cases of this direct *amparo* brought before the Collegiate Circuit Courts, the constitution confers the power of reviewing the decisions taken to the Supreme Court, only when constitutional issues are involved, In particular, the article 107, IX of Constitution sets forth:

> Decisions in direct amparo rendered by a Collegiate Circuit Court are not revisable unless the decision involves the unconstitutionality of a law or establishes a direct interpretation of a provision of the constitution, in which case it may be taken to the Supreme Court of Justice, limited exclusively to the decision of actual constitutional questions.

Nevertheless, the same constitutional provision states that the Collegiate Circuit Courts decisions in direct *amparo* are not revisable if they are based "on a precedent established by the Supreme Court of Justice as to the constitutionality of a law or the direct interpretation of a provision of the constitution."

Anyway, in all these cases of *amparo*, judicial review of legislation has an incidental character regarding a concrete judicial proceeding in which the constitutional question is raised and which brings about the use of the "recourse" of *amparo*, against the judicial decision which applied the unconstitutional statute.

Judicial review of legislation through the trial for *amparo*, therefore, has the general trends of the diffuse systems of judicial review according to the North American

---

307 H. Fix–Zamudio, "Algunos problemas que plantea el amparo contra leyes", *Boletín del Instituto de Derecho Comparado de México*, UNAM, 37, 1960, 15, 20.

308 H. Fix–Zamudio, "Aspectos comparativos del derecho de amparo en México y venezuela..." *loc. cit.* p. 358, 359; "Algunos problemas que plantea el amparo contra leyes...", *loc. cit.*, p. 22, 23.

309 *Cf.* H. Fix–Zamudio, "Algunos problemas que plantea el amparo contra leyes...", *loc. cit.*, p. 22

model,[310] even though with a few very important particular features which result from this unique judicial proceeding.

First of all, as we mentioned, the jurisdiction for a trial for *amparo* is reserved to the federal courts. Judicial review of the constitutionality of legislation in Mexico is not a power of all courts but attributed only to the federal courts.

Secondly, since the *amparo* trial is initiated either through a recourse of *amparo* in its first four aspects or through an action in the fifth aspect of the *amparo* against laws, it is always developed against a "public authority", whether it be the judge who has dictated the judicial decision or the administrative authority that has produced the administrative act which are both the object of the recourse of *amparo*; or the legislative authorities that have approved the statute which is the object of the *amparo* against laws action. This aspect reveals another substantial difference between the Mexican system and the general diffuse system, in which the parties in the process in where a constitutional question is raised, continue to be the same.[311]

As we have said, in the first four aspects of the trial for *amparo,* the proceedings are initiated through a recourse of *amparo* normally exercised against a judicial decision, the situation being different in the fifth aspect of the trial for *amparo,* so called *amparo* against laws, in which judicial review of constitutionality of legislation is sought through an "action of unconstitutionality", rather than through a recourse, where the action is exercised against the legislative bodies that approved the challenged statute.

In effect, as we have said, one of the five aspects of the trial for *amparo* is the so called "*amparo* against laws", whose peculiarity regarding the other aspects of the trial for *amparo* consists in the fact that in this case, it is a proceeding initiated through a direct action brought before a federal district court (Art. 107, XII) by a plaintiff, against a particular statute. The defendants being the supreme organs of "the state" which intervened in the process of formation of the statute, namely, the Congress of the Union, or the state Legislatures which produced it; the President of the Republic or the Governors of the states which enacted it, and the Secretaries of state which countersigned it and ordered its publication.[312] In these cases, the federal district courts decisions are revisable by the Supreme Court of Justice. (Art. 107, VIII,a).

The *amparo* against laws, therefore, is a direct action against a statute, and the existence of a concrete administrative act or judicial decision for its enactment or its application is not necessary to its exercise.[313] Nevertheless, the constitutional question involved in this action is not an abstract one, and that is why only the statutes that inflict a direct injury on the plaintiff, without the necessity of any other inter-

310 J.A.C. GRANT, "El control jurisdiccional de la constitucionalidad de las leyes: una contribución de las Américas a la ciencia política", *Revista de la Facultad de Derecho de México*, 45, México 1962, p. 657.

311 *Idem*, p. 657–661.

312 H. FIX–ZAMUDIO, "Algunos problemas que plantea el amparo...", *loc. cit.*, p. 21.

313 *Cf.* R.D. BAKER, *op. cit.*, p. 164.

mediate or subsequent state act, can be the object of this action.[314] Therefore, the object of this action is self–executing statutes, that is to say, statutes that with their sole enactment, cause personal and direct prejudice to the plaintiff. That is why, in principle, the action seeking the *amparo* against laws must be brought before the court within 30 days after their enactment. Nevertheless, the action can also be brought before the Court within 15 days after the first act of enactment of the said statute so as to protect the plaintiff's rights to sue (Art. 21. Amparo Law).[315]

Regarding the effects of the judicial decision on any of the aspects of the trial for *amparo*, in which judicial review of constitutionality is sought whether in a pure incidental way or through the action to request an "*amparo* against laws", the constitution has expressly established (since the institution of the trial for *amparo* in the middle of the last century) that the courts cannot "make any general declaration as to the law or act on which the complaint is based", the judgment affecting "only private individuals" and limited to affording them shelter and protection in a special case to which the complaint refers" (Art. 107, II).[316] Therefore, a decision in a "trial for *amparo*" in which judicial review of legislation is accomplished, can only have *inter partes* effects, and can never consist of general declarations with *erga omnes* effects.

Therefore, the courts in their decisions regarding the unconstitutionality of a statute do not annul or repeal it; therefore, the statute remains in the books and can be applied by the courts, the only effect of the declaration of its unconstitutionality being directed to the parties in a concrete process.

On the other hand, it must be said that the decisions of the trials for *amparo*, whether or not referred to judicial review, do not have general binding effects even regarding other courts, and are only obligatory to other courts in cases of established *jurisprudencia,* that is to say, of obligatory precedent. The constitution does not expressly establish when an obligatory precedent exists and refers to the special Organic law of the Constitutional Trial to specify "the terms and cases in which the *jurisprudencia* of the courts of the federal judicial power is binding, as well as the requirements for modifying it"(Art. 107, XIII, 1). According to that Organic law *jurisprudencia* is established by the Supreme Court of Justice or by the Collegiate Circuit Courts when five consecutive decisions to the same effect, uninterrupted by any incompatible rulings are rendered (Art. 192, 193) but it can be modified when the respective Court pronounces a contradictory judgment with a qualified majority of votes of its members(Art. 194).[317]

---

314 Self–executed Statutes (auto–aplicativas). *Cf.* R.D. BAKER, *op. cit.* p. 167; H. FIX–ZAMUDIO, "Algunos problemas que plantea el amparo...", *loc. cit.* p. 24.

315 *Cf.* H. FIX–ZAMUDIO, "Algunos problemas que plantea el amparo...", *loc. cit.*, p. 32. *Cf.* R.D. BAKER, *op. cit.* p. 171.

316 The principle is named the "Otero formula" due to its inclusion in the 1857 constitution under the influence of Mariano Otero. *Cf.* H, FIX–ZAMUDIO, "Algunos aspectos comparativos del derecho de amparo..." *loc. cit.*, p. 360; and H. FIX–ZAMUDIO, "Algunos problemas que plantea el amparo...", *loc. cit.*, p. 33, 37.

317 See the quotations in R.D. BAKER, *op. cit.* p. 263.

Nevertheless, as *jurisprudencia* can be established by the federal Collegiate Circuit Courts and by the Supreme Court, contradictory interpretations of the constitution can exist, having binding effects upon the lower courts. In order to resolve these conflicts, the constitution establishes the power of the Supreme Court or of the Collegiate Circuit Court to resolve the conflict, when the contradiction is denounced by the Chambers of the Supreme Court or another Collegiate Circuit Court; by the Attorney General or by any of the parties to the cases in which the *jurisprudencia* was established (Art. 107, XIII).[318] Anyway the resolution of the contradiction between judicial doctrines, has the sole purpose of determining one single *jurisprudencia* on the matter, and does not affect concrete juridical situations, derived from the contradictory judicial decisions adopted in the respective trials (Art. 107, XIII).[319]

Finally, regarding the practical effects of the trial for *amparo*, it must be stressed that the constitution establishes a particular preliminary remedy during the trial for *amparo*, which consists of the possible suspension of the application of the contested state act, which in certain aspects is similar to the injunction in the North American system but reduced to an *injunction pendente litis*.[320] In this respect, Article 107 of the constitution established that:

Contested acts may be subject to suspension in those cases and under conditions and guaranties specified by law, with respect to which account shall be taken of the nature of the alleged violation, the difficulty of remedying the damages that might be incurred by the aggrieved party by its performance, and the damages that the suspension might cause to third parties and the public interest (Art. 107, X).

The amparo suit, if against definitive judicial decisions of a District Court, must be filled before another District Court in the same District or before the Collegiate Circuit Courts when there is no other ordinary available recourse to modify it (Articles 40 and 158, Amparo Law). In all other cases, the action must be brought before the District judges with jurisdiction in the place where the challenged act is executed or is trying to be executed (Article 36 Amparo Law). In places where there is no District court, the First Instance courts can receive the complaint, being authorized to order the facts to be maintained as they are and to ask for the relevant reports on the case, before sending the files to the respective District Court (Article 38).

According to Article 114 the petition of amparo must be brought before the District Courts when they are filled: 1) against federal or local statutes, international treaties, national executive regulations or State's Governors regulations or any other administrative regulations which causes prejudices to the plaintiff by its enacting or due to their first applicatory act; 2) against acts issued by judicial, administrative or labor courts; 3) against acts issued by judicial, administrative or labor courts executed outside the trial or after its conclusion; 4) against execution of judicial acts regarding persons of assets which are of impossible to repair; 5) against acts issued within or outside the trial that affect persons not involved in it; 6). against federal

318 See the comments, in R.D. BAKER, *op. cit.*, p. 264.

319 See the comments in J.A.C. GRANT, *loc. cit.* p. 662.

320 J.A.C. GRANT, *loc. cit.*, p. 652, note 33.

statutes or authority acts; and 7) against the Public prosecutor resolutions confirming the not filling or desisting from criminal claims.

It must be also mentioned that according to a constitutional reform passed in 1983, based in the experience of the North American writ of certiorari, the Supreme Court was vested with a discretionary competency to select to review the cases of amparo of constitutional importance; and according to another constitutional reform on 1988, the Supreme Court was attributed the competency to decide in last instance all cases of amparo where the constitutionality of a statute were at stake. Both attributions allow the Supreme Court to give final interpretation of the Constitution in a uniform way[321].

As we can see, although having peculiarities that cannot be reproduced in any other legal system, the trial for *amparo* remains within its own particular trends, a means for judicial review that follows the features of the diffuse system of judicial review.

The above implies that in the case of Mexico, the amparo is not reduced to one single guarantee (action or recourse) of the protection of constitutional rights, but is rather a varied range of judicial procedures that make it more of a constitutional right than a specific guarantee.

Finally, it must be mentioned that regarding judicial review of constitutionality of statutes, the 1994 Mexican constitutional reform, for the first time in Mexico, introduced an abstract judicial review proceeding of statutes, by attributing to the Supreme Court the power to decide with general binding effect, actions regarding the constitutionality of statutes. In this respect, Article 105,II of the Constitution assigns to the Supreme Court of the nation the power to decide judicial actions raising contradictions between a general norm (regulation) and the Constitution, for instance, a federal statute, when filed within 30 days after its publishing, by a number equivalent to the 33% of the members of the Chamber of Representatives or of the Senate; by the Attorney General of the Republic; or against electoral statutes by the national representatives of the political parties. In these cases, the Supreme Court resolution can declare the invalidity of the statute with *erga omnes* effects when approved by not less than 8 of the 11 votes[322].

B. *The right to "amparo" in Venezuela*

As Héctor Fix Zamudio himself pointed out in 1970, when Venezuela incorporated Article 49 regulating the *right to* amparo in its 1961 Constitution, "... it definitively enshrined the right to amparo as a procedural instrument to protect all the constitutionally enshrined fundamental rights of the human person," in what he de-

---

321 See Joaquín BRAGE CAMAZANO, *La jurisdicción constitucional de la libertad (Teoría general, Argentina, México, Corte Interamericana de Derechos Humanos)*, Editorial Porrúa, Instituto Mexicano de Derecho Procesal Constitucional, México, 2005, p. 153–155.

322 See Joaquín BRAGE CAMAZANO, "El control abstracto de la constitucionalidad de las leyes en México" in Eduardo FERRER MAC GREGOR (Coordinador), *Derecho Procesal Constitucional,* Editorial Podrúa, MéxicoVol I, 2003, pp. 919 ff.

scribed as "one of the most outstanding achievements of the very advanced Magna Carta of 1961"[323].

In fact, the great contribution of the Venezuelan constitutional text of 1961, a concept that is followed under Article 27 of the 1999 Constitution, in relation to fundamental rights, was the establishment of the amparo as one more fundamental right, and not just as a sole dependent guarantee of the rest of the constitutional rights[324]. Therefore, the Constitution of Venezuela not only established an "action of amparo" to protect constitutional rights, but what it provided was "a constitutional right to amparo" and the subsequent obligation of all Tribunals to provide amparo to the people of the Republic in the enjoyment of the rights and freedoms enshrined in the Constitution, or which, when not listed in the text, are inherent to the human person.

That is why Article 1 of the Organic Law of Amparo of Constitutional Rights and Guarantees states the following:

> Any individual living in the Republic or artificial person domiciled therein, may request from the competent courts the amparo provided in Article 49 of the Constitution, of the enjoyment and exercise of constitutional rights and guarantees, even of those fundamental rights of the human person that are not expressly provided in the Constitution, in order that the infringed juridical situation or the situation most resembling such situation be reestablished immediately.
>
> The guarantee of personal freedom that regulates the constitutional habeas corpus, shall be governed by this Law[325].

---

323 See Héctor FIX ZAMUDIO, "Algunos aspectos comparativos del derecho de amparo en México y Venezuela", *Libro Homenaje a la Memoria de Lorenzo Herrera Mendoza,* UCV, Caracas, 1970, Volumen II, pp. 333–390.

324 See Héctor FIX–ZAMUDIO, "La teoría de Allan R. BREWER–CARÍAS sobre el derecho de amparo latinoamericano y el juicio de amparo mexicano" in *El Derecho Público a comienzos del Siglo XXI. Libro Homenaje al profesor Allan R. Brewer–Carías*, Volumen I, Instituto de Derecho Público, Editorial Civitas, Madrid, 2003, pp. 1125 *et seq.*

325 On the action of amparo in Venezuela, in general, see: Gustavo BRICEÑO V., *Comentarios a la Ley de Amparo,* Editorial Kinesis, Caracas, 1991; José Luis CASTILLO MARCANO *et al.*, *El amparo constitucional y la tutela cautelar en la justicia administrativa,* Fundación Estudios de Derecho Administrativo (FUNEDA), Caracas, 2000; Rafael J. CHAVERO GAZDIK, *El nuevo régimen del* amparo *constitucional en Venezuela,* Editorial Sherwood, Caracas, 2001; Rafael J. CHAVERO GAZDIK, *La acción de* amparo *contra decisiones judiciales*, Fundación Estudios de Derecho Administrativo (FUNEDA)–Editorial Jurídica Venezolana, Caracas, 1997; *El amparo constitucional en Venezuela (Doctrina, Jurisprudencia, Legislación)*, Volumen I, Instituto de Estudios Jurídicos del Estado Lara, Colegio de Abogados del Estado Lara, Diario de Tribunales 1987; *El amparo constitucional en Venezuela (Doctrina, Jurisprudencia, Legislación)*, Volumen II, Instituto de Estudios Jurídicos del Estado Lara, Colegio de Abogados del Estado Lara, Diario de Tribunales 1987; Gustavo José LINARES BENZO, *El proceso de amparo en Venezuela*, Editorial Jurídica Venezolana, Caracas, 1993; Gustavo José LINARES BENZO, *El Proceso de Amparo*, Universidad Central de Venezuela, Facultad de Ciencias Jurídicas y Políticas, Caracas, 1999; Otto MARÍN GÓMEZ, *La protección procesal de las garantías constitucionales de Venezuela. Amparo y Hábeas Corpus*, Universidad Central de Venezuela, Ediciones de la Biblioteca, Colección Ciencias Jurídicas y Políticas VI, Caracas,

By regulating and establishing the *action of* amparo of all constitutional rights and freedoms, even for the protection of personal freedom and safety (Article 38), the Organic Law of the Amparo of Constitutional Rights and Guarantees, in force since January 22, 1988[326], expressly recognized that the exercise of the right of amparo is not exhausted nor it is exclusively incurred by such procedural means, but that it can *also* be exercised through other actions or recourses established in the legal order.

This was definitively resolved by the Supreme Court decision of July 7, 1971 (Caso: *Tarjetas Banvenez*)[327] referred to by the same Supreme Court in decision dated June 1oth 1992, in which the Court stated:

> "The Amparo Law set forth two adjective mechanisms: the (autonomous) action for amparo and the jointly filing of such action with other actions or recourses, which differs in their nature and legal consequences. Regarding the latter, that is to say, the filing of such action of amparo jointly with other actions or recourses, the Amparo Law distinguishes tree mechanism: a) the action of amparo filed jointly with the popular action of unconstitutionality against statutes and State acts of the same rank and value (Article 3); b) The action of amparo filed jointly with the judicial review of administrative act recourse or against omissive conducts of Public Administration (article 5); and c) the amparo action filed jointly with ordinary judicial actions (article 6,5).

The Court has also sustained that the action for amparo in neither of these cases is an autonomous action of amparo, but a subordinate one, accessory to the action or recourse to which it has been joined, subject to its final decision. Being joined actions, the case must be heard by the competent court regarding the principal action"[328].

This decision, definitively clarified that the intention of the Amparo Law was to distinguish between the autonomous action for amparo and the amparo claim filed jointly with other existing actions, in which cases, the amparo is a claim dependant on the principal action, having the amparo decision a preliminary protective nature[329]

1983; Nicolás VEGAS ROLANDO, *El amparo constitucional y jurisprudencias*, Ediciones Librerías Destino, Caracas, 1991; Francisco José Utrera and Luis A. ORTIZ ÁLVAREZ, *El amparo constitucional contra sentencias,* Editorial Torino, Caracas, 1997; Hildegard RONDÓN DE SANSÓ, *Amparo Constitucional*, Caracas, 1988; Hildegard RONDÓN DE SANSÓ, *La acción de amparo contra los poderes públicos*, Editorial Arte, Caracas, 1994.

326 See *Gaceta Oficial* N° 33.891 of January 22, 1988. See Allan R. BREWER–CARÍAS and Carlos M. AYALA CORAO, *Ley Orgánica de Amparo sobre Derechos y Garantías Constitucionales,* Caracas, 1988. See also Allan R. BREWER–CARÍAS, *El derecho y la acción de amparo,* Tomo V, *Instituciones Políticas y Constitucionales*, Editorial Jurídica Venezolana, Caracas, 1998, pp. 163 *et seq.*

327 See the text in *Revista de Derecho Público,* N° 47, EJV, Caracas, 1991, pp. 169–174.

328 See in *Revista de Derecho Público,* N° 50, Editorial Jurídica Venezolana, Caracas, 1992, pp. 183–184.

329 See regarding the inadmisibility of the action, decision of First Court on Judicial Review of Administrative Action (CPCA: Corte Primera de lo Contenciosao Administrativo), Decem-

According to these provisions, Article 3 of the Amparo law provided the possibility for the claim of amparo to be filed jointly with the popular action of unconstitutionality of statutes, which is exercised before the Constitutional Chamber of the Supreme Tribunal of Justice. In these cases, when the popular action is founded on the violation of a constitutional right or guarantee, due to the nullity that such claim implies, the Organic Law authorizes the Supreme Tribunal to *suspend the effects of the disputed statute* in respect of the specific case, while the nullity popular action is decided.

On the other hand, Article 5 of the Amparo law expressly establishes that the claim of amparo against administrative acts and against Public Administration omissions may also be brought jointly with judicial review of administrative actions recourses. In such cases, when the cause of such recourse is the violation of a constitutional right by the challenged administrative act, the requirement of previously exhausting administrative procedures and the lapse for expiry that are common in judicial review of administrative actions recourses have been eliminated; and the courts are allowed to adopt immediate procedures for the abbreviation of lapses, as well as the power to suspend of the effects of the challenged act while the nullity judicial action is decided (Articles 5, and 6,5).

Finally, Article 6, Number 6, when establishing the causes of inadmissibility of the action of amparo, implicitly recognizes that the claim of amparo may also be brought jointly with other "ordinary judicial procedures" or "pre–existing judicial means," wherein the "violation or threat of violation of a constitutional right or guarantee may be alleged.". For instance, it can be filed jointly with the recourse of cassation, when the claim against the challenged judicial decision consists in its alleged violation of a constitutional right or guarantee. In such cases, the Cassation Chambers of the Supreme Tribunal shall follow the procedure and lapses established in the Organic Law of Amparo (Article 6,5), and the recourse will anyway have the effect of suspending the challenged decision.

In all these cases of amparo claims filed jointly with other judicial means, the Supreme Court of Justice has clearly set forth the proceeding rules, as follows:

> The amparo claims filed jointly with another action or recourse have all the inherent adjective character of the actions' joint proceedings, that is: it must be decided by only one court (the one competent regarding the principal action), and both claims (amparo and nullity or other) must be heard in only one proceeding that has two stages: the preliminary one regarding the amparo, and the contradictory one that necessarily include in its final decision, the preliminary one which ends in such time, as well as the decision on the requested nullity. In other words, if because the above analyzed characteristics the amparo order is reduced only and exclusively to the preliminary suspension of a challenged act, the decision which resolves the nullity requested leaves without effects the preventive preliminary measure, whether the challenged act is declared null or not.[330].

---

ber 14, 1992, en FUNEDA, *15 años de Jurisprudencia, Corte Primera de lo Contencioso–Administrativo 1977–1992. Amparo Constitucional,* Caracas, 1994, p. 121.

330 *Idem.* p. 171.

Of course, the action for amparo can also by brought before the first instance courts in an autonomous way, not being in such cases attached or dependent to any other proceeding. As the former Supreme Court of Justice pointed out in the already mentioned decision of July 10th, 1991 that undoubtedly:

> This action that is filed autonomously because of its re–establishing nature and its capability, sufficient and adequate nature to obtain the requested amparo mandamus, is a sufficient judicial mean in itself in order to return the things to the situation they had when the right was harmed and to make definitively disappear the offender act or fact, without the need to file any other judicial proceedings.
>
> That is why this Court has reiteratively sustained that in such cases, the plaintiff must invoke and demonstrate that it is a matter of flagrant, vulgar, direct and immediate constitutional harm, which must not be understood as saying that the constitutional rights and guaranties must not be regulated by statutes, but only that in order to decide, the courts must not base its ruling only on the violation of such statutes. On the contrary, it will not be a constitutional action for amparo but rather another type of recourse, for instance, the judicial review action against administrative acts, whose annulatory effects does not correspond with the restitutory effects of the amparo; and if such substitution be allowed, the amparo would arrive to substitute not only those actions but all the other procedural means set forth in the legal order, losing its extraordinary character[331].

Even regarding administrative acts, Article 5 of the Organic Amparo law states that:

> The action for amparo proceeds against any administrative act, material actions, factual actions (vía de hecho), abstentions or omissions that violate or threaten to violate constitutional rights and guarantees, provided that no other brief, summary and efficient mean exist according to the constitutional protection.

And of course, a judicial mean of that sort is precisely to joint the amparo claim to the judicial review action to challenge the administrative act, provided that a competent court of the judicial review of administrative actions jurisdiction exists in the place where the administrative acts has been issued.

From all that has been mentioned above, it may be said that the Venezuelan right to amparo as a constitutional protection set forth in Article 27 of the 1999 Constitution, has certain peculiarities that distinguish it from the majority of similar institutions of protection of the constitutional rights and guarantees established nowadays, both in Europe and in Latin America[332].

Therefore, pursuant to this constitutional norm and the Organic Amparo Law regulations, it may be stated that in Venezuela, the amparo is enshrined as *a right* of the inhabitants of the country to seek from courts that they protect and guarantee the enjoyment and exercise of all the rights and guarantees established by the Constitution or that are inherent to the human person, against any disruption, whether by public or private entities, by means of a procedure that shall be brief and summary, and that allows the judge to immediately reinstate the impaired juridical situation.

---

331 *Idem.* pp. 169–170. 95

332 See, in general, H. FIX ZAMUDIO, *La protección procesal de los derechos humanos ante las jurisdicciones nacionales,* Madrid, 1982, pp. 366.

Therefore, the Constitution does not establish 'one' action or recourse of amparo as a particular means of judicial protection, but rather a right to amparo or "right to be subject to amparo," as a fundamental right that may materialize and which in fact materializes, through an "*autonomous action of* amparo"[333] which can, in principle, be exercised before any court or tribunal, irrespective of their hierarchy (Article 7); or by means of ordinary legal actions, when by means of brief and summary proceedings, the judge is empowered to immediately re–establish infringed legal situations. In all such cases, it is not that the ordinary means substitute the constitutional right of protection (or diminish it), but that they can serve as the judicial means for protection.

Thus, the "right to amparo" can be ensured by a variety of existing legal means (actions and recourses), in which case, the "right to protection" is not identified with any specific legal action. But in the case of the "action for amparo" –which, as it has been said, is of a subordinate nature in the sense that it is admissible only when there is no other judicial means of protection or relief formally provided for in the legal system–, this subordinate "action for amparo" does appear as differentiated from other means for the legal protection of rights and guarantees, and for the defense of the Constitution itself.

Indeed, this leads us to point out the substantial difference that exists between the Venezuelan "right to protection"– and even the subsidiary "action for amparo" contemplated in the Constitution, and the Mexican "trial for *amparo*", which is really a mixture, under one name, as we have seen, of five legal actions which in the Venezuelan legal system are completely different. These actions that in Mexico are covered by the heading *juicio de amparo* are: firstly, the protection of personal liberty, which is basically the remedy of *habeas corpus*; secondly, what is known as the "*amparo* against laws", which complements the direct action for judicial review of unconstitutionality of laws; thirdly, the "*amparo* cassation", which is really the same as the recourse of cassation; fourthly, what is known as "administrative protection", which leads to judicial review of administrative actions; and fifthly, the Mexican system of protection also includes what is known as "agrarian *amparo*" for the protection of the rights of peasants.[334]

By contrast with the Mexican situation, the right to protection contemplated in the Venezuelan Constitution, as we have pointed out, firstly ensures the possibility of protection when fundamental rights are infringed by state acts by means of the action of unconstitutionality of statutes (popular action), or through the power attributed to any judge to not apply a statute when it is considered unconstitutional (diffuse system of judicial review); by means of the recourse of cassation before the Cassation Chambers of the Supreme Tribunal with respect to judicial decisions; and by means of the administrative actions that can be exercised against administrative

333 See Allan R. Brewer–Carías, "El derecho de amparo y la acción de amparo", *Revista de Derecho Público,* N° 22, Editorial Jurídica Venezolana, Caracas, 1985, pp. 51 *et seq.*

334 Héctor Fix–Zamudio, "Algunos aspectos comparativos del derecho de *amparo* en México y Venezuela", *Libro Homenaje a la Memoria de Lorenzo Herrera Mendoza,* Universidad Central de Venezuela, Caracas, 1970, Vol. II, pp. 344–356.

acts before the judicial review of administrative action Jurisdiction. Additionally, it ensures the possibility of protection of fundamental rights against infringement by other individuals through ordinary judicial means.

To ensure the effectiveness of all these ordinary judicial means to serve as means for protecting fundamental rights, the Amparo statute of 1988 has perfected them. For instance, in cases of the popular action seeking abstract judicial review of legislation, when its grounds are the infringement of a constitutional right or guarantee, an "amparo" joined petition can be filed, and due to the absolute nullity implied, seeking the Supreme Tribunal to decide the suspension of the effects of the challenged statute while the case is being decided.

In the procedure of the recourse of cassation, when the complaint against the challenged judicial decision is based on the violation of a fundamental right, the motives for the admissibility of the recourse could be widened, as well as the judicial decisions that could be impugned.

In the proceeding of judicial review of administrative action, when the grounds of the actions are the violation of fundamental rights, according to Article 5 of the Amparo Organic Statute, the expiry delay for the actions to be exercised is eliminated, due to the absolute nullity involved, and the judge is allowed to use his powers more freely to declare the emergency situation of the process, shortening delays, and to promptly suspend the effects of the challenged administrative act while the final decision of the case is produced.

However, as we have said, additional to all the ordinary means, the right to protection allows adequate protection to be achieved for constitutional rights and guarantees, by means of an "action for amparo" which has been regulated in the Amparo Organic Law, as a judicial means, completely different from the popular action for judicial review of unconstitutionality of statutes, the recourse of cassation, and from actions for judicial review of administrative actions, that can be brought before the first instance courts with jurisdiction in the site[335].

In this case, the "action for amparo" appears as a much broader action for protecting absolutely all constitutional rights and guarantees including the enjoyment and exercise of personal freedom.

Now, one of the features of this autonomous constitutional action, called the "action for amparo", is that it does not presuppose that other previous legal judicial or administrative means have to be exhausted before it can be exercised. This differentiates the institution of the "action for amparo" in Venezuela from the "recourse of *amparo* or the "constitutional complaint" developed in Europe, particularly in Germany and in Spain. In these countries, the protective remedy is really an authentic "recourse" that is brought, in principle, against judicial decisions. In Germany, for example, to bring a constitutional complaint for the protection of constitutional rights before the Federal Constitutional Tribunal, the available ordinary judicial

---

335 See: Allan R. BREWER–CARÍAS and Carlos M. AYALA CORAO, *Ley Orgánica de Amparo a los Derechos y Garantías Constitucionales,* Editorial Jurídica Venezolana, Caracas, 1988; Hildegard Rondón De Sansó, *Amparo Constitucional,* 1991.

means need to be previously exhausted, which definitively entails a recourse against a final judicial decision, even though, in exceptional cases, a direct complaint for protection may be allowed in certain specific cases and with respect to a very limited number of constitutional rights.[336] In Spain, all legal recourses need to be exhausted in order to bring a "*recurso de amparo*" of constitutional rights before the Constitutional Tribunal, and, particularly when dealing with protection against administrative activities, the ordinary means for judicial review of administrative decisions must be definitively exhausted. For this reason, the recourse for protection in Spain is eventually a means for judicial review of decisions taken by the Administrative Judicial review courts.[337]

On the contrary, the "action for amparo" in Venezuela is not conditioned to previously exhausting other legal means, and thus it does not result as recourse against judicial decisions either. It is, as it has been pointed out, a judicial action that it is only admissible when no other legal action in the legal system exists to seek the protection of fundamental rights and their immediate reestablishment by means of brief, summary proceedings.

In this sense, in order to adequately understand the character of the "action for amparo", as an autonomous action, it must be borne in mind the protective character of other judicial means, among which are the actions for judicial review of administrative acts. It is not the case that the action for amparo requires the previous exhaustion of the actions for judicial review of administrative acts, when these violate fundamental rights, but that the action for judicial review can itself be considered as a means for protection of fundamental rights, in which case a petition in this regard can be joined to it. Thus, only when no judicial means for protection exists, and in the case of administrative acts, when actions for their judicial review are not effective as a means for protection due to the particular circumstances of the case, the "action for amparo" would be admissible.

On the other hand, it should be noted that according to the Constitution, the right to protection may be exercised according to the law, before "the Courts", and thus, as it has been said, the organization of the legal and procedural system does not provide for one single judicial action to guarantee the enjoyment and exercise of constitutional rights to be brought before one single Court.

The legal system may, and indeed does, regulate systems for the protection of constitutional rights and guarantees by means of ordinary actions, through brief and summary proceedings in which the judge has power to re–establish the infringed subjective legal situations immediately, which distinguishes the system from those in Europe, particularly from the action for protection in Germany or in Spain which

---

336 K. SCHLAICH, "Procedures et techniques de protection des droits fondamentaux. Tribunal Constitutionnel Fédéral allemand", in L. Favoreu (ed.), *Cours constitutionnelles européenes et droits fondamentaux*, Paris, 1982, pp. 105–164.

337 See, J.L. GARCÍA RUÍZ, *Recurso de amparo en el derecho español*, Madrid, 1980. F. CASTEDO ÁLVAREZ, "El recurso de amparo constitucional" in Instituto de Estudios Fiscales, *El Tribunal Constitucional*, Madrid, 1981, Vol. I, pp. 179–208.

is one, single action, to be brought before one, single Court, and which serves as a mechanism for the protection of certain constitutional rights and guarantees.[338]

In Venezuela, according to Article 7 of the Organic Law on Amparo, the competent courts to decide amparo actions are the First Instance Courts with jurisdiction on matters related to the constitutional rights or guarantees violated, in the place where the facts, acts of omission have occurred. Regarding amparo of personal freedom and security the competent courts should be the Criminal First Instance courts (Article 40). Nonetheless, when the facts, acts or omissions harming or threatening to harm the constitutional right or guarantee occurs in a place where no First Instance court exists, the amparo action may be brought before and judge of the place, which must decide according to the law, and in a 24 hour delay it must send the files for consultation to the competent First Instance court (Article 9).

Only in cases in which facts, actions or omissions of the President of the Republic, his Cabinet members, the National Electoral Council, the Prosecutor General, the Attorney general and the General Comptroller of the Republic are involved, the power to decide the amparo actions correspond in only instance to the Constitutional Chamber of the Supreme Tribunal of Justice (Article 8).

Nonetheless, in all the other cases, the Constitutional Chamber of the Supreme Court has the power to review all "amparo" highest instance decisions by means of the extraordinary recourse of revision that the interested party can file before it, in which the Chamber can decide at its discretion, in a similar way as the North American writ of certiorari.

On the other hand, and independently of the autonomous action of amparo, the right to constitutional protection in Venezuela is expressed in several legal judicial means which may be brought before all the Courts, and which may serve as a protection by means of pre–existing actions and remedies, so long as provision is made for brief, summary proceedings with powers for the judge to restore the infringed subjective legal situations. For this reason, and given this all–inclusive characteristic, the "action for amparo" is not the only action or recourse admissible for protection but that, rather, it may also be obtained by other legal means regulated by the legal system.

However, whether by use of pre–established judicial means or through the autonomous action, the right to protection as expressed in the Venezuelan Constitution is to protect all the rights and guarantees that the Constitution establishes. This protection constitutes a fundamental guarantee of human rights, which in turn entails certain implications. Above all, the objective of the right to protection, according to the Constitution, is to protect the enjoyment and exercise of constitutional rights and guarantees, and thus, it applies not only to individuals as holders of such rights, but also to cases in which these rights are exercised by companies or corporations. There can be no doubt that, given the scope with which the Constitution declares the "right to amparo", the expression "all the inhabitants" cannot be understood to refer

---

338 *Cf.* H. FIX–ZAMUDIO, "El derecho de amparo en México y en España. Su influencia recíproca", *Revista de estudios políticos*, Nº 7, Madrid, 1979, pp. 254–255.

solely to human beings, rather, it also refers to all entities or organizations, since the rights established in the Constitution are moreover not only rights of individuals, but many of them are also rights of collective entities or artificial persons.

At the same time, however, the protection of the enjoyment and exercise of constitutional rights and guaranties is embodied in the Constitution not only regarding public actions, which may disrupt the enjoyment and exercise of such rights, but also regarding disruptions, which may originate from other private individuals. The Constitution makes no distinction in this respect, and thus the action for amparo is perfectly admissible against actions by individuals, the action for amparo has doubtlessly been conceived as a traditional means of protection against actions by the state and its authorities. However, despite this tradition of conceiving the action for protection as a means of protecting rights and guarantees against public actions, in Venezuela, the scope with which this is regulated by Article 27 of the Constitution allows the action for amparo to be brought against individual actions, that is to say, when the disruption of the enjoyment and exercise of rights originates from private individuals or organizations.

This also differentiates the Venezuelan system from that which exists in other systems such as Mexico or Spain, in which the "action for amparo" is solely conceived against public actions.[339] For this reason, as we have said, in Spain the recourse of amparo is expressed as a review of decisions by the administrative judicial court when reviewing administrative acts.[340]

On the other hand, in the case of protection from disruption originating from public authorities, it should be affirmed, without doubt, that as regulated by Article 27 of the Constitution, this protection is admissible against all public actions, that is to say, against all state acts as well as against any other action by public officials. The right to protection has, of course, been regulated, in many cases in this field, by judicial means already established in the legal system. For example, as far as unconstitutional statutes, which affect constitutional rights and guarantees, are concerned, it is admissible to bring a popular action before the Supreme Tribunal of Justice, which can be considered a means for protection. Also, when a judge decides not to apply a law, under Article 334 of the Constitution or Article 20 of the Civil Procedural Code, because he decides that it infringes a constitutional right, he also ensures protection of that right.[341] The same occurs with actions brought before the administrative judicial Tribunals against administrative acts, which constitute a means for the protection of constitutional rights and guarantees when the basis for impugning the administrative act is the violation of the enjoyment and exercise of such rights and guarantees, and the judicial suspension of the effects of the challenged act may

---

339 *Idem*, pp. 254–255. On the contrary in Argentina is accepted the recourse of "*amparo*" against individual actions. Kot case: *of 5.9.1958*. See G.R. CARRIO, *Algunos aspectos del recurso de amparo*, Buenos Aires, 1959, p. 13.

340 *Cf.* J. González PÉREZ, *Derecho procesal constitucional*, Madrid, 1980, p. 278.

341 See Allan R. BREWER–CARÍAS, *El control de la constitucionalidad de los actos estatales*, Caracas, 1978.

be obtained immediately, and is admissible against any type of administrative act, both express and implied.[342]

Additionally, it must be said that the subordinate action for amparo is admissible against any activity by the Public Administration, even when this does not constitute a formal administrative act and is thus not open to actions before the administrative jurisdiction. That is to say, it would be admissible, for example, against material acts by the administration; its *de facto proceedings*; its failure to act or to fulfill an obligation; in short, against any action or omission by the Administration, and even, of course, against specific acts which may not be contested before the administrative judicial courts.

Indeed, the subordinate action for amparo may also be admissible against actions by the legislative body against which there are no legal means for objection, and may even be brought against judicial decisions against which no legal means of appeal exist or have been contemplated, or the recourse of cassation could not be exercised.

We have said, however, that the action for amparo also constitutes a means for the protection of the enjoyment and exercise of *all* rights and guarantees established in the Constitution: individual, social, cultural, economic, environmental and political rights.

By virtue of the Constitutional provision, there is nothing to suggest that the right to protection in Venezuela constitutes a means for the protection of only certain rights, but that rather, it relates, on the contrary, to all rights and guarantees established in the Constitution. This, of course, leads to the assertion that the right to protection and the subordinate "action for amparo" are means for protecting, not only those rights and guarantees listed in the Constitution, but also all the rights inherent to the human person, even when not specified in the Constitution. As abovementioned, this give substantial importance to the series of human rights listed in the Universal Declaration of the Rights of Man, and in the International Conventions that regulate human rights, such as those of the American Human Rights Convention, or the International Covenants on Civil and Political, and Economic and Social Rights, which are, moreover, laws of the Republic, because they have been approved in Congress by special laws.[343] But, though limiting our comments to the rights described in the Constitution, however, we must stress the fact that what is termed *amparo* is the right to a judicial means for protecting the enjoyment and exercise of absolutely all those constitutional rights, which means that a difference is established with respect to other *amparo* institutions particular to Latin America.

In fact, if the situation in Latin America is analyzed comparatively, the following criteria can, in general, be identified. In the first place, the system that identifies *amparo* with judicial protection from arbitrary detention (*habeas corpus*) always

342 Allan R. BREWER–CARÍAS, "Tipos de acciones y recursos contencioso–administrativos y el tema de la legitimación", in *Conferencia sobre la reforma de la justicia administrativa en Costa Rica*, Corte Suprema de Justicia, Marzo, 1986.

343 See *Gaceta Oficial* Nº 31.256 de 14–6–77 and Nº 2.146 Extra. de 28–1–78.

entails a writ requiring that the person detained be shown. This was the legal tradition, for example, in Chile. Secondly, there is the system that identifies *amparo* as a means for the protection of all rights, except that of personal liberty, which is granted a special means of protection, such as the remedy of *habeas corpus*. This system, in fact, distinguishes between the two types of actions, the action for protection and the writ of *habeas corpus*, and is for example, the tradition in the Argentinean, and Brazilian systems.

Thirdly, *amparo* is also seen as a means for the protection of all rights and guarantees enshrined in the Constitution, and it has been the tradition in Central America, particularly in Guatemala, Honduras and Nicaragua, in contrast to the situation in Europe, for example, in which the remedy is established for the protection of certain rights only.[344] This happens, for example, in Spain, where the recourse of protection is reserved for the protection of a limited group of constitutional rights only, equivalent to what the Venezuelan Constitution has characterized as "individual rights."[345]

We have pointed out that *amparo* is conceived in Venezuela as the right to a legal means (action or remedy) for the protection of absolutely all constitutional rights and guarantees, not only, of course, of individual rights, but also of the social, cultural, environmental, political and economic rights declared in the Constitution. Also, as *amparo* is intended for the protection of all the rights and guarantees enshrined in the Constitution, this implies that what is known as the right of *habeas corpus* is really a part of the right to protection, or if preferred, one manifestation of the *amparo*.

That is why the right to seek protection against any deprivation or restriction to personal freedom is regulated in the Organic Amparo Law, setting forth that the action must bring before the First Instance Criminal court with jurisdiction in the place where the aggrieving act is enforced or where the aggrieved person is, court that must issue an habeas corpus mandamus (Article 39).

From the terms of Article 27 of the Constitution, it can be said that the objective protected by the right to amparo is the enjoyment and exercise of constitutional rights and guarantees, and of course, protection for the enjoyment and exercise of such rights and guarantees is admissible, not only when some *direct* violation of a constitutional rule occurs, but also of course, when there is a violation of the legal rules that regulate the enjoyment and exercise of such rights. We consider that there is no foundation whatsoever in Venezuela for wishing to restrict the exercise of the subordinate action for protection only to cases in which a "direct violation" of the Constitution occurs[346].

---

344 Allan R. BREWER–CARÍAS, *Garantías constitucionales de los derechos del hombre*, Caracas, 1976, p. 69.

345 Art. 53, ord. 2. Spanish Constitution 1978.

346 See the decision of the Supreme Court in Politico–Administrative Chamber of October 28, 1983, in *Revista de Derecho Público*, Nº 16, Editorial Jurídica Venezolana, Caracas, 1983, p. 169. See the comments of René DE SOLA, "Vida y vicisitudes del recurso de amparo en Venezuela", *Revista del Instituto Venezolano de Derecho Social*, 47, Caracas, 1985, p. 58, (also published in *Revista SIC*; 472, Caracas, 1985, 74.

In effect, we must bear in mind that the regulation of constitutional rights and guarantees in Venezuela is not uniform, and that the manner in which they are embodied in the Constitution gives rise to differing effects of such rights and guarantees.[347] In fact, we may identify, in the first place, the "absolute rights", among which are the right to life, the right not to be held incommunicado, not to be subjected to torture or other procedures that cause moral or physical suffering, which is the same thing as the right to personal integrity, and the right not to be condemned to prison for life, or to punishments that are defamatory or that restrict personal freedom for more than 30 years. These rights are expressed in the Constitution in such a way that it can be said that they are rights that can neither be limited nor regulated even by the legislator, and that are, moreover, the rights which may not be restricted by executive decision based on the powers attributed to the President of the Republic in cases of emergency or disturbances that may disrupt the peace of the Republic, or in serious circumstances which affect its economic or social life. With the exception of these absolute rights, all other rights and guarantees, by contrast, are liable to limitation or regulation by the Legislator, and may be subject to measures for their restriction or suspension (art. 241 Constitution).

A second type of constitutional rights comprises those whose exercise may be restricted by the President of the Republic, even though, in principle, the legislator may not limit them. This stems from the manner in which the Constitution expresses the rights, for example, to protection of honor, reputation and privacy; the right not to take an oath or to make self–incriminating statements; not to remain imprisoned once officially released from jail; not to be punished twice for the same crime; the right to equality and freedom from discrimination; the right to religious freedom and to freedom of thought; the right to petition and to receive timely response; the right to be judged by one's ordinary judges; the right to defense; the right of association; the right to health protection; the rights to education and to work; and the right to vote.

A third category of rights, stemming from the Constitution, is that composed of those rights which may be limited by the legislator, although in a restricted way. This category contains, for instance, the prisoner's right, before being sentenced, to be heard "as indicated by the law"; the right to inviolability of the home, except in cases of search "according to the law and the decision of the courts"; the right to inviolability of correspondence, except in cases of inspection or fiscal supervision of accounting documents "according to the law"; the right to take public office, with the only restrictions being conditions of aptitude "required by law."

The fourth category comprises a series of constitutional rights that can be regulated and limited by the legislator in a wider form. Among such rights would be the right not to be detained unless caught *in fraganti*; "in the cases and with the formalities established in the law"; the freedom of movement "with the condition established by law"; the right to exercise a cult under the "supreme inspection of the State

---

347 Allan R. BREWER–CARÍAS, *Instituciones políticas y Constitucionales*, Vol IV, *Derechos y garantías Constitucionales*, Universidad Católica del Táchira, Editorial Jurídica venezolana, Caracas–San Cristóbal, 1996.

according to the law"; the right to carry on economic activities with no other limitations than those established by statute by reasons of security, health or other social interests; the right to property, submitted to the "contributions, restrictions and obligations established by law based on public or social interests"; the right to political association and to public demonstration "according to the formalities established by law." In all such cases, the exercise of rights is definitively subject to what the legislator stipulates, and within quite considerable margins.

The fifth and final category of constitutional rights and guarantees is formed by those established in such a manner that their exercise is definitively subject to legal regulation. Among such rights would be, for example, that of using the organs for the administration of justice "under the terms and conditions established by the law"; that of joining associations "according to the law"; and the right to strike "under the conditions set by the law". In all such cases, the manner in which the Constitution expresses the rights and guarantees requires that they be regulated by the Law so as to be exercised at all. From this classification of rights and guarantees into five groups, according to the Constitution, it is evident that there is no sense in holding that the right to protection, and in particular, the subsidiary "action for amparo", can only be admissible when the Constitution is "directly violated", since many rights are not only embodied in the Constitution, but rather, by virtue of the Constitution itself, their exercise is subject to provisions and regulations established by the Legislator. The right to protection is thus also admissible against violations of laws, which regulate the enjoyment, and exercise of rights.

We have pointed out that the right to protection, as regulated by the Constitution, has the definitive aim of ensuring the *enjoyment and exercise* of constitutional rights and guarantees. Precisely for this reason, the Constitution grants the competent judge the power to immediately "re–establish the infringed juridical situation", and precisely for this reason, also provides that "the procedure should be brief and summary."

This aim of the remedy of ensuring the enjoyment and exercise of constitutional rights and guarantees entails that the judge, of course, has power to adopt preventive and cautionary measures, but bearing in mind that the legal means of protection and even the subordinate action for amparo, are not necessarily exhausted thereby.

In other words, the protection for the enjoyment and exercise of constitutional rights and guarantees does not only entail, nor is it exhausted by the adoption of some immediate measure, by means of a brief and summary proceeding which re–establishes the infringed legal situation, but rather that the action or remedy for amparo by means of legal proceedings needs the judge in the case of *amparo* to decide on the substantive issue and give a verdict as to the legality and legitimacy of the "violation" of the right in question, without prejudice to the fact that, by means of brief and summary mechanisms, decisions may be adopted during the proceedings to immediately re–establish the infringed legal situation.

In our opinion and after analyzing the Venezuelan right for amparo, the following conclusions can be formed:

First, the Constitution consecrates a *right to amparo*, and not any particular "action" or "remedy" before a particular Court. This right is established as a fundamental right of individuals and collective persons.

Second, the right to protection implies an *obligation* of all Courts to protect according to the law, against disturbances of the enjoyment and exercise of rights and guarantees. Thus, the development the legislator has made regarding this right to amparo may take the form, as has happened, of pre–existing actions or remedies, or may consist of a subordinate action for protection, which is admissible when pre–existing actions and remedies cannot be effective by means of a brief and summary procedure with powers for the judge to protect fundamental rights and immediately re–establish the infringed legal situation.

Third, the right to protection may thus be guaranteed by means of *actions and recourse* contemplated in the legal order (the popular action of unconstitutionality; the power of all judges to decide not to apply a law considered unconstitutional; actions for judicial review of administrative actions; the provisional system of *habeas corpus*), or by means of the subordinate and autonomous action for protection[348] and that can be brought before any court according to its subject of attributions.

Fourth, the right of amparo is admissible to guarantee the enjoyment and exercise of *all* constitutional rights and guarantees. It may be put into effect with respect to disturbances of individual rights, as well as those of social, economic, cultural environmental and political rights.

Fifth, the right to amparo seeks to assure protection of constitutional rights and guarantees against *any disturbance* in their enjoyment and exercise, whether this is originated by *private* individuals or by *public* authorities. In the case of disturbance by public authorities, the right of protection is admissible against legislative, administrative and judicial acts, by means of the actions and recourses contemplated in the legal order (the action of unconstitutionality, the recourse of cassation, or actions for judicial review of administrative actions) when they allow a legal situation which has been infringed, to be re–established by means of a brief and summary procedure, or by means of the subsidiary autonomous action for protection. Moreover, this action for protection is admissible against material acts or courses of action of the administration, thus it is not then admissible only against administrative acts.

Sixth, by virtue of the different ways in the Constitution for regulating fundamental rights, the right to amparo can be exercised to protect the enjoyment and exercise of constitutional rights and guarantees, *not only when there has been some direct violation of the Constitution*, but also when what has been violated are the legal developments which, by virtue of the Constitution, regulate, limit and even allow the exercise of such rights. Of course, protection must be exercised against an activity that directly violates a fundamental right established in the Constitution, whether it be regulated by statute or not, and whether or not the violation is contrary to what the law developing the right establishes.

---

348 Allan R. BREWER–CARÍAS, "La reciente evolución jurisprudencial en relación a la admisibilidad del recurso de amparo", *Revista de derecho público,* N° 19, Caracas, 1984, pp. 207–218.

Seventh, the decision of the judge as a consequence of the exercise of this right to amparo, whether this be pre–existing actions or recourses or by means of the subordinate and autonomous "action for protection", should not limit himself to precautionary or preventive measures, but should re–establish the infringed legal situation. To this end he should make a pronouncement on the substantive issue brought before him, namely the legality and legitimacy or otherwise the disturbance of the constitutional right or guarantee that has been reported as infringed.

Eighth, the Venezuelan system of judicial review, being a mixed one (can be exercised by all courts in whatever kind of judicial proceeding), where the diffuse system of judicial review has been fully developed, it is obvious that judicial review of legislation is a power that can be exercised by the courts when deciding action for amparo" of fundamental rights, when for instance, their violation is infringed by a public authority act based on a statute deemed unconstitutional. In such cases, if the judge gives the protection requested through an order similar to the writs of mandamus or to the injunctions, he must previously declare the statute based on which the challenged action was taken, inapplicable on the grounds of it being unconstitutional. Therefore, in such cases, judicial review of the constitutionality of legislation is also exercised when an action for amparo of fundamental rights is filed.

In this respect, some precisions must be made regarding the Venezuelan system of judicial review. Article 336 of the Constitution of 1999, following a constitutional tradition that can be traced back to the 1858 Constitution[349], sets forth the power of the Constitutional Chamber of the Supreme Tribunal, as Constitutional Jurisdiction, to review the constitutionality of statutes and other national, state or municipal normative acts and acts of government adopted by the President of the Republic, when requested by means of a popular action. That is to say, it provides for judicial review of the constitutionality of all state acts issued in direct application of the Constitution, and particularly of statutes.

This judicial review power of the constitutionality of state acts allows the Supreme Tribunal of Justice to declare them null and void with *erga omnes* effects when they violate the Constitution. It thus constitutes a concentrated system of judicial review of the constitutionality of statutes and other state acts with similar rank or value.

Moreover, Article 334 of the same Constitution, also following a legal tradition that can be traced back to the 1897 Civil Procedure Code, sets forth the power of all courts to declare statutes or other normative state acts inapplicable in a given case, when they consider them unconstitutional and, hence, sets preference to constitutional rules, providing a diffuse system of judicial review.

Therefore, as also happens in the Portuguese system and in many Latin American countries, the Venezuelan system of judicial review of the constitutionality of

349 See J. G. ANDUEZA, *La jurisdicción constitucional en el derecho venezolano*, Universidad Central de Venezuela, Caracas, 1955 p. 46.

statutes and other state acts, mixes the diffuse system of judicial review of the constitutionality of statutes with the concentrated systems.[350]

With respect to this mixed character of the Venezuelan system, the former Supreme Court has analyzed the scope of judicial review of the constitutionality of statutes, and has correctly pointed out that this is the responsibility:

> [N]ot only of the Supreme Tribunal of the Republic, but also of all the judges, whatever their rank and standing may be. It is sufficient that an official is part of the Judiciary for him to be a custodian of the Constitution and, consequently, to apply it's ruling preferentially over those of ordinary statutes. Nonetheless, the application of Constitution by the judges, only has effects in the concrete case at issue and, for that very reason, only affects the interested parties to the conflict. In contrast, when constitutional illegitimacy in a law is declared by the Supreme [Tribunal] when exercising its sovereign function, as the interpreter of the Constitution, and in response to the pertinent [popular] action, the effects of the decision extend *erga omnes* and have the force of law. In the first case, the review is incidental and special, and in the second, principal and general. When this happens –that is to say when the recourse is autonomous– the control is either formal or material, depending on whether the nullity has to do with an irregularity relating to the process of drafting the statute, or whether –despite the legislation having been correct from the formalist point of view– the intrinsic content of the statute suffers from substantial defects.[351]

Consequently, the Venezuelan system of judicial review is a mixed one, in which the diffuse system functions in parallel with the concentrated system of judicial review assigned to the Constitutional Chamber of the Supreme Tribunal of Justice.

As previously stated, Article 334 of the Constitution following what was set forth in Article 20 of the Civil Procedure Code since 1897, states:

> **Art. 334.** [...] In case of incompatibility between this Constitution and a statute or other norm, the constitutional provisions will be apply, being the courts in any case, even ex officio, the ones to decide therein[352]

According to this norm, the diffuse system of judicial review allows any judge, from the lowest judicial rank to the Supreme Tribunal of Justice, to decide not to

---

350 See in general, Allan R. BREWER–CARÍAS, *El control de la constitucionalidad de los actos estatales*, Caracas, 1977; and also "Algunas consideraciones sobre el control jurisdiccional de la constitucionalidad de los actos estatales en el derecho venezolano", *Revista de Administración Pública*, 76, Madrid, 1975, pp. 419–446.

351 See decisión of Federal Court (which in 1961 was substituted by the Supreme Court of Justice), June 19, 1953 *Gaceta Forense*, 1, 1953, pp. 77–78.

352 Article 334: En caso de incompatibilidad entre esta Constitución y una ley u otra norma jurídica, se aplicarán las disposiciones constitucionales, correspondiendo a los tribunales en cualquier causa, aún de oficio, decidir lo conducente". The text of article 20 of the Civil Procedure Code says: "Cuando la ley vigente, cuya aplicación se pida, colidiere con alguna disposición constitucional, los jueces aplicarán ésta con preferencia." The text was originally adopted in the 1897 Code (Art. 10), followed by the 1904 Code (Art. 10) and the 1916 Code (Art. 7). In the 1985 Code the only change introduced in relation to the previous text, is the word "judges" which substituted the word "Tribunals". See the text of the 1897, 1904 and 1916 Codes in *Leyes y Decretos Reglamentarios de los Estados Unidos de Venezuela*, Caracas, 1943, Vol. V.

apply a statute in a concrete case that conflicts with any provision of the Constitution when the application of that statute is demanded by a party to litigation. This is, no doubt, the basic consequence of the principle of the supremacy of the Constitution, as considered since the beginning of the last century by all the commentators of the Civil Procedure Code.

According to this power attributed to all judges, the diffuse system of judicial review in Venezuela can be characterized by the following trends:

Firstly, as we have stated, the power attributed to all judges to control the constitutionality of legislation is the natural consequence of the principle of the supremacy of the Constitution. The judges are bound by the Constitution and have the duty to apply it; therefore, if a law is unconstitutional, they cannot apply it and must give preference to the Constitution, because an unconstitutional law can have no value.

It must be said that this was the basic principle established ever since the beginning of Venezuelan constitutionalism, in the 1811 Constitution where it has been considered that an implicit diffuse judicial review system was adopted.[353]

In effect, Article 227 of the 1811 Constitution set forth:

> The present Constitution, the statutes to be adopted in its execution and the Treaties to be subscribed under the authority of the Union Government will be the supreme law of the state in the whole Confederation, and the authorities and inhabitants of the provinces are bound to religiously obey and observe them without excuse or pretext; but the statutes enacted against the text of the Constitution will have no value unless they fulfill all the required conditions for a just and legitimate revision and sanction.[354]

According to this norm, in the same sense as the North American model, unconstitutional laws were considered null and void, as they could have no effect whatsoever.

The guarantee of the Constitution in that case was the nullity of the unconstitutional act, and not its annulability. Thus the judges were not bound to apply unconstitutional laws and acts; on the contrary, as established in the 1830 Constitution, all public officials had the duty not to "obey or execute orders evidently contrary to the Constitution or the laws."[355]

Now concerning fundamental rights and freedoms, ever since the 1893 Constitution the *nullity* of the statutes which violated or harmed them, as their basic guarantee has been expressly established.[356] That is why the 1999 Constitution expressly set forth that:

---

353 H. J. LA ROCHE, *El control jurisdiccional de la constitucionalidad en Venezuela y Estados Unidos*, Maracaibo, 1971, p. 24; T. "El recurso de inconstitucionalidad en la Constitución venezolana de 1811", in *El pensamiento constitucional de Latinoamérica 1810–1830*, Congreso de Academias e Institutos Históricos, Actas y Ponencias, Caracas, 1962, Vol. 3, p. 208.

354 See in Allan R. BREWER–CARÍAS, *Las Constituciones de Venezuela*, Instituto de Estudios de Administración Local, Centro de Estudios Constitucionales, Madrid, 1985, p. 203.

355 Art. 186. See in Allan R. BREWER–CARÍAS, *Las Constituciones ..., cit.*, p. 353.

356 Art. 17. See in Allan R. BREWER–CARÍAS, *Las Constituciones..., cit.*, p. 531.

> **Art. 25**: Every act of the Public Power which violates or impairs the rights guaranteed by this Constitution is void, and the public officials and employees who order or execute it shall be held criminally, civilly or administratively liable, as the case may be, and orders of superiors manifestly contrary to the Constitution and the laws may not serve as an excuse.

Consequently, it can be said that since the 1811 Constitution, the diffuse system of judicial review of legislation, based on the principle of the supremacy of the Constitution and the nullity and infectivity of unconstitutional acts, has existed in Venezuela following the implicit North American constitutional trends, particularly until 1897, when it was expressly established as a power of all judges in the Civil Procedure Code.

It must be mentioned also that in the 1901 Constitution, following the approval of the 1897 Civil Procedure Code, the power of all judges to control the constitutionality of statutes was ratified. In that Constitution, competence to declare which disposition would prevail in a concrete case, when a lower judge *motu proprio* or at party instance, would have referred a constitutional question to the Supreme Court, was attributed to the Supreme Court. Nevertheless, it was expressly established that this referral did not have suspenssive effects on the procedure, and that the lower judge was empowered to decide the constitutional question if through the opportunity of adopting his own decision, the Supreme Court opinion was not received by the lower court.[357]

Anyway, historically and in the present constitutional system, Venezuela has always had, following the American model, a diffuse system of judicial review according to which all courts have the power to examine the constitutionality of statutes and not to apply them when considering them unconstitutional, giving preference to the Constitution. Of course, the expression "statute" (*ley*) used in the Constitution and in the Civil Procedure Code has always been interpreted in an extensive way, comprising not only formal statutes approved by Congress, but also all normative state acts, including executive regulations.

Following the general trends of all diffuse systems of judicial review, the Venezuelan system also has an incidental character, that is to say, the judge can only review the constitutionality of a statute and decide not to apply it, when deciding a concrete case brought before him by a party, in which the constitutional question is not, of course, the principal issue submitted for his decision, but only an incidental question regarding the law which the judge must apply for the resolution of the case as required by a party.

Therefore, the power of courts to control the constitutionality of legislation can only be exercised within a concrete adversary litigation (case and controversy), regarding the statute the application of which is demanded by a party, and when the constitutional issue is relevant to the case and necessary to be resolved in their decision. But in the Venezuelan system, the constitutional issue itself can be raised *ex officio* by the judge when deciding the concrete case so it is not necessarily required,

357 Art. 106, 8 in Allan R. BREWER–CARÍAS, *Las Constituciones ..., cit.*, pp. 579–580. See the comments regarding this norm in R. FEO, *Estudios sobre el Código de procedimiento civil venezolano*, Caracas 1904, Vol. I, pp. 32–33

as happens in the North American system, to be alleged by a party. Therefore, the Venezuelan diffuse system of judicial review although incidental, is not a control that is exclusively exercised through an "exception of unconstitutionality"[358] risen by a party. On the contrary, it can be exercised by the judge, *motu proprio* as stated since the 1901 Constitution (art. 106,8).

On the other hand, the nullity of unconstitutional laws, particularly those that violate fundamental rights; being the guarantee of the Constitution, the decision of the courts in the diffuse system of constitutional control has declarative effects. That is to say, the judge when deciding not to apply a statute in a concrete case declares it unconstitutional and, therefore, considers it unconstitutional ever since its enactment (*ab initio*), thus as never having been valid and as always having been null and void. Consequently, the decision of the court in the concrete case evidently has *ex–tunc* and *pro pretaerito* or retroactive effects, preventing the unconstitutional and inapplicable statute from having any effect in the case. Thus, the judge's decision is not a declaration "of nullity" of the statute he considered unconstitutional, but rather a declaration that the statute "is unconstitutional." In declaring the statute inapplicable to the concrete case, the court considers that the statute could never have produced effects in the particular case; as it has never existed. In other words, when the court declares that the statute is inapplicable to a particular case which was supposed to have been governed, in the past, by a statute whose applicability is demanded by one of the parties to the case, the judge is "ignoring" the –in his opinion– unconstitutional law, and thus considering it never having had effects on the particular case brought before him.

Of course, these declarative and *ex–tunc* effects of the decision, only refer to the concrete parties, in the concrete process in which the decision is adopted.

Thus, the decision only has *in casu et inter partes* effects,[359] as a consequence of the incidental character (*incidenter tantum*) control. Therefore, if a statute has been considered unconstitutional in a concrete judicial case decision, and the judge decided not to apply it to the case but gave preference to the Constitution, this does not mean that the law has been invalidated and is not enforceable and applicable elsewhere. According to the Civil Procedure Code, judges have no competence to make declarations of the nullity of the unconstitutional law, or to annul it, because these attributions are exclusively assigned in the Constitution to the Constitutional Chamber of the Supreme Tribunal. Thus, in the diffuse system of review, the decision in which the judge decides not to apply a statute in the concrete case only means that concerning that particular process and parties, the law must be considered unconstitutional, null and void, but with no effects regarding other cases, other judges or other individuals.

Therefore, the fact that a statute is declared inapplicable by reason of unconstitutionality by a judge in a particular case does not affect its validity nor is it equivalent to a declaration of nullity. The law as such continues to be valid, and will only lose

---

358 See a contrary opinion in H.J. LA ROCHE, *op. cit.*, pp. 137, 140, 150, 162; and in J.G. ANDUEZA, *op. cit.*, pp. 37–38.

359 See the Federal Court decision of June 19, 1953, in *Gaceta Forense* N° 1, 1953, pp. 77–78.

its general effects if repealed by another law (art. 177, 1961 Constitution) or if annulled by the Supreme Tribunal of Justice (art. 215,3,4 1961 Constitution).

In this regard, it must be mentioned that the Organic law on the Supreme Tribunal of 2004 has incorporated a new provision imposing the Chambers of the Supreme Court, after ruling any statute as unconstitutional following the diffuse method of judicial review, to send the case to the Constitutional Camber to allow the latter to rule the matter, and if it proceeds, the statute can be annulled with *erga omnes* effects (article 5,1o, 22).

In any case, in the Venezuelan procedural system, the *stare decisis* doctrine has no application at all, the judges being sovereign in their decisions, only submitted to the Constitution and the law. Therefore, decisions regarding the inapplicability of a law considered unconstitutional do not have binding effects, neither regarding the same judge who may change his legal opinion in other cases, nor regarding other judges or courts, except in cases of decision issued by the Constitutional Chamber with obligatory effects.

On the other hand, like the American or Argentinean systems, in the Venezuelan system of constitutional judicial control, the 1999 Constitution has created an extraordinary means or review recourse that can be filed against judicial decisions in which constitutional questions are involved that can be brought before the Constitutional Chamber of the Supreme Tribunal.

Before 1999, judge's decisions on matters of unconstitutionality were only subject to the ordinary means of appeal and to the recourse of cassation, following the general rules established in the Civil Procedural Code. It was only in the 1901 Constitution that the Federal Court was assigned the power to establish general criterion in constitutional matters referred to by lower courts, when a constitutional issue was raised in concrete judicial cases, which power was eliminated in the subsequent constitutional reform of 1904.

Nevertheless, before 1999, the possible contradictions that could arise between different court decisions, with the consequent uncertainty in the legal order, were corrected ever since 1858, through the establishment, in parallel with the diffuse system of judicial review, of a concentrated system of constitutional control assigned now to the Constitutional Chamber of the Supreme Tribunal of Justice.

As mentioned, one of the important reforms introduced to the judicial review system by the 1999 Constitution was to give the Constitutional Chamber of the Supreme Tribunal, the power to "review the definitive decisions issued by the courts on amparo matters and on judicial review of statutes or other norms" (Article 336,10).

This power of the Constitutional Chamber was conceived as an extraordinary power to review, at its discretion, by means of an extraordinary recourse similar to the application to the writ of certiorari, highest instance courts decisions issued in matters of judicial review of legislation, and specifically on matters of amparo.

The essential trend of this attribution is its discretionary character[360], that allows the Constitutional Chamber to choose the cases to be reviewed. As the same Constitutional Chamber of the Supreme Tribunal pointed it out in its decision N° 727 of April 8th, 2003, "in the cases of the decisions subject to revision, the Constitution does not provide for the creation of a third instance. What has set forth the constitutional provision is an exceptional and discretional power of the Constitutional Chamber that as such, must be exercised with maxim prudence regarding the admission of recourses for review final judicial decisions"[361].

In absence of the statute that must regulate the Constitutional Jurisdiction assigned to the Constitutional Chamber, it has been the same Constitutional Chamber the one that has modeled the framework of this recourse for revision of judicial decisions on constitutional matters. By the end of 2000, as a consequence of the Chamber rulings N° 1, 2, 44 and 714, the Supreme Court doctrine regarding the conditions that a judicial decision must have in order to be the object of the review recourse was as follows:

> 1°) The decision must have been issued in second instance, by means of an appeal or consultation, so that the review cannot be understood as a new instance.
>
> 2°) The constitutional revision is only admissible in order to preserve the uniformity of interpretation of constitutional norms and principles, or when it exists a deliberate violation of constitutional prescription, which will be analyzed by the Constitutional Chamber, in a facultative way
>
> 3°) As a consequence, and different to consultations, the recourse for revision is not *ipso jure* admissible, because it depends on the party's initiative, and not on the initiative of the courts that issued the decision, unless the Constitutional Chamber ex officio decides to accepted it bearing always in mind its purpose[362].

After, in decision N° 93 of February 6th, 2001(Case: *Olimpia Tours and Travel vs. Corporación de Turismo de Venezuela*), the Constitutional Chamber began to extend its own review powers, adding to the recourse for revision other judicial decisions different to those issued in matters of amparo or on judicial review of constitutionality, as follows:

> 1. The last instance definitive judicial amparo decisions of any kind, issued by the other Chambers of the Supreme Tribunal of Justice and by any court or tribunal of the country.

---

360 As mentioned, in a certain way similar to the *writ of cerciorari* in the Nort American system. See Allan R. BREWER–CARÍAS, *Judicial Review in Comparative Law, op. cit.*, p. 141; See also the comments of Jesús María CASAL, *Constitución y Justicia Constitucional,* Caracas 2002, p. 92.

361 Case: *Revisión de la sentencia dictada por la Sala Electoral en fecha 21 de noviembre de 2002*, in *Revista de Derecho Público*, N° 93–96, Editorial Jurídica Venezolana, Caracas, 2003.

362 See decisión of November 2, 2000 (Case: *Roderick A. Muñoz P. vs. Juzgado de los Municipios Carache, Candelaria y José Felipe Márquez Cañizales de la Circunscripción Judicial del Estado Trujillo*) in *Revista de Derecho Público*, N° 84, (octubre–diciembre), Editorial Jurídica Venezolana, Caracas, 2000, p. 367.

2. The last instance definitive judicial decisions of courts and of the other Chambers of the Supreme Tribunal on judicial review of constitutionality of statutes or State regulations.
3. The last instance definitive judicial decisions issued by the other Chambers of the Supreme Tribunal or by the other courts and tribunals putting aside or expressly or tacitly by–passing the interpretations of the Constitution ruled in any Constitutional Chamber's decision issued before the impugned ruling, thus making an erroneous constitutional judicial review by erroneously applying the Constitution.
4. The last instance definitive judicial decisions issued by the other Chambers of the Supreme Tribunal of by the other courts and tribunals which, according to the Constitutional Chamber's criteria, would incur in a grotesque error regarding the interpretation of the Constitution or simply would disregard the interpretation of the constitutional provision; cases in which it would also be an erroneous judicial review of constitutionality[363].

According to this doctrine, the Constitutional Chamber has extended its review power regarding judicial decisions, that in the Constitution is reduced to "amparo" and judicial review decisions, including other judicial decisions, even those issued by the other Chambers of the Supreme Tribunal (Civil, Criminal and Social Chambers, Electoral Chamber and Administrative judicial review Chamber) which is not authorized in the Constitution, and constitutes a violation to the constitutional right to *res judicata*, affecting legal stability and security

The Constitutional Chamber, in effect, after analyzing the due process of law guarantees regarding the extraordinary revision of judicial decisions, in decision N° 93 of February 6th, 2001 (Case: *Olimpia Tours and Travel vs. Corporación de Turismo de Venezuela*), alter analyzing its constitutional role as guarantor of the supremacy or the Constitution and as the interpreter of the Constitution, concluded saying that "there are no doubts about the Constitution interpretative powers of the Chamber, whose decisions are obligatory for the other Chambers and the rest of the courts of the Republic. Thus, all the other Chambers of the Supreme Tribunal and the other courts and tribunal are obligated to decide accordingly to the interpretation of constitutional provisions issued by the Chamber…The Constitution gives the Constitutional Chamber the superior and unique power regarding the interpretation of the Constitution.".

The conclusion from the argument developed by he Constitutional Chamber has been the affirmation of its powers to be "the maxim interpreter of the Constitution" with the power to issue obligatory interpretations, from which resulted its power to review, even ex officio, any judicial decision of any other Chamber of the Supreme Tribunal or of any court, when contrary to the constitutional interpretation set forth by the Chamber[364].

---

363 See in *Revista de Derecho Público*, N° 85–88, Editorial Jurídica Venezolana, Caracas, 2001, pp. 414–415. See also decisión N° 727 of April 8th, 2003 (Caso: *Revisión de la sentencia dictada por la Sala Electoral en fecha 21 de noviembre de 2002)*, en *Revista de Derecho Público*, N° 93–96, Editorial Jurídica Venezolana, Caracas, 2003

364 *Idem*. pp. 412–414.

This doctrine, particularly regarding to the others Chamber of the Supreme Tribunal decisions, has been incorporated in the Organic Law of the Supreme Tribunal (art. 5,4).

But just regarding the "amparo" definitive last instance judicial decisions, the power of the Constitutional Chamber of the Supreme Court to hear the extraordinary review recourse, is a very important instrument in order to provide uniformity to the judicial constitutional interpretation and enforcement of human rights made by ordinary courts.

2. The amparo action or recourse as a constitutional guarantee

A. *The actions of constitutional protection in Brazil*

Since 1934,[365] the Constitution of Brazil has expressly established the *mandado de segurança* as a special means for the protection of fundamental rights, other than personal liberty –which is protected through the recourse for *habeas corpus*. Thus, in the Brazilian constitutional system there are two main special actions for the constitutional protection of fundamental rights: the *mandado de segurança* and the *habeas corpus* actions. In particular, the *mandado de segurança* is intended to protect actual individual rights not protected through *habeas corpus*, whoever the authority responsible for the illegality or abuse of powers may be.[366]

But after the 1988 Constitution, additionally to the *mandado de segurança* and the *habeas corpus* recourses, other two specific recourses had been regulated: the *mandado de injunçao* and the *habeas data*[367].

Regarding the *habeas corpus,* it can be brought before the courts whenever anyone, suffers or feels threatened with suffering violence or duress in his or her freedom of movement because of illegal acts or abuses of power (Article 5, LXVIII of the Constitution). The right of movement (*ius ambuland)* is defined as the right of every person to enter, stay and leave national territory with his belongings (Article 5, XV). In principle, the action is brought before the Tribunals of First Criminal Instance, but actions may be heard by the Appeals Tribunals and even by the Supreme Federal Tribunal, if action is brought against the Tribunal of First Instance or against the Appeals Tribunal.

---

365 Art. 113,33 Constitution 1934. A. RÍOS ESPINOZA, Presupuestos constitucionales del mandato de seguridad", *Boletín del Instituto de Derecho Comparado de México*, UNAM, 46, 1963, p. 71. (Also published in H. FIX–ZAMUDIO, A. RÍOS ESPINOSA and N. ALCALÁ ZAMORA, *Tres estudios sobre el mandato de seguridad brasileño*, México 1963, pp. 71–96.

366 153,21 Constitution

367 See (in general): José Alfonso DA SILVA, *Mandado de injunçao e habeas data,* Sao Paulo, 1989; Dimar ACKEL FILHO, *Writs Constitutionais,* Sao Paulo, 1988; Nagib Slaibi Filho, *Anotaçoes a Constituiçao de 1988,* Río de Janeiro, 1989; Celso AGRÍCOLA BARBI, *Do Mandado de Segurança,* 7th Edition, Revista, aumentada e actualizada de acordo com o Código de Processo Civil de 1973 e legislação posterior, Editora Forense, Río de Janeiro 1993; J. CRETELLA JÚNIOR, *Comentários à ley do mandado de segurança (de acordo com a constituição de 5 de outubro de 1988*, 5th Edition, Editora Forense, Río de Janeiro 1992.

The second action of protection provided in the Constitution is the individual or collective *mandado de segurança*, regulated in Law N° 1533 of December 31 1951[368]. This action is devoted to protect certain and determined rights that are not protected by *habeas corpus* or *habeas data*, when the party responsible for the illegal action or abuse of power is a public authority or an agent of an artificial person exercising attributions of the Authorities (Article 5, LXIX).

This recourse, which may be brought before any tribunal according to its competence, is not admissible when there are administrative recourses that can be brought against the act in question, or if the decisions are judicial, when there are recourses provided under procedural law by means of which the act may be corrected. Neither is the writ of *segurança* admitted against statutes, even those that are self–applicable.

The collective *mandado de segurança* is conceived as a means of protecting collective interests, which may be brought before the courts by political parties represented in the National Congress, trade union organizations, and legally organized entities or associations for the defense of the interests of their members or associates (Article 5, LXX).

Additionally, Brazil has a distinctive regulation which is the *mandado de injunçao* similar to the writ of injunction, directed to protect the exercise of constitutional rights and freedoms and of the prerogatives inherent to nationality, the sovereignty of the people or citizenship when the lack of a regulatory state on the matter can make such rights unviable (Article 5, LXXI), The purpose of this action against a legislative or regulatory omission is to obtain the order of a judge imposing the obligation to the legislative body to carry out or comply with a determined act, the violation of which constitutes an impairment of a right.

If the regulatory omission is attributable to the highest authorities of the Republic, the competent Tribunal is the Supreme Federal Tribunal; in other cases the High Courts of Justice are competent. Whatever the case, the respective judge cannot surrogate the legislative body in the sense that it cannot legislate by means of the writ of *injunçao*, but can simply order or instruct that the right established in the Constitution that is unviable because of lack of regulation be conceded,.

Lastly, the 1988 Constitution introduced the *habeas data,* provided to assure firstly, that the information relative to the plaintiff found in records or databanks of governmental or public sector entities be heard; and secondly, for the rectification of data, when not achievable through judicial or administrative proceedings (Article 5, LXXII). *Habeas data* may therefore be defined as a constitutional action used to guarantee three aspects: the right of access to official records; the right to rectify such records, and the right to correct them. The recourse can be brought before any competent court, and even before the Supreme Federal Tribunal.

In Brazil there also exists an extraordinary recourse of constitutionality that can be filed before the Federal Supreme Tribunal, against the judicial decision issued on

368 See J. CRETELLA JUNIOR, *Coméntarios à Lei do mandado de segurança. De acordo com a Constitução de 5 de Octubre de 1988*, Editora Forense, Rio de Janeiro, 1992,

matters of protection of constitutional rights by the Superior Federal Court or by the Regional Federal Courts, when it is considered that the courts have made the decisions in a way inconsistent with the Constitution, or in which the court has denied the validity of a treaty or federal statute, or when the decisions has declared the unconstitutionality of a treaty or of a Federal Law; and when they deem a local government law or act that has been challenged as unconstitutional or contrary to a valid federal law[369].

In these cases the matter can reach the Federal Supreme Tribunal, which is the most important court on matters of judicial review (having Brazil a mixed system of judicial review) as happens with numerous Latin American that combine the diffuse system on judicial review with the concentrated one[370].

In effect, the Brazilian system of judicial review, in its origin, like the Argentinean, can be considered one of the Latin American systems that followed the North American model more closely[371]. It was after the 1934 Constitution, that a direct action of unconstitutionality was introduced. This action was conceived to be brought before the Federal Supreme Tribunal to impugned statutes. This is how the Brazilian system of judicial review began to be a mixed one.

In effect, the Federal Constitution of 1891 clearly influenced by the North American constitutional system[372] assigned the Supreme Federal Tribunal the power to review, through an extraordinary recourse, the decisions of the federal courts and of the courts of the Member States, in which the validity or the application of the treaties or Federal Laws was questioned, and the decisions were against; or in which the validity of laws or government acts of the states was questioned on the grounds of contravention to the Constitution or to federal laws; and the decisions considered the challenged laws or acts valid[373]. As a consequence of this express constitutional at-

369 Art. 199. III, b,c. Constitution.

370 See in general Mantel GONCALVES FERREIRA FILHO, "O sistema constitucional brasileiro e as recentes inovacoes no controle de constitucionalidade" in *Anuario Iberoamericano de Justicia Constitucional*, N° 5, 2001, Centro de Estudios Políticos y Constitucionales, Madrid, España, 2001; José Carlos BARBOSA MOREIRA, "El control judicial de la constitucionalidad de las leyes en el Brasil: un bosquejo", in *Desafíos del control de constitucionalidad*, Ediciones Ciudad Argentina, Buenos Aires, Argentina, 1996; Paulo BONAVIDES, "Jurisdicao constitucional e legitimidade (algumas observacoes sobre o Brasil)" en *Anuario IberoamerivanoIberoamericano de Justicia Constitucional* N° 7, Centro de Estudios Políticos y Constitucionales, Madrid, 2003; Enrique Ricardo LEWANDOWSKI, "Notas sobre o controle da constitucionalidade no Brasil", en Edgar CORZO SOSA, y otros, *Justicia Constitucional Comparada*, Ed. Universidad Nacional Autónoma de México, México D.F. 1993; Zeno VELOSO, *Controle jurisdicional de constitucionalidade*, Ed. Cejup, Belém, Brasil, 1999.

371 H. FIX–ZAMUDIO and J. CARPIZO, "Amerique latine" in L. FAVOREU and J.A. JOLOWICZ (ed.), *Le contrôle juridictionnel des lois*, Paris 1986, p. 121.

372 O.A. BANDEIRA DE MELLO, *A teoria das Constituiçoes rigidas*, Sao Paulo 1980, p. 157; J. Alfonso DA SILVA, *Sistema de defensa da Constituiçao brasileira*, Congreso sobre la Constitución y su Defensa, UNAM, México 1982, p. 29. (mimeo).

373 Art. 59, III, 1. 1981 Constitution.

tribution, the Federal Law 221 of 1894[374] assigned the power to judge upon the validity of obviously unconstitutional laws and executive regulations, and to decide their inapplicability in concrete cases, to all federal judges. Thus, the diffuse system of judicial review of legislation was established in Brazil at the end of the last century, and was perfected through the subsequent constitutional reforms of 1926, 1934, 1937, 1946 and 1967[375]. Therefore, we can say that the main feature of the Brazilian system of judicial review is its diffuse character, with all its consequences according to the American model.

As mentioned, in addition to the diffuse system of judicial review, a concentrated system of review was established in the 1934 Constitution, by attributing power to the Supreme Federal Tribunal to declare the unconstitutionality of member state Constitutions or laws (state laws) when required to do so by the Attorney General of the Republic.[376] Thus, a direct action of unconstitutionality was established as of 1934, to defend federal constitutional principles, against Member state acts,[377] later developed in subsequent Constitutions [378] up to its extension after the 1965 Constitutional Amendment, to control all normative acts of state, whether federal or of the Member States.[379]

Consequently, the Brazilian system can be considered a mixed one in which the diffuse system of judicial review operates in combination with a concentrated system.[380]

In the American model and in the Argentinean experience the powers of the courts to control the constitutionality of legislation were derived from the principle of constitutional supremacy as applied by the Supreme Court. Contrary to that, the diffuse system of judicial review arose in Brazil from express provisions in the 1891 Constitution, [381] and it is still based on constitutional norms. In this respect, as previously mentioned, the Constitution establishes the power of the Supreme Federal Tribunal to judge through extraordinary recourses, cases decided in the last resort by other courts or judges, first, when the challenged judicial decisions are against any disposition of the Constitution or denied the enforcement of a Treaty or federal law; second, when they declared the unconstitutionality of a Treaty or of a federal law;

---

374 Art. 13,10. Law 221 of 20 November 1984

375 O.A. BANDEIRA DE MELLO, *op. cit.*, pp. 158–237

376 Art. 12,2. 1934 Constitution.

377 J. Alfonso da Silva, *doc. cit.* p. 29

378 Also in the Law N° 2271 of 22 July 1954.

379 *Cf.* J. Alfonso DA SILVA, *doc. cit.*, p. 31

380 A. BUZAID, "La acción directa de inconstitucionalidad en el derecho brasileño", *Revista de la Facultad de Derecho*, UCAB, N° 19–22, Caracas 1964, p. 55; O.A. BANDEIRA DE MELLO, *op. cit.*, p. 157.

381 *Cf.*, J. Alfonso DA SILVA, *doc. cit.*, pp. 32, 34; J. Alfonso DA SILVA, *Curso de direito constitucional positivo*, Sao Paulo 1984, p. 17.

and third, when they deemed a law or other local government valid when such law challenges the Constitution or a federal law.[382]

According to this norm, not only is the diffuse system of judicial review established, but the power of the Supreme Tribunal to intervene in all proceedings in which constitutional questions have been resolved, is also established.

As we have mentioned, the diffuse system of judicial review in Brazil follows the general trends of the American model also developed in Argentina. Therefore, all the courts of first instance have the power not to apply laws (federal, state or Municipal laws) that they deem unconstitutional, when a party to the proceeding has raised the question of constitutionality. Thus, the judges have no *ex officio* power to judge the constitutionality of the laws, and can only exercise it when the question of constitutionality has been raised by the interested party as an exception or defense in the process.[383] The constitutional question, once raised, has a preliminary character regarding the final decision of the case, which the judge must decide beforehand.

Of course, the decision of the courts on constitutional matters has only *in casu et inter partes* effects, and the unapplied law is considered null and void *ab initio*. Thus, the decision has *ex tunc*, retroactive effects.[384]

The constitutional question can also be considered in a second instance, through the normal appeals process, in which case, when the court of second instance is a collegiate court, the decision upon matters of unconstitutionality of legislation must be adopted by a majority vote decision of its members.[385]

As already mentioned, the Brazilian Constitution, ever since the establishment of the constitutional review judicial system in 1891, has always expressly regulated the power of the Supreme Court to review lower courts decisions on matters of constitutionality, through an extraordinary recourse that can be brought before the Tribunal, by the party to the process who has lost the case.[386]

Finally it must be said that when deciding constitutional questions, the Supreme Federal Tribunal must adopt its decision with the vote of the majority of its members.[387] The decision, as the first instance one, when declaring the unconstitutionality of a law, has *inter partes* and *ex tunc* effects.[388] In such cases, the Tribunal in fact recognizes the *ab initio* unconstitutionality of the law, in a decision which has declarative effects, but does not annul or repeal the law, which continues in force and to be applicable.

---

382 Art. 119, III b,c, Constitution. J. Alfonso DA SILVA, *Sistema... doc. cit.*, p. 43; O.A. BANDEIRA DE MELLO, *op. cit.*, p. 215.

383 J. Alfonso DA SILVA, *Curso...* p. 18; J. Alfonso da Silva, *Sistema... doc. cit.*, pp. 33, 37, 58.

384 J. Alfonso DA SILVA, *Sistema... doc. cit.*, pp. 41,64; A. Buzaid, *loc. cit.*, p. 91.

385 This qualified vote was first established in the 1934 Constitution (Art. 179), and is always required. See O.A. BANDEIRA DE MELLO, *op. cit.*, p. 159.

386 J. Alfonso DA SILVA, *Sistema... doc. cit.*, p. 44

387 D.A. BANDEIRA DE MELLO, *op. cit.*, p. 218

388 J. Alfonso DA SILVA, *Sistema... doc. cit.*, pp. 69, 71

In the Brazilian system, an additional feature can be distinguished: once adopted by the Tribunal, the decision must be sent to the Federal Senate which has the power, according to the Constitution, to "suspend the execution of all or part of a statute or decree when declared unconstitutional by the Supreme Federal Tribunal through a definitive decision,[389] in which case the effects of the Senate decisions have, of course, *erga omnes* and *ex nunc* effects.[390]

Anyway, it must be said that in Brazil, like in the North American system, a presumption of constitutionality also exists regarding laws and other state acts. Consequently, only when the unconstitutionality of a law appears to be without doubt, the Tribunal can declare its unconstitutionality. Thus, in case of doubt, it must reject the question and consider the law constitutional, and applicable in the concrete case.[391]

From the above mentioned, it can be deducted that additionally to the diffuse and concentrated systems of judicial review, an indirect means for judicial review, through the actions for protection of fundamental rights and liberties, can also be identified in the Brazilian constitutional system.

Nevertheless, it has been traditionally considered that laws or any other normative act of state, cannot be the object of an action requesting either *habeas corpus* or a *mandado de segurança*[392]. In this respect, as happened with the Argentinean recourse for *amparo* until recent changes within the Supreme Court decisions, the abstract control of the constitutionality of laws is not possible through the exercise of the actions for a *mandado de segurança*, or *habeas corpus*. In other words, no direct action against laws can be exercised through the *mandado de segurança*, or *habeas corpus* actions, even if they are what the Mexican system calls auto–applicative or self executing laws.[393] Nevertheless, such actions can serve as an indirect means of judicial review, for the diffuse system, when they are exercised against an act of any authority when executed based on a law deemed unconstitutional. Thus, it is only the concrete situation that results from the execution or application of the law or normative act, the one that can be directly impugned by means of these actions for protection of fundamental rights, and only in an indirect way and in accordance with the diffuse method of review, that laws can be controlled by the courts on the grounds of their unconstitutionality.

---

389 Art. 42, VII Federal Constitution

390 J. Alfonso DA SILVA, *Sistema...*, *doc. cit.*, p. 73.

391 *Cf.* T.B. CAVALCANTI, *Do controle de constitutionalidade*, Rio do Janeiro, 1966, p. 69.

392 *Cf.* A. Alfonso DA SILVA, "*Sistema... doc. cit.*, p. 47; H. FIX–ZAMUDIO, "Mandato de seguridad y juicio de *amparo*", *Boletín del Instituto de Derecho Comparado de México*, UNAM; 46, 1963, pp. 11, 17. Also published in H. FIX–ZAMUDIO, A. Ríos Espinosa, N. ALCALÁ ZAMORA, *op. cit.*, pp. 3–69; A. RIOS ESPINOSA, *loc.cit.*, p. 88

393 H. FIX–ZAMUDIO, *loc. cit.*, p. 16; A. Alfonso DA SILVA, *Sistema... doc. cit.*, pp. 46,47.

B. *The action of "tutela" in Colombia*

During the constitution–making process of 1991, the intention of the drafters of the Colombian Constitution was to regulate the amparo as a constitutional right[394], in the same trend of the Mexican and Venezuelan systems of amparo.

Nonetheless, in the final version of the Constitution, the National Constituent Assembly abandoned the proposal to set forth the amparo as a constitutional right in itself, regulating the amparo action as a specific judicial mean for the protection of only some constitutional rights, changing its general Latin American denomination of "action of amparo" to "action of tutela"[395]. Thus, even though at the beginning of the application of the reform we identified the Colombian system more in the general category of the Mexican and Venezuela amparo[396], the statutory regulation and its very important application have molded the tutela as a specific mean for the protection of fundamental constitutional rights[397], which are not all the rights enshrined in the Constitution, regulating it in parallel to the habeas corpus recourse, regulated in the Criminal Code.

Additionally, the Constitution also regulated the popular actions in order to protect collective rights and interests related to public patrimony, public space, public

---

394 See the draft in Jorge ARENAS SALAZAR, *La tutela. Una acción humaniaria*, Librería Doctrina y Ley, Bogotá 1992, pp. 47. See the comments in Allan R. BREWER–CARÍAS, "El amparo a los derechos y libertades constitucionales y la acción de tutela a los derechos fundamentales en Colombia: una aproximación comparativa" en Manuel José CEPEDA (editor), ***La Carta de Derechos. Su interpretación y sus implicaciones***, Editorial Temis, Bogotá 1993, pp. 21–81; y en la obra colectiva ***La protección jurídica del ciudadano. Estudios en Homenaje al Profesor Jesús González Pérez***, Tomo 3, Editorial Civitas, Madrid 1993, pp. 2.695–2.748.

395 Both words, "amparo"and "tutela" have the same meaning in Spanish. See the proposal in *Idem*, p. 49 ff.

396 See Allan R. BREWER–CARÍAS

397 See, in general, in regard to the tutela in Colombia, Jorge ARENAS SALAZAR, *La Tutela Una acción humanitaria,* 1st Edition 1992, Ediciones Librería Doctrina y Ley, Santa Fe de Bogotá D.C., Colombia 1992; Manuel José CEPEDA, *La Tutela Materiales y Reflexiones sobre su significado*, Presidencia de la República, Consejería para el desarrollo de la Constitución, Imprenta Nacional de Colombia, Bogotá D.C. 1992; Oscar José DUEÑAS RUIZ, *Acción de Tutela, Su esencia en la práctica, 50 respuestas básicas*, Corte Suprema, Consejo de Estado, Legislación, Ediciones Librería del Profesional, Santa Fe de Bogotá D.C., Colombia 1992; Federico GONZÁLEZ CAMPOS, *La Tutela: Interpretación doctrinaria y jurisprudencial*, 2nd Edition, Ediciones Jurídicas Gustavo IBÁÑEZ, Santa Fe de Bogotá D.C., Colombia 1994; Manuel José CEPEDA, *Las Carta de Derechos. Su interpretación y sus implicaciones*, Temis Presidencia de la República Consejería para el Desarrollo de la Constitución, Santa Fe de Bogotá, Colombia 1993; Juan Manuel CHARRY U., *La acción de tutela,* Editorial Temis, Santa Fe de Bogotá 1992; Herán Alejandro OLANO CORREA et al., *Acción de Tutela (Práctica Forense y Jurisprudencia)*, 2nd Edition 1994, Tunja–Boyacá–Colombia 1994; Carlos Augusto PATIÑO BELTRÁN, *Acciones de Tutela cumplimiento populares y de grupo. Guía Práctica*, Editorial Leyer, Bogotá D.C., Colombia 2000; *Pensamiento Jurídico. La Acción de Tutela, Revista de Teoría del Derecho y Análisis Jurídico* N° 7, Universidad Nacional de Colombia, Facultad de Derecho, Ciencias Políticas y Sociales, Santa Fe de Bogotá D.C. 1997.

safety and public health, administrative morals, the environment, free economic competition and others of like nature defined by statute.

The "action of *tutela*", has been regulated in Decree N° 2.591 of 1991, as an action that everybody has in order to claim before the courts, at all times and at in any place, through a preferential and summary procedure, by himself or by some one on his behalf, the immediate protection of their fundamental constitutional rights, whenever they are harmed by the action or the omission of any public authority or by individuals. In the latter case, the individuals are only those in charge of rendering a public service whose conduct seriously and directly affects collective interests, regarding which the aggrieved party finds himself in a position of subordination or defenselessness.

The Constitution does not exclude any State act from the tutela action, which includes judicial acts that harm fundamental rights. That is why Article 40 of the Decree 2591 provided for the action of tutela against judicial decisions. Nonetheless, this Article 40 of the Decree was annulled by the Constitutional Court in its October 1, 1992 decision, considering it unconstitutional[398]. Nonetheless, as abovementioned, the Constitutional Court has developed the doctrine of arbitrariness in order to admit the tutela against judicial decisions when it is thought that they are issued as a result of a judicial *voie de fact* [399].

The Decree set forth that the action of tutela can also be filed in states of exception, and when such exception measures refer to rights, the action of tutela can be exercised at least to defend its essential contents.

> According to Article 86 of the Constitution, such action shall only proceed when the affected party does not have another means of judicial defense, unless it is used as a temporary measure to avoid irreparable damage. This does not mean that the remedy can only be brought before the courts after exhausting the ordinary means; but that the action of tutela is only available for constitutional protection, when there are no other judicial preferred and brief means to achieve such purpose. That is why, as stated in Article 6,2 of the Decree N° 2591, the action of tutela is inadmissible when the recourse of *habeas corpus* can be filed for the protection of the particular right.

For this reason, Decree N° 2.591 of 1991 established, among the causes of inadmissibility of such protection, that it shall not proceed "when other recourses or judicial means of defense are available unless being used as a temporary measure to avoid irreparable damage," in the understanding that "irreparable damage is that which can only be wholly repaired by means of indemnification" (Article 6,1).

Therefore, pursuant to Decree N° 2.591, Article 8, "even when the affected party has other means of judicial defense, the action of *tutela* shall proceed when used as a temporary mechanism to avoid irreparable harm". The statute also provides that

---

398 See the decision N° C–543 of September 24, 1992 in *Derecho Colombiano,* Bogotá 1992, pp. 471 to 499; and in Manuel José CEPEDA, *Derecho Constitucional Jurisprudencial. Las grandes decisiones de la Corte Constitucional*, Legis, Bogotá 001, pp. 1009 ff.

399 See the decisión N° T–231 of May 13, 1994 in Manuel José CEPEDA, *Derecho Constitucional Jurisprudencial. Las grandes decisiones de la Corte Constitucional*, Legis, Bogotá 001, pp. 1022 ff.

"when used as a temporary mechanism to avoid irreparable harm, the action of *tutela* may be brought together with the action of annulment and others that are admitted before the judicial review of administrative action jurisdiction. In these cases, the judge may determine that the particular act be not applied to the specific judicial situation the protection of which is being sought, for as long as the trial lasts."

The Constitution set forth that the action of *tutela* for the protection of fundamental constitutional rights can be brought "before the judges"; and accordingly, Decree 2.591 of 1991 attributes the power "to hear the action of *tutela*, to the judges and tribunals with jurisdiction over the place where the violation or threat of violation takes place" (Article 37).

Decree 1380 of 2000, regarding the courts with jurisdiction in the place where the violation or threatens have taken place, before which the action must be filed, establishes the following rules, depending the defendant party. If it is 1) against any national public authority, before the Districts Superior Courts; 2) against any national or departmental decentralized entity for public utilities, before the Circuit courts; 3) against district or municipal authorities and against individuals, before the municipal courts; 4) against any general administrative act issued by a national authority, before the Cundinamarca Judicial review of administrative actions; 5) against any judicial entity, before the respective superior court; and 6) against the Supreme Court of Justice, the *Consejo de Estado* or the Superior Council of the Judiciary, or its Disciplinary Chamber before the same Corporation in the corresponding Chamber.

As mentioned above, in Colombia the action of *habeas corpus* also set forth in the Constitution (Article 30) is regulated in the Criminal Code as a right that proceeds in order to protect ("amparo") personal freedom against any arbitrary act of any authority that tends to restrict it (Article 5). It can be filed when a person is captured violating its constitutional or legal guarantees, or its freedom deprivation is illicitly extended (Articles 430); before any criminal court in the place where the detainee is or where the person has been captured (Article 431).

Now, regarding the decisions on the actions of *tutela*, they are subject to appeal; and pursuant to Decree 2.591 of 1991, if no appeal has been filed, the decisions must be sent for their revision to the Constitutional Court (Article 31); the Court having discretionary power to determine which decisions of *tutela* will be reviewed (Article 33).

Since the 1991 Constitution, the Constitutional Court plays a very important role in matters of judicial review, being the Colombian system, like the Venezuelan and Brazilian ones, a mixed system[400], set forth as such since the 1910 Constitution. In it, the power attributed to all courts to declare the inapplicability of laws they deem contrary to the Constitution, was set forth in parallel with a concentrated system of

---

400 See in general Eduardo CIFUENTES MUÑOZ, "La Jurisdicción constitucional en Colombia" en *La Jurisdicción constitucional en Iberoamérica,* Ed Dykinson, Madrid, España, 1997; Luis Carlos Sácchica, *La Corte Constitucional y su jurisdicción,* Ed. Temis, Bogotá, Colombia, 1993

judicial review attributed to the then Supreme Court, also through the exercise of a popular action.[401].

It was in the 1910 Constitution that the role of "guardian of the integrity of the Constitution" which is still today in the Fundamental text on the hands of the Constitutional Court, was attributed for the first time to the Supreme Court of Justice[402]. It was also in that same Constitution that the principle of the diffuse system of judicial review acquired constitutional rank, as established in Article 7 of the 1991Constitution, which states:

> **Art. 215.** The Constitution is the norm of norms. In all cases of incompatibility between the Constitution and a statute, the constitutional provisions shall be applied.

Anyway, since 1910, the Colombian constitutional system has mixed both the diffuse and the concentrated systems of judicial review, attributing now the concentrated power to annul, with *erga omnes* effects, to the Constitutional Court in a similar way to the Venezuelan system, by means of a popular action.

Regarding Article 7 of the Constitution, it provides the basis of the diffuse system of judicial review, according to which all judges have the power to decide not to apply a law in a concrete process, when they deem it contrary to the Constitution. The system, as it has been developed, functions entirely according to the North American model, particularly, because it has been conceived as an "exception of unconstitutionality."

Of course, in these cases of diffuse constitutional control, the judges cannot annul the law or declare its unconstitutionality, nor can the effects of their decision be extended or generalized. On the contrary, as happens in all other diffuse judicial review systems, the court must limit itself to deciding not to apply the unconstitutional law to the concrete case, of course only when it is pertinent to the resolution of the case. That decision has effects only concerning the parties to the case. Therefore, as with similar systems elsewhere, the law whose application has been denied in a concrete case, continues to be in force and other judges can moreover continue to apply it. Even the judge who chose not to apply it in a concrete case, can change his mind in a subsequent process.[403]

The creation of the Constitutional Court as the ultimate guardian of the Constitution originated the attribution of the Court to review all the judicial decisions resolving actions for *tutela.* As opposed to the Venezuelan or Argentinean cases, in Colombia there is not a specific matter for a recourse of revision, but an attribution that must be automatically accomplished in a discretionary way. In effect, the Decree regulating the procedure set forth that when a *tutela* decision is not appealed, it always must be automatically sent for revision to the Constitutional Court (Article 31). In cases in which the decisions are appealed, the superior court's decision,

---

401 Concerning the mixed character of the system see: J. VIDAL PERDOMO, *Derecho constitucional general*, Bogotá 1985, p. 42; D.R. Salazar, *Constitución Política de Colombia*, Bogotá 1982, p. 305; E. SARRIA, *Guarda de la Constitución*, Bogotá, p. 78.

402 *Cf.* D.R. SALAZAR, *op. cit.*, p. 304.

403 *Cf.* L.C. SACHICA, *El control...cit.*, p. 65.

whether confirming or revoking the appealed decision, must also be automatically sent to the Constitutional Court for its revision (Article 32). .

For that purpose, the Constitutional Court must appoint two of its Magistrates in order to select, without express motivation and according to their criteria, the *tutela* decisions which are to be reviewed. Nonetheless, any of the Magistrates of the Court and the Peoples' defendant can request the revision of the excluded decision, when they deem that the review can clarify the scope of a right or avoid a grave prejudice. Also, according to Decree 262 of February 2000, the General Attorney of the Nation can ask for the revision of *tutela* decisions when he deems necessary to defend the legal order, the public patrimony and the fundamental rights and guarantees (Art. 7,12).

All the decisions not excluded from review in a delay of 30 days, must be reviewed by the Court in a three month delay (Article 33). For that purpose, the Constitutional Court must appoint three magistrates who will integrate the Chamber called to decide (Article 34). All the review decisions that modify or revoke the *tutela* decision, that unify the constitutional judicial doctrine (*jurisprudencia*) or that clarify the scope of constitutional provisions must be motivated; the others must just be justified (Article 35). The Constitutional Court review decisions only produce effects regarding the concrete case. They must immediately be notified to the first instance court, which at his turn must notify it to the parties, and adopt the necessary decisions in order to adequate its own decision to the Court ruling.

C. *The action of amparo in Dominican Republic*

In the case of the Dominican Republic, as has been already mentioned, there are no constitutional or legal provisions regulating the amparo recourse as a specific judicial mean for protection of constitutional rights. The Constitution only refers to the recourse of habeas corpus for the protection of personal freedom, which has been regulated by the 1978 Habeas Corpus Law (*Ley de habeas corpus*), and based on such regulations, the Supreme Court traditionally limited the procedure of habeas data to the protection of the right to physical freedom and safety, excluding any possibility of using the habeas corpus recourse in order to protect other constitutional rights.

Nevertheless, as has been mentioned, the Supreme Court by means of a decision of February 24, 1999 (Case: *Productos Avon S.A.*) based in the American Convention on Human Rights, admitted the amparo recourse for the protection of constitutional rights and determined that the competent courts to decide on the matter of amparo are the courts of first instance in the place in which the challenged act or omission has been produced. A few months latter, by means of Resolution of June, 10 1999, the Supreme Court determined that the competent fist instance courts are those deciding civil matters.

The amparo action has been successfully used for the protection of constitutional rights. Among the multiple cases, the following can be mentioned: For instance, a 2002 case in which the Court of First Instance of the National District ordered the National Citizenship Registry to issue the Identification Card to two boys born in the

Republic from Haitian illegally settled parents, arguing that the rejection of such documents constituted a violation of the boys identity and citizenship rights.

Other case decided by the same Court of First Instance of the National District originated in the order adopted by the Public prosecutor of the National District seizing of the Listin Diario Newspaper, which was considered contrary to the constitutional rights not to be applied statutes retroactively, to non discrimination, to freedom of press and to property rights[404].

It must be mentioned that in Dominican Republic, a mixed system of judicial review exists combining the diffuse method of judicial review with the concentrated one. Regarding the diffuse method, the 1844 Constitution, as well as the 2002 Constitution set forth that "all statutes, decrees, resolutions, regulations or acts contrary to the Constitution are null and void" (Article 46). From this express regulation of the consequences of the constitutional supremacy principle, all the Courts can declare an act unconstitutional and not applicable to the concrete case[405].

On the other hand, the Supreme Court of Justice has the exclusive power to hear the action of unconstitutionality of statutes that can be brought before the Court by the President of the Republic, the Presidents of the national Congress Chambers or by an interested party (Article 67,1).

D. *The action of amparo in Ecuador*

As it has been already analyzed, the 1988 Ecuadorian Constitution set forth the basic and extensive regulations not only regarding the action for amparo, but also regarding the action of habeas corpus and habeas data; which are statutorily developed in the 1997 Law on Constitutionality Control.

Regarding the amparo action, according to Article 46 of the Law, its purpose is to effectively protect the rights enshrined in the Constitution or in international declarations, covenants and instruments, in force in Ecuador, against any threat originated in an illegitimate act of public administration authorities that could have caused, have caused or can cause an imminent, grave and irreparable harm. It must be highlighted that in these cases, the amparo action can only be filed against actions from Public Administration, and not from other non executive entities of the State. The Constitution expressly excludes judicial decisions from the action of amparo.

The action can be filed in order to request the adoption of urgent measures directed to put an end to the harm or to avoid the danger of the protected rights. It can also be the object of an amparo action the omission in the issuing of an act or the absence of its enforcement.

---

404 See Samuel ARIAS ARZENO, "El Amparo en la República Dominicana: su Evolución Jurisprudencial", publicado en *Revista Estudios Jurídicos*, Vol. XI N° 3, Ediciones Capeldom, Septiembre–Diciembre 2002.

405 *Cf.* M. BERGES CHUPANI, "Report" in *Memoria de la Reunión de Cortes Superiores de Justicia de Ibero–America, El Caribe, España y Portugal*, Caracas, 1983, p. 380.

The action may also be brought if the act or omission were carried out by persons that render public services or act by delegation or concession of a public authority. Only in such cases, an amparo can be filed against a private person.

As mentioned, according to Article 47 of the Law on Constitutional Control, the competent courts to hear the amparo action are the first instance courts where the challenged act has been in effect.

All decisions granting amparo adopted by the first instance courts by means of an advisory procedure must obligatorily be sent to the Constitutional Tribunal in order to be confirmed or revoked. When the first instance decision denies the amparo action (as well as the habeas corpus or habeas data actions), it can be appealed before the same Constitutional Tribunal (Articles 12,3; 31and 52).

The Constitutional Tribunal of Ecuador, in substitution of the former Constitutional Guarantees Tribunal, was vested in the 1998 Constitution with the power to declare the nullity on the grounds of unconstitutionality of any statute, decree, regulation or ordinance, when an action is brought before the Tribunal by the President of the Republic, the National Congress, the Supreme Court, one thousand citizens or by any person provided a previous favorable report from the Peoples' Defendant (Article 18).

But this power to annul statutes with *erga omnes* effects (Article 22) in a concentrated way, is combined in Ecuador with the diffuse method of judicial review which attributed to all courts the power to declare the unconstitutionality of statutes applying the Constitution with preference. The judicial review system in Ecuador, is thus a mixed one[406].

In this respect, Article 272 of the Constitution sets forth:

> "The Constitution prevails over any other legal norm. All the organic or ordinary statutes, decrees–law, ordinances, regulations or resolution dispositions, must conform to its provisions and in case they enter in contradiction with it or alters their provisions, they will have no value".

As a consequence of this supremacy principle, Article 274 of the Constitution sets forth the diffuse method of judicial review allowing any court at parties petitions or *ex officio*, to declare the inapplicability of any norm contrary to the Constitution, as follows:

---

406 See in general Hernán SALGADO PESANTES, *Manual de Justicia Constitucional Ecuatoriana,* Corporación Editora Nacional, Quito, Ecuador, 2004; Hernán SALGADO PESANTES, "El control de constitucionalidad en la Carta Política del Ecuador" en *Una mirada a los Tribunales Constitucionales. Las experiencias recientes. Lecturas Constitucionales Andinas* N° 4, Ed. Comisión Andina de Juristas, Lima, Perú; Ernesto LÓPEZ FREIRE, "Evolución del control de constitucionalidad en el Ecuador" en *Derecho Constitucional para fortalecer la democracia ecuatoriana,* Ed. Tribunal Constitucional – Kas, Quito, Ecuador, 1999; Marco MORALES TOBAR, "Actualidad de la Justicia Constitucional en el Ecuador" en Luis LÓPEZ GUERRA (Coordinador). *La Justicia Constitucional en la actualidad,* Corporación Editora Nacional, Quito, Ecuador, pp. 77–165; Oswaldo CEVALLOS BUENO, "El sistema de control concentrado y el constitucionalismo en el Ecuador" en *Anuario Iberoamericano de Justicia Constitucional,* N° 6, 2002, Madrid, España, 2002.

> Any court or judge, in the cases they are hearing, at party's request or ex officio, may declare a legal provision contrary to the Constitution or to international treaties or covenants as inapplicable, notwithstanding its power to decide the controversy.

According to the same article, this declaration will not have obligatory force except in the case in which it is issued, that is to say, has only *inter partes* effects; and the court or tribunal must write a report on the declaration of unconstitutionality of the statute that must be sent to the Constitutional Tribunal in order for it to resolve the matter in a general and obligatory way, that is to say, with *erga omnes* effects.

Thus, in matters of amparo, if when granting the constitutional protection the competent judges applying the diffuse method of judicial review has adopted decisions declaring the unconstitutionality of statutes[407], they must also write the report on the question of constitutionality to be sent to the Constitutional Tribunal by the advisory proceeding for its confirmation or revocation (Art. 12,6).

E. *The "amparo" in Guatemala*

In Guatemala the 1985 Constitution set forth the "amparo" as a specific judicial mean to protect people against the threat of violation of their rights, or to restore the rule of such rights when the violation has already occurred. According to the Constitution, "there is no scope that is not subject to amparo, and it shall be admitted provided that the acts, resolutions, provisions or statutes carry an implicit threat, restriction or violation of the rights guaranteed by the Constitution and the statutes" (Article 265).

In particular, according to Article 10 of the 1986 Amparo, personal exhibition and constitutionality Law, the amparo is due to protect all situations susceptible to risk, a threat, restriction or violation of the rights recognized in the Constitution and the statutes of the republic, whether the situation comes from public law persons or entities or private law entities. Article 9 of the Amparo Law specifies that amparo can be brought against the State, comprising decentralized or autonomous entities, against those entities sustained with public funds created by statute or by virtue of a concession, or those that act by delegation of the State, by virtue of a contract, concession or similar. Amparo can also be filed against entities to which persons must be integrated by law and other recognized by statute, like the political parties, associations, societies, trade unions, cooperatives and similar.

Article 10 of the Amparo Law enumerates as examples, the following cases in which everybody has the right to ask for amparo:

> a) To ask to be maintained or to be restituted in the enjoyment of the rights and guarantees set forth in the Constitution or any other statute;
>
> b) In order to seek a declaration in a concrete case, that a statute, regulation, resolution or authority act does not oblige the plaintiff because it contradicts or restricts any of the rights guaranteed in the Constitution or recognized by any other statute'

407 See Hernán SALGADO PESANTES, *Manual de Justicia Constitucional Ecuatoriana,* Corporación Editora Nacional, Quito, Ecuador, 2004, p. 85.

c) In order to seek a declaration in a concrete case that a non legislative disposition or resolution of Congress, is not applicable to the plaintiff because it violates a constitutional right;

d) When an authority of any jurisdiction issues a regulation, accord or resolution of any kind that abuses of power or exceeds its legal attributions, or when it has no attributions or they are exercised in a way that the harm caused or that can be caused would be irreparable through any other mean of defense.

e) When in administrative activities the affected party is compelled to accomplish unreasonable or illegal formalities, task or activities, or when no suppressive mean or recourse exists;

f) When the petitions or formalities before administrative authorities are not resolved in the delay fixed by statutes, or in case that no delay exists, in a delay of 30 days once exhausted the procedure, or when the petitions are not admitted;

g) In political matters, when the rights recognized in the Constitution or statutes, are injured by political organizations;

h) In judicial and administrative matters, regarding which the statutes set forth procedures and recourses according to due process rules that can serve to adequately resolve them, if after the exhaustion of recourses by the interested party, the threat, restriction or violation to the rights recognized in the Constitution and guarantied by the statute, persist;

Article 263 of the Constitution and Article 82 of the Amparo Law also regulate the right to *habeas corpus* in favor of anyone who is illegally arrested, detained or in any other way prevented from enjoying personal freedom, threatened with losing such freedom, or suffering humiliation, even when their imprisonment or detention is legally founded. In such cases, the affected party has the right to request his immediate personal appearance (*habeas corpus*) before the court, either for his constitutional guarantee of freedom to be reinstated, for the humiliations to cease, or to terminate the duress to which was being subjected.

Pursuant to Articles 11 *et seq.* of the 1986 Law of Amparo, the competence to hear the amparo is attributed to all courts as follows:

1. To the *Constitutional Court*, as sole instance, in the cases of amparo brought against the Congress of the Republic, the Supreme Court of Justice, the President and the Vice President of the Republic (Article 11).
2. To the *Supreme Court of Justice*, in the cases of amparo brought against the Supreme Electoral Tribunal; Ministers or Vice Ministers of State when acting in the name of their Office; Chambers of the Courts of Appeal, Martial Courts, Courts of Second Instance of Accounts and Administrative judicial review Courts; the Attorney General; the Human Rights Commissioner; the Monetary Board; Ambassadors or Heads of Diplomatic Guatemalan Missions abroad; and the National Council of Urban and Rural Development.
3. To the ordinary Chambers of the *Court of Appeals*, in their respective jurisdictions, the amparos against: Vice Ministers of State and Director–Generals; judicial officials of any jurisdiction or branch of first instance; mayors and municipal corporations of departmental centers; the Head of the Comptroller General; the managers, heads or presidents of decentralized or autonomous State entities or their directors, councils or boards of directors of any kind; the Director–General of the Peoples' Registry; general assemblies and directors of professional associations; general assemblies and di-

rectors of political parties; consuls or heads of Guatemalan consulates overseas; regional or departmental councils of urban and rural development, and governors.

4. The *Judges of First Instance* in their respective jurisdictions, for amparos against: revenue administrators; minor judges; police chiefs and employees; mayors and municipal corporations not included in the previous article; all other officials, authorities and employees of any jurisdiction or branch not specified in previous articles; and private law entities.

The competent courts in matters of habeas corpus are the same mentioned above, except regarding the attributions assigned to the Constitutional Court that corresponds to the Supreme Court of Justice (Article 83).

In all the cases, amparo decisions are subjected to appeal before the Constitutional Court (Art 60), recourse that can be filed by the parties, the Public prosecutor and the Human Rights Commissioner (Article 63).

The Constitutional Court in its decision can confirm, revoke or modify the lower court resolution (Art. 67); and can also annul the whole proceeding when it is proved that in the proceedings the legal prescription had not been observed.

The judicial review system of Guatemala is also a mixed system, in which the Constitutional Court plays a principal role.

The Constitutional Court by means of the concentrated method of judicial review is empowered to hear actions of unconstitutionality against statutes, regulations or general dispositions (Article 133), that can be brought before the Court by the board of directors of the Lawyer's (Bar) Association (Colegio de Abogados), the Public prosecutor; the Human Rights Commissioner; or by any person with the help of three lawyers members of the Bar (Article 134). The statutes, regulations or general dispositions declared unconstitutional, will cease in their effects from the following day after the publication of the Constitutional Court decisions in the Official Gazette (Article 140). Thus, the Constitutional Court's decision has *erga omnes* effects.

But besides the Constitutional Court powers following the concentrated method of judicial review, in Guatemala the diffuse method of judicial review of legislation has also been traditionally set forth, derived from the principle of the supremacy of the Constitution. That is why Article 115 of the Amparo Law declared that all "statutes, governmental dispositions or any order regulating the exercise of rights guaranteed in the Constitution, shall be null and void if they violate, diminish, restrict or distort them. No statute can contravene the Constitution's disposition. The statutes that violate or distort the constitutional norms are null and void.

The consequence of this principles is the possibility of the parties to raise in any concrete case (including cases of amparo and habeas corpus), before any court, at any instance or in cassation, before the decision is issued, as an action or as an exception or incident, the question of the unconstitutionality of the statute in order to its inapplicability to the concrete case be declared (Article 116). In such cases, once raised the constitutional question before any court, it assumes the character of constitutional tribunal (Art. 120).

In cases of action of unconstitutionality in concrete cases, it can be brought before the competent court by the Public prosecutor or by the parties in 9 days. The court must decide in three days, and the decision can be appealed before the Constitutional Courts (Article 121). If the question of unconstitutionality of a statute supporting the claim is raised has an exception or incident, the competent court must resolve the matter (Article 123). The decision can also be appealed before the Constitutional court (Article 130).

F. *The recourse of amparo in Perú*

Article 200 of the Peruvian Constitution sets forth the action of *habeas corpus* against any action or omission by any authority, official or person that impairs or threatens individual freedom; the action of amparo to protect all other rights recognized by the Constitution impaired or threatened by any authority, official or person; and the action of *habeas data*, against any act or omission by any authority, official or person that impairs or threatens the rights referred to in Article 2, Subsections 5 and 6 of the Constitution; that is, to request and receive information from any public office, except when they affect personal intimacy or were excluded for national security; to assure that public or private informatics services will not release information that affects personal and familiar intimacy.

In 2004 the first Constitutional Procedural Code in Latin America was sanctioned in Peru (Law 28.237)[408], which repealed the previous statutes regulating the amparo and the habeas corpus recourses (Law 23.506 of 1982, and Law 25.398 of 1991).

This Code highlights the purposes of the habeas corpus, habeas data and amparo guaranties, which is to protect the constitutional rights, in order to restore things to the state they had previous to the violation or threat of violation of constitutional rights, or dispose the accomplishment of a legal order or of an administrative act (Article 1).

According to Article 2 of the Code, the constitutional remedies of habeas corpus, amparo and habeas data are admissible when the constitutional rights are threatened or violated by actions or obligatory acts omissions from any authority, public official or person. In case of a threat being invoked, it must be of certain and imminent execution.

The competent courts to hear the amparo recourses are the Civil Courts with jurisdiction on the place where the right was affected, or of the plaintiff or defendant residence (Article 51). But if the harm has been caused by a judicial decision, the amparo must be filed before the Civil Chamber of the respective Superior Court of Justice.

According to the same Code, the amparo shall only be admitted when previous procedures have been exhausted (Articles 5,4; 45). However, in case of doubt over

408 See: Samuel B. ABAD YUPANQUI *et al.*, *Código Procesal Constitucional*, Ed. Palestra, Lima 2004. See (in general): Alberto BOREA ODRIA, *Las garantías constitucionales: Habeas Corpus y* Amparo, Libros Peruanos S.A., Lima 1992; Alberto BOREA ODRÍA, *El* amparo *y el Hábeas Corpus en el Perú de Hoy,* Lima, 1985.

the exhausting of prior procedures, the Code requires that the amparo suit be given preference (Article 45).

Regarding the habeas corpus recourse, the competent judges are the Criminal ones (Article 28).

According to Article 202,2 of the Constitution, it is attributed to the Constitutional Tribunal the power to hear in last and definitive instance, the judicial decisions denying the habeas corpus, amparo and habeas data. Thus, all the habeas corpus, habeas data and amparo decisions can reach the Constitutional Tribunal of Perú, by means of a recourse of constitutional damage (*agravio*) that can be filed against the second instance judicial decision denying the claim (Article 18, Code). If this constitutional damage recourse is denied, the interested party can file before the Constitutional Tribunal a recourse of complaint (*queja*), in which case, if the Tribunal considered the complaint duly supported, it will the proceed to decide the constitutional damage recourse, asking from the superior court the envoy of the corresponding files (Article 19).

If the Constitutional Tribunal considers that the challenged judicial decision has been issued as a consequence of a defect or vice in the procedure that has affected its sense, will annul it and order the reposition of the procedure to the situation previous to when the defect happened. In cases in which the vice only affects the challenged decision, the Tribunal must repeal it and issue a substantive ruling (Article 20).

This Constitutional Tribunal of Peru, reinstalled in 1996, plays a very important role in the judicial review system, which nevertheless, is a mixed one, combining the diffuse system of judicial review with the concentrated one attributed to the Tribunal[409].

Article 138 of the 1993 Constitution sets forth the diffuse method of judicial review, providing:

> **Article 138**. The power to administer justice derives from the people and is exercised by the Judiciary, through its hierarchical organs according to the Constitution and the statutes. In any process, if an incompatibility exists between a constitutional norm and a legal norm, the

409 See in general Domingo GARCÍA BELAÚNDE, "La jurisdicción constitucional en Perú" en Domingo GARCÍA BELAÚNDE y Francisco FERNÁNDEZ SEGADO (Coord.), *La jurisdicción constitucional en Iberoamérica,* Ed. Dykinson, Madrid, España, 1977; Domingo GARCÍA BELAUNDE, "La jurisdicción constitucional y el modelo dual o paralelo" en *La Justicia Constitucional a fines del siglo XX, Revista del Instituto de Ciencias Políticas y Derecho Constitucional,* año VII, N° 6, Palestra editores, Huancayo, Perú; Domingo GARCÍA BELAUNDE (Coordinador) *La Constitución y su defensa,* Ed Jurídica Grijley, Lima, 2003, p. 96. César LANDA, *Teoría del Derecho procesal Constitucional,* Ed. Palestra, Lima, Perú, 2004; José PALOMINO MANCHEGO, "Control y magistratura constitucional en el Perú" in Juan VEGA GÓMEZ, and Edgar CORZO SOSA (Coordinadores.), *Instrumentos de tutela y justicia constitucional, Memoria del VII Congreso Iberoamericano de Derecho Constitucional,* Instituto de Investigaciones Jurídicas, UNAM, México. Aníbal QUIROGA LEÓN, "El derecho procesal constitucional peruano" en Juan VEGA GÓMEZ y Edgar CORZO SOSA (Coord.) *Instrumentos de tutela y justicia constitucional, Memoria del VII Congreso Iberoamericano de Derecho Constitucional,* Instituto de Investigaciones Jurídicas, UNAM, México, pp. 471 y ss.

courts must prefer the former. Likewise, must prefer the legal norm over the norms with inferior rank.

Thus, all courts can exercise judicial review of legislation in concrete cases, having their decisions in such cases *inter partes* effects[410].

Nonetheless, the Peruvian diffuse method of judicial review has a peculiarity that makes it unique in comparative law because the ordinary judges when deciding the inapplicability to a case of statutes based on constitutional arguments, according to Article 14 of the Organic Law on the Judiciary, must obligatorily send its decision to the Supreme Court of Justice. It is then the Supreme Court, through its Constitutional Law and Social Chamber, the one that eventually determines if the decision of the ordinary court was adequate or not, validating the non applicability of the statute to the concrete case.

But additional to the diffuse method of judicial review, in Peru a concentrated method is also set forth by attributing the Constitutional Tribunal the power to hear in unique instance the actions of unconstitutionality (Article 202,1) regarding norms of legal rank (statutes), legislative decrees, urgency decrees, treaties approved by Congress, Congress internal regulations, regional norms and municipal ordinances (Art. 77, Code).

This action can be brought before the Tribunal by: 1. The President of the Republic; 2. The Prosecutor General of the nation; 3. The Peoples defendant; 4. By a number equivalent to 25% of representatives to the Congress; 5. By 5.000 citizen whose signatures must be validated by the National Jury of Elections. If it is a local government regulation the action can be filed by 1% of the citizens of the corresponding; 6. The presidents of Regions with the vote of the Regional Coordinating Councils, or the provincial mayors with the vote of the local Councils, in matter of their jurisdiction; and 7. The professional associations *(Colegios)* in matters of their specialty (Article 203; Article 99 Code).

The decision of the Constitutional Tribunal, in these cases of the concentrated method of judicial review when declaring the unconstitutionality of a norm, must be published in the Official Gazzette. The day after such publication the statute will began to have no effects, and the decision of the Constitutional Tribunal will have no retroactive effects (Article 204). Thus, the decision has *erga omnes* and *ex nunc* effects, and the authority of *res judicata*, being obligatory to all public entities (Articles 81, 82 Code).

410 See Aníbal QUIROGA LEÓN, "Control difuso y control concentrado en el derecho procesal peruano" en *Revista Derecho* N° 50, diciembre de 1996, Facultad de Derecho de la Pontificia Universidad Católica del Perú, Lima, Perú, 1996, pp. 207 ff.

CHAPTER VII.

THE JUSTICIABLE CONSTITUTIONAL RIGHTS BY MEANS OF THE "AMPARO" AND HABEAS CORPUS ACTIONS

I. CONSTITUTIONAL RIGHTS AND JUSTICIABILITY

Justiciability is the quality or state of being appropriate or suitable for review by a court[411]. Regarding specific Latin American actions for protection of constitutional rights, justiciability is the quality of a right of being suitable to be protected.

Amparo and habeas corpus recourses are specific constitutional means set forth in the Constitutions for the protection of constitutional rights. Consequently, not all individual rights are justiciable by means of the amparo and habeas corpus recourses; but only certain rights, those enshrined in the Constitution what places them out of reach from the Legislative branch of government. There lays the importance that in the Latin American systems of judicial protection constitutional declarations of human rights have; and also lays one of the main differences between the North American injunction remedies and the Latin American amparo.

Both are extraordinary remedies, but injunctions are equitable remedies that can be filed for the protection of any personal or property rights, even those of statutory origin, provided that they cannot be effectively protected by ordinary common law courts. Amparo, on the contrary, is an action that can only be filed for the protection of rights of constitutional origin and rank.

The consequence of the need of constitutional rank for a right to be justiciable by means of amparo and habeas corpus is that the rights that are only set in statutes and other lower rank norms cannot be protected by mean of amparo and habeas corpus, and it is thus compulsory to seek their judicial protection by means of the ordinary remedies.

In this regard, the system on the United States can be mentioned regarding the protection of social rights that are not declared in the Constitution and that their character of fundamental right have been denied by the Supreme Court, as it is the case of the right to education, or to have a dwelling. For instance, all were referred in the case *San Antonio Independent School District et al. v. Rodriguez et al.*, 411 U.S. 1; 93 S. Ct. 1278; 36 L. Ed. 2d 16; (1973), decided by the Supreme Court on March 21, 1973, in which it was ruled that though education "is one of the most important services performed by the State (as was ruled in *Brown v. Bord of Education*), it is not within the limited category of rights recognized by this Court as guaranteed by the Constitution", thus denying such right the quality of "fundamental

411 Brian A. GARNER (Editor in Chief), *Black's Law Dictionary,* Wets Group, St. Paul, Minn. 2001., p. 391.

right". The decision was issued as a result of the attack to the Texas system of financing public education by Mexican–American parents whose children attend the elementary and secondary schools in an urban school district in San Antonio, Texas. They brought a class action on behalf of school children throughout the State who are members of minority groups or who are poor and reside in school districts having a low property tax base

The Court considered that:

> "[The] financing system did not impinge upon any fundamental right protected by the Constitution, so as to require application of the strict judicial scrutiny test under which a compelling state interest must be shown, since education, notwithstanding its undisputed importance, is not a right afforded explicit or implicit protection by the Constitution; even assuming that some identifiable quantum of education is a constitutionally protected prerequisite to the meaningful exercise of the right of free speech and the right to vote, nevertheless the strict judicial scrutiny rule is not applicable where the state's financing system does not occasion an absolute denial of educational opportunities to any of its children, and where there is no indication or charge that the system fails to provide each child with an opportunity to acquire the basic minimal skills necessary for the enjoyment of the rights of speech and of full participation in the political process".

In support of this decision, the Court referred to the case *Lindsaey v. Normet*, 405 U.S. 56 (1972) decided only the year before, in which it "firmly reiterates that social importance is not the critical determinant for subjecting state legislation to strict scrutiny" In that case, which denies constitutional rank to the right to have dwelling, the matter referred to the procedural limitations imposed on tenants in suits brought by landlords under Oregon's Forcible Entry and Wrongful Detainer Law. The tenants argued that the statutory limitations implied "fundamental interests which are particularly important to the poor," such as the "'need for decent shelter'" and the "'right to retain peaceful possession of one's home.'" The Supreme Court in the reference to this case, highlighted the following analysis made by Mr. Justice White, in his opinion for the Court, as instructive:

> "We do not denigrate the importance of decent, safe, and sanitary housing. But the Constitution does not provide judicial remedies for every social and economic ill. We are unable to perceive in that document any constitutional guarantee of access to dwellings of a particular quality or any recognition of the right of a tenant to occupy the real property of his landlord beyond the term of his lease, without the payment of rent... Absent constitutional mandate, the assurance of adequate housing and the definition of landlord–tenant relationships are legislative, not judicial, functions."

In a similar way, the court in its decision also referred to the case of *Dandridge v. Williams*, 397 U.S. 471 (1970), arguing that the Court's explicit recognition of the fact that the "administration of public welfare assistance . . . involves the most basic economic needs of impoverished human beings" provided no basis for departing from the settled mode of constitutional analysis of legislative classifications involving questions of economic and social policy. The Court then concluded that:

> "As in the case of housing, the central importance of welfare benefits to the poor was not an adequate foundation for requiring the State to justify its law by showing some compelling state interest. The Court refused to apply the strict–scrutiny test despite its contemporaneous

recognition in *Goldberg v. Kelly*, 397 U.S. 354,364 (1970) that "welfare provides the means to obtain essential food, clothing, housing, and medical care."

The lesson of these cases in addressing the question now before the Court is plain. It is not the province of this Court to create substantive constitutional rights in the name of guaranteeing equal protection of the laws. Thus, the key to discovering whether education is "fundamental" is not to be found in comparisons of the relative societal significance of education as opposed to subsistence or housing. Nor is it to be found by weighing whether education is as important as the right to travel. Rather, the answer lies in assessing whether there is a right to education explicitly or implicitly guaranteed by the Constitution.

Regarding the Latin American countries, there is no doubt regarding the constitutional rank of such rights, being the amparo the judicial mean for the protection of them, as rights declared in the Constitutions. Thus, when the Bolivian Amparo Law set forth that the amparo is devoted to protect rights and guaranties "recognized in the Constitution and the laws" (Article 94); the reference to "laws" must not be interpreted as an alternative (Constitution " or "laws), but in an accumulatively (Constitution and the laws). In the case of Guatemala, if it is true that Article 1 of the Amparo law refers to "rights inherent to persons protected by the Constitution, the laws and international agreements ratified by Guatemala", including "laws", it only refers to amparo as a "constitutional guaranty of defense"; thus, based on constitutional reasons.

II. AMPARO FOR THE JUSTICIABILITY OF CONSTITUTIONAL RIGHTS ONLY IN CASES OF CONSTITUTIONAL VIOLATIONS

Consequently, even in cases of rights enshrined in the Constitution, the amparo recourse is only admissible when the constitutional provision referred to the right has been violated.

Thus, it is not possible to file an action of amparo just basing it in the violation of the statutory provisions which regulate the right. It is, for instance, the case of property rights, widely regulated in the Civil Codes, regarding which all the conducts affecting those regulations in general terms had their own ordinary remedies. One example is the civil injunctions set forth in the Civil Code and the Civil Procedure Codes for the immediate protection of possession rights in cases of trespasses (*interdictos*) which are effective judicial remedies for the protection of a land owner or occupant rights. Thus, in cases of property trespass, the *interdicto of amparo* or of new construction are effective means for protection, and no amparo action can be filed in such cases.

As was decided by the Constitutional Chamber of the Supreme Tribunal of Justice of Venezuela,

"The amparo action protects one aspect of the legal situations of persons referred to their fundamental rights, corresponding the defense of subjective rights –different to fundamental rights and public liberties– to the ordinary administrative and judicial recourses and actions. For instance, it is not the same to deny a citizen the condition to have property rights, than to discuss property rights between parties, the protection of which corresponds to a specific judicial action of recovery (*reivindicación*). But if the right to defend its property means the denial of a fundamental right, then the proprietor is denied of his right, and must be protected.

> This means that in the amparo proceedings the court judge the actions of public entities or Individuals that can harm fundamental rights; but in no case can it review, for instance, the applicability or interpretation or ordinary law by the Administration or the courts, unless than from them a direct violation of the Constitution can be deducted. The amparo is not a new judicial instance, nor the substitution of ordinary judicial means for the protection of rights and interest; it is the reaffirmation of constitutional values, by mean of which the court hearing an amparo can decide regarding the contents or the application of constitutional provisions regulating fundamental rights, can review the interpretation made by public administration or judicial bodies, or determine if the facts from which constitutional violations are deducted constitute a direct violation of the Constitution"[412].

This relates the subject, of course, to the general condition of the extraordinary character of the amparo action, in the sense that it can only be filed when no other appropriate and effective ordinary judicial means of protection are legally provided. This condition is set forth in a similar way to the "inadequacy" condition provided for the equitable injunction remedies in North America, in the sense that they are only admissible when there is no adequate remedy at law[413].

This inadequacy, of course, can result from the factual situations that impede granting the protection as was resolved since the well know case of *Wheelock v. Nooman* (NY 1888), in which an injunction was granted to require the defendant to remove great boulders which he had left on the plaintiff's property beyond the terms of the license to do so. The plaintiff in the case could not easily remove the boulders and sued the cost of removal of the trespassing rocks because of their size and weight[414]. On the contrary, the remedy at law is adequate if the defendant left litter on the property because the plaintiff can pay for someone to remove the trash and then sue the defendant for the cost incurred, as was decided in *Connor v. Grosso* (Cal. 1953)[415].

But in other cases in the United States, the extraordinary character of the injunctive remedies derives from the fact that the law cannot provide an adequate remedy because of the nature of the right involved, which was the case of the constitutional claims in the case of school segregation which violated rights that require equitable intervention.

It is because of this nature of the rights that can be protected by means of amparo, as constitutional rights, that this specific action for protection can only be filed when the Constitution is directly infringed.

The Venezuelan First Court on Judicial Review of Administrative action Jurisdiction, in a decision of December 6, 1989, issued just after the Amparo Law was sanctioned (1988), fixed this doctrine, as follows:

---

412 Decision Nº 828 of July, 27, 2000 (case: *Seguros Corporativos (SEGUCORP), C.A. et al. vs. Superintedencia* de *Seguros*), in *Revista de Derecho Público*, Nº 83, Editorial Jurídica Venezolana, Caracas 2000, pp. 290 ff.

413 See Owen M. FISS and Doug RENDLEMAN, *Injunctions*, 2d Ed, The Foundation Press, Mineola, New Cork, 1984, p. 59.

414 See the reference in William M. TAB and Elaine W. SHOBEN, Remedies in a Nutshell, Thomson West, St. Paul, 2005, p. 24.

415 *Idem.*

> The amparo is admissible only in cases of violations of constitutional rights and guaranties. These rights and guaranties can be regulated in norms of inferior rank, but those are not the norms that can be alleged as violated, and reference must be made to the text that originates them. The extraordinary character of the amparo impedes that through it, the fulfillment or regulations and conditions set forth in statutory norms, those matters that can be discussed by other ordinary means be argued. If it were not conceived like this, the amparo jurisdiction would substitute any other, and the critics and fear would be raised by this new institution"[416].

Of course, and even if the constitutional right and guaranty can be regulated through statutory norms, the amparo action cannot be founded in the sole violation of such statutory provisions. As was subsequently ruled by the Supreme Court of Venezuela in decision of August 14, 1990, the amparo can only be filed because of direct and immediate contraventions of constitutional rights and guaranties; and for that purpose:

> It is necessary to demonstrate the sole harm to such norms and not to others of infra constitutional character. Thus, the action for amparo, is always of constitutional nature, it is justified in the measure that the rights or guaranties harmed or threatened are of such same rank. In conclusion, it is not enough to allege the violation of inferior rank norms, which are not the ones to be protected by amparo but for other means. Even if they apply constitutional provisions, it is indispensable, and also enough, to demonstrate the direct violation of a constitutional provision"[417] .

Consequently, as a matter of principle, all constitutional rights and guaranties are justiciable by mean of the amparo recourse, provided that the Constitution is directly infringed, notwithstanding the right to also be regulated by statutes. That is why, for instance, the Peruvian Code on Constitutional Jurisdiction is precise when it sets that the "amparo shall not be admitted in defense of a right that lacks direct constitutional founding or when it is does not directly refer to the protected constitutional aspects of such right." (Articles 5,1 and 38), which confirms the already mentioned principle of the amparo protection only regarding the violation of the Constitution provisions regarding the rights.

---

416 See in *Revista de Derecho Público,* N° 41, Editorial Jurídica Venezolana, Caracas, 1990, p. 99. This doctrine has been followed by the First Court on Judicial review of Adminsitrative action in the decisions of August 22, 1990 in FUNEDA *15 años de Jurisprudencia, op. cit., p.* 138; of September 16, 1992, in *Revista de Derecho Público,* N° 51, Editorial Jurídica Venezolana, Caracas, 1992, p. 151; ando f December 4, 1992, in *Revista de Derecho Público,* N° 52, Editorial Jurídica Venezolana, Caracas, p. 165 and in FUNEDA, *15 años de Jurisprudencia, op. cit., p.* 140.

417 See in *Revista de Derecho Público,* N° 44, Editorial Jurídica Venezolana, Caracas, 1990 p. 143. See also, Supreme Court of Justice decisions (Politico Adminsitrative Chamber) of November 8, 1990, in *Revista de Derecho Público,* N° 44, Editorial Jurídica Venezolana, Caracas, 1990, p. 141; of April 4, 1990, in *Revista de Derecho Público,* N° 42, Editorial Jurídica Venezolana, Caracas, 1990; p. 112; of January 31, 1989, *Revista de Derecho Público* N° 37, Editorial Jurídica Venezolana, Caracas, 198, p; of August 14, 1989, in *Revista de Derecho Público,* N° 39, Editorial Jurídica Venezolana, Caracas, 1989, p. 144; of March 4, 1993, in *Revista de Derecho Público,* nos 53–54, Editorial Jurídica Venezolana, Caracas, 1993, p. 254; ando f the First Court on Judicial Reviwe of Administrative Action of September 7, 1992, in FUNEDA en *15 años de Jurisprudencia, op. cit.,* p. 127.

III. AMPARO AND HABEAS CORPUS FOR THE PROTECTION OF ALL CONSTITUTIONAL RIGHTS

Almost all Latin American countries set forth the habeas corpus recourse for the protection of personal freedom and safety, and the amparo recourse for the protection of all the other constitutional rights and guarantees. The only exception in this pattern, are Mexico and Venezuela, where the personal freedom and safety are also protected through the general amparo suit or action, being thus the habeas corpus only a kind or a specie of the amparo. On the contrary, in all others Latin American Countries the habeas corpus is regulated as a separate action or recourse for the specific protection of personal freedom and safety.

The reason for the Mexican and Venezuelan exception is, precisely, the conception that those countries have of the amparo as a constitutional right and not exclusively as an adjective mean for protection of human rights.

But what is important regarding the amparo and habeas corpus recourses, is that in almost all the Latin American countries, by means of a general amparo suit or action or of both, amparo and habeas corpus recourses or actions, all constitutional rights are protected, without any exception. The exception in this regard are the countries where the amparo has been reduced to protect only certain constitutional rights, as is the case of the "tutela" action in Colombia and of the action for protection in Chile, conceived only for the protection of some constitutional rights qualified as "fundamental" or enumerated in the constitutional text. It is also the case of Mexico, where the amparo suit is established for the protection of only the "individual guarantees".

Thus two general systems can be distinguish in Latin America regarding the amparo: those in which all constitutional rights and guaranties can be protected through the amparo and habeas corpus recourse; and those where the amparo recourse is directed to protect only some constitutional rights, those qualified as "fundamental rights" or " individual guarantees".

In the first system, the rights protected in principle are those enshrined in the Constitutions, thus the use of the expression "constitutional rights", in order, first, to comprise the rights enumerated in the constitutional texts; second, those that even not being enumerated in the Constitutions are inherent to human beings; and third, those enumerated in the international instruments on human rights ratified by the State. In the words of the Argentinean Amparo Law (Article 1) and in the Uruguayan 1988 Amparo Law (Article 72), the constitutional protection refers to the rights and freedoms "expressly or implicitly recognized by the Constitution"

Is the case of Venezuela, where the action of amparo is conceived as a means for the protection of the enjoyment and practice of absolutely all the constitutional rights and guarantees, as well as those inherent to human beings not enumerated in the Constitution or in the international instruments on human rights; the expression "instruments" comprising not only treaties, conventions and covenants but also declarations. This is what is expressly set forth in Article 27 of the Constitution.

Consequently, all constitutional rights listed in Title III (Human Rights, Guarantees and Duties) of the Constitution as the citizenship rights, the civil (individual) rights, the political rights, the social and family rights, the cultural and educational rights, the economic rights, the environmental rights and the indigenous people rights, can be protected by means of the amparo action (Articles 19–129). And additionally, other rights and guaranties derived from other constitutional provisions not included in Title III on "Human Rights, Guarantees and Duties", like the constitutional guarantee of the independence of the Judiciary[418], or the constitutional guarantee to the legality of taxation (that taxes can only by set forth by statute)[419], can also be protected by means of amparo.

But as aforementioned, the amparo action in Venezuela is also admissible for the protection of all "constitutional rights and guaranties, even those inherent to persons that are not expressly enumerated in the Constitution or in international instruments on human rights" (Art. 27, Constitution). This declaration leaves no loophole regarding right or guarantee to be constitutionally protected; particularly because of the open clause enshrined in Article 22 of the Constitution.

This clause, extensively used by the Latin American supreme courts to identity rights and guaranties not expressly listed in the Constitution, has its antecedent in the IX Amendment of the United States Constitution, even though, in contrast, in the United States the Supreme Court has had little occasion to interpret it. One of the few cases, though, is the case *Griswold v. Connecticut* decided on June 7, 1965, 381 U.S. 479; 85 S. Ct. 1678; 14 L. Ed. 2d 510; 1965[420], in which Justice Goldberg, delivering the opinion of the Court, held the unconstitutionality of the Connecticut's birth–control law because it intruded upon the right of marital privacy, which was considered as embraced by the concept of liberty, even if it was not explicitly mentioned in the Constitution. The Court based its ruling precisely on the Ninth Amendment to the Constitution, declaring that:

> To hold that a right so basic and fundamental and so deep–rooted in our society as the right of privacy in marriage may be infringed because that right is not guaranteed in so many words by the first eight amendments to the Constitution is to ignore the **Ninth Amendment** and to give it no effect whatsoever. Moreover, a judicial construction that this fundamental right is not protected by the Constitution because it is not mentioned in explicit terms by one of the first eight amendments or elsewhere in the Constitution would violate the **Ninth Amendment,** which specifically states that "the enumeration in the Constitution, of certain rights, shall not be construed to deny or disparage others retained by the people
>
> Rather, the **Ninth Amendment** shows a belief of the Constitution's authors that fundamental rights exist that are not expressly enumerated in the first eight amendments and an intent that the list of rights included there not be deemed exhaustive. As any student of this Court's opinions knows, this Court has held, often unanimously, that the Fifth and Fourteenth Amendments protect certain fundamental personal liberties from abridgment by the Federal

---

418 Decision of the former Supreme Court of Justice, Political Administrative Chamber, dated march, 25, 1994 (Case *Arnoldo Echegaray*).

419 See Allan R. BREWER–CARÍAS, "Derecho y Acci6n de Amparo", *Instituciones Políticas y Constitucionales,* Vol. V., Caracas, 1998, pp. 209 y ss. See decision of the First Court on judicial review of Administrative Action, case *Fecadove*. See the reference in Rafael CHAVERO G, *El Nuevo régimen del amparo constitucional en Venezuela*, Caracas, 2001, p. 157.

420 U.S. LEXIS 2282

> Government or the States. See, e. g., Bolling v. Sharpe, 347 U.S. 497; Aptheker v. Secretary of State, 378 U.S. 500; Kent v. Dulles, 357 U.S. 116; Cantwell v. Connecticut, 310 U.S. 296; NAACP v. Alabama, 357 U.S. 449; Gideon v. Wainwright, 372 U.S. 335; New York Times Co. v. Sullivan, 376 U.S. 254. The **Ninth Amendment** simply shows the intent of the Constitution's authors that other fundamental personal rights should not be denied such protection or disparaged in any other way simply because they are not specifically listed in the first eight constitutional amendments...
>
> In sum, the **Ninth Amendment** simply lends strong support to the view that the "liberty" protected by the Fifth and Fourteenth Amendments from infringement by the Federal Government or the States is not restricted to rights specifically mentioned in the first eight amendments. *Cf.* United Public Workers v. Mitchell, 330 U.S. 75, 94–95.
>
> In determining which rights are fundamental, judges are not left at large to decide cases in light of their personal and private notions. Rather, they must look to the "traditions and [collective] conscience of our people" to determine whether a principle is "so rooted [there] . . . as to be ranked as fundamental." Snyder v. Massachusetts, 291 U.S. 97, 105. The inquiry is whether a right involved "is of such a character that it cannot be denied without violating those 'fundamental principles of liberty and justice which lie at the base of all our civil and political institutions' . . . ." Powell v. Alabama, 287 U.S. 45, 67. "Liberty" also "gains content from the emanations of . . . specific [constitutional] guarantees" and "from experience with the requirements of a free society." Poe v. Ullman, 367 U.S. 497, 517.

The Court thus concluded that:

> "The entire fabric of the Constitution and the purposes that clearly underlie its specific guarantees demonstrate that the rights to marital privacy and to marry and raise a family are of similar order and magnitude as the fundamental rights specifically protected. Although the Constitution does not speak in so many words of the right of privacy in marriage, I cannot believe that it offers these fundamental rights no protection. The fact that no particular provision of the Constitution explicitly forbids the State from disrupting the traditional relation of the family –a relation as old and as fundamental as our entire civilization– surely does not show that the Government was meant to have the power to do so. Rather, as the **Ninth Amendment** expressly recognizes, there are fundamental personal rights such as this one, which are protected from abridgment by the Government though not specifically mentioned in the Constitution."

In sum, the Supreme Court concluded affirming that "the right of privacy in the marital relation is fundamental and basic a personal right retained by the people" within the meaning of the Ninth Amendment", thus considering unconstitutional the Connecticut law that prohibits the use of contraceptives.

The application of open clause on human rights in Venezuela, similar to the Ninth Amendment, has already been analyzed, expanding the scope of the constitutional rights protected by means of amparo. The same has happened in the other Latin American Countries, which had developed both the amparo and habeas corpus recourses for the protection of all human rights declared in the Constitutions and in the International Treaties.

Is the case of Costa Rica, where Article 48 of the Constitution is absolutely clear when it guarantees the right of every person to file the action of habeas corpus to guarantee their freedom and personal integrity and the action for amparo to maintain or reestablish the enjoyment of all other rights conferred by this Constitution as well as those of a fundamental nature established in international instruments on human rights, enforceable in the Republic. In the same sense it is regulated in the Ecuadorian Law where amparo is set for "the judicial effective protection of all rights enshrined in the Constitution and those contained in the declarations, covenants, conventions and other international instruments in force in Ecuador (Article 46).

Other legislations, in order to precise the extension of the constitutional amparo and habeas corpus protection, tend to be exhaustive in the listing of the constitutional rights to be protected, as is the case of Peru. For instance, when distinguishing the amparo and habeas corpus actions, the Constitutional Procedure Code (Law 28.237 of 2004) expressly lists and identifies the following rights as protected by mean of the *habeas corpus*:

1. Personal integrity and the right not to be submitted to torture or inhuman or humiliating treatment, nor coerced to obtain declarations.
2. The right not to be forced to render oaths nor be compelled to declare or recognize their own guilt, that of their spouse, or their family members up to the fourth level of consanguinity or second of affinity.
3. The right not to be exiled or banished or confined except by final judicial decision.
4. The right not to be expatriated nor kept away from one's residence except by legal order or by application of the Immigration Law.
5. The right of the foreigner to whom political asylum has been granted, not to be expelled from the country to the country that is persecuting him, or under no circumstance if his freedom or safety is in danger through being expelled.
6. The right of nationals or resident foreigners to enter, transit or leave national territory, except by legal order or application of the Immigration or Health Law.
7. The right not to be detained except by written and justified judicial order, or by the police forces for having committed a flagrant crime; or if he or she has been detained, to be brought before the corresponding Court within 24 hours or as soon as possible.
8. The right to voluntarily decide to render military service, pursuant to the law governing such matter.
9. The right not to be arrested for debt.
10. The right not to be deprived of the national identity document, or to obtain a passport or its renewal within the Republic or overseas.
11. The right not to be held incommunicado, except in those cases established under the Constitution (Article 2, 24, g).
12. The right to be assisted by a freely chosen defense lawyer at the moment of being summonsed or arrested by the police or other authority, without exception.
13. The right to have removed the surveillance of one's domicile or suspended police trailing, when arbitrary and unjustified.
14. The right of the person on trial or condemned to be released from jail, if his or her freedom has been decided by a judge.
15. The right to have the correct procedure observed in the case of the processing or detention of persons, pursuant to Article 99 of the Constitution.
16. The right not to be subject to a forced disappearance.
17. The right of the person under arrest or imprisoned not to be subject to treatment that is unreasonable or disproportional, in respect of the form and conditions in which the order of detention or imprisonment is carried out.

The article adds that "*habeas corpus* shall also be admitted in defense of constitutional rights associated with individual freedom, especially when due process and the inviolability of the home are concerned."

As far as the action of amparo is concerned, pursuant to the same Peruvian Code on Constitutional Procedure, such action shall be admitted in defense of the following rights expressly listed in article 37:

1. To equality and not to be discriminated because of origin, sex, race, sexual orientation, religion, opinion, economic or social condition, language or any other;
2. To publicly exercise any religious creed;
3. To information, opinion and expression;
4. To contract freely;
5. To the artistic, intellectual and scientific creation;
6. To the inviolability and secrecy of private documents and communications;
7. To assembly;
8. To honor, intimacy, voice, image and to the rectification of incorrect or harmful information;
9. To associate;
10. To work;
11. To unionize, collectively bargain and go on strike;
12. To property and to inherit;
13. To petition before the competent authority;
14. To participate individually and collectively in the political life of the country;
15. To citizenship;
16. To effective judicial protection;
17. To education and the right of the parents to choose the school and participate in the education of their children;
18. To teach according to constitutional principles;
19. To social security;
20. To compensation and a pension;
21. To the freedom to lecture;
22. To have access to the media, pursuant to Article 35 of the Constitution;
22. To enjoy an environment that is balanced and appropriate for developing one's life;
23. To health; and
24. To others recognized by the Constitution.

Fortunately, the last item referred to all "the other rights recognized in the Constitution" resolves the problems that normally have the practice to list in some statutes, specific situations with the risk of leaving thinks behind.

The Guatemalan Amparo Law also tends to exhaust the cases in which the amparo action can be filed[421], when setting in Article 10 that its admission extends

421 See: Jorge Mario GARCÍA LA GUARDIA, "La Constitución y su defensa en Guatemala", en el libro editado por la UNAM, *La Constitución y su defensa,* México, 1984, pp. 717–719; and *La Constitución Guatemalteca de 1985,* México, 1992.

to any situation that presents a risk, a threat, a restriction or a violation of the rights recognized by "the Constitution and the laws of the Republic of Guatemala", whether such situation is caused by public or private law entities or individuals. Therefore, as it is listed in the same Article 10, every person shall have the right to request amparo, in the following cases, among others:

a) To be maintained or reinstated in the enjoyment of the rights and guarantees established in "the Constitution or any other law".
b) To seek a decision to declare, in specific cases, that a law, regulation, resolution or act of the authorities shall not be enforced against the plaintiff because it contravenes or restricts a right that is guaranteed by "the Constitution or any other law".
c) To seek a decision to declare in specific cases, that a provision or resolution (not merely legislative) of the Congress of the Republic is not applicable to the plaintiff since it violates a constitutional right.
d) When an authority of any jurisdiction issues a regulation, decision or resolution of any kind, abusing its power or exceeding its legal powers, or when such powers are non–existent or exercised in such a way that the harm caused or likely to be caused "cannot be corrected by any other legal means of defense".
e) When in administrative proceedings, the affected party is forced to comply with unreasonable or unlawful requirements, procedures or activities, or when "there is no means or recourse available to suspend their effect".
f) When petitions and procedures before administrative authorities are not resolved in the delay established by law, or, in absence of such delay, within thirty days following the exhaustion of the corresponding procedure; and also when petitions are not admitted for processing.
g) In political matters, when rights recognized by the law or by the by–laws of political organizations are infringed. Nevertheless, in purely electoral matters, the court analysis and examination shall be limited to legal aspects, accepting such questions of fact that are considered proven in the recourse of review.
h) In matters of judicial and administrative order, for which procedures and recourses are established by law, and by means of which such matters may be appropriately discussed in accordance with the legal principle of due process, if after the interested party has made use of the recourses established by law, there is still a threat, restriction or violation of the rights guaranteed by the Constitution and the law.

Even in the cases where this article of the Amparo law refers to rights protected in "the Constitution or the laws", the violation of the right must be a constitutional one. If it is just a legal one, the affected party has the ordinary means for protection, thus the amparo is not admitted when these ordinary means exists.

IV. AMPARO AND HABEAS CORPUS FOR THE PROTECTION OF ONLY SOME CONSTITUTIONAL RIGHTS

As already mentioned, in contrast with the general trend of the Latin American system of amparo and habeas corpus for the protection of all constitutional rights, in the case of Chile and Colombia, the specific action for protection of constitutional rights and freedoms is only established in the Constitution with respect to certain rights and guarantees which are listed as *fundamental*. These systems follow the general trend set by German and Spanish regulations on the amparo recourses.

1. The European antecedents

In Germany, in addition to the abstract judicial review of norms exercised by the Federal Constitutional Tribunal at the request of some State political organs, judicial review can also be exercised by the Constitutional Tribunal as a result of a constitutional complaint or "amparo" recourse that any person can bring before the Tribunal when he claims that one of his basic or fundamental rights has been directly violated by a normative state act. This "constitutional complaint", only constitutionalized in 1969 was originally established in the 1951 Federal Statute of the Constitutional Tribunal (Art. 90. Federal Constitutional Tribunal Law) and was conceived as a specific judicial means for the protection of fundamental rights and freedoms against any action of the state organs which violates them. Therefore, it is not a specific action only directed to obtain judicial review of legislation, but it can be used for that purpose, when exercised against a statute.

The constitutional complaint after the 1969 constitutional amendment is expressly established in Article 93, section 1, N° 4ª of the Constitution when attributing the Federal Constitutional Tribunal power to decide:

> On complaints of unconstitutionality, which may be entered by any person who claims that one of his basic (fundamental) rights or one of his rights under paragraph (4) of article 20, under articles 33, 38, 101, 103, or 104 has been violated by public authority.[422]

Therefore, the constitutional complaint can be brought before the Tribunal against any state act, whether legislative, executive or judicial, but in all cases, it can only be exercised once the ordinary judicial means for the protection of the fundamental rights that have been violated are exhausted (Art. 90, 2 Federal Constitutional Tribunal Law). Consequently, the constitutional complaint is a subordinate mean of judicial protection of fundamental rights,[423] and if there are other judicial recourses or actions that can serve the purpose of protecting fundamental rights, the constitutional complaint is not admissible, except when the Constitutional Tribunal considers the matter as being of general importance or when it considers that the claimant is threatened by a grave and irremediable prejudice if it is sent to the ordinary judicial means for protection (Art. 90, *2* Federal Constitutional Tribunal Law).

The most important feature of the German constitutional complaint, when comparing it with the Latin American amparo, is that it is set in the Constitution only for the protection of the rights listed in Article 93,1 of the Constitution, which are the following:

First, the fundamental rights (*Grundrechte*), enshrined in Articles 1 to 19 of the Constitution, which are the followings:

1. Man's dignity (Art. 1);
2. Freedom to develop its own personality (Art. 2–1);

---

422 See also Arts. 90–96 FCT Law.

423 Art. 19.4 of the Constitution establishes in general that "Should any person's rights be violated by public authority resource to the courts shall be open to him. If jurisdiction is not specified, recourse shall be to the ordinary courts."

3. Right to life and to physical integrity (Art. 2–2);
4. Equality (Art. 3);
5. Ideological and Religion freedom (Art. 4–1);
6. Freedom of cult (Art. 4–2);
7. Conscience objection (Art. 4–3 y Art. 12–a2);
8. Freedom of expression and to inform (Art. 5–1);
9. Freedom to teach and to research (Art. 5–3);
10. Marital freedom, family protection and non discrimination because of extra matrimonial birth (Art. 6);
11. Right to education (Art. 7);
12. Freedom of assembly (Art. 8);
13. Freedom of association (Art. 9);
14. Inviolability of communications secret (Art. 10);
15. Freedom of residence and of movement (Art. 11);
16. Freedom to freely choose a profession and the place of work (Art. 12);
17. Inviolability of domicile (Art. 13);
18. Private property rights and to inherit (Art. 14);
19. Right to German nationality (Art. 16–1);
20. Right to political asylum for aliens (Art. 16–2); and
21. Right to petition (Art. 17).

Additionally, it also can be protected by the constitutional complaint, the constitutional rights enshrined in Articles 20–4, 33, 38, 101, 103 and 104 of the same Constitution, which are the following:

21. Right to resist against who acts against the constitutional order (Art 20–4);
22. Equal rights and obligations of Germans in all Status of the Federation (Art. 33–1);
23. Right to have access in equal terms to public positions (Art. 33–2);
24. Right to vote and to be elected (Art. 38);
25. Prohibition of extraordinary courts and right to "natural judge" (Art. 101);
26. Right to be heard by courts (Art. 103–1);
27 Right to *non bis in ídem* principle (Art. 103–3); and
28 Judicial guarantees for deprivation of liberty (Art. 104).

In all these cases, the constitutional complaint can be exercised directly against a statute or any other normative state act on the grounds that it directly impairs the fundamental rights of the claimant. In that case, it leads directly to the exercise of a judicial review of normative state acts function by the Constitutional Tribunal. As a result of this constitutional complaint, if the statute is considered unconstitutional, it must be declared null (Art. 95, 3, B FCT Law).

The basic condition for the admissibility of constitutional complaints against laws is, of course, the fact that the challenged statute or normative state act, must personally affect the claimant's fundamental rights, in a direct and current way, without the need for any further administrative application of the norm. On the contrary, if this further administrative application is needed, he must wait for the administrative execution of the statute and complain against it. This direct prejudice caused by the normative act on the rights of the claimant, as a basic element for the admissibility of the complain, justifies the delay of one year after its publication established for the introduction of the action before the Tribunal (Art. 93, 1, B FCT Law).

It also explains the power of the Constitutional Tribunal to adopt provisional protective measures regarding the challenged statute, *pendente litis*, in the sense that the Tribunal can even theoretically, suspend the application of the challenged law (Art. 32 FCT Law).

Finally, regarding this constitutional complaint, Article 93, section 1, N° 4b of the Constitution, also empowers the constitutional tribunal to decide:

> On complaints of unconstitutionality, entered by communes (municipalities) or association of communes (municipalities) on the ground that their right to self–government under Article 28 has been violated by a law other than a Lander Law open to complaint to the respective land constitutional court.

Hence, the direct constitutional complaint against laws is not only attributed to individuals for the protection of their fundamental rights, but also to the local government entities, for the protection of their autonomy and right to self–government guaranteed in the Constitution, against federal statutes that could violate them. In these cases, it also results in a direct means of judicial review of statutes of legislation.

The 1978 Spanish Constitution, when setting forth the amparo recourse, in a certain way followed the features of the German constitutional complaint and also, of the amparo recourse originally established in the Republic in the thirties.

Thus, apart from the direct and incidental methods of judicial review, in the Spanish system a recourse of amparo has been created for constitutional protection also of fundamental rights, which can be brought before the Constitutional Tribunal by any person with direct interest in the matter, against state acts of a non legislative character (Art. 161,1,b, Constitution; and Art. 41,2 Organic Law 2/1979)

However, if the recourse for protection is based on the fact that the challenged state act is based on a statute that at the same time infringes fundamental rights or freedoms, the Tribunal must proceed to review its constitutionality through the procedural rules established for the direct action or recourse of unconstitutionality (Art. 52,2 Organic Law 2/1979).

The Spanish recourse of amparo, following the German constitutional complaint features, reduces the constitutional protection to only certain constitutional rights and freedoms also qualified as "fundamental", recognized in Article 14, in the first section of the Second Chapter (Arts. 15 a 20) and in the second paragraph of Article 30 of the Constitution, which are the following:

1. Equality before the law (Art. 14);
2. Right to life and physical and moral integrity (Art. 15);
3. Ideological, religious and freedoms and freedom of cult (Art. 16);
4. Right to personal freedom and safety (Art. 17);

5. Right to honor, personal and familiar intimacy and to one's image Arts. 18–1 and 18–4);
6. Inviolability of domicile (Art. 18–2);
7. Secrecy of communications (Art. 18–3);
8. Right to freely choose one's residence, to move within the territory and to freely leave Spain (Art. 19);
9. Right to freedom of expression and to freely propagate one's thought (Art. 20–1–a);
10. Right to produce and to literary, artistic, scientific and technical creations (Art. 20–1–b);
11. Freedom of teaching (chair) (Art. 20–1–c);
12. Right to communicate and to receive true information by any mean (Art. 20–1–d);
13. Right to meet and to demonstration (Art. 21);
14. Right to association (Art. 22);
15. Right to participate in public affairs (Art. 23–1);
16 Right to equal access to public functions or positions (Art. 23–2);
17. Right to obtain effective protection by courts and judges (Art. 24–1);
18. Right to have the ordinary and predetermined judge, to defense and to be assisted by a lawyer, to be inform of the accusation, to a public process without undue delays and with the guaranties of using the pertinent means of evidence for its defense, not to self incriminate, not to confess culpability and to the presumption of innocence (Art. 24–2;
19. Principle of criminal legality (*nullum crime sine legge*) (Art. 25–1);
20. Rights of the detainees to a pay work and to the benefits of social security, to have access to culture and to the integral development of one's personality (Art. 25–2);
21. Right to education and to the liberty to teach (Art. 27–1);
22. Freedom to create teaching centers, within the constitutional principles (Art. 27–6);
23. Freedom to freely unionized trade (Art. 28–1);
24. Right to strike (Art. 28–2);
25. Right to personal and collective petition (Art. 29); and
26. Right to conscience objection (Art. 30–2).

It must be said that notwithstanding the very ample enumeration of fundamental rights that can be protected by means of the amparo recourse before the Constitutional Tribunal, they are other constitutional rights not protected by the recourse which although constitutional, do not qualify as "fundamental rights".

This limitative approach to the justiciable rights by means of amparo is exceptionally followed in Latin America only in Chile and Colombia.

2. The Chilean "acción de protección" for the protection of some constitutional rights

In Chile, as in the majority of Latin American Countries, constitutional rights are protected by means of the action of habeas corpus, aimed at protecting any individual who is arrested, detained or imprisoned in breach of the Constitution; and by the recourse of protection, which is only aimed at guaranteeing the amparo of determined constitutional rights, in cases of arbitrary or illegal actions or omissions, or of privation, disturbance or threat in the legitimate exercise of the rights and guarantees established in Article 19, numbers 1, 2, 3 (paragraph 4), 4, 5, 6, 9 (final paragraph), 11, 12, 13, 15, 16 of the Constitution regarding to freedom to work and the right of freedom of choice and freedom of contract, and to what is established in the fourth paragraph and numbers 19, 21, 22, 23, 24 and 25. These rights are the following:

1. The right to life and to the physical and psychological integrity (19,1);
2. Equality before the law (19,2);
3. Right to be judged by one's natural judges (19,3);
4. Right to respect for private and public life and the honor of the individual and his family (19,4);
5. Right to the inviolability of home and all forms of private communication (19,5);
6. Freedom of conscience and of manifestation of all cults (19,6);
7. Right to choose the health system (19,9 fine);
8. Freedom of teaching (19,11);
9. Freedom to express opinions and to disseminate information (19,12);
10. Right to assemble (19,13).
11. Right to associate (19,15);
12. Freedom to work, and the right to free selection and contracting (19,16);
13. Right to affiliate to trade unions (19,19);
14. Economic freedom (19,21);
15. Right to a non–discriminatory treatment (19,22);
16. Freedom to acquire ownership (19,23);
17. Property right (19,24);
18. Right of authorship (19,25); and
19. Right to live in a contamination–free environment (20).

Apart from these constitutional rights and freedoms, the other rights enshrined in the Constitution have no specific means of protection, but rather their protection corresponds to the ordinary courts through ordinary judicial procedures.

3. The Colombian "action de tutela" for the protection of fundamental rights

In the case of Colombia, in similar way, the Constitution also sets forth two means of general protection of constitutional rights: the *habeas corpus* and the action of " tutela"; the latter designed in Article 86 of the Constitution for the immediate protection of "fundamental constitutional rights", which are not all the rights and guarantees enshrined in the Constitution.

In effect, Title II of the Constitution, on referring to "the rights, guarantees and duties", regulates them in several Chapters, as follows: Chapter 1, concerning "fundamental rights"; Chapter 2, concerning social, economic and cultural rights; and Chapter 3, concerning collective rights and the environment. From this it results that in principle, only the rights listed in Chapter I (Articles 11 to 41) as "fundamental rights" are the only constitutional rights that can be protected by the "action of tutela", being the other constitutional rights excluded from this means of protection, and thus, protected by the ordinary judicial mean.

On the other hand, Article 85 of the Constitution also defines which of the "fundamental rights" are of "immediate application," which, in principle, would imply that the action of tutela would only be admitted in these cases.

Such rights "of immediate application" and therefore susceptible of constitutional protection through the action of tutela, are the following:

1. Right to life (Article 11).
2. Right to not be disappeared, or be submitted to torture or inhuman or degrading treatment (Article 12).
3. Right to equality (Article 13).
4. Right to personality (Article 14)
5. Right to intimacy (Article 15).
6. Right to the free development of own personality (Article 16).
7. Prohibition of slavery, servitude, and human trade (Article 17).
8. Freedom of conscience (Article 18).
9. Freedom of cult (Article 19).
10. Freedom of expression (Article 20).
11. Right to honor (Article 21).
12. Right to petition (Article 23).
13. Freedom of movement (Article 24).
14. Right to exercise one's profession (Article 26).
15. Freedom to teach (Article 27).
16. Personal freedom (Article 28).
17. Right to due process and defense (Article 29)
18. Right to habeas corpus (Article 30).
19. Right to review judicial decisions (Article 31).
20. Right to not testify against oneself (Article 33).
21. Prohibition of deportation, life imprisonment, or confiscation penalties (Article 34).
22. Right to assemble (Article 37).
23. Right to political participation and to vote (Article 40).

Other rights enshrined in other articles of the Constitution can also be considered as fundamental rights, like the "fundamental rights" of children listed in Article 44 to life, physical integrity, health and social security

Apart from these constitutional expressly declared as fundamental rights and freedoms, other constitutional in principle, would not have constitutional protection under the "action of tutela", unless it is a right not expressly provided in the Constitution as being "fundamental", nature that the Constitutional Court can determine (Article 2, Decree of 1991). That is why, Decree N° 306 of 19–02–92 which regulates Decree 2.591 of 1991, expressly declares:

> **Article 2.** Pursuant to Article 1 of Decree 2.591 of 1991, the action of tutela only protects fundamental constitutional rights, and therefore, may not be used to enforce respect of rights that only have legal rank, or to enforce compliance with laws, decrees, regulations or any other regulation of an inferior level.

The Constitutional Court, in every case, has played a fundamental role in broadening protection by means of tutela to include rights not defined as "fundamental", such as the right to health, but interdependent of others such as the right to life. For that purpose in one of its first decisions, N° T–02 of May 8th, 1992, issued in a case regarding educational rights, the Constitutional Court fixed the following principal criteria to identify "fundamental rights":

Being the human persons the subject, reason and purpose of the 1991 Constitution, the "first and most important criteria for the tutela judge to determine the fundamental constitutional rights, is to determine if it is or not an essential right to human beings". Thus, "in order to verify if a constitutional fundamental right derives from the concept of essential rights to human being, the tutela judge must rationally research from Articles 5 and 94 of the Constitution". The first article sets forth the recognition by the State, without any discrimination, of the primacy of the inalienable rights of persons and protects the family as a basic institution of society. The second sets forth the open clause regarding human rights, in the sense that the listing of rights and guaranties in the Constitution and international conventions, cannot be understood as denial of others that being inherent to human persons, are not expressly therein.

Both articles, being interpreted on the lights of the American Convention on Human Right, allow to infer what can be considered inalienable, inherent and essential, as the Constitutional Court ruled: "something is inalienable because it is inherent, and something is inherent because it is essential", being also another characteristic of the constitutional fundamental rights, the existence of correlative duties.

The Constitutional Court in the same decision also developed ancillary criteria to determine the fundamental rights, such as the concept of rights of immediate application, which do not require previous statutory regulation for its enforcement; and the location of the corresponding articles in the Titles of the Constitution, even though the latter cannot be considered as crucial. Thus, the list of "fundamental rights" of Chapter I of Title II of the Constitution does not exhaust the "fundamental rights" and does not exclude other rights for being considered fundamental and justiciable by means of tutela[424].

But, as abovementioned, the Constitutional Court has also developed its criteria of the connection of the rights seeking protection by means of amparo with other fundamental rights, particularly applying such criteria in cases of economic, cultural and social rights. The Constitutional Court thus has ruled that the acceptance of the tutela action regarding these (economic, social and cultural) rights is only possible in cases in which also a violation of a fundamental right exists. In the decision N° T–406 of June 5th, 1992, the Court heard a tutela brought before a court in a case of public drainage flooding, seeking the protection of the right to public health, the right to a healthy environment and to the population's health. The action was rejected by the lower court which considered that no fundamental rights were involved in

---

424 See decision T–02 of May 8th, 1992, in Manuel José CEPEDA, *Derecho Constitucional Jurisprudencial. Las grandes decisiones de la Corte Constitucional,* Legis, Bogotá, 2001, pp. 49–54.

the case, but the Constitutional Court admitted the action considering that the right to have sewage system, in circumstances in which it could evidently affect constitutional fundamental rights, as human dignity, right to life, rights of the disabled, it must be considered as justiciable by means of tutela[425].

4. The mexican amparo suit for the protection of only the "individual guarantees"

In Mexico, as already mentioned, if it is true that the amparo suit has been regulated in the Constitution for the protection of all constitutional rights, these, according to the wording of Article 103,1 are only the "individual guarantees" declared and enumerated in Section I, Articles 1 to 29 of the Constitution.

The *jurisprudencia* or judicial obligatory doctrine traditionally established by the Supreme Court, in effect, has been that "the amparo suit was established... not to safeguard the entire body of the Constitution but to protect the individual guarantees" enumerated in the first twenty nine articles of the Constitution[426]

This constitutional interpretation has in reduced the scope of the amparo protection, only to the following "individual guaranties": prohibition of slavery and discrimination (Article 1); rights of the indigenous eoples (article 2); right to education, and right to educate; (Article 3); right to equal treatment; right to the protection of health; right to an adequate environment; right to dwelling; and minors rights (article 4); economic and occupation freedom and prohibition to render services without remuneration (Article 5); freedom of expression of ideas (Article 6); freedom of writing and publishing (Article 7); right to petition (Article 8); right to assemble and association (Article 9); right to bear arms (Article 10); right to movement and travel (Article 11); prohibition of nobility title (Article 12); right to natural judge (Article 13); guaranty of non retroactivity of laws, and due process of law rights (Article 14, 19, 20, 21, 23); rights regarding extradition (Article 15); personal freedom and detention and search guaranties (Article 16, 17, 18, 19, 22); right to justice and access to justice (Article 17, 21); freedom of religion (Article 24); right to privacy of correspondence, mail (Article 25); right to inviolability of home (Article 26); right to property and land ownership (Article 27); prohibition of monopolies (Article 28). Articles 1 and 29 regulate the suspension of guaranties.

This restricted scope of the amparo provoked multiple discussions and interpretations tending to extend it. In this regard, mention must be made of the opinion of Ignacio L. Vallarta, who served as President of the Supreme Court (1878–1882), and who sustained that the individual guaranties cannot be reduced to those enumerated in the first 29 articles of the Constitution, because they can also be declared in other

---

425 See decision T–406 of June 5th, 1992 in Manuel José CEPEDA, *Derecho Constitucional Jurisprudencial. Las grandes decisiones de la Corte Constitucional,* Legis, Bogotá, 2001, pp. 55–63.

426 See Suprema Corte de Justicia, *Jurisprudencia de la Suprema Corte*, Thesis 111, II, 246. See the referentes in Ignacio BURGOA, *El juicio de amparo*, Editorial Porrúa, México 191, p. 231, and Richard D. BAKER, *Judicial Review in Mexico. A Study of the Amparo Suit*, University of Texas, Austin and London, 1971, p. 112.

articles of the Constitution, provided that they contain and contain an explanation, a regulation, a limitation of extension of the individual guarantees. He wrote that:

> "in the case of individual guarantees, it will frequently be necessary to refer to texts other that those that define them in order to decide with certainty whether one of them has been violated. Because of the intimate connection that exists between the articles containing guarantees and others that, although they de not mention them, nonetheless presuppose them, explain them or complement them; because of the undeniable correlation that exists between them, [the guarantee] cannot be considered in isolation without weakening them, without contradicting their spirit, without frequently rendering their application impossible...for instance, in order to know if persons may be deprived of the property guaranteed by Article 27, under the form of taxation, it would be necessary to consider Article 31, which provides that [such] contribution be proportional and equitable; similarly, to determine whether the personal liberty defined in Article 5 is violated by requiring the performance of the public services, it would be necessary to [interpret] it in terms of the same article 31, which specifies certain limits on that liberty... [or] finally, in order to explain the competence to which Article 16 refers, it is necessary to examine Article 50, which established the constitutional distribution of powers between the three branches of government"[427].

According to this doctrine, as concluded by Vallarta, the amparo suit is admissible only in the cases defined in Article 103, "but it can be based on the concordance of the guaranties found in Section I of the Constitution with articles not included under that heading"[428]. This concordance doctrine has been the main tool for the extension of the constitutional protection of amparo, particularly regarding social guarantees referred to agrarian and labor matters included in Articles 27 and 123 of the Constitution, considered also as citizens' guarantees[429].

Nonetheless, constitutional rights not included in the firsts articles of the Constitution, according to the *jurisprudencia* of the Supreme Court, traditionally where not protected by means of amparo. In this regard, the Supreme Court maintained that "the violation of political rights does not give grounds for the admissibility of amparo because these [rights] are not individual guarantees"[430]. Nonetheless, also by means of the concordance doctrine in other cases the Supreme Court has given protection to political rights, by saying that "even when political rights are in question, if the act complained of may involve the violation of individual guarantees, a fact that cannot be judge *apriori*, the complaint... should be admitted"[431]; and that "although the Court has established that amparo is inadmissible against the violation of political rights, this jurisprudence refers to cases in which federal protection is sought against authorities exercising political functions and whose acts are directly

---

427 See Ignacio L. VALLARTA, *Cuestiones constitucionales. Votos del C. Ignacio L. Vallarta, presidente de la Suprema Corte de Justicia en los negocios más notables*, III, pp. 145–149. See the references in Ignacio Burgoa, *op. cit*, p. 253; Richard D. BAKER, *op. cit*, p. 113t

428 *Idem.*

429 See Ignacio BURGOA, *op. cit,* p. 263.

430 See Suprema Corte de la Nación, *Jurisprudencia de la Suprema Corte*, thesis 345, III, 645, *cit.*, by Richard D. BAKER, *op. cit.*, pp. 130, 156.

431 See Suprema Corte de la Nación, *Jurisprudencia de la Suprema Corte*, thesis 346, III, 656, *cit.*, by Richard D. BAKER, *op. cit.*, p. 157.

and exclusively related to the exercise of rights of that nature. It cannot be applied to cases in which amparo is sought against judicial decisions, that although affecting political rights, may also violate individual guarantees"[432]

V. THE QUESTION OF THE PROTECTION OF RIGHTS IN SITUATIONS OF EMERGENCY

One last issue must be mentioned regarding the justiciability of rights, and it is the question of the admissibility of amparo actions in situations of emergency.

For instance, Article 6,7 of the 1988 Venezuelan Amparo Law used to provide that the amparo action was inadmissible "in case of suspensions of rights and guarantees" when referred to the protection of such. This decision of suspension, according to Article 241 of the 1961 Constitution, could only be decided when in cases of interior or exterior conflict, a situation of emergency was declared. To the contrary, the American Convention on Human Rights provides that even in cases of emergency, the judicial guaranties of rights cannot be suspended. Thus, due to the prevalent rank that the American Convention on Human Rights has regarding internal law, as set forth in Article 23 of the 1999 Venezuelan Constitution, the abovementioned Venezuelan Amparo Law restriction was tacitly repealed. Thus, the prevalent regulation in Latin America is that the action for amparo can be filed even in states of emergency, as declared in Article 1st of the Decree regulating the action for tutela in Colombia. Also regarding the habeas corpus, in a similar sense, Article 62 of the Nicaraguan Law of Amparo sets forth that in case of suspension of the constitutional guaranties of personal freedom, the recourse of personal exhibition will remain in force.

The Peruvian Constitutional Procedure Code establishes the principle that during the emergency regimes, the amparo and habeas corpus as well as all the others constitutional proceedings, will not be suspended. According to Article 23 of the Code, when the recourses are filed in relation to the suspended rights, the court must examine the reasonability and the proportionality of the restrictive act, following these criteria:

1) If the claim refers to constitutional rights not suspended;
2) If referred to the suspended rights, the founding of the right's restrictive act does not have direct relation with the motives justifying the declaration of state of emergency;
3) If referred to the suspended rights, the right's restrictive act happens to be evidently unnecessary or unjustified bearing in mind the conduct of the aggrieved party or the factual situation briefly evaluated by the judge.

In particular, regarding the habeas corpus guarantee, the Argentinean Habeas Corpus Law provides that in case of state of siege when the personal freedom of a person is restricted, the habeas corpus proceeding is directed to prove, in the concrete case:

---

432 See Suprema Corte de la Nación, *Mendoza Eustaquio y otros, 10 S. J. (475) (1922), cit.* by Richard D. BAKER, *op. cit.*, pp. 130, 156.

1) The legitimacy of the declaration of state of siege;
2) The relation between the freedom depriving order and the situation that originates the declaration of state of siege;
3) The illegitimate worsened detention way and conditions which in no case can be effective in prisons.

On October 1986, the Inter–American Commission on Human Rights submitted to the Inter American Court of Human Rights a request for advisory opinion seeking the interpretation of Articles 25,1 and 7,6 of the American Convention on Human Rights, in order to determine if the writ of habeas corpus is one of the judicial guarantees that, pursuant to the last clause of Article 27,2 of that Convention, may not be suspended by a State Party to the Convention.

Article 27 of the Convention authorizes States, in time of war, public danger, or other emergency that threatens the independence or security of a State Party, to take measures derogating its obligations under the Convention; but with the express declaration that such does not authorize any suspension of the following articles:

> **Article 3** (Right to Juridical Personality), Article 4 (Right to Life), Article 5 (Right to Humane Treatment), Article 6 (Freedom from Slavery), Article 9 (Freedom from Ex Post Facto Laws), Article 12 (Freedom of Conscience and Religion), Article 17 (Rights of the Family), Article 18 (Right to a Name), Article 19 (Rights of the Child), Article 20 (Right to Nationality), and Article 23 (Right to Participate in Government), or *of the judicial guarantees essential for the protection of such rights.*

The Inter American Court on Human Rights issued its *Advisory Opinion OC–8/87* of January 30, 1987 (Habeas Corpus in Emergency Situations), declaring that since "in serious emergency situations it is lawful to temporarily suspend certain rights and freedoms the free exercise of which must, under normal circumstances, be respected and guaranteed by the State…it is imperative that "the judicial guarantees essential for (their) protection" remain in force. Article 27(2)"[433]; adding that these "judicial remedies that must be considered to be essential within the meaning of Article 27(2) are those that ordinarily would effectively guarantee the full exercise of the rights and freedoms protected by that provision and the denial of which or restriction would endanger their full enjoyment"[434].

The Court also advises that the guaranties must not only be essential but also *judicial,* expression that "can only refer to those judicial remedies that are truly capable of protecting these rights" before independent and impartial judicial bodies[435]; concluding that:

> 42. From what has been said before, it follows that writs of habeas corpus and of "amparo" are among those judicial remedies that are essential for the protection of various rights the derogation of which is prohibited by Article 27(2) and that serve, moreover, to preserve legality in a democratic society.

---

433 *Advisory Opinion OC–8/87* of January 30, 1987 (Habeas corpus in emergency situations), paragraph 27.

434 *Idem*, paragraph 29.

435 *Idem*, paragraph 30.

> 43. The Court must also observe that the Constitutions and legal systems of the States Parties that authorize, expressly or by implication, the suspension of the legal remedies of habeas corpus or of "amparo" in emergency situations cannot be deemed to be compatible with the international obligations imposed on these States by the Convention.

In the same year 1986, the Government of Uruguay also submitted to the Inter–American Court a request for an advisory opinion on the scope of the prohibition of the suspension of the judicial guaranties essential for the protection of the rights mentioned in Article 27,2 of the American Convention; resulting in the issue of the *Advisory Opinion* OC–9/87 of October 6, 1987 (Judicial Guarantees in States Of Emergency), in which the Court, following its aforementioned Advisory Opinion OC–8/97, empathized that "the declaration of a state of emergency… cannot entail the suppression or ineffectiveness of the judicial guarantees that the Convention requires the States Parties to establish for the protection of the rights not subject to derogation or suspension by the state of emergency"; "therefore, any provision adopted by virtue of a state of emergency which results in the suspension of those guaranties is a violation of the Convention"[436]. The conclusion of the Court then was:

> 1. That the "essential" judicial guarantees which are not subject to derogation, according to Article 27(2) of the Convention, include habeas corpus (Art. 7(6)), amparo, and any other effective remedy before judges or competent tribunals (Art. 25(1)), which is designed to guarantee the respect of the rights and freedoms the suspension of which is not authorized by the Convention[437].

The Inter American Court also concluded that the "essential" judicial guarantees which are not subject to suspension, "include those judicial procedures, inherent to representative democracy as a form of government (Art. 29©), provided for in the laws of the States Parties as suitable for guaranteeing the full exercise of the rights referred to in Article 27(2) of the Convention and the suppression of which or restriction entails the lack of protection of such rights"; and that "the above judicial guarantees should be exercised within the framework and the principles of due process of law, expressed in Article 8 of the Convention"[438].

This doctrine of Inter American Court is a very important one for the protection of human rights in Latin America, due to the unfortunate past experiences some countries have had in situations of emergency or of state of siege, particularly under military dictatorship or internal civil war cases; where there has been no effective judicial protection available to persons' life and physical integrity; where it has been impossible to prevent their disappearance or their whereabouts been kept secret; and other times no means have been effective to protect persons against torture or other cruel, inhumane, or degrading punishment or treatment.

Nonetheless, according to the Inter American Court on Human Rights doctrine following the provisions of the American Convention, the discussion that has been

---

436 *Advisory Opinion* OC–9/87 of October 6, 1987 (Judicial Guarantees in States Of Emergency), paragraphs 25, 26.

437 *Idem*. paragraph 41,1

438 *Idem*, paragraph 41,2 and 41,3.

held in the United States regarding the possibility to exclude the habeas corpus protection to the so called "combatant enemies" which had been kept for years in custody without any judicial guaranty to protect their rights, cannot be held.

The matter was decided by the Supreme Court in *Rasul v.Bush,* 542 U.S. 466; 124 S. Ct. 2686; 159 L. Ed. 2d 548; 2004 in a case referred to aliens that had been captured abroad, from 2002 and onward, by United States authorities during hostilities with the Taliban regime in Afghanistan, and that were held in executive detention at the Guantanamo Bay Naval Base in Cuba. They filed various habeas corpus actions in the United States District Court for the District of Columbia against the United States and some federal and military officials, alleging that they were being held in federal custody in violation of the laws of the United States, that they had been imprisoned without having been charged with any wrongdoing, permitted to consult counsel, or provided access to courts or other tribunals. The District Court's jurisdiction was invoked under the federal habeas corpus provision (28 USCS § 2241©(3)) that authorized Federal District Courts to entertain habeas corpus applications by persons claiming to be held in custody "in violation of the Constitution or laws or treaties of the United States." The District Court dismissed the actions for jurisdiction, on the ground that aliens detained outside the sovereign territory of the United States could not invoke a habeas corpus petition; and the United States Court of Appeals for the District of Columbia Circuit, in affirming, concluded that the privilege of litigation in United States courts did not extend to aliens in military custody who had no presence in any territory over which the United States was sovereign (355 US App DC 189,321 F3d 1134). On certiorari, the United States Supreme Court reversed and remanded, holding that the District Court had jurisdiction, under 28 USCS § 2241, to review the legality of the plaintiffs' detention.

Notwithstanding this Supreme Court decision, the Senate of the United States voted on November 2005 an amendment to a military budget bill, to strip captured "enemy combatants" at Guantánamo Bay, of the legal tool given to them by the Supreme Court when it allowed them to challenge their detentions in United States courts[439].

As mentioned before, a law banning the habeas corpus action could not even be proposed in Latin American Countries, due to its regulation in the Constitutions and in the Inter American Convention on Human Rights as a right that cannot be suspended even in situations of emergency. The same occurs, for instance, regarding personal freedom related to the length of administrative detention that in general is established in the Latin American Constitutions. Thus, no legal regulation or amendments can be approved extending that restrictive police custody, as for instance has occurred in Europe also due to the war against terrorism[440]. In Latin

439 See Eric SCHMITT, "Senate Approves Limiting Rights of U.S. Detainees", *The New York Times,* November 11, 2005.

440 As reported by Katrin BENNHOLD, in "Europe Takes Harder Line With Terror Suspects", *The New York Times,* April 17, 2006: "In December, France increased its period of detention without charge for terror suspects to six days from four; it retained rules that have allowed uncharged suspects to be denied access to a lawyer during the first three days.

America, on the contrary, due to the constitutional rank of the regulation, the only way to extend police custody length restriction is through a constitutional amendment or reform.

CHAPTER VIII.
THE QUESTION OF THE JUSTICIABILITY OF SOCIAL CONSTITUTIONAL RIGHTS BY MEANS OF THE "AMPARO" ACTION

I. THE QUESTION OF THE JUSTICIABILITY OF SOCIAL RIGHTS

The most important question on the justiciability of constitutional rights in Latin America refers to those rights of economic, social and cultural character. As was argued by the Colombian Constitutional Court in the already mentioned decision N° T–406 of June 5th, 1992:

> The majority of the economic, social and cultural rights imply the rendering of an activity by the State and thus, an economic expenditure that in general terms depends on political decisions. It is based on these propositions that it is sustained that the provisions setting forth such rights cannot only be subject to the existence of a legislation issued by Congress in order to assure their enforcement. Nonetheless, the new principles of the Social State and the new relations deriving from the Welfare State impose the questioning of that solution...
>
> The *raison d'étre* of these rights derives from the fact that its minimal satisfactions are an indispensable condition for the enjoyment of the civil and political rights. In other words, without the satisfaction of minimal conditions of existence, or in the sense of Article 1 of the Constitution, without respect to human dignity regarding the material conditions of existence, any aspiration of effectively ensuring the classical freedom and equalitarian rights enshrined in Chapter I of Title II of the Constitution, would be just simple and useless formalism...
>
> ...The judicial intervention in cases of economic, social and cultural rights is necessary when it is indispensable in order to assure the respect a constitutional principle or of a fundamental right.
>
> The Constitution is a present time legal (juridical) norm and has to be immediately applied and respected. From that, to sustain that the social, economic and cultural rights are reduced to a political responsibility link between the constituent and the legislator, is not only ingenuity regarding the existence of such link, but also an evident distortion regarding the sense and coherence that the Constitution must maintain. If the responsibility of the Constitu-

---

Italy last year extended custody to 24 hours from 12 and authorized the police to interrogate detainees in the absence of their lawyers. In 2003, Spain extended the period in which suspected terrorists can be held effectively incommunicado to a maximum 13 days, according to the advocacy group Human Rights Watch.

Britain has gone furthest. The latest law doubles the period during which a terror suspect can be held in custody without charge to 28 days. It was just 48 hours in 2001, and Prime Minister Tony Blair fought for an extension to three months. The new law followed one filed soon after the attacks of Sept. 11, 2001, that allowed foreign terror suspects to be held indefinitely without charge. The House of Lords declared that measure unlawful in late 2004.

> tion's efficiency would be in the hands of the legislator, the constitutional norm would not have any value and the validity of the constituent's will, would stay subject to the legislator's will[441].

Eventually the Constitutional Court of Colombia concluded its ruling saying that due to the fact that "the application of social, economic and cultural rights pose the political problem, not of generation of resources but of allocation of them, the admission of tutela regarding social, economic and cultural rights can only be accepted in cases where a violation of a fundamental right exists"[442].

Consequently, for instance, the Constitutional Court has protected the right to health of a military servicemen and to be treated in a military hospital, although he was not formally entitled to have such treatment because his military oath was yet to be given, considering that the right must be protected "when the health service is needed and is indispensable in order to preserve the right to life, in which cases the State is obligated to render it to persons in need"[443]. So when there are no such connections, the social right in itself cannot be protected by means of tutela, as for instance has been the case of the constitutional right to a dignified dwelling or housing, regarding which, the Constitutional Court has ruled that, "as happens with other rights of social, economic and cultural contents, no subjective right is given to persons to ask the State in a direct and immediate way, to plainly satisfy such right"[444]

For the same reason of the political character of the possible enforcement of social, economic and cultural rights, its justiciability has been widely discussed in contemporary constitutional law.

For instance, this has been the feature of the North American Supreme Court doctrine, even in the aftermath of the so called "The Rights Revolution" that shaped North America in the last decades of the XX Century. As Charles R. Repp has pointed out referring to the Supreme Court's scattered attention to individual rights in the thirties (when less than 10 percent of the Court's decisions involved individual rights other than property rights), and the revolutionary changes that occurred in the following decades:

> By the late sixties, almost 70 percent of its decisions involved individual rights, and the Court had, essentially, proclaimed it the guardian of the individual rights of ordinary citizen. In the process, the Court created and expanded a host of new constitutional rights, among them virtually all the rights now regarded as essential to the Constitution: freedom of speech and the press, rights against discrimination on the basis of race or sex, and the right to due process in criminal and administrative procedures[445]

---

441 See decision T–406 of June 5th, 1992 in Manuel José CEPEDA, *Derecho Constitucional Jurisprudencial. Las grandes decisiones de la Corte Constitucional,* Legis, Bogotá, 2001, p. 61.

442 *Idem*. p. 61

443 See Decision T–534 of September 24, 1992, in pp. 461 ff.

444 See Decision T–251 of June 5, 1995, in p. 486.

445 See Charles R. REPP, *The Rights Revolution. Lawyers, Activists, and Supreme Courts in Comparative Perspective*, The University of Chicago Press, Chicago and London, 1998, p. 2. See also, pp. 26 ff.

This very important "Rights Revolution" in the United States led the Supreme Court to guarantee civil rights that were not effectively protected before, like the non discrimination rights derived from the implementation of *Brown v. Board of Education* 347 U.S. 483 (1954) overturning the racial segregation in public schools; the extension of freedom of speech guaranteed in the First Amendment; restricting federal and state actions, from *Fiske v. Kansas* 274 U.S. 380 (1927); the due process of law rights of accused persons and prisoners, following *Mapp v. Ohio* 367 U.S 643 (1961) and *Gideon v. Wainwright* 372 U.S. 335 (1963); the women's rights regarding sex discrimination beginning in *Reed v. Reed* 404 U.S. 71 (1971 and in *Fontinero v. Richardson*, 411 U.S. 677 (1973).

But if it is true that in matters of judicial protection of civil and individual rights in the United States it is possible to talk about a Revolution, nothing similar can be said regarding social and cultural rights, many of them the Supreme Court had denied to even qualify them as fundamental rights, as happened with the right to education, to housing and to social welfare.

Nonetheless, in Latin America, the discussion is not whether social, economic and cultural rights like education, health, social welfare or housing are or are not fundamental constitutional rights, but even if they have such rank, the question is if they can be justiciable, that is to say, if they can be enforced by means of judicial actions against the State.

II. THE CASE OF THE RIGHT TO HEALTH IN LATIN AMERICAN CONSTITUTIONS AND THE STATE'S OBLIGATIONS

This is the main issue on the discussion in Latin America. Without doubts, the Constitutions of all Latin American countries recognized the constitutional and even the fundamental character and rank of social, economic and cultural rights, but not always the courts had decided actions for amparo of such rights, particularly when brought against the State.

One important constitutional right whose justiciability has been discussed in Latin America is the right to health, enshrined in all the Constitutions; justiciability that is conditioned, first, by the way the right is declared in the Constitutions; second regarding the scope given to the amparo action; and third by the concrete cases resolved by the Courts.

Not all the Latin American Constitutions set forth the right to health in the same way. Some refer to the matter as a public asset, as is the case of El Salvador, where the Constitution declares that "the health of the inhabitants of the republic is a public asset" (Art 65). In similar terms, it is set in the Constitution of Guatemala (Art. 95); and in both texts it is declared that the State and the individuals are obligated to take care of its preservation and reestablishment.

Nonetheless, in almost all Constitutions the "right to health" is listed as a constitutional right (Bolivia, Art. 7,a; Brazil, Art. 6 y 196; Ecuador Art. 46; Nicaragua, Art. 59); Venezuela, Art. 84), that corresponds to everybody in equal terms as it is expressed in the Constitution of Nicaragua (Art. 59); and is reaffirmed in the Constitution of Guatemala, by saying that "the enjoyment of health is a fundamental right of human beings, without any kind of discrimination" (Art. 93).

This constitutional formula of "right to health", though, in fact what reveals in a general declaration of principles regarding the commitment of the State and the society toward human beings, rather that a strict constitutional right, due to the absence of an *alter* party in the declaration. In fact nobody can be obligated to promise the health of a person, and conversely, nobody can have the "right" not become ill.

Nonetheless, it can be said that with this formula of the "right to health" in reality, what the Constitutions are setting forth is the constitutional right of everybody to the protection of health, or to be protected in their health, by the State. Thus, the State, as well as the whole society, has the obligation to watch for the maintenance and recuperation of people's health. That is why other Latin American Constitutions provide in a more precise way, the "right to the protection of health" (Honduras, Art. 145); or referrer to the right of everybody to the protection of their health" (Chile Art. 19,9; México, Art. 4; Perú, Art. 7); or the right "for their health to be taken care of or protected" (Cuba, Art. 50); or that everybody has to have the guarantee "to have access to the services for the promotion, protection and recovery of health" (Colombia, Art. 49). In Panama, Article 105 of the Constitution provides that:

> The individual, as part of the community, has the right to the promotion, protection, maintenance, restitution and rehabilitation of health, and the obligation to maintain it, understood as the complete physical, mental and social welfare".

In some cases, as it happens in the Venezuelan Constitution, both formulas have been put together, when Article 83 of the Constitution provides as follows: "Health is a fundamental social right... all persons have for their health to be protected". In similar sense, Article 68 of the Constitution of Paraguay referring to the "right to health", says: "In the interest of community, the State will protect and promote health as a fundamental right of persons".

But a right for health to be protected by the State, in fact, is a right to have access to the service that takes care of health. Nonetheless, only a few Constitutions assure the equalitarian right to have such access, in some cases without cost, regarding public health services. In the case of Chile, where the Constitution provides that "the State protects the free and equalitarian access to the actions for promotion, protection and recovery of health and of rehabilitation of the individuals" (Art. 19,9). The Cuban Constitution, in Article 50, sets forth that the State guarantees the rights of persons to have their health being taken care of and protected "with the rendering of free medical and hospital assistance".

In the case of Chile, in the same constitutional provision a distinction is made between the health public programs and services render, regarding which it is provided that "the public health programs and actions are free for all", but, "the public services of medical attention will be free for those who need them " (Art. 43). The Constitution also provides that "in no case the emergency attentions will be denied in public or private premises" (Art. 43). In similar sense the Constitution of Paraguay sets forth that "Nobody will be deprived of public assistance in order to prevent or treat diseases, pests or plague, or of help in cases of catastrophes or accidents" (Art. 68).

The Constitution of El Salvador provides that the State must "give free assistance to the sick who lacked resources, and in general to all inhabitants, when the treatment is an efficient mean to prevent the dissemination of a transmissible disease"; (Art. 66); and in Uruguay, the Constitution provides that "the State must freely provide the means for protection and of assistance only to those in need and to those without enough resources" (Art. 44). In other cases, the Constitutions refer to the statute to "define the terms through which the basis attention for all the inhabitants will be free and obligatory" (Colombia, Art. 49); or for the definition of "the rules and modes for the access to the health services" (México, Art. 4).

From all these constitutional regulations, additionally to the general duties imposed to everyone, the communities and society in general have the duty to preserve healthy conditions, in particular a series of constitutional duties are set forth regarding the State and public bodies, which in a certain way are the ones that can orient the scope of the justiciability of the right to health.

For instance, in the Panamanian Constitution it is set forth that "It is an essential State function to watch for the health of the population" (Art. 105); and the Constitution of Guatemala, provides as an "obligation of the State on health ad social assistance" that "The State must watch for the health and social assistance of all inhabitants. It will develop, through its institutions, actions for the prevention, promotion, recovery, rehabilitation, coordination and the complementary ones in order to seek the most complete physical, mental and social welfare" (Article 94).

The Venezuelan Constitution, after declaring health as a fundamental right, declares as an "obligation for the State, who must guarantee it as part of the right to life. The State must promote and develop policies devoted to raise the quality of life, the collective welfare and the access to the..." (Art. 83). In the Constitution of Honduras, Article 145 provides that "The state must maintain an adequate environment for the protection of people's helath".

And the Constitution of Cuba sets forth that the State guarantees the right of persons to have their health taken care of and protected" (Art. 50) "by means of rendering free medical and hospital assistance through the network of rural medical services, polyclinics, hospitals, prophylactic and special treatment facilities; by rendering free stomatology assistance; by means of the development of plans for sanitary and health education, periodical medical exams, general vaccination and other disease preventive measures".

In Ecuador, Article 42 of the Constitution prescribes that the State guarantees the right to health, and the promotion and protection of health, "by means of the development of the alimentary safety, the provision of drinking water and basic sanitation, the promotion of family, labor and community healthy environment and the possibility to have permanent an uninterrupted access to health services, according the equity, universality, solidarity, quality and efficiency principles".

Article 106 of the Panamanian Constitution provides that in matters of health; it is for the State basically to develop activities, integrating the prevention, restoration and rehabilitation, among other purposes for "the protection of the mother, the child and the adolescent by means of guaranteeing integral attention during the gestation, nursing, growth and development of youth and adolescence; the fighting of transmissible diseases by means of environmental sanitation, development of access to drinking water and to adopt measures for the immunization, prophylaxis and treatment, collectively and individually rendered to all the population; and to create, according to the needs of each region, facilities in which integral health services are rendered, and drugs are given to all the population. This health services and medication will be freely rendered to whom lacks economic resources".

In Bolivia the State has the "obligation to defend human persons by protecting the health of the population, to assure the continuity of subsistence and rehabilitation means of disabled persons; to commit the raise family group life conditions (Art. 158.I). The Constitution of Peru provides that "the State determines the health policy" (Art. 9); and in similar terms the Constitution of El Salvador prescribes that "The State will determine the national health policy and will control and supervise its application" (Art. 65). In Nicaragua, Article 59 of the Constitution provides that the State must establish basic conditions for health promotion, protection, recovery and rehabilitation, and that it must direct and organize health programs, services and actions and promote popular participation in its defense".

In Brazil, the State has the duty to guarantee health "through social and economic policies tending to reduce the risk of sickness and other risks and the universal and equalitarian access to actions and services for health promotion, protection and recovery" (Art. 196). In Ecuador, the State must promote "the culture for health and life, with emphasis on alimentary and nutrition education of mothers and children and in sexual and reproductive health, by means of society participation and the social media collaboration (Art. 43).

For such purpose, the State must formulate "a health national policy and will watch for its application; control the functioning of entities in the sector; recognize, respect and promote the development of traditional and alternative medicine, the exercise of which will be regulated by statute, and will promote the scientific and technological advancement in health are, subjected to bioethics principles. Will also adopt programs tending to eradicate alcoholism and other toxic manias" (Art. 44).

According to all these express constitutional provisions, in some case vaguely and in others very detailed and precise, the protection of health can be considered in general as a constitutional obligation of the State, which does not exclude the possibility for individual to render health care services. In this regard, for instance, the Chilean Constitution provides that "everyone has the right to choose the health care system to which want to belong, be it public or private" (Art. 19), which implies the right of individuals to render health care services. This is expressly set in the Brazilian Constitution by providing that "sanitary assistance is of free private initiative", but subjected to express constitutional restrictions such as the ones provided in Article 199, "private institutions may participate in a complementary way in the Unique Health System, according the rules set forth by it, by means of public law contract or agreement, favor being given the philanthropic institutions and non–profit entities"; that "it is forbidden that public funds be directed to help or subsidize profit–oriented private"; and that also "it is forbidden the direct or indirect participation of foreign companies or capital in the sanitary assistance in the country, except in cases provided by statute".

Anyway, except for this provision, in the other Latin American countries, it can be said that in general, no private initiative to render health care services is provided, and what is provided is the State's power to regulate all health care services. As it is provided in the Venezuelan Constitution: "The State shall regulate both public and private health care institutions" (Art. 85); or as is it provided in Article 19 of the Chilean Constitution, in which additionally to declaring that the coordination and control of the activities related to health corresponds to the State, it declares that "the State shall give preference to guarantee the execution of health assistance, whether undertaken by public or private institutions, in accordance with the form and conditions set by statute which may establish obligatory payments"

Article 44 of the Uruguayan Constitution provides that "The State must legislate on all questions related to public health and hygiene, tending to the physical, moral and social improvement of all inhabitants of the country". In Honduras, Article 149 assigns to the State the power to supervise all the private activities related to health. In Brazil, Article 197 of the Constitution, due to the public importance of health activities and services, empowers the public bodies directly or by third parties, to regulate, supervise and control them. Also, the Colombian Constitution provides in Article 49 that it is for the State to establish "the policies for the rendering of health care services by private entities, and to supervise and control them."

The general consequence of the Constitutions providing for State obligations to render health care services to answer individual's constitutional right to receive health care materializes in public utilities or public services. As provided expressly in the Colombian Constitution: "health care and environment sanitation are public services that the State has to meet (Article 49); and the Bolivian Constitution adds that "The social services and assistance are State functions" being the regulations related to public health of coactive and obligatory character (Art. 164).

In this regard, the majority of Latin American Constitutions contained the general principles regarding public and private health care services, integrated in a national or unique system (Chile, Art. 45: Paraguay, Art. 69; Venezuela, Art. 84; Brazil, Art. 198).

III. THE JUSTICIABILITY OF THE RIGHT TO HEALTH

The people's constitutional right to health –particularly due to the obligations imposed to the States to provide services for the maintenance and recovery of people's health– pose the question of its justiciability by means of the amparo recourses or actions. Being constitutional rights, in principle they can be enforced by courts through the specific means for the protection of human rights.

Nonetheless, this has only been expressly regulated in one Latin American country: Peru. The Peruvian Constitutional Procedure Code, which expressly provides that the amparo recourse can be filed for the defense of the right "to health" (Article 37,24). In the case of Chile, the Constitution refers to the recourse of protection only to protect the "right to choose the system of health" (Article 19,9). No other specific regulation exists regarding amparo and right to health, which does not exclude the judicial protection. On the contrary, as a matter of principle, amparo actions can be brought before the courts for the protection of the right to health.

Nonetheless, the decisions of the courts in this regard have not been as protective as the constitutional provisions can allow. In general terms, and taking into account judicial decisions of the Constitutional Courts or Constitutional Chambers of Supreme Courts, as well as other court decisions of Peru, Colombia, Costa Rica, Chile and Venezuela, it is possible to distinguish two general tendencies: First, of wide protection in three cases: in cases in which it exists a concrete legal relationship between the plaintiff and the public entity defendant party, like the one derived from the social security system paid by the individual; in cases in which the right to health is protected because of its connection with other fundamental rights as the right to life; and in cases in which the courts have denied the programmatic character to the right to health; and second, of limited protection in cases which impose the State obligations to render services of health care which surpass the resources originally set forth.

The first cases related to amparo decisions for protection of the rights to health in concrete legal situations usually derived from the social security obligations regarding insured persons. This is the case of the Constitutional Chamber of the Supreme Tribunal of Justice of Venezuela decision N° 487 of April 6th, 2001 (Case: *Glenda López y otros vs. Instituto Venezolano de los Seguros Sociales*), in which the Court started by pointing out that the right to health or to the protection of health is "an integral part of the right to life, set forth in the Constitution as a fundamental social right (and not simply as an assignments of State purposes), whose satisfaction mainly belongs to the State and its institutions, thorough activities intended to progressively raise the quality of life of citizens and the collective welfare". This implies, according to the Court's decision that "the right to health is not to be exhausted with the simple physical care of the illness of a person, but it must be extended to the appropriate care in order to safeguard the mental, social, environmental etc., integrity of persons, including the communities, as collective imperfect entities, in the sense that they do not have by–laws organizing them as artificial persons".

In the concrete case heard by the Court, the violation of the right to health (and also the threat regarding the right to life) was alleged by HIV/AIDS infected persons, as caused by the Venezuelan Institute for Social Security, which they considered was obligated to "give medical integral care to its affiliates". The Constitutional Chamber thus ruled that because the omission of the Institute "to provide the plaintiffs, in a regular and permanent way, the drugs for the treatment of HIV/SIDA prescribed by the specialist attached to the Hospital Domingo Luciani, and to practice the specialized medical exams directed to help the efficient treatment of HIV/AIDS"; the right to health and even the right to life of the plaintiff were put in danger[446].

446 Véase en *Revista de Derecho Público*, N° 85–88, Editorial Jurídica Venezolana, Caracas, 2001, pp. 139–141.

The second cases are related to the protection of the right to health as a consequence of the protection of the right to life, as has been decided in Colombia and Costa Rica.

As mentioned before, the Colombian Constitution does not include, among the fundamental rights protected by means of the action of tutela, the right to health or to the protection of health, so that the Constitutional Court has constructed the possibility of its protection establishing its connection to the right to life. In the decision N° T–484/92 of August 11, 1992[447], when deciding a revision recourse of a tutela decision against the Institute of Social Security, the plaintiff in the case, also infected with HIV/AIDS, claimed that it was infected while being covered by the Social Security program and had a favorable decision of the first instance Court which ordered the Institute to continue to render the plaintiff the health care services that we had been receiving. The Constitutional Court, when deciding, affirmed that "health is one of those assets that because of its inherent character to the dignified existence of man, is protected and especially, regarding persons that because of its economic, physical or mental conditions are in a manifest weakness condition" (Article 13, Constitution); being it a right that "seeks the assurance the fundamental right to life (Article 11 Constitution). Thus, the assistance nature imposes a primordial and preferential treatment by public entities and the legislator, in order for its effective protection". The Court, moreover, when connecting the right to health with the right to life, pointed out that:

The right to health comprises in its legal nature a bunch of elements that can be classified in two great blocks: First, those that identify it as an immediate condition to the right of life, thus, attacking peoples health is equivalent to attacking life itself. Thus conducts that harass the safe environment (Article 49,1), are to be treated in a concurrent manner with the health problems. Additionally, the recognition of the right to health forbids personal conducts that can cause damage to others, originating criminal and civil liabilities. Because all of these aspects, the right to health comes out as a fundamental right. The second block of elements place the right to health within an assistance character derived from the Welfare State, due to the fact that its recognition imposes concrete actions, developed through legislation, in order to render a public service not only for medical assistance, but also regarding hospital, pharmaceutical and laboratory rights. The threshold between the right to health as fundamental and assistance is imprecise and above all subject to the circumstances of each case (Article 13 Constitution), but in principle it can be asserted that the right to health is fundamental when related to the protection of life".

Based on the foregoing, regarding the concrete case of the petitioner infected with HIV/AIDS who was been treated by the health care services from the Institute of Social Security, the Court ratified the inferior decision's on tutela, bearing in mind that in the particular circumstance, the prevention of the right to health, was the condition for the protection of the his fundamental right to life.

447 File N° 2130, Case: *Alonso Muñoz Ceballos*,

In a similar sense, the Constitutional Chamber of the Supreme Court of Justice of Costa Rica, in decision N° 2003–8377 of August 8th, 2003[448], deciding an amparo recourse filed by the People's Defendant on behalf of the aggrieved person against the Costa Rican Institute of Social security because of the denial of the requested treatment for the disease known as Gaucher type 1, arguing that such denial "harmed the right to life and to health of the minor" who required the prescribed drug for "maintaining his life", the Constitutional Chamber after referring to the doctrine of the right of life in previous Court's decisions, including the right to health, concluded that "the Constitution provides in its Article 21 that he human life is inviolable, from which it derives the right every citizen has to health, thus corresponding to the State to ensure public health… (N° 5130–94 of 17:33 hrs on 7 September 1994)".

The Chamber added that "the preeminence of life and health, as superior values of people, is present and is of obligatory protection by the State, not only in the Constitution, but also in the various international instruments ratified by the country", making reference to Article 3 of the Universal Declaration on Human Rights, Article 4 of the American Convention on Human Rights; Article 1 of the American Declaration on Rights and Duties of Man; Article 6 of the International Covenant on Civil and Political Rights; Article 12 of the International Covenant on Economic, Social and Cultural Rights; and Articles 14 and 26 of the Convention on Chile Rights (Law 7184 of July 18, 1990).

Due to the responsibilities of the State derived from these norms, the Constitutional Chamber comes in to analyzing the mission and functions of the Costa Rican Institution of Social Security making reference to its previous decision n° 1997–05934 of September 23, 1997, in which "it was considered that the denial from the Costa Rican institutions on Social Security to provide patients infected with HIV/AIDS the adequate therapy harms their fundamental rights". Departing from this premise, the Chamber analyzes the concrete case of the protected Tania González Valle, being proved in the files that she was not receiving the prescript treatment. Regarding the arguments of the Institutions based on financial aspects, the Chamber pointed out that:

> "This Court is conscientious regarding the scattered financial resources of the social security system, nonetheless it considers that the principal challenge the Costa Rican Institution of Social Security faces in this stage of its institutional development, –where Costa Rica has achieved life standards qualities similar to those of developed countries–, is to optimize the management of available resources of the system of health insurance and reduce the administrative costs in order to efficiently invest these resources. The Chamber considers that the prescript drugs are undoubtfully onerous, nonetheless, due to the exceptional characteristics of the illness suffered, which is lethal, and due to the impossibility for her parents to contribute for the acquisition of the drugs, based on Articles 21 and 173 of the Constitution, and 24 and 26 of the Convention on the Child's Rights, it proceeds to confirm the recourse. The acceptance of the recourse implies that the Costa Rican Institution on Social Security must immediately provide Tania Gonzalez Valle with the drug "Cerezyme" (Imuglucerase) in the conditions prescribed by her doctor".

---

448 File. 03–007020–0007–CO, Case: *Tania González Valle*.

In Peru, the Constitutional Court in a decision of April 20, 2004[449], also ruled regarding the right to health when deciding an extraordinary revision recourse filed against an amparo decision issued by the Superior Court of Justice of Lima. The latter had partially adjudicated the amparo action brought against the Peruvian State (Ministery of Health), demanding for the plaintiff, an HIV/AIDS infected "integral health care by means of the constant provision of drugs needed to treat HIV/AIDS, as well as the performance of periodical exams and tests that the doctor orders".

The Constitutional Tribunal, referring to the rights that are protected by means of the action of amparo, admitted that "the right to health is not among the fundamental rights set forth in Article 2 of the Constitution, but is rather recognized in Articles 7 and 9 of the Constitution in the Chapter related to social and economic rights"; nonetheless, concluded in a "similar way decided by the Colombian Constitutional Court, that when the violation of the right to health compromises other fundamental rights, like the right to life, the right to physical integrity and the right to the free development of one's personality, such right acquires fundamental right character and, therefore, must be protected by means of amparo action *(STC N.° T– 499 Corte Constitucional de Colombia)".*

The nature of the economic and social rights, as is the case of the right to health, originates State obligations directed to provide social assistance. The Tribunal argued that the right health, as all the so called *prestacionales* ("rendering") rights, like social security, public health, housing, education and other public services, it represents "one of the social goals of the State through which individuals can achieve their complete auto determination". Individuals can then "demand" the accomplishment of State duties by "asking the State to adopt adequate measures in order to achieve the social goals". However, "not in all cases the social rights are by themselves legally enforceable, due to the need of a budget support for its accomplishment".

Notwithstanding the above mentioned, the Constitutional Tribunal pointed out that "there were not just programmatic provisions with mediate effects as has been traditionally considered when differentiating them from the so called civil and political rights of immediate efficacy, because the indispensable guarantee for the enjoyment of the civil and political rights is precisely its minimal satisfaction. Accordingly, without dignified education, health and life quality, it would be difficult to talk about freedom and social equality, which motivates both the Legislator and the Judiciary to think jointly and interdependently on the recognition of such rights. Their satisfaction also requires a minimum action from the State, by means of the establishment of public services to render health care in equal conditions for all the population.

In this regard, the Tribunal ruled that "the social rights must be interpreted as true citizen guaranties that bind the State within a vision that tends to reevaluate the legal validity of constitutional norms, thus of the enforcement of the Constitution". Thus, the enforcement of these rights implies the need to surpass the programmatic conception allowing the improvement of the social prescriptions of the Constitution, as well as the State obligation, to which it is necessary to impose quantified goals in

449 File N.° 2945–2003–AA/TC, Case: *Azanca Alhelí Meza García*

order to guaranty the force of the right". According to the Tribunal criteria, "this new vision of the social rights allows to recognize in its essential content, principles like solidarity and human being dignity respect, which are the funding of the Welfare State based on the rule of Law".

After analyzing these principles, the Tribunal considered as "erroneous the argument of the State defendant when arguing that the right to health and the national policy of health are just programmatic norms that more that a concrete right only signify a plan of action for the State"; adding that it would be naïve "to sustain that the social rights are reduced to be just a link for political responsibility between the Constituent and the legislator, which would be "an evident distortion regarding the Constitution's sense and coherence".

Regarding the right to health and its inseparable relation to the right to life, the Tribunal ruled that according to the Constitution "the defense of human beings and the respect of their dignity... presupposes the unrestricted enforcement of the right to life"; because "the exercise of any right, privilege, faculty or power has no sense or turns out to be useless in cases of non existence of physical life of somebody in favor of which it can be recognized". The Tribunal continued its ruling saying:

> 28. Health is a fundamental right due to its inseparable relation with the right to life, which is irresoluble, due to the fact that an illness can provoke death or in any case, the deterioration of life conditions. Thus the need to materialize actions tending to take care of life is evident, which supposed a health care oriented to attack the illness signs...

Since the right to the protection of health is recognized in Article 7 of the Constitution, persons have also a right to attain and preserve a plain physical and psychical condition; consequently, they have "the right to be assigned sanitary and social measures for nourishing, clothing, dwelling and medical assistance, according to the level allowed by public funds and social solidarity".

The Tribunal then considered the question of the justiciability of social rights, like the right to health, ruling that "they cannot be requested in the same way in all cases, due to the fact that it is not a matter of specific rendering, because its depend on budget allocations; on the contrary, that would suppose that each individual could judicially ask at any moment for an employment or for a specific dwelling or for health"; concluding that:

> 33. To judicially demand a social right will depend on various factors, such as seriousness and reasonability of the case, its relation to other rights and State's budget resources, provided that concrete actions can be proved for the accomplishment of social policies"...

The Tribunal then analyzed the State's actions in the case, due to the pleading of the plaintiff's rights which affects his own life, ruling that "if it is true that in developing countries it is difficult to demand immediate attention and satisfaction of social policies for the whole population, [this Tribunal] reaffirms that its justification is valid only when concrete State actions are observed for the achievement of the resulting effect; on the contrary, the lack of attention would result in an unconstitutional omission situation".

Regarding the public policies in matters of HIV/AIDS the Tribunal considered that "in general, regarding social rights such as the right to health, no rendering obligation results in it itself because it depends on the State's financial resources, which nevertheless, in no way can justify a prolonged inaction, because it would result in an unconstitutional omission". The conclusion in the case was "the granting of the legal protection to a social right as the right to health, due to the fact that in this particular case the conditions justifying it are fulfilled" not only "due to the potential damage to the right to life, but also because of the motives on which the legislation is based in the matter which has organized the means for maximum protection to the AIDS infected persons".

1. The right to health and the State's financial resources

In other cases, the justiciability of the right to health regarding HIV/AIDS treatment has been completely subordinated to the disposal of resources. This has been the sense of some 2000/2001 Chilean courts' decisions regarding action for protections suits. In one case, the action was filed against the Ministry of Health, for failing to provide medical treatment to a group of HIV patients, arguing violation to the right to life and the right to equal protection. The plaintiff asked to be treated with the same therapy that was been given to others HIV patients, which the Ministry had denied arguing that it lacked enough economic resources for providing it to all Chilean HIV patients. The Court of appeals of Santiago ruled that the obligation of the Ministry of Health, according to the Law regulating health care provisions (Law N° 2763/1979), was to provide health care in accordance with the resources that are available to it considering reasonable the explanation provided by the Ministry based on the lack of economic resources to provide the best available treatment to the plaintiffs. The decision was confirmed by the Supreme Court[450].

In another 2001 decision, the same Ministry of Health was sued for the same reasons by HIV patients on a more critical conditions, and even though the Court of appeals of Santiago ruled in favor of the petitioners, ordering the Ministry to provide them immediately with the best available treatment, the Supreme Court reversed the ruling, arguing that the Ministry had acted in accordance to the law[451].

2. The rejection to protect the right to health in an abstract way

Finally, it must be mentioned a recent ruling of the Venezuelan Constitutional Chamber of the Supreme Court, that while contradicting previous rulings, decided that the right to health was not able to be protected by means of amparo actions, but only through political mechanisms of control regarding public policies.

The Chamber in a decision N° 1002 of May 26, 2004 (Case: *Federación Médica Venezolana*), rejected an amparo action brought by the Venezuelan Medical Federation "defending diffuse society rights and interests, and in particular those of the physicians", seeking protection to health, against the "*omissive*" conduct of the Ministry of Health and Social Development and the Venezuelan Institute of Social Secu-

---

450 See the reference in Javier A. COURSO, "Judicialization pd Chilean Politics" in Rachel Sieder, Line Schjolden and Alan Angeli (Ed.), *The Judicializacion of Politics in Latin America*, Palgrave Macmillan, New York, 2005, pp. 119–120.

451 *Idem*. p. 120.

rity, because it failed to "directly provide an efficient service of health to the population in all the national territory, by means of promptly providing the necessary equipment and resources".

The Constitutional Chamber, in order to reject the claim, began by establishing a distinction that is not reflected in the Constitution, "between the civil and political rights and those of third generation", pointing out that:

> The dichotomy between civil and political rights and the economic, social and cultural ones was establish since the preparatory works of the two United nations Covenants, and particularly, in the 1951 decision of the General Assembly not to frame on both instruments the regulation of the two category of rights as an expression of the idea that the civil and political rights where rights that can be immediately enforced –because of implied abstention duties form the State–; whereas the economic, social and cultural rights were implemented by means of rules of that ought to be progressively developed –due to the fact that they implied positive obligations. Such criterion was also followed in the European Social Charter– in which's negotiation process existed the conviction that it would be difficult to guaranty the application of economic, social and cultural rights by means of judicial control– and in the American Convention on Human Rights".

The Constitutional Chamber, after recognizing the indivisibility of human rights, in the sense that the full enjoyment of the civil and political rights is impossible without the enjoyment of economic, social and cultural rights –as declared in the Teheran Conference on Human Rights and accepted by the General Assembly of United Nations in Resolution N° 32/130–; pointed out that such assertion did not vanish the incertitude regarding the role of States in economic, social and cultural rights and its obligations deriving form such rights. The doubt subsists, because as explained by the Constitutional Chamber, the implementation of economic, social and cultural rights "faces the debt crisis and the resulting impoverishment of Latin American countries, so the satisfaction of such rights depends on the availability of existing resources, the State being committed only to provide means in order to progressively achieve its goals".

But, as pointed out by the Chamber, due to the fact that the 1999 Venezuelan Constitution set forth not only the Welfare State based on the Rule but on the consideration of the economic, social and cultural rights as "fundamental rights", this situation imposes the need to do a theoretical effort to framework the protection of such rights, in order to not issue decisions that could be qualified as demagogic because of their impossibility to enforce.

The Constitutional Chamber began its argument by saying that the idea of the Welfare State based on the Rule of law refers to a State devoted to satisfying the basic needs of individuals, in order to the achievement of higher living standards in the population; but from that sole idea it is not possible to deduct rights, or consider that they are within the subjective sphere of citizens. From this idea what results is the aspiration to satisfy basic needs of individuals as a guiding principle of administrative activity. Regarding the justiciability of rights, the Constitutional Chamber added:

> In contrast, at least in the 1999 Constitution, the economic, social and cultural rights are declared as fundamental rights, which implies specific consequences, among them, –in prin-

> ciple– the applicability of the protection by means of amparo, because the Constitution, in contrast to what is establish in other legal orders, does not exclude certain rights from that guaranty, nor its immediate applicability, due to the fact that our constitutional order has a normative immediate value and application, rejecting what are known as programmatic rights.

Consequently, having such economic, social and cultural rights a fundamental rights character; they are undoubtedly judicially protected, because on the contrary, we will not be facing a right but a moral value aspiration".

But after affirming this, the Constitutional Chamber built the denial of such justiciability of social right, stating that "the point is to determine when one is asking for the enforcement of an economic, social or cultural right, and when one is asking that the Public Administration perform the Welfare State based on the Rule of Law State clause, given that the way s to ask in both cases differ". This distinction derives from the recognition of the political value of the State's activity devoted to satisfy the existence needs, and from the definition of the essential core of each of the rights that is stake". From this, the Chamber went to rule on the non justiciability of social rights, arguing that they were only submitted to political control, emphasizing that:

> In the first case we must begin affirming that the policy, is basically manifested itself, through acts, and also through application, design, planning, evaluation and follow–up regarding the government trends and public expenses, so that policy does not exhaust itself in the legal framework. In this context the acts are subjected to judicial review, but only regarding its legal elements (conformity of the concrete action to the law, and not in a general or abstract way). The of participation set forth in the Constitution and the laws (during the accomplishment of governmental and administrative functions, and in case of evident incapacity of Public Administration to plan in an efficient way its activity to satisfy the existence needs, citizens will withdraw the confidence given to their representatives by mean of election, as a sign of a process of de legitimization of political actors".
>
> ....the point is to emphasize the impossibility for the judge to challenge the opportunity and convenience of the Administration, of the government or of the legislation, or the material or technical impossibility that in some occasions exists of enforcing the judicial decisions that order the accomplishment of certain duties...
>
> ...in the public activity, the State has freedom to organize itself, which cannot be legitimately substituted by the Judiciary. It has it as a consequence of the accomplishment of its constitutional duties resulting from the nature of such functions, that is, as a derivation of the principle of separation of powers that sets forth a scope reserved to each power and excludes the substitution of wills, and that the Government–Judiciary relation prevents for judicial review to be the measure for the sufficiency of the rendering burden".

The Constitutional Chamber then went to quote the doctrine of the Spanish Constitutional Tribunal and of the German federal Constitutional Tribunal, regarding the absence of judicial review in political acts or political order acts, generalizing as follows:

> "Policies are in principle, outside the scope of judicial review, but not for that reason they escape control only that this applicable control is the political one also set forth in the Constitution. The State organs act under their own responsibility, which can be challenged in the political level, meaning that they cannot be unvested of the authorization in their political management. But that process of de–legitimating can not be qualified by the Judiciary, unless

when determining an administrative liability for damages caused by the political activity and putting aside that a fundamental right be affected by the decision, in which case, eventually, the control will not be regarding the political elements of the act and turn to be a control regarding its juridical elements…"

From the abovementioned, the Constitutional Chamber then concluded that:

> a) The economic, social and cultural rights have, as all rights, judicial protection; b) In order to know if one is facing one of such rights, it must exist a perfectly defined juridical relation where the harm to them comes from a change to the juridical sphere of a citizen or of collectivity; c) The State activity directed to satisfy the existence need is an activity with political contents; d) That such activity can manifest itself by acts or through policies; e) That such acts can be the object of judicial control in their juridical elements, not in the political; f) That the policies, in principle, can not be the object of judicial control but of political control; g) That such judicial impossibility cannot be understood as the rejection of the citizens right to action".

The Constitutional Chamber eventually ruled that "resulting from the principle of separation of powers, the Judiciary cannot substitute the Legislative or the Executive definition of social policies, the violation of which, could led to a government by judges", adding that "due to the fact that the economic, social and cultural policies depend on the existing resources, the Judiciary has the power to control in positive way, that bearing in mind the economic situation of the State, it has made a maximal use of the available resources –including legislative measures–; and in negative sense, the absolute absence of economic, social and cultural policies (which voided the essential core of the respective rights), as well as those policies openly directed to harm the juridical situation that protect the economic, social or cultural rights, cases that impose the State the burden of proof, also implying regarding the former, the analysis of the distribution of social spending".

Regarding the amparo action, the Constitutional Chamber concluded affirming that being "of a reestablish nature, the possibility to judicially control the economic, social and cultural policies are not comprised by this constitutional guaranty, but it is completely within the nature of the functions of the People's Defendant.

Finally, referring the right to health, and the claim of the *Federación Médica Venezolana* asking to the court to order the accomplishment of economic resources to the hospitals, and budget allocation for the acquisition of medical equipment and hospital materials, the Chamber rejected it considering that it is a very evident political activity, abstract in nature, which makes it "impossible to be the object of an amparo action directed to restore concrete juridical situations". In the proceedings of the public hearing on the case, the Chamber finally ruled that "social or third generation rights, contrary to those of first or second generation, have a specific structure" that originates certain differences which impose the precision on what can be referred the judicial protection regarding such rights, pointing out that:

> "Such rights, by themselves, are not in the subjective sphere of citizens due to the fact that, *ab initio*, they are guiding principles of the administrative activity; they are the basis of the Social and Justice State based on the Rule of law clause, and thus, they are elements defining the goals, in the sense that they qualified what must be considered of public interest.

Consequently, the enforcement of the third generations of rights is not possible, being the political control the only way to verify its accomplishment. Faced to the evident incapacity of Public Administration to efficiently plan its activities, the citizens will withdraw the confidence given to their representatives by means of suffrage, as demonstration of the de–legitimating of the actors"[452].

CHAPTER IX.
THE EXTRAORDINARY CHARACTER OF THE AMPARO ACTION AND THE GENERAL PROCEDURAL RULES OF THE SUIT

I. THE EXTRAORDINARY CHARACTER OF THE AMPARO

The most common characteristic of the Latin American amparo action, is its extraordinary character, in the sense that in general terms it is granted when there are no other adequate judicial means to obtain the immediate protection of the constitutional right that has been violated.

This characteristic also applies in the United States to the injunctions and to all other equitable remedies like the mandamus and prohibitions, in the sense that they are considered available only "after the applicant shows that the legal remedies are inadequate"[453] since they are reserved for extraordinary cases[454],

This main characteristic of the injunction as an extraordinary remedy has been established since the XIX Century in *In re Debs* 158 U.S. 564, 15 S.Ct 900, 39 L. Ed. 1092 (1895), in which, in words of Justice Brewer, who delivered the opinion of the court, it was decided that:

> "As a rule, injunctions are denied to those who have adequate remedy at law. Where the choice is between the ordinary and the extraordinary processes of law, and the former are sufficient, the rule will not permit the use of the latter" [455]

In Latin America, even though the common law distinction between remedies at law and equitable remedies does not exist, regarding the amparo action, –which comprises in only one institution all the drastic remedies established in North American law (injunctions, mandamus and prohibitions), it has the same general characteristic of extraordinary remedy. This is provided not only in the Latin American

---

452 See in *Revista de Derecho Público*, N° 97–98, Editorial Jurídica Venezuela, Caracas 2004, p. 143 ff

453 See in Owen M. FISS and Doug RENDLEMAN, *Injunctions*, The Foundation Press, Mineola New York, 1984, p. 59.

454 Exparte Collet, 337 U.S. 55, 69 S. Ct 944, 93 L. Ed. 1207, 10 A.L.R. 2D 921 (1949). See in John BOURDEAU et al, "Injunctions" in Kevin SCHRODER, John GLENN and Maureen PLACILLA, *Corpus Juris Secundum*, Volume 43A, Thomson West, 2004, p. 20.

455 See in Owen M. FISS and Doug RENDLEMAN, *Injunctions*, The Foundation Press, Mineola New York, 1984, p. 8.

sense that it is only established for the protection of constitutional rights and guaranties, but also in the sense that it is admissible only when there are no other adequate judicial means for obtaining the constitutional protection.

This extraordinary character of the Latin American amparo action, equivalent to the so called "subordinate" character of the North American injunction, implies then that the amparo is only admissible when there are no other judicial means for granting the constitutional protection, or in case they exist, are not adequate means for the immediate protection of the harmed or threatened constitutional rights. The questions of the non availability and of the inadequacy are, thus, two key factors regarding the admissibility of the action.

Only in a very few Latin American countries, the filing of the amparo action requires the obligatory previous exhaustion of ordinary existing judicial means, as it is established in Spain regarding its amparo action.

1. The question of the previous exhaustion of the ordinary judicial means

Actually, the general principle in Spain is that since the protection of constitutional rights and liberties is a task attributed to the courts, the filing of an amparo action before the Constitutional Tribunal can only be admitted when the ordinary judicial means have been exhausted, so that the Tribunal can only be asked to decide an amparo action when filed against the final judicial decision. The amparo action in Spain can then be considered as *subsidiaria* ("ancillary") in the sense that it can only be filed after a prior judgment has been issued[456].

In Latin America, this condition of the necessary prior exhaustion of the existing ordinary judicial or administrative means is only regulated in Mexico, Guatemala and Peru.

In Mexico, the condition of the previous exhaustion of the ordinary judicial means in order to file an amparo action, responds to the principle of the "definitive character of the challenged act" set forth in Article 103 of the Constitution and Article 73 of the Amparo Law, in the sense that when the amparo action is directed against a judicial act, it can only be filed against the definitive and final judicial rulings, regarding which there is no other judicial remedy available to obtain its modification or repeal (Art 73, XIII). The only exception to this condition is when the challenged act implies a danger of extinguishing life or deportation or any act forbidden in Article 20 of the Constitution. Regarding administrative acts the amparo action is inadmissible when they can be challenged by a recourse, suit or any other mean of defense, providing that the statutes allow for the suspension of the effects of the challenged acts without additional conditions to those set forth in the Amparo Law (Art. 73, XV). The general consequences of this "definitively" rule are the followings:

1. It is necessary that regarding the authority act challenged by means of amparo that all the recourses and means of defense that can modify or repeal it, be filled.

456 See Eduardo FERRER MAC GREGOR, *La acción constitucional de amparo en México y España. Estudio de derecho comparado*, Editorial Porrúa, México, 2002, pp. 292 ff.

2. The above mentioned judicial means must be exhausted, which means that it is not sufficient for them to be filed, but they must be pursued up to the final stage obtaining the definitive decision of the authority[457].

A similar principle is followed by the Guatemalan Amparo Law, by setting forth that "in order to file an amparo, except in the cases specified in this statute, it is necessary that the ordinary judicial and administrative recourses by mean of which the matters can be adequately resolved according to the due process principle, be exhausted"(Art. 19)[458]. It must be highlighted that in this case, the exhaustion rule refers not only to judicial recourses but also to administrative ones[459]. In the case of Brazil, Article 5,1 of the *mandado de segurança* Law also sets forth that it will not be admissible against acts against which administrative recourses with suppressive effects can be filed, independently of bail.

It must be said also regarding injunctions against administrative acts in the United States that they can only be filed after the available administrative remedy has been exhausted (*Zipp v. Geske & Sons, Inc*, 103 F. 3d 1379 (7th Cir. 1997)); the rule is not applied when the exhaustion of the remedy will cause imminent and irreparable harm (*State ex rel. Sheehan v. District Court of Minn. In and For Hennepin County*, 253 Minn. 462, 93 N.W.2d 1 (1958))[460].

In Peru, Articles 5 and 45 of the Constitutional Procedures Code also provide for the inadmissibility of the amparo action when the "previous means" were not exhausted beforehand; adding that in case of doubt regarding such exhaustion, the amparo will be preferred.

This "previous means" that must be exhausted are basically the administrative procedure challenging recourses, like the hierarchical one in order to obtain the decision of the peck of Public Administration hierarchy before filing the amparo. As was justified by the Constitutional Tribunal, "the need for the exhaustion of such [administrative] mean before filing the amparo, is founded in the need to give the Public Administration the possibility to review its own acts, in order to allow the possibility for the Administration to resolve the case, without the need to appear before the judicial organs"[461].

---

457 See Eduardo FERRER MAC GREGOR, *La acción constitucional de amparo en México y España. Estudio de derecho comparado*, Editorial Porrúa, México, 2002, pp. 315, 392 ff.; Richard D. BAKER, *Judicial Review in Mexico. A Study of the Amparo Suit*, University of Texas Press, Austin, 1971, p. 100

458 See the courts' decision in this sense in Jorge Mario GARCÍA LAGUARDIA, *Jurisprudencia constitucional. Guatemala., Honduras, México, Una Muestra*, Guatemala 1986, pp. 43, 45

459 In Honduras, for instance, regarding the habeas data action, article 40 of the Amparo law set forth that in only can be filed when exhausted the corresponding administrative procedure (art. 40).

460 See the reference in John BOURDEAU et al, "Injunctions" in Kevin SCHRODER, John GLENN and Maureen PLACILLA, *Corpus Juris Secundum*, Volume 43A, Thomson West, 2004, p.225.

461 See Exp 1042–AA–TC, decision of December 6, 2002, F.J. Nº 2). See the reference in Samuel B. ABAD YUPANQUI, *El proceso constitucional de amparo*, Gaceta Jurídica, Lima 2004, p. 234

This condition for the admissibility of the amparo action, considered as a Public Administration "privilege" that could in itself harm the constitutional right to obtain judicial protection, has some exceptions provided in Article 45 of the same Constitutional Procedure Code, when establishing that the exhaustion of the previous means would not be required in the following cases:

> 1) If a resolution, even if its not the last in the administrative procedure, has been executed before the exhaustion of the delay established in order to be considered as consented; 2) If because of the exhaustion of the previous mean the aggression could become irreparable; 3) If the previous mean is not regulated or has been unnecessarily initiated by the injured party; or 4) If the previous mean is not resolved within the delays fixed for its resolution.

The Constitutional Tribunal has extensively elaborated all these exceptions: regarding the first exception, it has considered that the amparo action is admissible in all cases in which the challenged resolution has been immediately executed by the Public Administration before any possibility for the affected party to challenge it in the administrative procedure[462]. Regarding the irreparability of the damage exception, it has been considered that that situation occurs when the exhaustion of the administrative means would impede the harmed right to be restored to the position exiting before the harm was caused[463]. This is the case, for instance, when a Municipal administrative decision to demolish a building, would be executed during the exhaustion of the administrative recourse. Regarding the last exception, it tends to avoid the perpetuation of undefined situations due to the lack of decision regarding administrative petitions[464].

Even though it is not expressly regulated, in cases of amparo actions filed against judicial decisions when the due process rights are being clearly and ostensibly harmed, the Constitutional Tribunal has also imposed the previous exhaustion of the ordinary judicial means in order to bring the amparo action before the competent court[465]; being consider the adequacy for the constitutional protection of the judicial ordinary means[466].

As aforementioned, only in Mexico, Guatemala and Peru it is imposed as a general condition for the filing of the amparo action –although with important excep-

---

462 See Samuel B. ABAD YUPANQUI, *El proceso constitucional de amparo*, Gaceta Jurídica, Lima 2004, pp. 246–250.

463 Exp. N° 1266–2001–AA/TC, decisión of September 9, 2002, El Peruano –Garantías Constitucionales– April 4, 2003, p. 6081. See the reference in Samuel B. ABAD YUPANQUI, *El proceso constitucional de amparo*, Gaceta Jurídica, Lima 2004, pp. 251–255

464 See Samuel B. ABAD YUPANQUI, *El proceso constitucional de amparo*, Gaceta Jurídica, Lima 2004, pp. 258–260

465 Exp. N° 1821–98, decision June 25, 1999, El peruano –Jurispurdencia–, November 7, 2001, p. 4501. See the reference in Samuel B. ABAD YUPANQUI, *El proceso constitucional de amparo*, Gaceta Jurídica, Lima 2004, p. 242.

466 See Luis R. SÁENZ DÁVALOS, "Las innovaciones del Código Procesl Constitucional en el recurso constitucional de amparo", in Susana CASTAÑEDA et al, *Introducción a los procesos constitucionales. Comentarios al Código Procesal Constitucional*, Jurísta Editores, Lima 2005, p. 135.of

tions– the need to previously exhaust all the existing ordinary judicial and administrative means.

In the other Latin American countries such condition has not been imposed; and the admissibility condition discussion is referred to the effective existence of adequate means for the immediate protection of the harmed or threatened constitutional rights. In these cases, the questions to be discussed in order to determine the admission of the amparo action refer to the availability or non availability of judicial or administrative means for protection of the harmed right; and to the adequacy or inadequacy of the existing judicial means for such protection, rather than to their imposed exhaustion.

2. The question of the non availability of other adequate judicial or administrative means for protection

In this regard, the general principles referred to the admissibility of the amparo action are very similar to the same question referred to the admission of the injunction remedy in North America, where one of its traditional and fundamental bases is the inadequacy of the existing legal remedies as the main prerequisite to granting an injunction (*Beacon Theatres, Inc. v. Westover*, 359 U.S. 500, 79 S.Ct. 948, 3L.Ed. 2d 988, 2 Fed. R. Serv. 2d 650 (1959))[467]. The North American judicial doctrine on the matter has been summarized as follows:

> "An injunction, like any other equitable remedy, will only be issued where there is no adequate remedy at law. Accordingly, except where the rule is changed by statute, an injunction ordinarily will not be granted where there is an adequate remedy at law for the injury complained of, which is full and complete. Conversely, a court of equitable jurisdiction may grant an injunction where an adequate and complete remedy cannot be had in the courts of law, despite the petitioner's efforts. Moreover, a court will not deny access to injunctive relief when procedures cannot effectively, conveniently and directly determine whether the petitioner is entitled to the relief claimed"[468].

This condition regarding injunctions has been also referred in the United States as to the "availability" or the "sufficiency" rule[469], and also to the "irreparable injury" rule, implying the admission of the injunction only when the harm "cannot be adequately repaired by the remedies available in the common law courts if the threatened harm is one that can be rectified by a legal remedy, then the judge will refuse to enjoin".[470]

---

467 See in John BOURDEAU et al, "Injunctions" in Kevin Schroder, John Glenn and Maureen Placilla, *Corpus Juris Secundum*, Volume 43A, Thomson West, 2004, p. 89

468 See in John BOURDEAU et al, "Injunctions" in Kevin Schroder, John Glenn and Maureen Placilla, *Corpus Juris Secundum*, Volume 43A, Thomson West, 2004, pp. 89–90; 119 ff.; 224 ff.

469 See in John BOURDEAU et al, "Injunctions" in Kevin Schroder, John Glenn and Maureen Placilla, *Corpus Juris Secundum*, Volume 43A, Thomson West, 2004, pp. 119 ff.

470 See Owen M. FISS and Doug RENDLEMAN, *Injunctions*, The Foundation Press, Mineola New York, 1984, p. 59.

This situation, as pointed out by Owen M. Fiss "makes the issuance of an injunction conditional upon a showing that the plaintiff has no alternative remedy that will adequately repair the injury. Operationally this means that as general proposition the plaintiff is remitted to some remedy other than an injunction unless he can show that his non injunctive remedies are inadequate"[471].

This term "inadequacy", according to Tabb and Shoben, "has a specific meaning in the law of equity because it is a shorthand expression for the policy that equitable remedies are subordinate to legal ones. They are subordinate in the sense that the damage remedy is preferred in any individual case if it is adequate"[472]. But in particular, regarding constitutional claims involving constitutional rights such as those for school desegregation, it has been considered that their protection precisely requires of the extraordinary protection that can be obtained by equitable intervention, as was decided by the Supreme Court regarding school desegregation in its second opinion in *Brown v. Board of Education* (S. Ct. 1955) and regarding the unconstitutional cruel and unusual punishment in the prison system in *Hutto v. Finney (S.Ct. 1978)*[473]

The same general principle of the availability and adequacy, even though with any relation whatsoever to the distinction between law and equitable remedies, is applied in some Latin American countries like Argentina, Uruguay, Colombia, Venezuela, Chile and Dominican Republic, where in general terms, the amparo action cannot be admissible if there exists another adequate judicial or administrative means for the immediate protection of the constitutional right.

This is the case of Argentina, where the amparo action is also considered as an extraordinary and residual judicial remedy reserved for the "delicate and extreme situations in which, because of the lack of other legal means, the safeguard of fundamental rights is in danger"[474]. The same expression regarding the "extraordinary or residual" character of the amparo action is used by the Uruguayan courts[475].

That is why, in Argentina, Article 43 of the Constitution provides that the amparo action is admissible "as long as it does not exist another more adequate judicial mean"; and Article 2,a of the Amparo Law provides that the amparo is inadmissible "when there exist other juridical or administrative recourses or remedies which allow to obtain the protection of the constitutional right or guaranty". Because in Argentina the amparo action is not admitted against judicial decisions, regarding the amparo against administrative acts, this article refers first, to the availability of judicial and administrative means for the protection, the latter (administrative recourses) to be exercised before the superior organs of Public Administration; and second, to

---

471 Owen FISS, *The Civil Rights Injunction*, Indiana University Press, 1978, p. 38.

472 See William M. TABB and Elaine W. SHOBEN, *Remedies*, Thomson West 2005, p. 15

473 See William M. TABB and Elaine W. SHOBEN, *Remedies*, Thomson West 2005, pp. 25–26

474 CSJN, 7/3/85, LL, 1985–C–140; íd., Fallos, 303"422; 306; 1253. See in Néstor Pedro SAGÜÉS, *Derecho procesal Constitucional,* Vol 3, *Acción de amparo*, Editorial Astrea Buenos Aires 1988, p. 166

475 J.L. Cont. Adm. 2° S. 194 del 9/9/92; tAC 7° S. 171 del 25/9/92; TAC 7° S. 27 del 28/2/90; J.L. Cont. Adm, 2° res. Del 10/10/91. See in Luis Alberto VIERA, *Ley de Amparo*, Ediciones Idea, Montevideo 1993, pp.145, 148, 149.

the adequacy of those means, in the sense that they must be adequate, sufficient and effective in order to protect the plaintiff. Therefore, even when other remedies exist, the amparo action is admissible when their use could provoke grave and irreparable harm or they cannot be adequate for the immediate protection required for the harmed or threatened constitutional right[476]. Being a condition of admissibility, it is for the plaintiff to allege and proof that there are no other adequate means for the protection of his rights[477]. As was decided by the Supreme Court:

> "It is indispensable for the admission of the exceptional remedy of amparo that those claimant judicial protection to prove, in due form, the inexistence of other legal means for the protection of the harmed right or that the use of the existing could provoke an ulterior irreparable harm"[478].

In Uruguay, in a more or less similar way, Article 2 of the Amparo law also provides that "the amparo action will only be admissible when no other judicial or administrative means exist permitting to obtain the same result established in Article 9,B (the precise determination of what must or not must be done) or when if in existence, because of the circumstances they were ineffective for the protection to the right". Is his admissibility condition what gives the amparo action in Uruguay its "extraordinary, exceptional, residual character, in the sense that it is admissible when the normal means for protections will be powerless".[479]

Also in Colombia, Article 86 of the Constitution provides that the amparo action can only be filed when the affected party does not have another judicial mean available for his protection; and Article 6,1 of the Tutela Law prescribes that the amparo action is inadmissible "when other judicial recourses or means of defense exists, unless when they are used as a transitory mechanism to prevent irreparable harms". In the later case, the question of the efficacy of the existing judicial means must be judged in concrete, according to the circumstances of the plaintiff' (Art, 6, 1).

It must be highlighted that the residual character of the Colombian tutela only refers to the existence of other judicial means, and not to administrative means or recourses considered in Colombia as optional for the plaintiff (Art. 9 Tutela law). Also in Costa Rica it is expressly provided in the Amparo Law that it is not necessary to file any administrative recourse prior to the filling of the amparo action (Art. 31)[480].

476 See José Luis LAZZARINI, *El juicio de amparo*, Ed. La Ley, Buenos Aires1987, p. 94.95, 122 ff., 139; Alí Joaquín SALGADO, *Juicio de amparo y acción de inconstitucionalidad*, Editorial Astrea, Buenos Aires, 1987, pp. 31 ff.

477 See Néstor Pedro SAGÜÉS, *Derecho Procesal Constitucional*, Vol 3, *Acción de Amparo*, Editorial Astrea, Buenos Aires, 1988, p. 170

478 Case *Carlos Alfredo Villar v. Banco de la República Argentina*. See he reference in Samuel B. ABAD YUPANQUI, *El proceso constitucional de amparo*, Gaceta Jurídica, Lima, 2004, pp. 223–224.

479 See Luis Alberto VIERA, *Ley de Amparo*, Ediciones Idea, Montevideo 1993, p. 20. See the court decisions reference regarding the "residually" rule in pp. 57, 131 ff; 154 ff.; and 158 ff.

480 See Rubén HERNÁNDEZ, *Derecho Procesal Constitucional*, Editorial juricentro, San José, 2001, p. 242

The other judicial means of protection that in Colombia instead of the tutela action are considered as serving for effective protection of fundamental rights, are the public action of unconstitutionality, the exception of unconstitutionality, the habeas corpus action, the action for compliance, the popular actions, the judicial review of administrative acts actions, the exception of illegality and the provisional suspension of the effects of administrative acts[481]. In any case, it is for the tutela judge to determine if there are other judicial means for protection, as it has been ruled by the Constitutional Court, when deciding that:

> "When the tutela judge finds that other judicial defense mechanisms exists are applicable to the case, he must evaluate if according to the facts expressed in the claim and the scope of the harmed or threatened fundamental right, the available remedies include all the relevant aspects for the immediate, complete and efficient protection of the violated rights, in matters of proof and of the alternate defense decision mechanism"[482].

As mentioned, the only exception to the rule imposing the need to file the other judicial existing means for protection before bringing a tutela action, is the possibility to use the tutela as a transitory protective mean in order to avoid harms considered irreparable (Art. 8), that is, harms that because of their imminence and gravity impose the immediate adoption of protection[483].

The same principle also applies in Venezuela, event without an express legal provision as those existing in the Argentinean, Colombian and Uruguayan laws. As it has been decided by the former Supreme Court of Justice in a decision dated March 8, 1990,

> "the amparo is admissible even in cases where although ordinary means exist for the protection of the infringed juridical situation, they would not be suitable, adequate or effective for the immediate restoration of the said situation"[484].

In similar sense, the Supreme Court in a decision dated December 11, 1990, ruled that:

> "The criteria of this High Court as well as the authors opinions, has been reiterative in the sense that the amparo action is an extraordinary or special judicial remedy that is only admissible when the other procedural means that could repair the harm, are exhausted, do not exist or would be inoperative. Additionally, Article 5 of the Amparo Law provides that the amparo action is only admissible when no brief, summary and effective procedural means exist in accordance with the constitutional protection".
>
> This objective procedural condition for the admissibility of the action, turns the amparo into a judicial mean that can only be admissible by the court once it has verified that the other

---

481 See Juan Carlos ESGUERRA PORTOCARRERO, *La protección constitucional del ciudadano*, Legis, Bogotá, 2004 p. 125.

482 See decisión &–100/94, march 9, 1994. See the reference in Samuel B. ABAD YUPANQUI, *El proceso constitucional de amparo*, *Gaceta Jurídica*, Lima, 2004, p. 229.

483 See Juan Carlos ESGUERRA PORTOCARRERO, *La protección constitucional del ciudadano*, Legis, Bogotá 2004 p. 127.

484 See in *Revista de Derecho Público*, N° 42, Editorial Jurídica Venezolana, Caracas, 1990, pp. 107–108. See also decision of First Court on Judicial Review of Administrative Actions dated September 5, 1991 in FUNEDA, *15 años de Jurisprudencia*, *op. cit.*, p. 130.

ordinary means are not effective or adequate in order to restore the infringed juridical situation. If other means exist, the court must not admit the proposed amparo action"[485].

The Supreme Court in another decision dated June 12, 1990, decided that the amparo action is admissible:

> "when there are no other means for the adequate and effective reestablishment of the infringed juridical situation. Consequently, one of the conditions for the admissibility of the amparo action is the non existence of other more effective means for the reestablishment of the harmed rights. If such means are adequate to resolve the situation, there is no need to file the special amparo action. But even if such means exists, if they are inadequate for the immediate reestablishment of the constitutional guaranty, it is also justifiable to use the constitutional protection mean of amparo"[486].

Of course, the question of the availability and of the adequacy of the existing judicial means for the admissibility or not of the amparo action, in the end is a matter of judicial interpretation and adjudication, decided always in the concrete case decision, when evaluating the adequacy question. For instance, in a decision of the First Court on administrative jurisdiction dated May 20, 1994 (case *Federación Venezolana de Deportes Equestres*) it was ruled that the judicial review of administrative acts actions were not adequate for the protection requested in the case, that seeks the participation of the Venezuelan Federation of Equestrian Sports in an international competition. The case required immediate decision, so the court ruled as follows:

> It is the opinion of this court that when the action was brought before it, the only mean that the claimant had in order to obtain the reestablishment of the infringed juridical situation was the amparo action, due to the fact that by means of the judicial review of administrative acts recourse seeking its nullity, they could never be able to obtain the said reestablishment of the infringed juridical situation that was to assist to the 1990 the international competitions"[487]

In contrary sense and after having established for years a judicial doctrine admitting the autonomous amparo action against administrative acts, in recent years, the Supreme Tribunal of Justice of Venezuela has been progressively imposing a restrictive interpretation on the matter, ruling on the adequacy of the judicial review action seeking the annulment of such acts before the Administrative Jurisdiction. This can be realized from the decision taken in a recent and polemic case referred to the expropriation of some premises of a corn agro–industry complex, which developed as follows:

---

485 See in en *Revista de Derecho Público,* N° 45, Editorial Jurídica Venezolana, Caracas, 1991, p. 112

486 See decision of the Politico Administrative Chamber of the Supreme Court of Justice of June 12, 1990, *Revista de Derecho Público* N° 43, Editorial Jurídica Venezolana, Caracas, 1990, p. 78. See also in *Revista de Derecho Público,* N° 55–56, Editorial Jurídica Venezolana, Caracas, 1993, pp. 311–313.

487 See the reference in Rafael CHAVERO G. *El nuevo amparo constitucional en Venezuela,* Ed. Sherwood, Caracas 2001, p. 354.

In August 2005, officers from the Ministry of Agriculture and Land and military officers and soldiers from the Army and the National Guard, surrounded the installation of the company *Refinadora de Maíz Venezolana, C.A. (Remavenca)*, and announces were publicly made regarding the appointment of an Administrator Commission that would taking over the industry. These actions where challenged by the company as a de facto action alleging the violation of the company rights to equality, due process and defense, economic freedom, property rights and to the non confiscation guaranty of property. A few days latter, the Governor of the State of *Barinas* where the industry is located, issued a Decree ordering the expropriation of the premises, and consequently the Supreme Tribunal declared the inadmissibility of the amparo action that was filed, basing its ruling on the following arguments:

> The criteria established up to now by this Tribunal, by which it has concluded on the inadmissibility of the autonomous amparo action against administrative acts has been that the judicial review of administrative act actions –among which the recourse for nullity, the actions against the administrative abstentions and recourse filed by public servants– are the adequate means, that is, the brief, prompt and efficient means in order to obtain the reestablishment of the infringed juridical situation, in addition to the wide powers that are attributed to the administrative jurisdiction courts in Article 29 of the Constitution.
>
> Accordingly, the recourse for nullity or the expropriation suit, are the adequate means to resolve the claims referred to supposed controversies in the expropriation procedure; those are the preexisting judicial means in order to judicially decide conflicts in which previous legality studies are required, and which the constitutional judge cannot consider.
>
> Thus, the Chamber considers that the claimants, if they think that the alleged claim persists, they can obtain the reestablishment of their allegedly infringed juridical situation, by means of the ordinary actions and to obtain satisfaction to their claims. So existing adequate means for the resolution of the controversy argued by the plaintiff, it is compulsory for the Chamber to declare the inadmissibility of the amparo action, according to what is set forth in Article 6,5 of the Organic Law[488].

Also even without statutory regulation, the same rule of admissibility has been adopted in Chile[489] and in Dominican Republic. In the latter country, the Supreme Court has ruled as follows:

> "According to the Dominican legal doctrine, as well as to the international doctrine and jurisprudence, the amparo action has a subordinate character, which implies that it can only be filed when the interested person does not have any other mean to

---

488 See decision of the Constitucional Chamber of the Supreme Tribunal of Justice N° 3375 of November 4, 2005, Case: *Refinadora de Maíz Venezolana, C.A. (Remavenca), y Procesadora Venezolana de Cereales, S.A. (Provencesa) vs. Ministro de Agricultura y Tierras y efectivos de los componentes Ejército y Guardia Nacional de la Fuerza Armada Nacional.*

489 See Humberto NOGUEIRA ALCALÁ, "El derecho de amparo o protección de los derechos humanos, fundamentales o esenciales en Chile: evolución y perspectivas", in Humberto Nogueira Alcalá (Editor), *Acciones constitucionales de amparo y protección: realidad y perspectivas en Chile y América Latina*", Editorial Universidad de Talca, Talca 2000, p. 27. In contrary sense, see Emilio PFEFFER URQUIAGA, "Naturaleza, caracteristicas y fines del recurso de protección", in Humberto Nogueira Alcalá (Editor), *Acciones constitucionales de amparo y protección: realidad y perspectivas en Chile y América Latina*", Editorial Universidad de Talca, Talca 2000, p. 153.

claim for the protection of the harmed or threatened right; the principle supposes that the amparo action cannot be filed when other procedures exists in parallel, in which the injured party has the possibility to claim for the protection of the same fundamental rights[490].

3. The question of the previous election of other remedies that are pending of decision, including amparo suits

The extraordinary character of the amparo suit not only implies that it can only be filed when the affected party does not have any other available ordinary judicial to obtain adequate protection for his harmed or threatened constitutional rights, but that the affected party in seeking protection when bringing an amparo suit, must not have a pending action or recourse brought before a court for the same purpose. This can be considered also as a general rule on the matter, similar to what is called in North American law, the "doctrine of the election of remedies" regarding the equitable defenses in the suit for injunctions. As Tabb and Shoben have pointed out: "The doctrine of elections of remedies provides that when an injured party has two available but inconsistent remedies to redress a harm, the act of choosing one constitutes a binding election that forecloses the other"[491].

In similar sense, the general rule in Latin America, as it is set forth in Article 73, XIV of the Mexican Amparo Law, is that the amparo suit is inadmissible when the claimant has brought before an ordinary court any recourse or legal defense seeking to modify, repeal or nullify the challenged act". So pending the decision on a judicial process in which the claimant has asked the same protective remedies, the amparo suit cannot be admissible[492]. The Peruvian Code on Constitutional procedures also establishes that the amparo action is inadmissible "when the aggrieved party has previously chosen other judicial processes seeking protection of his constitutional right" (Art 5, 3). The same has been decided by the Chilean courts regarding the action for protection.[493]

In Venezuela, Article 6,5 of the Amparo Law also provides that the suit is inadmissible "when the injured party has chosen other ordinary judicial means or has used other preexisting judicial means". In such cases, when the violation or threat of constitutional rights and guarantees has been alleged, the court must follow the procedure set forth in the Amparo Law (Arts. 23, 24 and 25), in order to provisionally suspend the effects of the challenged act.

---

490 Manuel A. VALERA MONTERO, *Hacia un nuevo concepto de Constitución. Selección y clasificación de decisiones de la Suprema Corte de Justicia de la República Dominicana en materia constitucional 1910–2004*, Santo Domingo, 2006, pp. 374–375.

491 See William M. TABB and Elaine W. SHOBEN, *Remedies*, Thomson West 2005, p. 56.

492 See Eduardo FERRER MAC–GREGOR, *La acción constitucional de amparo en México y España. Estudio de derecho comparado*, Editorial Porrúa, México, 2002, pp. 393.; Richard D. BAKER, *Judicial Review in Mexico. A Study of the Amparo Suit,* University of Texas Press, Austin, 1971, p. 100

493 See Juan Manuel ERRAZURIZ G. and Jorge Miguel OTERO A., *Aspectos procesales del recurso de protección*, Editorial Jurídica de Chile, Santiago, 1989, p. 114.

This inadmissibility clause is only applicable when in the other judicial action or recourse the constitutional violation has been alleged; so that the constitutional protection can be obtained. Thus, it is possible to obtain in an immediate way the effective protection of the constitutional rights, this justifies in such cases, the inadmissibility of the amparo action.

This inadmissibility clause has been applied in cases of the exercise of judicial review against administrative acts actions, when a protection of constitutional rights has been conjunctly requested, seeking the suspension of the effects of the challenged administrative acts. In these cases, the First Court on Administrative Jurisdiction in a decision dated May 11, 1992 (Case *Venalum*), ruled as follows:

> "It has been the criteria of this court that Article 6,5 of the Amparo law imposes the inadmissibility of the amparo action when the aggrieved party has chosen for the ordinary judicial means or has used the preexistent judicial means. The court has considered in previous cases that when the plaintiff is asking for the suspension of the challenged administrative act according to Article 136 of the Supreme Court Organic Law, that means the use of a parallel mean for protection that turns in inadmissible the amparo action, because such petition for a provisional remedy requested conjunctly with the nullity action, is in itself a cause of inadmissibility[494].

On the other hand, it most be highlighted that the inadmissibility clause only applies when the plaintiff has used other judicial means for protection exercised before the courts; so if only administrative recourses have been used, the inadmissible clause is not applied, because the administrative recourses are not judicial ordinary means that can impede the filing of the amparo action[495].

Nonetheless, in Argentina, even thought the same general rule of inadmissibly has been developed through judicial interpretation, it has also comprised the cases in which the injured party has chosen to use administrative means for defense. As was decided in the Hughtes Tool Company SA. case, "the sole fact that the plaintiff has chosen to file a petition or recourse before the Administration, provokes the inadmissibility of the amparo action, because a claim of this nature cannot be used to take the case from the authority intervening in the case because so asked by the

494 See en *Revista de Derecho Público,* N° 50, Editorial Jurídica Venezolana, Caracas, 1992, pp. 187–188. See also the decisions of the First Court of February 21, 1991, *Revista de Derecho Público,* N° 45, Editorial Jurídica Venezolana, Caracas, p. 146, and of September 24, 1991, en FUNEDA, *15 años de Jurisprudencia... cit.*, p. 105; of December 5, 1991 and April 1, 1993 in *Revista de Derecho Público,* N° 53–54, Editorial Jurídica Venezolana, Caracas, 1994, p. 263. See also decisión of the Politico Administrative Chamber of the Supreme Court of July 13, 1992 (*Case Municipio Almirante Padilla*), *Revista de Derecho Público,* N° 51, Editorial Jurídica Venezolana; Caracas, 1992, pp. 215–216; and decisión of November 11, 1993, Caso *UNET*, in *Revista de Derecho Público,* N° 55–56, Editorial Jurídica Venezolana, Caracas, 1993, p. 489.

495 See the decisión of the First Court on administrative jurisdiction has decided on a decision dated march 8, 1993 (Case: Federico Domingo) in *Revista de Derecho Público,* N° 53–54, Editorial Jurídica Venezolana, Caracas, 1994, p. 261. See also decision dated May 6, 1994 (Caso *Universidad Occidental Lisandro Alvarado*), en *Revista de Derecho Público,* N° 57–58, Editorial Jurídica Venezolana, Caracas, 1994. See Rafael CHAVERO G. *El nuevo amparo constitucional en venezuela*, Ed. Sherwood, Caracas 2001, pp. 250 ff.

same plaintiff"[496]. In other cases, the decision has been that "it is not legal nor logic for a plaintiff in parallel and simultaneously to use two means of different procedural nature, one ordinary and the other extraordinary because it would be incompatible and it would place the claimant in a position of privileged or advantage contrary to the principle of equality in the exercise of procedural rules"[497].

Finally, in order to assure the effective protection of rights, the courts in Argentina have developed the doctrine that even in cases in which the interested party has chosen to use other judicial means for the protection of the harmed constitutional rights other than the amparo action, a subsequent amparo action could be admissible when there is an excessive delay in the resolution of the previous procedure to be issued; delay that can provoke the grave and irreparable harm that can justify the filing on the amparo action in order to obtain the immediate protection needed[498].

On the other hand, in the legislation of Bolivia, Ecuador, Mexico and Venezuela the inadmissibility of the amparo action is specifically regulated in cases in which a previous amparo action has been previously filed. In this regard, in Bolivia the Amparo Law provides that the amparo action is inadmissible when a previous constitutional amparo action has been filed with identity on the person, the object and the cause (Art. 96, 2); and in Ecuador, the Amparo Law forbids the filing of more that one amparo action regarding the same matter and with the same object, before more than one court. That is why, those filing an amparo action must declare under oath in the written request that he has not filed before other courts another amparo action with the same matter and object (Art 57).

In Mexico, Article 73, III of the amparo law also provides the inadmissibility of the amparo action against statutes and acts that are the object of another amparo suit pending of resolution, filed by the same aggrieved party, against the same authorities and regarding the same challenged act, even if the constitutional violations are different.

Also in Venezuela, Article 6,8 of the Amparo law provides the inadmissibility of the action for amparo when a decision regarding another amparo suit has been brought before the courts regarding the same facts and is pending of decision[499].

---

496 See in Alí Joaquín SALGADO, *Juicio de amparo y acción de inconstitucionalidad*, Editorial Astrea, Buenos Aires 1987, pp. 33

497 See ST La Rioja, 27/1/71, J.A., 10–1971–782. See the reference in Néstor Pedro SAGÜÉS, *Derecho procesal Constitucional,* Vol 3, *Acción de amparo*, Editorial Astrea, Buenos Aires 1988, p. 187

498 See Alí Joaquín SALGADO, *Juicio de amparo y acción de inconstitucionalidad*, Editorial Astrea, Buenos Aires 1987, p. 34; José Luis lazzarini, *El juicio de amparo*, Ed. La Ley, Buenos Aires1987, p. 143.

499 See for instance decision of the Politico Administrative Chamber of the Supreme Court of Justice of October 13, 1993, in *Revista de Derecho Público*, N° 55–56, Editorial Jurídica Venezolana, Caracas, 1993, pp. 348–349.

II. THE CHARACTER OF THE AMPARO SUIT PROCEDURE

1. The brief character of the procedure

Being the amparo suit an extraordinary remedy for the immediate protection of constitutional rights, its main feature is the brief character of the procedure, which is justified because its purpose is to protect a person in cases of irreparable injuries or threats to his constitutional rights. Thus, this irreparable character of the harm or threat and the immediate need for protection are the key elements that conform the procedural rules of the amparo suit.

In this regard, the same principle applies to the North American injunctions, regarding which the judicial doctrine on the matter has established the following principles:

> "An injunction is granted only when required to avoid immediate and irreparable damage to a legally recognized rights, such as property rights, constitutional rights or contract rights. There must be some vital necessity for the injunction so that one of the parties will not be damaged and left without adequate remedy. This requirement cannot be met where there is no showing of any real or immediate threat that the petitioner will be wronged again. Except as is otherwise provided by statute, to warrant an injunction it ordinarily must be clearly shown that some act has been done, or is threatened, which will produce irreparable injury to the party asking for the injunction, regardless of whether the party may additionally prove that the activity sought to be enjoined is illegal per se...
>
> The very function of an injunction is to furnish preventive relief against irreparable mischief or injury, and the remedy will not be awarded where it appears to the satisfaction of the court that the injury complained of is not such a character. More specifically, a permanent, mandatory injunction, a preliminary, interlocutory or temporary injunction, a preliminary mandatory injunction, or a preliminary, interlocutory or temporary restraining order, will not, as a general rule, be grated where it is not shown that an irreparable injury is immediate impending and will be inflicted on the petitioner before the case can be brought to a final hearing, no matter how likely it may be that the moving party will prevail on the merits"[500].

In general terms, these same principles applies to the amparo suit, but with the particular feature that in Latin America they have given shape to specific and particular procedural rules that govern the judicial procedure of the amparo suit, characterized by being a brief judicial process that is justified because of its protective objective regarding constitutional rights against violations, that requires immediate protection.

Those rules are characterized by a few particular trends, mainly referred to the general brief configuration of the procedure and, in particular, to the rules governing the complaint to be filed; the proof activity of the parties; the defendant report needed because of the bilateral character of the process and the hearing of the case.

That is, even being the nature of the amparo suit procedure a brief an prompt one, the bilateral character of the procedure imposes the respect of the due process rules and the need to guarantee the right to self defense of the defendant. That is

---

500 See in John BOURDEAU et al, "Injunctions" in Kevin Schroder, John Glenn and Maureen Placilla, *Corpus Juris Secundum*, Volume 43A, Thomson West, 2004, pp. 76–78.

why no definitive amparo adjudication can be given without the participation of the defendant. That is why only in a very exceptional way, some legislation as the Colombian one, admits the possibility of granting the constitutional protection (tutela) *in limene litis*, that is, "without any formal consideration and without previous enquiry, if the decision is founded in an evidence that shows the grave and imminent violation of harm to the right" (Art. 18). In the Venezuelan Amparo Law, from which such provision was taken, also provided for the possibility for the amparo judge "to immediately restore the infringed juridical situation, without considerations of mere form and without any kind of brief enquiry", being required in such cases, that "the amparo protection be founded in an evidence which constitute a grave presumption of the violation of harm of violation" (Art. 22).

Nonetheless, this article of the Venezuelan Amparo Law was annulled by the former Supreme Court of Justice[501], considering that it violated in a flagrant way the constitutional right to defense, and denying to establish its constitutional interpretation as just as a provision which only established –although with incorrect wording– a provisional and not definitive judicial measure of protection[502].

2. The brief and prompt nature of the procedure

The Latin American statutes regulating the amparo suit not only provide for a specific judicial mean for the protection of constitutional rights, but also for specific rules of procedure particularly referred to the amparo suit, which differ from the general rules that govern the ordinary judicial procedure. These specific rules are conditioned by the brief and promptness nature of the amparo procedure, which is imposed by the need for the immediate protection of constitutional rights.

As it is provided in Article 27 of the Venezuelan Constitution: the procedure of the constitutional amparo action must be oral, public, brief, free of charge and not subject to formality". Regarding some of these principles, the First Court on Judicial review of administrative actions even before the enactment of the Amparo law in 1988 ruled that because of the brief character of the procedure, it must be understood as having "the condition of being urgent, thus it must be followed promptly and decided in the shorter possible time"; and additionally it must be summary, in the sense that "the procedure must be simple, uncomplicated, without incidences and complex formalities". In this sense, the procedure must not be converted in a procedural complex and confused situation, limited in time to resolve the multiple" and various challenges and questions opposed as previous stage"[503]. According to these

501 Decision dated May 21, 1996. See in *Gaceta Oficial Extra* N° 5071 May 29, 1996. See the comments in Allan R. BREWER–CARÍAS, "Derecho y Acción de Amparo", Vol. V, *Instituciones Políticas y Constitucionales*, Editorial Jurídica venezolana, Caracas, 1998, pp. 388–396; Rafael CHAVERO GAZDIK, *El nuevo régimen del amparo constitucional en Venezuela*, Edit. Sherwood, Caracas 2001, pp. 212, 266 ff., 410 ff.

502 See the comments in Allan R. BREWER–CARÍAS, "Derecho y Acción de Amparo", *Instituciones Políticas y Constitucionales*, Vol V, Editorial Jurídica venezolana, Caracas 1998, pp. 398.

503 See decision of January 17, 1985, in *Revista de Derecho Publico,* N° 21, Editorial Jurídica Venezolana, Caracas, 1985, p. 140

principles, the Amparo Law of 1988 provided for the brief, prompt and summary procedure that governed the amparo suit up to the enactment of the 1999 Constitution, when the Constitutional Chamber interpreted the Statute provision according to the new Constitution having re–written its regulations by constitutional interpretation[504].

III. THE PRINCIPLES GOVERNING THE PREFERRED CHARACTER OF THE PROCEDURE

The general principles governing these specific rules are often expressly enumerated in the Amparo Laws, as guidelines for their general judicial interpretation. For instance, in Colombia, these are "the principles of publicity, prevalence of substantial law, economy, promptness and efficacy" (Art 3); in Ecuador, "the principles of procedural promptness and immediate [response]" (*inmediatez*) (Art 59); in Honduras, the "principles of independence, morality of the debate, informality, publicity, prevalence of substantial law, free of charge, promptness, procedural economy, effectiveness, and due process" (Art. 45); in Peru, "the principles of judicial direction of the process, free of charge regarding the plaintiff acts, procedural economy, immediate and socialization" (Art. III).

In particular, as a key principle for interpretation of procedural rules, it must be highlighted the one provided in the Honduras Law regarding the need for the prevalence of substantial rules over formal provisions, in the sense that because in the procedure "the merits on the matter must prevail", the "procedural defects must not prevent the quick development of the procedure". Consequently, it is provided that "the parties can correct their own mistakes, if remediable" being the courts also authorized to ex officio correct them (Honduras, Art. 4,5; Guatemala, Art. 6; Paraguay, Art. 20; El Salvador, Art. 80). That is why the Peruvian Code specifies that "the judge and the Constitutional Tribunal must adjust the formalities set forth in this Code, to the attainment of the purposes of the constitutional processes" (Art. III) which is the immediate protection of constitutional rights.

For such purposes, in the Venezuelan Constitution is provided that "any time will be workable time and the courts will give preference to the amparo regarding any other matter" (Art. 27). These principles are set forth in almost all the Amparo Laws in Latin America, by expressly providing that the amparo action can be filed at any time (Colombia, Arts. 1 and 15; Honduras, Art. 16; Guatemala, Art. 5), even on holidays and out of labor hours (Costa Rica Art. 5; Ecuador, Art. 47; El Salvador Art. 79; Paraguay, Art.19).

---

504 See the decisión of the Constitucional Chamber of the Supreme Tribunal of Justice N° 7 dated February 1, 2000 (Case *José Amando Mejía*), in *Revista de Derecho Público*, N° 81, Editorial Jurídica Venezolana, Caracas, 2000, pp. 245 ff. See the comments in Allan R. BREWER–CARÍAS, *El sistema de justicia constitucional en la constitución de 1999 (Comentarios sobre su desarrollo jurisprudencial y su explicación, a veces errada, en la Exposición de Motivos),* Editorial Jurídica Venezolana, Caracas, 2000 and in Rafael CHAVERO GAZDIK, *El nuevo régimen del amparo constitucional en Venezuela*, Edit. Sherwood, Caracas, 2001, pp. 203 ff.

One of the abovementioned procedural principles is the preferred character of the amparo in the sense that the procedure must be followed with preference, which implies that when an amparo is filed, the courts must postpone all other matters of different nature (Guatemala, Art. 5; Honduras, Arts. 4,3; Peru; Venezuela, Art. 13), except the cases of habeas corpus" (Colombia, Art. 15; Brazil, Art. 17; Costa Rica, Art. 39; Honduras, Art 511).

The Amparo Laws also assigns the courts the task of directing the procedure, empowering them to act ex officio (El Salvador, Art. 5; Guatemala, Art. 6; Honduras, Art. 4,4; Peru, Art. III) even in matter of evidence; the inertia of the parties not being valid to justify any delay (Costa Rica, Art. 8; El Salvador, Art. 5). Additionally, the notifications made by the court can be done by any mean including technical, electronic or magnetic ones (El Salvador. Art. 79).

In the amparo procedure, as a general rule, the procedural terms cannot be extended, nor suspended nor interrupted, except in cases expressly set forth in the statute (Costa Rica, Arts. 8 and 39; El Salvador, Art. 5; Honduras 4; Peru, Art 33,8; Paraguay Art. 19). Any delay in the procedure is the responsibility of the courts (Costa Rica, Art. 8; Honduras, Art. 4,8; Peru, Art. 13).

Another general rule regarding the amparo suit procedure is that no incidents are allowed in it (Honduras, Art. 70; Uruguay, Art. 12; Panamá, Art. 2610; Paraguay, Art. 20; Uruguay, Art. 12); thus, neither excuse or recuse of judges are admitted or they are restricted (Argentina, Art.16; Colombia, Art. 39; Ecuador Art. 47, and 59; Honduras, Art. 18; Panamá, Art. 2610; Paraguay, Art. 20; Peru Art. 33, 1 and 2; Venezuela, Art. 11). Nonetheless, the Amparo law in some countries provides for specific and prompt procedure rules to resolve the situation regarding the cases of impeding situations of the competent judges to resolve the case (Costa Rica, Art. 6; Guatemala, Arts. 17, 111; Mexico, Art. 66; Panama, Art. 2610; Peru, Art. 52; Venezuela, Art. 11).

1. General provisions regarding the filing of the petition

The general principle on judicial procedure in Latin America, is that the petitions that are to be brought before the courts must always be filed in writing. That is why, all the Amparo Laws specify with detail the necessary content of the petition in matters of amparo.

Nonetheless, some exceptions have been established allowing the oral presentation of the amparo in cases of urgency (Venezuela, Arts. 16, 18; Colombia, Art. 14; Honduras, Art. 16; Peru, Art. 27), danger to life, deprivation of liberty without judicial process, deportation or exile (Mexico, Art. 117) or if the plaintiff is short of means (Guatemala, Art. 26 Honduras, Art. 22 –habeas corpus–). Nonetheless, is such cases, the petitions must be subsequently ratified in writing.

In other cases, it is allowed for the plaintiff to bring the petition before the court by telegram or radiogram (Brazil, Art. 4; Costa Rica, Art. 38) or by electronic means (Peru, Art. 27).

Since the normal way to bring the amparo action before the competent court is through a written text –as it is also required for the petition for injunction in North

America[505], the petitioner must express in it, in a clear and precise manner, all the necessary elements regarding the alleged right to relief and on the arguments for the admissibility of the action. Thus, according to what is established in the Amparo Laws in Latin America, in general terms, the petition or complaint must comprise the following:

1) The complete identification and information regarding the plaintiff (Argentina, Art 6,a; Bolivia, Art. 97,I; Colombia, Art. 14; El Salvador, Art. 14; Mexico, 116,1 and 166, 1; Nicaragua, Art. 27,1; Peru, Art, 42,2; Paraguay, Art.; 6,a; Venezuela, Art. 18, 1 and 2). If someone is acting on behalf of the plaintiff, also his identification; and if the plaintiff is an artificial person, its identification as well as the representative's complete identification (El Salvador, Art. 14,1; Guatemala Arts. 21,b and c; Honduras, Art. 49,2)

2) The individuation of the injurer party (Argentina, Art 6,b; Bolivia, Art. 97, II; Honduras, Art. 49, 2; Paraguay, Art. 6,b; Venezuela, Art. 18,2), and regarding public entities, the harming public authority, and if possible, the organ provoking the harm or threat (Colombia, Art. 14; Costa Rica, Art. 38; El Salvador, Art. 14; Guatemala, Art. 21,d; panama, Art. 2619,2; México, Arts. 116,III and 166,III; Nicaragua, Art. 27,2 and 55).

3) The detailed narration of the circumstances in which the harm or the threat has been caused (Argentina, Art., 6,c; Bolivia, Art. 97,III; Colombia, Art. 14; Costa Rica, Art. 38; El Salvador, Art. 14,5; Guatemala, Art. 21,e; Panama, Art. 2619,3; Paraguay, Art. 6,d; Honduras, Art. 49,5; Nicaragua, Art. 55; Peru, Art. 42,4; Venezuela, Art. 18,5), and in particular, the act, action, omission or fact causing the harm or threat (El Salvador, Art. 14,3; Honduras, Art. 49,3; Nicaragua, Art. 27,3; Peru, Art. 42,5; Mexico Arts. 116, IV and 166,IV).

4) The constitutional right or guaranty that has been violated, harmed or threatened (Bolivia, Art. 97,IV; Colombia, Art. 14; El Salvador, Art. 14,4; Panamá, Art. 2619,V; Honduras, Art. 49,6; Venezuela, Art. 18,4), with the precise indication of the articles of the Constitution containing the rights or guarantees (Guatemala, Art. 21,f; Mexico, Arts. 116, V and 166,VI; Nicaragua, Art. 27,4). The Tutela Law in Colombia exempts the need of identifying the article of the constitution providing that the harmed or threatened right is identified with precision (Art. 14). A similar provision is set forth in the Costa Rican Constitutional Jurisdiction Law (Art. 38).

5) The plaintiff must specify the concrete petition for the judicial order to be issue in protection of his rights that is requested from the court (Argentina, Art. 6,d; Bolivia, Art. 97,VI; Honduras, Art. 49,7; Peru. Art. 42,6; Paraguay, Art 6,d).

6) Finally, the plaintiff must base the conditions for the admissibility of the action, in particular, regarding the inadequacy of the other possible judicial remedies

505 See in John BOURDEAU et al, "Injunctions" in Kevin Schroder, John Glenn and Maureen Placilla, *Corpus Juris Secundum*, Volume 43A, Thomson West, 2004, pp.346 ff.

and the irreparable injury the plaintiff will suffer without the amparo suit protection[506].

In order to soften the consequences of not mentioning correctly all the abovementioned requirements that have to be complied with in the presentation of the petition, almost all the Latin American Amparo Laws, in protection of the injured party right to sue, provides that the courts are obliged to return to the plaintiff the petition that does not conform with those requirements in order for him to make the necessary corrections. That is to say, the petition will not be considered inadmissible because of the non compliance with the requirements of the Laws, and in order to have them corrected or mended the court must return it to the petitioner for him to correct it in a brief delay. And only if the petitioner does not make the corrections then the complaint will be rejected (Colombia, Art. 17; Costa Rica, Art. 42; El Salvador, Art. 18; Guatemala, Art. 22; Honduras, Art. 50; Mexico, Art. 146; Nicaragua, Art. 28; Peru, Art. 48; Paraguay, Art. 7; Venezuela, Art. 19).

2. General principles regarding evidence and burden of proof

As has been studied in previous chapters, the amparo suit is a specific judicial mean regulated in Latin America in order to obtain the immediate protection of constitutional rights and guaranties, when the aggrieved or injured parties have no other adequate judicial means for such purpose.

In any case, the violation of a constitutional right that can found an amparo action, in general terms must be a flagrant, vulgar, direct and immediate, caused by a perfectly determined act or omission, and the harm or injury caused to the constitutional rights must be manifestly arbitrary, illegal or illegitimate, consequence of a violation of the Constitution; all of which, in principle must be clear and ostensible from what the plaintiff argues before the court in his petition.

This conditions, similar to what is established in the United States regarding the injunctions[507], imposes to the plaintiff the burden to proof the existence of the right, the alleged violations of threat, and the illegitimate character of the action causing it, with clear and convincing evidence. That is why, for instance, all the Amparo Laws in Latin America require that all the circumstances of the case must be explained in the text of the petition, with all the evidences supporting it. Also some statutes impose the need for the petition to be filed attaching all the documentary evidence (Argentina, Art. 7; Bolivia, Art. 97,V; Guatemala, Art. 21,g; Panama, Art. 2619; Uruguay, Art. 5), and specifying all the other evidences to be presented (Argentina, Art. 7; Uruguay, Art. 5). In México the evidences must be shown in the hearing, except the documentary evidence that can be filed before (Art. 151).

In any case, the amparo suit is a brief and prompt procedure for the immediate protection of constitutional rights based in sufficient evidence, which cannot be in-

506 In similar way as in the injunction petition in the United States. See in John BOURDEAU et al, "Injunctions" in Kevin Schroder, John Glenn and Maureen Placilla, *Corpus Juris Secundum*, Volume 43A, Thomson West, 2004, pp. 346, 352.

507 See Kevin Schroder, John Glenn and Maureen Placilla (Editors), *Corpus Juris Secundum*, Vol. 43A, Thomson West, 2004, p 54.

volved in complex evidence activity. If the latter situation is the case, the Argentinean Amparo Law provides for the inadmissibility of the amparo action, by establishing it in cases "where in order to determine the invalidity of the [challenged] act, a mayor scope of debate or proof is required" (Art., 2d).

Accordingly, the courts have rejected amparo actions in complex cases where a mayor debate is needed, and in cases in which the evidences are difficult to be provided[508], which is considered incompatible with the brief and prompt character of the amparo suit that requires that the alleged violation be "manifestly" illegitimate and harming. Even though without the clear provision on the matter of the Argentinean Law, this same principle has been considered as applicable regarding the *mandado de seguranca* in Brazil, Uruguay[509] and Venezuela[510]

On the other hand, regarding the "evidence phase" in the process in the amparo suit, regulated in some Laws (El Salvador, Art, 29; Guatemala, Art. 35); some legislations, as is the case of Peru, discard its existence, providing that the evidences must be presented with the petition, and that they will be accepted if they do not require further procedural developments (Art. 9). The courts also have among their ex officio powers, the competence to obtain evidences (Costa Rica, Art. 47; Guatemala, Art. 36; Paraguay, Art. 11) if it does not cause an irreparable prejudice to the plaintiff (Venezuela Art. 17), or to do whatever they consider necessary without affecting the length of the procedure. In the latter case no previous notification to the parties is required (Peru, Art 9).

In principle, all evidences are admitted in the amparo suit, so the court can found its decision to grant or not the required protection in any evidence (Colombia, Art. 21). Nonetheless, some legislations forbid some evidences in the amparo suit, as is the case of confession (Argentina Art. 7; El Salvador, Arts. 29; Mexico, Art. 150; Paraguay, Art 12), and those considered contrary to morality or good costumes (México, Art. 150).

3. The decision regarding the admissibility of the petition

It can be considered as a general feature of the procedure of the amparo suit, the power of the competent court to decide at the beginning of the procedure upon the admission of the petition, when it accomplishes with all the admissibility conditions set fort in the Amparo Laws. Consequently, the courts are empowered to decide *in limine litis* about the inadmissibility of the action when the petition does not accomplish in a manifest way with the conditions determined in the statute (Argentina, Art. 3; Bolivia, Art. 98; Costa Rica, Art. 9; Mexico, Art. 145; Peru, Art. 47; Uruguay, Art. 2).

---

508 See José Luis LAZZARINI, *El juicio de amparo*, Ed. La Ley, Buenos Aires1987, p. 94–95, 173 ff.; Alí Joaquín SALGADO, *Juicio de amparo y acción de inconstitucionalidad,* Editorial Astrea, Buenos Aires, 1987, pp. 52; Néstor Pedro SAGÜÉS, *Derecho procesal Constitucional,* Vol 3, *Acción de amparo*, Editorial Astrea, Buenos Aires, 1988, pp. 231–239.

509 See Luis Alberto VIERA, *Ley de Amparo*, Ediciones Idea, Montevideo 1993, p. 17.

510 See Rafael CHAVERO G., *El nuevo amparo constitucional en Venezuela*, Ed. Sherwood, Caracas, 2001, p. 340.

4. The defendant (the injurer or aggrieving party) pleading or answer

In almost all the Latin American Laws regulating the amparo suit, after the decision of the court to admit the action, one of the main phases of the procedure refers to the need for the court to notify the aggrieving party in order to request it, a formal answer regarding the alleged violations of constitutional rights of the plaintiff. Due to the bilateral character of the procedure, as happens in the injunctive relief procedure in the United States, an amparo ruling must not be issued until the pleadings by the defendant have been joined[511]. In the cases of Bolivia and Ecuador, the Amparo Laws do not require the filing of an answer, which can be nonetheless be presented before the court in the hearing of the case (Bolivia, Art. 100; Ecuador, Art. 49).

Thus, after admitting the claim, the first procedural step the court must take is the request from the defendant and the formal answer of the petition formulated by the injured party, in which, in addition the defendant must put forward his counter evidences. This is what was established in the Venezuelan Amparo Law (Art. 24); which nonetheless has been eliminated by the Constitutional Chamber in its decision of 2000, interpreting the Amparo law according to the new 1999 Constitution, reshaping the amparo suit procedure[512].

In the other Latin American countries, the defendant's answer or pleading regarding the harm or threat alleged by the plaintiff to be sent to the court, must be sent in a very brief term (Argentina, Art. 8; Bolivia, Art. 100; Panama, Art. 2591) of hours (24h: El Salvador, Art. 21; 48h: Venezuela, Art. 23) or three days (Colombia, Art. 19; Costa Rica, Arts. 19, 43, 61; Paraguay, Art. 9), five days (Honduras, Arts. 26, 52; Mexico, Art. 147, 149; Peru, Art. 53) of ten days (Nicaragua, Art. 37). The omission by the court to request the defendant's answer produces the nullity of the process (Argentina, Art. 8).

The omission of the defendant to send his pleading answer to the court, implies that the facts alleged by the injured party facts and acts causing the harm or threat must be considered as certain (Colombia, Art. 19; Costa Rica, Art. 45[513]; El Salvador, Art. 22; Honduras (habeas corpus), Art. 26; Mexico, Art 149; Nicaragua, Art. 39); or that the constitutional right or guarantee that is allegedly be violated, must in fact be considered violated (Honduras, Art. 53) or that the plaintiff alleged facts must be considered as accepted by the defendant (Venezuela, Art. 23). In those cases, the consequence of the omission by the defendant to send his answer to the court is that the amparo should be granted (Argentina, Art. 20; Costa Rica, Art. 45; Honduras, Art. 53). In some cases, the effect of such omission is to grant a preliminary relief, suspending the effects of the challenged act (Guatemala, Art. 33).

---

511 See in John BOURDEAU et al, "Injunctions" in Kevin Schroder, John Glenn and Maureen Placilla, *Corpus Juris Secundum*, Volume 43A, Thomson West, 2004, pp.357 ff.

512 See Rafael CHAVERO G., *El nuevo amparo constitucional en Venezuela,* Ed. Sherwood, Caracas, 2001, pp.264 ff.

513 In cases of habeas corpus article 23 of the Costa Rican Law set forth that the facts could be considered as certain.

Notwithstanding, in certain cases, the court can insist on the remittance of the answer or ask for new information (Argentina, Arts. 20, 21; Colombia, Art. 21; Costa Rica, Art. 45; Peru, Art. 53)

5. The hearing in the amparo suit

In all the Latin American Amparo Laws, one of the most important steps on the procedure is the hearing that the court must convene, also in a very prompt term of days, with the participation of the parties (Argentina, Art. 9; Bolivia, Art. 100; Ecuador, Art. 49; Uruguay, Art. 6; Paraguay, Art. 10; Venezuela, Art. 26) The absence of the defendant in general terms does not produce the suspension of the hearing (Bolivia, Art. 100).

According to some Amparo laws, if the plaintiff does not assist to the hearing it is understood that he desisted his action, with payment of the costs (Argentina, Art. 10; Ecuador, Art. 50); and if it is the defendant the one who does not assist, the hearing is not suspended (Ecuador, Art. 5), and the evidences presented by the plaintiff will be accepted and the court then must proceed to decide (Art. 10).

In some Latin American Laws, it is set forth that the court must take its decision in the same hearing or trial (Bolivia Art. 100; Uruguay, Art. 6; Venezuela, or in the following days (Venezuela, Art. 24).

CHAPTER X.

THE PROTECTED PERSONS: THE INJURED PARTY IN THE AMPARO SUIT INDIVIDUAL AND COLLECTIVE ACTIONS AND THE GENERAL STANDING CONDITIONS

I. THE PARTIES IN THE AMPARO SUIT

The Latin American amparo is always conceived as a suit, that is, as a proceeding initiated by a party or parties, the injured or offended party, by mean of an action or a recourse brought before the competent court, against another party (the injurer or offender party) whose actions or omissions has violated or has caused harm to his constitutional rights.

The final outcome of the amparo suit is always a judicial order, similar to the North American writs of injunction, mandamus or error, directed to the injuring party ordering to do or to abstain from doing something or a decisions suspending the effects or annulling the damaging act causing the harm.

Thus, in general terms, it can be said that the amparo suit has similarities with the civil suit for an injunction that an injured party can bring before a court to seek for the enforcement or restoration of his violated rights or for the prevention of its violation. It also can be identified with a "suit for mandamus" brought by an injured party before a court against a public officer whose omission has caused harm to the plaintiff, in order to seek for a writ ordering the former to perform a duty which the law requires him to do but he refuses or neglects to perform. Also, the suit for amparo has similarities with some kind of "suit for writ of error" brought before the competent superior court by an injured party whose constitutional rights have been violated by a judicial decision, seeking the annulment or the correction of the judicial wrong or error.

What is clear in the Latin American amparo legislations, is that the amparo is not only the remedy, or the final court written order (writ) commanding the addressee to do or refrain from doing some specific act[514]. It is, above all, a suit that is specifically designed to protect constitutional rights following an adversary process according to the "cases or controversy" condition derived from Article III of the North American Constitution; which opposes one or multiple injured or complaining parties acting as plaintiffs, against one or multiple injuring parties acting as defendants, ending with a judicial decision or judicial order directed to protect the constitutional rights of the injured party. Also being considered as parties the interested third parties that can be harmed or benefited by the action and its results, as well as the Public Prosecutor (Attorney General) or the People's Defendant.

That is why in the amparo suit the procedural adversary principle or principle of bilateralism[515] prevails, in the sense that the judicial proceeding of the suit, although it has to be brief and speedy, must always assure the presence of both parties and the respect of the constitutional guaranties of defense. Thus, a judicial guarantee of constitutional rights as is the amparo suit can in no way transform itself in a proceeding violating the other constitutional guarantees like the right to defense. Except regarding preliminary judicial orders, the principle of *audi alteram partem* (hear the other party or listen to both sides) must then always be respected. That is why, for instance, the Supreme Court of Justice of Venezuela in a 1996 judicial review procedure, annulled Article 22 of the 1988 Amparo Law, which allowed the courts to adopt final decisions on amparo in cases of grave violations of constitutional rights, reestablishing the constitutional harmed right without any formal or summary inquiry and without hearing the plaintiff or potential injurer. Even if the Article could be constitutionally interpreted as only directed to allow the adoption of *inaudita partem* preliminary decisions or injunctions in the proceeding[516], the Supreme Court considered the Article as a vulgar and flagrant violation of the constitutional right to self defense[517], and annulled it.

---

514 Bryan A. Garner (ed), *Black's Law Dictionary,* Secod Pocket Edition, St. Paul, Minn. P. 2001

515 José Luis LAZZARINI, *El Juicio de Amparo*, Editorial La Ley, Buenos Aires, 1987, pp. 270 y ss.

516 As was asked to be decided by the Supreme Court. See Allan R. BREWER–CARÍAS, "Derecho y Acción de Amparo", *Instituciones Políticas y Constitucionales,* Vol V, Universidad Católica del Táchira, Editorial Jurídica Venezolana, Caracas, 1998, pp. 389 y ss.

517 Decision of the Supreme Court of Justice of May, 21 1996, in *Gaceta Oficial Extra*. N° 5071 of May, 29, 1996. See the comments in Allan R. BREWER–CARÍAS, "Derecho y Acción de Amparo", *Instituciones Políticas y Constitucionales*, Vol V, Universidad Católica del Táchira, Editorial Jurídica Venezolana, Caracas, 1998, pp. 389 y ss; and in Rafael CHAVERO, *El*

Accordingly, one of the most important aspects of the amparo suit legislations in Latin America, refers to the parties in the suit, which can only be initiated at the party's request. Thus, no case of *ex officio* amparo proceeding is possible or admissible.

The suit must the be initiates by mean of an action or recourse brought before a court by the injured party or parties, as the complainant or plaintiff, against the injurer party or parties, as defendants, called to the proceeding because they provoked the harm or violation to the constitutionals rights of the former. The initiation of the suit can be an action or recourse, the latter when exercised against an administrative act or a judicial decision which is to be challenged only after the exhaustion of the available administrative or judicial recourses. When through an action, the amparo can be brought directly before the courts against facts, acts or omissions, without the need to exhaust previous recourses.

This principle of bilateralism regarding the amparo, which always implies the existence of a controversy between two parties, always initiated by a complainant or injured party against an injurer party, can be considered as the common trend in Latin America. The only exception in this regard is Chile, where in the absence of a statutorily regulated amparo, it has been considered that the proceeding of the recourse for protection is not based on a controversy between parties, but on a request raised by a party before a court, being the procedural relation the one established between a complainant and a court, and not between an injured and an injurer party[518].

Regarding the plaintiff, the Latin American amparo legislations have detailed regulations in relation to who can be the specific aggrieved or injured party, in the sense of who has standing to sue for constitutional judicial protection; in relation to how can the injured party act in the judicial proceeding; and in relation to the conditions the constitutional right harms or violations most have for the action to be brought before the courts.

In respect to the defendants or injurer party, the Latin American amparo laws also set forth extensive regulations regarding the authorities that can be sued before the courts for constitutional violations, as well as the individuals or private persons that can be sued before the competent courts when responsible for the harm or the violation of a constitutional rights; how can all the injurer or offender parties act in the judicial proceeding; and also, the specific public or private acts or omissions that have caused those harms or violations in the plaintiff's constitutional rights.

Nuevo Régimen del Amparo Constitucional en Venezuela, Caracas, 2001, pp. 212, 266 y ss. and 410 y ss.

518 See for example Sergio LIRA HERRERA, *El recurso de protección. Naturaleza jurídica, doctrina, jurisprudencial, derecho comparad*, Santiago de Chile 1990, pp. 157 y ss.; Juan Manuel ERRAZUZIZ G. y Jorge Miguel OTERO A, *Aspectos procesales del recurso de protección*, Editorial Jurídica de Chile, Santiago, 1989, pp. 39, 40 y 157. In contrary sense, Enrique PAILLAS considers that in the recourse for protection the principle of bilateralism applies. See Enrique PAILLAS, *El recurso de protección ante el derecho comparado*, Editorial Jurídica de Chile, Santiago, 1990, pp. 105.

II. THE INJURED PARTY

In the amparo suit, the injured party, also named the claimant, the complainant or the petitioner, who in the proceeding is the plaintiff, is the person holder of a constitutional right that has suffered an actionable wrong, that is, whose constitutional right have been violated, thus having sufficient concrete interest in bringing the case before a court, and regarding the outcome of the controversy. Being the amparo action an action *in personam* for the protection of constitutional rights, the litigant must be the injured or aggrieved person. That is why, it is generally considered that the amparo action needs to be personalized, as attributed to the particular person enjoying the harmed right, that is, the person who has a justiciable interest in the subject matter of the litigation in his own right, or a personal interest in the outcome of the controversy. As ruled regarding injunctions in *Parkview Hospital v. Com., Dept. of Public Welfare*, 56 Pa. Commw. 218, 424 A. 2d 599 (1981): to bring an action "requires an aggrieved party to show a substantial, direct, and immediate interest is the subject matter of the litigation"[519]. Or as ruled in *Warth v. Seldin*, 422 U.S. 4909, 498–500 (1975): the plaintiff must "allege such a personal stake in the outcome of the controversy" as to justify the exercise of the court's remedial powers on his behalf, because he himself has suffered "some threatened or actual injury resulting from the putatively illegal action"[520].

It is in this sense that Article 23 of the Nicaraguan Amparo law provides that only the aggrieved party can file the amparo, defining as such, "any natural or artificial person being harmed or in a situation of imminent danger of being harmed by any disposition, act or resolution, and in general, by any action or omission from any public officer, authority or its agent, that violates or threats to violate the rights and guaranties enshrined in the Constitution".

A few questions must be emphasized regarding the injured or aggrieved party: first, the matter of standing to sue; second, the quality of the persons entitled to sue, in the sense of it being a physical person or human being and also artificial persons or corporation, including public law entities; third, the possibility for the Public Prosecutors or Peoples' Public Defendants to sue in amparo; and forth, regarding the third parties that can intervene in the proceedings on the side of the claimant.

1. Injured persons and standing

In the amparo suit, having the action a personal character, the plaintiff or injured party can only be the holder of the violated right; thus, the aggrieved party can only be the person whose constitutional rights have been injured or threatened of being

---

519 See the reference in Kevin SCHRODER et al, "Injunction", *Corpus Juris Secundum*, Thomson West, Volume 43A, 2004, p. 331, note 4.

520 M. Glenn ABERNATHY and Barbara A. PERRY, *Civil Liberties Under the Constitution*, University of South Carolina Press, 1993, p. 4

harmed[521]. Thus, nobody can sue in amparo alleging in his own name a right belonging to another[522].

As it was ruled by the former Supreme Court of Justice of Venezuela regarding the personal character of the amparo suit, which imposes for its admissibility:

> "A qualified interest of who is asking for the restitution or reestablishment of the harmed right or guaranty, that is, that the harm be directed to him and that, eventually, its effects affect directly and indisputably upon him, harming his scope of subjective rights guarantied in the Constitution. It is only the person that is specially and directly injured in his subjective fundamental rights by a specific act, fact or omission the one that can bring an action before the competent courts by mean of a brief and speedy proceeding, in order that the judge decides immediately the reestablishment of the infringed subjective legal situation"[523].

Thus the amparo action has been qualified as a "subjective action"[524], that can only be brought before the courts personally by the aggrieved party which having the personal, legitimate and direct interest[525], is the one that directly or through his duly appointed representative has the standing to sue[526].

Even though this is the general rule in Latin America, a few legislations authorized other persons different to the injured parties or their representatives, to file the amparo suit on their behalf. It is then possible to distinguish in matter of amparo, the *legitimatio* or standing *ad causam* from the *legitimatio* or standing *ad processum*[527].

---

521 See decisions of the former Politico–Administrative Chamber of the Supreme Court of Justice of June 18, 1992, *Revista de Derecho Público* N° 50, Editorial Jurídica Venezolana, Caracas, 1992, p. 135; and of August 13, 1992, *Revista de Derecho Público,* N° 51, Editorial Jurídica Venezolana, Caracas, 1992 p. 160

522 See decision of the former Politico–Administrative Chamber of the Supreme Court of Justice of February 14, 1990, in *Revista de Derecho Público,* N° 4l, Editorial Jurídica Venezolana, Caracas, 1990, p. 101

523 See decision of the former Politico–Administrative Chamber of the Supreme Court of Justice of August 27, 1993 (Case: *Kenet E. Leal*), in *Revista de Derecho Público,* N° 55–56, Editorial Jurídica Venezolana, Caracas, 1993, p. 322

524 See decision First Court on Judicial Review of Administrative Action, of November 18, 1993, in *Revista de Derecho Público,* nos. 55–56, Editorial Jurídica Venezolana, Caracas, 1993, pp. 325–327.

525 See decisios of the former Politico–Administrative Chamber of the Supreme Court of Justice of October 22, 1990 and October 22, 1992, in *Revista de Derecho Público,* N° 52, Editorial Jurídica Venezolana, Caracas, 1992, p. 140 and of November 18, 1993, in *Revista de Derecho Público,* N° 55–56, Editorial Jurídica Venezolana, Caracas, 1993, p. 327.

526 See decision of the First Court on Judicial Review of Administrative Action of August 21, 1992, in *Revista de Derecho Público,* N° 51, Editorial Jurídica Venezolana, Caracas, 1992, p. 161.

527 See in general, Alí Joaquín Salgado, *Juicio de amparo y acción de inconstitucionalidad*, Astrea Buenos Aires 1987, pp. 81 ff; Joaquín Brage Camazano, *La jurisdicción constitucional de la libertad*, Editorial Porrúa, México 2005, pp. 162 ff.; Sergio Lira Herrera, *El recurso de protección. Naturaleza jurídica. Doctrina. Jurisprudencia. Derecho Comparado*, Santiago 1990, pp;

The standing *ad causam* in the amparo suit refers to the person or entity that enjoys the particular constitutional right which has been violated. The standing *ad processum* refers to the particular capacity the persons has to act in the procedure (procedural capacity), that is, the ability to appear in court and to use the appropriate procedures in support of a claim, which can refer to his own rights or to the rights of others.

In conclusion, any person whose constitutional rights have been violated or threatened to be violated, has the right to seek protection form the courts by means of the action for amparo; whether being *natural persons* or human beings without distinction of being citizens, disabled or foreigners; or being *artificial* persons or entities. And the word persons is used in the sense of human beings or entities that are recognized by law as having rights and duties, including corporations or companies[528].

Exceptionally, though, in some countries the amparo suit has been admitted when filed by groups or communities without formal legal "personality" attributed by law, as has happened in Chile with the recourse for protection[529] in some cases filed by affected individual or collective entities without having personality (Case: RP, *Federación Chilena de Hockey y Patinaje*, C. de Santiago, 1984, RDJ, T, LXXXI, N° 3, 2da, P., Secc.5ta, p. 240)[530]

2. Natural persons: Standing ad causam and ad processum

The general principle in Latin America, is that all natural persons, as human beings, when their constitutional rights are arbitrarily or illegitimately harmed or threatened with violation, have the necessary standing to file the action for protection, as is expressly set forth in all the Amparo Laws, when referring to "persons" in general, comprising human beings and juridical or artificial persons, without distinctions,

Regarding the natural persons, of course, the expression is not equivalent to "citizens", being the latter those persons who by birth or naturalization are members of the political community represented by the State. But if it is true that the amparo is a judicial guarantee granted to all persons, citizens or foreigners; regarding the protec-

528 Argentina (article 5: "any individual or juridical persons"), Colombia (Article 1: "any person"); Ecuador (article 48: "natural or juridical persons"); El Salvador (article "3 and 12: "any person"; (Guatemala (article 8: "persons"), Honduras (article 41: "any aggrieved person"; article 44: "any natural or juridical person"), Mexico (article 39: affected person"); Panamá (article: 2615: "any person"); Peru (article 39: "the affected"); Uruguay (article 1: any physical or juridical person, public or private"); Venezuela (article 1: "natural or juridical persons").

529 The Chilean Constitution in matter of standing refers to "el que" (who), not mentioning "persons" (art. 20) See, Juan Manuel ERRAZURIZ and Jorge Miguel OTERO A., *Aspectos procesales del recurso de protección*, Editorial Jurídica de Chile, Santiago 1989, pp. 15, 50; 9.

530 Nonetheless, in other judicial decisions the contrary criteria has been sustained. See the reference in Sergio LIRA HERRERA, *El recurso de protección. Naturaleza jurídica. Doctrina. Jurisprudencia. Derecho Comparado,* Santiago 1990, pp. 144–145.

tion of political rights, like the right to vote, being the citizens the only persons entitled to those rights, only they have the right to sue in amparo for their protection.

As natural persons, foreigners also have the same general rights as nationals, having the needed standing to exercise the right to amparo. Only in Mexico an exception can be found regarding the decisions where the President of the Republic is constitutionally authorized to adopt measures expulsing foreigners, in which case it has been recognized that they cannot challenge such decisions vía amparo[531].

Except this particular case, the general trend in Latin America has been to apply an extensive interpretation regarding standing *ad causam*, allowing all affected persons to file the amparo suit. As an example of this trend, the interpretation of the Venezuelan Law of Amparo can be mentioned, regarding the expression of its Article 1 which entitles "all natural persons inhabitants of the Republic" (Art. 1) to file amparo suits. The main problem with this article resulted from the condition to be "inhabitant of the Republic", that is, to physically be in the territory of the Republic as resident, tourist or in any other situation, which was originally interpreted to deny the right to amparo to persons not living in the country. The Supreme Court of Justice, progressively widened the interpretation, admitting the amparo action filed by a person not inhabitant of the Republic, no matter his nationality or legal condition, providing, according to a decision of August 27, 1993, "that his constitutional rights and guaranties had been directly harmed or threatened by any act, fact or omission carried out, issued or produced in the Republic"[532].

The following year this same Supreme Court, by mean of the exercise of its diffuse judicial review powers, declared unconstitutional the limiting reference of Article 1 of the Law when stressing the character of "inhabitants of the Republic", ruling on the contrary, that any person whether or not living in the Republic whose rights are harmed in Venezuela, has enough standing to file an amparo action[533]

Minors, of course, also have standing *ad causam*, and through their representatives (parents or tutors) can file amparo actions for the protection and defense of their constitutional rights, and only exceptionally they are allowed to act personally. Is the case of México, were the Amparo law provided that a minor "can ask for amparo without the intervention of his legitimate representative when he is absent or impaired"; adding that "in such case, the court, without being impeded to adopt urgent measures, must appoint a special representative in order to intervene in the suit"(Art. 6).

The standing *ad processum* regarding natural persons, that is, the possibility to appear before the court, in principle corresponds to the same injured persons for the

---

531 See Eduardo FERRER MAC–GREGOR, *La acción constitucional de amparo en México y España*, Editorial Porrúa, México 2002, p. 230.

532 See in *Jurisprudencia Ramírez & Garay*, Tomo CXXVI, p. 667. See the references in Allan R. BREWER–CARÍAS, "Derecho y Acción de Amparo", Vol V, *Instituciones Políticas y Constitucionales,* Editorial Jurídica Venezolana, Caracas, 1998, p. 319

533 Decision of December 13, 1994 (Case: *Jackroo Marine Limited*). See the reference in Rafael CHAVERO, *El Nuevo Régimen del Amparo Constitucional en Venezuela*, Caracas, 2001, pp. 98–99,

defense of their own rights. Thus, as a matter of principle, no other person can judicially act on behalf of the injured person, except when legally prescribed, for instance in the case of minors or incapacitated that must act in court through their representatives.

A general exception for this principle refers to the action of habeas corpus, in which case, generally, being the injured person impeded to act personally because he is under detention or has his freedom restrained, normally the Law authorizes anybody to file the action on his behalf[534]. In México, the Law imposes the injured party the obligation to expressly ratify the filing of the amparo suit, to the point that if the complaint is not ratified it will be considered as not filed (Art. 17). In some cases, as is the case of Guatemala (art. 86) and Honduras (art. 20), the courts even have *ex officio* power and the obligation to initiate the habeas corpus suit, in cases where they happen to have knowledge of the facts.

But regarding the amparo suit, as mentioned, the principle of its personal character prevails, in the same sense as the rule of standing to seek injunctive relief in the United States, which only is attributed to the person affected[535]. Thus, the injured party is the one that in principle can file the action, as is expressly set forth for instance in Ecuador[536]. In Costa Rica, even though the Amparo Law provides that the action can be filed by anybody (Article 33), the Constitutional Chamber has interpreted that it refers to anybody that has been injured in his constitutional rights[537]; and in case of an amparo action filed by a person different form the injured party, in order for the proceeding to continue, the latter must approve the filing. Otherwise, there would be lack of standing[538].

Some Amparo Laws, in order to guarantee the constitutional protection, set forth the possibility for other persons to act on behalf of the injured party, and file the action in his name. It can be any lawyer or a relative as established in Guatemala (Article 23), it can be anybody, as for instance in Colombia, where anyone can act on behalf of the injured party when the latter is in a situation of inability to assume his own defense (Article 10)[539]. What the Legislator wanted to assure in this case, was the possibility for an effective protection of the rights, for instance, in cases of

---

534 Argentina (article 5: anybody on his behalf'); Bolivia (article 89: anybody in his name); Guatemala (art 85: any other person); Honduras Art. 19: any person); Mexico (article 17: any other person in his name); Nicaragua (article 52: any inhabitant of the republic); Peru: (article 26: anybody in his favor); Venezuela (article 39: anybody acting on his behalf).

535 See Kevin SCHRODER et al, "Injunctions" in *Corpus Juris Secundum*, Vol. 43A, West 2004, p. 229

536 See Hernán SALGADO PESANTES, *Manual de Justicia Constitucional Ecuatoriana,* Corporación Editora Nacional, Quito 2004, p. 81

537 Decisión 93–90. See the reference in Rubén HERNÁNDEZ VALLE, *Derecho Procesal Constitucional,* Editorial Juricentro, San José, 2001, p. 234.

538 Decisión 5086–94. See the reference in Rubén HERNÁNDEZ VALLE, *Derecho Procesal Constitucional,* Editorial Juricentro, san José2001, p. 235.

539 See Carlos Augusto PATIÑO BELTRÁN, *Acciones de tutela, cumplimiento, populares y de grupo*, Editorial Leyer, Bogotá 2000, p. 10i

physical violence infringed by parents regarding their children, in which case a neighbor is the person that can intervene filing an action for tutela. Otherwise, in such cases, the action for protection could not be filed, particularly because the parents are the legal representatives of their children[540]

Also, in Ecuador, any spontaneous agent justifying the impossibility of the affected party to do so can file the action in his name, which nonetheless must be ratified within the three subsequent days (Art. 48). In Honduras the Amparo Law authorizes anyone to act on behalf of the injured party, without needing a power of attorney, in which case Article 44 provides that the criteria of the affected party shall prevail (Art. 44). In Uruguay (Art. 3) and Paraguay (Art 4), the Amparo Laws provides that in cases where the affected party, by himself of through his representative, cannot file the action, then anybody can do it on his behalf, being subjected the acting person to liability if initiating the amparo with fraud malice or frivolity (Article 4). In similar sense the Peruvian Code also set forth a general rule on the matter, that:

> **Article 41**. Any person can appear in court in the name of another person without procedural representation, when it is impossible for the latter to file the action on his own behalf, whether because his freedom is being concurrently affected, has a founded fear or threat, there is a situation of imminent danger or any other analogous cause. Once the affected party is in the possibility of acting, he must ratify the claim and the procedural activity followed by the person acting in fact.

Another aspect to be pointed out is that being the amparo suit a judicial process, some Latin American Amparo Laws impose the need for the parties in the amparo suit to act personally or through formal representatives, and in any case to formally appoint an attorney to assist them, as set forth in the Panamanian Judicial Code (Art. 22618). In Venezuela, according to what is provided in the Attorneys Law (*Ley de Abogados*), in all judicial processes the parties must be assisted by lawyers, which was also considered to be applicable to the amparo suit"[541]. Nonetheless, in more recent decisions, the Constitutional Chamber of the Supreme Tribunal, due to the non formalistic character of the amparo proceeding, has ruled that even though the injured party does not need to be assisted by an attorney when filing the action, it must appointed one in the course of the proceeding or the court must appoint one to act on his behalf[542]

---

540 See Juan Carlos ESGUERRA PORTOCARRERO, *La protección constitucional del ciudadano*, Lexis, Bogotá 2005, p. 122.

541 See for instantes decisions of the First Court on Judicial Review of Administrative Action of November 18, 1993 (*Caso: Carlos G. Pérez*), *Revista de Derecho Público,* N° 55–56, Editorial Jurídica Venezolana, Caracas, 1993, pp. 353–354; of September 14, 1989, *Revista de Derecho Publico* N° 40, Editorial Jurídica Venezolana, Caracas, 1989, p. 105; and of March 4, 1993 and March 25, 1993, *Revista de Derecho Público,* N° 53–54, Editorial Jurídica Venezolana, Caracas, 1993, p. 258 v

542 See decision of July, 19 2000 (Case: *Rubén Guerra*). See the reference and comments in Rafael CHAVERO, *El Nuevo Régimen del Amparo Constitucional en Venezuela*, Caracas, 2001, pp. 129–135.

3. Artificial persons: Standing at causam and ad processum

As mentioned before, artificial persons also have the right to file amparo actions when their constitutional rights have been violated. If it is true that "human rights" are of the exclusivity of human beings, they are constitutional rights that are not only attributed to human beings but to all other persons, with rights and obligations, like associations, foundations, corporations or companies. These artificial persons, like human beings, also have constitutional rights such as the right to non discrimination, the due process of law guaranties, the right to defense or property rights.

The action of tutela in the Constitution of Colombia can only be used for the protection of immediately applicable "fundamental rights", which in principle are individual rights, artificial persons, however, may file the action of tutela for the protection of rights such as that of petition (Article 22), due process and defense (Article 29) and review of judicial decisions (Article 31).

Thus, in case of violations of those rights, the entities have the needed standing *ad causam* to file the action of amparo, as is accepted in almost all Latin American Amparo laws[543]. Even in the Dominican Republic, were the amparo suit was admitted by the Supreme Court, even without constitutional or legal provision, precisely in a suit brought before the Court by a commercial company (Productos Avon SA)[544]. Of course, like all artificial persons, they must act by means of their directors or representatives as regulated in their by–laws (México, Article 8).

The main question regarding the artificial persons as injured parties with standing to file amparo suits refers to the possibility for the public artificial persons or entities that are part of the State general organization to file amparo suits.

It is clear that historically, the amparo suit, being a specific judicial mean for the protection of constitutional rights, was originally conceived as a constitutional guarantee for individuals or private persons facing public officers or public entities; that is, as a guarantee for protection against the State. So initially, it was unconceivable that a public entity could file an amparo against other public or private entity; but currently it is accepted in most Latin American Countries that public entities can be holders of constitutional rights and file actions of amparo for their protection, as is the case, for instance, of Argentina[545], Uruguay (where it is expressly regulated in the Amparo Law when referring to "public or private artificial persons") or Venezuela. Among the amparo cases decided in Argentina as a consequence of the emergency economic measures adopted by the Government in 2001, freezing all deposits in saving and current accounts in all the Banks, and converting them from US dollars into Argentinean devaluated pesos, one that must be mentioned is the *Case San*

---

543 In Ecuador, the standing of artificial persons to file an amparo action has been denied by Marco MORALES TOBAR in "La acción de amparo y su procedimiento en el Ecuador", *Estudios Constitucionales. Revista del Centro de Estudios Constitucionales*, Año 1, Nº 1, Universidad de Talca, Santiago, Chile 2003, pp. 281–282.

544 See for instante, Juan DE LA ROSA, *El recurso de amparo, Estudio Comparativo*, Santo Domingo, 2001, p. 69.

545 See José Luis LAZZARINI, *El juicio de Amparo*, Ed. La Ley, Buenotes 1987, p. 238–240; 266.

Luis, decided by the Supreme Court on March 5, 2003, in which not only the Court declared the unconstitutionality of the Executive but in the case, "ordered the Central Bank of the Argentinean Nation the reimbursement to the Province of San Luis of the amounts of North American dollars deposited, or its equivalent in pesos at the value in the day of payments, according to the rate of selling of the free market of exchange". The interesting aspect of the suit was that it was filed by the Province of San Luis against the National State and the Central Bank of the Argentinean Nation, that is, a Federated State (Provincia de San Luis) against the National State for the protection of the constitutional rights to property of the former[546].

In other countries, on the contrary, as in the case of Peru, the Code of Constitutional Procedure expressly declares the inadmissibility of the amparo suit when referring to "conflicts between public law internal entities. The constitutional conflicts between those entities, whether public powers of the State, organs of constitutional level of importance, local or regional governments, will be settled through the corresponding constitutional procedures" (Article 5,9). The Code substituted the Law 25011 provision that declared inadmissible actions of amparo, but "when filed by the public offices, including public enterprises, against public powers of the State and the organs created in the Constitution, against acts accomplished in the regular exercise of their functions" (Article 5,4, Code)[547].

Thus, and particularly because of the assumption of economic activities by public entities in the same level of activities as private persons, the amparo also protect them, when their constitutional rights are illegitimately harmed. In some countries, as is the case of Mexico, it is expressly admitted for public corporations to file amparo suits but only when their economic interests (*intereses patrimoniales*) are harmed (Article 9). In no other way can a public entity in México, for instance a State, a Municipality or a public corporation file an amparo suit, because it would otherwise result in a conflict between authorities that cannot be resolved through this judicial action[548]. The Supreme Court has decided that "it is absurd to pretend that a public dependency of the Executive could invoke the violation of individual guaranties seeking protection against acts of other public entities also acting within the Executive branch of government"[549]. In another decision the Supreme Court has ruled that: "it is not possible to concede the extraordinary remedy of amparo to organs of the state against acts of the state itself manifested through other of its agen-

---

546 See the comments in Antonio María HERNÁNDEZ, *Las emergencias y el orden constitucional*, Universidad Nacional Autónoma de México, Rubinzal–Culsoni Editores, México, 2003, pp. 119 y ss.

547 See the comments regarding this provision in the repealed Law 2501, in Victor Julio ORCHETO VILLENA, Jurisdicción y procesos constitucionales, Editorial Rhodas, Lima, p. 169.

548 See Eduardo FERRER MAC–GREGOR, *La acción constitucional de amparo en México y España*, Editorial Porrúa, México 2002, p. 244–245; Richard D. BAKER, *Judicial Review in México. A Study of the Amparo Suit*, University Press of Texas, Austin 1971 pp. 107–109

549 See Tesis jurisprudencial 916, *Apéndice al Semanario Judicial de la Federación*, 1917–1988, Segunda Parte, Salas y Tesis Comunes, p. 1500. See the reference in Eduardo FERRER MAC–GREGOR, *La acción constitucional de amparo en México y España*, Editorial Porrúa, México 2002, p. 245, note 427.

cies, since this would establish a conflict of sovereign powers, whereas the amparo suit is concerned only with the complaint of private individual directed against an abuse of power"[550]

In some countries, discussions have arisen regarding the possibility of the exercise of the amparo suit between public entities in a federal system in order to protect the constitutional guarantee of political autonomy and self government. In Germany, for example, a constitutional complaint may be brought before the Federal Constitutional Tribunal by municipalities or groups of municipalities when alleging that their right to constitutional autonomy or self government, recognized in the Constitution (Article 28–2) has been violated by a federal legal provision. In the case of violations by a law of the *Lander,* such recourse shall be brought before the Constitutional Tribunal of the respective *Lander* (Article 93,1,4 of the Constitution). A similar situation, albeit debatable, is to be found in Austria with regard to the constitutional recourse. Whatever the case, of course it would not be an amparo for the protection of fundamental rights, but rather of a specific constitutional guarantee of the autonomy of local entities.

In the case of Mexico, Article 103, III and 107 of the Constitution set forth the amparo suit in case of controversies arisen "because laws or acts of federal authority infringe or restrict the States sovereignty"; provision that could be understood as establishing the action of amparo for the protection of the distribution of power between the federal and state level of the State, that is, for the protection of the federated States constitutional autonomy regarding the invasions from the federal State. Nonetheless, the Supreme Court has denied such possibility arguing that:

> "the amparo suit was established in Article 103 of the Constitution not for the protection of all the constitutional text, but for the protection of individual guarantees; and what is established in Section III must be understood in the sense that a federal law can only be challenged in the amparo suit when it invades or restricts the sovereignty of the States, when there is an affected individual which in a concrete case claims against the violation of his constitutional guarantees"[551].

The same discussion has been raised in Venezuela, also a federal state, regarding the guarantee of the political autonomy of the States and Municipalities, recognized and guaranteed in the Constitution, in order to determine if their violation could give rise to constitutional protection through an action of amparo. In this sense, in 1997 several Municipalities brought an action of unconstitutionality against a national statute limiting the income that higher–level state and municipal officials could have; action to which the claimants joined an action of amparo for the protection of the constitutional autonomy impaired by the Law. In the end the constitutional protection was denied by the then Supreme Court of Justice, in a decision of October 2, 1997 in which the Court ruled that if "it is undoubted that artificial persons, and

550 See Tesis 450, III, pp. 868–868. See the reference in Richard D. BAKER, *Judicial Review in México. A Study of the Amparo Suit,* University Press of Texas, Austin 1971 p.108

551 See Tesis jurisprudencial 389, *Apéndice al Semanario Judicial de la Federación,* 1917–1995, Tribunal Pleno, p. 362. See the reference in Eduardo FERRER MAC–GREGOR, *La acción constitucional de amparo en México y España,* Editorial Porrúa, México 2002, p. 246, note 425.

consequently, political–territorial entities can be holders of the majority of rights enshrined in the Constitution, as for instance, the rights to defense, non discrimination of property" they are also "holders of public powers and prerogatives, public functions exclusively directed to obtain constitutional goals"; and that if it is true that those prerogatives are also guarantied in the Constitution, these institutional guaranty cannot be equivalent to the guaranty of constitutional rights; thus not admitting the amparo as a means for protection of such guaranties. Additionally, the Court ruled that being the amparo an extraordinary action that "can only be filed when no other efficient means for constitutional protection exists", due to the fact that in Venezuela the Constitution sets forth a series of recourses directed to impede the miss knowledge or invasion of public prerogatives between territorial entities, the amparo cannot be used for those purpose. The Court concluded affirming that:

> "the territorial entities, as artificial persons, can have standing to sue in amparo; but only regarding the protection in strict sense of constitutional rights and guaranties, thus excluding from the amparo the protection of their prerogatives and powers, as well as to resolve the conflicts among those entities between themselves or regarding other Public Power entities"[552]

The Constitutional Chamber latter, in a decision N° 1595 of November 2000, confirmed the ruling rejecting an amparo action, this time filed by a State of the Federation against the Ministry of Finance which, it was alleged, affected their financial autonomy, arguing as follows:

> "The object of the amparo is the reinforced protection of constitutional rights and guaranties, which comprises the rights enumerated in the Constitution, some of which are outside of Title III (see for instance articles 143,260 and 317 of the Constitution), as well as those set forth in international treaties on human rights ratified by the Republic, and any other inherent to human persons.
>
> The aforementioned does not imply to restrict the notion of constitutional rights and guaranties only to the rights and guaranties of natural persons, because also artificial persons are holders of fundamental rights, Even the public law artificial persons can be holders of rights.
>
> But what has been said allows to conclude that the political–territorial entities as the States and the Municipalities, can only file amparo suits for the protection of the rights and liberties they can be holders of, as the right to due process, or the right to equality or to the retroactivity of the law. Conversely, they cannot file an amparo in order to protect the autonomy the Constitution recognized to them or the powers or competencies derived from the latter.
>
> The autonomy of a public entity only enjoys protection through amparo when the Constitution recognizes it as a concretion of one funded fundamental right, like the universities autonomy regarding the right to education (Article 109 of the Constitution).
>
> In the concrete case, the claimants have not invoked a constitutional right of the States which could have been violated, but the autonomy the Constitution assures, and in particular, "the guaranty of the financial autonomy regulated in Articles 159; 164, section 3; and 167, sections 4 and 6 of the Constitution".
>
> Nonetheless, under the concept of constitutional guaranty there cannot be submitted contents completely strange to the range of constitutionally protected public freedoms, as is pre-

552 See the reference and comments in Rafael CHAVERO, *El Nuevo Régimen del Amparo Constitucional en Venezuela*, Caracas, 2001, pp. 122– 123

> tended, due to the fact that the guarantee is closely related with the right. The guarantee can be understood as the constitutional reception of the rights or as the existing mechanisms for its protection. Whether in one or other sense the guarantee is consubstantial to the right, thus it is not adequate to use the concept of guarantee to expand the amparo's scope of protection, including in it any power or competency constitutionally guaranteed. The latter would conduct to the denaturalization of the amparo, which would lose its specificity and convert it in a mean for the protection of all the Constitution"[553].

The restrictive criteria has been also followed by the Constitucional Chamber of Costa Rica, arguing that "the object and matter of the amparo is not to guarantee in an abstract way the enforcement of the Constitution, but the threats and violations of the enjoyment of fundamental rights of persons…and in the case examined that situation is not present". The case referred to an alleged violation of the official procedures followed to facilitate the operation of a cellular mobile network by a company, concluding the Chamber that "the violation of Constitutional norms cannot be demanded through an amparo action"[554].

On the other hand, in systems such as Brazil's, where the *mandado de segurança* can only be brought against the State and not against individuals, it is argued that the State itself or its agencies cannot file the suit[555].

III. STANDING AND THE PROTECTION OF COLLECTIVE AND IFFUSE CONSTITUTIONAL RIGHTS

Constitutional rights are commonly identified with individual or civil rights that corresponds to individuals who enjoy them in a personalized way. That is why the amparo action, as a judicial mean for the protection of constitutional rights, has also been traditionally characterized as a personal action that can only be brought before the competent courts by the particular person holder of the rights or his representatives. Some legislations like the Brazilian one, regarding the *mandado de securança* set forth that in case of rights threatened or violated covering a few persons, any of them can file the action (Article 1,2). In Costa Rica, also, regarding the constitutional right to rectification and response in cases of offenses, the Constitutional Jurisdiction Law provides that when the offended are more than one person, any of them can file the action; and in cases in which the offended could be identified with a group or an organized collectivity, the standing to sue must be exercised by their authorized representative (Article 67).

Nonetheless, some rights are collective by nature in the sense that they correspond to a group more or less defined of persons, in which case its violations affects not only the right of each of the individuals who enjoy them, but also the group of

553 Case *State Mérida and other v. Ministry of Finances*, in *Revista de Derecho Público*, N° 84, Editorial Jurídica venezolana, Caracas, pp 315 ff.

554 See Vote 285–90. See the reference in Rubén HERNÁNDEZ VALLE, *Derecho Procesal Constitucional,* Editorial Juricentro, San José 2001, p. 235

555 See Celso AGRÍCOLA BARBI, *Do mandado de Seguranca*, Editora Forense, Río de Janeiro, 1993, pp. 68 ff; José Luis LAZZARINI, *El Juico de Amparo*, Editorial La Ley, Buenos Aires, 1987, pp. 267–. 268.

persons or collectivity to which the individuals belongs. In these cases, the amparo action can also be filed by the group or association of persons representing their associates, even if those associations do not have the formal character of an artificial person. That is why, for instance, the Amparo Law of Paraguay, when defining standing to sue in matters of amparo, additionally to physical or artificial persons, refers to political parties duly registered, entities with guild or professional identities and societies or associations that without being given the character of artificial persons, according to their by–laws their goals are not contrary to public good (*bien público*) (Art. 5). In Argentina, the Amparo Law also provides the standing to file amparo actions by these associations that without being formally artificial persons can justify, according to their by–laws that they are not against "public or collective interest" (*bien público*) (Article 5).

In Venezuela, the 1999 Constitution expressly sets forth the constitutional right of everybody to have access to justice, not only to seek for the enforcement of specific personal rights and interests, but even to enforce "collective or diffuse interests" (Art. 26); which opened the possibility of amparo actions that can be filed on behalf of collective or diffuse interest.

The Constitutional Chamber of the Supreme Tribunal of Justice in a decision N° 656 of May 5, 2001 (Case: *Defensor del Pueblo vs. Comisión Legislativa Nacional*, defined the diffuse and the collective interests or rights, as concepts established not for the protection of a number of individuals that can be considered as representing the entire or an important part of a society, which are affected on their constitutional rights and guarantees destined to protect the public welfare by an attack to their quality of life. The Constitutional Chamber defined the collective rights, when the "damage is specifically located in a groups that can be determined as such, even if it is not quantifiable or individualized, as would be that case of the inhabitants of an area of the country affected by an illegal construction that creates problems with the public services in the area". These focused specific interests are the collective ones, which "refer to a determined and identified sector of the population (even though not quantified), individually, within the group there exists or might exist a legal bond uniting them. This is the case of damages to professional groups, to groups of neighbors, to labor unions, to the inhabitants of a certain area, etc."

In a different sense, regarding the diffuse rights, they affect the population as a whole because they are intended to assure the people, in a general way, an acceptable quality of life (basic conditions of existence). When they are affected, the quality of life of the entire community or society in its different scopes diminishes, and an interest arises in each member of that community and of the other components of society, in preventing that situation to occur, and that it be repaired if that situation already occurred. Thus, the Constitutional Chamber has ruled, in these cases:

> "it is a diffuse interest (that originates rights), since it spread among all the individuals of a society, even though from time to time the damage to the quality of life may be limited to groups that are able to be individualized as sectors that suffer as social entities. It can be the case of the inhabitants of a given sector or people pertaining to a same category, or the member of professional groups, etc. Nevertheless, those affected shall be no specified individuals,

> but a totality or groups of individuals or corporations, since the damaged goods are not susceptible of exclusive appropriation by one subject …
>
> Despite the concept that rules the diffuse interest or right as part of the defense of the citizenship, it is aimed at satisfying social or collective needs, before the personal ones. Since the damage is general (to the population or broad parts of it), the diffuse right or interest unites individuals who do not know each other, who individually lack of connection or legal relations among them, who at the beginning are undetermined, but united only because of the same situation of damage or danger they are involved in as members of a society and due to the right that arises in everyone to the protection of their quality of life, set forth in the Constitution…
>
> The common damage to the quality of life, which concerns any component of population or society as such, despite the legal relations they may have with other of these undetermined members, is the content of the diffuse right or interest.

In this sense, damages to the environment or to the consumers, for example, even in the case that they occur in a certain place, have expansive effects that harm the inhabitants of large sectors of the country and even the world, and respond to the undetermined obligation of protecting the environment or the consumers. Thus according to the doctrine of the Constitutional Chamber,

> The diffuse interests are the wider ones, where the damaged good is the most general good, since it concerns the entire population and, contrary to the collective interests or rights, they arise from an obligation of uncertain object; while in the collective ones, the obligation may be concrete, yet not demandable by individualized persons.
>
> Consumers are all the inhabitants of the country. The damage to them as such responds to a *supra* individual or *supra* personal right, and to an uncertain obligation in favor of them, from those managing goods and services. Their quality of life diminishes, whether they realize it or not, since many massive communicational mechanisms shall annul or alter the conscience of the damage. Their interest, or the one of those affected, for example, due to the damages to the environment, is diffuse and so is the right raised to preventing or impeding the damage.
>
> The interest of the neighbors, whose neighborhood is worsened in its public services by a construction, for example, responds as well to a supra personal legal right, yet it can be determined, located in specific groups, and it is the interest that allows a collective action. That is the collective interest. It gives origin to collective rights and may refer to a certain legal object.
>
> The truth in both cases (diffuse and collective interest) is that the damage is suffered by the social group equally, even if some members do not consider themselves damaged, since they consent the damage. This concept differs from the personal damage directed to a personal legal right. This difference does not impede the existence of mixed damages, the same fact damaging a personal legal right and a supra individual one."[556]

Now, regarding the standing to bring before courts action for amparo seeking the protection of collective and diffuse constitutional rights, the same Constitutional Chamber of the Supreme Court, for instance, has admitted the filing of an action of *amparo* to protect political electoral rights filed by one voter exercising his own right, even having granted precautionary measures with *erga omnes* effects "to both

556 See decision of the Constitutional Chamber N° 656 of 06–05–01 (Case: *Defensor del Pueblo vs. Comisión Legislativa Nacional*.

individuals and corporations who have brought to suit the constitutional protection, and to all voters as a group"[557].

The Constitutional Chamber, with this same orientation, has interpreted Article 26 of the Constitution in a wide way regarding the action of *amparo* of collective or diffuse interests by stating that:

> "Consequently, any individual with legal capacity to bring suit, who is going to impede a damage to the population or parts of it where he belongs to, is entitled to bring to suit grounded in diffuse or collective interests, and where he had suffered personal damages, he shall claim for himself (jointly) the compensation of such. This interpretation, grounded in Article 26, extends the standing to companies, corporations, foundations, chambers, unions and other collective entities, whose object is the defense of the society, as long as they act within the boundaries of their corporate object, aimed at protecting the interests of their members regarding their object. Article 102 of the Organic Law of Urban Planning follows this orientation.
>
> In the Venezuelan legislation, currently, an individual shall not bring to suit a compensation for the damaged collectivity, when claiming diffuse interests. Such claim corresponds to entities such as the Public Prosecutor or the Defender of the People.
>
> When the damages harm groups of individuals that are legally bound or pertain to the same activity, the action grounded in collective interests, whose purpose is the same as the one of the diffuse interests, shall be brought to suit by the corporations that gather the damaged sectors or groups and even by any member of that sector or group as long as he acts in defense of that social segment…
>
> Due to the foregoing, it is not necessary for whoever brings a suit grounded on diffuse or collective interests, if it is a diffuse one, to have a bond previously established with the offender. It is necessary that he acts as a member of the society, or its general categories (consumers, users, etc.), and invokes his right or interest shared with the citizenship, since he participates with them in the damaged factual situation because of the infringement or detriment of the fundamental rights concerning the collectivity, which generates a common subjective right that despite being indivisible, may be enforced by anyone in the infringed situation, since the legal order acknowledges those rights in Article 26 of the Constitution. It is a legal interest guaranteed in the Constitution. It cannot be appropriated individually and exclusively by any individual, since anyone damaged is able to enforce it, unless it is restricted by law, which can be claimed to whoever owes the obligation of certain object.
>
> Even though it is a general right or interest enjoyed by the plaintiff, which allows various plaintiffs, he himself shall be threatened, shall have suffered the damage or shall be suffering it as a part of the citizenship, whereby whoever is not residing in the country, or is not damaged shall lack of standing; this situation separates these actions from the popular ones.
>
> Whoever brings suit based on collective rights or interests, shall do it in his condition of member of the group or sector damaged, therefore, he suffers the damage jointly with others, whereby he assumes an interest of his own and gives him or her the right to claim the end of the damage for himself and the others, with whom shares the right or interest. It shall be a group or sector not individualized, otherwise, it would be a concrete party.

---

557 Decision of the Constitutional Chamber N° 483 of 05–29–2000 (Case: *"Queremos Elegir" y otros*), *Revista de Derecho Público*, N° 82, 2000, Editorial Jurídica Venezolana, pp. 489-491. In the same sense, decision of the same Chamber N° 714 of 13–07–2000 (Case: *APRUM*).

In both cases, if the action is admitted, a legal benefit will arise in favor of the plaintiff and his common interest with the society or collectivity of protecting it, maintaining the quality of life. The defense of society's interests is guaranteed.

The plaintiff is given the subjective right to react against the damaging act or concrete threat, caused by the offender's violation of the fundamental rights of the society in general.

Whoever is entitled to act shall always plea for an actual interest, which does not terminate for the society in one single process.

If an individual brings suit grounding his action in diffuse rights or interests, yet the judge considers that it is about them, he shall subpoena the Defender of the People or the entities established by law in particular subjects, and shall notify through an edict all the parties in interest, whether there are processes in which the law excludes and grants representation to other individuals. All these legitimate interested parties shall intervene as third party claimants, if the judge admits them as such taking into consideration the existence of diffuse rights and interests.[558]

The Constitutional Chamber has also determined the general conditions of standing in these cases of collective or diffuse rights, in a decision N° 1948 of February 17, 2000 (Case: *William O. Ojeda O. vs. Consejo Nacional Electoral*), in which it ruled that is necessary that the following elements be combined:

"1. That the plaintiff sues based not only on his personal right or interest, but also on a common or collective right or interest.
2. That the reason of the claim (or the action of amparo filed) be the general damage to the quality of life of all the inhabitants of the country or parts of it, since the legal situation of all the member of the society or its groups has been damaged when their common quality of life was worsened.
3. That the damaged goods not be susceptible of exclusive appropriation by one subject (as the plaintiff).
4. That it concern an indivisible right or interest that involves the entire population of the country or a group of it.
5. That a bond exists, even if it is not a legal one, between whoever demands in general interest of the society or a part of it (social common interest), raised from the damage or danger in which collectivity is (as such). This damage or danger and the possibility of it happening are known by the judge due to common knowledge.
6. That a necessity of satisfying social or collective interests exist, before the individual ones.
7. That a person is obliged to an undetermined obligation, the enforcement of which is general."[559]

One of the most important issues regarding these collective and diffuse amparo actions relates to the standing of the "representative". The Constitutional Chamber, on the matter, has ruled the following criteria:

---

558 See decision of the Constitutional Chamber N° 656 of 06–05–2001, Case: *Defensor del Pueblo vs. Comisión Legislativa Nacional.*

559 Decision N° 1.048 of the Constitutional Chamber dated 02–17–00, Case: *William Ojeda vs. Consejo Nacional Electoral.*

"Any person capable in procedure that tends to impede harms to the population or sectors of it to which he appertains, can file actions in defense of diffuse or collective interest...This interpretation founded in Article 26 (of the Constitution), extend standing to the associations, societies, foundations, chambers, trade unions and other collective entities, devoted to defend society, provided they act within the limits of their societal goals referred to watch for the interest of their members".

The Chamber added that:

"Those who file actions regarding the defense of diffuse interest do not need to have any previously established relation with the offender, but has to act as a member of society, or of its general categories (consumers, users, etc.) and has to invoke his right or interest shared with the population's, because he participates with all regarding the harmed factual situation due to the noncompliance of the diminution of fundamental rights of everybody, which give birth to a communal subjective right, that although indivisible, is actionable by any one place within the infringed situation"[560].

But in spite of all the aforementioned progressive decisions regarding the protection of collective and diffuse rights, like the political ones, in a recent decision dated November 21, 2005, the Constitutional Chamber has set back, and in the case, originated by a claim filed by the director of a political association named "Un Solo Pueblo" against the threat of violations of the political rights of the aforesaid political party and of all the other supporters of the calling of a recall referendum regarding the President of the Republic, ruled that:

"The action of amparo was filed for the protection of constitutional rights of an undetermined number of persons, whose identity was not indicated in the filing document, in which they are not included as claimants.

It is the criteria of this Chamber, those that could result directly affected in their constitutional rights and guaranties by the alleged threat attributed to the Ministry of Defense and the General Commanders of the Army and the National Guard are, precisely, the persons that are members or supporters of "Un solo Pueblo", or those who prove they are part of one of the groups that promoted the recall referendum; in which case they would have standing to bring before the constitutional judge, by themselves or through representatives, seeking the reestablishment of the infringed juridical situation or impeding the realization of the threat, because the *legitimatio ad causam* exists in each one of them, not precisely as constitutionally harmed of aggrieved.

Due to the foregoing, the Chamber considers that Mr. William Ojeda, who said he acted as Director of the political association called "Un Sólo Pueblo", quality that he furthermore has not demonstrated, lacks of the necessary standing to seek for constitutional amparo of the constitutional rights set forth in Articles 19, 21 and 68 of the Constitution regarding the members, supporters and participants of the mentioned political association as well as the political coalition that proposed the recall referendum of the President of the Republic, and consequently, this Chamber declares the inadmissibility of the amparo action filed"[561].

560 Decisión of the Constitutional Chamber of June 30, 2000 (Case *Defensoría del Pueblo).* See the reference and comments in Rafael CHAVERO, *El Nuevo Régimen del Amparo Constitucional en Venezuela*, Caracas, 2001, pp. 110–114.

561 See Case: *William Ojeda vs. Ministro de la Defensa y los Comandantes Generales del Ejercito y de la Guardia Nacional*, in *Revista de Derecho Público*, N° 104, Editorial Jurídica Venezolana, Caracas, 2005.

Besides the foregoing inconsistencies in judicial doctrine, "Collective suits" of amparo for the protection of diffuse rights have been expressly constitutionalized in Argentina, where the Constitution provides in Article 43, that the amparo suit can be filed by "the affected party, the People's Defendant and the registered associations that tend to those goals":

> Against any form of discrimination and regarding the rights for the protection of environment, the free competition, the user and the consumer, as well as the rights of collective general incidence, the affected party, the People's Defendant and the registered associations that tend to those goals, could file this action.

Regarding the associations that can file the collective amparo suits, the Supreme Court of Argentina has also considered that they do not require formal registration[562].

Three specific collective actions result from this article: amparo against any form of discrimination; amparo for the protection of the environment; and amparo for the protection of free competitions, the user and the consumer. That is why regarding discrimination, the object of this amparo is not a discrimination regarding a particular individual but a group of persons between which a nexus or common trend exists which originates the discrimination.[563],

On the other hand, regarding the protection of the environment, it was formalized the trend that began to be consolidated after a 1983 case in which an amparo was filed for the protection of the ecologic equilibrium regarding the protection of dolphins. The Supreme Court accepted in that case, the possibility for anybody individually or in representation of his family, to file an amparo action when pursuing the maintenance of the ecological equilibrium, due to the right any human being has to protect his habitat[564].

In Peru, Article 40 of the Constitutional Procedure Code authorizes any person to file the amparo suit "in cases referred to threats or violation of environmental rights or other diffuse rights that enjoy constitutional recognition, as well as the non lucrative entities whose goals are the defense of such rights".

In Brazil, Article 5, LXIII of the Constitution sets forth the *mandado de securanca colectivo* , as a sort of *mandado de seguranca* for the protection of actual rights not protected by habeas–corpus or habeas–data, when the responsible of the illegality or abuse of power is a public authority or an agent of a artificial person acting in exercise of public power attributions, but that can be filed by: a) political parties with representation in national Congress, b) trade unions, class institutions or associations legally established and functioning at least for one year in defense of

---

562 Decisions 320:690, Case: *Asociación Grandes Usuarios and Decision 323:1339*, Asociación Benghalensis. See the referentes in Joaquín Brage Camazano, *La jurisdicción constitucional de la libertad*, Editorial Porrúa, México 2005, pp. 92–93.

563 See Joaquín BRAGE CAMAZANO, *La jurisdicción constitucional de la libertad*, Editorial Porrúa, México 2005, pp. 94.

564 See Alí Joaquín SALGADO, *Juicio de amparo y acción de inconstitucionalidad*, Astrea Buenos Aires 1987, pp. 81–89.

the interests of its members. This *mandado de securanca* is thus not intended to protect individual rights, but diffuse or collective rights.

It must also be mentioned, that since 1985 a "collective civil action" has been developed in Brazil, with similar trends as the Class Actions of the United States, very widely used for the protection of group rights, like consumers though limiting the standing to the public entities (national, state and municipal) and to associations[565].

In Ecuador, Article 48 of the Amparo Law also authorizes any person, natural or artificial to file the amparo action, "when it is a matter of protection of the environment". Thus, any person, including the indigenous communities through their representative, can file the amparo suit[566]

It also must be mentioned the case of Costa Rica, where the collective amparo has also been admitted in matters of environment by the Constitutional Chamber of the Supreme Court. Article 50 of the Constitution, in effect, provides that "any person has the right to a healthy and ecologically equilibrated environment"; thus, it has standing to denounce the acts which infringe that right and to claim the reparation of the harm caused". Even though not expressly referring to the amparo suit, the Constitutional Chamber did refer to a similar norm of the previous Constitution (Article 89) which gave standing to anybody "to file amparo actions for the defense of the right to the conservation of the natural resources of the country. Even tough it does not exist a direct and clear suit for the claimant as in the concrete case of the State against an individual, all inhabitants, regarding the violations of Article 89 of the Constitution, suffer a prejudice in the same proportion as if it where a direct harm, thus it is accepted that an interest exists in his favor that authorizes him to file an action for the protection of such right to maintain the natural equilibrium of the ecosystem"[567].

Even in the Dominican Republic, where no constitutional provision exists regarding the amparo suit, the Supreme Court not only has created it but, accordingly, the courts have admitted that any person legally capable and with interest in the general enforcement of collective human rights, as the right to education, can file an action for amparo due that the matter is not only and exclusively a private one[568].

In Mexico, contrary to the current tendency of other countries, the amparo suit continues to have an essential individual character, based in the personal and direct

565 See Antonio GIDI, "Acciones de grupo y "amparo colectivo" en Brasil. La protección de derechos difusos, colectivos e individuales homogéneos", in Eduardo FERRER MAC–GREGOR (Coordinator), *Derecho Procesal Constitucional*, Colegio de Secretarios de la Suprema Corte de Justicia de la Nación, Editorial Porrúa, Tomo III, México 2003, pp. 2.538 ff.

566 Hernán SALGADO PESANTES, *Manual de Justicia Constitucional Ecuatoriana,* Corporación Editora Nacional, Quito 2004, p. 76.

567 Decision 1700–03. See the reference Rubén HERNÁNDEZ VALLE, *Derecho Procesal Constitucional,* Editorial Juricentro, San José, 2001, pp.239–240.

568 See decisión 406–2 of June 21, 2001, First Instante Court of San Pedro Macoris. See the reference in Miguel A. VALERA MONTERO, *Hacia un Nuevo concepto de constitucionalismo*, Santo Domingo, 2006, pp. 388–389.

interest[569]. The only cases in which the amparo in certain way protects collective interest are those related to the agrarian amparo, for the protection of peasants and of collective agrarian land owners[570].

In Colombia, the general principle is also that the action for tutela is a personal and private action, that can only be filed by the holder of the individual right protected by the constitutional norm. Thus it is not a public or popular action. The tutela action can only be exercised in person, seeking the protection of a personal, fundamental right, of constitutional rank of the person on whose behalf it is filed[571]. That is why, Article 6,3 of the Tutela Law expressly provides that the action of tutela is inadmissible when the rights seeking to be protected are "collective rights, as the right to peace and others referred to in Article 88 of the Constitution", particularly because for that purposes a special judicial means for protection is established called "popular actions". Article 6,3 of the Tutela Law added that the foregoing will not prevent that the holder of rights threatened to be violated or that have been violated can file a tutela action in situations compromising collective rights and interest and of his own threatened or violated rights, when it is a matter to prevent an irremediable harm".

According to Article 88 of the Constitution, the diffuse or "collective" rights are protected not by the tutela action, but by means of the "popular actions" or the group actions. The former are those established in the Constitution for the protection of rights and interests related to public property, public space, public security and health, administrative morale, environment, economic free competition and others of similar nature. All these are diffuse rights, and for its protections, the law 472 of 1998 has regulated these popular actions.

This statute also regulates other sort of actions, for the protection of rights in cases of harms suffered by a plural number of persons. These group actions are similar to the class actions of North American Law.

Regarding the popular actions, they can be filed by any person, the Non Governmental Organizations, the Popular or Civic Organizations, the public entities with control functions, when the harm or threat is not initiated by their activities, the General Prosecutor, the Peoples 'Defendant and the District and Municipal prosecutors, and the mayors and public officers that because of their functions they must defend and protect the abovementioned rights (Art. 12).

Regarding the group actions set forth for the protection of a plurality of persons in cases of suffering harm in their rights in a collective way, the Law 472 of 1998 establishes these actions basically with indemnizatory purposes, and they can only be filed by 20 individuals, acting all of them on their own behalf. Thus, these are not

---

569 See Eduardo FERRER MAC–GREGOR, *Juicio de amparo e interés legítimo: la tutela de los derechos difusos y colectivos*, Editorial Porrúa, México 2003, p. 56.

570 See Eduardo FERRER MAC–GREGOR, *La acción constitucional de amparo en México y España*, Editorial Porrúa, México 2002, p. 233 ff.

571 Juan Carlos EZQUERRA PORTOCARRERO, *La protección constitucional del ciudadano,* Lexis, Bogotá, 2005, p. 121.

actions directed to protect the whole population or collectivity, but only a plurality of persons that have the same rights, and seek for its protection.

These group actions have some similarities with the class actions regulated in Rule 23 of the Federal Rules of Civil Procedure filed for the protection of civil rights, that is, the "civil rights class actions". According to that Rule, in cases of a class of persons who have question of law or fact common to the class, but have so numerous members that joining all of them would be an impracticable task, then the action can be filed by one or more of its members as representative plaintiff parties on behalf of all, provided that the claims of the representative parties are typical of the claims of the class and that such representatives parties will fairly and adequately protect the interests of the class. (Rule 23, Class Actions, a).

The class actions have been applied in cases of violation of civil rights, particularly regarding to the right of non discrimination. It was the case decided by the Supreme Court *Zablocki, Milwaukee County Clerk v. Redhail* case of January 18, 1978, 434 U.S. 374; 98 S. Ct. 673; 54 L. Ed. 2d 618, as a result of a class action brought before a federal court under 42 U.S.C.S. § 1983, by Wisconsin residents holding that the marriage prohibition set forth in Wisconsin State § 245.10 (1973) violated the equal protection clause, U.S. Const. amend. XIV. According to that statute, Wisconsin residents were prevented from marrying if they were behind in their child support obligations or if the children to whom they were obligated were likely to become public charges. The Court found that the statute violated equal protection in that it directly and substantially interfered with the fundamental right to marry without being closely tailored to effectuate the state's interests.

Another Supreme Court decision, *Lau et al. v. Nichols et al.*, dated January 21, 1974, 414 U.S. 563; 94 S. Ct. 786; 39 L. Ed. 2d 1; 1974 also decided in favor of a class, on discrimination violations. In the case, non–English speaking students of Chinese ancestry brought a class suit in a federal court of California against officials of the San Francisco Unified School District, seeking relief against alleged unequal educational opportunities resulting from the officials' failure to establish a program to rectify the students' language problem. The Supreme Court eventually held that the school district, which received federal financial assistance, violated dispositions that ban discrimination based on race, color, or national origin in any program or activity receiving federal financial assistance, and furthermore violated the implementing regulations of the Department of Health, Education, and Welfare, by failing to establish a program to deal with the complaining students' language problem.

IV. THE PEOPLES' DEFENDANT STANDING ON THE AMPARO SUIT

As the amparo suit has been instituted in Latin America as a specific judicial means for the protection of constitutional rights, another general tendency in Latin American constitutionalism is for the creation in the Constitution or Legislation (Costa Rica) of a specific autonomous State entity or body with the objective of protecting and seeking for the protection of constitutional rights, called the Defendant of the People (People's Defendant) or of Human Rights.

In some cases, the institution follows in general lines the classical Scandinavian Ombudsman, initially conceived as a parliamentary independent entity for the protection of citizens' rights regarding Public Administration. In other Latin American countries, it is more conceived as an autonomous institution, from both parliament and the Executive as well as from the Judicial Power.

In the first group, closer to the European model, the Argentinean Constitution in the chapter referred to the Legislative Power (Art. 86) establishes the Defendant of the People for the protection of human rights regarding Public Administration. It is conceived as an independent entity in the scope of the Congress, acting with functional autonomy and without receiving instructions from any authority. Its mission is the defense and protection of human rights guaranteed in the Constitutions and statues against Public Administration facts, acts or omissions, and to control the exercise of administrative functions. The Peoples defendant is nominated by the Congress, by 2/3 of the votes of the members present in the voting and can only be removed in the same way.

In the Constitution of Paraguay, the Peoples' Defendant is a parliamentary commissioner for the protection of human rights, for the channeling of popular claims and for the protection of communitarian interests, without having any judicial or executive functions (Art. 276). It is elected by the Chamber of Representatives, from a proposal by the Senate, with the vote of 2/3 of its members.

In Guatemala, the Constitution establishes a Procurator on Human Rights as a parliamentary commissioner, elected by Congress from a proposal made by a Commission on Human Rights integrated by representatives of the political parties in Congress. His mission is to defend human rights and to supervise Public Administration (Article 274). The Law on amparo in Guatemala gives the Public Prosecutor and the Procurator on Human Rights sufficient standing to file amparo actions "for the defense of the interests assigned to them" (Article 25).

In the majority of the Latin American Constitutions, the Peoples' defendant or the Procurator for the Defense of Human Rights are created without any specific reference to Public Administration, thus they face all State organs, for the protection of human rights. This is the case of Colombia, Ecuador and El Salvador, even though in the last two countries, it is regulated attached to the Public Prosecutor's Office (*Ministerio Público*).

In Colombia, the Peoples' Defendant, elected by the representative Chamber of Congress from a proposal formulated by the president of the Republic, is created as part of the Public Prosecutor Office (Article 281), with the specific mission of watching for the promotion, exercise and divulgation of human rights. Within its powers is to invoke the right to habeas corpus and to file actions for tutela, without prejudice of the interested party rights. The Tutela Law also authorizes the Peoples' Defendant to file these actions on behalf of anyone when asked to do so, in cases of the person being in a non protective situation (Articles 10 and 46), or regarding Colombians residing outside the country (Article 51). In such cases, the Peoples' Defendant will be considered party in the process together with the injured party (Article 47).

In El Salvador, the Procurator for the Defense of Human Rights in part of the Public Ministry, together with the Public Prosecutor and the Attorney General of the

Republic (Art. 191), all elected by the Legislative Assembly by a 2/3 vote of its members. Within its functions are to watch for the respect and guarantee of human rights and to promote judicial actions for their protection (Article 194).

Other countries have a Peoples Defendant as a complete independent and autonomous institution regarding the classical branches of government, as is the case of Ecuador, with the Peoples' Defendant, also elected by the Congress with the vote of the 2/3 of its members (Article 96). Among its functions are to defend and encourage the respect of the fundamental constitutional rights, to watch for the quality of the public services and to promote and support the habeas corpus and amparo actions at the person's request. The Law regulating the matter in Ecuador also authorizes the Peoples' defendant to file habeas corpus and amparo actions (Articles 33 and 48).

In Mexico, the Constitution has also established that Congress and the state legislatures must create entities for the protection on human rights, receiving grievances regarding administrative acts or omissions of any authority except the judicial power, that violate such rights. At the national level, the entity is named National Commission on Human Rights. Nonetheless, the Amparo Law authorizes the Federal Public Prosecutor to file action for amparo in criminal and family cases, but not in civil or commercial cases (Article 5, 1,IV),

In Bolivia, the Constitution also creates the Peoples' Defendant for the purpose of watching for the enforcement and respect of the persons' rights and guarantees regarding administrative activities on all the public sector, as for the defense, promotion and divulgation of human rights (Article 127). The Peoples defendant does not receive instructions from the public powers and is elected by Congress (Article 128). Among its functions are to file the actions of amparo and habeas corpus without needing any power of attorney. (Article 129).

In Peru, the Constitution also creates the Peopels' Defendant Office as an autonomous organ, the head of which is elected by Congress also with 2/3 votes of its members (article 162), for the purpose of defending persons and community human and fundamental rights, to supervise for the accomplishment of public administration duties and the rendering of public services to the people. The Constitutional Procedure Code authorizes the People' Defendant, in exercising its competencies, to file amparo actions (Article 40).

In Nicaragua the Constitution only establishes that the National Assembly will appoint the Procurator for the defense of Human Rights (Article 138,30).

The tendency to create an independent and autonomous organ of the State for the protection of human rights has reached the extreme regulation in the 1999 Venezuelan Constitution, which establishes a *penta* separation of powers, between the Legislative, Executive, Judicial, Electoral and Citizens branches of government, creating within the Citizens Power the Peoples' Defendant. Also the Public Prosecutor Office and the General Comptroller Office form part of the Citizens Power (Article 134).

The Peoples' Defendant is created for the promotion, defense and supervision of the rights and guaranties set forth in the Constitution and in the international treaties on human rights, as well as for the citizens' legitimate, collective and diffuse interests (Article 281). In particular, according to Article 281 of the Constitution, it also has among its functions to watch for the functioning of public services power and to promote and protect the peoples' legitimate, collective and diffuse rights and interests against arbitrariness or deviation of power in the rendering of such services, being authorized to file the necessary actions to ask for the compensation of the damages caused from the malfunctioning of public services. It also has among its functions, the possibility of filing actions of amparo and habeas corpus.

In Venezuela, the Constitutional Chamber has admitted the standing of the Defender of the People to file actions for *amparo* on behalf of the citizens as a whole, as was the case of the action filed against the Congress'pretension to appoint the Electoral National Council members without fulfilling the constitutional requirements. In the case, decided on June, 6, 2001, the Constitutional Chamber, when analyzing Article 280 of the Constitution, pointed out that:

> "As a matter of law, the Defender has standing to bring to suit actions aimed at enforcing the diffuse and collective rights or interests; not being necessary the requirement of the acquiescence of the society it acts on behalf of for the exercise of the action. The Defender of the People is given legitimate interest to act in a process defending a right granted to it by the Constitution itself, consisting in protecting the society or groups in it, in the cases of Article 281 *eiusdem*.
>
> ...The forgoing, according to this Chamber criteria, makes clear that the issue of the protection of diffuse and collective rights and interests may be raised by the Defender of the People, through the action of amparo, and it is declared this way.
>
> As for the general provision of Article 280 *eiusdem*, regarding the general defense and protection of diffuse and collective interests, this Chamber considers that the Defender of the People is entitled to act to protect those rights and interests , when they correspond in general to the consumers and users (6, Article 281), or to protect the rights of Indian peoples (paragraph 8 of the same Article), since the defense and protection of such categories is one of the faculties granted to said entity by Article 281 of the Constitution in force. It is about a general protection and not a protection of individualities.
>
> Within this frame of action, and since the political rights are included in the human rights and guarantees of Title III of the Constitution in force, which have a general projection, among which the ones provided in Article 62 of the Constitution can be found, it must be concluded that the Defender of the People on behalf of the society, legitimated by law, is entitled to bring to suit an action of amparo tending to control the Electoral Power, to the citizen's benefit, in order to enforce Articles 62 and 70 of the Constitution, which were denounced to be breached by the National Legislative Assembly..." (right to citizen participation).
>
> Due to the difference between diffuse and collective interests, both the Defender of the People, within its attributions, and every individual residing in the country, except for the legal exceptions, are entitled to bring to suit the action (be it of amparo or an specific one) for the protection of the former ones; while the action of the collective interests is given to the Defender of the People and to any member of the group or sector identified as a component of that specific collectivity, and acting defending the collectivity. Both individuals and corporations whose object be the protection of such interests may raise the action, and the standing in all these actions varies according to the nature of the same, that is why law can limit the action in specific individuals or entities. However, in our Constitution, in the provisions of Arti-

cle 281 the Defender of the People is objectively granted the procedural interest and the capacity to sue"[572].

V. THE QUESTION OF OTHER PUBLIC (STATE) INSTITUTIONS STANDING ON THE AMPARO SUIT

Another important issue regarding standing in filing amparo suits is to determine if other State entities can file amparo actions on behalf of the people, in defense of collective or diffuse rights. In contrast with what has occurred in the United States, it can be said that in general terms, beside the Peoples' Defendant standing, no other public entity can assume the defense of the rights of the peoples by means of filing amparo suits.

In the United States, in the Supreme Court decision *In Re Debs*, 158 U.S. 565, 15 S.Ct. 900,39 L.Ed. 1092 (1895), the standing of the Attorney General for the protection of the State's general interest as the property on the mail in injunctive proceedings, was admitted, even being a party against the members of a railway trade union which threatened the functioning of railways. A few years before, the Congress had approved the Sherman Antitrust Act which granted authority to the Attorney General to commence injunctive proceedings to prevent restraints to trade.

Half a century later, after the Supreme Court decision in *Brown v. Board of Education of Topeka,* 347 U.S. 483 (1954); 349 U.S. 294 (1955) declared the dual school system ("separate but equal") unconstitutional, by means of the Civil Rights Act of 1957, the Congress authorized the Attorney General to bring injunctive suits to implement the Fifteenth Amendment referred to right to vote in a non discriminatory basis. As referred by Owen R. Fiss:

> "The very next congressional initiative, the Civil Rights Act of 1960, was in large part intended to perfect the Attorney General's injunctive weaponry on behalf of voting rights. In each of the subsequent civil rights acts, those of 1964 and 1968 the pattern was repeated; the Attorney General was authorized to initiate injunctive suits to enforce wide range of rights – public accommodations (e.g. restaurants), state facilities (e.g. parks), public schools, employments, and housing"[573].

Thus, after *Brown*, it can be said that the United States ceased to participate in civil rights proceedings just as *amicus curia*, and in his name the Attorney General began to play prominent role acting in civil rights proceedings even before having specific authorization from Congress. As mentioned by Fiss: "The civil rights era forced the Attorney General and the courts to re–examine the non–statutory powers of the United States to sue to enforce the Constitution"[574]".

The standing of the Attorney General was finally generally admitted regarding the protection of human rights in the case *United States v. City of Philadelphia*, 644

---

572 Decision of the Constitutional Chamber N° 656 of 06–05–2001, Case: *Defensor del Pueblo vs. Comisión Legislativa Nacional.*

573 See Owen M. FISS, *The Civil Rights Injunction,* Indiana University Pres, Bloomington & London, 1978, p. 21

574 See Owen M. FISS and Doug RENDLEMAN, *Injunctions*, Second Edition, University Casebook Series, The Foundation Press, Mineola, New York, 1984, p. 35.

F.2d. 187 (3d Cir. 1980), in which the United States authority to sue a city and its officials for an injunction against the violation of the XIV Amendment rights of individual because of police brutality, was admitted; the United States was considered as suing as class representative for the city of Philadelphia. The United States Court of Appeals, Third Circuits ruled in the matter, as follows:

Article II section 3 of the Constitution charges the Executive to "take care that the Laws be faithfully executed." Independent of any explicit statutory grant of authority, provided Congress has not expressly limited its authority, the Executive has the inherent constitutional power and duty to enforce constitutional and statutory rights by resort to the courts. When Federal courts have upheld executive standing without explicit congressional authority, they have looked to other provisions of the Constitution, such as the commerce clause (See, e. g., Sanitary District of Chicago v. United States, 266 Us. 405,45 S. Ct. 176, 69 L. Ed. 352 (1925); In re debs, 158 U.S. 564 15 S. Ct. 900, 39 L. Ed. 1092 (1895) and cases cited infra, p 218. and the fourteenth amendment (See United States v. Brand Jewelers, 318 F. Supp. 1293 (S.D.N.Y. 1970) and to a general statutory scheme defining federal rights but lacking the specific remedy of executive suit (See, e. g., Wyandotte Transp. Co. v. United States, 389 U.S. 191, 88 S. Ct. 379, 19 L. Ed. 2d. 407 (1967); United States v. American Bell Telephone Co., 128 U.S. 315, 9 S. Ct. 90, 32 L. Ed. 450 (1888); United States v. San Jacinto Tin Co., 125 U.S. 273, 8 S. Ct. 850, 31 L. Ed. 747 (1888)). In addition, 28 U.S.C. § 518 (b) affords the Attorney General statutory authority to "conduct and argue any case in a court of the United States in which the United States is interested." The Supreme Court has held that this statute confers on the Executive general authority to initiate suits "to safeguard national interests." (United States v. California, 332 U.S. 19, 27, 67 S. Ct. 1658, 1662, 91 L. Ed. 1889 (1946)). Moreover, the Supreme Court has held that the Executive's general constitutional duty to protect the public welfare "is often of itself sufficient to give it standing in court." (In re Debs, 158 U.S. 564, 584, 15 S. Ct. 900, 906, 39 L. Ed. 1092 (1895).

Thus, the standing of the Attorney General in the United States as well as of other public agencies has been admitted to file injunctions seeking the protection of some constitutional rights of citizens. For example, the standing of the United States and of the Secretary of Education, has been recognized to seek an injunction against a university to stop the release of student records in violation of a federal statute (*United States v. Miami University*, 294 F. 3d 797, 166 Ed. Law Rep. 464 2002 FED App. 0213P (6th Cir. 2002)[575]. In general terms, the standing of the United States, the States and the Municipalities has been accepted in all cases in which they act in its capacity as protectors of the public interest, like public welfare, public safety or public health. That is why actions for injunction in cases of the illegal practice of medicine, and other allied professions had been brought by the attorney general, a State board of health or a county attorney[576],

575 See the reference in Kevin SCHRODER et al, "Injunction", *Corpus Juris Secundum*, Thomson West, Volume 43A, 2004, p. 252.

576 See the referentes to specific cases in Kevin Schroder et al, "Injunction", *Corpus Juris Secundum*, Thomson West, Volume 43A, 2004, p.271 ff.

Contrary to this North American tendency, in the Latin American countries except for the already mentioned standing assigned to the Peoples' Defendant, no other public officer or agency can claim the representation of collective or diffuse rights in order to file an amparo suit. This has even been expressly ruled in Venezuela, where the Constitutional Chamber of the Supreme Court deciding an amparo suit initiated by a Governor of one of the federated States, in a decision of November 21, 2000 ruled the following:

The States and Municipalities cannot file actions for diffuse and collective rights and interest, except if a statute expressly authorizes them.

The collective and diffuse rights and interests pursue to maintain in all the population or sectors of it, an acceptable quality of life, in those matters related to the quality of life that must be rendered by the State of by individuals. They are rights and interest that can coincide with individual rights and interests, but that according to Article 26 of the Constitution and unless the statute denies the action, can be claimed by any person invoking a right or interest shared with the people in general or a sector of the population, and who fears or has suffered, being part of such collectivity, a harm in his quality of life.

Now, being for the State to maintain the acceptable quality of life conditions, its bodies or entities cannot ask from it to render an activity; thus, within the structure of the State, the only institution that can file such actions is the Peoples' Defendant due to the fact that it represents the people and not the State, as well as other public entities when a particular statute gives them such actions[577].

In this sense, the Venezuelan Constitutional Chamber has denied the standing to file collective actions for amparo to the governors or mayors. In an action for judicial review of a statute with a joint amparo claim, of May 6, 2001, the Chamber decided that:

> [The] actions in general grounded in diffuse or collective rights and interests may be filed by any Venezuelan person or legal entity, or by foreign persons residing in the country, who have access to the judicial system through the exercise of this action. The Venezuelan State, as such, lacks of it, since it has mechanisms and other means to cease the damage to those rights and interests, specially through administrative procedures; but the population in general is entitled to bring them in the way explained in this decision, and those ones can be brought by the Defender of the People, since as for Article 280 of the Constitution, the Defendant of the People is in charge of the promotion, defense and guardianship of the legitimate, collective and diffuse interest of the citizens. According to this Chamber, said provision does not exclude or prohibit the citizens the access to the judicial system in defense of the diffuse and collective rights and interests, since Article 26 of the Constitution in force sets forth the access to the judicial system to every person, whereby individuals are entitled to bring to suit as well, unless a law denies them the action. Within the structure of the State, since it does not have those attributions granted, the only one who is able to protect individuals in matters of collective or diffuse interest is the Defender of the People (in any of its scopes: national, state, county or special). The Public Prosecutor (except in the case that a law grants it), Mayors, or

577 Case *William Dávila. Gobernación Estado Mérida.* See the comments in Rafael CHAVERO, *El Nuevo Régimen del Amparo Constitucional en Venezuela*, Caracas, 2001, p. 115.

Municipal auditors lack both such attribution and the action, unless the law grants them both)."[578]

VI. THE INJURED THIRD PARTY

As in all suits, and particularly in matters of amparo and protection of constitutional rights, it is possible that third parties not originally connected with the suit, have some personal interest in the action filed because the omission, the particular situation or the challenged act, also affects their constitutional rights, coinciding whether with the claimant or plaintiff or with the allegations of the defendants.

Injured third parties, thus, may be added in the proceedings so that their rights in the subject matter may be also determined and enforced by the corresponding court when coinciding with the plaintiff allegations. Of course the general rule is the same as in the injunctions proceeding in the United States: persons with a unity of interest in the subject matter of the suit and who are entitled to, and seek the same character of relief, may join the plaintiff claim[579]. Consequently, a person is allowed to intervene in an amparo proceeding adhering to the plaintiff claim and in defense of it because they have a direct interest in the matter that can be affected with the final decision; claim that cannot be modified nor expand by the third party.

Some Latin American Amparo Laws refer specifically to the intervention of third parties, as is the case of Guatemala where Article 34 of the Law establishes the obligation of

> "the authority, the person denounced or the claimant, if they arrive to know of any person with direct interest in the subject matter or the suspension of the challenged act, resolution or procedure, whether because they are party in the proceedings of because they have any other legal relation with the exposed situation; to tell the foregoing to the court, indicating name and address and in a brief way, the relation with such interest. In this case the court must hear the referred person, as well as the Public prosecutor, considered as a party".

In Mexico, Article 5 of the Amparo Law, in addition to the aggrieved person or persons and to the challenged authority or authorities, are declared also as parties in the amparo suit, "the affected third party or parties", having the possibility to intervene in such character, the following:

a) The counterpart of the injured when the claimed act is issued in a non criminal trail or controversy, or any of the parties in the same trail when the amparo is filed by a person strange to the procedure:

b) The offended or the persons that according to the law, have right to have the damage repaired or to demand for civil liability derived from the commitment of the crime, in amparo suits filed against criminal judicial decisions, when the latter affects the reparation or the liability;

c) The person or persons that have argued in their own favor regarding the challenged act against which the amparo is filed, when being acts adopted by authorities other than judi-

578 Decision of the Constitutional Chamber N° 656 of June 5, 2001, Case: *Defensor del Pueblo vs. Comisión Legislativa Nacional.*

579 See the comments in reference in Kevin SCHRODER et al, "Injunction", *Corpus Juris Secundum*, Thomson West, Volume 43A, 2004, p. 332.

cial of labor; or that without arguing in their favor, they have direct interest in the subsistence of the challenged act.

In the case of Peru, the Constitutional Procedural Code following the universal procedural rules, provides that when in the suit for amparo, it appears for the court the need to incorporate third parties not initially summoned, the judge must incorporate them if from the suit or the answer it is evident that the final decision will affect other parties (Art. 43). Additionally, Article 54 of the Code provides the right to anybody having legal and relevant interest in the outcome of the trail to be incorporated to the procedure and be declared as third interested party, being incorporated to the proceedings at the stage as it is.

Finally, regarding third parties, and without prejudice to what has being said about the intervention of the Peoples' Defendants in the amparo suits, before the extension of this public officer, it has been a legal tradition in Latin American regulations referred to habeas corpus and amparo, to consider the Public Prosecutor (Ministerio Público) in its character of general guarantor for the respects of constitutional rights in the judicial proceedings, as a *bona fide* third party that must be summoned to allow its participation in the proceedings.

In this respect, for instance, the Argentinean Habeas Corpus Law regulates the intervention of the Public Prosecutor, for which purpose the court once received the complaint, must notify its representatives, which will have in the proceedings the same rights given to all those that intervene in it, without any need to notify them for the accomplishment of any procedural act. The Public Prosecutor can file arguments and make the appeals considered necessary (Article 21).

The same occurs in México, where the Amparo Law guarantees the Public prosecutor its right to intervene in the procedure (Article 5, I, IV). In similar sense the Venezuelan Law of Amparo allows the intervention of the Public prosecutors in all amparo suits, but points out that its non intervention cannot affect the continuity or validity of the procedure (Article 14).

In similar sense regarding the participation of the Public Prosecutor as third party in good faith, in the United States, particularly in matters of judicial protection of civil rights, the participation of the Attorney General in injunctive proceedings as *amicus curiae* has been even encouraged by the courts. In the Texas prison case *Estelle v. Justice,* 426 U.S. 925; 96 S. Ct. 2637: 49 L. Ed. 2d 380 (1976) the matter was definitively resolved: the trial Judge in the case invited the Attorney general to participate as *"litigating amicus"*, with the same rights normally associated with the party, for instance to present evidence and to cross–examine witnesses. This participation was challenged by the State but finally was accepted.

However, since the expansion of injunctive process for the protection of civil rights, beginning with school desegregation cases following the Supreme Court's decisions in *Brown v. Board of Education of Topeka,* (1955), the Attorney General has had a very important role intervening in what has been called "structural injunctions". Through them, on civil rights massive violation matters, the courts have undertaken to judicially supervise the authorities' institutional policies and practices, in many cases with the active participation of the Attorney General in the litigation as *amicus curiae*. As defined by Tabb and Shoben:

Structural injunctions are modern phenomenon born of necessity from development in Constitutional law where the Supreme Court has identified substantive rights whose enforcement requires substantial judicial supervision. These rights concern the treatment of individuals by institutions, such as the right not to suffer inhumane treatment in prisons or public mental hospital. Enforcement of such rights by injunction has become an implicit part of the Constitutional guarantee of protecting individual liberties from inappropriate government action[580].

CHAPTER XII

THE DAMAGING OR INJURING PARTY IN THE AMPARO SUIT, AND THE ACTS OR OMISSIONS CAUSING THE HARM OR THE THREATS TO CONSTITUTIONAL RIGHTS

The amparo suit is governed by the principle of bilateralism, in the sense that not only the procedure must be initiated by a plaintiff that must in principle be the party whose constitutional rights and guaranties have been injured or threatened, but in principle, it must also always exist a defendant party, that is, the party whose actions or omissions are those precisely causing the harm or threats. This means that the judicial decision the plaintiff is seeking through the amparo suit, must always be directed to somebody that must be individuated[581].

This is similar to what occurs in the United States, regarding injunctions, referring to its individuated character, which implies that in general terms the resulting judicial order must be "addressed to some clearly identified individual, not just the general citizenry"[582]

I. THE QUESTION OF THE INDIVIDUATION OF THE DEFENDANT

The general principle regarding amparo, then, is that in the complaint, the plaintiff must clearly identify the authority, public officer, person or entity against whom the action is filed, that is the defendant, as is set forth in the Amparo Laws (Argentina, Art. 6,b; Bolivia, 97,II; Colombia, Art. 14; Costa Rica, Art. 38; El Salvador, Art. 14,2; Guatemala Art. 21,d; Honduras, Art. 21; 49,4; México 116, III; 166,III; Nicaragua, Art. 27,2; Panama, Art. 2619,2; Paraguay, Art. 6,c; Peru, Art. 42,3; Venezuela Art. 18,3).

580 See William M. TABB and Elaine W. SHOBEN, *Remedies,* Thomson West, 2005, pp. 87–88.

581 The only exception to the principle of bilateralism is the case of Chile, where the offender is not consider a defendant party but only a person whose activity is limited to inform the court and give it the documents it have. That is why in the Regulation set forth by the Supreme Court it is said that the affected state organ, person of public officer just "can" appear as party in the process. See Juan Manuel ERRAZURIZ G. and Jorge Miguel OTERO A, *Aspectos procesales del recurso de protección,* Editorial Jurídica de Chile 1989, p. 27.

582 See Owen M. FISS, *The Civil Rights Injunction,* Indiana University Press, 1978, p. 12

Nonetheless, some legislations although establishing that the need for the identification of the defendant, provide that this condition only applies "when it is possible" (Argentina, Art. 6,b; Colombia 14; Nicaragua, Art. 25; 55; Venezuela Art. 18, 3); and some Laws as the Paraguayan one, even establish that when the identification of the defendant is not possible, it is for the judge to provide the necessary measures in order to establish the procedural bilateral relation.

Thus, from the beginning of the procedure when the action is filed, or latter in the proceeding, the bilateral character of the amparo suit implies that in principle, a procedural relation must be established between the injured party and the injurer one, which must participate in the process. This implies the individuation character of the suit, equivalent to its personal character.

In this regard, the former Supreme Court of Justice of Venezuela in a decision of December 15, 1992 pointed out that:

> "The amparo action set forth in the Constitution, and regulated in the Organic Amparo law, has among its fundamental characteristic its basic personal or subjective character, which implies that a direct, specific and undutiful relation must exist between the person claiming for the protection of his rights, and the person purported to have originated the disturbance, who is to be the one with standing to act as defendant or the person against whom the action is filed. In other words, it is necessary, for granting an amparo, that the person signaled as the injurer be in the end, the one originating the harm"[583].

But as mentioned, in some situations, it is not possible for the plaintiff or for the judge, to clearly identify the defendant. The important aspect to clearly determine is the fact or action causing the harm, in which case, even without the identification of the exact authority or public officer who had produced it, the constitutional protection must be given. In Argentina this question has been analyzed, and it has been considered as a general principle, that the individuation of the author of the challenged act or omission will only be requested, when possible, because "preferably the amparo tends to focus on the damaging act and only in an accessory way in its author"[584]. In other words, that once the injurer act has been proved, the sole fact that its author has not been determined, cannot impede the decision to repair the harm, "due to the fact that the amparo action tends to restore the aggrieved constitutional rights, more than to individualize its author"[585].

That is why, in the *Angel Siri* Argentinean leading case, in which and without statutory regulations, the Supreme Court in Argentina admitted the amparo action, the Court protected the owner of a newspaper that was shoot down by the government, notwithstanding that in the files there was no clear evidence regarding the authority that closed it, nor the motives of the decision[586].

---

583 See decision of the Politico Administrative Chamber of the Supreme Court of Justice of December 16, 1992 (Caso *Haydée Casanova*), *Revista de Derecho Público*, N° 52, Editorial Jurídica Venezolana, Caracas, 1992, p. 139.

584 See Alí Joaquín SALGADO, *Juicio de amparo y acción de inconstitucionalidad*, Astrea, Buenos Aires, 1987, p. 92

585 José Luis LAZZARINI, *El juicio de amparo*, La Ley, Buenos Aires, 1987, p. 274.

586 See José Luis LAZZARINI, *El juicio de amparo*, La Ley, Buenos Aires, 1987, pp. 275–276.

Nonetheless, in case of absence of individuation of the author of the injuring action, the court must to adopt the necessary measures in order to determine it, and eventually, for the purpose of preserving the bilateral character of the process, designate a public defendant in the case. The Uruguayan Amparo law in this regard expressly provides the possibility to file the action in urgent cases even without knowing with precision about the person responsible for the harm fact, in which case, the court must publish public notices to identify it, and in case of the responsible not showing, the court must appoint an ex officio defendant (Art. 7).

Nonetheless, in other cases of absence of individuation of the injurer party, the claim has been rejected when it is determined that what the plaintiff pretends is to force the court to do the job. It was the case decided by the Argentinean Supreme Court rejecting an amparo actions filed by the former President of the Republic *Juan D. Perón* case, asking for the return of the body of his dead wife. In that case, the Supreme Court ruled about the need for a "minimal individuation of the author of the act originating the claim", due to the fact that:

> "the general principles of procedural law do not suffer any exception due to the exceptional character of the amparo, and must be respected, in order to eventually assure the exercise of the right to defense, from which the counterpart must not be deprived... This is evident from the text of the suit in which it is affirmed that the act provoking the claim has been executed 'by disposition of the former Provisional Government' without adding any other reference or explanation regarding the pointed public officer or entity. It is evident that the minimal requirements of individuation of the defendant, referred above, have not been accomplished in the case. On the contrary what is revealed in the files of this case, is that in lieu of seeking protection to his constitutional guarantees harmed by a an illegal State act, the plaintiff has intended to use the amparo procedure with the purpose of obtaining from the judges the order to practice the necessary inquiries regarding the facts, which are not proved or specified with precision. And it is clear that the performance of the instruction phase can not be achieved by means of this amparo remedy, whose incorporation to Argentinean positive law has purposes different to the one pursued in this case"[587].

Anyway, with the aforementioned exceptions, the principle of the individuation of the defendant rules in amparo maters. If the aggrieving party is a natural person (human being), whether a public officer or an individual, it must be identified in the usual way, being necessary in any case, to be the person originating the harm or threat to the plaintiff's rights. Being the aggrieving party an artificial person which needs to act through its representatives, whether it be a public entity or a corporation, the action for amparo must be filed against it, identifying with precision the entity and its representative, when possible. In the latter case, the action can be filed against the entity or corporation itself, or personally against the representative itself (public officer or manager), if the harm or threat has been personally provoked by the latter, independently of the artificial person or entity for which he is acting.

That is, as it has been decided by the Venezuelan courts, the aggrieving party must always be directly responsible for the conduct violating the constitutional

587 Fallos: 248–537, referred in José Luis LAZZARINI, *El juicio de amparo*, La Ley, Buenos Aires, 1987, p.275

rights and guaranties of the aggrieved party[588]; consequently, if a person is denounced as aggrieving without being so, the amparo action must be rejected[589] As decided by the Fist Court on Judicial review of Administrative Action in a decision of July 13, 1993:

"Among the basic characteristics of the amparo action, it is its subjective character, which requires for its admissibility that the threat of violation of a constitutional right be immediate, possible and realizable by the person identify as aggrieving, which means that in the case of a once materialized violation, it must be executed directly by the accused, that is, a direct relation must exist between the person asking for the protection to his rights and the person identified as aggrieving who will be the one with standing, and this being the person against whom the action is filed. This leads to affirm that for the admissibility of the amparo action, it is necessary that the person identified as aggrieving eventually be the one causing the purported harm and the one which would be obliged to follow the amparo order in case of the granting of the protection petition.

This essentially personal and subjective character of the amparo action results from the very reading of Article 18,3 of the Amparo Law which imposes on the plaintiff the burden of sufficiently identifying the aggrieving party, when possible. It is also evident from Article 32,a, where it is set forth the need for the decision to expressly mention "the authority, private body or person against whose acts or resolution the amparo is conceded; because on the contrary it could happen that processes could be filed against persons different to those that supposedly caused the harm, which will be contrary to the spirit, purpose and raison d'êter of the Amparo Law. Anyway, the problem of the precise identification of the aggrieving party has been raised regarding amparo actions against Public Administration activities, in order to avoid that the amparo actions be unnecessarily filed against the Republic as a legal person. The necessary identity between the 'aggrieved party and the person accused as being the aggrieving –which must be the one provoking the constitutional harm– has been repeatedly ruled by this Chamber, particularly in order to avoid the filing of amparo processes against the Republic, and to encourage the filing against the specific public officer who produced the purported harm act, fact or omission. In this sense it was decided in ruling of August 1°, 1991 (Case: *María Pérez, N° 391*) where it was said that "the constitutional amparo action, because of its special nature, is an action directly filed against the administrative authority which harms or threatens to harm the constitutional right"[590].

That is why Article 27 of the Venezuelan Amparo Law provides that in case of amparo against public officials, the court deciding on the merits must notify its decision to the competent authority "in order for it to decide the disciplinary sanctions against the public official responsible of the violation or the threat against a constitutional right or guarantee". This implies that in the filing of the action of amparo in

---

588 See decisions of the First Court on Judicial Review of Administrative Action of May 12, 1988, *Revista de Derecho Público,* N° 34, Editorial Jurídica Venezolana, Caracas, 1988, p. 113; and of June 16, 1988, *Revista de Derecho Público,* N° 35, Editorial Jurídica Venezolana, Caracas, 1988, p. 138.

589 See decision of the Politico Administrative Chamber of the Supreme Court of Justice of November 22, 1993, *Revista de Derecho Público,* N° 55–56, Editorial Jurídica Venezolana, Caracas, 1993, pp. 487–489

590 See decisión of the Politico–Administrative Chamber of the Supreme Court of Justice of December 15, 1992 (Caso *Haydee Casanova*), *Revista de Derecho Público,* N° 52, Editorial Jurídica Venezolana, Caracas, 1992, p. 139.

cases of Public Administration activities, "the person acting on behalf of (or representing) the entity who caused the harm or threat to the rights or guarantees must be identified, which is, the signaled person who has the exact and direct knowledge of the facts"[591].

But the requirement to identify the individual or natural person representative of the entity causing the harm, does not imply that the action must always be filed against such individual; it can be directly filed against the entity in itself. This has been for instance, the general trend in civil right injunctions in the United States, particularly when filed through class actions where the lost of individuation in the act and beneficiary has also provoked its address "to the office rather than the person"[592].

This is also the sense of aggrieving authority in the Mexican system where the responsible authority is conceived in institutional rather than personal terms, in the sense that the institution involved remains responsible regardless of the changes in personas[593]. In this sense it has been decided by the Supreme Court of Mexico, ruling that the discharge, transfer, promotion, demotion, death, or other removal of the individual who has actually ordered or executed the act object of the complaint, or any transfer of jurisdiction over the matter in contest, is no bar to the suit[594].

Thus, the amparo suit against artificial persons can be filed against the organ or directly against the person in charge of it. In the former case, the person in charge can be changed, that is for instance the case of public entities, where the public official can be changed, but this circumstance does not change the bilateral relation between aggrieved and aggrieving parties. As it has been decided by the Venezuelan First Court on Judicial review of Administrative Action in a decision of September 28, 1993 regarding an amparo action filed against the dean of a Law Faculty, in which case the person in charge as Dean was changed:

> "the heading of the position does not change its organic unity. If the dean of the Faculty changes, it will always be a subjective figure that substitutes the preceding one. That is why in a decision of September 11, 1990 this Court ruled that the circumstance of the head of an organ mentioned as aggrieving being changed does not alter the procedural relation originated with the amparo action. To the latter it must in this case be added that it would have no sense to rule that the procedural relation be continued with the person that doesn't occupy anymore the position, because in case the constitutional amparo is granted, then the ex public official would not be in a position to reestablish the factual infringed situation. As much, the former public officer could be liable for the damages caused, but as it is known, the amparo action

---

591 See decision of the First Court on Judicial Review of Administrative Action of June 16, 1988, *Revista de Derecho Público,* N° 35, Editorial Jurídica Venezolana, Caracas, 1988, p. 138

592 See Owen M. FISS, *The Civil Rights Injunction*, Indiana University Press 1978, p. 15

593 See Richard D. BAKER, *Judicial Review in Mexico. A Study of the Amparo Suit*, Texas University Press, Austin1971, p. 209

594 Suprema Corte, *Jurisprudencia de la Suprema Corte*, Tesis 183, II, p. 365; also Suprema Corte, *Montufar Miguel*, 17 *S.J.* 798 (1925). See the references in Richard D. BAKER, *Judicial Review in Mexico. A Study of the Amparo Suit*, Texas University Press, Austin1971, p. 208–109, note 36

has the only purpose of reestablishing the harmed legal situation, and that can only be assured by the current public official"[595].

Consequently, according to the Venezuelan judicial doctrine on the matter, in cases in which the aggrieved party identifies with precision as aggrieving the public official responsible for the harm, it is this one and only him who must act in the procedure, in which case no notice must be made to its superior or to the Attorney general[596]. Conversely, if the action is for instance filed against a Ministerial entity as an organ of the Republic, the action must be understood to be filed against the latter, being in such cases the Attorney general the entity that must act as the judicial representative of it[597]. On the contrary, if the amparo suit is exercised against a perfectly identified and individuated organ of Ministerial entity and not against the Republic, the judicial representative of the latter has no procedural role to play[598]. That is, if the amparo action is directed against an individuated administrative authority, for instance, a Ministry, the representative of the Republic can not act on his behalf[599]. In such cases, it is the individuated person or public officer that must personally act as aggrieving party[600].

---

595 See decision of the First Court on Judicial Review of Administrative Action of September 28, 1993, *Revista de Derecho Público*, N° 55–56, Editorial Jurídica Venezolana, Caracas, 1993, p. 330.

596 See decisions of the First Court on Judicial Review of Administrative Actions of May 12, 1988, *Revista de Derecho Público,* N° 34, Editorial Jurídica Venezolana, Caracas, 1988, p. 113; and of September 7, 1989, *Revista de Derecho Público* N° 40, Editorial Jurídica Venezolana, Caracas, 1989, p. 107. Also decision of the Politico Administrative Chamber of the Supreme Court of Justice of March 16, 1989, *Revista de Derecho Público,* N° 38, Editorial Jurídica Venezolana, Caracas, 1989, p. 110.

597 See decision of the First Court on Judicial Review of Administrative Actions of September 7, 1989, *Revista de Derecho Público,* N° 40, Editorial Jurídica Venezolana, Caracas, 1989, p. 107.

598 See decision of the First Court on Judicial Review of Administrative Actions of November 21, 1990, *Revista de Derecho Público,* N° 44, Editorial Jurídica Venezolana, Caracas, 1990, p. 148.

599 See decisions of the First Court on Judicial Review of Administrative Actions of October 10, 1990, *Revista de Derecho Público,* N° 44, Editorial Jurídica Venezolana, Caracas, 1990, p. 142; and of July 30, 1992, *Revista de Derecho Público,* N° 51, Editorial Jurídica Venezolana, Caracas, 1992, p. 164; and decisions of the Politico Administrative Chamber of the Supreme Court of Justice of August 1, 1991, *Revista de Derecho Público,* N° 47, Editorial Jurídica Venezolana, Caracas, 1991, p. 120, and of December 15, 1992, *Revista de Derecho Público,* N° 52, Editorial Jurídica Venezolana, Caracas, 1992, p. 139.

600 See decision of the Politico Administrative Chamber of the Supreme Court of Justice of March 8, 1990, *Revista de Derecho Público,* N° 42, Editorial Jurídica Venezolana, Caracas, 1990, p. 114; and of the First Court on Judicial Review of Administrative Actions of November 21, 1990, *Revista de Derecho Público,* N° 44, Editorial Jurídica Venezolana, Caracas, 1990, p. 148. Igualmente en FUNEDA, *15 años de Jurisprudencia, cit.,* p. 164; and of July, 14, 1988, FUNEDA, *15 años de Jurisprudencia, cit.*, p. 177.

II. THE DEFENDANT IN THE AMPARO SUIT: AUTHORITIES AND INDIVIDUALS

One of the most important aspects regarding the damaging, aggrieving or injurer party in the amparo suit, that is, the defendant, is related to whether the amparo can only be filed against public authorities or can it also be filed against particulars or individuals. That is, whether the specific judicial means of amparo is only established for the protection of constitutional rights and guaranties against public entities and authorities harms or threats, that is, in general terms, against the State, or it can also be used against private individuals' actions harming or threatening such rights.

The former position can be considered as the general trend in Latin America, following the historical fact that the amparo suit was originally created to protect individuals against the State. Nonetheless, nowadays, in the majority of the countries, this situation does not exclude the admission of the amparo suit for the protection of constitutional rights against individual's actions, as is the case in Argentina, Bolivia, Chile, Dominican Republic, Peru, Venezuela and Uruguay, as well as, although in a more restrictive way, in Colombia, Costa Rica Ecuador, and Guatemala.

III. THE AMPARO AGAINST PUBLIC AUTHORITIES: PUBLIC ENTITIES AND PUBLIC OFFICERS

In general terms, all Latin American countries establish that the amparo action shall be filed against public entities and public officials, following the original features of the amparo as a special judicial means for the protection of human rights, facing the State. But this situation, as mentioned before, has changed to the point that, nowadays, the countries that only admit the amparo suit against public entities or officers, excluding the suit against individuals or private persons, are the minority, as is the case in Brazil, El Salvador, Panama, Mexico and Nicaragua. In all the other Latin American countries, additionally to the amparo suit against public entities and officers, the action for constitutional protection can be filed against private parties.

Regarding civil rights injunctions, the United States can also be included in the former group. If it is true that in this country, injunctions, as general judicial means for rights' protection can be filed against any person as "higher public officials or private persons"[601] causing the harm to a right, in matters of constitutional or civil rights guaranties, it has been considered that it is only admissible regarding public entities. As explained by, M. Glenn Abernathy and Barbara A. Perry:

> "Limited remedies for private interfere with free choice. Another problem in the citizen's search for freedom from restriction lies in that many types of interference stemming from private persons do not constitute actionable wrongs under the law. Private prejudice and private discrimination do not, in the absence of specific statutory provisions, offer grounds for judicial intervention on behalf of the sufferer. If one is denied admission to membership in a social club, for example, solely on the basis of his race or religion or political affiliation, he may

601 See M. Glenn ABERNATHY and Barbara A. PERRY, *Civil Liberties under the Constitution*, Sixth Edition, University of South Carolina Press, 1993, p. 8.

understandably smart under the rejection, but the courts cannot help him (again assuming no statutory provision batting such distinctions). There are, then, many types of restraints on individual freedom of choice which are beyond the authority of courts to remove or ameliorate.

It should be noted that the guarantees of rights in the United States Constitution only protect against governmental action and do not apply to purely private encroachments, except for the Thirteenth Amendment's prohibition of slavery. Remedies for private invasion must be found in statutes, the common law, or administrative agency regulations and adjudications"[602].

In Latin America, as mentioned before, only Brazil, El Salvador, Panama, Mexico and Nicaragua leave the amparo action to be filed no more than against the State, that is, public entities and public officials. This was the situation at the origin of the amparo suit in Mexico, as it currently remains when Article 103 of the Constitution provides that the amparo shall be filed against infraction to constitutional guarantees committed by an "authority", in the sense that it must always be a responsible authority. Accordingly, Article 11 of the Amparo Law points out that "The authority responsible is the one who edicts, promulgates, orders, executes or tries to execute the statute or the claimed act". This article has been interpreted in the sense that authorities are not only those superior ones which order the acts, but also those subordinate ones that execute or try to execute them; the amparo being admitted against any of them"[603].

This term "authority" could be interpreted in the wider sense of any public entity of public official regardless its powers of functions. This is the sense given, for instance, to the Amparo laws of Argentina, Peru or Venezuela. But in Argentina, the notion of "authority" regarding the amparo suit, even though apparently wider, has in fact a restrictive meaning, when it refers only to those public officers with power to decide. As was defined in the *case Campos Otero Julia* (1935), this term is understood as "an organ of the State legally vested with the powers of decision and command necessary for imposing upon individuals either its own determinations or those that emanate form some other State organs"[604]. This definition was expanded to include "all those persons who dispose of public power (*fuerza pública*) by virtue of either legal or *de facto* circumstances, and who, consequently find themselves in a position to perform acts of a public character, due to the fact that the power they have is public"[605].

---

602 See M. Glenn ABERNATHY and Barbara A. PERRY, *Civil Liberties under the Constitution*, Sixth Edition, University of South Carolina Press, 1993, p. 6.

603 See "Autoridades para efectos del juicio de amparo" (*Apéndice al Semanario Judicial de la federación, 1917–1988*, Segunda parte, tesis 300, p. 519. See the reference in Eduardo FERRER MAC-GREGOR, *La acción constitucional de amparo en México y España. Estudio de derecho comparado*, Editorial Porrúa, México, 2002, p. 254.

604 See Suprema Corte, *Campos Otero Julia*, 45, S.J. 5033 (1935). See the reference in Richard D. BAKER, *Judicial Review in Mexico. A Study of the Amparo Suit*, Texas University Press, Austin, 1971, p. 94

605 See "Autoridades para efectos del juicio de amparo" (*Apéndice al Semanario Judicial de la Federación*, 1917–1988, Segunda parte, tesis 300, p. 519. See the reference in EDUARDO FERRER MAC–GREGOR, *La acción constitucional de amparo en México y España. Estudio de*

Three aspects must be emphasized regarding the judicial doctrine on the notion of "authority" in Mexico: First, the idea of the *de facto* public officer, in the sense that even if the offender is not the legitimate holder of the public office whose authority is exercised, the amparo must be admitted because the harm is caused by some one that pretends to be exercising public power, the citizens having the right to legitimate confidence in those who exercise public power.

Second, that because the definition of "authority" refers to those public entities that are in a position to make a decision and to impose or execute them by a coactive use of public power, in many cases, the courts had rejected the amparo suit against public entities considering that they do not have the power to decide, like those with purely staff or consultative nature[606]. According to this interpretation, for instance, many decentralized public entities like *Petróleos Mexicanos,* the National Commission on Electricity, the Human Rights' Defendant of the UNAM and the Autonomous Universities were initially excluded from the category of "authorities"[607]. Nonetheless, progressively the amparo suit has been admitted against some of these entities based on the decision powers they have in concrete cases[608].

Third, that from a procedural point of view, all the authorities materially involved in the aggrieving action must be identified by the plaintiff in his action and be notified by the court; not only those who ordered the action, but those who have decided it and that have to execute or apply it. As decided by the Supreme Court: if in the amparo claim it is only mentioned the responsible authority adopting the act – the authority who orders– and the suspension of the act is requested, this cannot be granted because the situation will be of acts consented; on the contrary, if there are only mentioned as responsible authorities those who have executed the act, then the suspension can be granted, but the case must be discontinued because the facts resulted from a consented act[609].

In contrast with this restrictive interpretation on the concept of authority regarding the Mexican amparo suit, in Argentina, for instance, the amparo action can be

---

derecho comparado, Editorial porrúa, México 2002, p, 253. Also see Suprema Corte, *Jurisprudencia de la Suprema Corte*, thesis 179, II, 360. see the referente in Richard D. BAKER, *Judicial Review in Mexico. A Study of the Amparo Suit*, Texas University Press, Austin, 1971, p. 94.

606 Richard D. BAKER, *Judicial Review in Mexico. A Study of the Amparo Suit*, Texas University Press, Austin, 1971, p. 95.

607 See the references to the judicial decisions in Eduardo FERRER MAC–GREGOR, *La acción constitucional de amparo en México y España. Estudio de derecho comparado*, Editorial Porrúa, México, 2002, pp. 255–256.

608 Se Eduardo Ferrer MAC–GREGOR, *La acción constitucional de amparo en México y España. Estudio de derecho comparado*, Editorial Porrúa, México 2002, p. 257

609 See the Supreme Court jurisprudencia on "Actos Consumados. Suspensión "improcedente" y actos derivados de actos consentidos" en Apéndice al Semanario Judicial de la federación, 1917–1995, Primera sala, tesis 1090, p. 756; y Tribunal Pleno, Tesis 17, p. 12. See the references in Eduardo FERRER MAC–GREGOR, *La acción constitucional de amparo en México y España. Estudio de derecho comparado*, Editorial Porrúa, México 2002, p. 255, notes 450 and 451.

filed against "any public authority act or omission" (Art. 1), being interpreted the term "public authority", in a wide sense including all sorts of public entity or officials of all branches of government. It must be said that the expression "public authority" in Article 1 of the the Amparo Law was incorporated because of the intention of the 1964 legislator to not regulate the amparo against individuals, which nonetheless was already admitted by the Supreme Court and later expressly regulated in the Civil Procedure Code. Even though the expression could also be interpreted in a restrictive way referring only to public officers with *imperium*, that is, those with power to command and to edict obligatory decisions and to require the use of public force to execute them, the general trend is to interpret it in a wide sense comprising any agent, employee, public official, magistrate of government agent acting in that condition, including individuals accomplishing public functions, like the public services concessionaries[610]. In some cases it has even been considered that actions of a Provincial Constituent Assembly violating constitutional rights can be challenged via the amparo action[611]

In similarly wide sense, the term "public authorities" is also conceived for the purpose of the amparo protection, for instance, in Bolivia (Art. 94), Colombia (Art.1), El Salvador (Art. 12), Peru (Art. 2), Uruguay (Art. 2) and Venezuela (Art. 2). In Brazil, Article 1 of the statute regulating the *mandado de segurança* provides that this action can be filed against any violation provoked by "authorities, no matter its category and functions"; and in Nicaragua the expression refers to "any public official, authority of its agents" (Art. 3). Some legislations, in order to dissipate any doubts, are enumerative and include any act from any of the branches of government, including delegated, decentralized or autonomous entities, municipal corporations or those supported with public founds or that act by delegation of a State organ by means of a concession, contract or resolution (Guatemala Art. 9, Honduras Art. 41).

The only Latin American country where the amparo action regarding authorities is statutorily reduced expressly to those of the Executive branch of government is Ecuador, where Article 46 of the Amparo Law only admits the amparo against "public administration authorities"(Art. 46).

But besides this specific exception, in contrast, it can be said that in almost all other Latin American countries, the amparo action is established as a specific judicial means for the protection of constitutional rights and guaranties against any acts, facts or omissions of any public authority (public entities or public officials), which can be part of any of the branches of government, whether executive, legislative, judicial or control.

---

610 See Néstor Pedro SAGÜÉS, *Derecho procesal Constitucional, Vol 3, Acción de amparo*, Editorial Astrea Buenos Aires 1988, pp.91–93; Joaquín BRAGUE CAMAZANO, *La Jurisdicción constitucional de la libertad (Teoría general, Argentina, México, Corte Interamericana de Derechos Humanos)*, Editorial Porrúa, México 2005, p. 97. José Luis LAZZARINI, *El juicio de amparo,* Editorial La Ley, Buenos Aires 1987, pp. 208–209

611 See Alí Joaquín SALGADO, *Juicio de amparo y acción de inconstitucionalidad*, Editorial Astrea, Buenos Aires, 1987, pp. 24–25.

As set forth in the Guatemalan Amparo law, *"no sphere shall be excluded from amparo"* and the action will be admitted against acts, resolutions, dispositions and statutes of authority which could imply a threat, a restriction or a violation of the rights guarantied in the Constitution and in statutes" (Art. 8).

It is also the case in Venezuela, where Article 2 of the Amparo law provides that the action can be filed against "any fact, act or omission of any of the National, States, of Municipal Public Powers (branches of government); which means that the constitutional protection can be filed against any public action, that is, any formal state act, any material action and any factual activity (*vía de hecho*) (Art. 5); as well as against any omission from public entities.

This universality of the amparo suit has been developed by judicial decisions doctrine. For instance, in the case Aura Loreto Rangel, the First Court on Judicial review of Administrative Action of November 11, 1993, it was ruled that:

> "From what Article 2 of the Amparo law sets forth, it results that there is no conduct type, regardless of its nature or character, or from their authors, which can be excluded per se from the amparo judge revision in order to determine if it harms or not constitutional rights or guarantees"[612].

The same criterion has been adopted by the Political Administrative Chamber of the Supreme Court of Justice in a decision of may 24, 1993 as follows:

> The terms on which the amparo action is regulated in Article 49 of the Constitution (now Article 27) are very extensive. If the extended scope of the rights and guarantees that can be protected and restored through this judicial mean is undoubted; the harm cannot be limited to those produced only by some acts. So, in equal terms it must be permitted that any harming act –whether an act, a fact or an omission– with respect to any constitutional right and guarantee, can be challenged by means of this action, due to the fact that the amparo action is the protection of any norm regulating the so called subjective rights of constitutional rank, it cannot be sustained that such protection is only available in cases in which the injuring act has some precise characteristics, whether from a material or organic point of view. The *jurisprudencia* of this Court has been constant regarding both principles. In decision N° 22, dated January 31, 1991 (Case*: Anselmo Natale*), it was decided that 'there is no State act that could not be reviewed by amparo, the latter understood not as a mean for judicial review of constitutionality of State acts in order to annul them, but as a protective remedy regarding public freedoms whose purpose is to reestablish its enjoyment and exercise, when a natural or artificial person, or group or private organization, threaten to harm them or effectively harm them (See, regarding the extended scope of the protected rights, decision of December 4, 1990, Case *Mariela Morales de Jimenez*, N° 661)[613].

In another decision dated February 13, 1992, the First Court ruled:

> "This Court observes that the essential characteristic of the amparo regime, in its constitutional regulation as well as in its statutory development, is its universality.., so the protection it assures is extended to all subjects (physical or artificial persons), as well as regarding all

612 See in *Revista de Derecho Público,* N° 55–56, Editorial Jurídica Venezolana, Caracas, 1993, p. 284.

613 See in *Revista de Derecho Público,* N° 55–56, Editorial Jurídica Venezolana, Caracas, 1993, pp. 284–285.

constitutionally guaranteed rights, including those that without being expressly regulated in the Constitution, are inherent to human beings. This the departing point in order to understand the scope of the constitutional amparo... Regarding Public Administration, the amparo against it is so extended that it can be filed against all acts, omissions and factual actions, without any kind of exclusion regarding some matters that always related to the public order and social interest"[614]

Notwithstanding this general principle of the universality of the amparo, a series of exceptions can be identified in various legislations, regarding some particular and specific State activities that are expressly excluded. In this regard, we will analyze the situation regarding the amparo against legislative, executive and judicial acts as well as the particular exceptions established in the statutory regulations of the amparo suit.

1. The Amparo against legislative actions

Congress and parliamentary commissions are public authorities, and by means of its actions they can harm constitutional rights and guaranties; that is, legislative bodies, from national Congress down to municipal councils, can be a source of interference with personal freedom[615]. Against such legislative actions or omissions that injure constitutional rights or guarantees, amparo suits can be brought before the competent courts.

A. *Amparo against parliamentary bodies' and their commissions' decisions*

Regarding parliamentary bodies (Chambers) and its commissions, in Argentina, Costa Rica[616] and Venezuela, for instance, the amparo action has been admitted against their acts when they harm constitutional rights.

In Argentina, it was the case of the parliamentary enquiries developed in 1984 regarding the facts occurred during the previous de facto government, in which the parliamentary commission ordered the breaking into law offices of various lawyers and the seizure of documents. In the court decisions, particularly in the Case *Klein* decided in 1984, without questioning the powers of the parliamentary commissions to make inquiries, it was ruled that they cannot, without formal statutory provisions, validly restrict individual rights, in particular, to break into the personal domicile of people and to seize their personal documents. It was thus decided that the order, could only be taken based on a statutory provision, not by the sole decision of the commissions, and eventually based in a judicial order[617]

---

614 See in *Revista de Derecho Público,* N° 49, Editorial Jurídica Venezolana, Caracas, 1992, pp. 120–121.

615 See *Stuab v. City of Baxley*, 355 U.S. 313 (1958). See the comments in M. Glenn ABERNATHY and Barbara A. PERRY, *Civil Liberties under the Constitution,* University of South Carolina Press, 1993, pp. 12–13.

616 See Rubén HERNÁNDEZ VALLE, *Derecho Procesal Constitucional*, Editorial Juricentro, San José 2001, pp. 211–214

617 See the comments on the First Instance decision of 1984 (1ª *InstCrimCorrFed*, Juzg N° 3, 10–9–84, ED 110–653) in Néstor Pedro SAGÜÉS, *Derecho procesal Constitucional,* Vol 3,

In Venezuela, a similar situation can be identified regarding the privative attributions of legislative bodies. Although the 1961 Constitution (Art. 159) set forth that they were not to be reviewed by other branches of government, regarding the former Congress and their commissions, the Supreme Court admitted the amparo action against their acts, in a decision dated January 31, 1991 (Caso: *Anselmo Natale*), ruling as follows:

> "The exclusion of judicial review regarding certain parliamentary acts –except in cases of extra limitation of powers– set forth in Article 159 of the Constitution, as a way to prevent, due to the rules of separation of powers, that the executive and judicial branches could invade or interfere in the orbit of the legislative body which is the trustee of the popular sovereignty, is restricted to determine the intrinsic regularity of such acts regarding the Constitution, in order to annul them, but it does not apply when it is a matter of obtaining the immediate reestablishment of the enjoyment and exercise of harmed rights and guarantees set forth in the Constitution"[618].

Consequently, after ruling –as has been above mentioned– that "it cannot exist any State act excluded from revision by means of amparo, the purpose of which is not to annul State acts but to protect public freedoms and restore its enjoyment when violated or harmed", the Supreme Court decided as follows:

> The Chamber considers that the constitutional amparo, understood in this way, can be filed by any person, natural or artificial, even against acts excluded from judicial control as those set forth in Article 159 of the Constitution as established in that provision, alleging a harm or violation of constitutional rights or guarantees, or those that being inherent to human beings, are not listed expressly in it"[619].

In the case of México, Article 73, VIII of the Amparo Law expressly excludes from the amparo suit, the resolutions and declarations of the Federal Congress and its Chambers, as well as of the State Legislative bodies and heir Commissions, regarding the election, suspension or dismissal of public officers, in cases in which the corresponding Constitutions confer them the power to resolve the matter in a sovereign or discretionary way[620]. There are also excluded from the amparo suit, the decisions adopted by the Representative Chamber of by the Senate in cases of impeachments, which Article 110 of the Constitution declares as non challenging ones[621].

Acción de amparo, Editorial Astrea Buenos Aires 1988, pp. 95–97; Joaquín Brague Camazano, *La Jurisdicción constitucional de la libertad (Teoría general, Argentina, México, Corte Interamericana de Derechos Humanos)*, Editorial Porrúa, México 2005, p. 98. José Luis Lazzarini, *El juicio de amparo,* Editorial La Ley, Buenos Aires 1987, pp. 216–216.

618 See in *Revista de Derecho Público,* N° 45, Editorial Jurídica Venezolana, Caracas, 1991, p. 118

619 See in *Revista de Derecho Público,* N° 45, Editorial Jurídica Venezolana, Caracas, 1991, p. 118. See also decision of the First Court on Judicial review of Administrative action of June 18, 1992 See in *Revista de Derecho Público,* N° 46, Editorial Jurídica Venezolana, Caracas, 1991, p. 125.

620 See Richard D. BAKER, *Judicial Review in Mexico. A Study of the Amparo Suit*, Texas University Press, Austin 1971, p. 98

621 See Eduardo FERRER MAC–GREGOR, *La acción constitucional de amparo en México y España. Estudio de derecho comparado*, Editorial Porrúa, México 2002, p. 378.

In the United States, the general rule is that injunctions may not be directed against Congress; and injunctions have been rejected for instance to suspend a congressional subpoena, where the complainant had an adequate remedy to protect his rights in connection with a hearing[622].

B. *Amparo against laws (statutes)*

One of the most important issues regarding the Latin American amparo refers to the possibility of filing the amparo action against statutes, which if it is true that it is accepted in some countries like Mexico, Venezuela and Guatemala, is excluded –in some cases expressly– in others, like Argentina, Brazil, Colombia, Chile, Costa Rica, El Salvador, Panama, Peru and Uruguay. But regardless of the acceptance in some countries, the admissibility of the amparo action against laws has been progressively restricted, allowing in some countries its filing only against self–executing statutes (Mexico), or only regarding the acts which apply the particular statute, not being in general, admitted directly against the statute itself, except in Guatemala.

In effect, in Mexico, Article 1,I of the Amparo Law establishes that the amparo can be filed against statutes that violate the constitutional guarantees. In such cases, the amparo action can be filed directly against self executing or self applicable statutes (laws) when considered contrary to the Constitution, giving rise in such cases, to a judicial means of judicial review of constitutionality of the statutes. In these cases, the action can be filed directly against the statute, without any need for an administrative or judicial act of application of the statute, because the statute in itself is the one that causes direct harm to the constitutional guarantees of the plaintiff[623]. In these cases, the action has to be filed within 30 days following their enforcement. In such cases, the defendants are the supreme institutions of the State that had intervened in the drafting of the statute, that is, the Congress of the Union or the legislatures of the States that passed the statute, the President of the Republic or State Governors that ordered its execution and the Executive Secretariats that approved it and ordered its enactment.

Consequently, the amparo against laws in Mexico, is considered a judicial means for the direct control of the constitutionality of such statutes, even if it is not brought in an abstract manner, since the claimant must have been directly harmed by the legislation, without the need for another state act for the application of the statute. On the contrary, when the statute in itself does not cause direct and personal harm to the claimant, that is, the statute is not self executing, the amparo action is inadmissi-

622 See U.S. –Mins et al. V. McCarty, 209 F. 2d 307 (D.C. Cir. 1953), in John Bourdeau et al, "Injunctions" in Kevin Schroder, John Glenn and Maureen Placilla, *Corpus Juris Secundum*, Volume 43A, Thomson West, 2004, p. 230.

623 See Garza Flores Hnos., Sucs., 28 S.J. 1208 (1930). See the reference in Richard D. Baker, *Judicial Review in Mexico. A Study of the Amparo Suit*, Texas University Press, Austin1971, p. 167

ble, unless it is filed against the State acts that apply it to a specific person[624]. As it is expressly set forth in Article 73,VI, the amparo suit is inadmissible "against statutes, treaties or regulations that, by its sole passing, they do not cause harm to the plaintiff, but need a subsequent act of its application in order for the prejudice to initiate". In these cases, of statutes that are not self–executing, the amparo action must be filed within 15 days following the issuing of the first act of its execution or application.

The main aspect to be stressed on the matter, of course, is the distinction between the self executing and not self executing laws. Following the doctrine established in the case of *Villera de Orellana María de los Angeles y coags*., the former are those immediately obligatory, in which provisions the persons to whom are applicable are clearly and unmistakably identified, being *ipso jure* subjected to an obligation which implies the accomplishment of acts not previously required, resulting a prejudicial modification of the person's rights[625].

The Mexican solution is similar to the United States exceptions to the doctrine of non–interference, according to which injunctions, if not admitted in principle against legislative acts, are admitted against municipal ordinances and regulations, when by its mere passage they immediately produce some irreparable loss or injury to the plaintiff[626].

According to the universality character of the system set forth in the Venezuelan Constitution regarding the acts that can be challenged by means of amparo, one of the most distinguishable innovations of the 1988 Amparo Law was the regulation of the amparo against statutes and other normative acts, complementing the general mixed system of judicial review[627]. In this regard, Article 3 of the Amparo law establishes the following:

> **Artículo 3º** The amparo action is also admissible when the violation or the threats of violation derives from a norm contrary to the constitution. In this case, the resulting judicial decision resolving the filed action, must take notice of the inapplicability of the challenged norm and the court must inform its decision to the Supreme Court.
>
> The action of amparo may also be brought together with the popular action of unconstitutionality of laws and other state normative acts, in which case, if it deems it necessary for the constitutional protection, the Supreme Court of Justice may suspend the application of the norm in respect of the specific juridical situation whose violation is alleged, whilst the suit for its annulment lasts.

---

624 See Eduardo FERRER MAC–GREGOR, *La acción constitucional de amparo en México y España. Estudio de derecho comparado*, Editorial Porrúa, México 2002, p, 387

625 Suprema Corte de Justicia, 123 S.J. 783 (1955). See the comments in Richard D. BAKER, *Judicial Review in Mexico. A Study of the Amparo Suit*, Texas University Press, Austin, 1971, p. 168–173e

626 See. *Larkins v. City of Denison*, 683 S.W. 2d 754 (Tex. App. Dallas 1984). See the reference to this and other court decisions on the matter in John Bourdeau et al, "Injunctions" in Kevin Schroder, John Glenn and Maureen Placilla, *Corpus Juris Secundum*, Volume 43A, Thomson West, 2004, pp. 257–260

627 See Allan R. BREWER–CARÍAS, "Derecho y Acción de Amparo", Vol V, *Instituciones Políticas y Constitucionales,* Editorial Jurídica Venezolana, Caracas, 1998, pp. 227 ff.

This article sets forth two ways through which an amparo pretension can be filed before the competent court: in an autonomous way, or exercised together with the popular action of unconstitutionality of statutes. In the latter case, the amparo pretension is subordinated to the principal action for judicial review, producing only the possibility for the court to suspend the application of the statute pending the unconstitutionality suit. In this case, the situation is similar to the one of the popular action of unconstitutionality in the Dominican Republic when the amparo pretension is filed together with it[628].

But in the former case, Article 3 of the Venezuelan Amparo Law sets forth a direct amparo action against statutes, different to the popular action of unconstitutionality whose nullity results have *erga omnes* effects, seeking only the inapplicability of the statute to a concrete case with *inter partes* effects[629]. But even thought the clear wording of the article, it can be said that the amparo action against laws has in fact been eliminated in Venezuela as a consequence of the interpretation made by the former Supreme Court of Justice, imposing the need of the action to be always and only directed against the State acts applying the statute and not directly against it. In a decision dated May 24, 1993, the Politico Administrative Chamber of the Supreme Court issued a decision that has been the leading case on the matter, ruling that:

> Thus, it seem that there is no doubt that Article 3 of the Amparo law does not set forth the possibility of filing an amparo action directly against a normative act, but against the act, fact or omission that has its origin in a normative provision which is considered by the claimant as contrary to the Constitution and for which, due to the presumption of legitimacy and constitutionality of the former, the court must previously resolve its inapplicability to the concrete case argued. It is obvious, thus, that such article of the Amparo law does not allow the possibility of filing this action for constitutional protection against a statute or other normative act, but against the act which applies or executes it, which is definitively the one that in the concrete case can cause a particular harm to the constitutional rights and guaranties of a precise person"[630].

The Court, in its decision, admitted the distinction between the self executing and not self executing statutes, ruling that the former imposes an immediate obligation for the persons to whom it is issued, with its promulgation; and on the contrary, the latter requires an act for its later execution, in which case its sole promulgation cannot produce a constitutional violation"[631]. But even though it admits the distinction, the Supreme Court concluded its ruling declaring the impossibility for a real

---

628 See Eduardo Jorge PRATS, *Derecho Constitucional*, Vol. II, *Gaceta Judicial*, Santo Domingo 2005, p. 399.

629 See Allan R. BREWER–CARÍAS, "Derecho y Acción de Amparo", Vol V, *Instituciones Políticas y Constitucionales*, Editorial Jurídica Venezolana, Caracas 1998, pp. 224 ff; Rafael Chavero, *El nuevo régimen del amparo constitucional en Venezuela*, Editorial Sherwood, Caracas, 2001, pp. 553 ff.

630 See in *Revista de Derecho Público*, N° 55–56, Editorial Jurídica Venezolana, Caracas, 1993, pp. 287–288

631 See in *Revista de Derecho Público*, N° 55–56, Editorial Jurídica Venezolana, Caracas, 1993, p. 285.

normative act to directly and by itself, harm the constitutional orbit of a concrete and particular situation of an individual.

But by rejecting the possibility of direct harms that a statute can cause to particular constitutional rights, the Court in principle admitted the possibility for the unconstitutional statute to cause threats to those same persons' rights, ruling that in such case the threats ought to be "imminent, possible and realizable" in order for an amparo action to be admitted. But in the same decision, such possibility was rejected with the following argument:

> "In case of an amparo action against a norm, the concretion of the possible harm would not be 'immediate', because it will always be the need for a competent authority to execute or apply it in order for the statute to effectively harm the claimant. It must be concluded that the probable harm produced by the norm will always be a mediate and indirect one, due to the need for the statute to be applied to the concrete case. So that the harm will be caused by mean of the act applying the illegal norm.
>
> The same occurs with the third condition, in the sense that the probable and imminent threat will never be made by the possible defendant. If it would be possible to sustain that the amparo could be admissible against a statute whose constitutionality is challenged, it would be necessary to accept as aggrieved party the legislative body issuing it, being the party to participate in the process as defendant. But it must be highlighted that in the case in which the possible harm could be realized, it would not be the legislative body the one called to execute it, but rather the public officer that must apply the norm in all the cases in which an individual is located in the situation regulated.
>
> If it is understood that the object of the amparo action is the statute, then the conclusion would be that the possible defendant (the public entity enacting the norm whose unconstitutionality is alleged) could not be the one that could make the threat. The concrete harm would be definitively made by a different entity or person (the one applying the unconstitutional norm to a specific and concrete case)[632].

From the above mentioned, the Venezuelan Supreme Court concluded rejecting the amparo action against statutes and normative acts, not only because it considered that the Amparo laws does not set forth such possibility –bypassing its text–, but because even being possible to bring the extraordinary action against a normative act, it would not comply with the imminent, possible and realizable conditions of the threats set forth in Article 6,2 of the Amparo Law.

In Guatemala the amparo against laws is established in a direct form, being the Constitutional Courts empowered to "declare in specific cases that a statute, a regulation, resolution or act of the authorities does not bind the claimant, since it contravenes or restricts any of the rights guaranteed by the Constitution or recognized by any Law (Article 10,b Guatemala Law). This same judicial power, but only regarding to executive regulations, is established in Honduras (Article 41,b Law). In both cases, the judicial decisions on amparo suspend the application of the statute, the executive regulation, resolution or challenged act in respect of the claimant, and if

632 See in *Revista de Derecho Público,* N° 55–56, Editorial Jurídica Venezolana, Caracas, 1993, pp. 288 a 290.

applicable, the re–establishment of the juridical situation affected or the cessation of the measure (Article 49,a Guatemala)[633].

In other Latin American countries, the possibility of bringing an action of amparo against statutes is expressly excluded. This is the case of Costa Rica, where the Law on Constitutional Jurisdiction provides that the amparo action against statutes and other regulatory provisions is not admissible, except when challenged together with the acts individually applying it, or when dealing with automatically enforced regulations, in such a way that their prescriptions become automatically enforceable simply by their enactment, without the need for other regulations or acts that develop them or render them applicable to the claimant (Art 30,a Costa Rica Law). Nonetheless, in these cases, the amparo against the self executing statute is not directly decided by the Constitutional Chamber, and instead, it is converted into a direct action on judicial review of the constitutionality of the challenged statute[634]. In such cases, the President of the Constitutional Chamber must suspend the procedure and give the plaintiff 15 days in order for him to formalize a direct action on judicial review of constitutionality against the statute (Art. 48 Costa Rica Law). So, only after the statute is annulled by the Constitutional Chamber, the amparo action will be decided.

In Uruguay, in similar sense, the amparo against statutes is excluded regarding statutes and State acts of similar rank (Art. 1,c Law 16011), being the only means to challenge the constitutionality of a statute, the judicial action file to obtain a declaration of its unconstitutionality in a concrete case by the Supreme Court. In such cases, the amparo pretension can only have a suppressive effect regarding the application of the statute to the plaintiff pending the Supreme Court decision on the unconstitutionality of the statute[635]

In Argentina, even with its longstanding tradition on judicial review of legislation by means of the diffuse method of judicial review, the amparo against statutes is not admitted[636]. Nonetheless, if in an amparo action against State acts, the statute in which the challenged act is based is considered unconstitutional, the amparo judge, by means of the diffuse method of judicial review can decide upon the inapplicability of the statute in the case. In this regard, Article 2,d of the Amparo Law when setting forth that the amparo action is not admissible "when for the purpose of determining the invalidity of the challenged act it is required the declaration of the unconstitutionality a the statute", has been considered as not being in force because it

---

633 See Edmundo ORELLANA, *La justicia constitucional en Honduras*, Universidad Nacional Autónoma de Honduras, Tegucigalpa, 1993, p. 102, note 26.

634 See Rubén HERNÁNDEZ, *Derecho Procesal Constitucional*, Editorial Juricentro, San José, 2001, pp. 45, 208–209, 245, 223.

635 See Luis Alberto VIERA, *Ley de Amparo*, Ediciones Idea, Montevideo 1993, pp. 23,

636 See José Luis LAZZARINI, *El juicio de amparo*, Editorial La Ley, Buenos Aires 1987, p. 214; Néstor Pedro SAGÜÉS, *Derecho procesal Constitucional,* Vol 3, *Acción de amparo*, Editorial Astrea Buenos Aires 1988, p. 97.

contradicts Article 31 of the Constitution (supremacy clause)[637]. Additionally, Article 43 of the 1994 Constitution, now regulating the amparo action, has expressly solved the discussion by setting forth that "In the case, the judge can declare the unconstitutionality of the norm in which the act or omission is based". After discussions based in previous legislation, regarding the admissibility in the judicial doctrine of the amparo against self executing statutes[638], in similar sense to the Argentinean solution, the Peruvian Constitutional Procedure Code has established as follows: "When it is argued that the acts causing threats or violation are based in the application of a norm not compatible with the Constitution, the decision declaring the claim founded must additionally decide on the inapplicability of such norm" (Article 43). In this case, also, the court in order to decide must use its judicial review powers through the diffuse method.

In other countries, the amparo action against statutes is just declared as inadmissible in the legislation or considered as such by the courts: as is the case in Chile[639], Uruguay (Art. 1,c Amparo Law), Panamá and El Salvador[640]. In Brazil, the *mandado de segurança* is also excluded against laws or legal provisions when they have not been applied through an administrative act[641]. In Colombia, the tutela action is also excluded regarding all "acts of a general, impersonal and abstract nature" (Art 6,5); and in Nicaragua, the amparo action is not admissible "against the process of drafting the statute, its promulgation or publication or any other legislative act or resolution" (Article 51, Law).

2. Amparo against executive and administrative acts and actions

The general terms, it can be said that the amparo action was born seeking the protection from executive authorities, in particular, against administrative acts issued by public officers or facts or omissions accomplished by them; that is, against acts, facts or omissions from the entities or bodies forming Public Administration at all its levels (national, state, municipal). These acts, facts or omissions are always considered as produced by public authorities, particularly from the executive branch of government and its decentralized or deconcentrated bodies.

In general terms it can be said that in all Latin American countries the amparo actions are admitted against executive and administrative acts causing harms or threats to constitutional rights and guarantees, including acts issued by the Head of

637 See Néstor Pedro SAGÜÉS, *Derecho procesal Constitucional,* Vol 3, *Acción de amparo*, Editorial Astrea Buenos Aires 1988, pp. 243–258

638 See Samuel B. ABAD YUPANQUI, *El proceso constitucional de amparo*, Gaceta Jurídica, Lima 2004, pp. 352–374

639 Humberto NOGUEIRA ALCALÁ, "El derecho de amparo o protección de los derechos humanos, fundamentales o esenciales en Chile: evolución y perspectivas", in Humberto Nogueira Alcalá (Editor), *Acciones constitucionales de amparo y protección: realidad y perspectivas en Chile y América Latina*", Editorial Universidad de Talca, Talca 2000, p. 45.

640 See Edmundo ORELLANA, *La Justicia Constitucional en Honduras*, Universidad Nacional Autónoma de Honduras, Editorial Universitaria, Tegucigalpa 1993, p 102, note 26.

641 See José Luis LAZZARINI, *El juicio de amparo*, La Ley, Buenos Aires, 1987, pp. 213–214.

the Executive, that is, the President of the Republic, in contrary sense to what happens in the United States where in principle, the coercive remedy of an injunction cannot be directed against the President[642]. The only express exceptions on these matters are the Mexican amparo suit against executive acts of expulsion of foreigners from the territory (Art. 33)[643], and in Uruguay, the amparo action against executive regulations[644].

Regarding in particular the amparo against administrative acts, Article 5 of the Venezuelan Amparo Law[645] provides that:

> The action of amparo shall be admitted against any administrative act, material action, irreversible facts, abstentions or omissions that violate or threaten to violate a constitutional right or guarantee, when there is no brief, summary and efficient procedure available, in accordance with the constitutional protection.
>
> When an action for amparo is brought against administrative acts of particular effects or against abstentions or denials of Public Administration, it can be filed before the Judicial review of administrative action jurisdiction, together with the judicial review recourse seeking the nullity of administrative acts or against the omission. In such cases, in a brief, summary and effective way, if it deems necessary for the constitutional protection, pending the suit, the court may suspend the effects of the challenged act, as guarantee of the violated constitutional right.
>
> In such cases of exercising the amparo action together with the judicial review recourse against the administrative act based on violation of a constitutional right, there will be no delay for the exercise of the recourse, which can be brought even after those statutorily estab-

642 See Sloan v. Nixon, 60 F.R.D. 228 (S.D.N.Y. 1973), aff'd, 93 F.2d 1398 (2d Cir. 1974), judgment aff'd, 419 U.S. 958, 95 S. Ct. 218, 42 L. Ed. 2d 174 (1974). See the reference in John BOURDEAU et al, "Injunctions" in Kevin Schroder, John Glenn and Maureen Placilla, *Corpus Juris Secundum*, Volume 43A, Thomson West, 2004, p. 229.

643 See Eduardo FERRER MAC–GREGOR, *La acción constitucional de amparo en México y España. Estudio de derecho comparado*, Editorial Porrúa, México 2002, p. 377.

644 See Luis Alberto VIERA, *Ley de Amparo*, Ediciones Idea, Montevideo 1993, pp. 99,

645 **Artículo 5.** *La acción de amparo contra actos administrativos, vías de y hecho y conductas omisivas de la Administración.* La acción de amparo procede contra todo acto administrativo, actuaciones materiales, vías de hecho, abstenciones u omisiones que violen o amenacen violar un derecho o una garantía constitucionales, cuando no exista un medio procesal breve, sumario y eficaz, acorde con la protección constitucional.

Cuando la acción de amparo se ejerza contra actos administrativos de efectos particulares o contra abstenciones o negativas de la Administración, podrá formularse ante el Juez Contencioso–Administrativo competente, si lo hubiere en la localidad, conjuntamente con el recurso contencioso administrativo de anulación de actos administrativos o contra las conductas omisivas, respectivamente, que se ejerza. En estos casos, el Juez, en forma breve, sumaria, efectiva y conforme a lo establecido en el artículo 22, si lo considera procedente para la protección constitucional, suspenderá los efectos del acto recurrido como garantía de dicho derecho constitucional violado, mientras dure el juicio.

Parágrafo Único. Cuando se ejerza la acción de amparo contra actos administrativos conjuntamente con el recurso contencioso–administrativo que se fundamente en la violación de un derecho constitucional, el ejercicio del recurso procederá en cualquier tiempo, aun después de transcurridos los lapsos de caducidad previstos en la Ley y no será necesario el agotamiento previo de la vía administrativa.

lished lapses have elapsed, and it will not be necessary the exhaustion of the administrative recourses.

This regulation can be considered as one of the most comprehensive in all Latin American Amparo laws regarding amparo actions against administrative acts, regulating the possibility of exercising the amparo action in two ways: in an autonomous way or together with a nullity recourse for judicial review of the act. Regarding the latter, the former Supreme Court of Justice in the decision of July, 10, 1991 (Caso: *Tarjetas Banvenez*), clarified that in such case, the action is not a principal one, but subordinated and ancillary regarding the principal recourse to which it has been attached, and subjected to the final nullifying decision that has to be issued in it[646]. That is why, in such cases, the amparo pretension that must be founded in a grave presumption of the violation of the constitutional right, has a preventive and temporal character, pending the final decision of the nullity suit, consisting in the suspension of the effects of the challenged administrative act. This provisional character of the amparo protection pending the suit, is thus subjected to the final decision to be issued in the nullity judicial review procedure against the challenged administrative act[647].

The main difference between both procedures according to the Supreme Court doctrine is that:

> In the first case of the autonomous amparo action against administrative acts, the plaintiff must allege a direct, immediate and flagrant violation to the constitutional right, which in its own demonstrates the need for the amparo order as a definitive means to restore the harmed juridical situation. In the second case, given the suspensive nature of the amparo order which only tends to provisionally stop the effects of the injuring act until the judicial review of administrative action confirming or nullifying it is decided, the alleged unconstitutional violations of constitutional provisions can be formulated together with violations of legal or statutory provisions developing the constitutional ones, because it is a judicial review action against administrative acts, seeking their nullity, they can also be founded on legal texts. What the court cannot do in these cases of filing together the actions, in order to suspend the effects of the challenged administrative act, is to found its decision only in the legal violations alleged, because that would mean to anticipate the final decision on the principal nullity judicial review recourse[648].

The Supreme Court then concluded affirming that the final distinction between both lies, first, in their purpose: in the autonomous action of amparo against administrative acts it has a restorative character, and in the case of the amparo filed together with the judicial review action against the challenged act, it has a nullifying character. Second, in the first case the alleged and proved constitutional right violation must be a direct, immediate and flagrant one; in the second case, what has to be proved is the existence of a grave presumption of the constitutional violation. And third, in the first case, the judicial decision issued is a definitive constitutional pro-

---

646 See the text in *Revista de Derecho Público,* N° 47, Editorial Jurídica Venezolana, Caracas, 1991, pp. 169–174 See also the comments in *Revista de Derecho Público,* N° 50, Editorial Jurídica Venezolana, Caracas, 1992, pp. 183–184

647 *Idem.* pp. 170–171

648 *Idem.,* pp. 171–172.

tection one; in the second case, it has only preventive character of suspension of the effects of the challenged act pending the principal judicial review process[649].

In some way similar to the Venezuelan solution, in Article 8 of the Colombian Tutela Law[650] it can also be found a regulation regarding the "tutela as a transitory mean" of protection, as follows:

First, it is provided that even in case the injured party would have another judicial means of protection, the action for tutela will be admitted when used as a transitory means in order to prevent an irreparable damage. In such cases, the court will expressly rule in its decision that the protection [order] will be in force only during the term the competent judicial court will use in order to decide on the merits of the action brought by the injured party. In any case, the affected party must file such action in the maximum delay of 4 month from the tutela decision. In case that the action is not filed, the tutela decision will cease in its effects.

Second, in cases in which the tutela is used as a transitory means in order to prevent an irreparable injury, the action for tutela can also be filed together with the nullifying action before the judicial review of administrative action (contencioso–administrativo) jurisdiction. In these cases, if the court deems it justified, it could order, pending the process, the non application of the particular act regarding the concrete juridical situation whose protection is being demanded.

Finally, regarding executive and administrative acts and actions, mention must be made of the Argentinean restriction regarding the possible filing of the amparo action, in matters related to national defense and to public services (public utilities).

Article 2,b of the Amparo Law declares inadmissible the amparo action against "acts issued in express application of the Law 16.970", which is the so called Law of

---

649 *Idem.*, p. 172. See also regarding the nullity of article 22 of the Organic Amparo law the Supreme Court decisión dated May 21, 1996, in Allan R. BREWER–CARÍAS, *Acción y Derecho de* Amparo, Tomo V, *Instituciones Políticas y Constitucionales*, Editorial Jurídica Venezolana, Caracas, 1996, pp. 392 y ss.

650 **Artículo 8º La tutela como mecanismo transitorio.** Aún cuando el afectado disponga de otro medio de defensa judicial, la acción de tutela procederá cuando se utilice como mecanismo transitorio para evitar un perjuicio irremediable.

En el caso del inciso anterior, el juez señalará expresamente en la sentencia que su orden permanecerá vigente sólo durante el término que la autoridad judicial competente utilice para decidir de fondo sobre la acción instaurada por el afectado.

En todo caso el afectado deberá ejercer dicha acción en un término máximo de cuatro (4) meses a partir del fallo de tutela.

Si no se instaura, cesarán los efectos de éste.

Cuando se utilice como mecanismo transitorio para evitar un daño irreparable, la acción de tutela también podrá ejercerse conjuntamente con la acción de nulidad y de las demás procedentes ante la jurisdicción de lo contencioso administrativo. En estos casos, el juez si lo estima procedente podrá ordenar que no se aplique el acto particular respecto de la situación jurídica concreta cuya protección se solicita, mientras dure el proceso.

National Defense. For this exception to be applied, it has been considered that the challenged act must in a clear and exact way rely on the provisions of such law[651].

On the other hand, also in Argentina, the Amparo Law sets forth the inadmissibility of the amparo action in cases in which "the judicial intervention could directly or indirectly place in a compromising situation the regularity, continuity and efficacy of rendering a public service for the development of the essential activities of the State" (Article 2,c). Due to the general expressions used in the article (compromising, directly, indirectly, regularity, continuity, efficacy, rendering, public service), this provision has been highly criticized, being considered that with it "it is difficult to see an amparo against the State to be granted"[652], particularly, due to the fact that any administrative activity of the State can always be related to a public service[653]. Nonetheless, the final decision corresponds to the court, and if it is true that in practice the exception has hardly been used[654], in some important matters it was alleged. It happened for instance in the amparo actions filed in 1985 against the Central Bank of the Republic decision suspending for a few months delay the payments of the deposits in foreign currency. Even though some courts rejected amparo actions in the matter[655], in the "Peso" Case the Federal National Chamber on judicial review of administrative actions of Buenos Aires decided to reject the arguments asking for the rejection of the amparo action based in the consideration of the matter as related to a "public service", considering that the Central bank activities have not the elements to be considered as a public service in the sense of public utility[656]. A few years latter, regarding similar decisions of the Central Bank on the non payments of deposit in foreign currencies, in the cases referred to as the "Corralito", there was no allegation whatsoever considering those Central Bank decisions, which were adopted on situation of state of economic emergency, as public service activities. In such cases, the amparo actions were admitted and granted, but with multiple judicial incidents[657].

651 See Case *Diario El Mundo c/ Gobierno nacional*, CNFed, Sala 1 ContAdm, 30/4/74, JA, 23–1974–195. See the comments in Néstor Pedro SAGÜÉS, *Derecho procesal Constitucional,* Vol 3, *Acción de amparo*, Editorial Astrea Buenos Aires 1988, pp. 212–214.

652 José Luis LAZZARINI, *El juicio de amparo*, La Ley, Buenos Aires, 1987, p. 231.

653 Néstor Pedro SAGÜÉS, *Derecho procesal Constitucional,* Vol 3, *Acción de amparo*, Editorial Astrea Buenos Aires 1988, pp. 226 ff.

654 See José Luis LAZZARINI, *El juicio de amparo*, La Ley, Buenos Aires, 1987, p. 233; Néstor Pedro SAGÜÉS, *Derecho procesal Constitucional, Vol 3, Acción de amparo*, Editorial Astrea Buenos Aires 1988, p. 228

655 See Cfed B. Blanca, 13/8/85, ED, 116–116. See the comments in Alí Joaquín SALGADO, *Juicio de amparo y acción de inconstitucionalidad*, Editorial Astrea 1987, p. 51, note 59.

656 See CNFedConAdm, Sala IV, 13/6/85, ED, 114–231. See the comments in Alí Joaquín SALGADO, *Juicio de amparo y acción de inconstitucionalidad*, Editorial Astrea, 1987, p. 50, note 56

657 See for instance the *Smith* and the *San Luis* cases, 2002, in Antonio María HERNÁNDEZ, *Las emergencias y el orden constitucional*, Universidad Nacional Autónoma de México, México 2003, pp. 71 ff. And 119 ff. In Duch cases, the Laws and Decrees of Economic Emergency were declared unconstitutional.

3. Amparo against judicial acts and decisions

There is a general acceptance of the amparo action as a specific judicial means for constitutional rights protection against administrative acts (including those administrative acts issued by courts and tribunals), but the same cannot be said regarding judicial decisions on jurisdictional matters. In some countries, their Amparo Laws expressly reject and consider inadmissible the filing of amparo actions against judicial decisions, issued applying jurisdictional power[658]. This is the case of Argentina (Art. 2,b)[659], Bolivia (Art. 96,3), Costa Rica (Art. 30,b)[660], Chile[661], Dominican Republic[662], Ecuador[663], Nicaragua (Art. 51,b), Paraguay (Art. 2,a) and Uruguay (Art. 2,a)[664]. In El Salvador and Honduras, the exclusion is in particular referred to judicial acts issued "in judicial matters that are purely civil, commercial or labor–related, and in respect of definitive decisions in criminal matters" (El Salvador, Art. 13; Honduras Art. 45,6). In Brazil, the *mandado de seguranca* Statute excludes it against judicial decisions when according to the procedure statutes it exists a judicial recourse against them, or when they can be modified by means of correction (Art. 5,II).

On the contrary, in other Latin American countries, the amparo action can be filed against judicial decisions, as is the case in Mexico, where the direct amparo suit finds its broadest application (amparo cassation)[665], and is also the case in Gua-

---

658 Administrative acts issued by courts can be challenged by means of amparo. See for exaple, regarding Argentina, Néstor Pedro SAGÜÉS, *Derecho procesal Constitucional, Vol 3, Acción de amparo*, Editorial Astrea Buenos Aires 1988, pp.197 ff.

659 See Joaquin BRAGUE CAMAZANO, *La Jurisdicción constitucional de la libertad (Teoría general, Argentina, México, Corte Interamericana de Derechos Humanos)*, Editorial Porrúa, México 2005, p. 98. José Luis LAZZARINI, *El juicio de amparo,* Editorial La Ley, Buenos Aires 1987, pp. 218–223; Alí Joaquín SALGADO, *Juicio de amparo y acción de inconstitucionalidad*, Astrea, Buenos Aires, 1987, p. 46.

660 See Rubén HERNÁNDEZ VALLE, *Derecho Procesal Constitucional*, Editorial Juricentro, San José 2001, pp. 45, 206, 223, 226.

661 See Juan Manuel ERRAZURIZ G. and Jorge Miguel OTERO A., *Aspectos procesales del recurso de protección,* Editorial Jurídica de Chile, Santiago 1989, p. 103. Nonetheless, some authors considers that sthe recourse for protection is admisible against judicial decisions when issued in an arbitrary way and in violation of due process rights.See Humberto NOGUEIRA ALCALÁ, "El derecho de amparo o protección de los derechos humanos, fundamentales o esenciales en Chile: evolución y perspectivas", in Humberto Nogueira Alcalá (Editor), *Acciones constitucionales de amparo y protección: realidad y perspectivas en Chile y América Latina*", Editorial Universidad de Talca, Talca 2000, p. 45

662 See Eduardo Jorge PRATS, *Derecho Constitucional*, Vol. II, Gaceta Judicial, Santo Domingo 2005, p. 391.

663 Hernán SALGADO PESANTES, *Manual de Justicia Constitucional Ecuatoriana,* Corporación Editora nacional, Quito 2004, p. 84.

664 See Luis Alberto VIERA, *Ley de Amparo*, Ediciones Idea, Montevideo 1993, pp. 50, 97.

665 See Richard D. BAKER, *Judicial Review in Mexico. A Study of the Amparo Suit,* Texas University Press, Austin 1971, p. 98.

temala (Art. 10,h), Honduras (Arts. 9,3 and,10,2,*a*), Panama (Art. 2615)[666], Peru and Venezuela.

The general principle in this cases, as set forth in the Peruvian Code on Constitutional Procedures, is that the amparo is admitted against definitive judicial resolutions when "they manifestly impair the effective procedural protection, including access to justice and due process" (Art. 4)[667]. In the case of Venezuela, in a similar way to what it was established in the Peruvian legislation prior to the Code, Article 4 of the Amparo law provides that "the action of amparo shall also be admitted when a Tribunal of the Republic, acting outside its competence, pronounces a resolution or decision or orders an action that impairs a constitutional right". Since no court has power to unlawfully cause harm to constitutional rights or guarantees, the amparo against judicial decisions is admitted when a court decision directly harms the constitutional rights of the plaintiff, normally related to the due process of law rights. As was decided by the Cassation Chamber of the former Supreme Court of Justice in a decision of December 5, 1990, the amparo against judicial decisions is admitted "when the decision in itself injures the juridical conscience, when harming in a flagrant way individual rights that cannot be renounced or when the decision violates the principle of juridical security (judicial stability), deciding against *res judicata*, or when issued in a process where the plaintiff's right to defense has not been guaranteed, or in any way the due process guarantee has been violated"[668].

In Colombia, Article 40 of the the Decree N° 2.591 of 1991, due to the fact that the Constitution did not exclude it, also established the possibility of bringing an action of amparo against judicial actions, when the impairment of the right is a direct consequence of them, adding that "when the right invoked is that of due process, the tutela shall be brought together with the appropriate recourse," that is, together with the recourse of appeal". Notwithstanding the statutory admissibility of tutela against judicial decisions, the Constitutional Court in ruling C–543 of October 1, 1992, declared the aforementioned Article 40 of Decree 2.591 unconstitutional, and hence null and void, considering it contrary to the principle of intangibility of the *res judicata*.[669] Nonetheless, one year later, and after numerous judicial decisions on the matter, the same Constitutional Court admitted the tutela action against judi-

666 With no suspensive effects. See Boris BARRIOS GONZÁLEZ, *Derecho Procesal Constitucional*, Editorial Portobelo, Panama 2002, p. 159

667 See Samuel B. ABAD YUPANQUI, *El proceso constitucional de amparo*, Gaceta Jurídica, Lima, 2004, p. 326

668 *Case José Díaz Aquino*, also refered to in decisión dated December 14, 1994 of the same cassation Chamber. See the reference in Alan R. BREWER–CARÍAS, "Derecho y Acción de Amparo", *Instituciones Políticas y Constitucionales* Vol V, Editorial Jurídica Venezolana, Caracas, 1998, pp. 261 ff; Rafael CHAVERO, *El nuevo régimen del amparo constitucional en Venezuela*, Editorial Sherwood, Caracas, 2001, pp. 483 ff.

669 See in Manuel José CEPEDA ESPINOSA, *Derecho Constitucional jurisprudencial. Las grandes decisiones de la Corte Constitucional*, Legis, Bogotá 2001, pp. 1009 ff.

cial decisions when they constitute a *vía de hecho* (voi de fait) or factual action[670], being considering as such:

> The ostensible and grave violation of the rules governing the process in which the challenged decision was issued, up to the point that because the flagrant disregard of the due process and other constitutional, the plaintiff's constitutional rights had been directly violated by the challenged act.
>
> This means that the via de hecho is in fact the arbitrary exercise of the judicial function, in such terms that the deciding court has decided not according to law –which thus has been violated– but only according to its personal will"[671]

According to this doctrine, applicable to almost all the other cases in which the amparo action is admissible against judicial decisions, it can be said that for granting the amparo, the challenged judicial decision must have been issued in grave and flagrant violation of the due process of law guaranties, thus constituting not a lawful decision but an unlawful one or *vía de hecho*, that is, an action with no legal support whatsoever.

In a certain way regarding injunctions on judicial matters, it can be said that in the United States, injunction can also be granted when for instance, it clearly appears that the prosecution of law actions will result in fraud, gross wrong or oppression, and that justice clearly requires equitable interference. As has been decided by the courts:

> "The power of a court of equity to interfere with the general right of a person to sue and to restrain the person from prosecuting the action will be exercised only where it appears clearly that the prosecution of the law action will result in a fraud, gross wrong, or oppression, and that conscience and justice clearly require equitable interference. Accordingly, an action at law may be restrained under these restrictive rules where a person is attempting to, or would, through the instrumentality of an action at law, obtain an unconscionable advantage of another"[672]

On the other hand, some restrictions have been established in the Amparo law admitting the amparo actions against judicial decisions. Besides the need to the exhaustion of the available ordinary judicial recourses against the challenged decision, the decisions of the Supreme Court (Mexico, Panama, Art 2.615; Venezuela, Art 6,6) or the Constitutional Tribunal (Peru) had been expressly excluded form the

---

670 See decision S–231 dated May 13, 1994, in Manuel José CEPEDA ESPINOSA, *Derecho Constitucional jurisprudencial. Las grandes decisiones de la Corte Constitucional*, Legis, Bogotá, 2001, pp. 1022 ff.

671 See SU–1218 decision of November 21, 2001. See in Juan Carlos ESGUERRA, *La protección constitucional del ciudadano,* Legis, Bogotá 2004, p. 164. See Eduardo CIFUENTES MUÑOZ, "Tutela contra sentencias (El caso colombiano)", in Humberto Nogueira Alcalá (Editor), *Acciones constitucionales de amparo y protección: realidad y perspectivas en Chile y América Latina*", Editorial Universidad de Talca, Talca 2000, pp. 307 ff.

672 See Miles v. Illinois Cent. R. Co. 315 U.S. 698, 62 S. Ct. 827, 86 L. Ed. 1129, 146 A.L.R 1104 (1942); Langenau Mfg. Co. v. City of Cleveland, 159 Ohio St. 525, 50 Ohio *Op.* 435, 112 N.E. 2d 658 (1953); Kardy v. Shook, 237 Md. 524, 207 A2d 83 (1965). See in John BOURDEAU et al, "Injunctions" in Kevin Schroder, John Glenn and Maureen Placilla, *Corpus Juris Secundum*, Volume 43A, Thomson West, 2004, pp. 114–115.

amparo action. In some cases, the judicial amparo decision itself cannot be the object of another amparo suit (Honduras, Art 45,2; Mexico, Art. 73,II[673]); in the same sense that in the United States, an injunction against an injunction, sometimes referred to as a counter injunction, should not be issued[674]. In other countries, on the contrary, the amparo actions are admitted even against amparo judicial decisions (Colombia[675], Perú[676], Venezuela[677] because those decisions, in their selves, can also additionally violate constitutional rights, different to those claimed in the initial suit.

4. Amparo against acts of other constitutional entities

In contemporary Latin American constitutional law, additionally to the three classic branches of government, the separation of powers principle has given origin to other State organs, not dependent on the Legislative, Executive or Judicial branches, with certain types of autonomy and independence. It is the case, for instance of the Electoral bodies, in charge of governing the electoral processes, the Peoples' Defendant or Human Rights Defendants Office, the Public Prosecutor Offices, the General Audit entities (Contraloría General) and the Council of the Judiciary for the government and administration of courts and tribunals. Being State organs, their acts, facts and omissions can also be challenged by means of amparo actions when violating constitutional rights.

Nonetheless, regarding these State entities, some exceptions have been established regarding the justicablility of their actions by means of amparo actions. For instance, in Costa Rica (Art. 30,d)[678], Mexico (Art. 73,VII)[679], Nicaragua (Art. 51,5),

673 See Eduardo FERRER MAC–GREGOR, *La acción constitucional de amparo en México y España. Estudio de derecho comparado*, Editorial Porrúa, México 2002, p, 379

674 See Sellers v. Valenzuela, 249 Ala. 620, 32 So. 2d 520 (1947). See in John BOURDEAU et al, "Injunctions" in Kevin Schroder, John Glenn and Maureen Placilla, *Corpus Juris Secundum*, Volume 43A, Thomson West, 2004, pp. 87.

675 See Juan Carlos ESGUERRA, *La protección constitucional del ciudadano,* Legis, Bogotá 2004, p. 164

676 See Samuel B. ABAD YUPANQUI, *El proceso constitucional de amparo*, Gaceta Jurídica, Lima 2004, pp. 327, 330

677 See Allan R. BREWER–CARÍAS, "Derecho y Acción de Amparo", Vol. V, *Instituciones Políticas y Constitucionales*, Editorial Jurídica Venezolana, Caracas, 1998, pp. 263 ff.

678 See Rubén HERNÁNDEZ VALLE, *Derecho Procesal Constitucional*, Editorial Juricentro, San José 2001, pp. 228–229. Other matters decided by the Tribunal Supremo de Elecciones like citizenship, personal capacity or personal status matters, are justiciables by means of amparo. See José Miguel VILLALOBOS, "El recurso de amparo en Costa Rica" in", in Humberto Nogueira Alcalá (Editor), *Acciones constitucionales de amparo y protección: realidad y perspectivas en Chile y América Latina*", Editorial Universidad de Talca, Talca 2000, pp 222–223.

679 See Eduardo FERRER MAC–GREGOR, *La acción constitucional de amparo en México y España. Estudio de derecho comparado*, Editorial Porrúa, México 2002, p. 378; See Richard D. BAKER, *Judicial Review in Mexico. A Study of the Amparo Suit*, Texas University Press, Austin, 1971, pp. 98, 152.

Panamá (Art. 2.615)[680], Peru (Art. 5,8)[681] and Uruguay (Art. 1,b), the amparo suit is excluded regarding acts of the electoral bodies, in similar sense as the injunctions are excluded in the United States regarding actions of the election officers in the performance of their duties[682].

On the other hand, regarding the Council of the Judiciary (Consejo de la Magistratura), the Peruvian Amparo Law excludes the acts of that entity from being challenged through the amparo action, when referred to the dismissal or ratification of judges, when the decisions are duly motivated and issued after the interested party being heard (Art. 5,7)[683].

5. The amparo action and the political questions

In has been a traditional judicial doctrine in the United States to consider as non justifiable the so called "political questions" mainly related to the "separation of powers" and particularly with "the relationship between the judiciary and the co–ordinate branches of the Federal Government."[684] It is considered that the preemptive political nature of these questions imposes their solution in the political branches of government rather than in the courts. That is why, the exemption not only applies to judicial review in general, but also to injunctions.

The main source of questions considered as political and thus non justiciable by the Supreme Court are related to foreign affairs which involves –as the Supreme Court stated in *Ware* v. *Hylton* (1796)– "considerations of policy, considerations of extreme magnitude, and certainly entirely incompetent to the examination and decision of a Court of Justice."[685] Decisions concerning foreign relations therefore, as stated by Justice Jackson in *Chicago and Southern Air Lines v. Waterman Stamship Co.* (1948):

> Are wholly confined by our constitution to the political departments of the government. ... They are decisions of a kind for which the Judiciary has neither aptitude, facilities nor re-

680 See Boris BARRIOS GONZÁLEZ, *Derecho Procesal Constitucional*, Editorial Portobelo, Panama 2002, p. 161

681 Nonetheless, the amparo action can be admitted if the decision of the Jurado Nacional de Elecciones does not have jurisdiccional nature or if jurisdiccional, it violates the effective judicial protection (due process). See Samuel B. ABAD YUPANQUI, *El proceso constitucional de amparo*, Gaceta Jurídica, Lima 2004, pp. 128, 421, 447.

682 See Boyd v. Story, 350 Ark. 56, 84 S.W.3d 444 (2002). See in in John BOURDEAU et al, "Injunctions" in Kevin Schroder, John Glenn and Maureen Placilla, *Corpus Juris Secundum*, Volume 43A, Thomson West, 2004, pp. 238–239.

683 See Samuel B. ABAD YUPANQUI, *El proceso constitucional de amparo*, Gaceta Jurídica, Lima 2004, p. 126.

684 Baker v. Carr, 369 U.S. 186 (1962). See in See M. Glenn ABERNATHY and Barbara A. PERRY, *Civil Liberties under the Constitution*, Sixth Edition, University of South Carolina Press, 1993, pp. 6–7.

685 *Ware v. Hylton*, 3 Dallas, 199 (1796)

sponsibility and which has long been held to belong in the domain of political power not subject to judicial intrusion or inquiry.[686]

Even though developed mainly in the foreign affairs sphere, the Supreme Court has also considered certain matters relating to the government of internal affairs, a political question, and thus non justiciable; like the decision as to whether a state must have a republican form of government, which in *Luther* v. *Borden* (1849) was considered a "decision binding on every other department of the government, and could not be questioned in a judicial tribunal."[687]

Any way and even though that through the decisions of the Supreme Court, a list of "political questions" that the Court has considered as non–justifiable can be elaborated, the ultimate responsibility in determining them corresponds to the Supreme Court.

As the Court said in *Baker* v. *Carr* (1962):

> Deciding whether a matter has in any measure been committed by the constitution to another branch of government, or whether the action of that branch exceeds whatever authority has been committed, –said the Court– is itself a delicate exercise in constitutional interpretation, and is a responsibility of this Court as ultimate interpreter of the constitution...[688].

Following the United States tradition, in Argentina, the Supreme Court of Justice has developed the same exception to judicial review and to the amparo action, concerning political questions, even though the Constitution does not expressly establish anything on the matter. These political questions are related to the "acts of government" of "political acts" doctrine developed in continental European law, and within which it can be mentioned the following: the declaration of state of siege; the declaration of federal intervention in the provinces; the declaration of "public use" for means of expropriation; the declaration of war; the declaration of emergency to approve certain direct tax contributions; acts concerning foreign relations; the recognition of new foreign states or new foreign state governments; the expulsion of aliens, etc.[689] In general, within these political questions there are acts exercised by the political powers of the state in accordance with powers exclusively and directly attributed to them in the constitution, which can be considered the key element for their identification.

---

686 Chicago *and Southern Air Lines v. Waterman Steamship Co.*, 333 US 103 (1948) p. 111.

687 Luther v. Borden 48 U.S. (7 Howard), 1,(1849). See in M. Glenn ABERNATHY and Barbara A. PERRY, *Civil Liberties under the Constitution*, Sixth Edition, University of South Carolina Press, 1993, pp. 6–7

688 Baker v. Carr, 369 U.S. 186 (1962).

689 See José Luis LAZZARINI, *El juicio de amparo*, La Ley, Buenos Aires, 1987, p. 190 ff.; Néstor Pedro SAGÜÉS, *Derecho procesal Constitucional,* Vol 3, *Acción de amparo*, Editorial Astrea, Buenos Aires, 1988, pp. 270 ff.; Alí Joaquín SALGADO, *Juicio de amparo y acción de inconstitucionalidad*, Astrea, Buenos Aires, 1987, p. 23.

Apart from Argentina, only in Peru the issue of the political questions as non justiciable matter by means of amparo has been considered by the Constitutional Tribunal[690].

6. The amparo against executive and administrative omissions

In general terms, the amparo action can be filed in all Latin American countries, not only against positive acts or actions from public officers or authorities (and also from individuals) that cause harm or threat upon constitutional rights and guarantees, but also against the omissions of such entities or persons when they do not comply with their general obligations to decide petitions, which can also cause such harms of threats. In particular, the amparo action has been frequently used to challenge Public Administration omissions or abstentions to act; but in the countries where amparo is admissible against individual, it also can be filed against their omissions harming or threatening constitutional rights.

Regarding public officers omissions, the amparo action in Latin America is generally filed in order to obtain from the court an order directed against a public officer in order for him to act in a matter with respect to which he has authority or jurisdiction. The amparo action against omissions in these cases is similar to the North American mandamus or mandatory injunction[691], defined as "a writ commanding a public officer to perform some duty which the laws require him to do but he refuses or neglects to perform". Thus mandamus cannot be used if the public officer has any discretion in the matter; "but if the law is clear in requiring the performance of some ministerial (nondiscretionary) function, then mandamus may properly be sought to nudge the reluctant or negligent official along in the performance of his or her duties"[692]. As it was decided by the Supreme Court in Wilbur v. United States, 281 U.S. 206, 218 (1930):

> "Where the duty in a particular situation is so plainly prescribed as to be free from doubt and equivalent to a positive command it is regarded as being so far ministerial that its performance may be compelled by mandamus, unless there be provision or implication to the contrary, But where the duty is not thus plainly prescribed but depends upon a statute the con-

---

690 See Samuel B. ABAD YUPANQUI, *El proceso constitucional de amparo*, Gaceta Jurídica, Lima 2004, pp. 128 ff.

691 In the United Status, it has been considered that while as a general rule courts will not compel by injunction the performance by public officers of their official duties (Bellamy v. gates, 214 Va. 314, 200 S.E. 2d 533, (1973)), a court may compel public officers or boards to act in a matter with respect to which they have jurisdiction or authority (Erie v. State By and Through State Highway Commission, 154 Mont. 150, 461 P 2d 207 (1969)). See in in John BOURDEAU et al, "Injunctions" in Kevin Schroder, John Glenn and Maureen Placilla, *Corpus Juris Secundum*, Volume 43A, Thomson West, 2004, pp. 221, 222, 244.

692 See M. Glenn Abernathy and Barbara A. Perry, *Civil Liberties under the Constitution*, Sixth Edition, University of South Carolina Press, 1993, p. 8. One of the important features of the writ of mandamus in North America y that the writ does not issue to purely private persons, but can only be directed to public officials or persons performing some quasi–public functions. Idem, p. 8.

struction or application of which is not free from doubt, it is regarded as involving the character of judgment or discretion which cannot be controlled by mandamus"[693].

In Latin America, for an omission to be the object of an amparo action, it must produce a direct violation of a constitutional right of the plaintiff, who in cases of illegalities in some countries like Venezuela, will only be allowed to use other judicial remedies, as the judicial review of administrative omission action before the special courts of the matter (contencioso–administrativo).

According to the judicial doctrine established by the former Supreme Court of Justice of Venezuela, the amparo action against omissive conducts of Public Administration, must comply with the following two conditions:

> "a) That the alleged omissive conduct be absolute, which means that Public Administration has not accomplished in any moment the due function; and b) that the omission be regarding a generic duty, that is, the duty a public officer has to act in compliance with the powers attributed to him, which is different to the specific duty that is the condition for the judicial review of administrative omissive action. Thus, only when it is a matter of a generic duty, of procedure, of providing in a matter which is inherent to the public officer position, he incurs in the omissive conduct regarding which the amparo action is admissible[694].

From this Venezuelan judicial doctrine results that the important condition for the admissibility of the amparo action against public officer omissions, is the one related to the nature of his duties, being only admissible when the matters refer to generic duties and not to specific ones. As defined by the same former Supreme Court in a decision dated February, 11, 1992:

> "In cases of Public Administration abstentions or omissions a distinction can be observed regarding the constitutional provisions violated when they provide for generic or specific duties. In the first case, when a public entity does not comply with its generic obligation to respond [a petition] of continuing the procedure or recourse filed by an individual, it violates the constitutional right to obtain prompt answer [to petitions] set forth in Article 67 of the Constitution; whereas when the inactivity is produced regarding a specific duty imposed by a statute in a concrete and ineludible way, no direct constitutional violation occurs. Condition in the latter case that the Court has been imposing for the filing of the judicial review of administrative omissions recourse…
>
> From the aforementioned reasons the Court deems conclusive that the inactivity of Public Administration to accomplish a specific legal duty precisely infringes in a direct and immediate way the legal (statutory) text regulating the matter, in which case the Constitution is only violated in a mediate and indirect way. For the amparo judge, in order to detect if an abstention of the aggrieved entity effectively harms a constitutional right or guarantee, it must first, rely himself on the supposedly unaccomplished statute in order to verify if the abstention is regarding an specific obligation. In which case it must deny the amparo action and give to the

---

693 See the reference in See M. Glenn ABERNATHY and Barbara A. PERRY, *Civil Liberties under the Constitution*, Sixth Edition, University of South Carolina Press, 1993, p. 8

694 See thye decisions of the former Supreme Court of Justice, Politico Adminsitrative Chamber, dated November 5, 1992 (Caso *Jorge E. Alvarado*), in *Revista de Derecho Público,* N° 52, Editorial Jurídica Venezolana, Caracas, 1992, p. 187; and November 18, 1993, in *Revista de Derecho Público,* N° 55–56, Editorial Jurídica Venezolana, Caracas, 1993, p. 295

plaintiff another remedy, as the judicial review action against Public Administration omissions[695].

In these cases, the judicial order of mandamus eventually consists in commanding the public officer to perform the duty the Constitution requires him to do which he refuses or neglects to perform, that is, to promptly decide the petitions individuals had filed before him[696]. In general terms, then, the court order cannot substitute the public officer decision[697]; and only in cases when a specific statute provides what is called the "positive silence" (the presumption that after the exhaustion of a particular delay, it is considered that Public Administration has decided accordingly to what has been asked in the particular petition), then the judicial order impliedly gives positive effects to the official abstention or omission[698]

IV. THE AMPARO AGAINST INDIVIDUALS OR PRIVATE PERSONS

If it is true that the amparo action, as a specific means for the protection of constitutional rights and guarantees was originally conceived for the protection of individuals against the State and its public officials, it has been progressively admitted against private persons, corporations or institutions whose actions can also cause harm or threats regarding constitutional rights of others. As was ruled in the Argentinean *Samuel Kot Case,* in which the Supreme Court of the Nation began to admit the amparo against acts of individuals, by saying that:

> "There is nothing in the letter and spirit of the Constitution that allows for the assertion that the protection of constitutional rights is circumscribed only to attacks of the State, since, sustained the High Court, what is to be kept in mind is not only the origin of the impairment of constitutional rights but the rights themselves, because the same attention is not paid to the aggressors as to the rights aggrieved"[699].

Nonetheless, not in all Latin American countries amparo actions against individuals are admitted. In Mexico, for instance, the amparo suit is not admitted against violations caused by acts of private individuals, so the constitutional protection

---

695 See in *Revista de Derecho Público,* N° 53–54, Editorial Jurídica Venezolana, Caracas, 1993, pp. 272–273.

696 See the former venezuelan Supreme Court decisión dated August 26, 1993 (*Caso Inversiones Klanki*), *Revista de Derecho Público,* N° 55–56, Editorial Jurídica Venezolana, Caracas, 1993, p. 294.

697 See for instante in Argentina, Néstor Pedro SAGÜÉS, *Derecho procesal Constitucional, Vol 3, Acción de amparo*, Editorial Astrea Buenos Aires 1988, pp. 73 ff.

698 See the venezuelan former Supreme Court decision dated December 20, 1991 (Caso *BHO, C.A.*), en *Revista de Derecho Público,* N° 48, Editorial Jurídica Venezolana, Caracas, 1991, pp. 141–143

699 See José Luis LAZZARINI, *El juicio de amparo*, La Ley, Buenos Aires, 1987, p. 228; Joaquín BRAGE CAMAZO, La jurisdicción constitucional de la libertad (Teoría general, Argentina, México, Corte Interamericana de derechos humanos), Editorial Porrúa, México, 2005, p. 99; Néstor Pedro SAGÜÉS, *Derecho procesal Constitucional,* Vol 3, *Acción de amparo*, Editorial Astrea Buenos Aires 1988, pp. 13, 512, 527 ff.

through the amparo suit is established exclusively against the authorities[700]. Similarly, when regulating the *mandado de segurança,* the Constitution of Brazil provides for its admission to protect constitutional rights and freedoms "when the party responsible for the illegality or abuse of power is a public authority or an agent of a legal entity exercising attributions of the Authorities," thus excluding this recourse of protection against the actions of private individuals[701]. Similar provisions are set forth in the Amparo law regulations in Panamá (Art. 50 Constitution; Art 2608 Judicial Code), El Salvador (Art. 12) and Nicaragua (Art. 23).

As mentioned above, in other Latin American countries, after the Argentinean *Kot Case*, the amparo against individual's actions or omissions causing harm or threats to constitutional rights of other individuals has been admitted, although in some countries in a restrictive way. In general terms it is admitted in Argentina, even though the 1966 Law 16.986 only refers to the amparo action against the State, that is "against every act or omission of the authorities" (Article 1); the amparo against individuals being regulated in articles 321,2 and 498 of the Code of Civil and Commercial Procedure.

In Venezuela, the amparo action against acts of individuals, is expressly provided in the 1988 Organic Law of Amparo[702], where Article 2 provides:.

> [The amparo action] shall be admitted against any fact, act or omission originated by citizens, legal entities, private groups or organizations that have violated, violate or threaten to violate any of the guarantees or rights that are entitled to the amparo of this Law.

In a similar manner, Uruguay's 1988 Law 16.011 of Amparo admits, in general, the action of amparo "against any act, omission or fact of the state or public sector authorities, as well as individuals, that is deemed to currently or imminently, manifestly and unlawfully impair, restrict, alter or threaten any of the rights and freedoms expressly or implicitly recognized by the Constitution" (Art. 1)703. A similar provision is set forth in Article 2 of the Peruvian Code of Constitutional procedures704 and in the Bolivian Constitution (Art. 19).

Also in Chile, it has been interpreted that the action for protection of constitutional rights and freedoms against arbitrary or unlawful acts or omissions that perturb or threaten when legally exercised (Article 20), being established without making any distinction as to the origin of such acts or omissions, can also be brought

---

700 See Eduardo FERRER MAC–GREGOR, *La acción constitucional de amparo en México y España. Estudio de derecho comparado,* Editorial Porrúa, México 2002, p, 251; Joaquín Brage Camazo, La jurisdicción constitucional de la libertad (Teoría general, Argentina, México, Corte Interamericana de derechos humanos), Editorial Porrúa, México, 2005, 184.

701 See Celso AGRÍCOLA BARBI, *Do mandado de segurança,* Editora Forense, Rio de Janeiro 1993, p. 92.

702 Allan R. BREWER–CARÍAS, *Instituciones Políticas y Constitucionales,* Vol V, *Derecho y Acción de Amparo,* Editorial Jurídica Venezolana, Caracas 1998, pp. 96, 128.

703 See Luis Alberto VIERA, *Ley de Amparo,* Ediciones Idea, Montevideo 1993, pp. 63, 157.

704 See Samuel B. ABAD YUPANQUI, *El proceso constitucional de amparo,* Gaceta Jurídica, Lima 2004, pp. 389 ff.

against acts or omissions of individuals[705]. Similar interpretation was adopted by the Supreme Court of the Dominican Republic regarding the admissibility of the amparo against individuals[706].

Other Latin American countries, such as Colombia, Costa Rica Ecuador and Guatemala admit the amparo action when filed against individuals, but in a restricted way, only regarding the individuals that are in a position of superiority regarding citizens or in some way exercises public functions or activities or are rendering public services or public utilities[707]. In this regard, the Costa Rican Law of Constitutional Jurisdiction restricts the amparo against individual[708] as follows:

> **Article 57**. The recourse of amparo shall also be admitted against actions or omissions of individual subjects of the law when they act or should act in exercise of public functions or authority, or are by right or in fact in a position of power before which ordinary jurisdictional remedies are clearly insufficient or belated for guaranteeing the rights and freedoms referred to in Article 2,a of this Law.

In similar terms it is provided in the Guatemalan Law on Amparo (Art. 9) and in Colombia where the Constitution expressly refers to the law for the establishment of "the cases in which the action of tutela may be filed against private individuals entrusted with providing a public service or whose conduct may affect seriously and directly the collective interest or in respect of whom the applicant may find himself/herself in a state of subordination or vulnerability" (Art. 86). Was in compliance with this constitutional mandating that the Decree 2.591 of 1991 (Article 42) establishes that the action of tutela shall be admitted against acts or omissions of private individuals[709] in the following cases:

1. When the person against whom action is brought is in charge of the public service of education, in protection of the rights enshrined in Articles 13, 15, 16, 18, 19, 20, 23, 27, 29, 37 and 38 of the Constitution.
2. When the person against whom action is brought is in charge of rendering a public health service, to protect the rights to life, intimacy, equality and autonomy.
3. When the person against whom action is brought is in charge of rendering public services.

---

705 See Humberto NOGUEIRA ALCALÁ, "El derecho de amparo o protección de los derechos humanos, fundamentales o esenciales en Chile: evolución y perspectivas", in Humberto Nogueira Alcalá (Editor), *Acciones constitucionales de amparo y protección: realidad y perspectivas en Chile y América Latina*", Editorial Universidad de Talca, Talca 2000, p. 41

706 See Eduardo Jorge PRATS, *Derecho Constitucional*, Vol. II, Gaceta Judicial, Santo Domingo 2005, p. 390.

707 In a similar way to the injunctions admitted in the United Status against public services corporations. See in John BOURDEAU et al, "Injunctions" in Kevin Schroder, John Glenn and Maureen Placilla, *Corpus Juris Secundum*, Volume 43A, Thomson West, 2004, p. 182 ff.

708 See Rubén HERNÁNDEZ VALLE, *Derecho Procesal Constitucional*, Editorial Juricentro, San José 2001, pp. 275, 281 ff.

709 See Juan Carlos ESGUERRA, *La protección constitucional del ciudadano,* Legis, Bogotá 2004, p. 151.

4. When the request is directed against a private organization, against who effectively controls such organization or is the real beneficiary of the situation that caused the action, provided the claimant is in a position of subordination or defenselessness before such organization.
5. When the person against whom action is brought violates or threatens to violate Article 17 of the Constitution.
6. When the private entity is the one against which the request for habeas data would have been brought, pursuant to Article 15 of the Constitution.
7. When requesting the rectification of incorrect or erroneous information. In this case it is necessary to attach the transcription of the information or copy of the publication and of the rectification requested that was not published in such a way that its effectiveness be assured.
8. When the individual acts or should act in exercise of his or her public functions, in which case the same régime that regulates public authorities shall be applied.

When the request is for the tutela of the life or safety of the person who is in a position of subordination or defenselessness with respect to the matter against which action was brought. The minor who brings an action of tutela shall be presumed defenseless.

Finally, also in Ecuador, the amparo actions is admitted against entities that though not public authorities, they render public services by delegation or concession and in general against individuals but only when their actions or omissions cause harm or threats to constitutional rights and affect in a grave and direct way common, collective or diffuse interests (Art. 95,3)[710]. In this regard, for instance, amparo actions can be filed against political parties or their officials when their conduct violates the rights of other persons, as it has also being admitted in the United States[711].

V. THE PARTICIPATION OF THIRD PARTIES FOR THE DEFENDANT IN THE AMPARO SUIT

In the amparo suit, the injurer or damaging parties are those authorities, public officials, private persons, entities or corporations duly individuated whose actions or omissions are those precisely causing the harm or threats to the constitutional rights and guaranties of the plaintiff. Nonetheless, third parties can also act in the process, defending the injurer party position. It happens with those persons that, for instance, are beneficiaries of the authority act challenge. In this sense the Mexican Amparo Law provides that besides the injured and the injurer, are also considered party in the amparo suit, the persons that have obtained challenged act in their favor or those that could have direct interest in the act's endurance (Art. 5, III, c)[712]. In similar

710 Hernán Salgado Pesantes, *Manual de Justicia Constitucional Ecuatoriana*, Corporación Editora Nacional, Quito, 2004, p. 77.

711 *Maxey v. Washington State Democratic Committee*, 319 F. Supp. 673 (W.D. Wash. 1970), in John BOURDEAU et al, "Injunctions" in Kevin Schroder, John Glenn and Maureen Placilla, *Corpus Juris Secundum*, Volume 43A, Thomson West, 2004, p. 240.

712 See Eduardo FERRER MAC–GREGOR, *La acción constitucional de amparo en México y España. Estudio de derecho comparado*, Editorial Porrúa, México 2002, pp. 249–250.

sense in the Norte American procedure on injunctions, it is considered that all persons whose interest will necessarily be affected by the decree in a suit for injunction are properly joined as defendants[713].

Due to the general bilateral procedural rule, the principle applies in all Latin American countries, except in Chile, where, as mentioned, the bilateralism of the procedure is not admitted[714]. In some cases even the need for the participation of third parties for the defendant is necessary, as is the case in Venezuela on the amparo actions against judicial decisions, in which the party beneficiary of the challenged ruling must obligatorily be notified to participate in the procedure as defendant of the challenged decision.[715]

CHAPTER XIII

THE MOTIVES FOR THE AMPARO SUIT: THE INJURY OR THE THREAT OF VIOLATION TO THE PLAINTIFF'S CONSTITUTIONAL RIGHTS

The amparo action, as a specific judicial means for the protection of constitutional rights and guaranties, can be filed by the plaintiff when he is personally affected in his own rights, in a direct and present way; or when he is threatened to be harmed in those rights in an imminent way.

The personal character of the amparo suit is then related to the direct harm caused to the plaintiff or to the threat that affects such rights (which must be an imminent one).

I. THE GENERAL PERSONAL AND DIRECT CHARACTER OF THE INJURY

The claimant or plaintiff in the amparo suit must have suffered a direct, personal and present injury in his constitutional rights or must have been threatened in them.

That is, in cases of injury it must personally affect the claimant, in a direct and present way regarding his constitutional rights. If it harms only statutory established rights, or another person's rights or only affects the plaintiff in an indirect way, the action is inadmissible.

The Mexican Constitution, in this regard, refers to the need for the plaintiff to have "a personal and direct" harm (Art. 107,I), in the sense that his personal consti-

713 Silva V. ROMNEY, 473 F. 2d 287 (1st Cir. 1973); Greenhouse v. Greco, 368 F. Supp. 736 (W.D. La. 1973). See the reference in John BOURDEAU et al, "Injunctions" in Kevin Schroder, John Glenn and Maureen Placilla, *Corpus Juris Secundum*, Volume 43A, Thomson West, 2004, pp. 332–333.

714 See Juan Manuel ERRAZURIZ G. and Jorge Miguel OTERO A., *Aspectos procesales del recurso de protección*, Editorial Jurídica de Chile 1989, p. 149.

715 See Rafael CHAVERO, *El nuevo régimen del amparo constitucional en Venezuela*, Editorial Sherwood, Caracas 2001, pp. 489.

tutional rights must have been directly affected. That is why the claimant must be the 'affected" person (Argentina: Article 5; Peru: Article 39), the "aggrieved" person (Nicaragua, Article 23) or the one who "suffers" the harm (Brazil: Article 1). Consequently if the harm does not affect the plaintiff in his constitutional rights, in a personal and direct way, the action is considered inadmissible[716].

The foregoing means, first, that the rights that must be directly affected or harmed for the amparo action to be admissible must be of constitutional order, and second, that the harm must directly and personally affect the plaintiff. Consequently, rights just recognized in statutes without constitutional rank, cannot be protected by means of amparo actions, and this is one of the main distinctions between the North American injunctions and the amparo.

In this sense, in Venezuela the courts have ruled that the harm caused must always be the result of a violation of a constitutional right that must be "flagrant, vulgar, direct and immediate, which does not mean that the right or guarantee are not due to be regulated in statutes, but it in not necessary for the court to base its decision in the latter to determine if the of the violation of the constitutional right has effectively occurred"[717].

In other words, only direct and evident constitutional violations can be protected by means of amparo; thus, for instance, as ruled in 1991 by the Venezuelan courts, the internal electoral regime of political parties or of professional associations could not be the object of an amparo action funded in the right to vote set forth in the Constitution, "which only applies to the national electoral process [not being applied] to the internal electoral process of the political parties", concluding that the amparo only protects constitutional rights and guaranties and not legal (statutory) ones, and much less the ones contained in association's by–laws"[718]. In other decisions, the courts declared inadmissible amparo actions for the protection of rights when the allegations were only founded "in legal (statutory) considerations", as the right to work commonly conditioned by statutes regarding dismissals. Thus, the amparo is not the judicial mean for the protection of such right if the violation is only referred to the labor Law provisions"[719].

716 See Eduardo FERRER MAC–GREGOR, *La acción constitucional de amparo en México y España*, Editorial Porrúa, México 2002, pp. 386–387.

717 See Supreme Court of Justice, Case *Tarjetas Banvenez*, July 10, 1991, in *Revista de Derecho Público,* N° 47, Editorial Jurídica Venezolana, Caracas, 1991, pp. 169–170. See also decisión of may 20, 1994, Corte Primera de lo Contencioso Administrativa (Case *Federación Venezolana de Deportes Ecuestres)*; in *Revista de Derecho Público,* N° 57–58, Editorial Jurídica Venezolana, Caracas, 1994, p.

718 See decision of August, 8, 1991, *Revista de Derecho Público,* N° 47, Editorial Jurídica Venezolana, Caracas, 1991, p. 129.

719 See decision of October 8, 1990, *Revista de Derecho Público,* N° 44, Editorial Jurídica Venezolana, Caracas, 1990, pp. 139–140. In similar sense, the violation of the right to self defense because the right to cross examination of a witness was denied according to article 349 of the Procedural Civil Code, cannot be founded in article 68 of the Constitution because that would signify to analyze the violation of norms of statutary rank and not of constitutional rank. See decision of the Politico Administrative Chamber of the Supreme Court of Justice of

As mentioned, the violation of the constitutional right must be a direct violation caused by a concrete action or omission which the claimant must allege and must proof. The courts in Venezuela have ruled in this regard that

> "the amparo action can only be directed against a perfectly and determined act or omission, and not against a generic conduct; against an objective and real activity and not against a supposition regarding the intention of the presumed injurer, and against the direct and immediate consequences of the activities of the public body or officer. It is necessary, though, that the denounced actions directly affect the subjective sphere of the claimant, consequently excluding the generic conducts, even if they can affect in a tangential way on the matter.
>
> That is why the amparo action is not a popular action for denouncing against the illegitimacy of the public entities of control over convenience or opportunity, but a protector remedy of the claimant sphere when it is demonstrated that it has been directly affected"[720].

In another decision, the Supreme Court of Justice ruled abut the need that:

> The violation of the constitutional rights and guaranties be a direct and immediate consequence of the act, fact or omission, not being possible to attribute or assign to the injurer agent different results to those produced or to be produced. The right's violation must be the product of the harming act"[721].

The main consequence of being the injury a direct and immediate one regarding the claimant is that he has to prove his assertions, that is to say, in the amparo action the injured party has the burden to proof the personal and direct harm. Similar to the rules on injunctions, as resolved by the North American courts, according to which, "the party seeking an injunction, whether permanent or temporary, must establish some verifiable injury"[722].That is why, regarding documental proofs, the claimant must always present them with the filling of the action (Amparo Laws: Argentina, Article 7; Uruguay, Article 5).

II. THE ARBITRARY, ILLEGAL AND ILLEGITIMATE MANIFEST INJURY

On the other hand, the harm or injury caused to a constitutional right in order for an amparo action to be admitted, must be manifestly arbitrary, illegal or illegitimate, and consequence of a violation of the Constitution.

In this regard, for instance, the Argentinean Amparo Law, is precise in indicating that for an amparo action to be admissible it must be filed against any "manifestly arbitrary or illegal" act or omission of a public authority, that "harms, restricts, alters or threatens the constitutional rights and guaranties" (Art. 1). This feature of the challenged official action or omission to be manifestly illegal or arbitrary, is a consequence of the presumption of validity that as a general principle of public law, all

---

November 8, 1990, *Revista de Derecho Público,* N° 44, Editorial Jurídica Venezolana, Caracas, 1990, pp. 140–141

720 See decisión of December 2, 1993, *Revista de Derecho Público,* N° 55–56, Editorial Jurídica Venezolana, Caracas, 1993, pp. 302–303

721 See decisión of August 14, 1992, *Revista de Derecho Público,* N° 51, Editorial Jurídica Venezolana, Caracas, 1992, p. 145

722 See Kevin Schroder, John Glenn and Maureen Placilla (Editors), *Corpus Juris Secundum,* Vol. 43A, Thomson West, 2004, p 54.

official acts have. The Uruguayan Amparo law refers to acts issued with "manifest illegitimacy" (Art. 1); and the Brazilian Law, in similar sense, also set forth expressly that the *mandado de segurança* is established for the protection of constitutional rights when being violated "*ilegalmente ou com abuso do poder*" (Art 1)[723].

The challenged act or omission, thus, must be manifestly contrary to the legal order (*legalidad*), that is, the rules of law contained not only in the Constitution, but also in statutes and regulations; or it must be manifestly illegitimate, because it lacks of any legal support; or because it is manifestly arbitrary, that is, an act not reasonable or unjust; in other words, contrary to justice or to reason[724]. The same principle applies in the United States imposing to the plaintiff in civil right injunctions the burden to prove the alleged violations in order to destroy the presumption that the official acts are valid, which has been considered a limitation on judicial power to protect rights. As M. Glenn Abernathy and Perry have commented:

> "The courts do not automatically presume that all restraints on free choice are improper. The burden is thrown on the person attacking acts to prove that they are improper. This is most readily seen in cases involving the claim that an act of the legislature is unconstitutional...Judges also argue that acts of administrative officials should be accorded some presumption of validity. Thus a health officer who destroys food alleged by him to be unfit for consumption is presumed to have good reason for his action. The person whose property is so destroyed must bear the burden of proving bad faith on part of the official, if an action is brought as a consequence"[725].

Consequently, when expressly established in the statutes or not, the same principle applies in Latin America, in the sense that in the amparo action, the act or omission challenged by the plaintiff because it harms his rights, must be manifestly illegal, illegitimate, arbitrary or issued with abuse of power, which implies the need for the claimant on the contrary, to build his arguments upon reasonable basis, and to prove that the challenged act or omission of the public official is an unreasonable one.

III. THE ACTUAL AND REAL CHARACTER OF THE INJURY

Another general condition of the injury in order to be protected by the amparo action is its actual character, as is expressly provided in the Argentinean (Article 1) and Uruguayan (Amparo, Art 1) Laws, in the sense that the harm must be presently occurring and must not have ceased. In similar sense as it is the rule regarding the injunctions in the United States:

---

723 The principle is also referred to in Chile and Ecuador. Juan Manuel ERRAZURIZ G. and Jorge Miguel OTERO A., *Aspectos procesales del recurso de protección,* Editorial Jurídica de Chile, Santiago, 1989, pp. 51–55; Hernán SALGADO PESANTES, *Manual de Justicia Constitucional Ecuatoriana*, Corporación Editora Nacional, Quito 2004, p. 79.

724 See Alí Joaquín SALGADO, *Juicio de amparo y acción de inconstitucionalidad*, Astrea, Buenos Aires 1987, pp. 28–29.

725 See M. Glenn ABERNATHY and Barbara A. PERRY, *Civil Liberties under the Constitution*, University of South Carolina Press, 1993, p. 5

> "A petitioner is not entitled to an injunction where no injury to the petitioner is shown from the action sought to be prevented. Ordinarily, a person, in order to be entitled to injunctive relief, whether prohibitory or mandatory in its nature, must establish an actual and substantial, serious, injury, or an affirmative prospect of such an injury"[726].

The actual character of the injury regarding the amparo suit, as argued by the Venezuelan courts, signifies that the injury "must be alive, must be present in all its intensity", in other words, the actual character of the harm "refers to the present character, not to the past, nor to facts already happened, which appertain to the past, but to the present situation which can be prolonged in an in definitive length of time"[727].

In this regard, Article 6,1 of the Amparo law of Venezuela establishes as a cause of inadmissibility of the amparo action, that the violation would have not ceased, that is, "it must be actual, recent, alive"[728]. The principle is the same in Argentina, where if the harm has ceased, the claim by mean of amparo must be declared inadmissible[729]. In Honduras (Art. 46,6 Constitutional Justice Law) and Nicaragua (Art. 51,3, Amparo Law) prescribes that the recourse for amparo is inadmissible when the effects of the challenged act have ceased, in which case the court could reject *in limene* (*de plano*) the claim. Also in México, Article 73,XVI of the Amparo law declares inadmissible the amparo action when the challenged acts have ceased in their effects, or when even those acts subsist, they cannot produce material or legal effects whatsoever, because they have lost their object or substance. In Peru, the Constitutional procedure Code also prescribes the inadmissibility of the amparo action when at the moment of its filing the threat or the violation of the constitutional rights has ceased (Art. 5,5).

In this regard, the First Court on Judicial Review of administrative actions of Venezuela resolved the inadmissibility of an action for amparo because, during the proceedings, the challenged act was repealed[730]. The Supreme Court also decided that in the proceedings of an amparo suit the harm must not have ceased before the judge decision; on the contrary, if the harm has ceased, the judge must declare *in limine litis*, the inadmissibility of the action[731]. For instance, in the case of an

---

726 See Kevin Schroder, John Glenn and Maureen Placilla (Editors), *Corpus Juris Secundum*, Vol. 43A, Thomson West, 2004, p 66.

727 See decision of the First Court on Judicial Review of Administrative Action of May 7, 1987 (Caso: *Desarrollo 77 C.A.*), in FUNEDA *15 años de Jurisprudencia cit.*, p. 78.

728 See decision of the First Court on Judicial Review of Administrative Action of November 13, 1988, in FUNEDA, *15 años de la Jurisprudencia, cit.*, p. 134

729 Alí Joaquín SALGADO, *Juicio de amparo y acción de inconstitucionalidad,* Astrea, Buenos Aires 1987, p. 27

730 See decision of the First Court on Judicial Review of Administrative Action of August 14, 1992 in *Revista de Derecho Público,* N° 51, Editorial Jurídica Venezolana, Caracas, 1992, p. 154.

731 See decisions of the Politico Administrative Chamber of the former Supreme Court of Justice of December 15, 1992, *Revista de Derecho Público* N° 52, Editorial Jurídica Venezolana, Caracas, 1992, p. 164; and of May 27, 1993, *Revista de Derecho Público,* nos 53–54, Edito-

amparo against the omission of a court to decide a case, which as alleged harms the rights of somebody, if before the filing of the action or during the proceeding the challenged court has decided, from that moment on the harm can be considered to have ceased[732]

In similar sense, the Constitutional Chamber of Costa Rica has determined that it has not jurisdictional present interest to examine the circumstances for the suspension [of the effects on an act], when [the act has been repealed], and thus, when the affected party has been reestablished in the enjoyment of his rights before filing the recourse[733]. But regarding the actual character of the harm, it is possible to consider that when new a fact modifies to such an extreme an already known and declared situation as not being present at the moment the harm occurred, then the new argument could provoke different or contradictory results regarding the previous ones. This could occur, for instance, when the amparo judge, that must know regarding an specific, actual and determined situation, could determine the existence of a new fact that had not occurred at the moment of the filing, and that could alter or modify that situation, in which case, the action can be admitted and decided protecting the plaintiff, even if it had been beforehand rejected[734].

Regarding the actual character of the harm for granting the amparo or constitutional protection, the rule in federal cases in the United States is that an actual controversy must exist not only at the time the action was initiated, but at all stages of the proceeding, even at appellate or certiorari review. Nonetheless, in the important case *Roe v. Wade,* 410 U.S. 113 (1973), in which the Supreme Court expanded the women's right to privacy, striking down states laws banning abortion. The Court recognized that even if this right of privacy was not explicitly mentioned in the Constitution, it was guaranteed as a constitutional right for protecting "a woman's decision whether or not to terminate her pregnancy", even though admitting that the states legislation could regulate the factors governing the abortion decision at some point in pregnancy based on "safeguarding health, maintaining medical standards and in protecting potential life".

But the point in the case was that, pending the procedure, the pregnancy period of the claimant came to term, so the injury claimed lost its present character. Nonetheless, the Supreme Court ruled in the case that

---

rial Jurídica Venezolana, Caracas, 1993, p. 264. *Cfr.* Decision of the First Court on Judicial Review of Administrative Actions of December 12, 1992 (Caso *Allan R. Brewer–Carías*), *Revista de Derecho Público,* N° 49, Editorial Jurídica Venezolana, Caracas, 1992, pp. 131–132

732 See Rafael CHAVERO G., *El nuevo régimen del amparo constitucional en Venezuela,* Editorial Sherwood, caracas 2001, pp. 237–238.

733 Decision N° 1051–97, in Rubén HERNÁNDEZ VALLE, *Derecho Procesal Constitucional,* Editorial Juricentro, San José 2001, pp. 244–245.

734 *Cfr.* decision of the Politico Administrative Chamber of the former Supreme Court of Justice of August 5, 1992, *Revista de Derecho Público,* N° 51, Editorial Jurídica Venezolana, Caracas, 1992, p. 145.

> "[When], as here, pregnancy is a significant fact in the litigation, the normal 266–day human generation period is so short that pregnancy will come to term before the usual appellate process is complete. If that termination makes a case moot, pregnancy litigation seldom will survive much beyond the trial stage, and appellate review will be effectively denied. Our law should not be that rigid. Pregnancy comes more than once to the same woman, and in the general population, if man is to survive, it will always be with us. Pregnancy provides a classic justification for a conclusion of non mootness. It truly could be 'capable of repetition, yet evading review'"[735].

In Peru, even though the same general rule is established regarding the inadmissibility "when at the filing of the action the harm or threat to a constitutional rights has ceased", it has been considered that when the harm or threat ceases after the action has been filed, the Constitutional Procedure Code allows the continuation of the proceedings, taking into account the harm produced, and that the amparo be granted[736].

On the other hand, as established in the Amparo laws of México (Art. 73, IX) and Honduras (Art. 46,5), in cases of injuries or harms produced to constitutional rights, the amparo action can only be filed when the injury is a reparable one or the harm is reversible; thus, the amparo action is inadmissible when the challenged act provoking the harm has already been accomplished or has already been completed (*consumado*) in an irreparable way. That is, amparo actions cannot be the adequate remedy regarding fait accompli.

In México, the classical example regarding this condition of admissibility of the amparo suit, has been the situation of an executed death sentence[737], in which case it will be wholly irrelevant to file an amparo action. The non admissibility condition applies to all cases "when it is materially or juridically impossible to return the injured party to the position occupied prior to the violation"[738]; or when in general terms the challenged act is in fact irreparable because it is "physically impossible to turn back the things to the stage they had before the violation"[739].

---

735 See M. Glenn ABERNATHY and Barbara A. PERRY, *Civil Liberties under the Constitution*, University of Scout carolina Press, 1993, pp. 4–5

736 See Luis SANZ DÁVALOS, "Las innovaciones del Código Procesal constitucional en el proceso constitucional de amparo", in Susana CASTAÑEDA et al, *Introducción a los procesos constitucionales. Comentarios al Código Procesal Constitucional,* Jurista Editores, Lima 1005, p 126.

737 Tesis 32, II, 90. Supreme Corte, Jurisprudencia de la Suprema Corte. See the reference in Richard D. BAKER, *Judicial Review in Mexico. A Study of the Amparo Suit*, University of Austin Press, Austin 1971, p. 95, note 11.

738 See Robert D. BAKER, *Judicial Review in Mexico. A Study of the Amparo Suit*, University of Austin Press, Austin 1971, p.96

739 Tesis "Actos consumados de modo irreparable", Apéndice al Semanario Judicial de la federación 1917–1988, Segunda Parte, salas y Tesis Comunes, pp. 106–107. See the referente in Eduardo FERRER MAC–GREGOR, *La acción constitucional de amparo en México y España*, Edit. Porrúa, México 2002, p. 388, notes 232 and 233.

This is also the general condition for the admissibility of the injunctions in the United States, as has been decided by the courts, constructing the following judicial doctrine:

> The purpose of an injunction is to restrain actions that have not yet been taken and, therefore, an injunction will not lie to restrain an act already completed at the time the action is instituted, since the injury has already been done. There is no cause for the issuance of an injunction unless the alleged wrong is actually occurring or is actually threatened or apprehended with reasonable probability and a court cannot enjoin an act after it has been completed. An act which has been completed, such that it no longer presents a justiciable controversy, does not give grounds for the issuance of an injunction[740].

IV. THE RESTORATIVE NATURE OF AMPARO SUIT AND THE REPARABLE CHARACTER OF THE INJURY

In general terms, regarding violations of constitutional rights, the amparo action in Latin America has a restorative character, tending to restitute the affected right to the situations existing when the right was harmed, eliminating the detrimental act or fact, or to restore the personal situation of the plaintiff to one closer to the existing before the injury. Regarding threats to rights, the amparo action has a preventive character, in the sense that it seeks to impede the injury to be produced or completed.

In this sense, regarding constitutional rights that has been violated, the amparo action has similarities with the so called reparative injunctions in the United States, which seeks to eliminate the effects of a past wrong or to compel the defendant to engage in a course of action that seeks to correct those effects[741]. As has been explained by Owen M. Fiss:

> To see how it works, let us assume that a wrong has occurred (such as an act of discrimination). Then the missions of an injunction –classically conceived as a preventive instrument– would be to prevent the recurrence of the wrongful conduct in the future (stop discriminating and do not discriminate again). But in *United States v. Louisiana* (380 U.S. 145, (1965)), a voting discrimination case, Justice Black identified still another mission for the injunction – the elimination of the effects of the past wrong the past discrimination). The reparative injunction –long thought by the nineteenth–century textbook writers, such as High (*A Treatise on the Law of Injunction* 3, 1873) to be an analytical impossibility– was thereby legitimated. And in the same vein, election officials have been ordered not only to stop discriminating in the future elections, but also to set aside a past election and to run a new election as a means of removing the taint of discrimination that infected the first one (*Bell v. Southwell*, 376 F.2de 659 (5TH Cir. 1976)). Similarly, public housing officials have been ordered both to cease discriminating on the basis of race in their future choices of sites and to build units in the white areas as a means of eliminating the effects of the past segregative policy (placing public housing projects only in the black areas of the city)(*Hills v. Gautreaux*, 425 U.S. 284 (1976)).[742]

---

740 See Kevin Schroder, John Glenn, Maureen Placilla (Editors), *Corpus Juris Secundum*, Vol 43A, Thomson West, 2004, p. 73.

741 Seen Owen M. Fiss, *The Civil Rights Injunction*, Indiana University Press 1978, p.7.

742 Seen Owen M. Fiss, *The Civil Rights Injunction*, Indiana University Press 1978, pp.7–10

Accordingly, as also decided by the former Supreme Court of Justice of Venezuela, in 1996:

> One of the principal characteristics of the amparo action is to be a restorative (restablecedor) judicial means, the mission of which is to restore the infringed situation or, what is the same, to put the claimant again in the enjoyment of his constitutional rights which has been infringed. The abovementioned characteristic of this judicial means, besides been recognized by court decisions doctrine and by legal writers, is set forth in the Amparo Law, when establishing in Article 6,3, as a motive for the inadmissibility of the action, "when the violation of the constitutional rights and guarantees, turns on in an evident irreparable situation, being impossible to restore the infringed legal situation. It is understood that the acts that by means of the amparo can not be turn up thinks to the stage they had before the violation are irreparable"[743].

Due to this restorative character of the amparo, no new juridical situations can be created by means of this judicial action, nor is it possible to modify those in existence[744]. The Constitutional Chamber of the Supreme Tribunal of Justice, in a decision of January 20, 2000 ruled in this sense that a claimant cannot pretend to obtain the claimed asylum right by means of an amparo action, which through he pretended to obtain the Venezuelan citizenship but without following the established procedure. The Court ruled in the case, that:

> "This amparo action has been filed in order to seek a decision from this court, consisting in the legalization of the situation of the claimant, which would consist in the constitution or creation of a civil and juridical status the petitioner did not have before filing the complaint for amparo".

Thus this petition was considered "contrary to the restorative nature of the amparo"[745].

In another decision issued on April 4, 1999, the former Supreme Court in a similar sense, declared inadmissible an amparo action in a case in which the claimant was asking to be appointed as judge in a specific court or to be put in a juridical situation that he did not have before the challenged act was issued. The Court decided that in the case, it was impossible for such purpose to file an amparo action, declaring it inadmissible, thus ruling as follows:

> "This Court must highlight that one of the essential characteristics of the amparo action is it reestablishing effects, that is, literally, to put one thing in the stage it possessed beforehand, in its natural stage, which for the claimant means to be put in the situation he had before the production of the claimed violation. The foregoing means that the plaintiff claim must be directed to seek 'the reestablishment of the infringed juridical situation'; the amparo actions are

743 See decisión of February 6, 1996, case: Asamblea legislativa del Estado Bolívar. See in Rafael CHAVERO, *El nuevo régimen del amparo constitucional en Venezuela*, Ed. Sherwood, Caracas 2001, pp. 185, 242–243.

744 See decisions of the Politico Administrative Chamber of the former Supreme Court of Justice, of October 27, 1993 (Case *Ana Drossos*), and November 4, 1993 (Case *Partido Convergencia*), in *Revista de Derecho Público,* nos 55–56, Editorial Jurídica Venezolana, Caracas, 1993, p. 340.

745 See Case *Domingo Ramírez Monja*. See the reference in Rafael CHAVERO, *El nuevo régimen del amparo constitucional en Venezuela*, Ed. Sherwood, Caracas 2001, p. 244.

> inadmissible when the reestablishment of the infringed situation is not possible; when through them the claimant seeks a compensation of damages, because the latter cannot be a substitution of the harmed right; nor when the plaintiff pretends the court to create a right or a situation that did not exist before the challenged act, fact or omission. All this is the exclusion for the possibility for the amparo to have constitutive effects"[746].

What in the suit for amparo can certainly be done is to restore things to the stage they had at the moment of the injury, making the challenged and proved infringing fact or act regarding a constitutional right or guarantee, to disappear. Thus when the violation to a constitutional right turns up to be an irreparable situation, the amparo actions is inadmissible. This is congruent with what Article 29 of the Venezuelan Constitution and Article 1 of Amparo Law provide in that the amparo action seeks to "the immediate restoring of the infringed juridical situation or to the situation more similar to it"[747].

In this regard, the former Supreme Court of Justice declared inadmissible an amparo action against a undue tax collecting act, once paid, considering that in such case it was not possible to restore the infringed juridical situation[748]; and the First Court on Judicial review of administrative action on a decision of September 7, 1989, declared inadmissible an amparo action referred to maternity protection rights (pre and post natal leave) filed after the childbirth, ruling that:

> "It is impossible for the plaintiff to be restored in her presumed violated rights to enjoy a pre and post natal leave during 6 month before and after the childbirth, because we are now facing an irremediable situation that can not be restored, due that it is impossible to date back the elapsed time"[749].

In similar sense, the former Supreme Court of Justice in a decision of November 1, 1990, considered inadmissible an amparo action, when the only way to restore the infringed juridical situation was declaring the nullity of an administrative act, which the amparo judge cannot do in its decision[750].

---

746 Decision of April 21, 1999, Case *J. C. Marín*. See the reference in Rafael CHAVERO, *El nuevo régimen del amparo constitucional en Venezuela*, Ed. Sherwood, Caracas, 2001, pp. 244–245

747 See First Court on Judicial review of Administrative Action, decision of January 14, 1992, in *Revista de Derecho Público,* N° 49, Editorial Jurídica Venezolana, Caracas, 1992, p. 130; and decision of the former Supreme Court of Justice, Politico Administrative Chamber, of March 4, 1993, in *Revista de Derecho Público,* N° 53–54, Editorial Jurídica Venezolana, Caracas, 1993, p. 260.

748 CSJ–CP 21–3–88– *Revista de Derecho Público,* N° 34, Editorial Jurídica Venezolana, Caracas, 1988, p. 114

749 See decision of First Court on Judicial Review of Administrative Actions of September 17, 1989, *Revista de Derecho Público* N° 40, Editorial Jurídica Venezolana, Caracas, 1989, p. 111.

750 See decisions of the Politico Administrative Chamber of the former Supreme Court of Justice of November 1, 1990, *Revista de Derecho Publico,* N° 44, Editorial Jurídica Venezolana, Caracas, 1990, pp. 152–153; *Cfr.* decision of the First Court on Judicial Review of Administrative Actions of September 10, 1992, *Revista de Derecho Público,* N° 51, Editorial Jurídica Venezolana, Caracas, 1992, p. 155.

The abovementioned can be considered the general trend regarding the amparo regulations in Latin America. In México, Article 73,X of the Amparo Law prescribes that the amparo in inadmissible against acts adopted in a judicial or administrative proceeding, when due to the change of the juridical situation, the violations claimed in the proceeding must be considered as completed in an irreparable way. It is also the general trend regarding the tutela in Colombia where the Law provides that the action is inadmissible "when it is evident that the violation originated a completed harm, unless the action or omissions harming the rights continues".

In conclusion, in general terms, the amparo suit imposes the need for the harm to possibly be amended, or if it has not been initiated, to be restored by a judicial order impeding its execution, or if it has continuous effects, for its suspension in case it has not been initiated; and regarding those effects already accomplished, the possibility to date back things to the stage before the harm commenced. What the amparo judge cannot do is create situations that were inexistent at the moment of the action's filing; or to correct harms to rights when it is too late to do so. As resolved by the First Court on Judicial Review of administrative action of Venezuela, regarding a municipal order for the demolition of a building, in the sense that if the demolition was already executed, the amparo judge cannot decide the matter, because of the irreparable character of the harm[751].

The First Court also ruled in a case decided in February 4, 1999 regarding a public university position contest that, "the pretended aggrieved party is seeking to be allowed to be registered itself in the public contest for the Chair of Pharmacology in the School of Medicine José María Vargas, but at the present time, the registration was impossible due to the fact that the delay had elapsed the previous year, and consequently the harm produced must be considered as irreparable, declaring the inadmissible the action for amparo"[752].

Another example that can also be mentioned refers to the right to the protection of health, different to a possible right to have one's health restored. The former Supreme Court of Justice, in a decision of March 3, 1990, ruled as following:

> "The Court considers that the infringed juridical situation is reparable by means of amparo, due to the fact that the plaintiff can be satisfied in his claims through such judicial means. From the judicial procedure point of view, it is possible for the protection of health the possibility for the judge to order the competent authority to assume precise conduct for the medical protection of the claimant conduct. The claim of the petitioner is to have a particular and adequate health care, which can be obtained via the amparo action, seeking the reestablishment of a harmed right, and this can be obtained by means of amparo. In this case, the

751 See the January 1st, 1999 decision (Case: *B. Gómez*). See the reference in Rafael Chavero, *El nuevo régimen del amparo constitucional en Venezuela*, Ed. Sherwood, Caracas, 2001, p. 242.

752 See Case *C. Negrín*. See the reference in Rafael CHAVERO, *El nuevo régimen del amparo constitucional en Venezuela*, Ed. Sherwood, Caracas, 2001, p. 243.

claimant is not seeking her health to be restored to the stage it had before, but to have a particular health care, which is perfectly valid"[753].

In Peru, the Constitutional Procedure Code also prescribes that the amparo action, as well as all constitutional proceedings, are inadmissible when at the moment of its filing, the violation of the constitutional rights has become irreparable (Art. 5,5). Nonetheless, being the purpose of the constitutional processes to protect constitutional rights, reestablishing the thighs to the stage they had before the constitutional rights violation or threat or prescribing the accomplishment of a legal mandate or an administrative act, the Code establishes that if after the filing of the claim, the aggression or threat has ceased because of a voluntary decision of the aggressor, or if the harm turns up to be irreparable, the court, taking into account the injury, will grant the claim indicating the scope of its decision and ordering the defendant to refrain from performing again the actions or omissions that provoked the filing of the suit.

V. THE PREVENTIVE NATURE OF AMPARO SUIT AND THE IMMINENT CHARACTER OF THE THREAT

The amparo suit is not only the effective judicial means for the restoration of the injured constitutional rights that has been harmed, similar to the reparative or restorative civil rights injunctions, but it is also the effective judicial means for the protection of such rights and guaranties when threatened to be violated or harmed. This latter amparo suit is then similar to the preventive civil rights injunctions which, in this case, "seeks to prohibit some discrete act or series of acts from occurring in the future"[754], and is designed "to avoid future harm to a party by prohibiting or mandating certain behavior ay another party. The injunction is 'preventive' in the sense of avoiding harm"[755].

All the amparo laws on Latin America expressly refers to the possibility of filing the amparo suit not only against actual violation of constitutional rights but also and basically against threats (*amenaza*) of harming or injuring constitutional rights and guaranties; threats that in general terms must also be real and certain, but additionally, must be immediate, imminent, possible and realizable (Nicaragua, Articles 51, 57, 79; Peru, Article 2; Venezuela, Articles 2; 6,2).

---

753 See in *Revista de Derecho Público,* N° 42, Editorial Jurídica Venezolana, Caracas, 1990, p. 107

754 See Owen M. FISS, *The Civil Rights Injunction*, Indiana University Press, 1978, p. 7

755 See William M. TABB and Eliane W. SHOBEN, *Remedies*, Thomson West, 2005, p. 22. The last sentence is very important from the terminological point of view when comparing the injunctions with the amparo suits: in Spanish the word "*preventivo*" is used in procedural law (*medidas preventivas o cautelares*) to refers to the "temporary": or "preliminary" orders or restraints that in North America the judge can issue during the proceeding. So the preventive character of the amparo and of the injunctions cannot be confused with the "*medidas preventivas*" or temporary or preliminary measures that the courts can issue during the trial for the immediate protection of rights, facing the prospect of an irremediable harm that can be caused.

As decided by the Venezuelan courts: to threaten means to provoke fear to others or to make others feel in danger regarding their rights; conversely, a violation is a situation in which a fact has already been accomplished, so no threat is possible[756]. In this regard, the Colombian Constitutional Court has drawn the distinction between harm and threat, as follows:

> "The harm has implicit the concept of injury or prejudice. A right is harmed when its object is damaged. A right is threatened when that same object, without being destroyed, is put in a situation of suffering a decrease"[757].
>
> "Harm and threat of fundamental rights are two different concepts clearly distinguishable: the former needs an objective verification that the tutela judges must do, by proving its empirical occurrence and their constitutional repercussions; the latter, conversely, adds subjective and objective criteria, conforming itself not by the intention of the public officer or the individual, but by the result the action or omission can have regarding the spirit of the affected person. Thus, in order to determine the constitutional hypothesis of the threat, the confluence of subjective and objectives elements are needed: the fear of the plaintiff that feels his fundamental rights are in danger of perish and the validation of such perception by means of external objective elements, the significance of which is the one offered by the temporal and historical circumstances in which the facts are developing"[758]

A threat is then, a potential harm or violation, that is imminent and to occur soon, regarding which the same Constitutional Court of Colombia has said:

> "A threat to a fundamental constitutional right has multiple expressions: it can be referred to the specific circumstances of a person regarding the exercise of the right; to the existence of positive and unequivocal signs regarding the intention of a person capable to execute acts that can violate the right; or be represented in the challenge of someone (attempt), with direct repercussion on the right; also it can be constituted by non deliberated acts that, according to its characteristics, can lead the amparo court to be convinced that if no order is issued, impeding the conduct to continue, the violation of the right will be produced; also it can correspond to an authority omission whose extension in time allows the risk to appear or to increase; its configuration is also feasible in case of the existence of a norm –authorization or mandate– contrary to the Constitution, the application of which in the concrete case would be in itself an attack or a disregard of the fundamental"[759]

Of course there are some constitutional rights that if they are not protected against threats, they could lose all sense in their selves. It happens with the right to life, in the sense that if someone has received imminent death threats, the only way

---

756 Decision First Court on Judicial Review of Administrative Actions of July 16, 1092, *Revista de Derecho Público,* Nº 51, Editorial Jurídica Venezolana, Caracas, 1992, p. 155

757 Decision T–412 of June 17, 1992. See he references in Juan Carlos ESGUERRA PORTOCARRERO, *La protección constitucional del ciudadano,* Legis, Bogotá 2005, p. 147; and in Federico GONZÁLEZ CAMPOS, *La tutela. Interpretación doctrinaria y jurisprudencial,* Ediciones Jurídicas Gustavo IBÁÑEZ, Bogotá, 1994, pp. 46–47.

758 Decision T–439 of July 2, 1992. See he references in Juan Carlos ESGUERRA PORTOCARRERO, *La protección constitucional del ciudadano,* Legis, Bogotá, 2005, p. 148

759 See decision T– 349 of August 27, 1993. See the references in Rafael CHAVERO, *El nuevo régimen del amparo constitucional en Venezuela,* Ed. Sherwood, Caracas, 2001, pp. 238–239.

to guarantee the right to life is by avoiding the concretion of the threats, for instance, providing the person with due police protection.

According to Article 2 of the Venezuelan Amparo Law, the threats that can be protected by the amparo suits, must be imminent, adding Article 6,1 of the same Law that the action for amparo will not be admitted when the threat of violation of a constitutional right has ceased, or when the threat against a constitutional right or guarantee is not "immediate, possible and feasible (Art. 6,2)[760]. Regarding these general conditions, the Venezuelan former Supreme Court of Justice, ruled that they must be concurrent conditions when referred to the constitutional protection against harms that will soon be done by someone to the rights of others[761].

In similar sense, the Constitutional Chamber of the Supreme Court of Costa Rica has ruled that "according to Article 29 (of the Constitutional Jurisdiction Law), the amparo against a threat regarding a fundamental right can only be granted if the threat is certain, real, effective and imminent; thus, those probable prejudices not capable of being objectively apprehended cannot be protected by amparo,"[762]

In this regard, the *jurisprudencia* of the Supreme Court of México has developed as a non admissibility cause for the amparo suit, when the action refers to "future and probable acts"[763]. This refers to acts that have not yet occurred, thus referring to injuries that not only do not presently exist but may never be inflicted; in other words, "simple futurity is not in itself a sufficient bar to the suit. If the execution of the act is imminent and certain, although not formally completed or in process, the amparo suit is admissible"[764]. In the same sense in Ecuador, regarding the "imminent" character of the harm prescribed in Article 95 of the Constitution must be to occur in the near future, as a true potential injury that is not a mere conjecture. Addi-

760 *Cfr.* See decisions of the Politico Administrative Chamber of the former Supreme Court of Justice of June 9, 1988, *Revista de Derecho Público,* N° 35, Editorial Jurídica Venezolana, Caracas, 1988, p. 114; and of August 14, 1992, *Revista de Derecho Público,* N° 51, Editorial Jurídica Venezolana, Caracas, 1992, pp. 158–159; and of the First Court on Judicial Review of Administrative Actions of June 30, 1988, *Revista de Derecho Público,* N° 35, Editorial Jurídica Venezolana, Caracas, 1988, p. 115.

761 See decisions of the Politico Administrative Chamber of the Supreme Court of Justice of June 24, 1993, *Revista de Derecho Público,* N° 55–56, Editorial Jurídica Venezolana, Caracas, 1993, p. 289; and of March 22, 1995 (Case: *La Reintegradora*), in Rafael CHAVERO, *El nuevo régimen del amparo constitucional en Venezuela*, Ed. Sherwod, Caracas 2001, p. 239

762 See Vote 295–93. See the references in Rubén HERNÁNDEZ VALLE, *Derecho Procesal constitucional*, Editorial Juricentro, 2001, p. 222.

763 Tesis jurisprudencial 74, *Apéndice al Semanario Judicial de la Federación*, 1917–1988, Segunda parte, salas y tesis Comunes, p. 123. See the reference in Eduardo FERRER MAC–GREGOR, *La acción constitucional de amparo en México y España,* Edit. Porrúa, México, 2002, p.395.

764 Tesis 44 and 45. *Jurisprudencia de la Suprema Corte*, pp. 110, 113. See the referencie in Richard D. BAKER, *Judicial Review in México. A study of the Amparo Suit*, University of Texas Press, Austin, 1971, p. 96, note 12.

tionally, the harm must be concrete and real and the claimant must prove how it affects his rights[765].

In the same sense, in Mexico the courts have ruled regarding the imminent character of the harm that they are those that have been sufficiently proved that they will occur, because for instance, previous actions had been taken or they will ineludible be consequence of past facts also proved[766]. This distinguishes the imminent actions from those already existing or from those just to be occurring in the future. What is certain is that if the amparo action were only to be admitted against existing facts, the affected party, even though having complete knowledge of the near occurrence of a harm, in order to file the amparo action, would have to patiently wait for the act to be issued, with all its harming consequences.

But what is basically needed for the amparo against threats regarding constitutional rights is its imminent character. This rule has also been developed in the United States as an essential requirement for preventive injunctions, in the sense that courts will order them only when the threatened harm is imminent, in order to prohibit future conduct; and not when the harm is considered remote, potential or speculative. *In Reserve Mining Co. v. Environmetal Protection Agency* 513 F.2d, 492 (8th Cir 1975), the Circuit Court did not grant the requested injunction ordering Reserve Mining Company to cease discharging wastes from its iron ore processing plant in Silver Bay, Minnesota, into the ambient air of Silver bay and the waters of lake Superior, because even though the plaintiff has established that the discharges give rise to a "potential threat to the public health…no harm to the public health has been shown to have occurred to this date and the danger to health is not imminent. The evidence calls for preventive and precautionary steps. No reason exists which requires that Reserve terminate its operations at once"[767]. In other classically cited case, *Fletcher v. Bealey*, 28 Ch. 688 (1885), referred to waste deposits in the plaintiff land by the defendant, the judge ruled that being the action brought to prevent continuing damages, for a *quia timet* action, two ingredients are necessary:

> "There must, if no actual damage is proved, be proof of imminent danger, and there must also be proof that the apprehended damage will, if it comes, be very substantial. I should almost say it must be proved that it will be irreparable, because, if the danger is not proved to be so imminent that no one can doubt that, if the remedy is delayed, the damage will be suffered, I think it must be shown that, if the damage does occur at any time, it will come in such a way and under such circumstances that it will be impossible for the Plaintiff to protect himself against it if relief is denied to him in a *quia timet* action"[768].

---

765 See Hernán SALGADO PESANTES, *Manual de Justicia Constitucional Ecuatoriana*, Corporación Editora nacional, Quito 2004, p.80.

766 Joaquin BRAGE CAMAZANO, *La Jurisdicción Constitucional de la Libertad. Teoría general, Argentina, México, Corte Interamericana de Derechos Humanos*, Ed. Porrúa, México, 2005, pp. 171–173

767 See the comments in Owen M. FISS and Doug RENDELMAN, *Injunctions*, The Foundation Press, Mineola New York, 1984, pp. 116 ff.

768 See the reference in Owen M. FISS and Doug RENDELMAN, *Injunctions*, The Foundation Press, Mineola New York, 1984, pp. 11o–111.

As happens also regarding injunctions in the United States, the amparo in Latin American Countries cannot be granted "merely to allay the fears and apprehensions or to soothe the anxieties of individuals, since such fears and apprehensions may exist without substantial reasons and be absolutely groundless or speculative"[769]. The amparo, as the injunction, is an extraordinary remedy "designed to prevent serious harm, is not to be used to protect a person from mere inconvenience or speculative and insubstantial injury"[770].

As mentioned, the imminence of the harm must be certain, so that for example, the Mexican courts have ruled that mere possibility for the authorities to exercise their powers of investigation and control, cannot be sufficient for the filing of an amparo action[771]. In this same sense it is regulated, regarding the tutela action, in Article 3 of Decree 306–92 of Colombia".

> **Article 3:** *When it does not exist threat to a fundamental constitutional right*: It will be understood that a fundamental constitutional right will not be threaten by the only fact of the opening of an administrative enquiry by the competent authority, subjected to the procedure regulated by law.

In the same sense, the Supreme Court of Justice of Venezuela ruled in 1989 that

> "the opening of a disciplinary administrative inquiry is not enough to justify the protection of a party by means of the judicial remedy of amparo, moreover if the said proceeding, in which all needed defenses can be exercised, may conclude in a decision discarding the incriminations against the party with the definitive closing of the disciplinary process, without any sanction to the party"[772].

On the other hand, the threats regarding which constitutional rights can be protected by the amparo suit must be proven by the claimant, as threats against his rights that are precisely made by the defendant. That is why, the Argentinean courts for instance, have rejected an amparo action against non proved threats, for instance, when a mother filed a complaint asking the police protection to avoid an order of seizure of a minor, issued by a foreign court, because the existence of the order was not proved, nor sufficient elements for judging the case were alleged in order to prove that the local authorities were going to fail to apply the legal dispositions that

---

769 See Kevin Schroder, John Glenn and Maureen Placilla (Editors), *Corpus Juris Secundum*, Vol. 43A, Thomson West, 2004, p. 57

770 Kevin Schroder, John Glenn and Maureen Placilla (Editors), *Corpus Juris Secundum*, Vol. 43A, Thomson West, 2004, pp. 57–58.

771 See *Semanario Judicial de la Federación*, Tomo I, Segunda parte–2, p. 697. See the reference in Joaquín BRAGE CAMAZANO, *La Jurisdicción Constitucional de la Libertad. Teoría general, Argentina, México, Corte Interamericana de Derechos Humanos*, Ed. Porrúa, México 2005, p. 173, note 269

772 See decision of the Politico Administrative Chamber of October 26, 1989 (Case *Gisela Parra Mejía*). See the reference in Rafael CHAVERO, *El nuevo régimen del amparo constitucional en Venezuela*, Ed. Sherwood, Caracas 2001, pp. 191, 241,

apply to the execution in the country of foreign judicial decisions, which prescribes enough guarantees for the defense of rights and to protect internal public order[773].

The proof of the harm can also be based on previous acts or conducts of the defendant, or on his past pattern of conduct. One example, in the United States, as resumed by Tabb and Shoben, is the case *Galella v. Onassis* (S.D.N.Y. 1972) originated in the claim of the wife of J. F. Kennedy, the former President of the United States, seeking for an injunction against a professional free–lance photographer to restrain him from violating her rights of privacy. "The evidence showed that the photographer had repeatedly engaged in harassing behavior of the Onassis family in order to obtain pictures, but each time the invasive behavior was different. Based upon the pattern of past conduct, the court concluded that the photographer's behavior would continue indefinitely in the future. The evidence on imminency was very strong because the photographer had even sent an advertisement to customers announcing future anticipated pictures of Onassis. Even though the pattern of behavior was varied in the types of invasive conduct, the overall nature of it was harassing. With sufficient evidence, even an unpredictable pattern can establish imminency"[774].

The threat must also be attributed to the defendant; on the contrary, the amparo action must be rejected. It was the case of an amparo action brought before the former Venezuelan Supreme Court of Justice in 1999, against the President of the Republic, denouncing as injuring acts possible measures to be adopted by the National Constituent Assembly convened by the President, once it were installed. The Court rejected the action not only because "the reasons alleged by the plaintiff were of eventual and hypothetical nature, which contradicts the need of an objective and real harm or threat to constitutional rights or guarantees" in order for the amparo to be admissible; but said, regarding the alleged defendant in the case, the following:

> "This court must say, that the action for constitutional amparo serves to give protection against situations that in a direct way could produce harms regarding the plaintiff's constitutional rights or guarantees, seeking the restoration of its infringed juridical situation. In this case, the person identified as plaintiff (President of the Republic) could not be by himself the one to produce the eventual harm which would condition the voting rights of the plaintiff, and the fear that the organization of the constituted braches of government could be modified, would be attributed to the members of those that could be elected to the National Constituent Assembly not yet elected. Thus in the case there does not exist the immediate relation between the plaintiff and the defendants needed in he amparo suit"[775].

Another aspect to be mentioned is the possibility to file an amparo action against the legislator based on the threat to constitutional rights provoked by statutes or legislative acts, which is related to the main subject of the amparo against laws. In this

773 See the references in Néstor Pedro SAGÜES, *Derecho Procesal Constitucional, Acción de Amparo*, Vol 3, Astrea, Buenos Aires, 1988, pp. 117; and in Rafael Chavero, *El nuevo régimen del amparo constitucional en Venezuela*, Ed. Sherwood, Caracas 2001, pp. 190 and 239.

774 See William M. TABB and Eliane W. SHOBEN, *Remedies*, Thomson West, 2005, p. 29

775 See decision of April 23, 1999 (Case: *A. Albornoz*). See the reference in Rafael CHAVERO, *El nuevo régimen del amparo constitucional en Venezuela*, Ed. Sherwood, Caracas, 2001, p. 240.

regard, the former Supreme Court of Justice of Venezuela, in a restrictive, has ruled that a statute or a legal norm, in itself, cannot originate a valid possible, imminent and feasible threat, to allow the filing of an amparo action. In a decision of May 24, 1993, the Politico–Administrative Chamber of the Supreme Court ruled:

> It is indisputable that a legal norm violating the Constitution can also harm persons situated in the juridical situation it regulates, so in such case, the harm could be considered 'possible', according to Article 6,2 of the Amparo law.
>
> Nonetheless, when an amparo action is filed against a norm, –that is, when the object of the action is the norm in itself–, the concretion of the possible alleged harm would not be "immediate", due to the fact that there would be always necessary for the competent authority to proceed to the execution or application of the norm, in order to harm the plaintiff. One must conclude that the probable harm caused by a norm will always be mediate and indirect, needing to be apply to the concrete case. Thus, the injury will be caused through and by means of an act applying the disposition that is contrary to the rule of law.
>
> The same occurs with the third condition set forth in the Law; the threat, that is, the probable and imminent harm, will never be feasible –that is, concreted– by the defendant. If it could be sustained that the amparo could be filed against a disposition the constitutionality of which is challenged, then it would be necessary to accept as defendant the legislative body or the public officer which had sanctioned it, being the latter the one that would act in court defending the act. It can be observed that in case the possible harm would effectively arrive to be materialized, it would not be the legislative body or the sate organ which issued it, the one that will execute it, but the public official for whom the application of the norm will be imposing in all the cases in which an individual would be in the factual situation established in the norm.
>
> If it is understood that that the norm can be the object or an amparo action, the conclusion would be that the defendant (the public entity sanctioning the norm the unconstitutionality of which is alleged) could not be the one entity conducting the threat; but that the harm would be in the end concretized or provoked by a different entity (the one applying to the specific and concrete case the unconstitutional provision).
>
> Thus the amparo against law and other normative acts must be discarded, not only because the Amparo law does not establish such possibility, but also because even though being possible to file the extraordinary action against a normative act of general effects, the court must declare its inadmissibility because the conditions set fort in Article 6,2 of the Amparo law are not covered"[776].

Accordingly, the former Supreme Court rejected the possibility to fill amparo actions against laws, restricting the scope of the Amparo Law in our opinion without major basic arguments, and facing the possibility for the constitutional protection to be needed, ruled as follows:

> "Nonetheless, this High Court considers necessary to point out that the previous conclusion does not signify the impossibility to prevent the concretion of the harm –objection that could be drawn from the thesis that the amparo can only proceed if the unconstitutional norm is applied–, due to he fact that the imminently aggrieved person, must not necessarily wait for the effective execution of the illegal norm, because since he faces the threat having the conditions established in the Law, he could seek for amparo for his constitutional rights. In such

776 See decision of the Politico Administrative Chamber of May 25, 1993 in *Revista de Derecho Público,* N° 55–56, Editorial Jurídica Venezolana, Caracas, 1993, pp. 289–290

case, thou, the amparo would not be directed against the norm, but against the public officer that has to apply it. In effect, being imminent the application to an individual of a normative disposition contrary to any of the constitutional rights or guaranties, the potentially affected person could seek from the court a prohibition directed to the said public officer plaintiff, compelling not to apply the challenged norm, once evaluated by the court as being unconstitutional"[777].

VI. THE NON CONSENTED CHARACTER OF THE INJURY

The injury to a constitutional right or guarantee that can permit an individual to seek constitutional judicial protection by means of an amparo action, must not only be actual, possible, real and imminent, and not provoked by the plaintiff himself[778], but must not be a consented harm or injury; that is, the complainant must not have expressly or tacitly consented to the challenged act or the harm caused to his right.

Regarding the express consent, it exists, as ruled in the Venezuelan Amparo Law, when there are "unequivocal signs of acceptance" (Art. 6,4)[779] of the act, the facts or the omissions causing the injury, in which case the amparo action is inadmissible.

This case of inadmissibility of the amparo action is also expressly regulated in the Amparo Laws of México, against expressly consented acts or acts consented as consequence of "expression of will that implies such consent" (article 73, XI); in Nicaragua, against "acts that have been consented by the claimant in an express way" (Article 51,4); and in Costa Rica, "when the action or omission would be legitimately consented by the aggrieved person"(Article 30,ch).

In certain aspects, this inadmissibility clause for the amparo suit referred to the express consent of the plaintiff, has some equivalence with the equitable defense in the United Stated injunctions called *estopell*, which refers to actions of the plaintiff prior to the filing of the suit, that are inconsistent with the rights it asserts in his claim.

The classic example of *estopell*, as referred to by Tabb and Shoben, "is that a plaintiff cannot ask equity for an order to remove a neighbor's fence built over the lot line if the plaintiff stood by and watched the fence construction in full knowledge of the location of the lot line. The plaintiff silence with knowledge of the facts is an action inconsistent with the right asserted in court"[780].

The other clause of inadmissibility in the amparo suit refers to the tacit consent of the plaintiff regarding the act, fact or omission causing the injury to his rights, which happens when a precise delay of time has elapsed without the claim being brought before the courts.

777 *Idem.*, p. 290.

778 See Hernán SALGADO PESANTES, *Manual de Justicia Constitucional Ecuatoriana*, Corporación Editora Nacional, Quito 2004, p. 80.

779 The Venezuelan Law qualifies this express consent as "tacit".

780 See William M. TABB and Eliane W. SHOBEN, *Remedies*, Thomson West, 2005, pp. 50–51

This clause for the inadmissibility of the amparo suit is also equivalent to what in North American procedure for injunction is called laches, which as resumed by Tabb and Shoben, "bars a suitor in equity who has not acted promptly in bringing the action; it is reflected in the maxim: 'Equity aids the vigilant, not those who slumber in their rights'"[781].

As argued in *Lake Development Enterprises, Inc. v. Kojetinsky*, 410 S.W. 2d 361, 367–68 (Mo. App. 1966):

> ""Laches" is the neglect, for an unreasonable and unexplained length of time under circumstances permitting diligence, to do what in law, should have been done. There is no fixed period within which a person must assert his claim or be barred by laches. The length of time depends upon the circumstances of the particular case. Mere delay in asserting a right does not of itself constitute laches; the delay involved must work to the disadvantage and prejudice of the defendant. Laches is a question of fact to be determined from all the evidence and circumstances adduced at trial"[782].

The difference between the doctrine of laches regarding injunctions and the Latin American concept of tacit consent referred to amparo suits, basically lays in the fact that the delay to file the action for amparo in Lain America, is in general expressly established in the Amparo Laws, so the exhaustion of the delay without the filing of the action, is what is considered to be a tacit consent regarding the act, the fact or the omission causing the injury.

In this regard, and only with few exceptions, as Ecuador[783] and Colombia (where for instance, the tutela law establishes that the action for tutela can be filed in any moment, Art. 11), the Amparo Laws in Latin America set forth a delay, considering that it is tacitly understood that the injured party has consented the acts, when the recourses or actions are not filed within the delays set forth in the statutes. The established delay varies in the legislation in a number of days counted from the date of the challenged act or from the day the injured party has known about the violation: Argentina, 15 days (Art. 2,e); Brazil, 120 days (Art. 18); Guatemala, 30 days (Art. 20); Honduras, 2 months; México, 15 days as a general rule, but with many other delays with different length of time (Arts. 21, 22 and 73,XII); Nicaragua, 30 days (Art. 26; 51,4); Peru, 60 days (Arts. 5,10; 44); Uruguay, 30 days (Art 4); Venezuela, 6 months (Art. 6,4). In the cases of Dominican Republic and Chile, where the delay (15 days) has been regulated by Supreme Court, discussions have arisen regarding the constitutionality of such norms, due to the criteria that a delay of such type must be only established by the Legislator[784]

---

781 See William M. TABB and Eliane W. SHOBEN, *Remedies*, Thomson West, 2005, p. 48.

782 See the reference Owen M. FISS and Doug RENDELMAN, *Injunctions*, The Foundation Press, Mineola New York, 1984, pp. 102–103.

783 See Hernán SALGADO PESANTES, *Manual de Justicia Constitucional Ecuatoriana*, Corporación Editora Nacional, Quito 2004, p. 81

784 See Juan Manuel ERRAZURIZ and Jorge Miguel OTERO A., *Aspectos procesales del recurso de protección*, Editorial Jurídica de Chile, Santiago 1989, p. 130; Miguel A. VALERA MONTERO, *Hacia un nuevo concepto de Constitución*, Santo Domingo, 2006, p. 404.

In Costa Rica, the Constitutional Jurisdiction Law establishes that the amparo recourse can be filed at any time while the violation, threat, injury or restriction endures, and up to 2 months after the direct effects regarding the injured party, have ceased (Arts. 35, 60). This delay can also be suspended if the interested party decides to file an administrative recourse against the particular act (Art. 31). Regarding this clause of inadmissibility of the amparo action, the former Supreme Court of Justice of Venezuela ruled in a decision of October 24, 1990, that:

> "Being the amparo action a special, brief, summary and effective judicial remedy for the protection of constitutional rights...it is logic for the Legislator to prescribe a correct proportion of time between the moment in which the harm is produced and the moment the aggrieved party is to file the action. To let pass more that 6 months from the moment in which the injuring act is issued for the exercise of the action is the demonstration of the acceptance of the harm from the side of the aggrieved party; the indolence must be sanctioned, impeding the use of the judicial remedy that has its justification on the urgent need to reestablish a legal situation"[785].

Of course, as a general rule in this matter, the exhaustion of the delay without filing the amparo action, although considered as a tacit consent regarding the injury, does not prevent the interested person from filing any other recourse or action against the act provoking the harm, as it is expressly regulated in the Costa Rican Law (Art. 36)[786].

A particular aspect can be mentioned, regarding the situation in cases of wrongs that are continuous in nature. In the United States, it is considered that laches cannot be urged as a defense to a suit to enjoin a wrong which is continuing in its nature (Pacific Greyhound Lines v. Sun Valley Bus Lines, 70 Ariz. 65, 216 P. 2d 404, 1950; Goldstein v. Beal, 317 Mass. 750, 59 N.E. 2d 712, 1945)[787]. A similar rule has been applied for instance, in Venezuela, where the Fist Court on Administrative Judicial review actions in a decision of October 22, 1990 (Case: *María Cambra de Pulgar*) in which when deciding on a defense on inadmissibility of an action, ruled:

> "In spite that a number of the facts indicated had been produced more that 6 months ago, they have been described in order to reveal a supposed chain of events that, due to their constancy and re incidence, allows presuming that the plaintiff is threatened with those facts being repeated. This character of the threat is what the amparo intends to stop. According to what the plaintiff point out, no tacit consent can be produced from his part ... Consequently, there are no grounds for the application to any of the inadmissibility clauses set forth in the Amparo Law"[788].

---

785 See in *Revista de Derecho Público,* N° 44, Editorial Jurídica Venezolana, Caracas, 1990, p. 144.

786 See the comments in Ruben HERNÁNDEZ VALLE, *Derecho procesal Constitucional*, Editorial Juricentro, 2001, pp. 226–229, 243.

787 See the references in Kevin Schroder, John Glenn and Maureen Placilla (Editors), *Corpus Juris Secundum*, Vol. 43A, Thomson West, 2004, p. 329

788 See decision of October 22, 1990, in *Revista de Derecho Público,* N° 44, Editorial Jurídica Venezolana, Caracas, 1990, pp. 143–144

VII. EXCEPTIONS TO THE TACIT CONSENT RULE

On the other hand, since there are constitutional question involved, the Laws establish various exceptions regarding the caducity or lapsing of the action. For instance, in Honduras, it is expressly regulated that the action can be filed after the exhaustion of the delay, when the impossibility to bring the action before the court is duly proved (Art. 46,3). In similar sense it is regulated in Article 4 of the Uruguayan Law when the plaintiff has been impeded by "just cause" to file the action.

In México, in particular, regarding the amparo against laws, the action can be filed not only against the statute, but also after the exhaustion of the delay, against the first concrete act that applies it; so the tacit consent rule applies in this case, only when the latter is not challenged in the delay set forth in the Amparo Law (Art. 73,XII)[789]. But additionally to this particular exception, Article 22 of the Amparo Law of Mexico establishes other general exception to the tacit consent rule, in cases of authority acts endangering the life, the personal freedom, deportation, any other acts prohibited in Article 22 of the Constitution, or the forced incorporation to the army[790]. In these cases the amparo action can be brought before the courts at any time. Also the amparo action can be filed at any time, in cases of the protection of peasants rights related to communal land (Art. 217).

In Costa Rica, Article 20 of the Constitutional Jurisdiction Law also establishes as an exception regarding the delay, in cases in which the amparo action is filed against the risk of an unconstitutional law or regulation to be applied in concrete cases, as well as in cases of a manifest possibility of acts harming the plaintiff rights could be issued or occur.

In Venezuela, the Amparo Law also provides a few exceptions regarding the tacit consent rule, when the amparo action is filed together or jointly with another nullity action, in which cases the general 6 month delay established for the filing of the action does not apply. This is the rule in cases of harms or threats originated in statutes or regulations, and in administrative acts or public administration omissions, when the amparo action is filed jointly with the popular action for judicial review of unconstitutionality of statutes, or with the judicial review action against administrative actions or omissions.

Regarding the judicial review popular action against statutes, it is conceived in the Organic Law of the Supreme Tribunal as an action that can be filed at any time, so if a petition for amparo is filed together with the popular action, no delay is applicable. This is why, no tacit consent can be understood when the harm is provoked by a statute.

Similarly, the tacit consent rule does not apply either in cases of administrative acts or omissions, when the amparo action is filed together with the judicial review

---

789 See Eduardo FERRER MAC–GREGOR, *La acción constitucional de amparo en México y España*, Editorial Porrúa, México 2002, p. 391; Richard D. BAKER, *Judicial Review in Mexico. A Study of the Amparo Suit*, University of Austin Press, Austin 1971, p. 172.

790 Eduardo FERRER MAC–GREGOR, *La acción constitucional de amparo en México y España*, Editorial Porrúa, México 2002, p. 331

action against administrative acts or omissions, in which case, due to the constitutional complaint, the latter can be filed at any moment, as is expressly provided in the Amparo Law (Art. 5).

Finally, mention must be done to the exception regarding the tacit consent rule regarding actions or omissions established in Article 6,4 of the Venezuelan Amparo Law, in cases when the violations of constitutional rights infringes "public order and good conduct", an exceptional situation that must derive from a rule of law[791].

This concept of "public order" in the Venezuelan legal system refers to situations where the application of a state concerns the general and indispensable legal order for the existence of the community, which cannot be bequeathed; and it does not apply in cases that only concern the parties in a contractual or private controversy. As ruled by the Cassation Chamber of the Supreme Court in Venezuela, in a decision of April 3, 1985, "the concept of public order tend to make the general interest of the Society and of the State to win over the individual particular interest, in order to assure the enforcement and purpose of some institutions"[792].

For instance, as a matter of general principle, public order provisions in public law are those establishing competencies or attributions to the public entities[793], including the Judiciary, and those concerning the taxation powers of public entities. In private law, for instance, all the provisions referring to the status of persons (for instance: *patria potestas*, divorce, adoption) are norms in which public order and good customs are involved[794].

But in many cases it is the lawmaker itself that has expressly declared in a particular statute that its provisions are of "public order" character, in the sense that its norms cannot be modified through contracts. That is the case for instance, of the 2004 Consumers and Users Protection Law[795], where Article 2 sets forth that its provisions are of public order and may not be renounced by the parties.

Regarding the amparo action and the exception to the tacit consent rule, the First Court of Administrative Judicial Review, has ruled as follows:

> "It is true that the tacit or express consent does not extinguish the action when the violation infringes the public order or the good customs, and that Article 14 of the Amparo Law qualifies the action, whether in its principal or incidental aspects up to the judicial decision execution, as "eminent public order". A textual interpretation could lead to the absurd of con-

---

791 See decision of the Politico Administrative Chamber of March 22, 1988, in *Revista de Derecho Público,* N° 34, Editorial Jurídica Venezolana, Caracas, 1988, p. 114.

792 See the reference in decisión of the Politico Administrative Chamber of February 1, 1990 (*Case Tuna Atlántica C.A.*) and of June 30, 1992, in *Revista de Derecho Público,* N° 60, Editorial Jurídica Venezolana, Caracas, 1992, p. 157.

793 See for instante, decisión of the Constitucional Chamber of the Supreme Tribunal of March 1, 2001 (Case: *Alcalde del Municipio Baruta, Bingos*). See the reference in Rafael CHAVERO G., *El nuevo régimen del amparo constitucional en Venezuela*, Editorial Sherwood, Caracas 2001, 187.

794 Allan R. BREWER–CARÍAS, *Contratos Administrativos*, Editorial Jurídica Venezolana, Caracas, 1992, pp. 265–268.

795 *Official Gazette*, N° 37.930, May 4th 2004.

sidering that, because all matters of amparo are of public order, the express consent (configured by the delay exhaustion) does not extinguish the action; but such interpretation contradicts the logic of the system and the nature of amparo, which is a brief and speedy mean regarding actual harms. Thus, it must be interpreted that the extinction of the amparo action due to the elapse of the delay (express consent, according to the legislator), is produced in all cases, except when the way through which the harm has been produced, is of such gravity that it constitutes an injury to the juridical conscience. It would be the case, for instance, of flagrant violations to individual rights that cannot be denounced by the affected party; deprivation of freedom; submission to physical or psychological torture; maltreatment; harms to human dignity and other extreme cases"[796].

Consequently not all violations of constitutional rights and guarantees are considered in their selves as having public order concern, but only those where the juridical or legal conscience of society is harmed, like when human dignity is injured in a flagrant and grave way, as happens with freedom deprivation and infringement of tortures. In such cases, no tacit consent can be admitted, and the amparo judicial protection must be admitted even tough the delay for filing the action would have been exhausted.

CHAPTER XIV

JUDICIAL ADJUDICATIONS IN THE "AMPARO" SUIT: PRELIMINARY MEASURES AND DEFINITIVE RULINGS: PREVENTIVE AND RESTORATIVE DECISIONS

The final purpose of filing an amparo action is for the plaintiff to obtain a judicial adjudication from the competent court, seeking for the immediate protection of his harmed or threatened constitutional right or guarantee, which in general terms, using the same wording used for the North American injunctions, can consist on:

"Restrain action or interference of some kind; to furnish preventive relief against irreparable mischief or injury; or to preserve the status quo. It is a remedy designed to prevent irreparable injury by prohibiting or commanding certain acts. The function of injunctive relief is to restrain motion and to enforce inaction. An injunction is designed to prevent harm, not

796 See the decision of the First Court on Judicial Review of Administrative Actions of October 13, 1988, in *Revista de Derecho Público,* N° 36, Editorial Jurídica Venezolana, Caracas, 1988, p. 95. This opinion was followed exactly by the Politico Administrative Chamber of the Supreme Court of Justice, decision of November 1, 1989, in *Revista de Derecho Público,* N° 40, Editorial Jurídica Venezolana, Caracas, 1989, p. 111; and by the Cassation Chamber of the same Supreme Court of Justice, in decision of June 28, 1995, (Exp. N°. 94–172). See the reference in Rafael CHAVERO G., *El nuevo régimen del amparo constitucional en Venezuela*, Editorial Sherwood, Caracas, 2001, p. 188, note 178. See other judicial decision on the matter in pp. 214 and 246.

redress harm; it is not compensatory. The remedy grants prospective, as opposed to retrospective, relief; it is preventative, protective or restorative, but not addressed to past wrongs"[797].

Thus, if it is true that the general purpose of both institutions can be considered the same, and that both have an extraordinary character in procedural law, there is a basic distinction between them, regarding their protective object: the North American injunction is a judicial equity remedy that can serve for the protection of any kind of personal or property right that in a particular circumstance cannot be adequately protected by remedies at law. In contrast, the Latin American Amparo is conceived as a specific judicial means for the exclusive protection of constitutional rights and guarantees. That is why the general rules governing the injunctions in North America are set forth in the general procedural statutes. Instead, in Latin America, the general rules for the amparo suit are set forth in the Constitutions.

As in the injunctive procedure, two general sort of judicial adjudications can also be issued in the amparo suit for the protection of the claimed constitutional rights or guaranties: preliminary measures that can be issued since the beginning of the procedure and that are in general subject to the final court ruling; and definitive preventive or restorative adjudications ending the process.

I. PRELIMINARY MEASURES IN THE AMPARO SUIT

The preliminary, interlocutory and temporal judicial measures that a Latin American court can adopt in any judicial process before full trial on the merits, generally regulated in the Procedural Codes and applicable to the amparo processes are what in Spanish are called "*medidas preventivas*" or "*medidas cautelares*" issued in an interlocutory way, the expressions "*preventiva*" or "*cautelar*" being used in to describe "preliminary" procedural decisions in contrast to definitive or final adjudications. Thus, the Spanish expression "*preventiva*", is not used exclusively in the English sense of "preventive" as to prevent or to avoiding harm. In the North American system, the "preventive injunction" is a definitive injunction and not a "preliminary" one. In other words, as explained by Tabb and Shoben:

> "The classic form of injunctions in private litigation is the preventive injunction. By definition, a preventive injunction is a court order designed to avoid future harm to a party by prohibiting or mandating certain behavior by another party. The injunction is "preventive" in the sense of avoiding harm. The wording may be either prohibitory ("Do not trespass") or mandatory ("Remove the obstruction")[798].

The preliminary judicial measures, of course, can also have "preventive" effects in the sense of preserving the *status quo*, but only in a temporary or preliminary basis, pending the procedure. As the same authors Tabb and Shoben have said:

> "Upon a compelling showing by the plaintiff, the court may issue a coercive order even before full trial on the merits. A preliminary injunction gives the plaintiff temporary relief

797 See the reference to the corresponding judicial decisions in John BOURDEAU et al, "Injunctions" in Kevin Schroder, John Glenn and Maureen Placilla, *Corpus Juris Secundum*, Volume 43A, Thompson West, 2004, p. 20.

798 See William M. TABB and Elaine W. SHOBEN, *Remedies*, Thomson West, 2005, p. 22

pending trial on the merit. A temporary restraining order affords immediate relief pending the hearing on the preliminary injunction. Both of these types of interlocutory relief are designed to preserve the status quo to prevent irreparable harm before a court can decide the substantive merits of the dispute. Such orders are available only upon a strong showing of the necessity for such relief and may be conditioned upon the claimant posting a bond or sufficient security to protect the interests of the defendant in the event that the injunction is later determined to have been wrongfully issued"[799].

So, in order to avoid confusions, we are going to use the English expression "preliminary" measures to identify what in Spanish is called "*medidas preventivas o cautelares*" as interlocutory and temporal judicial protective measures that are issued pending the suit, which are similar to the North American "preliminary injunctions" also issued as interlocutory and temporal relief pending the trial. In both cases, the preliminary measures are different from the final judicial protective (permanent injunction) decisions consisting in preventive or restorative adjudication[800].

That is why, in general terms, the amparo suit in Latin America does not have a "cautelar" in the sense of preliminary nature, but tends to protect in a definitive way the constitutional right or guarantee alleged as harmed or threatened. Nonetheless, some terminological confusion can be identified in some countries in which it has been given to the amparo action a "cautelar" nature, based on the distinction between "cautelar" measures and "cautelar actions". Nonetheless, in those cases, the leveling of the amparo action as "cautelar" is not in the sense of just having a "preliminary" nature, but in the sense of deciding only about the immediate protection of a constitutional right without resolving the other matters of a controversy. This can be seen in Ecuador and Chile, where the amparo suit has been considered to have "cautelar" nature, but in a sense not equivalent to a "preliminary" nature. The Constitutional Court of Ecuador, for instance, has decided as followed:

> "That the amparo action set forth in Article 95 of the Constitution is in essence, preliminary (*cautelar*) regarding the constitutional rights, not allowing [the court] to decide on the merits or to substitute the proceedings set forth in the legal order for the resolution of a controversy, but only to suspend the effects of an authority act which harms those rights; and the decisions issued in the amparo suit do not produce *res judicata*, so the authority, once corrected the incurred defects, may go back to the matter and issue a new act, providing it is adjusted to the constitutional and legal provisions"[801]

In similar way, in Chile the action for protection has been considered to have a "*cautelar*" nature, not in the sense of "preliminary" measures, but as tending to obtain a definitive protective adjudication regarding constitutional rights[802].

---

799 See William M. TABB and Elaine W. SHOBEN, *Remedies*, Thomson West, 2005, p. 4

800 See John BOURDEAU et al, "Injunctions" in Kevin Schroder, John Glenn and Maureen Placilla, *Corpus Juris Secundum*, Volume 43A, Thompson West, 2004, pp. 24 ff.

801 See the text and comments in Hernán SALGADO PESANTES, *Manual de Justicia Constitucional Ecuatoriana*, Corporación Editora Nacional, Quito, 2004, p. 78.

802 See Eduardo Soto KLOSS, *El recurso de protección. Orígenes, doctrina y jurisprudencia*, Editorial Jurídica de Chile, Santiago 1982, p. 248; Juan Manuel ERRAZURIZ and Jorge Miguel OTERO A., *Aspectos procesales del recurso de protección*, Editorial Jurídica de Chile, Santiago, 1989, pp. 34–38.

But putting aside these terminological clarifications, in the amparo procedure, preliminary measures can be adopted by the courts pending the final adjudication, in order to preserve the *status quo*, avoiding harms or restoring the plaintiff situation to the original situation, during the development of the procedure. The Latin American Laws vary in the regulatory scope of the preliminary measures, in the sense that in some cases they are enumerated in a restrictive way, and in others, the range of power for preliminary protective measures is unlimited.

1. The suspension of the effects of the challenged act

The preliminary judicial measures can consist in the suspension of the effects of the challenged acts. This is considered to be the most traditional preliminary measure, having its origin in the traditional conception of the amparo as a judicial mean for the protection of constitutional rights against State acts.

Two legal regulations can be distinguished in this matter of the suspension of the effects of the challenged acts, regarding the automatic suspension or the need for a court decision on the matter.

In the specific case of Costa Rica, the suspension of the effect of the challenged act can be considered an automatic preliminary effect of the filing of the amparo action, but in the other cases, it is properly a preliminary protective decision that the court must take.

In effect, in Costa Rica, when the amparo action is filed against a statute or other normative act, the application of them to the plaintiff is automatically suspended. In concrete challenged acts, their effects are also automatically suspended (Art. 41). The court can also adopt any other adequate conservatory or security measure in order to prevent material risks or avoid the production of other harms consequence of the facts occurred, (Art. 41). Being the suspension of the challenged act an automatic consequence of the filing of the amparo petition, it is for Public Administration to ask the court to order the execution of the challenged act. For such purpose, the same Article 41 of the Amparo Law provides that in grave exceptional cases the court can order the execution or the continuation of the execution of the challenged act, at the request of Public Administration. This power that can be exercised ex officio, in cases when the suspension of the effects of the act may cause or threaten to cause effective and imminent damages and prejudices to the public interest, bigger that those that could be caused to the aggrieved party. The court can issue the preliminary measures that it considers adequate for the protection of rights and liberties of the aggrieved party and to prevent that the effects of an eventual resolution granting the amparo in his favor become illusory (Art. 41)[803].

Except in this exceptional case, the suspension of the effects of the challenged act is set forth as a preliminary protective measure that the competent court can issue.

---

803 See Rubén HERNÁNDEZ VALLE, *Derecho Procesal Constitucional*, Editorial Juricentro, San José 2001, pp. 248–254.

The initial regulations on the matter began with the amparo suit Laws in Mexico, where the suspension of the challenged act is the classic preliminary measure on matters of amparo, which can be decided ex officio or at the request of the party (Art. 122). The decision to suspend the effect of the challenged act can be granted when it means a danger of deprivation of life, deportation, expulsion or other conducts prohibited in Article 22 of the Constitutions; or an act that if executed would make physically impossible for the plaintiff to enjoy the individual guarantee claimed. The suspension will consist 1) In ordering the end of the acts that are endangering the life, or that allows the deportation or the expulsion of the plaintiff, or the execution of any of those forbidden in Article 22 of the Constitution; or 2) in ordering that things be maintained in the stage they are, the court having to adopt the adequate measures in order to avoid the consummation of the challenged acts (Art. 123).

Additionally, the suspension can only be decided, when requested by the party; when the harm caused to the aggrieved would be difficult to repair if the act is executed; or when because of the suspension no prejudice is provoked to the social interest, nor the public order norms are contravened. It is understood that the latter is produced when the suspension for instance, implies the continuation of vicious or criminal activities or related to drug production or trafficking, alcoholism or that prevent the adoption of measures to fight grave diseases (Arts. 124, 130)[804].

In a more precise way, the suspension of the effects of the challenged act has been regulated as a preliminary measure in Articles 31 ff. of the Nicaraguan Amparo Law, as follows:

1) Three days after the filing of the petition, the court ex officio or at the party's request can suspend the effects of the challenged act (Art. 31).

2) The suspension will be ex officio decided when the challenged act if executed would make physically impossible to restore the plaintiff in the enjoyment of his right, or when a notorious lack of jurisdiction of the authority or public officer against the action is filed, or when the challenged act is one of those that no authority can legally execute (Art. 32).

3) If the suspension is requested by the party, it will be granted when the following circumstances concur: a) That the suspension not cause harm to the general interests nor be contrary to public order provisions; b) That the damages and prejudices that could be caused to the aggrieved party with the execution of the act be deemed by the court as difficult to repair; c) That the petitioner post sufficient bond or guarantee in order to repair the damages or compensate the prejudices that the suspension could cause to third parties, in case the amparo action is rejected (Art. 33).

---

804 See Richard D. BAKER, *Judicial Review in Mexico. A Study of the Amparo Suit,* University of Texas Press, Austin 1971, p. 233 ff.; Joaquín BRAGE CAMAZANO, *La jurisdicción constitucional de la libertad (Teoría general, Argentina, México, Corte Interamericana de derechos humanos*), Editorial Porrúa, México 2005, p. 197.

4) Once the suspension order is issued, the court must establish the situation according to which things must remain, and adopt the adequate measures for the conservation up to the end of the procedure, of the matter object of the amparo, (Art. 34).

5) The suspension will lose its effects if a third interested party gives sufficient bond in order to restore things to the stage it was before the challenged act and to pay the damages and prejudices that occur to the plaintiff in case the amparo is granted (Art. 35).

In similar sense to the Nicaraguan regulations, the Guatemalan Amparo Law also sets forth the provisions for what is called the "provisional amparo" decision, consisting in the suspension of the challenged acts (Art. 23 ff). The same principles can be found in the Honduran Amparo Law (arts. 57 ff).

In other Amparo Laws such as in El Salvador, the general provision is the possibility for the court to decide on "the immediate provisional suspension of the challenged act when its execution could cause irreparable harm or damages of difficult reparation by the definitive ruling"(Art. 20). The Law also sets forth that the provisional suspension can only refer to acts with positive effects (Art. 19), thus no suspension is admitted regarding acts with negative effects, that is, for instance, acts denying a petition, because the suspension would be equivalent to provisionally granting the original petition.

Also in Brazil, in the mandado de segurança regulations it is set forth as a provisional measure the possibility for the court to suspend the challenged act when from the evidences filed it could result the inefficacy of the definitive measure in case it is granted (Art. 7,2)[805].

In Colombia, Article 7 of the Tutela Law provides for the "provisional measures for the protection of a right", as follows:

> **Art. 7.** From the filing of the petition, when the court considers it expressly necessary and urgent for the protection of a right, it will suspend the application of the concrete act that threatens or harms it.
>
> Nonetheless, at party's request or *ex offico*, the execution or the continuation of the execution can be decided in order to avoid certain and imminent prejudices to public interest. In any case, the court must order what it considers necessary to protect the rights and to prevent that the effects of an eventual decision in favor of the plaintiff become illusory".
>
> The court, *ex officio* and at the request of a party, according to the circumstances of the case, can also issue any conservatory or security measure tending to protect the right or to avoid further damages produced by the facts.

In Venezuela, when the amparo action is filed jointly with the judicial review popular action for nullity against statutes or with the judicial review of administrative actions recourse, the amparo petition has always a preliminary (*cautelar*) character, and consequently, the decision granting the amparo pending the principal suit is always of a preliminary character of suspension of the effects of the challenged act. Thus, in the case of statutes it is the Constitutional Chamber the competent one

805 See José Luis LAZZARINI, *El juicio de amparo*, Ed. La Ley, Buenos Aires 1987, p. 319

for deciding the suspension of the application of the statute, in such cases, with *erga omnes* effects[806]; and regarding administrative acts, the courts of the Administrative Jurisdiction are the ones that can decide the matter of suspension of the effects of the administrative challenged act pending the judicial review suit[807].

2. The order not to adopt innovative actions

In Argentina Amparo law refers to the preliminary measures in an indirect way in Article 15, referring to non innovative measures and to the suspension of the effects of the challenged act; the former tending to the maintenance of the *status quo*, thus, paralyzing the facts that even with the filing of the action, pending the brief procedure of the amparo action, could continue to prejudice the integral repairing of the harmed constitutional right. The measure, as all the preliminary measures, tends to assure the result of the definitive decision ending the amparo suit, and to ensure that it will have the same efficacy as if it would have been issued at the moment of the filing of the action[808].

In similar way the Amparo Law of Paraguay also authorizes the competent court, ex officio or at the party's request, to order non innovation orders at any moment, in case that the execution has begin or of imminent grave harm. In such cases, when the violation of the rights and guarantees appears in an evident way and the harm could result irreparable, the court must order the suspension of the challenged act, order the accomplishment of the omitted act, or order the preliminary convenient measures (Art. 8).

3. The other preliminary protective measures

In other Latin American countries, the preliminary measures that the court can issue in the amparo suit, are referred in a wider sense, in that the judge can order at any moment the "preliminary measures" for the protection of the rights (Costa Rica, Art. 21[809]; Uruguay, Art. 7[810]); as is the case in the Bolivian Law, which authorizes the court to issue "the necessary preliminary decisions" in order to avoid the completion of the threat, to restrict or suspend a constitutional right or guarantee in

---

806 See Rafael CHAVERO G. *El nuevo amparo constitucional en Venezuela,* Ed. Sherwood, Caracas 2001, pp. 468 ff. 327 ff.; Allan R. BREWER–CARÍAS, "Derecho y Acción de Amparo, Vol V, *Instituciones Políticas y Constitucionales*, Editorial Jurídica venezolana, Caracas, 1998, pp. 277 ff.

807 See Allan R. BREWER–CARÍAS, "Derecho y Acción de Amparo, Vol V, *Instituciones Políticas y Constitucionales* Editorial Jurídica venezolana, Caracas, 1998, pp. 281 ff.

808 See José Luis LAZZARINI, *El juicio de amparo*, Ed. La Ley, Buenos Aires 1987, pp. 314–315; Alí Joaquín SALGADO, *Juicio de amparo y acción de inconstitucionalidad,* Editorial Astrea, Buenos Aires 1987, pp. 109; Néstor Pedro SAGÜÉS, *Derecho procesal Constitucional, Vol 3, Acción de amparo*, Editorial Astrea Buenos Aires 1988, p. 460.

809 See Rubén HERNÁNDEZ, *Derecho Procesal Constitucional*, Editorial Juricentro, San José, 2001, pp. 248, 252

810 See Luis Alberto VIERA, *Ley de Amparo*, Ediciones Idea, Montevideo, 1993, pp. 41, 206.

which the petition is founded and that at the court's criteria could create an irreparable situation by means of the amparo" (Art. 99).

4. The conditions for the issuing of preliminary protective measures

In the Peruvian Code on Constitutional Procedures, which is the most recent of all the Latin American legislation referred to the amparo suit, the preliminary protective measures have found a precise regulation, particularly regarding the conditions that need to be accomplished for its issuing, as follows:

> **Article 15**. Preliminary measures. In the constitutional processes, preliminary measures can be adopted as well as the suspension of the harming act. In order for it issuance, the appearance of good right, the danger in the delay and the adequacy of the petition to guarantee the efficacy of the claim, must be required. They can be issued without the knowledge of the other party and the appeal is only granted without suspensive effects. Its justification, formality and execution will depend on the content of the constitutional claim and the final decision securing..."

This article is the only one that can be found in the Latin Amparo Laws expressly establishing the conditions for the issuance of preliminary measures, which in the other countries have been constructed through judicial doctrine[811]. The main conditions refer, first, to what is called the *fumus boni juris* or the need for the petitioner to prove the existence of his right or guarantee set forth in the Constitution that can be violated or threatened. And second, to what is called the *periculum in mora* or the need to prove that the delay in granting the preliminary protection will make the harm irreparable. Additionally it also exists a condition called *periculum in dammi*, referred to the need to prove the imminence of the harm that can be caused; and the need to balance the collective and particular interest involved in the case[812].

As was ruled by the Supreme Tribunal of Justice of Venezuela, in a decision N° 488 dated March 3, 2000:

> "In order for an anticipated protective measure to be granted it is necessary to examine the existence of three essential elements due to its preliminary content, and always balancing the collective or individual interest; such conditions are:
>
> 1. *Fumus Boni Iuris*, that is, the reasonable appearance of the existence of good right in hands of the petitioner alleging its violation, appearance that must derive from the documents attached to the petition.
>
> 2. *Periculum in mora*, that is, the danger that the definitive ruling could result illusory, due to the necessary delay in resolving the incident of the suspension.
>
> 3. *Periculum in Damni*, that is, the imminence of the harm caused by the presumptive violation of the fundamental rights of the petitioner and its irreparability. These elements are

---

811 See Samuel B. ABAD YUPANQUI, *El proceso constitucional de amparo*, Gaceta Jurídica, Lima, 2004, pp. 491, 422 ff. 501 ff.

812 As for instante has been decided by the Venezuelan First Court on Adminsitrative Jurisdiction, Case: *Video & Juegos Costa Verde, C.A. vs. Prefecto del Municipio Maracaibo del Estado Zulia*, in *Revista de Derecho Público*, N° 85–98, Editorial Jurídica Venezolana, Caracas 2001, p. 291

> those that basically allow seeking for the necessary anticipatory protection of the constitutional rights and guarantees".[813]

In general terms, these conditions for the issuance of the preliminary protective measures in the amparo suit are the same as those expected to be tested when issuing the preliminary injunctions in the United States. As has been summarized by Tabb and Shoben:

> "Most circuits follow the traditional test for a preliminary injunction. That test has four prerequisites for the issuance of a preliminary injunction. They are: 1) a probability of prevailing on the merits; 2) an irreparable injury if the relief is delayed; 3) a balance of hardship favoring the plaintiff; 4) a showing that the injunction would not adverse to the public interest. The burden of proof on each of these four elements rests with the movant"[814].

5. The inaudita pars issuing of the preliminary protective measures

Due to the extraordinary character of the amparo action, the preliminary protective measures requested by the plaintiff, if the abovementioned prerequisites are fulfilled, can be decided and issued by the court in an immediate way, without a previous hearing of the potential defendants, that is, *inadi alteram parte* or *inaudita pars*, as it is expressly provided in the Peruvian Constitutional Procedures Code (Art. 15)[815]. Nonetheless, many Amparo laws provide for the need of an immediate notification of the corresponding authority when the suspension of effects of his acts is decided as a preliminary protective measure (Colombia, Art. 7; Mexico, Art. 123,II; El Salvador, Art. 24; Honduras, Art. 6o).

In a similar sense, in the United States, the preliminary injunctions and restraining orders can be issued in cases of great urgency and when an immediate threat of irreparable injury exists which forecloses the opportunity to give reasonable notice to the plaintiff, in which the court must balance the harm sought to be preserved against the rights of notice and hearing.[816]

Due to this character of being decided without previous hearing the potential defendant, the preliminary decision is adopted at the responsibility and risk of the plaintiff, as is provided in the Honduras Law (Art. 58); the court being empowered to ask for the posting of a bond in order to guarantee the damages that can be caused by the measure, in particular, regarding third parties (Mexico, Art. 124 ff.; Honduras, Art. 58; Paraguay, Art. 8).

---

813 Case *Constructora Pedeca, C.A. vs. Gobernación del Estado Anzoátegui*, in *Revista de Derecho Público*, Nº 81, Editorial Jurídica Venezolana, Caracas, 2000, p. 459.

814 See William M. TABB and Elaine W. SHOBEN, *Remedies*, Thomson West, 2005, p. 63.

815 See Samuel B. ABAD YUPANQUI, *El proceso constitucional de amparo*, Gaceta Jurídica, Lima, 2004, pp. 508.

816 See the reference to the corresponding judicial decisions in John BOURDEAU et al, "Injunctions" in Kevin Schroder, John Glenn and Maureen Placilla, *Corpus Juris Secundum*, Volume 43A, Thompson West, 2004, pp. 339 ff.

The preliminary measures in the amparo process, as happens with the injunctions[817], are essentially modifiable or revocable by the court, particularly at the request of the defendant or of third parties (Colombia, Art. 7; Honduras, Art. 61; Guatemala, Art. 30). In Mexico, even third parties can place a bond requesting the revocation of the preliminary measure of suspension of challenged acts effects, in order to restore things to how they were before the guarantee was violated an to pay the damages and prejudices that could be caused to the petitioner, in case the amparo is granted (Art. 126).

II. THE DEFINITIVE JUDICIAL ADJUDICATION IN THE AMPARO SUIT

The purpose of the amparo suit is for the injured or aggrieved party (the plaintiff), to obtain a judicial protection (*amparo, tutela, protección*) of his constitutional rights or guarantees that have been harmed or threatened by an aggrieving or injurer party (the defendant). The final result of the process, characterized by its bilateral frame which imposes the need for the defendants to have the right to participate and to be heard[818], is thus a formal judicial decision or order issued by the court in order to protect threatened rights or to restore the harmed one. This order, like the North American injunction:

> "Is a court order commanding or preventing virtually any type of action, or commanding someone to undo some wrong or injury. It is a judicial order requiring a person to do or refrain from doing certain acts, for any period of time, no matter its purpose. This is to say, an injunction is a writ framed according to the circumstances or the case commanding an act which the court regards as essential in justice, or restraining an act which it deems contrary to equity and good conscience"[819].

In similar sense, the function of the amparo court's decision is, on the one hand, to prevent the defendant from inflicting further injury on the plaintiff, similarly the "preventive injunction" in the United States, that can be prohibitory or mandatory; or on the other hand, to correct the present by undoing the effects of a past wrong, similarly the "restorative or reparative injunction" in the United States[820].

But the amparo judicial order in Latin America, where the distinction between equitable and law extraordinary remedies does not exist, is not only similar in its purposes and effects to the North American injunction, but also to the other non eq-

817 See the reference to the corresponding judicial decisions in John BOURDEAU et al, "Injunctions" in Kevin Schroder, John Glenn and Maureen Placilla, *Corpus Juris Secundum*, Volume 43A, Thomson West, 2004, pp. 406 ff; 421.

818 Similarly, regarding definitive injunctions, they only can be granted if process issues and service is made on the defendant. See the reference to the corresponding judicial decisions in John Bourdeau et al, "Injunctions" in Kevin Schroder, John Glenn and Maureen Placilla, *Corpus Juris Secundum*, Volume 43A, Thomson West, 2004, p. 339.

819 See the reference to the corresponding judicial decisions in John BOURDEAU et al, "Injunctions" in Kevin Schroder, John Glenn and Maureen Placilla, *Corpus Juris Secundum*, Volume 43A, Thomson West, 2004, p. 19.

820 See William M. TABB and Elaine W. SHOBEN, *Remedies*, Thomson West, 2005, pp. 86–89; John BOURDEAU et al, "Injunctions" in Kevin Schroder, John Glenn and Maureen Placilla, *Corpus Juris Secundum*, Volume 43A, Thomson West, 2004, pp. 28 ff.

uitable extraordinary remedies, like the mandamus and prohibition legal remedies. That is, the amparo order can not only be prohibitory, that is, issued to restrain an action or that certain acts be forbidden (to command a person to refrain from doing a specific act), but also mandatory, that is, to compel an action; that is, like the writ of mandamus, it can compel the execution of some act (command a person to do a specific act), and likewise, the mandatory injunction can also require undoing an act, restoring the statu quo. The amparo judicial order can also be similar to the writ of prohibition, when the order is directed to a court, what normally happens in the cases of amparo actions filed against judicial decisions[821].

Regarding for instance the Venezuelan amparo process, where the courts have very extensive powers that allow them, in similar way to the North American and British judges[822], to provide for remedies in order to effectively protect constitutional rights, in that they can issue orders to do, to refrain from doing, or to undo; or prohibitions[823].

1. The preventive and restorative nature of the amparo

The contents of the final adjudication in the amparo suit is a very extensive one, and in general consists, as is set forth in Article 86 of the Colombian Constitution, in an order directed to the person or persons "against whom the tutela is filed, in order to act or to refrain from act"; or as it is set forth in a more generic way in the Amparo Law, the decision must establish "the order and precise definition of the conduct to be accomplished in order to make effective the tutela" (Colombia, Art. 29,4[824]); the "precise conduct to be accomplished" (Argentina, Art. 12,b[825]; Honduras, Art. 63,3[826]; Mexico, Art. 77,III; Nicaragua, Art. 45; Paraguay, Art. 16,b; Peru, Art. 17,5; Uruguay, Art. 9,b[827]; Venezuela, Art. 32,b[828]). That is why in general

---

821 See for the reference to the North American remedies, William M. TABB and Elaine W. SHOBEN, *Remedies*, Thomson West, 2005, pp. 86 ff; and in John BOURDEAU et al, "Injunctions" in Kevin Schroder, John Glenn and Maureen Placilla, *Corpus Juris Secundum*, Volume 43A, Thompson West, 2004, pp. 21 ff.; 28 ff.

822 Véase F. H. LAWSON, *Remedies of English Law,* Londres, 1980, p. 175; B. SCHWARTZ y H.W. R. WADE, *Legal control of government,* Oxford, 1978, p. 205.

823 See Allan R. BREWER–CARÍAS, "Derecho y Acción de Amparo, Vol V, *Instituciones Políticas y Constitucionales* Editorial Jurídica Venezolana, Caracas 1998, pp. 143 ff.

824 Juan Carlos ESGUERRA PORTOCARRERO, *La protección constitucional del ciudadano*, Legis, Bogotá, 2004 p. 153

825 See Néstor Pedro SAGÜÉS, *Derecho procesal Constitucional,* Vol 3, *Acción de amparo*, Editorial Astrea Buenos Aires, 1988, p. 434; Alí Joaquín SALGADO, *Juicio de amparo y acción de inconstitucionalidad*, Editorial Astrea, Buenos Aires, 1987, p. 100; José Luis LAZZARINI, *El juicio de amparo*, Ed. La Ley, Buenos Aires, 1987, pp. 345, 359.

826 Edmundo ORELLANA, *La justicia constitucional en Honduras*, Universidad Nacional Autónoma de Honduras, Tegucigalpa, 1993, pp. 181, 208, 216.

827 See Luis Alberto VIERA, *Ley de Amparo*, Ediciones Idea, Montevideo, 1993, p. 52, 207 ff.

828 Rafael CHAVERO G. *El nuevo amparo constitucional en Venezuela,* Ed. Sherwood, Caracas, 2001, p. 185 ff., 327 ff.; Allan R. BREWER–CARÍAS, "Derecho y Acción de Amparo, Vol V,

terms the Honduran Law states that the court, when issuing its decision, must always bear in mind that its "purpose is to guarantee the aggrieved party the complete enjoyment of his fundamental rights and to return things, when possible, to the stage they had previous to the violation" (Art. 63).

That is, the order can be of a restorative nature, consisting in seeking for the reestablishment of the juridical situation of the plaintiff to the stage it had before the violation or to the most similar one; and can be of a preventive nature, compelling the defendant to do or refrain from doing acts in order to maintain the plaintiff in the situation of enjoyments of is rights. As it is expressly provided in Article 80 of the Mexican Amparo Law:

> **Article 80.** When the claimed act is of a positive character, the decision granting the amparo will have the purpose to restore the aggrieved party in the complete enjoyment of the harmed constitutional guarantee, reestablishing things to the stage they had before the violation; when the claimed act is of negative character, the effect of the amparo will be to compel the responsible authority to act in the sense to respect the guarantee and to accomplish what the same guarantee implies.

The same provision is set forth in Article 49 of the Costa Rican Constitutional Jurisdiction Law; as well as in Article 46 of the Nicaraguan Amparo Law. Its content has been explained by Baker as follows:

> "When the act complained of is of a positive character, the writ of amparo has the form of a prohibitory injunction plus whatever additional elements that may be necessary to repair damages already inflicted. The latter is to be accomplished by reproducing the situation that existed before the Constitution was violated. When the act is negative in character, the writ takes the form of an order directing the responsible authority to actively comply with the provisions of the violated constitutional guarantee. In both cases, the purpose of the judgment is to restore to the complaint the full and unimpaired enjoyment of his constitutional rights. Consistent with this purpose, monetary damages are not appropriate remedies in amparo"[829].

Accordingly, it can be said that one of the main characteristic of the amparo in all Latin American countries is its restorative or reestablishing purpose. In this regard, for example, the Colombian Tutela Law provided that "when the claim is directed against an authority action, the tutela decision has the purpose of guaranteeing the aggrieved party the complete enjoyment of his right and when possible, to return the situation to the stage previous to the violation" (Art. 23). A similar provision is established in El Salvador (Art. 35), Costa Rica (Art. 49) and in Peru (Art. 1), where Article 55,3 of the Constitutional Procedures Code provides as one of the contents of the amparo decision "the restitution or reestablishment of the aggrieved party in the complete enjoyment of his constitutional rights ordering that things will revert to the stage they had before the violation", as well as the order for the conduct to be accomplished for the effective compliance with the decision (Art. 55,4).

Instituciones Políticas y Constitucionales Editorial Jurídica Venezolana, Caracas, 1998, pp. 399 ff.

829 See Richard D. BAKER, *Judicial Review in Mexico. A Study of the Amparo Suit,* University of Texas Press, Austin, 1971, p. 238.

In other perspective, in Guatemala, the Amparo law regarding the effects of the amparo decision states that it will suspend, regarding the claimant, the application of the challenged statute, regulation, resolution or act, and being the case, the reestablishment of the affected juridical situation or the ending of the measure" (Art. 49,a; Ecuador, Art. 51). Also in Colombia, according to Article 29,6 of the Tutela Law, "when the violation or threat of harming derives form the application of a norm incompatible with the fundamental rights, the resulting judicial decision resolving the action must also order the inapplicability of the challenged norm in the concrete case". In a similar sense it is stated in the Honduran Constitutional Justice Law (Art. 63,2)

But the amparo decision also can have protective character when issued against omissions or actions. In cases in which the harm to the constitutional right is caused by a negative of action or an omission from a public authority, in which cases, as set forth in the Colombian Tutela Law, "the decision will order the issuance of the act or the accomplishment of the adequate actions, for which purpose it must establish a prompt delay" (Art. 23). A similar provision is established in the El Salvador Amparo Law (Art. 35) and in the Ecuatorian Amparo law (Art. 51). Also, the Guatemalan Amparo Law sets forth that in such cases the amparo decision will establish a term for the delay to be ended, if the case is only a matter of delay in resolving" (Art. 49,b; Costa Rica, Art 49); and in cases where the amparo is filed against an omission of the authority to issue a regulation of a statute, the court will decide determining the basis and elements to be apply in the case according to the general principles of law (Art. 49,c). Additionally, in Costa Rica, in such cases, the judicial order must establish a term of two months for the authority to issue the regulation (Art. 49)

In cases referred to mere conduct or material activity or threats, according to the Costa Rican Constitutional Jurisdiction Law (Art. 49) and Colombian Tutela Law (Art. 23), the amparo or tutela decision will "order its immediate ending, as well as measures to prevent any new violation or threat, disturbance or restriction". Also, in cases where if by the moment where the tutela protection is granted, the challenged act has ceased in its effects or has produced them, making impossible to restore the plaintiff in the enjoyment of his rights, the court will warn the public authority not to cause again in any way, the actions or omissions which originated the tutela suit (Colombia, Art. 24). In a similar way it is stated in the Peruvian Constitutional Procedures Code (Art. 1).

2. The question of the annulling content of the amparo decision

In general terms it can be said that the amparo suit in Latin America does not have annulling purposes regarding the State acts that can cause or provoke the harm or threats to constitutional rights, corresponding the decisions to annul statutes to the Constitutional Jurisdiction and to the Administrative Jurisdictions when administrative acts are targeted.

In effect, if the amparo action is filed directly against statutes, as in some countries it is possible in cases of self executing laws (Mexico[830], Guatemala[831], Honduras[832]), the amparo judge, when granting the amparo has no power to annul the statute, and in order to protect the harmed or threatened right it only declares its inapplicability to the plaintiff, as is also the case in Venezuela[833]. In countries where the concentrated method of judicial review exists, the annulment of statutes with general or *erga omnes* effects, is a judicial power reserved to the Constitutional Jurisdictions (Constitutional Courts or Tribunal); and in countries with the diffuse method of judicial review, if it is true that there is not such judicial power to annul statutes, the courts are only empowered to declare their unconstitutionality regarding the concrete case. Thus, in countries with the diffuse method of judicial review, in general terms when the competent courts in an amparo suit grants the constitutional protection, they have the power to declare the unconstitutionality of the applicable statute in the concrete case.

Nonetheless, the case of Costa Rica must be mentioned because the Constitutional Chamber of the Supreme Court is the competent court to decide the amparo suits and the nullity actions against statutes, Article 48 of the Constitutional Jurisdiction Law provides that when the amparo is filed against a statute norm or when the Constitutional Chambers determines that the challenged acts are founded in a statute, it will decide to suspend the procedure and ask for the petitioner to file a petition in a term of 15 days, for judicial review of the unconstitutionality of the statute (Art. 48).

In Venezuela, regarding the possibility for the Chambers of the Supreme Tribunal to exercise the diffuse control of the constitutionality of legislation when deciding in a concrete case, the Law regulating the Tribunal provides that the other Chambers must notify the Constitucional Chamber for it to proceed to examine in an abstract way the constitutionality of the statute and eventually declare its nullity (Articles 5, 1,22; and 5,5)[834].

In cases where the amparo action is filed against administrative acts, again, in general terms the amparo decision cannot annul the corresponding administrative act, but only suspend its application to the plaintiff, corresponding to the Administrative Jurisdiction the exclusive power to annul such acts, as is the case in Venezue-

---

830 See Eduardo FERRER MAC–GREGOR, *La acción constitucional de amparo en México y España. Estudio de derecho comparado*, Editorial Porrúa, México, 2002, pp. 262–263; Richard D. BAKER, *Judicial Review in Mexico. A Study of the Amparo Suit,* University of Texas Press, Austin, 1971, p. 270

831 See in Jorge Mario GARCÍA LAGUARDIA, *Jurisprudencia constitucional. Guatemala., Honduras. México, Una Muestra*, Guatemala, 1986, pp. 23, 24, 92, 93.

832 See Edmundo ORELLANA, *La justicia constitucional en Honduras*, Universidad Nacional Autónoma de Honduras, Tegucigalpa, 1993, pp. 208, 221.

833 Rafael CHAVERO G. *El nuevo amparo constitucional en Venezuela,* Ed. Sherwood, Caracas 2001, pp. 468 ff.

834 See Allan R. BREWER–CARÍAS, *Ley Orgánica del Tribunal Supremo de Justicia*, Editorial Jurídica Venezolana, Caracas, 2004, p. 40.

la[835]. In this regard, the case of Peru must be highlighted because its Constitutional Procedures Code expressly provides that the amparo decision must contain "the declaration of the nullity of the decision, act or resolution that has impeded the complete exercise of the constitutional rights protected with the ruling, and in the case, the extension of its effects" (Art. 55)[836]. Also in Costa Rica, according to Article 49 of the Constitutional Jurisdiction Law, it is considered that in case of amparo actions against administrative acts, the granting of the amparo implies the annulling effects of the decision.

Finally, regarding the amparo action when filed against judicial decisions, the effects of the ruling granting the amparo protection are also the annulment of the challenged judicial act or decision, as happens in Venezuela[837].

3. The non compensatory character of the amparo decision

Similarly to the North American injunction[838], in general terms, the Latin American amparo suit and decision have not a compensatory character in the sense that the function of the courts in such suit is not to condemn the defendant to pay the plaintiff any sort of compensation for damages caused. For instance in the case of an illegitimate administrative order to demolish a building issued by a municipal authority, if executed, even if it violates the constitutional right to property, it cannot be the object of an amparo action due to the irreparable character of the harm. Consequently, the amparo judge is not competent to condemn the public entity to pay damages. The amparo judge, in such cases, could only have the possibility to prevent the harm, for instance by suspending the demolition before its execution, but never to condemn the entity to the payment of compensation. The amparo suit, as mentioned, is in general terms a preventive and restorative process, but not a compensatory one[839].

---

835 Rafael CHAVERO G. *El nuevo amparo constitucional en Venezuela,* Ed. Sherwood, Caracas 2001, pp. 358 ff.; Allan R. BREWER–CARÍAS, "Derecho y Acción de Amparo, Vol V, *Instituciones Políticas y Constitucionales,* Editorial Jurídica Venezolana, Caracas, 1998, pp. 144; 400.

836 See Samuel B. ABAD YUPANQUI, *El proceso constitucional de amparo*, Gaceta Jurídica, Lima, 2004, p. 186

837 See Rafael CHAVERO G. *El nuevo amparo constitucional en Venezuela,* Ed. Sherwood, Caracas, 2001, p. 511; Allan R. BREWER–CARÍAS, "Derecho y Acción de Amparo, Vol V, *Instituciones Políticas y Constitucionales* Editorial Jurídica Venezolana, Caracas, 1998, p. 297.

838 See John BOURDEAU et al, "Injunctions" in Kevin Schroder, John Glenn and Maureen Placilla, *Corpus Juris Secundum*, Volume 43A, Thomson West, 2004, p. 20

839 See José Luis LAZZARINI, *El juicio de amparo*, Ed. La Ley, Buenos Aires1987, pp. 346–347; Néstor Pedro SAGÜÉS, *Derecho procesal Constitucional,* Vol. 3, *Acción de amparo*, Editorial Astrea Buenos Aires, 1988, p. 437; Rafael CHAVERO G. *El nuevo amparo constitucional en Venezuela,* Ed. Sherwood, Caracas 2001, pp. 185, 242, 262, 326, 328; Allan R. BREWER–CARÍAS, "Derecho y Acción de Amparo, Vol V, *Instituciones Políticas y Constitucionales,* Editorial Jurídica Venezolana, Caracas, 1998, p. 143.

Nonetheless, if it is true that this is the general principle, some Latin American Amparo Laws give compensatory character to the amparo suit a. This is the case of Bolivia, Colombia and Costa Rica.

In Bolivia, Article 102,II of the Law, regarding the content of the amparo decision, states that when granting the amparo the court will determine the existence of civil and criminal liability, fixing the amount of the damages and prejudices to be paid. Also, in Guatemala, Article 59 of the Law refers to the damages and prejudices, stating that when the court in its decision condemns to the payment of damages and prejudices, it must fix its amount or at least establish the basis for its determination (Art. 59).

Bolivia and Guatemala are the only Latin American Amparo Laws that provide for a direct compensatory character of the amparo decision. In other legislations, such as Colombia and Costa Rica the compensation in the amparo decision is only established in an abstract way.

In effect, in Costa Rica, Article 51 of the Constitutional Jurisdiction Law provides that "always when an amparo is granted the court, in abstract, will condemn for the compensation of damages and prejudices", and the settlement belongs in the stage of the execution of the decision. When the amparo action is filed against authorities, the condemnation will be issued against the State or against the entity where the defendant works, and jointly with the latter if he has acted with dolus or guilt, without excluding all other administrative, civil or criminal liabilities. Also, in case when the amparo process is pending and the challenged State act is revoked, stopped or suspended, the amparo will be granted only to the effects of the corresponding decision awarding compensation (Art. 52). In these cases the settlement will be made by the Administrative Jurisdiction courts[840].

In cases where the amparo action is filed against individuals, Article 53 of the same Law provides that when granting the amparo, the court must also condemn the person or responsible entity to compensate for the damages and prejudices, the settlement of which will be made in the civil judicial execution of the decision mean.

Also in Colombia, Article 25 of the Tutela Law provides that when the affected party has not other means, and the violation of his rights is manifest and a clear and indisputable consequence of an arbitrariness, in the decision granting the tutela the court can, ex officio, order in an abstract way the compensation of the damages caused, provided it is needed in order to assure the effective enjoyment for the right. Similarly to what is provided in the Costa Rican Law, Article 23 of the Colombian Law establishes that the condemn will be issued against the entity where the defendant works, and jointly with the latter if he has acted with dolus or guilt, without excluding all other administrative, civil or criminal liabilities. The settlement of the

840 See Rubén HERNÁNDEZ, *Derecho Procesal Constitucional*, Editorial Juricentro, San José, 2001, p. 268; José Luis VILLALOBOS, El recurso de amparo en Costa Rica", in Humberto Nogueira Alcalá (Editor), *Acciones constitucionales de amparo y protección: realidad y perspectivas en Chile y América Latina*", Editorial Universidad de Talca, Talca, 2000, p. 229.

compensation corresponds to the Administrative Jurisdiction courts in an incidental procedure that must take place within the following six months[841].

Also, in case where the tutela process is pending and the challenged State act is revoked, stopped or suspended, the tutela will be granted only to the effects of the corresponding decision awarding the compensation (Art. 26).

Except in these cases of Bolivia, Colombia and Costa Rica, in all other Latin American countries, the judicial actions tending to seek for compensation from the defendant, because of its liability as a consequence of the constitutional right harm or threat, must be filed before the civil or administrative judicial jurisdiction by means of the ordinary judicial remedies established for that purpose. This is provided in some Latin American Amparo Laws (El Salvador, Art. 35; Panama, Art. 2627). The Venezuelan Amparo Law also expressly provides that in cases of granting an amparo, the court must send copy of the decision to the competent authority where the public officer causing the harm works, in order to impose the corresponding disciplinary measures (Art. 27).

Finally, regarding the economic consequences of the amparo suit, in general terms in the Latin American Laws it is provided that the party against whom the decision is directed is due to pay the costs of the process (Argentina, Art. 14; Bolivia, Art. 102,III; Colombia, Art. 25; Costa Rica, Arts. 51, 53; El Salvador, Art. 35; Guatemala, Arts. 44, 45, 100; Honduras, Art. 105; Paraguay, Art. 22; Peru, Art. 56). Only in Venezuela the order to pay the costs is provided regarding the amparo suits only against individuals and not against public authorities (Art. 33).

4. The effects of the definitive judicial ruling on the amparo suit

The question of the effects of the amparo ruling refers to various aspects: first, to the scope of the effects of the judicial decision granting the amparo, whether *inter partes* or general effects; second, to the *res judicata* effects of the decision; and finally, to the extent of the compulsory effects of the ruling, regarding the consequences of the disobedience of the judicial orders.

A. *The* inter partes *effects and its exceptions*

The general rule regarding the amparo judicial decisions effects, is that it only has *inter partes* effects, that is, between the parties that have been involved in the suit, that is, the plaintiff or plaintiffs, the defendant or defendants and the third parties that have participated in the process on the side or any the aforementioned.. As it is established in the Mexican Amparo Law: "the decisions in the amparo suits only refers to the individuals or corporations, private or public which filed the actions, limiting their scope to protect them in the case, without making general declarations regarding the statute or act causing the suit" (Art. 76). In the same sense it is set forth in Article 44 of the Nicaraguan Law.

841 See Juan Carlos ESGUERRA PORTOCARRERO, *La protección constitucional del ciudadano*, Legis, Bogotá, 2004, p. 155

Thus, and as in the case of the injunctions in North America[842], the decision rendered binds only the parties to the suit, and only regarding the controversy. This is the most important consequence of the personal character of the amparo, which is an action mainly devoted for the protection of personal constitutional rights or guarantees. Other aspects refer to the general content of the ruling on constitutional questions, which in North America implies that in cases decided by the United States Supreme Court, because of the doctrine of precedent (*stare decisis*), all courts are obliged to apply the same constitutional rule in cases with a similar controversy[843]. The same rule exists in Latin America, in cases where the Supreme Courts or Constitutional Courts rulings, regarding the constitutional interpretation, have been entrusted with obligatory general effects, as is the case in Venezuela with the Constitutional Chamber rulings (Art. 336 of the Constitution) and of Peru, with the Constitutional Tribunal decisions (precedents, Art. VII of the Code on Constitutional procedures).

Thus, as a general rule, regarding the particular ruling in the amparo suit, the decision is only binding on the parties to the suit, including third parties. Those are the beneficiaries and the obliged parties.

But of course, progressively, the amparo suit in many cases has acquired a collective nature, for instance, in cases of violation of environmental rights and other diffuse and collective rights[844], in which cases, as happens in the class actions in the United States[845], the definitive ruling can benefit other persons different to those that have actively participated in the procedure as plaintiff.

The Venezuelan regulations can be highlighted in this regard. In principle, the court decisions have been constant in granting the action of *amparo* a personal character where the standing belongs firstly to "the individual directly affected by the infringement of constitutional rights and guarantees."[846]

Nonetheless, by virtue of the constitutional acknowledgment of the legal protection of diffuse or collective interests, the Constitutional Chamber of the Supreme Tribunal has also admitted the possibility of employing the action of *amparo* to assure the enforcment of those collective interests, including for instance, that of voters in their political rights. In such cases, the Chamber has granted precautionary

842 See the reference to the corresponding judicial decisions in John BOURDEAU et al, "Injunctions" in Kevin Schroder, John Glenn and Maureen Placilla, *Corpus Juris Secundum*, Volume 43A, Thomson West, 2004, pp. 414; 417.

843 See M. Glenn ABERNATHY and Barbara A. PERRY, Civil Liberties under the Constitution, University of South Carolina Press, 1993, p. 5.

844 See Rafael CHAVERO G. *El nuevo amparo constitucional en Venezuela,* Ed. Sherwood, Caracas, 2001, pp. 333 ff.

845 See M. Glenn ABERNATHY and Barbara A. PERRY, Civil Liberties under the Constitution, University of South Carolina Press, 1993, p. 6

846 See for example, decision of the Constitutional Chamber dated 03–15–2000, *Revista de Derecho Público*, N° 81, Editorial Jurídica Venezolana, 2000, pp. 322–323.

measures with *erga omnes* effects "for both individuals and corporations who have instituted an action for constitutional protection and to all voters as a group."[847]

The Constitutional Chamber, has decided that "any individual is entitled to bring suit based on diffuse or collective interests" and has extended "standing to companies, corporations, foundations, chambers, unions and other collective entities, whose object is the defense of society, as long as they act within the boundaries of their corporate objects, aimed at protecting the interests of their members regarding those objects."[848]

In addition, the Peoples' Defendant has the authority to promote, defend, and guard constitutional rights and guarantees "as well as the legitimate, collective or diffuse interests of the citizens" (Art. 280 and 281,2 of the Constitution); consequently, the Constitutional Chamber has admitted the standing of the Peoples' Defendant to bring to suit in an action of *amparo* on behalf of the citizens as a whole group. In one case the Defender of the People acted against a threat by the National Legislative Commission to appoint Electoral National Council members without fulfilling constitutional requirements.

In that case, the Constitutional Chamber, decided that "the Defender has standing to bring actions aimed at enforcing diffuse and collective rights or interests" without requiring the acquiescence of the society on whose behalf he acts, but this provision does not exclude or prevent citizens' access to the judicial system in defense of diffuse and collective rights and interests, since Article 26 of the Constitution in force provides access to the judicial system to every person, whereby individuals are entitled to bring suit as well, unless a law denies them that action.[849]. In all those cases, consequently, the judicial ruling benefits all the persons enjoying the collective rights or interest involved.

B. *The question of the scope of the* res judicata *effects*

As all definitive judicial decisions, the amparo decision in Latin America has in general *res judicata* effects, which provides stability, and is binding not only for the parties in the suit or its beneficiaries, but regarding the court itself which cannot modify its ruling (immutability). *Res judicata* implies then, the impossibility for a new suit to take place regarding the same matter already decided, or that a decision be taken in different sense than the one already decided in a previous process.

In contrast, as a general rule, the injunction ruling in North America does not have, in general, this *res judicata* effect since the injunction orders can be modified by the court. As it has been summarized regarding the judicial doctrine on the matter:

---

847 Decision of the Constitutional Chamber N° 483 of 05–29–2000 (Case: *"Queremos Elegir" y otros*), *Revista de Derecho Público*, N° 82, Editorial Jurídica Venezolana, 2000, pp 489–491. In the same sense, decision of the same Chamber N° 714 of 13–07–2000 (Case: *APRUM*).

848 See decision of the Constitutional Chamber N° 656 of 06–05–2001 (Case: *Defensor del Pueblo vs. Comisión Legislativa Nacional).*

849 Decision of the Constitutional Chamber N° 656 of 06–05–2001, (Case: *Defensor del Pueblo vs. Comisión Legislativa Nacional).*

"Injunctions are different from other judgments in the context of *res judicata* because the parties are often subject to the court's continuing jurisdiction, and the court must strike a balance between the policies of *res judicata* and the right of the court to apply modified measures to changed circumstances "[850].

But in Latin America, although the *res judicata* effects have been admitted regarding the amparo decisions, discussions have developed in many countries following a traditional distinction established between the "material" and the "formal" *res judicata*, in order to determine which one applies to the amparo ruling.

In general terms, the concept of "formal res judicata" applies to judicial decisions that even when enforced, they do not impede for a new process between the same parties to be developed, due to the fact that in such cases the matter has not been decided on the merits and on the defenses; while "material *res judicata*" exists when the judicial decision has decided on the merits, not being allowed for other processes to develop regarding the same matter.

The matter in the amparo suit is the illegitimate and manifest harm or threat caused by an identified aggrieving party to the constitutional right or guarantees of the plaintiff; matter that is to be resolved in a brief and prompt procedure. Thus, the merits on the matters are reduced to determining the existence of such illegitimate and manifest violation of the right, regardless of other matters that can be resolved or in some cases must be resolved between the parties in other processes.

As it is set forth in the Argentina Amparo Law:

Article 13. The definitive decision declaring the existence or nonexistence of an arbitrary or manifestly illegal harm, restriction, alteration or threat regarding a constitutional right and guarantee, produces res judicata regarding the amparo, and the exercise of the actions or recourses that could correspond to the parties subsist, in spite of the amparo.

A similar provision is set forth in Article 17 of the Paraguayan Law; and in Article 11 of the Uruguayan Law[851].

This provision, regarding the effects of the *res judicata*, has been considered interpreted in two ways: On the one hand, Lazzarini has considered it establishes the "material res judicata" effects regarding the protective amparo decision, arguing that the allusion the article makes regarding other actions or recourses, are referred to criminal actions tending to punish the offenses causing the harm, or to civil actions tending to obtain compensation, but not to other actions in which the amparo could be again reargued[852]. On the other hand, Sagües has considered that even being the amparo suit a bilateral process, due to its brief and prompt character with the consequent restrictions regarding proofs and formalities, there can not be a decision on the merits of the matter, so no material *res judicata* can be produced, but only a formal one, being possible for the merits to be resolved through the ordinary judicial means,

---

850 See the reference to the corresponding judicial decisions in John BOURDEAU et al, "Injunctions" in Kevin Schroder, John Glenn and Maureen Placilla, *Corpus Juris Secundum*, Volume 43A, Thomson West, 2004, p. 416. See also Owen M. FISS and Doug RENDLEMAN, Injunctions, The Foundation Press, 1984, pp. 497–498, 526.

851 See Luis Alberto VIERA, *Ley de Amparo*, Ediciones Idea, Montevideo, 1993, p. 40

852 See José Luis LAZZARINI, *El juicio de amparo*, Ed. La Ley, Buenos Aires, 1987, pp. 356 ff.

only if the parties allege a violation to their due process rights occurred (for instance, regarding evidences) in the amparo process[853].

In the Venezuelan Amparo Law, in a similar way to the Argentinean provision, and with the same different approach regarding the material or formal *res judicata* effects[854], Article 36 establishes:

> **Article 36.** The definitive amparo decision will produce legal effects regarding the right or guarantee that has been the object of the process, without prejudice of the actions or recourses that legally correspond to the parties.

In this regard, the First Court on Administrative Jurisdiction, in a decision dated October 16, 1986 (*Case Pedro J. Montilva*), decided that if in a case "the action of amparo is filed with the same object, denouncing the same violations, based on the same motives and with identical object as the previous one and directed against the same person, then it is evident that in such case, the res judicata force applies in order to avoid the rearguing of the case, due to the fact that the controversy to be resolved has the same subjective and objective identity than the one already decided"[855].

According to this doctrine, and according to Article 36 of the Law, the *res judicata* in the amparo suit only refers to what has been argued and decided in the case regarding the violation of harm produced to a constitutional right or guarantee. Thus, the amparo decision in general terms does not resolve all the possible merits of the matter but only the aspect of the violation or harm of the rights or guarantees, which is the only aspect regarding which the decision can produce res judicata effects. That is why the decision only has restorative effects, due to the fact that by means of the amparo suit, as it has been resolved by the Supreme Court of Venezuela, "non of the three types of judicial declarative, constitutive or to condemn decision can be obtained, nor, of course, the interpretative decision"[856]. For example, if an amparo decision is issued against an administrative act because it causes harm to constitutional rights, it only has restorative or reestablishing effects suspending the application of the challenged act, but it does not have annulling effects. Consequently, the amparo decision in such cases, does not have res judicata effects regarding the judicial review action that can be filed against the administrative act before the Administrative Jurisdiction courts.[857]

That is, in matters of amparo suit, in many cases the amparo decision regarding the violation of the right by the illegitimate action of omissions, resolves definitively

---

853 See Néstor Pedro SAGÜÉS, *Derecho procesal Constitucional,* Vol 3, *Acción de amparo*, Editorial Astrea Buenos Aires, 1988, pp. 449 ff.

854 See Rafael CHAVERO G. *El nuevo amparo constitucional en Venezuela,* Ed. Sherwood, Caracas, 2001, pp. 338 ff.; Gustavo LINARES BENZO, *El proceso de amparo en Venezuela*, Caracas, 1999, p. 121 f.

855 See in *Revista de Derecho Público,* N° 28, EJV, Caracas, 1986, p. 106

856 See decisión of the Politico–Administrative Chamber of July 15, 1992, in *Revista de Derecho Público,* N° 51, EJV, Caracas, 1992, p. 171.

857 See Allan R. BREWER–CARÍAS, "Derecho y Acción de Amparo, Vol V, *Instituciones Políticas y Constitucionales* Editorial Jurídica Venezolana, Caracas, 1998, pp. 346 ff.

the matter, not being necessary to discuss any other legal matter through any other process. In such cases, it can be said that the amparo ruling has material res judicata effects. But in other cases, after the amparo decision has been issued, other legal questions can remain pending to be resolved in other processes, and that is why the amparo decision is issued "without prejudice of the actions or recourses that could legally correspond to the parties". Is has been said that the amparo decision has formal res judicata effects, which do not refer to the matter of the right's violation ruling.[858]

These effects of the amparo decision also exists regarding the amparo suit against individuals, and a case can illustrate the matter: in 1987 a controversy arose in a private Caracas University (Santa María), regarding the position for the Head of the institution (Rector), a position that was disputed by two professors that argued they where appointed by the University bodies. The First Court on Administrative Jurisdiction in a decision dated December 17, 1987, issued an amparo decision on the matter filed by one of the *Rectores* in order to assure legal security to the university community, due to the fact that the matter regarding who was the Head of the University could not remain indefinitely unresolved, ruled considering legitimate the designation of one of the Rectores, "until the controversy regarding the legitimacy of the bodies that made the appointments be resolved by the judicial competent court"[859]. According to this decision, a civil action was needed to be resolved in order to resolve the merits.

The different approaches to the *res judicata* regarding amparo decisions have been expressly resolved, for instance, in the El Salvador Amparo Law, which prescribes the following:

> **Article 81**. The definitive amparo decision produces *res judicata* effects against any person of public officer, had he intervened or not in the process, only regarding the matter of the challenged act being or not constitutional or contrary to the constitutional provisions. With all, the content of the decision does not constitute in itself a declaration, recognition or constitution of private rights of individuals or of the state; consequently the decision can not be opposed as a *res judicata* defense regarding any action that could be afterward filed before the courts of the Republic".

In similar terms it is set forth in the Honduran Law (Art. 72), and in the Guatemalan Law, which provides that "the decisions issued in the amparo suits have declarative effects and do not originate the res judicata defense, without prejudice of the provisions derived from the *jurisprudencia* on the matter (Art. 190).

Finally, in Peru, the Code of Constitutional Procedures does not resolve the discussion, just declaring that "In the constitutional processes, only the final decision deciding the merits acquire the *res judicata* authority" (Art. 6)[860]. But the Peruvian Code is one of the few that expressly regulates the effects of the *res judicata* au-

858 See in this respect, Juan Manuel ERRAZURIZ and Jorge Miguel OTERO A., *Aspectos procesales del recurso de protección*, Editorial Jurídica de Chile, Santiago 1989, pp. 195 ff, 202.

859 See in *El Universal,* Caracas, December 27, 1987, p. 2–5.

860 See Samuel B. ABAD YUPANQUI, *El proceso constitucional de amparo*, Gaceta Jurídica, Lima 2004, pp. 194 ff.

thority regarding the preliminary orders or measures issued during the procedure, in the sense that they will be automatically extinguished. Nonetheless, if the final decision grants the amparo, the effects of the preliminary measures will be kept being converted if definitive (Art. 16).

III. THE OBLIGATORY CHARACTER OF THE AMPARO RULINGS AND THE PUNISHMENT FOR CONTEMPT

The amparo ruling, as all judicial decisions, is binding upon the parties and all other public officers that must apply them, and the defendant must immediately obey by it as it is expressed in the Amparo Laws (Bolivia, Art. 102; Colombia, Arts. 27, 30; Costa Rica, Art. 53; Ecuador, Art, 58; Honduras, Art. 65; Nicaragua, Art. 48; Peru, Arts. 22, 24; Venezuela, Arts. 29, 30).

In order to execute the decision, the courts, ex officio or at the party's request, must adopt all the measures directed to its accomplishment, being empowered in the Guatemalan Law to issue orders and mandamus to the authorities and public officers of Public Administration or obligated persons (Art. 55). The amparo courts are also empowered to use public enforcement units to assure the accomplishment of its decisions (Guatemala, Art. 105; Ecuador, Art. 61; El Salvador, Art. 61; Nicaragua, Art. 77).

But the amparo judges in Latin America do not have direct power to punish for disobedience, in other words, they do not have contempt power, which in contrast is one of the most important futures of the injunctive relief system in the United States. This is particularly important regarding criminal contempt, which was established since the *In Re Debs* case (158 U.S. 564, 15 S.Ct. 900, 39 L.Ed. 1092 (1895), where according to Justice Brewer who delivered the court's opinion, it was ruled:

> "But the power of a court to make an order carries with it the equal power to punish for a disobedience of that order, and the inquiry as to the question of disobedience has been, from time immemorial, the special function of the court. And this is no technical rule. In order that a court may compel obedience to its order it must have the right to inquire whether there has been any disobedience thereof. To submit the question of disobedience to another tribunal, be it a jury or another court, would operate to deprive the proceedings of half its efficiency...In Watson v. Williams, 36 Miss. 331, 341, it was said: "The power to fine and imprison for contempt, from the earliest history of jurisprudence, has been regarded as the necessary incident and attribute of a court, without which it could no more exist than without a judge. It is a power inherent in all courts of record, and coexisting with them by the wise provisions of the common law. A court without the power effectually to protect itself against the assaults of the lawless, or to enforce its orders, judgments, or decrees against the recusant parties before it, would be a disgrace to the legislation, and a stigma upon the age which invented it".[861]

These contempt powers are precisely what gave to the injunction in the United States its effectiveness regarding any disobedience, being empowered the same court to vindicate their own power by imposing criminal or economic sanctions by

861 See Owen M. FISS and Doug RENDLEMAN, "Injunctions", The Foundation Press, 1984, p. 13. See also William M. TABB and Elaine W. SHOBEN, *Remedies*, Thomson West, 2005, pp. 72 ff

means of imprisonment and fines. The Latin American courts, in contrast do not have such powers, or they are very weak.

In effect, even though the disobedience of the amparo ruling is punishable in the Amparo Latin American Laws, it is not the power of the same amparo court to apply the sanctions. In general terms, the sanctioning powers are attributed to Public Administration of to criminal court. So, in case of disobedience, the court must seek for the initiation of an administrative disciplinary procedure against the disobedient public officer that must be developed by the corresponding superior organ in Public Administration (Colombia, Art. 27; Peru, Art. 59; Nicaragua, Art. 48). Regarding the application of criminal sanctions, the amparo court in cases of disobedience, must seek for the initiation of a criminal procedure against the disobedient to be brought before the competent criminal courts (Bolivia, Art. 104; Colombia, Arts. 27, 52, 53; Costa Rica, Art. 71; Ecuador, Art. 58; El Salvador, Art. 37, 61; Guatemala, Arts. 32, 54, 92; Honduras, Art. 62; Panama, Art. 2632; Mexico, Arts. 202, 209; Nicaragua, Art. 77; Venezuela, Art. 31). Therefore, the amparo judge in Latin America does not have the power to impose directly to those that disobey their orders, disciplinary or criminal sanctions, and only in some countries there have been improvements in the legislations, granting the same amparo courts the powers to impose successive fines (*astreintes*) up to the accomplishing of the order to those disobeying them (Colombia, Art. 27; Guatemala, Art. 53; Nicaragua, Art. 66; Peru, Art. 22[862]) and in some cases, to impose administrative arrests (Colombia, Art. 27).

IV. THE REVISION OF THE AMPARO DECISIONS BY A CONSTITUTIONAL COURT OR THE SUPREME COURT

The amparo decisions, except in the cases where the competent court that issued them is the highest court in the country, as happens in Costa Rica (Constitutional Chamber of the Supreme Court of Justice), Nicaragua (Constitutional Chamber of the Supreme Court of Justice) and El Salvador (Constitutional Chamber of the Supreme Court of Justice), can be appealed according the general rules established in the procedural codes. Due to the general rule of double instance, the decisions cannot normally arrive to their revision by the Supreme Court of the Constitutional Court, except when an extraordinary means for revision is established, in some cases similar to the writ for certiorari in the United States.

In effects, whether or not they involve constitutional issues, the United States Supreme Court is authorized to review all the decisions of the federal courts of appeals, and of the specialized federal courts, and all the decisions of the supreme courts of the states involving issues of federal law, but on a discretionary basis, when considering a petition for a writ of certiorari.

In effect, in all such cases where there is no right of appeal established and where the mandatory appellate jurisdiction of the Supreme Court is not established, they can reach the Supreme Court as petitions for certiorari, where a litigant who has lost in a lower court, petitions a review in the Supreme Court, setting out the reasons

862 See Samuel B. ABAD YUPANQUI, *El proceso constitucional de amparo*, Gaceta Jurídica, Lima, 2004, p. 136.

why review should be granted.[863] This method of seeking review by the Supreme Court is expressly established in the cases set forth in the 28 US Code, according to the Supreme Court's Rule N° 17,1 establishing that the rules governing review on certiorari are, "not a matter of right, but of judicial discretion, and will be granted only when there are special and important reasons therefore".

According to this Rule, consequently, in order to promote uniformity and consistency in federal law, the following factors might prompt the Supreme Court to grant certiorari: 1. Important questions of federal law on which the court has not previously ruled; 2. Conflicting interpretations of federal law by lower courts; 3. Lower courts decisions that conflict with previous Supreme Court decisions; and 4. Lower court departures from the accepted and usual course of judicial proceedings.[864]

Of course, review may be granted on the basis of other factors, or denied even if one or more of the above mentioned factors is present. The discretion of the Supreme Court is not limited, and it is the importance of the issue and the public interest considered by the Court in a particular case, which leads the Court to grant certiorari and to review some cases.

Although in different ways in Argentina, Bolivia, Brazil, Colombia, Honduras, Mexico and Venezuela, the Constitutional Courts, the Constitutional Chambers of the Supreme Courts or the latter, can finally review the amparo decisions.

In effect, in Argentina, even thought the actions of amparo are in general exercised before the judges of first instance, the cases can reach the Supreme Court of the Nation, by means of an extraordinary recourse when in the judicial decision a matter of judicial review of constitutionality is resolved[865]. This is, undoubtedly, the judicial mean through which the Supreme Court normally decides upon the final interpretation of the Constitution when reviewing the constitutionality of state acts, and consequently it is the most important mean for judicial review.

But of course, the "extraordinary recourse" is quite different to the American request for writ of *certiorari*, in the sense that the Supreme Court of the Nation does not have discretionary powers in accepting extraordinary recourses. On the contrary, in such cases it is a mandatory jurisdiction, exercised as a consequence of a right the parties have to introduce the extraordinary recourse. In these cases the Supreme Court does not act as a mere third instance court, particularly because the Court does not review the motives of the judicial decision under consideration, regarding the facts. Its power of review is concentrated only in aspects of law regarding constitutional questions.

In Brazil there also exists an extraordinary recourse of constitutionality that can be filed before the Federal Supreme Tribunal, which is the most important court on

863 See L. BAUM, *The Supreme Court*, Washington, 1981, p. 81.

864 See. R.A. ROSSUM and G.A. TARR, *American Constitutional Law*, New York, 1983, p. 28.

865 See Elias GUASTAVINO, *Recurso extraordinario de inconstitucionalidad,* Ed. La Roca, Buenos Aires, Argentina, 1992.

matters of judicial review[866], against the judicial decision issued on matters of protection of constitutional rights by the Superior Federal Court or by the Regional Federal Courts, when it is considered that the courts have made the decisions in a way inconsistent with the Constitution, or in which the court has denied the validity of a treaty or federal statute, or when the decisions has declared the unconstitutionality of a treaty or of a Federal Law; and when they deem a local government law or act that has been challenged as unconstitutional or contrary to a valid federal law (Art. 199,III,b,c) .

The general judicial procedural system in Venezuela is also governed by the by–instance principle, so that judicial decisions resolving cases on judicial review are subject to the ordinary appeal. The cases could only reach the Cassation Chambers of the Supreme Tribunal through cassation recourses (Art. 312 and ff. CCP). Because this situation could lead to possible dispersion of the judicial decision on constitutional matters, the 1999 Constitution, also provided a corrective procedure by granting the Constitutional Chamber of the Supreme Tribunal of Justice, the power to:

> "Review final judicial decisions issued by the courts of the Republic on amparo suits and when deciding judicial review of statutes, in the terms established by the respective organic law." (Art. 336,10 C)

Regarding this provision, it must be pointed out that it is neither an appeal nor a general second or third procedural instance. It is an exceptional faculty of the Constitutional Chamber to review, upon its judgment and discretion, through an extraordinary recourse (in similar sense as the *writ of certiorary*) exercised against *last instance* decisions in which constitutional issues are decided by means of judicial review or in *amparo* suits.

It is a reviewing non obligatory power that can be exercised in an optional way[867]. The Chamber has the power to choose the cases in which it considers convenient to decide because of the constitutional relevance of the matter.

In Colombia, the creation of the Constitutional Court as the ultimate guardian of the Constitution originated the attribution of the Court to review all the judicial decisions resolving actions for tutela. As opposed to the Venezuelan or Argentinean cas-

---

866 See in general Manoel Goncalves FERREIRA FILHO, "O sistema constitucional brasileiro e as recentes inovacoes no controle de constitucionalidade" in *Anuario Iberoamericano de Justicia Constitucional*, N° 5, 2001, Centro de Estudios Políticos y Constitucionales, Madrid, España, 2001; José Carlos BARBOSA MOREIRA, "El control judicial de la constitucionalidad de las leyes en el Brasil: un bosquejo", in *Desafíos del control de constitucionalidad*, Ediciones Ciudad Argentina, Buenos Aires, Argentina, 1996; Paulo BONAVIDES, "Jurisdicao constitucional e legitimidade (algumas observacoes sobre o Brasil)" en *Anuario Iberoamerivano de Justicia Constitucional* N° 7, Centro de Estudios Políticos y Constitucionales, Madrid, 2003; Enrique Ricardo LEWANDOWSKI, "Notas sobre o controle da constitucionalidade no Brasil", en Edgar CORZO SOSA, y otros, *Justicia Constitucional Comparada*, Ed. Universidad Nacional Autónoma de México, México D.F. 1993; Zeno VELOSO, *Controle jurisdicional de constitucionalidade,* Ed. Cejup, Belém, Brasil, 1999.

867 See Allan R. BREWER–CARÍAS, *Judicial Review in Comparative Law*, *op. cit*. p. 141; See the comments of Jesús María CASAL, *Constitución y Justicia Constitucional*, Caracas 2003, p. 92

es, in Colombia there is not a specific recourse for revision, but an attribution that must be automatically accomplished in a discretionary way. In effect, the Decree regulating the procedure sets forth that when a tutela decision is not appealed, it must be automatically sent for revision to the Constitutional Court (Article 31). In cases where the decisions are appealed, the superior court's decision, whether confirming or revoking the appealed decision, must also be automatically sent to the Constitutional Court for its revision (Article 32). .

In Bolivia, according to the Constitution (Article 120,7), and to the Law of the Constitutional Tribunal (Articles 7,8; 93; 102,V), all judicial decisions issued on amparo or habeas corpus suits must be sent ex officio to the Constitutional Tribunal in order to be reviewed. The revision, in the case of Bolivia, is also different to the Argentinean, Brazilian, and Venezuelan extraordinary recourses for revision, and more similar to the situation in Colombia where it is not a recourse, but an obligatory revision that the Constitutional Tribunal must do, to which the decisions must be sent by the courts.

In Honduras, a procedure of two instances is also established and in all cases an obligatory consultation of the amparo decisions is provided. Regarding the decisions issued by the department courts, they must be sent in consultation before the Appellate Courts; and regarding these decision issued by the Appellate Courts, they can be subject to review by the Constitutional Chamber of the Supreme Court by means of the parties' request for study.

In such cases the Constitutional Chamber has also discretionary power to resolve the admissibility of the request (Article 68). Regarding the decisions adopted in first instance by the Appeals Courts in questions of amparo, they must also be sent for consultation before the Constitutional Chamber of the Supreme Court (Article 69).

Finally, the case of Mexico must be also mentioned. Through the constitutional reform of 1983, the Supreme Court was vested with a discretionary competency to select to decide, requesting them from the Circuit courts, ex officio or at the request of the General Prosecutor of the Republic, the cases of amparo of constitutional relevance; Later, by means of another constitutional reform in 1988, power was attributed to the Supreme Court to decide in last instance all cases of amparo suits where the constitutionality of a statute is at stake. Both attributions allow the Supreme Court to give final interpretation of the Constitution in a uniform way[868].

---

868 See Joaquín BRAGE CAMAZANO, *La jurisdicción constitucional de la libertad (Teoría general, Argentina, México, Corte Interamericana de Derechos Humanos)*, Editorial Porrúa, Instituto Mexicano de Derecho Procesal Constitucional, México 2005, pp. 153–155.

III
CONSTITUTIONAL COURTS AS POSITIVE LEGISLATORS IN COMPARATIVE LAW (2010)

This is the original text of the *General Report* I wrote for the XVIII *International Congress Congress of Comparative Law,* organized by the International Academy of Comparative Law and held in Washington, DC, on July 2010.[*]

INTRODUCTION
HANS KELSEN, JUDICIAL REVIEW, AND THE NEGATIVE LEGISLATOR

At the beginning of the twentiest century, Hans Kelsen, in his very well–known article "La garantie juridictionnelle de la constitution (La justice constitutionnelle)," published in 1928, in the *Revue du droit public et de la science politique en France et a l'étranger*, began to write for non–German–speaking readers about constitutional courts as "negative legislators."[1] As Kelsen was one of the most important constructors of modern public law of the twentieth century, it is indeed impossible to

* This text of my General Report was published in 2011, as part of my book: *Constitutional Courts as Posiyive Legislators. A Comparative Law Study*, Cambridge University Press, New York 2011, pp. 5–191, which contained also all the national Reports I received for the purpose of the Congres. An abrige version of the report was published in the book: Karen B. Brown y David V. Snyder (Editors), *General Reports of the XVIIIth Congress pf the International Academy of Comparative Law– Rapports Généraux du XVIIIème Congrès de l'Académie Internationale de Droit Comparé*, Springer, 2012, pp. 549–569.

1 See Hans KELSEN, "La garantie juridictionnelle de la constitution (La justice constitutionnelle)," *Revue du droit public et de la science politique en France et a l'ètranger*, Librairie Général de Droit et de Jurisprudence, Paris 1928, pp. 197–257. See also the Spanish text in Hans KELSEN, *La garantía jurisdiccional de la Constitución (La justicia constitucional)*, Universidad Nacional Autónoma de México, Mexico City 2001.

write about the opposite assertion – on constitutional courts as positive legislators – without referring to his thoughts on the matter.[2]

In his article, while sharing his experience on the establishment and functioning of the Constitutional Court of Austria in 1920, conceived of as an important part of the concentrated system of judicial review that he had introduced for the first time in Europe,[3] Kelsen began to explain the role of such constitutional organs established outside of the judicial branch of government, but with jurisdictional powers to annul statutes they deemed unconstitutional.

The Austrian system, which was established the same year as that in Czechoslovakia,[4] according to Kelsen's own ideas,[5] sharply contrasted with, at that time, the already well–established and well–developed diffuse system of judicial review adopted in the United States, where for more than a century, courts and the Supreme Court had already developed a very active role as constitutional judges.[6]

It is true that the classic distinction of the judicial review systems in the contemporary world, between the concentrated systems of judicial review and the diffuse systems of judicial review,[7] has developed and has changed, and is difficult to apply in many cases clearly and sharply.[8] Consequently, in almost all democratic coun-

---

2 As all the national reporters, in one way or another, have done in their national reports for subject IV.B.2 of the eighteenth International Congress of Comparative Law, Washington, D.C., July 2010. See the text of all national reports in Part 2 of this book.

3 See generally Charles EISENMANN, *La justice constitutionelle et la Haute Cour Constitutionelle d'Autriche* (reprint of the 1928 edition, with H. Kelsen's preface), Economica, Paris 1986; Konrad Lachmayer, *Austrian National Report*, p. 1.

4 See Zdenek KÜHN, *Czech National Report*, p. 1.

5 Kelsen called constitutional justice his "most personal work." See Theo ÖHLINGER, "Hans Kelsen y el derecho constitucional federal austriaco: Una retrospectiva crítica," *Revista Iberoamericana de Derecho Procesal Constitucional*, N° 5, Instituto Iberoamericano de Derecho Procesal Constitucional, Editorial Porrúa, Mexico City 2006, p. 219.

6 For the purpose of this general report, the expression "constitutional courts" refers generally to constitutional tribunals or courts – specifically established in many countries as constitutional jurisdictions, with powers to annul with *erga omnes* effects unconstitutional statutes, as well as to supreme courts or tribunals also acting as constitutional jurisdictions, or any court or tribunal when acting as constitutional judges.

7 See generally Mauro CAPPELLETTI, *Judicial Review in Contemporary World*, Bobbs–Merrill, Indianapolis 1971, p. 45; Mauro Cappelletti and J. C. Adams, "Judicial Review of Legislation: European Antecedents and Adaptations," *Harvard Law Review* 79, N° 6, April 1966, p. 1207; Mauro CAPPELLETTI, "El control judicial de la constitucionalidad de las leyes en el derecho comparado," *Revista de la Facultad de Derecho de México* 61, 1966, p. 28; Allan R. Brewer–Carías, *Judicial Review in Comparative Law*, Cambridge University Press, Cambridge 1989; Allan R. BREWER–CARÍAS, *Étutes de droit pubic comparé*, Bruylant, Brussels 2000, pp. 653 ff.

8 See, e.g., Lucio PEGORARO, "Clasificaciones y modelos de justicia constitucional en la dinámica de los ordenamientos," *Revista Iberoamericana de Derecho Procesal Constitucional*, N° 2, Instituto Iberoamericano de Derecho Procesal Constitucional, Editorial Porrúa, Mexico City 2004, pp. 131 ff.; Alfonse CELOTTO, "La justicia constitucional en el mundo: Formas y modalidades," *Revista Iberoamericana de Derecho Procesal Constitucional*, N° 1, Instituto

tries, a convergence of principles and solutions on matters of judicial review has progressively occurred,[9] to the point that nowadays it is possible to say that there are no means or solutions that apply exclusively in one or another system.[10] Nonetheless, this fact, in my opinion, does not deprive the distinction of its basic sense.

In effect, and in spite of criticisms of the concentrated–diffuse distinction,[11] the distinction remains very useful, particularly for comparative law analysis, and it is not possible to consider it obsolete.[12] The basis of the distinction, which can always be considered valid, is established between, on the one hand, constitutional systems in which all courts are constitutional judges and have the power to review the constitutionality of legislation in decisions on particular cases and controversies, without such power necessarily being expressly established in the Constitution, and on the other hand, constitutional systems in which a constitutional jurisdiction is established assigning its exercise to a constitutional court, tribunal or council or to the supreme or high court or tribunal of the country, as the only court with jurisdictional

---

Iberoamericano de Derecho Procesal Constitucional, Editorial Porrúa, Mexico City 2004, pp. 3 ff.

9 See, e.g., Francisco FERNÁNDEZ SEGADO, *La justicia constitucional ante el siglo XXI. La progresiva convergencia de los sistemas americano y europeo–kelseniano*, Librería Bonomo Editrice, Bologna 2003, pp. 40 ff.

10 On the effort to establish a new basis for new distinctions, see Louis FAVOREU, *Les cours constitutionnelles*, Presses Universitaires de France, 1986; Michel FROMONT, *La justice constitutionnelle dans le monde*, Dalloz, Paris 1996; D. ROUSSEAU, *La justice constitutionnelle en Europe*, Montchrestien, Paris 1998.

11 See Francisco FERNÁNDEZ SEGADO, "La obsolecencia de la bipolaridad 'modelo Americano–modelo europeo–kelseniano' como criterio analítico del control de constitucionalidad y la búsqueda de una nueva tipología explicativa," in *La justicia constitucional: Una visión de derecho comparado*, Ed. Dykinson, Madrid 2009, vol. 1, pp. 129–220; Guillaume TUSSEAU, *Contre les "modèles" de justice constitutionnelle: Essai de critique métodologique*, Bononia University Press, Universitá di Bologna, Bologna 2009 (bilingual French–Italian edition); Guillaume TUSSEAU, "Regard critique sur les outils méthodologique du comparatisme. L'example des modèles de justice constitutionnelle," *IUSTEL: Revista General de Derecho Público Comparado*, Nº 4, Madrid, January 2009, pp. 1–34.

12 In fact, what can be considered obsolete is the distinction that derives from an erroneous denomination that has been given to the two systems, particularly by many in Europe, contrasting the so–called American and European systems. This ignores that the "European system," which cannot be reduced to the existence of a specialized Constitutional Court, was present in Latin America a few decades before its introduction in the Czechoslovak Constitution and that the "American system" is not at all endemic to countries with common law systems, having been spread since the nineteenth century into countries with Roman law traditions. See Allan R. BREWER–CARÍAS, *Judicial Review in Comparative Law*, Cambridge University Press, Cambridge 1989; Vicki C. Jackson and Mark Tushent, *Comparative Constitutional Law*, 2nd ed., Foundation Press/Thomson West, New York 2006, pp. 465 ff., 485 ff. Also, as has been pointed out by Francisco Rubio Llorente, it is impossible to talk about a European system, when within Europe there are more differences between the existing systems of judicial review than between any of them and the American system. See Francisco Rubio Llorente, "Tendencias actuales de la jurisdicción constitucional en Europa," in *Manuel Fraga: Homenaje académico*, Fundación Canovas del Castillo, Madrid 1997, vol. 2, p. 1416.

power to annul statutes contrary to the Constitution – such courts or the assignment of power to them must be expressly provided for in the Constitution. This is the basic ground for the distinction that still exists in comparative law, even in countries where both systems function in parallel, as it happens in many Latin American countries.[13] It is in this sense that this book refers to the concentrated system and the diffuse system of judicial review.[14]

In this sense, the concentrated system of judicial review, after being adopted since the nineteenth century in many Latin American countries, was adopted in Europe following Kelsen's ideas set forth in the 1920 constitutions of Czechoslovakia and Austria based on the principle of constitutional supremacy and its main guarantee, that is, the nullity and the annulability of statutes and other State acts with similar rank, when they are contrary to the Constitution. Given the general fear regarding the Judiciary and the prevailing principle of the sovereignty of parliaments, the system materialized through the creation of a special constitutional court established outside of the judicial branch of government with the power not only to declare the unconstitutionality of statutes that violate the Constitution but also to annul them with *erga omnes* effects, that is, to expel them from the legal order.

Kelsen's initial arguments were developed to confront the problems that such powers of judicial review in the hand of a new constitutional organ different from the Legislator could arise in Europe regarding the principle of separation of powers and, in particular, its incidence in legislative functions. But the fact was that the system, by that time and without the need to create a separate constitutional court, was already in existence, with similar substantive trends in some Latin American countries such as Colombia and Venezuela, where the annulment powers regarding unconstitutional statutes had been granted since 1858 to supreme courts of justice.[15]

On the other hand, at the time when the concentrated system of judicial review was formulated in Europe, it contrasted sharply with the diffuse or decentralized system of judicial review that had developed in the United States since the 1808 Supreme Court case *Marbury v. Madison*, 1 Cranch 137 (1803), which beginning in the nineteenth century also spread to many Latin American countries, including Ar-

---

13 As is, for instance, the case of Brazil, Colombia, Dominican Republic, Ecuador, Guatemala, Mexico, Nicaragua, Peru, and Venezuela, as well as Portugal, and in a certain way Greece, and Canada. See Allan R. BREWER–CARÍAS, "La jurisdicción constitucional en América Latina," in Domingo García Belaúnde and Francisco Fernández Segado (coords.), *La jurisdicción constitucional en Iberoamérica*, Dykinson S.L. (Madrid), Editorial Jurídica Venezolana (Caracas), Ediciones Jurídicas (Lima), Editorial Jurídica E. Esteva (Uruguay), Madrid 1997, pp. 117–161.

14 See Allan R. BREWER–CARÍAS, *Constitutional Protection of Human Rights in Latin America: A Comparative Study of Amparo Proceeding*, Cambridge University Press, New York 2009, pp. 81 ff.

15 On the origins of the Colombian and Venezuelan systems, see Allan R. BREWER–CARÍAS, *El sistema mixto o integral de control de la constitucionalidad en Colombia y Venezuela*, Universidad Externado de Colombia, Pontificia Universidad Javeriana, Bogotá 1995. See Sandra MORELLI, *Colombian National Report II*, p. 2.

gentina, Brazil, Colombia, and Venezuela,[16] and was adopted in some European countries, including Norway,[17] Denmark, Sweden, and Greece.[18]

Summarizing, when Kelsen formulated his arguments in support of the concentrated system of judicial review in Europe, the same system had already existed for more than six decades in Latin America, and the diffuse system had existed for almost a century in North America and later also in Latin America and in some European countries.

But the fact is that it was through Kelsen's proposals and writings that judicial review developed in Europe, eventually contributing to end the principle of parliamentary sovereignty. Kelsen himself not only drafted the proposal to incorporate the new Constitutional Court in the 1920 Austrian Constitution but also was a distinguished member of that tribunal for many years, where he acted as its judge rapporteur. He was then key in implementing the concentrated system of judicial review that over the following decades, and particularly after World War II, developed throughout Europe. Even in France, with its traditional and initial a priori concentrated system of judicial review, the result of the jurisprudence of the Constitutional Council has been considered the "symbolic end of the sovereignty of the law," given the current consideration of the law as "the expression of the general will *within the respect of the Constitution.*"[19]

The basic thoughts of Kelsen on the matter, as already mentioned, directed at non–German–speaking readers, were expressed in his 1928 article "The Jurisdictional Guarantee of the Constitution (Constitutional Justice),"[20] in which he considered the general problem of the legitimacy of the concentrated system of judicial review. In particular, he analyzed the compatibility of the system with the principle of separation of powers, based on the fact that an organ of the State other than the

---

16 See Allan R. BREWER–CARÍAS, "La jurisdicción constitucional en América Latina," in Domingo García Belaúnde–Francisco Fernández Segado (coords.), *La jurisdicción constitucional en Iberoamérica*, Dykinson S.L. (Madrid), Editorial Jurídica Venezolana (Caracas), Ediciones Jurídicas (Lima), Editorial Jurídica E. Esteva (Uruguay), Madrid 1997, pp. 117–161.

17 See Eivind AMITH, *Norway National Report*, p. 1.

18 See Julia ILIOPOULOS–Strangas and Stylianos–Ioannis G. KOUTNATZIS, *Greek National Report*, pp. 2–3.

19 See Bertrand MATHIEU, *French National Report*, p. 5.

20 See Hans KELSEN, "La garantie juridictionnelle de la constitution (La justice constitutionnelle)," *Revue du droit public et de la science politique en France et a l'ètranger*, Librairie Général de Droit et de Jurisprudence, Paris 1928, pp. 197–257. See also Hans KELSEN, "Judicial Review of Legislation: A Comparative Study of the Austrian and the American Constitutions," *Journal of Politics* 4, N° 2, Southern Political Science Association, May 1942, pp 183–200; "El control de la constitucionalidad de las leyes: Estudio comparado de las Constituciones Austríacas y Norteamericana," *Revista Iberoamericana de Derecho Procesal Constitucional*, N° 12, Editorial Porrúa, Mexico 2009, pp. 3–17; "Le contrôle de constitutionnalité des lois. Une étude comparative des Constitutions autrichienne et américaine," *Revue française de droit constitutionnel*, N° 1, Presses Universitaires de France, Paris 1999, pp. 17–30.

Legislator could annul statutes without the decision to do so being considered an invasion of the Legislator's domain.

In this regard, after arguing that "to annul a statute[] is to establish a general norm, because the annulment of a statute has the same general character of its adoption," and after considering that to annul a statute is "the same as to adopt it but with a negative sign, and consequently in itself, a legislative function," Kelsen considered that the court that has the power to annul statutes is, consequently, "an organ of the Legislative branch."[21] Nonetheless, Kelsen finished by affirming that, although the "activity of the constitutional jurisdiction" is an "activity of the Negative Legislator," this does not mean that the constitutional court exercises a "legislative function," because that would be characterized by the "free creation" of norms. The free creation of norms, however, does not exist in the case of the annulment of statutes, which is a "jurisdictional function" that can only be "essentially accomplished in application of the norms of the Constitution," that is, "absolutely determined in the Constitution."[22] His conclusion was that the constitutional jurisdiction accomplishes a "purely juridical mission, that of interpreting the Constitution," with the power to annul unconstitutional statutes the principal guarantee of the supremacy of the Constitution.[23]

As I argued a few years ago, in reality, constitutional courts do not "repeal" a statute in annulling it, and the annulment they can pronounce is not based on discretionary powers but on constitutional and legal criteria, on the application of a superior rule, embodied in the Constitution. Thus, in no way do they exercise a legislative function. The function of a constitutional court, as argued by Kelsen, is thus jurisdictional; the same that is assigned to an ordinary court but characterized as a guarantee of the Constitution. And, if it is true that constitutional judges in many cases decide political issues when considering the constitutionality of legislative acts, they do so by legal methods and criteria, in a process initiated by a party with the required standing.[24] Only exceptional constitutional courts are authorized to initiate *ex officio* constitutional proceedings.

Eventually, Kelsen, in the same article, summarized the "result" of judicial review in the concentrated system, highlighting that, to guarantee the Constitution, it is indispensable for the unconstitutional statute to be annulled by a constitutional court ruling, that has as a matter of principle and in the interest of legal security, *ex nunc, pro futuro* effects (i.e., nonretroactive effects), a rule that nonetheless could be

---

21 See Hans KELSEN, *La garantía jurisdiccional de la Constitución (La justicia constitucional)*, Universidad Nacional Autónoma de México, Mexico City 2001, p. 54.

22 *Id.*, pp. 56–57. See Allan R. BREWER–CARÍAS, *Études de droit public comparé*, Bruylant, Brussels 2003, p. 682.

23 See Hans KELSEN, *La garantía jurisdiccional de la Constitución (La justicia constitucional)*, Universidad Nacional Autónoma de México, Mexico City 2001, p. 57.

24 See Allan R. BREWER–CARÍAS, *Études de droit public comparé*, Bruylant, Brussels 2003, p. 685. See also A. PÉREZ GORDRO, *El Tribunal Constitucional y sus funciones*, Barcelona 1982, p. 41. See the comment of Laurence CLAUS and Richard S. KAY, *U.S. National Report*, pp. 4, 6.

mitigated. Kelsen also considered that the annulment of a statute did not produce the rebirth of old statutes abrogated by the annulled one, a decision that nonetheless he considered could be assigned to the constitutional court, evidencing in such case the "legislative character" of its function.[25]

My purpose in this study is to analyze in comparative law all those situations in which constitutional courts interfere not only with the Legislator and its legislative functions but also with the "constitutional legislator," that is, with the Constituent Power,[26] by assuming, in one way or another, the role of positive legislators. For such purpose, I divide this general report into five chapters. The first analyzes the general aspects of judicial review of the constitutionality of legislation exercised by constitutional courts, as well as the courts' relation with the Legislator. The second chapter examines cases in which the constitutional courts interfere with the Constituent Power, by enacting constitutional rules and even mutating[27] the Constitution. The third chapter explores the role of constitutional courts that interfere with the Legislator regarding existing legislation, assist the Legislator, complement statutes and add provisions to them through constitutional interpretation, and determine the temporal effects of legislation. The fourth chapter analyzes the role of constitutional courts that interfere with the Legislator regarding absolute and relative legislative omissions and, in some cases, act as provisional legislators. The fifth chapter discusses the role of constitutional courts as legislators on matters of judicial review.

---

25 See Hans KELSEN, *La garantía jurisdiccional de la Constitución (La justicia constitucional)*, Universidad Nacional Autónoma de México, Mexico City 2001, pp. 82–86.

26 I will use the expression "Constituent Power" in order to refer to the will of the people (original constituent power) when approving a Constitution (for instance through a referendum), or to a Constituent Assembly when sanctioning a Constitution, or to any organs of the state with constitutional power to review or change the Constitution. See generally, Pedro de Vega, *La Reforma Constitucional y la Problemática del Poder Constituyente,* Ed. Tecnos, Madrid 2000; Allan R. BREWER–CARÍAS, *Poder Constituyente Originario y Asamblea Nacional Constituyente,* Editorial Jurídica Venezolana, Caracas 1998.

27 The expresión "constitutional mutation" is used in order to refer to the changes made to the content of a constitutional provision when without formally "reforming" its text, by means of a judicial interpretation it result with a different meaning. See Salvador O. NAVA GOMAR, "Interpretación, mutación y reforma de la Constitución. Tres extractos," in Eduardo Ferrer Mac–Gregor (coord.), *Interpretación Constitucional*, vol. II, Editorial Porrúa, Universidad Nacional Autónoma de México, México 2005, pp. 804 ss. See also generally on the subject, Konrad HESSE, "Límites a la mutación constitucional," in *Escritos de derecho constitucional*, Centro de Estudios Constitucionales, Madrid 1992, pp. 79–104; and Rogelia CALZADA CONDE, "Poder Constituyente y mutación constitucional: especial referencia a la interpretación judicial," in *Jornadas de Estudio sobre el Título Preliminar de la Constitución,* Ministerio de Justicia/Secretaría General Técnica/Centro de Publicaciones, Madrid 1988, vol. 11., pp. 1.097–1.111.

CHAPTER 1
JUDICIAL REVIEW OF LEGISLATION AND THE LEGISLATOR

I. THE SYSTEMS OF JUDICIAL REVIEW AND THE ROLE OF CONSTITUTIONAL COURTS

The result of Kelsen's proposals and their applications in Europe was the development of the concentrated system of judicial review, which attributed specially created constitutional bodies (constitutional courts, tribunals or councils) generally conceived of outside the Judiciary with the power to annul, with *erga omnes* effects, unconstitutional statutes –this was the initial pattern followed after World War II in Germany, Italy, France, Spain, and Portugal. The system developed as the result of a compromise between the need for a judicial review system derived from the notion of constitutional supremacy and the traditional European idea of the separation of powers, which had denied the courts any power to invalidate statutes.

But in spite of the importance of Kelsen's contributions, it is improper to identify the concentrated system of judicial review as a whole with a so–called "European model," because there are also concentrated systems of judicial review in which the exclusive and original jurisdiction to annul statutes, without the creation of a special court or tribunal, has fallen to the existing supreme courts of justice, located at the apex of the Judicial Power, as has been the case, since the nineteenth century, in many Latin American countries.[28] In addition, in many Latin American countries, the judicial review system has developed as a mixed system, combining the diffuse

28 The "European model" is referred to the concentrated system of judicial review when the constitutional jurisdiction is assigned to a special constitutional court. Other countries without special constitutional courts also follow the concentrated system of judicial review by assigning the constitutional jurisdiction to existing supreme courts. In this sense, the concentrated system of judicial review has been adopted in Brazil, Bolivia, Colombia, Costa Rica, Chile, Dominican Republic, Ecuador, El Salvador, Guatemala, Honduras, Mexico, Nicaragua, Panama, Paraguay, Peru, Uruguay, and Venezuela. But only in Bolivia, Colombia, Chile, Guatemala, Peru, and Ecuador is the constitutional jurisdiction assigned to special constitutional courts or tribunals. In the other countries, it is exercised by the existing supreme courts. Only in Bolivia, Costa Rica, Chile, Ecuador, El Salvador, Honduras, Panama, Paraguay, and Uruguay does the system remain exclusively concentrated. In the other countries it has been mixed with the diffuse system, functioning in parallel. See Allan R. BREWER–CARÍAS, *Judicial Review in Comparative Law*, Cambridge University Press, Cambridge 1989; and Allan R. BREWER–CARÍAS, *Constitutional Protection of Human Rights in Latin America: A Comparative Study of Amparo Proceeding*, Cambridge University Press, New York 2009.

and the concentrated methods that function in parallel,[29] as is also the case in Portugal,[30] Greece,[31] and Canada.[32]

In addition, we must remind that before Kelsen's ideas took root in Europe, also since the nineteenth century, the other main system of judicial review, the diffuse or decentralized one, was developed in the United States as a consequence of the same principle of the supremacy of the Constitution. According to this diffuse system, all judges and courts are empowered to act as constitutional judges, in the sense that when applying the law, they are allowed to decide the law's constitutionality; therefore, they are empowered to decide not to apply a statute that they consider unconstitutional when deciding a particular judicial case or controversy, giving priority to the Constitution. In this system, the courts are empowered not to formally annul statutes with *erga omnes* effects but to only declare their unconstitutionality with *inter partes* effects.

Although the system was first implemented in the United States, and was followed in many common law countries, it cannot be considered a system peculiar to the common law system, and thus incompatible with the civil or Roman law tradition.[33] As mentioned already, it had existed and developed since the nineteenth century in parallel with the concentrated system in many Latin American countries,[34] all of them being part of the Roman law family of legal systems, as well as in some European countries.

In any case, an important aspect to bear in mind is that in diffuse systems of judicial review, when the final decision in a case reaches the supreme court or tribunal, according to the principle of *stare decisis*, the practical effects of the non–application of a statute declared unconstitutional are similar to the practical effects of its annulment, in the sense that even if the statute continues to appear in the books, in practice it is considered null and void.

---

29 As in Brazil, Colombia, Dominican Republic, Guatemala, Mexico, Nicaragua, Peru, and Venezuela. See *Id.*

30 See Allan R. BREWER–CARÍAS, *Judicial Review in Comparative Law*, Cambridge University Press, Cambridge 1989; Joaquim DE SOUSA RIBEIRO and Esperança MEALHA, *Portuguese National Report*, p. 1.

31 See Julia Iliopoulos–Strangas and Stylianos–Ioannis G. Koutnatzis, *Greek National Report*, pp. 6–7.

32 See Kent ROACH, *Canadian National Report*, p. 1.

33 See Allan R. BREWER–CARÍAS, *Judicial Review in Comparative Law*, Cambridge University Press, Cambridge 1989; Vicki C. Jackson and Mark Tushent, *Comparative Constitutional Law*, 2nd ed., Foundation Press and Thomson West 2006, pp. 465 ff., 485 ff.

34 The diffuse system of judicial review has been adopted in Argentina, Brazil, Colombia, Dominican Republic, Guatemala, Mexico, Nicaragua, Peru, and Venezuela. Only in Argentina does it remain exclusively diffuse. In the other countries, the diffuse system is combined with the concentrated one. See Allan R. BREWER–CARÍAS, *Judicial Review in Comparative Law*, Cambridge University Press, Cambridge 1989; and *Constitutional Protection of Human Rights in Latin America: A Comparative Study of Amparo Proceeding*, Cambridge University Press, New York 2009.

In addition, even in countries with the diffuse system of judicial review that have not developed the *stare decisis* doctrine, the effects of the supreme court decisions on matters of judicial review are similar, because of the authority that the legal and judicial communities give to supreme court decisions. This is the case in the Netherlands,[35] and also the case in Argentina, where the Supreme Court, since its early decisions, has progressively imposed the doctrine of *stare decisis.*[36] It has been considered as a *de facto stare decisis* doctrine[37] regarding the interpretation of the Constitution and of federal laws, which aims to provide litigants with some degree of certainty as to how the law must be interpreted, a requirement the court finds embedded in the due process clause of the Constitution. In the Argentine *García Aguilera* case decided in 1870, barely eight years after the court's establishment, the Supreme Court held, in a since then oft–repeated statement, that "lower courts are required to adjust their proceedings and decisions to those of the Supreme Court in similar cases,"[38] from which they can depart only if they give "valid motives."[39]

In all the systems of judicial review – whether concentrated or diffuse, hybrid or mixed – what is clear is that the main role of constitutional courts is to interpret and apply the Constitution to test the constitutionality of statutes and thus preserve the Constitution's supremacy. Thus, constitutional courts are always subordinate to a constitution, not having in principle any power to modify or mutate it or to usurp powers assigned to other State organs. Their essential function is to guarantee the supremacy and integrity of the Constitution by declaring unconstitutional or annulling State acts that violate it, all while being obliged to obey the Constitution by exercising the powers expressly attributed to them in it. Constitutional courts, therefore, are not allowed to assume constituent powers (e.g., issuing decisions that illegitimately modify or mutate the Constitution) or to usurp powers attributed to other constituted powers or organs of the State, like the Executive or the Legislative branches. The contrary is to be considered as a case of the pathology of judicial review.

Regarding other key principles, in general terms, in the exercise of their functions, constitutional courts do so in the course of judicial processes normally initiated by an interested party with due standing in cases or controversies. In the diffuse system it must be a party to the particular case or process, and in the the concentrated system it must be a petitioner with a specific interest to file direct actions on the

---

35 See J. UZMAN, T. BARKHUYSEN, and M. L. VAN EMMERIK, *Dutch National Report*, p. 18.

36 Néstor P. SAGÜES has called this "Argentinean *stare decisis*." See Néstor P. SAGÜES, "Los efectos de las sentencias constitucionales en el derecho argentino," in *Anuario Iberoamericano de Justicia Constitucional*, Centro de Estudios Políticos y Constitucionales, N° 12, 2008, Madrid 2008, pp. 345–347; *Argentinean National Report II*, p. 3.

37 See Alejandra RODRÍGUEZ GALÁN and Alfredo Mauricio VÍTOLO, *Argentinean National Report I*, p. 3.

38 Fallos 9:53 (1870), in Alejandra Rodríguez Galán and Alfredo Mauricio Vítolo, *Argentinean National Report I*, p. 4 (footnote 11).

39 See Néstor P. SAGÜES, *Argentinean National Report II*, p. 3.

unconstitutionality of statutes before constitutional courts.[40] As mentioned by Zdenek Kühn, in reference to the Constitutional Court of the Czech Republic, "unlike its short–lived federal predecessor (the Constitutional Court of Czechoslovakia) the Czech Constitutional Court does not have the power to provide generally binding interpretation of the Constitution which would have no connection to either abstract constitutional review or constitutional complaint."[41]

So even in cases of constitutional courts with express constitutional powers to interpret in an abstract way the Constitution, that is, without any reference to a particular action, omission, or decision of a State body, a factual dispute must always exist, for example between two constitutional bodies regarding the interpretation of the Constitution. This is, for instance, the case of Slovakia, where article 128 of the Constitution expressly states that "the Constitutional Court shall give an interpretation of the Constitution or constitutional law if the matter is disputable." The same Constitutional Court of Slovakia has stated that the "Constitutional Court does not decide if the state bodies did break the Constitution by the wrong interpretation" or decide on the constitutionality "of the action, omission or decision of state body, which led to origination of the dispute. The court only provides the interpretation of the disputed part of a constitutional statute."[42]

In Slovakia, petitions for the abstract interpretation of the Constitution can be filed only by some public officials or State bodies[43] and, as mentioned, when a dispute occurs between two State bodies standing against each other with different opinions on the interpretation of a constitutional provision.[44] As a result of the exercise of this competency, the decisions of the Constitutional Court of Slovakia directly complement the normative text of the Constitution, its wording having identical legal power and binding effect as the text of the Constitution itself.[45] This power of judicial review has been used especially since 1993, after the establishment of the Slovak Republic, having an important influence on the shaping of constitutional

40 See generally Richard S. Kay (ed.), *Standing to Raise Constitutional Issues: Comparative Perspectives, XVIth Congress of the International Academy of Comparative Law, Académie Internationale de Droit Comparé, Brisbane 2002*, Bruylant, Brussels 2005.

41 See Zdenek KÜHN, *Czech National Report*, p. 2.

42 The Court has also said: "It follows that the decisions on interpretation of the Constitutional Court of the Slovak Republic does not have and can not have any legal effects in connection with actions, omissions or decisions of state bodies that led to origination of the dispute alike in the cases of proceeding according to art. 125a and art. 152 of the Constitution." See Decision N° II. ÚS 69/99. See Ján SVÁK and Lucia BERDISOVÁ, *Slovakian National Report*, p. 3 (footnote 2).

43 By at least one–fifth of the Members of the National Council of the Slovak Republic, the President of the Slovak Republic, the Government of the Slovak Republic, a court, the Attorney General, or the Public Defender of Rights.

44 "Constitutionally relevant dispute on interpretation of the constitution is a dispute on rights or duties between bodies of the state which have such rights and duties prescribed in the constitution." See Decision N° I. ÚS 30/97. See Ján SVÁK and Lucía BERDISOVÁ, *Slovakian National Report*, p. 3 (footnote 3)

45 See Ján SVÁK and Lucia BERDISOVÁ, *Slovakian National Report*, p. 3.

order of the new State, for instance in matters related to the position and authority of the President of the Slovak Republic.

In Canada, the Constitution can also be interpreted by constitutional courts in an abstract way, without the need for any live cases and controversies. An important feature of the Canadian system of judicial review, is the statutory powers of the federal government to refer abstract legal and constitutional questions to the Supreme Court on a "reference procedure" including those involving the constitutionality of legislation. It has been through this reference procedure that the courts have developed the most important roles as positive legislators, in some cases mutating the Constitution.[46]

A deformation of this possibility of a constitutional court to interpret with binding effects a constitution in an abstract way, that is, without any particular case or dispute involved, at the request of the government or at the request of any individual, has been developed by the Constitutional Chamber of the Supreme Tribunal of Venezuela, without any constitutional or legal support. The Chamber, in effect, has "created" a "recourse for the abstract interpretation of the Constitution," whose indiscriminate use has had catastrophic consequences for democracy, given way to an institutional path contrary to democracy and the rule of law.[47] The result has been the reinforcement of an authoritarian government that has developed over the past decade despite its initial electoral origin (1998).[48] This deformation of judicial review powers is also a case of the pathology of judicial review.

In other cases, as an exception to the rule of standing, in some cases constitutional courts can issue rulings also for the abstract interpretation of the Constitution by acting *motu proprio*, that is, without the request of any specific party, whether an individual or a State entity. This is the case, for instance, of the Constitutional Courts in Croatia and in Serbia. In Croatia, the Constitutional Court has cautiously avoided using this power, showing a considerable measure of deference, except in cases where an obviously unconstitutional act has unconstitutionally regulated the Constitutional Court itself.[49] In the case of Serbia, in contrast, the Constitutional Court has often initiated proceedings *ex officio* to assess the constitutionality of statutes, which in practice blurs the difference between requests for judicial review filed

---

46 See Kent ROACH, *Canadian National Report*, pp. 1, 9.

47 See generally Allan R. BREWER–CARÍAS, "Le recours d'interprétation abstrait de la Constitution au Vénézuéla," in *Renouveau du droit constitutionnel. Mélanges en l'honneur de Louis Favoreu*, Paris 2007, pp. 61–70; Brewer–Carías, *Crónica de la "in"justicia constitucional: La Sala Constitucional y el autoritarismo en Venezuela*, Editorial Jurídica Venezolana, Caracas 2007.

48 See generally Allan R. BREWER–CARÍAS, *Dismantling Democracy. The Chávez Authoritarian Experiment*, Cambridge University Press, New York 2010; BREWER–CARÍAS, "El juez constitucional al servicio del autoritarismo y la ilegítima mutación de la Constitución: el caso de la Sala Constitucional del Tribunal Supremo de Justicia de Venezuela (1999–2009)," in *Revista de Administración Pública*, N° 180, Centro de Estudios Constitucionales, Madrid 2009, pp. 383–418.

49 See Decision N° U–I–39/2002, Official Gazette *Narodne novine*, N° 10/2002; Sanja Barić and Petar Bačić, *Croatian National Report*, p. 7.

by authorities (initiatives) having the needed standing. In addition, when the Court declines to start a procedure on an initiative, it usually states its opinion on the constitutionality of the challenged act. Only when it rejects an initiative for formal reasons does the court not assess the constitutionality of the act in the reasoning of the decision. However, the court can, in any case, put the proceeding in motion independently, even when the initiative has been filed having formal inaccuracies.[50]

In other cases, as in Venezuela, the Constitutional Chamber of the Supreme Tribunal has also assumed *ex officio* judicial review powers but in this case without any constitutional or legal authorization, in what can also be considered a case of the pathology of judicial review.[51]

The general principle in any case is that, in general terms, in exercising judicial review, constitutional courts do not act as advisory institutions, without the request of a particular party based on a particular interest, even if the action of unconstitutionality is conceived as an *actio popularis*, that is, a popular action that can be filed by any citizen. In Australia, for example, the High Court held in 1921:

The Parliament could not confer on a court jurisdiction to give advisory opinions even when such opinions were confined to the validity of enacted legislation and when the determination of the court was "final and conclusive." Under such an arrangement there was no "matter" within the meaning of the Constitution, because there was no "immediate right, duty or liability to be established by the determination of the Court," which would be obliged to make a "declaration of the law, divorced from any attempt to administer that law.[52]

Also in Hungary, in the early phase of court operations, the Constitutional Court declared that it did not undertake answering hypothetical constitutional questions, and in several decisions, it entered to consider how abstract the question raised was. On the one hand, the Court, interpreting its competence narrowly, requires necessary closeness between the statement of facts and the related provision of the Constitution, and it provides interpretation of the Constitution only to resolve a "particular constitutional problem."[53] On the other hand, the Court demands certain distance; it

50 See Boško Tripković, *Serbian National Report*, p. 6.

51 See Allan R. Brewer–Carías, "Régimen y alcance de la actuación judicial de oficio en materia de justicia constitucional en Venezuela," *Estudios Constitucionales: Revista Semestral del Centro de Estudios Constitucionales* 4, N° 2, Universidad de Talca, Santiago, Chile 2006, pp. 221–250.

52 See *In re Judiciary and Navigation Acts (Advisory Opinions* case) (1921) 29 CLR 257; Cheryl Saunders, *Australian National Report*, p. 4.

53 The Court refused to make a statement about the possibility of raising interest rates on housing loans, because it would have meant interpreting the "constitutional provision in some abstract way unrelated to any individual problem, or . . . a possibility for unbound interpretation." See Decision N° 31/1990, in Lóránt Csink, Józef Petrétei, and Péter Tilk, *Hungarian National Report*, p. 7 (footnote 24).

requires that the issue not be closely related to the case and that the decision not become factual,[54] because the Court is not a counsel but the judge of Parliament.[55]

II. CONTROL OF CONSTITUTIONALITY AND CONTROL OF CONVENTIONALITY

In democratic regimes, all judicial review methods have as their main purpose the guarantee of the supremacy of the Constitution. Consequently, when constitutional courts exercise judicial review, they have the task of comparing statutes or primary legislation with the provisions of the Constitution. That is why judicial review is, fundamentally, a constitutional control of legislation or the exercise of judicial control over the constitutionality of legislation.

Nonetheless, the constitutions of many countries, by giving constitutional or supralegal rank to international treaties, also allow the courts, within their constitutional functions of judicial review, the possibility of exercising what can be called "control of conventionality" of statutes, in the sense of guaranteeing the subjection of primary legislation to international conventions, particularly on matters of human rights.[56] This is the case, for instance, in Argentina and Venezuela, where international treaties on human rights have been given constitutional hierarchy, that is, the same rank as constitutional provisions.[57]

In Argentina, even before the 1994 constitutional reform that formally gave "constitutional hierarchy" to a series of enumerated international documents, particularly on matters of human rights (article 75.22), the Supreme Court in *Ekmekdjián*

---

54 Upon this, the Court did not interpret whether the petition for the dismissal of the director of public radio can be considered to violate freedom of the press; it could have given, therefore, a statement–of–fact answer for the dispute of the Prime Minister and the President of the Republic. See Decision N° 36/1992, in Lóránt Csink, Józef Petrétei and Péter Tilk, *Hungarian National Report*, p. 7 (footnote 26).

55 See Decision N° 16/1991, in Lóránt Csink, Józef Petrétei, and Péter Tilk, *Hungarian National Report*, p. 7.

56 See, e.g., Ernesto REY CANTOR, *El control de convencionalidad de las leyes y derechos humanos*, Editorial Porrúa, Mexico City 2008; Juan Carlos HITTERS, "Control de constitucionalidad y control de convencionalidad. Comparación (Criterios fijados por la Corte Interamericana de Derechos Humanos), in *Estudios Constitucionales* 7, N° 2, Santiago de Chile 2009, pp. 109–128; Fernando SILVA GARCÍA, "El control judicial de las leyes con base en tratados internacionales sobre derechos humanos," in *Revista Iberoamericana de Derecho Procesal Constitucional*, N° 5, Instituto Iberoamericano de Derecho Procesal Constitucional, Editorial Porrúa, Mexico City 2006, pp. 231 ff; Víctor BAZÁN, "Corte Interamericana de derechos humanos y Cortes Supremas o Tribunales Constitucionales latinoamericanos: el control de convencionalidad y la necesidad de un diálogo interjurisdiccional crítico," in *Revista Europea de Derechos Fundamentales*, N°. 16/2, 2010, pp. 15–44.

57 See Allan R. BREWER–CARÍAS, "La aplicación de los tratados internacionales sobre derechos humanos en el orden interno," *Revista Instituto Interamericano de Derechos Humanos*, N° 46, San José, Costa Rica, 2007, pp. 219–271.

v. Sofovich (1992),[58] on the right to correction (rectification) and response regarding published informations, recognized that international treaties have precedence over internal legislation. Decisions in this vein multiplied after the 1994 constitutional reform in which the Court held that constitutional review includes, as well, comparing internal laws and regulations with international conventions, with the power to declare such laws "unconventional,"[59] that is, contrary to an international convention. In this regard, for instance, the Court compared the provision of the American Convention on Human Rights that guarantees the right to appeal before a superior court as one of the due process rules (article 8.2.h), with provisions of the Argentine criminal legal system that, in some cases, establish a single–instance trial by limiting review of the judgment before the Penal Cassation Court. Consequently, the Supreme Court in the *Casal* case (2005) held that the only way to square the requirement established in the American Convention with the Argentine criminal legal system was to interpret article 456 of the Criminal Procedural Code as allowing an ample review of the prior ruling.[60]

In Venezuela, all international treaties on human rights have the same constitutional hierarchy as the Constitution (article 23) and even prevail in application over the same Constitution if those treaties establish more favorable provisions for the exercise of particular rights. Thus, the Constitutional Chamber of the Supreme Tribunal, during the first years of enforcement of the 1999 Constitution, on many occasions annulled statutes because they were contrary to the American Convention on Human Rights, for instance on matters of the right to political participation and the right to appeal before a superior court in all judicial processes.[61] Unfortunately, this constitutional provision of article 23 of the Constitution, in more recent years, has been illegitimately mutated by the same Constitutional Chamber, adopting at the request of the Attorney General, denying the general power of all court to give preference to international treaties on human rights over internal law, and even deciding in 2008 that the rulings of the Inter–American Court on Human Rigths are non–executable in the country.[62]

---

58 See Fallos 315:1492 (1992). See Alejandra RODRÍGUEZ GALÁN and Alfredo Mauricio VÍTOLO, *Argentinean National Report I*, p. 14 (footnote 55). See Néstor Pedro Sagües, *Argentinean National Report II*, p. 19.

59 See *Mazzeo*, Fallos 330 (2007). See Alejandra RODRÍGUEZ GALÁN and Alfredo Mauricio VÍTOLO, *Argentinean National Report I*, p. 14 (footnote 57).

60 Fallos, 328:3399 (2005). See Alejandra RODRÍGUEZ GALÁN and Alfredo Mauricio VÍTOLO, *Argentinean National Report I*, p. 14 (footnote 59).

61 See Decision N° 87 of March 13, 2000. "*C. A. Electricidad del Centro (Elecentro) v. Superintendencia para la Promoción y Protección de la Libre Competencia (Procompetencia)*," *Revista de Derecho Público*, N° 81, Editorial Jurídica Venezolana, Caracas 2000, pp. 157 ff. See Carlos Ayala Corao, "Las consecuencias de la jerarquía constitucional de los tratados relativos a derechos humanos," in *Rumbos del Derecho Internacional de los Derechos Humanos, Estudios en Homenaje al Profesor Antonio Augusto Cancado Trindade*, vol. 5, Sergio Antonio Fabris Editor, Porto Alegre, Brazil, 2005.

62 See Decision N° 1.939 of December 18, 2008, Attorney General Office case, http://www.tsj.gov.ve/decisiones/scon/Diciembre/1939–181208–2008–08–1572.html. See

In effect, in Decision N° 1.939 of December 18, 2008, the Constitutional Chamber of the Supreme Tribunal, in deciding a recourse of interpretation of a decision adopted by the Inter–American Court on Human Rights filed by the Attorney General, rejected the general prevalence of international treaties on human rights regarding internal law, except only when the matter is decided by the Chamber itself.[63] On the other hand, the constitutional rank of international treaties on human rights was proposed to be eliminated in a draft constitutional reform proposal made by a Presidential Council desgned by the President in 2007.[64] Eventually, the proposal was not included in the constitutional reform submitted to popular vote, which that year was rejected by the people. However, what the authoritarian regime was not able to attain thorugh a constitutional reform, in a certain way was carried out by the Constitutional Chamber of the Supreme Court.[65]

As mentioned before, in the same decision, and contrary to the express provision of the same article 23 of the Constitution that established the "direct and immediate application by the courts and other bodies of the State" of human rights treaties, the Constitutional Chamber decided to reserve to itself the power to determine which provisions of treaties would prevail in the internal legal order.[66] With this unconstitutional decision, the Constitutional Chamber illegitimately mutated the Constitution: according to article 23, the authority to apply international treaties on human rights corresponds not only to the Constitutional Chamber but also to all the courts of the Republic when acting as constitutional judges, for instance, when exercising the diffused control of the constitutionality of statutes or when deciding cases of amparo. The intention of the Constitutional Chamber to resereve for itself this aspect of judicial review is not in accordance to the Constitution and to the judicial review system it establishes.

In any case, and referring to the same sort of control of "conventionality" of statutes in democratic countries, this control has developed in all European countries where European Union law, and particularly the European Convention of Human

---

comments in Allan R. BREWER–CARÍAS, "La interrelación entre los Tribunales Constitucionales de América Latina y la Corte Interamericana de Derechos Humanos, y la cuestión de la inejecutabilidad de sus decisiones en Venezuela," in Armin von Bogdandy, Flavia Piovesan, and Mariela Morales Antonorzi (coords.), *Direitos humanos, democracia e integração jurídica na América do Sul*, Juris Editora, Rio de Janeiro 2010, pp. 661–701.

63 See the case *Gustavo Alvarez Arias*, http://www.tsj.gov.ve/decisiones/scon/ Diciembre/1939–181208–2008–08–1572.html.

64 See *Consejo Presidencial para la Reforma de la Constitución de la República Bolivariana de Venezuela, "Modificaciones propuestas."* The complete text was published as *Proyecto de Reforma Constitucional. Versión atribuida al Consejo Presidencial para la reforma de la Constitución de la república Bolivariana de Venezuela*, Editorial Atenea, Caracas, July 1, 2007.

65 See Allan R. BREWER–CARÍAS, *Reforma constitucional y fraude a la Constitución. Venezuela 1999–2009*, Academia de Ciencias Políticas y Sociales, Caracas 2009, pp 249–261.

66 See *Revista de Derecho Público*, N° 93–96, Editorial Jurídica Venezolana, Caracas 2003, pp. 135 ff.

Rights, have prevalence over national law.[67] In particular, the case of the Netherlands must be highlighted. There, as no judicial review of the constitutionality of statutes is allowed in the Constitution, judicial review has developed only as a control of the "conventionality" of such statutes to ensure their subjection to international conventions, specifically on matters of human rights.

In effect, according to article 120 of the Dutch Constitution, "The constitutionality of Acts of Parliament and treaties shall not be reviewed by the courts," which means that judicial review of primary legislation is prohibited, the courts being banned not only from determining the unconstitutionality of statutes but also from declaring them incompatible with the Kingdom Charter.[68] Nonetheless, article 94 of the same Constitution establishes that "Statutory regulations in force within the Kingdom shall not be applicable if such application is in conflict with provisions of treaties that are binding on all persons or of resolutions by international institutions," thus leading to the very important development of the system of judicial review of "conventionality" of statutes, particularly on matters of human rights.

Thus, the Dutch system is referred to as a system of "constitutional fundamental rights review by the judiciary" or as "fundamental rights review of parliamentary legislation," that is, regarding the powers of the courts and particularly of the Hoge Raad (High Court) to review acts of Parliament for their compliance with convention rights if the treaty is ratified and insofar as the individual provisions are self–executing.[69] This means that, in the Netherlands, statutes can be reviewed by the courts for their consistency with the written provisions of international law, particularly the UN International Covenant on Civil and Political Rights and the European Convention for the Protection of Human Rights and Fundamental Freedoms (European Convention on Human Rights), which has become the most important civil rights charter for the Netherlands.[70]

Such judicial review has also developed regarding European Union law, which also contains provisions on fundamental rights, in the sense that, because international treaties have precedence over national law, the courts must examine whether national law is compatible with the law of the European Union and, if necessary,

67 In the case of Poland, as mentioned by Marek Safjan, "The national court, denying application of a national norm which is contradictory to the European law or interpreting creatively a national norm in the spirit of a European norm *de facto* applies in the legal system a new, earlier non–existent, norm, thus becoming in a way a positive legislator on the level of a specific case." See Marek Safjan, *Polish National Report*, p. 16. Also in Slovakia, according to article 154c of the Constitution, having international treaties, particularly the European Convention of Human Rights, precedence over laws, the courts (including the Constitutional Court) exercise control of conventionality, by giving preference to convention. See Ján SVÁK and Lucia BERDISOVÁ, *Slovak National Report*, pp. 11, 12.

68 See J. Uzman, T. BARKHUYSEN, and M. L. VAN EMMERIK, *Dutch National Report*, pp. 2, 5.

69 *Id.*, pp. 1, 2, 9, 12, 22.

70 *Id.*, p. 7.

either construe national law consistently with European Union law or set it aside if such an interpretation proves impossible under national constitutional law.[71]

In Greece, although the Constitution has no explicit provision for the control of the conventionality of statutes, the courts have held that international treaties have supralegislative status (article 28.1 of the Constitution), which is sufficient basis to exercise control of conventionality if the treaty in question is self–executing, such as the European Convention on Human Rights. In the same sense of the control of constitutionality, if Greek courts find that a statutory provision is inconsistent with international law, that provision cannot be applied in the pending case. However, unconventional legislation remains in effect and thus can be applied in a future occasion.[72]

The situation in the United Kingdom must also be mentioned. The British Constitution is not a single and overarching written document like the constitutions of other contemporary democratic states. In addition, it is not possible in principle to formally distinguish a constitutional statute from an ordinary statute. Nonetheless, the British Constitution undoubtedly exists, and it is possible to attach the label "constitutional" to some legal[73] and nonlegal rules,[74] called "conventions of the Constitution," which are considered binding rules of political morality and called the "common law constitution," as a set of legal principles and rules that have been laid down over time, typically by judges.[75] It is possible, therefore, to identify a judicial process of controlling the subjection of statutes to these conventions, which can be called "constitutional review."[76] As it has been summarized by John Bell:

> Britain has neither "specific constitutional or statutory provisions that empower constitutional judges, by means of interpreting the Constitution, to adopt obligatory decisions on constitutional matters" nor specific decisions on constitutional matters. But this would be too simplistic an approach. The nature of a common law constitution is that the basic "rules of recognition" (H. L. A. Hart) are not contained in statute, but are in the common law. The principles are rather like the "fundamental principles recognized by the laws of the Republic" in French law, which are not laid down by statute, but which are judicially identified, even if formally not created by judges. There do arise a number of issues on which ordinary judges have to take decisions which are binding and which could be characterized as constitutional.[77]

---

71 *Id.*, pp. 2, 31, 32.

72 See Julia Iliopoulos–Strangas and Stylianos–Ioannis G. Koutnatzis, *Greek National Report*, p. 10.

73 An example is the agreement reached by the Prime Ministers of the British Empire in 1931 for the U.K. Parliament to not legislate for Dominions without consent of their parliaments. See John BELL, *British National Report*, p. 1.

74 One example is the Nolan principles (1995), which govern standards in public life and introduce a set of values governing the holders of a range of public offices. See John BELL, *British National Report*, p. 2.

75 See John BELL, *British National Report*, p. 1.

76 *Id.*, p. 2.

77 *Id.*, p .3.

In this respect, regarding the conventions to the British Constitution, it is also possible to call this process of constitutional review – of course, in its own historical context – a judicial control of conventionality.

But in other constitutional matters, given the recent evolution of the British Constitution by the creation of a Supreme Court in 2009, it is also possible to distinguish constitutional review powers exercised by the courts. This is the case on matters of devolution, regarding the control of the validity of the legislation of the three devolved assemblies (Wales, Scotland, and Northern Ireland) that can be referred to the Supreme Court by the British Secretary of State, the British Attorney General, or the national Attorneys General (or equivalent), or by the national courts before which the issue is raised.[78]

But the most important recent developments in the United Kingdom on matters of constitutional review have been regarding the compatibility of British statutes with European Union law, that is, on matters of control of conventionality. An example is the matter decided on the compatibility of a British statute concerning the limits for fishing with European Union law, which was raised and decided by the lowest tier of criminal law courts, the Magistrates' Court.[79] But most important in this process of developing constitutional review in the United Kingdom is the example of the protection and interpretation of human rights, particularly after the Human Rights Act was passed in 1998 to implement the European Convention on Human Rights. The Act is considered by John Bell as a major "constitutional statute on fundamental rights" and can lead "to either the narrowing of the scope of legislation by means of an interpretation, which makes the statute compatible with the Convention, or a declaration of incompatibility, which empowers a minister to amend or repeal an incompatible statutory provision."[80] In addition, the question concerning the compatibility of British law with EU law can be raised before the British courts, and if the matter does not give rise to a serious difficulty in interpretation, the courts can apply European law directly and refuse to apply a British statute.[81] Compatibility with EU law is the only area in which British judges have the power to strike down legislation of Parliament, an approach that was definitively adopted after the European Court of Justice specifically stated that the British courts ought not to apply a British act of Parliament that was incompatible with European legislation.[82]

In any case, the court's decision in these cases does not annul an act of Parliament. As expressed by John Bell:

78 *Id.*, p. 2.

79 *Id.*, p. 3.

80 See N. BAMFORTH, "Parliamentary Sovereignty and the Human Rights Act 1998," [1998] Public Law 572. See John BELL, *British National Report*, p. 3.

81 Case 283/81, *Srl CILFIT v. Minister of Health*, [1982] ECR 3415. See John BELL, *British National Report*, p. 3 (footnote 14).

82 See *R v. Secretary of State for Transport, ex parte Factortame Ltd.*, [1990] 2 AC 85; *R v. Secretary of State for Transport, ex parte Factortame Ltd (N° 2)*, [1991] 1 AC 603; *R v. Secretary of State for Employment, ex parte Equal Opportunities Commission*, [1995] 1 AC 1. See John BELL, *British National Report*, p. 3 (footnotes 15–16).

> The Government has to decide whether to propose an amendment of the law to bring it into line with the Convention or to take other action to maintain the incompatibility, e.g. by registering a formal derogation from the Convention. This is the nearest that English judges come to a constitutional review.[83]

As Lord Bingham highlighted in the case A (FC) v. Secretary of State for the Home Department:

> The effect is not, of course, to override the sovereign legislative authority of the Queen in Parliament, since if primary legislation is declared to be incompatible the validity of the legislation is unaffected (section 4(6)) and the remedy lies with the appropriate minister (section 10), who is answerable to Parliament.[84]

This case of the House of Lords was issued to decide the challenge filed by a number of individuals regarding their detention without trial on the basis of them being a danger to national security, according to the Anti–Terrorism, Crime, and Security Act of 2001. The House of Lords declared the corresponding provision incompatible with articles 5 and 14 of the European Convention.

This control of "conventionality" of statutes, therefore, as is the case in the Netherlands, is the most common constitutional review procedure in the United Kingdom; it has been applied in numerous cases and is considered the most significant constitutional function that the new Supreme Court will have in the future.[85]

In Sweden, there is a very weak diffuse method of judicial review that has developed after the constitutional reform of 1979, which established the power of judicial review only when Parliament has issued an unconstitutional statute due to a "manifest error."[86] It has only been after the beginning of the Europeanization of Swedish law in the late 1990s that some sort of judicial review has been developed, mainly as a result of the progressive subordination of Swedish law to European law and particularly to the European Convention on Human Rights. Consequently, the most important cases of judicial review have been cases of control of conventionality decided by the courts, which have compared national legislation with the provisions of the European Convention on Human Rights.[87]

Finally, also regarding the control of conventionality of statutes, the situation of France must be highlighted. In France, the Cour de Cassation and the Conseil d'État have developed control of conventionality of statutes besides and in parallel to the traditional *a priori* judicial review power of legislation exercised by the Constitutional Council. As it has been summarized by Bertrand Mathieu, it has been due to

---

83 See John BELL, *British National Report*, p. 3.

84 See [2004] HL 56. See John BELL, *British National Report*, p. 5 (footnote 25).

85 See John Bell, *British National Report*, p. 6.

86 Chapter 11, article 14 of the Instrument of Government. See Joakim NERGELIUS, *Swedish National Report*, pp. 17–18.

87 See *Lassagard* case, Administrative Court of Appeal of Jönköping, 1996, which declared that the absence of judicial review in the particular case (agricultural subsidy) was contrary to article 6 of the ECHR; see also *Lundgren* case, Supreme Court, 2005, in which the extension of a criminal judicial procedure was also considered contrary to article 6 of the ECHR. See Joakim NERGELIUS, *Swedish National Report*, pp. 21–29.

the requirements imposed by international law, particularly by European Union law and the law of the European Convention on Human Rights that, first, the Cour de Cassation and, later, the Conseil d'État, have proceeded to reject the application of laws deemed *inconventionnelles*, that is, contrary to the conventions. The jurisprudence in such cases have been constructed not only on the basis of article 55 of the Constitution, which assigns the treaties or international agreements regularly ratified or approved superior authority regarding the laws, but also because of the refusal of the Conseil Constitutionnel to examine the *conventionalité de la loi* in accordance with its attributions on matters of control of the constitutionality of statutes.

The consequence of this situation on matters of judicial review has been a clear division of tasks: the control of the constitutionality of laws in an abstract and *a priori* way is exercised by the Conseil Constitutionnel when requested by political authorities,and the control of conventionality of laws is exercised by the ordinary judicial or administrative judges, in specific cases and controversies, particularly regarding fundamental rights and freedoms, which the Conseil Constitutionnel has refused to examine. On this situation, Bertrand Mathieu has referred to the paradox that exists in France between the traditional theory and platonic assertion of constitutional preeminence, and the jurisdictional impotence regarding constitutional provisions.[88]

III. THE INTERPRETATION OF THE CONSTITUTION AND THE INFLUENCE OF THE CONSTITUTIONAL COURTS ON CONSTITUTIONAL AND LEGAL REFORMS

The main tool of constitutional courts is the power to interpret the Constitution to ensure its application, enforceability, and supremacy by adapting the Constitution when changes and time require such task but without assuming the role of a constituent power or of the Legislator – they cannot on a discretionary political basis create legal norms or provisions that cannot be deducted from the Constitution itself.[89]

That is why, as a matter of principle, constitutional courts are considered "negative legislators" particularly when deciding to annul statutes,[90] and they cannot act as "positive legislators" in the sense of creating *ex novo* pieces of legislation or introducing "reforms" to statutes. In the words of Laurence Claus and Richard S. Kay, "We will treat judges as engaged in positive lawmaking when they originate a scheme of law as opposed to merely considering, revising or rejecting schemes conceived by other legislative actors" or "for a constitutional court to be positive lawmaker under this terminology would involve the court in considering, propounding, and creating a scheme of regulation of its own conception."[91]

---

88 See Bertrand MATHIEU, *French National Report*, p. 3.

89 See Jorge CARPIZO, *El Tribunal Constitucional y sus límites*, Grijley, Lima 2009, pp. 56, 68.

90 In this sense, in some countries, as in Chile, it has been said that the Constitutional Tribunal can act only as negative legislator. See Francisco ZÚÑIGA URBINA, "Control de constitucionalidad y sentencia," *Cuadernos del Tribunal Constitucional*, Nº 34, Santiago de Chile 2006, pp. 107, 109.

91 See Laurence CLAUS and Richard S. KAY, *U.S. National Report*, pp. 3, 5.

That is, constitutional courts cannot innovate in the legal order in a discretionary way, as they do not have the authority to create new law.[92] As the Federal Supreme Tribunal of Brazil has explained with respect to its decisions that annul statutes:

> The Federal Supreme Tribunal, when exercising the abstract judicial review of objective law positivized in the Constitution of the Republic, act as a virtual Negative Legislator, so its declaration of unconstitutionality comprise an exclusion judgment of control that, based on the attributions assigned to the Tribunal, consists in removing from the positive legal order, the State invalid expression non conformed with the model included in the Constitution of the Republic.[93]

In another case, the same Brazilian Federal Supreme Tribunal, in reviewing Law N° 9.504/97 on the free use of television and radio programs by political parties challenged because considered contrary to the principle of equality, argued:

> The declaration of unconstitutionality in the way it was requested, would modify the system of the law, altering it sense, which is a legal impossibility, because the Judicial Power, when controlling the constitutionality of normative acts, only acts as negative legislator and not as positive legislator.[94]

The consequence of this classical approach is that, constitutional courts being negative legislators, the direct effect of the constitutional courts' decisions excluding from the legal order pieces of legislation, is that the Legislator, in response, very frequently decides to reform the legislation or to enact a new piece of legislation, to comply with the constitutional court criteria.[95] Also, constitutional reforms have occurred after decisions adopted by constitutional courts to follow the doctrine they established.

For instance, in Argentina, Law N° 26,025 was passed to modify the rules applicable to the Supreme Court's appellate jurisdiction (article 117 of Constitution), after the Supreme Court ruled on the unconstitutionality of previous legislation that provided that all cases ordering the government to pay social security benefits were to be appealed before the Supreme Court. Because the rule actually delayed the payment of pensions to elderly people, in *Itzcovich* case (Fallos 2005), the Court

---

92 See Luis Roberto BARROSO et al., "Notas sobre a questão do legislador positivo," *Brazilian National Report III*, pp. 19–20; Néstor Pedro Sagües has mentioned that constitutional jurisdiction transforms itself into positive legislation, when it generates infraconstitutional provisions compatible with the Constitution, with the excuse of controlling the constitutionality of the legal order, in *Argentina National Report II*, p. 3.

93 STF, *DJ*, June 18, 1993, Rcl 385 QO/MA, Rel. Min. Celso de Mello, in Luis Roberto BARROSO et al., "Notas sobre a questão do legislador positivo," *Brazilian National Report III*, p. 9.

94 See STF, *DJ*, December 10, 1999, ADI 1.822/DF, Rel. Min. Moreira Alves, in Luis Roberto BARROSO et al., "Notas sobre a questão do legislador positivo," *Brazilian National Report III*, p. 15.

95 For instance, in the Netherlands, legislation was issued after the *Dutch Citizenship* case (Supreme Court judgment of October 12, 1984, NJ 1985/230). See J. UZMAN, T. BARKHUYSEN, and M. L. VAN EMMERIK, *Dutch National Report*, p. 21.

declared that the appeal procedure had become unconstitutional in that it affected petitioner's right to a speedy trial.[96]

Something similar happened on matters of marriage law. Although the Argentinean Constitution recognizes the right to marriage, the Civil Code established that divorce did not entail the right to a new marriage, a clause whose constitutionality the courts upheld several times. However, in 1986, the Supreme Court applied what was called a "dynamic", or living constitution, approach considering in *Sejean* case[97] that changes to society's perception of a topic require giving new scope to the right to human dignity, and thus it declared unconstitutional the statute that had been in force for almost a century. This decision was the prelude to reforming the law of civil marriage, which, following the Supreme Court decision, allowed for the possibility of a subsequent marriage.[98]

With respect to Portugal, as mentioned by Joaquim de Sousa Ribeiro, it is a fact that, "even though the Constitutional Court does not play a part in the law making process, many amendments made to existing legislation are the result of its ruling, either to incorporate or to set aside the Court's ruling on the subject."[99]

IV. THE QUESTION OF CONSTITUTIONAL COURTS AS POSITIVE LEGISLATORS

In any case, in the contemporary world, the truth is that judicial review has progressively evolved, surpassing the former rigid character of courts only being negative legislators,[100] as a result of the development of new principles that, at the time of Kelsen's proposals, were not on the agenda of constitutional courts and judges.[101]

That is why, for instance, in Brazil, the Federal Supreme Tribunal in some cases has considered the same notion of negative legislator that it defended in many previous decisions an "ancient dogma" and a "myth."[102]

Consequently, new principles have developed; for example, the principle of preservation of statutes, derived from the presumption of constitutionality they have,

---

96 See Fallos: 328:566 (2005). See Alejandra RODRÍGUEZ GALÁN and Alfredo Mauricio VÍTOLO, *Argentinean National Report I*, pp. 13–14 (footnote 54).

97 See Fallos 308:2268 (1986). See Alejandra RODRÍGUEZ GALÁN and Alfredo Mauricio VÍTOLO, *Argentinean National Report I*, p. 15 (footnote 61).

98 See Alejandra RODRÍGUEZ GALÁN and Alfredo Mauricio VÍTOLO, *Argentinean National Report I*, p. 5.

99 See Joaquim de SOUSA RIBEIRO and Esperança MEALHA, *Portuguese National Report*, p. 9.

100 See Francisco FERNÁNDEZ SEGADO, "Algunas reflexiones generales en torno a los efectos de las sentencias de inconstitucionalidad y a la relatividad de ciertas fórmulas estereotipadas vinculadas a ellas," *Anuario Iberoamericano de Justicia Constitucional*, Centro de Estudios Políticos y Constitucionales, Nº 12, 2008, Madrid 2008, p. 195.

101 That is why Francisco Javier DÍAZ REVORIO, referring to the European system of judicial review has said, "We are debtors of Kelsen, but not 'slaves' of his ideas," in *Las sentencias interpretativas del Tribunal Constitucional*, Lex Nova, Valladolid 2001, p. 305.

102 See Luis Roberto BARROSO et al., "Notas sobre a questão do legislador positivo," *Brazilian National Report III*, p. 22.

has empowered constitutional courts to interpret statutes according to or in harmony with the constitution,[103] in order to avoid any legislative vacuum, bypassing the need to declare statutes unconstitutional. This is today one of the main tools of constitutional courts when interpreting the constitution, which they have used in some cases, to fill permanently or temporarily the vacuums that annulling the statute could originate.

Another important role that has progressively developed during the past decades, far from the role of declaring null unconstitutional statutes, is the power of constitutional courts on matters of judicial review, not regarding existing legislation, but regarding the absence of statutes or the omissions or abstention incurred by the Legislator when sanctioning statutes.[104]

That is, constitutional courts also control the omissions of the Legislators to produce the legislation that they have the constitutional obligation to sanction. These omissions can be absolute or relative, and judicial review, in both cases, has contributed to the development of new trends in the control of constitutionality of statutes, which converts constitutional courts into a sort of legislative assistant. Nonetheless, in some cases, where judicial review of legislative omissions is not effectively developed, control of those omissions is only possible in an indirect way, by claiming State liability for the absence of a legislative act.[105]

In contrast, the same change of the scope of judicial review has occurred in diffuse or decentralized systems of judicial review, where, in practice, as was stated by Christopher Wolfe, supreme courts, "once a distinctively judicial power, essentially different from legislative power, [have] become merely another variant of legislative power"; considering that, although the Court had never proclaimed it, for the legal profession, "judicial review is an essentially legislative activity"; as such, the controversy is "generally restricted to how this power should be employed, actively or with restraint."[106]

That is why it is sometimes difficult to understand, particularly for non–American lawyers, the exact extent of the expression that any nominee to the U.S. Supreme Court must repeat again and again before the Senate in confirmation hearings: "the task of a judge is not to make law; it is to apply the law."[107] This approach

103 See Francisco Javier DÍAZ REVORIO, *Las sentencias interpretativas del Tribunal Constitucional*, Lex Nova, Valladolid 2001, p. 288; See Joaquim de SOUSA RIBEIRO and Esperança MEALHA, *Portuguese National Report*, p. 7.

104 These judicial review powers do not correspond with Kelsen's pattern of judicial review as negative legislation. See Francisco Javier DÍAZ REVORIO, *Las sentencias interpretativas del Tribunal Constitucional*, Lex Nova, Valladolid 2001, p. 278.

105 This is what has been envisaged in Greece. See Julia Iliopoulos–Strangas and Stylianos–Ioannis G. Koutnatzis, *Greek National Report*, p. 5.

106 See Christopher WOLFE, *The Rise of Modern Judicial Review: From Constitutional Interpretation to Judge–Made Law*, Basic Books, New York 1986, p. 3; Wolfe, *La transformación de la interpretación constitucional*, Civitas, Madrid 1991, p. 15.

107 This was what Judge Sonia Sotomayor said in the confirmation hearing before the Senate on July 13, 2009. See Peter BAKER and Neil A. LEWIS, "Sotomayor Vows 'Fidelity to the Law' as Hearings Start," *New York Times*, July 14, 2009, p. A15.

has been considered a "myth" that, as it has been said by Geoffrey R. Stone, must be exposed before there can be a serious discussion about the proper role of U.S. judges:

> Faithfully applying our Constitution's 18th– and 19th–century text to 21st–century problems requires not only careful attention to the text, fidelity to the framers' goals and respect for precedents, but also awareness of the practical realities of the present. Only with such awareness can judges, in a constantly changing society, hope to keep faith with our highest law.
>
> This does not mean judges are free to make up the law as they go along. But it does mean that constitutional law is not a mechanical exercise of just "applying the law."[108]

In any case, it is a fact in the contemporary world that constitutional courts have progressively assumed a more important role assisting the Legislator in its functions and even creating norms that they can deduct from the constitution.[109] In some cases, they are more than auxiliaries to the Legislator; they substitute for it, assuming the role of positive legislators by issuing temporary or provisional rules to be applied on specific matters.

This has occurred, for instance, in many cases by means of the application of the principle of progressiveness and the prevalence of fundamental rights, like the right to equality and nondiscrimination, in the interest of the protection of citizens' rights and guarantees, in which cases the interference of the courts in the legislative function has been considered legitimate and according to the constitutional principles and values.

Nonetheless, the legislative agenda of constitutional courts has also included other areas of activism, sometimes with political purposes. For example, in many cases, as has been the case in the former Socialist countries of Eastern Europe, constitutional courts have had an important role implementing, developing, and strengthening the Constitution, and particularly the newly established democratic regime and the rule of law principles.[110]

But in other countries, quite far from the protection of fundamental rights and the consolidation of democratic principles, the danger of constitutional courts encroaching on the legislative power to contribute to the dismantling of the principle of separation of powers is not just a "phantom," as Hamilton pointed out in another context two centuries ago.[111] On the contrary, it has been a tragic reality, particularly in

---

108 See Geoffrey R. STONE, "Our Fill–in–the–Blank Constitution," Op–Ed, *New York Times*, April 14, 2010, p. A27.

109 See Iván ESCOBAR FORNOS, "Las sentencias constitucionales" in *Estudios Jurídicos*, vol. 1, Ed. Hispamer, Managua 2007, p. 489.

110 For instance, in the process of transformation of the former Socialist States into contemporary democratic States subjected to the rule of law. See, for instance, Marek SAFJAN, *Polish National Report*, pp. 7, 10; Sanja Barić and Petar Bačić, *Croatian National Report*, pp. 18, 21, 28; Boško Tripković, *Serbian National Report*, pp. 1, 14.

111 He said in Paper N° 81 of *The Federalist*, "The Judiciary Continued, and the Distribution of the Judiciary Authority," that "It may in the last place be observed that the supposed danger of judiciary encroachments on the legislative authority, which has been upon many occasions

countries ruled by authoritarian governments. In some countries, constitutional courts have assumed with absolute impunity the task of supporting and legitimizing unconstitutional statutes and government acts, in many cases usurping the constituent and legislative powers, of course without any sort of argument to support the partisan judicial decisions taken supposedly in the best interest of the country or for the good of the nation.[112]

Worse, in those cases, it is not a matter of considering "the Judge as Legislator for Social Welfare,"[113] as was the case in the United States at the beginning of the twentieth century, which Benjamin Cardozo considered a necessity,[114] but a matter of the court being an instrument to support an authoritarian government,[115] and even to restrict constitutional freedoms, which cannot be accepted. This happened, for instance, regarding freedom of expression in Venezuela, in 2001, when the constitutional court *ex officio* restricted the citizens' right to response and to rectification regarding the President of the Republic's media statements;[116] and in 2008, when the same constitutional court decided to confiscate the assets of a private TV station.[117]

---

reiterated, is in reality a phantom." See Clinton Rossiter (ed.), *The Federalist Papers*, Penguin Books, New York 2003, pp. 483–484.

112 See Christopher WOLFE, *The Rise of Modern Judicial Review: From Constitutional Interpretation to Judge–Made Law*, Basic Books, New York 1986, p. 101; *La transformación de la interpretación constitucional*, Civitas, Madrid 1991, p. 144.

113 *Id.* pp. 223 ff. and 305 ff.

114 Benjamin CARDOZO recognized "without hesitation that judges must and do legislate," though "only between gaps" of the law. See Benjamin CARDOZO, *The Nature of the Judicial Process*, Yale University Press, 1921, pp. 10, 113, 165. See the references in Christopher WOLFE, *The Rise of Modern Judicial Review: From Constitutional Interpretation to Judge–Made Law*, Basic Books, New York 1986, pp. 230, 231, 315, 316.

115 As it has been the case in Venezuela during the past years. See the comments on the most relevant Constitutional Chamber of the Supreme Tribunal decision in Allan R. BREWER–CARÍAS, *Crónica de la "in"justicia constitucional: La Sala Constitucional y el autoritarismo en Venezuela*, Edigtorial Jurídica Venezulana, Caracas 2007; BREWER–CARÍAS, *Reforma constitucional y fraude a la Constitución (1999–2009)*, Academia de Ciencias Políticas y Sociales, Caracas 2009.

116 See Decision N° 1013 of June 12, 2001, *Elías Santana* case. See http://www.tsj.gov.ve/ decisiones/scon/Junio/1013–120601–00–2760%20.htm. See the comments in Allan R. BREWER–CARÍAS et al., *La libertad de expresión amenazada (Sentencia 1013)*, Instituto Interamericano de Derechos Humanos, Editorial Jurídica Venezolana, Caracas and San José 2001; "El juez constitucional vs. la libertad de expresión: La libertad de expresión del pensamiento y el derecho a la información y su violación por la Sala Constitucional," in Allan R. BREWER–CARÍAS, *Crónica de la "in"justicia constitucional. La Sala Constitucional y el autoritarismo en Venezuela*, Caracas 2007, pp. 419–468. See also Daniela UROSA MAGGI, *Venezuelan National Report*, pp. 16–17.

117 See decision of the Constitutional Chamber N° 956 of May 25, 2007 in Allan R. BREWER–CARÍAS, "El juez constitucional en Venezuela como instrumento para aniquilar la libertad de expresión plural y para confiscar la propiedad privada: El caso RCTV," *Revista de Derecho Público*," N° 110, Editorial Jurídica Venezolana, Caracas 2007, pp. 7–32.

In any case, in all the countries that have developed systems to control the constitutionality of statutes, discussions have developed regarding the limits of judicial review, the extent of the effects of the constitutional courts, decisions, and the degree of interference allowed in constitutional states by constitutional courts regarding legislative functions. These discussions have always existed and will continue to exist. They began in all countries with the adoption of judicial review of legislation, and they will continue to exist with constitutional courts, which are the supreme interpreters of the Constitution and have the power to guarantee its supremacy, to interpret statutes according to the Constitution's provisions, to guarantee the enforcement of fundamental constitutional rights, and to resolve conflicts between the different constitutional organs of the State.

The fact is, at the beginning of the twenty–first century, that there is no doubt that constitutional courts are no longer confined to be negative legislators in the traditional way, because their role is no longer reduced when controlling the constitutionality of statutes, to declare their unconstitutionality, or to annul them when contrary to the Constitution. Constitutional courts have progressively assumed a more active role when reviewing legislative acts vis–à–vis the Constitution.

Nonetheless, what is essential to bear in mind even in cases of new roles and powers is that constitutional courts are, above all, subjected to the Constitution, and as such, they are constituted organs of the State.[118] Thus, they are also subjected to the principle of separation of powers and consequently they are not legislators, as the legislative function is assigned in the Constitution to the legislative body. They can assist the legislators in accomplishing their functions, but they cannot substitute for the legislators and enact legislation.[119] The legislative organs of the States that are contemporary democracies, integrated by representatives elected by universal suffrage, are called to enact legislation through a constitutionally prescribed procedure and are subject to political accountability before the electors. This legislative framework of State action cannot be substituted for by constitutional courts' attempts to legislate in place of the legislators.[120] On the contrary, they risk being considered "illegitimate oligarchies."[121]

---

118 As stated by the Constitutional Tribunal of Peru: "the fact of the Constitutional Tribunal being the supreme interpreter of the Constitution, does not change its character of constituted power, and as all of them, subjected to the limits established in the Constitution." Decision of February 2, 2006, STC 0030–2005. See Fernán ALTUVE FEBRES, *Peruvian National Report II*, pp. 27–28. See also Rubén HERNÁNDEZ VALLE, *Costa Rican National Report*, p. 43.

119 See Humberto NOGUEIRA ALCALÁ, "La sentencia constitucional en Chile: Aspectos fundamentales sobre su fuerza vinculante," *Anuario Iberoamericano de Justicia Constitucional*, Centro de Estudios Políticos y Constitucionales, N° 12, 2008, Madrid 2008, p. 315.

120 As mentioned by Rubén HERNÁNDEZ VALLE, "the activity of the courts is not to create law, but to interpret law. Consequently, Constitutional Courts cannot substitute the Legislator will, because constitutional interpretation, in spite of being conditioned by evident political components, is always juridical interpretation." See Rubén HERNÁNDEZ VALLE, *Costa Rican National Report*, p. 42.

121 See P. MARTENS, "Les cours constitutionelles: des oligarchies illegitimes?" in *La Republic des judges*, Actes du Colloque Organize par le Jeune Barreau de Liège le 7 Février 1997, pp.

That is why, for instance, one can find declarations from constitutional courts themselves explaining their limits, as the Federal Supreme Tribunal of Brazil did in deciding a direct action of unconstitutionality involving article 45.1 of the Constitution, which established the integration of the House of Representatives. The Court said that the only organ that could establish the number of Federal Representatives for each of the Member States was the National Congress, through the corresponding legislation:

> The absence of a complementary law (*vacum juris*) that constitutes the necessary normative instrument cannot be filled by any other State act, specially one with jurisdictional character like this Court. The admission of such possibility would imply to transform the Federal Supreme Tribunal, when exercising the concentrated control of constitutionality, into a positive legislator, a role that the Court refuses itself to assume.[122]

But in spite of this self–restraint approach, it is possible to find examples of such illegitimate oligarchies in other countries, like Venezuela, where the Constitutional Chamber of the Supreme Tribunal has attributed to itself a general power called normative jurisdiction, according to which:

> in specific cases where a constitutional infraction arises, the Chamber has exercised jurisdiction in a normative way, giving immediate enforcement to constitutional provisions, establishing its scope or ways of exercise, even in the absence of statutes directly developing them.[123]

It is true that this normative jurisdiction has been mainly used regarding programmatic constitutional provisions referring to fundamental rights, to allow their immediate enforcement, but unfortunately, it has also been used for other purposes by the authoritarian government that has existed in the country since 1999.[124] In any case, the Venezuelan Constitutional Chamber has based its normative jurisdiction on article 335 of the Constitution, which confers to it the role of guaranteeing the supremacy and effectiveness of constitutional provisions and principles and of issuing binding interpretations of the same, arguing that this provision of the Constitution:

53–72, quoted by Christian BEHRENDT, "L'activité du judge constitutionnel comme législateur–cadre positif," summary of the thesis published in *Revue Européenne de Droit Public*, 2010, p. 16.

122 See STF, *DJ*, May 19, 1995, ADI 267 MC/DF, Rel. Min. Celso de Mello. See Luis Roberto BARROSO et al., "Notas sobre a questão do legislador positivo," *Brazilian National Report III*, pp. 14. In another case, the Federal Supreme Tribunal reviewed the electoral law (Lei N° 9.504/97).

123 See Decision N° 1571 of August 22, 2001, case *Asodeviprilara*; http://www.tsj.gov.ve/decisiones/scon/Agosto/1571–220801–01–1274%20.htm; Daniela UROSA MAGGI, *Venezuelan National Report*, p. 3.

124 See generally Allan R. BREWER–CARÍAS, *Dismantling Democracy: The Chávez Authoritarian Experiment*, Cambridge University Press, New York 2010.

> allows the normative jurisdiction particularly regarding programmatic provisions that exists in the Constitution, which would by timely suspended up to when the Legislator could be so kind to develop them, remaining in the meantime without effects.[125]

For such purpose of exercising its normative jurisdiction, which in its broader sense is an example of a case of the pathology of judicial review, the constitutional court in Venezuela has even rejected the general procedural law principle that requires the courts to act only at the request of a party with standing, assuming it *ex officio*, without any specific party request or judicial controversy developed on the deciding matter.[126]

That is why, as with any power attributed to a State organ with no possibility of itself being controlled, judicial review can also be distorted and abused without any possibility for the citizens or other constitutional organs of the State to control their actions.

The main question that remains to be anwered on this matter of abuse of constitutional jurisdiction remains, *Quis custodies ipso custodiem*?[127] There is no answer, because there are no State organs that can control constitutional jurisdictions, nor can citizens by means of electoral processes.

Constitutional jurisdiction, therefore, is the only State organ not subjected to checks and balance or control, so the abuse of its functions are out of the reach of the enforcement of constitutional provisions. That is why George Jellinek said that the only guarantee regarding the guardian of the Constitution eventually lies in its "moral conscience";[128] and Alexis de Tocqueville was accurate in his observations of the U.S. Federal Constitution:

> The peace, the prosperity, and the very existence of the Union are vested in the hands of the seven Federal judges. Without them the Constitution would be a dead letter. . . .
>
> Not only must the Federal judges be good citizens, and men of that information and integrity which are indispensable to all magistrates, but they must be statesmen, wise to discern the

---

125 See Decision N° 1571 of August 22, 2001, case *Asodeviprilara*; http://www.tsj.gov.ve/decisiones/scon/Agosto/1571-220801-01-1274%20.htm; Daniela UROSA MAGGI, *Venezuelan National Report*, pp. 3–4.

126 See Allan R. BREWER–CARÍAS, "Régimen y alcance de la actuación judicial de oficio en materia de justicia constitucional en Venezuela," *Estudios Constitucionales: Revista Semestral del Centro de Estudios Constitucionales* 4, N° 2, Universidad de Talca, Santiago, Chile 2006, pp. 221–250; Daniela UROSA MAGGI, *Venezuelan National Report*, pp. 4, 5, 22.

127 See Jorge CARPIZO, *El Tribunal Constitucional y sus límites*, Grijley, Lima 2009, pp. 44, 47, 51; Allan R. BREWER–CARÍAS, "*Quis Custodiet Ipsos Custodes*: De la interpretación constitucional a la inconstitucionalidad de la interpretación," *Revista de Derecho Público*, N° 105, Editorial Jurídica Venezolana, Caracas 2006, pp. 7–27; *VIII Congreso Nacional de Derecho Constitucional, Perú*, Fondo Editorial 2005, Colegio de Abogados de Arequipa, Arequipa, September 2005, pp. 463–489.

128 See George JELLINEK, *Ein Verfassungsgerichtshof fur Österreich*, Alfred HOLDER, Vienna 1885, quoted by Francisco FERNÁNDEZ SEGADO, "Algunas reflexiones generales en torno a los efectos de las sentencias de inconstitucionalidad y a la relatividad de ciertas fórmulas estereotipadas vinculadas a ellas," *Anuario Iberoamericano de Justicia Constitucional*, Centro de Estudios Políticos y Constitucionales, N° 12, 2008, Madrid 2008, p. 196.

signs of the times, not afraid to brave the obstacles that can be subdued, nor slow to turn away from the current when it threatens to sweep them off, and the supremacy of the Union and the obedience due to the laws along with them.

The President, who exercises a limited power, may err without causing great mischief in the state. Congress may decide amiss without destroying the Union, because the electoral body in which the Congress originates may cause it to retract its decision by changing its members. But if the Supreme Court is ever composed of imprudent or bad men, the Union may be plunged into anarchy or civil war.[129]

In the same sense, Alexander Hamilton, warned about the "authority of the proposed Supreme Court of the United States," and particularly the following:

> [Its] power of construing the laws according to the *spirit* of the Constitution, will enable that court to mould them into whatever shape it may think proper; especially as its decisions will not be in any manner subject to the revision or correction of the legislative body.

He concluded:

> [T]he legislatures of the several States, can at any time rectify, by law, the exceptionable decisions of their respective courts. But the errors and usurpations of the Supreme Court of the United States will be uncontrollable and remediless.[130]

This is important to bear in mind, particularly in democratic regimes, where the conversion of constitutional courts into legislators violates the principle of separation of powers and transforms them into State organs not subject to political liability. In other words, the blurring of the limits between interpretation and normative jurisdiction "could transform the guardian of the Constitution into sovereign."[131]

The truth is that, in many countries, given the political regime or the condition of the members of constitutional courts, the important instruments designed to guarantee the supremacy of the Constitution, the enforcement of fundamental rights, and the functioning of the democratic regime have been the most diabolical instruments of authoritarianism, legitimizing the actions contrary to the Constitution taken by the other branches of government,[132] and sometimes on their own initiative by the obsequious servants of those in power. These cases, of course, make a mockery of judicial review, because as Mauro Cappelletti affirmed a few decades ago, judicial re-

---

129 See Alexis DE TOCQUEVILLE, *Democracy in America*, ch. 8, "The Federal Constitution," trans. Henry Reeve, revised and corrected, 1899, http://xroads.virginia.edu/HYPER/DETOC/1_ch08.htm See also Jorge CARPIZO, *El Tribunal Constitucional y sus límites*, Grijley, Lima 2009, pp. 46–48.

130 See Alexander HAMILTON, N° 81 of *The Federalist*, "The Judiciary Continued, and the Distribution of the Judiciary Authority"; Clinton Rossiter (Ed.), *The Federalist Papers*, Penguin Books, New York 2003, pp. 480. See also Laurence CLAUS and Richard S. KAY, *U.S. National Report*, p. 10.

131 See Francisco FERNÁNDEZ SEGADO, "Algunas reflexiones generales en torno a los efectos de las sentencias de inconstitucionalidad y a la relatividad de ciertas fórmulas estereotipadas vinculadas a ellas," *Anuario Iberoamericano de Justicia Constitucional*, Centro de Estudios Políticos y Constitucionales, N° 12, 2008, Madrid 2008, p. 161.

132 See Néstor Pedro SAGÜES, *La interpretación judicial de la Constitución*, LexisNexis, Buenos Aires 2006, p. 31.

view is incompatible with authoritarianism and not tolerated by authoritarian regimes that are enemies of freedom.[133] This illness of judicial review, that is also a case of the pathology of judicial review, occurs when constitutional courts, as docile instruments of governments, openly assume the role of the legislator, usurping its powers and functions or, even worse, assuming the role of the constituent power by mutating the Constitution in an illegitimate way.[134] Unfortunately, this has been the case of constitutional courts acting at the service of authoritarian governments, and the Constitutional Chamber of the Supreme Tribunal of Justice in Venezuela is an example. In many aspects, that example shows how serious the illness is that is affecting constitutional jurisdiction and turning constitutional justice into unconstitutional justice.[135]

CHAPTER 2

CONSTITUTIONAL COURTS' INTERFERENCE WITH THE CONSTITUENT POWER

Constitutional courts, being constitutional organs leading with constitutional questions, in many cases interfere not with the ordinary Legislator, but with the constitutional legislator, that is with the constituent power, by enacting constitutional rules when resolving constitutional disputes between state organs or even by legitimately making changes to a constitution by means of adapting its provisions and giving them concrete meaning.

I. CONSTITUTIONAL COURTS' RESOLUTION OF DISPUTES OF CONSTITUTIONAL RANK AND ENACTMENT OF CONSTITUTIONAL RULES

The principle of the supremacy of the Constitution, particularly regarding rigid Constitutions, implies that the Constitution and all constitutional rules can be enacted only by the constituent powers established and regulated in the same constitution. This constituent power can be the people, directly expressing their will (e.g., by means of a referendum) or an organ of the State acting as a derived constituent pow-

133 See Mauro CAPELLETTI, "¿Renegar de Montesquieu? La expansión y legitimidad de la justicia constitucional," *Revista Española de Derecho Constitucional* 6, N° 17, Madrid 1986, p. 17; Francisco EGUIGUREN and Liliana SALOMÉ, *Peruvian National Report I*, p. 7.

134 See regarding the case of the Constitutional Chamber in Venezuela, Allan R. BREWER–CARÍAS "El juez constitucional al servicio del autoritarismo y la ilegítima mutación de la Constitución: el caso de la Sala Constitucional del Tribunal Supremo de Justicia de Venezuela (1999–2009)," in *Revista de Administración Pública*, N° 180, Madrid 2009, pp. 383–418; "La ilegítima mutación de la Constitución por el juez constitucional y la demolición del Estado de derecho en Venezuela," in *Revista de Derecho Político*, N° 75–76, Homenaje a Manuel García Pelayo, Universidad Nacional de Educación a Distancia, Madrid, 2009, pp. 289–325.

135 See generally Allan R. BREWER–CARÍAS, *Crónica de la "in"justicia constitucional. La Sala Constitucional y el autoritarismo en Venezuela*, Editorial Jurídica Venezolana, Caracas 2007.

er. The consequence is that no constituted power of the State by itself can enact constitutional rules, except when expressly authorized by a constitution to participate in a constitution–making process.

Nonetheless, in contemporary constitutional law, there are cases in which constitutions authorize, exceptionally and indirectly, organs of the State to enact constitutional rules. For instance, this is the case of parliaments when the constitution has authorized them to enact laws with constitutional rank (i.e., constitutional laws). In other cases, constitutions expressly authorize constitutional courts to enact constitutional rules when deciding conflicts regarding attributions of State organs, for instance on matters of political decentralization. This is particularly true in federal States, which are always constructed on a constitutional system of territorial distribution of powers between the federal (national) and state level, and even in some cases, a municipal level.

When resolving conflicts of competencies between constitutional organs, constitutional courts without a doubt enact constitutional rules. It is in this sense that Konrad Lachmayer, with respect to Austria, says that, since 1925, article 138.2 of the Constitution has enabled the Constitutional Court to act as a positive legislator, giving positive powers to the court in the sensitive area of the division of competences between the Federation and the states (*Länder*). The provision reads as follows: "The Constitutional Court furthermore determines at the request of the Federal Government or a state Government whether a legislative or executive act is part of the competence of the Federation or the States." This means that the Constitutional Court has the final say on the question of whether ultimate authority belongs to the Federation or to the states (*Länder*).

Because in the Austrian concept of a federal state, concurring competences between the federal level of government and the states do not exist, but only exclusive competencies according to a strict separation of powers, the decisions of the Constitutional Court, established in article 138.2 of the Constitution, is understood to be an authentic interpretation of the Constitution, meaning that the Constitutional Court, when deciding conflicts between constitutional entities, "enacts constitutional law."[136]

In other federal states with the same concentrated system of judicial review as Austria, constitutional courts are also empowered to decide on constitutional conflicts between the Federation and the states, and consequently to determine the territorial level of government to which correspond the competence in conflict. This is the case, for instance, of Venezuela, where the Constitutional Chamber of the Supreme Tribunal is empowered to arbitrate constitutional controversies raised between national, state, and municipal bodies (article 336.9 of the Constitution)[137] in a system in which, in addition to exclusive competencies of the three levels of government, there are also concurrent competencies. The decision of the Constitutional

---

136 See Konrad LACHMAYER, *Austrian National Report*, pp. 1–2.

137 See, e.g., Decision N° 2401 of October 8, 2004, "*Gobernador del Estado Carabobo v. Poder Ejecutivo Nacional*," *Revista de Derecho Público*, N° 99–100, Editorial Jurídica Venezolana, Caracas 2004, p. 317.

Chamber, when determining the level of government that possesses the competency, undoubtedly has constitutional value.

Nonetheless, this judicial review power can become an instrument for illegitimately mutating the Constitution in a way contrary to its provisions. This happened precisely in Venezuela, in particular, regarding the distribution of competencies between the various territorial levels of government (municipalities, states, and national government), which can be changed only by means of a constitutional reform.[138] Specifically, it happened regarding the competency referred to the conservation, administration and use of roads and national highways, and administration and use of national ports and airports of commercial use, which the Constitution assigns in an "exclusive" way to the states (article 164.10). In 2007, by proposing a constitutional reform, the National Executive intended to centralize this competence of the states,[139] but it was rejected by the people in referendum. Nonetheless, what could not be achieved through popular vote was achieved by the Constitutional Chamber of the Supreme Tribunal in Decision N° 565 of April 15, 2008,[140] issued deciding an autonomous recourse for constitutional interpretation filed by the attorney general. In such ruling, the "exclusive attribution" of the states was converted into a "concurrent" competency that the National Government can revert it in its favor. With this interpretation, the Constitutional Chamber illegitimately mutated the Constitution; usurped popular sovereignty; and changed the federal form of government by mutating the territorial distribution system of powers between the National Power and the states.

The U.S. Supreme Court can also be mentioned regarding the delimitation of the powers of the federal government in relation to the states. In this regard, since 1937,

---

138 See Allan R. BREWER–CARÍAS, "Consideraciones sobre el régimen de distribución de competencias del poder público en la Constitución de 1999," in Fernando Parra Aranguren and Armando Rodríguez García (eds.), *Estudios de Derecho Administrativo: Libro Homenaje a la Universidad Central de Venezuela, Facultad de Ciencias Jurídicas y Políticas, con ocasión del Vigésimo Aniversario del Curso de Especialización en Derecho Administrativo*, vol. I, Tribunal Supremo de Justicia, Caracas 2001, pp. 107–136.

139 See Allan R. BREWER–CARÍAS, *Hacia la consolidación de un estado socialista, centralizado, policial y militarista: Comentarios sobre el sentido y alcance de las propuestas de reforma constitucional 2007*, Editorial Jurídica Venezolana, Caracas 2007, pp. 41 ff.; BREWER CARÍAS, *La reforma constitucional de 2007 (Comentarios al proyecto inconstitucionalmente sancionado por la Asamblea Nacional el 2 de Noviembre de 2007)*, Editorial Jurídica Venezolana, Caracas 2007, pp. 72 ff.

140 See Constitutional Chamber, Decision N° 565 of April 15, 2008, case: *Attorney General of the Republic, interpretation recourse of article 164,10 of the 1999 Constitution of 1999*, http://www.tsj.gov.ve/decisio–nes/scon/Abril/565–150408–07–1108.htm. See also Daniela Urosa Maggi, *Venezuelan National Report*, pp. 15–16. See the comments in Allan R. BREWER–CARÍAS, "La ilegítima mutación de la Constitución y la legitimidad de la jurisdicción constitucional: la 'reforma' de la forma federal del Estado en Venezuela mediante interpretación constitucional," in *Memoria del X Congreso Iberoamericano de Derecho Constitucional*, Instituto Iberoamericano de Derecho Constitucional, Asociación Peruana de Derecho Constitucional, Instituto de Investigaciones Jurídicas–UNAM y Maestría en Derecho Constitucional–PUCP, IDEMSA, Lima 2009, vol. 1, pp. 29–51.

the Supreme Court has developed an expansive constitutional interpretation of congressional authority, according Congress broad authority to regulate under constitutional provisions like the commerce clause of the U.S. Constitution. Article 1, section 8, of the Constitution states, "The Congress shall have the power . . . to regulate Commerce with foreign Nations, and among the several States, and with the Indian Tribes," This provision was initially interpreted in *Gibbon v. Ogden*, 22 U.S. (9 Wheat) I (1824), in which Chief Justice John Marshall, writing for the Court, defined *commerce* to include "all phases of business" and "among the several States" to refer to interstate effects, even if commerce occurs within a state. This clause, "the focus of most of the Supreme Court decisions that have considered the scope of congressional power and federalism,"[141] led to the adoption of very important Supreme Court decisions that were issued after the invalidation of various important pieces of New Deal legislation, like *National Labor Relations Board v. Jones & Laughlin Steel Corp.*, 301 U.S. 1 (1937), *United States v. Darby* 312 U.S. 199 (1941), and *Wickard v. Filburn*, 317 U.S. 111 (1942).

In these decisions, the Supreme Court ceased to distinguish between commerce and other kind of business, such as mining, manufacturing, and production, allowing Congress to exercise control over all business; ceased to distinguish between direct and indirect effects of interstate commerce, allowing Congress to regulate any activity that cumulatively had an effect on interstate commerce; and ceased to consider the Tenth Amendment as a limit on congressional power. Under the test developed, during the following decades, according to Erwin Chemerinsky, it has been difficult to imagine anything that Congress cannot regulate under the commerce clause, so long as it does not violate another constitutional provision.[142] By means of the case law on matters related to the federal State, the Supreme Court's decisions, without doubt, eventually have enacted constitutional rules.

However, in enacting rules about constitutional disputes regarding constitutional distribution of powers in federal States, constitutional courts are not authorized to enact constitutional rules or to give constitutional rank to provisions adopted by constitutional organs of the State not authorized to enact constitutional rules. The contrary would be a violation of a constitution, as occurred also in Venezuela, where the Constitutional Court gave constitutional rank and even supraconstitutional rank to provisions that the people had not approved. In effect, after the popular approval of the 1999 Constitution, the National Constituent Assembly adopted a set of "constitutional transition" provisions, not approved by the people, by means of a decree of the "Regime of Transition of the Public Power."[143] In the decree, the Constituent Assembly dismissed all heads of the branches of government, including members of the Supreme Tribunal, and appointed new ones, changing the content of the transition provisions contained in the text of the Constitution. The decree was challenged before the Constitutional Chamber of the Supreme Tribunal of Justice, which issued

---

141 See Erwin CHEMERINSKY, *Constitutional Law: Principles and Policies*, Aspen Publishers, New York, 2006, pp. 243 ff.

142 *Id.*, pp. 259–260.

143 *Gaceta Oficial* N° 36.859, December 29, 1999.

Decision N° 6, of January 27, 2000,[144] ruling that the National Constituent Assembly had "supraconstitutional" power to create constitutional provisions without popular approval, admitting the existence in the country of two parallel transitional constitutional regimes: the one contained in the transition provisions of the Constitution approved by the people and those approved by the National Constituent Assembly without popular approval. In this way, the Chamber illegitimately changed the Constitution, thus violating popular sovereignty and giving birth to a long period of constitutional instability that still has not ended. This constitutional mutation was ratified by the same Constitutional Chamber in Decision N° 180 of March 18, 2000.[145]

II. CONSTITUTIONAL COURTS AND JUDICIAL REVIEW OF PROVISIONS OF THE CONSTITUTION AND OF CONSTITUTIONAL REFORMS AND AMENDMENTS

Constitutional courts can also enact constitutional rules when they are empowered to review the Constitution itself, as is the case in Austria, where the Constitutional Court is empowered to confront the Constitution with its own basic principles, like the principle of democracy, the federal state, the rule of law, separation of powers, and the general system of human rights. Exercising this power, the Austrian Constitutional Court declared in 2001 a constitutional provision itself as unconstitutional, annulling it.[146] The reason for this decision was the ongoing policy of the Austrian legislator to (indirectly) legitimize unconstitutional provisions, which the Constitutional Court had annulled, by creating new constitutional provisions mirroring the former unconstitutional ones. In this case, the Constitutional Court declared void a constitutional provision excluding parts of the Public Procurement Act from its compliance with the Constitution. The scope of review by the Court was limited to the basic principles of the Constitution, holding that the democracy principle and the *Rechtsstaat* principle were violated by exempting constitutional compliance with a significant aspect of legislation (public procurement) in a general manner.[147]

In the same sense, constitutional courts can enact constitutional rules when exercising judicial review over constitutional amendments. For instance, in Colombia, according to article 379 of the Constitution, all constitutional review procedures,

---

144 See *Milagros Gómez et al.* case, in *Revista de Derecho Público*, N° 81, Editorial Jurídica Venezolana, Caracas, 2000, pp. 81 ff., http://www.tsj.gov.ve/decisiones/scon/Enero/06–270100–00011.htm. See also Daniela UROSA MAGGI, *Venezuelan National Report*, p. 14.

145 See Allan BREWER–CARÍAS et al. case, in http://www.tsj.gov.ve/decisiones/scon/Marzo/180–280300–00–0737%20.htm. See the comments in Allan R. BREWER–CARÍAS, *Golpe de estado y proceso constituyente en Venezuela*, Universidad Nacional Autónoma de México, Mexico City 2002, pp. 367 ff.; BREWER–CARÍAS, "El juez constitucional al servicio del autoritarismo y la ilegítima mutación de la Constitución: El caso de la Sala Constitucional del Tribunal Supremo de Justicia de Venezuela (1999–2009)," *Revista de Administración Pública*, N° 180, Madrid 2009, pp. 383–418. See also Daniela UROSA MAGGI, *Venezuelan National Report*, p. 14.

146 See, e.g., Constitutional Court, Decision VfSlg 16.327/2001; Konrad Lachmayer, *Austrian National Report*, p. 6 (footnote 20).

147 *Id.*, p. 9.

including the convening of popular referendum or constituent assemblies are subject to judicial review by the Constitutional Court, which can declare them unconstitutional if they violate rules of procedure.[148] In Ecuador, article 433 of the Constitution assigns the Constitutional Court the power to determine which constitutional review procedure (reform or amendment) must be applied. The Constitution of Bolivia allows the Constitutional Tribunal to decide on actions of unconstitutionality filed against the procedures of partial reform of the Constitution.[149]

Greek courts also have affirmed their power to engage in judicial review of constitutional amendments, although without specifying the exact constitutional basis or engaging in any meaningful scrutiny of constitutional amendments.[150]

The situation is completely different in cases where constitutional courts exercise judicial review powers regarding reforms or amendments of the Constitution on their merits, not only on matters of procedure. This happens for instance, when the constituent powers try to change constitutional clauses that, according to the express terms of the Constitution, are declared as principles or provisions that cannot be modified or changed. For instance, the Constitution of Brazil establishes: "No proposal of amendment shall be considered which is aimed at abolishing: I. The federative form of State; II. The direct, secret, universal and periodic vote; III. The separation of the Government Powers; IV. Individual rights and guarantees" (article 64, para. 4).

Nonetheless, the powers of a constitutional court to exercise judicial review of the merits of constitutional reforms or amendments, even in cases of clauses that the Constitution stipulates as not modifiable, must be expressly established as one of its competency, as has been established in many countries regarding review on procedural matters concerning constitutional reforms or amendments. On the contrary, the exercise by the constitutional court of judicial review powers not authorized in the Constitution as to the merits of constitutional reforms or amendments would eventually lead the Court to substitute itself for the constituent power. This is what happened, for instance, in Colombia in a decision N° C–141 issued by the Constitutional Court on February 26, 2010, in which the Court annulled Law N° 1,354 of 2009, which convened a referendum to approve reforms to article 197 of the Constitution

---

148 See Mario Alberto CAJAS SARRIA, "Acerca del control judicial de la reforma constitucional en Colombia," *Revista Iberoamericana de Derecho Procesal Constitucional*, N° 7, Instituto Iberoamericano de Derecho Procesal Constitucional, Editorial Porrúa, Mexico 2007, pp. 19 ff.

149 See Allan R. BREWER–CARÍAS, *Reforma constitucional y fraude a la Constitución. Venezuela 1999–2009*, Academia de Ciencias Políticas y Sociales, Caracas 2009, pp. 78 ff.; BREWER–CARÍAS, "La reforma constitucional en América Latina y el control de constitucionalidad," in *Reforma de la Constitución y control de constitucionalidad. Congreso Internacional, Pontificia Universidad Javeriana, Bogotá Colombia, junio 14 al 17 de 2005*, Pontificia Universidad Javeriana, Bogotá, 2005, pp. 108–159.

150 See Supreme Special Court Judgment N° 11/2003, *DtA* 2009, 553 (555–556); Julia Iliopoulos–Strangas and Stylianos–Ioannis G. Koutnatzis, *Greek National Report*, p. 11 (footnote 85).

to allow the reelection for a third period of the President of the Republic.[151] In this case, the Court, in addition to considering various procedural vices affecting the popular initiative of the legislation, and the legislative process followed in the approval of the challenged law, also considered the existence of "vices or excesses in the exercise of the power of constitutional reform." Referring to jurisprudence established since 2003 "under the name of the theory of substitution, the Court confirmed that "it is not feasible any constitutional reform ignoring structural principles or defining elements of the Constitution of 1991," and it affirmed its power to exercise judicial review even regarding the law convening a constitutional reform referendum. As to Law 1,354 of 2009, the Court "found that it ignores some structural axes of the Political Constitution like the principle of separation of powers and the system of checks and balances, the rule of alternation and presidential terms, the right to equality and the general and abstract nature of the laws."[152] The general conclusion of the Constitutional Court's Decision of 2010 to declare the unconstitutionality and to annul Law N° 1,354 was that it was not just "a matter of mere procedural irregularities but of substantial violations of the democratic principle, one of whose essential components is the respect of the forms provided so that the people can express itself."[153]

Regarding this decision of the Constitutional Court, Sandra Morelli has considered it "nothing less than surprising that to find the national body responsible for guarantying the supremacy of the Constitution and its preservation, in sharp contrast with the content of Article 247 of the Constitution that limit[s] its competence to consider vices of procedure when exercising control of constitutionality on the laws convening a constitutional referendum, and that it does it raising the issue that the proposed constitutional reform would constitute a substitution of the constitutional system, in a way that only the primary constituent would be legitimized for such purpose." According to Morelli, "the Colombian constitutional court, on the one hand, is curtailing the powers to reform of the constituted bodies, and on the other, referring to powers, the mutations of the constitution."[154]

In India, the Supreme Court has changed the Constitution on matters of constitutional amendments by establishing substantive limitations on the power of the parliament to amend the Constitution, not provided for in article 368 of the Constitution. In this respect, the Indian Supreme Court, in *Kesvananda Bharti v. State of Kerala*, interpreted an "implied" limitation on the power of Parliament to amend the Constitution, in the sense that it cannot amend the basic features or basic structure of

151 Initially the Court published Communiqué N° 9, on February 26, 2010, containing the basic ruling. See http://www.corteconstitucional.gov.co/comunicados/N°%2009%20Comunicado%2026%20de%20febrero%20de%202010.php. See also Sandra Morelli, *Colombian National Report*, pp. 13–16; Germán Alfonso LÓPEZ DAZA, *Colombian National Report I*, p. 6. The full text of the decision was later published in 2011. See in http://www.corteconstitucional.gov.co/ relatoria/2010/c–141–10.htm.

152 *Id.*, p. 19.

153 *Id.*, p. 20.

154 *Id.*, p. 22.

the Constitution.[155] Consequently, judicial review is interpreted as a basic feature of the Constitution,[156] which means that even a constitutional amendment cannot remove the power of judicial review, thus converting the Supreme Court, according to Surya Deva, to "probably the most powerful court in any democracy."[157]

Finally, a case in Venezuela must be mentioned in which the Constitutional Chamber of the Supreme Tribunal of Justice refused to control the constitutionality of a constitutional review procedure that was challenged on grounds of its unconstitutionality. The 1999 Venezuelan Constitution establishes three different and precise procedures for constitutional reforms: the "Constitutional Amendment," the "Constitutional Reform," and the "National Constituent Assembly," depending on the degree and importance of the proposed reforms, the latter being needed for major reforms aiming to transform the State. In 2007, at the initiative of the President of the Republic, the National Assembly sanctioned a "Constitutional Reform" directed to transform the Democratic Decentralized Social State established in the 1999 Consitution into a Socialist, Centralized and Militaristic State.[158] The reform procedure that was followed was challenged before the Constitutional Chamber, but it refused to hear the popular actions filled against it on the grounds that they were "not allowed to be proposed" (*improponibles*) pending the definitive approval of the reform, renouncing to be the guardian of the Constitution'supremacy.[159] Nonetheless, it was the people in the December 7, 2007 referendum who rejected the unconstitutional reform.[160]

---

155 See Surya DEVA, *Indian National Report*, pp. 5–6.

156 See *Waman Rao v. Union of India*, AIR 1981 SC 271; *S P Sampath Kumar v. Union of India*, AIR 1987 SC 386; *L Chandra Kumar v. Union of India,* AIR 1997 SC 1125. See Surya Deva, *Indian National Report*, p. 6 (footnote 41).

157 See Surya Deva, *Indian National Report*, p. 6.

158 See on the reform proposal Allan R. BREWER–CARÍAS, *Hacia la consolidación de un Estado Socialista, Centralizado, Policial y Militarista. Comentarios sobre el sentido y alcance de las propuestas de reforma constitucional 2007,* Colección Textos Legislativos, N° 42, Editorial Jurídica Venezolana, Caracas 2007; BREWER–CARÍAS, *La reforma constitucional de 2007 (Comentarios al Proyecto inconstitucionalmente sancionado por la Asamblea Nacional el 2 de noviembre de 2007)*, Colección Textos Legislativos, N° 43, Editorial Jurídica Venezolana, Caracas 2007; BREWER–CARÍAS, *Reforma constitucional y fraude a la Constitución (1999–2009)*, Academia de Ciencias Políticas y Sociales, Caracas 2009.

159 See Allan R. BREWER–CARÍAS, "El juez constitucional vs. la supremacía constitucional o de cómo la jurisdicción constitucional en Venezuela renunció a controlar la constitucionalidad del procedimiento seguido para la 'reforma constitucional' sancionada por la Asamblea Nacional el 2 de noviembre de 2007, antes de que fuera rechazada por el pueblo en el referendo del 2 de diciembre de 2007," in Eduardo Ferrer Mac–Gregor y César de Jesús Molina Suárez (Coordinarores), *El juez constitucional en el Siglo XXI,* Universidad nacional Autónoma de México, Suprema Corte de Justicia de la Nación, México 2009, Tomo I, pp. 385–435.

160 See the comments in Allan R. BREWER–CARÍAS, "La reforma constitucional en Venezuela de 2007 y su rechazo por el poder constituyente originario," in José Ma. Serna de la Garza (coord.), *Procesos Constituyentes contemporáneos en América latina. Tendencias y perspectivas*, Universidad Nacional Autónoma de México, México 2009, pp. 407–449.

III. CONSTITUTIONAL COURTS' ADAPATION OF THE CONSTITUTION AND THE QUESTION OF LEGITIMATE CHANGES TO THE CONSTITUTION

The situation is different when constitutional courts adapt constitutional provisions through interpretation. Undoubtedly, one of the main roles of constitutional courts during judicial review of statutes is to interpret the Constitution and to adapt its provisions according to constitutional principles and values, particularly on matters of protecting fundamental rights. In such cases, according to Laurence Claus and Richard S. Kay, constitutional courts "engage in positive constitutional lawmaking," particularly when the rule they "formulate, creates 'affirmative' public duties."[161] Consequently, it is possible to accept judge–made constitutional "mutations," this expression understood to mean "change[s] in the interpretation of a constitutional provision, the meaning of which is altered in spite of the maintenance of the same wording of the Constitution."[162] But in this there are some risks. As I wrote a few years ago, if it is true that "constitutional courts, certainly, can be considered as a phenomenal instrument for the adaptation of the Constitution, and the reinforcement of the rule of law," then it is also true that "they can also be a diabolic instrument of constitutional dictatorship, not subjected to control, when they validate constitutional violations made by authoritarian regimes or when separation of powers is not assured."[163]

These constitutional mutations, when reinforcing the rule of law, generally take place as a consequence of enforcing the fundamental values and principles of the Constitution, particularly the protection of fundamental rights and the strengthening of democratic rule. Nonetheless, they have also occurred in other constitutional matters related to the general organization of the State.

1. Adapting the Constitution on Matters of Fundamental Rights Guarantees

Regarding the protection of fundamental rights, the mutation of the Constitution in many countries has resulted from constitutional courts "discovering" fundamental rights that were not expressly listed in a constitution, and consequently enlarging the scope of the constitutional provisions. In this regard, constitutional courts always

161 See Laurence Claus and Richard S. Kay, *U.S. National Report*, p. 6.

162 See Salvador O. NAVA GOMAR, "Interpretación, mutación y reforma de la Constitución: Tres extractos," in Eduardo Ferrer Mac–Gregor (coord.), *Interpretación constitucional*, vol. 2, Editorial Porrúa, Universidad Nacional Autónoma de México, Mexico City 2005, pp. 804 ff. See also Thomas BUSTAMANTE and Evanlida de GODOI BUSTAMANTE, *Brazilian National Report*, p. 28. See generally Konrad HESSE, "Límites a la mutación constitucional," in *Escritos de derecho constitucional*, Centro de Estudios Constitucionales, Madrid 1992, pp. 79–104.

163 See Allan R. BREWER–CARÍAS, "La reforma constitucional en América Latina y el control de constitucionalidad," in *Reforma de la Constitución y control de constitucionalidad. Congreso Internacional junio 14 al 17 de 2005*), Pontificia Universidad Javeriana, Bogotá, 2005, pp. 108–159.

have had an additional duty over that of the ordinary judge, in that they must defend the Constitution and its foundational values at a given time.[164]

This is why it is considered legitimate for constitutional courts, in their interpretative process, to adapt a constitution to the current values of society and the political system, precisely "to keep the constitution alive."[165] To that end, because a constitution is not a static document, constitutional courts must be creative in effectively applying constitutions that may have been written, for instance, in the nineteenth century, particularly when controlling the constitutionality of legislation according to the evolving social needs and institutions of the country.

This also occurs in the case of more recent constitutions, where fundamental rights sometimes are expressed in a vague, and elusive way, with provisions expressed in ambiguous, but worthy, terms, such as *liberty*, *democracy*, *justice*, *dignity*, *equality*, *social function*, and *public interests*.[166] This leads to the need for judges to have an active role when interpreting what have been called a constitution's "precious ambiguities"[167] and "majestic generalities."[168]

It is precisely in these matters, as mentioned by Laurence Claus and Richard S. Kay, that the U.S. Supreme Court's elaboration of constitutional principles and values "provides perhaps the most salient example of positive lawmaking in the course of American constitutional adjudication." For instance, the Court interpreted the equal protection clause of the Fourteenth Amendment to expound the nature of equality; it argued about the constitutional guarantee of due process (Amendments V

---

164 This has been particularly true, for instance, in the process of the transformation in the former socialist States of Eastern Europe to contemporary democratic States subject to the rule of law. See, e.g., Marek SAFJAN, *Polish National Report*, pp. 7, 10; Sanja Barić and Petar Bačić, *Croatian National Report*, pp. 18, 21, 28; Boško Tripković, *Serbian National Report*, pp. 1, 14.

165 See Mauro CAPPELLETTI, "El formidable problema del control judicial y la contribución del análisis comparado," *Revista de Estudios Políticos* 13, Madrid 1980, p. 78; "The Mighty Problem of Judicial Review and the Contribution of Comparative Analysis," *Southern California Law Review*, 53, 1980, p. 409 ff.

166 See Mauro CAPPELLETTI, "Nécessité et légitimité de la justice constitutionnelle," in Louis Favoreu (ed.), *Cours constitutionnelles européenes et droit fundamentaux*, Economica, Presses Universitaires d'Aix–Marseille, 1982, p. 474.

167 "If it is true that precision has a place of honor in the writing of a governmental decision, it is mortal when it refers to a constitution which wants to be a lively body." S. M. HUFSTEDLES, "In the Name of Justice," *Stanford Lawyers* 14, N° 1 (1979), pp. 3–4, quoted by Mauro Cappelletti, "Nécessité et légitimité de la justice constitutionnelle," in Louis Favoreu (ed.), *Cours constitutionnelles européennes et droit fondamentaux*, Economica, Presses Universitaires d'Aix–Marseille, 1982, p. 474; L. FAVOREU, *Le contrôle juridictionnel des lois et sa légitimité. Développements récents en Europe Occidentale*, Association Internationale des Sciences Juridiques, Colloque d'Uppsala 1984, (mimeo), p. 32.

168 See *W. Va. State Bd. of Educ. v. Barnette*, 319 U.S. 624, 639 (1943). See Laurence CLAUS and Richard S. KAY, *U.S. National Report*, p. 12 (footnote 33).

and XIV), and the open clause of Amendment IX, to construct a sense of liberty.[169] As Geoffrey R. Stone has pointed out regarding the text of the U.S Constitution:

> It defines our most fundamental rights and protections in an open–ended terms: "freedom of speech," for example, and "equal protection of laws," "due process of law," "unreasonable searches and seizures," "free exercise" of religion and "cruel and unusual punishment." These terms are not self–defining; they did not have clear meaning even to the people who drafted them. The framers fully understood that they were leaving it to future generations to use their intelligence, judgment and experience to give concrete meaning to the expressed aspirations.[170]

In particular, for instance, it was in *Brown v. Board of Education of Topeka*, 347 U.S. 483 (1954), that this process of mutating the U.S. Constitution began for matters of fundamental rights. It is important to bear in mind that the 1789 U.S. Constitution and the 1791 amendments did not establish the principle of equality and that the Fourteenth Amendment (1868) included only the equal protection clause, which until the 1950s had been interpreted differently.

This process converted the Court, according to Claus and Kay, into "the most powerful sitting lawmaker in the nation,"[171] by having used old but renewed means of relief, particularly equitable remedies, to move beyond prohibitory to mandatory relief. This is one of the most striking developments in modern constitutional law, and it produced changes impossible to imagine a few years earlier. As aforementioned, these means were broadly applied in *Brown v. Board of Education of Topeka*, 347 U.S. 483 (1954), where the Supreme Court held that racial segregation in public education was a denial of the "equal protection of the laws," which, under the Fourteenth Amendment, no state was to deny to any person within the state's jurisdiction. The Court needed to answer various questions to find segregation unconstitutional, such as whether the ruling should order that African American children "forthwith be admitted to schools of their choice" or whether the court should "permit an effective gradual adjustment" to systems.[172] Eventually, these inquiries led the Supreme Court, in May 1954, to declare racial segregation incompatible with the Fourteenth Amendment. It issued the final ruling in the case in May 1955, two and a half years after the initial argument.[173]

In effect, in *Brown*, the Supreme Court changed the meaning of the Fourteenth Amendment. Chief Justice Warren said:

---

169 See Laurence Claus and Richard S. Kay, *U.S. National Report*, pp. 12–13.

170 See Geoffrey R. Stone, "Our Fill–in–the–Blank Constitution," op–ed, *New York Times*, April 14, 2010, p. A27.

171 See Laurence Claus and Richard S. Kay, *U.S. National Report*, p. 20. On the different stages in the process of law regarding those clauses, see *id.*, pp. 13–14. The authors argue that "the law of liberty and equality in America is now, in large measure, ultimately created and shaped by the Supreme Court," p. 14.

172 *Brown v. Bd. of Educ.*, 345 U.S. 972, 972 (1953). See Laurence Claus and Richard S. Kay, *U.S. National Report*, p. 26 (footnote 89).

173 *Brown v. Bd. of Educ.*, 345 U.S. 972, 972 (1953). See Laurence Claus and Richard S. Kay, *U.S. National Report*, p. 27 (footnote 91).

> In approaching this problem we cannot turn the clock back to 1868 when the Amendment was adopted, or even to 1896 when *Plessy v. Ferguson* was written. We must consider public education in the light of its full development and its present place in American life throughout the Nation. Only in this way can it be determined if segregation in public schools deprives these plaintiffs of the equal protection of the laws.

This assertion led Chief Justice Warren to conclude:

> [I]n the field of public education the doctrine of "separate but equal" has no place. Separate educational facilities are inherently unequal. Therefore, we hold that the plaintiffs, and others similarly situated from whom the actions have been brought are by reason of the segregation complained of, deprived of the equal protection of the laws guaranteed by the Fourteenth Amendment.

In other contexts, particularly in France, where the Constitution does not make a declaration of fundamental rights, the role of the Constitutional Council during the past decades must be highlighted, beginning with the important decision adopted on July 16, 1971, concerning freedom of association.[174] In that case, the Constitutional Council accepted the positive legal value of the Preamble to the 1958 Constitution with all its consequences,[175] which conformed with what Louis Favoreu called the *bloc de constitutionnalité*.[176]

Consequently, regarding the particular law establishing a procedure to control the acquisition of legal capacity by association, the Constitutional Council considered it against the Constitution,[177] arguing that the Preamble to the 1946 Constitution referred to the "fundamental principles recognized by the laws of the Republic," among which the principle of liberty of association was to be included. The Council, in accordance with such principle, considered that associations were to be constituted freely and able to develop their activities with the only condition of filing a declaration before the Administration, that was not submitted to a previous authorization by either administrative or judicial authorities. Thus, the Constitutional Council decided that fundamental constitutional principles were included not only in the Preamble of the 1958 Constitution but also in the Preamble of the 1946 Constitution,

---

174 See L. FAVOREU and L. PHILIP, *Les grandes décisions du Conseil Constitutionnel*, Dalloz, Paris 1984, p. 222–237; Bertrand MATHIEU, *French National Report*, p. 2.

175 See L. FAVOREU, "Rapport général introductif," in *Cours constitutionnelles europées et droit fondamentaux*, Economica, Presses Universitaires d'Aix–Marseille, 1982, pp. 45–46.

176 See L. FAVOREU, "Le principe de Constitutionalité. Essai de definition d'apres la jurisprudence du Conseil Constitutionnel," *Recueil d'Étude en Hommage a Charles Eisenman*, Paris 1977, p. 34. On comparative law, see also Francisco ZÚÑIGA URBINA, "Control de constitucionalidad y sentencia," *Cuadernos del Tribunal Constitucional*, N° 34, Santiago de Chile 2006, pp. 46–68.

177 See the Constitutional Council decision in L. FAVOREU and J. PHILIP, *Les grandes décisions du Conseil Constitutionnel*, Dalloz, Paris 1984, p. 222. See the comments of the July 16, 1971, decisions in J. RIVERO, "Note," *L'Actualité Juridique. Droit Administratif*, Paris, 1971, p. 537; J. RIVERO, "Principles fondamentaux reconnus par les lois de la République; une nouvelle catégorie constitutionnelle?" *Dalloz 1974*, Chroniques, Paris 1974, p. 265; J. E. BRADSLEY, "The Constitutional Council and Constitutional Liberties in France," *American Journal of Comparative Law* 20, N° 3 (1972), p. 43; B. Nicholas, "Fundamental Rights and Judicial Review in France," *Public Law*, 1978, p. 83.

and through it in the Declaration of Rights of Man and Citizens of 1789. Thus, the limits imposed on associations by the proposed bill establishing prior judicial control of the Declaration were considered unconstitutional. In this way, according to Jean Rivero:

> The liberty of association, which is not expressly established either in the Declaration or by the particularly needed principles of our times, but which is only recognized by a Statute of 1 July 1901, has been recognized by the Constitutional Council decision, as having a constitutional character, not only as a principle, but in relation to the modalities of its exercise.[178]

This sort of adaptation of the French Constitution was also developed by the Constitutional Council in the well–known *Nationalization* case in 1982, which applied the article concerning the right of property in the Declaration of the Rights of Man and Citizen of 1789 and declared the right to property as having constitutional force. In its decision of January 16, 1982,[179] even though the article of the 1789 Declaration concerning property rights was considered obsolete, and so its interpretation could not result in a completely different sense from the one defined in 1789,[180] the Constitutional Council stated:

> Taking into account that if it is true that after 1789 and up to the present, the aims and conditions of the exercise of the right to property have undergone an evolution characterized both, by a notable extension of its application to new individual fields and by limits imposed by general interests, the principles themselves expressed in the Declaration of Rights of Man have complete constitutional value, particularly regarding the fundamental character of the right to property, the conservation of which constitutes one of the aims of political society, and located on the same rank as liberty, security and resistance to oppression, and also regarding the guarantees given to the holders of that right and the prerogatives of public power.[181]

In this way, the Constitutional Council not only created a constitutional right by giving the 1789 Declaration constitutional rank and value but also adapted the "sacred" right to property established two hundred years earlier to the limitable right of our times, thus allowing the Council to declare unconstitutional certain articles in the Nationalization statute regarding the banking sector and industries of strategic importance (especially in electronics and communications).

The role of constitutional courts in adapting the Constitution to guarantee fundamental rights not expressly established in the Constitution, even in the absence of open constitutional clauses like the Ninth Amendment to the U.S. Constitution, has

178 See J. Rivero, "Les garanties constitutionnelles des droits de l'homme en droit français," in *IX Journées Juridiques Franco–Latino Américaines*, Bayonne, May 21–23, 1976 (mimeo), p. 11.

179 See L. Favoreu and L. Philip, *Les grandes décisions du Conseil Constitutionnel*, Dalloz, Paris 1984, pp. 525–562.

180 See L. Favoreu, *Le contrôle juridictionnel des lois et sa légitimité. Développements récents en Europe Occidentale*, Association Internationale des Sciences Juridiques, Colloque d'Uppsala 1984 (mimeo), p. 32.

181 See L. Favoreu and L. Philip, *Les grandes décisions du Conseil Constitutionnel*, Dalloz, Paris 1984, p. 526; L. Favoreu, "Les décisions du Conseil Constitutionnel dans l'affaire des nationalisations," *Revue du Droit Public et de la Science Politique en France et à l'Étranger* 98, N° 2, Paris 1982, p. 406.

been commonly accepted, mainly because of the principle of progressiveness in the protection of fundamental rights.[182]

In Switzerland, for instance, before the 1999 constitutional reform was sanctioned, which included an extended declaration of fundamental rights, the Federal Supreme Court interpreted the previous 1874 Constitution, which included only a few fundamental rights, as allowing for very important unwritten fundamental rights, including the guarantee of property (1960);[183] freedom of expression (1961);[184] the right to personal freedom within the meaning of a right to physical and mental integrity (1963);[185] freedom of language (1965);[186] the right to existence and care, including a minimum of governmental assistance in case of need (1995);[187] freedom of assembly and freedom of expression, which encompass the right to hold public demonstrations (1970);[188] and the freedom to demonstrate.[189] Also, before the 1999 constitutional reform, the Federal Supreme Court recognized the freedom to elect and vote as a constitutional right;[190] most important, it enforced the right of women to participate in the Landsgemeinde (assembly of the citizens as the highest legislative body) of the Canton Appenzell–Innerrhoden,[191] where the Cantonal Constitution provided that only men could participate in such an assembly. All these rights were later included in the 1999 Constitution.

In Germany, the Federal Constitutional Tribunal has also developed an important process of interpreting the constitution to protect fundamental rights. Ines Härtel refers to a 2008 decision adopted by the Federal Constitutional Tribunal regarding the searches of computers. in which the Tribunal created a "new" basic right on the "warranty of confidentiality and integrity in information technology systems." In this case, in the course of the judicial review process of a provision of a North Rhine–Westphalia law regarding the change of the statute by the Federal Office for the Protection of the Constitution, the Tribunal ruled on the protection of general personal rights provided in article 2, section 1, in conjunction with article 1, section

---

182 See Pedro NIKKEN, *La protección internacional de los derechos humanos: Su desarrollo progresivo*, Instituto Interamericano de Derechos Humanos, Ed. Civitas, Madrid 1987; Mónica PINTO, "El principio *pro homine*: Criterio hermenéutico y pautas para la regulación de los derechos humanos," in *La aplicación de los tratados sobre derechos Humanos por los tribunales locales*, Centro de Estudios Legales y Sociales, Buenos Aires 1997, p. 163.

183 See Supreme Court, in ZBl 62/1961, 69, 72; Tobias Jaag, *Swiss National Report*, p. 11 (footnote 49).

184 See BGE 87 I 114, 117; Tobias Jaag, *Swiss National Report*, p. 11 (footnote 51).

185 See BGE 89 I 92, 97 ff.; Tobias Jaag, *Swiss National Report*, p. 11 (footnote 56).

186 See BGE 91 I 480, 485 ff. This includes the right to use one's native language. See Tobias Jaag, *Swiss National Report*, p. 12 (footnote 59).

187 See BGE 121 I 367, 370 ff.; Tobias Jaag, *Swiss National Report*, p. 12 (footnote 61).

188 See BGE 96 I 219, 223 ff.; Tobias Jaag, *Swiss National Report*, p. 11 (footnote 52).

189 See BGE 100 I a 392, 400 ff.; Tobias Jaag, *Swiss National Report*, p. 11 (footnote 53).

190 *Cf.* BGE 121 I 138, 141 ff.; Tobias Jaag, *Swiss National Report*, p. 12 (footnote 64).

191 See BGE 116 I a 359 ff.; Tobias Jaag, *Swiss National Report*, p. 13 (footnote 66).

1, of the Constitution,[192] in particular within the tension between liberty and security that affects the handling of personal data and information.

In Poland, the Constitutional Tribunal has developed judicial activism regarding the expansion of human rights, particularly after 1989, with the fall of the country's totalitarian system and the need to build the structures of a democratic state of law. The Constitutional Tribunal was pushed to interpret the standards of rights and freedoms not directly expressed in the Constitution, and to complement existing constitutional provisions, according to the new democratic values and system. Consequently, the Tribunal derived such fundamental rights as the right to the protection of human life before birth,[193] the right to trial,[194] the right to privacy,[195] ban on retroactivity,[196] the rule of protection of duly acquired rights,[197] the protection of business and legal security,[198] and the principle of proportionality, for instance in the imposition of sanctions.[199]

Also in Poland, the Court has been charged with giving specific content to programmatic clauses established in the Constitution, particularly during the transformation from an authoritarian socialist State to one of democratic rule of law. In this process, the broad catalog of general rules established in the Constitution related to social and economic rights, and the definition of the economic system as a "social market economy" (article 20 of the Constitution) were developed by the Constitutional Court. That is why, regarding these rules, Judge Marek Safjan said, that "if these rules are not to remain a pure ideology and constitutional decorum, expressing the 'wishful thinking' attitude of the authors of the Constitution, the Constitutional Court by turning rules into norms, and seeking at least a minimal normative content in the so–called program norms," has exercised "an increasingly stronger influence on the directions of state policy in these dimensions."[200] For such purpose, the Court

192 See BVerfG, Reference Nº 1 BvR 370/07 from February 27, 2008, available at http://www.bverfg.de/entscheidungen/rs20080227_1bvr037007.html; I. Härtel, *German National Report*, p. 12.

193 See Decision of May 28, 1997, K 26/96, OTK ZU 1997/2/19; Marek Safjan, *Polish National Report*, p. 9 (footnote 22).

194 See Decision of January 7, 1992, K 8/91, OTK ZU 1992, part 1, pp. 76–84; of June 27, 1995, K4/94, OTK 1993, part 2, pp. 297–310; Marek Safjan, *Polish National Report*, p. 9 (footnote 23).

195 See Decision of June 24, 1997, K21797, OTK ZU 1997/12/23; Marek Safjan, *Polish National Report*, p. 9 (footnote 24).

196 See Decision of August 22, 1990, K7/90, OTK 1990, pp. 42–58; Marek Safjan, *Polish National Report*, p. 9 (footnote 25).

197 See Decision of February 25, 1992 K3/9, OTK 1992, part 1, item 1; Marek Safjan, *Polish National Report*, p. 9 (footnote 26).

198 See Decision of July 15, 1996, K5/96, OTK ZU 1996, part 2, pp. 16–28; Marek Safjan, *Polish National Report*, p. 9 (footnote 28).

199 See Decision of April 26, 1995, K11/94, OTK 1995, part 1, item 12; Marek Safjan, *Polish National Report*, p. 9 (footnote 29).

200 See Marek Safjan, *Polish National Report*, p. 12. On decisions establishing positive normative content from the so–called program norms, see, e.g., National Health Fund of January 7,

following the superior values in the Constitution, has filled in these concepts, pinpointing and determining their boundaries. As Judge Safjan explains:

> It is characteristic for each Constitution to employ a large number of "open" norms having undefined (fuzzy) normative scope, expressing fundamental legal values and creating "axiology of the Constitution." This search for a normative content hidden in the general, undefined constitutional expressions, as well as decoding other – more precise and concrete – norms out of them, setting limits to the application of rules and establishing a special "hierarchy" between the colliding rules and values – is inscribed into the nature of interpretation of the Constitution and is closely connected with the essence of the function of each constitutional court.[201]

With respect to the principle of proportionality, the Constitutional Court of Croatia also has developed this principle, determining that the State must draft legislation related to individual rights and liberties, including in their regulation, appropriate and proportional solutions in the scope of their limitations. The 1990 Constitution refers only to the proportionality principle in article 17 on the restriction of rights and freedoms during a state of emergency, without establishing it as a clear general principle of Croatian Constitutional Law. Consequently, during regular or normal circumstances, article 16 applies, which states only that rights and freedoms can be restricted by law only "to protect freedoms and rights of others, public order, public morality and health."[202] Because the legislators had displayed what was considered political immoderateness by disproportionately restricting rights and freedoms, the Constitutional Court gradually started to apply the proportionality principle in all matters, clearly indicating to legislators the limitations that they could impose on rights and freedoms to protect the general well–being of individuals and their communities.[203]

In Greece, the Council of State, which rules on matters of judicial review, has explicitly recognized the constitutional rank of the proportionality principle as a corollary of rule of law.[204] In contrast, since 1998, the Council of State has construed the constitutional principle of gender equality to allow positive measures that aim to establish true equality between men and women.[205] After a long debate between

---

2004, K14703, OTK ZU 2004/1A/1; the protection of consumer (biofuels) of April 21, 2004, K33/03, OTK ZU 2004/4A/31; the protection of tenants judgments of January 12, 2001, P11/98, OTK ZU2000/1/3; and April 19, 2005, K 4/05, OTK ZU 2005/4A/37; and the social market economy of January 29, 2007, P5/05,2007/1A/1. See Marek Safjan, *Polish National Report*, p. 12 (footnote 37).

201 See Marek Safjan, *Polish National Report*, p. 7.

202 In the 2000 constitutional amendment, the principle was also incorporated in article 17: "Every restriction of freedoms or rights shall be proportional to the nature of the necessity for restriction in each individual case."

203 See Sanja Barić and Petar Bačić, *Croatian National Report*, pp. 23 ff.

204 See Council of State Judgment N° 2112/1984, *ToS* 1985, 63 (64); Julia Iliopoulos–Strangas and Stylianos–Ioannis G. Koutnatzis, *Greek National Report*, p. 14.

205 See Council of State (Full Bench) Judgment N° 1933/1998, *ToS* 1998, 792 (793). After the 2001 amendments, the Constitution explicitly allows the "adoption of positive measures for

constitutional scholars and the courts, the Council of State ultimately followed the *Areios Pagos* court by extending the scope of a statutory provision to groups of persons who had been unconstitutionally excluded. In addition, especially since 1993, the Council of State has derived the principle of sustainable development from the Greek Constitution's environmental clauses (article 24) and in connection with European Union law. On this basis, the Council of State has emphasized that the sole constitutionally permissible form of economic development is sustainable development that incorporates the needs of future generations. With the 2001 constitutional amendments, the Greek Constitution explicitly established the principle of sustainable development (article 24.1.1)[206]

Regarding the same matter of constitutional courts mutating constitution provisions on fundamental rights, in Portugal, the Constitutional Tribunal, in Decision N° 474/95, established that, although the wording of article 33 of the Constitution prohibited, at that time, only extradition for crimes for which the death penalty was legally possible, the principles of the Constitution also prohibited extradition for crimes punishable by life imprisonment. Furthermore, the Court's ruling provides the keystone for the interpretation of the conditions that must be fulfilled to allow for extradition of persons charged with crimes for which a sentence of death or life imprisonment is possible.[207] The consequence of this mutation was an amendment to the Constitution introduced in 1997 on the wording of article 33.4 of the Constitution, concerning extradition for crimes punishable under the applicant state's law by a sentence or security measure which deprives or restricts freedom in perpetuity or for an undefined duration.

In India, the Supreme Court has introduced important changes in the Constitution, particularly by expanding the scope of fundamental rights. For instance, article 21 of the Constitution establishes, "No person shall be deprived of his life or personal liberty except according to procedure established by law." The Supreme Court ruled in 1970, reversing a previous position, that the expression "procedure established by law" in the article refers to a procedure that must be "right, just and fair." Thus, the Court gave itself the authority to judge whether a procedure laid down by the Legislator conformed to the principles of natural justice,[208] which is especially remarkable because the constituent assembly, after a long debate, had expressly rejected the due process clause.[209]

---

promoting equality between men and women" (art. 116, sec. 2). See Julia Iliopoulos–Strangas and Stylianos–Ioannis G. Koutnatzis, *Greek National Report*, p. 16 (footnote 123).

206 See Julia Iliopoulos–Strangas and Stylianos–Ioannis G. Koutnatzis, *Greek National Report*, p. 22.

207 See Ruling N° 384/05, summary of which can be found in *Bulletin on Constitutional Case–Law*, Venice Commission, Edition 2005, vol. 2, pp. 269–271, in Joaquim de Sousa Ribeiro and Esperança Mealha, *Portuguese National Report*, pp. 9–10.

208 *Maneka Gandhi v. Union of India*, AIR 1879 SC 597. See Surya Deva, *Indian National Report*, p. 4 (footnote 24).

209 See Surya Deva, *Indian National Report*, p. 4.

In contrast, regarding the right to life under article 21 of the Indian Constitution, the Supreme Court has interpreted it to include the right to health,[210] the right to livelihood,[211] the right to free and compulsory education up to fourteen years of age,[212] the right to an unpolluted environment[213] and to clean drinking water,[214] the right to shelter,[215] the right to privacy,[216] the right to legal aid,[217] the right to a speedy trial,[218] and various rights of persons under trial (convicts and prisoners).[219] The Court extended the meaning of *life* by, among other things, reading nonjusticiable directive principles of State policy into fundamental rights. As Surya Deva affirmed, the effect of this judicial extension of fundamental rights had a direct bearing on the power of judicial review: the more fundamental rights are recognized, the broader would be the scope for judicial review.[220]

In the Slovak Republic, the Constitutional Court has played an important role in mutating and complementing the Constitution to guarantee the protection of fundamental rights. This has happened, for instance, on matters of the right to personal freedom and physical integrity, particularly regarding the extension of the duration of pretrial detentions without the basis of a decision of the court,[221] and on matters of the right to enter and leave the territory of the Slovak Republic freely, which is

---

210 See *Parmanand Kataria v. Union of India*, AIR 1989 SC 2039; *Paschim Banga Khet Mazdoor Samity v. State of West Bengal*, (1996) 4 SCC 37; Surya Deva, *Indian National Report*, p. 5 (footnote 28).

211 See *Olga Tellis v. Bombay Municipal Corporation*, AIR 1986 SC 180; *DTC Corporation v. DTC Mazdoor Congress*, AIR 1991 SC 101. In *id.*, p. 5 (footnote 29).

212 See *Unni Krishnan v. State of AP*, (1993) 1 SCC 645. In *id., p.* 5 (footnote 30).

213 See, e.g., *Indian Council for Enviro Legal Action v. Union of India*, (1996) 3 SCC 212; *M C Mehta v. Union of India*, (1996) 6 SCC 750; *Vellore Citizens Welfare Forum v. Union of India*, (1996) 5 SCC 647; *Narmada Bachao Andolan v. Union of India* (2000) 10 SCC 664. In *id.*, p. 5 (footnote 31).

214 See *A P Pollution Control Board II v. M V Nayudu*, (2001) 2 SCC 62. In *id.*, p. 5 (footnote 33).

215 See *Gauri Shankar v. Union of India*, (1994) 6 SCC 349. In *id.*, p. 5 (footnote 32).

216 See *Kharak Singh v. State of UP*, AIR 1963 SC 1295; *Govind v. State of MP*, AIR 1975 SC 1378; *R Raj Gopal v. State of Tamil Nadu*, (1994) 6 SCC 632; *PUCL v. Union of India*, AIR 1997 SC 568; *'X' v. Hospital Z*, (1998) 8 SCC 296. In *id.*, p. 5 (footnote 34).

217 See *M H Hoskot v. State of Maharashtra* AIR 1978 SC 1548; *Hussainara Khatoon v. State of Bihar* AIR 1979 SC 1369; *Khatri v. State of Bihar* AIR 1981 SC 928; *Suk Das v. Union Territory of Arunachal Pradesh* AIR 1986 SC 991. In *id.*, p. 5 (footnote 35).

218 See *Hussainara Khatoon (I) to (VI) v. Home Secretary, Bihar* (1980) 1 SCC 81; *Kadra Pahadiya v. State of Bihar* AIR 1982 SC 1167; *Common Cause v. Union of India* (1996) 4 SCC 33 and (1996) 6 SCC 775; *Rajdeo Sharma v. State of Bihar* (1998) 7 SCC 507 and (1999) 7 SCC 604. In *id.*, p. 5 (footnote 36).

219 See *Sunil Batra v. Delhi Administration* AIR 1978 SC 1675; *Prem Shankar v. Delhi Administration* AIR 1980 SC 1535; *Munna v. State of UP* AIR 1982 SC 806; *Sheela Barse v. Union of India* AIR 1986 SC 1773. In *id.*, p. 5 (footnote 37).

220 See Surya Deva, *Indian National Report*, p. 5.

221 See decisions I. ÚS 6/02, I. ÚS 100/04, II. ÚS 111/08, II. ÚS 8/96; Ján Svák and Lucia Berdisová, *Slovak National Report*, pp. 12–13.

guaranteed in the Constitution. In the latter case, the Court interpreted this right in such a way that it deduced an obligation of State bodies to actively participate in its protection. According to the Court, the constitutional provision means not only that State bodies are not allowed to create obstacles to the free return of a citizen to the territory of the Slovak Republic but also that State bodies are obliged to actively help citizens to return to the territory. Consequently, the bodies of the Slovak Republic (e.g., the Ministry of Foreign Affairs) have an obligation to help citizens to return to Slovak Republic when they have been kept abroad against their will, even if that obligation is not enumerated in the law and State bodies did not have the explicit requirement to do so.[222]

Of course, all these constitutional mutations are considered legitimate because they follow the basic principle of the progressive protection of human rights. On the contrary, they represent also a case of the pathology of judicial review when courts make such mutations to reduce the scope of protection of fundamental rights, as in Venezuela, where the Constitutional Chamber of the Supreme Tribunal of Justice, in Decision N° 1.939 of December 18, 2008,[223] ignored the decisions of the Inter–American Court on Human Rights by declaring that its rulings condemning the Venezuelan State for violations of human rights are unenforceable in Venezuela. This also occurred with the decision of the Chamber issued on August 5, 2008, in the case of the former judges of the First Court on Contentious Administrative Jurisdiction who were illegitimately dismissed without any sort of judicial guarantees (*Apitz Barbera et al. [First Court on Contentious Administrative Matters] v. Venezuela*[224]). In its decision, the Constitutional Chamber accused the Inter–American Court on Human Rights of usurping the power of the Supreme Tribunal.[225] This decision contradicted article 31 of the Constitution, which established the right of access to international protection in matters of human rights, with the State being obligated to carry out the decisions of such international bodies. But the Constitutional Chamber did not stop there. In an evident usurpation of powers, it requested that "the National Executive . . . proceed to denounce the Convention, in view of the evident usurpation of functions in which the Inter American Court on Human Rights

222 See Decision N° II. ÚS 8/96; Ján Svák and Lucia Berdisová, *Slovak National Report*, pp. 12.

223 See *Gustavo Álvarez Arias et al.* In fact, the case can be identified as "*Venezuelan Government vs. Inter–American Court on Human Rights.*" See http://www.tsj.gov.ve/ decisiones/scon/Diciembre/1939–181208–2008–08–1572.html. See the comments in Allan R. BREWER–CARÍAS, *Reforma constitucional y fraude a la Constitución (1999–2009)*, Academia de Ciencias Políticas y Sociales, Caracas 2009, pp. 253 ff.

224 See.http://www.adc–sidh.org/images/files/apitzbarberaingles.pdf. Judgment of August 5, 2008 (*(Preliminary Objection, Merits, Reparations and Costs)*

225 The issue had been affirmed by the Constitutional Chamber in its known Decision N° 1.942 of July 15, 2003, in which, when referring to the International Courts, the Chamber stated that, in Venezuela, "above the Supreme Court of Justice and according to article 7 of the Constitution, there is no jurisdictional body, unless stated otherwise by the Constitution or the law, and even in this last possible case, any decision contradicting the Venezuelan constitutional order, lacks of application in the country." See "Impugnación de artículos del Código Penal, Leyes de desacato," *Revista de Derecho Público*, N° 93–96, Editorial Jurídica Venezolana, Caracas 2003, pp. 136 ff.

has incurred into with the ruling object of this decision." With this, the Venezuelan State continued in its process of separating from the American Convention on Human Rights and avoiding the jurisdiction of the Inter–American Court on Human Rights, using the Supreme Tribunal for this purpose.

Another case in which the Constitutional Chamber of the Supreme Tribunal of Venezuela changed constitutional provisions affecting fundamental rights is refer to the political right to participation by means of referendum, established in article 72 of the 1999 Constitution as a political right of the people to revoke or repeal the mandates of all popular elected offices. The petition for such a referendum must derive from popular initiative, and the mandate is considered revoked when "a number of electors equal or higher than those who elected the official, vote in favour of the revocation."[226] Nevertheless, in a clearly unconstitutional way, the Constitutional Chamber, in Decision N° 2750 of October 21, 2003,[227] abstractly interpreting article 72 of the Constitution, endorsed a resolution of the National Electoral Council (Resolution N° 030925–465 of September 25, 2003) and decided against the Constitution by adding to the provision that the revocation of the mandate can proceed only if votes to revoke, even if greater than those cast for the election, "do not result to be lower than the number of electors that voted against the revocation." As to the revoked public official, the Chamber considered that, "if the option of his permanence obtains more votes in the referendum, he should remain in office." In this way, the Chamber illegitimately changed the nature of the revocation referendum, turning it into a "ratifying" referendum of mandates.[228]

---

226 This was ratified by the Constitutional Chamber in several decisions: Decision N° 2750 of October 21, 2003, case: *Carlos Enrique Herrera Mendoza (Interpretación del artículo 72 de la Constitución* (Exp. 03–1989), *Revista de Derecho Público*, N° 93–96, Editorial Jurídica Venezolana, Caracas 2003; and Decision N° 1139 of June 5, 2002, case: *Sergio Omar Calderón Duque and William Dávila Barrios*, *Revista de Derecho Público*, N° 89–92, Editorial Jurídica Venezolana, Caracas 2002, p. 171. The same criterion was followed in Decision N° 137 of February 13, 2003, case: *Freddy Lepage Scribani et al.* (Exp. 03–0287).

227 See Carlos E. HERRERA MENDOZA, *Interpretación del artículo 72 de la Constitución, Revista de Derecho Público*, N° 93–96, Editorial Jurídica Venezolana, Caracas 2003.

228 This mutation had a precise purpose in 2004: to avoid revocation of the mandate of the President of the Republic (Hugo Chávez). He had been elected in August 2000 with 3,757,744 votes, so a greater number of votes in a revocation referendum twould have been enough to revoke his mandate. The number of votes in favor of the revocation of the mandate of the President of the Republic, cast in the August 15, 2004 revocation referendum, was 3,989,008, reason for which his mandate could be considered constitutionally revoked. Nonetheless, the National Electoral Council, because more votes were cast against his revocation of the President mandate, on August 27, 2004 decided instead to "ratify" the President of the Republic in his position until the culmination of the constitutional term in January 2007. See *El Nacional*, Caracas, 08–28–2004, pp. A–1 and A–2. See the comments in Allan R. BREWER–CARÍAS, "La Sala Constitucional vs. El derecho ciudadano a la revocatoria de mandatos populares o de cómo un referendo revocatorio fue inconstitucionalmente convertido en un 'referendo ratificatorio,'" in *Crónica sobre la "in"justicia constitucional: La Sala Constitucional y el autoritarismo en Venezuela*, Colección Instituto de Derecho Público, Universidad Central de Venezuela, N° 2, Editorial Jurídica Venezolana, Caracas 2007, pp. 350 ff.

The position of the Venezuelan Supreme Tribunal on the Constitution contradicts the general one of constitutional courts: they cannot substitute for the constituent power by deducing concepts in a way that goes against what is written in the Constitution, nor can they interpret the Constitution in a way so as to arrive at concepts that could be contrary to the constitutional text and its fundamental values. As Jorge Carpizo has pointed out:

> [C]onstitutional courts cannot usurp the functions of the Constituent Power, and consequently, they cannot create provisions or principles that could not be referred to the Constitution; they can deduct implicit principles from those expressly included, like human dignity, liberty, equality, juridical security, social justice, Welfare State.[229]

In the same sense, as Sandra Morelli has pointed out, constitutional courts cannot be "above the Constitution," and they cannot "appropriate the Constitution for themselves, in an abusive way," such as by invading the field of the Legislator or of the Constituent Power. The contrary would open the door to "irresponsible judicial totalitarianism."[230]

2. The Mutation of the Constitution on Institutional Matters

But constitutional mutations by constitutional courts have not occurred only in the field of fundamental rights; they have also occurred with respect to other key constitutional matters, including the organization and functioning of the State.

For instance, the German Federal Constitutional Tribunal also issued a decision mutating the Constitution, in the case *AWACS–Urteil* on July 12, 1994.[231] The Tribunal reviewed the constitutionality of the deployment, in peacetime, of missions of German Armed Forces to foreign countries. The decision referred to the modalities surrounding the deployment, and the Tribunal concluded that the deployment of troops to foreign countries required the consent of the legislative branch. Although this assertion is reasonable – the Tribunal considered it "a requirement that derives directly from the Constitution" – the truth is that it was not expressly established in the Constitution, and the Legislator had sanctioned no legislative development on the matter. In this case, the Tribunal not only mutated the Constitution but even issued a detailed substitute legislation (provisional measures) contained in the decision, ordering the Legislator and the Executive to proceed according to it until a statute was adopted to establish in a more detailed way "the formal participation of

229 See Jorge CARPIZO, *El Tribunal Constitucional y sus límites*, Grijesly Ed., Lima 2009, pp. 56, 68.

230 See Sandra MORELLI, *La Corte Constitucional: Un papel por definir*, Academia Colombiana de Jurisprudencia, 2002; *Colombian National Report II*, p. 3.

231 See BVferG, July 12, 1994, BVeffGE 90, 585–603; Christian BEHRENDT, *Le judge constitutionnel, un législateur–cadre positif. Un analyse comparative en droit francais, belge et allemande*, Bruylant, Brussels 2006, pp. 352–356; I. HÄRTEL, *German National Report*, p. 20.

the Legislator in the adoption of decisions related with the use of German troops in military missions."[232]

In Austria, the Constitutional Court has also filled in the fundamental principles of the Constitution, which has had substantial influence on the interpretation of Austrian constitutional law.[233] The most important example is the principle of *Rechtsstaat* (rule of law), from which various concepts have been derived, including the principle of legality and, from it, the principle of clarity, which obliges the legislator to provide clear and detailed provisions, the principle of comprehensibility of legislative acts,[234] and the principle of effective legal protection,[235] which obliges Parliament to provide sufficient and adequate legal protection to individuals. Through these interpretations, the Court created new constitutional limitations on Parliament, which had to adapt its legislation to the Court's new standards.

In the same line, the Austrian Court has sometimes even created a new constitutional framework for Parliament to follow when enacting legislation in areas not expressly provided for in the Constitution, such as the privatization process. In four main judgments,[236] the Court established an obligatory framework for privatizing state functions exercised by specific organizations, thus intervening in the legislative function and governmental policy and defining the functions and tasks of the State itself. The Court derived the rules from different provisions of the Constitution, requiring, for instance, the application in all privatization processes of the principles of rationality, efficiency, and legality, as well as the principle of the hierarchical structure of Public Administration. In contrast, according to these rules, the State is only authorized to privatize singular tasks, not an entire area of State functions; and in any case, the State has to provide effective control mechanisms with regard to private organizations performing the tasks of State authorities. Finally, the Court defined core areas of State functions that cannot be privatized at all, including foreign affairs, internal affairs, jurisdiction (judicial system), and criminal law. In this way, the Court created a new understanding of the Constitution and imposed it on all State authorities.[237]

---

232 See BVferG, July 12, 1994, BVeffGE 90, 286 (390), in Christian BEHRENDT, *Le judge constitutionnel, un législateur–cadre positif. Un analyse comparative en droit francais, belge et allemande*, Bruylant, Brussels 2006, p. 354.

233 See Konrad Lachmayer, *Austrian National Report*, p. 8.

234 See VfSlg 12.420/1990, in Konrad Lachmayer, *Austrian National Report*, p. 8 (footnote 24).

235 See VfSlg 11.196/1986; Konrad Lachmayer, *Austrian National Report*, p. 8 (footnote 25).

236 See "Austro Control" decision VfSlg 14.473/1996, "Bundeswertpapieraufsicht" (Federal Bond Authority) decision VfSlg 16.400/2001, "E–Control" decision VfSlg 16.995/2003, "Zivildienst–GmbH" (Compulsory Community Service Ltd) decision VfSlg 17.341/2004; Konrad Lachmayer, *Austrian National Report*, p. 11 (footnote 31).

237 See Konrad Lachmayer, *Austrian National Report*, p. 11.

Also regarding the limits of privatization, the Greek Council of State has held that the principles of popular sovereignty and separation of powers do not allow conferring police powers to privatize legal entities.[238]

In the Slovak Republic, where the Constitutional Court has the exceptional attribution of rendering abstract interpretations of the Constitution in cases of disputes between two State bodies with different interpretations of a constitutional provision, the Court has issued important decisions that have mutated and complemented the Constitution. This has happened, for instance, regarding the position and authority of the President of the Republic within the general organization of the State. In the original text of the Constitution of the Slovak Republic, inspired by the classical parliamentary form of the government, the President had the relatively weak position of a *porvoir neuter*. It was the Constitutional Court that directly strengthened the President's position through interpretation of the Constitution, affirming in 1993 that, "even if the Government of the Slovak Republic ("government") is the highest executive body (art. 108), the constitutional position of the President of Slovak Republic is in fact dominant towards the constitutional position of the government."[239] The question debated was whether the President had the right or the constitutional obligation to appoint members of the government on the basis of a motion by the Prime Minister. The Court added that, "to create inner balance within the executive power, the Constitution of the Slovak Republic assigns the President of the Slovak Republic only the obligation to deal with the motion of the Prime Minister, it is not his obligation to comply with it.[240] This decision of the Court had serious consequences for the constitutional system of the Slovak Republic, as it strengthened the position of the President, and made the Court, as mentioned by Ján Svák and Lucia Berdisová, "the direct creator of the constitutional system of the Slovak Republic."[241]

This constitutional mutation was latter reaffirmed in the matter of the competence to appoint the Chief of the General Staff of the Army, which a law had vested in the government. Nonetheless, with article 102 of the Constitution establishing the competence of the President to appoint and recall "higher state officials," the Court interpreted "higher state official" in deciding that there is no "obstacle that could keep the President from the execution of his competence towards Chief of the General Staff of the army as a higher state official."[242]This decision, issued in connection with the direct interpretation of the Constitution by the Court, is considered to have "de facto transformed classical parliamentary form of government into some

238 See Council of State (Full Bench) Judgment N° 1934/1998, *ToS* 1998, 598 (602–603) (concerning enforcement of no–parking zones); Julia Iliopoulos–Strangas and Stylianos–Ioannis G. Koutnatzis, *Greek National Report*, p. 16 (footnote 125).

239 See Decision N° I. ÚS 39/93; Ján Svák and Lucia Berdisová, *Slovak National Report*, p. 4.

240 *Id.*

241 *Id.*

242 See Decision N° PL. ÚS 32/95; Ján Svák and Lucia Berdisová, *Slovak National Report*, p. 5.

kind of semi–presidential form, and yet without the change of the normative text of the Constitution."[243]

In Canada, where the Supreme Court also has the exceptional power to issue reference judgments at the request of public officials and entities of the State, among the most important Supreme Court decisions on constitutional matters are those in which the Court has created and declared constitutional rules. In particular, in the 1981 *Patriation Reference*,[244] the Court laid down the basic rules governing the patriation of Canada's Constitution from the United Kingdom; and in the 1998 *Quebec Secession Reference*,[245] the Supreme Court dealt with the possible secession of Quebec from Canada. These two cases were decided at the request of the federal government, which has statutory powers to refer questions of law, including those involving the constitutionality of legislation, directly to the Supreme Court of Canada.[246] In the decisions, the Supreme Court laid down some basic rules for guiding constitutional change and warned of potential constitutional crises that could arise from arguably unconstitutional acts, such as an attempt by the federal government to change the powers of the provincial legislatures without their consent or a similarly unilateral decision by the Quebec legislature to declare its sovereignty and secession from Canada.

IV. THE PROBLEM OF ILLEGITIMATE MUTATIONS OF THE CONSTITUTION

If constitutions are superior laws that support the validity of all the legal order, one of the institutional solutions to ensure their enforcement is the existence of a constitutional court, that must act as its guardian, with powers to annul unconstitutional State acts or to declare their unconstitutionality.

In democracies, these courts have always been the main institutional guarantee of freedom and of the rule of law. As such guardian, and as it in any rule–of–law system, the submission of the constitutional court to a constitution is absolute, not subject to discussion,[247] because it would be inconceivable that the constitutional judge can violate the Constitution that he or she is called on to apply. As a matter of principle, it is possible to imagine that other bodies of the State could violate the Constitution (e.g., Parliament), but not its guardian. For such purpose and to ensure that this does not occur, a constitutional court must have absolute independence and autonomy, because on the contrary, a constitutional court subject to the will of the political power, becomes the most atrocious instrument of authoritarianism instead of the guardian of the Constitution. Thus, in the hands of judges subject to political

243 *Id.*

244 [1981] 1 S.C.R. 753, in Kent Roach, *Canadian National Report*, p. 9.

245 [1998] 2 S.C.R. 217, in Kent Roach, *Canadian National Report*, p. 9.

246 See Kent Roach, *Canadian National Report*, p. 9.

247 See Néstor Pedro SAGÜES, *La interpretación judicial de la Constitución*, LexisNexis, Buenos Aires 2006, p. 32. In article 204 of the Portuguese Constitution, it is expressly set forth that "in matters brought before them for decision, the courts shall not apply any rules that contravene the provisions of this Constitution or the principles contained there."

power, the best constitutional justice system is a dead letter for individuals and an instrument for defrauding the Constitution.

Unfortunately, the latter is what has been occurring in Venezuela since 2000. The Constitutional Chamber of the Supreme Tribunal, far from acting within the expressed constitutional attributions, has been adopting decisions that in some cases contain unconstitutional interpretations of the constitution,[248] not only about its own powers of judicial review but also about substantive matters. It has changed or modified constitutional provisions, in many cases to legitimize and support the progressive building of the authoritarian State. That is to say, it has distorted the content of the Constitution, through illegitimate and fraudulent "mutation," which in some cases the people have rejected through referendum.[249]

One of the most important instruments for accomplishing these mutations of the Constitution is the already–mentioned creation of a recourse for abstract interpretation of the Constitution, in which case constitutional interpretations is not made deciding a particular case or controversy or deciding other means of judicial review, but abstractly.

This has happened in many cases of autonomous requests for interpretation filed at the request of the same national executive through the attorney general for the purpose of strengthening authoritarianism, the most notorious of which have being the following:

First, regarding article 6 of the Constitution that establishes the fundamental principles of republican government, in an immutable way, expressly including the democratic, elective, and alternate character of the government; principles that have been incorporated in Venezuelan constitutions since 1830. In particular, the principle of alternation in government, as pointed out by the Electoral Chamber of the Supreme Tribunal of Justice in Decision N° 51 of March 18, 2002,[250] implies "the successive exercise of a position by different persons, belonging or not to the same party," conceived to face the desire to remain in power. Nevertheless, in Decision N° 53 of February 3, 2009, the Constitutional Chamber confused "alternate govern-

---

248 See Allan R. BREWER–CARÍAS, "*Quis Custodiet Ipsos Custodes*: De la interpretación constitucional a la inconstitucionalidad de la interpretación," in *VIII Congreso Nacional de derecho Constitucional, Perú*, Fondo Editorial 2005, Colegio de Abogados de Arequipa, Arequipa, September 2005, pp. 463–489; and BREWER–CARÍAS, *Revista de Derecho Público*, N° 105, Editorial Jurídica Venezolana, Caracas 2006, pp. 7–27. See also Allan R. BREWER–CARÍAS, *Crónica sobre la "in"justicia constitucional: La Sala Constitucional y el autoritarismo en Venezuela*, Editorial Jurídica Venezolana, Caracas 2007; BREWER–CARÍAS, *Reforma constitucional y fraude a la Constitución*, Academia de Ciencias Políticas y Sociales, Caracas 2009.

249 As mentioned, constitutional mutation occurs when the content of a constitutional standard is modified in such a way that, even when the standard maintains its content, it receives a different meaning. See Néstor Pedro SAGÜES, *La interpretación judicial de la Constitución*, LexisNexis, Buenos Aires 2006, pp. 56–59, 80–81, 165 ff.

250 See Allan R. BREWER–CARÍAS, "El juez constitucional vs. la alternabilidad republicana (La reelección continua e indefinida)," *Revista de Derecho Público*, N° 117, Editorial Jurídica Venezolana, Caracas 2009, pp. 205–211.

ment" with "elective government" to conclude that the principle of alternation implies only "the periodic possibility to choose government officials or representatives." The result was not only to mutate the Constitution, eliminating the principle of alternating government, but to allow a referendum that took place on February 15, 2009, for the people to vote for a "constitutional amendment" to allow for continuous reelection for elective positions. The 2009 amendment was approved in the referendum, and the Constitution was then formally changed to eliminate the principle of alternate government, which by the way was conceived as unmodifiabale in article 6 of the Constitution.[251]

Second, article 67 of the 1999 Constitution expressly establishes that "the financing of political associations with Government funds will not be allowed," a provision that in 1999 radically changed the previous regime of public financing of political parties.[252] This express constitutional prohibition regarding public financing of political parties was also one of the matters referred to in the 2007 proposed constitutional reform,[253] which sought to modify article 67 to provide that "the State will be able to finance electoral activities." As already mentioned, the 2007 constitutional reform proposal was rejected by popular vote in a referendum of December 2, 2007;[254] but the Constitutional Chamber of the Supreme Court of Justice, in Decision N° 780 of May 8, 2008, also illegitimately mutated the Constitution, contrary to the popular will. The Chamber ruled that the constitutional prohibition only "limit[ed] the possibility to provide resources for the internal expenses of the different forms of political associations, but...said limitation is not extensive to the electoral campaign, as a fundamental stage of the electoral process." That is, the Constitutional Chamber, again, usurped the constituent power, substituted itself for the people, and reformed the provision, thus expressly allowing for government financing of the electoral activities of the political parties and associations, contrary to what the Constitution provides for.

Finally, the decision of the Constitutional Chamber to modify article 203 of the Constitution must be mentioned, as here the Chamber mutated an important consti-

---

251 *Id.*

252 As was established in article 230 of the Organic Law of Suffrage and Political Participation of 1998. See Allan R. BREWER–CARÍAS, "Consideraciones sobre el financiamiento de los partidos políticos en Venezuela," in *Financiamiento y democratización interna de partidos políticos: Memoria del IV Curso Anual Interamericano de Elecciones*, San José, Costa Rica, 1991, pp. 121–139; BREWER–CARÍAS, "Regulación jurídica de los partidos políticos en Venezuela," in *Estudios sobre el Estado constitucional (2005–2006)*, Cuadernos de la Cátedra Fundacional Allan R. Brewer Carías de Derecho Público, Universidad Católica del Táchira, N° 9, Editorial Jurídica Venezolana. Caracas, 2007, pp. 655–686.

253 See *Proyecto de exposición de motivos para la reforma constitucional, Presidencia de la República, Proyecto Reforma Constitucional: Propuesta del presidente Hugo Chávez Agosto 2007; Proyecto de Reforma Constitucional, Prepared by the President of the Bolivarian Republic of Venezuela, Hugo Chávez Frías*, Editorial Atenea, Caracas, August 2007, p. 19.

254 See Allan R. BREWER–CARÍAS, "La proyectada reforma constitucional de 2007, rechazada por el poder constituyente originario," in *Anuario de Derecho Público 2007*, Universidad Monteavila, Caracas 2008, pp. 17–65.

tutional rule of procedure for the approval of organic laws. Article 203 of the Constitution, in effect, defines the various types of organic law[255] and establishes in general terms that, to reform an organic law, a special quorum of two–thirds of the votes of members of the National Assembly is required. The Constitutional Chamber, in Decision N° 34 of January 26, 2004,[256] ruled that such a special quorum was not necessary to initiate the discussion of organic law drafts to reform existing organic laws that have such denomination in the Constitution, thus illegitimately changing a constitutional procedural condition regarding the approval of statutes.

Constitutional mutations have also occurred in other countries through judicial decisions, particularly on matters of presidential reelections, which in Latin American constitutional history has always provoked political conflicts because of the traditional general prohibition on reelection. Sometimes, the prohibition has been embodied in provisions considered immutable, as was the case in Honduras, where attempts by former President Manuel Zelaya in 2009 to change the constitutional prohibition on reelection by means of a constitutional assembly provoked one of the most bitter political conflicts in the region in the past decades.[257]

A similar constitutional provision prohibiting the continuous reelection of the President of the Republic is also established in article 147 of the Constitution of Nicaragua, which nonetheless was "reformed" by the Supreme Court of the country in Decision N° 504 of October 19, 2009, when ruling on an amparo action filed against a decision of the Supreme Electoral Council, in which the Council rejected a request to apply the principle to equality to all public officials on matters of election. In the case, no specific candidacy was involved, and the decision consisted in a rejection of the petition due to the lack of attributions of the Supreme Electoral Council to decide on such matter. In the decision, nonetheless, the Supreme Court, incomprehensibly declared article 147 of the Constitution "inapplicable," mutating in an illegitimate way the Constitution, by eliminating from its text the entrenched prohibition on reelection.[258]

---

255 According to article 203, "organic laws" are those qualitied as such in the text of the Constitution itself, as well as those enacted for the purpose of organizing the branches of government, or for the regulation of constitutioonal rights, or which serve as normative framework of other statutes.

256 See *Vestalia Araujo* case, interpretation of article 203 of the Constitution, at http://www.tsj.gov.ve/decisiones/scon/Enero/34–260104–03–2109%20.htm. See also Daniela UROSA MAGGI, *Venezuelan National Report*, p. 14.

257 See Allan R. BREWER–CARÍAS, "Reforma constitucional, asamblea nacional constituyente y control judicial contencioso administrativo: El caso de Honduras (2009) y el precedente venezolano (1999)," *Revista Aragonesa de Administración Pública*, N° 34 (June 2009), Gobierno de Aragón, Zaragoza 2009, pp. 481–529. In 2010, the Constitution of Honduras was changed in order to establish the possibility of the reelection of the President of the Republic.

258 See Sergio J. CUAREZMA TERÁN and Francisco ENRÍQUEZ CABISTÁN, *Nicaragua National Report*, p. 43.

CHAPTER 3
CONSTITUTIONAL COURTS' INTERFERENCE WITH THE LEGISLATOR ON EXISTING LEGISLATION

Leaving aside the relation between constitutional courts and the constituent power, the most important and common role of constitutional courts has been developed with respect to legislation, controlling its submission to the Constitution. This role is performed by the courts, not only acting as the traditional "negative" Legislator but also as a jurisdictional organ of the State designed to complement or assist legislative organs in their main function of establishing legal rules.

This role has been assumed by the courts since the initial conception of the diffuse system of judicial review in the United States, deciding not to apply statutes when considered contrary to the Constitution, thus giving preference to the latter; or in the concentrated system of judicial review, which has extended throughout the world during the last century, in which constitutional courts have the power to annul unconstitutional statutes. In all systems, in accomplishing their functions, constitutional courts have always, in some way, assisted the Legislator. At the beginning, in a limited manner, they provided only for the nullity or inapplicability of statutes declared contrary to a Constitution; subsequently, they broadly interpreted the Constitution, and the statutes in conformity with it, giving directives or guidelines to the Legislator to correct the legislative defects.

I. CONSTITUTIONAL COURTS' INTERPRETATION OF STATUTES IN HARMONY WITH THE CONSTITUTION

During the past decades, given the increasing role of constitutional courts not only as the guarantors of the supremacy of a constitution but also as its supreme interpreter through decisions with binding effects on courts, public officials, and citizens, courts have move beyond their initial role as negative legislators, ruled by the traditional unconstitutionality and invalidity–nullity dichotomy.[259] In that trend, their powers have progressively extended, and courts have assumed a more active role interpreting constitutions and statutes, in order not only to annul or not to apply them when unconstitutional but also to preserve the Legislator's actions and the statutes it has enacted, thus interpreting them in harmony with the Constitution.

Thus, when a statute can be interpreted accordingly or contrary to the constitution, courts often make efforts to preserve its validity by choosing to interpret it in harmony with the Constitution and by rejecting interpretations that could result in the statute being declared unconstitutional. This is a general principle currently applied in comparative law.

---

259 See F. FERNÁNDEZ SEGADO, *Spanish National Report*, pp. 8 ff.

This role of courts has been a classical principle in the U.S. Supreme Court judicial review doctrine, formulated by Justice Brandeis:

> When the validity of an act of Congress is drawn in question, and even, if a serious doubt of constitutionality is raised, it is a cardinal principle that this Court will first ascertain whether a construction of the statute is fairly possible by which the question may be avoided.[260]

This approach to judicial review, followed in all countries, responds to the principle of conservation or preservation of legislation (norm preservation) when issued by the democratically elected representative body of the State, whose legislative acts are covered by their presumption of constitutionality.[261] This principle has led to two lines of action: (1) by overestimating the presumption, in which the validity of the legislation is assumed until a decision is adopted, and (2) by preserving the piece of legislation by interpreting it according to the Constitution.

In the first case, in Greece, for example, courts traditionally have failed to meaningfully and consistently scrutinize the constitutionality of legislation, instead emphasizing the need to respect legislative prerogatives and considering the mere existence of legislation that restricts constitutional rights a sufficient basis to uphold its constitutionality.[262]

In the second case, it has been the practice of constitutional courts in all judicial review systems to issue so–called interpretative decisions, which the Constitutional Tribunal of Spain has defined as those

> that reject an unconstitutionality action, that is to say, that declare the constitutionality of the challenged statutory provision, provided that it be interpreted in the sense that the Constitutional Tribunal considered according to the Constitution, or not to be interpreted in the sense that it is considered not according.[263]

Of course, in this regard, interpretative decisions are those that interpret statutes in harmony with the Constitution to preserve their enforcement and to avoid declaring them contrary to the Constitution, a notion that cannot be applied when the

---

260 See *Ashwander v. TVA*, 297 U.S. 288, 346–48 (1936). The principle was first formulated in *Crowell v. Benson*, 285 U.S. 22, 62 (1932). See "Notes. Supreme Court Interpretation of Statutes to avoid constitutional decision," *Columbia Law Review*, Vol. 53, N° 5, New York, May 1953, pp. 633–651.

261 This presumption implies the following (1) the protection of the statutes, as well as of the functions of the Legislator and its independence; (2) in case of doubt, the unconstitutionality must be rejected; (3) if two criteria exist regarding the interpretation of a statute, the one in harmony with the Constitution must be chosen; (4) when two interpretations, one contrary to the Constitution and the other according to it, the latter must be chosen. See Iván Escobar Forns, "Las sentencias constitucionales y sus efectos en Nicaragua," in *Anuario Iberoamericano de Justicia Constitucional*, Centro de Estudios Políticos y Constitucionales, N° 12, 2008, Madrid 2008, pp. 105–106. See also I. Härtel, *German National Report*, p. 6.

262 See Julia Iliopoulos–Strangas and Stylianos–Ioannis G. Koutnatzis, *Greek National Report*, p. 12.

263 See Decision STC 5/1981, February 13, 1981, FJ 6 in Francisco Javier Díaz Revorio, *Las sentencias interpretativas del Tribunal Constitucional*, Lex Nova, Valladolid 2001, p. 67; José Julio Fernández Rodríguez, *La justicia constitucional europea ante el Siglo XXI*, Tecnos, Madrid 2007, p. 129.

courts interpret the Constitution according to a statute to also avoid the declaration of the statute's unconstitutionality. As has been indicated for Greece, if it is true that to avoid reaching a holding of unconstitutionality, Greek courts have regularly interpreted statutory law as conforming to the Constitution, in so doing, "they have occasionally interpreted the Constitution to be in accordance with statutory law rather than conversely or they have exceeded the permissible limits of interpretation to avoid reaching a judgment of unconstitutionality." This refers to the case in which the Council of State construed the statutorily required "permission" of the Orthodox Church for the construction of religious sites of other denominations – against the wording of the statutory law in force at the time – to be a mere nonbinding opinion for the executive branch.[264] On the basis of this interpretation, Julia Iliopoulos–Strangas and Stylianos–Ioannis G. Koutnatzis state that the Council of State found no violation of religious freedom according to the Greek Constitution and the European Convention on Human Rights. In construing statutory legislation contrary to its wording, however, the Council of State substituted its own formulation for that of Parliament, arguably engaging in positive legislation.[265]

In any case, the technique to interpret statutes in harmony or in conformity with the Constitution to preserve their validity has been also applied in cases of the control of "conventionality" of statutes, regarding their conformity with international treaties. With respect to the Netherlands, J. Uzman, T. Barkhuysen, and M. L. van Emmerik stated:

> [T]he courts generally assume that unless Parliament expressly deviates from its international obligations, it must clearly have intended any provision in its Act to be consistent with a given treaty. This assumption is the basis for the courts' usual practice to interpret national law as far as possible in a way consistent with the rights laid down in conventions such as the ECtHR. And it is this practice that has given rise to a few of the most celebrated but also deeply notorious (some might even say activist) Supreme Court judgments.[266]

The technique, in principle, cannot be considered invasive regarding the attributions of the Legislator, and on the contrary, being conceived to help the Legislator, its purpose is to preserve its normative products and, in a certain way, from a practical point of view, to avoid unnecessary legislative vacuums that result from the declaration of a statute as invalid or null.[267] In any case, this judicial review technique of interpretative decisions in which the unconstitutionality of a statute is rejected has helped mold constitutional courts into important constitutional institutions that assist and cooperate with the legislator in its legislative functions.

---

264 See Council of State (Full Bench) Judgment N° 1444/1991, N° *V* 1991, 626 (627); Julia Iliopoulos–Strangas and Stylianos–Ioannis G. Koutnatzis, *Greek National Report*, p. 13 (footnote 94).

265 See Julia Iliopoulos–Strangas and Stylianos–Ioannis G. Koutnatzis, *Greek National Report*, p. 13.

266 See J. Uzman, T. Barkhuysen, and M. L. van Emmerik, *Dutch National Report*, pp. 8, 24, 32, 37.

267 See this assertion regarding the Italian and Spanish judicial review practice in Francisco Javier DÍAZ REVORIO, *Las sentencias interpretativas del Tribunal Constitucional*, Lex Nova, Valladolid 2001, p. 92; F. FERNÁNDEZ SEGADO, *Spanish National Report*, p. 5.

Constitutional courts have widely used these sorts of interpretative decisions.[268] In Italy, for instance, the Constitutional Court has disregarded the interpretation proposed by the *a quo* judge in the remittal ordinance regarding the unconstitutionality of a legal provision and instead has recommended a different interpretation of the same provision, one that is compatible with the Constitution. In other words, "with the interpretative decision of rejection, the question raised is declared groundless, on condition that one interprets the provision challenged in the sense indicated in it."[269] The Court's decision imposes on the *a quo* judge a negative obligation in that he or she is obliged to not insist on attributing to the provision the meaning disregarded by the Court.

Nonetheless, as interpretation is a delicate function, many times accomplished on the border between constitutionality and unconstitutionality, constitutional courts have also established limits or self–restraint regarding interpretative decisions with respect to the wording of the text to be interpreted and the intention of the Legislator when sanctioning the law.[270] In this regard, for instance, the Spanish Constitutional Tribunal has summarized the scope of interpretative decisions in decision STC 235/2007 of November 7, 2007, as follows:

> a) The effectiveness of the norms preservation principle must not ignore or configure the clear text of legal provisions, due to the fact that the Tribunal cannot reconstruct provisions against their evident sense in order to conclude that such reconstruction is the constitutional norm;
>
> b) The interpretation accordingly cannot be a contra legem interpretation, the contrary would imply to disfigure and manipulate the legal provisions; and
>
> c) It is not the attribution of the Tribunal to reconstruct a norm that is explicit in the legal provision, and, consequently, to create a new norm and the assumption by the Constitutional Tribunal of a function of Positive Legislator that institutionally it does not have.[271]

It must also be mentioned that the technique of interpreting the law in harmony with the Constitution to avoid a declaration of unconstitutionality has also been applied in France, by means of *a priori* judicial review, which has been traditionally exercised by the Constitutional Council. The technique is used to consider whether the Legislator has respected the Constitution in interpreting the law according to it.[272] In these cases, the Constitutional Council has a double task: on the one hand, it interprets the statute according to the Constitution; on the other hand, it addresses a directive to the Legislator on the conditions of the exercise of its attributions and,

---

268 See Francisco Javier Díaz Revorio, *Las sentencias interpretativas del Tribunal Constitucional*, Lex Nova, Valladolid 2001, pp. 59 ff.; F. Fernández Segado, *Spanish National Report*, p. 25 ff.; I. Härtel, *German National Report*, pp. 6–7.

269 See Gianpaolo Parodi, *Italian National Report*, p. 3.

270 See BVerfGE, 69,1 (55); 49, 148 (157), in I. Härtel, *German National Report*, p. 6 (footnote 33).

271 See Francisco Fernández Segado, *Spanish National Report*, p. 34.

272 E.g., Decisions 2000–435 DC, 2001–454 DC, 2007–547 DC, in Bertrand Mathieu, *French National Report*, p. 13.

eventually, a directive to the authorities who must apply the law on how they must perform their duties.[273]

As Lóránt Csink, Józef Petrétei, and Péter Tilk highlighted in referring to Hungary, by setting constitutional requirements regarding the law, the Constitutional Court necessarily gives a narrow interpretation of the norm, thus reducing the possible constitutional meanings. In these cases, the Court does not annul the challenged law but modifies its meaning, and in some cases, it creates a new norm – one that may result in a Court order "to neglect significant parts of the norm," even contradicting "the will of the legislator."[274] In these cases, the Court chooses one possible interpretation from the alternatives, not necessarily the same one the Legislator thought of; that is, the Court interprets the law extensively by determining a requirement that totally alters the effect of the law or gives a new statement that was not originally in the norm, thus creating a new norm.[275] The Constitutional Court's decision establishing new content for a provision is the result of a constitutional interpretation in order to make the law constitutional.[276]

Regarding all these functions of constitutional courts in interpreting statutes in harmony with the Constitution, their interference with the Legislator, and their legislative functions regarding existing and in–force legislation, they can be studied through two courses of action: by complementing legislative functions as provisional Legislators or adding rules to existing Legislation through interpretative decisions and by interfering with the temporal effects of existing legislation.

II. CONSTITUTIONAL COURTS COMPLEMENTING THE LEGISLATOR BY ADDING NEW RULES (AND NEW MEANING) TO THE EXISTING LEGISLATIVE PROVISION

Through interpretation, constitutional courts frequently create new legislative rules by altering meaning or adding what is considered lacking in the provision so that it is in harmony with the Constitution.

These additive decisions have been extensively studied particularly in Italy, where it is possible to find the widest variety of decisions issued by the Constitutional Court in declaring unconstitutional a statutory provision. They have been widely studied, analyzed, and classified under the general category of "manipulative" decisions. As Gianpaolo Parodi has explained in the Italian National Report, these decisions of acceptance of unconstitutionality, despite leaving the text of the provision unaltered, transform its normative meaning, at times reducing and at other times extending its sphere of application, not without, especially in the second case, introducing a new norm into the legal system or creating new norms. In this regard,

---

273 See Bertrand MATHIEU, *French National Report*, p. 13.

274 See Decision 48/1993 (VII.2) and Decision 52/1995 (IX.15), in Lóránt Csink, Józef Petrétei, and Péter Tilk, *Hungarian National Report*, p. 4 (footnote 10).

275 See Decision 41/1998 (X.2), Decision 60/1994 (XII.24), and Decision 22/1997 (IV.25), in Lóránt Csink, Józef Petrétei, and Péter Tilk, *Hungarian National Report*, p. 4 (footnote 12).

276 See Lóránt Csink, Józef Petrétei, and Péter Tilk, *Hungarian National Report*, p. 4.

one speaks of manipulative (or manipulating) decisions, and among them, the typically additive and substitutive decisions.[277]

The difference between interpretative decisions and manipulative decisions has also been established by Parodi as follows:

> The first of the two, indeed, preferably makes reference to the subject of the ruling: a norm obtainable in an interpretative way from a legislative statement, rather than a provision, or one of its segments (in this sense, the notion fits both the interpretative decisions of acceptance in a strict sense, and the "non textual" decisions of partial acceptance); the notion of manipulative decision usually throws light on a peculiar effect of the ruling: of alteration and, precisely, manipulation of the meaning *prima facie* of the provision contested, which, on the textual plane remains unaltered.[278]

Within the additive decisions (*sentenze additive*), it is possible to distinguish additive decisions of principle, because the principles formulated in the Court's decision are established to guide "both the legislator, in the necessary normative activity subsequent to the ruling, aimed at remedying the unconstitutional omission; and ordinary judges, so that, while waiting for the legislative intervention, they find, with integration of law, a solution for the controversies submitted to them."[279]

In these cases, as pointed out by the Italian Constitutional Court in 1991, although a declaration of constitutional illegitimacy of a legislative omission leaves to the Legislator its undeniable competence to discipline the matter, even retroactively, through general legislation, "it gives a principle to which the ordinary judge is able to make reference to place a remedy in the meantime to the omission at the time of identification of the rule for the concrete case."[280]

In many cases, through additive decisions, constitutional courts establish that the challenged provision is lacking something for it to be in accordance with the Constitution; deciding that, from that moment on, the provision must be applied as if that something is not missing. As the Constitutional Tribunal of Peru has said, by means of additive decisions:

> [T]he unconstitutionality of a provision or of part of it is declared, in which the needed part for it to result in harmony with the Constitution has been omitted (in the part in which the provision does not establish that). In such cases, the whole provision is declared unconstitutional, but only its omission, so after the declaration of its unconstitutionality it will be obligatory to include within it the omitted aspect.[281]

These decisions, frequently issued to guarantee the right to equality and to non-discrimination,[282] eventually transform an unconstitutional provision into a constitu-

---

277 See Gianpaolo PARODI, *Italian National Report*, p. 6.

278 See Gianpaolo PARODI, *Italian National Report*, pp. 6–7.

279 See Gianpaolo PARODI, *Italian National Report*, p. 10.

280 See Decision N° 295/1991, in Gianpaolo PARODI, *Italian National Report*, p. 10.

281 See Decision of January 3, 2003 (Exp. N° 0010–2002A1–TC), in Fernán ALTUVE FEBRES, *Peruvian National Report II*, p. 13.

282 See Francisco Javier DÍAZ REVORIO, *Las sentencias interpretativas del Tribunal Constitucional*, Lex Nova, Valladolid 2001, pp. 183, 186, 203, 204, 274, 299, 300; José Julio FERNÁNDEZ RODRÍGUEZ, *La inconstitucionalidad por omisión: Teoría general. Derecho comparado.*

tional one by adding to the norm what is lacking, or even by substituting something into the provision. In other words, without affecting the challenged provision, they extend or expand its normative content by establishing that such content must include something that is not expressly established in its text.[283] Although these decisions, in a certain way, change the scope of legislative rules regardless of any amended wording, as mentioned by Joaquim de Sousa Ribeiro, "the Court's ruling does not put up a norm *ex nihilo*. Those decisions only put forward a solution imposed by the Constitution provisions and principles by extending a rule already chosen by the legislator."[284]

Of course, the additive rulings as expressed by the Italian Constitutional Court cannot imply a discretional appraisal regarding the challenged provision, in that the Constitutional Court cannot intervene when it is a matter of choosing between a plurality of solutions, all of which are admissible – in that case, the discretion corresponds only to the Legislator.[285] However, they cannot refer to matters that must exclusively be regulated by the Legislator, such as criminal matters.[286]

One example of these additive decisions is one issued by the Constitutional Court of Italy in 1969 regarding the constitutionality of article 313.3 of the Criminal Code, in which the prosecution for insults against the Constitutional Court itself was subjected to previous authorization from the Ministry of Justice and Grace. The Court considered that such authorization contradicted the independence of the Court, arguing that the provision was unconstitutional, deducting that the authorization was to be given by the same Court,[287] and forcing the provision – according to Díaz Revorio – to say something that it was not capable of saying and even eliminating

El caso español, Civitas, Madrid 1998, pp. 232 ff.; Joaquin BRAGE CAMAZANO, "Interpretación constitucional, declaraciones de inconstitutionalidad y arsenal sentenciador (Un suscinto inventario de algunas sentencias 'atípicas')," in Eduardo Ferrer Mac–Gregor (coord.), Interpreación Constitucional, Ed. Porrúa, Vol. I, México 2005, pp. 192 ff.; Joaquim de SOUSA RIBEIRO and Esperança MEALHA, *Portuguese National Report*, p. 8.

283 See Francisco Javier DÍAZ REVORIO, *Las sentencias interpretativas del Tribunal Constitucional*, Lex Nova, Valladolid 2001, pp. 28, 32, 33, 45, 97,146, 165, 167, 292.

284 See Joaquim de SOUSA RIBEIRO and Esperança MEALHA, *Portuguese National Report*, p. 9.

285 See Decision Nos. 109 of April 22, 1986, and125 of January 27, 1988, in Francisco Javier DÍAZ REVORIO, *Las sentencias interpretativas del Tribunal Constitucional*, Lex Nova, Valladolid 2001, p. 273 (footnote 142); Francisco FERNÁNDEZ SEGADO, "Algunas reflexiones generales en torno a los efectos de las sentencias de inconstitucionalidad y a la relatividad de ciertas fórmulas estereotipadas vinculadas a ellas," in *Anuario Iberoamericano de Justicia Constitucional*, Centro de Estudios Políticos y Constitucionales, N° 12, 2008, Madrid 2008, p. 164–165.

286 See Patricia Popelier, *Belgian National Report*, pp. 13–14; Iván ESCOBAR FORNS, "Las sentencias constitucionales y sus efectos en Nicaragua," in *Anuario Iberoamericano de Justicia Constitucional*, Centro de Estudios Políticos y Constitucionales, N° 12, 2008, Madrid 2008, pp. 110.

287 See Decision N° 15, February 12, 1969, in Francisco Javier DÍAZ REVORIO, *Las sentencias interpretativas del Tribunal Constitucional*, Lex Nova, Valladolid 2001, pp. 151–152.

the part of it considered incompatible with the independence of the Court.[288] Another decision of this sort of the Italian Constitutional Court was issued in 1989 regarding a provision of the Criminal Code that sanctioned those refusing to serve in the military because of conscience with prison terms of two to four years. The Constitutional Court, asked to review the provision, ruled that the sanction was contrary to the constitutional right to equality because the same Criminal Code established a sanction of only six months to two years in a similar situation for those who were called to serve in the military but refused to serve without motives or because of nonserious motives. The consequence was a declaration of unconstitutionality of the provision "in the part in which the minimal sanction is established in two years instead of six months, and in the part in which the maximal sanction is established in four years instead of two years."[289] The result was that the Constitutional Court substituted the sanction of two to four years with another one of six months to two years.

In Germany, one of the typical additive decisions adopted by the Federal Constitutional Court is one regarding the Political Parties Law, which lowered the parties' required threshold of votes with regard to the reimbursement of election campaign costs from 2.5 percent to 0.5 percent.[290]

In Spain, an example of additive or substitutive decision is the one issued by the Constitutional Tribunal in 1988 when deciding on the constitutionality of article 7.4 of the Inter–Territorial Compensation Fund established for financing projects of the Autonomous Communities of the State, which established that, in some cases, the decision regarding the project proposals needed approval "of the Government Council of the Autonomous Communities." The Tribunal considered that this was unconstitutional, because to determine which organ of the Autonomous Communities was to intervene in the approval was a matter corresponding to their own autonomy, and the Court ruled that the reference to the Government Councils must be understood as a reference to the Autonomous Communities, without specific reference to any of their organs.[291]

Another example from the Spanish Constitutional Tribunal is the decision issued in 1993 regarding the benefit of Social Security pensions to the "daughters and sisters" of a holder of a retirement pension, which the Tribunal considered unconstitutional because, contrary to the constitutional guarantee of equality, it excluded "sons

---

288 See Francisco Javier DÍAZ REVORIO, *Las sentencias interpretativas del Tribunal Constitucional*, Lex Nova, Valladolid 2001, p. 152.

289 See Decision Nº 409 of July 6, 1989, in Francisco Javier DÍAZ REVORIO, *Las sentencias interpretativas del Tribunal Constitucional*, Lex Nova, Valladolid 2001, p. 153.

290 See BVerfGE 24, 300 (342 f.), in I. Härtel, *German National Report*, p. 19.

291 See decision STC 183/1988, October 13, 1988, in Francisco Javier DÍAZ REVORIO, *Las sentencias interpretativas del Tribunal Constitucional*, Lex Nova, Valladolid 2001, pp. 154–155.

and brothers" from the benefit, extending the benefits to the latter.[292] In the same sense is a 1992 decision of the Constitutional Tribunal regarding the Urban Tenants Law, whose article 58.1 established that upon the death of a tenant, his spouse could subrogate in his rights and duties. The Court considered that the absence in the provision of any reference to those living *more uxorio* in a marital–like relationship with the deceased tenant was contrary to the right to equality and thus unconstitutional; the result was that the provision was also to be applied to them.[293] Regarding all these cases, as mentioned by F. Fernández Segado, it is possible to consider the Spanish Constitutional Tribunal as a "real positive legislator."[294]

In Portugal, additive decisions have been issued by the Constitutional Tribunal in applying the principle of equality in the sense that, if a norm grants favors to certain groups of persons while excluding or omitting others in violation of an equal protection clause, the exclusion or omission is considered unconstitutional. If the Court has no power to bring about an equal solution for the excluded group, in what has been considered rare cases, the Court's ruling, by itself, has made possible the inclusion of certain groups under the scope of rules that omitted or excluded them. For instance, as pointed out by Sousa Ribeiro, in Ruling N° 449/87, the Court held unconstitutional a norm that established different allowances for a widower and widow in case of death caused by work accident. Furthermore, it stated that the only solution that would comply with the Constitution would be one that granted equal treatment to both, meaning that the favor granted to the widow should be extended to the widower. In addition, in Ruling N° 359/91, the Court considered and ruled on a request from the Ombudsman for not only a successive abstract review of the rules laid down by the Civil Code concerning the transmission of the position of the tenant in the event of divorce when interpreted as not applicable to *de facto* unions, even if the couple in question had underage children, but also a review of the "unconstitutionality by omission of a legislative measure which expressly states that those rules are applicable, with the necessary adaptations, to *de facto* unions of couples with underage children." In this decision, the Court issued a declaration with generally binding force of the unconstitutionality of that interpretation for breaching the principle of nondiscrimination against children born outside wedlock, but it did not find unconstitutionality by omission. As a result of the Court's decision, the rules of the Civil Code were thereafter understood as including such *de facto* unions.[295] According to Sousa Ribeiro, such decisions can be considered additive decisions, as their implementation changes the scope of legislative rules regardless of any amendment to the wording of such rules.[296]

---

292 See Decision STC 3/1993, January 14, 1993, in Francisco Javier DÍAZ REVORIO, *Las sentencias interpretativas del Tribunal Constitucional*, Lex Nova, Valladolid 2001, pp. 177, 274; F. FERNÁNDEZ SEGADO, *Spanish National Report*, p. 42.

293 See Decision STC 222/1992, December 11, 1992, in Francisco Javier DÍAZ REVORIO, *Las sentencias interpretativas del Tribunal Constitucional*, Lex Nova, Valladolid 2001, pp. 181, 182, 275; F. FERNÁNDEZ SEGADO, *Spanish National Report*, p. 41.

294 See F. FERNÁNDEZ SEGADO, *Spanish National Report*, p. 48.

295 See Joaquim DE SOUSA RIBEIRO and Esperança MEALHA, *Portuguese National Report*, p. 8.

296 See Joaquim DE SOUSA RIBEIRO and Esperança MEALHA, *Portuguese National Report*, p. 9.

Also in Greece, regarding violations of the constitutional equality principle due to the unconstitutional exclusion of persons or groups from a State benefit or the preferential treatment of one person or group at the expense of another, in exercising the diffuse method of judicial review, civil courts have regularly extended preferential treatment to remedy a violation of the equality principle – regardless of whether the discriminatory legislation accords preferential treatment as a general rule or exceptionally.[297] The extension to judges, of legislation concerning remuneration of higher public servants[298] is usually considered a common manifestation of this jurisprudence. Ordinary administrative courts have generally followed the same approach, invoking in their reasoning the European Court of Justice's case law on the principle of equal pay for male and female workers for equal work or work of equal value.[299] More recently, the Council of State has aligned its jurisprudence with that of the Areios Pagos Court, also extending preferential treatment in cases of violation of the constitutional equality principle, as in cases of gender discrimination in social security legislation.[300] Accordingly, as affirmed by Julia Iliopoulos–Strangas and Stylianos–Ioannis G. Koutnatzis, "in extending the applicability of discriminatory, and thus unconstitutional, legislation, Greek courts exercise legislative power in a positive sense."[301]

In a similar way, in South Africa, the Constitutional Court, referring to a 1991 statute (reformed in 1996) that assigned the spouse of a permanent resident in the country the right to automatically obtain a residence permit, considered it discriminatory and unconstitutional because it did not include foreigners in homosexual relationships. The Court complemented the text to include after the word *spouse* the phrase "or the same sex partner in a stable condition."[302]

In Canada, it is also possible to find similar additive judicial review decisions, also on matters of family law and regarding the right to equality, thus supported by

---

297 See, e.g., Areios Pagos Judgment Nos. 3/1990, *NoV* 1990, 1313 (1314); 7/1995 (Full Bench), *EErgD* 1996, 494 (495); 1578/2008, *EErgD* 2009, 180 ff.; Julia Iliopoulos–Strangas and Stylianos–Ioannis G. Koutnatzis, *Greek National Report*, p. 18 (footnote 140).

298 See, e.g., Areios Pagos Judgment N° 40/1990, *EEN* 1990, 579 ff. (579); Julia Iliopoulos–Strangas and Stylianos–Ioannis G. Koutnatzis, *Greek National Report*, p. 18 (footnote 144).

299 See, e.g., Athens Administrative Court of First Instance Judgment Nos. 10391/1990, *DiDik* 1991, 1309 (1309–1310); 3151/1992, *DiDik* 1993, 350 (351). See also Athens Administrative Court of Appeals Judgment N° 3717/1992, *DiDik* 1993, 138 (138–139); Julia Iliopoulos–Strangas and Stylianos–Ioannis G. Koutnatzis, *Greek National Report*, p. 19 (footnote 146).

300 See, e.g., Council of State Judgment Nos. 1467/2004 (Full Bench), *Arm* 2004, 1049 (1050); 3088/2007 (Full Bench), *DtA* 2009, 540 (541); see also Council of State Judgment N° 2180/2004 (Full Bench), *NoV* 2005, 173 (174–175) (extending to pilots remuneration provisions for the cabin crew). See Julia Iliopoulos–Strangas and Stylianos–Ioannis G. Koutnatzis, *Greek National Report*, p. 19 (footnote 148).

301 See Julia Iliopoulos–Strangas and Stylianos–Ioannis G. Koutnatzis, *Greek National Report*, p. 19.

302 See Iván Escobar Fornos, "Las sentencias constitucionales y sus efectos en Nicaragua," in *Anuario Iberoamericano de Justicia Constitucional*, Centro de Estudios Políticos y Constitucionales, N° 12, 2008, Madrid 2008, pp. 111–112.

constitutional values, in which the Court may read in or add words to legislation to cure a constitutional defect. A famous example is the decision issued by the Supreme Court in *Vriend v. Alberta*, where the Court, though considering Alberta's human rights code unconstitutional because it violated equality rights by failing to protect gays and lesbians from discrimination, decided to add or read into the provision the inclusion of sexual orientation as a prohibited grounds of discrimination rather than striking down the legislation.[303] A similar use of the power was the decision of the Ontario Court of Appeal to strike down the definition of marriage as a union of a man and a woman and to substitute the gender–neutral concept of a union between persons to allow for same–sex marriages, considering that religious views about marriage could not justify excluding same–sex couples from the civil institution of marriage.[304] Although such remedies are not used in a routine fashion to cure all constitutional defects, they, according to Kent Roach, "amount to judicial amendments or additions to legislation."[305]

In Poland, the Constitutional Tribunal has developed these kinds of judgments, which are not directly established in the Constitution or in the governing statute. As mentioned by Marek Safjan, "the Tribunal adopts one of the following formulas: 'provision X complies with the Constitution under the condition that it will be understood in the following way . . . ', or 'provision X understood as follows . . . complies with the Constitution' or 'provision X understood in the following way . . . does not comply with the Constitution. . . '. The so called partial judgments usually go further because they directly determine the normative elements included in the provision, which do not comply with a hierarchically higher act (e.g. 'provision X up to an extent in which it envisages that . . . does not comply with the Constitution')."[306] As an example of these decisions,[307] which have been compared with laparoscopic surgery versus an invasive operation, is the case on interpreting the Civil Code to regulate the liability of the State for damage inflicted to an individual by public functionaries.[308] Issuing an interpretative judgment, and therefore avoiding derogation of a Civil Code provision, the Tribunal established a totally new regime of *ex delicto* liability for damages of the State, on the basis of an objective premise of illegality and eliminating the fault of the functionary as a premise of public authority liability.[309]

---

303 See *Vriend v. Alberta* [1998] 1 S.C.R. 493; Kent Roach, *Canadian National Report*, pp. 6, 14 (footnotes 5 and 27).

304 See *Halpern v. Ontario* (2003) 65 O.R. (3d) 161 (C.A.); Kent Roach, *Canadian National Report*, pp. 7, 14 (footnotes 6 and 29).

305 See Kent Roach, *Canadian National Report*, p. 7.

306 See Marek Safjan, *Polish National Report*, pp. 13–14.

307 The Polish Supreme Court has opposed this practice of the Constitutional Tribunal, arguing that the process of interpretation is strictly connected with the process of application of a given norm, not with the procedure of its evaluation from the point of view of its conformity with a hierarchically higher act. See Marek Safjan, *Polish National Report*, p. 14.

308 See decision of the Constitutional Tribunal of December 4, 2001, in the case SK18/00, OTK ZU 2001/8/256, in Marek Safjan, *Polish National Report*, p. 14 (footnote 43).

309 See Marek Safjan, *Polish National Report*, pp. 14, 15.

In Hungary, additive decisions can also be found as a consequence of the Constitutional Court's decisions declaring partial nullity of laws, called mosaic annulment. In this regard, Lóránt Csink, Józef Petrétei, and Péter Tilk point out that the Court has always tried to annul the least possible from the law, that is, only to annul what is necessary to restore constitutionality. For this purpose, as they argued, partial annulment pushed the Court far from negative legislation, as the text that remained in force after the annulment often had a different and sometimes contradictory meaning from the one before constitutional review. This has been the case, for instance, when some words have been annulled, with the result of expanding the scope of grantees of a tax law, either in the field of substantive law[310] or in the field of procedure law;[311] when certain texts of a law restrain a fundamental right concerning the publicity of declarations of properties of local government deputies;[312] and when the competence to determine compensation in matters of criminal law was removed from the minister of justice to the courts, just annulling some words of the Criminal Procedure Code.[313] Another case refers to a decision declaring unconstitutional a comma in a sentence containing an enumeration because it resulted in a different meaning of the sentence, a meaning that was not in conformity with the Constitution.[314]

In the Czech Republic, the Constitutional Court has issued interpretative decisions that read text differently or add sense to constitutional provisions. A typical example, mentioned by Zdenek Kühn, is the judgment in the *Clearance of Defense Counsel* case of January 28, 2004, regarding a law mandating that, in criminal cases in which classified information might be discussed, the defense attorneys are subject to a security clearance. As a result, no defense attorney was available for the defendant in the criminal case before the district court, and the defendant was effectively denied of his or her right to legal aid. Therefore, the district court petitioned the Constitutional Court to annul the law if it included also the "defense attorneys" among those who were subject to a security clearance. The Court rejected this reading of the law and found, against its clear wording, that defense attorneys in criminal

---

310 See Decision 87/2008 (VI.18). The decision found it discriminatory that only one group of contributors enjoyed tax preferences. The Court annulled the regulation in a way that the preference would also pertain to the members of the other group; Lóránt Csink, Józef Petrétei and Péter Tilk, *Hungarian National Report*, p. 5 (footnote 18).

311 See Decision 73/2009 (VII.10). The Court found it unconstitutional that the law did not grant the possibility of reducing or releasing tax liabilities of individuals. Such a possibility is the result of mosaic annulment. See Lóránt Csink, Józef Petrétei, and Péter Tilk, *Hungarian National Report*, p. 5 (footnote 19).

312 See Decision 83/2008 (VI.13). The decree of the local government allowed only Hungarian citizens to check the declarations and only after certifying their identity. These texts have been annulled. See Lóránt Csink, Józef Petrétei, and Péter Tilk, *Hungarian National Report*, p. 5 (footnote 20).

313 See Decision 66/1991 (XII.21) See in Lóránt Csink, Józef Petrétei, and Péter Tilk, *Hungarian National Report*, p. 5.

314 See Decision 16/1999. (VI.11), in Lóránt Csink, Józef Petrétei, and Péter Tilk, *Hungarian National Report*, p. 5.

proceedings are not subject to this type of clearance. Aware of the controversial nature of its reasoning, the Court added the second part to its verdict, creating a new exception to the clear wording of the law. Hence, the verdict of the judgment includes two parts:

> I. The petition is rejected.
>
> II. Clearance of defense attorney in criminal proceedings for purposes of access to classified information through a security clearance by the National Security Office is inconsistent with Art. 37 par. 3, Art. 38 par. 2, and Art. 40 par. 3 of the Charter of Fundamental Rights and Freedoms and with Art. 6 par. 3 let. c) of the Convention on Protection of Human Rights and Fundamental Freedoms.[315]

In this case, the Constitutional Court explained why it included the second part based on the principle of the primacy of constitutionally consistent interpretation over unconstitutional interpretations, adding that "for these reasons, in these proceedings on review of norms, given a negative verdict with interpretative arguments, the Constitutional Court placed the fundamental constitutional principle, arising from a number of significant grounds, in the verdict section of the judgment."[316]

In another case, the *Permanent Residence Case* of 1994, the Constitutional Court annulled the requirement that the Czech citizens who were allowed to claim restitution of their property have permanent residence in the Czech Republic. The Court found the requirement discriminatory and annulled the rule that set the deadline for claiming restitution. The law thus lost much of its clarity because the effect of annulling the deadline was doubtful. The problem was explained in the Court's reasoning:

> However, if the consequences of legalizing this unconstitutional condition are to be repaired, it is not only necessary to cancel the condition itself, but ...it is also necessary to ensure that the new wording of . . . the Act [after annulment] can realistically be brought to life. This can be achieved only by opening the period . . . for exercising a claim before the court *for those citizens for whom the condition of permanent residence in the country* has heretofore made impossible the exercise of their right to issuance of a thing.[317]

However, in that case, as explained by in Zdenek Kühn, it was far from clear what the annulment of the deadline effectively meant. In any case, the answer to the law's interpretation could have been found not in the law's text but in the Court's justification of its judgment. Only in referring to the Court's judgment did it become clear that the deadline was newly opened only for those who were prohibited to do so under the earlier version of the law (those citizens who had no permanent residence in the Czech Republic) and when the period of time commenced.[318]

---

315 See Decision Pl. ÚS 41/02 of January 28, 2004, published as N. 98/2004 Sb. See http://angl.concourt.cz/angl_verze/doc/p–41–02.php; Zdenek Kühn, *Czech National Report*, p. 9 (footnote 41).

316 See Zdenek Kühn, *Czech National Report*. p. 9.

317 See Decision Pl. ÚS 3/94 of July 12, 1994, published in Czech as 164/1994 Sb. See http://angl.concourt.cz/angl_verze/doc/p–3–94.php; Zdenek Kühn, *Czech National Report*, p. 10 (footnote 47).

318 See Zdenek Kühn, *Czech National Report*, pp. 8–9.

The Constitutional Court of Croatia has also developed additive decisions, creating policies by way of strengthening the rule of law and protection of human rights. An important case highlighted by Sanja Barić and Petar Bačić is the one referred to the annulment in 1998 of some provisions of the Pension Adjustment Act, in which the Court considered unconstitutional the fact that, since 1993, the Government ceased to adjust pensions according to increased inflation and cost of living, even though it continued to do so with wages. The result was that during four years (1993–1997) wages increased twice as much as pensions (the average pension was half the average wage), which meant that the standard of living for retired persons was half the one corresponding to the average working population. Therefore, the Constitutional Court ruled that "this legal arrangement…changed the social status of retired persons to such an extent that it created social inequality of citizens" and that the contested provisions "contravene[d] with basic constitutional provisions of article 3 of the Constitution of the Republic of Croatia, which guarantee equality, social justice, and the rule of law; and with article 5 of the Constitution, which states that laws are to be in conformity with the Constitution."[319] As a consequence of the Court decision, retired persons were to receive the unpaid pensions for the period 1993–1997, and six years later, the Croatian Parliament sanctioned the Law on the Enforcement of the Constitutional Court's Ruling, dated May 12, 1998.[320]

In many countries, these decisions have been considered invasive regarding legislative attributions because, through them, the Constitutional Court, by interpretation, proceeds to supplant the Legislator, affecting at length the system of separation of powers. They have also been considered judicial decisions adding a *quid novi* that transforms the negative into positive, so that a Tribunal converts itself from a judge of the constitutionality of statutes into a constitutional "cleaner" of the same, thus invading the sphere of other branches and adding legislative norms, or positive legislation.[321]

In some way, a similar position is found in the Netherlands regarding the control of conventionality of statutes. The Supreme Court ruled in 1980, in the *Illegitimate Child Case*, that Article 959 of the Civil Procedure Code was to be interpreted in the light of Articles 8 and 14 of the European Convention, to ignore the difference established regarding the procedural treatment between cases concerning the custody of legitimate and illegitimate children, thus allowing the relatives of an orphan born out of wedlock to appeal a decision of the local magistrate withholding custody,

---

319 See Decision N° U–I–283/1997. of May 12, 1998; Sanja Barić and Petar Bačić, *Croatian National Report*, p. 15.

320 See Decision on the Promulgation of the Law on the Enforcement of the Constitutional Court's Ruling, dated May 12, 1998, Official Gazette "*Narodne novine*," N° 105/2004; Sanja Barić and Petar Bačić, *Croatian National Report*, p. 15 (footnote 30).

321 See the opinions of M. A. García Martínez, F. Rubio Llorente, G. Silvestri, T. Ancora, and G. Zagrebelsky, in Francisco Javier Díaz Revorio, *Las sentencias interpretativas del Tribunal Constitucional*, Lex Nova, Valladolid 2001, p. 254 (footnotes 70–76).

which the Civil Procedure Code granted only to legally recognized kin.[322] On the basis of the interpretation already adopted by the European Court of Human Rights regarding the Convention, the Supreme Court accepted the right to appeal for relatives of children born outside of marriage. The same approach was followed in the 1982 *Parental Veto on Underage Marriage Case*, where the Supreme Court spontaneously introduced the duty for parents to justify their decision not to let their underage children enter marriage.[323] Where refusing their consent would be evidently unreasonable, the courts were allowed to substitute the parents' withheld permission, ignoring Article 1:36 (2) of the Civil Code, which prohibited the courts from allowing a marriage where one of the parents objected to it. Again, this judgment was backed up by several decisions of the European Commission on Human Rights,[324] which eventually led to the adoption of more self–restraint on matters of control of conventionality, in the sense that the Court more recently recognized that it was not empowered to set aside national provisions for their inconsistency with Convention law, purely on the basis of its own interpretation of the Convention but only on the prevailing interpretation offered by the European Court.[325]

Also in the area of family law, in the Netherlands, the Supreme Court has developed its own ability to regulate certain areas of the law by means of the exercise of its power of judicial review of "conventionality" of statutes. In effect, in the *Spring Cases*,[326] the Court considered the provisions of Dutch law that stated that when a child was born to unmarried parents or parents who had never been married before or did not have any intention of doing so in the near future, such parents could exercise no parental authority at all, being able to only obtain shared guardianship; the Court found that this violated Articles 8 and 14 of the European Convention. From that decision, the Court set aside certain provisions of the Civil Code and interpreted others so that they might be read consistently with the Convention, and it eventually elaborately tried to regulate the conditions under which a request for joint parental authority was to be granted by the courts; it devoted an entire page in the case re-

322 See Supreme Court judgment of 18 January 1980, *NJ* 1980/463 (*Illegitimate Child*); Jerfi Uzman; Tom Barkhuysen and Michiel L. van Emmerik, *Dutch National Report*, p. 14 (footnote 37).

323 See Supreme Court judgment of 4 June 1982, *NJ* 1983/32 (*Parental Veto on Underage Marriage*); Jerfi Uzman, Tom Barkhuysen, & Michiel L. van Emmerik, *Dutch National Report*, p. 14 (footnote 39).

324 See Jerfi Uzman, Tom Barkhuysen and Michiel L. van Emmerik, *Dutch National Report*, p. 14.

325 See Supreme Court judgment of 19 October 1990, *NJ* 1992/129 (*Gay Marriage*); Supreme Court judgment of 10 August 2001, *NJ* 2002/278 (*Duty of Support*); Jerfi Uzman; Tom Barkhuysen and Michiel L. van Emmerik, *Dutch National Report*, p. 16 (footnote 46).

326 See Joint Supreme Court decisions of 21 March 1986, *NJ* 1986/585–588 (*Spring Decisions*); Jerfi Uzman; Tom Barkhuysen and Michiel L. van Emmerik, *Dutch National Report*, p. 15 (footnote 43) and p. 24.

ports to describe the conditions and provide lower courts with a "manual" for how to work through such difficult cases.[327]

In Latin America, a typical additive and substitutive decision can be found in Peru, in the decision adopted by the Constitutional Tribunal in 1997 regarding article 337 of the Civil Code, where, for purposes of a spouse seeking divorce, it "understood that the term '*sevicia*' [extreme cruelty] must be substituted by the phrase 'physical and physiological violence, that is, not only referred to physical cruelty.'"[328] In Costa Rica, the Constitutional Chamber of the Supreme Court has issued additive decisions on matters of citizenship, as when interpreting that, when article 14.4 of the Constitution establishes that when foreign women marry Costa Ricans, they are Costa Ricans by naturalization if they lost their nationality, the word *woman* must be read as *person* to include men, thus overcoming the discrimination that results from the word "woman" regarding foreign men married to a Costa Rican females. The Court said:

> In order to avoid inequalities and future discriminations that could come from the application of the Constitution, exercising the attributions the Constitution assigns the Chamber, it is resolved that when statutes uses the terms "men" or "women," they must be understood as synonymous to the word "person," eliminating all possible "legal" discrimination because of gender; a correction that must be applied by all public officials when requested to take any decision that would require to apply provisions in which such terms are used.[329]

In another case, the Constitutional Chamber of the Supreme Court of Costa Rica, interpreting the Currency Law, considered the matter of the essential contents of contracting freedom and concluded in relation to contractual obligations established in foreign currencies that the exchange rate to be applicable in case of payment in national currency, to avoid the violation of property rights, must be the market rate, that is, the effective commercial value of the foreign currency at the moment of payment, and not the official rate, as indicated in article 6 of the Currency Law. Consequently, the Court established how the provision of the Currency Law was to be read.[330]

In Venezuela, a few examples of additive decisions issued by the Constitutional Chamber can be identified. One of them pertains to a provision of the Organic Law of the Attorney General of the Republic (article 90), in which it is established, in judicial process in which the Republic is a party, the need for consent from the Attorney General regarding the bail to be requested to lift some precautionary measures. In Decision N° 1104 of May 23, 2006, the Chamber declared the partial nullity of this provision because it violated the right to defense and due process, and it established a new wording for the challenged provision, in the sense that the bail

327 See Jerfi Uzman; Tom Barkhuysen and Michiel L. van Emmerik, *Dutch National Report*, p. 24.

328 See Decision of April 29, 1997 (Exp. N° 0018–1996–1–TC), in Fernán Altuve Febres, *Peruvian National Report II*, pp. 14–15.

329 See Decision Voto 3435–92, in Rubén Hernández Valle, *Costa Rican National Report*, p. 38.

330 See Decision Voto 3495–92, in Rubén Hernández Valle, *Costa Rican National Report*, p. 39.

must be approved by the corresponding judge and not the Attorney General.[331] Another example is the Organic Law of Public Defense, an institution established in the Constitution as part of the judicial system. Nonetheless, article 3 of the Law specified that the Public Defense Service was to depend on the Public Defender's office, which was considered unconstitutional and annulled by the Chamber, which established in Decision N° 163 of February 28, 2008, that the provision was to be read in the sense of attaching the Service to the Supreme Tribunal of Justice, not to the Peoples' Defender Office.[332] In addition, in the same decision, the Chamber annulled *ex officio* the provisions establishing the attribution of the Peoples' Defender to appoint the Head of the Public Defense Service, providing for another regime of appointment by the Supreme Tribunal; and it annulled the provision establishing the approval by the People's Defender of the Budget of the Public Defense Service, changing the wording of the Law to attribute that function to the Supreme Tribunal.[333]

This technique of additive rulings on matters of judicial review can also be identified in countries with a diffuse system of judicial review, like Argentina, where the Supreme Court has issued additive decisions on monetary matters. In the *Massa* case,[334] regarding the compulsory conversion of foreign currency into pesos through various emergency legal provisions, the Court ruled that the regime did not violate property rights recognized in the Constitution providing that a conversion of 1.40 pesos to one U.S. dollar be ensured, with a stabilization coefficient and an annual interest rate of 4 percent. This was a judicial addition to the legal emergency regime to avoid it being declared unconstitutional.[335] In human rights cases, the Supreme Court has also issued additive rulings, like in the *Portillo* Case (1989), where the Court was required to rule on the constitutionality of mandatory military service. The petitioner claimed that, to the extent that military service might require the killing of another individual, it affected the petitioner's deep religious beliefs in violation of the free exercise of religion clause of the Constitution. The Court held that, in peacetime, compliance with military service as established by Congress violated such a clause, but it still required the petitioner to serve time in alternative civil ser-

---

331 See Decision N° 1104 of May 23, 2006, *Carlos Brender* case; http://www.tsj.gov.ve/decisiones/scon/Mayo/1104–230506–02–1688.htm. See also Daniela Urosa Maggi, *Venezuelan National Report*, p. 27.

332 See Decision N° 163 of February 28, 2008, *Ciro Ramón Araujo* case. See http://www.tsj.gov.ve/decisiones/scon/Febrero/163–280208–07–0124.htm. See also Daniela Urosa Maggi, *Venezuelan National Report*, pp. 27–28.

333 *Id.*, p. 28.

334 See Fallos 329:5913 (2006); Alejandra Rodríguez Galán and Alfredo Mauricio Vítolo, *Argentinean National Report I*, p. 17 (footnote 71). See also the *Bustos* case, Fallos 327:4495 (2004). *Id.*, p. 17 (footnote 70).

335 See Néstor P. Sagües, "Los efectos de las sentencias constitucionales en el derecho argentino," in *Anuario Iberoamericano de Justicia Constitucional*, Centro de Estudios Políticos y Constitucionales, N° 12, 2008, Madrid 2008, p. 339; Néstor Pedro Sagües, *Argentinean National Report II*, p. 19.

vice, thus redefining the concept of "national defense" despite the fact that Congress did not provide for such an alternative.[336]

Even in France, where the judicial review system until 2009 was reduced to the *a priori* review of legislation not yet in force, the Constitutional Council has exercise its attributions, adding provisions to the reviewed statute and modifying the scope of application of the law. For example, in Decision 82–141 DC of July 27, 1982 regarding the control of constitutionality of the draft statute on TV communications (*communications audiovisielle*), the Council extended the scope of the right to response, interpreting the phrase "without lucrative purpose" to establish the titleholder of the right. As mentioned by Bertrand Mathieu, in this case, the Council has said what the law is, instead of the Legislator, which established the right to response in television communications only to a category of persons. By eliminating those restrictions, the Council extended the scope of the right, substituting itself for the will of the Legislator. The Constitutional Council considered that the Constitution established such right of response without it being reserved to some persons.[337]

III. CONSTITUTIONAL COURTS COMPLEMENTING LEGISLATIVE FUNCTIONS BY INTERFERING WITH THE TEMPORAL EFFECTS OF LEGISLATION

One of the most common interferences of the Constitutional Courts regarding legislative functions is the power of the Courts to determine the temporal effects of legislation enacted by the Legislator. In general terms, in comparative law, three different situations can be distinguished: first are cases in which the Constitutional Court determines when an annulled legislation will cease to have effects at some point in the future; second are cases in which the Constitutional Court, by assigning retroactive or nonretroactive effects to its decisions, determines the date on which legislation ceases to have effects; third are cases in which the Constitutional Court, when declaring null an unconstitutional statute, decides to bring back previously repealed legislation.

The matter, for instance, has been expressly regulated in the Constitution of the Republic of South Africa of 1996, which provides the following:

> Article 172. Powers of courts in constitutional matters.
>
> 1. When deciding a constitutional matter within its power, a court:
>   a) must declare that any law or conduct that is inconsistent with the Constitution is invalid to the extent of its inconsistency; and
>   b) may make any order that is just and equitable, including

336 See Fallos 312:496 (1989); Alejandra Rodríguez Galán and Alfredo Mauricio Vítolo, *Argentinean National Report I*, p. 15 (footnote 63).

337 See Bertrand Mathieu, *French National Report*, p. 16. See the decision in http://www.conseil–constitutionnel.fr/conseil–constitutionnel/francais/les–decisions/depuis–1958/decisions–par–date/1982/82–141–dc/decision–n–82–141–dc–du–27–juillet–1982.7998.html.

i. an order limiting the retrospective effect of the declaration of invalidity; and
ii. an order suspending the declaration of invalidity for any period and on any conditions, to allow the competent authority to correct the defect.

1. The power of the Constitutional Court to determine when annulled legislation will cease to have effects: Postponing the effect of the Court's ruling

The first of the cases in which constitutional courts interfere with the legislative function, by modulating the temporal effects of its decision declaring unconstitutional or null a statute, is when the Court establishes *vacatio sentenciae*, determining when annulled legislation will cease to have effects by postponing the beginning of the effects of its own decision and thus extending the application of the invalidated statute.

In principle, it is a general rule in systems of judicial review in which the constitutional courts have power to annul unconstitutional statutes,[338] as was, for instance, established since the beginning in the 1920 Austrian Constitution (article 140.3), that the Constitutional Court's decisions must be published in an Official Journal. This means, that in principle, as the Court's decisions have *erga omnes* effects as products of the negative legislator, the judicial review decision annulling a statute begins to have effects since the date of its publication, unless the Court establishes another date to avoid legislative vacuums, giving time to the Legislator to enact a new legislation to replace the annulled one. In the Austrian Constitution, the Court can postpone the effects of its decision for a term of up to six months, and in the constitutional reform of 1992 this was extended to eighteen months (art. 140.5).[339] In these cases of extending the beginning of the effects of the Court's decisions, the annulled statute remains in force until the extinction of the term or the intervention of the Legislator by enacting a statute to replace the annulled one. Consequently, as the Court has the power to extend the effects of an annulled statute, it can be said that, since the beginning of the concentrated system of judicial review in Europe, the Austrian Constitutional Court was "a corrective jurisdictional legislator and not only a simple negative jurisdictional legislator."[340]

---

338 Although in some countries like Portugal, "The Court has never postponed the effects of its ruling by safeguarding effects produced after the declaration of unconstitutionality (and according to the prevailing opinion on this subject the effects of annulment could not be postponed)." See Joaquim de Sousa Ribeiro and Esperança Mealha, *Portuguese National Report*, p. 6.

339 See Francisco Javier Díaz Revorio, *Las sentencias interpretativas del Tribunal Constitucional*, Lex Nova, Valladolid 2001, p. 266; Francisco Fernández Segado, "Algunas reflexiones generales en torno a los efectos de las sentencias de inconstitutionalidad y a la relatividad de ciertas fórmulas estereotipadas vinculadas a ellas," in *Anuario Iberoamericano de Justicia Constitucional*, N° 12, 2008, Centro de Estudios Políticos y Constitucionales, Madrid 2008, pp. 174, 188.

340 See Otto Pfersmann, "Preface," in Christian Behrendt, *Le judge constitutionnel, un législateur–cadre positif. Un analyse comparative en droit francais, belge et allemande*, Bruylant, Brussels 2006, p. xxxiii; Konrad Lachmayer, *Austrian National Report*, p. 7.

In Greece, article 100.4, para. 2, of the Constitution, provides that the Supreme Special Court invalidates unconstitutional statutory provisions "as of the date of publication of the respective judgment, or as of the date specified in the ruling," thus implicitly recognizing that the Supreme Special Court can establish a different date for the beginning of the effects of the invalidation of the unconstitutional statute.[341]

This also occurs in Belgium, where the Constitutional Court (formerly the Arbitration Court), according to its Organic Law (article 8.2), has the power to provisionally maintain the effects of an invalidated statutory provision – in this case, not for a specific period of time but for the time the Court determines.[342] This term has been established in different ways according to the Court appreciation of facts, for instance, as referred to by Christian Behrendt, to the publication of the Court decision in the *Moniteur*, to the end of the academic year, to the end of the fiscal year, and to the nomination of the Officials of an organ of the State.[343] In such cases, the effects of the annulled provision cease automatically, thus creating a legislative vacuum, which the Legislator is compelled to fill. This was the case of a 2002 statute modifying the rules for the publication of the *Moniteur* and establishing its exclusive electronic publication, reducing the physical (paper) publication for public consultation to only three copies. Because of the discriminatory character of the reform, impeding the access of some citizens to the Official Journal, the Court in 2004 declared invalid the statute but provided that it was to continue to have effects (*delai d'abrogation*) until July 31, 2005, imposing on the Legislator the obligation to determine alternative rules to overcome the inequalities.[344] That is why, in some cases, the Constitutional Court has determined that the term during which the unconstitutional statute must remain in force extends up to the moment in which the corresponding Legislator issues a new legislation on the matter.[345]

In the Czech Republic, the Constitutional Court has postponed the effects of a decision issued in 2000 to offer the legislature time to enact a new law that would enact a mechanism for just terms in rent.[346] Nonetheless, the most celebrated example is the case of the annulment of the law on judicial review of administrative acts, which did not fit the requirements of the Czech Constitution and, above all, the Eu-

341 See Julia Iliopoulos–Strangas and Stylianos–Ioannis G. Koutnatzis, *Greek National Report*, p. 20 (footnote 152).

342 See Christian Behrendt, *Le judge constitutionnel, un législateur–cadre positif. Un analyse comparative en droit francais, belge et allemande*, Bruylant, Brussels 2006, p. 87, 230, 235, 286, 309; P. Popelier, *Belgian National Report*, pp. 4–7.

343 See Christian Behrendt, *Le judge constitutionnel, un législateur–cadre positif. Un analyse comparative en droit francais, belge et allemande*, Bruylant, Brussels 2006, p. 236.

344 See CA arrêt 106/2004, June 16, 2004. See also the references in Christian Behrendt, *Le judge constitutionnel, un législateur–cadre positif. Un analyse comparative en droit francais, belge et allemande*, Bruylant, Brussels 2006, pp. 313–320.

345 Arrêt 45/2004; Christian Behrendt, *Le judge constitutionnel, un législateur–cadre positif. Un analyse comparative en droit francais, belge et allemande*, Bruylant, Brussels 2006, p. 87, 235, 309–321.

346 See judgment of June 21, 2000, Pl. ÚS 3/2000, *Rent Control I*, published as N° 231/2000 Sb.; Zdenek Kühn, *Czech National Report*, p. 12 (footnote 57).

ropean Convention of Human Rights. The Constitutional Court repeatedly urged the legislature to enact a new and constitutionally consistent law. Finally, as mentioned by Zdenek Kühn, the Court lost its patience and annulled all of part 5 of the Code of Civil Procedure related to administrative judiciary. It noted that the law as a whole suffered serious constitutional deficits, even though there were many provisions that would be included in a new law, stating:

> After taking into account all calls made by the Court to both the legislature and the executive branch, and after considering the current state of work on the reform of administrative judiciary, the Court decided to delay the effects of its judgment until December 31, 2002. As it would take some time before enacting the law and its entering into force, it is clear that it is the task for this legislature to enact a new law.[347]

Eventually, the legislature, which delayed the enactment of the new law on administrative judiciary for almost ten years, enacted a new law.

In France, the constitutional law N° 2008–724 of July 23, 2008 reforming article 62 of the Constitution on the judicial review system established that in the case of statutory provisions declared unconstitutional according to article 61–1 (exception of unconstitutionality), the decision has effect since its publication, as the Constitutional Council is authorized to fix another ulterior date. In Croatia, to avoid legal uncertainties occurring in the period between the adoption and publication of a repeal decision by the Constitutional Court, article 55.2 of the 2002 Constitutional Act on the Constitutional Court states:

> The repealed law or other regulation, or their repealed separate provisions, shall lose legal force on the day of publication of the Constitutional Court decision in the Official Gazette Narodne novine, unless the Constitutional Court sets another term.[348]

The same general principle has been applied in Germany, although without such a clear provision as those in Belgium, France, or Croatia. Article 35 of the Federal Constitutional Court of Germany only establishes regarding the execution of its decision that, in individual cases, the Court can establish how such execution will take place. Given this provision, it can be considered usual practice for the Federal Constitutional Court to establish a term for its decision to by applied, which is fixed according to different rules, for instance, a precise date or a particular fact like the end of the legislative term.[349] One recent case, highlighted by I. Härtel, concerns the inheritance tax statutory provision.[350] In some aspects the provision was unconstitu-

---

347 See the judgment of June 27, 2001, Pl. ÚS 16/99, *Part Five of the Code of Civil Procedure – Administrative Judiciary*, published as N° 276/2001 Sb.; Zdenek Kühn, *Czech National Report*, p. 14 (footnote 63) (the Court was referring to the fact of parliamentary elections, which were due in June 2002).

348 See Sanja Barić and Petar Bačić, *Croatian National Report*, p. 17.

349 See BVferG, May 22, 1963 (Electoral Circuits), in Christian Behrendt, *Le judge constitutionnel, un législateur–cadre positif. Un analyse comparative en droit francais, belge et allemande*, Bruylant, Brussels 2006, pp. 299–300. See BVferG, November 7, 2006 (Inheritance Tax); I. Härtel, *German National Report*, p. 7.

350 See BVerfG, court order from 2006–11–7, reference number: 1 BvL 10/02; I. Härtel, *German Report*, pp. 7–8.

tional, but the Tribunal did not annul it but referred it to the Legislator to reform it in conformity with the Constitution, thus maintaining the applicability of the unconstitutional statute until a new legislative regulation could be established. As I. Härtel said: "The continuing implementation was seen as necessary to prevent a situation of legal uncertainty during the interim period, especially affecting, and potentially complicating, the regulations regarding succession of property during a transferor's lifetime. The *BVerfG* has therefore, as a kind of 'emergency legislator,' created a law–like condition (*Steiner*, ZEV 2007, 120 (121)); it has 'invented' a new decision type (*Schlaich/Korioth*, Das Bundesverfassungsgericht, 7th ed. 2007, margin number 395)."[351]

In Italy, the Constitution clearly establishes that when the Constitutional Court declares unconstitutional a statutory provision, it ceases in its effects the day after its publication (article 136, Constitution), which implies that the Constitutional Court cannot postpone the annulment effects or extend the application of the annulled provision.[352] Nonetheless, it is possible to identify in the jurisprudence important cases of deferring the effects in time of a declaration of unconstitutionality. As mentioned by Gianpaolo Parodi, "in these cases, the Court declared the unconstitutional character of legislative provisions by the state successive to the constitutional law no. 3/2001 and detrimental to the new regional attributions, explaining that the state discipline censured would not have ceased to find application until the arrangement and the coming into force of the new regional regulations and setting aside the administrative procedures in progress and founded on the first, even if not yet exhausted, to avoid that, due to the situation of normative void determined by the ruling of acceptance, the guarantee of constitutional rights might result compromised."[353]

In Canada, the Supreme Court has also developed innovative remedies of delaying or suspending the declaration of invalidity for periods of six to eighteen months to provide legislatures an opportunity to enact new constitutional legislation so that there are no lacunae in the legal regime. It was first used in the case *Manitoba Language Reference*, where in the Province of Manitoba all laws were unconstitutional because they had not been translated into French. The Court delayed the declaration of invalidity under s. 52(1) of the Constitution Act (which says that laws inconsistent with the Constitution are of no force and effect) and justified the use of a suspended declaration of invalidity on the basis that the immediate striking down of all of Manitoba's laws would offend the rule of law. The practical effect of this decision, however, was that Manitoba translated all of its laws over a period of time supervised by the court.[354] Since that time, as mentioned by Kent Roach, "the use of

---

351 See I. Härtel, *German National Report*, p. 8.

352 In the 1997 proposed reform of the Constitution, which was not approved, one of the reforms aimed to allow the Constitutional Court to postpone the effects of annulment for up to one year. See Francisco Javier Díaz Revorio, *Las sentencias interpretativas del Tribunal Constitucional*, Lex Nova, Valladolid 2001, p. 125 (footnote 166).

353 On the subject of education, see Const. C., Judgment Nos. 370/2003; 13 and 423/2004. See also Gianpaolo Parodi, *Italian National Report*, p. 13.

354 See *Manitoba Language Reference* [1985] 1 S.C.R. 721; Kent Roach, *Canadian National Report*, p. 7 (footnote 8).

suspended declarations of invalidity has increased, though the Court formally maintains that the remedy should only be used in cases where an immediate declaration of invalidity will threaten the rule of law or public safety or deprive people of benefits simply because the benefit has been extended in an unconstitutionally under inclusive manner."[355] Kent Roach also mentions that the South African Constitution follows the Canadian example and specifically provides for suspended declarations of invalidity (article 172). It must be noted, that, although it may have that practical effect, the suspended declaration of invalidity is not a mandatory order that the legislature enact new legislation. The legislature is legally free to do nothing. In such an event, the court's declaration of invalidity takes effect once the period of delay has expired.[356]

In Brazil, in contrast, in the 2006 Law N° 11.417 developing the provision of article 103–B of the Constitution, when regulating the institution known as *súmula vinculante* and establishing the general principle of the immediate effects of the decisions of the Federal Supreme Tribunal, it authorizes the Tribunal to decide for the effects to start in another moment, taking into account legal security reasons or exceptional public interest.[357] The same sort of regulation is found in article 190.3 of the Polish Constitution, where regarding the decisions of the Constitutional Tribunal, after establishing that they shall take effect from the day of its publication, it authorizes the Constitutional Tribunal to specify another date for the end of the binding force of a normative act, a period that may not exceed eighteen months for a statute or twelve months for any other normative act.[358] As has been said by Marek Safjan, "no other organ, except for the constitutional court, may order application of norms declared unconstitutional, which is paradoxical considering that the fundamental role of any constitutional court is to eliminate unconstitutional statutes and not to let them remain in force."[359]

In Spain, the Organic Law on the Constitutional Tribunal has no express provision on this matter, as the Tribunal ruled in Decision 45/1989 that it could not postpone the beginning of the effects of its nullity decision "due to the fact that the Organic Law does not empower the Tribunal, in a different way to what occurs in another system, to postpone or put off the moment of the effectiveness of the nullity."[360] Nonetheless, in subsequent decisions, the Constitutional Tribunal, without legal support, has assumed the power to postpone the beginning of the effects of its

355 See *Schachter v. Canada* [1992] 2 S.C.R. 679; Kent Roach, *Canadian National Report*, p. 8 (footnote 9).

356 See Kent Roach, *Canadian National Report*, p. 8.

357 See Jairo Gilberto Schäfer and Vânia Hack de Almeida, "O controle de constitutionalidade no dereitto brasileiro e a possibilidade de modular os efeitos da decisão de inconstitutionalidade," in *Anuario Iberoamericano de Justicia Constitucional*, N° 12, 2008, Centro de Estudios Políticos y Constitucionales, Madrid 2008, p. 384.

358 See Marek Safjan, *Polish National Report*, p. 4 (footnote 13).

359 *Id.*, p. 6.

360 See STC 45/1989, February 20, 1989, in F. Fernández Segado, *Spanish National Report*, pp. 16–17.

nullity decisions, as was the case of the Law 6/1992 establishing the territorial area of the Santoja y Noja Marsh, considered unconstitutional because it interfered with the competencies of the Autonomous Communities. To avoid any lack of protection regarding the environment, the Tribunal postponed the effects of its annulment up to the moment that the corresponding Autonomous Community exercised its legislative attributions.[361] Although the power the Tribunal assumed was proposed to be incorporated in the 2007 reform of the Organic Law, it was not passed, evidence of the role of the Tribunal as positive legislator on matters of judicial review.[362]

Something similar is accepted in Mexico, where the Supreme Court is empowered to postpone the effects of a decision annulling a statute according to its evaluation of the effects of the legislative vacuum produced by the annulment. No maximum term is established in these cases.[363] In Peru, the Constitutional Tribunal applied *vacatio senenciae* when annulling in 2002 the Fujimori Government's antiterrorist laws, "to allow the democratic legislator in a short and reasonable delay," to issue legislation on procedural matters that could rationally allow for retrials in cases of those already condemned for treason.[364] In Colombia, the Constitutional Court has often postponed the effects of its decisions annulling statutes.[365]

Finally, it must be mentioned that this possibility of postponing the date on which the effects of a decision begin has also been applied in countries with a diffuse system of judicial review, as in Argentina, where the Supreme Court, to avoid chaotic consequences from the immediate application of its declaration of unconstitutionality of a statutory provision, postponed the beginning of the effects for one year after the decision was published.[366] In other cases, the Supreme Court has clearly ruled for future cases, expanding the scope of protection of the declaratory judgments (*acción declarativa de certeza*), regulated by Article 322 of the National Code of Federal Civil and Commercial Procedure. For instance, in the *Rios* case, decided

---

361 See STC 195/1998, October 1, 1998, in F. Fernández Segado, *Spanish National Report*, p. 18.

362 See the critic of F. Fernández Segado, *Spanish National Report*, pp. 13, 17.

363 See Tesis Jurisprudencial P./J 11/2001, in SJFG, Vol. XIV, Sept. 2001, p. 1008. See the reference in Héctor Fix Zamudio and Eduardo Ferrer Mac–Gregor, *Las sentencias de los Tribunales Constitucionales*, Ed. Porrúa, Mexico City 2009, p. 69; and "Las sentencias de los tribunales constitucionales en el ordenamiento mexicano," in *Anuario Iberoamericano de Justicia Constitucional*, N° 12, 2008, Centro de Estudios Políticos y Constitucionales, Madrid 2008, pp. 247–248.

364 See Domingo García Belaúnde and Gerardo Eto Cruz, "Efectos de las sentencias constitucionales en el Perú," in *Anuario Iberoamericano de Justicia Constitucional*, N° 12, 2008, Centro de Estudios Políticos y Constitucionales, Madrid 2008, pp. 283–284; Francisco Eguiguren and Liliana Salomé, *Peruvian National Report I*, p. 10.

365 See, e.g., Decision C–221 of 1997; C–700 of 1999; C–442/01; C–500/01; C–737/01; Germán Alfonso López Daza, *Colombian National Report I*, p. 11 (footnote 26).

366 See *Rosza* case, *Jurisprudencia Argentina*, 2007–III–414, in Néstor P. Sagües, "Los efectos de las sentencias constitucionales en el derecho argentino," in *Anuario Iberoamericano de Justicia Constitucional*, Centro de Estudios Políticos y Constitucionales, N° 12, 2008, Madrid 2008, p. 352.

in 1987, a statute provision providing that only political parties could present candidates to federal elections was challenged because it violated the right to elect and be elected for public office. Even though at the time of the decision the election had passed, the Supreme Court accepted the case, to establish precedent that settles the matter for future cases, thus reaffirming its role as final interpreter of the Constitution and its pretense to expand the effect of its rulings beyond the case being heard.[367]

In the same trend, in the Netherlands, regarding the control of conventionality of statutes, the Supreme Court has postponed the effects of some of its decisions, "true prospective" ones, when the Court does not apply its new interpretation in the case at hand but postpones it.[368]

2. The power of the Constitutional Court to determine when annulled legislation will cease to have effects: retroactive or nonretroactive effects of its own decisions

But regarding the effects of the judicial decisions declaring a statute unconstitutional, another aspect of the temporal effects of the annulment is the retroactive or nonretroactive effects given to the Constitutional Court's decisions. The Court can determine the point in the past at which an annulled legislation ceased to have effects.

This Constitutional Court ruling depends on the nature of the judicial review decision, and it varies according to the system adopted in the given country. If the Court decisions are considered declarative by nature, with *ex tunc* or *ab initio* effects, the judicial review decisions declaring the unconstitutionality of statutes have retroactive effects, and the result is that the statute is considered as if it never had produced effects. If the decisions of the Court declaring a statute unconstitutional are considered constitutive, with *ex nunc* or *pro futuro* effects, the judicial review decisions declaring the statute unconstitutional have nonretroactive effects, not affecting the effects produced by the statute up to its annulment. In some countries, a rule has been established in the statute regulating the Constitutional Court, and in others, the decision to opt for a solution corresponds to the Constitutional Court itself when having the power to determine when the effects of the annulled legislation ceased. In any case, any rigidity on the matter has passed.

A. *The Possibility of Limiting the Retroactive* Ex Tunc *Effects Regarding Declarative Decisions*

In the case of a classical diffuse system of judicial review, as in the United States, the Supreme Court decisions declaring the unconstitutionality of statutes have in principle declarative effects, in the sense of considering the statute null and

---

367 See Fallos 310:819 (1987); Alejandra Rodríguez Galán and Alfredo Mauricio Vítolo, *Argentinean National Report I*, p. 10.

368 See Supreme Court judgment of 12 May 1999, *NJ* 2000/170 (*Labour Expenses Deduction*); J. Uzman, T. Barkhuysen, and M.L. van Emmerik, *Dutch National Report*, p. 26 (footnote 79).

void, as if "it had never been passed"[369] or had never "been made";[370] that is, they are generally considered to have *ex tunc* or retroactive effects. Nonetheless, this initial doctrine has been progressively relaxed, given the possible negative or unjust effects that could be produced by the Court's decisions regarding the effects that the unconstitutional statute has already produced. This was, for instance, specifically highlighted by Justice Clark in *Linkletter v. Walker* (1965), in applying a new constitutional rule to cases previously finalized. The Court said:

> Petitioner contends that our method of resolving those prior cases demonstrates that an absolute rule of retroaction prevails in the area of constitutional adjudication. However, we believe that the constitution neither prohibits nor requires retrospective effect. As Justice Cardozo said, we think the federal constitution has no voice upon the subject. Once the premise is accepted that we are neither required to apply, nor prohibited from applying a decision retrospectively, we must then weigh the merits and demerits in each case by looking to the prior history of the rule in question, its purpose and effect, and whether retrospective operation will further or retard its operation.[371]

Therefore, considering that "the past cannot always be erased by a new judicial decision,"[372] the principle of the retroactive effects of the Supreme Court decisions in constitutional matters has been applied in a relative way. "The questions – said the Supreme Court in *Chicot County Drainage District v. Baxter State Bank* (1940) – are among the most difficult of those that have engaged the attention of courts, state and federal, and it is manifest from numerous decisions that an all–inclusive statement of a principle of absolute retroactive invalidity cannot be justified."[373] The Supreme Court in any case has abandoned the absolute rule[374] and has recognized its authority to give or to deny retroactive effects to its ruling on constitutional issues; the Supreme Courts of the states have done the same during recent decades.

For instance, in criminal matters, the Courts have given full retroactive effects to their rules when they benefit the prosecuted. In particular, they have given retroactive effects to decisions in the field of criminal liability, for example, allowing prisoners on application for *habeas corpus* to secure their release on the grounds that they are held under authority of a statute that, subsequent to their conviction, was held unconstitutional.[375] The Court has also given retroactive effects to its decisions on constitutional matters, when it considers the rules essential to safeguard against the conviction of innocent persons, such as the requirement that counsel be fur-

---

369 See *Norton v. Selby County*, 118 U.S. 425 (1886), p. 442. See the critics to this ruling in J. A. C. Grant, "The Legal Effect of a Ruling That a Statute Is Unconstitutional," *Detroit College of Law Review*, 1978, Nº 2, p. 207, in which he said: "An unconstitutional act may give rise to rights. It may impose duties. It may afford protection. It may even create an office. In short, it may not be as inoperative as though it had never been passed." See also Laurence Claus and Richard S. Kay, *U.S. National Report*, p. 21 (footnote 21).

370 See *Vanhorne's Lessee* v. *Dorrance* case (1795), 2 Dallas 304.

371 See *Linkletter v. Walker*, 381 U.S. 618 (1965).

372 See *Chicot County Drainage District v. Baxter State Bank*, 308 U.S. 371 (1940), p. 374.

373 *Id.*

374 See Laurence Claus and Richard S. Kay, *U.S. National Report*, p. 21.

375 See *Ex parte Siebold*, 100 U.S. 371 (1880).

nished at the trial (*Gideon v. Wainwright*, 327 U.S. 335, 1963), or when the accused is asked to plead (*Arsenault* v. *Massachusetts*, 393 U.S. 5, 1968), or when it is sought to revoke the probation status of a convicted criminal because of his or her subsequent conduct (*McConnell v. Rhay*, 393 U.S. 2, 1968), as well as the rule requiring proof beyond a reasonable doubt (*Ivan v. City of New York*, 407 U.S. 203, 1972). Its ruling concerning the death penalty has also been made fully retroactive (*Witherspoon v. Illinois*, 391 U.S. 510, 1968).[376]

In other criminal cases, the position of the Court has been to give no retroactive effects to its rulings on constitutional issues when it also benefits the prosecuted. As J. A. C. Grant said, in 1977, the Supreme Court held that any change in the interpretation of the Constitution that has the effect of punishing acts that were not penalized under the earlier interpretation cannot be applied retroactively; as it is stated in *Marks v. United States* (1977), "the notion that persons have a right to fair warning of that conduct which will give rise to criminal penalties, is fundamental to our concept of constitutional liberty."[377]

Therefore, the rule of retroactiveness of the effects of the Court's decisions in criminal cases is not absolute and has been applied by the Court in considering the justice of its application in each case. Consequently, when the decision has not, for instance, affected the "fairness of a trial" but only the rights to privacy of a person, the Court has denied the retroactive effects of its ruling.

It must also be mentioned that, even in cases of rules related to the idea of the type of trial necessary to protect against convicting the innocent, the rules established by the Supreme Court have been made wholly prospective when to give them retroactive effect would impose what the Court considers unreasonable burdens on the government brought about at least in part by its reliance on previous rulings of the Supreme Court. This happened in *De Stefano v. Woods* (392 U.S. 631 (1968)), which established that state criminal trials must be by jury, and in *Adam v. Illinois* (405 U.S. 278 (1972)), which established the right to counsel at the preliminary hearing whose retroactivity the Court said "could seriously disrupt the administration of our criminal laws." In contrast, in civil cases, it has been considered that the new rule established in a court decision on constitutional matters cannot disturb property rights or contracts previously made. In this respect, the Supreme Court in *Gelpcke v. Dubuque* (68 U.S. (1 Wall) 175 (1864)) considered that a decision of the Supreme Court of Iowa was to be given prospective effect only:

> The sound and true rule is, that if the contract, when made, was valid by the laws of the state as then expounded . . . and administered in its courts of justice, its validity and. obligation cannot be impaired by any subsequent action of legislation, or decision of its courts altering the construction of the law.

In other countries that have adopted the diffuse system of judicial review, following the U.S. model, as is the case of Argentina, the same modality of mitigating

376 See J. A. C. Grant, *loc. cit.*, p. 237.

377 See *Marks v. United States*, 430 U.S. 188 (1977), p. 191; J. A. C. Grant, *loc. cit.*, 238.

the retroactive effects of the decisions declaring the unconstitutionality of statutes has been adopted.[378]

The same mitigating process regarding the general rule of the retroactive effects of the judicial review decisions has also been developed in countries, like the Netherlands, regarding the control of conventionality of statutes. Departing from the initial general rule of the retroactive effect of the Supreme Court rulings on the matter, since the 1970s, as referred to by J. Uzman, T. Barkhuysen, and M. L. van Emmerik. These have embraced a lawmaking duty, openly discussing the consequences of judicial review decisions and giving in some cases prospective effects –called qualified prospective decisions– when the Court immediately applies its new interpretation or rule but limits the possibilities for other parties than those in the case at hand to appeal to the new rule. An example is the 1981 *Boon v. Van Loon* case, where the Court changed its case law on the ownership of pensions in divorce law[379] but explicitly limited the temporal effect of its new course to the case at hand and future cases. Where the divorce had already been pronounced, no appeal to the new rule would be possible.[380]

However, it must be mentioned that not all countries following the concentrated system of judicial review have adopted the constitutive effects of the decision annulling the unconstitutional statute. In Germany, for instance, the proclaimed principle is the contrary one. As a matter of principle, the decisions of the Federal Constitutional Tribunal when annulling a statute have *ex tunc* and *eo ipse* effects, considering that the annulled statute should never have produced legal effects.[381] Nonetheless, in practice the reality is another, and it is not common to find decisions annulling statutes with purely *ex tunc* effects, except if with the *ex tunc* annulment of the statute the situation of conformity with the Constitution is immediately reestablished.[382] In contrast, the Law regulating the functions of the Federal Constitutional Tribunal establishes in article 95.1 the possible *ex tunc* effects on criminal matters, prescribing that "new proceedings may be instituted in accordance with the provisions of the Code of Criminal Procedure against a final conviction based on a rule which has been declared incompatible with the Basic Law or null and void in accordance with Article 78 above or on the interpretation of a rule which the Federal Constitutional Court has declared incompatible with the Basic Law." In article 95.2, it adds that, "in all other respects, subject to the provisions of Article 95 (2) below or

378 See *Itzcovich* case, *Jurispudencia Argentina* 2005–II–723, in Néstor P. Sagües, "Los efectos de las sentencias constitucionales en el derecho argentino," in *Anuario Iberoamericano de Justicia Constitucional*, Centro de Estudios Políticos y Constitucionales, N° 12, 2008, Madrid 2008, p. 351.

379 See Supreme Court judgment of 27 November 1981, *NJ* 1982/503 (*Boon v. Van Loon*); J. Uzman, T. Barkhuysen, and M. L. van Emmerik, *Dutch National Report*, p. 42 (footnote 138).

380 See J. Uzman, T. Barkhuysen, and M. L. van Emmerik, *Dutch National Report*, pp. 41–42.

381 See I. Härtel, *German National Report*, p. 10.

382 See Francisco Fernández Segado, *Spanish National Report*, pp. 8, 14.

a specific statutory provision, final decisions based on a rule declared null and void pursuant to Article 78 above shall remain unaffected."[383]

In Poland, the decisions of the Constitutional Tribunal annulling statutes according to article 190.4 of the Constitution imply, in addition to the ban on application of the unconstitutional norm in the future, an opportunity to modify past decisions issued, for instance, by courts and administrative organs on the basis of the provisions found unconstitutional, before the judgment was passed. Such provision states that the Constitutional Tribunal's decision "shall be a basis for re–opening proceedings, or for quashing the decision or other settlement in a manner and on principles specified in provisions applicable to the given proceedings."[384]

In Portugal, the effects given to the annulment decisions of the Constitutional Tribunal are also retroactive, although article 282.4 of the Constitution limits the retroactivity of the decision when motives of juridical security, equity, or public interests prevent application of the retroactive principle.[385] Also in Brazil, decisions delivered by the Supreme Federal Tribunal applying the concentrated method of judicial review of the constitutionality of laws normally have *ex tunc* or retroactive effects. Nevertheless, as pointed out by Thomas Bustamante, "the Supreme Court may restrict the effects of the pronouncement of unconstitutionality of a law to deliver *ex nunc* or *pro futuro* decisions or even to determine that the pronouncement of unconstitutionality will produce effects only after a deadline to be set by the Court. There are, however, some requirements for delivering such manipulative decisions: (i) there must be reasons of legal certainty or of (ii) exceptional social interest and, apart from that, (iii) the restriction or the exception to the retroactive efficacy of the decision must be established by a vote of at least two thirds of the members of the Court (in its plenary sitting)."[386]

B. *The Possibility of Retroactive Effects for* Ex Nunc *Constitutive Decisions*

In the concentrated system of judicial review, the initial principle adopted according to Kelsen's thoughts in the Austrian 1920 Constitution was the one of the

383 Cf. Francisco Fernández Segado, "Algunas reflexiones generales en torno a los efectos de las sentencias de inconstitucionalidad y a la relatividad de ciertas fórmulas estereotipadas vinculadas a ellas," in *Anuario Iberoamericano de Justicia Constitucional*, Centro de Estudios Políticos y Constitucionales, N° 12, 2008, Madrid 2008, pp. 190–191.

384 See Marek Safjan, *Polish National Report*, p. 5.

385 See María Fernanda Palma, "O legislador negativo e o interprete da Constitucão," in *Anuario Iberoamericano de Justicia Constitucional*, Centro de Estudios Políticos y Constitucionales, N° 12, 2008, Madrid 2008, pp. 174, 329; Francisco Fernández Segado, "Algunas reflexiones generales en torno a los efectos de las sentencias de inconstitucionalidad y a la relatividad de ciertas fórmulas esterotipadas vinculadas a ellas," in *Anuario Iberoamericano de Justicia Constitucional*, Centro de Estudios Políticos y Constitucionales, N° 12, 2008, Madrid 2008, p. 174; Iván Escobar Fornos, *Estudios Jurídicos*, Vol. I, Ed. Hispamer, Managua 2007, p. 493; Joaquim de Sousa Ribeiro and Esperança Mealha, *Portuguese National Report*, pp. 6.

386 See Law N° 9.882 of December 3, 1999: art. 11; and Law N° 9.868 of November 10, 1999: art. 27; in Thomas Bustamante and Evanlida de Godoi Bustamante, *Brazilian National Report*, p. 26.

constitutive effects of the constitutional courts decision annulling a statute, in the sense that its annulment, similar to the effects of the repeal, implied that the statute produced effects up to the moment in which its annulment was established.[387] According to this rule, the statute whose nullity is declared and established is considered, in principle, by the Court as having been valid up to that moment. That is why in these cases the decision of the Court has *ex nunc* and *pro futuro* or prospective effects, in the sense that, in principle, they do not go back to the moment of the enactment of the statute considered unconstitutional, and the effects produced by the annulled statute until annulment are considered valid. The legislative act declared unconstitutional by the Constitutional Court in concentrated systems of judicial review, therefore, are considered a valid act until its annulment by the court, having produced complete effects until the moment when the court annuls it. Only the interested party that initiated a concrete case of judicial review of a legislative act (*Anlassfall*) can benefit from an exemption to the *ex nunc* rule.[388] Nevertheless, only in Austria does the Court have powers to annul statutes or decrees already repealed, that consequently are without formal validity (Art. 139, 4; Art. 140, 4), which, in principle, supposes some retroactive effects of the judicial review and is an exception to the *ex nunc* effects.

Other countries that, though they follow the general principle of nonretroactive effects of annulments, have reached the same practical effects,[389] even when the contrary (nonretroactive effect) is expressly established in the Constitution, as is the case in Italy with article 136 of the Constitution. The Constitutional Court has interpreted this provision in the sense that the declaration of unconstitutionality of a statute makes it inapplicable to all trials pending decision with *res judicata* force, in the same sense as if it were a *ius superveniens*.[390] Nonetheless, regarding cases already decided, particularly in criminal cases, the retroactive effects of the annulment are accepted when a judicial condemnation has been pronounced on the basis of a statute declared unconstitutional, in which case its execution and its criminal effects must cease (Art. 30, Statute N° 87, 1953). Another indirect exception of the *ex nunc* effects of the decision results from the possibility of annulment of statutes already repealed.

In Spain, according to the provisions of the Constitution, the Constitutional Tribunal's declaration of unconstitutionality or declaration of nullity of a statute means its annulment, and the declaration has *ex nunc*, *pro futuro* effects.[391] That is why the Constitution expressly establishes that "the decisions already adopted in judicial

---

387 See Hans Kelsen, "El control de la constitucionalidad de las leyes. Estudio comparado de las constituciones austriaca y americana," in Revista Iberoamericana de Derecho procesal Constitucional, N° 12, Editorisl Porrúa, Mexico 2009, pp.7–8..

388 See Konrad Lachmayer, *Austrian National Report*, pp. 7–8.

389 See Gianpaolo Parodi, *Italian National Report*, p. 13.

390 See Decision N° 3491, 1957. See the reference in F. Rubio Llorente, *La Corte Constitucional italiana*, Universidad Central de Venezuela, Caracas 1966, p. 30.

391 See J. Arosemena Sierra, "El recurso de inconstitucionalidad," in *El Tribunal Constitucional*, Instituto de Estudios Fiscales, Madrid 1981, Vol. I, p. 171.

proceedings will not lose their *res judicata* value" (article 161.1.a). The Organic Law of the Tribunal also establishes, "The decisions which declare the unconstitutionality of statutes, dispositions or acts with force of law[,] will not allow the review of judicial proceedings ended by decisions with *res judicata* force in which the unconstitutional act would have been applied" (article 40.1). However, as is the general trend in the concentrated system in granting nonretroactive effects to judicial review decisions, the exception to the *ex nunc* effects is established regarding criminal cases, where a limited retroactive effect is allowed and is extended to administrative justice decisions in cases of administrative sanction cases.[392]

A similar situation can be found in Peru, where the general principle established in article 204 of the Constitution and article 89 of the Constitutional Procedural Code is that the decisions annulling statutes have *pro futuro* effects and are not retroactive. Nonetheless, the same provisions of the Code as applied by the Constitutional Tribunal establish that, in taxation cases, the nullity can produce retroactive effects, which can also be determined by the Constitutional Tribunal.[393] Regarding annulment of statutes in criminal matters, the same principle is also applied by interpretation of article 103 of the Constitution (principle of retroactivity of the law), which allows for the exceptional retroactive effects of the laws in criminal matters.[394]

In France, in the constitutional reform sanctioned on matters of judicial review in 2008 (Constitutional Law 2008–724, of July 23, 2008), it was established that the Constitutional Council's decisions declaring unconstitutional a provision according to article 61–1 of the Constitution are considered repealed since the publication of the decision, as the Constitutional Council is authorized to determine when and how the effects that the annulled provision has produced in the past can be affected.[395]

In the case of Croatia, where decisions of the Constitutional Court have *ex nunc* effect, the final judicial decisions for a criminal offense grounded on the legal provi-

392 See Francisco Javier Díaz Revorio, *Las sentencias interpretativas del Tribunal Constitucional*, Ed. Lex Nova, Valladolid 2001, pp. 104–105, 126–127; Francisco Fernández Segado, "Algunas reflexiones generales en torno a los efectos de las sentencias de inconstitucionalidad y a la relatividad de ciertas fórmulas esterotipadas vinculadas a ellas," in *Anuario Iberoamericano de Justicia Constitucional*, Centro de Estudios Políticos y Constitucionales, N° 12, 2008, Madrid 2008, pp. 192–194.

393 See Decision STC 0041–2004–AI/TC, FJ 70, in Domingo García Belaúnde and Gerardo Eto Cruz, "Efectos de las sentencias constitucionales en el Perú," in *Anuario Iberoamericano de Justicia Constitucional*, Centro de Estudios Políticos y Constitucionales, N° 12, 2008, Madrid 2008, pp. 281–282.

394 See Decision STC 0019–2005–AI/TC, FJ 52, in Domingo García Belaúnde and Gerardo Eto Cruz, "Efectos de las sentencias constitucionales en el Perú," in *Anuario Iberoamericano de Justicia Constitucional*, Centro de Estudios Políticos y Constitucionales, N° 12, 2008, Madrid 2008, pp. 281–283.

395 See Francisco Fernández Segado, "Algunas reflexiones generales en torno a los efectos de las sentencias de inconstitucionalidad y a la relatividad de ciertas fórmulas esterotipadas vinculadas a ellas," in *Anuario Iberoamericano de Justicia Constitucional*, Centro de Estudios Políticos y Constitucionales, N° 12, 2008, Madrid 2008, p. 175.

sion that has been repealed due to its unconstitutionality do not produce legal effects from the day the Constitutional Court's decision takes effect, and the criminal judicial ruling may be changed by the appropriate application of the provisions in renewed criminal proceedings. Regarding noncriminal offence cases, since 2002, the right to demand the issuing of a new individual act or decision is conferred only to those individuals and legal persons who submitted to the Constitutional Court a proposal to review the constitutionality of the provision of a law. In such cases, the request for changing the individual act should be submitted within a term of six months from the publication of the Court's decision.[396] In Serbia, the general principle of the effects of the Constitutional Court decisions when annulling a law are *ex nunc*. Nonetheless, there are some exceptions to the *pro futuro* effects, as decisions can affect individual legal relationships retroactively. As referred to by Boško Tripković, the Court's decision can have retroactive consequences, although not *ex tunc*, in the sense that everyone whose right has been violated by a final or legally binding individual act adopted on the basis of a law determined unconstitutional by a decision of the Constitutional Court is entitled to demand from the competent authority a revision of that individual act. Nevertheless, this right to revision has certain restrictions: first, proposals for revision may be submitted within six months from the day of the publication of the Constitutional Court's decision in the Official Gazette; second, the revision is restricted to acts delivered within two years before the submission of the proposal or initiative for judicial review (Article 60 of the Law on Constitutional Court).[397]

In the Slovak Republic, article 41b of Act N° 38/1993 regulating the Proceedings before the Court states, as mentioned by Ján Svák and Lucia Berdisová, "if a judgment issued in a criminal proceeding based on the regulation that is in inconformity with the Constitution has not been executed, then the ruling of the Constitutional Court on inconformity is a reason for a retrial." The valid decisions issued in civil and administrative proceedings remains unaffected, but obligations imposed by such a decision cannot be subject to enforcement.[398]

The legislative provision does not clearly establish the *ex nunc* effects of the Constitutional Court's decision, as this is a matter in which the case law of the Constitutional Court has settled the rules to be applicable. In effect, in one case, the Constitutional Court had to decide whether it would protect legal certainty and thus not allow the retroactive effect of the ruling (decision on *ex nunc* effect) or would protect the principle of constitutionality and so not allow any application of the regulation that is known to be unconstitutional (decision on *ex tunc* effect); being both, the principle of legal certainty and the principle of constitutionality, fundamental principles of rule of law. Finally, the Constitutional Court decided that it would protect the principle of constitutionality because it was inadmissible to apply the principle of legal certainty absolutely, and it decided that the ruling had ex *tunc* sub-

---

396 See Sanja Barić and Petar Bačić, *Croatian National Report*, p. 8.

397 See Boško Tripković, *Serbian National Report*, p. 17.

398 See Ján Svák and Lucia Berdisová, *Slovak National Report*, p. 6. See also Decision III. ÚS 164/07. *Id.*, p. 8.

stantive effect. This means that a judge of the ordinary court cannot apply a regulation that is in inconformity with the Constitution. The Constitutional Court thus *de facto* set up a doctrine on the substantial effects of the rulings on inconformity between legal regulation, which is not yet deeply developed.[399]

In other countries, the nonretroactive effects of annulment have been expressly established in the Constitutions, without the aforementioned exception, as in the case of Ecuador[400] and Chile.[401]

In Bolivia, the same principle of the *ex nunc* effects of the Constitutional Tribunal decisions annulling a statute applies but with the exception regarding cases of formal *res judicata* and on criminal matters if the retroactivity affects harms the legal situation of the condemned.[402] In Nicaragua, article 182 of the Constitution assigns retroactive effects to the annulment decisions of statutes by the Supreme Court, although on matters of amparo, the same Constitution produces only *pro futuro* effects.[403]

In many other cases, like in Venezuela, although the general rule in principle has been *ex nunc*, nonretroactive effects of the Constitutional Chamber's decisions annulling statutes, the Law on the Supreme Tribunal expressly leaves to the Constitutional Chamber the power to determine the temporal effects of its judicial review decisions, which depending on the case, can have retroactive effects or not.[404] The same occurs in Brazil, where the Constitution empowers the Federal Constitutional Tribunal to always decide the temporal effects of its decisions and to determine

---

399 In the opinion of Ján Svák and Lucia Berdisová, the Constitutional Court of the Czech Republic advocates a bit more "sophisticated" doctrine. That is, the court prefers *ex tunc* substantive effects of the rulings on inconformity of legal regulation on the proceedings that are not validly decided only if the *ex nunc* effect would infringe the fundamental rights and freedoms of aggrieved persons. And so a judge of an ordinary court can apply unconstitutional regulation if the fundamental rights and freedoms will not be infringed. See, e.g., decision of the Constitutional Court of the Czech Republic N° IV.ÚS 1777/07 and other decisions mentioned there. See Ján Svák and Lucia Berdisová, *Slovak National Report*, p. 8 (footnote 11).

400 See Hernán Salgado Pesantes, "Los efectos de las sentencias del Tribunal Constitucional del Ecuador," in *Anuario Iberoamericano de Justicia Constitucional*, Centro de Estudios Políticos y Constitucionales, N° 12, 2008, Madrid 2008, p. 362.

401 Art. 94.3. See Humberto Nogueira Alcalá, "La sentencia constitucional en Chile: Aspectos fundamentales sobre su fuerza vinculante," in *Anuario Iberoamericano de Justicia Constitucional*, Centro de Estudios Políticos y Constitucionales, N° 12, 2008, Madrid 2008, p. 297.

402 See Decision S.C 1426/2005–R of November 8, 2005, in Pablo Dermisaky Peredo, "Efectos de las sentencias constitucionales en Bolivia," in *Anuario Iberoamericano de Justicia Constitucional*, Centro de Estudios Políticos y Constitucionales, N° 12, 2008, Madrid 2008, p. 86.

403 See Iván Escobar Fornos, "Las sentencias constitucionales y sus efectos en Nicaragua," in *Anuario Iberoamericano de Justicia Constitucional*, Centro de Estudios Políticos y Constitucionales, N° 12, 2008, Madrid 2008, p. 101.

404 See Allan R. BREWER–CARÍAS, "Algunas consideraciones sobre el control jurisdiccional de la constitucionalidad de los actos estatales en el derecho venezolano," *Revista de Administración Pública*, N° 76, Madrid 1975, pp. 419–446; BREWER–CARÍAS, *Justicia constitucional: Procesos y procedimientos constitucionales*, Universidad Nacional Autónoma de México, Mexico City 2007, pp. 343 ff.

when they begin,[405] and in Costa Rica, where, to sustain legal security, the Law on the Constitutional Jurisdiction empowered the Constitutional Chamber of the Supreme Court to determine the temporal effects of the judicial review decision. In Mexico, the exception to the nonretroactive effects of Supreme Court decisions annulling statutes refers to criminal matters when it benefits the prosecuted.[406]

In Colombia, the Law regulating the Judicial Power (article 45) provided that the Constitutional Court decisions have *pro futuro* effects, except if the Court decided the contrary. In addition, article 51 of Law N° 1836 of the Constitutional Court prevented the Court from giving retroactive effects to its decisions, if they were to affect formal *res judicata*,[407]a provision that the Court declared unconstitutional because it limited its functions. The Court argued that, according to the Constitution, the Court is the sole arbiter to determine the effects of its own decisions.[408] Consequently, the Constitutional Court has the powers to determine the temporal effects of its own decisions and, for instance, to give retroactive effects to them, a matter that it has found that not even the Legislator can regulate.

3. The power of Constitutional Courts to revive repealed legislation

As a matter of principle, as Hans Kelsen wrote in 1928, judicial review decisions declaring null a statutory provision adopted by a Constitutional Court do not imply the revival of the former legislation that the annulled statute repeals; that is, they do not reestablish the legislation already repealed.[409] Nonetheless, the contrary principle is the one applied in Portugal, where the declaration of unconstitutionality with general binding force has negative force of law, as it directly annuls the unconstitutional rule, thus producing as a consequence that "the legal provisions which had been amended or repealed by the norm declared unconstitutional are revived from the date on which the decision of the Constitutional Court becomes effective, unless the Constitutional Court determines otherwise (article 282 (1 and 4) of the Constitu-

---

405 See Jairo Gilberto Schäfer and Vânia Hack de Almeida, "O controle de constitucionalidade no dereito brasileiro e a possibilitade de modular os effeitos de decisão de inconstitucionalidade," in *Anuario Iberoamericano de Justicia Constitucional*, Centro de Estudios Políticos y Constitucionales, N° 12, 2008, Madrid 2008, pp. 383–384.

406 See Tesis Jurisprudencial P/J. 74/79, in Héctor Fix Zamudio and Eduardo Ferrer Mac–Gregor, *Las sentencias de los Tribunales Constitucionales*, Ed. Porrúa, Mexico City 2009, p. 69; and "Las sentencias de los Tribunales Constitucionales en el ordenamiento mexicano," in *Anuario Iberoamericano de Justicia Constitucional*, Centro de Estudios Políticos y Constitucionales, N° 12, 2008, Madrid 2008, p. 248.

407 See Humberto Nogueira Alcalá, "La sentencia constitucional en Chile: Aspectos fundamentales sobre su fuerza vinculante," in *Anuario Iberoamericano de Justicia Constitucional*, Centro de Estudios Políticos y Constitucionales, N° 12, 2008, Madrid 2008, p. 297.

408 See Decision C–113 of 1993, in Iván Escobar Fornos, "Las sentencias constitucionales y sus efectos en Nicaragua," in *Anuario Iberoamericano de Justicia Constitucional*, Centro de Estudios Políticos y Constitucionales, N° 12, 2008, Madrid 2008, p. 112; and in *Estudios Jurídicos*, Vol. I, Ed. Hispamer, Managua 2007, p. 511.

409 See Hans Kelsen, *La garantía jurisdiccional de la Constitución (La justicia constitucional)*, Universidad Nacional Autónoma de México, Mexico City 2001, p. 84.

tion."[410] In Belgium, the revival of the repealed legal provisions as a consequence of the annulment of a statute is the general rule.[411] In Austria, the annulment of statutes by the Constitutional Court can have the consequence that other statutes previously repealed by the annulled one will restart their validity beginning on the day in which the annulment is effective, unless the Tribunal decides otherwise (Article 140.6).

This is a matter that in other countries has been decided by the Constitutional Tribunal. For instance, in Poland, in a decision concerning pension regulation, the Constitutional Tribunal directly ordered the restoration of the provision that had earlier been in force and did not contain elements considered unconstitutional.[412] In Mexico, the Supreme Tribunal has decided, particularly in electoral matters, that the nullity of a statute implies the revival of the legislation that was in force before the annulled statute was sanctioned. The decision was adopted to avoid a legislative vacuum, which could affect the legal security on the matter.[413] In Costa Rica, the Constitutional Chamber, when annulling statutes on forestry, tenancy, and monetary matters, decided to revive the legislation that the annulled statute had repealed.[414]

IV. THE DEFORMATION OF THE INTERPRETATIVE PRINCIPLE: CONSTITUTIONAL COURTS' REFORMING OF STATUTES AND INTERPRETING THEM WITHOUT INTERPRETING THE CONSTITUTION

Constitutional courts are interpreters of the Constitution, not interpreters of statutes, except when they do so in connection or in contrast with the Constitution. That is, constitutional courts can only interpret statutes when interpreting the Constitution, to declare a statute unconstitutional, to reject its alleged unconstitutionality, or to establish an interpretation of the statute according to or in harmony with the Constitution. That is, when interpreting statutes, the Constitutional Court is always obliged to do so by interpreting the Constitution, as their function is not to interpret

410 See Joaquim de Sousa Ribeiro and Esperança Mealha, *Portuguese National Report*, pp. 6–7; and Jairo Gilberto Schäfer and Vânia Hack de Almeida, "O controle de constitucionalidade no dereito brasileiro e a possibilitade de modular os effeitos de decisão de inconstitucionalidade," in *Anuario Iberoamericano de Justicia Constitucional*, Centro de Estudios Políticos y Constitucionales, N° 12, 2008, Madrid 2008, p. 377.

411 See Christian Behrendt, *Le judge constitutionnel, un législateur–cadre positif. Un analyse comparative en droit francais, belge et allemande*, Bruylant, Brussels 2006, pp. 280, 281, 436–437.

412 Decision of 20 December 1999, K 4/99; Marek Safjan, *Polish National Report*, p. 5 (footnote 12).

413 See Tesis Jurisprudencial P./J. 86/2007, SJFG, Vol. 26, December 2007, p. 778. See the reference in Héctor Fix Zamudio and Eduardo Ferrer Mac–Gregor, *Las sentencias de los Tribunales Constitucionales*, Ed. Porrúa, Mexico City 2009, pp. 63–64, 74; and "Las sentencias de los Tribunales Constituticonales en el ordenamiento mexicano," in *Anuario Iberoamericano de Justicia Constitucional*, Centro de Estudios Políticos y Constitucionales, N° 12, 2008, Madrid 2008, p. 252.

414 See Iván Escobar Fornos, *Estudios Jurídicos*, Vol. I, Ed. Hispamer, Managua 2007, p. 513; and in "Las sentencias constitucionales y sus efectos en Nicaragua," in *Anuario Iberoamericano de Justicia Constitucional*, Centro de Estudios Políticos y Constitucionales, N° 12, 2008, Madrid 2008, p. 114.

statutes in isolation, without any interpretation of the Constitution, as this last task generally corresponds to ordinary courts.

As Iván Escobar Fornos has pointed out, "a constitutional judge cannot interpret or correct a statute unless it is done regarding its constitutionality; corresponding the task of interpreting the law to ordinary courts."[415] In such cases, constitutional ccourts interpret the Constitution and the law, but the sole interpretation of a statute when no interpretation of the Constitution is made is no more that a legislative reform of a statute by the Constitutional Court. As explained by Francisco Díaz Revorio:

> In order for an interpretative decision to be within the functions of the constitutional court, it is necessary that the interpretation, or the normative content that the constitutional court establishes in harmony with the Constitution, be really the consequence of the constitutional requirement, and the result of a "new" provision without constitutional foundation.[416]

In the same sense, it must be emphasized that constitutional courts are not allowed to create law *ex novo* or to reform statutes, even in matters of judicial review. As the Constitutional Tribunal of Bolivia said in 2005, constitutional courts

> only establish the sense and scope of legal provisions, without creating of modifying a new legal text. In this sense, the provision interpreted by the Courts does not constitute itself in a new legal provision, due to the fact that the judicial authority by mean of interpretation does not create different provisions.[417]

In the same sense, the Constitutional Tribunal of Peru has said:

> [I]n a different way as the Congress that can ex novo create law within the constitutional framework, the interpretative decisions [of the Constitutional Tribunal] can only determine a provision of law from a direct derivation of constitutional provisions as a *secundum constitutionem* interpretation.[418]

Nonetheless, despite these self–imposed limits, in many cases, a clear interference of the constitutional courts regarding legislative functions, surpassing the assistance or cooperative framework, has ended in extending the text of the interpreted statutes far beyond its literal meaning, modifying the intention or purpose of the original legislator, which are the two main limits of interpretative decisions.[419] Consequently, in many cases, interpretative decisions adopted by constitutional courts

---

415 See Iván Escobar Fornos, *Estudios Jurídicos*, Vol. I, Ed. Hispamer, Managua 2007, p. 497; and "Las sentencias constitucionales y sus efectos en Nicaragua," in *Anuario Iberoamericano de Justicia Constitucional*, Centro de Estudios Políticos y Constitucionales, N° 12, 2008, Madrid 2008, pp. 104.

416 See Francisco Javier Díaz Revorio, *Las sentencias interpretativas del Tribunal Constitucional*, Lex Nova, Valladolid 2001, pp. 296–297.

417 See Decision S.C 1426/2005–R. of November 8, 2005, in Pablo Dermizaky Peredo, "Efectos de las sentencias constitucionales en Bolivia," in *Anuario Iberoamericano de Justicia Constitucional*, Centro de Estudios Políticos y Constitucionales, N° 12, 2008, Madrid 2008, p. 86.

418 See Decision of February 2, 2006. STC 0030–2005; Fernán Altuve Febres, *Peruvian National Report II*, pp. 27–28.

419 See Francisco Fernández Segado, *Spanish National Report*, p. 20.

have hidden decisions of clear normative content;[420] in them, the Constitutional Court assumes a clear role as positive legislator and even denaturalizes the will of the Legislator. This has been noticed, for instance, in Germany[421] and in Spain.

Referring to the Spanish Constitutional Tribunal's practice of interpreting statutes according to the Constitution, Francisco Fernández Segado has highlighted its "abusive and perverted use," as in decision STC101/2008 of July 24, 2008,[422] where the Tribunal decided an action of unconstitutionality of an article of the Regulation of the Senate, reformed in 2007, after the reform of the Organic Law 6/2007 of the Tribunal. In the latter, a new procedure was established for the appointment by the King of the Members of the Constitutional Tribunal (article 16.1), which stated: "The Magistrates proposed by the Senate will be selected among the candidates nominated by the Legislative Assemblies of the Autonomous Communities in the terms provided by the Regulation of the Chamber [Senate]." The statute's provision was binding in that the Senate, in such case, has no discretion in the selection of the four candidates it must select, which ought to be selected among those nominated by the Autonomous Communities. Nonetheless, an exception was introduced in the Senate's Regulation (article 184.b) allowing the Senate to choose the candidate only when the said Legislative Assemblies would not propose "enough candidates" (*candidatos suficientes*) in the prescribed term, a condition hardly to be applied because in Spain there are exist seventeen Legislative Assemblies, each of which can propose up to two candidates each (a total of thirty–four candidates).[423] Eventually, when deciding the action of unconstitutionality, the Tribunal dismissed it, changing the unequivocal will expressed by the Legislator, and established that the expression "enough candidates" referred not only to a numerical matter but also to a subjective matter regarding the suitability (*idoneidad*) of the candidates according to their evaluation by the Senate. This allowed the parliamentary groups of the Senate to propose candidates in a way contradicting the provision of article 26.1 of the Organic Law of the Tribunal. That is, through an interpretative decision, the Constitutional Court produced a new norm *contra legem*.[424]

A case of this sort – also a case of the pathology of judicial review – can also be identified in Venezuela. In effect, according to Articles 335 and 336 of the Consti-

420 See Francisco Javier Díaz Revorio, *Las sentencias interpretativas del Tribunal Constitucional*, Lex Nova, Valladolid 2001, p. 97.

421 See, e.g., Helmut Simón, "La jurisdicción constitucional," in Benda et al., *Manual de derecho constitucional*, Instituto Vasco de Administración Pública, Marcial Pons, Madrid 1996, pp. 853–854.

422 See Francisco Fernández Segado, "Algunas reflexiones generales en torno a los efectos de las sentencias de inconstitucionalidad y a la relatividad de ciertas fórmulas esterotipadas vinculadas a ellas," in *Anuario Iberoamericano de Justicia Constitucional*, Centro de Estudios Políticos y Constitucionales, N° 12, 2008, Madrid 2008, p. 167.

423 That is why Francisco Fernández Segado considers it a case of "science fiction," in Francisco Fernández Segado, *Spanish National Report*, p. 35.

424 See the comments in Francisco Fernández Segado, *La justicia constitucional: Una visión de derecho comparado*, Ed. Dykingson, Madrid 2009, Vol. III, pp. 1031 ff.; F. Fernández Segado, *Spanish National Report*, pp. 35–38.

tution, the Supreme Tribunal is the "highest and final interpreter" of the Constitution, as its role is to ensure a "uniform interpretation and application" of the Constitution and "the supremacy and effectiveness of constitutional norms and principles." For such purpose, the 1999 Constitution created the Constitutional Chamber within the Supreme Tribunal, as constitutional jurisdiction (Articles 266,1 and 262), with the exclusive powers to annul statutes (Article 334). To implement the concentrated method of judicial review, the Constitution provides for different means or recourse to the courts, including the popular action for unconstitutionality of statutes, which any citizen can file directly before the Constitutional Division.

In addition, as argued herein, the Constitutional Chamber, without any constitutional or legal support, created in Decision 1077 of September 22, 2000,[425] a recourse for the abstract interpretation of the Constitution, through which any citizen, including public Officers and the Attorney General, can fill a petition to obtain from the Supreme Tribunal a declarative ruling to clarify the content of legal or constitutional provisions. In these cases, the Constitutional Chamber can establish binding interpretations of the Constitution and of a provision of a statute related to the interpretation of the Constitution, but it is not empowered to establish in isolation binding interpretations of statutory provisions without any parallel interpretation of a constitutional provision. That is, a petition of interpretation regarding a particular statute must be filed only before the Politico–Administrative Chamber of the Supreme Tribunal or the other Chambers; it cannot be filed before the Constitutional Chamber. Consequently, the latter cannot issue interpretations of a statute without interpreting the Constitution; if it does, it is illegitimately interpreting the Constitution.

Nonetheless, the latter occurred in Venezuela, with Decision N° 1541 of June 14, 2008 of the Constitutional Chamber.[426] In that case, a petition to interpret article 258 of the Constitution, filed by the Attorney General of the Republic, the Constitutional Chamber without interpreting such provision –which needed no interpretation at all– decided to interpret article 22 of the 1999 Protection and Promotion of the Investment Law, according to the sense that the Attorney General proposed and asked, that is, to deny that such article contained a general open offer of consent given by the Venezuelan State to submit disputes regarding investment to international arbitration. Article 258 of the Constitution, whose "interpretation" was requested, in fact and legally, required no interpretation at all. It states: "The law shall promote arbitration, conciliation, mediation and any other alternative means of dispute resolution." As there is nothing obscure, ambiguous, or inoperative in this provision, it is obvious that the real purpose of the official petition of constitutional interpretation filed by the representative of the Executive was not to obtain a clarifying interpretation of Article 258 of the Constitution, but to obtain an interpretation of Article 22 of the In-

425 See Decision N° 1,077 of September 22, 2000, *Servio Tulio León Briceño* case, *Revista de Derecho Público*, N° 83, Editorial Jurídica Venezolana, Caracas 2000, pp. 247 ff.

426 See Decision 1541 of June 14, 2008, in *Official Gazette* N° 39055 of October 17, 2008.

vestment Law so that it would not contain the State's unilateral consent for international arbitration. In particular, the Attorney General requested from the Constitutional Chamber a declaration that "Article 22 of the 'Investment Law' may not be interpreted in the sense that it constitutes the consent of the State to be subjected to international arbitration" and "that Article 22 of the Investment Law does not contain a unilateral arbitration offer, in other words, it does not overrule the absence of an express declaration made in writing by the Venezuelan authorities to submit to international arbitration, nor has this declaration been made in any bilateral agreement expressly containing such a provision."[427] As was said in the Dissent Vote in the decision, the petition of interpretation eventually had the purpose of obtaining from the Constitutional Chamber a "legal opinion" by means of *a priori* judicial review, which does not exist in Venezuela, thus implying the exercise of a "legislative function" by the Constitutional Chamber.[428]

In another case decided by the same Constitutional Chamber, by means of Decision N° 511 of April 5, 2004,[429] the Court established *ex officio*, that is, without any relation with the particular case at hand, the rules of procedure applicable in the proceedings to be followed by any of the other Chambers of the Supreme Tribunal of Justice when they decide to assume or take over any judicial cause and process from lower courts for their decision (*avocamiento*) at the Supreme Tribunal. In this case, the Chamber did not interpret any constitutional provision, because this exceptional takeover proceeding (*avocamiento*) regarding cases from lower courts is not a constitutional institution and is regulated only in the Organic Law of the Supreme Tribunal. Thus, usurping legislative functions in this case, the Constitutional Court acted as a direct and *ex officio* positive legislator and created rules of procedure without interpreting the Constitution.

Nonetheless, the extreme case of the pathology of judicial review regarding the relation of constitutional courts with the Legislator and its existing legislation occurs when the former proceeds to "reform" pieces of legislation, openly acting as positive legislator. In effect, one of the most elemental principles in constitutional law is that statutes can be reformed only by other statutes, and consequently, only the Legislator's action can reform statutes. The contrary would be an action contrary to the Constitution, whether it is the Executive that pretends to reform acts of Parliament or any other organ of the State different from the Legislator itself.

In this regard, one of the most astonishing decisions issued by the Constitutional Chamber of the Venezuelan Supreme Tribunal of Justice to "reform" statutes was issued in 2007. Here, the Chamber, *ex officio* and in *obiter dictum*, regarding a provision of the Income Tax Law that in the particular case it was resolving and was not even challenged on unconstitutional grounds, decided to reform that law. In ef-

427 *Id.*

428 *Id.*

429 See Decision N° 511 of April 5, 2004, *Maira Rincón Lugo* case; http://www.tsj.gov.ve/decisiones/scon/Abril/511–050404–04–0418..%20.htm. See also Daniela Urosa Maggi, *Venezuelan National Report*, pp. 18–19.

fect, in Decision N° 301 of February 27, 2007,[430] after rejecting a popular action of unconstitutionality filed in 2001 against articles 67, 68, 69, 72, 74, and 79 of the 1999 Income Tax Law,[431] because of the petitioners' lack of standing, instead of sending the file to the general court's Archives, the Chamber proceeded, after deciding the inadmissibility of the action, and without any judicial debate or discussion on the issue, to reform *ex officio* another article of the Law (article 31), which had not even been challenged by petitioners.

The decision provoked bitter protests in public opinion and in the National Assembly, which, in a unanimous resolution, "categorically rejected" the Constitutional Chamber's decision, considering it "unconstitutional, contrary to the social and collective fundamental rights and social ethics," and declared it "without any legal effects." In addition, the National Assembly publicly praised for the disobedience of the Chamber decision, and "exhorted the Venezuelan people and specifically, the tax payers, as well as the National Tax Service (*Seniat*) to continue with the process of tax returns as it is established in the statute."[432] The Vice President of the National Assembly qualified the Chamber decision reforming an article of the Income Tax Law as one in which the Constitutional Jurisdiction "usurped legislative powers."[433] In fact, in this case, the Constitutional Chamber usurped the legislative function by reforming an article of the Tax Law in an *obiter dictum* of a decision in which the Chamber declared inadmissible an action of unconstitutionality filed against other articles of the same Taxation Law.[434]

Many other decisions of the Constitutional Chamber reforming provisions of legislation have been issued during the past decade, for instance on matters of procedural terms applicable in civil procedure trials: the Chamber partially annulled a provision of the Civil Procedural Law and created new wording that establishes a different way of counting procedural terms.[435] On the same matters of procedural

430 See *Adriana Vigilanza y Carlos A. Vecchio* case, Exp. N° 01–2862; *Gaceta Oficial* N° 38.635 of March 1, 2007, at http://www.tsj.gov.ve/decisiones/scon/Febrero/301–270207–01–2862.htm. See also Daniela Urosa Maggi, *Venezuelan National Report*, pp. 22–23.

431 See Decree Law N° 307, *Gaceta Oficial* N° 5.390 Extra. of October 22, 1999.

432 See in *Gaceta Oficial* N° 38.651 March 26, 2007.

433 Resolution of March 22, 2007; *El Universal*, Caracas March 23, 2007, p. 1–1; *El Nacional*, Caracas, March 23, 2007, p. 4.

434 See the general comment on this decision in Allan R. BREWER–CARÍAS, "El juez constitucional en Venezuela como legislador positivo de oficio en materia tributaria," *Revista de Derecho Público*, N° 109, Editorial Jurídica Venezolana, Caracas 2007, pp. 193–212.

435 See Decision N° 80 of February 1, 2001, case *Article 197 of the Civil Procedural Code*; *Revista de Derecho Público*, N° 85–89, Editorial Jurídica Venezolana, Caracas 2001, pp. 90 ff., at http://www.tsj.gov.ve/decisiones/scon/Febrero/80–010201–00–1435%20.htm. See the comments in Allan R. BREWER–CARÍAS, "Los primeros pasos de la Jurisdicción Constitucional como 'legislador positivo' violando la Constitución, y el régimen legal de cómputo de los lapsos procesales," in *Crónica sobre la "in"justicia constitucional: La Sala Constitucional y el autoritarismo en Venezuela*, Colección Instituto de Derecho Público, Universidad Central de Venezuela, N° 2, Editorial Jurídica Venezolana, Caracas 2007, pp. 511 ff. See also Daniela Urosa Maggi, *Venezuelan National Report*, p. 24.

terms applicable in criminal procedure trials, the Court modified the Criminal Procedure Code to establish a new way of counting the terms but without annulling the provision.[436] On matters of judicial holidays established in the same Civil Procedural Code, the Court partially annulled the specific provision of the Code eliminating one of the two holiday terms established in it, thus usurping the discretional options to be established on the matter in legislation that is attributed to the National Assembly.[437] In other cases, also regarding procedural rules, when deciding a nullity action against provisions of the Rural Land Law, in which the notice to the interested parties to participate in the respective trial was established by a publication in newspapers, the Court reformed the provisions by adding that the notice was also to be delivered personally to interested parties.[438]

In other cases, the Constitutional Chamber of the Supreme Tribunal has "reformed" the Amparo Law, establishing a new procedure to be applied in the amparo proceedings, and the same Organic Law of the Supreme Tribunal establishes a new set of procedural rules to be applied in judicial review, assuming an active role as positive legislator. In effect, in the first two decisions the Constitutional Chamber adopted after its installment in 2000, the Chamber modified, *ex officio*, articles 7 and 8 of the Organic Law on Amparo, redistributing the competencies of the courts, including its own competencies on matter of amparo,[439] that is, to decide the specific action or complaint for the protection of fundamental rights. Since then, such competencies have been ruled by the Chamber's decision, not by what is provided for in the Organic Law. Another notorious case was Decision N° 7 of February 1, 2000,[440] where the Chamber, on the occasion of ruling in a particular case of amparo, also in an *obiter dictum* and *ex officio*, by means of interpreting articles 27 and 49 of the Constitution that establish the oral trial in the amparo proceeding for the protection of fundamental rights and the basic rules of due process, decided to "adapt" the 1988 Amparo Law to the new 1999 Constitution, completely "reforming" the law by establishing a completely new set of rules of procedure that since have been applied in all amparo cases. The ones established in the Amparo Law have not been applied,

436 See Decision N° 2560 of August 5, 2005, *Article 172 of the Organic Civil Criminal Code* case; http://www.tsj.gov.ve/decisiones/scon/Agosto/2560–050805–03–1309.htm. See also Daniela Urosa Maggi, *Venezuelan National Report*, pp. 21–22.

437 See Decision N° 1264 of June 11, 2002, *Article 201 of the Civil Procedure Code* case; http://www.tsj.gov.ve/decisiones/scon/Junio/1264–110602–00–1281.htm. See also Daniela Urosa Maggi, *Venezuelan National Report*, pp. 24–25.

438 See Decision N° 2855 of November 20, 2002, *Articles 40 and 42 of the Rural Land Law* case; http://www.tsj.gov.ve/decisiones/scon/Noviembre/2855–201102–02–0311..htm. See also Daniela Urosa Maggi, *Venezuelan National Report*, p. 21.

439 See Decision N° 1, *Emery Mata Millán* case, at http://www.tsj.gov.ve/decisiones/scon/Enero/01–200100–00–002.htm; and Decision N° 2, of January 20, 2000, *Domingo Ramírez Monja* case, at http://www.tsj.gov.ve/decisiones/scon/Enero/02–200100–00–001.htm; *Revista de Derecho Público*, N° 84, Editorial Jurídica Venezolana, Caracas, 2000, pp. 225 ff. and 235 ff. See Daniela Urosa Maggi, *Venezuelan National Report*, p. 12.

440 Case: *José A. Mejía y otros, Revista de Derecho Público*, N° 81, Editorial Jurídica Venezolana, Caracas 2000, pp. 349 ff. See also http://www.tsj.gov.ve/ decisiones/scon/Febrero/07–010200–00–0010.htm; Daniela Urosa Maggi, *Venezuelan National Report*, pp. 4–5.

though that law remains "in effect" without having been annulled or repealed.[441] Without doubt, in this case, the Chamber exceeded its functions as the highest interpreter of the Constitution and openly proceeded as a positive legislator, "reforming" the text of a statute.[442] Consequently, since 2000, on matters of amparo procedure and of distribution of jurisdiction between the different courts, the applicable "law" in Venezuela is decision N° 7 of 2000 of the Constitutional Chamber of the Supreme Tribunal that "reformed" the 1988 Amparo Law.[443]

Another decision of the Constitutional Chamber reforming statutes has been issued regarding the rules of procedure concerning actions for judicial review of the constitutionality of statutes. The Organic Law on the Supreme Tribunal of Justice was sanctioned by the National Assembly in 2004, establishing the rules of procedure regarding actions filed before the Court claiming for the nullity of statutes (article 21.9 ff.). In Decision N° 1645 of August 19, 2004, a few months after the publication of the Organic Law, the Constitutional Chamber, without declaring any statutory provision unconstitutional, in exercising its normative jurisdiction, proceeded to reform the new law and to establish a completely new judicial procedure.[444]

---

441 See Daniela Urosa Maggi, *Venezuelan National Report*, p. 5.

442 See the general comment on this decision in Allan R. BREWER–CARÍAS, "El juez constitucional como legislador positivo y la inconstitucional reforma de la Ley Orgánica de Amparo mediante sentencias interpretativas," in Eduardo Ferrer Mac–Gregor y Arturo Zaldívar Lelo de Larrea (coords.), *La ciencia del derecho procesal constitucional: Estudios en homenaje a Héctor Fix–Zamudio en sus cincuenta años como investigador del derecho*, Instituto de Investigaciones Jurídicas, Universidad Nacional Autónoma de México, Mexico City 2008, Vol. V, pp. 63–80.

443 See Humberto Enrique Tercero Bello Tabares, "El procedimiento de Amparo Constitucional, según la sentencia N° 7 dictada por la Sala Constitucional del Tribunal Supremo de Justicia, de fecha 01 de febrero de 2000. Caso *José Amando Mejía Betancourt y José Sánchez Villavicencio*," *Revista de Derecho del Tribunal Supremo de Justicia*, N° 8, Caracas 2003, pp. 139–176; María Elena Toro Dupuy, "El procedimiento de amparo en la jurisprudencia de la Sala Constitucional del Tribunal Supremo de Justicia (Años 2000–2002)," *Revista de Derecho Constitucional*, N° 6, Editorial Sherwood, Caracas 2003, pp. 241–256.

444 See Decision 1645 of August 19, 2004, *Gregorio Pérez Vargas* case; http://www.tsj.gov.ve/decisiones/scon/Agosto/1645–190804–04–0824.htm. This decision was ratified and complemented with new procedural rules in Decision 1795 of July 19, 2005. *Promotora San Gabriel* case, http://www.tsj.gov.ve/decisiones/scon/Julio/1795–190705–05–0159.htm; Daniela Urosa Maggi, *Venezuelan National Report*, p. 10. See the comments in Allan R. BREWER–CARÍAS, *Ley Orgánica del Tribunal Supremo de Justicia*, Editorial Jurídica Venezolana, Caracas 2004.

CHAPTER 4
CONSTITUTIONAL COURTS' INTERFERENCE WITH THE LEGISLATOR REGARDING LEGISLATIVE OMISSIONS

As aforementioned, one of the most important contemporary trends in the transformation of judicial review of legislation, particularly in concentrated systems, has been the development of the possibility for constitutional courts to exercise their power to control the constitutionality of statutes, interpreting them according to the Constitution without being obliged to decide on the nullity of the unconstitutional provisions.

The same sort of control is also exercised regarding the constitutionality of the conduct of the Legislator, not related to statutes duly enacted, but regarding the absence of such statutes or the omissions the statutes contain when the Legislator does not comply with its constitutional obligation to legislate on specific matters or when the Legislator has passed legislation it in an incomplete or discriminatory way. It is important to highlight in all these cases that judicial review decisions adopted by constitutional courts are issued completely separate from the need to annul existing statues, as it is impossible in these cases to characterize the constitutional courts as negative legislators. On the contrary, in many of these cases, constitutional courts act openly as positive legislators, often with the possibility to issue declarations of unconstitutionality of certain legal provisions without annulling them. In some ways, this is similar to what occurs in diffuse systems of judicial review, where the courts have no power at all to annul statutes.

Two sorts of legislative omissions can generally be distinguished: absolute and relative omissions.[445] Absolute omissions exist in cases of the absence of any legislative provision adopted with the purpose of applying the Constitution or executing a constitutional provision, in which case a situation contrary to the Constitution is created. Relative omissions exist when legislation has been enacted but in a partial, incomplete, or defective way from the constitutional point of view. As pointed out by Luís Fernández Revorio, absolute omissions are related to the "silences of the legislator" that create situations contrary to the Constitution; relative omissions are

445 See José Julio Fernández Rodríguez, *La inconstitucionalidad por omisión: Teoría general. Derecho comparado. El caso español*, Civitas, Madrid 1998, pp. 33, 114 ff. According to Thomas Bustamante, "While a complete omission takes place when the legislator does not produce any law although there is a genuine constitutional obligation of regulating some constitutional issue, a partial omission occurs when the legislative authority regulates a situation in an unconstitutional way because it does not cover situations that should have been included in the statute." See Thomas Bustamante and Evanlida de Godoi Bustamante, *Brazilian National Report*, p. 11.

related to the "silences of the statutes," which also create the same unconstitutional situation.[446]

Both sorts of legislative omissions have been subjected to judicial review by constitutional courts, though not uniformly.

I. CONSTITUTIONAL COURTS' FILLING THE GAP OF ABSOLUTE LEGISLATIVE OMISSIONS

Regarding judicial review of absolute legislative omissions, the matter can be decided by the constitutional courts through two judicial means: when deciding a direct action for the unconstitutionality of an omission by the Legislator and when deciding a particular action or complaint for the protection of fundamental rights filed against an omission of the Legislator that prevents the possibility of enforcing such right.

1. Direct action against absolute legislative omissions

The origin of the direct action seeking judicial review of unconstitutional absolute legislative omissions is found in the 1974 Constitution of the former Yugoslavia, which assigned the Constitutional Guaranties Tribunal the power to decide on cases of lack of legislative development of constitutional provisions that impeded the complete execution of the Constitution (article 377).[447]

Two years later, and influenced by the former Yugoslavian institution,[448] the direct action against absolute legislative omissions was incorporated in the 1976 Constitution of Portugal. It assigned the Council of the Revolution, as a political organ assisting the President of the Republic, the necessary powers to verify failures of the Legislator to comply with the Constitution by enacting the necessary statutes to implement the provisions of the new Constitution (article 279, Constitution),[449] and particularly in view of changing prerevolutionary legislation and implementing legislative provisions of the Constitution than banned organizations with fascist ideology.[450]

---

446 See Francisco Javier Díaz Revorio, *Las sentencias interpretativas del Tribunal Constitucional*, Ed. Lex Nova, Valladolid 2001, p. 171.

447 See José Julio Fernández Rodríguez, *La inconstitucionalidad por omisión: Teoría general. Derecho comparado. El caso español*, Civitas, Madrid 1998, pp. 244–246.

448 See Jorge Campinos, "Brevísimas notas sobre a fiscalizacão da constitucionalidade des leis em Portugal," in Giorgo Lombardi (coord.), *Constituzione e giustizia constitutionale nel diritto comparato*, Maggioli, Rimini 1985; and *La Constitution portugaise de 1976 et sa garantie*, Universidad Nacional Autónoma de México, Congreso sobre La Constitución y su Defensa (mimeo), Mexico City, August 1982, p. 42.

449 See generally Jorge Miranda, "L'inconstitutionalité par omisión dans le droit portugais," in *Revue Européene de Droit Public*, Vol. 4, N° 1, 1992, pp. 39 ff.; José Julio Fernández Rodríguez, *La inconstitucionalidad por omisión: Teoría general. Derecho comparado. El caso español*, Civitas, Madrid 1998, pp. 249 ff.

450 See Francisco Javier Díaz Revorio, *Las sentencias interpretativas del Tribunal Constitucional*, Ed. Lex Nova, Valladolid 2001, pp. 257–260.

Up to the sanctioning of the 1982 First Revision of the Constitution, which definitively established this "constitutional control of omission," control of absolute omissions was exercised by the then Council of the Revolution in two occasions and basically as a political means of control.[451] In 1977, through *Parecer* 8/1977 of March 3, 1977, the Council "recommended" that the Assembly of the Republic adopt legislative measures to enforce Article 46.4 of the 1976 Constitution regarding organizations with fascist ideology, establishing as the main condition for the exercise of such control, first, that the constitutional norm could not be self–executing (i.e., it could not require implementation to be applied), and second, that the competent body to adopt the legislative measures must have violated its obligation of issuing legislative provisions to a degree that it obstructed the observance of the Constitution by the very party for whom the constitutional obligation was intended.[452]

In a second case, in *Parecer* 11/1977, April 14, 1978, the Council of the Revolution recommended that the competent legislative bodies adopt legislative measures to guarantee the applicability of Article 53 of the Constitution to domestic servants, conferring to those workers the right to rest and to recreation by limiting the length of the workday and establishing the weekly rest period as well as periodic paid holidays. On this second occasion, the essential contribution of the decision was the extensive interpretation of the Constitutional Commission regarding the initiative to request control of the omission.[453]

Following these previous experiences on judicial review, the 1982 Constitution created the Constitutional Tribunal and established its power to exercise judicial review of legislative omissions regarding the enactment of provisions necessary to make enforceable constitutional mandates (article 283). The standing to sue in these cases was given to the President of the Republic or the Ombudsman at the national level, and to the Presidents of the Regional Assemblies in cases of violation of the rights of the autonomous regions. The decisions of the Tribunal in these cases are only of declarative character and with nonbinding effects, so the Court "cannot substitute itself for the legislator by creating the missing rules nor can it urge them to act by indicating the timing for or the content of such action."[454] In these cases of judicial decisions on legislative omissions, the Tribunal can only inform the competent legislative organ of its findings.

The Portuguese Constitutional Tribunal issued only seven important decisions exercising this judicial review mean of control of legislative omissions.[455] Its first

---

451 See M. Gonzalo, "Portugal; El Consejo de la Revolución, su Comisión Constitucional y los Tribunales ordinarios como órganos de control de la constitucionalidad," in *Boletín de Jurisprudencia Constitucional*, Cortes Generales, 8, Madrid 1981, pp. 630, 640.

452 See José Julio Fernández Rodríguez, *La inconstitucionalidad por omisión: Teoría general. Derecho comparado. El caso español*, Civitas, Madrid 1998, pp. 265–266.

453 See José Julio Fernández Rodríguez, *La inconstitucionalidad por omisión: Teoría general. Derecho comparado. El caso español*, Civitas, Madrid 1998, pp. 265–266.

454 See Joaquim de Sousa Ribeiro and Esperança Mealha, *Portuguese National Report*, pp. 10–11.

455 See Joaquim de Sousa Ribeiro and Esperança Mealha, *Portuguese National Report*, p. 10.

decision was Decision N° 182/1989 of February 1, 1989, on the noncompliance of article 35.4 of the Constitution on the use of computers and the prohibition of third–party access to files containing personal data, given the lack of a legislative measure defining personal data.[456] Another case was Decision N° 474/2002, on the noncompliance of article 59.1–e of the Constitution, given the omission of legislative measures needed to provide social benefits for Public Administration workers who involuntarily found themselves unemployed.[457] In both cases, although the Legislator is not constitutionally obliged to initiate any legislative procedure, the result of the Tribunal's decision was the sanctioning of the needed legislation (Law 10/91 and Law 11/2008).[458]

After the Portuguese constitutional experience, the direct action for judicial review of absolute unconstitutional legislative omissions has been established in only some other countries, mainly in Latin America, including Brazil, Ecuador, and Venezuela.

The first country to follow the Portuguese trends on the matter was Brazil, where judicial review of absolute legislative omissions through a direct action was incorporated in the 1988 Constitution (Articles 102.I.a and 103), which gave power to the Federal Supreme Tribunal to decide the actions filed against the unconstitutionality of legislative omissions, thus impeding the enforcement of a constitutional provision. In this case, also, the action can be filed only by a limited number of State officials or organs, namely the President of the Republic, the Board of the Federal Senate, and the Board of the House of Representatives, and the Board of a Legislative Assembly of a State.

The ruling of the Tribunal declaring unconstitutional a legislative omission to enforce a provision of the Constitution does so without annulling any act and without issuing a direct order to Congress. The Tribunal only must inform the competent organ for it to adopt the necessary measures. In this sense, in a case of an action intended to establish that the value of the minimum wage was unconstitutional because it could not meet the basic needs of a person, the Supreme Federal Tribunal held that, while deciding on these omissive actions, "the Supreme Court can do no more than notify the competent legislative body which should have enacted a normative act, in order to make this body of the Republic aware of the unconstitutionality and to enable it to regulate the matter required by the Constitution, without the

---

456 See José Julio Fernández Rodríguez, *La inconstitucionalidad por omisión: Teoría general. Derecho comparado. El caso español*, Civitas, Madrid 1998, pp. 268–269; Joaquim de Sousa Ribeiro and Esperança Mealha, *Portuguese National Report*, p. 10.

457 See Joaquim de Sousa Ribeiro and Esperança Mealha, *Portuguese National Report*, p. 10.

458 See Joaquim de Sousa Ribeiro and Esperança Mealha, *Portuguese National Report*, pp. 10–11.

interference of the Judiciary."[459] Consequently, the judicial decision in these cases is also declarative, without *erga omnes* and binding effects.[460]

In contrast, in many cases, the Federal Supreme Court has stipulated a deadline for the omission to be filled and has established the self–applicability of the constitutional rule in the event the deadline expired.[461] For instance, in the action filed by the Mato Grosso State Legislature against the unconstitutionality of the omission by the National Congress in drafting the federal supplementary law referred to by Section 4 of Article 18 of the Constitution –related to the creation, merger, consolidation, and subdivision of Municipalities– the Tribunal stipulated a deadline of eighteen months for it to take all the legislative steps necessary to comply with the constitutional provision.[462]

Another Latin American country that has adopted the system of judicial review of absolute legislative omissions is Venezuela, which, in article 336.7 of the 1999 Constitution has empowered the Constitutional Chamber of the Supreme Tribunal of Justice to declare the unconstitutionality of municipal, state, or national legislative organ omissions, when they failed to issue indispensable rules or measures to guarantee the enforcement of the Constitution, or when they issued them in an incomplete way; and to establish the terms, and if necessary, the guidelines for their correction.

This provision gave extended judicial power to the Constitutional Chamber of the Supreme Tribunal, as Constitutional Jurisdiction, to control "legislative silence and legislative abnormal functioning,"[463] surpassing the trends of the Portuguese and Brazilian antecedents, first, by not limiting the standing to file the action to high public officials but configuring it as an *actio popularis*, and second, by granting express powers to the Court to establish the terms and, if necessary, the guidelines for the correction of the omission.

In many cases, the Constitutional Chamber has been asked to rule on omissions of the National Assembly in sanctioning statutes that it is obliged to enact within a fixed term established in the 1999 Constitution – for instance, the Organic Law on Municipal Power was due to be sanctioned within two years following the approval

---

459 See STF, ADI 1439–MC, Rel. Min. Celso de Mello, DJ de 30–5–2003, in Thomas Bustamante and Evanlida de Godoi Bustamante, *Brazilian National Report*, p. 12.

460 See Marcia Rodrígues Machado, "Inconstitutionalidade por omissão," *Revista da Procuradoria Greal de São Paulo*, N° 30, 1988, pp. 41 ff.; Héctor Fix Zamudio and Eduardo Ferrer Mac–Gregor, *Las sentencias de los Tribunales Constitucionales*, Ed. Porrúa, Mexico City 2009, pp. 38–39; José Julio Fernández Rodríguez, *La inconstitucionalidad por omisión: Teoría general. Derecho comparado. El caso español*, Civitas, Madrid 1998, pp. 285; Marcelo Figuereido, *Brazilian National Report II*, p. 3.

461 See Marcelo Figuereido, *Brazilian National Report II*, p. 4.

462 See ADI 3682/MT, May 9, 2007, in Thomas Bustamante and Evanlida de Godoi Bustamante, *Brazilian National Report*, p. 12; Marcelo Figuereido, *Brazilian National Report II*, p. 7.

463 See decision of the Political–Administrative Chamber N° 1819 of August 8, 2000, case: *Rene Molina v. Comisión Legislativa Nacional*.

of the Constitution. Even though the Chamber issued two decisions in the case,[464] the National Assembly failed to adjust the statute until 2005.[465] In these cases, as it is the general situation regarding constitutional control of legislative omissions, the Constitutional Chamber had not itself became a positive legislator and abstained from deciding in place of the legislative body, that is, it had not legislated itself. Nonetheless, according to the Constitution, the Constitutional Chamber always has the power when declaring the unconstitutionality of a legislative omission "to establish the terms" of the statute to be sanctioned "and[,] if necessary, the guidelines" for the correction of the legislative omissions. That is why, in other cases, the Constitutional Chamber has issued provisional legislation filling the existing vacuum on, for instance, tax matters related to the distribution of competencies between the National and the State level of governments. It occurred when deciding a conflict between the national Law on Tax Stamps and the Ordinance on Tax Stamps of the Metropolitan District of Caracas, by resolving in Decision N° 978 of April 2003[466] to establish the legal regime as strictly applicable on the matter pending the issue of the national legislation on the coordination of tax competencies (article 164.4 of the Constitution).

In addition, in Venezuela, the Constitutional Chamber has been asked to decide not only cases of absolute omissions of the National Assembly to enact statutes that it had the constitutional obligation to sanction, but also other nonnormative acts that the National Assembly must adopt. This was the case, for instance, of the appointment of the members of the National Electoral Council, which the National Assembly must do by a majority of two–thirds of the representatives following a complex procedure involving civil society and citizen participation.[467] In 2004, the National Assembly, after completing almost all the steps of the procedure, failed to appoint the Members of the National Electoral Council, because the official party did not have the necessary votes to appoint its candidates (two–thirds) without any compromise with the opposition parties. In the face of the omission of the National Assembly, a citizen requested that the Constitutional Chamber control the unconstitutionality of the omission and sought a decision of the Constitutional Chamber compelling the National Assembly to accomplish its constitutional duty, which no other

---

464 See decisions of the Constitutional Chamber N° 1347 of May 27, 2003; N° 3118 of October 6, 2003 *Revista de Derecho Público*, N° 93–96, Editorial Jurídica Venezolana, Caracas 2003, pp. 108 ff. and 527 ff.; and N° 1043 of May 31, 2004, *Revista de Derecho Público*, N° 97–98, Editorial Jurídica Venezolana, Caracas 2004, pp. 270 ff. and 409 ff.

465 The Organic Law was published in *Official Gazette* N° 38327 of December 2, 2005. See the reference in Allan R. BREWER–CARÍAS et al., *Ley Orgánica del Poder Público Municipal*, Editorial Jurídica Venezolana, Caracas 2005, p. 17.

466 Decision N° 978 of April 30, 2003, *Banco Bolívar* case; http://www.tsj.gov.ve/decisiones/scon/Abril/978–300403–01–1535%20.htm. See also Daniela Urosa Maggi, *Venezuelan National Report*, pp. 17–18.

467 See Allan R. BREWER–CARÍAS, "La participación ciudadana en la designación de los titulares de los órganos no electos de los Poderes Públicos en Venezuela y sus vicisitudes políticas," *Revista Iberoamericana de Derecho Público y Administrativo*, Vol. 5, N° 5,2005, San José, Costa Rica 2005, pp. 76–95.

organ of the State could assume. Instead, what the petitioner obtained from a Constitutional Chamber of the Supreme Tribunal, packed with Magistrates completely controlled by the Executive, was the direct appointment of the members of the National Electoral Council by the Constitutional Court itself, without complying with the requirements and conditions established in the Constitution. Without doubt, in this case, the Constitutional Court usurped the National Assembly's exclusive powers; acted as positive Legislator and in violation of the Constitution; and through its decision, guaranteed the complete control of the Electoral branch of government by the National Executive.[468]

In other countries, like Costa Rica, the Law on Constitutional Jurisdiction assigns the Constitutional Chamber of the Supreme Court the power to decide actions of unconstitutionality "against the inertia, the omissions and the abstentions of public authorities" (article 73.f).[469]

More recently, in the 2008 Constitution of Ecuador, the direct action for judicial review of legislative omissions was expressly established (article 436.10), assigning the Constitutional Court the power to "declare the unconstitutionality in which the institutions of the State or public authorities incurred because of omissions in complying total or partially the mandates contained in constitutional provisions, within the terms established in the Constitution or in the term considered reasonable by the Constitutional Court." The same provision empowers the Constitutional Court provisionally to "issue the omitted provision or to execute the omitted act according to the law," once the term has elapsed and the omission persists. It is unique in comparative law that constitutional power, even provisional, is given to the Constitutional Court to substitute for the Legislator.

In Hungary, article 49 of the 1989 Amendment of the Constitution establishes that the Constitutional Court *ex officio* or on anyone's petition can decide on the unconstitutionality of legislative omissions when a legislative organ has failed to fulfill its legislative tasks, instructing the organ that committed the omission to set a deadline to fulfill its task. The Hungarian Constitutional Court has interpreted this competence expansively and has practiced it not only in the cases of unconstitutional failures of fulfillment of legislative obligations resulting from particular legal authorization, but also when the Legislator failed to establish a statute necessary for the emergence of a fundamental right, designated in the Constitution.[470] As men-

---

468 See Decisions Nos. 2073 of August 4, 2003 (case: *Hermánn Escarrá Malaver y oros*) and 2341 of August 25, 2003 (case: *Hermánn Escarrá M. y otros*), in Allan R. BREWER–CARÍAS, "El secuestro del Poder Electoral y la confiscación del derecho a la participación política mediante el referendo revocatorio presidencial: Venezuela 2000–2004," in *Boletín Mexicano de Derecho Comparado*, Instituto de Investigaciones Jurídicas, Universidad Nacional Autónoma de México, N° 112. Mexico City, January–April 2005, pp. 11–73.

469 See José Julio Fernández Rodríguez, *La inconstitucionalidad por omisión: Teoría general. Derecho comparado. El caso español*, Civitas, Madrid 1998, pp. 300–302.

470 An example of such a case is Decision 37/1992 (VI.10). Under Article 61, section (4), of the Constitution, a majority of two–thirds of the votes by the members of Parliament present is required to pass an Act on the supervision of public radio, television, and the public news agency, as well as on the appointment of the directors thereof, on the licensing of commer-

tioned by Lóránt Csink, Józef Petrétei, and Péter Tilk, in exercising this attribution, the Constitutional Court establishes not only the unconstitutionality of the omission of legislation – for instance, by making it impossible for the exercise of a fundamental right – but also the contents of the rules to be sanctioned, which the Legislator must respect.[471]

Regarding Croatia, where the Constitutional Court has powers to proceed *ex officio* on matters of control of constitutionality, the 2002 constitutional reform empowered the Court to adopt reports about any kind of unconstitutionality (and illegality) it has observed and to send them to the Croatian Parliament. Until November 2009, it had adopted six reports addressing important issues that emerged in practice, such as the right to reasonable duration of a trial and the unconstitutionality of regulations on parking fees.[472]

In Bolivia, even in the absence of constitutional or legal provisions, the Constitutional Tribunal created its own power to exercise judicial review control on Legislative omissions. In Decision S.C. 0066/2005 of September 22, 2005, the Court, after verifying its own powers of judicial review, argued that, "when the Legislator does not develop a constitutional provision in a particular and precise way, or it develops the provision in a deficient or incomplete way turning the constitutional mandate inefficient, or impossible to be applied because of such omission or deficiency, the Constitutional Tribunal has the attribution to judge the constitutionality of such acts, providing for the Legislator to develop the constitutional provision as imposed by the Constitution."[473] In the case of the National Congress's failure to appoint the members of the Supreme Court of Justice, the Constitutional Tribunal of Bolivia issued a decision in 2004 ruling on the unconstitutionality of the Executive's provisional appointment of the magistrates. To avoid creating a more severe situation of unconstitutionality, the Tribunal postponed the effects of its decision for a term of sixty days, exhorting the Legislator to perform its duties but without usurping its functions.[474]

---

cial radio and television, and on the prevention of monopolies in the media sector. However, until 1996, Parliament failed to adopt a comprehensive Act on radio and television. Likewise, under Article 68, section (5), of the Constitution, a majority of two–thirds of the votes by members of Parliament present is required to pass an Act on the rights of national and ethnic minorities. Decision 35/1992 (VI.10) established an unconstitutional omission as the representation of national and ethnic minorities had not been regulated to the extent and in the manner required by the Constitution; Lóránt Csink, Józef Petrétei, and Péter Tilk, *Hungarian National Report*, p. 5 (footnote 18).

471 See Lóránt Csink, Józef Petrétei, and Péter Tilk, *Hungarian National Report*, pp. 5–6.

472 See Sanja Barić and Petar Bačić, *Croatian National Report*, pp. 12–13.

473 See Pablo Dermizaky Peredo, "Efectos de las sentencias constitucionales en Bolivia," in *Anuario Iberoamericano de Justicia Constitucional*, Centro de Estudios Políticos y Constitucionales, N° 12, 2008, Madrid 2008, p. 79.

474 See Decision S.C. 0129/2004–R, of November 10, 2004, in Pablo Dermizary Peredo, "Efectos de las sentencias constitucionales en Bolivia," in *Anuario Iberoamericano de Justicia Constitucional*, N° 12, 2008, Centro de Estudios Políticos y Constitucionales, Madrid 2008, p. 78.

In other cases, also without a specific means of judicial review to control absolute legislative omissions, the constitutional courts have developed judicial control through other general means of judicial review, as in the case of Mexico, but only by means of the recourse for the solution of constitutional controversies between constitutional organs of the State. Nonetheless, this thesis was abandoned in 2006, in a decision resolving a constitutional controversy in which the Court considered inappropriate such judicial review to control legislative omissions.[475]

2. The protection of fundamental rights against absolute legislative omissions by means of actions or complaints for their protection

The other means for controlling unconstitutional legislative omissions are specific actions or complaints for the protection of fundamental rights that can be filed against the harms or threats that such omissions can cause. This is the case, for example, in many Latin American countries, where amparo actions are filed against omissions of the Legislator or for specific actions for the protection of fundamental rights that have been established.[476] Therefore, in some countries, at least theoretically, it is possible to file amparo actions to protect fundamental rights against legislative omission when such omissions prevent the effective enforcement of a fundamental right.[477]

In particular, mention must be made of the important writ of injunction (*mandado de injunção*) in Brazil, established in Article 5.LXXI, of the Constitution, which is to be "granted whenever the lack of regulatory provision makes the exercise of constitutional rights and liberties, as well as rights inherent in nationality, sovereign status and citizenship, unfeasible." According to the Federal Supreme Tribunal, the writ of injunction does not authorize the Tribunal to fill the gap left by the legislative omission, so the Tribunal cannot enact a normative rule;[478] its function is limited to declaring the delay to develop the normative rule and to notify the Legislator, and the decision has only *inter partes* effects.

---

475 See Decision 56/2006, in Héctor Fix Zamudio and Eduardo Ferrer Mac–Gregor, *Las sentencias de los Tribunales Constitucionales*, Ed. Porrúa, Mexico City 2009, pp. 71, 72; and "Las sentencias de los tribunales constitucionales en el ordenamiento mexicano," in *Anuario Iberoamericano de Justicia Constitucional*, Nº 12, 2008, Centro de Estudios Políticos y Constitucionales, Madrid 2008, pp. 252. See also Eduardo Ferrer Mac–Gregor, "La Corte Suprema di Giustizia del Messico quale Tribunale constituzionale," in Luca Mezetti (coord.), *Sistemi e modelli di giustizia costitutionale*, Cedam, Padua 2009, p. 618.

476 On the amparo proceedings against authorities' omissions in Latin American countries, see particularly Allan R. BREWER–CARÍAS, *Constitutional Protection of Human Rights in Latin America: A Comparative Study of Amparo Proceeding*, Cambridge University Press, New York 2009, pp. 324 ff.

477 In Venezuela, amparo actions have been filed against omissions of the Legislator regarding certain administrative acts. See Allan R. BREWER–CARÍAS, *La justicia constitucional: Procesos y procedimientos constitucionales*, Universidad Nacional Autónoma de México, Mexico City 2007, pp. 153 ff.

478 See Decision STF 168/RS, Reporting Justice J. Ministro Pertence, DJU, on April 20 1990, in Marcelo Figuereido, *Brazilian National Report II*, p. 4.

In the first writ of injunction decided in 1989, the Tribunal considered that the action attempts to obtain from the Judiciary a declaration of unconstitutionality of an omission in regulating a right, with a view to notify the entity responsible for that regulation to take action.[479] However, there are cases in which the Tribunal has given a broader scope to this procedural remedy. In Case 283 of 1991, the Tribunal recognized a state of negligence of Congress in regulating provisions established by the Temporary Provisions of the Constitution related to compensation for the victims of abuses committed by the military dictatorship via Secret Acts of the Ministry of Defense, which banned a large number of people from exercising certain economic activities. Because the Temporary Provisions required the passing of a federal statute to regulate such compensation, the victims could not exert their constitutional rights. In the face of this specific situation, the Supreme Federal Tribunal not only ruled that there was an unconstitutional omission but also established a deadline of forty–five days for Congress to pass the statute. The Tribunal determined, moreover, that if parliamentary negligence remained after that deadline, the applicant would be automatically entitled to claim compensation according to the general rules of the Civil Code.[480]

In another relevant case, the Constitution guaranteed a tax privilege to certain social institutions, excluding them from taxation by contributions to the social security, "as long as these entities complied with the conditions established in law" (article 197.5). The Constitution left to the ordinary legislator the task to establish the conditions to be complied to claim immunity from the contributions. Accordingly, the Federal Government understood that such entities could claim no fiscal immunity until Congress passed a law listing such conditions. The Supreme Federal Tribunal, after holding that there was an unjustifiable legislative omission, fixed a deadline of six months for Congress to pass a law eliminating that omission. Furthermore, it determined that, if no law was passed before that deadline, the claimant would be automatically entitled to claim the fiscal benefit.[481]

It must also be mentioned that, in some cases, the Brazilian Federal Supfreme Tribunal has supplied the missing rule through analogy until the Legislator can enact legislation. This was the case in the application of social security rules regarding special pension in the private sector to civil servants working at the Health Department of the public sector (MI 721/DF, March 8, 2007) and in the application to the provisions of a statute (Law 7.783/1989) that governs the right to strike in the private sector (MI 670/ES, October 25, 2007) to civil servants of a State.[482]

---

479 STF, MI 107–QO, Rel. Min. Moreira Alves, DJ de 21–09–1990; Thomas Bustamante and Evanlida de Godoi Bustamante, *Brazilian National Report*, p. 17.

480 STF, MI 283, Rel. Min. Sepúlveda Pertence, DJ de 14–11–1991; Thomas Bustamante and Evanlida de Godoi Bustamante, *Brazilian National Report*, p. 17.

481 STF, MI 232, Rel. Min. Moreira Alves, DJ de 27–03–1992; Thomas Bustamante and Evanlida de Godoi Bustamante, *Brazilian National Report*, pp. 17–18.

482 See Marcelo Figuereido, *Brazilian National Report II*, p. 6–7; Thomas Bustamante and Evanlida de Godoi Bustamante, *Brazilian National Report*, p. 19; Luis Roberto Barroso et al., "Notas sobre a questão do legislador positivo," *Brazilian National Report III*, pp. 28 ff., 32.

The same general approach of the constitutional court complementing the Legislator, particularly on matters of protecting fundamental rights, can be found in other countries. For example, in Argentina, the Supreme Court's ruling in the *Badaro* cases concerned automatic adjustment of pensions. In effect, because the Constitution provides for "mobile" pensions (article 14 *bis*), in *Badaro I*,[483] the Supreme Court considered that Congress's inaction with respect to the increase of pensions, which had been seriously reduced as a result of high inflation, violated the constitutional mandate. Therefore, the Court urged Congress to pass legislation within a reasonable time to solve that problem. The Court emphasized that it is not only a power but also a duty of Congress to give effect to the constitutional guarantee of pension mobility, for which it must legislate and adopt measures to guarantee the full enjoyment of the right. Eventually, in view of the lack of action by Congress, in *Badaro II*,[484] the Court, in reurging Congress to enact legislation, resolved to grant the petitioner's request and adopted criteria for readjusting pensions until Congress decided to act.[485]

In another important case, regarding the environment, the Supreme Court in *Mendoza*,[486] decided a complaint filed by a group of neighbors of a settlement known as Villa Inflamable – located on the outskirts of Buenos Aires – against the National Government, the province of Buenos Aires, the government of the City of Buenos Aires, and forty–four private companies, alleging damages caused by multiple diseases that their children and themselves had suffered as a result of the pollution of the water basin Matanza–Riachuelo." In two landmark rulings, the first in 2006 and the other in 2008, the Court ordered the defendants to present an environmental recovery program, entrusted the Matanza–Riachuelo Basin Authority in its implementation, and established detailed court–monitored guidelines on compliance to avoid interprovincial conflicts, all of them matters traditionally within the realm of legislatures and the executive of both federal and provincial levels.[487]

In Germany, with respect to a complaint for constitutional protection of fundamental rights (*Verfassungsbeschwerde*),[488] the decision of the Constitutional Federal Tribunal N° 26/1969 of January 29, 1969, regarding article 6.5 of the Constitution, which establishes that the law must ensure for children born outside of marriage the same conditions of children born to married parents, in their physical, spiritual, and social development. The Federal Constitutional Tribunal considered that article 1712 of the Civil Code was insufficient regarding the constitutional provision and

---

483 Fallos 329:3089 (2006); Alejandra Rodríguez Galán and Alfredo Mauricio Vítolo, *Argentinean National Report I*, p. 16 (footnote 68).

484 Fallos 330:4866 (2007); Alejandra Rodríguez Galán and Alfredo Mauricio Vítolo, *Argentinean National Report I*, p. 17 (footnote 69).

485 See also Néstor Pedro Sagües, *Argentinean National Report II*, pp. 12–13.

486 Fallos 329:2316 (2006) and Fallos 331:1622 (2008); Alejandra Rodríguez Galán and Alfredo Mauricio Vítolo, *Argentinean National Report I*, p. 17 (footnote 72).

487 See Alejandra Rodríguez Galán and Alfredo Mauricio Vítolo, *Argentinean National Report I*, p. 17.

488 See generally Francisco Fernández Segado, "El control de las omisiones legislativas por el Bundesverfassungsgericht," *Revista de Derecho*, N° 4, Universidad Católica del Uruguay, Konrad Adenauer Stiftung, Montevideo 2009, pp. 137–186.

exhorted the Legislator to reform it according to the conditions set forth in article 6.5 of the Constitution before the end of the legislative term (Autumn 1969), which in fact occurred on August 19, 1969, with the promulgation of the reform.[489] Regarding this decision, Ines Härtel has reported the following:

> The BVerfG has already admonished the Legislator several times to fulfill explicit constitutional obligations through law. The constitutional obligations mentioned are oftentimes those which can only rely on weak forces in society in their realization; an example would be the task of the Legislator to create equal conditions between illegitimate and legitimate children in their physical and emotional development and consequently in their social standing (BVerfGE 8, 210 (216); 17, 148 (155); 25, 167 (173–188)) The respective decision states: "If the Legislator does not accomplish the order assigned to him by Constitution in Art. 6 Sec. 5 GG to reform Illegitimacy Law . . . until the ending of the current (fifth) legislative period of the Bundestag, it is the will of the Constitution to realize as much as possible of the Legislation.[490]

In India, an important case regarding ragging (bullying) at universities must be mentioned. In the exercise of its power under Articles 32 and 142 of the Constitution, in 2001, the Supreme Court decided on public interest litigation initiated in 1998 by Vishwa Jagriti Mission, a spiritual organization, seeking to curb the menace of ragging in educational institutions.[491] The Court, deciding in favor of the protection of fundamental rights, issued several guidelines, not only defining ragging but also contemplating possible causes of ragging, prescribing detailed steps to curb this practice, and outlining diverse modes of punishment that educational authorities could take. The Court also ruled that "failure to prevent ragging shall be construed as an act of negligence in maintaining discipline in the institution," and said, if "an institution fails to curb ragging, the UGC/Funding Agency may consider stoppage of financial assistance to such an institution till such time as it achieves the same." Because ragging continued to be reported in the media, the Indian Supreme Court engaged in its fight to curb ragging, directly appointing, in November 2006, a Committee to suggest remedial measures to tackle the problem of ragging in educational institutions. In May 2007, the Supreme Court ordered that several recommendations of the Committee be implemented without any further lapse of time, establishing, among other things, that "punishment to be meted out has to be exemplary and justifiably harsh to act as a deterrent against recurrence of such incidents."[492] The Court did not leave the task of monitoring the guidelines to the executive branch of the government, ruling that the "Committee constituted pursuant to the order of this Court shall continue to monitor the functioning of the anti–ragging committees and the squads to be formed. They shall also monitor the implementation of the recommendations to which reference has been made above." In 2007, the Supreme Court

---

489 See José Julio Fernández Rodríguez, *La inconstitucionalidad por omisión: Teoría general. Derecho comparado. El caso español*, Civitas, Madrid 1998, pp. 313–315.

490 See I. Härtel, *German National Report*, p. 19.

491 *Vishwa Jagriti Mission v. Central Government* AIR 2001 SC 2793; Surya Deva, *Indian National Report*, p. 9 (footnote 58).

492 See *University of Kerala v. Council of Principals of Colleges of Kerala*, order dated 16 May 2007; Surya Deva, *Indian National Report*, p. 10 (footnote 61).

gave further directions while dealing with specific instances of ragging in two colleges that were investigated by the Raghavan Committee;[493] and in 2009, in *University of Kerala v. Council of Principals of Colleges of Kerala*,[494] it directed all state governments as well as universities to act in accordance with the guidelines formulated by the Committee, considering ragging as a human rights abuse and thus expressly justifying the Court's exercise of power under Article 32 of the Constitution.[495]

In a similar trend, and through judicial means progressively developed for the protection of fundamental rights, the U.S. Supreme Court has filled the gap of legislative omissions, particularly in issuing equitable remedies, like injunctions,[496] through which a court of equity can adjudicate extraordinary relief to an aggrieved party, consisting of an order by the court commanding the defendant or injuring party to do something or to refrain from doing something.[497] These are called coercive remedies because they are backed by the contempt power, or the power of the court to directly sanction a disobedient defendant. Although they are not conceived of as only for the protection of constitutional rights, but for the protection of any right, they have been specifically effective for the protection constitutional rights, particularly preventive injunctions, which are designed to avoid future harm to a party by prohibiting or mandating certain behavior by another party (mandatory injunctions or prohibitory injunctions), and structural injunctions. The latter were developed by the courts after *Brown v. Board of Education* (347 U.S. 483 (1954); 349 U.S. 294 (1955)), in which the Supreme Court declared the dual school system discriminatory, using injunction as an instrument of reform, by means of which the courts in certain cases undertake the supervision over institutional State policies and practices to prevent discrimination. As described by Owen S. Fiss:

> Brown gave the injunction a special prominence. School desegregation became one of the prime litigative chores of courts in the period of 1954–1955, and in these cases the typical remedy was the injunction. School desegregation not only gave the injunction a greater currency, it also presented the injunction with new challenges, in terms of both the enormity and the kinds of tasks it was assigned. The injunction was to be used to restructure the educational systems throughout the nation. The impact of Brown on our remedial jurisprudence – giving primacy to the injunction – was not confined to schools desegregation. It also extended to civil rights cases in general, and beyond civil rights to litigation involving electoral reappointments, mental hospitals, prisons, trade practices, and the environment. Having desegregated the schools of Alabama, it was only natural for Judge Johnson to try to reform the mental

493 See J. Venkatesan, "SC Issues Guidelines to Check Ragging," *The Hindu*, May 9, 2009, http://www.thehindu.com/2009/05/09/stories/2009050957401100.htm; Surya Deva, *Indian National Report*, p. 10 (footnote 62).

494 See *University of Kerala v. Council of Principals of Colleges of Kerala*, order dated 11 February 2009, para. 2; Surya Deva, *Indian National Report*, p. 10 (footnote 63).

495 See Surya Deva, *Indian National Report*, p. 10.

496 See Allan R. BREWER–CARÍAS, *Constitutional Protection of Human Rights in Latin America*, Cambridge University Press, New York 2009, pp. 69 ff.

497 See William Tabb and Elaine W. Shoben, *Remedies*, Thomson West, St. Paul MN 2005, p. 13.

> hospitals and then the prisons of the state in the name of human rights – the right to treatment or to be free from cruel and unusual punishment – and to attempt this Herculean feat through injunction. And he was not alone. The same logic was manifest in actions of other judges, North and South.[498]

In effect, deciding these equitable remedies for the protection of fundamental rights, the Supreme Court in the United States has also created complementary judicial legislation, for instance invoking the Fourth, Fifth, and Sixth Amendments to the Constitution, regarding the conditions for lawful search and arrest in connection with investigation and prosecution of crime. The Court's decisions have resulted in a substantial and relatively complex body of law controlling police behavior, which allows courts to reverse the convictions of defendants who have not been treated in accordance with the judicially produced rules. In contrast, law enforcement agencies interested in securing convictions have an interest in compliance, so police departments have adopted procedures and trained their personnel to follow the rules.[499]

On matters of racial segregation in public education, declared contrary to the equal protection clause set forth in the Fourteenth Amendment, the Supreme Court rulings in *Brown v. Board of Education* required the courts to be involved in the process of administering desegregation plans, which became clear three years later in *Swann v. Charlotte–Mecklenburg Board of Education*,[500] where the Supreme Court approved a detailed decree issued by a district court, based on the recommendation of an expert in educational administration, containing measures like "the design of oddly shaped attendance zones, the pairing or clustering of black and white schools to permit a more reasonable racial balance, compulsory transportation of students to schools outside their neighborhoods, reassignment of teachers and other personnel to reduce the racial character of individual schools and requiring that new schools be constructed in locations that would not contribute to the persistence of segregation."[501] As mentioned by Laurence Claus and Richard S. Kay, the following twenty years witnessed numerous instances of federal judges attempting to reconcile the constitutional imperative with the practical realities of operating a school system, a task often made more difficult by passive or active resistance from local authorities. The practical and political questions associated with managing a desegregation regime returned regularly to the Supreme Court, whose judgments, from that

---

498 See Owen M. FISS, *The Civil Rights Injunctions*, Indiana University Press, Bloomington 1978, pp. 4–5; Owen M. Fiss and Doug Rendelman, *Injunctions*, Foundation Press, Mineola – New York 1984, pp. 33–34. Thus, structural injunctions can be considered a modern constitutional law instrument specifically developed for the protection of human rights, particularly in state institutions; an instrument that has been considered "an implicit part of the Constitutional guarantee of protecting individual rights from inappropriate government action." See William M. Tabb and Elaine W. Shoben, *Remedies*, Thomson West, St. Paul MN 2005, pp. 87–88.

499 See also Laurence Claus and Richard S. Kay, *U.S. National Report*, p. 23.

500 See *Swann v. Charlotte–Mecklenburg Bd. of Educ.*, 402 U.S. 1 (1971); Laurence Claus and Richard S. Kay, *U.S. National Report*, p. 30 (footnote 101).

501 *Id.* at 19–25. See Laurence Claus and Richard S. Kay, *U.S. National Report*, p. 30 (footnote 102).

point on, were largely concerned with defining limits to the broad judicial mandate sketched out in *Brown* and other decisions. The kinds of issues involved were illustrated by the Supreme Court's 1995 judgment in *Missouri v. Jenkins*,[502] one of its last significant statements on the remedial authority of federal courts in desegregation cases. The district court, in that case, had found that unconstitutional segregation had reduced the quality of the education offered in the affected schools. Over a ten–year period, the district court judge had, consequently, ordered that class size be reduced, that full–time kindergarten be instituted, that summer programs be expanded, that before– and after–school tutoring be provided, and that an early childhood development program be established. The district court also ordered a major capital improvement program and salary increases for teachers and other school employees.[503]

A similar situation occurred in the United States on matters related to the operation of prisons, based on the provision of the Eighth Amendment's prohibition of cruel and unusual punishment, and resulted in long–term supervision of numerous institutions. In litigation challenging the constitutionality of aspects of the Arkansas correctional institutions, federal judges ordered through structural injunctions, among other things, the closing of institutions, the maximum number of inmates in a particular facility and in individual cells, detailed procedures for determining disciplinary violations, and limits on the punishments administered. They required the employment of full–time psychiatrists or psychologists, affirmative action to recruit more minority personnel, and mandatory training of employees to improve race relations in the prisons. The practice of using armed inmates as "trusty" guards was prohibited. Inmates were to be provided with educational opportunities and a fair procedure for filing grievances. The courts retained jurisdiction for more than ten years.[504] Mental hospitals have been the subject of similar decrees,[505] and in somewhat more contained proceedings, so has the process of apportioning legislative representation.[506]

In Canada, similar to the Latin American amparo proceeding for the protection of constitutional rights, article 24.1 of the Charter establishes the right of anyone, when the rights or freedoms guaranteed by the Charter have been infringed or denied, "to apply to a court of competent jurisdiction to obtain such remedy as the court considers appropriate and just." According to that provision, the courts have the power to issue a wide variety of remedies where they find that the rights of individuals have been violated, including declarations and injunctions requiring the government to

---

502 See *Missouri v. Jenkins*, 515 U.S. 70 (1995). See Laurence Claus and Richard S. Kay, *U.S. National Report*, p. 31 (footnote 104).

503 *Id.* at 74–80. Laurence Claus and Richard S. Kay, *U.S. National Report*, p. 31.

504 See *Hutto v. Finney*, 437 U.S. 678 (1978); Laurence Claus and Richard S. Kay, *U.S. National Report*, p. 32 (footnote 107).

505 See *Wyatt v. Stickney*, 344 F. Supp. 373 (1972). See Laurence Claus and Richard S. Kay, *U.S. National Report*, p. 32 (footnote 108).

506 See *Branch v. Smith*, 538 U.S. 254 (2003); Laurence Claus and Richard S. Kay, *U.S. National Report*, p. 32 (footnote 109).

take positive actions to comply with the Constitution and to remedy the effects of past constitutional violations. In a leading case related to minority language, the court also issued structural injunctions or interdicts requiring the government, in particular, to provide instruction and facilities. In Canada, the Constitution Act of 1867 provided that both French and English be used in the legislatures and courts of Canada and Quebec, and the provincial constitutions, such as the Manitoba Act of 1870, provided similar rights. In 1985, the Supreme Court confronted a law that purported to abolish the bilingualism obligations of Manitoba, where the French–speaking population had become a minority. Nonetheless, the Court decided that the unilingual laws were unconstitutional but held that immediate invalidation of most of Manitoba's laws was not appropriate because it would produce a legal vacuum that would threaten the rule of law. The Court then decided that it would give the unilingual laws temporary validity for the period of time that was necessary to translate them into French; it retained jurisdiction over the case for a number of years and, during that time, heard various motions concerning the extent of the constitutional obligations for bilingualism.[507] The Court's actions in this regard have been considered a form of remedial activism, somewhat similar to the American and Indian experience of courts maintaining jurisdiction over public institutions such as schools and prisons in the 1970s and 1980s to ensure that they satisfied constitutional standards.[508]

However, legislative omissions have also given rise in Canada to important acts of judicial activism on matters of criminal justice, given the absence of legislative response to enact statutory standards for speedy trials and the prosecutor's disclosure of evidence to the accused. In 1993, however, the Court acted decisively by holding that the Charter requires pretrial disclosure to the accused of all relevant evidence held by the prosecutor,[509] and it held that the right to a trial in a reasonable time would be violated by pretrial delays of more than a year.[510] Another example would be the Supreme Court's decision that holds that it will generally violate the Charter to extradite a person to face the death penalty.[511] Although framed in negative terms that would potentially prevent extradition, the practical effect of the decision is to require the government to take positive steps to seek assurances from states that they will not seek or impose the death penalty on a person extradited from Canada.[512]

---

507 *Reference re Manitoba Language Rights* [1985] 1 S.C.R. 721; [1985] 2 S.C.R. 347; [1990] 3 S.C.R. 1417n; [1992] 1 S.C.R. 212. See Kent Roach, *Canadian National Report*, p. 18 (footnote 48).

508 See Kent ROACH, *Canadian National Report*, p. 18.

509 See *R. v. Stinchcombe* [1991] 3 S.C.R. 326; Kent Roach, *Canadian National Report*, p. 11 (footnote 18).

510 See *R. v. Askov* [1990] 2 S.C.R. 1199; Kent Roach, *Canadian National Report*, p. 12 (footnote 19).

511 See *United States v. Burns and Rafay* [2001] 1 S.C.R; Kent Roach, *Canadian National Report*, p. 12 (footnote 21).

512 See Kent Roach, *Canadian National Report*, p. 12.

In a certain way, in the United Kingdom, where the basic principle is that the court does not substitute itself for the legislature, it is also possible to identify important activities developed by the courts on matters of constitutional review regarding the protection of human rights, by issuing decisions with guidelines that supplement the jurisdiction of the Legislator or the administration. For example, referring to cases of the judges making the law in areas where there was inadequate previous precedent or statute, John Bell mentioned the case regarding the sterilization of intellectually handicapped adults, in which the House of Lords laid down principles that would govern the approval of such cases;[513] and the case decided in *Airedale NHS Trust v. Bland*[514] regarding the situation of a man who was in a permanent vegetative state and being fed through a tube. In the latter case, the House of Lords decided the circumstances, establishing policies on medical treatment for doctors could lawfully accede to the wishes of the man's parents that the feeding stop and that he be allowed to die. That is, in such cases, judicial decisions have provided rules for future application in the absence of any authoritative pronouncement by government.

In the Czech Republic, the Constitutional Court has filled the gap resulting from the Legislator's omission. The best and most controversial example mentioned by Zdenek Kühn is the one provided by the rent–control saga. In effect, in 2000, the Constitutional Court found unconstitutional rent control as practiced by Czech law, and it annulled the decree of the Ministry of Finance that regulated rent increases in apartment houses. The Court delayed the annulment to offer the legislature time to enact a new law with a mechanism to put rents to just terms, but the legislature declined to deal with the issue. The Court continued to annul decrees that dealt with the issue, and it used more and more compelling arguments to urge the legislature to enact a proper law.[515] In 2006, finally, the Court again criticized the legislative "activity, or rather, inactivity," which resulted in "freezing of controlled rent, which further deepens the violation of property rights of the owners of those apartments to which rent control applied. . . . By not passing them, the legislative assembly evoked an unconstitutional situation."[516] That is why the Constitutional Court rejected the petition but at the same time gave a rather unique verdict N° 1, according to which "[t]he long–term inactivity of the Parliament of the Czech Republic, consisting of failure to pass a special legal regulation defining cases in which a landlord is entitled to unilaterally increase rent, payment for services relating to use of an apartment, and to change other conditions of a lease agreement, is unconstitutional and vio-

513 See *Re F (Mental Patient: Sterilisation)* [1990] 2 AC 173; John Bell, *British National Report*, p. 7 (footnote 33).

514 See [1993] 1 All ER 821; John Bell, *British National Report*, p. 7.

515 See decision of November 20, 2002, Pl. ÚS 8/02, *Rent Control II*, published as N° 528/2002 Sb.; and see decision of March 19, 2003, Pl. ÚS 2/03, *Rent Control III*, published as N° 84/2003 Sb; Zdenek Kühn, *Czech National Report*, p. 14 (footnote 58).

516 See decision of February 28, 2006, Pl. ÚS 20/05, *Rent Control IV*, at http://angl.concourt.cz/angl_verze/doc/p–20–05.php; Zdenek Kühn, *Czech National Report*, p. 13 (footnote 59).

lates" a number of constitutional rights.[517] The unique verdict was accompanied by a similarly unique reasoning in which the Court directed general courts to increase rents themselves, instead of entirely passive legislature; that is, the Court ordered general courts to make the law instead of the legislature. In this regard, the Court openly held that it must deviate from its role of negative legislator, expressing the following:

> Based on these facts [legislative inactivity], the Constitutional Court, in its role of protector of constitutionality, cannot limit its function to the mere position of a "negative" legislator, and must, in the framework of a balance of the individual branches of power characteristic of a law–based state founded on respect for the rights and freedoms of man and of citizens . . . , create space for the preservation of the fundamental rights and freedoms. Therefore, the general courts, even despite the absence of the envisaged specific regulations, must decide to increase rent, depending on local conditions, so as to prevent the abovementioned discrimination. In view of the fact that such cases will involve the finding and application of simple law, which is not a matter for the Constitutional Court, . . . the Constitutional Court refrains from offering a specific decision–making procedure and thereby replacing the mission of the general courts. It merely states that it is necessary to refrain from arbitrariness; a decision must be based on rational arguments and thorough weighing of all the circumstances of a case, the application of natural principles and the customs of civic life, the conclusions of legal learning and settled, constitutionally consistent court practice.[518]

The Constitutional Court, in addition, clearly explained in its decision its role in cases of absolute omissions by the Legislator, expressing the following:

> As a consequence of the inactivity of the legislative assembly it can evoke an unconstitutional situation, if the legislature is required to pass certain regulations, does not do so, and thereby interferes in a right protected by the law and by the constitution. . . . [W]e can conclude that under certain conditions the consequences of a gap (a missing legal regulation) are unconstitutional, in particular when the legislature decides that it will regulate a particular area, states that intention in law, but does not pass the envisaged regulations. The same conclusion applies to the case where Parliament passed the declared regulations, but they were annulled because they did not meet constitutional criteria, and the legislature did not pass a constitutional replacement, although the Constitutional Court gave it a sufficient period of time to do so.
>
> The relationship between the legislative and judicial branches arises from the separation of powers in the state, as established in the Constitution. A material analysis necessarily leads us to conclude that this separation is not a purpose in and of itself, but pursues a higher purpose. From its very beginnings it was subjected by the constitutional framers to an idea based above all on service to the citizen and to society. Every power has a tendency to concentration, growth and corruption; absolute power to an uncontrollable corruption. If one of the branches of power exceeds its constitutional framework, its authority, or, on the contrary, does not fulfill its tasks and thus prevents the proper functioning of another branch (in the adjudicated case, of the judicial branch), the control mechanism of checks and balances, which is built into the system of separation of powers, must come into play. . . . [G]eneral courts err if they refuse to provide protection to the rights of those who have turned to them with a demand for justice, if they deny their complaints merely with a formalistic reasoning and refer-

517 *Id.*

518 *Id.*

> ence to the inactivity of the legislature (the non–existence of the relevant legal regulations), after the Constitutional Court, as protector of constitutionality and review thereof, opened the way for them through its decisions. The Constitutional Court has repeatedly declared the unequal position of one group of owners of rental apartments and buildings to be discriminatory and unconstitutional, and the long–term inactivity of the Parliament of the CR to be incompatible with the requirements of a law–based state. The Constitutional Court, by the will of the constitutional framers, is responsible for the maintenance of the constitutional order in the Czech Republic, and therefore it does not intend to abandon this obligation, it calls on the general courts to fulfill their obligations.[519]

Finally, the case of the Constitutional Court of Colombia must be mentioned, particularly regarding a new constitutional situation that the Court has created to decide specific actions of *tutela* (*amparo*) for the protection of fundamental rights filed by displaced persons within Colombia due to the situation of violence suffered for years, particularly in rural areas and specifically on the occasion of deciding on the factual lack of enforcement of the *tutela* rulings. In such cases of massive violations of human rights, the Court has created what it has called an *estado de cosas inconstitucionales* (factual state of unconstitutionality), which it has used to substitute itself for the ordinary judges, the Legislator, and the Administration in the definition and coordination of public policies, a power that the Constitutional Court has exercised *ex officio*. This was referred to, among other decisions, in Decision N° 007 of January 26, 2009, where the Court ruled on the "[c]oordination with the territorial entities of public policies of attention to the displaced population" and ordered a series of public actions to be executed by a variety of public administration entities.[520] In Decision N° T–025/04, the Court specified the conditions required to declared a factual state of unconstitutionality, such as "(i) the massive and widespread infringement of various constitutional rights affecting a significant number of people; (ii) the prolonged omission of the authorities in the fulfillment of its obligation to guarantee the rights; the adoption of unconstitutional practices, such as incorporating the action of *tutela* as part of the procedure to ensure the violated right; … (iv) the failure to issue legislative, administrative, or budgetary measures to avoid infringement of Rights; (v) the existence of a social problem whose solution compromises the involvement of several entities, requires the adoption of complex and coordinated actions[,] and demands level of resources requiring important additional budgetary effort; (vi) if all people affected by the same problem would resort to the *tutela* for the protection of their rights, there would be greater judicial congestion."[521]

With these sorts of decisions, as mentioned by Sandra Morelli, the Constitutional Court has "abandoned its role as guarantor of fundamental constitutional rights of an individual in a particular case, to assume another role, that of formulating or contributing to formulate public policies, adding its implementation, and monitoring its implementation to guarantee the satisfaction of needs of displaced populations according to available resources and subject to compliance of procedural requirements

---

519 See Zdenek Kühn, *Czech National Report*, p. 14.

520 See Sandra Morelli, *Colombian National Report II*, p. 5.

521 *Id.*, p. 8.

that the same Court assumed the role to regulate."[522] This, of course, has nothing to do with the role of the constitutional judge in taking over responsibilities of the legislature and the public administration and in ordering specific actions to public entities and public officials. Sandra Morelli has considered this a "historical betrayal that the Colombian Constitutional Court undertakes, when instead of protecting each displaced individual that had filed action of *tutela* regarding their fundamental rights, even by way of guarantee of the right to equality, ventures into the strange category of the factual state of unconstitutionality and via the general way, without any need to bring an action of *tutela*, assumes the role of supreme administrative authority."[523]

II. CONSTITUTIONAL COURTS' FILLING THE GAP OF RELATIVE LEGISLATIVE OMISSIONS

Apart from the aforementioned cases of specific judicial review to ensure judicial review of *absolute* legislative omissions, judicial review of relative legislative omissions has been extensively developed in the past decades in all democratic countries, particularly in cases in which the matter is not the absence of legislation but the existence of poor, deficient, or inadequate regulation according to the constitutional provisions.[524] This can lead to the evaluation of the omission and the declaration of the unconstitutionality of the provision containing the omission, as commonly happens in countries with a diffuse system of judicial review.

But in countries with a concentrated system of judicial review, although constitutional courts have the power to annul statutes considered unconstitutional, including those that omit fundamental aspects imposed by the Constitution, in cases of relative legislative omissions being considered unconstitutional, the constitutional courts have also developed the practice of declaring the omission unconstitutional without annulling the provision. In the decisions, the courts send to the Legislator guidelines or instructions to correct the unconstitutionality, thus orienting the Legislator's future activities.[525]

Of course, in all these cases, the purpose of the constitutional courts' controlling the unconstitutionality of relative legislative omissions is not to allow the courts to create new legislative provision; that is, the purpose is not to usurp the Legislator's

522 *Id.*, p. 10.

523 *Id.*, p. 11.

524 See Francisco Javier Díaz Revorio, *Las sentencias interpretativas del Tribunal Constitucional*, Ed. Lex Nova, Valladolid 2001, pp. 293, 294; Héctor Fix Zamudio and Eduardo Ferrer Mac–Gregor, *Las sentencias de los Tribunales Constitucionales*, Ed. Porrúa, Mexico City 2009, pp. 34, 37, 71; Víctor Bazan, "Jurisdicción constitucional local y corrección de las omisiones inconstitucionales relativas," *Revista Iberoamericana de Derecho Procesal Constitucional*, N° 2, Instituto Iberoamericano de Derecho Procesal Constitucional, Editorial Porrúa, Mexico City 2004, pp. 189 ff.

525 See José Julio Fernández Rodríguez, *La inconstitucionalidad por omisión: Teoría general. Derecho comparado. El caso español*, Civitas, Madrid 1998, pp. 227 ff.

functions.[526] Nonetheless, in many cases, the result of these judicial decisions has been the encroachment of legislative attributions when orienting or instructing the Legislative body as to how it must fill the omission to make it conform with the Constitution.[527]

1. Constitutional Courts and equality rights: deciding on the unconstitutionality of statutes without declaring their nullity

As in countries with a diffuse system of judicial review, in countries with a concentrated system of judicial review, constitutional courts have also declared statutory provisions unconstitutional but without annulling them. Instead, in these cases, constitutional courts have limited their activity to declaring unconstitutional the challenged provision only regarding the part that is not in accord with the Constitution. Instead of annulling the provision, in some cases, the courts referred to the Legislator for it to produce the needed legislation,[528] and in others cases, the constitutional court issued directives, guidelines, recommendations, and even orders to the Legislator to correct the unconstitutional legislative omissions. In all these cases, the constitutional court assists and collaborates with the Legislator.

An important note is that, in almost all the cases of relative legislative omissions that are declared unconstitutional but not annulled, the protection of fundamental constitutional rights have always been involved, particularly the right to equality and nondiscrimination.[529]

In concentrated systems of judicial review, the ability of constitutional courts to declare a legal provision unconstitutional without annulling it has been expressly established in the legislation governing the constitutional court's functions, as in Germany, where in 1970 the reform of the Law related to the Federal Constitutional Tribunal (BVerfG) established a specific function of the Tribunal in specific cases: to give preference to the constitutional interpretation of a statute and to "declare a law to be compatible or *incompatible* with the Basic Law," without the need to declare the provision "to be null and void" (article 31.2).[530] A similar reform was proposed in 2005 in Spain in relation to the Organic Law of the Constitutional Tribunal that established the contrary principle: "when a [Constitutional Tribunal's] decision

---

526 See Héctor Fix Zamudio and Eduardo Ferrer Mac–Gregor, *Las sentencias de los Tribunales Constitucionales*, Ed. Porrúa, Mexico City 2009, p. 34.

527 *Id.*, pp. 36–37; 75, 88.

528 See Christian Behrendt, *Le judge constitutionnel, un législateur–cadre positif. Un analyse comparative en droit francais, belge et allemande*, Bruylant, Brussels 2006, p. 124.

529 See F. Fernández Segado, *Spanish National Report*, pp. 9, 25, 39–42. P. Popelier has pointed out that, in Belgium, "the principle of equality and non discrimination constitutes the reference norm in more than 85% of the decisions adopted by the Constitutional Courts." See P. Popelier, *Belgian National Report*, p. 3.

530 See Christian Behrendt, *Le judge constitutionnel, un législateur–cadre positif. Un analyse comparative en droit francais, belge et allemande*, Bruylant, Brussels 2006, p. 93; See I. Härtel, *German National Report*, pp. 7–9; Francisco Javier Díaz Revorio, *Las sentencias interpretativas del Tribunal Constitucional*, Ed. Lex Nova, Valladolid 2001, p. 260; F. Fernandez Segado, *Spanish National Report*, p. 6.

declares the unconstitutionality of a provision, it must in addition declare the nullity of the challenged provisions."[531] The reform of the Law was not approved in Spain,[532] which did not prevent the Constitutional Tribunal from overcoming the rigidity of the dichotomy and issuing decisions of unconstitutionality without nullity.

An important case resolved by the Spanish Constitutional Tribunal was Decision N° 116/1987, regarding Law 37/1984 of October 22, 1984, which established social rights and benefits to military and police officers for services accomplished during the Civil War, excluding professional military who enrolled in the Armed Forces after 1936. Because of that exclusion, the Constitutional Tribunal considered the Law contrary to the principle of equality, annulled the exclusion, and extended the application of the provision to those who had been excluded.[533] Another important decision was Decision N° 45/1989, where the Constitutional Tribunal found unconstitutional a provision of Law 48/1985 on Income Tax that made the joint tax return for family members compulsory, which implied heavier tax obligations for a person integrated in a family group than for a person with the same income but not part of a family group.[534] The Constitutional Tribunal in this case considered the issue of the dichotomy unconstitutionality–nullity, arguing that, although the text of article 40.1 of the Tribunal's Law was contradictory, it was not necessary for that dichotomy to be applied, particularly in cases of judicial review of an omission, in which case "the nullity as an strictly negative measure[] is manifestly incapable of reordering the Income Tax regime in a way compatible with the Constitution." The Tribunal concluded that it was for the Legislator, "according to the decision, to make the needed modifications or adaptations of the legal regime, according to its normative powers."[535] As Francisco Fernández Segado has pointed out:

> with the decision 45/1989, the Tribunal not only moved away from the legal text, giving birth to decisions of unconstitutionality without nullity, situating itself in the wake of the BVerfG [German Federal Constitutional Tribunal], but in addition categorically breached the binomial unconstitutionality/ nullity characteristic of the vision of the constitutional judge as "negative legislator."[536]

The same technique has been applied in Nicaragua, where the Supreme Court, in a decision recognizing the unconstitutionality of articles 225 and 228 of the Civil Code prohibiting and restricting cases of paternity inquiry, decided not to annul the

531 See Francisco Javier Díaz Revorio, *Las sentencias interpretativas del Tribunal Constitucional*, Ed. Lex Nova, Valladolid 2001, p. 301.

532 See F. Fernández Segado, *Spanish National Report*, p. 6

533 See F. Fernández Segado, *Spanish National Report*, p. 10.

534 See STC 45/1989, of February 20, 1989, para. 11.; F. Fernández Segado, *Spanish National Report*, p. 12.

535 *Id.* See also STC 13/1992, February 6, 1992, fund. jur. 17; STC 16/1996, February 1, 1996 fund. jur. 8; and STC 68/1996, April 18, 1996, fund. jur. 14, in F. Fernandez Segado, *Spanish National Report*, pp. 12–13.

536 See F. Fernández Segado, *Spanish National Report*, p. 12.

articles and maintained them with effects pending new legislation to be approved by Congress, in order to avoid graver problems that a legal vacuum could produce.[537]

In Switzerland, where judicial review of cantonal laws is allowed, the Federal Court has also decided cases in relative legislative omissions but has refused to assume the role of legislator. In the *Hegetschweiler* case,[538] on the appeal of a married couple, the Supreme Court concluded that a cantonal regulation related to income and property taxes for married couples was unconstitutional because married couples owed higher taxes than unmarried couples who lived together in the same household and had similar financial means; this was considered a breach of the equal treatment precept (Article 8.1, Constitution). The subject matter of the appeal for an abstract control of norms was a new rule that represented an improvement over the previous legal situation. As mentioned by Tobias Jaag, if the Supreme Court had annulled the contested rule, the former rule would have again entered into effect, unless the Court had established a substitute rule. The Supreme Court rejected the appeal and limited itself to stating that the contested rule was not in full conformity with the Constitution; in this manner, the cantonal legislator was asked to remedy the unconstitutional situation. For the couple who appealed, the outcome was most dissatisfactory.[539]

In another case issued in 1986, the Supreme Court found that a cantonal regulation imposing a lower retirement age for women than for men was in breach of the constitutional right to equal treatment of women and men. The Supreme Court, however, left it at that, reasoning that the cantonal legislator needed time to establish the constitutional status.[540] In the same sense, the Supreme Court protected the complaint of a federal official that a rule permitting only women, not men, to take early retirement after thirty–five years of service violated the right to equal treatment of women and men. The Court did not view itself as having competence, however, to issue a correct rule; the petition of the federal official for permission to take early retirement was therefore rejected.[541] In a similar case relating to the equal treatment of boys and girls during school lessons, the Court explicitly held: "it would, however, be out of the question for the Supreme Court, on its own initiative, to create a rule in lieu of the cantonal legislator."[542]

In general terms, the main result of constitutional courts exercising judicial review powers regarding statutes with unconstitutional provisions has been the as-

537 See decisions of November 22, 1957, B.J. p. 18730 (1873?), and of June 16, 1986, B.J. p. 105; Iván Escobar Fornos, "Las sentencias constitucionales y sus efectos en Nicaragua," in *Anuario Iberoamericano de Justicia Constitucional*, Centro de Estudios Políticos y Constitucionales, Nº 12, 2008, Madrid 2008, p. 102.

538 See BGE 110 Ia 7; Tobias Jaag, *Swiss National Report*, p. 8 (footnote 37).

539 See Tobias Jaag, *Swiss National Report*, p. 8.

540 See Supreme Court in ZBl 87/1986, 482 ff.; Tobias Jaag, *Swiss National Report*, p. 9 (footnote 40).

541 See BGE 109 Ib 86, 88 ff.; Tobias Jaag, *Swiss National Report*, p. 9 (footnote 41).

542 See Supreme Court, in ZBl 86/1985, 492, 495; Tobias Jaag, *Swiss National Report*, p. 9 (footnote 42).

sumption by constitutional courts of a new role as aides to the Legislator; they direct requests, recommendations, and instructions for the legislative organ to issue additional legislation to surpass the constitutional doubts that result from the relative legislative omission.[543]

Even in countries like Switzerland, where there is no judicial review of federal legislation but only regarding cantonal legislation, this does not preclude the Federal Supreme Court from criticizing a federal legislative rule, thereby signaling to the legislators that an amendment of the law is required.[544] For instance, during the past years, several cantonal voting systems have been held unconstitutional because they did not guarantee equal treatment of the voters (equal right to vote). In these cases, the Supreme Court contented itself with declaring that the voting systems were unconstitutional and asking the cantonal legislators to amend the rule that was objected to.[545]

These instruction or directives sent by constitutional courts to the Legislator are in some cases nonbinding recommendations and in other cases obligatory.[546]

2. Constitutional Courts' issuing nonbinding directives to the legislator

In general terms, regarding noncompulsory judicial recommendations – known as exhortative decisions, delegate decisions, or *sentenze indiritzzo* in Italy[547]– the Constitutional Court declares the unconstitutionality of a provision but does not introduce the norm to be applied through interpretation, leaving this task to the Legislator. In Italy, these decisions are also called "principles' additive decisions,"[548] such as Decision N° 171 of 1996, issued by the Constitutional Court to declare unconstitutional a provision of the Law regulating the right to strike in public services. The provision did not provide for previous notice and a reasonable term in strikes of lawyers and advocates.[549]

---

543 See Héctor Fix Zamudio and Eduardo Ferrer Mac–Gregor, *Las sentencias de los Tribunales Constitucionales*, Ed. Porrúa, Mexico City 2009, pp. 39, 89.

544 See BGE 103 Ia 53, 55; Tobias Jaag, *Swiss National Report*, p. 7 (footnote 29).

545 See BGE 131 I 74, p. 84 ff.; 129 I p. 185, 205 ff.; Tobias Jaag, *Swiss National Report*, p. 7 (footnote 44, 45).

546 In this sense, Christian Behrendt, in analyzing the situation in Germany, Belgium, and France, distinguishes between what he calls permissive, not binding interferences or *lignes directives*, and the enabling obligatory interferences, or injunctions. See Christian Behrendt, *Le judge constitutionnel, un législateur–cadre positif. Un analyse comparative en droit francais, belge et allemande*, Bruylant, Brussels 2006, pp. 253 ff.

547 See L. Pegoraro, *La Corte e il Parlamento. Sentenze–indirizzo e attivitá legislativa*, Cedam, Padua 1987, pp. 3 ff.; Francisco Javier Díaz Revorio, *Las sentencias interpretativas del Tribunal Constitucional*, Ed. Lex Nova, Valladolid 2001, p. 268; Néstor Pedro Sagües, *Argentinean National Report II*, pp. 4–7.

548 Francisco Javier Díaz Revorio, *Las sentencias interpretativas del Tribunal Constitucional*, Ed. Lex Nova, Valladolid 2001, pp. 279–284, 305.

549 See A. Vespaziani, "Una sentenza additiva di principio reguardo allo 'sciopero' degli avvocati," in *Giurisprudenza costitutionalle*, 1996, Vol. IV, pp. 2718 ff. Francisco Javier Díaz

In other cases, the instruction directed to the Legislator can be conditional with respect to the constitutional court. In Italy, for instance, when dealing with an unconstitutional statute, the Constitutional Court can recommend that the Legislator introduce legislation to eliminate the constitutional doubts. Through the *doppia pronuncia* formula, if the Legislator fails to execute the recommendations of the Court, in a second decision, the Court can declare unconstitutional the impugned statute.[550]

This sort of exhortative judicial review is also accepted in Germany, where it is called "appellate decisions."[551] Here, the Federal Constitutional Tribunal in cases of unconstitutional statutes can issue "an admonition to the Legislator," which contains legislative directives "addressed to the Legislator which can be of norm–requesting as well as norm–demanding nature still considered constitutional, in its impacts and effects, to improve or alternatively replace it,"[552] for which purpose it must give the Legislator a term to do so. Once the term is exhausted, the provision becomes unconstitutional, and the Tribunal must rule on the matter. An example of this type of decision is one issued by the Federal Constitutional Tribunal regarding a survivor's pension. A statute provided that a widow would always obtain the pension of her late husband, but the widower would obtain his wife's pension in case of her death only if she had primarily provided for the family and earned the family income before or if she had been a public official. The Federal Constitutional Court found that the provision was in process of becoming unconstitutional because of social changes that have taken place particularly on the role of women in the family, asking the Legislator to issue according to its powers to legislate the necessary provisions to prevent the unconstitutionality.[553]

In other cases, the Federal Constitutional Tribunal has limited itself to issue directives to the Legislator but leaving the Legislator to make the political decision. This was the case of the decision issued regarding a statute of March 18, 1965, on the reimbursement of electoral expenses of political parties. The Tribunal also developed some conditions to be followed only if the Legislator decided to implement the reimbursement system.[554]

Revorio, *Las sentencias interpretativas del Tribunal Constitucional*, Ed. Lex Nova, Valladolid 2001, pp. 281–282 (footnote 164).

550 See Iván Escobar Fornos, *Estudios Jurídicos*, Vol. I, Ed. Hispamer, Managua 2007, p. 504.

551 See Francisco Javier Díaz Revorio, *Las sentencias interpretativas del Tribunal Constitucional*, Ed. Lex Nova, Valladolid 2001, pp. 264; Iván Escobar Fornos, *Estudios Jurídicos*, Vol. I, Ed. Hispamer, Managua 2007, p. 505.

552 See I. Härtel, *German National Report*, pp. 17–18.

553 See BVerfGE 39, 169 ff.; I. Härtel, *German National Report*, pp. 18; Francisco Javier Díaz Revorio, *Las sentencias interpretativas del Tribunal Constitucional*, Ed. Lex Nova, Valladolid 2001, pp. 265 (footnote 115).

554 See BVerfG, decision of July 19, 1966, BVerfGE 20, 56 (114–115), in Christian Behrendt, *Le judge constitutionnel, un législateur–cadre positif. Un analyse comparative en droit francais, belge et allemande*, Bruylant, Brussels 2006, pp. 176–179, 185 ff.

In France, the Constitutional Council has also issued directives to the Legislator, which even without normative direct effects can establish a framework for future legislative action.[555] They have persuasive effect only because the Constitutional Council always is able to exercise review of the constitutionality of a subsequent law.

A similar technique, called signalizations, has been applied in Poland, through which the Constitutional Tribunal directs the Legislator's attention to problems of general nature.[556]

In Belgium,[557] the Constitutional Court has also applied this technique. In particular, in a 1982 case referring to regional taxation legislation on environmental matters, as to the definition of *pollutant payer*, the former Court of Arbitration issued directives to the regional Legislators establishing the conditions under which *pollutant payer* was not in conformity with the Constitution's principle of equality.[558] Also in an interesting decision issued by the same former Court of Arbitration in 2004, on the taxation regime for donations to nonprofit associations established in a federal law, the Court sent directives to a regional Legislator that was different from the one that had incurred in an unconstitutionality, that is, to the regional legislator that the Court considered competent to issue legislation on the matter.[559]

In Serbia, Article 105 of the Law on the Constitutional Court empowers the Constitutional Court to give its opinion or to point out the need to adopt or revise laws, or to implement other measures relevant for the protection of constitutionality and legality, which are used to put some pressure on the National Assembly to bring laws for implementation of constitutional provisions or to correct existing unconstitutional rules. In these cases, the court can act *ex officio*, but the opinions do not have binding force. The most important notifications and opinions issued by the Court were connected to noncompliance with deadlines stipulated in constitutional laws for the enforcement of the Constitution.[560]

In the Czech Republic, the Constitutional Court in some cases has also provided a detailed analysis of the law that will fit the constitutional test of the Court after the original law has been annulled.[561] Nonetheless, those guidelines are not binding, and

---

555 See Decision 83–164 DC; Bertrand Mathieu, *French National Report*, p. 10.

556 See, e.g., signalization concerning protection of tenants of June 29, 2005, OTK ZU 2005/6A/77; Marek Safjan, *Polish National Report*, p. 16 (footnote 45).

557 See P. Popelier, *Belgian National Report*, p. 8.

558 See CA arrêt 79/93 of November 9, 1993, in Christian Behrendt, *Le judge constitutionnel, un législateur–cadre positif. Un analyse comparative en droit francais, belge et allemande*, Bruylant, Brussels 2006, pp. 175–176, 191 ff.

559 See CA arrêt 45/2004 of March 17, 2004, in Christian Behrendt, *Le judge constitutionnel, un législateur–cadre positif. Un analyse comparative en droit francais, belge et allemande*, Bruylant, Brussels 2006, pp. 175–176, 230–237.

560 See Boško Tripković, *Serbian National Report*, pp. 9–10.

561 See Decision *Anonymous Witness* of October 12, 1994, Pl. ÚS 4/94, at http://angl.concourt.cz/angl_verze/doc/p-4-94.php; Zdenek Kühn, *Czech National Report*, p. 12 (footnote 53).

practice shows that the Legislator frequently does not follow the Court's reasoning.[562]

In France, the Constitutional Council – which until 2009 could only review statutes' constitutionality before they were promulgated by the National Assembly – has necessarily issued decisions that have interfered with the legislative function.[563] Consequently, on many occasions, the Council has issued decisions containing non-obligatory directives to the Legislator to sufficiently correct the draft legislation submitted. One example of such a decision on economic matters is the one adopted in 1982 on the occasion of the control exercised by the Constitutional Council regarding the Nationalization Law, particularly referring to the provisions on compensation regarding the nationalized enterprise stocks. The Council argued that it was necessary for the Legislation to be approved to take into account the corresponding compensation and the phenomenon of monetary depreciation.[564]

On institutional matters, in another decision in 2000, the Constitutional Council issued directives to the Legislator when reviewing a statute on election age. The statute lowered the age to be elected in European elections for non–French candidates to eighteen years but kept the age of twenty–three years for French citizens. The Council expressed that if the Legislator was to reduce the age to be elected, it must do so for all candidates.[565]

In Mexico, in the first decision the Supreme Court adopted to resolve a direct action of a statute's unconstitutionality (37/2001), in addition to declaring the provision unconstitutional, the Court exhorted the Legislator to legislate on the matter, fixing a term of ninety days to do so.[566]

In countries with diffuse systems of judicial review, exhortative rulings have also been issued by Supreme Courts. This is the case in Argentina, in the *Verbitsky* case, where the Supreme Court decided a collective *habeas corpus* petition, without declaring unconstitutional any legal provision of the Province of Buenos Aires. It then exhorted authorities to sanction new legal provisions to take care of the overcrowding and dreadful situation in the penitentiary system.[567] Another important case was

---

562 See Zdenek Kühn, *Czech National Report*, p. 12.

563 See Bertrand Mathieu, *French National Report*, p. 6.

564 See Decision 132 DC of January 16, 1982 (*GD*. N° 31. Loi de nationalization), in Christian Behrendt, *Le judge constitutionnel, un législateur–cadre positif. Un analyse comparative en droit francais, belge et allemande*, Bruylant, Brussels 2006, pp. 173–175.

565 See CC, Decision 426 DC of March 30, 2000, in Christian Behrendt, *Le judge constitutionnel, un législateur–cadre positif. Un analyse comparative en droit francais, belge et allemande*, Bruylant, Brussels 2006, pp. 176.

566 See Héctor Fix Zamudio and Eduardo Ferrer Mac–Gregor, "Las sentencias de los tribunales constitucionales en el ordenamiento mexicano," in *Anuario Iberoamericano de Justicia Constitucional*, N° 12, 2008, Centro de Estudios Políticos y Constitucionales, Madrid 2008, p. 252.

567 See CSIJ, Fallos 328:1146, in Néstor P. Sagües, "Los efectos de las sentencias constitucionales en el derecho argentino," in *Anuario Iberoamericano de Justicia Constitucional*, Centro de Estudios Políticos y Constitucionales, N° 12, 2008, Madrid 2008, p. 340; Néstor Pedro Sagües, *Argentinean National Report II*, pp. 7–11.

Rosza, where the Supreme Court, after declaring unconstitutional a decision of the Judiciary Council of the Nation regarding the provisional appointment of judges, exhorted the Congress and the executive to enact a new "constitutionally valid" regime, provided guidelines for the new regime to follow, and granted Congress one year to implement the new system.[568]

In other cases, the Argentinean Supreme Tribunal, after declaring the unconstitutionality of some statutory provisions, has issued guidelines to Congress for future legislation that indicate the constitutional path that Congress should take on certain affairs. Moreover, in some decisions, it has changed the clear legislative intent – through judicial interpretation – to make the law adequate with the Court's interpretation of the Constitution. These actions show the Court's increasing involvement in realms previously left to the political branches of government. For instance, in the cases *Castillo*[569] and *Aquino* (2004),[570] the Supreme Court declared unconstitutional the Labor Risks Law (Law 24.557), particularly its procedural contents (a matter constitutionally reserved to provincial legislation) and the limits of compensation for labor injuries. The Court found that its provisions denied workers their right to complete restitution. In addition, the Court's rulings demanded congressional action to modify the system in accordance with Court–established guidelines.

In *Vizzoti*, the Supreme Court ruled that the limits to the base salary used to calculate termination compensation provided for in the Employment Law were unreasonable, in light of the constitutional obligation to protect workers against unjustified firings. The Court then provided Congress with guidelines for valid limits, indicating that "the Court's decision does not entail undue interference with congressional powers, nor a violation of the separation of powers, being only the duly exercise of the constitutionally–mandated judicial review over laws and governmental action."[571] In other cases of judicial review of conventionality, regarding the American Convention of Human Rights, as in the *Cantos* case (2003),[572] the Argentinean Supreme Court demanded that Congress pass legislation to comply with the binding rulings of the Inter–American Court of Human Rights.

568 Decision of May 23, 2007, *Jurisprudencia Argentina*, 2007–III–414, in Néstor P. Sagües, "Los efectos de las sentencias constitucionales en el derecho argentino," in *Anuario Iberoamericano de Justicia Constitucional*, Centro de Estudios Políticos y Constitucionales, N° 12, 2008, Madrid 2008, p. 341. See also Néstor Pedro Sagües, *Argentinean National Report II*, pp. 11–12. See also Fallos 330:2361 (2007), in Alejandra Rodríguez Galán and Alfredo Mauricio Vítolo, *Argentinean National Report I*, p. 13.

569 See Fallos 327:3610 (2004); Alejandra Rodríguez Galán and Alfredo Mauricio Vítolo, *Argentinean National Report I*, p. 13.

570 See Fallos 327:3753 (2004); Alejandra Rodríguez Galán and Alfredo Mauricio Vítolo, *Argentinean National Report I*, p. 13.

571 See Fallos 327:3677 (2004); Alejandra Rodríguez Galán and Alfredo Mauricio Vítolo, *Argentinean National Report I*, p. 13; Néstor Pedro Sagües, *Argentinean National Report II*, p. 20.

572 See Fallos 326:2968 (2003); Alejandra Rodríguez Galán and Alfredo Mauricio Vítolo, *Argentinean National Report I*, p. 15 (footnote 60).

In Colombia, the Constitutional Court has also assumed similar exhortative powers with respect to Congress. After declaring unconstitutional a few articles of Law 600 of 2000 (Articles 382–389) on *habeas corpus*, the Court exhorted Congress to legislate on the matter according to the criteria established in the ruling, and it gave Congress a term in which it needed to legislate.[573]

A similar position has been adopted by the Supreme Court of the Netherlands, despite the ban on judicial review of statutes' constitutionality established in Article 120 of the Constitution. In the 1989 *Harmonization Act* case, the Supreme Court, though maintaining that it was clearly not entitled to review whether an Act of Parliament was compatible with legal principles, made it clear that – had it been allowed to do so – it would have ruled that the 1988 Harmonization Act violated the principle of legal certainty. The Court thus gave the legislature some "expert advice," and the latter, taking the hint, eventually changed the law. As mentioned by J. Uzman, T. Barkhuysen, and M. L. van Emmerik, "the ban on judicial review of legislation then does not prevent the judiciary to engage in a dialogue with the legislature, be it that such occasions remain rare."[574]

In some cases, this dialogue has led the Supreme Court, as in the *Labour Expenses Deduction* case,[575] to rule that it would not – for the time being – intervene because doing so would entail choosing from different policy options. The Court made clear that it might think otherwise if the legislature knowingly persisted in its unlawful course.[576] But in no case can these judicial decisions consist of the Supreme Court giving orders to Parliament to produce legislation by means of injunctions, even if the legislative omission renders the legislation incompatible with the European Union law.[577]

3. Constitutional Courts' issuing binding orders and directives to the legislator

In contrast, in many other cases of judicial review, particularly those referring to relative legislative omissions, constitutional courts have progressively assumed a more positive role regarding the Legislator, issuing not only directives, but also orders or instructions, for the Legislator to reform or correct pieces of legislation in the sense indicated by the Court. This has transformed constitutional courts into a sort of auxiliary Legislator, imposing on the Legislator certain tasks and establishing a precise term for their performance.

This judicial review technique has been used in Germany, where the Federal Constitutional Tribunal, in many cases, after having determined the incompatibility of a legal provision with the Constitution, without declaring its nullity, declares the

573 See Germán Alfonso López Daza, *Colombian National Report I*, p. 11.

574 See J. Uzman, T. Barkhuysen, and M. L. van Emmerik, *Dutch National Report*, p. 6.

575 See Supreme Court judgment of 12 May 1999, *NJ* 2000/170 (*Labour Expenses Deduction*). See J. Uzman, T. Barkhuysen, and M. L. van Emmerik, *Dutch National Report*, p. 26 (footnote 79).

576 See J. Uzman, T. Barkhuysen, and M. L. van Emmerik, *Dutch National Report*, p. 42.

577 See Supreme Court judgment of 21 March 2003, *NJ* 2003/691 (*State v. Waterpakt*); J. Uzman, T. Barkhuysen, and M. L. van Emmerik, *Dutch National Report*, p. 38.

obligation of the Legislator to resolve the unconstitutional condition and to improve or abolish the law.[578] An early example of this sort of injunctive decision regarding the Legislator was adopted in 1981 with respect to a provision of the Civil Code (Article 1579) that established the regime of alimony, specifically the possibility of it reduction or suppression for equitable reasons and in particular, the exceptions to the reduction based on the impossibility for the holder of the pension to carry on remunerative work due to the attention to be given to the child the former spouse had. This exception was challenged in a particular judicial case that reached the Tribunal, which found that, though motivated by educational and family reasons, the rigidity of the provision prevented the courts from adjusting it to individual circumstances, violating article 2.1 of the Constitution (individual freedom). Consequently, the Tribunal decided that "the Legislator must establish a new regime taking into account the principle of proportionality. The Legislator is free to decide whether to adopt an additional provision or to modify the second part of article 1579."[579]

In another case, on professional conflicts of interest as contrary to the fundamental right of everyone to choose his or her profession, the Tribunal also issued orders to the Legislator but without leaving it any alternative. The Tribunal found a specific legal conflict of interest (preventing tax counsels from exercising commercial activities) unconstitutional in certain situations, concluding that, "[f]ollowing the principle of proportionality, the Legislator must establish transitory dispositions for the cases in which to immediately end commercial activities could signify a heavy burden. It is for the Legislator to fix the content of these transitory provisions."[580] Another classic example is the Federal Constitutional Tribunal decision in a case of reimbursement for electoral expenses in the electoral campaign of 1969, in which article 18 of the Political Parties Law was considered contrary to article 38 of the Constitution, which guaranteed the equality of candidates in elections. The Constitutional Tribunal ordered the Legislator to substitute the provision declared unconstitutional by issuing another according to the Constitution; it even indicated to the Legislator what not to do to avoid aggravating the unconstitutional inequalities.[581]

Other important cases in which the Federal Constitutional Tribunal has established "legislative programmes" in certain decisions include the *Numerus–Clausus* decision,[582] the decision concerning professors,[583] the decision on abortion, and the

578 See I. Härtel, *German National Report*, p. 9.

579 See BVerfG, decision of July 14, 1981, BVerfGE 57, 381, in Christian Behrendt, *Le judge constitutionnel, un législateur–cadre positif. Un analyse comparative en droit francais, belge et allemande*, Bruylant, Brussels 2006, pp. 263–268.

580 See BVerfG, decision of February 15, 1967, BVerfGE 21, 183, in Christian Behrendt, *Le judge constitutionnel, un législateur–cadre positif. Un analyse comparative en droit francais, belge et allemande*, Bruylant, Brussels 2006, pp. 259–262.

581 See BVerfG, decision of March 9, 1976, BVerfGE 41, 414, in Christian Behrendt, *Le judge constitutionnel, un législateur–cadre positif. Un analyse comparative en droit francais, belge et allemande*, Bruylant, Brussels 2006, pp. 275–278.

582 See BVerfGE 33, 303; I. Härtel, *German National Report*, p. 14 (footnote 89).

583 See BVerfGE 35, 79; I. Härtel, *German National Report*, p. 14 (footnote 90).

decision on alternative civilian service.[584] For instance, in the *Numerus–Clausus* decision and the decision concerning professors, the Tribunal structured the basic rights as participation rights, which guarantee state services, and deducted from this a limitation of university places, and instruction to the Legislator on how to arrange the *Numerus–Clausus*.[585]

A similar sort of decision of the Constitutional Court can be found in Belgium, one of the most illustrative cases being the one related to the electoral constituency of Bruxelles–Hal–Vilvorde Province, in which in a decision issued in 2003, after finding that the enlargement of the constituency coincided with the one of the Province, the Constitutional Court urged the Legislator to put an end to the unconstitutionality found, establishing in the case a term for the Legislature to do so.[586]

This last technique of issuing orders to the Legislator that impose a term or deadline for it to take the necessary legislative action has been developed in many countries, reinforcing the character of constitutional courts as direct collaborators of the Legislators. In Germany, this technique is considered the general rule in the Federal Constitutional Tribunal's decisions containing injunctions to the Legislator, whether those injunctions establish a fixed date, or the occurrence of a fact not yet determined, a reasonable term, or in the near future.[587] The power of the Tribunal has been deducted from article 35 of the Law regulating its functions (BVerfG),[588] which states that "in its decision the Federal Constitutional Tribunal may state by whom it is to be executed; in individual instances it may also specify the method of execution." According to I. Härtel, "the setting of a deadline is meant to provide a form of pressure against the Legislator and thereby serve the enactment of justice found by the BVerfG."[589] In a recent case on inheritance tax, the Federal Constitutional Court declared unconstitutional the current capital–transfer tax and fixed a deadline of December 31, 2008, for the Legislator to restore a legal condition in conformity with the Constitution.[590] The unconstitutional statute, which had been considered valid until said resolution, therefore maintained validity for more than another year, which was justified by the Tribunal, which pointed out that, in the case of a violation of the principle of equity (Art. 3.1 Constitution) several possibilities for correcting the unconstitutional condition are available to the Legislator, so that the regulation under review is not annulled but simply declared incompatible with the Constitution.[591] Another classical example of these decisions is one issued by the

---

584 See BVerfGE 48, 127; I. Härtel, *German National Report*, p. 14 (footnote 91).

585 See I. Härtel, *German National Report*, p. 15.

586 See CA N° 73/2003 du 26 mai 2003, in P. Popelier, *Belgian National Report*, p. 4.

587 See I. Härtel, *German National Report*, pp. 7–8; Christian Behrendt, *Le judge constitutionnel, un législateur–cadre positif. Un analyse comparative en droit francais, belge et allemande*, Bruylant, Brussels 2006, pp. 288 ff.

588 See I. Härtel, *German National Report*, p. 9.

589 *Id.*, p. 9.

590 BVerfG, court order from 2006–11–7, reference number: 1 BvL 10/02. I. Härtel, *German National Report*, p. 7.

591 I. Härtel, *German National Report*, p. 8.

Federal Constitutional Tribunal in 1998 on an individual's freedom to exercise a particular profession, where it considered a provision of a statute contrary to article 12.1 of the Constitution. The Tribunal argued, "Nonetheless, the violation of the Constitution does not lead to the annulment of the provision due to the fact that the Legislator has various possibilities to put an end to the declared unconstitutionality," thus limiting the Tribunal "only to verify[ing] the incompatibility of the unconstitutional provision with article 12,1 of the Constitution." The Tribunal also indicated, "The Legislator is oblige[d] to replace the questioned provision with a regulation in harmony with the Constitution before January 1, 2001."[592]

In a similar sense, in Austria, the Constitutional Court has the power to issue such guidelines for the Legislator that establish the rules to be applied in future legislation. One of the most important decisions of the Constitutional Court, as summarized by Ulrich Zellenberg[593] and referred to by Konrad Lachmayer, relates to the creation of self–governing corporations that exist besides local, municipal self–government, playing an important role in Austrian administration. In a series of decisions, the Constitutional Court established the conditions that the Legislator must meet to create such self–governing bodies, particularly in the field of social insurance. In decision VfSlg 8215/1977, the *Salzburger Jägerschaft* (Salzburg Hunting Association) case, the Court ruled on the requirements with which the Legislator must comply to establish self–governing corporations; it provided rules ensuring state–supervision over administrative affairs and within the autonomous sphere of competencies. In decision VfSlg 8644/1979, the Constitutional Court added the need to provide for a democratic way of nominating the officials of the self–governing corporation. In VfSlg 17.023/2003, the Constitutional Court subjected the action of the self–governing corporation to the principle of efficiency. In decision VfSlg 17.869/2006, the Austrian Constitutional Court restricted the self–governing bodies to enact regulations only with regard to persons within their sphere of competence; that is, they must not address persons who are not its members.[594]

In Croatia, the Constitutional Court also instructed the Legislator in general terms as to how to enact legislation, particularly on matters of the restriction of human rights. This was the case in Decision N° U–I–673/1996, of April 21, 1999, which repealed several provisions of the Law on Compensation for Property Expropriated during the Yugoslav Communist Rule.[595] In that case, as mentioned by Sanja Barić and Petar Bačić, the Court found that some restrictions to the right to dispose

---

592 BVerfG, decision of November 10, 1998, BVerfGE 99, 202, in Christian Behrendt, *Le judge constitutionnel, un législateur–cadre positif. Un analyse comparative en droit francais, belge et allemande*, Bruylant, Brussels 2006, p. 295.

593 Ulrich Zellenberg, "Self–Government and Democratic Legitimacy," Vol. 3, *ICL–Journal* 2/2009, 123 (http://www.icl–journal.com); Konrad Lachmayer, *Austrian National Report*, p. 10 (footnote 28).

594 See Konrad Lachmayer, *Austrian National Report*, p. 10.

595 See Decision and Resolution of the Constitutional Court, N° U–I–673/1996, dated April 21, 1999, Official Gazette "*Narodne novine*," 39/1999; Decision U–I–902/1999, of January 25, 2000, Official Gazette "*Narodne novine*," 14/2000; Sanja Barić and Petar Bačić, *Croatian National Report*, p. 24 (footnote 65).

of property were disproportionate to the goal the Law attempted to achieve and contradicted the constitutional provisions on the restriction of human rights and freedoms. The Court seized the opportunity to instruct the legislators on future practice by emphasizing that any limitation of human rights and freedoms, be it necessary and Constitution based, represented "an exceptional state, because it does not abide by the general rules regarding constitutional rights and freedoms." The Constitutional Court decided: "Because of this, not only must these restrictions be based on the Constitution, but they also have to be proportional to the target goal and purpose of the law. In other words, this goal and purpose must be achieved with as little interference in the constitutional rights of citizens as possible (if the restrictions can be gradated, of course)."[596]

In France, given the traditional *a priori* judicial review of legislation exercised by the Constitutional Council, one of the most important means to ensure the enforcement of the Council's decisions are the directives called *réserves d'interprétation* or *réserves d'application.* By means of these directives, the Council establishes the conditions for the law to be enforced and applied, and the directives are aimed at the administrative authorities who must issue the regulations of the law and to the judges who must apply the law.[597]

Finally, in Colombia, the Constitutional Court has also ruled on the unconstitutionality of relative omissions by the Legislator and has exhorted Congress to sanction the corresponding statute. This was, for example, the case of the decision of the Constitutional Court issued when reviewing article 430 of the Labor Code, which prohibits strikes in public services. The Court in Decision N° C–473/94 reviewed the omission of the Legislator regarding the sanctioning of the legislation concerning the right to strike in essential public services, and "exhort[ed] Congress to legislate in a reasonable term" the corresponding legislation on the matter in accordance with the Constitution.[598]

III. CONSTITUTIONAL COURTS AS PROVISIONAL LEGISLATORS

In many other cases, in addition to constitutional courts issuing orders for the Legislator to enact legislation in a specific way and on a fixed or determined date, which occurs particularly on matters of legislative omissions, constitutional courts have also assumed the role of being provisional Legislators by including in their decisions provisional measures or regulations to be applied in the specific matter considered unconstitutional, until the Legislator sanctions the statute it is obliged to produce. In these cases, the court immediately stops the application of the unconstitutional provision, but to avoid the vacuum that annulment can create, the court

596 See Sanja Barić and Petar Bačić, *Croatian National Report*, p. 25.

597 See Bertrand Mathieu, *French National Report*, p. 10.

598 See Germán Alfonso López Daza, *Colombian National Report I*, p. 10; Mónica Liliana Ibagón, "Control jurisdiccional de las omisiones legislativas en Colombia," in Juan Vega Gómez and Edgar Corzo Sosa, *Instrumentos de tutela y justicia constitucional: Memoria del VII Congreso Iberoamericano de Derecho Constitucional*, Universidad Nacional Autónoma de México, Mexico City 2002, pp. 322–323.

temporarily establishes certain rules to be applied until new legislation is enacted.[599] Constitutional courts, in these cases, in some way act as "substitute legislators," not to usurp their functions but to preserve their legislative freedom.[600]

This technique has also been applied in Germany, on the basis of an extensive interpretation of the same article 35 of the Federal Constitutional Tribunal's Law, from which the Tribunal deducted that it has the power to enact general rules to be applied pending the sanctioning by the Legislator of the legislation on the matter in harmony with the Constitution. In these cases, the Tribunal has assumed an "auxiliary" legislative power, acting as a "parliamentary reparation enterprise" and "eroding the separation of powers."[601]

The most important and interesting case ruled by the Federal Constitutional Tribunal in this regard has been the one rendered in 1975, referring to the reform of the Criminal Code regarding the partial decriminalization of abortion.[602] The Tribunal found unconstitutional the provision (Article 218a of the Criminal Code) requiring the Legislator to establish more precise rules; it further found that, "[i]n the interest of the clarity of law (*Rechtsklareit*), it seems suitable, according to article 35 of the Federal Constitutional Tribunal Law, to establish a provisory regulation that must be applicable until the new provisions would be enacted by the Legislator." The result was the inclusion in the Tribunal's decision of a detailed "provisional legislation" on the matter, which was immediately applicable and did not fix any precise date for the Legislator to act.[603] Fifteen years later, in 1992, a new statute was approved regarding help to pregnant women and to families, which was challenged because it was contrary to article 1 of the Constitution, which guarantees human dignity. In 1993, the Federal Constitutional Tribunal issued a new decision on the matter of abortion,[604] finding much of the reform contrary to the Constitution and establishing itself, in an extremely detailed way, as "real legislator" on all the rules applicable to

599 See Christian Behrendt, *Le judge constitutionnel, un législateur–cadre positif. Un analyse comparative en droit francais, belge et allemande*, Bruylant, Brussels 2006, pp. 333 ff.

600 See Otto Bachof, "Nuevas reflexiones sobre la jurisdicción constitucional entre derecho y política," in *Boletín Mexicano de Derecho Comparado*, XIX, N° 57, Mexico City 1986, pp. 848–849.

601 See the references to the opinions of W. Abendroth, H.–P. Scheider, and R. Lamprech works in Christian Behrendt, *Le judge constitutionnel, un législateur–cadre positif. Un analyse comparative en droit francais, belge et allemande*, Bruylant, Brussels 2006, p. 341 (footnotes 309 and 310).

602 BVerfG, decision of February 25, 1975, BVerfGE 39, 1, (68), in Christian Behrendt, *Le judge constitutionnel, un législateur–cadre positif. Un analyse comparative en droit francais, belge et allemande*, Bruylant, Brussels 2006, pp. 342 ff.; I. Härtel, *German National Report*, p. 14.

603 *Id.*

604 BVerfG, decision of May 28, 1993 (*Schwangerrschaftsabbruch II*), February 25, 1975, BVerfGE 88, 203, in Christian Behrendt, *Le judge constitutionnel, un législateur–cadre positif. Un analyse comparative en droit francais, belge et allemande*, Bruylant, Brussels 2006, pp. 346 ff.

abortion in the country.[605] Of course, the Tribunal based its decision on article 35 of the Law, which has been considered insufficient to support this sort of detailed substitutive legislation.[606]

In Switzerland, the Supreme Court has also provided for rules to fill the gap due to legislative omissions concerning enforcement of constitutional rights. For instance, regarding the proceedings on the detention of foreigners, the Supreme Court concluded that the Swiss legal system did not sufficiently protect the right of asylum seekers to protection of their freedom. After mentioning that the Legislator must act immediately, it ruled that it was "not prevented from establishing principles, for a transitional period until the effective date of a new rule of law, such that at least . . . the right to freedom pursuant to Article 5 clause 1 of the EHRC will be guaranteed to a sufficient extent."[607] On matters of expropriation, because the respective Law was tailored to the classic case of the compulsory deprivation of property, it does not establish the rules regarding limitations on property that are tantamount to an expropriation (quasi expropriation), and it has developed the conditions and modalities of these forms of expropriation.[608] Even today, the Supreme Court case law in these areas continues to play the role of legislative rules.[609]

In other cases, also mentioned by Tobias Jaag, the Supreme Court has also filled the gap produced by other relative legislative omissions. For instance, in deviation from the Planning and Construction Law of the Canton of Zurich, the Federal Supreme Court approved a zone for public buildings outside of the construction zone to enable sports facilities to be erected. The Court held the legislative rule to be manifestly incomplete to the extent that, contrary to its meaning, it failed to make distinctions that "according to all reason . . . were to be drawn."[610] For the introduction of the *numerus clausus* at universities, the Supreme Court, in the absence of a legislative rule, formulated strict requirements.[611] For telephone monitoring within the scope of criminal investigations, the Supreme Court likewise developed rules by requiring that affected persons be notified and providing for exceptions from this requirement.[612]

---

605 See the whole text of the regulation in Christian Behrendt, *Le judge constitutionnel, un législateur–cadre positif. Un analyse comparative en droit francais, belge et allemande*, Bruylant, Brussels 2006, pp. 348–351 ff.

606 See the references in Christian Behrendt, *Le judge constitutionnel, un législateur–cadre positif. Un analyse comparative en droit francais, belge et allemande*, Bruylant, Brussels 2006, p. 352.

607 See BGE 123 II 193, 201 ff.; Tobias Jaag, *Swiss National Report*, p. 1 (footnote 57).

608 See BGE 91 I 329 ff. (substantive expropriation); BGE 94 I 286 ff. (appropriation of rights of neighbors); Tobias Jaag, *Swiss National Report*, p. 16 (footnote 89).

609 For instance, a decision issued in 2008, on compensation based on aircraft noise: BGE 134 II 49 ff. and 145 ff.; Tobias Jaag, *Swiss National Report*, p. 16 (footnote 90).

610 See BGE 108 Ia 295, 297; Tobias Jaag, *Swiss National Report*, p. 17 (footnote 91).

611 See BGE 121 I 22 ff.; Tobias Jaag, *Swiss National Report*, p. 17 (footnote 92).

612 See BGE 109 Ia 273, 298 ff.; Tobias Jaag, *Swiss National Report*, p. 17 (footnote 92).

In India, and as a consequence of deciding direct actions for the protection of fundamental rights established in article 32 of the Constitution, the Supreme Court has assumed the role of provisional legislator on matters related to police arrest and detention. Surya Deva summarized the case as follows. In August 1986, a nongovernmental organization (NGO) addressed a letter to the Chief Justice of India drawing his attention to certain deaths reported in police lockups and custody. The letter, along with some other similar letters, was treated as a writ petition under Article 32 of the Constitution, for which purpose the Supreme Court issued notices to all state governments and to the Law Commission, with a request to make suitable suggestions. After making reference to constitutional and statutory provisions and international conventions, the Supreme Court, in *D K Basu v. State of West Bengal*,[613] issued eleven requirements, as follows:

> We, therefore, consider it appropriate to issue the following requirements to be followed in all cases of arrest or detention till legal provisions are made in that behalf as preventive measures:
>
> 1. The police personnel carrying out the arrest and handling the interrogation of the arrestee should bear accurate, visible and clear identification and name tags with their designations. The particulars of all such personnel who handle interrogation of the arrestee must be recorded in a register.
> 2. That the police officer carrying out the arrest of the arrestee shall prepare a memo of arrest at the time of arrest and such memo shall be attested by one witness, who may either be a member of the family of the arrestee or a respectable person of the locality from where the arrest is made. It shall be countersigned by the arrestee and shall contain the time and date of arrest.
> 3. A person who has been arrested or detained . . . shall be entitled to have one friend or relative or other person known to him or having an interest in his welfare being informed, as soon as practicable, that he has been arrested and is being detained at the particular place. . . .
> 4. The time, place of arrest, and venue of custody of an arrestee must be notified by the police where the next friend or relative of the arrestee lives outside the district or town through the Legal Aid Organization in the district, and the police station of the area concerned, telegraphically, within a period of 8 to 12 hours after arrest.
> 5. The person arrested must be made of aware of this right to have someone informed of his arrest or detention as soon as he is put under arrest or is detained. . . .
> 8. The arrestee should be subject to medical examination by a trained doctor every 48 hours during his detention in custody. . . .
> 9. Copies of all the documents . . . should be sent to the Magistrate for his record.
> 10. The arrestee must be permitted to meet his lawyer during interrogation, though not throughout the interrogation.[614]

The Court observed that these requirements, which flow from Articles 21 and 22 of the Constitution, must be complied with by all government agencies and that any breach will render the concerned official liable for departmental action, as well as for contempt of court. Even though the requirements were seemingly intended to be

613 See (1997) 1 SCC 416; Surya Deva, *Indian National Report*, pp. 6–7.

614 *Id.*

a temporary stop–gap arrangement, they continue to be the main rules applicable to dealing with details of arrest and detention.

Another important decision in this same line regarding the protection of human rights was the one adopted in the *Vishaka v. State of Rajasthan* case,[615] on matters of sexual harassment of women at the workplace. The Supreme Court decided on petitions filed before it by social activists and nongovernmental organizations for the enforcement of the rights of working women under Articles 14, 19, and 21 of the Constitution (the right to equality, the right to carry on any profession or trade, and the right to life and liberty, respectively). The Supreme Court, though acknowledging that the primary responsibility for protecting these rights of working women lies with the legislature and executive, in cases of sexual harassment that resulted in the violation of fundamental rights of women workers, found that "an effective redressal requires that some guidelines should be laid down for the protection of these rights *to fill the legislative vacuum*" and consequently, it not only laid down a detailed definition of sexual harassment but also imposed a duty on the employer or other responsible persons in workplaces or other institutions "to prevent or deter the commission of acts of sexual harassment and to provide the procedures for the resolution, settlement or prosecution of acts of sexual harassment by taking all steps required." The Court also issued guidelines covering several different aspects, including taking preventive steps, initiating criminal proceedings under the criminal law, taking disciplinary action, establishing a complaint mechanism, and spreading awareness of the guidelines. The Supreme Court concluded by directing that "the above guidelines and norms would be strictly observed in all work places for the preservation and enforcement of the right to gender equality of the working women. These directions would be binding and enforceable in law until suitable legislation is enacted to occupy the field," having been extended to be applied in nonstate entities such as private companies.[616]

In these sorts of judicial review decisions, where the constitutional courts issue provisional regulations by interpreting the Constitution, it is possible to mention one decision issued by the Federal Supreme Tribunal of Brazil, through a *súmula vinculante* in which the Tribunal, after adopting a few decisions regarding the prohibition of nepotism in the Judiciary, concluded that, for the implementation of such practice, no formal law needed to be sanctioned because it can be deducted from the principles contained in article 37 of the Constitution. The Tribunal declared that the practice of nepotism (i.e., the appointment of a spouse, partner, or parent of the director or chief executive) in any of the branches of government of the Union, the States, the federal District, and the Municipalities violates the Constitution.[617] Another important case for the Brazilian Federal Supreme Tribunal was the decision adopted when analyzing the constitutionality of the demarcation of indigenous peo-

---

615 See AIR 1997 SC 3011; Surya Deva, *Indian National Report*, p. 8 (footnote 49).

616 *Id.*, p. 9.

617 See *Súmula Vinculante* N° 13, STF, *DJ* 1°.set.2006, ADC 12 MC/DF, Rel. Min. Carlos Britto; Luis Roberto Barroso et al., "Notas sobre a questão do legislador positivo," *Brazilian National Report III*, pp. 33–37.

ple's land in the area of Raposa Serra do Sol, in Roraima State. After many discussions and political conflicts, the Tribunal decided to sustain the constitutionality of the demarcation made by the Federal Union, but it determined for the demarcation of indigenous peoples' land a detailed set of rules establishing the conditions to always be met in all future demarcation process; this resulted in a decision with *erga omnes* effects.[618]

In Venezuela, it is possible to find cases where the Constitutional Chamber of the Supreme Tribunal of Justice, in the absence of corresponding statutes, has issued decisions containing legislation. In Decision N° 1682 of August 15, 2005, answering a recourse of interpretation of article 77 of the Constitution, the Constitutional Chamber, in exercising its normative jurisdiction, established that the *de facto* stable relations between men and women have the same effects as marriage. The Constitutional Chambers established that the decision applied to all of the legal regime regarding such *de facto* stable relations and determined the civil effects of marriage applicable to them, including matters of pensions, use of partner's name, economic regime, and succession rights, thereby completely substituting itself for the Legislator.[619]

In another case, the Constitutional Chamber has also legislated, this time *ex officio*, and in a decision issued in an amparo proceeding regarding the process of in vitro fertilization. In Decision N° 1456 of July 27, 2006, in effect, the Chamber also exercised its normative jurisdiction to determine *ex officio* the legislative provisions on the matter, including rules on parenthood, assisted reproduction, nonconsensual fertilization, retributive donation, surrogate mothers, and rules on succession.[620] In this case, the Chamber not only acted as positive legislator in establishing all the provisions applicable in case of in vitro fertilization or assisted reproduction, but also ordered the application of the new rules to the particular case involved in the decision, thus giving retroactive effects to the legislative provisions it created, in violation of article 24 of the Constitution, which prohibits the retroactivity of laws.

In all these cases of judicial means established or developed for controlling legislative omissions, it is always important to have in mind the warning given by Justice Cardozo about this problem: "[L]egislative inaction – or the inability of groups to win the necessary votes to pass desired legislation – may lead to attempts to have the judiciary accomplish by judicial review what the legislature has refused to do."[621]

---

618 See STF, *DJ* 25.set.2009, Pet 3388/RR, Rel. Min. Carlos Britto; Luis Roberto Barroso et al., "Notas sobre a questão do Legislador Positivo," *Brazilian National Report III*, pp. 43–46.

619 See Decision 1682 of July 15, 2005, *Carmela Manpieri, Interpretation of article 77 of the Constitution* case; http://www.tsj.gov.ve/decisiones/scon/Julio/1682–150705–04–3301.htm. See also Daniela Urosa Maggi, *Venezuelan National Report*, p. 19.

620 See Decision N° 1456 of July 27, 2006, *Yamilex Núñez de Godoy* case; http://www.tsj.gov.ve/decisiones/scon/Julio/1456–270706–05–1471.htm. See also Daniela Urosa Maggi, *Venezuelan National Report*, pp. 19–20.

621 See Christopher Wolfe, *The Rise of Modern Judicial Review. From Constitutional Interpretation to Judge–Made Law*, Basic Books, New York 1986, p. 238; *La transformación de la interpretación constitucional*, Civitas, Madrid 1991, p. 325.

CHAPTER 5

CONSTITUTIONAL COURTS AS LEGISLATORS ON MATTERS OF JUDICIAL REVIEW

One particular aspect in which it is possible to identify interferences of constitutional courts in the legislative function is precisely in matters of legislation on judicial review, particularly in countries with concentrated systems of judicial review, in which not only constitutional courts have created rules of procedure in spite of the existence of a special statute establishing them, but also they have assumed new powers of judicial review and created new actions that can be filed before the courts.

I. CONSTITUTIONAL COURTS CREATING THEIR OWN JUDICIAL REVIEW POWERS

1. The judge–made law regarding the diffuse system of judicial review

In the diffuse, or decentralized, system of judicial review, being a power attributed to all courts, judicial review has always been deduced from the principle of the supremacy of the Constitution and of the duty of the courts to discard statutes contrary to the Constitution, always preferring the latter. Such power of the courts, consequently, does not need an express provision in the Constitution that instructs courts to give preference to the Constitution. As Chief Justice Marshall definitively stated in *Marbury v. Madison* (1 Cranch 137 (1803)):

> Those who apply the rule to particular cases, must of necessity expound and interpret that rule . . . so, if a law be in opposition to the constitution . . . the court must determine which of these conflicting rules governs the case: This is the very essence of judicial duty. If then, the courts are to regard the constitution, and the constitution is superior to any ordinary act of the legislature, the constitution, and not such ordinary act, must govern the case to which they both apply.

Consequently, because of this essential link between supremacy of the Constitution and judicial review, in the United States, judicial review was a creation of the courts – this was also the case in Norway (1820);[622] in Greece (1897);[623] and in Argentina, a few decades later, where judicial review was also a creation of the respective Supreme of High Court, based on the principles of supremacy of the Constitution and judicial duty in applying the law.

In Argentina, the first case in which judicial review was exercised for a federal statute was the *Sojo* case (1887), concerning the unconstitutionality of a law that

---

622 See Eivind Smith, *Norway National Report*, p. 1.

623 See Julia Iliopoulos–Strangas and Stylianos–Ioannis G. Koutnatzis, *Greek National Report*, p. 2.

tried to extend the original jurisdiction of the Supreme Court,[624] similar to *Marbury v. Madison*. In Argentina, the Supreme Court has also developed in case law the contours of its judicial review powers, including binding effects –what has been called an "Argentinean *stare decisis*" effect[625] – and in some cases of protection of collective rights, *erga omnes* effects.[626]

2. The extension of judicial review powers to ensure the protection of fundamental rights

But most important, particularly regarding the protection of fundamental rights and liberties, constitutional courts in many Latin American countries, in their character of supreme interpreter of the Constitution, in the absence of legislation, have created the action of amparo as a special judicial means for the protection of fundamental rights. This was the case also in Argentina, where, in the 1950s, when constitutional rights, other than physical and personal freedom protected by the *habeas corpus* action, were protected only through ordinary judicial means, the courts found that *habeas corpus* could not be used for such purpose. That is why, for instance, in 1933, the Supreme Court of the Nation in the *Bertotto* case[627] rejected the application of the *habeas corpus* proceeding to obtain judicial protection of other constitutional rights. This situation radically changed in 1957 as a result of the decision of the *Angel Siri* case, where the petitioner requested amparo for the protection of his freedom of press and his right to work (because of the closing of the newspaper, *Mercedes*, which he directed in the province of Buenos Aires). This case eventually led the Supreme Court, in a decision of December 27, 1957, to admit the action of amparo, because it found that the courts needed to protect all constitutional rights, even in the absence of a statutory regulation on such action.[628] This important decision was followed by another, the *Samuel Kot* case, of October 5, 1958, where the Supreme Court extended the scope of the amparo proceeding to include the protec-

---

624 See H. Quiroga Lavié, *Derecho constitucional*, Buenos Aires 1978, p. 481. Before 1863, the first Supreme Court decisions were adopted in constitutional matters but referred to provincial and executive acts.

625 See Néstor P. Sagües, "Los efectos de las sentencias constitucionales en el derecho argentino," in *Anuario Iberoamericano de Justicia Constitucional*, Centro de Estudios Políticos y Constitucionales, N° 12, 2008, Madrid 2008, p. 347.

626 See *Halabi* case, Fallos 332: (2009); Alejandra Rodríguez Galán and Alfredo Mauricio Vítolo, *Argentinean National Report I*, p. 12.

627 See the references to the *Bertotto* case in Joaquín Brage Camazano, *La jurisdicción constitucional de la libertad (Teoría general, Argentina, México, Corte Interamericana de Derechos Humanos)*, Editorial Porrúa, Instituto Mexicano de Derecho Procesal Constitucional, Mexico City 2005, p. 66.

628 See the reference to the *Siri* case in José Luis Lazzarini, *El juicio de amparo*, La Ley, Buenos Aires, 1987, pp. 26 ff., 373 ff.; Alí Joaquín Salgado, *Juicio de amparo y acción de inconstitucionalidad*, Ed. Astrea, Buenos Aires, 1987, p. 5; Néstor Pedro Sagües, *Derecho procesal constitucional: Acción de amparo*, Vol. 3, 2nd ed., Editorial Astrea, Buenos Aires, 1988, pp. 9 ff. See also Alejandra Rodríguez Galán and Alfredo Mauricio Vítolo, *Argentinean National Report I*, p. 7; Néstor Pedro Sagües, *Argentinean National Report II*, pp. 13–14.

tion of constitutional rights against individuals, not only against authorities.[629] In 1958, the amparo action was regulated in a federal statute, and in the 1994 constitutional reform, it was incorporated in the Constitution (article 43). Nonetheless, before the constitutional reform took place recognizing collective rights like the right to a clean environment and consumers' rights, the Supreme Courts in *Verbitsky* (2005) and *Halabi* (2009) introduced another important reform to the *habeas corpus* and amparo proceeding by recognizing collective protection and class actions.[630] In particular, for class actions, the Supreme Court developed the main rules concerning new class actions, explaining how the courts must act in face of legislative silence on the matter and defining their character, standing conditions, and requirements for representation.[631]

In India, the most important remedy used for judicial review is that established in articles 32 and 226 of the Constitution to enforce fundamental rights, which provides that the Supreme Court shall have the power for such purpose to issue directions or orders or writs, including writs in the nature of *habeas corpus*, mandamus, prohibition, *quo warranto*, and certiorari, whichever may be appropriate. The Court has interpreted this remedial provision widely so as to liberalize the standing requirements,[632] thus enabling the courts to entertain voices (including in the form of judicial review petitions) from a larger populace, and on occasion even from civil society organizations, which has approached the Court for the enforcement of collective or diffused rights. This has given rise to what is called public interest litigation (PIL) in India, which has led to the Court's expansive interpretation of fundamental rights and matters related to them; thus, it has led to the courts acting as legislators.[633]

In 1999, the Dominican Republic was still the only Latin American country without a constitutional provision establishing the amparo, a situation that did not impede the Supreme Court of Justice from allowing it, applying for that purpose the American Convention on Human Rights. That occurred in a decision of February 24, 1999, in the *Productos Avon S.A.* case, when the Supreme Court, on the basis of

629 See the references to the *Samuel Kot Ltd.* case of September 5, 1958, in S. V. Linares Quintana, *Acción de amparo*, Buenos Aires, 1960, p. 25; José Luis Lazzarini, *El juicio de amparo*, La Ley, Buenos Aires, 1987, pp. 243 ff.; Alí Joaquín Salgado, *Juicio de amparo y acción de inconstitucionalidad*, Ed. Astrea, Buenos Aires, 1987, p. 6.; Susana Albanese, *Garantías judiciales: Algunos requisitos del debido proceso legal en el derecho internacional de los derechos humanos*, Ediar S. A. Editora, Comercial, Industrial y Financiera, Buenos Aires, 2000; Augusto M. Morillo et al., *El amparo: Régimen procesal*, 3rd ed., Librería Editora Platense SRL, La Plata 1998, 430 pp.; Néstor Pedro Sagües, *Derecho procesal constitucional*, Vol. 3, *Acción de amparo*, 2nd ed., Editorial Astrea, Buenos Aires, 1988.

630 See *Verbitsky* case, Fallos 328:1146 (2005); and *Halabi* case, Fallos 332:(2009); Alejandra Rodríguez Galán and Alfredo Mauricio Vítolo, *Argentinean National Report I*, p. 9.

631 See Néstor Pedro Sagües, *Argentinean National Report II*, pp. 14–19.

632 See *S P Gupta v. Union of India* AIR 1982 SC 149; *PUDR v. Union of India* AIR 1982 SC 1473; *Bandhua Mukti Morcha v. Union of India* (1984) 3 SCC 161; Surya Deva, *Indian National Report*, p. 2.

633 See Surya Deva, *Indian National Report*, pp. 2, 4–5.

the American Convention on Human Rights, admitted the amparo recourse for the protection of constitutional rights, assigned the power to decide on amparo matters to the courts of first instance,[634] and established the general procedural rules for the proceeding. Later, the amparo action was regulated in a statute (2006), and in the constitutional reform of 2009, it was incorporated in the Constitution (article 72). In these cases, the principle of prevalence of human rights declared in the Constitution led the Supreme Courts to create this specific judicial mean of protection, so it was extended in all Latin America.[635]

The Courts, nonetheless, can interpret the judicial review powers attributed to them in the Constitution and adapt their implementation or expand their scope, as has occurred in Brazil with the *mandado de injunçào*, to effectively control the relative omissions of the Legislator. In Brazil this can be found in a leading case deciding on the application to civil servants of the rules of strike in the private sector.[636] This has led Luís Roberto Barroso to say that, because of this change in its jurisprudence, the Federal Supreme Tribunal, with constitutional authorization, "has given a step, a long step, in the sense of acting as positive legislator."[637]

In the Slovak Republic, the constitutional complaint for the protection for fundamental rights, given the delay established for the entry in force of the constitutional amendment of article 127 establishing the complaint (December 31, 201), was "created" by the Court despite the previous means of protection repealed as of July 1, 2001. As it has been summarized by Ján Svák and Lucia Berdisová, from July 1, 2001, until December 31, 2001, there did not exist a national means by which natural or legal persons could have pleaded the infringement of their fundamental rights and freedoms before the Constitutional Court. The Constitutional Court filled this vacuum of protection with extensive interpretation of article 124 of the Constitution, which states that "the Constitutional Court shall be an independent judicial authority vested with the mandate to protect constitutionality." The Court deduced from this article that it does have the competence to deal with individual motions by natural persons and legal persons that are pleading infringement of their constitutional rights (no matter how they were called – petition or complaint) even in the period of time from July 1, 2001, until December 31, 2001.[638] The Constitutional Court argued:

> The Constitutional Court is according to art. 124 of the Constitution the judicial authority for protection of constitutionality. This article constitutes the competence of the Constitutional Court to protect mainly fundamental rights and freedoms guaranteed by the Constitution.

---

634 See Samuel Arias Arzeno, "El amparo en la República Dominicana: Su evolución jurisprudencial," *Revista Estudios Jurídicos*, Vol. XI, N° 3, Ediciones Capeldom, 2002.

635 See Allan R. BREWER–CARÍAS, *Constitutional Protection of Human Rights in Latin America: A Comparative Study on Amparo Proceeding*, Cambridge University Press, New York 2009, p. 68.

636 See STF, DJ 31.out.2008, MI 708/DF, Rel. Min. Gilmar Mendes; Luis Roberto Barroso et al., "Notas sobre a questão do legislador positivo," *Brazilian National Report III*, pp. 28–33.

637 See Luis Roberto Barroso et al., "Notas sobre a questão do Legislador Positivo," *Brazilian National Report III*, p. 33.

638 See Ján Svák and Lucia Berdisová, *Slovak National Report*, p. 9.

> The Constitutional Court is led by this imperative even after the nullification of the paragraphs about petition (from July 1, 2001) until the entry into force of art. 127 of the Constitution (January 1, 2002) and so it is entitled and obliged to provide individual protection of fundamental rights and freedoms while the court also relies on art. 1 of the Constitution, which states that Slovak Republic is the state governed by the rule of law. That is why fundamental rights and freedoms cannot be even temporarily deprived of judicial protection as to art. 124 of the Constitution in connection with other articles that guarantee fundamental rights and freedoms.[639]

The Constitutional Court thus acted as if the institute of petition had been repealed not from July 1, 2001, but from January 1, 2002.

In Venezuela, the Constitutional Chamber, in Decision N° 656 of June 30, 2000, admitted the direct amparo action for the protection of diffuse and collective rights and interests established in the Constitution[640] and established the standing conditions for the filing of the action in Decision N° 1395 of November 21, 2000.[641] It ruled a year later on the rules of procedure to be applicable in such cases in Decision N° 1571 of August 22, 2001.[642]

3. The need for the express provision in the constitution of judicial review powers of the constitutional jurisdiction and its deviation

Particularly in concentrated systems of judicial review, the idea of the supremacy of the constitution and the duty of the courts to say which law is applicable in a particular case[643] has a limitation: the power to judge the unconstitutionality of legislative acts and other state acts of similar rank or value is reserved to a supreme court of justice or to a constitutional court or tribunal. Thus, in the concentrated system of judicial review, all courts have the power only to act as a constitutional judge and to decide on the constitutionality of other norms applicable to the case, regarding acts

---

639 Decision of the Constitutional Court N° III. ÚS 117/01. The Court similarly justifies its decision in III. ÚS 124/01: In the period of time from July 1, 2001, to December 31, 2001, the competence of the Constitutional Court was founded on the art. 124 in connection with art. 1 of the Constitution and it was so "in order to provide protection of constitutionality including protection of guaranteed fundamental rights and freedoms of natural persons and legal persons." See also II. ÚS 80/01, III. ÚS 100/01, III. ÚS 116/01; Ján Svák and Lucia Berdisová, *Slovak National Report*, p. 9 (footnote 14).

640 See Decision N° 656 of June 30, 2000, *Dilia Parra Guillen (Peoples' Defender)* case, at http://www.tsj.gov.ve/decisiones/scon/Junio/656–300600–00–1728%20.htm. See also Daniela Urosa Maggi, *Venezuelan National Report*, p. 11.

641 See Decision N° 1395 of November 21, 2000, *William Dávila* case, *Revista de Derecho Público*, N° 84, Editorial Jurídica Venezolana, Caracas, 2000, pp. 330 ff.; Daniela Urosa Maggi, *Venezuelan National Report*, p. 12.

642 See Decision N° 1571 of August 22, 2001, *Asodeviprilara* case; http://www.tsj.gov.ve/decisiones/scon/Agosto/1571–220801–01–1274%20.htm; Daniela Urosa Maggi, *Venezuelan National Report*, p. 12.

643 See W. K. Geck, "Judicial Review of Statutes: A Comparative Survey of Present Institutions and Practices," *Cornell Law Quarterly*, 51, 1966, p. 278.

other than statutes or acts adopted in direct execution of the Constitution.[644] Consequently, the concentrated system of judicial review, based also on the supremacy of the Constitution, when reserving constitutional justice functions regarding certain state acts to a constitutional jurisdiction, cannot be developed by deduction through the work of the supreme court decisions, as happened in many countries with the diffuse system of judicial review.

On the contrary, of course, because of the limits that the system imposes on the duty and power of all judges to say which law is applicable in the cases they are to decide, only when prescribed *expressis verbis* through constitutional regulations is it possible to establish the concentrated system of judicial review. The Constitution, as the supreme law of the land, is the only text that can establish limits on the general power and duty of all courts to say which is the law applicable in a particular case and to assign that power and duty in certain cases regarding certain state acts to a specific constitutional body, whether the supreme court of justice or a constitutional court or tribunal.

Therefore, the concentrated system of judicial review must be established and regulated expressly in the Constitution,[645] as constitutional courts are always constitutional bodies, that is, state organs expressly created and regulated in the Constitution, whether they be the supreme court of justice of a given country or a specially created constitutional court, tribunal, or council.

The consequence of the express character of the system of judicial review is that, in principle, on the one hand, only the Constitution can determine the judicial review powers of constitutional courts not being allowed to create without constitutional support different means of judicial review; and on the other hand, only the legislation issued by the Legislator can develop the rules of procedure and the way constitutional courts can exercise their powers of judicial review.

The practice in many countries, nonetheless, has been different – sometimes they adapt their own judicial review powers, and other times they create them.

As aforementioned, one of the main characteristics of the concentrated judicial review system is that the constitutional court exclusively can make constitutional attributions on matters of judicial review of legislation. Such power can only be given to specific constitutional organs by means of a constitutional provision. Consequently, contrary to the diffuse method of judicial review, the concentrated judicial review powers of the constitutional courts cannot be created by the courts themselves, that is, they cannot be the product of judge–made law. That is why in all con-

644 See Manuel García Pelayo, "El 'Status' del Tribunal Constitucional," *Revista Española de Derecho Constitucional*, 1, Madrid 1981, p. 19; Eduardo García de Enterría, *La Constitución como norma y el Tribunal Constitucional*, Madrid 1981, p. 65. In particular, in concentrated systems, the tribunals or courts empowered with administrative justice functions can always act as constitutional judge regarding administrative acts. See C. Frank, *Les fonctions juridictionnelles du Conseil d'État dans l'ordre constitutionnel*, Paris 1974.

645 See Allan R. BREWER–CARÍAS, *Judicial Review in Comparative Law*, Cambridge University Press, Cambridge 1989, pp. 185 ff.; Jorge Carpizo, *El Tribunal Constitucional y sus límites*, Grijley Ed., Lima 2009, p. 41.

stitutional systems where a concentrated system of judicial review has been established, it is the Constitution that creates or regulates the constitutional jurisdiction attributing to a specific constitutional court the power of judicial review regarding legislation; the courts are not allowed themselves to create new judicial review powers not attributed to them in the Constitution.

But constitutional courts, in some cases, have extended or adapted their constitutional powers. For instance, they created the technique of exercising judicial review in declaring statutes unconstitutional but without annulling them, as well as the technique of extending the application of the unconstitutional statute for a term and issuing directives to the Legislator for it to legislate in harmony with the Constitution. This technique was developed in Germany, as mentioned by I. Härtel, "without statutory authorization, in fact *contra legem*, as the BVerfG assumed until 1970 the compelling connection between the unconstitutionality and the invalidity of a norm."[646] In the reform of the Federal Constitutional Tribunal Law sanctioned in 1970, the Legislator officially recognized the judge–made law (Articles 31, 79), thereby allowing the Tribunal to declare a provision unconstitutional without annulling it, a matter that still is discussed.[647] That is why – referring to the decision of the Federal Constitutional Tribunal on the inheritance tax case,[648] where the Tribunal declared unconstitutional the current capital–transfer tax and fixed a deadline of December 31, 2008, for the Legislator to restore a legal condition in conformity with the Constitution – Härtel also pointed out, "The BVerfG has therefore as a kind of 'emergency Legislator' created a law–like condition; it has 'invented' a new decision type."[649] The same can be said regarding the powers that the Federal Constitutional Tribunal has assumed, for example, issuing provisional legislative rules and measures with substitute legislation as a consequence of the declaration of unconstitutionality of certain provisions. The Constitutional Court in these cases, through judge–made law, has assumed a role that principally corresponds to the Legislator.[650]

In Spain, the same process of judge–made law has been developed by the Constitutional Tribunal, which can declare provisions unconstitutional without annulling them, despite a provision to the contrary in the Organic Law of the Constitutional

646 See I. Härtel, *German National Report*, p. 8; Francisco Fernández Segado, "Algunas reflexiones generales en torno a los efectos de las sentencias de inconstitucionalidad y a la relatividad de ciertas fórmulas esterotipadas vinculadas a ellas," in *Anuario Iberoamericano de Justicia Constitucional*, Centro de Estudios Políticos y Constitucionales, N° 12, 2008, Madrid 2008, p. 162.

647 See Christian Behrendt, *Le judge constitutionnel, un législateur–cadre positif. Un analyse comparative en droit francais, belge et allemande*, Bruylant, Brussels 2006, pp. 93, 94; F. Fernández Segado, *Spanish National Report*, p. 6.

648 BVerfG, court order from 2006–11–7, reference number: 1 BvL 10/02. See I. Härtel, *German National Report*, p. 8.

649 See I. Härtel, quoting Steiner, *ZEV* 2007, 120 (121) and Schlaich/Korioth, *Das Bundesverfassungsgericht*, 7th ed. 2007, margin number 395, *German National Report*, p. 9.

650 See Christian Behrendt, *Le judge constitutionnel, un législateur–cadre positif. Un analyse comparative en droit francais, belge et allemande*, Bruylant, Brussels 2006, p. 354.

Tribunal, which states: "[W]hen the decision declares the unconstitutionality, it will also declare the nullity of the challenged provisions" (article 39.1). Spain's Constitutional Tribunal also tried to legitimate this *contra legem* procedural technique in the draft reform of its Organic Law in 2005, which was not sanctioned as drafted.[651]

But in other cases, constitutional courts have created their own judicial review powers not established in the Constitution. As aforementioned, in concentrated systems of judicial review, constitutional courts as Constitutional Jurisdiction cannot exist and cannot exercise their functions of judicial review of legislation without an express constitutional provision that establishes them. That is, as a matter of principle, in democratic regimes governed by the rule of law and the principle of separation of powers, all the powers of constitutional courts must be expressly provided for in the Constitution or in the law as prescribed in the Constitution. Therefore, within the concentrated system of judicial review, it is not possible for the constitutional court to create its own judicial review powers or to expand those established in the Constitution.[652] Constitutional courts are an exception regarding the general power of the courts to apply and guarantee the supremacy of the Constitution, being the Constituent Power the one that in order to preserve the Constitution, can exclude or restrict ordinary courts from that task. Being then an exception, and because of the assignment to a constitutional court of the monopoly of Constitutional Jurisdiction, it must be expressly created in the Constitution with expressly established powers.

Nonetheless, in some countries, it is possible to find a deformation of this principle, as in Venezuela,[653] where the Constitutional Chamber of the Supreme Tribunal of Justice, despite the powers established in article 336 of the Constitution, has created new powers of judicial review not envisaged in the Constitution. In particular, without any constitutional or legal support, the Constitutional Chamber of the Supreme Tribunal created in 2000 a recourse for the abstract interpretation of the Constitution, based on the interpretation of its Article 335, which grants the Supreme Tribunal the character of "superior and final interpreter of the Constitution."[654] Alt-

651 See F. Fernández Segado, *Spanish National Report*, p. 6, 11.

652 See, e.g., Francisco Eguiguren and Liliana Salomé, *Peruvian National Report I*, p. 17; Sanja Barić and Petar Bačić, *Croatian National Report*, p. 3.

653 See Allan R. BREWER–CARÍAS, "La ilegítima mutación de la constitución por el juez constitucional: La inconstitucional ampliación y modificación de su propia competencia en materia de control de constitucionalidad," in *Libro Homenaje a Josefina Calcaño de Temeltas*, Fundación de Estudios de Derecho Administrativo (FUNEDA), Caracas 2009, pp. 319–362.

654 The recourse was created by Decision N° 1077 of September 22, 2000, *Servio Tulio León* case; *Revista de Derecho Público*, N° 83, Editorial Jurídica Venezolana, Caracas 2000, pp. 247 ff. The procedural rules regarding the recourse were established in decision of the same Constitutional Chamber, N° 1415 of November 22, 2000, *Freddy Rangel Rojas* case. See the comments to these decisions in Allan R. BREWER–CARÍAS, "*Quis Custodiet Ipsos Custodes*: De la interpretación constitucional a la inconstitucionalidad de la interpretación," in *VIII Congreso Nacional de derecho Constitucional, Perú*, Fondo Editorial 2005, Colegio de Abogados de Arequipa, Arequipa, September 2005, pp. 463–489; *Revista de Derecho Público*, N° 105, Editorial Jurídica Venezolana, Caracas 2006, pp. 7–27; Allan R. BREWER–CARÍAS, "Le recours d'interprétation abstrait de la Constitution au Vénézuéla," in *Renouvau*

hough in the Constitution the only recourse of interpretation established is the recourse of interpretation of statutes that can be filed before the various Chambers of the Supreme Tribunal, and only in cases expressly provided for in each statute (Article 266.6), the Constitutional Chamber created this recourse, providing as the only condition for standing that the petitioner must invoke an actual, legitimate, and juridical interest in the interpretation that is needed regarding his or her particular and specific situation. For such purpose, the Constitutional Chamber has held that the petition must always point to "the obscurity, the ambiguity or contradiction between constitutional provisions," and the decisions of the Chamber have *erga omnes* and *ex nunc* effects.[655] This sort of recourse seeking the abstract interpretation of statutes gives the Constitutional Court powers to issue bindings "opinions," which generally are not related to a specific case or controversy, which in general terms is considered a function outside the scope of constitutional courts.

To create this recourse, the Chamber based its decision on Article 26 of the Constitution, which establishes the people's right to have access to justice, considering therefore that "citizens do not require a statutory provision establishing the recourse for constitutional interpretation, to file it." On the basis of that argument, the Chamber found that no constitutional or legal provision was necessary to allow the development of such recourse.[656] Three years later, the National Assembly sanctioned the Organic Law of the Supreme Tribunal, which regulated the general means for judicial review, as it was the will of the Legislator to exclude from the powers of the Constitutional Chamber the ability to decide on recourses of abstract interpretation of the Constitution. Nonetheless, the Constitutional Chamber has continued to develop the regulation of the recourse in subsequent decisions, for the purpose of issuing declarative ruling of mere certainty on the scope and content of a constitutional provision.[657]

This extraordinary interpretive power, though theoretically an excellent judicial means for the interpretation of the Constitution, unfortunately has been extensively abused by the Constitutional Chamber to distort important constitutional provisions,

---

du droit constitutionnel: Mélanges en l'honneur de Louis Favoreu, Dalloz, Paris 2007, pp. 61–70.

655 Of the Constitutional Chamber, see Decision N° 1309 of June 19, 2001, case: *Hermann Escarráa*, and Decision N° 1684 November 4, 2008, case: *Carlos Eduardo Giménez Colmenárez, Revista de Derecho Público*, N° 116, Editorial Jurídica Venezolana, Caracas 2008, pp. 66 ff

656 See Decision N° 1077 of the Constitutional Chamber of September 22, 2000, case: *Servio Tulio León Briceño, Revista de Derecho Público*, N° 83, Caracas, 2000, pp. 247 ff. This criterion was ratified later in decision N° 1347, dated September 11, 2000, *Revista de Derecho Público*, N° 84, Editorial Jurídica Venezolana, Caracas 2000, pp. 264 ff.

657 See, e.g., Decision N° 1347 of the Constitutional Chamber, dated November 9, 2000, *Revista de Derecho Público*, N° 84, Editorial Jurídica Venezolana, Caracas 2000, pp. 264 ff.; Decision N° 2651 of October 2003 (case: *Ricardo Delgado (Interpretación artículo 174 de la Constitución)), Revista de Derecho Público*, N° 93–96, Editorial Jurídica Venezolana, Caracas 2003, pp. 327 ff.

to interpret them in a way contrary to the text, or to justify constitutional solutions according to the will of the Executive, because the initiative to file many recourses has been in the hands of the Attorney General. This was the case, for instance, with the various Constitutional Chamber's decisions regarding the consultative and repeal referenda between 2002 and 2004, where the Chamber confiscated and distorted the people's constitutional right to political participation.[658] One of the last notoriously politically motivated decisions of the Constitutional Chamber that has been issued using these powers was in answering a petition filed by the Attorney General, not for the purpose of interpreting the Constitution but for the purpose of interpreting a decision of the Inter–American Court of Human Rights that condemned the Venezuelan State for violations of due process rights and judicial guarantees of various superior judges who were illegally dismissed.[659] The result of this process before the Supreme Court was that by means of Decision N° 1.939 of December 18, 2008, the Constitutional Chamber did not "interpret" anything, particularly because judicial decisions are not to be interpreted but to be applied, but just considered the international Court decision was unenforceable in Venezuela, recommending the Executive to denounce the American Convention on Human Rights.[660]

In another case, the Constitutional Chamber created a judicial review power expanding the scope of an existing provision of the Constitution, as it has happened regarding the general power of review the Constitution grants the Constitutional Chamber regarding final decisions adopted by the courts on matters of amparo proceedings and in cases when the diffuse method of judicial review is applied (article 336.10). Even though the express scope of this discretional power of review regarding judicial decisions issued by inferior courts granted to the Constitutional Chamber is precise, the Chamber has modified the Constitution and has assumed, first,

658 See Decision Nos. 1139 of June 5, 2002, *Sergio Omar Calderón Duque y William Dávila Barrios* case; N° 137 of February 13, 2003, *Freddy Lepage y otros* case; N° 2750 of October 21, 2003, *Carlos E. Herrera Mendoza* case; N° 2432 of August 29, 2003, *Luis Franceschi y otros* case; and N° 2404 of August 28, 2003, *Exssel Alí Betancourt Orozco, Interpretación del artículo 72 de la Constitución* case. See the comments on these decisions in Allan R. BREWER–CARÍAS, *La Sala Constitucional versus el estado democrático de derecho: El secuestro del poder electoral y de la Sala Electoral del Tribunal Supremo y la confiscación del derecho a la participación política*, Los Libros de El Nacional, Colección Ares, Caracas 2004.

659 See decision of the Inter–American Court of Human Rights of August 5, 2008, *Apitz Barbera y otros ("Corte Primera de lo Contencioso Administrativo") vs. Venezuela* case, at http://www.corteidh.or.cr. Excepción Preliminar, Fondo, Reparaciones y Costas, Serie C N° 182.

660 Decision N° 1.939 of December 18, 2008, *Attorney General Office* case, at http://www.tsj.gov.ve/decisiones/scon/Diciembre/1939–181208–2008–08–1572.html. See the comment on this decision in Allan R. BREWER–CARÍAS, "La interrelación entre los Tribunales Constitucionales de América Latina y la Corte Interamericana de Derechos Humanos, y la cuestión de la inejecutabilidad de sus decisiones en Venezuela," in *Anuario Iberoamericano de Justicia Constitucional*, Centro de Estudios Políticos y Constitucionales, N° 13, Madrid 2009, pp. 99–136. See also Daniela Urosa Maggi, *Venezuelan National Report*, pp. 7–8.

powers of review regarding any judicial decision in which a court departs from the interpretation given to a constitutional provision by the same Constitutional Chamber or regarding which the Chamber considers that constitutional principles have been violated by the judicial decision; and second, powers of review on the same grounds of decisions issued by other Chambers of the Supreme Tribunal, consequently assuming a *de facto* superior hierarchy in the Judiciary that the Constitution has not conferred on it.[661] Three years later, the Organic Law of the Supreme Tribunal was sanctioned (2004), and this modification of the Constitution was not included by the National Assembly, a fact that did not prevent the Constitutional Chamber, through a new decision issued the same year, 2004,[662] to insist that the rule it established in 2001, despite the provisions of the Organic Law, was to continue to apply.

Another judicial review power that the Constitutional Chamber has assumed without any constitutional support is the incidental concentrated means of judicial review, which is found in countries where a concentrated system of judicial review is established exclusively – this is nonexistent in countries adopting a mixed system of judicial review where the concentrated method is combined with the diffuse method, as happens in many Latin American countries. Nonetheless, despite Venezuela having a mixed system of judicial review, the Constitutional Chamber in a clearly contradictory way has created the possibility of this incidental means of judicial review for the Constitutional Chamber to decide on the annulment of an unconstitutional statute, which is completely contradictory with the diffuse judicial review powers of all courts.[663]

II. CONSTITUTIONAL COURTS CREATING PROCEDURAL RULES ON JUDICIAL REVIEW PROCESSES

One of the specific matters in which judicial review of legislative omissions has taken place has been in the cases where constitutional courts have created rules of procedures for the exercise of their constitutional attributions when those have not been established in the legislation regulating their functions. For such purpose, constitutional courts, such as the Constitutional Tribunal of Peru, have claimed to have procedural autonomy in exercising their extended powers to develop and complement their decisions, but the procedural rules applicable in the judicial review pro-

661 See Decision N° 93 of February 6, 2001, *Corpoturismo* case, *Revista de Derecho Público*, N° 85–88, Editorial Jurídica Venezolana, Caracas 2001, pp. 406 ff., at http://www.tsj.gov.ve/decisiones/scon/Febrero/93–060201–00–1529%20.htm. See also Daniela Urosa Maggi, *Venezuelan National Report*, p. 6.

662 See Decision N° 1992 of September 8, 2004, *Peter Hofle* case; http://www.tsj.gov.ve/decisiones/scon/Septiembre/1992–080904–03–2332%20.htm. See also Daniela Urosa Maggi, *Venezuelan National Report*, p. 7.

663 See Decision 2588 of December 11, 2001, *Yrene Martínez* case, in http://www.tsj.gov.ve/decisiones/scon/Diciembre/2588–111201–01–1096.htm; Decision 806 of April 24, 2002, *Sintracemento* case (annulment of article 43 of the Organic Law of the Supreme Tribunal), at http://www.tsj.gov.ve/decisiones/scon/Abril/806–240402–00–3049.htm; Daniela Urosa Maggi, *Venezuelan National Report*, p. 9.

cess are not expressly regulated in statutes.[664] Nonetheless, the Constitutional Tribunal of Peru has established some limits to its procedural autonomy; its exercise cannot expand judicial review powers of the Tribunal that are not expressly established in the Constitution.[665]

In Germany, the same principle of procedural autonomy (*Verfahrensautonomie*) has been used to explain the powers developed by the Federal Constitutional Tribunal to complement procedural rules of judicial review. This was the case, for instance, with the application of article 35 of the Law of the Federal Constitutional Tribunal, which establishes that the Court can establish how such execution will take place. On the basis of this provision, for instance, the Federal Constitutional Court established a term for its decision to be applied, which is fixed according to different rules, for instance, a precise date like the end of the legislative term.

In other cases, judicial interference on legislative matters related to rules of procedures on matters of judicial review has been more intense. For instance, in Colombia, the Constitutional Court has assumed the exclusive competency to establish the effects of its own decisions, considering unconstitutional and annulling the provisions of the Law (Decree 2,067 of 1991) regulating its organization an functions in which the Legislator established rules regarding such effects (Articles 21 and 22).[666]

In Venezuela, the Constitutional Chamber of the Supreme Tribunal of Justice, in the absence of legislative rules, has established procedural rules, according to the authorization provided in article 19 of its Organic Law to establish a more convenient procedure for accomplishing its constitutional justice functions, "provided that they have legal basis." Consequently, in these cases, it has invoked its normative jurisdiction to establish the procedural rules for judicial review when not regulated in statutes. This has happened, precisely, on matters of judicial review regarding absolute legislative omission and the *habeas data* proceeding.

Regarding judicial review of absolute omissions, though established in the Constitution (article 336.7), its procedure was not regulated in the 2004 Organic Law of the Supreme Tribunal; consequently, the Constitutional Chamber in Decision N° 1556 of July 9, 2002, established the regulation on the matter to be applied until the National Assembly approved the statute establishing the procedural rules.[667]

Regarding the procedural rules on matters of *habeas data* – through which any person can have access to information about him– or herself gathered in official or private registries; has the right to know the use and purpose of such information; and has the right to ask for its updating, rectification, or destruction when erroneous or

664 See Resolution of the Constitutional Tribunal, Exp. N° 0020–2005–AI/TC, FJ 2; Francisco Eguiguren and Liliana Salomé, *Peruvian National Report I*, p. 14; Fernán Altuve–Febres, *Peruvian National Report II*, pp. 22–23.

665 See Francisco Eguiguren and Liliana Salomé, *Peruvian National Report I*, p. 17.

666 See Decision C–113/93; Germán Alfonso López Daza, *Colombian National Report I*, p. 9.

667 See Decision N° 1556 of July 9, 2002, *Alfonzo Albornoz and Gloria de Vicentini* case, at http://www.tsj.gov.ve/decisiones/scon/Julio/1556–090702–01–2337%20.htm. See also Daniela Urosa Maggi, *Venezuelan National Report*, pp. 10–11.

in cases where it illegitimately affects those rights[668] – in 2001, the Constitutional Chamber assumed exclusive jurisdiction to decide direct *habeas data* actions.[669] The Chamber ruled that it would establish the corresponding procedure for the exercise of its functions: in 2003, in Decision N° 2551 of November 24, 2003,[670] the Chamber based its ruling on the provision of Article 102 of the Law of the Supreme Court of Justice of 1976, which authorized the Supreme Court to establish the rules of procedure in all those cases not expressly regulated by the Legislator. In 2004, the new Organic Law of the Supreme Tribunal was sanctioned, repealing the former 1976 Organic Law of the Supreme Court without providing specific rules of procedure for the *habeas data* action. Thus, the Constitutional Chamber proceeded to modify its previous ruling and reformed the rules of procedure applicable to the *habeas data* actions in Decision N° 1511 of November 9, 2009.[671] The foundation for this decision was the immediate applicability of article 27 of the Constitution establishing the amparo proceeding and the attribution to the Chamber of guaranteeing and interpreting the Constitution. The Court reasoned that it had acted "in order to fill the existing vacuum existing in relation to this highly innovative constitutional action of habeas data."[672]

FINAL REMARKS

From all of what I have said, and after analyzing the role of constitutional courts as positive legislators in comparative law – leaving aside the cases for the pathology of judicial review that are directed not to reinforcing democratic principles and evolution but to dismantling democracy using in an illegitimate way a democratic tool[673] – it is possible to deduce the following two conclusions.

First, as noted at the beginning of this study, there is no longer a sharp distinction between two models of judicial review. In the contemporary world there is the experience of judicial review systems in a transformation, convergence, and mixture that

---

668 See Allan R. Brewer–Carías, *La Constitutición de 1999: Derecho constitucional venezolano*, Editorial Jurídica Venezolana, Caracas 2004, Vol. II, pp. 759 ff.

669 See Decision N° 332 of March 14, 2001, *Insaca* case; http://www.tsj.gov.ve/decisiones/scon/Marzo/332–140301–00–1797%20.htm. See also Daniela Urosa Maggi, *Venezuelan National Report*, p. 12.

670 Case: *Jaime Ojeda Ortiz*; http://www.tsj.gov.ve/decisiones/scon/Septiembre/2551–240903–03–0980.htm. See also Daniela Urosa Maggi, *Venezuelan National Report*, p. 13.

671 See *Mercedes Josefina Ramírez, Acción de Habeas Data* case; http://www.tsj.gov.ve/decisiones/scon/Noviembre/1511–91109–2009–09–0369.html See in Daniela Urosa Maggi, *Venezuelan National Report*, p. 13.

672 See Allan R. Brewer–Carías, El proceso constitucional de las acciones de habeas data en Venezuela: las sentencias de la Sala Constitucional como fuente del Derecho Procesal Constitucional," in Eduardo Andrés Velandia Canosa (coord.), *Homenaje al Maestro Héctor Fix Zamudio. Derecho Procesal Constitucional. Memorias del Primer Congreso Colombiano de Derecho Procesal Constitucional* Mayo 26, 27 y 28 de 2010, Bogotá 2010, pp. 289–295.

673 On Venezuela, see Allan R. Brewer–Carías, *Dismantling Democracy in Venezuela: The Chávez Authoritarian Experiment*, Cambridge University Press, New York, 2010.

was not possible to envision one hundred years ago, when the confrontation between the diffuse and concentrated methods of judicial review began to be imagined.

Second, the clear and simple system of the concentrated judicial review model, based on the binomial unconstitutionality–invalidity, or unconstitutionality–nullity, exercised by a Constitutional Court as a negative legislator, is nowadays difficult to defend.[674]

In fact, contemporary constitutional comparative law shows the existence of constitutional courts that have progressively assumed roles that decades ago corresponded only to the Constituent Power or to the Legislator; in some cases, they have discovered and deduced constitutional rules, particularly on matters of human rights not expressively enshrined in the Constitution and that could not be considered to have been the intention of an ancient and original Constituent Power. In other cases, constitutional courts have progressively been performing legislative functions, complementing the Legislator in its role of lawmaker and, in many cases, filling the gaps resulting from legislative omissions, sending guidelines and orders to the Legislator, and even issuing provisional legislation.

Nonetheless, the important results of a comparative law approach to the subject of constitutional courts as positive legislators are the common trends that can be found in all countries and in all legal systems; trends that are more numerous and important than the possible essential and exceptional differences, which confirms the importance of comparative law. That is why, in matters of judicial review, constitutional courts in many countries – to develop their own competencies and exercise their powers to control the constitutionality of statutes, to protect fundamental rights, and to ensure the supremacy of the Constitution – have progressively begun to study and analyze similar work developed in other Courts and in other countries, thus enriching their rulings.

Today, it is common to find in constitutional courts' decisions constant references to decisions issued on similar matters or cases by other constitutional courts. So it can be said that, in general, there is no aversion to using foreign law to interpret, when applicable, the Constitution. On matters of fundamental rights, for instance, the process of the internationalization of the constitutionalization of such rights in the way it has occurred during the past sixty years has resulted in a globalization process regarding the general applicable regime, which is indistinctively used

---

674 The model, as defined by Judge Marek Safjan, in the *Polish National Report*, was characterized as follows: "It is not the competence of the constitutional court to make laws or to bring into the legal order any normative elements, which have not been established before under an appropriate legislative procedure; therefore, the constitutional court may not replace the legislator in this process. The constitutional review is based on a coherent structure of a hierarchical legal system and the constitutional court has to operate within this order, drawing its own competence from the constitutional legislator. Judgments passed by the constitutional court cannot contain anything that has not been already proclaimed by the supreme norm laid down in the Constitution whereas the role of the constitutional review will always be limited to the application of law – although placed at the highest level of the normative hierarchy – and cannot involve creation of norms." See Marek Safjan, *Polish National Report*, p. 1.

to control the constitutionality or the conventionality of statutes, producing uniform principles of constitutional law never seen before.

Consequently, on the matter of judicial review, it is simply incomprehensible to pretend that the judicial solutions in a given country – on matters of the right to equality and nondiscrimination, or the right to privacy or due process, or the right not to be subject to torture – could be considered an endemic matter exclusively to a particular country, and that in the interpretation of the Constitution of the country, it is impossible to rely on judicial solutions to the same problems in other countries. This is at least a general trend that, with the exception of some judges and scholars in the United States, is possible to identify in comparative law, as a subject like the one studied in this General Report demonstrates. Consequently, in general terms, for a public comparative law scholar, it is incomprehensible that nominees to the U.S. Supreme Court have the almost–inevitable duty to express in their confirmation hearings before the Senate, for example, that "American Law does not permit the use of foreign law or international law to interpret the Constitution," and this a "given" question regarding which "[t]here is no debate."[675] A different matter is the possible use of foreign law in the U.S. universities for academic purposes. Regarding this assertion, Justice Ruth Bader Ginsburg has said that she "frankly [doesn't] understand all the brouhaha lately from Congress and even from some of my colleagues about referring to foreign law," explaining that the controversy was based in the misunderstanding that citing a foreign precedent means the court considers itself bound by foreign law as opposed to merely being influenced by such power as its reasoning holds. That is why she formulated the following question: "Why shouldn't we look to the wisdom of a judge from abroad with at least as much ease as we would read a law review article written by a professor?"[676]

And this is precisely what is now common in all constitutional jurisdictions all over the world: constitutional courts commonly consider that, with respect to foreign law, when they have to decide on the same matter and on the basis of the same principles, in the same way that they would study the matter through others authors' opinions and analysis from books and articles, they can also rely on courts' decisions from other countries, which can be useful because those courts dealt not only with a theoretical proposition, but also with a specific solution already applied to resolve a particular case.

675 Judge Sonia Sotomayor, at the confirmation hearing before the Senate, on July 15, 2009. See "Sotomayor on the Issues," *New York Times*, July 16, 2009, p. A18.

676 See Adam Liptak, "Ginsburg Shares Views on Influence of Foreign Law on Her Court, and Vice Versa," in *New York Times*, April 12, 2009, p. 14.

IV

JUDICIAL REVIEW AND AMPARO PROCEEDING IN LATIN AMERICA AND IN THE PHILIPPINES (2008)

This Paper was written for the preparation of two Lectures that I delivered at Fordham Law School, New York City in 2008. The first Lecture, on *Judicial Review in Latin America. A general overview,* was delivered at the Constitutional Comparative Law Course of Professor Ruti G. Teitel, on February 11, 2008; and the second Lecture, on *The Latin American "Amparo". A General Overview,* was delivered in the *Latin America Workshop on Human Rights & Legal Theory*, Leitner Center for International Law and Justice, on April 4th, 2008.

PART I:

JUDICIAL REVIEW AND AMPARO PROCEEDING IN LATIN AMERICA. A GENERAL COMPARATIVE CONSTITUTIONAL LAW OVERVIEW

Judicial review of the constitutionality of legislation an judicial protection of constitutional rights have been developing in Latin America since the 19th century, where the two main judicial review systems known in comparative law[1] have been applied, that is, the diffuse (decentralized) and the concentrated (centralized) methods of judicial review. In some cases, one of these methods have been established as the only one existing in some countries, in other cases, they have been adopted in a mixed or parallel way, coexisting for the purpose of guarantying the supremacy of

1 See in general M. Cappelletti, *Judicial Review in the Contemporary World*, Indianapolis 1971, p. 45 and M. Cappelleti and J.C. Adams, "Judicial Review of Legislation: European Antecedents and Adaptations", in *Harvard Law Review*, 79, 6, April 1966, p. 1207.

the Constitutions. This last solution has been followed in many Latin American countries, in the same sense that was it was also followed in Europe, in Portugal.[2]

The main criteria for classifying these systems of judicial review or control of the constitutionality of State acts, particularly of statutes, is basically based on the number of courts that carry out that task of exercising constitutional justice, in the sense that judicial review can be assigned to all the courts of a given country (diffuse method), or to only one single court (concentrated system), whether the Supreme Court or a special Constitutional Court created for such purpose.

In the first case, that is, in the diffuse method, when all the courts of a given country are empowered to act as constitutional judges controlling the constitutionality of statutes, the system has been identified as the "American system", because it was first adopted in the United States, particularly after the well known *Marbury* v. *Madison* case U.S. (1 Cranch), 137; 2 L. Ed. 60 (1803). Notwithstanding, the system is not only specific to countries with common law systems, since it has also been developed in countries with Roman or civil law traditions, precisely like those in Latin America. This method of judicial review has also been called as diffuse or decentralized,[3] because in it, the judicial control powers belongs to all the courts, from the lowest level up to the Supreme Court of the country, allowing them not to apply a statute in the particular case they have to decide, when they consider it unconstitutional and void, thereby giving prevalence to the Constitution.[4]

Since the 19th Century this diffuse method has been applied in almost all Latin American countries, as is the case of Argentina (1860), Brazil (1890), Colombia (1850), Dominican Republic (1844), Mexico (1857), Venezuela (1897), and also since the 20th Century in Ecuador, Guatemala, Nicaragua, and Peru.[5] Only in Argentina, the method strictly follows the American model. In the other countries it exists, but applied in combination with the concentrated method of judicial review.

Following the American model, when applying the diffuse method of judicial review of legislation, the decisions of the courts only have *inter partes* effect, that is, related to a particular case where the decision has been issued and to the parties in the process. So the courts do not annul the statutes considered unconstitutional, but only declare them void and unconstitutional, and not applicable to the case.

---

2 See Allan R. BREWER–CARÍAS, *Judicial Review in Comparative Law*, Cambridge University Press, Cambridge 1989; *Études de Droit Public Comparé*, Bruylant, Bruxelles 2001, pp. 855 ff.

3 See M. Cappelletti, "El control judicial de la constitucionalidad de las leyes en el derecho comparado", in *Revista de la Facultad de Derecho de México,* N° 61, 1966, p. 28.

4 See Allan R. Brewer Carías, *Judicial Review in Comparative Law,* Cambridge University Press, Cambridge 1989.

5 See Allan R. BREWER–CARÍAS, "La jurisdicción constitucional en América Latina", in Domingo García Belaúnde and Francisco Fernández Segado (Coord.), *La jurisdicción constitucional en Iberoamérica*, Dykinson S.L. (Madrid), Editorial Jurídica Venezolana (Caracas), Ediciones Jurídicas (Lima), Editorial Jurídica E. Esteva (Uruguay), Madrid 1997, pp. 117–161.

In the second method of judicial review, that is the concentrated one, when the power to control the constitutionality of legislation is given to a single judicial organ of the State, whether it is the Supreme Court or a special Constitutional Court created for such particular purpose, it has been identified as the "Austrian" system, because in Europe, it was first established in Austria in 1920, due to the influence of Hans Kelsen,[6] who proposed the creation of the Constitutional Court. It has also been called the "European system" because after World War II it was followed in other European countries, as was the case of Germany, Italy, France, Portugal and Spain, countries where Constitutional Tribunal or Courts were created. It is a concentrated system of judicial review, as opposed to the diffuse system, because the power to control the constitutionality of statutes is given only to one single Constitutional Court or Tribunal, that must decide on the matter in an objective way without any reference to a particular case or controversy, with powers, in general, to declare the nullity of the challenge statutes with general, *erga omnes* effects.

But before Kelsen's proposals and before the European experiences, and even though without the creation of special Constitutional Courts or Tribunals, the concentrated method of judicial review also was established since the middle of the 19th Century in Latin America by assigning to the existing Supreme Court of the countries, the power to nullify statutes on grounds of unconstitutionality. This was the case in Colombia and in Venezuela where an authentic concentrated system of judicial review exercised by means of a popular action has existed since 1858, initially in the hands of the Supreme Courts and more recently, through a Constitutional Court in Colombia or a Constitutional Chamber of the Supreme Tribunal of Justice in Venezuela, having the monopoly of annulling statutes on the grounds of their unconstitutionality.

This concentrated system has been adopted in all Latin American counties, except Argentina. In Bolivia, Costa Rica, Chile, Ecuador, El Salvador, Honduras, Panama, Paraguay and Uruguay, the system is conceived as exclusively concentrated; and on these countries, only in Bolivia, Ecuador and Chile, the concentrated judicial review power is exercised by a Constitutional Tribunal or Court that have been specially created. In the other countries it is the Supreme Court the one exercising judicial review powers, in some cases through a Constitutional Chamber.

In the other Latin American countries, the system has moved to a mixed one, combining the diffuse and the concentrated methods of judicial review. It is the case of Brazil, Colombia, the Dominican Republic, Guatemala, Mexico, Nicaragua, Peru and Venezuela. In this latter group, only in Colombia, Guatemala, Peru and Dominican Republic, a Constitutional Court or Tribunal has been crated; and in Nicaragua, El Salvador and Venezuela what has been created is a Constitutional Chamber within the Supreme Court of Justice.

6 See H. Kelsen, "La garantie juridictionnelle de la Constitution (La Justice constitutionnelle), *Revue du droit public et de la science politique en France et à l'étranger,* Paris 1928, pp. 197–257; Allan R. Brewer Carías, *Judicial Review in Comparative Law*, Cambridge University Press, Cambridge 1989.

In the concentrated system of judicial review, the petition for judicial review of legislation can be brought before the Court, whether by means of a direct action filed against the statute, in which case its constitutionality is the only matter in discussion in the proceeding, without any reference or relation to a particular case or controversy; or whether by means of an incidental constitutional question or request that must be raised in a particular case or controversy, where, on the contrary, the main issue of litigation is not the constitutional question, but what constitutes the merits of the case.

Other distinction can be made in the concentrated system regarding the direct actions of unconstitutionality, referred, first, to the standing to sue, which can be a limited one, as occurs in many countries (reserved to High Officials) or can be open to the citizenship, through a popular action (*action popularis*) as is the case in Colombia, Ecuador, El Salvador, Nicaragua, Panama and Venezuela. And second, to the moment of the filling of the action, which can be prior to the enactment of the particular challenged statute (*a priori* control) like for instance in Europe was the case of France (up to 2009); or after the statute has come into effect (*a posteriori* control), like in Europe has been the cases of Germany, Italy and Spain. In Latin America, in all the counties having a concentrated system of judicial review, the control is always *a posteriori* one, although in some countries both possibilities have been established, as is the case of Colombia, Ecuador and Venezuela, in similar way that was established in Europe, in Spain and Portugal.

But in addition to judicial review of the constitutionality of legislation, Latin American countries have also developed the amparo proceeding (suit, action or recourse of amparo of *tutela* or *protección*) which is one of the most distinguishable features of Latin American constitutional law, established as an extraordinary judicial remedy specifically conceived for the protection of constitutional rights against harms or threats inflicted by authorities or individuals,[7] which has also influenced similar actions in other counties.[8] This remedy was introduced in Latin America since the 19th century, particularly in 1857, in México, as the *juicio de amparo*, which according to the unanimous opinion of all the Mexican scholars, had its ori-

7. See Héctor Fix–Zamudio and Eduardo Ferrer Mac–Gregor (Coord.), *El derecho de amparo en el mundo*, Edit. Porrúa, México 2006; Allan R. BREWER–CARÍAS, *El amparo a los derechos y libertades constitucionales. Una aproximación comparativa*, Cuadernos de la Cátedra de Derecho Público, N° 1, Universidad Católica del Táchira, San Cristóbal 1993, 138 pp.; also published by the Inter American Institute on Human Rights, (Interdisciplinary Course), San José, Costa Rica, 1993, (mimeo), 120 pp. and in *La protección jurídica del ciudadano. Estudios en Homenaje al Profesor Jesús González Pérez*, Tomo 3, Editorial Civitas, Madrid 1993, pp. 2.695–2.740; Allan R. BREWER–CARÍAS, *Mecanismos nacionales de protección de los derechos humanos (Garantías judiciales de los derechos humanos en el derecho constitucional comparado latinoamericano)*, Instituto Interamericano de Derechos Humanos, San José 2005; and Allan R. BREWER–CARÍAS, *Constitutional Protection of Human Rights in Latin America. A Constitutional Comparative Law Study on the amparo proceeding*, Cambridge University Press, New York 2009.

8 It has been the case of the Philippines with the Writ of Amparo. See Allan R. BREWER–CARÍAS, The Latin American Amparo Proceeding and the Writ of Amparo in The Philippines," in *ity University of Hong Kong Law Review*, Volume 1:1 October 2009, pp 73–90

gins in the American judicial review of constitutionality of statutes system, as was described by Alexis de Tocqueville (*Democracy in America,* 1835),[9] a few years after *Malbury v. Madison* U.S. (1 Cranch), 137; 2 L. Ed. 60 (1803).

Nonetheless, the fact is that in a quite different way to the model, the amparo suit evolved, on the one hand, in México, into a unique and very complex *juicio de amparo*, exclusively found in that country where in addition to protect individuals against authorities and all their acts, is the instrument *par excellence* in order to seek judicial review of legislation, in addition to other judicial means; and on the other hand, in all the other Latin American countries, as an extraordinary judicial action, recourse or petition established exclusively for the protection of constitutional rights.

Being both, the judicial review proceedings in order to control the constitutionality of legislation and the amparo as a mean for the protection of constitutional rights, judicial institutions that since the 19th century are essential parts of their constitutional systems; in order to analyze them in Latin America I am going to analyze the subject in three parts::

First, Judicial Review and Amparo in countries having only a diffuse system of judicial review, which is only the case of Argentina;

Second, Judicial Review and Amparo in countries having only a concentrated system of judicial review, which is the case of Costa Rica, El Salvador, Honduras and Panama in Central America; and of Bolivia, Ecuador, Chile, Paraguay and Uruguay in South America;

And ***Third***, countries having a mixed system of judicial review, that is, at the same time the diffuse and the concentrated ones, which is the case of México in North America; of Dominican Republic in the Caribbean; of Guatemala and Nicaragua in Central America; and of Brazil, Colombia, Peru and Venezuela in South America.

I. JUDICIAL REVIEW AND AMPARO IN COUNTRIES ONLY APPLYING THE DIFFUSE METHOD OF JUDICIAL REVIEW OF LEGISLATION: THE CASE OF ARGENTINA

In Latin America, Argentina is the only country where the diffuse method of judicial review remains as being the only one applied in order to control the constitutionality of legislation.

The Argentinean system of judicial review system,[10] is perhaps the one that more closely follows the United States model, also derived from the supremacy clause

---

9 See Alexis De Tocqueville, *Democracy in America* (Ed. by J.P. Mayer and M. Lerner), The Fontana Library, London, 1968, Vol. 1, p. 120–124.See Robert D. Baker, *Judicial Review in México. A Study of the Amparo Suit*, University of Texas Press, Austin 1971, pp. 15, 33; Eduardo Ferrer Mac–Gregor, *La acción constitucional de amparo en México y España, Estudio de Derecho Comparado*, 2nd Edition, Edit. Porrúa, México D.F. 2000; Héctor Fix–Zamudio, *Ensayos sobre el derecho de amparo, Universidad Nacional Autónoma de México*, Editorial Porrúa, México 2003.

established in the 1860 Constitution which as in the United States, does not expressly confer any judicial review power upon the Supreme Court or the other courts. So in the case of Argentina, judicial review was also a creation of the Supreme Court, based on the same principles of supremacy of the Constitution and judicial duty when applying the law.

The first case in which judicial review power was exercised was the *Sojo* case (1887) concerning the unconstitutionality of a federal statute that tried to extend the original jurisdiction of the Supreme Court[11] as also happened in the *Marbury* v. *Madison* case U.S. (1 Cranch), 137; 2 L. Ed. 60 (1803), in which the Constitution was considered as the supreme law of the land and the courts were empowered to maintain its supremacy over the statutes which infringed it.[12]

Therefore, through the work of the courts, in the Argentinean system of judicial review, all the courts have the power to declare the unconstitutionality of treaties[13] and legislative acts[14] whether at national or provincial levels.

So in a similar way as the United States system of judicial review, the Argentinean system has also an incidental character, in the sense that the question of constitutionality is not the principal matter of a process. The question has to be raised

---

10 See in general Néstor Pedro Sagüés, *Derecho procesal Constitucional*, Ed. Asrea, Buenos Aires 2002; Ricardo Haro, *El control de constitucionalidad*, Editorial Zavalia, Buenos Aires, Argentina, 2003; Juan Carlos Hitters, "La jurisdicción constitucional en Argentina", in Domingo García Belaunde and Francisco Fernández Segado (Coord.), *La jurisdicción constitucional en Iberoamérica*, Ed. Dykinson, Madrid, España, 1997; Maximiliano Toricelli, *El sistema de control constitucional argentino*, Editorial Lexis Nexis Depalma, Buenos Aires, Argentina, 2002.

11 See A.E. Ghigliani, *Del control jurisdiccional de constitucionalidad*, Buenos Aires 1952., p. 5; R. Bielsa, *La protección constitucional y el recurso extraordinario. Jurisdicción de la Corte Suprema*, Buenos Aires 1958, p. 41, 43, 179 who speaks about a "pretorian creation" of judicial review by the Supreme Court, p. 179. See Jorge Reinaldo Vanossi and P.F. Ubertone, "Control jurisdiccional de constitucionalidad", in *Desafíos del control de constitucionalidad*, Ediciones Ciudad Argentina, Buenos Aires, Argentina, 1996 (also printed as *Institutuciones de defense de la Constitución en la Argentina*, Universidad Nacional Autónoma de México, Congreso Internacional sobre la Constitución y su defense, México 1982); H. Quiroga Lavie, *Derecho constitucional*, Buenos Aires 1978, p. 481. Previously in 1863 the first Supreme Court decisions were adopted in constitutional matters but referred to provincial and executive acts. See. A.E. Ghigliani, *Idem*, p. 58.

12 See. A.E. Ghigliani, *Idem*, p. 58.

13 In particular, regarding the unconstitutionality of Treaties and the posibility of the Courts to control them, A.E. Ghigliani, *Del control jurisdiccional de constitucionalidad*, Buenos Aires 1952, p. 62; Jorge Reinaldo Vanossi, *Aspectos del recurso extraordinario de inconstitucionalidad*, Buenos Aires 1966, p. 91, and *Teoría constitucional*, Vol. II, Supremacía y control de constitucionalidad, Buenos Aires 1976, p. 277.

14 See Néstor.Pedro Sagües, *Recurso Extraordinario*, Buenos Aires 1984, Vol. I, p. 91; Jorge Reinaldo Vanossi and P.F. Ubertone, "Control jurisdiccional de constitucionalidad", in *Desafíos del control de constitucionalidad*, Ediciones Ciudad Argentina, Buenos Aires, Argentina, 1996; J.R. Vanossi, *Teoría constitucional*, Vol. II, Supremacía y control de constitucionalidad, Buenos Aires 1976, p. 155.

by a party in a particular judicial controversy, case or process, normally through an exception, at any moment before the decision in the case is adopted by the court.

Thus, in the particular case[15] a party can raise the question of unconstitutionality of the statute to be applied, alleging that the statute which is considered invalid injures his own rights. Consequently, in Argentina, as in the United States, the question of unconstitutionality cannot be raised *ex officio,*[16] except in cases where "public order" is involved.[17]

In addition, it has been considered that the constitutional question raised in the case, particularly due to the presumption of constitutionality of all statutes, must be of an unavoidable character, in the sense that its decision must be alleged to be essential to the resolution of the case which depends on it. For that purpose the constitutional question must be clear and undoubted.[18]

Finally, it must be said that in the Argentinean system, the Supreme Court of the Nation has developed the same exception to judicial review established in the United States system, concerning the political questions. Even though the Constitution does not expressly establish anything on the matter, these political questions are related to the "acts of government" or "political acts" exercised by State political bodies in accordance with powers exclusively and directly attributed to them in the Constitution.[19]

The courts in Argentina, as in the United States, when deciding constitutional questions regarding statutes, do not have the power to annul or repeal a law. This power is reserved to the legislative body, so the only thing the courts can do is to refuse or reject its application in the particular case when they consider it unconstitutional. The statute, therefore, when considered unconstitutional and non–

---

15 Article 100 of the Constitution; R. Bielsa, *Idem.*, p. 213, 214; A.E. Ghigliani, *Del control jurisdiccional de constitucionalidad*, Buenos Aires 1952., pp. 75, 80; J.R. Vanossi and P.F. Ubertone, *Idem.*, p. 23; .M. Lozada, *Derecho Constitucional Argentino,* Buenos Aires 1972, Vol. I, p. 342.

16 R. Bielsa, *Idem.*, p. 198, 214; H. Quiroga Lavie, *Derecho constitucional*, Buenos Aires 1978, p. 479.

17 G. Bidart Campos, *El derecho constitucional del poder*, Vol. II, Chap. XXIX; J.R. Vanossi, *Teoría constitucional*, Vol. II, Supremacía y control de constitucionalidad, Buenos Aires 1976, p. 318, 319; J.R. Vanossi and P.E. Ubertone, "Control jurisdiccional de constitucionalidad", in *Desafíos del control de constitucionalidad*, Ediciones Ciudad Argentina, Buenos Aires, Argentina, 1996; .R. Bielsa, *Idem*, 255; H. Quiroga Lavie, *Idem,* p. 479.

18 A.E. Ghigliani, *Del control jurisdiccional de constitucionalidad*, Buenos Aires 1952, p. 89; S.M. Losada *Derecho Constitucional Argentino,* Buenos Aires 1972, Vol. I, p. 341; H. Quiroga Lavie, *Derecho constitucional,* Buenos Aires 1978, p. 480. Thus when an interpretation of the statute avoiding the consideration of the constitutional question is possible, the court must follow this path. See A.E. Ghigliani, *Idem*, p. 91.

19 A.E. Ghigliani, *Idem.*, p. 85; H. Quiroga Lavie, *Idem*, p. 482; S.M. Losada, *Derecho Constitucional Argentino,* Buenos Aires 1972, Vol. I, p. 343; J.R. Vanossi and P.E. Ubertone, "Control jurisdiccional de constitucionalidad", in *Desafíos del control de constitucionalidad*, Ediciones Ciudad Argentina, Buenos Aires, Argentina, 1996.

applicable by the judge, is considered void, with no effect whatsoever,[20] but only in the particular case, remaining valid and generally applicable, so in principle, even the same court, can change its criteria about the unconstitutionality of the statute and apply it in the future.[21]

Being a federal state, the Argentinean Judiciary is regulated through national and provincial statutes, and the Supreme Court of Justice, which is the only judicial body created in the Constitution, is the "final interpreter" or "the defendant of the Constitution", having also two sorts of jurisdiction: original and appellate ones.[22] It has been through the appellate jurisdiction and by means of the "extraordinary recourse" in cases decided by the National Chambers of Appeals and by the Superior Courts of the Provinces that the constitutional cases can reach the Supreme Court, with similar results to the request for *writ of certiorari* before the United States Supreme Court can be achieved.

Nonetheless, the main difference between both extraordinary means is that contrary to the United States system, the Supreme Court of Argentina does not have discretionary powers in accepting extraordinary recourses, which in the case is a mandatory jurisdiction, exercised as a consequence of a right the parties have to file them.

When deciding these extraordinary recourses, the Supreme Court does not act as a third instance court, its power of review only concentrated on matters regarding constitutional questions.[23]

That is why, in a different way to the appeal, the extraordinary recourse must be motivated and founded on constitutional reasons, and one of the important conditions for its admissibility is that the constitutional question raised, must have been discussed in the proceeding before the lower courts. Therefore, the Supreme Court has rejected the recourse when the constitutional issue has not been discussed and decided in the lower courts.[24]

Another aspect that must be highlighted is that in the Argentinean system, the Supreme Court decisions on judicial review on constitutional issues in principle are not obligatory for the other courts or for the inferior courts;[25] that is, they do not have *stare decisis* effects. In the 1949 constitutional reform, an attempt was made to give binding effects on the national and provincial courts to the interpretation adopt-

---

20 A.E. Ghigliani, *Idem,* p. 95; R. Bielsa, *La protección constitucional y el recurso extraordinario. Jurisdicción de la Corte Suprema,* Buenos Aires 1958, pp. 197, 198, 345; N.P. Sagües, *Derecho procesal Constitucional,* Tomo I, Cuarta edición, 2002, p. 156.

21 A.E. Ghigliani, *Idem,* p. 92, 97; R. Bielsa, *Idem,* p. 196; N. P. Sagües, *Idem,* p. 177.

22 R. Bielsa, *La protección constitucional y el recurso extraordinario. Jurisdicción de la Corte Suprema,* Buenos Aires 1958, pp. 60–61, 270; J.R. Vanossi and P.F. Ubertone, "Control jurisdiccional de constitucionalidad", in *Desafíos del control de constitucionalidad,* Ediciones Ciudad Argentina, Buenos Aires, Argentina, 1996.

23 R. Bielsa, *Idem,* p. 222; N. P. Sagües, *Idem,* p. 270; pp. 185, 221, 228, 275.

24 R. Bielsa, *Idem,* p. 190, 202–205, 209, 245, 252.

25 R. Bielsa, *Idem,* pp. 49, 198, 267; A.E. Ghigliani, *Del control jurisdiccional de constitucionalidad,* Buenos Aires 1952, pp. 97, 98.

ed by the Supreme Court of Justice regarding articles of the Constitution,[26] but this provision was later repealed and the situation today is the absolute power of all courts to render their judgment autonomously with their own constitutional interpretation. Nonetheless, the fact is that the Supreme Court has progressively imposed the doctrine of the binding effects of its decisions,[27] developing what has been called "*de facto stare decisis*" doctrine regarding the interpretation of the Constitution and of federal laws, aiming to provide litigants with some degree of certainty as to how the law must be interpreted, a requirement the Court finds embedded in the due process clause of our Constitution. In the *García Aguilera* case decided in 1870, barely eight years after the court's establishment, the Supreme Court held, in a since then oft–repeated statement, that "lower courts are required to adjust their proceedings and decisions to those of the Supreme Court in similar cases,"[28] from which they can only depart if they give "valid motives."

But in addition to judicial review, the Constitution of Argentina in an article that was included in the constitutional reform of 1994, establishes three specific actions for the protection of human rights protection: the "amparo", the habeas data and the habeas corpus actions (Article 43).[29]

Regarding the "amparo" action, the Constitution provides that any person may file a prompt and summary proceeding against any act or omission attributed to of public authorities or to individuals, for the protection of the rights and guaranties recognized by the Constitution, the treaties or the statutes, which can only be brought before a court if there is no other more suitable judicial mean.

The same article 43 of the Constitution also provides for a collective action of "amparo" that can be filed by the affected party, the people's defendant and non–profit associations, in order to protect collective rights, like the rights to a proper environment and to free competition, and the user and consumer rights, as well as the rights that have general collective impact.

In the case of Argentina, these three specific remedies for the protection of all human rights are regulated in three separate statutes: the "amparo" Action Law (*Ley*

---

26 Article 95 of the 1949 Constitution. See C.A. Ayanagaray, *Efectos de la declaración de inconstitucionalidad,* Buenos Aires 1955, p. 11; R. Bielsa, *Idem,* p. 268.

27 Néstor P. Sagües has called the "Argentinean stare decisis." See Néstor P. Sagües, "Los efectos de las sentencias constitucionales en el derecho argentino," in *Anuario Iberoamericano de Justicia Constitucional,* Centro de Estudios Políticos y Constitucionales, N° 12, 2008, Madrid 2008, p. 345–347.

28 Fallos 9:53 (1870).

29 See Juan F. Armagnague et al., *Derecho a la información, hábeas data e Internet,* Ediciones La Roca, Buenos Aires 2002; Miguel Ángel Ekmekdjian et al., *Hábeas Data. El derecho a la intimidad frente a la revolución informática,* Edic. Depalma, Buenos Aires 1998; Osvaldo Alfredo Gozaíni, *Derecho Procesal Constitucional, Hábeas Data. Protección de datos personales. Ley 25.326 y reglamentación (decreto 1558/2001),* Rubinzal–Culzoni Editores, Santa Fe, Argentina 2002.

de acción de amparo, Ley 16986/1966), the Habeas Corpus Law (*Ley 23098/1984*) and the Personal Data Protection Law (*Ley 25366/2000*).[30]

But, as aforementioned, even though the "amparo" action was regulated for the first time in the 1994 Constitution, in practice it was created four decades before by the Supreme Court in the *Angel Siri* Case of 27 December 1957[31] in which the power of ordinary courts to protect fundamental rights of citizens against violation from public authorities actions was definitively admitted. At that time, the Constitution only provided for the habeas corpus action (Article 18) which was regulated in the provisions of the Criminal Procedural Code (Title IV, Section II, Book IV) and established for the protection of physical and personal freedom against illegal or arbitrary detentions.[32] Regarding other constitutional rights, they were only protected through the ordinary judicial means, so the courts considered that the habeas corpus could not be used for such purpose.

That is why, for instance, in 1950 the Supreme Court of the Nation in the *Bartolo* Case, rejected the application of the *habeas corpus* proceeding to obtain judicial protection of constitutional rights other than personal freedom, ruling that "nor in the text, or in its spirit, or in the constitutional tradition of the habeas corpus institution, can be found any basis for its application for the protection of the rights of property or of freedom of commerce and industry", concluding that against the infringements of such rights, the statutes set forth administrative and judicial remedies."[33]

This situation radically changed in 1957 as a result of the decision of the *Angel Siri* case, who was the director of a newspaper (Mercedes) in the Province of Buenos Aires, which was shut down by the Government. He filed a petition requesting "amparo" for the protection of his freedom of press and his right to work, which was rejected by the corresponding criminal court, arguing that the petition was filed as a habeas corpus action which was only established for the protection of physical and personal freedom and not of other constitutional rights. By means of an extraordinary recourse, the case arrived before the Supreme Court, which in a decision of December 27, 1957 repeal the lower court decision, and admitted the action of "amparo", following these arguments: First, that in the case, the violation of the

30 See in general, José Luis Lazzarini, *El Juicio de Amparo*, La Ley, Buenos Aires, 1987; Néstor Pedro Sagües, *Derecho Procesal Constitucional. Acción de Amparo*, Vol 3., Editorial Astrea, Buenos Aires 1988, and "El derecho de amparo en Argentina", in Héctor Fix–Zamudio and Eduardo Ferrer Mac–Gregor, *El derecho de amparo en el mundo*, Edit. Porrúa, México 2006, pp. 41–80.

31 See. G. R. Carrio, *Algunos aspectos del recurso de amparo*, Buenos Aires 1959, p. 9; J. R. Vanossi, *Teoría constitucional*, Vol. II, Supremacía y control de constitucionalidad, Buenos Aires 1976, p. 277.

32 See: Néstor Pedro Sagües, *Derecho Procesal Constitucional. Hábeas Corpus*, Volume 4, 2nd Edition, Editorial Astrea, Buenos Aires 1988, p. 116.

33 See the references to the *Barolo* Case in Joaquín Brage Camazano, *La jurisdicción constitucional de la libertad (Teoría general, Argentina, México, Corte Interamericana de Derechos Humanos)*, Editorial Porrúa, Instituto Mexicano de Derecho Procesal Constitucional, México 2005, p. 66.

constitutional guaranty of freedom of press and the right to work was duly argued; second, that the arbitrary governmental violation affecting those rights was proved; and third, that those rights needed to be protected by the courts, concluding that for such purpose the absence of a statutory regulation on "amparo" could not be a valid argument to reject the judicial protection. In brief, the Supreme Court considered in its decision that the constitutional rights and guaranties of the peoples, once declared in the Constitution, needed always to be judicially protected, regardless of the existence of a regulatory statute on the matter.[34]

The second important decision of the Argentinean Supreme Court on "amparo" matters was issued a year later, in the *Samuel Kot* Case, of October 5th, 1958. In this case the plaintiff was the owner of an industry, which had been occupied by workers on strike. After an "amparo" petition that was filed before a lower court was rejected, once the procedure reached the Supreme Court, the "amparo" was admitted, and the Court ordered the restitution of the occupied premises to its owner. The Court decided that in any case when in a manifest way the illegitimacy of a restriction to any of the essential constitutional rights clearly appears, and when the resolution of the case through the judicial ordinary means could cause grave and irreparable damages, then the courts must immediately re–establish the harmed right by means of the "amparo" action, even applying the habeas corpus procedure.

But beside admitting the "amparo" action without constitutional or legal provision, the other very important issue decided by the Supreme Court in this *Kot Case* was that the "amparo" was not only intended to protect rights against acts of authorities, but also against private individuals' illegitimate actions when if seeking protection by means of the ordinary judicial procedure, serious and irreparable harm could affect the claimant.[35]

After these decisions, the "amparo" action developed through judicial interpretation up to the enactment of the 1966 Amparo Law 16.986,[36] which in spite of the

---

34 See the reference to the *Siri* Case in José Luis Lazzarini, *El juicio de amparo*, La Ley, Buenos Aires, 1987, pp. 26 ff y 373 ff.; Alí Joaquín Salgado, *Juicio de amparo y acción de inconstitucionalidad*, Ed. Astrea, Buenos Aires 1987, pp. 5; Néstor Pedro Sagües, *Derecho Procesal Constitucional. Acción de Amparo*, Volume 3, 2nd Edition, Editorial Astrea, Buenos Aires 1988, pp. 9 ff.

35 See the references to the *Samuel Samuel Kot Ltd.* Case of 5 September, 1958, in S.V. Linares Quintana, *Acción de amparo*, Buenos Aires 1960, p. 25; José Luis Lazzarini, *El juicio de amparo*, La Ley, Buenos Aires, 1987, pp. 243 ff; Alí Joaquín Salgado, *Juicio de amparo y acción de inconstitucionalidad*, Ed. Astrea, Buenos Aires 1987, pp. 6.; Susana Albanese, *Garantías Judiciales. Algunos requisitos del debido proceso legal en el derecho internacional de los derechos humanos*, Ediar S.A. Editora, Comercial, Industrial y Financiera, Buenos Aires 2000; Augusto M. Morillo et al., *El amparo. Régimen procesal*, 3rd Edition, Librería Editora Platense SRL, La Plata 1998, 430 pp.; Néstor Pedro Sagües, *Derecho Procesal Constitucional*, Vol. 3, *Acción de Amparo*, 2nd Edition, Editorial Astrea, Buenos Aires 1988.

36 See José Luis Lazzarini, *El juicio de amparo*, Buenos Aires, 1987; Néstor Pedro Sagüés, *Derecho Procesal Constitucional. Acción de Amparo*, Buenos Aires, 1988; Néstor Pedro Sagüés, "El derecho de amparo en Argentina", in Héctor Fix–Zamudio and Eduardo Ferrer Mac–Gregor (Coord.), *El derecho de amparo en el mundo*, Universidad Nacional Autónoma de México, Editorial Porrúa, México 2006, pp. 41–80.

doctrine set forth in the *Kot case*, only referred to the action of "amparo" against acts of the State, leaving aside the "amparo" against individuals that nonetheless, was is filed in accordance to the Civil and Commercial Procedure Code of the Nation (Article 32,1, Sub–sections 2 and 498).[37]

According to this 1966 Law, the "amparo" action can be brought before the competent judge of first instance (Article 4) for the protection of all constitutional rights and freedoms against acts or omissions of public authorities, but not against judicial decisions or against statutes, which are excluded from the "amparo" action.

This action is thus basically directed, in Argentina, to be filed against administrative actions or omission, and can only be filed when no other judicial or administrative recourses or remedies exist to assure the claimed protection. So that if they exist, they must be previously exhausted, unless it is proved that they are incapable of redressing the damage and their processing can lead to serious and irreparable harm. This can also be considered as a common trend of the amparo action in Latin America, as an extraordinary remedy, similar to what happens with the injunction procedure in the United States.

As mentioned, the amparo action is filed before the first instance courts and also in this case, the cases can only reach the Supreme Court by means of an extraordinary recourse which can only be filed when in the judicial decision a matter of judicial review of constitutionality is resolved,[38] in a similar way as constitutional questions can reach the Supreme Court in the United States.

In the Argentinean system of judicial review, even though the amparo action is also an important tool to raise constitutional questions, discussions have raised regarding the applicability of the diffuse method of judicial review by the courts, precisely when deciding actions for amparo.

In the initial development of the amparo, and in spite of the diffuse system of judicial review followed in Argentina, the Supreme Court, in a contradictory way, established the criteria that the courts, when deciding amparo cases, have no power to decide on the constitutionality of legislation, reducing their powers to decide only on acts or facts that could violate fundamental rights. Thus, the amparo could not be granted when the complaint contained the allegation of unconstitutionality of a statute on which the relevant acts or facts were based.[39] This doctrine was incorporated in the Law 16.986 of 18 October 1966 on the recourse for amparo, in which it was expressly established that the "action for amparo will not be admissible when the decision upon the invalidity of the act will require.... the declaration of the unconstitutionality of statues, decrees or ordinances." (Article 2,d).

---

37 J. L. Lazzarini, *Idem*, p. 229.

38 See Elias Guastavino, *Recurso extraordinario de inconstitucionalidad*, Ed. La Roca, Buenos Aires, Argentina, 1992; Lino Enrique Palacio, *El recurso extraordinario federal. Teoría y Técnica*, Abeledo–Perrot, Buenos Aires, 1992.

39 See the *Aserradero Clipper SRL case* (1961), J. R. Vanossi, *Teoría constitucional*, Vol. II, Supremacía y control de constitucionalidad, Buenos Aires 1976, p. 286.

But one year later, in 1967, the Supreme Court, without expressly declaring the unconstitutionality of this provision, in the *Outon* case,[40] decided its inapplicability and accepted the criteria that when considering amparo cases, the courts have the power to review the unconstitutionality of legislation.[41]

But in spite of Argentina being the only Latin American country that has kept the diffuse method of judicial review as the only one applicable in order to control the constitutionality of legislation, the diffuse method of judicial review is also applied in Brazil, Colombia, Dominican Republic, Ecuador, Guatemala, Mexico, Nicaragua, Peru and Venezuela but with the main difference that it is applied within a mixed system of judicial review (diffuse and concentrated).

II. JUDICIAL REVIEW AND AMPARO IN COUNTRIES APPLYING ONLY THE CONCENTRATED METHOD OF JUDICIAL REVIEW OF LEGISLATION

Other Latin American countries, do not apply at all the diffuse method of judicial review, having adopted only the concentrated one, as is the case of Bolivia, Ecuador, Chile, Costa Rica, El Salvador, Honduras, Panama, Paraguay and Uruguay. Some countries have attributed the power to decide on the unconstitutionality of statutes to the existing Supreme Court, as is the case in Costa Rica, El Salvador, Honduras, Panama, Paraguay and Uruguay; and others, as in Europe, to a special Constitutional Tribunal created for such purpose, [42] as is the case in Bolivia, Ecuador and Chile. In the former group, in some countries, a special Constitutional Chamber of the Supreme Court has been created for the purpose of being the Constitutional Jurisdiction (Costa Rica, El Salvador, Honduras and Paraguay).

The Supreme Court of Constitutional Tribunal can be reach on matters of judicial review trough a direct action or in an incidental way by means of a referral of the constitutional question made by a lower court ex officio or at a party request. In general the action of unconstitutionality of statutes is subjected to standing rules limiting it to some High Officials of the State (Bolivia, Chile and Costa Rica). In some countries a popular action is provided (Panama, Ecuador and El Salvador) and

---

40 *Outon* Case of 29 March 1967. J. R. Vanossi, *Idem,* p. 288.

41 G. J. Bidart Campos, *Régimen legal del amparo*, 1969; G. J. Bidart Campos, "El control de constitucionalidad en el juicio de amparo y la arbitrariedad o ilegalidad del acto lesivo", *Jurisprudencia argentina*, 23–4–1969; N. P. Sagües, "El juicio de amparo y el planteo de inconstitucionalidad", *Jurisprudencia argentina*, 20–7–1973; J. R. J. R. Vanossi, *Idem*, pp. 288–292; José Luis Lazzarini, *El juicio de amparo*, La Ley, Buenos Aires, 1987, pp. 80, 86; Alí Joaquín Salgado, *Juicio de amparo y acción de inconstitucionalidad*, Ed. Astrea, Buenos Aires 1987, p. 58; Joaquín Brage Camazano, *La jurisdicción constitucional de la libertad (Teoría general, Argentina, México, Corte Interamericana de Derechos Humanos)*, Editorial Porrúa, Instituto Mexicano de Derecho Procesal Constitucional, México 2005, pp. 71, 117.

42 See Allan R. BREWER–CARÍAS, "La jurisdicción constitucional en América Latina", in Domingo García Belaúnde and Francisco Fernández Segado (Coord.), *La jurisdicción constitucional en Iberoamérica*, Dykinson S.L. (Madrid), Editorial Jurídica Venezolana (Caracas), Ediciones Jurídicas (Lima), Editorial Jurídica E. Esteva (Uruguay), Madrid 1997, pp. 117–161.

in Uruguay the action is given to the interested party. Only in Uruguay, no direct action exists, and the Supreme Court can only be reach in the incidental way. Only in Ecuador an incidental mean of judicial review is provided, imposing the courts to raise before the Constitutional Court, ex officio or at a party request, the questions of constitutionality of statutes.

In all the countries with only an exclusive concentrated system of judicial review, except in Paraguay and Uruguay where it has inter partes effects, the effects of the Supreme Court of Constitutional Tribunal decision on the unconstitutionality of statutes, have annullatory, erga onmes effects.

Finally, being a concentrated system of judicial review, in these countries some mechanism have been established in order to assure that the decisions on other constitutional matters different to judicial review, like those adopted in amparo proceedings for the protection of constitutional rights, can reach the higher constitutional court. For such purpose, in Bolivia, an automatic review power of the Constitutional Court has been set forth and in Honduras, a recourse for revision is provided.

In these countries with only a concentrated system of judicial review, another distinction can be made specifically regarding the judicial competencies on matter of amparo, in the sense that in some of these countries, the concentrated method on matters of constitutionality is an absolute one, also including the amparo proceeding, as is the case in Costa Rica and El Salvador, where the power to decide the "amparo" action has also been concentrated in a "Constitutional Jurisdiction", as it also happens with the "amparo" actions in Europe. In Latin America, this is an exceptional trend, not being in general terms the Supreme Courts or the Constitutional Tribunals the only ones empowered to decide on matters of amparo. On the contrary, in the majority of the Latin American countries with or without concentrated system of judicial review, the "amparo" jurisdiction corresponds to a variety of courts and judges.

That is why, for the purpose of studying the concentrated method of judicial review as the only one applied in some countries, a distinction must be made between countries where the "amparo" proceedings are also attributed to the single court exercising the concentrated power of judicial review, and countries where there are attributed to the whole Judiciary, independently of the concentrated method of judicial review.

1. The Absolute Concentrated Systems of Judicial Review and Amparo

The first group of countries refers to those where the competence on all constitutional matters, including amparo, is reserved to one single court. This is the system followed in Europe, in Germany[43], Austria[44] and Spain[45] where the "amparo" re-

43 See I. V. Munch. "El recurso de amparo constitucional como instrumento jurídico y político en la República Federal de Alemania", in Revista *de Estudios Políticos*, N° 7, Madrid, 1979, pp. 269–289; Klaus Schlaich, "El Tribunal constitucional alemán", in L. Favoreu et al., *Tribunales Constitucionales Europeos Derechos Fundamentales*, Madrid, 1984, pp. 133–232.

courses can only be filed before the same Constitutional Courts or Tribunals that have the exclusive power to decide on matters of judicial review. In Latin America, this system is only followed in Costa Rica and El Salvador, where the Constitutional Chambers of the Supreme Courts, have the monopoly of the concentrated systems of judicial review in order to annul statutes on the grounds of unconstitutionality, and are also the sole and exclusive courts to hear and decide on matters of "amparo" and habeas corpus.

A. *The Constitutional Chamber in Costa Rica with exclusive powers on matters of judicial review, and the amparo action*

The concentrated system of judicial review was established in Costa Rica in the 1989 Constitutional reform, when the Constitutional Chamber of the Supreme Court was created with the exclusive power to declare the unconstitutionality of statutes and other State acts, with nullifying effects (Article 10). For this purpose, the Chamber can be reached through the following means set forth in the Law on Constitutional Jurisdiction (article 73):

First, by means of a direct action of unconstitutionality that can be brought before the Chamber against any statute or executive regulation, or international treaty considered contrary to the Constitution, and even against constitutional amendments approved in violation of the constitutional procedure.

This principal unconstitutionality action can only be brought before the Constitutional Chamber by the General Comptroller, the Attorney General, the Public Prosecutor and the Peoples' Defendant (Article 75). Nonetheless, the action can also be brought before the Chamber in a similar way to a popular action in cases involving the defense of diffuse or collective interests filed against executive regulation or self executing statutes which do not require additional public actions for its enforcement.[46]

Second, the action can also be exercised in an incidental way before the Constitutional Chamber when a party raises the constitutional question in a particular judicial case, even in cases of habeas corpus and "amparo", as a mean for the protection of the rights and interest of the affected parties (Article 75).

In all these cases of actions, the decisions of the Chamber when declaring the unconstitutionality of the challenged statute have nullifying and general *erga omnes* effects.

---

44 See F. Ermacora, "El Tribunal Constitucional Austríaco", in the *Tribunal Constitucional*, Dirección General de lo Contencioso del Estado, Instituto de Estudios Fiscales, Madrid, 1981, Volumen I, pp. 409–459.

45 See Joan Oliver Araujo, *El recurso de amparo*, Palma de Mallorca, 1986; Antonio Moya Garrido, *El recurso de amparo según la doctrina del Tribunal Constitucional*, Barcelona, 1983; José L. Cascajo Castro and Vicente Gimeno Sendra, *El recurso de amparo*, Madrid, 1985; Antonio Cano Mata, *El recurso de amparo*, Madrid, 1983.

46 See Rubén Hernández Valle, *El Control de la Constitucionalidad de las Leyes*, San José, 1990.

Third, in addition to the direct or incidental action of unconstitutionality, the other important mean for judicial review is the judicial referrals on constitutional matters that any courts can raise *ex officio* before the Constitutional Chamber when they have doubts regarding the constitutionality of the statutes they must apply for the resolution of the case (Article 120). In these cases, the lower court must prepare a resolution on the constitutional questions that must be sent to the Constitutional Chamber. The judicial procedure of the case must be suspended until the Constitutional Chamber decision is taken, having obligatory character and *res judicata* effects (articles 104 and 117).

On the other hand, the Constitution of Costa Rica has also expressly regulated the right of persons to file recourses of habeas corpus and "amparo" in order to seek for the protection of their constitutional rights, attributing to the same Constitutional Chamber the exclusive competency to decide on the matter.[47]

In this regard, Article 48 of the Constitution provides that "every person has the right to the habeas corpus recourse in order to guarantee his personal freedom and integrity, and to the "amparo" recourse in order to be reestablished in the enjoyment of the rights declared in the Constitution, as well as those fundamental rights set forth in international instruments on human rights applicable in the Republic."

In Costa Rica, both the habeas corpus and the "amparo" recourses are also regulated in a single statute, the Constitutional Jurisdiction Law (*Ley de la Jurisdicción Constitucional, Ley Nº 7135*) of October 11, 1989.[48] According to article 29 of this Law, the recourse of "amparo" can be filed against any provision, decision or resolution and, in general, against any public administration action, omission or material activity which is not founded in an effective administrative act and has violated or threatened to violate the constitutional rights.

As in Argentina, the law excludes the "amparo" action against statutes or other regulatory provisions. Nonetheless, they can be challenged together with the individual acts applying them, or when containing self executing or automatically applicable provisions, in the sense that their provisions become immediately obligatory simply upon their sanctioning. But in such cases, the Chamber must decide the matter of the unconstitutionality of the statute, not in the "amparo" proceeding, but in a general way following the procedure of the action of unconstitutionality.

The Law also excludes the "amparo" action against judicial resolutions or other authorities' acts when executing judicial decisions, and against the acts or provisions in electoral matters issued by the Supreme Tribunal of Elections (Article 30).

Regarding individuals, Costa Rica's Law as in Argentina, admits the possibility of the "amparo" actions to be filed against any harming actions or omissions from

---

47 See, in general, Rubén Hernández Valle, *La tutela de los derechos fundamentales*, Editorial Juricentro, San José 1990; Rubén Hernández Valle, "El recurso de amparo en Costa Rica", in Héctor Fix–Zamudio and Eduardo Ferrer Mac–Gregor (Coord.), *El derecho de amparo en el mundo*, Universidad Nacional Autónoma de México, Editorial Porrúa, México 2006, pp. 257–304.

48See in general, Rubén Hernández Valle, "El recurso de amparo en Costa Rica", in Héctor Fix–Zamudio and Eduardo Ferrer Mac–Gregor, *Idem,* Edit. Porrúa, México 2006, pp. 257–304

individuals, but in this case, in a limited way only referred to persons or corporations exercising public functions or powers that by law or by fact place them in a position of power against which ordinary judicial remedies are clearly insufficient to guaranty the protection of fundamental rights and freedoms (Article 57).

B. *The Constitutional Chamber of the Supreme Court in El Salvador with exclusive powers on judicial review, and the amparo action*

In El Salvador, the concentrated judicial review system established in the Constitution was the result of the creation of the Constitutional Chamber of the Supreme Court by the Constitutional reform of 1991–1992, with the exclusive power to declare the unconstitutionality of statutes, decrees and regulations challenged by means of a direct action, having the power to annull them with general *erga omnes* effects.

But in the case of El Salvador, contrary to the Costa Rican regulation, ann similar to Colombia, Nicaragua, Panama and Venezuela, the action in order to file petitions regarding the unconstitutionality of statutes, is not restricted in its standing, but is conceived as a popular action that can be brought before the Chamber by any citizen (Articles 2 and 10, Law).

In addition in El Salvador, Article 247 of the Constitution also sets forth the two common specific judicial means for the protection of all constitutional right: the "amparo" and the habeas corpus actions, the latter also for the protection of personal freedom. As in Costa Rica, the only competent court to hear and decide on this matter is the Constitutional Chamber of the Supreme Court of Justice, also establishing a concentrated judicial system of "amparo" (Article 247)[49]. The only exception to this rule exists in matters of habeas corpus when the aggrieving action takes place outside the capital, San Salvador, cases in which the habeas corpus recourse can be filed before the Chambers of Second Instance (article 42). In such cases, and only if they deny the liberty of the aggrieved party, can the case be reviewed by the Constitutional Chamber.

The regulation of the "amparo" and habeas corpus action in El Salvador is also set forth, along with the other constitutional processes, in one single statute: the 1960 Statute on Constitutional Proceedings (*Ley de Procedimientos Constitucionales*) of 1960, as amended in 1997.[50]

According to this Law, the action of "amparo" can be filed against any actions or omissions of any authority, public official or decentralized bodies. Regarding judicial decisions, contrary to Argentina and Costa Rica, the action can also be filed but just against judicial definitive decisions issued by the Judicial Review of Adminis-

49 See Manuel Arturo Montecino Giralt, "El amparo en El Salvador", in Héctor Fix–Zamudio and Eduardo Ferrer Mac–Gregor (Coord.), *El derecho de amparo en el mundo*, Universidad Nacional Autónoma de México, Editorial Porrúa, México 2006, pp. 333–380.

50 See in general, Manuel A. Montecino Giralt, "El amparo en El Salvador", in Héctor Fix–Zamudio and Eduardo Ferrer Mac–Gregor, *El derecho de amparo en el mundo*, Edit. Porrúa, México 2006, pp. 333–380.

trative Action courts when violating the rights guaranteed in the Constitution or which impeding its exercise (Article 12).

The Law expressly refers to the extraordinary character of the action of "amparo", also providing, as in Argentina, that it can only be filed when the act against which it is formulated cannot be reparable by means of other remedies.

2. The Concentrated Systems of Judicial Review Combined With the Amparo Proceeding Before a Variety of Courts

With the exception of the two abovementioned cases of Costa Rica and El Salvador where all constitutional judicial matters are concentrated in one single Constitutional Chamber of the Supreme Court, in all the other Latin American countries with concentrated systems of judicial review, the actions or recourses of "amparo" and habeas corpus are regulated in a diffuse way in the sense that they can be filed before a wide range of courts, generally the first instance courts, as is the case of Bolivia, Brazil, Colombia, Chile, Dominican Republic, Ecuador, Guatemala, Honduras, Mexico, Panama, Paraguay, Peru, Uruguay and Venezuela.

So, even in countries where a concentrated system of judicial review has also been established as the only method to control the constitutionality of legislation, as is the case of Bolivia, Ecuador, Chile, Honduras, Panama, Paraguay and Uruguay, the jurisdiction to decide "amparo" and habeas corpus actions is attributed to multiple courts.

A. *The Plurinational Constitutional Tribunal in Bolivia, and the actions of constitutional amparo, freedom (habeas corpus) and of protection of privacy (habeas data)*

In Bolivia, since the 1994 constitutional reform, the judicial review system has also been configured as an exclusively concentrated one,[51] corresponding, to the Plurinational Constitutional Tribunal, established in article 132 of the 2008 Constitution, the exclusive power to declare the nullity of statutes considered unconstitutional, also with general (*erga omnes*) effects.[52] For such purpose, the action of the unconstitutionality of a juridical norm (for instance, of a statute or of a general executive acts) can be brought before the Constitutional Tribunal by means of a direct

---

51 See in general José Antonio Rivera Santibañez, "La jurisdicción constitucional en Bolivia. Cinco años en defensa del orden constitucional y democrático", in *Revista Iberoamericana de Derecho Procesal Constitucional,* N° 1, enero, junio 2004, Ed. Porrúa, 2004; José Antonio Rivera Santibañez, "El control constitucional en Bolivia", in *Anuario Iberoamericano de Justicia Constitucional.* Centro de Estudios Políticos y Constitucionales N° 3, 1999, pp. 205–237; José Antonio Rivera Santivañez, "Los valores supremos y principios fundamentales en la jurisprudencia constitucional", in *La Justicia Constitucional en Bolivia 1998–2003,* Ed. Tribunal Constitucional–AECI, Bolivia, 2003. pp. 347 ff.; Benjamín Miguel Harb, "La jurisdicción constitucional en Bolivia", in *La Jurisdicción Constitucional en Iberoamérica,* Ed. Dykinson, Madrid, España, 1997, pp. 337 ff.

52 Jorge Asbún Rojas, "Control constitucional en Bolivia, evolución y perspectivas", in *Jurisdicción Constitucional,* Academia Boliviana de Estudios Constitucionales. Editora El País, Santa Cruz, Bolivia, 2000, p. 86.

action of abstract character, that can by filed by any individual or collective person. According to the Constitutional Tribunal Law, it is also possible for the parties in a particular case or *ex officio* by the judge to raise the question of unconstitutionality of statutes before the Constitutional Tribunal by means of an incidental recourse, when the decision of a particular case depends upon its constitutionality (Article 59).

So with the exception of decisions on the cases of actions of constitutional "amparo", actions of freedom (*acción de libertad* or habeas corpus) and action of protection of privacy (habeas data), the ordinary courts cannot rule on constitutional matters, and must refer the control of constitutionality of statutes to the Constitutional Tribunal.

The Constitution of Bolivia in effect, regulates the action of freedom (habeas corpus), the action of constitutional "amparo" and the action for the protection of privacy (articles 125 to 131). The first of such actions can be filed for the protection of life in cases of being in danger, and also personal freedom when somebody claims they are being illegally persecuted, detained, prosecuted or held (Article 125).

Regarding the action of constitutional "amparo", Article 128 of the Constitution conceived it as an action for the protection of all constitutional rights declared in the Constitution and in statutes, which can also be filed against any illegal or undue acts or omissions from public officials or private individuals or collective persons that restrict, suppress or threaten to restrict or withhold such rights (Article 128)[53]. In this cases the action can only be filed when there is no other mean or legal recourse available for the immediate protection of the restricted, suspended or threatened right or guaranty.

Law 1.836 of 1998 of the Constitutional Tribunal (*Ley Nº 1836 del Tribunal Constitucional*) enacted in 1998, provides that the constitutional "amparo" can be brought before the highest Courts in the Department capitals or before the District Judges in the Provinces (Article 95) and shall be admitted "against any unlawful resolution, act or omission of an authority or official, provided there is no other procedure or recourse available to immediately protect the rights and guaranties", which, as established in Argentina and El Salvador, confirms its extraordinary character. Judicial decisions are excluded from the "amparo" action when they can be modified or suppressed by means of other recourses (Article 96,3).

The Law also admits, like in Argentina, the filing of the "amparo" action "against any unlawful act or omission of a person or group of private individuals that restricts, suppresses or threatens the rights or guaranties recognized by the Constitution and the Laws" (Article 94).

Regarding the action for protection of privacy, article 130.I of the 2008 Constitution has established if in order to ensure that any individual or collective person deeming being undue and illegitimately prevented of knowing, objecting or obtain-

53 See José Antonio Rivera Santibáñez, "El amparo constitucional en Bolivia", in Héctor Fix–Zamudio and Eduardo Ferrer Mac–Gregor (Coord.), *El derecho de amparo en el mundo*, Universidad Nacional Autónoma de México, Editorial Porrúa, México 2006, pp. 81–122.

ing the erase or rectification of data anyway registered in public or private archives or databases, affecting his fundamental right to personal and family personal privacy, or his own image, honor and reputation.

In Bolivia, according to the Constitution (Article 202,6) the decisions adopted in all these actions of freedom, constitutional amparo and protection of privacy can be reviewed by the Plurinational Constitutional Tribunal. For such purpose the Law of the Constitutional Tribunal (Article 7,8), establishes that all those judicial decisions must be sent to the Constitutional Tribunal in order to be reviewed. But in this case of Bolivia, similar to the situation in Colombia, but different to the provisions in Argentina, Brazil, and Venezuelan where an extraordinary recourse for revision is provided, the power of the Constitutional Tribunal to review the "amparo," habeas corpus and habeas data decisions is exercised, not because of an extraordinary recourse, but because of an obligatory review duty, for which purpose the decisions must automatically be sent by the courts to the Constitutional Tribunal. Through this power, the Tribunal can guaranty the uniformity of the constitutional interpretation.

The action of constitutional "amparo" and the action of freedom (habeas corpus) have been regulated in one single statute along with other constitutional procedures, the Constitutional Tribunal Law.[54]

B. *The Constitutional Court in Ecuador, and the actions for amparo, habeas corpus and habeas data*

Since the approval of the 2008 Constitution, Ecuador abandoned the mixed system of judicial review, transforming its system into an exclusive concentrated one.

In effect, before the 2008 Constitution, a mixed system of judicial review of legislation existed in the country, combining the diffuse and the concentrated methods, which were developed bases on a similar provision to the one included in the current article 424 of the 2008 Constitution, which prescribes not only that "The Constitution is the superior norm and prevails over any other legal norm," but that "The norms and acts of the public power must conform to the constitutional provisions and in contrary case they will have no juridical efficacy". Nonetheless, and notwithstanding the permanence of the same provision, the system has been radically changed, eliminating the diffuse method of judicial review.

In effect, Article 425 of the Constitution begins by establishing the hierarchy of all norms, providing that in case of conflict, the Constitutional Court and all judges and authorities are empowered to decide, and to apply the provision with superior hierarchy. Although this provision could lead to consider that the Constitution had maintained the diffuse method of judicial review, the fact is that the general power of all judges to decide not to apply provisions considered unconstitutional has been eliminated, by instead establishing an incidental mean for the exercise of its concentrated judicial review powers by the Constitutional Court.

---

54 See in general, José A. Rivera Santivañez, *Jurisdicción constitucional. Procesos constitucionales en Bolivia*, Ed. Kipus, Cochabamba 2004, and "El amparo constitucional en Bolivia", in Héctor Fix–Zamudio and Eduardo Ferrer Mac–Gregor, *Idem,* Edit. Porrúa, México 2006, pp. 81–122.

In effect, article 428 of the same 2008 Constitution established that when a judge, whether ex officio or at a party's request, deems that a legal provision is contrary to the Constitution or to an international instruments on human rights establishing more favorable rights that those recognized in the Constitution, is stead of deciding giving preference to the constitutional provision, it must suspend the procedure and refer the files to the Constitutional Court, which in a term of no more than 45 days, must decide upon the constitutionality of the provision. Consequently, the powers of the courts to declare the inapplicability of the legal provision contrary to the Constitution or to international treaties or covenants when deciding cases or controversies, was eliminated. In the previous regime, what was established as a complement to the diffuse method of judicial review, was that in all cases of diffuse judicial review decisions, the courts were to produce a report on the issue of unconstitutionality of the statute, that was due to be sent to the Constitutional Tribunal in order for it to decide the matter in a general and obligatory way, that is to say, with *erga omnes* effects.

Regarding the direct concentrated method of judicial review, the 2008 Constitution assigns the Constitutional Court, created in substitution of the Constitutional Tribunal at its turn created in 1998 in substitution of a original Constitutional Guarantees Tribunal,[55] the power to decide when requested through "public actions on unconstitutionality" filed against all normative acts of general character issued by organs and authorities of the State, having as it effect the invalidity of the challenged provision (article 425,1). In the previous regulations, the standing to file these actions was reduced to the President of the Republic, the National Congress, the Supreme Court, one thousand citizens or by any person having a previous favorable report from the Peoples' Defendant (Article 18, 1997 Constitutional Control Law).

The Constitution of Ecuador also provides for the three fundamental judicial means designed for the protection of human rights: the habeas corpus, habeas data and action for protection ("amparo").

The habeas corpus recourse, provided in article 89 of the Constitution can be files by any person who thinks that he has been illegally, arbitrarily or illegitimately deprived of his freedom by order of public authorities or persons, and also, in order to protect the life and physical integrity of persons deprived of freedom.

Regarding the protection action it is also conceived as a judicial remedy, in order to provide direct and effective protection (amparo) of the rights recognized in the Constitution, that can be filed when such rights were infringed by actions or omis-

---

55 See in general Hernán Salgado Pesantes, "El control de constitucionalidad en la Carta Política del Ecuador", in *Una mirada a los Tribunales Constitucionales. Las experiencias recientes*. Lecturas Constitucionales Andinas N° 4, Ed. Comisión Andina de Juristas, Lima, Perú; Ernesto López Freire, "Evolución del control de constitucionalidad en el Ecuador", in *Derecho Constitucional para fortalecer la democracia ecuatoriana,* Ed. Tribunal Constitucional – Kas, Quito, Ecuador, 1999; Marco Morales Tobar, "Actualidad de la Justicia Constitucional en el Ecuador", in Luis López Guerra, (Coord.). *La Justicia Constitucional en la actualidad,* Corporación Editora Nacional, Quito, Ecuador, pp. 77–165; Oswaldo Cevallos Bueno, "El sistema de control concentrado y el constitucionalismo en el Ecuador", in *Anuario Iberoamericano de Justicia Constitucional*, N° 6, 2002, Madrid, España, 2002.

sions of any public non judicial authority; against public policies that deprive the enjoyment or exercise of constitutional rights;[56] or when the violation, being provoked by individuals providing public services or acting by delegation or concession, cause grave damage to the affected person; or when the latter is in situation of subordination, defenseless or discrimination. From this provision, it result that the amparo action is not admissible against judicial decisions, and the competent courts to hear the "amparo" action are the first instance courts (Article 47, Constitutional Control Law).

The Constitution also provides in article 92 for the action of habeas that can be filed by any person in order to know the existence and to have access to documents, genetic data, personal database or reports regarding itself or regarding his assets, located in public or private entities; as well as to know the use that is made of the same, the purpose and origin of personal information, and the term of the file or database.

These three remedies, habeas corpus, habeas data and the action of protection ("amparo") have been also regulated in one single statute along with other constitutional proceedings: the Constitutional Control Law (*Ley de Control Constitucional*, Ley N° 000 RO/99) of July 2, 1997.[57]

Finally, it must be mentioned that for the purpose of unifying the jurisprudence in constitutional matters, according to the the Constitutional Control Law, all the decisions granting "amparo" claims must obligatorily be sent to the Constitutional Tribunal in order to be confirmed or repeal. In cases of decisions denying the "amparo" action (as well as the habeas corpus or habeas data actions), they can be appealed before the same Constitutional Court (Articles 12,3; 31; 52).

Also, in matters of "amparo" when the constitutional protection is granted by the competent courts applying the diffuse method of judicial review declaring the unconstitutionality of statutes,[58]according to the Law they must send the report on the question of constitutionality to the Constitutional Tribunal for its confirmation (Article 12,6).

---

56 Hernán Salgado Pesantes, "La garantía de amparo en Ecuador", in Héctor Fix–Zamudio and Eduardo Ferrer Mac–Gregor (Coord.), *El derecho de amparo en el mundo*, Universidad Nacional Autónoma de México, Editorial Porrúa, México 2006, pp. 305–331.

57 See in general, Rafael Oyarte martínez, *Manual de Amparo Constitucional. Guía de litigio constitucional*, CLD–Konrad Adenauer, Quito 2003; Hernán Salgado Pesantes, *Manual de Justicia Constitucional Ecuatoriana*, Corporación Editora Nacional, Quito 2004, and "La garantía de amparo en Ecuador", in Héctor Fix–Zamudio and Eduardo Ferrer Mac–Gregor, *Idem*, Edit. Porrúa, México 2006, pp. 305–331.

58 See Hernán Salgado Pesantes, *Manual de Justicia Constitucional Ecuatoriana*, Corporación Editora Nacional, Quito, Ecuador, 2004, p. 85.

C. *The Constitutional Tribunal in Chile, and the recourses for protection and of habeas corpus*

According to the concentrated judicial review system established in Chile[59] since 1990, and according to the provisions of the 2005 Constitutional Reform, the question of unconstitutionality of statutes can reach the Constitutional Tribunal (Article 82), by two means: a direct action that can be brought before the Tribunal by some public entities and high officials like the President of the Republic, the Senate, the Representative Chamber and the General Comptroller; or by means of a referral of a constitutional question made by any court at the request of any of the parties when the resolution of the case depends on the constitutionality of the provision, in which cases, the decision regarding the inapplicability of a statutory provision in a particular case has only *inter partes* effects. Only when the Constitutional Tribunal decides an action of unconstitutionality of statutes, does the ruling annulling the statute have general *erga omnes* effects (article 82,7).

In Chile, Articles 20 and 21 of the Constitution, in addition to the habeas corpus recourse and with antecedents in the Constitutional Act N° 3 (Decree–Law 1.552) of 1976, also establishes the "amparo" recourse called recourse for protection (*recurso de protección*) conceived, as in Colombia, to protect only certain constitutional rights and freedoms, which are enumerated in some paragraph of article 19 of the Constitution, basically referred to civil and individual rights, freedom of economic rights and the right to live in an environment free of contamination. In this regard, the Chilean provisions, follow the same pattern of the German and Spanish constitutional regulations regarding the "amparo" recourse, established only the protection of "fundamental rights". The consequence of these rules is that all the other constitutional rights not enumerated or listed as protected by the recourse for protection, must be enforced by means of the ordinary judicial procedures

The Chilean "*recurso de protección*" is the only action for amparo constitutionally established in Latin America which has not yet been statutorily regulated, which of course has not prevented it exercise,[60] particularly in cases where there is an urgent need for the protection. The recourse is only regulated by a Supreme Court regulation: *Auto acordado de la Corte Suprema de Justicia sobre tramitación del Recurso de Protección de Garantías Constitucionales, 1992.*[61]

---

59 See in general Raúl Bertelsen Repetto, *Control de constitucionalidad de la ley,* Editorial Jurídica de Chile, Santiago, Chile, 1969; Francisco Zúñiga Urbina, *Jurisdicción constitucional en Chile,* Tomo II, Ed. Universidad Central de Chile, Santiago, 2002; Humberto Nogueira Alcalá, "El Tribunal Constitucional chileno", in *Lecturas Constitucionales Andinas*, N° 1, Ed. Comisión Andina de Juristas, Lima, Perú, 1991; Lautaro Ríos Álvarez Álvarez, "La Justicia Constitucional en Chile", in *La Revista de Derecho,* N° 1, Ed. Facultad de Derecho, Universidad Central, Santiago, Chile, 1988; Teodoro Rivera, "El Tribunal Constitucional", in *Revista Chilena de Derecho*, Volumen 11 N° 23, Santiago, Chile, 1984.

60 See in Enrique Paillas, *El recurso de protección ante el derecho comparado,* Santiago de Chile, 1990, pp. 80 ff.

61 See in general, Eduardo Soto Kloss, *El recurso de protección. Orígenes, docgtrina, jurisprudencia,* Editorial Jurídica de Chile, Santiago 1982; Humberto Nogueira Alcalá, "El derecho y acción constitucional de protección (amparo) de los derechos fundamentales en Chile a ini-

The recourse for protection must be brought before the Courts of Appeals, which can immediately adopt the rulings they consider appropriate for re–establishing the rule of law and assuring the due protection of the affected party's rights (Article 20).[62]

The Chilean Constitution (Article 21) also provide for the habeas corpus recourse for the protection of personal freedom and safety, naming it in this case, as the "amparo" recourse.

One aspect that must be highlighted regarding the Chilean recourse for protection is that when deciding the case, the courts cannot adopt any decision on judicial review of legislation which is reserved to the Constitutional Tribunal. Consequently, when deciding a recourse of protection, if the court considers that the applicable statute is unconstitutional, it cannot decide on the matter, but has to refer the case to the Constitutional Tribunal for its decision.

D. *The Constitutional Chamber of the Supreme Court of Justice in Honduras, and the actions for amparo and habeas corpus*

Article 320 of the Honduran Constitution sets forth the general rule on judicial review in the country declaring that "in cases of incompatibility between a constitutional norm and an ordinary statutory one, the courts must apply the former."

In the same sense as it is established in the Constitutions of Colombia, Guatemala and Venezuela, this constitutional provision of Honduras without doubts establishes the diffuse method of judicial review.[63] Nonetheless, the 2004 Law on Constitutional Justice (*Ley de Justicia Constitucional*),[64] failed to regulate such method in

---

cios del Siglo XXI", in Héctor Fix–Zamudio and Eduardo Ferrer Mac–Gregor, *Idem,* Edit. Porrúa, México 2006, pp. 159–211.

62 See in general Pedro Aberastury et al., *Acciones constitucionales de amparo y protección: realidad y prospectiva en Chile y América Latina,* Editorial Universidad de Talca, Talca 2000, Chile; Juan Manuel Errazuriz Gatica et al., *Aspectos procesales del recurso de protección,* Editorial Jurídica de Chile, Santiago de Chile 1989; Sergio Lira Herrera, *El recurso de protección. Naturaleza Jurídica, Doctrina, Jurisprudencia, Derecho Comparado*, Editorial Jurídica de Chile, Santiago de Chile 1990; Enrique Paillas, *El recurso de protección ante el derecho comparado,* Editorial Jurídica de Chile, Santiago de Chile 1990; Humberto Nogueira Alcalá, "El derecho y acción constitucional de protección (amparo) de los derechos fundamentales en Chile a inicios del Siglo XXI", in Héctor Fix–Zamudio and Eduardo Ferrer Mac–Gregor (Coord.), *El derecho de amparo en el mundo,* Universidad Nacional Autónoma de México, Editorial Porrúa, México 2006, pp. 159–211.

63 See Allan R. BREWER–CARÍAS, "El sistema de justicia constitucional en Honduras", in *El sistema de Justicia Constitucional en Honduras (Comentarios a la Ley sobre Justicia Constitucional),* Instituto Interamericano de Derechos Humanos, Corte Suprema de Justicia. República de Honduras, San José, 2004, pp. 27 ff.

64 See Allan R. BREWER–CARÍAS, "La reforma del sistema de justicia constitucional en Honduras", in *Revista Iberoamericana de Derecho Procesal Constitucional. Proceso y Constitución* (Directores Eduardo Ferrer Mac–Gregor y Aníbal Quiroga León), N° 4, 2005, Editorial Porrúa, México, pp. 57–77; and "El sistema de justicia constitucional en Honduras", in *El sistema de Justicia Constitucional en Honduras (Comentarios a la Ley sobre Justicia Constitucio-*

the country, and, instead, limited itself to established only an exclusive concentrated method of judicial review of legislation by attributing to the Constitutional Chamber of the Supreme Court the monopoly to annul statutes on the grounds of their unconstitutionality. According to this power, the Constitutional Chamber can declare the unconstitutionality of statutes "on grounds of form or in its contents" (Articles 184; 315,5).

For such purpose, the constitutional questions can reach the Constitutional Chamber also through two means: First, through an action of unconstitutionality that can be brought before the Constitutional Chamber by persons with personal interest against statutes and constitutional amendments when approved contrary to the formalities set forth in the Constitution and against approbatory statutes of international treaties sanctioned without following the constitutional formalities (Article 17). It is also admissible against statutes that contravene the provisions of an international treaty or convention in force (article 76).

Second, the questions of constitutionality can also reach the Constitutional Chamber in an incidental way, as an exception raised by a party in any particular case (Article 82), or by the referral of the case that any court can make before the Chamber, before deciding the case (Article 87).

In both cases, whether through the action of unconstitutionality or by means of the incidental constitutional question, the decision of the Constitutional Chamber regarding the unconstitutionality of statutes also has general *erga omnes* effects (Article 94).

The Constitution of Honduras also provides for two separate actions for the protection of human rights: "amparo" and habeas corpus, that must be filed according to what is provide in the already mentioned general statute on constitutional proceedings, the Constitutional Judicial Review statute (*Ley sobre la Justicia Constitucional*) of 2004.[65]

Regarding the recourse of "amparo", Article 183 of the Constitution declares the right of any person to file the recourse, in order to be restored in the enjoyment of all rights declared or recognized in the Constitution, and in addition, in treaties, covenants and other international instruments of human rights (Article 183 Constitution, Article 41,1 Law), against public authority actions or facts, comprising statutes, judicial decisions or administrative acts and also omissions or threats of violation (Articles 13 and 41, Law). In this cases, and depending on the rank of the injurer's public authority, the action of "amparo" that can be filed before a variety of courts,.

Regarding individuals, as in Colombia, Costa Rica and Ecuador, the action can be filed against their actions only when issued exercising delegated public powers,

---

nal), Instituto Interamericano de Derechos Humanos, Corte Suprema de Justicia. República de Honduras, San José, 2004, pp. 1–148.

65 See in general, Francisco D. Gómez Bueso, "El derecho de amparo en Honduras", in Héctor Fix–Zamudio and Eduardo Ferrer Mac–Gregor, *Idem,* Edit. Porrúa, México 2006, pp. 409–460; and Allan R. BREWER–CARÍAS, "El sistema de justicia constitucional en Honduras", in *El sistema de justicia constitucional en Honduras (Comentarios a la ley sobre Justicia Constitucional)*, Instituto Interamericano de Derechos Humanos, San José 2004, pp, 107–140.

that is, against institutions maintained by public funds and those acting by delegation of a State entity by virtue of a concession, contract or other valid resolution (Article 42)[66]..

The Constitution of Honduras, like the solution in Guatemala, also expressly admits the "amparo" against statutes, establishing the right of any party to file the action for amparo, in order to have a judicial declaration ruling that its provisions do not oblige the plaintiff and are not applicable when they contravene, diminish or distort any of the rights recognized in this Constitution"

In the case of Honduras, the "amparo" decisions are subject to an obligatory review by the corresponding superior court, and those issued by the Appellate Courts also subject to review by the Constitutional Chamber of the Supreme Court, but in this case on a discretionary basis, by means of the parties' request (articles 68, 69, Law). Thus, the Constitutional Chamber can always be the last resort to decide upon the matters of "amparo".

On the other hand, by means of the "amparo" action is possible to consider that in Honduras the diffuse method of judicial review can be applied, in the sense that in a contrary sense to the other Latin American regulations in concentrated systems, the Constitution allows the courts to decide that a statute is not to be enforced against the claimant nor is it applicable in a specific case when such statute contravenes, diminishes or distorts a right recognized by this Constitution," (183,2 Constitution)

E. *The Supreme Court of Justice of Panama, and the actions for amparo and habeas corpus*

The judicial review system of Panama, is also conceived as a concentrated one, attributing to the Supreme Court of Justice the exclusive power (Article 203,1) to protect the integrity of the Constitution and to control the constitutionality of legislation also by means of two different methods: a direct popular action or by means of a question of constitutionality that can be raised by the parties to the case as an incident before a lower court, or *ex officio* by the respective court.[67]

Regarding the action of unconstitutionality, in similar terms as in Colombia, El Salvador, Nicaragua and Venezuela, it is conceived as a popular action that can be

---

66 See Francisco Daniel Gómez Bueso, "El derecho de amparo en Honduras", in Héctor Fix–Zamudio and Eduardo Ferrer Mac–Gregor (Coord.), *El derecho de amparo en el mundo,* Universidad Nacional Autónoma de México, Editorial Porrúa, México 2006, pp. 409–460.

67 See in general on the Panamanian system of judicial review, Carlos Bolívar Pedreschi,. *El control de la constitucionalidad en Panamá.* Ediciones Guadarrama, España, 1965; Edgardo Molina Mola, *La jurisdicción constitucional en Panamá.* Edit. Biblioteca Jurídica Dike, Colombia, 1998; Rigoberto González Montenegro, *Los desafíos de la justicia constitucional panameña*, Instituto de Estudios Políticos e Internacionales, Panamá 2002; Allan R. Brewer–Carias, "El sistema panameño de justicia constitucional a la luz del Derecho Comparado," in *Revista Novum Ius*, Edicion N° 15°, Editada por los Miembros de la Asociación Nueva Generación Jurídica publicación estudiantil de la Facultad de Derecho y Ciencias Políticas de la Universidad de Panamá, Panamá, 2010. pp. 130–168

brought before the Supreme Court by anybody in order to denounce the unconstitutionality of statutes, decrees, decisions or acts founded in substantive or formal questions (Article 2559).

In both cases, the Supreme Court's decision is final, definitive, obligatory and with general but non retroactive effects, and must be published in the *Official Gazette* (article 2573 Judicial Code).

On the other hand, following the general trend of Latin America, the Constitution of Panama also distinguishes two specific judicial means for the protection of constitutional rights: the habeas corpus and the "amparo" recourses.

Regarding the recourse of "amparo", the Constitution of Panama set forth the right of any person to have revoked any order to do or to refrain from doing issued by any public servant violating the rights and guaranties set forth in the Constitution (Article 50).

Thus, the "amparo" is also conceived in Panamá for the protection of constitutional rights only against authority actions and is not admitted against individual unconstitutional actions. The action can be filed before the ordinary first instance courts, except in cases of high rank officials, in which cases the Supreme Court is the competent one.[68]

Panama together with Paraguay, are the only two countries where the statutory regulation regarding habeas corpus and "amparo" are set forth in the general procedural code, the Judicial Code (*Código Judicial, Libro IV Instituciones de garantía*), Articles 2574–2614 (habeas corpus) and 2615–2632 (*amparo de garantía constitucionales*) of 1987.[69]

According to the Code, the "amparo of constitutional guaranties" can be brought before the courts against any acts that harm or injure the fundamental rights and guaranties set forth in the Constitution (Article 2615) and also against judicial decisions when all the existing judicial means to challenge them have been exhausted; but it cannot refer to judicial decisions adopted by the Electoral Tribunal or by the Supreme Court of Justice or any of its Chambers.

F. *The Constitutional Chamber of the Supreme Court of Justice in Paraguay, and the recourses for amparo, habeas corpus and habeas data*

Since 1992, the Constitution of Paraguay establishes a concentrated system of judicial review attributing to the Constitutional Chamber of the Supreme Court of

---

68 See: Lao Santizo P., *Acotaciones al amparo de garantías constitucionales panameño*, Editorial Jurídica Sanvas, San José, Costa Rica 1987; Arturo Hoyos, "El proceso de amparo de derechos fundamentales en Panamá", in Héctor Fix–Zamudio and Eduardo Ferrer Mac–Gregor (Coord.), *Idem*, pp. 565–580.

69 See in general, Arturo Hoyos, "El proceso de amparo de derechos fundamentales en Panamá", in Héctor Fix–Zamudio and Eduardo Ferrer Mac–Gregor, *Idem*, Edit. Porrúa, México 2006, pp. 565–580.

Justice, the exclusive power to decide on all matters dealing with judicial review of legislation.[70]

According to this method, the Supreme Court of Justice has the power to decide actions and exceptions seeking to declare the unconstitutionality and inapplicability of statutes contrary to the Constitution. For such purpose, when a judge hearing a particular case considers the applicable statute contrary to the Constitution, he must send the files, even *ex officio*, to the Constitutional Chamber of the Supreme Court of Justice, in order for the Court to decide the question of unconstitutionality when evident (Article 582 Code).

The main distinctive feature of the Paraguayan concentrated judicial review system is that contrary to all the other countries with the same concentrated system, there is not a direct action of unconstitutionality that can be filed before the Chamber, so that the constitutional questions regarding the unconstitutionality of statutes can only reach the Supreme Court in an incidental way. That is why the Supreme Court decisions only declare in the particular case the inapplicability of the statute provisions, having only *inter partes* effects regarding the particular case (Article 260, Constitution)[71], being this provision, together with the Uruguayan one, an exception regarding the general pattern in the other Latin American countries.

On the other hand, the Constitution of Paraguay also regulates in a very detailed way three judicial means for the protection of constitutional rights: the "amparo", the *habeas corpus* (Article 133)[72] and the habeas data recourses (Article 135).

Regarding the petition for "amparo", according to Article 134 of the Constitution, it can be filed by anyone who considers himself seriously affected in his rights or guaranties by a clearly illegitimate act or omission, either by governmental authorities or individuals, or who may be in imminent danger that his constitutional rights and guaranties may be curtailed, and whom, in light of the urgency of the matter cannot obtain adequate remedy through regular legal means. In all such cases, the affected person may file a petition for "amparo" before a competent judge[73].

The "amparo" petition, originally regulated in the 1971 Law N° 341 of Amparo (*Ley 341/71 reglamentaria del "amparo")*, since 1988 has been regulated in a sec-

---

70 See in general, Norbert Lösing, "La justicia constitucional en Paraguay y Uruguay", in *Anuario de Derecho Constitucional Latinoamericano* 2002. Ed. KAS, Montevideo, Uruguay, 2002; Luis Lezcano Claude, *El control de constitucionalidad en el Paraguay*, Ed. La Ley Paraguaya S.A. Asunción, Paraguay, 2000.

71 L.M. Argaña, "Control de la Constitucionalidad de las Leyes en Paraguay", in *Memoria de la Reunión de Presidentes de Cortes Supremas de Justicia en Iberoamérica, el Caribe, España y Portugal,* Caracas 1982, pp. 550, 551, 669, 671.

72 See: Evelio Fernández Arévalos, *Habeas Corpus Régimen Constitucional y legal en el Paraguay*, Intercontinental Editora, Asunción, Paraguay 2000.

73 See Jorge Seall–Sasiain, "El amparo en Paraguay", in Héctor Fix–Zamudio and Eduardo Ferrer Mac–Gregor (Coord.), *El derecho de amparo en el mundo*, Universidad Nacional Autónoma de México, Editorial Porrúa, México 2006, pp. 58–591.

tion of the Civil Procedure Code (articles 565–588)[74], which, as in Argentina and Costa Rica, provides that it is not admissible against judicial decisions and resolutions, nor in the procedure of formation, sanction and promulgation of statutes, or when the matter refers to the individual freedom protected by the recourse of habeas corpus (Article 565,a,b).

According to Article 566 of the Code, the petition for "amparo" can be filed before any first instance court with jurisdiction in the place where the act or omission could have effect. Nonetheless, regarding electoral questions and matters related to political organization, the competent court will be those of the electoral jurisdiction (Article 134 Constitution).

G. *The Supreme Court of Justice in Uruguay, and the actions for amparo and habeas corpus*

Since 1934, Article 256 of the Uruguayan Constitution,[75] has assigned the Supreme Court of Justice the exclusive and original power to declare the unconstitutionality of statutes and other State acts with force of statutes, whether founded on formal or substantive reasons as a consequence of an action of unconstitutionality that can be filed before the Court by all those who deem that their personal and legitimate interests have been harmed (Article 258)[76]. Thus, regarding the quality to sue (standing), the Uruguayan regulation has similarities with the Honduran one.

The constitutional question can also be submitted to the Supreme Court in an incidental way by a referral made *ex officio* or as a consequence of an exception of unconstitutionality raised by a party in a particular case by an inferior court (Article 258).

In all cases, similar to the Paraguayan solution where the question on the constitutionality of statutes referred only to particular cases, the decisions of the Supreme Court on matters of constitutionality only refer to the particular case in which the question is raised (Article 259)[77] and also has *inter partes* effects.

---

74 See in general, Jorge Seall–Sasian, "El amparo en Paraguay", in Héctor Fix–Zamudio and Eduardo Ferrer Mac–Gregor, *Idem*, Edit. Porrúa, México 2006, pp. 581–591

75 Originally the system was established in 1934, and later in 1951. See H. Gross Espiell, *La Constitución y su Defensa*, Congreso, printed for the International Congress on La Constitución y su Defensa, Universidad Nacional Autónoma de México, México 1982, pp. 7, 11. The system remained in the 1966 Constitution, in the "Acta Institucional N° 8 de 1977"and in the "Acta Institucional N° 12 de 1981". *Idem*, pp. 16, 20.

76 Article 258. See H. Gross Espiell, "La Constitución y su Defensa", *Idem*,. 28, 29; J.P. Gatto de Souza, "Control de la Constitucionalidad de los Actos del Poder público en Uruguay", in *Memoria de la Reunión de Presidentes de Cortes Supremas de Justicia en Iberoamérica, el Caribe, España y Portugal*, Caracas 1982, pp. 661, 662.

77 This principle is clear regarding the incidental mean of judicial review where the question of constitutionality is raised in a particular case, but originates doubts regarding the action of unconstitutionality. According to the Law N° 13747 of 1969 which regulates the procedures in matters of judicial review, the decision of the Supreme Court impedes the application of the challenged norms declared unconstitutional regarding the plaintiff, and authorizes its use

Regarding the amparo action, the Constitution of Uruguay, if it is true that it does not expressly and specifically provide for it, nonetheless it has been deducted from Articles 7,72 and 332 of the 1966 Constitution, that declare the general right of all inhabitants of the Republic "to be protected in the enjoyment of their life, honor, freedom, safety, work and property". In contrast, the Constitution expressly provide for the action of habeas corpus (Article 17) to protect any undue imprisonment.

Nonetheless, the "amparo" recourse has been regulated in the 1988 *Amparo* Law N° 16011 (*Ley de amparo*),[78], which establishes that any person, human or artificial, public or private, except in those cases where an action of *habeas corpus* is admitted, may bring an action of "amparo" against any act, omission or fact of the public sector authorities, as well as of private individuals that in a illegitimate and evident unlawful way, currently or imminently, impair, restrict, alter or threaten any of the rights and freedoms expressly or implicitly recognized by the Constitution (Article 72).

This action of "amparo" for the protection of all constitutional rights and freedoms may be brought before the judges of first instance in the place where the act, fact or omission under dispute have produced effect (Article 3).[79]

However, Law N° 16.011, like in Argentina, Costa Rica and in Paraguay, excludes all judicial acts issued in judicial controversies from the action of "amparo". The acts of the Electoral Court, and the statutes and decrees of departmental governments that have force of statute in their jurisdiction (Article 1) are also excluded, as in Costa Rica and Panama,

This action of "amparo" in the Uruguayan system, as in Argentina, is only admitted when there are no other judicial or administrative means available for obtaining the same result of protection or "amparo", or when, if they exist, they are clearly ineffective for protecting the right (Article 2).

In the proceeding of the "amparo" action, constitutional questions regarding the unconstitutionality of statutes may also arise, but as in Paraguay, the ordinary court cannot resolve them and must refer the matter to the Supreme Court of Justice, as a

---

as an exception in all other judicial proceedings, including the judicial review of Public administration activities. See H. Gross Espiell, "La Constitución y su Defensa", *Idem,* p. 29.

78 See in general, José R. Saravia Antúnez, Recurso de Amparo. Práctica Constitucional, Fundación Cultura Universitaria, Montevideo 1993; Héctor Gros Espiell, "El derecho de amparo en Uruguay", in Héctor Fix–Zamudio and Eduardo Ferrer Mac–Gregor, *Idem,* Edit. Porrúa, México 2006, pp. 633–648.

79 See in general Luis Alberto Viera et al., *Ley de Amparo. Comentarios, Texto Legal y Antecedentes legislativos a su sanción. Jurisprudencia sobre el amparo,* 2nd Edition, Ediciones IDEA, Montevideo 1993; Miguel Ángel Semino, "Comentarios sobre la acción de amparo en el Derecha uruguayo", in *Boletín de la Comisión Andina de Jurista,* N° 27, Lima, 1986; Héctor Gross Espiel, "El derecho de amparo en el Uruguay", in Héctor Fix–Zamudio and Eduardo Ferrer Mac–Gregor (Coord.), *El derecho de amparo en el mundo,* Universidad Nacional Autónoma de México, Editorial Porrúa, México 2006, pp. 633–648.

consequence of the concentrated method of judicial review of legislation that exists.[80]

III. JUDICIAL REVIEW AND AMPARO IN COUNTRIES APPLYING THE MIXED SYSTEM OF JUDICIAL REVIEW OF LEGISLATION

Except in the case of Argentina which remains the most similar to the "American model",[81] the judicial review system in all the other Latin American countries applying the same diffuse method of judicial review has moved from the original exclusive diffuse one towards a mixed one, by also adopting the concentrated method. This is the case of Brazil, Colombia, Dominican Republic, Guatemala, Mexico, Nicaragua, Peru and Venezuela. This transition towards the mixed system has happened even in Mexico, a country that with the peculiarities of its *juicio de amparo*, also moved in 1994 from the original diffuse system of judicial review initially and precisely established since 1857 with the amparo suit, to the current mixed system of judicial review by attributing to the Supreme Court the power to annul, with general effects, statutes directly challenged by some high officials

This mixed system mean that in all these countries, for the resolution of particular cases or controversies, all the courts are empowered to decide upon the unconstitutionality of legislation, and to not apply for the resolution of the case the statutes they considered contrary to the Constitution, giving preference to the latter. At the same time, the Supreme Court (Brazil, Dominican Republic, Mexico), its Constitutional Chamber (Nicaragua, Venezuela) or the Constitutional Court or Tribunal (Colombia, Guatemala, Peru) are also empowered to decide upon the unconstitutionality of statutes, when requested through a direct action that can be filed by some high public officials (Brazil, Dominican Republic, Guatemala, Mexico, Peru), or by any citizen through a popular action (Colombia, Nicaragua, Venezuela). In all these cases, the Court or Tribunal has the power to annul, with general effects, the challenged statutes.

---

80 See in general José Korseniak, "La Justicia constitucional en Uruguay", in *La Revista de Derecho,* año III, enero–junio 1989, Facultad de Derecho, Universidad Central, 1989; Héctor Gross Espiell, "La jurisdicción constitucional en el Uruguay", in *La Jurisdicción Constitucional en Iberoamérica*, Ed. Universidad Externado de Colombia, Bogotá Colombia, 1984; Eduardo Esteva G. "La jurisdicción constitucional en Uruguay", in Domingo García Belaunde and Francisco Fernández Segado (Coord.), *La Jurisdicción Constitucional en Iberoamérica,*. Ed. Dykinson, Madrid 1997; Norbert Lösing, "La justicia constitucional en Paraguay y Uruguay", in *Anuario de Derecho Constitucional Latinoamericano 2002,* Ed. Kas, Montevideo 2002.

81 See A. E. Ghigliani, *Del control jurisdiccional de constitucionalidad*, Buenos Aires 1952, who speaks about "Northamerican filiation" of the judicial control of constitutionality in Argentinian law, p. 6, 55, 115; R. Bielsa, *La protección constitucional y el recurso extraordinario. Jurisdicción de la Corte Suprema*, Buenos Aires 1958, p. 116; J.A.C. Grant, "El control jurisdiccional de la constitucionalidad de las Leyes: una contribución de las Américas a la ciencia política", in *Revista de la Facultad de Derecho de México*, Universidad Nacional Autónoma de México, T. XII, N° 45, México 1962, p. 652; C.J. Friedrich, *The Impact of American Constitutionalism Abroad*, Boston 1967, p. 83.

Finally, being a mixed system of judicial review where the concentrated method is applied by a Supreme Court of a Constitutional Tribunal, also in these countries some mechanism have been established in order to assure that the decisions on constitutional matters whether by applying the diffuse method of judicial review by lower courts, or those adopted in amparo proceedings for the protection of constitutional rights, can reach the higher constitutional court. For such purpose, in Colombia an automatic review power of the Constitutional Court or Tribunal has been set forth; in Brazil and Venezuela, an extraordinary recourse for revision before the Supreme Court has been establish; in Guatemala and Nicaragua, an appeal has been provided; and in a very exceptional way, a discretionary power of revision has been established in Mexico.

Additionally, in all these countries, the amparo proceeding for the protection of constitutional rights has also been regulated, generally following the diffuse judicial pattern by attributing competence to decide the cases to a variety of courts, mainly the first instance courts, and not to a single one. The only exception is Nicaragua, where the Supreme Court is the only competent court to decide upon amparo matters.

1. The Federal Tribunal in Brazil, and the mandado de segurança, mandado de injunção, habeas corpus and habeas data

The mixed system of judicial review of the constitutionality of legislation , since the 19th Century has been developing in Brazil, combining the diffuse and the concentrated method of judicial review.

The diffuse method, clearly influenced by the United States constitutional system,[82] was introduced in the 1891 Federal Constitution by empowering the Supreme Federal Tribunal to review, through an extraordinary recourse, the decisions of the federal courts and of the courts of the States in which the constitutionality of treaties or federal statutes were questioned (article III, I, 1891 Constitution). As a consequence of this express constitutional attribution, the Federal Law N° 221 of November 20, 1984 (Article 13,10) expressly assigned to all federal courts the power to judge upon the validity of statutes and executive regulations when they considered them unconstitutional, and to decide upon their inapplicability when deciding a particular case.[83]

According to this diffuse system of judicial review in Brazil, all the courts of first instance have the power to decide not to apply laws (federal, state or municipal) that they deem unconstitutional when a party to the proceeding has raised the ques-

---

82 See O.A. Bandeira de Mello, *A teoria das Constituiçoes rigidas*, Sao Paulo 1980, p. 157; J. Alfonso da Silva, *Sistema de defensa da Constituiçao brasileira,* Congreso sobre la Constitución y su Defensa, Universidad nacional Autónoma de México, México 1982, p. 29. (mimeo).

83 Thus, the diffuse system of judicial review of legislation was established in Brazil at the end of the 19th century, and was perfected through the subsequent constitutional reforms of 1926, 1934, 1937, 1946 and 1967. See O.A. Bandeira De Mello, *Idem,* pp. 158–237.

tion of constitutionality,[84] or when the challenged particular authority act, in cases of *mandado de segurança* or the *habeas corpus* recourses, is alleged to be issued in execution of a statute deemed unconstitutional In these cases, the question must be examined before the final decision of the case is adopted in a decision with *inter partes* effects on the case.[85]

The constitutional question can also be decided, in the appellate jurisdiction, in which case, if the court of second instance is a collegiate court, the decision upon matters of unconstitutionality of legislation must be adopted by a majority vote.[86]

But, the most distinctive feature of the Brazilian diffuse method of judicial review (Article 119, III,b,c), is that since its constitutional creation in 1894, the power of the Supreme Tribunal to intervene in all proceedings in which constitutional questions are resolved was also established when requested through an extraordinary recourse. In these cases, the Supreme Court's decisions have to be sent to the Federal Senate which has the power to "suspend the execution of all or part of a statute or decree when declared unconstitutional by the Supreme Federal Tribunal through a definitive decision" (Article 42, VII Federal Constitution) in which case the effects of the Senate's decisions has *erga omnes* and *ex nunc* effects.[87].

This diffuse system of judicial review, initially established in an exclusive way, in 1934 was transformed into a mixed system, when in addition, the Constitution established the concentrated method of judicial review by empowering the Federal Supreme Tribunal to declare the unconstitutionality of Member States' Constitutions or statutes when requested by means of a direct action of unconstitutionality that could be filed directly before the Tribunal by the Attorney General of the Republic (Article 12,2).

This direct action of unconstitutionality, originally established to defend federal constitutional principles against Member States acts, was extended through subsequent constitutional and statutory reforms (including the 1965 constitutional amendment and the Law N° 2271 of 22 July 1954), in order to allow the constitutional control over Federal and Member States statutes.[88.] In these reforms the standing to sue was also extended, so that now, the action of unconstitutionality can be

84 J. Alfonso Da Silva, J. Alfonso Da Silva, *Curso de direito constitucional positivo*, Sao Paulo 1984, p. 18.

85 J. Alfonso da Silva, *Sistema de defensa da Constituiçao brasileira,* Congreso sobre la Constitución y su Defensa, Universidad Nacional Autónoma de México, México 1982, pp. 41,64.

86 This qualified vote was first established in the 1934 Constitution (Article 179), and is always required. See O.A. Bandeira De Mello, *A teoria das Constituiçoes rigidas*, Sao Paulo 1980, p. 159.

87 Article 119, III b,c, Constitution *Cf.* J. Alfonso Da Silva, *Sistema de defensa da Constituiçao brasileira,* Congreso sobre la Constitución y su Defensa, Universidad Nacional Autónoma de México, México 1982, pp. 32, 34, 43, 73; J. Alfonso Da Silva, *Curso de direito constitucional positivo*, Sao Paulo 1984, pp. 17, 18; O.A. Bandeira De Mello, *A teoria das Constituiçoes rigidas*, Sao Paulo 1980, p. 215; H. Fix–Zamudio and J. Carpizo, "Amerique Latine", in L. Favoreu and J.A. Jolowicz (ed.), *Le contrôle juridictionnel des lois*, Paris 1986, p. 121.

88 See J. Alfonso Da Silva, *Sistema de defensa da Constituiçao brasileira,* Congreso sobre la Constitución y su Defensa, Universidad Nacional Autónoma de México, México 1982, p. 31.

filed by the President of the Republic, by the boards of the Senate and of the Representative Chamber, as well as of the Legislative Assemblies of the States; by the States' governors and by the Attorney General of the Republic. In addition, it can be filed by the Federal Council of the Federal Bar (*Ordem dos advogados de Brasil*), the political parties represented in Congress, and the trade unions confederations and class entities (article 103, constitution). The decisions of the Supreme Tribunal resolving the actions when declaring the unconstitutionality of statutes have, *erga omnes* effects.[89]

Consequently, since 1934, the Brazilian system of judicial review can be considered as a mixed one in which the diffuse method of judicial review operates in combination with a concentrated one,[90] being one of its particular trends, ever since its establishment in 1891, the power assigned to the Supreme Tribunal to review lower courts' decisions on matters of constitutionality through an extraordinary recourse that can be brought before the Tribunal against judicial decision issued on matters of constitutionality by the Superior Federal Court or by the Regional Federal Courts, when their decisions are considered to be inconsistent with the Constitution; and in cases in which the courts have denied the validity of treaties or federal statutes, or have declared their unconstitutionality; or when a local government law or act has been challenged as unconstitutional for being contrary to a valid federal law (Article 199. III, b,c. Constitution).

On the other hand, in Brazil, Article 5 of the Constitution establishes four actions for the protection of constitutional rights and guaranties: in addition to the habeas corpus,[91] and habeas data recourses, it provides for the *mandado de segurança* and

---

89 See, José Carlos Barbosa M, "El control judicial de la constitucionalidad de las leyes en el derecho brasileño: Un bosquejo", in Eduardo Ferrer Mac–Gregor (Coord.), *Derecho Procesal Constitucional*, Tomo III, Editorial Porrúa, México 2003, Tomo III, p. 1999.

90 See A. Buzaid, "La accion directa de inconstitucionalidad en el derecho brasileño", in *Revista de la Facultad de Derecho*, UCAB, Nº 19–22, Caracas 1964, p. 55; O.A. Bandeira De Mello, *A teoria das Constituiçoes rigidas*, Sao Paulo 1980, p. 157. See in general Mantel Goncalves Ferreira Filho, "O sistema constitucional brasileiro e as recentes inovacoes no controle de constitucionalidade", in *Anuario Iberoamericano de Justicia Constitucional*, Nº 5, 2001, Centro de Estudios Políticos y Constitucionales, Madrid, España, 2001; José Carlos Barbosa Moreira, "El control judicial de la constitucionalidad de las leyes en el Brasil: un bosquejo", in *Desafíos del control de constitucionalidad,* Ediciones Ciudad Argentina, Buenos Aires, Argentina, 1996; Paulo Bonavides, "Jurisdicao constitucional e legitimidade (algumas observacoes sobre o Brasil)", in *Anuario IberoamerivanoIberoamericano de Justicia Constitucional* Nº 7, Centro de Estudios Políticos y Constitucionales, Madrid, 2003; Enrique Ricardo Lewandowski, "Notas sobre o controle da constitucionalidade no Brasil", in Edgar Corzo Sosa et al., *Justicia Constitucional Comparada*, Ed. Universidad Nacional Autónoma de México, México D.F. 1993; Zeno Veloso, *Controle jurisdicional de constitucionalidade*, Ed. Cejup, Belém, Brasil, 1999.

91 The habeas corpus can be brought before the courts whenever anyone suffers or feels threatened with suffering violence or duress in his or her freedom of movement because of illegal acts or abuses of power (Article 5, LXVIII of the Constitution). The right of movement (*ius ambuland*) is defined as the right of every person to enter, stay and leave national territory with his belongings (Article 5, XV). In principle, the action is brought before the Tribunals of First Criminal Instance, but actions may be heard by the Appeals Tribunals and even by

the *mandado de injunção*, both which are the most similar to the amparo decisions. The procedural rules regarding the *mandado de segurança* are set forth in *Lei* N° 1.533, of December 31, 1951; and *Lei* N° 4.348, of June 26, 1964.[92]

The *mandado de segurança* and the recourse for *habeas corpus* were set forth in the 1934 Constitution;[93] and the *mandado de injunçao* and the recourse of *habeas data* established in the 1988 Constitution,[94] being Brazil the first Latin American country to have constitutionalized this latter to guaranty the right to have access to official records and the rights to rectify or correct the information they contain (Article 5, LXXII).

The *mandado de segurança* was expressly provided for the protection of fundamental rights, except for personal freedom and the right to free movement which are protected by the recourse for *habeas corpus* (Article 153, 21). According to the Law N° 1533 of December 31 1951, it is only admitted against illegal or abuse of power actions adopted by public authority or corporations when exercising public attributions (Article 5, LXIX). The *mandado de segurança*, as is the case of the "amparo" action in Argentina, cannot be filed against statutes, even being of auto–applicative or self–executing nature.[95]

The 1988 Constitution also provided for a *mandado de segurança* of a collective nature, conceived as a mean for protecting collective interests that can be brought before the courts by political parties represented in the National Congress, and by trade union and other legally organized entities or associations for the defense of the interests of their members or associates (Article 5, LXX).

---

the Supreme Federal Tribunal if action is brought against the Tribunal of First Instance or against the Appeals Tribunal.

92 See in general, J. Cretella Junior, *Comentários à la Lei do mandado de segurança*, Forense, Rio de Janeiro, 1992; José Afonso de Silva, "El mandamiento de seguridad en Brasil", in Héctor Fix–Zamudio and Eduardo Ferrer Mac–Gregor, *Idem*, pp. 123–157.

93 Article 113,33 Constitution 1934. See A. Ríos Espinoza, Presupuestos constitucionales del mandato de seguridad", in *Boletín del Instituto de Derecho Comparado de México,* Universidad Nacional Autónoma de México, N° 46, México 1963, p. 71. Also published in H. Fix–Zamudio, A. Ríos Espinosa and N. Alcalá Zamora, *Tres estudios sobre el mandato de seguridad brasileño,* México 1963, pp. 71–96.

94 See in general. José Alfonso Da Silva, *Mandado de injunçao e habeas data*, Sao Paulo, 1989; Dimar Ackel Filho, *Writs Constitutionais*, Sao Paulo, 1988; Nagib Slaibi Filho, *Anotaçoes a Constituiçao de 1988*, Río de Janeiro, 1989; Celso Agrícola Barbi, Do *Mandado de Segurança*, 7th Edition de acordo com o Código de Processo Civil de 1973 e legislação posterior, Editora Forense, Río de Janeiro 1993; J. Cretella Júnior, *Comentários à ley do mandado de segurança (de acordo com a constituição de 5 de outubro de 1988*, 5th Edition, Editora Forense, Río de Janeiro 1992; José Alfonso Da Silva, "El mandamiento de seguridad en Brasil", in Héctor Fix–Zamudio and Eduardo Ferrer Mac–Gregor (Coord.), *El derecho de amparo en el mundo*, Universidad Nacional Autónoma de México, Editorial Porrúa, México 2006, pp. 123–157.

95 See H. Fix–Zamudio, "Mandato de seguridad y juicio de amparo", in *Boletín del Instituto de Derecho Comparado de México*, Universidad Nacional Autónoma de México, N° 46, México 1963, pp. 11, 17.

This *mandado de segurança* can be brought before a variety of courts, and only if there are no other administrative recourses that can be filed against the challenged act, or if against judicial decisions, when no other recourses are provided in procedural law to obtain for their modification.

The *mandado de injunçao* was established to protect constitutional rights against the omissions of State authorities to regulate their exercise, particularly referring to constitutional rights related to nationality and citizenship when the lack of legislative or regulatory provisions make them unenforceable (Article 5, LXXI). So the action is filed in order to obtain a court order directed to the legislative or regulatory bodies to produce determined regulatory acts, the absence of which affects or harms the specific right.[96] In these cases, the courts cannot surrogate themselves in the powers of the legislative body, in the sense that they cannot "legislate" by means of this writ of *injunçao*, and are restricted to order or instruct for the protection of the constitutional right when unenforceable because of the lack of regulation.

2. The Constitutional Court in Colombia, and the actions for "tutela" and habeas corpus

The system of judicial review also established since the 19th century in Colombia, has always been a mixed system of judicial review of legislation, which in a very similar way to the Venezuelan one, mixed the diffuse and concentrated methods of judicial review.[97]

Regarding the diffuse method of judicial review it was consolidated since the 1910 Constitution, which expressly attributed to all courts the power to declare the inapplicability of statutes deemed contrary to the Constitution. As in all cases where the diffuse method is applied, the courts cannot annul the statutes, the declaration of their unconstitutionality only being referred to the particular case, in the sense that the court must limit the ruling to not apply the unconstitutional statute to the case, with *inter partes* effects.

This method was developed in parallel with a concentrated method of judicial review by attributing the former Supreme Court of Justice and now the Constitutional Court, the power to annul statutes with general effects on the grounds of their unconstitutionality, when requested by means of a popular action. It was also in the 1910 Constitution that the role of the Supreme Court as "guardian of the integrity of the

---

96 If the regulatory omission is attributable to the highest authorities of the Republic, the competent court to decide the mandado de injunçao is the Supreme Federal Tribunal. In other cases, the High Courts of Justice are the ones competent to do so.

97 See in general Eduardo Cifuentes Muñoz, "La Jurisdicción constitucional en Colombia", in F. fernández Segado and Domingo García Belaúnde, *La Jurisdicción constitucional en Iberoamérica*, Ed Dykinson, Madrid, España, 1997; Luis Carlos Sáchica, *La Corte Constitucional y su jurisdicción*, Ed. Temis. Bogotá Colombia, 1993. Concerning the mixed character of the system see: J. Vidal Perdomo, *Derecho constitucional general*, Bogotá 1985, p. 42; D.R. Salazar, *Constitución Política de Colombia*, Bogotá 1982, p. 305; E. Sarria, *Guarda de la Constitución*, Bogotá p. 78.

Constitution" was consolidated, a role that today is accomplished by the Constitutional Court.[98]

On the other hand, for the immediate protection of constitutional rights, the 1991 Constitution created the "action for tutela," using a word that in Spanish has the same general meaning as "amparo" and as "protección".

This action for "*tutela*", is referred in Article 86 of the Constitution as a preferred and summary proceeding that can be used for the immediate protection of certain constitutional rights (like in Chiile) that are those listed in the Constitution as "fundamental rights" or that are considered as such because of their connection with them. The Constitution refers to the action for *tutela* providing that it can be filed against public officials' violations and also against individual or corporations whose activities may particularly affect collective interest.

The action can only be filed when the injured party has no other judicial mean for the protection of his rights, unless when the tutela action is used as a transitory mean to prevent irreparable damages.

The *tutela* action, created by the 1991 Constitution was immediately regulated in the decree–law N° 2591 of November 19, 1991, and subsequently developed by decree N° 306 of February 19, 1992 and decree N° 382 of July 12, 2000.[99]

In addition to the habeas corpus recourse, which is regulated in the Criminal Code, the Constitution also provide for a "popular action" established for the protection of collective rights and interests when related to the protection of public property, public space use, public safety and public health, administrative behavior, the environment, free economic competition and others of the same nature defined by statute.

In particular, regarding the "action of *tutela*", its statutory regulation issued by Decree N° 2.591 of 1991, [100] and its very important application by the courts, have

---

98 See Allan R. Brewer–Carías, *El Sistema mixto o integral de control de la constitucionalidad en Colombia y Venezuela*, Universidad Externado de Colombia (Temas de Derecho Público N° 39) y Pontificia Universidad Javeriana (Quaestiones Juridicae N° 5), Bogotá 1995.

99 See in general, Manuel José Cepeda, *La Tutela. Materiales y reflexiones sobre su signifycado*, Imprenta nacional, Bogotá1992; Juan Carlos Esguerra Portocarrero, *La protección constitucional del ciudadano*, Legis, Bogotá 2004; Julio César Ortiz Gutierrez, "La acción de tutela en la Carta Politica de 1991. El derecho de amparo y su influencia en el ordenamiento constitucional de Colombia", in Héctor Fix–Zamudio and Eduardo Ferrer Mac–Gregor, *Idem*, Edit. Porrúa, México 2006, pp. 213–256.

100 See, in general, in regard to the tutela in Colombia, Jorge Arenas Salazar, *La Tutela Una acción humanitaria,* 1st Edition 1992, Ediciones Librería Doctrina y Ley, Santa Fe de Bogotá D.C., Colombia 1992; Manuel José Cepeda, *La Tutela Materiales y Reflexiones sobre su significado*, Imprenta Nacional, Bogotá 1992; Oscar José Dueñas Ruiz, *Acción de Tutela, Su esencia en la práctica, 50 respuestas básicas, Corte Suprema, Consejo de Estado, Legislación*, Ediciones Librería del Profesional, Santa Fe de Bogotá D.C., Colombia 1992; Federico González Campos, La Tutela: *Interpretación doctrinaria y jurisprudencial*, 2nd Edition, Ediciones Jurídicas Gustavo Ibáñez, Santa Fe de Bogotá 1994; Manuel José Cepeda, *Las Carta de Derechos. Su interpretación y sus implicaciones,* Temis, Bogotá 1993; Juan Manuel

molded an effective judicial mean for the protection of fundamental constitutional rights, which can be filed before the courts[101] at all times and in any place for the immediate protection of fundamental constitutional rights, whenever they are harmed by the action or the omission of any public authority or by certain individuals. In the latter case, they must be those rendering a public service, whose conduct can seriously and directly affects collective interests, and regarding which the aggrieved party finds himself in a position of subordination or defenselessness.

The Constitution does not exclude any State act from the tutela action, so Article 40 of the Decree 2591 expressly provided for the action for tutela against judicial decisions. Notwithstanding, the following year this article was annulled by the Constitutional Court by a decision issued on October 1, 1992, considering it unconstitutional[102] because it was contrary to the general principle of *res judicata* effects of the judicial rulings, as an expression of the due process rights. With this Constitutional Court ruling, all arbitrary judicial decisions were left out of specific control. But in spite of the annulment of the article, this situation was amended by the same Constitutional Court through the development of the so called doctrine of arbitrariness, precisely conceived to allow the admission of the tutela actions against judicial decisions when issued as a result of courts arbitrary ruling or *voie de fait.* [103]

According to Article 86 of the Constitution, the action for tutela can only be admitted when the affected party does not have any other preferred and brief mean for judicial defense (Article 6,2 of the Decree N° 2591), and in such cases, when filed "to obtain temporary judicial relief to avoid irreparable harm", being understood as irreparable damage those " that can only be wholly repaired by means of compensation" (Article 6,1). The Tutela Law also provides, similar to the Venezuelan "amparo"

Charry U., *La acción de tutela*, Editorial Temis, Bogotá 1992; Julio César Ortiz Gutierrez, "La acción de tutela en la Carta política de 1991. El derecho de amparo y su influencia en el ordenamiento constituicional de Colombia", in Héctor Fix–Zamudio and Eduardo Ferrer Mac–Gregor (Coord.), *El derecho de amparo en el mundo*, Universidad Nacional Autónoma de México, Editorial Porrúa, México 2006, pp. 213–256.

101 The Constitution sets forth that the action of tutela for the protection of fundamental constitutional rights can be brought "before the judges"; which according to Decree 2.591 of 1991 are those with jurisdiction in the place where the violation or threat of violation have taken place (Article 37). In another Decree N° 1380 of 2000, regarding the courts with jurisdiction to decide the tutela actions, it was established that they must be file: before the Districts' Superior Courts when against any national public authority; before the Circuit courts when against any national or departmental decentralized entity for public services; before the municipal courts when against district or municipal authorities and against individuals; before the Cundinamarca Judicial review of administrative actions when against any general administrative act issued by a national authorities; before the respective superior court when against any judicial decision; and before a Corporation in its corresponding Chamber when against the Supreme Court of Justice, the Consejo de Estado or the Superior Council of the Judiciary, or its Disciplinary Chamber.

102 See the decision N° C–543 of September 24, 1992 in *Derecho Colombiano*, Bogotá 1992, pp. 471 to 499; and in Manuel José Cepeda, *Derecho Constitucional Jurisprudencial. Las grandes decisiones de la Corte Constitucional*, Legis, Bogotá 2001, pp. 1009 ff.

103 See the decision N°. T–231 of May 13, 1994, in *Idem*, pp. 1022 ff.

regulations, that in these cases "when used as a preliminary protective relief to avoid irreparable harm, the action of *tutela* may be brought conjunctly with the actions for annulment filed against administrative acts before the judicial review of administrative action jurisdiction (*contencioso administrativo*).

In all these cases, the judge may determine that the challenged administrative act "would not be applied to the specific protected situation pending the final decision on the nullity of the challenged act." (Decree N° 2.591, Article 8).

The creation of the Constitutional Court in 1991 as the ultimate guardian of the Constitution also originated the attribution to the Court of the power to review all the judicial decisions resolving actions for tutela. But, contrary to the Venezuelan or Argentinean regulations on this matter, the competence of the Constitutional Court in Colombia in the case is not the result of the filing of a specific recourse for review, but, as in Bolivia, is an attribution that must be automatically accomplished by the Court, although in a discretionary way (Article 33). For such purpose, in all cases where tutela decisions are not appealed, they must always be automatically sent for revision before the Constitutional Court (Article 31). But even in cases in which the tutela decisions are appealed, the matter must also reach the Constitutional Court because the superior court's decision, whether confirming or revoking the appealed decision, must also be automatically sent for review before the Constitutional Court (Article 32). In all these cases, the Constitutional Chamber has discretionary powers to determine which decision of tutela will be examined (Article 33).

These Constitutional Court review decisions only produce effects regarding the particular case; thus the first instance court must be immediately notified, and in its turn, must notify the parties and adopt the necessary decisions in order to conform their own initial ruling to the Constitutional Court decision.

3. The Constitutional Tribunal in the Dominican Republic, and the actions for amparo, habeas corpus and habeas data

The Dominican Republic also has a mixed system of judicial review which combines the diffuse method of judicial review with the concentrated one. Regarding the former, since 1844, the Constitution sets forth that "all statutes, decrees, resolutions, regulations or acts contrary to the Constitution are null and void" (article 6, 2010 Constitution). From this express supremacy clause the courts developed their general power to declare statutes unconstitutional and not applicable when resolving particular cases,[104] which has been expressly regulated in article 1888 of the 2010 Constitution that empowers all courts to decide the exception of constitutionality in the cases they must decide. On the other hand, regarding the concentrated method of judicial review, the Constitutional Tribunal created in article 184 of the 2010 Constitution has the exclusive power to hear and decide action of unconstitutionality against statutes, decrees, regulations, resolutions and ordinances that can be filed by the President of the Republic, on third of the members of the Senate or of the Chambers of representatives, and also by any party with a legitimate interest legally pro-

104 See M. Berges Chupani, "Informe", in *Memoria de la Reunión de Cortes Superiores de Justicia de Ibero–America, El Caribe, España y Portugal*, Caracas 1983, p. 380.

tected (Article 185,1) In such cases, the Constitutional Tribunal decisions have *erga omnes* effects.

The previous Constitutions of the Dominican Republic only established the judicial guaranties for the protection of personal safety by means of the action of habeas corpus (Article 8) for the protection of personal freedom, which was initially regulated by the 1978 Habeas Corpus Law (*Ley de habeas corpus*). Since 2002 it was regulated in the Procedural Criminal Code (Ley 76–02) (articles 381–392).[105] Based on such regulations, the Supreme Court traditionally limited the procedure of habeas corpus for the protection of physical freedom and safety, excluding any possibility of using it in order to protect other constitutional rights. Apart from the Cuban Constitution, the Dominican Constitution was then the only Latin American one which did not expressly regulate the "amparo" action as a specific judicial mean for the protection of the other constitutional rights. As aforementioned, the other Constitution that does not expressly provide for the amparo action is the Uruguayan one, but the action has been deducted from other guaranties established in it.

Nonetheless, the omission on the Dominican Republic Constitution did not prevented the Supreme Court of Justice from admitting the "amparo" action, applying for that purpose the American Convention on Human Rights. It occur in a decision of February 24, 1999 in the *Productos Avon S.A.* Case, when the Supreme Court, based on the American Convention on Human Rights, admitted the "amparo" recourse for the protection of constitutional rights, in a case involving a judicial decision, assigning the power to decide on amparo matter, to the courts of first instance;[106] and establishing the general procedural rules for the proceeding.

This judicial doctrine regarding the admissibility of the "amparo" recourse leads to the sanctioning, in 2006, of the Law 437–06 establishing the recourse for amparo (*Ley N° 437–06 que establece el Recurso de Amparo)*, "against any act or omission from public authorities of from any individual, which in an actual and imminent way and with manifest arbitrariness and illegality, harms, restrict, alter of threat the rights and guaranties recognized explicit or implicit in the Constitution" (article 1). Nonetheless, and even though the amparo recourse was admitted by the Supreme Court in 1999 as a public law institution in a case brought before the Court against a judicial decision, the 2006 Law expressly excluded the amparo recourse against "jurisdictional acts issued by any court within the Judicial Power" (Judiciary) (article 3,a); also providing that no judicial process before any court can be suspended by the exercise of the action for amparo (article 5).

---

105 See in general, Juan de la Rosa, *El recurso de amparo*, Edit. Serrales, Santo Domingo, 2001.

106 Since then, the amparo action was successfully used for the protection of constitutional rights. Among the multiple cases is a very interesting 2002 case in which the Court of First Instance of the National District ordered the National Citizenship Registry to issue the Identification Card to two boys born in the Republic from illegally settled Haitian parents, arguing that the rejection of such documents constituted a violation of the boys' identity and citizenship rights. The matter finally reached the Inter American Court on Human Rights. See Samuel Arias Arzeno, "El Amparo en la República Dominicana: su Evolución Jurisprudencial", in *Revista Estudios Juridicos*, Vol. XI, N° 3, Ediciones Capeldom, Septiembre–Diciembre 2002.

The courts of first instance are the competent on matters of amparo (article 6), being the recourse an "autonomous action" which imply that in the Dominican Republic, the amparo action is not subjected to the previous exhaustion of other recourses or judicial means establish to challenge the act or omission (article 4).

The 2010 Constitution has definitively incorporated the amparo action within its provisions, establishing in its article 72 that everybody has such action in order to file claims before the courts for the immediate protection of his fundamental rights, not protected through habeas corpus, when harmed or threatened by actions or omissions of public authorities or by individuals, for making effective the enforcement of a statute or the execution of an administrative act, or for guarantying diffused or collective rights.

The 2010 Constitution, in addition, set forth for the action of habeas data, that anybody can file in order to know the existence and to have access to the data concerning itself incorporated in registries or public or private databanks; providing that in case of falsely or discrimination, he can request for it suppression, rectification, updating or confidentiality (article 70).

4. The Constitutional Court in Guatemala, and the amparo

The judicial review system of Guatemala is also a mixed system which combines the diffuse and concentrated methods. The former has been traditionally set forth in Guatemala, derived from the principle of the supremacy of the Constitution, expressly provided in Article 115 of the Amparo Law when it declares that all "statutes, governmental dispositions or any order regulating the exercise of rights guarantied in the Constitution shall be null and void if they violate, diminish, restrict or distort them. No statute can contravene the Constitution's disposition. Statutes that violate or distort the constitutional norms are null and void."

On the other hand, the consequence of this principle is the possibility of the parties to raise in any particular case (including cases of "amparo" and habeas corpus), before any court, at any instance or in cassation, but before the decision on the merits is issued, the question of the unconstitutionality of the statute in order to obtain a declaration of its inapplicability to the particular case. (Articles 116 and 120)

The question of unconstitutionality can be brought and raised as an action or as an exception or incident in the particular case, before the competent court by the Public prosecutor or by the parties. The decision which must be issued in three days, can be appealed before the Constitutional Courts (Article 121). If the question of unconstitutionality of a statute supporting the claim is raised has an exception or incident, the competent court must also resolve the matter (Article 123); and the decision can also be appealed before the Constitutional court. (Article 130)

The concentrated method of judicial review is exercised by the Constitutional Court which is empowered to hear actions of unconstitutionality filed against statutes, regulations or general dispositions. (Article 133) This action can be brought before the Court by the Public Prosecutor and the Human Rights Commissioner; and also by the board of directors of the Lawyer's (Bar) Association (*Colegio de*

Abogados), and by any person with the help of three lawyers who are members of the Bar. (Article 134).

The statutes, regulations or general dispositions declared unconstitutional, will cease in their effects from the following day after the publication of the Constitutional Court decisions in the *Official Gazette* (Article 140), the decision of the Constitutional Court having general *erga omnes* effects.

On the other hand, in Guatemala, Article 265 of the Constitution sets forth the "amparo", as a specific judicial mean with the purpose of protecting the people's constitutional rights against the violations or the threats to their rights in order to restore their effectiveness. The Constitution emphatically states that "there is no scope that could escape from the "amparo" as constitutional protection, since it is possible to file the action against acts, resolutions, provisions or statutes which explicitly or implicitly threatens, restricts or violates the rights guarantied by the Constitution and the statutes" (Article 265).[107]

For such protection, the constitutional provision only refers to actions from public authorities, but this has not prevented the admission of the "amparo" for the protection of all rights declared in the Constitution and also in statutes, as well as against individual actions.

The regulation of the action of "amparo" in Guatemala is also set forth in a general statute, the 1986 Amparo, Personal Exhibition and Constitutionality Statute (Decree N° 1–86, *Ley de amparo, exhibición personal y de constitucionalidad*).[108]

According to Article 10 of this Law, the "amparo" is established to protect all rights against any situation provoking any risk, threat, restriction or violation, whether from authorities or private entities. Notwithstanding, regarding the latter, Article 9 of the Amparo Law restrict the "amparo" action only against private entities that are supported with public funds or that have been created by statute or by virtue of a concession, or those that act by delegation of the State, by virtue of a contract or a concession. Amparo can also be filed against entities to which certain individuals are legally compelled to be part of them (professional corporations) and other that are recognized by statute, like political parties, associations, societies, trade unions, cooperatives and similar.

Article 10 of the Amparo Law enumerates a few examples according to which everybody has the right to ask for "amparo",[109] including, like in Honduras, the

---

107 See Jorge Mario García Laguardia, "Las garantías jurisdiccionales para la tutela de los derechos humanos en Guatemala: Hábeas corpus y amparo", in Héctor Fix–Zamudio and Eduardo Ferrer Mac–Gregor (Coord.), *El derecho de amparo en el mundo*, Universidad Nacional Autónoma de México, Editorial Porrúa, México 2006, pp. 381–408.

108 See in general, Jorge Mario García Laguardia, "Las garantías jurisdiccionales para la tutela de los derechos humanos en Guatemala. Habeas courpus y amparo", in Héctor Fix–Zamudio and Eduardo Ferrer Mac–Gregor, *Idem*, Edit. Porrúa, México 2006, pp. 381–408.

109 Article 10: a) To ask to be maintained or to be restituted in the enjoyment of the rights and guaranties set forth in the Constitution or any other statute; b) In order to seek a declaration in a particular case, that a statute, regulation, resolution or authority act does not oblige the plaintiff because it contradicts or restricts any of the rights guarantied in the Constitution or

"amparo" against statutes which is conceived as a mean to obtain in a judicial decision in a particular case, a declaration that a statute, regulation, resolution or act of any authority does not oblige the plaintiff or injured party because it contradicts or restricts any of the rights guarantied in the Constitution or recognized by any statute. (Article 10,b).

Article 263 of the Constitution and Article 82 of the Amparo Law also regulate the right to *habeas corpus* in favor of anyone who is illegally arrested, detained or in any other way prevented from enjoying personal freedom, threatened with losing such freedom, or suffering humiliation, even when their imprisonment or detention is legally founded. In such cases, the affected party has the right to request his immediate personal appearance (*habeas corpus*) before the court, either for his constitutional guarantee of freedom to be reinstated, for the humiliations to cease, or to terminate the duress to which he was being subjected.

The competent courts to hear and to decide on amparo matters vary regarding the challenged acts,[110] and in all the cases, the amparo decisions are subjected to appeal before the Constitutional Court (Art 60), which can be filed by the parties, the Public prosecutor and the Human Rights Commissioner (Article 63). The Constitutional Court in its decision can confirm, revoke or modify the lower court resolution (Article 67); and can also annul the whole proceeding when it is proved that the formalities had not been observed.

5. The Supreme Court of the Nation in México, and the "juicio de amparo"

Regarding judicial review of constitutionality of statutes, since the 1994 constitutional reform, the Mexican system has moved from an original exclusive diffuse system into a mixed system of judicial review by the incorporation of the concen-

---

recognized by any other statute; c) In order to seek a declaration in a particular case that a non legislative disposition or resolution of Congress is not applicable to the plaintiff because it violates a constitutional right; d) When an authority of any jurisdiction issues a regulation, accord or resolution of any kind that abuses power or exceeds its legal attributions, or when it has no attributions or they are exercised in a way that the harm caused or that can be caused would be irreparable through any other mean of defense. e) When in administrative activities the affected party is compelled to accomplish unreasonable or illegal formalities, task or activities, or when no suppressive mean or recourse exists; f) When the petitions or formalities before administrative authorities are not resolved in the delay fixed by statutes, or in case that no delay exists, in a delay of 30 days once exhausted the procedure, or when the petitions are not admitted; g) In political matters when the rights recognized in the Constitution or statutes are injured by political organizations; h) In judicial and administrative matters, regarding which the statutes set forth procedures and recourses according to due process rules that can serve to adequately resolve them, if after the exhaustion of threat by the interested party, the threat, restriction or violation to the rights recognized in the Constitution and guarantied by the statute persist.

110 For instance, according to Articles 11 et seq. of the 1986 Law of Amparo, the Constitutional Court, is competent in the cases of amparo brought against the Congress of the Republic, the Supreme Court of Justice, the President and the Vice President of the Republic, an the The Supreme Court of Justice must decide the cases of amparo brought against the Supreme Electoral Tribunal; Ministers or Vice Ministers of State when acting in the name of their Office.

trated method exercised by the Supreme Court by means of an abstract judicial review proceeding of statutes, with the power to decide in these cases with general binding effect.

According to article 105,II of the Constitution, in these cases, in order for the Supreme Court of the Nation to decide, a judicial action must be filed against federal statutes on the grounds of their unconstitutionality, the standing to sue being limited to members of Congress in number equivalent to the 33% of the members of the Chamber of Representatives or of the Senate; and to the Attorney General of the Republic. In the cases of actions against electoral statutes, the national representatives of the political parties also have standing to sue.

In all these cases, as mentioned, the Supreme Court can declare the invalidity of the statute with general *erga omnes* effects when approved by no less than 8 of the 11 votes.[111]

But the most important feature of the Mexican system of judicial review, related to the diffused method of judicial review, is the amparo suit (*juicio de amparo*) that can also be initiated be means of an action brought before the courts of the Federation for the protection of all individual guaranties declared in the Constitution, but only against actions accomplished by authorities, such as statutes, judicial decisions or administrative acts, and not against private individual actions. Since its introduction in the 1847 Acts of Constitutional Reform (article 25) as the duty of federal courts to provide protection to citizens against State actions, the *juicio de amparo* has developed allowing the courts to decide, always in particular cases or controversies, without making general declarations concerning the challenged act.

This "amparo" suit is also set forth to resolve any controversy arising from statutes' and authorities' acts which violate individual guaranties; and to resolve any controversy produced by federal statutes' or authorities' acts harming or restricting the States' sovereignty, or by States' statutes of authorities' acts invading the sphere or federal authority (Article 1,1 of the Amparo Law).

In all these cases of "amparo", the judicial protection is granted by means of a quick and efficient procedure witch in the various expressions of the "amparo" suit, follows the same general procedural trends: the absence of formalisms; the role of the judges as intermediaries between the parties; the inquisitorial character of the procedure which grants the judge a wide range of powers to conduct and direct it, that can also to be exercised *ex officio*; and the concentration of the procedure steps in only one hearing.[112]

---

111 See José Brage Camazano, "El control abstracto de la constitucionalidad de las leyes en México", in Eduardo Ferrer Mac Gregor (Coordinador), *Derecho Procesal Constitucional,* Editorial Porrúa, México, Vol. I, 2003, pp. 919 ff.

112 See Héctor Fix–Zamudio, *Ensayos sobre el derecho de amparo*, Universidad Nacional Autónoma de México, Editorial Porrúa, México 2003; Héctor Fix–Zamudio and Eduardo Ferrer Mac–Gregor, "El derecho de amparo en México", in Héctor Fix–Zamudio and Eduardo Ferrer Mac–Gregor (Coord.), *El derecho de amparo en el mundo*, Universidad Nacional Autónoma de México, Editorial Porrúa, México 2006, pp. 461– 521.

Article 107 of the Constitution regulates in a very extensive and detailed way the procedural rules for the exercise of the "amparo" action, and the competent courts to hear the cases. In this basic regulation, the traditional Mexican rule established is that in deciding the cases, the courts can not make any general declaration as to the statute or act on which the complaint is based.The "amparo" suit has also been regulated in Mexico in a specific "amparo" statute which develops Articles 103 and 107 of the Constitution *(Ley de amparo reglamentaria de los artículos 103 y 107 de la Constitución Política)* of 1936, which has been amended many times.[113]

But this trial of amparo, if it is true that is the only judicial mean that can be used for the judicial protection of constitutional rights and guaranties as well as for judicial review of the constitutionality of legislation, in its substance is a collection of various proceedings assembled in a very complex procedural institution, comprising at least five different judicial processes that in all other countries with a civil law tradition are different ones. These five different aspects, contents or expressions of the trial for *amparo*, as systematized by Professor Héctor Fix–Zamudio,[114] are the following:

The first aspect of the *juicio de amparo* is the so called "amparo" for the protection of freedom (*amparo de la libertad*), which is a judicial mean for the protection of fundamental rights established in the Constitution. This trial for "amparo" is equivalent to the *habeas corpus* proceeding for the protection of personal liberty, but in Mexico can also serve for the protection of all other fundamental rights or guaranties established in Articles 1 to 29 when violated by an act of an authority.[115]

The second aspect of the trial for amparo is the amparo against judicial decisions (Article 107, III, V Constitution) called "*amparo judicial*" or "*amparo casación*", filed by a party in a particular case alleging that the judge, when deciding, has incorrectly applied the pertinent legal provision. In this case, the amparo is a recourse to challenge judicial decisions very similar to the recourse of cassation that exists in procedural law in all civil law countries which are filed before the Supreme Courts of Justice to control the legality or constitutionality of judicial decisions. The institu-

---

113 See in general, Hector Fix–Zamudio, *Ensayos sobre el derecho de amparo*, Universidad nacional Autónoma de México, Editorial Porrúa, México 2003; Ignacio Burgoa, *El Juicio de Amparo*, Ediorial Porrúa, México1991; Eduardo Ferrer Mac–Gregor, *La acción constitucional de amparo en México y España*, Editorial Porrúa, México 2002; Héctor Fix–Zamudio and Eduardo Ferrer Mac–Grego, "El derecho de amparo en México", in Héctor Fix–Zamudio and Eduardo Ferrer Mac–Gregor, *Idem,* Edit. Porrúa, México 2006, pp. 461–521.

114 See H. Fix–Zamudio, *El juicio de amparo*, México 1964, p. 243, 377; H. Fix–Zamudio, "Reflexiones sobre la naturaleza procesal del amparo", in *Revista de la Facultad de Derecho de México*, 56, 1964, p. 980; H. Fix–Zamudio, "Lineamientos fundamentales del proceso social agrario en el derecho mexicano", in *Atti della Seconda Assemblea. Istituto di Dirito Agrario Internazionale a Comparato,* Vol. I, Milán 1964, p. 402; Eduardo Ferrer Mac–Gregor, *La acción constitucional de amparo en México y España, Estudio de Derecho Comparado*, 2nd Edition, Edit. Porrúa, México 2000; Ignacio Burgoa O., *El juicio de amparo*, Twenty–eighth Edition, Editorial Porrúa S.A., México 1991.

115 See Robert D. Baker, *Judicial Review in México. A Study of the Amparo Suit*, University of Texas Press, Austin 1971, p. 92.

tion is elsewhere called *recurso de casación*, according to the French tradition, and is filed before the Court on cassation or before the Cassation Chambers of the Supreme Court as an extraordinary judicial mean to challenge definitive and final judicial decisions founded on violations of the Constitution, or of statutes or of the judicial procedural formalities. By this judicial mean, the Supreme Courts assures the uniformity of judicial interpretation and application of the law. In Mexico this well known extraordinary judicial recourse is regulated as one of the modalities or expressions of the *juicio de amparo*.

The third aspect of the trial for amparo is the so–called administrative amparo (*amparo administrativo*) through which it is possible to challenge administrative acts that violate the Constitution or the statutes (Article 107, IV Constitution), resulting in this case, in a judicial mean for judicial review of administrative action. This means is equivalent to the *contencioso–administrativo* recourses (Judicial review of administrative actions) that, also following the French influence, exists in many of the civil law countries.These recourses are commonly filed before special courts (*contencioso administrativo)* specifically established for the purpose to control the legality and constitutionality of Public Administration's actions and, in particular, of administrative acts, seeking their annulment.[116] In Mexico, on the contrary, the administrative amparo is the judicial mean established to control the legality of administrative action and for the protection of individual constitutional rights and guaranties against administrative acts, substituting what in other countries is the *jurisdicción contencioso administrativa.*[117]

The fourth aspect of the trial for amparo is the so called agrarian amparo (*amparo agrario*) which is set up for the protection of peasants' rights against acts of public authorities, particularly referring to collective rural property rights (Article 107, II.).

And finally, the fifth aspect of the trial for amparo, is the so called amparo against laws *(amparo contra leyes),* as a judicial mean directed to challenge statutes that violate the Constitution, resulting in this case, in a judicial review mean of the constitutionality of legislation. It is exercised in a direct way against statutes without the need for any additional administrative or judicial act of enforcement or of application of the statute considered unconstitutional; which implies that the challenged statute must have a self executing character.

All of these five "amparo" proceedings are developed before a variety of courts, so for instance, when the petition of "amparo" is filed against federal or local statutes, international treaties, national executive regulations or State's Governors'

116 Even in some Latin American countries, like Colombia, a Consejo de Estado has been created following the Conseil d'État French model, as the head of a Judicial Review of Administrative Action separate Jurisdiction. In the other countries, the head of the Jurisdiction has been located in the Supreme Court, and the main purpose of it, as mentioned, is to challenge administrative acts seeking their annulment when considered unconstitutional or illegal. The important trend of such Jurisdiction is that it is not only devoted to protect human or constitutional rights, but in general, the legality of the administrative actions.

117 An exception has always been the Tribunal Fiscal de la Federación.

regulations or any other administrative regulations, it must be filed before the District Courts (article 114 Amparo Law).[118]

From all these five aspects or expressions of the "amparo" suit, the conclusion is that in Mexico, the "amparo" is not really one single adjective guaranty (action or recourse) for the protection of constitutional rights, but is rather a varied range of judicial processes and procedures all used for the protection of constitutional guaranties. It is a unique judicial proceeding which, with all its procedural peculiarities, cannot be reproduced in any other legal system. It was initially established following the United States judicial review model,[119] also as a mean for judicial review of the constitutionality of statutes following the features of the diffuse method of judicial review of legislation[120], but it eveolved in a quite different way

Regarding the amparo against statutes, always filed against "public authorities"[121], is a mean for judicial review of the constitutionality of legislation, sought through an "action of unconstitutionality" that is filed before a federal District Court (Article 107, XII). The defendants in the case are the organs of the State that have intervened in the process of formation of the statute, namely, the Congress of the Union or the state Legislatures which have sanctioned it; the President of the Republic or the Governors of the states which have enacted it, and the Secretaries of state which have countersigned it and ordered its publication.[122] In these cases, it is provided that the federal district courts decisions are reviewable by the Supreme Court of Justice (Article 107, VIII,a).

The *amparo* against statutes, therefore, is a direct action filed against a statute when it directly affects the plaintiff's guaranties, without the need of any other intermediate or subsequent administrative or judicial act, that is, a statute that with its sole enactment causes personal and direct prejudice to the plaintiff. [123]

---

118 H. Fix–Zamudio, "Algunos problemas que plantea el amparo contra leyes", in *Boletín del Instituto de Derecho Comparado de México,* Universidad Nacional Autónoma de México, México 1960, pp. 15, 20.

119 J.A.C. Grant, "El control jurisdiccional de la constitucionalidad de las leyes: una contribución de las Américas a la ciencia política", in *Revista de la Facultad de Derecho de México,* N° 45, México 1962, p. 657.

120 H. Fix–Zamudio, "Algunos problemas que plantea el amparo contra leyes", in *Boletín del Instituto de Derecho Comparado de México,* Universidad Nacional Autónoma de México, México 1960,p. 22, 23.

121 This aspect, particularly regarding judicial review of statutes, reveals another substantial difference between the Mexican system and the general diffuse system of judicial review, in which the parties in the particular process where a constitutional question is raised, continue to be the same.

122 H. Fix–Zamudio, "Algunos problemas que plantea el amparo contra leyes", in *Boletín del Instituto de Derecho Comparado de México,* Universidad Nacional Autónoma de México, México 1960, p. 21.

123 That is why, in principle, the action seeking the amparo against laws must be brought before the court within 30 days after their enactment, or within 15 days after the first act of execution of the said statute so as to protect the plaintiff's rights to sue. Article 21 Amparo Law.

Regarding the effects of the judicial decision on any of the aspects of the trial for *amparo*, including the cases of judicial review of constitutionality of legislation, since the initial 19th Century provision for the trial for *amparo*, the Constitution has expressly emphasized that the courts cannot "make any general declaration as to the law or act on which the complaint is based". Consequently, the judgment can "only affect private individuals" and is limited to protect them in the particular case to which the complaint refers (Article 107,II).[124] Therefore, the decision in a *juicio de amparo* in which judicial review of legislation is accomplished, as it happens with the decisions of the Supreme Courts in Paraguay and Uruguay, only has *inter partes* effects, and can never consist in general declarations with *erga omnes* effects.

Therefore, the courts, in their amparo decisions regarding the unconstitutionality of statutes, can not annul or repeal them; and similarly to all legal systems with the diffuse method of judicial review, the statute remains in the books and can be applied by the courts, the only effect of the declaration of its unconstitutionality being directed to the parties in the particular process.

As a consequence, the decisions of the trials for *amparo* do not have general binding effects, being only obligatory to other courts when a precedent is established by means of *jurisprudencia* (Article 107, XIII, 1 Constitution), which according to that Amparo Law is attained when five consecutive decisions to the same effect, uninterrupted by any incompatible ruling, are rendered by the Supreme Court of Justice or by the Collegiate Circuit Courts.[125] Nonetheless, the *jurisprudencia* can be modified when the respective Court pronounces a contradictory judgment with a qualified majority of votes of its members (Article 139).[126]

It must also be highlighted that according to a constitutional reform passed in 1983, the Supreme Court of Mexico was vested with a discretionary power to review the cases of "amparo" of constitutional importance (*facultad de atracción*),

---

See H. Fix–Zamudio, *Idem*, pp. 24, 32; Robert D. Baker, *Judicial Review in México. A Study of the Amparo Suit*, University of Texas Press, Austin 1971, pp. 164, 171, 176.

124 The principle is named the "Otero formula" due to its inclusion in the 1857 constitution under the influence of Mariano Otero. See H, Fix–Zamudio, *Idem*, p. 33, 37.

125 Article 192, 193. See in Robert D. Baker, *Judicial Review in México. A Study of the Amparo Suit*, University of Texas Press, Austin 1971, pp. 256, 257.

126 Nevertheless, as *jurisprudencia* can be established by the federal Collegiate Circuit Courts and by the Supreme Court, contradictory interpretations of the constitution can exist, having binding effects upon the lower courts. In order to resolve these conflicts, the constitution establishes the power of the Supreme Court or of the Collegiate Circuit Court to resolve the conflict, when the contradiction is denounced by the Chambers of the Supreme Court or another Collegiate Circuit Court; by the Attorney General or by any of the parties to the cases in which the jurisprudencia was established (Article 107, XIII). Anyway the resolution of the contradiction between judicial doctrines, has the sole purpose of determining one single *jurisprudencia* on the matter, and does not affect particular juridical situations, derived from the contradictory judicial decisions adopted in the respective trials (Article 107, XIII). See the comments in J.A.C. Grant, "El control jurisdiccional de la constitucionalidad de las leyes: una contribución de las Américas a la ciencia política", in *Revista de la Facultad de Derecho de México*, 45, México 1962, p. 662.

with some similarities to the writ of certiorari. Nevertheless, Collegiate Circuit Courts' decisions in direct *amparo* are not reviewable by the Supreme Court if they are based "on a precedent established by the Supreme Court of Justice as to the constitutionality of a statute or the direct interpretation of a provision of the Constitution".

Also, according to another constitutional reform sanctioned in 1988, the Supreme Court was also attributed the power to decide in last instance all cases of "amparo" where the decision involves the unconstitutionality of a federal statute or establishes a direct interpretation of a provision of the Constitution (article 107,IX).

Both attributions allow the Supreme Court to give final interpretation of the Constitution in a uniform way,[127] its decisions limited to resolve upon the actual constitutional questions.

6. The Constitutional Chamber of the Supreme Court of Justice in Nicaragua, and the recourses for amparo and habeas corpus

The system of judicial review established in Nicaragua is also a mixed one, combining the diffuse and the concentrated methods. Regarding the diffuse method, the Constitution assigns to all courts (Article 182 of the Constitution) when resolving particular cases, the general power to decide upon the unconstitutionality of statutes, of course, with only *inter partes* effects.

On the other hand, the Constitution also assigns the Supreme Court of Justice the power to decide upon the unconstitutionality of statutes, decrees or regulations when challenged by means of an action of unconstitutionality which, as in Colombia, El Salvador, Panamá and Venezuela, is also conceived as a popular action that can be brought directly by any citizen (Article 2 of the Amparo Law). When deciding such popular action, the Supreme Court's decision declaring the unconstitutionality of the challenged statute, has general effects, preventing its application by the courts (Articles 18 and 19).

But in the Nicaraguan system, the question of the unconstitutionality of a statute, decree or regulation, can also be raised before the Constitutional Chamber of the Supreme Court by means of recourse of cassation and also, as mentioned, through a recourse of "amparo" filed by the corresponding party in the procedure of a case. In the former case, the Supreme Court, in addition to the cassation ruling regarding the challenged judicial decision, can also declare its nullity. And in the case of "amparo" recourses, as mentioned, they can serve as a judicial mean for judicial review of legislation, and the Supreme Court has the exclusive power to decide on the matter. So in these cases, in addition to the constitutional protection granted to the party in accordance to the "amparo" petition, the Supreme Court can also declare

127 See Joaquin Brage Camazano, *La jurisdicción constitucional de la libertad (Teoría general, Argentina, México, Corte Interamericana de Derechos Humanos)*, Editorial Porrúa, Instituto Mexicano de Derecho Procesal Constitucional, México 2005, p. 153–155.

the unconstitutionality of the statute, decree or regulation, also with general effects (Article 18)[128]

The Amparo Law also provides that in any judicial decision other than "amparo", issued applying the diffuse method of judicial review with express declaration of the unconstitutionality of a statute, if such decision cannot be challenged by means of a cassation recourse, the respective court must send it to the Supreme Court in order for this Court to ratify the unconstitutionality of the statute, decree or regulation and declare its inapplicability.[129]

According to these means, in order to guarantee the uniformity of jurisprudence in constitutional matters, the Supreme Court in Nicaragua always has the power to review judicial decisions on constitutional matters.

On the other hand, the Constitution of Nicaragua provides for a recourse for "amparo", as well as the habeas corpus recourse established for the protection of people's freedom, physical integrity and safety (Articles 188 and 189 of the Constitution), both regulated in one general "amparo" statute (*Ley de amparo*) of 1988.[130]

Regarding the "amparo" action, the Constitution only provides that "the persons whose constitutional rights have been violated or are in peril of being violated, can file the recourse of personal exhibition or the recourse of "amparo". No constitutional provision exists regarding the origin of the violation, so that if it is true that the recourse could then be brought against violations provoked by public officials and individuals, the latter case has not been regulated. Like in Costa Rica and El Salvador, Nicaragua has also established a concentrated judicial system of "amparo" by granting the Supreme Court of Justice the exclusive power to decide the "amparo" actions (Article 164,3), but with the difference that in those countries, the judicial review system is an exclusively concentrated one, exercised by the Constitutional Chamber of the Supreme Courts. In Nicaragua, the judicial review system is a mixed one.

According to the Law, the recourse of amparo in Nicaragua is set forth against any provision, act or resolution, and in general against any action or omission from any official, authority or agent that violates or an attempt to violate the rights declared in the Constitution (Article 45), and is not admitted against violations or threats committed by individuals.

Regarding the procedure of the Nicaraguan concentrated "amparo", it is also different from the one in Costa Rica and El Salvador, particularly because the recourse for "amparo", although being decided by the Supreme Court, is not directly filed before it, but before the Courts of Appeals. So in Nicaragua, the procedure on the

---

128 Nonetheless, in these cases, the decision does not have retroactive effects in the sense that it cannot affect third party rights acquired from those statutes or regulations (Articles 20 and 22).

129 In such cases the decisions also cannot affect third party rights acquired from those statutes or regulations (Articles 21 and 22).

130 See in general, Iván Escobar Fornos, "El amparo en Nicaragua", in Héctor Fix–Zamudio and Eduardo Ferrer Mac–Gregor, *Idem,* Edit. Porrúa, México 2006, pp. 523–563

"amparo" suit has two steps: one that must be accomplished, including the possible suspension of the effects of the challenged act, before the Courts of Appeals; and the second that must be accomplished before the Supreme Court where the files must be sent for the final decision. The Courts of Appeals are also empowered to reject the recourses, in which cases the plaintiff can bring the case before the Supreme Court also by means of an action of "amparo" (Article 25 Law)[131].

7. The Constitutional Tribunal in Peru, and the recourses for amparo, habeas corpus and habeas data

The judicial review system of the constitutionality of legislation has also being conceived in Peru as a mixed one,[132] since it combines the diffuse system of judicial review with the concentrated one attributed to the Constitutional Tribunal[133]. The former is expressly set forth in Article 138 of the 1993 Constitution which provides that "in any process, if an incompatibility exists between a constitutional provision and a statute, the courts must prefer the former" (Article 138), having of course their decisions, in such cases, only *inter partes* effects.

But in the case of Peru, the diffuse method of judicial review has a peculiarity in the sense that all the courts' decisions regarding the inapplicability of statutes based on constitutional arguments must obligatorily be sent for revision to the Supreme Court of Justice and not to the Constitutional Tribunal. This provision, sanctioned before the Constitutional Procedures Code was enacted, has remained in force, empowering the Supreme Court, through its Constitutional Law and Social Chamber, to

---

131 See Iván Escobar Fornos, "El amparo en Nicaragua", in Héctor Fix–Zamudio and Eduardo Ferrer Mac–Gregor (Coord.), *El derecho de amparo en el mundo*, Universidad Nacional Autónoma de México, Editorial Porrúa, México 2006, pp. 523–563.

132 See Aníbal Quiroga León, "Control difuso y control concentrado en el derecho procesal Perúano", in *Revista Derecho* N° 50, diciembre de 1996, Facultad de Derecho de la Pontificia Universidad Católica del Perú, Lima, Perú, 1996, pp. 207 ff.

133 See in general Domingo García Belaunde, "La jurisdicción constitucional en Perú", in D. García Belaúnde, y F. Fernández Segado (Coord.), *La jurisdicción constitucional en Iberoamérica*, Ed. Dykinson, Madrid, España, 1977; Domingo García Belaunde, "La jurisdicción constitucional y el modelo dual o paralelo", in *La Justicia Constitucional a fines del siglo XX, Revista del Instituto de Ciencias Políticas y Derecho Constitucional,* año VII, N° 6, Palestra editores, Huancayo, Perú; Domingo García Belaunde (Coordinador) *La Constitución y su defensa*, Ed Jurídica Grijley, Lima, 2003, p. 96. César Landa, *Teoría del Derecho procesal Constitucional*, Ed. Palestra, Lima, Perú, 2004; José Palomino Manchego, José, "Control y magistratura constitucional en el Perú", in Juan Vega Gómez, and Edgar Corzo Sosa (Coord.), *Instrumentos de tutela y justicia constitucional, Memoria del VII Congreso Iberoamericano de Derecho Constitucional*, Instituto de Investigaciones Jurídicas, Universidad Nacional Autónoma de México, México; Domingo García Belaúnde and Gerardo Eto Cruz, "El proceso de amparo en el Perú", in Héctor Fix–Zamudio and Eduardo Ferrer Mac–Gregor (Coord.), *El derecho de amparo en el mundo*, Universidad Nacional Autónoma de México, Editorial Porrúa, México 2006, pp. 593–632.

determine if the decision of the ordinary court on constitutional matters was adequate or not (Article 14, Organic Law of the Judiciary)[134].

But in addition to the diffuse method of judicial review, a concentrated method is also set forth in the Constitution of Peru, by attributing the Constitutional Tribunal the power to hear in unique instance the actions of unconstitutionality (Article 202,1) that can be filed against statutes, legislative decrees, urgency decrees, treaties approved by Congress, Congressional internal regulations, regional norms and municipal ordinances (Article 77, Code).

This action can be brought before the Constitutional Tribunal by high public officials, as the President of the Republic, the Prosecutor General, the Peoples Defendant; by a number equivalent to 25% of representatives to the Congress; and also, by 5,000 citizen whose signatures must be validated by the National Jury of Elections. When the challenged act is a local government regulation, the action can be filed by 1% of the citizens of the corresponding entity. The Presidents of Regions with the vote of the Regional Councils, or the provincial mayors with the vote of the local Councils can also file actions of unconstitutionality in matter of their jurisdiction; and also the professional associations (*Colegios)* in matters of their specialty (Article 203; Article 99 Code).

The decision of the Constitutional Tribunal, in all these cases of the concentrated method of judicial review when declaring the unconstitutionality of a statute or normative provision, produces general *erga omnes* effects, from the day of its publication in the *Official Gazzette* (Article 204, Constitution; Articles 81,82 Code).

The Constitution of Peru in its enumeration of the constitutional guaranties also provides for the three actions for constitutional protection: the habeas corpus, the "amparo" and the habeas data actions (Article 200). [135]

The action of *habeas corpus* that can be filed against any action or omission by any authority, official or person that impairs or threatens individual freedom, and the action of *habeas data* can be filed against any act or omission by any authority, official or person that impairs or threatens the rights to request and receive information from any public office, except when they affect personal privacy or were excluded for national security. The action of habeas data can also de filed to assure that public or private information services will not release information that affects personal and familiar privacy. (Article 2, 5 and 6).

All these actions (habeas corpus, "amparo" and habeas data) have been regulated in the Constitutional Procedural Code sanctioned in 2004 (Ley N° 28237, *Código*

---

134 Quiroga León, Aníbal, "El derecho procesal constitucional Perúano", in Juan Vega Gómez and Edgar Corzo Sosa (Coord.) *Instrumentos de tutela y justicia constitucional, Memoria del VII Congreso Iberoamericano de Derecho Constitucional*, Instituto de Investigaciones Jurídicas, Universidad Nacional Autónoma de México, México, pp. 471 ff.

135See in general, Samuel B. Abad Yupanqui, *El proceso constitucional de amparo*, Gaceta Jurídica, Lima 2004; Domingo García Belaúnde and Gerardo Eto Cruz, "El proceso de amparo en el Perú", in Héctor Fix–Zamudio and Eduardo Ferrer Mac–Gregor, *Idem,* Edit. Porrúa, México 2006, pp. 593–632

Procesal Constitucional)[136], which in addition to regulate all the juducial review procedures, provide that in matters of "amparo", the competent courts to hear the proceeding are the Civil Courts with jurisdiction on the place where the right is affected, or where the plaintiff or defendant have their residence. (Article 51) When the harm is caused by a judicial decision, the competent court is always the Civil Chamber of the respective superior court of justice.

Article 200 of the Constitution also establishes the action of "amparo" to protect all other rights recognized by the Constitution which are impaired or threatened by any authority, official or private individuals in order to restore things to the situation they had previous to the violation (Article 1). As in Paraguay, according to the Constitution, the action of "amparo" is not admissible against statutes or against judicial decisions, but with the difference that in Peru, the exclusion refers only to judicial decisions issued in a regular proceeding.

According to the same Code, the "amparo" action shall only be admitted when previous procedures have been exhausted (Articles 5,4; 45); and in any case, when doubts exists over the exhaustion of prior procedures. (Article 45)

All judicial decisions denying the habeas corpus, "amparo" and habeas data can be review by the Constitutional Tribunal, which has the power to hear the cases in last and definitive instance (Article 202,2 Constitution). In addition, all the other decisions can also reach the Constitutional Tribunal of Peru by means of a recourse of constitutional damage (*agravio*) that can be filed against all second instance judicial decision denying the claim (Article 18, Code). If this constitutional damage recourse is denied, the interested party can also file before the Constitutional Tribunal a recourse of complaint (*queja*), in which case, if the Tribunal considered the complaint duly supported, it will proceed to decide the constitutional damage recourse, asking the superior court to send the corresponding files. (Article 19).

If the Constitutional Tribunal considers that the challenged judicial decision has been issued as a consequence of a procedural error or vice affecting its sense, it can annul it and order the reposition of the procedure to the situation previous to when the defect happened. In cases in which the vice only affects the challenged decision, the Tribunal must repeal it and issue a substantive ruling. (Article 20)

8. The Constitutional Chamber of the Supreme Tribunal of Justice in Venezuela, and the amparo proceeding

The other country with a mixed system of judicial review established since the 19th Century[137] is Venezuela, where the diffuse method is also expressly regulated in

---

136 The Code repealed the previous statutes regulating the amparo and the habeas corpus recourses (Law 23.506 of 1982, and Law 25.398 of 1991). See Samuel B. Abad Yupanqui et al., *Código Procesal Constitucional*, Ed. Palestra, Lima 2004; Alberto Borea Odria, *Las garantías constitucionales: Habeas Corpus y Amparo,* Libros Perúanos S.A., Lima 1992; Alberto Borea Odría, *El amparo y el Hábeas Corpus en el Perú de Hoy*, Lima, 1985.

137 With respect to this mixed character of the Venezuelan system, the former Supreme Court has analyzed the scope of judicial review of the constitutionality of statutes and has correctly pointed out that this is the responsibility: "not only of the Supreme Tribunal of the Republic,

Article 334 of the 1999 Constitution, following a legal tradition that can be traced back to the 1897 Civil Procedure Code, by granting all courts, even *ex officio*, the power to declare statutes inapplicable for the resolution of a given case when they consider them unconstitutional and, hence, giving preference to constitutional rules.[138]

On the other hand, Article 336 of the same 1999 Constitution, also following a constitutional tradition that can be traced back to the 1858 Constitution,[139] establishes the concentrated method of judicial review by granting to the Constitutional Chamber of the Supreme Tribunal, as Constitutional Jurisdiction, the power to decide with nullifying effects upon the constitutionality of statutes and other national, state or municipal normative acts and acts of government adopted by the President of the Republic when requested, as is also established in Colombia, El Salvador, Nicaragua and Panama, by means of a popular action. This concentrated method of judicial review of the constitutionality of statutes and other similar State acts allows the Supreme Tribunal of Justice to declare them null and void with general *erga omnes* effects when they violate the Constitution.

Within this mixed system of judicial review, in addition, the Constitution also establishes a constitutional right for amparo[140]or for protection by the courts that eve-

---

but also of all the judges, whatever their rank and standing may be. It is sufficient that an official is part of the Judiciary for him to be a custodian of the Constitution and, consequently, to apply its ruling preferentially over those of ordinary statutes. Nonetheless, the application of the Constitution by the judges, only has effects in the particular case at issue and, for that very reason, only affects the interested parties in the conflict. In contrast, when constitutional illegitimacy in a law is declared by the Supreme [Tribunal] when exercising its sovereign function, as the interpreter of the Constitution, and in response to the pertinent [popular] action, the effects of the decision extend erga omnes and have the force of law. In the first case, the review is incidental and special, and in the second, principal and general. When this happens –that is to say when the recourse is autonomous– the control is either formal or material, depending on whether the nullity has to do with an irregularity relating to the process of drafting the statute, or whether –despite the legislation having been correct from the formalist point of view– the intrinsic content of the statute suffers from substantial defects." See Federal Court (which in 1961 was substituted by the Supreme Court of Justice), decision June 19, 1953, *Gaceta Forense*, 1, 1953, pp. 77–78

138 See in general, Allan R. Brewer–Carías, *El control de la constitucionalidad de los actos estatales,* Caracas 1977; and also "Algunas consideraciones sobre el control jurisdiccional de la constitucionalidad de los actos estatales en el derecho venezolano", in *Revista de Administración Pública,* N° 76, Madrid 1975, pp. 419–446.

139 See J. G. Andueza, *La jurisdicción constitucional en el derecho venezolano*, Caracas 1955 p. 46.

140 Regarding this constitutional provision, Héctor Fix Zamudio pointed out in 1970 that Article 49 of the 1961 Constitution, "definitively enshrined the right to amparo as a procedural instrument to protect all the constitutionally enshrined fundamental rights of the human person", in what he described as "one of the most outstanding achievements of the very advanced Magna Carta of 1961. See Héctor Fix Zamudio, "Algunos aspectos comparativos del derecho de amparo en México y Venezuela", *Libro Homenaje a la Memoria de Lorenzo Herrera Mendoza*, UCV, Caracas 1970, Volumen II, pp. 333–390. This trend has been followed in Article 27 of the 1999 Constitution. See Héctor Fix–Zamudio, "La teoría de Allan

rybody have for the protection of all the rights and freedoms enshrined in the Constitution and in international treaties, or which, even if not listed in the text, are inherent to the human person.[141]

As in Guatemala and Mexico, the Constitution does not set forth a separate action of habeas corpus for the protection of personal freedom and liberty, instead it establishes that the action for "amparo" regarding freedom or safety, may be exercised by any person in which cases "the detainee shall be immediately transferred to the court, without delay".

Additionally, the Venezuelan Constitution has also set forth the habeas data recourse, guaranteeing the right to have access to the information and data concerning the claimant contained in official or private registries, as well as to know about the use that has been made of the information and about its purpose, and to petition the competent court for the updating, rectification or destruction of erroneous records and those that unlawfully affect the petitioner's right (Article 28).

The "amparo" action is regulated in a Statute on Amparo for the protection of constitutional rights and guaranties sanctioned in 1988 (*Ley Orgánica de Amparo sobre derechos y garantías constitucionales*).[142]

This right to amparo can be exercised through an "autonomous action for amparo"[143] that in general is filed before the first instance court (Article 7 Amparo

R. BREWER–CARÍAS sobre el derecho de amparo latinoamericano y el juicio de amparo mexicano", in *El Derecho Público a comienzos del Siglo XXI. Libro Homenaje al profesor Allan R. Brewer–Carías*, Volumen I, Instituto de Derecho Público, Editorial Civitas, Madrid 2003, pp. 1125 ff.

141 On the action of amparo in Venezuela, in general, see Gustavo Briceño V., *Comentarios a la Ley de Amparo*, Editorial Kinesis, Caracas 1991; Rafael J. Chavero Gazdik, *El nuevo régimen del amparo constitucional en Venezuela*, Editorial Sherwood, Caracas 2001; Gustavo José Linares Benzo, *El Proceso de Amparo*, Universidad Central de Venezuela, Facultad de Ciencias Jurídicas y Políticas, Caracas 1999; Hildegard Rondón De Sansó, *Amparo Constitucional*, Caracas 1988; Hildegard Rondón De Sansó, *La acción de amparo contra los poderes públicos*, Editorial Arte, Caracas 1994; Carlos M. Ayala Corao and Rafael J. Chavero Gazidk, "El amparo constitucional en Venezuela", in Héctor Fix–Zamudio and Eduardo Ferrer Mac–Gregor (Coord.), *El derecho de amparo en el mundo*, Universidad Nacional Autónoma de México, Editorial Porrúa, México 2006, pp. 649–692.

142 See in general, Allan R. BREWER–CARÍAS, *Instituciones políticas y constitucionales, Vol. V, El derecho y la acción de amparo*, Universidad Católica del Táchira, Editorial Jurídica Venezolana, Caracas–San Cristóbal 1998; Hildegard Rondón de Sansó, *Amparo constitucional*, Caracas 1988; Gustavo J. Linares Benzo, *El proceso de amparo*, Universidad Central de Venezuela, Caracas 1999; Rafael J. Chavero Gazdik, *El Nuevo regimen del amparo constitucional en Venezuela*, Editorial Sherwood, Caracas 2001; Allan R. BREWER–CARÍAS, Carlos Ayala Corao and Rafael J. Chavero G., *Ley Orgánica de Amparo sobre derechos y garantías constitucionales,* Editorial Jurídica Venezolana, Caracas 2007; Carlos Ayala Corao and Rafael Chavero G., "El amparo constitucional en Venezuela", in Héctor Fix–Zamudio and Eduardo Ferrer Mac–Gregor, *Idem,* Edit. Porrúa, México 2006, pp. 649–692.

143 See Allan R. BREWER–CARÍAS, "El derecho de amparo y la acción de amparo", in Revista *de Derecho Público*, N° 22, Editorial Jurídica Venezolana, Caracas 1985, pp. 51 ff.

Law);[144] or by means of pre existing ordinary or extraordinary legal actions or recourses to which an "amparo" petition can be joined, and the judge is empowered to immediately re–establish the infringed legal situation. In all such cases, it is not that the ordinary means substitute the constitutional right of protection (or diminish it), but that they can serve as the judicial mean for protection since the judge is empowered to protect fundamental rights and immediately re–establish the infringed legal situation.[145]

This last possibility does not presuppose in Venezuela that for the filing of an autonomous "amparo" action, all other pre–existing legal judicial or administrative means have to be exhausted, as is the case for instance, of the recourse for amparo or the "constitutional complaint" developed in Europe, particularly in Germany and in Spain.[146]

---

144 According to the Constitution, the right to protection may be exercised, according to the law, before "the Courts", and thus, as it has been said, the organization of the legal and procedural system does not provide for one single judicial action to guaranty the enjoyment and exercise of constitutional rights to be brought before one single Court. In Venezuela, according to Article 7 of the Organic Law on Amparo, the competent courts to decide amparo actions are the First Instance Courts with jurisdiction on matters related to the constitutional rights or guaranties violated, in the place where the facts, acts of omission have occurred. Regarding amparo of personal freedom and security, the competent courts should be the Criminal First Instance courts (Article 40). Nonetheless, when the facts, acts or omissions harming or threatening to harm the constitutional right or guaranty occurs in a place where no First Instance court exists, the amparo action may be brought before and any judge of the site, which must decide according to the law, and in a 24 hour delay it must send the files for consultation to the competent First Instance court (Article 9). Only in cases in which facts, actions or omissions of the President of the Republic, his Cabinet members, the National Electoral Council, the Prosecutor General, the Attorney general and the General Comptroller of the Republic are involved does the power to decide the amparo actions correspond to the Constitutional Chamber of the Supreme Tribunal of Justice (Article 8).

145 Allan R. BREWER–CARÍAS, "La reciente evolución jurisprudencial en relación a la admisibilidad del recurso de amparo", in *Revista de derecho público*, Nº 19, Caracas 1984, pp. 207–218.

146 In these countries, the protective remedy is really an authentic "recourse" that is brought, in principle, against judicial decisions. In Germany, for example, to bring a constitutional complaint for the protection of constitutional rights before the Federal Constitutional Tribunal, the available ordinary judicial means need to be previously exhausted, which definitively entails a recourse against a final judicial decision, even though, in exceptional cases, a direct complaint for protection may be allowed in certain specific cases and with respect to a very limited number of constitutional rights. See K. Schlaich, "Procedures et techniques de protection des droits fondamentaux. Tribunal Constitutionnel Fédéral allemand", in L. Favoreu (ed.), *Cours constitutionnelles européenes et droits fondamentaux,* Paris 1982, pp. 105–164. In Spain, all legal recourses need to be exhausted in order to bring a "recurso de amparo" of constitutional rights before the Constitutional Tribunal, and, particularly when dealing with protection against administrative activities, the ordinary means for judicial review of administrative decisions must be definitively exhausted. For this reason, the recourse for protection in Spain is eventually a means for judicial review of decisions taken by the Administrative Judicial review courts. See J.L. García Ruíz, *Recurso de amparo en el derecho español,* Ma-

This right for "amparo" has been regulated in the 1988 Organic Law of Amparo,[147] expressly providing for its exercise, not only by means of an autonomous action for "amparo", or by the filing of the amparo petition jointly with the popular action of unconstitutionality against statutes and State acts of the same rank and value (Article 3); with the judicial review of administrative actions recourses against administrative acts or against omissions from Public Administration (article 5); or with another ordinary judicial actions (article 6,5).[148]

The same Supreme Court has also ruled that in these latter cases, the action for "amparo" is not an autonomous action, "but an extraordinary one, ancillary to the action or recourse to which it has been joined, thus subject to its final decision. Being joint actions, the case must be heard by the competent court regarding the principal one"[149].

Regarding the first mean for protection, that is, the autonomous action for "amparo", in principle it can be brought before the first instance courts[150], having a re–establishing nature and "is a sufficient judicial mean in itself in order to return the things to the situation they were when the right was violated and to definitively make the offender act or fact disappear. In such cases, the plaintiff must invoke and demonstrate that it is a matter of flagrant, vulgar, direct and immediate constitution-

---

drid 1980. F. Castedo Álvarez, "El recurso de amparo constitucional", in Instituto de Estudios Fiscales, *El Tribunal Constitucional*, Madrid 1981, Vol. I, pp. 179–208.

147 See *Gaceta Oficial* N° 33.891 of January 22, 1988. See Allan R. BREWER–CARÍAS, Carlos M. Ayala Corao and Rafael Chavero G., *Ley Orgánica de Amparo sobre Derechos y Garantías Constitucionales*, Caracas 2007. See also Allan R. BREWER–CARÍAS, *Instituciones Políticas y Constitucionales*, Tomo V, *El derecho y la acción de amparo*, Editorial Jurídica Venezolana, Caracas 1998, pp. 163 et seq.

148 See the Supreme Court decision of July 7, 1991 (Case*: Tarjetas Banvenez*), in *Revista de Derecho Público*, N° 47, Editorial Jurídica Venezolana, Caracas 1991, pp. 169–174.

149 See in *Revista de Derecho Público,* N° 50, Editorial Jurídica Venezolana, Caracas 1992, pp. 183–184. See Allan R. BREWER–CARÍAS, "Observaciones críticas al Proyecto de Ley de la Acción de Amparo de los Derechos Fundamentales (1985)"; "Proyecto de Ley Orgánica sobre el Derecho de Amparo (1987)"; and "Propuestas de reforma al Proyecto de Ley Orgánica de Amparo sobre Derechos y Garantías Constitucionales (1987)", in *Estudios de Derecho Público, Tomo III, (Labor en el Senado 1985–1987)*, Ediciones del Congreso de la República, Caracas 1989, pp. 71–186; 187–204; 205–229

150 Regarding amparo of personal freedom and security the competent courts should be the Criminal First Instance courts (Article 40). Nonetheless, when the facts, acts or omissions harming or threatening to harm the constitutional right or guarantee occurs in a place where no First Instance court exists, the amparo action may be brought before and judge of the place, which must decide according to the law, and in a 24 hour delay it must send the files for consultation to the competent First Instance court (Article 9). Only in cases in which facts, actions or omissions of the President of the Republic, his Cabinet members, the National Electoral Council, the Prosecutor General, the Attorney general and the General Comptroller of the Republic are involved, the power to decide the amparo actions correspond in only instance to the Constitutional Chamber of the Supreme Tribunal of Justice (Article 8).

al harm, and the courts must decide based on the violation of the Constitution and not only on the violation of statutes.[151]

In all these other cases of "amparo" petitions filed jointly with other judicial means, contrary to the Mexican system, they do not substitute the ordinary or extraordinary judicial means by naming them all as "amparo"; only providing that the "amparo" claim can be filed jointly with those other judicial means"[152].

From all these regulations it results that the Venezuelan right for "amparo", as it happened with the Mexican system, also has certain peculiarities that distinguish it from the other similar institutions for the protection of the constitutional rights and guaranties established in Latin America.[153] Beside the adjective consequences of the "amparo" being a constitutional right, it can be characterized by the following trends:

First, the right of "amparo" can be exercised in Venezuela for the protection of all constitutional rights, not only of civil individual rights. Consequently, the social, economic, cultural, environmental and political rights declared in the Constitution and in international treaties are also protected by means of "amparo". The habeas corpus *is* an aspect of the right to constitutional protection, or one of the expressions of the *amparo*.

Second, the right to "amparo" seeks to assure protection of constitutional rights and guaranties against any disturbance in their enjoyment and exercise, whether originated by public authorities or by private individuals without distinction[154].

---

151 Decision of July 7, 1991. See the text in *Revista de Derecho Público*, N° 47, Editorial Jurídica Venezolana, Caracas 1991, pp. 169–174.

152 In this regard, the Supreme Court of Justice has clearly set forth the proceeding rules as follows: "The amparo claims filed jointly with another action or recourse have all the inherent adjective character of the actions' joint proceedings, that is: it must be decided by only one court (the one competent regarding the principal action), and both claims (amparo and nullity or other) must be heard in only one proceeding that has two stages: the preliminary one regarding the amparo, and the contradictory one, which must include in its final decision, the preliminary one which ends in such time, as well as the decision on the requested nullity. In other words, if because of the above analyzed characteristics the amparo order [for instance when the amparo is filed conjunctly with other action] is reduced only and exclusively to the preliminary suspension of a challenged act, the decision which resolves the requested nullity leaves without effects the preventive preliminary measure, whether the challenged act is declared null or not." *Idem*, p. 171.

153 See, in general, H. Fix Zamudio, *La protección procesal de los derechos humanos ante las jurisdicciones nacionales,* Madrid, 1982, pp. 366.

154 The Constitution makes no distinction in this respect, and thus the action for amparo is perfectly admissible against actions by individuals, the action for amparo has doubtlessly been conceived as a traditional means of protection against actions by the state and its authorities. However, despite this tradition of conceiving the action for protection as a means of protecting rights and guarantees against public actions, in Venezuela, the scope with which this is regulated by Article 27 of the Constitution allows the action for amparo to be brought against individual actions, that is to say, when the disruption of the enjoyment and exercise of rights originates from private individuals or organizations. This also differentiates the Venezuelan system from that which exists in other systems such as México or Spain, in which the "action

And in the case of disturbance by public authorities, the "amparo" is admissible against statutes, against legislative, administrative and judicial acts, and against material or factual courses of action of Public Administration or public officials.

Third, the decision of the judge, as a consequence of the exercise of this right to "amparo", whether through the pre–existing actions or recourses or by means of the autonomous action for "amparo", is not limited to be of a precautionary or preliminary nature, but to re–establish the infringed legal situation by deciding on the merits, that is, the constitutionality of the alleged disturbance of the constitutional right.

Fourth, since the Venezuelan system of judicial review is a mixed one, judicial review of legislation can also be exercised by the courts when deciding action for "amparo" when, for instance, the alleged violation of the right is based on a statute deemed unconstitutional. In such cases, if the protection requested is granted by the courts, it must previously declare the statute inapplicable on the grounds of it being unconstitutional. Therefore, in such cases, judicial review of the constitutionality of legislation can also be exercised when an action for "amparo" of fundamental rights is filed.

Finally, in the Venezuelan systems of judicial review and of "amparo", according to the 1999 Constitution an extraordinary review recourse can be filed before the Constitutional Chamber of the Supreme Court against judicial final decisions issued in "amparo" suits and also, against any judicial decision issued when applying the diffuse method of judicial review resolving the inapplicability of statutes because they are considered unconstitutional (Article 336,10).

The essential trend of this attribution of the Constitutional Chamber is its discretionary character[155] that allows it to choose the cases to be reviewed. As the same Constitutional Chamber of the Supreme Tribunal pointed it out in its decision N° 727 of April 8th, 2003, "in the cases of the decisions subject to revision, the Constitution does not provide for the creation of a third instance. What has set forth the constitutional provision is an exceptional and discretional power of the Constitutional Chamber that as such, must be exercised with maxim prudence regarding the admission of recourses for review final judicial decisions."[156]

---

for amparo" is solely conceived against public actions. For this reason, in Spain the recourse of amparo is expressed as a review of decisions by the administrative judicial court when reviewing administrative acts. See J. González Pérez, *Derecho procesal constitucional*, Madrid, 1980, p. 278.

155 As mentioned, in a certain way similar to the *writ of cerciorari* in the North American system. See Jesús María Casal, *Constitución y Justicia Constitucional,* Caracas 2002, p. 92.

156 See *Revisión de la sentencia dictada por la Sala Electoral en fecha 21 de noviembre de 2002* Case, in *Revista de Derecho Público*, N° 93–96, Editorial Jurídica Venezolana, Caracas 2003. See decision of November 2, 2000,*Roderick A. Muñoz P.* Case, in *Revista de Derecho Público*, N° 84, (octubre–diciembre), Editorial Jurídica Venezolana, Caracas 2000, p. 367

FINAL REMARKS

Any system of judicial review can be considered in its own context as the ultimate result of the process of consolidation of the rule of law. That is why, due to the general consolidation of democracy in contemporary world, it has had a very important development, being perhaps the most important trend of today's constitutional law. In particular, in Latin America, without doubts, it has been because of the consolidation of democracy, which during the past five decades is possible to find a very important, wide and varied catalogue of judicial review means such as the one previously analyzed.

Judicial review, consequently, is the most important instrument that democratic countries have in order to guarantee the supremacy of the Constitution, the rule of law and the enforcement of constitutional rights. Of course, in order to ensure such functions, Constitutional Courts or Tribunals, or the Supreme Courts or Tribunals need to be effectively independent and autonomous entities, at the exclusive service of the Constitution. On the contrary, if the power vested upon the Supreme Courts or the Constitutional Tribunals is exercised against the democratic principles, instead of being instruments to sustain the rule of law, they can constitute the most powerful instrument for the consolidation of authoritarian governments.

Consequently, it is evident that the sole regulation in a Constitution, of various methods of judicial review and of the corresponding actions and recourses, is not enough to guarantee the subjection of State powers to the Constitution, and particularly, to preserve the constitutional division and separation of powers, which still is the most important principle of democracy. The condition for such functions to be performed has always being the existence of a real, independent and autonomous judiciary, and in particular, of the adequate institutions (Constitutionals Court or Supreme Tribunals) disposed for controlling the constitutionality of State acts and capable of controlling the exercise of political power and of annulling unconstitutional State acts.

Unfortunately, in some Latin American countries like for instance, my own country, Venezuela, notwithstanding the formally marvelous system of judicial review enshrined in the Constitutions that I have previously described, which combines all the imaginable instruments and methods for that purpose; due to the concentration of state power developed during the past decade in the National Assembly and in the Executive, and due to the political control exercised upon the Supreme Tribunal of Justice, the rule of law has been progressively demolished, and the authoritarian elements enshrined in the 1999 Constitution, have been progressively developed and consolidated, precisely through the decisions of the Constitutional Chamber of the Supreme Tribunals, being the result, the progressive weakening of the rule of law.[157] In such cases, the politically controlled Constitutional judge (Constitutional Chamber of the Supreme Tribunal of Justice), instead of being the guarantor of constitutionalism, of democracy and of the rule of law, unfortunately has been the instrument used by the Government in order to cover up with some sort of "constitutional" or "legality" prints of camouflage, the authoritarian regime that has been developed.

PART II:
THE LATIN AMERICAN AMPARO PROCEEDING AND THE WRIT OF AMPARO IN THE PHILIPPINES

This Paper on the "The Latin American Amparo Proceeding and the Writ of Amparo in the Philippines," was written for the *Second Distinguish Lecture*, Series of 2007, which I was invited to deliver in Manila in March 2008, in an event organized by the Supreme Court of the Philippines, the Judicial Academy and the Philippine Association of Law Schools. The text was published as "The Latin American Amparo Proceeding and the Writ of Amparo in The Philippines," in the *City University of Hong Kong Law Review,* Volume 1:1 October 2009, pp 73–90

INTRODUCTION

The *amparo* proceeding is a Latin American extraordinary judicial remedy specifically conceived for the protection of constitutional rights. It can be filed by the injured person against harms or threats inflicted to such rights, not only by authorities but also by individuals.

Although being indistinctly called as an 'action,' a 'recourse' or a 'suit' of *amparo*, it has always been configured as a whole judicial proceeding that normally concludes with a judicial order or writ of 'protection'.[158] That is why, in Latin Amer-

---

157 See Allan R. BREWER–CARÍAS, *Dismantling Democracy in Venezuela: The Chávez Authoritarian Experiment*, Cambridge University Press, New York 2010.

158 In Spanish, *amparo, protección* or *tutela* are all used to express the same meaning, See Héctor Fix–Zamudio and Eduardo Ferrer Mac–Gregor (Coord), *El Derecho de Amparo en el Mundo* (Editorial Porrúa, México 2006); Allan R BREWER–CARÍAS, *El Amparo a los Derechos y Libertades Constitucionales: Una Aproximación Comparativa,* (Universidad Católica del Táchira, San Cristóbal 1993) 138; Allan R BREWER–CARÍAS, *Mecanismos Nacionales de Protección de los Derechos Humanos (Garantías Judiciales de los Derechos Humanos en el Derecho Constitucional Comparado Latinoamericano)* (Instituto Interamericano de Derechos Humanos, San José 2005); and Allan R BREWER–CARÍAS, *Constitutional Protection of Human Rights in Latin America: A Comparative Study on of the Amparo Proceeding* (Cambridge University Press, New York 2009).

ica, *amparo* is not merely a writ or a judicial protective order but a whole judicial proceeding.

This remedy has a long tradition in Latin America. It was introduced in the 19th century in Mexico and from there it spread to other countries. Although similar remedies were established during the 20th century in European countries[159] such as Austria,[160] Germany,[161] Spain[162] and Switzerland,[163] the institution remains more of a Latin American one, adopted in addition to the other two classical protective remedies of constitutional rights, the *habeas corpus* and *habeas data* actions.

The consequence of this development is that *amparo* influenced the introduction of a similar, although more restrictive remedy, in the Philippines, that is, the 'writ of *amparo*' created in 2007 by the Supreme Court of Philippines by means of the Rule on the Writ of *Amparo*, in order to reinforce the protection of the rights to life, to liberty and security.[164]

This article begins, in Part II, by highlighting the principal trends of the *amparo* proceeding in Latin America within the process of progressive protection of constitutional rights since the 19th century. Part III then offers an overview of the birth of the institution in Mexico and its evolution in Latin America. Considering that the recently established writ of *amparo* in the Philippines is inspired by the *amparo* proceedings in Latin America, Part IV compares and then contrasts the two institutions. Part V highlights various distinctive features of the *amparo* proceeding in Latin America.

---

159 See Allan R BREWER–CARÍAS, *Judicial Review in Comparative Law* (Cambridge University Press, Cambridge 1989); Fix–Zamudio and Mac–Gregor (2006) (n 158) 761 ff, 789 ff and 835 ff.

160 Article 144, Law of the Constitutional Tribunal. See F Ermacora, 'Procédures et Techniques de Protection des Droits Fundamentaux: Cour Constitutionnelle Autrichienne' in L Favoreu (ed), *Cours Constitutionnelles Européennes et Droit Fundamentaux* (Economica;Presses Universitaires d'Aix–Marseille, Paris 1982) 189.

161 Article 93(1)/(4)(a), Federal Constitutional Tribunal Law. See F Sainz Moreno, 'Tribunal Constitucional Federal Alemán' in Cortes Generales, *Boletín de Jurisprudencia Constitucional,* N° 8 (Boletín Oficial del Estado, Madrid 1981) 603; G Müller, 'E1 Tribunal Constitucional Federal de la República Federal de Alemania' (1965) 4 *Revista de la Comisión Internacional de Juristas* 222.

162 See Article 161(1)(b), Constitution; Article 41(2), Constitutional Tribunal Organic Law 2/1979. See Encarna Carmona Cuenca, 'El Recurso de Amparo Constitucional y el Recurso de Amparo Judicial' in *Revista Iberoamericana de Derecho Procesal Constitucional,* N° 5 (Instituto Iberoamericano de Derecho Procesal Constitucional, Editorial Porrúa, México 2006) 3–14.

163 Articles 84–88, Law of Judiciary Organization. See A Grisel, 'Réflexions sur la juridiction constitutionnelle et administrative en Suisse' in *Etudes et Documents*, N° 28 (Conseil d'Etat, Paris 1976) 255; E Zellweger, 'El Tribunal Federal Suizo en Calidad de Tribunal Constitucional' (1966) 7 *Revista de la Comisión Internacional de Juristas* 122; W J Wagner, *The Federal States and their Judiciary* (Mouton Co, The Hague 1959) 109.

164 'The Rule on the Writ of Amparo' in Resolution AM N° 07–9–12–SC of the Supreme Court of the Philippines of 25 September 2007. The Resolution was amended on 16 October 2007 and took effect on 24 October 2007.

I. PROGRESSIVE PROTECTION OF CONSTITUTIONAL RIGHTS

The Latin American system of constitutional protection of constitutional rights can be identified through a few basic yet important trends. The first being the long–standing tradition the countries have had of inserting in their constitutions a very extensive declaration of human rights, comprising not only civil and political rights, but also social, cultural, economic and environmental rights. This trend, for instance, can be contrasted with the relatively limited content of the United States (US) Bill of Rights, and also with the content of the 1987 Philippines Constitution, that merely enumerates civil rights.

This Latin American declarative trend began almost 200 years ago with the adoption in 1811 of the 'Declaration of Rights of the People' by the Supreme Congress of Venezuela, four days before the declaration of the Venezuelan Independence from Spain.[165] That is why, although having been a Spanish colony for three centuries, no Spanish constitutional influence can be found at the beginning of the 19th century Latin American modern state, which was conceived following the American and the French 18th century constitutional revolutionary principles.

However, in parallel to this declarative tradition, the second feature of the Latin American constitutional system regarding human rights has been the unfortunate process of their violations, which continues to occur in some countries where authoritarian governments have been installed defrauding democracy and the constitution.[166]

The third trend of the Latin American system of constitutional protection of human rights has been the progressive and continuous incorporation in the constitutions of 'open clauses' of rights, in the same sense as the IX Amendment to the US Constitution referring to the existence of other rights 'retained by the people' that are not enumerated in the constitutional text.[167] A similar clause can be found in all Latin American constitutions (except in Cuba, Chile, Mexico and Panama), in an even wider sense referring to others rights 'inherent to the human being' or to 'human dignity,' or derived from the 'nature of the human person.'

The fourth feature, also related to the progressive expansion of the content of the constitutional declarations of rights, is the express incorporation in the constitutions, in addition to the rights listed therein, of the rights enumerated in international treaties and conventions. For such purpose, the constitutions not only have given inter-

---

165 See Allan R BREWER–CARÍAS, *Las Constituciones de Venezuela,* Vol I (Academia de Ciencias Políticas y Sociales, Caracas 2008), 549 ff.

166 See, e.g., Allan R BREWER–CARÍAS, 'Constitution Making in Defraudation of the Constitution and Authoritarian Government in Defraudation of Democracy: The Recent Venezuelan Experience' in *Lateinamerika Analysen 19*, 1/2008, (GIGA,German Institute of Global and Area Studies, Institute of Latin American Studies, Hamburg 2008), 119–142.

167 For instance, in *Griswold v Connecticut* 381 US 479; 85 S Ct 1678, the Supreme Court declared that, even if it was not explicitly mentioned in the constitution, the right to marital privacy was to be considered as a constitutional right, embraced by the concept of liberty, and constitutionally protected. See also *Snyder v Massachusetts*, 291 US 97, 105; and *Poe v Ullman*, 367 US 497, 517.

national treaties and covenants the traditional statutory rank, similar to the US and to many countries in the world, but in many cases, the constitutions have given such international treaties supra–legal rank, constitutional rank and even supra–constitutional rank. In the latter case, some constitutions even grant pre–emptive status to international human rights treaties vis–a–vis the constitution itself, whenever they provide for more favourable rules for their exercise. This is the case, for example, of the Venezuelan Constitution.[168]

Regarding the hierarchy of international human rights treaties in some Latin American countries, even in the absence of express constitutional provisions, such treaties have also acquired constitutional value and status through constitutional interpretation. For example, when the constitutions themselves establish that constitutional rights must always be interpreted according to what it is set forth in those international human rights treaties. This is the case, for instance, with the Colombian Constitution[169] and of the Peruvian Constitutional Procedural Code.[170]

Within this process of internationalisation of human rights, a particular international treaty on the matter has had an exceptional impact in the Continent: it is the 1969 American Convention on Human Rights.[171] The importance of the Convention derives not only from the content of the declaration of rights, but also from the judicial guarantees established for the protection of human rights, even at the international level by the creation of the Inter American Court of Human Rights (IACHR), whose jurisdiction has been recognised by the Member States.[172]

This Convention was signed on 22 November 1969 and was ratified by all Latin American countries, except Cuba. The only American country that did not sign the Convention was Canada, and even though the US signed the Convention in 1977, it has not yet ratified it. This has also been the case of many Caribbean states, in particular, of Antigua and Barbuda, Bahamas, Belize, St Kitts and Nevis, St Lucia, St Vincent and the Grenadines. Trinidad and Tobago ratified the Convention on 3 April 1977, but denounced it on 28 May 1991.[173]

The importance of ratification of this Convention by all Latin American countries is that it has contributed to develop a very rich minimal standard on civil and political rights, common to all countries.

In addition to the above mentioned features, that characterise the Latin American constitutional system of protection of human rights, the other main feature of the system is the express provision in the constitutions of the judicial guarantee of hu-

168 Venezuelan Constitution, Article 23.

169 Columbian Constitution, Article 93.

170 Peruvian Constitutional Procedural Code, Article V.

171 See the text in Pedro Nikken, *Código de Derechos Humanos* (Editorial Jurídica Venezolana, Caracas 2006) 111 ff.

172 See Sergio García Ramírez (Coord), *La Jurisprudencia de la Corte Interamericana de Derechos Humanos* (Universidad Nacional Autónoma de México, Corte Interamericana de Derechos Humanos, México 2001) 1.200.

173 See http://www.oas.org/juridico/english/Sigs/b–32.html accessed 11 September 2009.

man rights. This is achieved by creating a specific judicial remedy for their protection, called the *amparo* proceeding, with different procedural rules to those provided in the general civil procedural code, in cases of protection of personal or property rights.

The judicial protection of human rights can be guaranteed in two ways. First, by means of ordinary or extraordinary suits, actions, recourses or writs prescribed in the general procedural codes. Second, through specific and separate judicial suits, actions or recourses particularly established for the protection of the constitutional rights and freedoms. Both options have been adopted in Latin American countries to protect human rights.

The provision of *amparo* remedy contrasts, for example, with the US constitutional system, where the protection of human rights is assured through the general judicial actions and equitable remedies that are also used to protect any other kind of personal or property rights or interests. In Latin America, on the contrary, and in part due to the traditional deficiencies of the general judicial means for granting effective protection to constitutional rights, the *amparo* proceeding has been developed to assure such protection.

II. BIRTH AND EVOLUTION OF THE AMPARO PROCEEDING

The *amparo* proceeding was first introduced in Mexico in 1857, being inspired, according to the unanimous opinion of all the Mexican scholars, by the American system of judicial review of constitutionality of statutes which was established just a few decades earlier in *Marbury v Madison*.[174]

Notwithstanding this influence, it can be said that the US model was only partially followed. The *amparo* suit in Mexico has evolved into a unique and very complex institution exclusively found in that country. In Mexico, the *amparo* suit, in addition to being the main instrument for the protection of human rights (*amparo libertad*), consists of a wide range of other protective judicial actions that can be filed against the state, which in all the other countries are always separate actions or recourses. The Mexican *amparo* suit, for instance, comprises actions for judicial review of the constitutionality and legality of statutes (*amparo contra leyes*), actions for judicial review of administrative actions (*amparo administrativo*), actions for judicial review of judicial decisions (*amparo casación*), and actions for protection of peasant's rights (*amparo agrario*). That is why the Mexican *amparo*, without doubt, has a comprehensive and unique character not to be found in any other Latin American country. Nonetheless, the Mexican *amparo* remains the most commonly referred to proceeding outside Latin America.[175]

After its introduction in Mexico, the *amparo* proceeding subsequently spread across all Latin America in the 19th century giving rise to the evolution of a very different specific judicial remedy established only for the purpose of protecting hu-

174 (1 Cranch) 137; 2L Ed 60 (1803)

175 See Héctor Fix–Zamudio, *Ensayos Sobre el Derecho de Amparo* (Editorial Porrúa, Mexico 2003).

man rights and freedoms and becoming in many cases more protective than the original Mexican institution.[176]

In addition to the *habeas corpus* recourse, and of course influenced by the initial Mexican institution, *amparo* was introduced in the second half of the 19th century in the constitutions of Guatemala (1879), El Salvador (1886) and Honduras (1894); and during the 20th century, in the constitutions of Nicaragua (1911), Brazil (*mandado de securança*, 1934), Panama (1941), Costa Rica (1946), Venezuela (1961), Bolivia, Paraguay, Ecuador (1967), Peru (1976), Chile (*recurso de protección*, 1976), and Colombia (*acción de tutela*, 1991).[177]

Since 1957, the *amparo* action was admitted through court decisions in Argentina.[178] The action was regulated by a special statute in 1966 and subsequently included in the 1994 Constitutional reform.[179] In the Dominican Republic the Supreme Court has also admitted the *amparo* action since 2000,[180] which in 2006 was regulated by a special statute.[181]

The consequence of this constitutional process is that in all the Latin American countries but Cuba, the *habeas corpus*, the *habeas data* and the *amparo* actions are regulated as specific judicial means exclusively designed for the protection of constitutional rights.

Except the Dominican Republic, the provisions for the action are expressly set forth in the constitutions;[182] and in all the countries, except Chile, the proceeding has

---

176 See Joaquín Brague Camazano, *La Jurisdicción Constitucional de la Libertad. Teoría General, Argentina, México, Corte Interamericana de Derechos Humanos* (Editorial Porrúa, México 2005) 156 ff.

177 See BREWER–CARÍAS (2009) (n 158); Fix–Zamudio and Mac–Gregor (2006) (n 158).

178 See the references to the *Samuel Kot Ltd case* (decision of 5 October 1958) in S V Linares Quintana, *Acción de Amparo* (Ed. Bibliográfica Argentina, Buenos Aires 1960) 25; José Luis Lazzarini, *El juicio de amparo* (La Ley, Buenos Aires 1987) 243 ff.

179 Constitution of Argentina, Article 43. See Oswaldo Alfredo Gozaíni, *Derecho Procesal Constitucional: Amparo* (Rubinzal–Culzoni Editores, Buenos Aires 2004) 245 ff.

180 See the reference to the *Productos Avon SA* case (decision of 24 February 1999) in *Iudicum et Vita, Jurisprudencia Nacional de América Latina en Derechos Humanos*, N° 7, Tomo I (Instituto Interamericano de Derechos Humanos, San José, Costa Rica 2000) 329 ff; Allan R BREWER–CARÍAS, 'La Admisión Jurisprudencial de la Acción de Amparo en Ausencia de Regulación Constitucional o Legal en la República Dominicana' in Ibid, 334; and Juan de la Rosa, *El Recurso de Amparo, Estudio Comparativo* (Editora Serrallés, Santo Domingo 2001) 69.

181 Law N° 437–06 (2006).

182 ARGENTINA: Constitución Nacional de la República Argentina, 1994; BOLIVIA: Constitución Política de la República de Bolivia, 2008); BRAZIL: Constituição da República Federativa do Brasil, 1988 (Last reform, 2005); COLOMBIA: Constitución Política de la República de Colombia, 1991 (Last reform 2005); COSTA RICA: Constitución Política de la República de Costa Rica, 1949 (Last reform 2003); CUBA: Constitución Política de la República de Cuba, 1976 (Last reform, 2002); CHILE: Constitución Poliítica de la República de Chile, 1980 (Last reform, 2005); ECUADOR: Constitución Política de la República de Ecuador, 2008; EL SALVADOR: Constituticón de la República de El Salvador, 1983 (Last reform, 2003); GUATEMALA: Constitución Poliítica de la República de Guatemala, 1989

been the object of statutory regulation as well.[183] Generally, these statutes are special ones enacted specifically to provide for the *amparo* proceedings. Nonetheless, in some countries, the special legislation also contains regulations regarding other judicial means for the protection of the constitution like the judicial review proceedings, and the petitions for *habeas corpus* and *habeas data*, as is the case in Bolivia, Guatemala, Peru, Costa Rica, Ecuador, El Salvador and Honduras. [184] Only in Panama and in Paraguay is the *amparo* proceeding regulated as a specific chapter of the General Procedural Judicial Code. [185]

In some constitutions, like the Guatemalan, Mexican and Venezuelan ones, the *amparo* action is conceived to protect all constitutional rights and freedoms including the protection of personal liberty. In such case, the *habeas corpus* is considered as a type of *amparo*, named for instance, recourse for personal exhibition (Guatema-

---

(Last reform 1993); HONDURAS: Constitución Política de la República de Honduras, 1982 (Last reform, 2005); MÉXICO: Constitución Política de los Estados Unidos Mexicanos, 1917 (Last reform, 2004); NICARAGUA: Constitución Política de la República de Nicaragua, 1987 (Last reform 2005); PANAMA: Constitución Política de la República de Panamá, 1972 (Last Reform, 1994); PARAGUAY: Constitución Política de la República de Paraguay, 1992; PERÚ: Constitución Política del Perú, 1993 (Last reform, 2005); REPÚBLICA DOMINICANA: Constitución Política de la República Dominicana, 2002; URUGUAY: Constitución Política de la República Oriental del Uruguay, 1967 (Last reform, 2004); VENEZUELA: Constitución de la República Bolivariana de Venezuela, 1999 (Amended 2009).

183 ARGENTINA: Ley N° 16.986, Acción de Amparo, 1966; BOLIVIA: Ley N° 1836, Ley del Tribunal Constitucional, 1998; BRAZIL: Lei N° 1.533, Mandado de Segurança, 1951; COLOMBIA: Decretos Ley N° 2591, 306 y 1382, Acción de Tutela, 2000; COSTA RICA: Ley N° 7135, Ley de la Jurisdicción Constitucional, 1989; CHILE: Auto Acordado de la Cortre Suprema de Justicia Sobre Tramitación del Recurso de Protección, 1992; ECUADOR: Ley N° 000, RO/99, Ley de Control Constitucional, 1997; EL SALVADOR: Ley de Procedimientos Constitucionales, 1960; GUATEMALA: Decreto N° 1–86, Ley de Amparo, Exhibición Personal y Constitucionalidad, 1986; HONDURAS: Ley Sobre Justicia Constitucional, 2004; MÉXICO: Ley de Amparo, Reglamentaria de Los Artículos 103 y 107 de la Constitución Política, 1936; NICARAGUA: Ley N° 49, Amparo, 1988; PANAMA: Código Judicial, Libro Cuarto: Instituciones de Garantía, 1999; PARAGUAY: Ley N° 1.337/88, Código Procesal Civil, Titulo II, El Juicio de Amparo, 1988; PERÚ: Ley N° 28.237, Código Procesal Constitucional, 2005; REPÚBLICA DOMINICANA: Ley N° 437–06 que Establece el Recurso de Amparo, 2006; URUGUAY: Ley N° 16.011, Acción de Amparo, 1988; VENEZUELA: Ley Orgánica de Amparo Sobre Derechos y Garantías Constitucionales, 1988. See the text of all these laws in Allan R Brewer–Carías, *Leyes de Amparo de America Latina* (Instituto de Administración Pública de Jalisco, Guadalajara, Mexico 2009).

184 In Peru, for instance, the Code on Constitutional proceedings repealed the previous statutes regulating the *amparo* and the *habeas corpus* recourses (Law 23.506 of 1982, and Law 25.398 of 1991). See Samuel B Abad Yupanqui et al, *Código Procesal Constitucional* (Editorial Palestra, Lima 2004).

185 See Allan R Brewer–Carías, 'Ensayo de Síntesis Comparativa sobre el Régimen del Amparo en la Legislación Latinoamericana' in *Revista Iberoamericana de Derecho Procesal Constitucional,* N° 9 (Instituto Iberoamericano de Derecho Procesal Constitucional, Editorial Porrúa, México 2008) 311–321.

la)[186] or *amparo* for the protection of personal freedom (Venezuela).[187] But in general, in all other Latin American countries,[188] in addition to the *amparo* action, a different recourse of *habeas corpus* has always been expressly established in the constitutions for the specific protection of personal freedom and integrity.

In recent times, in some countries such as Argentina, Ecuador, Paraguay, Peru and Venezuela, in addition to the *amparo* and *habeas corpus* recourses, the constitutions have also provided for a separate recourse called *habeas data*, by which any person can file a suit in order to obtain personal information regarding the content of the data referred to himself contained in public or private registries or data banks, and in case of false, inaccurate or discriminatory information, *habeas data* empowers the person to seek for suppression, rectification, confidentiality and updating of the information.[189]

As a result of this human rights protective process, the constitutional regulations regarding the protection of constitutional rights in Latin America are established in three different ways. First, by providing for three different remedies: the *amparo,* the *habeas corpus* and the *habeas data*, as is the case of Argentina, Brazil, Ecuador, Paraguay and Peru. Second, by establishing two remedies: the *amparo* and the *habeas corpus*, as is the case of Bolivia, Colombia, Costa Rica, Chile, the Dominican Republic, El Salvador, Honduras, Nicaragua, Panama and Uruguay, or the *amparo* and the *habeas data* as is the case of Venezuela. Third, by just establishing one general *amparo* action comprising the protection of personal freedom as is the case of Guatemala and Mexico.

In general terms, the rights to be protected by means of the *amparo* proceedings are all those declared in the constitution or those considered as having constitutional status. Only in an exceptional way have some constitutions reduced the protective scope of the *amparo* protection to only some constitutional guarantees or fundamental rights as is the case of Colombia, Chile and Mexico. This is the trend that has also been followed in Germany and Spain with the individual recourse for the protection or the *amparo* recourse, and more recently in the Philippines, with the writ of *amparo* conceived to protect only the right to life, liberty and security.

186 The Decree Nº 1–86 contained the Law on Amparo, Personal Exibition and Constitutionality, 1986. See Jorge Mario García La Guardia, 'La Constitución y su Defensa en Guatemala' in *La Constitución y su Defensa* (Universidad Nacional Autónoma de México, México 1984) 717–719.

187 The Organic Law on Amparo of the Constitutional Rights and Guaranties, 1988, contains the provisions regarding *habeas corpus*. See Allan R BREWER–CARÍAS et al, *Ley Orgánica de Amparo Sobre Derechos y Garantías Constitucionales* (Editorial Jurídica Venezolana, Caracas 2007).

188 As is the case of Argentina, Bolivia, Brazil, Colombia, Costa Rica, Chile, the Dominican Republic, Ecuador, El Salvador, Honduras, Nicaragua, Panama, Paraguay, Peru and Uruguay,

189 See, e.g., José Afonso da Silva, *Curso de Direito Constitucional Positivo* (Malheiros, Sao Paulo 2004); Oswaldo Alfredo Gozaíni, *Derecho Procesal Constitucional: Habeas Data* (Rubinzal–Culzoni Editores, Buenos Aires 2002); Miguel Ángel Ekmerkdjian and Calogero Pizzolo, *Hábeas Data*, (Depalma, Buenos Aires 1998).

As mentioned before, the American Convention on Human Rights, which now–a–days in Latin America is not only an international law text but also a text with internal law value, has played an important role regarding the consolidation of the *amparo* proceeding. In this sense, *amparo* is conceived in the Convention as a 'right to judicial protection', that is, the right of everyone to have 'a simple and prompt recourse, or any other effective recourse, before a competent court or tribunal for protection (*que la ampare*) against acts that violate his fundamental rights recognised by the Constitution or laws of the State or by this Convention.'[190]

In order to guarantee this right, the Convention imposes on the Member States the duty 'to ensure that any person claiming such remedy shall have his rights determined by the competent authority provided for by the legal system of the state', to develop 'the possibilities of judicial remedy', and 'to ensure that the competent authorities shall enforce such remedies when granted'.

In the words of the IACHR, this provision of the Convention is a 'general provision that gives expression to the procedural institution known as "*amparo*", which is a simple and prompt remedy designated for the protection of all of the rights recognised in the Constitution and laws of the Member States and by the Convention.'[191] The Convention also provides for the recourse of *habeas corpus* for the protection of the right to personal freedom and security, in cases of lawful arrests or detentions. [192]

Examining the *habeas corpus* and the *amparo* recourses, the IACHR has declared that the '*amparo* comprises a whole series of remedies and that *habeas corpus* is but one of its components,' so that in some instances '*habeas corpus* is viewed either as the *amparo* of freedom or as an integral part of *amparo*.'[193] In any case, the *amparo* in the Convention has been considered by the IACHR, as 'one of the basic pillars not only of the American Convention, but of the rule of law in a democratic society'[194].

Consequently, the IACHR has ruled that the Convention imposes 'the duty on the Member States to organise the governmental apparatus and, in general, all the structures through which public power is exercised, so that they are capable of juridically ensuring the free and full enjoyment of human rights.'[195]

190 American Convention on Human Rights, OAS Treaty Series N° 36, 1144 UNTS 123 (entered into force 18 July 1978) Article 25(1).

191 See Advisory Opinion OC–8/87 (30 January 1987) (*habeas corpus* in emergency situations) [32] in Ramírez (2001) (n 172) 1.008 ff.

192 American Convention on Human Rights (n 190) Article 7.

193 See Advisory Opinion OC–8/87 (n 191) [34] in Ramírez (2001) (n 172) 1.008 ff.

194 See *Castillo Páez case* (Peru) (1997) [83]; *Suárez Roseo case* (Ecuador) (1997) [65] and *Blake case* (Guatemala) (1998) [102] in Ramírez (2001) (n 172) 273 ff., 406 ff. and 372 ff. See also the Advisory Opinion OC–8/87 (n 191) [42] and the Advisory Opinion OC–9/87 (6 October 1987) (Judicial Guarantees in Status of Emergency) [33] in Ramírez (2001) (n 172) 1.008 ff and 1.019 ff.

195 *Velásquez Rodríguez case* (decision of 29 July 1988) [166], in Ramírez (2001) (n 172) 58 ff.

III. COMPARATIVE ANALYSIS OF THE AMAPRO PROCEEDING IN LATIN AMERICA AND THE PHILIPPINES WRIT OF AMPARO

In order to compare the Latin American *amparo* proceeding with the Philippines writ of *amparo*, it is important to compare the general principles of the American Convention on Human Rights comparing them and the Latin American national statutes.[196] It is also important to determine how the member States have conducted themselves 'so as to effectively ensure the free and full exercise of human rights.'[197] Referring to *amparo* as a judicial guaranty of human rights, the IACHR has ruled that 'for such a remedy to exist, it is not sufficient that it be provided for by the Constitution or by statute or that it be formally recognised, but rather it must be truly effective in establishing whether there has been a violation of human rights and in providing redress.'[198] In this regard, of course, the existence of an autonomous and independent judiciary is essential.

From what is provided in Article 25 of the Convention regarding the *amparo* action, the following elements characterize such action in Latin America.

First, under the Convention, the *amparo* action is conceived for the protection of all constitutional rights, not only those listed in the Convention, the Constitutions of the Member States and in statutes, but also all those rights that can be considered inherent to the human person and human dignity.

However, it should be noted that if it is true that this is the rule, not all the Latin American countries follow this general trend of the Convention, in the sense that in some countries not all constitutional rights can be protected by the *amparo* actions. This is the situation, as already mentioned, in the case of Germany and Spain regarding the individual protection action or the *amparo* recourse, which are only established to protect 'fundamental rights', that is, basically, civil rights and individual liberties. In Latin America it is also the case in respect of the Constitutions of Chile and Columbia which have reduced the list of rights that can be protected by means of the actions for *tutela* or *protección*, also to those considered as 'fundamental rights'. This is also the position in the case of Mexico where the *amparo* suit is conceived only for the protection of 'individual guarantees.'

Nonetheless, this restrictive configuration of the *amparo* is nowadays exceptional in Latin America in that the *amparo* proceeding is being used to protect all constitutional rights, including the social and economic rights. And even in those countries where the restrictive approach exists (e.g., Colombia), the restriction has been overcome through constitutional interpretation, allowing the courts to develop the doc-

---

196 See Allan R BREWER–CARÍAS, 'El amparo en América Latina: La Universalización del Régimen de la Convención Americana sobre los Derechos Humanos y la Necesidad de Superar las Restricciones Nacionales,'in *Etica y Jurisprudencia*, 1/2003 (Universidad Valle del Momboy, Facultad de Ciencias Jurídicas y Políticas, Centro de Estudios Jurídicos "Cristóbal Mendoza", Valera, Estado Trujillo 2004) 9–34.

197 *Velásquez Rodríguez case* (n 195) [167].

198 Advisory Opinión OC–9/87 (n 191) [24]; *Comunidad Mayagna (Sumo) Awas Tingni case* [113]; *Ivcher Bronstein case* [136]; *Cantoral Benavides case* [164]; *Durand y Ugarte case* [102] in Ramírez (2001) (n 172) 1019 ff, 710 ff, 768 ff, 452 ff, 484 ff.

trine of the interrelation, universality, indivisibility, connection and interdependence of human rights, with the result that almost all constitutional right can be protected by the action of *tutela*.[199] That is how, for instance, the right to health has been protected because of its connection to the right to life.[200]

In the case of the Philippines, in a certain way established in order to supplement the inefficiency of the traditional writ of *habeas corpus*,[201] the Rule on the Writ of *Amparo* was sanctioned by the Supreme Court in 2007. In the words of Chief Justice Reynato Puno announcing the Rule on 25 September 2007, the writ of *amparo* has the purpose of protecting the constitutional right to life, liberty and security, mainly by providing 'the victims of extralegal killings and enforced disappearances the protection they need and the promise of vindication for their rights', so that 'the sovereign Filipino people should be assured that if their right to life and liberty is threatened or violated, they will find vindication in our courts of justice.'[202]

The writ of *amparo* was created by the Supreme Court as a remedy available to any person only for the protection of the rights to life, liberty and security when violated or threatened with violation by an unlawful act or omission of a public official or employee, and a private individual or entity.[203] In addition, the Supreme Court also created the writ of *habeas data*,[204] as a remedy available to any person, whose right to privacy also limited to life, liberty or security is violated or threatened by an unlawful act or omission of a public official or employee, or of a private individual or entity engaged in the gathering, collecting or storing of information regarding the person, family, home and correspondence of the aggrieved party'.[205]

Even though, according to the Philippines Constitution, the Supreme Court is empowered to 'promulgate rules concerning the protection and enforcement of constitutional rights',[206] the writ of *amparo* was not established for the protection of all constitutional rights, that is, all the human or fundamental rights declared in the Constitution, but only the rights to life, liberty and security.

Second, the Latin American *amparo* proceeding is conceived as not only a judicial means for the protection of constitutional rights, but is also conceived as a human right in itself in some countries. Therefore, the judicial guarantee can also be obtained through various other judicial means, for instance, under the Mexican and Venezuelan legal systems.

---

199 See Juan Carlos Esguerra Portocarrero, *La Protección Constitucional del Ciudadano* (Legis, Bogotá 2004); Julio César Ortiz Gutierrez, 'La Acción de Tutela en la Carta Política de 1991: El Derecho de Amparo y su Influencia en el Ordenamiento Constitucional de Colombia' in Fix–Zamudio and Mac–Gregor (n 158) 13–256.

200 See decision T–406 of 5 June in Manuel José Cepeda, *Derecho Constitucional Jurisprudencial. Las Grandes Decisiones de la Corte Constitucional* (Legis, Bogotá 2001) 55–63.

201 Rule 102, Revised Rules of Court.

202 See the text available at News, Inquirer.net <http://www.inquirer.net/> (31 December, 2007)

203 Section 1, Rule on the Writ of *Amparo*.

204 The Rule on the Writ of *Habeas Data* (entered into force 2 February 2008).

205 *Ibid,* Article 1, The Rule on the Writ of *Habeas Data*

206 Philippines Constitution, Article VIII, Section 5(5).

This right to *amparo* or to protection is considered in the Convention as a 'fundamental' one, to the point that it cannot be suspended or restricted in cases of state of emergency.[207] Applying it, the IACHR has considered the suspension of both *habeas corpus* and *amparo* in emergency situations as completely 'incompatible with the international obligations imposed on the States by the Convention'.[208] The IACHR has emphasised that 'the declaration of a state of emergency... cannot entail the suppression or ineffectiveness of the judicial guaranties that the Convention requires the Member States to establish for the protection of the rights not subject to derogation or suspension by the state of emergency' and 'therefore, any provision adopted by virtue of a state of emergency which results in the suspension of those guaranties is a violation of the Convention.'[209]

This doctrine of the IACHR has been very important regarding the protection of human rights in Latin America, particularly when considering the unfortunate past experiences that some countries have had situations of emergency or of state of siege, especially under former military dictatorship or internal civil war cases. In such cases, no effective judicial protection was available to safeguard people's life and physical integrity, to prevent their disappearance or their whereabouts to be kept secret, to protect persons against torture or other cruel, inhumane, or degrading punishment or treatment.

On the other hand, considering *amparo* as a specific judicial remedy for the protection of human rights, the internal legislations in the countries have always conceived the *amparo* action as an extraordinary remedy, which is only available when there are no other effective judicial means available for the immediate protection of human rights. Moreover, the internal regulations provide that if a previous action has been filed seeking the protection of the constitutional right, then the extraordinary mean cannot be filed.

No similar provision is found in the Rule on the Writ of *Amparo* of the Philippines. These rules though contain an indirect provision as a condition of inadmissibility of the writ of *amparo* in cases 'when a criminal action has been commenced.' In these situations, the Rules then provide that 'no separate petition for the writ shall be filed', and expressly establishes that 'the reliefs under the writ shall be available by motion in the criminal case.'[210]

Being a judicial mean for the protection of rights, the Convention refers to *amparo* as an action that can be brought before the 'competent courts', in the sense of considering the protection of human rights as an essential function of the judiciary. That is why, in almost all Latin American countries, the jurisdiction for *amparo* cases corresponds in general terms to all the first instance courts, the only exception being the cases in which the competence on *amparo* is assigned to one single court. For instance, in Costa Rica, El Salvador and Nicaragua, the Constitutional Chamber

---

207 Article 27 of the Convention

208 Advisory Opinión OC–8/87 (n 191) [37], [42] and [43].

209 Advisory Opinion OC–9/87 (n 194).

210 Rule on the Writ of *Amparo* of the Philippines, Section 22.

of the Supreme Courts of these countries is the only court with exclusive power to decide the *amparo* cases.[211] Similarly, the individual action for protection and the *amparo* recourse in Germany and Spain can only be filed before the respective Constitutional Court or Tribunal.

In the Philippines, following the general Latin American trend, the petition for the writ of *amparo* can be filed before a variety of courts, namely the Regional Trial Court of the place where the threat, act or omission was committed or any of its elements occurred, or with the Court of Appeals, the Supreme Court, or any justice of such courts.[212]

As mentioned before, in order to guarantee the effective protection of human rights in any case, what is essential and necessary is that the courts empowered to decide *amparo* must really be independent and autonomous ones. *Amparo* will be no more than an illusion if the general conditions prevailing in the country, particularly regarding the judiciary, cannot assure its effectiveness. This is the case, as was ruled by the IACHR, 'when the judicial power lacks the necessary independence to render impartial decisions or the means to carry out its judgments; or in any other situation that constitutes a denial of justice, as there is an unjustified delay in the decision; or when, for any reason, the alleged victim is denied access to a judicial remedy.'[213]

The third element provided by the Convention regarding the action for *amparo* is that it must be a 'simple, prompt and effective' instrument.[214] The simplicity implies that the procedure must lack the dilatory procedural formalities of ordinary judicial means, imposing the need to grant immediate constitutional protection. Regarding the prompt character of the recourse, the IACHR, for instance, has argued about the need for a reasonable delay for the decision, not considering 'prompt' recourses those resolved after 'a long time'.[215] The effective character of the recourse refers to the capability to produce the results for which it has been created.[216] In the words of the IACHR, 'it must be truly effective in establishing whether there has been a violation of human rights and in providing redress.'[217]

For these purposes, many Latin American *Amparo* Laws expressly provide for some general procedural principles to avoid unnecessary delays. For instance, in Colombia, the Tutela Law refers to 'the principles of publicity, prevalence of substantial law, economy, promptness and efficacy';[218] in Ecuador, the Law refers to 'the principles of procedural promptness and immediate [response]' (*inmediatez*);[219] in Honduras, mention is made to the 'principles of independence, morality of the

211 See BREWER–CARÍAS (n 158).

212 Section 3, Rule on the Writ of *Amparo*.

213 Advisory Opinion OC–9/87 (n 194) [24].

214 *Suárez Romero case* [66] in Ramírez (2001) (n 172) 406 ff.

215 *Ivcher Bronstein case* [140]. *Ibid* 768 ff.

216 *Velásquez Rodríguez case* [66] *Ibid* 58 ff.

217 Advisory Opinion OC–9/87 (n 194) [24].

218 Article 3, Colombia Tutela Law

219 Article 59, Ecuador Law

debate, informality, publicity, prevalence of substantial law, freedom, promptness, procedural economy, effectiveness, and due process;'[220] and in Peru, the Code refers to 'the principles of judicial direction of the process: freedom regarding the plaintiff's acts, procedural economy, immediacy and socialization' (Article III). It is in this sense that Article 27 of the Venezuelan Constitution also expressly provides that the procedure of the constitutional *amparo* action must be oral, public, brief, free and not subject to formality.

For these reasons, in the *amparo* proceeding, as a general rule, the procedural terms cannot be extended, nor suspended, nor interrupted, except in cases expressly set forth in the statute; any delay in the procedure being the responsibility of the courts. Similarly, in the *amparo* proceeding, no procedural incidents are generally allowed,[221] and in some cases no recuse or motion to recuse the judges are admitted or they are restricted. In fact, some *amparo* laws provide for specific and prompt procedural rules regarding the cases in which the competent judge is impeded from resolving the case. Section 11 of the Philippines Rule on the Writ of *Amparo* embodies this spirit in that it is very precise in enumerating the different pleadings and motions that are prohibited on matters of the *amparo* procedure.[222]

The fourth element of the *amparo* remedy, as mentioned before, is that it is conceived to protect everybody's rights (in the very broadest sense of the term), without distinction or discrimination of any kind, whether individuals, nationals or foreigners. The protective tendency for the implementation of *amparo* has also gradually allowed interested parties to act in representation of diffuse or collective rights, like the right to safe environment or to health, the violation of which affects the community as a whole, as has been expressly established in the constitutions of Argentina, Brazil, Colombia, Costa Rica and Venezuela.[223]

Though the American Convention on Human Rights declares human rights in the strict sense of the term as rights belonging to human persons, the internal regulations of the countries have also assured private corporations or entities the right to file *amparo* actions for the protection of their constitutional rights, such as the right to non–discrimination, right to due process or right to own defence.[224]

---

220 Article 45, Honduras Law

221 See Honduras Law: Article 70; Uruguay Law: Article 12; Panama Law: Article 2610; Paraguay Code: Article 586; Uruguay Law: Article 12.

222 Section 11, Rule on the Writ of *Amparo*: '1. Motion to dismiss; 2. Motion for extension of time to file return, opposition, affidavit, position paper and other pleadings; 3. Dilatory motion for postponement; 4. Motion for a bill of particulars; 5. Counterclaim or cross–claim; 6. Third–party complaint; 7. Reply; 8. Motion to declare respondent in default; 9. Intervention; 10. Memorandum; 11. Motion for reconsideration of interlocutory orders or interim relief orders; and 12. Petition for certiorari, mandamus or prohibition against any interlocutory order'.

223 Argentina Consttution: Article 43; Brazil Constitution: Article 5, LXIII; Costa Rica Constitution: Article 50; Colombia Constitution: Article 88; Venezuela Constitution: Article 24.

224 See Brewer–Carías (n 158) 188.

The fifth feature of the constitutional *amparo* protection guaranteed in the Convention is its universal scope in the sense that it can be filed against any act, omission, fact or action that violates or threatens to violate them, without specifying the origin or the author of the harm or threat. This implies that the *amparo* action can be brought before the courts against any person, that is, not only against the State or public authorities, but also against private individuals and corporations.

Consequently, and in contrast with for instance the Spanish *amparo* action conceived to protect against only authorities, the *amparo* against individuals has been broadly admitted in the majority of Latin American countries, following a trend that began fifty years ago in Argentina, where the Supreme Court admitted such possibility.[225] Nowadays, the *amparo* action against individuals is expressly recognised in the constitutions of Argentina, Bolivia, Paraguay and Peru.[226] In other countries, such as Costa Rica, Nicaragua, the Dominican Republic, Uruguay and Venezuela, *amparo* against individuals is provided in the Laws on *Amparo*,[227] or it has been accepted by courts' decisions (Chile).[228] In other constitutions, it is admitted only regarding certain individuals, such as those who act as agents exercising public functions, or who exercise some kind of public prerogatives, or who are in a position of control, for example, when rendering public services by means of a concession.[229]

Only in Brazil, El Salvador, Guatemala, Mexico and Panama, the possibility to file an *amparo* action against private individuals has been excluded;[230] a situation that is distant from the orientation of the American Convention on Human Rights.

On this point, the Philippines petition for the writ of *amparo* follows the general trends of the Latin American *amparo* in that it is a remedy available to any person for the protection of the right to life, liberty and security when violated or threatened

---

225 See *Samuel Kot* case (n 178). See the references in Quintana (n 178) 25; Lazzarini (n 178) 16 ff; Alí Joaquín Salgado, *Juicio de Amparo y Acción de Inconstitucionalidad* (Editorial Astrea, Buenos Aires 1987) 6; Susana Albanese, *Garantías Judiciales: Algunos Requisitos del Debido Proceso Legal en el Derecho Internacional de los Derechos Humanos* (S A Editora, Buenos Aires, 2000); Augusto M. Morillo et al, *El Amparo Régimen Procesal* (3rd edn Librería Editora Platense SRL, La Plata 1998) 430; Néstor Pedro Sagües, *Derecho Procesal Constitucional,* Vol 3, *Acción de Amparo* (2nd edn Editorial Astrea, Buenos Aires 1988) 12 ff.

226 Argentina Constitution: Article 43; Bolivia Constitution: Article 19; Paraguay Constitution: Article 134; Peru Constitution: Article 200.

227 Costa Rica Law: Article 57; Nicaragua Law: Article 23; Dominican Republic Law: Article 1; Peru Code: Article 2; Uruguay Law: Article 1; Venezuela Law: Article 2.

228 See Humberto Nogueira Alcalá, 'El Derecho de Amparo o Protección de los Derechos Humanos, Fundamentales o Esenciales en Chile: Evolución y Perspectivas' in Humberto Nogueira Alcalá (ed), *Acciones Constitucionales de Amparo y Protección: Realidad y Perspectivas en Chile y América Latina* (Editorial Universidad de Talca, Talca 2000) 41.

229 Colombia Law: Articles 5 and 42; Ecuador Constitution: Article 95; and Honduras Law: Article 42.

230 Brazil Constitution: Article 5, LXIX; El Salvador Law: Article 12; Guatemala Constitution: Article 265; Mexico Constitution: Article 103; Panama Constitution: Article 50.

with violation by an unlawful act or omission, not only of a public official or employee, but also of a private individual or entity.[231]

IV. DISTINCTNESS OF THE AMPARO WRIT IN LATIN AMERICA

If *amparo* is a judicial means for the protection of human rights, it is a petition or action that can be filed against any public act that violates them, and therefore, no act must be excluded from the possibility to be challenged through the *amparo* action.

Nevertheless, a tendency towards excluding certain public acts from the purview of *amparo* remedy can also be identified in Latin America in different areas. In some countries, the exclusion refers to actions of certain public authorities, such as the electoral bodies, whose acts are expressly excluded from the recourse of *amparo*.[232] In other cases, like in Peru, an exclusion from the scope of constitutional protection of the *amparo* proceeding is provided only with respect to the acts of the National Council of the Judiciary.

In other cases, the exclusion refers to certain State acts, e.g., against judicial decisions, as is the case of Argentina, Uruguay, Costa Rica, the Dominican Republic, Panama, El Salvador, Honduras, Nicaragua and Paraguay. On the contrary, in many other countries the *amparo* proceeding is admitted against judicial decisions, as is the case of Colombia, Honduras, Guatemala, Mexico, Panama, and Venezuela.[233]

The case of Colombia must be highlighted, because in spite of the *tutela* action being admitted against judicial decisions, the Constitutional Court in 1992 considered that possibility as contrary to the principle of *res judicata*, and consequently annulled the article of the statute which provided for it.[234] However, in spite of this annulment, all the main courts of the country (Supreme Court, Constitutional Court and Council of State) progressively began to admit the action of *tutela* against judicial decisions in cases of arbitrary decisions.[235] Similarly, in Peru, the *amparo* action against judicial decisions is admitted when they are issued outside a regular procedure.

Another general feature of the Latin American *amparo* recourse, as well as the *habeas corpus*, is that as judicial means for the protection of constitutional rights, they have a personal or subjective character which implies that in principle they must be filed by the injured party. This implies that no one else can file an action for *amparo* alleging in his/her own name a right belonging to another.

Nonetheless, some Latin American *amparo* statutes authorise persons other than different to the injured parties or their representatives to file the *amparo* suit on their

---

231 Section 1, Rule on the Writ of *Amparo*.

232 As is the case of Costa Rica, Mexico, Nicaragua, Panama, Peru and Uruguay

233 See BREWER–CARÍAS (n 158) 320 ff.

234 See Decision C–543/92 (24 September 1992). See Manuel José Cepeda Espinosa, *Derecho Constitucional Jurisprudencial: Las Grandes Decisiones de la Corte Constitucional* (Legis, Bogotá 2001) 1009 ff.

235 Decision T–231 (13 May 1994) *Ibid* 1022 ff.

behalf, particularly, regarding minors. In this case, the Mexican Law exceptionally allows minors to act personally in cases when their representatives are absent or impaired.[236] In Colombia, when the representative of a minor is in a situation of inability to assume his defence, anyone can act on behalf of the injured party.[237]

Except in these cases where the representatives of incapacitated natural persons are called to act on their behalf, the general rule of standing is that the injured persons must act in their own defence and no other person can judicially act on their behalf, except when acting through legally appointed representatives.

Nonetheless, a general exception to this principle refers to the action of *habeas corpus*, in which case, since generally the injured person is physically prevented from acting personally because of detention or restrained freedom, the *amparo* laws authorise anybody to file the action on his/her behalf (e.g., Argentina, Bolivia, Guatemala, Honduras, México, Nicaragua, Peru, Venezuela).

In this same sense, some *amparo* laws, in order to guarantee the constitutional protection, also establish the possibility for other persons to act on behalf of the injured party and file the action in his/her name. It can be any lawyer or relative as established in Guatemala,[238] or it can be anybody, as is set forth in Paraguay,[239] Ecuador, Honduras, Uruguay and Colombia, where anyone can act on behalf of the injured party when the latter is in a situation of inability to assume his own defence.[240] The same principle is established in the Peruvian Code on Constitutional Procedures.[241] In México, the Law imposes on the injured party the obligation to expressly ratify the filing of the *amparo* suit, to the extent that if the complaint is not ratified it will be considered as not filed.[242] In the Philippines, although the Rule on the Writ of *Amparo* provides that the petition must be filed by the aggrieved person, section 2 lays down that another 'qualified person or entity' is entitled to file the petition, that is, any member of the immediate family (spouse, children and parents of the aggrieved party) or any ascendant, descendant or collateral relative of the aggrieved party. Also any concerned citizen, organisation, association or institution can also file the petition if there is no known member of the immediate family or relative of the aggrieved.

CONCLUSION

As readers may note from the above discussion, the *amparo* proceeding in Latin America, that derives not only from the provisions of the constitutions but also from

236 Mexico Constitution, Article 6.

237 Colombia Constitution, Article 10.

238 Article 23, Guatemala Law.

239 Article 567, Paraguay Code.

240 Article 10, Colombia Law.

241 Article 41, Peru Code.

242 Article 17, Mexico Law.

the statutes on *amparo*, contain a unique and impressive set of norms for the protection of constitutional rights.

The formal regulations of *amparo* are important but not enough to assure the effectiveness of the said remedy, which really depends on the existence of an effective independent and autonomous judiciary which may only be possible in democratic societies.

This is the basic condition for the enjoyment of constitutional rights and for their protection, to the point that the judicial protection of human rights can be achieved in democratic regimes even without the existence of formal constitutional declarations of rights or of the provisions for extraordinary means or remedies. Conversely, even with extensive declarations of rights and the provision of the *amparo* proceeding in the constitutions to assure their protection, the effectiveness of it depends on the existence of a democratic political system based on the rule of law, the principle of the separation of powers, the existence of a checks and balances between different branches of the government, and on the possibility for the State powers to be effectively controlled, among other, by means of the judiciary. Only in such situations, it is possible for a person to effectively have his rights protected.

In the case of the Philippines, the sole fact that the Supreme Court has adopted two extraordinary judicial means (i.e., writs of *amapro* and *habeas data*) for the purpose of protecting the constitutional right to life, liberty and security, is an important sign of its independence and autonomy. At the same time, it must also be highlighted that the very important protective judicial are only devoted to protect just a few, although fundamental, constitutional guarantees, that is, the rights to life, liberty, security and privacy. Thus, some constitutional rights provided for in the Constitution of the Philippines, are out of the scope of the protection offered by *amparo* and *habeas data*.

Even though the Rules adopted by the Supreme Court of Philippines have been and are of great importance and constitute a great beginning regarding the protection of constitutional rights it remains in the hand of the same Supreme Court to enlarge the protection, because it is empowered by the Constitution to 'promulgate rules concerning the protection and enforcement of constitutional rights'.[243] The Latin American experience on these matters, without doubt, can be very useful for such purposes, as I have tried to explain.

243 Article VIII, Section 5,5, Phillipines Constitution.

V
JUDICIAL REVIEW AND AMPARO PROCEEDING IN VENEZUELA (2008-2011)

PART I.

JUDICIAL REVIEW IN VENEZUELA

Paper prepared for the "Seminar on Judicial Review in the Americas . . . and Beyond," Duquesne University School of Law, Pittsburgh, Pennsylvania (November 2006); published in *Duquesne Law Review*, Volume 45, Number 3, Spring 2007, pp. 439-465

INTRODUCTION

Judicial review of constitutionality[1] is the power assigned to the courts to decide upon the constitutionality of statutes and other gorvenmental acts; therefore, it can only exist in legal systems in which there is a written and rigid Constitution, imposing limits to the state organs, and particularly to Parliament. That is why judicial review of the constitutionality of state acts has been considered as the ultimate result of the consolidation of the *rule of law*, extensively developed in the Americas due to the democratization process.

In his welcoming letter to the Seminar on "Judicial Review in the Americas . . . and Beyond," Professor Robert S. Barker referred to the fact that, since the United States Supreme Court decision of *Marbury v. Madison*[2] two hundred years ago, "ju-

1. See Allan R. Brewer-Carías, *Judicial Review in Comparative Law,* Cambridge University Press, Cambridge 1989, p. 215.
2. 5 U.S. 137 (1803).

dicial review of the constitutionality of statutes has been an integral part of the law and politics of the United States." To this we must add that in a certain way, that has also been the situation in all Latin American countries, particularly since democracy has been reinforced in the political systems of our countries, even with all its inconsistencies.

We must not forget when we talk about judicial review that, above all, it is an institutional tool which is essentially linked to democracy; democracy understood as a political system not just reduced to the fact of having elected governments, but where separation and control of power and the respect and enforcement of human rights is possible through an independent and autonomous judiciary. And precisely, it has been because of this process of reinforcement of democracy in Latin American countries that judicial review of the constitutionality of legislation and other governmental actions has become an important tool in order to guarantee the supremacy of the Constitution, the rule of law, and the respect of human rights. It is in this sense that judicial review of the constitutionality of state acts has been considered as the ultimate result of the consolidation of the *rule of law*, when precisely in a democratic system the courts can serve as the ultimate guarantor of the Constitution, effectively controlling the exercise of power by the organs of the state.[3]

On the contrary, as happens in all authoritarian regimes even having elected governments, if such control is not possible, the same power vested, for instance, upon a politically controlled Supreme Court or Constitutional Court, can constitute the most powerful and diabolical instrument for the consolidation of authoritarianism, the destruction of democracy, and the violation of human rights.[4]

Unfortunately this is what has been happening in my country, Venezuela, where after decades of democratic ruling through which we constructed one of the most formally complete systems of judicial review in South America, that same system has been the instrument through which the politically controlled judiciary, and particularly the subjected Constitutional Chamber of the Supreme Tribunal, have been consolidating the authoritarian regime we now have.

With this important warning, allow me to try to explain the general trends governing the very comprehensive judicial review system established in Venezuela, in many aspects, since the nineteenth century, and to try to classify it within a constitutional comparative law framework.

---

3. See Hans Kelsen, "La garantie juridictionnelle de la Constitution (La Justice constitutionnelle)," in *Revue du droit public et de la science politique en France et à l'étranger*, T. XLV, 1928, pp.197-257

4. See Allan R. Brewer-Carías, «*Quis Custodiet ipsos Custodes*: De la interpretación constitucional a la inconstitucionalidad de la interpretación», in *VIII Congreso Nacional de derecho Constitucional, Perú*, Fondo Editorial 2005, Colegio de Abogados de Arequipa, Arequipa, Sept. 2005, pp. 463-489.

I. A GENERAL OVERVIEW OF THE SYSTEMS OF JUDICIAL REVIEW AND THE VENEZUELAN SYSTEM

This guarantee can always be analyzed according to the criteria established a few decades ago by Mauro Cappelletti[5] who, following the trends of the so-called "North American" and "European" systems, distinguished between the "diffuse" (decentralized) and "concentrated" (centralized) methods of judicial review of the constitutionality of legislation. The former is exercised by all the courts of a given country, while the latter is only assigned to a Supreme Court or to a court specially created for that purpose such as a Constitutional Court or Tribunal.

In the diffuse, or decentralized, method, all the courts are empowered to judge the constitutionality of statutes, as is the case in the United States of America, where the "diffuse method"[6] was born. That is why it is also referred as the "American model," initiated with *Marbury v. Madison*[7] in 1803, later followed in many countries with or without a common law tradition. It is called "diffuse" or decentralized because judicial control is shared by all courts, from the lowest level up to the Supreme Court of the country. In Latin America, the only country that has kept the diffuse method of judicial review as *the only* judicial review method available is Argentina. In other Latin American countries, the diffuse method coexists with the concentrated method.[8]

The "concentrated" or centralized method of judicial review, in contrast with the diffuse method, empowers only one single court to control the constitutionality of legislation, utilizing annulatory powers. This can be achieved by a Supreme Court or a constitutional court created specially for that particular purpose. The concentrated or centralized system is also called the "Austrian" or "European" model because it was first established in Austria in 1920, and later developed in Germany, Italy, Spain, Portugal and France. This method has also been adopted in many Latin American countries, in some cases as *the only* form of judicial review applied.[9] In other countries, as mentioned, it is applied conjunctly with the diffuse method.[10]

It has been this mixture, or parallel functioning, of the diffuse and concentrated methods, which has given rise to what can be considered the "Latin American" model of judicial review. This model can be identified in Brazil, Colombia, the Dominican Republic, Ecuador, Guatemala, Mexico, Nicaragua, Perú and Venezuela.

---

5. See Mauro Cappelletti, *Judicial Review in the Contemporaly World*, Indianapolis, 1971; "El control judicial de la constitucionalidad de las leyes en el derecho comparado," in *Revista de la Facultad de Derecho de Mexico*, Nº 61, Mexico 1966. See *also* Allan R. Brewer-Carías, *Judicial Review in Comparative Law*, Cambridge University Press, Cambridge 1989.
6. See Mauro Cappelletti, "El control judicial de la constitucionalidad de las leyes en el derecho comparado", *Revista de la Facultad de Derecho de México*, No. 61, México 1966, p. 28.
7. 5 U.S. 137 (1803).
8. Such is the case in Brazil, Colombia, the Dominican Republic, Ecuador, Guatemala, Me-xico, Nicaragua, Perú and Venezuela.
9. This concentrated method of judicial review is the only method applied in Costa Rica, El Salvador, Bolivia, Chile, Honduras, Panama, Paraguay and Uruguay.
10. See *supra* note 8.

On the one hand, all courts are entitled to decide upon the constitutionality of legislation by autonomously deciding upon a statute's inapplicability in a particular case, with inter partes efects; and on the other hand, the Supreme Court or a Constitutional Court or Tribunal has been empowered to declare the total nulity of statutes contrary to the Constitution.[11] The Venezuelan judicial review system is precisely one of the latter, combining the diffuse and the concentrated methods of judicial review since the nineteenth century.[12]

In effect, article 7 of the 1999 Venezuelan Constitution[13] declares *expressis verbis* that its text is "the supreme law" of the land and "the ground of the entire legal order." This provision assigns to all judges the duty "of guaranteeing the integrity of the Constitution"[14] with the power to decide not to apply a statute that is deemed to be unconstitutional when deciding a concrete case. Article 335 of the Constitution also assigns the Supreme Tribunal of Justice the duty of guaranteeing "the supremacy and effectiveness of the constitutional rules and principles," as "the maximum and final interpreter of the Constitution," with the duty to seek for "its uniform interpretation and application."[15]

Additionally, the Constitutional Chamber of the Supreme Tribunal of Justice[16] is the "Constitutional Jurisdiction", exclusively empowered to declare the nullity of *certain state acts* on the grounds of their unconstitutionality, in particular, statutes and other state acts issued in direct execution of the Constitution.[17] The Tribunal also is empowered to judge the unconstitutionality of the omissions of the legislative organ.[18]

---

11. See Allan R. Brewer-Carías, "La jurisdicción constitucional en América Latina," in Domingo García Belaúnde and Francisco Fernández Segado, *La jurisdicción constitucional en Iberoamérica*, Edit. Dickinson, Madrid 1997, pp. 117-61.

12. See Allan R. Brewer-Carías, *El sistema mixto o integral de control de la constitucionalidad en Colombia y Venezuela,* Bogotá 1995; Manuel Arona Cruz, "El control de la constitucionalidad de los actos jurídicos en Colombia ante el Derecho Comparado," in *Archivo de Derecho Publico y Ciencias de la Administración*, Vol. VII 1984-1985, *Derecho Publico en Venezuela y Colombia*, Instituto de Derecho Publico, UCV, Caracas 1986, pp. 39-114; Allan R. Brewer-Carías, *El sistema de justicia constitucional en la Constitución de 1999,* Editorial Jurídica Venezolana, Caracas 2000.

13. The text of the Constitution of 12-30-99 was initially published in *Gaceta Oficial* N° 36.860 dated 12-30-99. Subsequently, it was published with corrections in *Gaceta Oficial* N° 5.453 Extraordinary dated 03-24-00. See the comments in Allan R. Brewer-Carías, *La Constitución de 1999,* Editorial Jurídica Venezolana, Caracas, 2 Vols, Caracas 2004.

14. Art. 334.

15. Art. 335.

16. Art. 266, par. 1° y 336.

17. See Allan R. Brewer-Carías, *Instituciones Políticas y Constitucionales,* Vol.VI, *La Justicia Constitucional,* Editorial Jurídica Venezolana, Caracas 1996, pp. 131 ff.; Allan R. Brewer-Carías, *Judicial Review in Comparative Law,* Cambridge University Press, Cambridge 1998, p. 190; and Allan R. Brewer-Carías, *El control concentrado de la constitucionalidad de las leyes (Estudio de Derecho Comparado),* Editorial Jurídica Venezolana, Caracas 1994, p. 19.

18. Art. 336.

Other state acts, such as administrative acts and regulations, are also subject to judicial review by the "Administrative Jurisdiction." These courts are empowered to annul administrative acts because of their illegality or unconstitutionality.[19]

Also, according to article 29 of the Constitution, the courts have a duty to protect all persons in their constitutional rights and guaranties, when deciding an action for protection, or "*amparo*." Such an action can be brought before the court against any illegitimate harm or threat to such rights.

Based on all the aforementioned constitutional provisions, judicial review of constitutionality in Venezuela can be exercised not only through the diffuse and concentrated methods, but also through a variety of other means.[20] Judicial review may occur through any of the following means:

(1) The diffuse method of judicial review of the constitutionality of statutes and other normative acts, exercised by all courts;

(2) The concentrated method of judicial review of the constitutionality of certain state acts, exercised by the Constitutional Chamber of the Supreme Tribunal of Justice;

(3) The protection of constitutional rights and guarantees through the actions for *amparo*;

(4) The concentrated method of judicial review of Executive regulations and administrative actions, exercised by special courts controlling their unconstitutionality and illegality (*contencioso adminsitrativo*);

(5) The judicial review powers to control the constitutionality of legislative omissions;

(6) The concentrated judicial review power to resolve constitutional conflicts between the State organs;

(7) The protection of the Constitution through the abstract recourse for interpretation of the Constitution; and

(8) The Constitutional Chamber's power to remove from ordinary courts jurisdiction over particular cases.

According to a long Venezuelan tradition that can be traced back to the nineteenth century,[21] all the principles of the mixed or comprehensive system of judicial review had been gathered in the 1999 Constitution.

---

19. Art. 259C.

20. See decision N° 194 of the Constitutional Chamber dated Feb. 15, 2001, in *Revista de Derecho Público*, N° 85-88, Editorial Jurídica Venezolana, Caracas 2001, pp. 416 ff.

21. See Allan R. Brewer-Carías, "La justicia constitucional en la nueva Constitución," in *Revista de Derecho Constitucional* N° 1, Edigtorial Sherwood, Caracas Sep.-Dec. 1999, pp. 35-44; Allan R. Brewer-Carías, *El Sistema de justicia constitucional en la Constitución de 1999,* Editorial Jurídica Venezolana, Caracas 2000; and Allan R. Brewer-Carías, "Standing to raise constitutional issues in Venezuela," in Richard S. Kay (Ed), *Standing to raise constitutional issues: comparative perspectives, XVIth Congress of the International Academy of Comparative Law,*

II. THE DIFFUSE METHOD OF JUDICIAL REVIEW

Since 1897, the Venezuelan Civil Procedure Code has regulated the diffuse method of judicial review,[22] which is currently set forth in Article 20. This article prescribes:

In the case in which a law in force, whose application is requested, collides with any constitutional provision, judges shall apply the latter with preference.

The principle of the diffuse method of judicial review also has been more recently set forth in article 19 of the Criminal Procedure Organic Code, as follows:

Control of the Constitutionality. The control of the supremacy of the Constitution corresponds to the judges. In case that a statute whose application is requested would collide with it, the courts shall abide [by] the constitutional provision.

Based on this author's proposal,[23] article 334 of the 1999 Constitution consolidated the diffuse method of judicial review of the constitutionality of legislation,[24] as follows:

In case of incompatibility between this Constitution and a law or other legal provision, constitutional provisions shall be applied, corresponding to all courts in any case whatsoever, even at their initiative, the pertinent decision.

Through this article, the diffuse method of judicial review acquired constitutional rank in Venezuela as a judicial power that can even be exercised *ex officio* by all courts,[25] including the different Chambers of the Supreme Tribunal of Justice.[26]

This constitutional provision follows the general trends shown in comparative law regarding the diffuse method: it is based on the principle of constitutional supremacy, according to which unconstitutional acts are considered void and hold no value. Therefore, each and every judge is entitled to decide the unconstitutionality of the statute they are applying in order to resolve the case. This power can be exer-

---

Académie Internationale de Droit Comparé, Brisbane 2002, Bruylant, Bruxelles 2005, pp. 67-92.

22. This was expressly established in the Civil Procedure Code of 1897. See Allan R. Brewer-Carías, *Judicial Review in Comparative Law*, Cambridge University Press, cambridge 1989, pp. 127 ff.; Allan R. Brewer-Carías, *Instituciones Políticas y Constitucionales,* Vol. VI, *La Justicia Constitucional,* Editorial Jurídica Venezolana, Caracas 1996, pp. 86 ff.

23. See the proposed draft for this article, in Allan R. Brewer-Carías, *Debate Constituyente (Aportes a la Asamblea Nacional Constituyente), Vol. II, (9 Sept. – 17 Oct. 1999)*, Caracas 1999, pp. 24-34.

24. For instance, as it previously happened in other countries like Colombia, from 1910 (art. 4); Guatemala, in 1965 (art. 204); Bolivia, in 1994 (art. 228); Honduras, in 1982 (art. 315) and Peru, in 1993 (art. 138). See Allan R. Brewer-Carías, *Debate Constituyente (Aportes a la Asamblea Nacional Constituyente), Vol.III (18 Oct.-30 Nov. 1999)*, Caracas 1999, pp. 94-105.

25. This has been a feature of the Venezuelan system. See Allan R. Brewer-Carías, *Instituciones Políticas y Constitucionales, Vol VI, La Justicia Constitucional, op. cit.*, p. 101.

26. See decision N° 833 of the Constitutional Chamber dated Feb. 25, 2001, Case: Instituto Autónomo de Policía Municipal de Chacao, in *Revista de Derecho Público*, No. 85-88, Editorial Jurídica Venezolana, Caracas 2001, pp. 369-371.

cised at the judge's own initiative, or *ex officio*. The decision of the judge has only an *inter partes* effect in each specific case and, therefore, is declarative in nature.[27]

The general judicial procedural system in Venezuela is governed under the "by-instance principle," so that judicial decisions resolving cases on judicial review are subject to ordinary appeal. Therefore, the cases could only reach the Cassation Chambers of the Supreme Tribunal through cassation recourses.[28] Because this situation could lead to possible dispersion of the judicial decision on constitutional matters, the 1999 Constitution specifically set forth a corrective procedure. The Constitution granted the Constitutional Chamber of the Supreme Tribunal of Justice the power to review final judicial decisions issued by the courts of the Republic on *amparo* suits and when deciding judicial review of statutes in the terms established by the respective organic law.[29]

Regarding this provision, it must be pointed out that it is neither an appeal nor a general second or third procedural instance. Instead, it is an exceptional faculty of the Constitutional Chamber to review, upon its judgment and discretion, through an extraordinary recourse, similar to a writ of certiorari. Such review is exercised against last instance decisions in which constitutional issues are decided by means of judicial review, or in *amparo* suits.

It is a reviewing, non-obligatory power that can be exercised optionally.[30] The Constitutional Chamber is empowered to choose the cases in which it considers convenient to decide due to the constitutional importance of the matter. The Chamber also has the power to give a general binding effect to its interpretation of the Constitution, similar to the effect of *stare decisis*.[31]

Nonetheless, the Constitutional Chamber has distorted its review power regarding judicial decisions, extending it far beyond the precise cases of judicial review and *amparo* established in the Constitution. The Chamber has extended its review power over any other judicial decision issued in any matter when it considers it contrary to the Constitution — a power that the Chamber has proceeded to exercise without any constitutional authorization, even *ex officio*. For instance, the Chamber will step in and rule that a judicial decision was contrary to the Constitutional Chamber's interpretation of the Constitution, or that a decision was affected by a grotesque error regarding constitutional interpretation.[32]

---

27. See Allan R. Brewer-Carías, *Judicial Review in Comparative Law,* Cambridge Univ. Press, Cambridge 1989, p. 127 ff.
28. Arts. 312 and ff. CCP.
29. Art. 336, 10 C.
30. In a certain way, the remedy is similar to the so-called writ of certiorari in the North American system. See Allan R. Brewer-Carías, *Judicial Review in Comparative Law*, Cambridge Univ. Press, Cambridge 1998, p.141. See the comments of Jesús María Casal, *Constitución y Justicia Constitucional*, Caracas 2003, p. 92.
31. Art. 335.
32. See decision N° 93 of February 6, 2001 (Caso: *Olimpia Tours and Travel vs. Corporación de Turismo de Venezuela*), in *Revista de Derecho Público*, N° 85-88, Editorial Jurídica Venezolana, Caracas, 2001, pp. 414-415. See also Allan R. Brewer-Carías, "*Quis Custodiet ipsos Custo-*

III. THE CONCENTRATED METHOD OF JUDICIAL REVIEW

The second traditional method of judicial review in Venezuela is the judicial power to annul unconstitutional statutes and other state acts of similar rank, which has been granted exclusively to the Supreme Court of the country since 1858. According to the 1999 Constitution, this power is now attributed to one of the Chambers of the Supreme Tribunal of Justice — the Constitutional Chamber — as Constitutional Jurisdiction.[33]

This method of judicial review can be exercised in three ways: (1) when the Chamber is requested through a popular action to decide upon the unconstitutionality of statutes already in force, (2) in some cases, in an obligatory way, or (3) when deciding on the matter in a preventive way before the publication of the challenged statute. In all of these cases, the Constitutional Chamber has the power to annul the unconstitutional challenged statutes with *erga omnes* effects.

1. The Concentrated Method of Judicial Review through the Popular Action

The second traditional method of exercising judicial review in Venezuela has been the judicial power to annul statutes and other state acts of similar rank issued in direct and immediate execution of the Constitution. This power is granted solely to the Constitutional Chamber of the Supreme Court of Justice, as the Constitutional Jurisdiction.[34]

According to article 334 of the Constitution of 1999, following a tradition that began in 1858,[35] the court retains competence in the following matters:

> [To] [d]eclare the nullity of the statutes and other acts of the organs exercising public power issued in direct and immediate execution of the Constitution or being ranked equal to a law, [which] corresponds exclusively to the Constitutional Chamber of the Supreme Court of Justice.

This judicial review power to annul state acts on the grounds of their unconstitutionality refers to: (1) *National laws or statutes* and other acts which have the force of laws; (2) *State constitutions and statutes, municipal ordinances,* and other acts of the legislative bodies issued in direct and immediate execution of the Constitution; (3) *State acts with rank equal to statutes* issued by the National Executive; and (4) *State acts issued in direct and immediate execution* of the Constitution by any State organ exercising the public power.

Since the 1858 Constitution, constitutional jurisdiction was assigned to the Supreme Court of Justice in Plenary Session.[36] Therefore, one of the novelties of the 1999 Constitution was to assign constitutional jurisdiction to just one of the Cham-

---

des: De la interpretación constitucional a la inconstitucionalidad de la interpretación," in *VIII Congreso Nacional de derecho Constitucional, Perú,* Fondo Editorial 2005, Colegio de Abogados de Arequipa, Arequipa, septiembre 2005, pp. 463-89.

33. Arts. 266,1; 334 and 336 of the Constitution.

34. Arts. 266,1; 334 and 336 of the Constitution.

35. See Allan R. Brewer-Carías, *Instituciones Políticas y Constitucionales, Vol. VI La Justicia Constitucional,* Editorial Jurídica Venezolana, Caracas 1996, pp. 131 ff.

36. *Id.*

bers of the Supreme Court of Justice — the Constitutional Chamber.[37] This chamber, like all of the other chambers, has the mission of:

> Guaranteeing the supremacy and effectiveness of the constitutional rules and principles: it shall be the last and maximum interpreter of the Constitution and guardian of its standard interpretation and application.[38]

The specificity of the Constitutional Chamber in these cases, according to article 335 of the Constitution, is that:

> The interpretations made by the Constitutional Chamber on the content or the scope of the constitutional rules are binding [on] the other Chambers of the Supreme Court and other courts of the Republic.

The most important feature of the concentrated method of judicial review under the Venezuelan system is that the standing necessary to raise an action resides in all individuals, being an *actio popularis*.[39] Consequently, according to article 5 of the Organic Law of the Supreme Tribunal of Justice, any individual or corporation with legal capacity is entitled to file a nullification action against the abovementioned state acts on grounds of the act's unconstitutionality.[40]

According to the doctrine of the Supreme Tribunal, the objective of the popular action is that anybody has the necessary standing to sue.[41] On August 22, 2001, the Constitutional Chamber of the Supreme Tribunal ruled:

> any individual having capacity to sue has procedural and legal interest to raise [the popular action], without requiring a concrete historical fact [of] harm [to] the plaintiff's private legal sphere. The claimant is a guardian of the constitutionality and that guardianship entitles him to act, whether [or not] he suffered a harm from the unconstitutionality of a law. This kind of popular action is exceptional.[42]

This concentrated method of judicial review has traditionally been used in an extensive way, particularly by states and municipalities against national statutes, and conversely, by the Federal government against state and municipal legislation. Also, individuals have used this method against national, state and municipal statutes for the protection of individual rights.

---

37. Arts. 262; 266,1.

38. Art. 335, first paragraph.

39. See Allan R. Brewer-Carías, *Instituciones Políticas y Constitucionales, Vol. VI La Justicia Constitucional,* Editorial Jurídica Venezolana, Caracas 1996, pp. 137 ff.

40. *Id.* at 144.

41. According to this criterion, therefore, as the Supreme Court in Plenary Session has said, the popular action "may be exercised by any and all citizens with legal capacity." Decision dated Nov. 19, 1985, in *Revista de Derecho Público*, N° 25, Editorial Jurídica Venezolana, Caracas 1986, p. 131.

42. Decision N° 1077, Case: *Servio Tulio León Briceño,* in *Revista de Derecho Público*, No. 83, Editorial Jurídica Venezolana, Caracas 200o, pp. 247 ff.

2. The Obligatory Concentrated Method of Judicial Review of the "State of Exception" Decrees

Under the concentrated method of judicial review, particular emphasis must be made regarding the "state of exception" decrees that can be issued by the President of the Republic. Pursuant to article 339 of the Constitution, these executive decrees declaring a "state of emergency" shall be submitted by the President of the Republic before the Constitutional Chamber of the Supreme Tribunal in order for its constitutionality to be reviewed. Additionally, article 336,6 set forth that the Constitutional Chamber is entitled to, "Review, in any case, even *ex officio*, the constitutionality of decrees declaring states of exception issued by the President of the Republic."[43]

This judicial power of obligatory judicial review is also a novelty introduced by the 1999 Constitution. This model followed the precedent of Colombia,[44] but added the Constitutional Chamber's power to exercise judicial review *ex officio*.

By exercising this control, the Constitutional Chamber can decide not only the constitutionality of the decrees declaring "states of exception," but also the constitutionality of its content. This control is exercised pursuant to the provisions of article 337 and the Constitution. In particular, in case of restriction of constitutional guaranties, the Chamber must verify that the decree effectively contains a *regulation* regarding "the exercise of the right whose guarantee is restricted."[45]

3. The Preventive Judicial Review of the Constitutionality of Some State Acts

In addition to the *actio popularis* and these cases of obligatory review, the concentrated method of judicial review can also be exercised by the Constitutional Chamber of the Supreme Tribunal in a preventive way regarding statutes that have been sanctioned but are not yet published. This preventive control can occur in three cases established as an innovation in the 1999 Constitution: (1) cases regarding international treaties, (2) cases involving organic laws, and (3) cases regarding non-promulgated statutes, at the request of the President of the Republic.

In the traditional system of judicial review in Venezuela, the sole mechanism of preventive concentrated judicial review of statutes was the Supreme Tribunal of Justice's power to decide the unconstitutionality of a statute that is already sanctioned, but not yet promulgated because of a presidential veto.[46]

Presently, the Constitution of 1999 has expanded preventive control of constitutionality to cover treaties, organic laws, and non-promulgated statutes when requested by the President of the Republic.

---

43 Art. 336,6.

44. Art. 241,7.

45. Art. 339.

46. See Allan R. Brewer-Carías *Instituciones Políticas y Constitucionales, Vol. VI La Justicia Constitucional,* Editorial Jurídica Venezolana, Caracas 1996, pp. 134 ff.

A. *Preventive Judicial Review of International Treaties*

With regard to international treaties, there is the preventive judicial review method, foreseen in Article 336,5 of the Constitution, which grants the Constitutional Chamber faculty to:

> Verify, at the President of the Republic's or the National Assembly's request, conformity with the Constitution of the international treaties subscribed by the Republic before their ratification.

It is important to point out that this provision originated in the European constitutional systems, like those existing in France[47] and Spain, and subsequently adopted in Colombia.[48] This system is now incorporated in the Venezuelan system of judicial review, and permits the preventive judicial review of international treaties subscribed by the Republic, thereby avoiding the possibility of subsequent challenge of the statutes approving the treaty.

In this case, if the treaty turns out not to be in conformity with the Constitution, it cannot be ratified, and an initiative for constitutional reform to adapt the Constitution to the treaty may result. On the other hand, if the Constitutional Chamber decides that the international treaty conforms to the Constitution, then a popular action of unconstitutionality against the approving statute could not subsequently be raised.

B. *The Preventive Judicial Review of the Organic Laws*

The second mechanism of the preventive judicial review method refers to organic laws. According to article 203 of the Constitution, the Constitutional Chamber must decide, before their promulgation, the constitutionality of the "organic" character of the *organic laws* when qualified this way by the National Assembly.

Article 203 of the Constitution defines the organic laws in five senses: (1) those the Constitution itself qualities as such;[49] (2) the organic laws issued in order to or-

---

47. See Allan R. Brewer-Carías, *Implicaciones constitucionales de los procesos de integración regional*, Editorial Jurídica Venezolana, Caracas 1998, pp. 75 ff.

48. *Id.* at 590.

49. This happens in the following cases: Organic Law of Frontiers (art. 15), Organic Law of Territorial Division (art. 16), Organic Law of the National Armed Force (art. 41), Organic Law of the Social Security System (art. 86), Organic Law for the Land Planning (art. 128), Organic Law Establishing the Limits to Public Officer's Emoluments (art. 147), Organic Law of Municipal Regime (art. 169), Organic Law on the Metropolitan Districts (arts. 171 and 172), Organic Law ruling officers ineligibility (art. 189), Organic Law Concerning the Nationalization of Activities, Industries or Services (art. 302), Organic Law of the Nation Defense Council (art. 232), Organic Law Ruling the remedy of reviewing decisions adopted on actions of *amparo* and on diffuse judicial review (art. 336), Organic Law of State of Emergency (art. 338 and Third,2 Transitional clause), Organic Law on Refugees and Asylum (Fourth,2 Transitional clause), Organic Law on the Peoples Defendant (art,5 Transitional clause), Organic Law on Education (Sixth Transitional clause), Organic Law on Indian Peoples (Seventh Transitional clause), Labor Organic Law (Fourth,3 Transitional clause), Labor Procedural Organic Law (Fourth,4 Transitional clause) and Tributary Organic Code (Fifth Transitional clause)

ganize public branches of government (Public Powers);[50] (3) those intended to "develop the constitutional rights," which implies that all laws issued to develop the content of articles 19 to 129 shall be Organic Laws; (4) those organic laws issued to "frame other laws;"[51] and (5) those Organic Laws named "organic" by the National Assembly, when they are admitted by 2/3 vote of the present members before initiating the discussion.

This last case of laws, qualified as such by the National Assembly, are those that shall be *automatically* sent, before their promulgation, to the Constitutional Chamber of the Supreme Tribunal of Justice. The Tribunal will make a decision regarding the constitutionality of the laws' organic character.

C. *Judicial Review of Statutes Sanctioned Before their Promulgation*

The third mechanism of preventive judicial review of constitutionality set forth in article 214 of the Constitution is established in cases when the President of the Republic raises before the Constitutional Chamber the constitutional issue against sanctioned statutes before their promulgation.[52] Thus, control over the constitutionality of sanctioned but not promulgated statutes is set forth in a different way than the traditional so-called "presidential veto" of statutes, which involves a devolution to the National Assembly.[53]

IV. JUDICIAL REVIEW THROUGH THE ACTION FOR AMPARO OF CONSTITUTIONAL RIGHTS AND GUARANTEES

Beside the classical diffuse and concentrated methods of judicial review, with the aforementioned variations, in Venezuela, as in all other Latin American countries, there is a third method of judicial review. This method is a specific action established in the Constitution for protection of constitutional rights, which can also serve to control the constitutionality of statutes and other governmental actions applicable to the case.

---

50. Such as the Organic Law of the Public Administration (art. 236, paragraph 20); Organic Law of the Attorney General for the Republic (art. 247); Organic Law of the Judicial Power, Organic Law of the Supreme Tribunal of Justice (art. 262); Organic Law of the Electoral Power (art. 292 and Eighth Transitional clause); Organic Law of the Citizen Power, comprising the Organic Law of the General Controller of the Republic, Organic Law of the General Prosecutor of the Republic and Organic Law of the Peoples Defender (Ninth Transitional clause); Organic Law of Municipal regime (art 169 and First Transitional clause) and Organic Law ruling the States Legislative Councils (art. 162).

51. For example, the Taxation Organic Code that shall frame all specific tax laws, or the Organic Law on the Financial Administration of the state that shall frame the annual or pluri-annual budget laws, or the specific laws referred to public credit operations.

52. The Constitutional Chamber considered that it is an exclusive standing of the President of the Republic. See decision N° 194 of Feb. 15, 2001.

53. Art. 214 of the Constitution.

The action or suit for protection, or *amparo*, as a specific judicial means for the protection of *all constitutional rights and guarantees*[54] has been constitutionalized in Venezuela since the 1961 Constitution. This provision implies the obligation of all the courts to protect persons in the exercise of their constitutional rights and guarantees. In the *amparo* suit decisions, judicial review of the constitutionality of legislation can also be exercised by the courts as part of their rulings.

Article 27 of the Constitution of 1999 establishes:

> Every individual is entitled to be protected by the courts in the enjoyment and exercise of rights, even those which derive from the nature of man that are not expressly set forth in this Constitution or in the international treaties on human rights.

The *amparo* suit is governed by an informal, oral proceeding that shall be public, brief and free of charge. The judge is entitled to immediately restore the affected legal situation, and the court shall issue the decision with preference to all other matters.

As per the Organic Law on A*mparo* of Constitutional Rights and Guarantees of 1988,[55] in principle, all courts of first instance are competent to decide *amparo* suits.

Standing to file the action of *amparo* corresponds to every individual whose constitutional rights and guarantees are affected[56] — even those inherent rights that are not expressly provided for in the Constitution or in the international treaties on human rights that are ratified by the Republic. In Venezuela, such treaties rank on the same level as the Constitution, and they even prevail in the internal order as long as they establish more favorable rules on the enjoyment and exercise of rights than those established under the Constitution and other laws.[57]

In Venezuela, the action of *amparo* may be instituted against state organs, against corporations and even against individuals whose actions or omissions may infringe or threaten constitutional rights and guarantees. In all cases of *amparo* proceedings, if the alleged violation of the constitutional right involves a statutory provision, in his decision, the *amparo* judge can decide that the statute is unconstitutional and not apply it to the case.

---

54. See Allan R. Brewer-Carías, *Instituciones Políticas y Constitucionales, Vol.V, Derecho y la Acción de Amparo*, Editorial Jurídica Venezolana, Caracas 1998, pp. 19 ff.

55. See *Gaceta Oficial* No.33.891 dated Jan. 22, 1988. See *generally* Allan R. Brewer-Carías & Carlos M. Ayala Corao, *La Ley Orgánica de Amparo sobre Derechos y Garantías Constitucionales*, Editorial Jurídica Venezolana, Caracas 1988.

56. Individual, political, social, cultural, educative, economic, Indian and environmental rights and their guarantees are listed in articles 19 through 129 of the Constitution. In Venezuela, there exists no limitation established in other countries (e.g. Germany, and Spain), which reduces the action of amparo to protect just "fundamental rights". See Allan R. Brewer-Carías, *El Amparo a los derechos y garantías constitucionales (una aproximación comparativa)*, Editorial Jurídica venezolana, Caracas 1993.

57. Art. 23 C.

Generally, "the individual directly affected by the infringement of the constitutional rights and guarantees" has standing in an action for *amparo*.[58] But by virtue of the constitutional acknowledgement of the legal protection of diffuse or collective interests, the Constitutional Chamber of the Supreme Court has admitted the possibility of exercising the action of *amparo* to enforce collective and diffuse rights. For instance, those rights related to an acceptable quality of life and also those pertaining to the political rights of voters, admitting precautionary measures with *erga omnes* effects.[59]

In such cases the Constitutional Chamber has admitted that:

> any individual with legal capacity to bring suit, who is going to prevent damage to the population or parts of it to which he belongs, is entitled to bring the [*amparo*] suit grounded in diffuse or collective interests . . . . This interpretation, based on article 26, extends standing to companies, corporations, foundations, chambers, unions and other collective entities, whose object be the defense of the society, as long as they act within the boundaries of their corporate object, aimed at protecting the interests of their members regarding their object.[60]

On the other hand, regarding the general defense and protection of diffuse and collective interests, the Constitutional Chamber has also admitted the standing of the Defender of the People.[61]

---

58. See, *e.g.*, decision of the Constitutional Chamber dated Mar. 15, 2000, *Revista de Derecho Público*, N° 81, Editorial Jurídica Venezolana, Caracas 2000, pp. 322-23.

59. Decision of the Constitutional Chamber N° 483 of May 29, 2000 (Case: *"Queremos Elegir" y otros*), *Revista de Derecho Público*, N° 82, Editorial Jurídica Venezolana, Caracas 2000, pp 489-491. In the same sense, decision of the same Chamber N° 714 of July 13, 2000 (Case: *APRUM*), in *Revista de Derecho Público*, No. 83, Editorial Jurídica Venezolana, Caracas 2000, pp. 319 ff.

60. See decision of the Constitutional Chamber N° 487 of April 6, 2001, Case: *Glenda López,* in *Revista de Derecho Público*, N° 85-88, Editorial Jurídica Venezolana, Caracas 2001, pp. 453 ff. In these cases, as stated by the Constitutional Chamber in a decision dated February 17, 2000 (N° 1.048, Case: *William O. Ojeda O. vs. Consejo Nacional Electoral*), in order to enforce diffuse or collective rights or interests, it is necessary that the following elements be combined: 1. That the plaintiff sues based not only on his personal right or interest, but also on a common or collective right or interest. 2. That the reason for the claim filed on the action of amparo, be the general damage to the quality of life of all the inhabitants of the country or parts of it, since the legal situation of all the members of the society or its groups has been damaged when their common quality of life was unimproved. 3. That the damaged goods are not susceptible of exclusive appropriation by one subject (such as the plaintiff). 4. That the claim concerns an indivisible right or interest that involves the entire population of the country or a group of it [and] that a necessity of satisfying social or collective interests exists, before the individual ones. See in *Revista de Derecho Público*, N° 83, Editorial Jurídica Venezolana, Caracas 2000, pp. 375 ff.

61. The Chamber has granted the Peoples' Defender standing: "to act to protect those rights and interests, when they correspond in general to the consumers and users (6, article 281), or to protect the rights of Indian peoples (paragraph 8 of the same article), since the defense and protection of such categories is one of the faculties granted to said entity by article 281 of the Constitution in force. It is about a general protection and not a protection of individualities. Within this frame of action, and since the political rights are included in the human rights and guarantees of Title III of the Constitution in force, which have a general projection, among which the one set forth in article 62 of the Constitution can be found, it must be concluded that the De-

In order to seek uniformity of the application and interpretation of the Constitution, article 336 of the Constitution also grants the Constitutional Chamber of the Supreme Tribunal the power to review, in a discretionary way, all final decisions issued in *amparo* suits. The extraordinary rcourse can also be raised against judicial decisions applying the diffuse method of judicial review, being the review power of the Constitutional Chamber of facultative, non-obligatory character.

V. THE JUDICIAL REVIEW OF THE CONSTITUTIONALITY EXECUTIVE REGULATIONS AND OTHER NORMATIVE ADMINISTRATIVE ACTS

The forth method of judicial review of constitutionality is the concentrated method, also established in the Constitution, which applies to Executive regulations and other normative administrative actions. For such purposes, Article 259 of the Constitution sets forth the "Administrative Jurisdiction" exercised by Judicial Review Courts of Administrative action (*contencioso-administrativo*), in the following way:

> The Administrative Jurisdiction corresponds to the Supreme Tribunal of Justice and to the other courts determined by law. The courts of the Administrative Jurisdiction have the power to annul general or individual administrative acts contrary to law, even because of deviation of power. Additionally, the courts may condemn the Administration to pay compensation of damages caused because the Administration liability; decide claims for the fulfillment of public services and arrange what is necessary to restore the subjective legal situation damaged by the activity of the Administration.

Therefore, pursuant to this constitutional article, judicial review also corresponds to the courts of Administrative Jurisdiction when exercising their faculty of annulment of administrative acts, when contrary to statutes, executive regulations or other sources of administrative law.[62] Similar to judicial review of constitutionality, decisions annulling administrative acts, both normative and specific ones, have *erga omnes* effects.[63]

The difference between the "Constitutional Jurisdiction" (*Juisdicción Constitucional*), attributed to the Constitutional Chamber of the Supreme Court of Justice, and the "Administrative Jurisdiction" (*Jurisdicción contencioso-administrativa*), attributed to the special courts for judicial review of administrative

---

fender of the People is entitled on behalf of the society, to bring to suit an action of *amparo* tending to control the Electoral branch of government, to the citizen's benefit, in order to enforcing articles 62 and 70 of the Constitution, which were denounced to be breached by the National Legislative Assembly… (right to citizen participation). See decision of the Constitutional Chamber N°487 of April 6, 2001, Case: *Glenda López*, in *Revista de Derecho Público*, N° 85-88, Editorial Jurídica Venezolana, Caracas 2001, pp. 453 ff..

62. See Allan R. Brewer-Carías, *Instituciones Políticas y Constitucionales*, *Vol. VII*, *La Justicia Contencioso-Administrativa,* Editorial Jurídica venezolana, Caracas 1997, pp. 26 ff.

63. *Id.*

actions,[64] resides in the state acts subjected to control. On the one hand, Constitutional Jurisdiction is in charge of nullifying actions *against unconstitutional statutes and other acts of similar rank or issued in direct and immediate execution of the Constitution.* On the other hand, Administrative Jurisdiction is in charge of deciding *nullity actions against unconstitutional or illegal administrative acts or regulations.*

Therefore, as per article 266,5 of the Constitution, the Political-Administrative Chamber of the Supreme Court is entitled:

> To declare the total or partial nullity of bylaws (regulations) and other general or individual administrative acts of the National Executive, when it proceeds.

Regarding the standing to challenge administrative acts on the grounds of unconstitutionality and illegality, when referring to normative administrative acts or regulations, anybody can bring an action before the court by means of the popular action of nullity. Consequently, a simple interest in the legality or constitutionality is enough for any citizen to be sufficiently entitled to raise the nullity action for unconstitutionality or illegality against regulations and other normative administrative acts.[65] This simple interest has been defined by the First Administrative Court, in a decision dated March 22, 2000, as "the general right granted by law upon every citizen to access the competent courts to raise the nullity of an unconstitutional or illegal administrative general act."[66]

As to the administrative acts of particular effects, the standing to challenge such acts before the Administrative Jurisdiction courts corresponds solely to those who have a personal, legitimate and direct interest in the annulment of the act.[67] This has been the general rule on the matter even though some decisions have been issued by the Politico-Administrative Chamber of the Supreme Tribunal, giving standing to any person with only a legitimate interest.[68]

Additionally, in the case of the Administrative Jurisdiction, even before the new Constitution took effect in 1999, the possibility of protecting collective interests was also made available. In particular, it is now widely accepted that a collective or diffuse right exists against city-planning acts.[69]

---

64. See the author's proposal before the National Constituent Assembly. See Allan R. Brewer-Carías, *Debate Constituyente (Aportes a la Asamblea Nacional Constituyente), Vol. II, (9 Sept. – 17 Oct. 1999)*, Caracas 1999, pp. 245 ff.

65. See Allan R. Brewer-Carías, *Instituciones Políticas y Constitucionales, Vol. VII, La Justicia Contencioso-Administrativa,* Caracas 1997, pp. 74 ff.

66. See decision of the First Administrative Court dated Mar. 22, 2000, case: *Banco de Venezolano de Crédito v. Superintendencia de Bancos, Revista de Derecho Público*, N° 81, Editorial Jurídica Venezolana, Caracas 2000, pp. 452-53.

67. Art. 5, Law.

68. See decision of the Supreme Court of Justice in Political-Administrative Chamber of April 13, 2000, case: *Banco Fivenez vs. Junta de Emergencia Financiera, Revista de Derecho Público*, N° 82, Editorial Jurídica Venezolana, Caracas, 2000, pp. 582-83.

69. See Allan R. Brewer-Carías, *Instituciones Políticas y Constitucionales, Vol. VII, La Justicia Contencioso-Administrativa,* Editorial Jurídica venezolana, Caracas 1997, pp. 130 and ff.

Nonetheless, despite very impressive advances regarding judicial review of administrative actions experienced in the past decades, due to the political control of the Judiciary during the past seven years, the role of the Administrative Jurisdiction in controlling Public Administration has dramatically diminished in Venezuela, affecting the rule of law.[70]

VI. JUDICIAL REVIEW OF LEGISLATIVE OMISSIONS

The fifth judicial review method established in the 1999 Constitution refers to legislative omissions, empowering the Constitutional Chamber to review the unconstitutional omissions of the legislative organ.[71] This is another new institution in matters of judicial review established by the 1999 Constitution. In Article 336, the Constitution grants the Constitutional Chamber faculty:

> To declare the unconstitutionality of municipal, state or national legislative organ omissions, when they failed to issue indispensable rules or measures to guarantee the enforcement of the Constitution, or when they issued them in an incomplete way; and to establish the terms, and if necessary, the guidelines for their correction.

This provision has given extended judicial power to the Constitutional Chamber, which surpasses the trends of the initial Portuguese antecedent on the matter, where only the President of the Republic, the Ombudsman or the Presidents to the Autonomous Regions had standing to require such decisions.[72] On the contrary, the Venezuelan Constitution of 1999 does not establish any condition whatsoever for standing; whereby regarding normative omissions,[73] standing has been treated similarly as in *popular actions*.

In many cases, the Chamber has been asked to rule on omissions of the National Assembly in sanctioning statutes, like the Organic Law on Municipalities which, according to the Transitory dispositions of the 1999 Constitution, was due to be sanctioned within two years following its approval. Even though the Chamber issued two decisions in the case, the National Assembly failed to sanction the statute until 2005.[74] In these cases, fortunately, the Chamber has not itself decided (in this case to legislated) in place of the legislative body, as it has done regarding the election of the National Electoral Council. There, due to the failure of the National Assembly to elect those members with the needed two-thirds majority vote, the Consti-

70. See Allan R. Brewer-Carías, "La progresiva y sistemática demolición institucional de la autonomía e independencia del Poder Judicial en Venezuela 1999-2004", en el libro: *XXX Jornadas J.M Dominguez Escovar, Estado de derecho, Administración de justicia y derechos humanos*, Instituto de Estudios Jurídicos del Estado Lara, Barquisimeto, 2005, pp. 33-174.

71. This institution has its origins in the Portuguese system. See Allan R. Brewer-Carías, *Judicial Review in Comparative Law*, Cambridge Univ. Press, Cambridge 1989, p. 269.

72. *Id.*

73. It has been called by the Constitutional Chamber: "legislative silence and the legislative abnormal functioning," decision N° 1819 of Aug. 8, 2000, of the Political-Administrative Chamber, case: *Rene Molina vs. Comisión Legislativa Nacional.*

74. See the reference in Allan R. Brewer-Carías et al, *Ley Orgánica del Poder Público Municipal*, Editorial Jurídica Venezolana, Caracas 2005.

tutional Chamber, which has been completely controlled by the Executive, directly appointed them in violation of the Constitution. Through that decision, the Constitutional Chamber guaranteed the complete control of the Electoral body by the Executive.[75]

VII. JUDICIAL REVIEW OF THE CONSTITUTIONAL CONTROVERSIES BETWEEN THE STATE ORGANS

The sixth judicial review method refers to the power attributed to the Constitutional Chamber of the Supreme Tribunal to "decide upon constitutional controversies aroused between any organ of the branches of government (public power)."[76]

This judicial review power refers to controversies between any of the organs that the Constitution foresees, whether in the horizontal or vertical distribution of the public power. In particular, "constitutional" controversies — those whose decision depends on the examination, interpretation and application of the Constitution — refers to the distribution of powers between the different state organs, especially those distributing the power between the national, state and municipal levels.

The "administrative" controversies that can arise between the Republic, the states, municipalities or other public entities are to be decided by the Political-Administrative Chamber of the Supreme Tribunal[77] as an Administrative Jurisdiction.

As the Supreme Court of Justice specified, in order to identify the constitutional controversy, it is required:

> That the parties of the controversy are those who have been expressly assigned faculties for those actions or provisions in the constitutional text itself, that is, the supreme state institutions, whose organic regulation is set forth in the constitutional text, different from others, whose concrete institutional frame is establish by the ordinary legislator. . .

On the contrary, "we are not in [the] presence of a constitutional controversy when the parties to same are not organs of the branches of government (public power), with attributes established in the constitutional text."[78]

---

75. See decisions N° 2073 of Aug. 4, 2003 (Caso: *Hermánn Escarrá Malaver y oros*) and N° 2341 of August 25, 2003 (Caso: *Hermánn Escarrá M. y otros*) in Allan R. Brewer-Carías, *La Sala Constitucional versus el Estado Democrático de Derecho. El secuestro del poder electoral y de la Sala Electoral del Tribunal Supremo y la confiscación del derecho a la participación política*, Los Libros de El Nacional, Colección Ares, Caracas 2004, p. 172; "El secuestro del Poder Electoral y la confiscación del derecho a la participación política mediante el referendo revocatorio presidencial: Venezuela 2000-2004," in *Boletín Mexicano de Derecho Comparado*, Instituto de Investigaciones Jurídicas, Universidad Nacional Autónoma de México, N° 112. México, enero-abril 2005 pp. 11-73.

76. Art. 336.

77. Art. 266, para. 4°.

78. Decision of the Political-Administrative Chamber N°1468 of June 27, 2000 of the Political-Administrative Chamber, in *Revista de Derecho Público*, N° 82, Editorial Jurídica Venezolana, Caracas 2000, pp. 744 ff..

In any case, the standing to raise a remedy in order to settle a constitutional controversy only corresponds to one of the branches of government (public power) party to the controversy.[79]

VIII. RECOURSE OF CONSTITUTIONAL INTERPRETATION

Finally, regarding the jurisdiction of the Constitutional Chamber, mention must be made of the faculty to decide abstract recourses of interpretation of the Constitution. This is a judicial means that the Constitutional Chamber has created from the interpretation of article 335 of the Constitution, which grants the Supreme Tribunal the character of "maximum and final interpreter of the Constitution."

In effect, the 1999 Constitution only grants the Supreme Tribunal of Justice power to "decide the recourses of interpretation on the content and scope of the *legal texts*,"[80] a faculty that is to be exercised "by the different Chambers [of the Tribunal] pursuant to the provisions of this Constitution and the law."[81] No reference is made in the Constitution to recourse for the interpretation of the Constitution itself.

Nonetheless, before the Supreme Tribunal of Justice Organic Law was sanctioned in 2005, and without any constitutional or legal support, the Constitutional Chamber of the Supreme Tribunal created an autonomous "recourse of interpretation of the Constitution."[82] The court's ruling was founded on article 26 of the Constitution, which established the right to access justice, from which it was deduced that although said action was not set forth in any statute, it was not forbidden, either. Therefore, it was decided that "citizens do not require statutes establishing the recourse for constitutional interpretation, in particular, to raise it."[83]

In order to raise this recourse for constitutional interpretation, the Constitutional Chamber has nonetheless considered that a particular interest shall exist in the plaintiff. The court ruled that:

> a public or private person shall have a current legitimate legal interest, grounded in a concrete and specific legal situation, which necessarily requires the interpretation of constitutional rules applicable to the case, in order to cease the uncertainty impeding the development and effects of said legal situation.[84]

In decision N° 1077 dated August 22, 2001, the Constitutional Chamber ruled that:

---

79. See dissenting vote of Justice Héctor Peña Torrelles, Case: *José Amando Mejía y otros*. (Decision Feb. 1, 2000)

80. Art. 266,6.

81. Art. 266,C.

82. Decision N° 1077 of the Constitutional Chamber dated Sept. 22, 2000, case: *Servio Tulio León Briceño*, See in *Revista de Derecho Público*, N° 83, Editorial Jurídica Venezolana, Caracas 2000, pp. 247 ff.

83. This criterion was ratified later in decision (N° 1347 dated Sept. 11, 2000), in *Revista de Derecho Público*, No. 84, Editorial Jurídica Venezolana, Caracas 2000, pp. 264 ff.

84. *Id.*

> The purpose of such recourse for constitutional interpretation would be a declaration of certainty on the scope and content of a constitutional provision, and would form an aspect of citizen participation, which may be made as a step prior to the action of unconstitutionality, since the constitutional interpretation could clear doubts and ambiguities about the supposed collision. It is about a preventive guardianship [of the Constitution].

The Chamber added that the petition for interpretation might be inadmissible "if it does not specify which is the obscurity, ambiguity or contradiction between the provisions of the constitutional text."[85] The petition, if applicable, must also specify "the nature and scope of the applicable principles," or "the contradictory or ambiguous situations aroused between the Constitution and the rules of its transitory regime."[86] The interpretation of the Constitution made by the Constitutional Chamber in these cases has binding effects.[87]

This extraordinary interpretive power, although theoretically an excellent judicial means for the interpretation of the Constitution, unfortunately has been extensively abused by the Constitutional Chamber to distort important constitutional provisions, to interpret them in a way contrary to the text, or to justify constitutional solutions according to the will of the Executive. This was the case, for instance, with the various Constitutional Chamber decisions regarding the consultative and repeal referendums between 2002 and 2004, where the Chamber confiscated and distorted the peoples' constitutional right to political participation.[88]

IX. THE CONSTITUTIONAL CHAMBER'S POWER TO TAKE AWAY JURISDICTION FROM LOWER COURTS IN PARTICULAR CASES

Finally, mention must be made to the figure of the "*avocamiento*," that is, the authority of the Constitutional Chamber to remove cases from the jurisdiction of lower courts, at any stage of the procedure, in order for the cases to be decided by the Chamber itself.

---

85. Case: *Servio Tulio León Briceño*, in *Revista de Derecho Público*, N° 83, Editorial Jurídica Venezolana, Caracas 2000, pp. 247 ff.

86. *Id.*

87. Decision N° 1347 of the Constitutional Chamber dated Nov. 9, 2000, in *Revista de Derecho Público*, N° 84, Editorial Jurídica Venezolana, Caracas 2000, pp. 264 ff.

88. See decisions: N° 1139 of June 5, 2002 (Caso: *Sergio Omar Calderón Duque y William Dávila Barrios*); N° 137 of Feb. 13, 2003 (Caso: *Freddy Lepage y otros*); N° 2750 of Oct. 21, 2003 (Caso: *Carlos E. Herrera Mendoza*); N° 2432 of Aug. 29, 2003 (Caso: *Luis Franceschi y otros*); and N° 2404 of Aug. 28, 2003 (Caso: *Exssel Alí Betancourt Orozco, Interpretación del artículo 72 de la Constitución*), in Allan R. Brewer-Carías, *La Sala Constitucional versus el Estado Democrático de Derecho. El secuestro del poder electoral y de la Sala Electoral del Tribunal Supremo y la confiscación del derecho a la participación política*, Los Libros de El Nacional, Colección Ares, Caracas 2004, p. 172; "El secuestro del Poder Electoral y la confiscación del derecho a la participación política mediante el referendo revocatorio presidencial: Venezuela 2000-2004," in *Boletín Mexicano de Derecho Comparado*, Instituto de Investigaciones Jurídicas, Universidad Nacional Autónoma de México, N° 112. México, enero-abril 2005 pp. 11-73.

This extraordinary judicial power was initially established in the 1976 Organic Law of the Supreme Court of Justice as a competence attributed only to the Politico-Administrative Chamber of the Supreme Court, which the Chamber used in a self-restricted way.[89] However, the Constitutional Chamber has now assumed for itself the *avocamiento* power in matters of *amparo* cases,[90] and eventually annulled the former Organic Law provision.[91]

In 2004, the new Organic Law of the Supreme Tribunal granted to all the Chambers of the Tribunal a general power to remove cases from the jurisdiction of lower courts, *ex officio* or through a party petition, and when convenient, to decide the cases.[92]

This power has been highly criticized as a violation of due process rights, and particularly, the right to a trial on a by-instance basis by the courts. It has allowed the Constitutional Chamber to intervene in any kind of process, including cases being tried by the other Chambers of the Supreme Tribunal, with very negative effects.[93] For instance, this Constitutional Chamber power was used to annul a decision issued by the Electoral Chamber of the Supreme Tribunal,[94] which protected the citizens' rights to political participation. There, the Electoral Chamber suspended the effects of a National Electoral Council decision,[95] objecting the presidential repeal referendum petition of 2004.

In this way,[96] the Constitutional Chamber interrupted the process which was normally developing before the Electoral Chamber of the Supreme Tribunal, took the case away from that Chamber, and annulled its ruling. Instead, the Constitutional Chamber decided the case according to the will of the Executive, restricting the peoples' right to participate through petitioning referendums.[97]

---

89. See Roxana ORIHUELA, *El avocamiento de la Corte Suprema de Justicia,* Editorial Jurídica Venezolana, Caracas 1998.

90. See decisión N° 456 of Mar. 15, 2002 (Case: *Arelys J. Rodríguez vs. Registrador Subalterno de Registro Público, Municipio Pedro Zaraza, Estado Carabobo*), in *Revista de Derecho Público,* N° 89-92, Editorial Jurídica Venezolana, Caracas 2002.

91. See decisión N° 806 of April 24, 2002 (Case: *Sindicato Profesional de Trabajadores al Servicio de la Industria Cementera),* in *Revista de Derecho Público,* N° 89-92, Editorial Jurídica Venezolana, Caracas 2002, pp. 179 y ss.

92. Arts. 5,1,48; and 18,11.

93. See Allan R. Brewer-Carías, «*Quis Custodiet ipsos Custodes*: De la interpretación constitucional a la inconstitucionalidad de la interpretación», in *VIII Congreso Nacional de derecho Constitucional, Perú,* Fondo Editorial 2005, Colegio de Abogados de Arequipa, Arequipa, Sept. 2005, pp. 463-89.

94. See decisions N° 24 of Mar. 15, 2004 (Exp. AA70-E 2004-000021; Exp. x-04-00006); and N° 27 of Mar. 29, 2004 (Case: *Julio Borges, César Pérez Vivas, Henry Ramos Allup, Jorge Sucre Castillo, Ramón José Medina y Gerardo Blyde vs. Consejo Nacional Electoral*) (Exp. AA70-E-2004-000021- AA70-V-2004-000006).

95. See Resolution N° 040302-131 of Mar. 2, 2004.

96. See Decision No. 566 of April 12, 2004.

97. See Allan R. BREWER-CARÍAS, *La Sala Constitucional versus el Estado Democrático de Derecho. El secuestro del poder electoral y de la Sala Electoral del Tribunal Supremo y la confisca-*

CONCLUSION

As abovementioned, judicial review has played a very important role in the contemporary world and can be considered as the ultimate result of the consolidation of the *rule of law*. Judicial review can contribute to the consolidation of democracy, which ensures control over the exercise of state powers and guarantees the respect of human rights. When exercised for those purposes, judicial review powers are the most important instruments for a Supreme Court or a Constitutional Tribunal to guarantee the supremacy of the Constitution.

But when used against democratic principles for circumstantial political purposes, the judicial review powers attributed to a Supreme Court or to a Constitutional Tribunal can constitute the most powerful instrument for the consolidation of an authoritarian government.

Consequently, the provision of various methods of judicial review and the corresponding actions and recourses established in a Constitution is not, alone, a guarantee of constitutionalism and of the enjoyment of human rights. Nor does the mere existence of such provisions guarantee that there will be control of state powers, particularly, that there will be the division and separation of powers, which today still remains the most important principle of democracy.

The most elemental condition for this control is inevitably the existence of an independent and autonomous judiciary and, in particular, the existence of adequate institutions for controlling the constitutionality of state acts (Constitutional Courts or Supreme Tribunals) — institutions capable of controlling the exercise of political power and of annulling unconstitutional state acts.

Unfortunately, in Venezuela — notwithstanding the marvelous, formal system of judicial review enshrined in the Constitution, which I have intended to describe, combining all the imaginable instruments and methods for that purpose – due to the concentration of all state power in the National Assembly and in the Executive branch of government, and due to the very tight political control that is exercised over the Supreme Tribunal of Justice, the *rule of law* has been progressively demolished with the complicity of the Constitutional Chamber. Consequently, the authoritarian elements that were enshrined in the 1999 Constitution have been progressively developed and consolidated, precisely through the decisions of the Constitutional Chamber, weakening the democratic principle.

That is why, unfortunately, the politically controlled Constitutional Chamber of the Supreme Tribunal of Justice in Venezuela, instead of being the guarantor of con-

---

ción del derecho a la participación política, Los Libros de El Nacional, Colección Ares, Caracas 2004; and "El secuestro del Poder Electoral y la confiscación del derecho a la participación política mediante el referendo revocatorio presidencial: Venezuela 2000-2004," in *Boletín Mexicano de Derecho Comparado*, Instituto de Investigaciones Jurídicas, Universidad Nacional Autónoma de México, N° 112. México, enero-abril 2005 pp. 11-73.

stitutionalism, of democracy, and of the *rule of law*, has instead been the a façade of "constitutionality" or "legality," camouflaging the authoritarian regime we now have installed in the country

PART II

AMPARO PROCEEDING IN VENEZUELA: CONSTITUTIONAL LITIGATION AND PROCEDURAL PROTECTION OF CONSTITUTIONAL RIGHTS AND GUARANTEES

Paper written for the Seminar on *Constitutional Litigation: Procedural Protections of Constitutional Guarantees in the Americas . . . and Beyond*, organized by Professor Robert S. Barker, Duquesne University School of Law, Pittsburgh, Nov. 5 and 6, 2010, published in *Duquesne Law Review*, Volume 49, Number 2, Spring 2011, pp. 161-241.

INTRODUCTION

The amparo proceeding is an extraordinary judicial remedy specifically conceived for the protection of constitutional rights against harms or threats inflicted by authorities or individuals. It is a Latin American procedural means for constitutional litigation that normally concludes with a judicial order or writ of protection (*amparo, protección* or *tutela*), that has been indistinctly called an action, recourse or suit of amparo.[98]

This constitutional litigation means was introduced in the American continent during the nineteenth century, and although similar remedies were established in the twentieth century in some European countries, like Austria, Germany, Spain and Switzerland, and also in Canada, it has been adopted by all Latin American countries, except in Cuba, being considered as one of the most distinguishable features of Latin American constitutional law.[99] As such, it has influenced the introduction of a

98. See Héctor FIX-ZAMUDIO and Eduardo FERRER MAC-GREGOR (Coord.), *El derecho de amparo en el mundo*, Edit. Porrúa, México, 2006; Allan R. BREWER-CARÍAS, *El amparo a los derechos y libertades constitucionales. Una aproximación comparativa*, Cuadernos de la Cátedra de Derecho Público, n° 1, Universidad Católica del Táchira, San Cristóbal, 1993; also published in *La protección jurídica del ciudadano. Estudios en Homenaje al Profesor Jesús González Pérez*, Tomo 3, Editorial Civitas, Madrid, 1993, pp. 2.695–2.740; and Allan R. BREWER-CARÍAS, *Mecanismos nacionales de protección de los derechos humanos (Garantías judiciales de los derechos humanos en el derecho constitucional comparado latinoamericano)*, Instituto Interamericano de Derechos Humanos, San José, 2005.

99. See generally Allan R. BREWER-CARÍAS, *Constitutional Protection of Human Rights in Latin America, A Comparative Study of the Amparo Proceedings* (Cambridge University Press 2009), pp. 77ff.

similar remedy in the Philippines, the writ of amparo, which was created by the Supreme Court in 2007.[100]

This specific remedy, providing for the protection of fundamental rights, contrasts with the constitutional system of the United States, where the effective protection of human rights is effectively assured, following the British procedural law tradition, through the general judicial actions and equitable remedies, particularly the injunctions, which are also used to protect any other kind of personal or property rights or interests.

The amparo proceeding was first introduced in Mexico in 1857 as the *juicio de amparo*, evolving in that country into a unique and very complex institution exclusively found in Mexico. Not only was it designed to guarantee judicial protection of constitutional guarantees against the State acts or actions, but to perform multipurpose judicial roles, including actions and procedures that in all other countries are separate processes, like judicial review, cassation review and judicial review of administrative actions.

In the rest of Latin America the amparo gave rise to a very different specific judicial remedy established with the *exclusive* purpose of protecting human rights and freedoms, becoming in many cases, more protective than the original Mexican institution. The institution has been described in various ways, always meaning the same, such as: *Amparo* (Guatemala); *Acción de amparo* (Argentina, Ecuador, Honduras, Paraguay, Uruguay, Dominican Republic, Venezuela); *Acción de tutela* (Colombia); *Proceso de amparo* (El Salvador, Peru); *Recurso de amparo* (Bolivia, Costa Rica, Nicaragua, Panama); *Recurso de protección* (Chile) or *Mandado de segurança* and *mandado de injunçao* (Brazil).[101] In all of the Latin American countries, the provisions for the action are embodied in the constitutions; and in all of them, except Chile, the actions of amparo have been expressly regulated by statutes, particularly in special statutes related to constitutional litigations, with the exception of Panama and Paraguay where the amparo action is regulated in the general procedural codes (*Código Judicial, Código Procesal Civil*).

I. THE RIGHT TO AMPARO IN VENEZUELA

Within a mixed system of judicial review, since 1961, the Venezuelan Constitution establishes a "constitutional right for amparo" or to be protected by the

100. See generally Allan R. BREWER-CARÍAS, *The Latin American Amparo Proceeding and the Writ of Amparo in The Philippines*, 1.1 CITY UNIV. HONG KONG L. REV. 73-90 (Oct. 2009).

101. See generally Allan R. BREWER-CARÍAS, *Ensayo de síntesis comparativa sobre el régimen del amparo en la legislación latinoamericana*, in *Revista Iberoamericana de Derecho Procesal Constitucional*, N° 9 enero-junio 2008, Editorial Porrúa, Instituto Iberoamericano de Derecho Procesal Constitucional, México 2008, pp. 311-321; Eduardo Ferrer Mac-Gregor, *Breves notas sobre el amparo latinoamericano (desde el derecho procesal constitucional comparado)*, in Héctor FIX-ZAMUDIO and Eduardo FERRER MAC-GREGOR, *El derecho de amparo en el mundo*, Edit. Porrúa, México, 2006, 3–39.

courts,[102] that according to article 27 of the 1999 Constitution everybody has for the protection of all the rights, freedoms and guarantees enshrined in the constitution and in international treaties, or which, even if not listed in the text, are inherent to the human person. The constitution does not set forth a separate action of habeas corpus for the protection of personal freedom and liberty; which are also protected by the action for amparo. In this latter case of amparo for the protection of personal freedom or safety, it can be exercised by any person in which cases "the detainee shall be immediately transferred to the court, without delay" [103]

Additionally, the Venezuelan Constitution has also set forth the habeas data recourse, in order to guarantee the right to have access to the information and data concerning the claimant, contained in official or private registries. The habeas data recourse also provides the right to know about the use that has been made of such information concerning its purpose, and to petition the competent court for the updating, rectification or destruction of erroneous records that unlawfully affect the petitioner's rights.

The amparo proceeding has been regulated in the Organic Law on Amparo for the protection of constitutional rights and guarantees that was sanctioned in 1988 (*Ley Orgánica de Amparo sobre derechos y garantías constitucionales*).[104] According to its provisions, the right to amparo can be exercised through an "autonomous action for amparo"[105] that is generally filed before the first instance courts,[106] with a

102. Venez. Const. Art. 27 (1999); Venez. Const. Art. 49 (1961). See generally, on the action of amparo in Venezuela, Allan R. BREWER-CARÍAS, *Instituciones Políticas y Constitucionales, Tomo V, El derecho y la acción de amparo*, Editorial Jurídica Venezolana, Caracas, 1998; Gustavo BRICEÑO V., COMENTARIOS A LA LEY DE AMPARO, Edit. Kinesis, Caracas, (1991); RAFAEL J. CHAVERO GAZDIK, *El nuevo régimen del amparo constitucional en Venezuela*, Editorial Sherwood, Caracas, 2001; Gustavo José LINARES BENZO, *El Proceso de Amparo*, Universidad Central de Venezuela, Facultad de Ciencias Jurídicas y Políticas, Caracas, (1999); Hildegard RONDÓN DE SANSÓ, *Amparo Constitucional*, Caracas, (1988); Hildegard RONDÓN DE SANSÓ, *La acción de amparo contra los poderes públicos*, Editorial Arte, Caracas, (1994); Carlos M. AYALA CORAO and Rafael J. CHAVERO GAZIDK, *El amparo constitucional en Venezuela*, in Héctor FIX-ZAMUDIO and Eduardo FERRER MAC-GREGOR (COORD.), *El derecho de amparo en el mundo*, Universidad Nacional Autónoma de México, Editorial Porrúa, México, 2006, 649–92.

103. Venez. Const. Art. 27 (1999).

104. See *Gaceta Oficial* N° 33.891 of January 22, 1988. On this Law, *see* Allan R. BREWER-CARÍAS, Carlos M. AYALA CORAO & Rafael CHAVERO G., LEY ORGÁNICA DE AMPARO SOBRE DERECHOS Y GARANTÍAS CONSTITUCIONALES, Editorial Jurídica Venezolana, Caracas, 2007.

105. See Allan R. Brewer-Carías, *El derecho de amparo y la acción de amparo*, in *Revista de Derecho Público*, n.° 22, Editorial Jurídica Venezolana, Caracas, 1985, 51 ff.

106. According to Article 7 of the Organic Law on Amparo, the competent courts to decide amparo actions are the courts of First Instance with competence on matters related to the constitutional rights or guarantees violated, in the place where the facts, acts or omission occurred. Venez. Amparo Law, Art. 7. Regarding amparo of personal freedom and security, the competent courts should be the criminal first instance courts. Venez. Amparo Law, Art. 40. Nonetheless, when the facts, acts or omissions harming or threatening to harm the constitutional right or guarantee occurs in a place where no First Instance court exists, the amparo action may be brought before any judge of the site, which must decide according to

reestablishing nature, in general regarding flagrant, vulgar, direct and immediate constitutional harm to the plaintiff's rights. The constitutional protection can also be claimed by means of other preexisting ordinary or extraordinary legal actions or recourses already established in the legal system to which an amparo petition is joined. This can be the popular action of unconstitutionality of statutes, the judicial review of administrative actions' recourses, and any other "ordinary judicial procedures" or "preexisting judicial means," through which the "violation or threat of violation of a constitutional right or guaranty may be alleged."[107] In these cases, in which a competent judge is empowered to immediately reestablish the infringed legal situation, it is not that the ordinary means substitute the constitutional right of protection (or diminish it), but instead that they can serve as the judicial means for constitutional litigation because the judge is empowered to protect fundamental rights and immediately reestablish the infringed legal situation.[108]

These regulations result in the Venezuelan right for amparo, which has certain peculiarities that distinguish it from the other similar institutions for the protection of the constitutional rights and guarantees established in Latin America.[109] Besides the adjective consequences of the amparo being a constitutional right in Venezuela, it can be characterized by the following trends:

First, the right of amparo can be exercised for the protection of all constitutional rights, not only of civil individual rights. Consequently, the social, economic, cultural, environmental and political rights declared in the constitution and in international treaties are also protected by means of amparo. The habeas corpus provision is an aspect of the right to constitutional protection, or one of the expressions of the amparo.

Second, the right to amparo seeks to assure protection of constitutional rights and guarantees against any disturbance in their enjoyment and exercise, whether originated by public authorities or by private individuals, without distinction. In addition, in the case of disturbance by public authorities, the amparo is admissible against statutes; against legislative, administrative and judicial acts and against material or factual courses of action of Public Administration or public officials.

Third, the decision of the judge, as a consequence of the exercise of this right to amparo, whether through the preexisting actions or recourses or by means of the

---

the law. Such judge must also, in a twenty-four hour delay, send the files for consultation to the competent First Instance court. Venez. Amparo Law, Art. 9. Only in cases in which facts, acts or omissions of the President of the Republic, his cabinet members, the National Electoral Council, the Prosecutor General, the Attorney General and the General Comptroller of the Republic are involved does the power to decide the amparo actions correspond to the Constitutional Chamber of the Supreme Tribunal of Justice. Venez. Amparo Law, Art. 8.

107. Venez. Amparo Law, Arts. 3, 4, 5

108. See Allan R. BREWER-CARÍAS, *La reciente evolución jurisprudencial en relación a la admisibilidad del recurso de amparo*, in *Revista de derecho público*, N° 19, Caracas, 1984, pp. 207–218.

109. See *generally* H. FIX-ZAMUDIO, LA PROTECCIÓN PROCESAL DE LOS DERECHOS HUMANOS ANTE LAS JURISDICCIONES NACIONALES, Madrid, 1982, 366.

autonomous action for amparo, is not limited to being of a precautionary or preliminary nature, but to reestablish the infringed legal situation by deciding on the merits, that is, the constitutionality of the alleged disturbance of the constitutional right.

Fourth, because the Venezuelan system of judicial review is a mixed one, judicial review of legislation can also be exercised by the courts when deciding an action for amparo when, for instance, the alleged violation of the right is based on a statute deemed unconstitutional. In such cases, if the protection requested is granted by the courts, it must previously declare the statute inapplicable on the grounds of it being unconstitutional. Therefore, in such cases, judicial review of the constitutionality of legislation can also be exercised when an action for amparo of fundamental rights is filed.

Finally, in the Venezuelan systems of judicial review and of amparo, according to article 336.10 of the 1999 Constitution, an extraordinary review recourse can be filed before the Constitutional Chamber of the Supreme Court against judicial final decisions issued in amparo proceedings, and also by any court when applying the diffuse method of judicial review resolving the inapplicability of statutes because they are considered unconstitutional.

Following these main general trends, I will analyze the amparo proceeding in Venezuela, studying the rules regarding the injured party; the justiciable rights; the conditions of the injury; the reparable character of harms and the restorative character of amparo; the imminent character of threats and preventive character of the amparo; the injuring party; the conditions of the injuring public actions and omissions; the admissibility condition and the extraordinary condition of the action; the rules of procedure; the preliminary protective measures; and the final decision. In each case where it proceeds I have made the corresponding comparisons with civil rights injunctions in the United States.

II. THE INJURED PARTY IN THE AMPARO PROCEEDING

One of the most distinguishable principles regarding the amparo proceeding as an extraordinary judicial means for the protection of constitutional rights is the principle of bilateralism, which implies the need for the existence of a controversy between two or more parties. The main consequence of this principle is that the amparo proceeding can only be initiated at a party's request, which excludes any case of *ex officio* amparo proceeding.[110]

Consequently, in order to initiate this proceeding, an action must be brought before a court by a plaintiff as the injured party, against the injuring party or parties, who, as defendants, must be called to the procedure as having caused the harm or the violation to the constitutional rights of the former.[111]

The injured party, in principle, is the person having the constitutional right that has been violated, a situation that gives him a particular interest in bringing the case

110 See ALLAN R. BREWER-CARÍAS, CONSTITUTIONAL PROTECTION OF HUMAN RIGHTS IN LATIN AMERICA,. A COMPARATIVE STUDY OF THE AMPARO PROCEEDINGS, *supra* note 2, at 179.

111. *Id.*

before a court. That is why the amparo action has been considered as an action *in personam* (*personalisima*) through which the plaintiff, seeking the protection of constitutional rights, must be the actual injured or aggrieved person.

Because the action has a personal character (*acción personalísima*), the plaintiff, as the person whose constitutional rights have been injured or threatened of being harmed,[112] is the titleholder of the harmed or violated right[113] and is the injured party with justiciable interest in the subject matter of the litigation, which can be a natural person (citizens or foreigner), or an artificial person (associations, foundations, corporations or companies). For this purpose the plaintiff can act directly, *in personam,* or through his representative.[114] Thus, nobody can file an action for amparo alleging in his own name a right belonging to another,[115] the general exception being the action of habeas corpus, in which case, because generally the injured person is physically prevented from acting personally because of detention or restrained freedom, the Amparo Law authorizes anybody to file the action on his behalf.[116]

On the other hand, as not all constitutional rights are individual, and to the contrary, some are collective by nature, in the sense that they correspond to a more or

---

112. See Decision of the former Venezuelan Supreme Court of Justice, Politico Administrative Chamber n.° 571 of Aug. 13, 1992, in REVISTA DE DERECHO PÚBLICO, n.° 51, Editorial Jurídica Venezolana, Caracas, 1992, pp. 160-61.

113. Regarding injunctions in the United States the court in *Parkview Hospital v. Commw. Dep't of Pub. Welfare*, held that bringing an action "requires an aggrieved party showing a substantial, direct and immediate interest in the subject matter of the litigation." 424 A.2d 599, 600 (Pa. Commw. Ct. 1981). See also 43A C.J.S. *Injunctions* § 299. See also *Warth v. Seldin*, 422 U.S. 490, 498-500 (1975) (the plaintiff must "'allege such a personal stake in the outcome of the controversy'" as to justify the exercise of the court's remedial powers on his behalf, because he himself has suffered "'some threatened or actual injury resulting from the putatively illegal action.'"). See M. GLENN ABERNATHY AND BARBARA A. PERRY, CIVIL LIBERTIES UNDER THE CONSTITUTION 4 (6th ed. 1993). That is why standing to seek injunctive relief in the United States is only attributed to the person affected. See Ala. Power Co. v. Ala. Elec. Co-op., 394 F.2d 672 (5th Cir. 1968); 43A C.J.S. *Injunctions* § 200 (2004).

114. As it was ruled by the former Supreme Court of Justice of Venezuela regarding the personal character of the amparo suit, imposing for its admissibility: A qualified interest of who is asking for the restitution or reestablishment of the harmed right or guaranty, that is, that the harm be directed to him and that, eventually, its effects affect directly and indisputably upon him, harming his scope of subjective rights guaranteed in the Constitution. It is only the person that is specially and directly injured in his subjective fundamental rights by a specific act, fact or omission the one that can bring an action before the competent courts by mean of a brief and speedy proceeding, in order that the judge decides immediately the reestablishment of the infringed subjective legal situation. See decision N° 460 of Aug. 27, 1993, *Kenet E. Leal* case, in *Revista de Derecho Público*, N° 55-56, Editorial Jurídica Venezolana, Caracas, 1993, p. 322; and decision of the Venezuelan First Court on Judicial Review of Administrative Actions, Nov. 18, 1993 (*Gobernación del Estado Miranda* case), in REVISTA DE DERECHO PÚBLICO, N° 55–56, Editorial Jurídica Venezolana, Caracas, 1993, pp. 325–327.

115. See decision of the former Venezuelan Supreme Court of Justice, Politico Administrative Chamber, N° 72 of Feb. 14, 1990, *Carlos Coll* case, in *Revista de Derecho Público*, n.° 4l, Editorial Jurídica Venezolana, Caracas, 1990, p. 101.

116. Venez. Amparo Law, Art. 41 (anybody acting on his behalf).

less defined group of persons, their violations affect not only the personal rights of each of the individuals who enjoy them, but also, the whole group of persons or collectivity to which the individuals belong. In these cases the amparo action can also be filed by the group or the association of persons representing their associates, even if they do not have the formal character of an artificial person. For such purpose, the Venezuelan constitution expressly sets forth the constitutional right of everybody to have access to justice, to seek for the enforcement not only of personal rights, but also of "collective" and "diffuse" rights.[117] This has been the case, for instance, of amparo actions filed for the protection of electoral rights, in which case, any citizen, invoking the general voters' rights, can file the action.[118] In other words, the Constitutional Chamber has admitted that: "Any capable person that tends to impede harm to the population or sectors of it to which he appertains, can file actions in defense of diffuse or collective interest," extending the "standing to the associations, societies, foundations, chambers, trade unions and other collective entities devoted to defend society, provided that they act within the limits of their societal goals referring to the protection of the interests of their members."[119]

In these cases, the Constitutional Chamber has determined that the action filed must be based "not only on the personal right or interest of the claimant, but also on

117. Venez. Const. Art. 26. The Constitutional Chamber has referred to the diffuse and collective interests or rights as concepts established for the protection of a number of individuals that can be considered as representing the entire, or at least an important part of a society, which are affected on their constitutional rights and guarantees destined to protect the public welfare by an attack to their quality of life. See decision of the Constitutional Chamber n° 656 of June 30, 2000, *Defensor del Pueblo vs. Comisión Legislativa Nacional* case, available at http://www.tsj.gov.ve/decisiones/scon/Junio/656-300600-00-1728%20.htm. See also decision of the same Constitucional Chamber n° 379 of Feb. 26, 2003, *Mireya Ripanti et vs. Presidente de Petróleos de Venezuela S.A. (PDVSA)* case, in REVISTA DE DERECHO PÚBLICO, n° 93–96, Editorial Jurídica Venezolana, Caracas, 2003, pp. 152 ff.

118. In these cases, the Chamber has even granted precautionary measures with *erga omnes* effects "to both individuals and corporations who have brought to suit the constitutional protection, and to all voters as a group." See Decision of the Constitutional Chamber n° 483 of May 29, 2000, *"Queremos Elegir" y otros* case, in REVISTA DE DERECHO PÚBLICO, n° 82, 2000, Editorial Jurídica Venezolana, pp. 489–491. In the same sense, see the decision of the same Chamber n° 714 of July 13, 2000, *APRUM* case, in REVISTA DE DERECHO PÚBLICO, n° 83, Editorial Jurídica Venezolana, Caracas, 2000, pp. 319 ff.

119. The Chamber added that: "Those who file actions regarding the defense of diffuse interest do not need to have any previously established relation with the offender, but has to act as a member of society, or of its general categories (consumers, users, etc.) and has to invoke his right or interest shared with the population's, because he participates with all regarding the harmed factual situation due to the noncompliance of the diminution of fundamental rights of everybody, which gives birth to a communal subjective right, that although indivisible, is actionable by any one place within the infringed situation." See decision of June 30, 2000, *Defensoría del Pueblo* case, available at http://www.tsj.gov.ve/decisiones/scon/Junio/656-300600-00-1728%20.htm. See the comments in RAFAEL CHAVERO, EL NUEVO RÉGIMEN DEL AMPARO CONSTITUCIONAL EN VENEZUELA, *supra* note 5, pp. 110–114.

a common or collective right or interest."[120] Consequently, in these cases, a bond or relation must exist, "even if it is not a legal one, between whoever demands in the general interest of the society or a part of it (social common interest), and the damage or danger caused to the collectivity."[121]

These collective actions have some similarities with the civil rights class actions developed in the United States,[122] which have been very effective for the protection of civil rights in cases of discrimination.[123]

---

120. That is, the reason of the claim or the action for amparo must be "the general damage to the quality of life of all the inhabitants of the country or parts of it, since the legal situation of all the members of the society or its groups have been damaged when their common quality of life was worsened." Thus, the damage "concerns an indivisible right or interest that involves the entire population of the country or a group of it." Decision nº 1048 of Aug. 17, 2000, *William O. Ojeda O. vs. Consejo Nacional Electoral* case, available at http://www.tsj.gov.ve/decisiones/scon/agosto/1053-310800-00-2397%20.htm.

121. See Decision nº 1048 of Aug. 17, 2000, *William O. Ojeda O. vs. Consejo Nacional Electoral* case, http://www.tsj.gov.ve/decisiones/scon/agosto/1053-310800-00-2397%20.htm. In spite of all the aforementioned progressive decisions regarding the protection of collective and diffuse rights, like the political ones, in a decision dated Nov. 24, 2005, the Venezuelan Constitutional Chamber has reverted its ruling, and in a case originated by a claim filed by the director of a political association named "Un Solo Pueblo" against the threat of violations of the political rights of the aforesaid political party and of all the other supporters of the calling of a recall referendum regarding the President of the Republic, the Chamber ruled that: "The action of amparo was filed for the protection of constitutional rights of an undetermined number of persons, whose identity was not indicated in the filing document, in which they are not included as claimants. It is the criteria of this Chamber, those that could result directly affected in their constitutional rights and guaranties by the alleged threat attributed to the Ministry of Defense and the General Commanders of the Army and the National Guard are, precisely, the persons that are members or supporters of "*Un Solo Pueblo*," or those who prove they are part of one of the groups that promoted the recall referendum; in which case they would have standing to bring before the constitutional judge, by themselves or through representatives, seeking the reestablishment of the infringed juridical situation or impeding the realization of the threat, because the *legitimatio ad causam* exists in each one of them, not precisely as constitutionally harmed or aggrieved. Due to the foregoing, the Chamber considers that Mr. William Ojeda, who said he acted as Director of the political association called "*Un Sólo Pueblo*," a quality that he furthermore has not demonstrated, lacks the necessary standing to seek for constitutional amparo of the constitutional rights set forth in Articles 19, 21 and 68 of the constitution regarding the members, supporters and participants of the mentioned political association as well as the political coalition that proposed the recall referendum of the President of the Republic, and consequently, this Chamber declares the inadmissibility of the amparo action filed." See Decision nº 3550 of Nov. 24, 2005, *Willian Ojeda vs. Ministro de la Defensa y los Comandantes Generales del Ejercito y de la Guardia Nacional* case, in REVISTA DE DERECHO PÚBLICO, nº 104, Editorial Jurídica Venezolana, Caracas, 2005, pp. 231 ff.

122. Regulated in Rule 23 of the Federal Rules of Civil Procedure filed for the protection of civil rights, according to which, in cases of a class of persons whom have "questions of law or fact common to the class," but have so many members that joining all of them would be an impracticable task, then the action can be filed by one or more of its members as representative plaintiff parties on behalf of all, provided that the claims of the representative parties are

Although being of a personal character, even in cases of actions for the protection of collective and diffuse rights, the People's Defendant was created in Venezuela as an independent and autonomous separate branch of government for the protection of human rights,[124] having enough standing to file amparo actions on behalf of the community or groups of persons.[125] For example, standing is extended to cases

---

"typical of the claims . . . of the class" and that such "representative parties will fairly and adequately protect the interests of the class." FED. R. CIV. P. 23(a).

123. It was the case decided by the Supreme Court in *Zablocki v. Redhail*, as a result of a class action brought before a federal court under 42 U.S.C. § 1983, by Wisconsin residents holding that the marriage prohibition set forth in Wisconsin Statute § 245.10 violated the equal protection clause of the Fourteenth Amendment of the United States Constitution. 434 U.S. 374, 375-77 (1978). According to that statute, Wisconsin residents were prevented from marrying if they were behind in their child support obligations or if the children to whom they were obligated were likely to become public charges. *Zablocki*, 434 U.S. 377. The Court found that the statute violated equal protection in that it "directly and substantially" interfered with the fundamental right to marry, without being closely tailored to effectuate the state's interests. *Id.* at 382, 387. Another Supreme Court decision, *Lau v. Nichols*, also decided in favor of a class on discrimination violations. 414 U.S. 563 (1974). In the case, non-English-speaking students of Chinese ancestry brought a class suit in a federal court of California against officials of the San Francisco Unified School District, seeking relief against alleged unequal educational opportunities resulting from the officials' failure to establish a program to rectify the students' language problem. *Lau*, 414 U.S. at 564-65. The Supreme Court eventually held that the school district, which received federal financial assistance, violated statutes that ban discrimination based on race, color, or national origin in any program or activity receiving federal financial assistance, and furthermore violated the implementing regulations of the Department of Health, Education, and Welfare by failing to establish a program to deal with the complaining students' language problem. *Id.* at 568-69.

124. The 1999 Venezuelan Constitution, in this regard, establishes a separation of powers, distinguishing five branches of government, separating the Legislative, Executive, Judicial, Electoral and Citizens branches; creating the People's Defendant within the Citizens Power, in addition to the Public Prosecutor Office and the General Comptroller Office. VENEZ. CONST. ART. 134 (1999). The People's Defendant was created for the promotion, defense and supervision of the rights and guarantees set forth in the constitution and in the international treaties on human rights, as well as for the citizens' legitimate, collective and diffuse interests. VENEZ. CONST. ART. 281 (1999). In particular, according to Article 281 of the constitution, it also has among its functions to watch for the functioning of public services power and to promote and protect the peoples' legitimate, collective and diffuse rights and interests against arbitrariness or deviation of power in the rendering of such services, being authorized to file the necessary actions to ask for the compensation of the damages caused from the malfunctioning of public services. VENEZ. CONST. ART. 281 (1999). It also has among its functions, the possibility of filing actions of amparo and habeas corpus.

125. The courts have declared that the Defender has standing to bring to suit actions aimed at enforcing the diffuse and collective rights or interests; not being necessary the requirement of the acquiescence of the society it acts on behalf of for the exercise of the action. See Decision n° 1051 of Aug. 2, 2000 of the Venezuelan First Court on Judicial Review of Administrative Actions, *Henry Lima et al. case*, in REVISTA DE DERECHO PÚBLICO, n° 83, Editorial Jurídica Venezolana, Caracas, 2000, pp. 326-27.

of the protection of indigenous peoples' rights, the right to the environment and the citizens' right to political participation.[126]

III. THE JUSTICIABILE CONSTITUTIONAL RIGHTS AND GUARANTEES THROUGH THE AMPARO PROCEEDING

As a matter of principle in Venezuela, all rights and guarantees enshrined in the constitution or those that have acquired constitutional rank and value are justiciable[127] rights by means of the amparo action. That is, they have to be, in spite of being regulated in statutes, out of the reach of the legislator in the sense that they cannot be eliminated, or diminished through statutes.

---

126. The Constitutional Chamber of the Supreme Tribunal of Venezuela admitted the standing of the Defender of the People to file actions for amparo on behalf of the citizens as a whole, as was the case of the action filed against the legislative body pretension to appoint the Electoral National Council members without fulfilling the constitutional requirements. In the case, decided on June 30, 2000, the Constitutional Chamber, when analyzing Article 280 of the constitution, in its decision n° 656 pointed out that "the protection of diffuse and collective rights and interests may be raised by the Defender of the People, through the action of amparo," adding the following: "As for the general provision of Article 280 *eiusdem*, regarding the general defense and protection of diffuse and collective interests, this Chamber considers that the Defender of the People is entitled to act to protect those rights and interests, when they correspond in general to the consumers and users (6, Article 281), or to protect the rights of Indian peoples (paragraph 8 of the same Article), since the defense and protection of such categories is one of the faculties granted to said entity by Article 281 of the Constitution in force. It is about a general protection and not a protection of individualities. Within this frame of action, and since the political rights are included in the human rights and guaranties of Title III of the Constitution in force, which have a general projection, among which the ones provided in Article 62 of the Constitution can be found, it must be concluded that the Defender of the People on behalf of the society, legitimated by law, is entitled to bring to suit an action of amparo tending to control the Electoral Power, to the citizen's benefit, in order to enforce Articles 62 and 70 of the Constitution, which were denounced to be breached by the National Legislative Assembly…(right to citizen participation). Due to the difference between diffuse and collective interests, both the Defender of the People, within its attributions, and every individual residing in the country, except for the legal exceptions, are entitled to bring to suit the action (be it of amparo or an specific one) for the protection of the former ones; while the action of the collective interests is given to the Defender of the People and to any member of the group or sector identified as a component of that specific collectivity, and acting defending the collectivity. Both individuals and corporations whose object be the protection of such interests may raise the action, and the standing in all these actions varies according to the nature of the same, that is why law can limit the action in specific individuals or entities. However, in our Constitution, in the provisions of Article 281 the Defender of the People is objectively granted the procedural interest and the capacity to sue." See Decision of the Constitutional Chamber n° 656 of June 30, 2000, *Defensor del Pueblo vs. Comisión Legislativa Nacional* case, available at http://www.tsj.gov.ve/decisiones/scon/Junio/656-300600-00-1728%20.htm. See *also* Decision n° 379 of February 26, 2003, *Mireya Ripanti et vs. Presidente de Petróleos de Venezuela S.A. (PDVSA)* case, in REVISTA DE DERECHO PÚBLICO, n° 93–96, Editorial Jurídica Venezolana, Caracas, 2003, pp. 152 ff.

127. "Justiciability" being defined as "The quality or state of being appropriate or suitable for review by courts;" and "Justiciable," as "capable of being disposed of judicially." BLACK'S LAW DICTIONARY 882 (8th ed. 2004).

The consequence of this principle is that the purpose of the amparo actions is to protect individuals against violations of the "constitutional" provision regarding their right; not being able to file an action for amparo simply based on the violation of the "statutory" provisions that regulate the constitutional right. For instance, as it happens with the right to property, regarding which an amparo action for its protection can be admitted when, for example, arbitrary administrative acts prevent or impede in absolute terms the use of property. On the contrary, it is not admitted for the protection of property, for instance, against trespassing. In these cases, the ordinary civil judicial expedite actions (*interdictos*) are the ones that should be filed.[128]

In general terms, this implies the extraordinary character of the amparo action, in the sense that it can only be filed when no other appropriate and effective ordinary judicial means for protection are legally provided or when if such protections are provided, they are ineffective.

This condition of admissibility of the amparo actions is very similar to the so-called "inadequacy" condition established in the United States regarding the equitable injunction remedies, in the sense that they are only admissible when there are no adequate remedies in law to assure the protection; or when the law cannot provide

128. Property rights are not only established in the constitutions but are also extensively regulated in the Civil Code. The latter not only contains substantive regulations regarding the exercise of such rights, but it also provides for adjective ordinary remedies in case those rights are affected. In particular, the Civil Code and the Civil Procedure Codes establishes some sort of civil injunctions to guarantee immediate protection in cases of trespasses (*interdictos*) for instance of possession rights, which are effective judicial remedies for the protection of land owners or occupant rights. Thus, in cases of property trespass, the *interdicto de amparo* or of new construction are effective judicial means for protection of property rights, not being possible to file an amparo action in such cases. In this regard, the Constitutional Chamber of the Supreme Tribunal of Justice of Venezuela, in a case decided in 2000, argued as follows: "The amparo action protects one aspect of the legal situations of persons referred to their fundamental rights, corresponding the defense of subjective rights – different to fundamental rights and public liberties – to the ordinary administrative and judicial recourses and actions. For instance, it is not the same to deny a citizen the condition to have property rights, than to discuss property rights between parties, the protection of which corresponds to a specific ordinary judicial action of recovery (reivindicación). This means that in the amparo proceedings the court judges the actions of public entities or individuals that can harm fundamental rights; but in no case can it review, for instance, the applicability or interpretation or statutes by Public Administration or the courts, unless from them a direct violation of the Constitution can be deduced. The amparo is not a new judicial instance, nor the substitution of ordinary judicial means for the protection of rights and interest; it is an instrument to reaffirm constitutional values, by mean of which the court, hearing an amparo, can decide regarding the contents or the application of constitutional provisions regulating fundamental rights; can review the interpretation made by Public Administration or judicial bodies, or determine if the facts from which constitutional violations are deduced constitute a direct violation of the Constitution."See Decision N° 828 of July 27, 2000, *Seguros Corporativos (SEGUCORP), C.A. et al. vs. Superintedencia de Seguros* case, in *Revista de Derecho Público*, n° 83, Editorial Juridica Venezolana, Caracas, 2000, pp. 290 ff.

an adequate remedy because of the nature of the right involved, as was the case regarding school segregation.[129]

The rights protected by the amparo action are the "constitutional rights," that comprise of first, rights expressly declared in the constitution. Second, are those rights that are not enumerated in the constitution and are inherent to human beings. Third, are the rights enumerated in international instruments on human rights ratified by the state, that in Venezuela have constitutional rank being applied with preference in all cases in which they provide more favorable conditions for the enjoyment of the right.[130] Consequently, all the rights listed in Title III of the constitution, which refer to human rights, guarantees and duties, are protected by the amparo action. Those rights include citizenship rights, civil (individual) rights, political rights, social and familial rights, cultural and educational rights, economic rights, environmental rights and the rights of indigenous peoples enumerated in Articles 19 to 129. Additionally, all other constitutional rights and guarantees derived from other constitutional provisions can also be protected even if not included in Title III, such as the constitutional guarantee of the independence of the judiciary, or the constitutional guarantee of the legality of taxation (that taxes can only by set forth by statute).[131] Also, regarding the protected rights, through the open clause of constitutional rights, the constitution admits the amparo action for the protection of those other constitutional rights and guaranties not expressly listed in the constitution, but that can be considered inherent to human beings.[132]

The most important question regarding the justiciability of constitutional rights refers to the scope of the protection of social rights, and in particular the right of the people to have their health protected by the state,[133] and the obligation of the state to provide public health services. In this regard, the Constitutional Chamber of the Supreme Tribunal of Justice of Venezuela in a decision (*Glenda López y otros vs.*

129. See OWEN M. FISS & DOUG RENDLEMAN, INJUNCTIONS, 59 (2nd ed. 1984). This inadequacy condition, of course, normally results from the factual situations regarding the case or from the nature of the right, which in some cases impedes or allows the granting of the protection. In this sense, for instance, it was resolved since the well-known case of *Wheelock v. Nooman*, 15 N.E. 67 (N.Y. 1888), in which case the defendant, having left on the plaintiff's property great boulders beyond the authorization he had, the injunction was granted in order to require such defendant to remove them. Wheelock, 15 N.E. at 67-70. The plaintiff in the case could not easily remove the boulders and sued the cost of removal of the trespassing rocks because of their size and weight. *Id.* at 69. On the contrary, in another case, the remedy at law was considered adequate because the litter the defendant left on the property could be removed by the plaintiff paying for someone to remove the trash, in which case he could simply sue the defendant for the cost incurred. *Connor v. Grosso*, 529 P.2d 435 (Cal. 1953).

130. Venez. Const. Art. 23.

131. See BREWER-CARÍAS, *Instituciones Políticas y Constitucionales,* Tomo V, *El derecho y la acción de amparo, supra* note 5, at 209. See Decision of the First Court on Judicial Review of Administrative Action, *Fecadove* case, in Rafael CHAVERO G., *El nuevo régimen del amparo constitucional en Venezuela, supra* note 5, at p. 157.

132. Venez. Const. Art. 22.

133. Venez. Const. Art. 83.

Instituto Venezolano de los Seguros Sociales) pointed out that the right to health or to the protection of health is:

> an integral part of the right to life, set forth in the Constitution as a fundamental social right (and not simply as an assignment of State purposes) whose satisfaction mainly belongs to the State and its institutions, through activities intended to progressively raise the quality of life of citizens and the collective welfare.[134]

This, according to the Court's decision, implies that "the right to health is not to be exhausted with the simple physical care of a person, but must be extended to the appropriate treatment in order to safeguard the mental, social, environmental integrity of persons, including the community."[135]

IV. THE INJURY IN THE AMPARO PROCEEDING

The injuries violating constitutional rights, against which the amparo action is established, can consist of harms or threats affecting those rights. Harms are always damages affecting or destroying the object of the right; and threats are injuries that, without destroying such object, put the enjoyment of the right in a situation of danger or of suffering a detriment.

In order to be protected by means of the amparo proceeding, these injuries–harms or threats–caused to constitutional rights, must be evident, actual and real, that is, they must affect personally and directly the rights of the plaintiff, in a manifestly arbitrary, illegal and illegitimate way, which the plaintiff must not have consented to.

In addition to these general conditions, specifically regarding harms, they must have a reparable character. Regarding threats, they must affect the rights in an imminent way. That is why the type of injuries inflicted on constitutional rights furthers the purpose for the amparo proceeding: if harms, being reparable, the amparo has a restorative effect; and if threats, being imminent, the amparo has a preventive effect.

Regarding the general conditions with which the injuries to constitutional rights must comply in order for an amparo actions to be admitted, the following are established in the Amparo Law. First, it must have a personal and direct character, in the sense that it must personally affect the plaintiff. Second, it must be actual and real. Third, it must be manifestly or ostensibly arbitrary, illegal and illegitimate. Fourth, it must be evidenced in the case. Finally, it must not be consented to by the plaintiff.

The first condition of the injury inflicted upon the plaintiff's constitutional rights, in order for an amparo action to be admitted, is that the plaintiff must have suffered

---

134 Decision of the Constitutional Chamber of the Supreme Tribunal of Justice of Venezuela nº 487 of Apr. 6, 2001, *Glenda López y otros vs. Instituto Venezolano de los Seguros Sociales* case, in *Revista de Derecho Público*, Nº 85-88, Editorial Juridica Venezulana, Caracas, 2001, pp. 139 ff.

135 *Id.*

a "direct, personal and present harm or threat in his constitutional rights."[136] That is, the plaintiff must be personally affected. Consequently, the amparo action cannot be filed when the affected rights belong to another person, separate from the claimant or only affects the plaintiff in an indirect way.

If the harm does not affect the constitutional rights of the plaintiff in a personal and direct way, the action must be considered inadmissible. The action is also inadmissible when the harm or threat is not attributed to the person identified as the injuring party, that is, when the injury is not personally caused by the defendant.[137]

However, in addition to directly affecting the constitutional rights of the plaintiff, the injury must be "actual," in the sense that at the moment of the filing of the action, the harm or threat must be presently occurring and must not have ceased or concluded.

This same rule is also applied in the United States regarding injunctions, in the sense that for a person to be entitled to injunctive relief, he or she must establish an actual, substantial and serious injury, or an affirmative prospect of such an injury. Consequently, a petitioner is not entitled to an injunction where no injury to the petitioner is shown from the action sought to be prevented.[138]

In other words, the injury must be real, in the sense that it must have effectively occurred; a fact that must be clearly demonstrated by the plaintiff in his petition. That is why the Venezuelan courts have ruled that:

---

136. For example, it has been ruled by the courts in Venezuela that: "[i]t is necessary, though, that the denounced actions directly affect the subjective sphere of the claimant, consequently excluding the generic conducts, even if they can affect in a tangential way on the matter." See Decision of the First Court on Juricial Review of Administrative Actions of Dec. 2, 1993, in *Revista de Derecho Público*, n° 55–56, Editorial Jurídica Venezolana, Caracas, 1993, pp. 302–303.

137. In this sense, for instance, it was decided by the former Supreme Court of Justice in 1999, in an amparo filed against the President of the Republic, denouncing as the injuring acts, possible measures to be adopted by the National Constituent Assembly that the President had convened, once installed. The Court rejected the action considering that "the reasons alleged by the plaintiff were of eventual and hypothetical nature, which contradicts the need of an objective and real harm or threat to constitutional rights or guaranties" in order for the amparo to be admissible. Regarding the alleged defendant in the case, the Court ruled as follows:

    This court must say that the action for constitutional amparo serves to give protection against situations that in a direct way could produce harm regarding the plaintiff's constitutional rights or guaranties, seeking the restoration of its infringed juridical situation. In this case, the person identified as plaintiff (President of the Republic) could not be by himself the one to produce the eventual harm which would condition the voting rights of the plaintiff, and the fear that the organization of the constituted branches of government could be modified, would be attributed to the members of those that could be elected to the National Constituent Assembly not yet elected. Thus in the case there does not exist the immediate relation between the plaintiff and the defendants needed in the amparo suit.

    See the reference to the Decision of Apr. 23, 1999 (*A. Albornoz* case), in Rafael CHAVERO, *El nuevo régimen del amparo constitucional en Venezuela*, *supra* note 5, at p. 240.

138. See Boyle v. Landry, 401 U.S. 77 (1971).

The amparo action can only be directed against a perfectly and determined act or omission, and not against a generic conduct; against an objective and real activity and not against a supposition regarding the intention of the presumed injurer, and against the direct and immediate consequences of the activities of the public body or officer.[139]

This actual and real character of the injury necessary to sustain an amparo suit implies that it cannot be a past injury, or one likely to occur in the future. In this sense the Venezuelan courts have argued that the injury "must be alive, must be present in all its intensity," in the sense that "referring to the present, not to the past; it does not refer to facts that already had happened, which appertain to the past, but to present situations, which can be prolonged during an indefinite length of time."[140]

Based precisely on this condition, the former Supreme Court of Justice of Venezuela rejected the possibility of filing amparo actions against statutes, in cases in which they are not directly applicable, needing additional acts for their execution.[141]

On the other hand, this same condition that the harm or threat be actual implies that it must not have ceased or concluded, as could happen, for instance, when, in the course of the procedure, the challenged act is repealed.[142] Consequently, in order to grant the amparo protection, the Venezuelan courts have ruled that the harm must

---

139. Decision of the former Supreme Court of Justice, Politico Administrative Chamber, of Dec. 2, 1993, in which the Court added, "that is why the amparo action is not a popular action for denouncing the illegitimacy of the public entities of control over convenience or opportunity, but a protector remedy of the claimant sphere when it is demonstrated that it has been directly affected," in *Revista de Derecho Público*, n° 55–56, Editorial Jurídica Venezolana, Caracas, 1993, pp. 302–303. In another decision, the same former Supreme Court of Justice ruled about the need that: "The violation of the constitutional rights and guaranties be a direct and immediate consequence of the act, fact or omission, not being possible to attribute or assign to the injurer agent different results to those produced or to be produced. The right's violation must be the product of the harming act." Decision n° 398 of Aug. 14, 1992, in *Revista de Derecho Público*, n° 51, Editorial Jurídica Venezolana, Caracas, 1992, p. 145.

140. See Decision of the First Court on Judicial Review of Administrative Actions, May, 7 1987, *Desarrollo 77 C.A.* case, in FUNEDA 15 *Años de Jurisprudencia de la Corte Primera de lo Contencioso Adminsitrativo* 1977–1992, Caracas, 1994, p. 78. In this sense, Article 6,1 of the Amparo Law establishes for the admissibility of the amparo action, that the violation "must be actual, recent, alive." Venez. Amparo Law, Art. 6.1.

141. The Court ruled: "When an amparo action is filed against a norm, that is, when the object of the action is the norm in itself, the concretion of the possible alleged harm would not be "immediate," due to the fact that it would always be necessary for the competent authority to proceed to the execution or application of the norm, in order to harm the plaintiff. One must conclude that the probable harm caused by a norm will always be mediate and indirect, needing to be applied to the concrete case. Thus, the injury will be caused through and by means of an act applying the disposition that is contrary to the rule of law." Decision n° 315 of the former Supreme Court of Justice, Politico Administrative Chamber, May 24, 1993, in *Revista de Derecho Público*, n° 55–56, Editorial Jurídica Venezolana, Caracas, 1993, pp. 289–90.

142. In this regard, the First Court on Judicial Review of Administrative Actions of Venezuela resolved the inadmissibility of an action for amparo because, during the proceedings, the challenged act was repealed. Decision of Aug. 14, 1992, *José V. Colmenares* case, in *Revista de Derecho Público*, n° 51, Editorial Jurídica Venezolana, Caracas, 1992, p. 154.

not have ceased before the judge's decision is adopted. On the contrary, if the harm has ceased, the judge *in limine litis* must declare the inadmissibility of the action.[143] For instance, in the case of amparo actions against judicial omissions, if before the filing of the action or during the proceeding, the court has issued its decision, the harm can be considered as having ceased[144] and the amparo action must be declared inadmissible. The same principle applies in the United States regarding the actual character of the harm for granting the injunctive protection because the rule in federal cases is that an actual controversy must exist, not only at the time of the filing of the action, but at all stages of the proceeding, even at appellate or certiorari review stages.[145]

Nonetheless, this principle of the actual character of the injury has some exceptions. For instance, in Venezuela, the exception involves the effects already produced by a challenged act. Because additional suits are necessary in order to establish civil liabilities and compensation, even if the effects of the challenged act have ceased, the amparo protection can be granted in order for the responsible person to be judicially determined, allowing the subsequent filing of an action seeking compensation.

In order for an amparo action to be admitted, in addition to the injury being a direct, real and actual one, the harm or threat to the constitutional right must be manifestly arbitrary, illegal or illegitimate. Regarding public authorities' acts, this general condition of admissibility of the amparo action derives from the general public

143. Decision n° 651 of Dec. 15, 1992, in *Revista de Derecho Público* n° 52, Editorial Jurídica Venezolana, Caracas, 1992, p. 164; See First Court on Judicial Review of Administrative Action, Decision of Dec. 12, 1992; *Allan R. Brewer-Carías* case, in *Revista de Derecho Público*, n° 49, Editorial Jurídica Venezolana, Caracas, 1992, pp. 131–132; Decision n° 210 of the Former Supreme Court, Politico Administrative Chamber of May 27, 1993, in *Revista de Derecho Público*, n° 53–54, Editorial Jurídica Venezolana, Caracas, 1993, p. 264.

144. See CHAVERO, *El nuevo régimen del amparo constitucional en Venezuela*, *supra* note 5, at 237–38.

145. Nonetheless, in the important case *Roe v. Wade*, the Supreme Court expanded women's right to privacy, striking down states' laws banning abortion. 410 U.S. 113 (1973). The Court recognized that even if this right of privacy was not explicitly mentioned in the constitution, it was guaranteed as a constitutional right for protecting "a woman's decision whether or not to terminate her pregnancy," even though admitting that the states' legislation could regulate the factors governing the abortion decision at some point in pregnancy based on "safeguarding health, maintaining medical standards and in protecting potential life." *Roe*, 410 U.S. at 153. The point in the case was that, pending the procedure, the pregnancy period of the claimant came to term, so the injury claimed lost its present character. See *id.* Nonetheless, the Supreme Court ruled in the case that: "[when], as here, pregnancy is a significant fact in the litigation, the normal 266-day human generation period is so short that pregnancy will come to term before the usual appellate process is complete. If that termination makes a case moot, pregnancy litigation seldom will survive much beyond the trial stage, and appellate review will be effectively denied. Our law should not be that rigid. Pregnancy comes more than once to the same woman, and in the general population, if man is to survive, it will always be with us. Pregnancy provides a classic justification for a conclusion of nonmootness. It truly could be capable of repetition, yet evading review."*Id.* at 125. See ABERNATHY & PERRY, *supra* note 16, at 4-5.

law principle of the presumption of validity that benefit the state's acts, which implies that in order to overcome such a presumption, the plaintiff must demonstrate that the injury caused is manifestly illegal and arbitrary. The same principle applies in the United States, imposing on the plaintiff in civil right injunctions against administrative officials, the burden to prove the alleged violations in order to destroy the presumption of validity of official acts.[146]

The consequence of this condition is that the challenged act or omission must be manifestly contrary to the legal order, that is, contrary to the rules of law contained in the constitution, the statutes and the executive regulations. It must be manifestly illegitimate and lacking any legal support, or manifestly arbitrary by resulting from an unreasonable or unjust decision, which is contrary to justice or to reason.

The condition of the injury–harm or threats–to be manifestly arbitrary, illegal and illegitimate and to affect in a direct and immediate way the plaintiff rights, implies that for the filing of the amparo action, it must be evident, thus, directly imposing on the plaintiff the burden to prove his assertions. That is, the plaintiff has the burden to overcome the presumption of validity and must base his arguments on a reasonable basis by proving the unreasonable character of the public officer's challenged act or omission, and that it has personally and directly harmed his rights. Also in this matter, the rule in the amparo proceeding is similar to the rules on matters of injunctions, as they have been resolved by the United States' courts, according to which, "the party seeking an injunction, whether permanent or temporary, must establish some demonstrable injury."[147]

Consequently, in the amparo proceeding, it is for the plaintiff to prove the harm or the threats caused to his rights as being caused precisely by the defendant. This implies that when the proof of the harms or threats can be established by means of written evidence (documents, for instance), they must always be filed with the complaint in order to illustrate this to the court.[148]

Finally, the injury to constitutional rights which allows the filing of an amparo action must not only be actual, possible, real and imminent, but must also be an injury that has not been consented to by the plaintiff, who, in addition, must not have provoked it. That is, the plaintiff must not have expressly or tacitly consented to the challenged act or the harm caused to his rights. On the contrary, the amparo action would be considered inadmissible. The Amparo Law in this matter distinguishes

---

146. ABERNATHY & PERRY, *supra* note 16, at 5. As M. Glenn Abernathy and Perry have commented: "The courts do not automatically presume that all restraints on free choice are improper. The burden is thrown on the person attacking such acts to prove that they are improper. This is most readily seen in cases involving the claim that an act of the legislature is unconstitutional . . . . Judges also argue that acts of administrative officials should be accorded some presumption of validity. Thus a health officer who destroys food alleged by him to be unfit for consumption is presumed to have good reason for his action. The person whose property is so destroyed must bear the burden of proving bad faith on part of the official, if an action is brought as a consequence." See ABERNATHY & PERRY, *supra* note 16, at 5.

147. See 43A C.J.S. *Injunctions* § 36 (2010) (citing Mt. Emmons Min. Co. v. Town of Crested Butte, 690 P.2d 231 (Colo. 1984).

148. Venez. Amparo Law, Art. 18.6.

two sorts of possible ways of consenting conducts: the express consent and the tacit consent, each with some exceptions.

Express consent, as established in article 6.4 of the Venezuelan Amparo Law, exists when there are "unequivocal signs of acceptance" by the plaintiff, of the acts, facts or omissions causing the injury, in which case the amparo action is inadmissible.[149] In certain aspects, this inadmissibility clause for the amparo proceeding when an express consent of the plaintiff exists also has some equivalence to the United States injunctions procedure with the equitable defense called "estoppel." Estoppel refers to actions of the plaintiff prior to the filing of the suit, when being inconsistent with the rights he is asserting in his claim.[150]

Apart from the cases of express consent, the other clause of inadmissibility in the amparo proceeding occurs in cases of tacit consent by the plaintiff regarding the act, fact or omission causing the injury to his rights. Tacit consent occurs when the precise term, legally established to file the complaint, has elapsed without the action being brought before the courts. This clause for the inadmissibility of the amparo suit is equivalent to the United States procedure for injunction called "laches," which seeks to prevent a plaintiff from obtaining equitable relief when he has not acted promptly in bringing the action, which is summarized in the phrase, that "equity aids the vigilant, not those who slumber in their rights."[151] The difference between the doctrine of "laches" and the Venezuelan Law concept of tacit consent, basically lies in the fact that the term to file the amparo action is expressly established in the Amparo Law[152] so the exhaustion of the term without the filing of the action results in tacit consent regarding the act, the fact or the omission causing the injury.

The sense of this clause of inadmissibility of the amparo action was summarized by the former Supreme Court of Justice of Venezuela when ruling as follows:

Since the amparo action is a special, brief, summary and effective judicial remedy for the protection of constitutional rights . . . it is logical for the Legislator to prescribe a precise length of time between the moment in which the harm is produced

---

149 Venez. Amparo Law, Art. 6.4 (six months).

150. See William M. TABB & Elaine W. SHOBEN, REMEDIES, 50-51 (3d ed. 2005). The classic example of estoppel, as referred to by Tabb and Shoben: is that a plaintiff cannot ask equity for an order to remove a neighbor's fence built over the lot line if the plaintiff stood by and watched the fence construction in full knowledge of the location of the lot line. The plaintiff's silence with knowledge of the facts is an action inconsistent with the right asserted in court.*Id.*

151. *Id.* at 48. As the court stated in Lake Dev. Enter. Inc. v. Kojetinsky, 410 S.W.2d 361, 367–68 (Mo. App. 1966): "'Laches' is the neglect, for an unreasonable and unexplained length of time under circumstances permitting diligence, to do what in law, should have been done. There is no fixed period within which a person must assert his claim or be barred by laches. The length of time depends upon the circumstances of the particular case. Mere delay in asserting a right does not of itself constitute laches; the delay involved must work to the disadvantage and prejudice of the defendant. Laches is a question of fact to be determined from all the evidence and circumstances adduced at trial."*Id.*

152. Venez. Amparo Law, Art. 6.4 (six months).

and the moment the aggrieved party has to file the action. To let more than 6 months pass from the moment in which the injuring act is issued for the exercise of the action is the demonstration of the acceptance of the harm from the side of the injured party. His indolence must be sanctioned, impeding the use of the judicial remedy that has its justification in the urgent need to reestablish a legal situation.[153]

However, regarding the effect of tacit consent, an exception has been established in the Venezuelan Amparo Law in cases of violations affecting "public order" provisions,[154] which refer to situations where the application of a statute may concern the general and indispensable legal order for the existence of the community. The exception, of course, cannot be applied in cases only concerning the parties in a contractual or private controversy.

This notion of "public order" is important because even when the term to sue has elapsed without the action being filed, the courts can admit the action because of reasons of "public order," not considered applicable in the case of tacit consent. As was decided by the Venezuelan First Court of Administrative Judicial Review:

The extinction of the amparo action due to the elapse of the term to sue... is produced in all cases, except when the way through which the harm has been produced is of such gravity that it constitutes an injury to the juridical conscience. It would be the case, for instance, of flagrant violations to individual rights that cannot be denounced by the affected party; deprivation of freedom; submission to physical or psychological torture; maltreatment; harms to human dignity and other extreme cases.[155]

---

153. Decision n° 555 of Oct. 24, 1990, in *Revista de Derecho Público*, n° 44, Editorial Jurídica Venezolana, Caracas, 1990, p. 144.

154. Venez. Amparo Law, Art. 6.4. See Decision n° 177 of the former Supreme Court of Justice, Politico Administrative Chamber, of June 30, 1992, in REVISTA DE DERECHO PÚBLICO, n° 50, Editorial Jurídica Venezolana, Caracas, 1992, p. 157. Public order has been defined by the Constitutional Chamber of the Supreme Tribunal of Justice as "a value destined to maintain the necessary harmony basic for the development and integration of society." See Decision n° 1104 of May 25, 2006 of the (quoting Decision N° 144 of March 20, 2000), in *Revista de Derecho Público*, n° 106, Editorial Jurídica Venezolana, Caracas 2006, p. 146. Consequently the concept of public order allows the general interest of the Society and of the State to prevail over the individual particular interest, in order to assure the enforcement and purpose of some institutions. For such purpose in many cases, it is the legislator itself that has expressly declared in a particular statute that its provisions are of "public order" character, in the sense that its norms cannot be modified through private agreements between parties. See Decision n° 105 of former Supreme Court of Justice, Politico Administrative Chamber, Mar. 22, 1988, IN *Revista de Derecho Público*, n° 34, Editorial Jurídica Venezolana, Caracas, 1988, p. 114.

155. See the decision of First Court on Judicial Review of Administrative Action of Oct. 13, 1988, in *Revista de Derecho Público*, n° 36, Editorial Jurídica Venezolana, Caracas, 1988, p. 95; decision n° 293 of the former Supreme Court of Justice, Politico Administrative Chamber, of Nov. 1, 1989, in *Revista de Derecho Público*, n° 40, Editorial Jurídica Venezolana, Caracas, 1989, p. 111. See *also* the Cassation Chamber of the same Supreme Court of Justice, of June 28, 1995, (Exp. n° 94–172), in Rafael CHAVERO G., *El nuevo régimen del amparo constitucional en Venezuela*, *supra* note 5, at p. 188, note 178, 214 & 246.

Consequently, in such cases where no tacit consent can be considered as having been produced, the amparo is admitted even though the term to file the action would have been exhausted.

Another general exception to the rule of tacit consent refers to situations where the harms inflicted on the rights are of a continuous nature, that is, when they are continuously occurring. In the same sense, in the United States, it is considered that "laches" cannot be alleged as a defense to challenge a suit for an injunction "to enjoin a wrong which is continuing in its nature."[156]

For instance, the Venezuelan courts have ruled regarding a defense argument on the inadmissibility of an amparo action because the term of six months to file the action had elapsed, that in the particular case:

In spite that the facts show that the challenged actions occurred more that six months ago, they have been described revealing a supposed chain of events that, due to their constancy and re-incidence, allows to presume that the plaintiff is presently threatened by those repeated facts. This character of the threat is what the amparo intends to stop. According to what the plaintiff points out, no tacit consent can be produced from his part ... Consequently, there are no grounds for the application to any of the inadmissibility clauses set forth in the Amparo Law.[157]

In Venezuela, the Amparo Law also provides a few exceptions regarding the tacit consent rule. When the amparo action is filed conjointly with another nullity action, the general six-month term established for the filing of the action does not apply. This is the rule in cases of harms or threats that have originated in statutes or regulations, and in administrative acts or public administration omissions, when the amparo action is filed jointly with the popular action for judicial review of unconstitutionality of statutes,[158] or with the judicial review action against administrative actions or omissions.[159]

156. 43A C.J.S. *Injunctions* § 297 (2004) (citing Pacific Greyhound Lines v. Sun Valley Bus Lines, 216 P.2d 404, (Ariz. 1950); Goldstein v. Beal, 59 N.E.2d 712 (Mass. 1945).

157. See Decision of First Court on Judicial Review of Administrative Action of Oct. 22, 1990, *María Cambra de Pulgar* case, in REVISTA DE DERECHO PÚBLICO, nº 44, Editorial Jurídica Venezolana, Caracas, 1990, pp. 143–44.

158. Regarding the judicial review popular action against statutes, it is conceived in the Organic Law of the Supreme Tribunal as an action that can be filed at any time. If a petition for amparo is filed together with the popular action, no delay is applicable. Venez. Amparo Law, Art. 21. See Allan R. BREWER-CARÍAS, *Ley Orgánica del Tribunal Supremo de Justicia*, Editorial Jurídica Venezolana, Caracas, 2006, p. 255. This is why no tacit consent can be understood when the harm is provoked by a statute.

159. Similarly, the tacit consent rule does not apply either in cases of administrative acts or omissions, when the amparo action is filed together with the judicial review action against administrative acts or omissions, in which case, due to the constitutional complaint, the latter can be filed at any moment, as is expressly provided in the Amparo Law. Venez. Amparo Law, Art. 5.

V. THE REPARABLE CHARACTER OF THE HARMS AND THE RESTORATIVE CHARACTER OF THE AMPARO PROCEEDING

As previously mentioned, the injury inflicted upon constitutional rights, necessary to file an amparo action can be the result of harms or threats, which must fulfill the general conditions previously mentioned. In addition, two other conditions must be fulfilled by the injury, depending on whether a harm or threat is at issue. The harm inflicted on a person's rights must be a reparable one and the amparo proceeding seeks to restore the enjoyment of that right, thus having a restorative character. If the injury to a person's rights is caused by a threat, the threat must be imminent. The amparo tends to prevent or impede the violation from occurring in the case of threats, and has a preventive character.

In cases involving harms, the amparo proceeding seeks to restore the enjoyment of the plaintiff's injured right and reestablish the situation that existed when the right was harmed. This is accomplished by eliminating or suspending if necessary, the detrimental act or fact. In this regard, the amparo action also has similarities with the reparative injunctions in the United States, which seek to eliminate the effects of a past wrong or to compel the defendant to engage in a course of action that seeks to correct those effects.[160]

However, in some cases, due to the factual nature of the harm that has been inflicted, the restorative effect cannot be obtained, in which case, the amparo decision must place the plaintiff's right "in the situation closest or more similar to the one that existed before the injury was caused."[161]

160. As has been explained by Owen M. Fiss: "To see how it works, let us assume that a wrong has occurred (such as an act of discrimination). Then the mission of an injunction – classically conceived as a preventive instrument– would be to prevent the recurrence of the wrongful conduct in the future (stop discriminating and do not discriminate again). But in *United States v. Louisiana*, a voting discrimination case, Justice Black identified still another mission for the injunction—the elimination of the *effects* of the past wrong (the past discrimination). The reparative injunction –long thought by the nineteenth-century textbook writers, such as High to be an analytical impossibility– was thereby legitimated. And in the same vein, election officials have been ordered not only to stop discriminating in the future elections, but also to set aside a past election and to run a new election as a means of removing the taint of discrimination that infected the first one. Similarly, public housing officials have been ordered to both cease discriminating on the basis of race in their future choices of sites and to build units in the white areas as a means of eliminating the effects of the past segregative policy (placing public housing projects only in the black areas of the city)."Owen M. Fiss, *The Civil Rights Injunction*, 10 (1978) (citing United States v. Louisiana, 380 U.S. 145 (1965); 29 U.S.C. §§ 101-115) (internal citations omitted).

161. In this sense, it has been decided by the former Venezuelan Supreme Court of Justice ruling that "one of the principal characteristics of the amparo action is to be a restorative (*restablecedor*) judicial means, the mission of which is to restore the infringed situation or, what is the same, to put the claimant again in the enjoyment of his infringed constitutional rights." See Decision of Feb. 6, 1996, *Asamblea Legislativa del Estado Bolívar* case; in CHAVERO, *El nuevo régimen del amparo constitucional en Venezuela*, *supra* note 5, at, 185, 242–43.

Due to the restorative character of the amparo, the specific conditions of the harms must be fulfilled for an amparo petition to be granted and they must have a reparable character. Consequently, as is established in the Venezuelan Amparo Law, that amparo actions are inadmissible, "when the violation of the constitutional rights and guaranties turns out to be an evident irreparable situation, and is impossible to restore."[162] In these cases, the Amparo Law defines the irreparable harms as those that, by means of the amparo action, cannot revert to the status existing before the violation had occurred.[163]

The main consequence of this reparable character of the harm is the restorative effect of the amparo proceeding, through the amparo action, and it is not possible to create new juridical situation for the plaintiff, nor is it possible to modify the existing legal situations.[164]

In this sense, the Venezuelan Constitutional Chamber of the Supreme Tribunal of Justice denied a request formulated by means of an amparo action for the plaintiff to obtain asylum because it was seeking to obtain Venezuelan citizenship without accomplishing the established administrative conditions and procedures. The Court ruled "this amparo action has been filed in order to seek a decision from this court, consisting in the legalization of the situation of the claimant, which would consist in the creation of a civil and juridical status that the petitioner did not have before filing the complaint for amparo." Thus the petition was considered "contrary to the restorative nature of the amparo."[165]

Consequently, the restorative effect of the amparo proceeding imposes the need for the harm to be of a reparable character in order for the courts to restore things to

---

162 Venez. Amparo Law, Art. 6.3.

163. Venez. Amparo Law, Art. 6.3.

164. See Decisions of the Politico Administrative Chamber of the former Supreme Court of Justice, nº 462 of Oct. 27, 1993, *Ana Drossos* case, and of nº 582 of Nov. 4, 1993, *Partido Convergencia* case, in *Revista de Derecho Público*, nº 55–56, Editorial Jurídica Venezolana, Caracas, 1993, pp. 340-42.

165. See Decision dated January 20, 2000, *Domingo Ramírez Monja* case, in RafaeL CHAVERO, *El nuevo régimen del amparo constitucional en Venezuela, supra* note 5, at p. 244. In another decision issued on Apr. 21, 1999, *J. C. Marín* case, the former Supreme Court in a similar sense, declared inadmissible an amparo action in a case in which the claimant was asking to be appointed as judge in a specific court or to be put in a juridical situation that he did not have before the challenged act was issued. The Court decided that in the case, it was impossible for such purpose to file an amparo action, declaring it inadmissible, thus ruling as follows: "This Court must highlight that one of the essential characteristics of the amparo action is its reestablishing effects, that is, literally, to put one thing in the situation it had beforehand, which for the claimant means to be put in the situation he had before the production of the claimed violation. The foregoing means that the plaintiff's claim must be directed to seek 'the reestablishment of the infringed juridical situation'; since the amparo actions are inadmissible when the reestablishment of the infringed situation is not possible; when through them the claimant seeks a compensation of damages, because the latter cannot be a substitution of the harmed right; nor when the plaintiff pretends to the court to create a right or a situation that did not exist before the challenged act, fact or omission. All this is the exclusion for the possibility for the amparo to have constitutive effects."*Id.* at 244-45.

the status or situation they had been in at the moment of the injury, enjoining the infringing fact or act. On the contrary, when the violation of a constitutional right turns out to be of an irreparable character, the amparo action is inadmissible.

This is congruent with the main objective of the amparo proceeding, which is found in Article 27 of the Venezuelan Constitution and Article 1 of Amparo Law, in that it seeks to "immediately restore the infringed situation or to place the claimant in the situation more similar to it."[166] This is also a general condition for the admissibility of injunctions in the United States where the courts have established that because "the purpose of an injunction is to restrain actions that have not yet been taken", an injunction cannot be filed to restrain an already completed action at the time the action is brought.[167]

In this same sense, for instance, the former Venezuelan Supreme Court declared inadmissible an amparo action against an illegitimate tax-collecting act after the tax was paid because it was not possible to restore the infringed situation.[168] Regarding women's pregnancy rights, the Venezuelan courts have declared an amparo action inadmissible that seeks to protect maternity leave rights when filed after childbirth, ruling that:

It is impossible for the plaintiff to be restored in her presumed violated rights to enjoy a maternity leave during six month before and after the childbirth, because we are now facing an irremediable situation that cannot be restored, due to the fact that it is impossible to date back the elapsed time.[169]

In other cases, the same former Venezuelan Supreme Court of Justice considered amparo actions inadmissible when the only way to restore the infringed juridical situation was by declaring the nullity of an administrative act, which the amparo judge cannot do in his decision.[170]

---

166. See First Court on Judicial Review of Administrative Action, Decision of Jan. 14, 1992, in *Revista de Derecho Público*, nº 49, Editorial Jurídica Venezolana, Caracas, 1992, p. 130; Decision nº 162 of the former Supreme Court of Justice, Politico Administrative Chamber, of Mar. 4, 1993, in *Revista de Derecho Público*, nº 53-54, Editorial Jurídica Venezolana, Caracas, 1993, p. 260.

167. As quoted in the *C.J.S.*: "There is no cause for the issuance of an injunction unless the alleged wrong is actually occurring or is actually threatened or apprehended with reasonable probability and a court cannot enjoin an act after it has been completed. An act that has been completed, such that it no longer presents a justiciable controversy, does not give grounds for the issuance of an injunction." 43A C.J.S. INJUNCTIONS § 55 (2004) (citing Ex parte Connors, 855 So. 2d 486 (Ala. 2003); Patterson v. Council on Probate Judicial Conduct, 577 A. 2d 701 (Conn. 1990); Kay v. David Douglas School Dist., 738 P. 2d 1389, (Or. 1987); County of Chesterfield v. Windy Hill, Ltd., 559 S.E.2d 627 (Va. 2002).

168. See Decision of the former Supreme Court of Justice, of Mar. 21, 1988, in *Revista de Derecho Público*, nº 34, Editorial Jurídica Venezolana, Caracas, 1988, p. 114.

169. See Decision of the First Court on Judicial Review of Administrative Actions of Sept. 7, 1989, in *Revista de Derecho Público*, nº 40, Editorial Jurídica Venezolana, Caracas, 1989, pp. 110-11.

170. See Decision nº 573 of the former Supreme Court of Justice, Politico Administrative Chamber of Nov. 1, 1990, in *Revista de Derecho Publico*, nº 44, Editorial Jurídica Venezolana,

From these regulations it can be determined that the amparo proceeding regarding violations is restorative in nature and imposes the need for the illegitimate harm to be possibly stopped or amended in order for the plaintiff's situation to be restored by a judicial order; or if having continuous effects, for its suspension when not being initiated. Regarding effects that have already been accomplished, an amparo action implies the possibility to set things back to the stage they had been before the harm was initiated. Consequently, the amparo judge cannot create situations that were nonexistent at the moment of the action's filing; or correct the harms that have infringed upon rights after it is too late.[171]

In this regard, with respect to the right to the protection of health, the former Venezuelan Supreme Court of Justice ruled that:

The Court considers that the infringed situation is reparable by means of amparo, due to the fact that the plaintiff can be satisfied in his claims through such judicial mean. From the judicial procedure point of view, for the protection of health it is possible for the judge to order the competent authority to assume precise conduct for the medical treatment of the claimant's conduct. The petitioner's claim is to have a particular and adequate health care, which can be obtained via the amparo action, seeking the reestablishment of a harmed right. In this case, the claimant is not seeking her health to be restored to the stage it had before, but to have a particular health care, which is perfectly valid.[172]

VI. THE IMMINENT CHARACTER OF THE THREATS AND THE PREVENTIVE CHARACTER OF THE AMPARO AGAINST THREATS

However, the amparo proceeding is not only a judicial device that seeks to restore harmed constitutional rights, it is also a judicial means established for the protection of constitutional rights against illegitimate threats that violate those rights. It is in these cases that the amparo proceeding has a preventive character by avoiding harm, similar to the United States' preventive civil rights injunctions that seek "to

---

Caracas, 1990, pp. 152–153; *Cfr.* First Court on Judicial Review of Administrative Action, decision of Sept. 10, 1992, *Consejo Nacional de Universidades* case, in *Revista de Derecho Público*, nº 51, Editorial Jurídica Venezolana, Caracas, 1992, p. 155.

171. As decided by the First Court on Judicial Review of Administrative Action of Venezuela, regarding a municipal order for the demolition of a building, in the sense that if the demolition was already executed, the amparo judge cannot decide the matter because of the irreparable character of the harm. See the decision of January 1, 1999, *B. Gómez* case, in Rafael CHAVERO, *El nuevo régimen del amparo constitucional en Venezuela*, *supra* note 5, p. 242. The First Court also ruled in a case decided in February 4, 1999, *C. Negrín* case, regarding a public university position contest that: "[t]he pretended aggrieved party is seeking to be allowed to be registered himself in the public contest for the Chair of Pharmacology in the School of Medicine José María Vargas, but at the present time, the registration was impossible due to the fact that the delay had elapsed the previous year, and consequently the harm produced must be considered as irreparable, declaring inadmissible the action for amparo." *Id.* at 243.

172. See Decision nº 109 of Mar. 8, 1990, *Luz M. Serna* case, in *Revista de Derecho Público*, nº 42, Editorial Jurídica Venezolana, Caracas, 1990, p. 107.

prohibit some act or series of acts from occurring in the future,"[173] and designed "to avoid future harm to a party by prohibiting or mandating certain behavior by another party."[174]

It would be absurd for the affected party to have complete knowledge of the near occurrence of the harm, or to patiently wait for the harming act to occur in order to file the amparo action. On the contrary, one has the right to file the action to obtain a judicial order prohibiting the action from being accomplished, thus avoiding the harm altogether.

The main condition for filing the type of amparo action against threats (*amenaza*) to constitutional rights is expressly provided in the Amparo Law.[175] The threat must be real, certain, immediate, imminent, possible and realizable.

On the other hand, there are some constitutional rights that specifically need to be protected against threats, such as the right to life in cases of imminent death threats, because on the contrary, they could lose all sense. In this case, the only way to guarantee the right to life is to avoid materialization of the threats, for instance, by providing the person with effective police protection.

If the main condition for the admissibility of the amparo action against harms to constitutional rights is their reparable character; regarding threats, the specific characteristic of the threat at issue must have an imminent character.

This condition is also expressly established in the Amparo Law,[176] which provides that in order to file an amparo action against threats, the threats must not only be real, certain, possible and realizable, but additionally, they must have an immediate and imminent character, provoking fear in persons or making persons feel in danger for their rights. On the contrary, "harm" refers to situations in which a fact has already been accomplished, so no threat is possible.

Consequently, in order to file an amparo action against a threat, it must consist of a potential harm or violation that is imminent in the sense that it may occur soon. This same rule requiring the imminent character of the threat is applied in the United States, as an essential condition for granting preventive injunctions. This means that the courts will order injunctions only when the threat is imminent and prohibits future conduct, but not when the threat is considered remote, potential or speculative.[177]

173. See FISS & RENDLEMAN, *supra* note 32, at 7.

174. See TABB & SHOBEN, *supra* note 53, at 22. In Spanish the word "preventive" is used in procedural law (*medidas preventivas o cautelares*) to refer to the "temporary" or "preliminary" orders or restraints that in the United States the judge can issue during the proceeding. So the preventive character of the amparo and of the injunctions cannot be confused with the "*medidas preventivas*" or temporary or preliminary measures that the courts can issue during the trial for the immediate protection of rights, facing the prospect of an irremediable harm that can be caused.

175. Venez. Amparo Law, Art. 2 & 6.2.

176. *Id.*

177. In *Reserve Mining Co. v. Environmental Protection Agency*, the Circuit Court did not grant the requested injunction ordering Reserve Mining Company to cease discharging wastes

In the same sense as the amparo, injunctions in the United States cannot be granted "merely to allay the fears and apprehensions or to soothe the anxieties of individuals, since such fears and apprehensions may exist without substantial reasons and be absolutely groundless or speculative."[178] Injunctions, similar to the amparo, are extraordinary remedies "designed to prevent serious harm, and are not to be used to protect a person from mere inconvenience or speculative and insubstantial injury."[179]

This condition is also generally established in Venezuela, in the sense that threats that can be protected by the amparo suits must be imminent,[180] so the action for amparo is inadmissible when the threat or violation of a constitutional right has ceased or ended[181] or when the threat against a constitutional right or guarantee is not "immediate, possible and feasible.[182]

---

from its iron ore processing plant in Silver Bay, Minnesota into the ambient air of Silver Bay and the waters of Lake Superior because even though the plaintiff has established that the discharges give "rise to a potential threat to the public health . . . no harm to the public health has been shown to have occurred, that the danger to health is not imminent but that it did call for preventive and precautionary steps; that no reason existed which required that the company terminate its operations at once . . ." 514 F.2d 492 (8th Cir. 1975); *see* FISS & RENDLEMAN, *supra* note 32, at 116. In another classically cited case, Fletcher v. Bealey, 28 Ch. 688 (1885), which referred to waste deposits in the plaintiff's land by the defendant, the judge ruled that since the action is brought to prevent continuing damages, for a quia-timet action, two ingredients are necessary: "There must, if no actual damage is proved, be proof of imminent danger, and there must also be proof that the apprehended damage will, if it comes, be very substantial. I should almost say it must be proved that it will be irreparable, because, if the danger is not proved to be so imminent that no one can doubt that if the remedy is delayed, the damage will be suffered, I think it must be shown that, if the damage does occur at any time, it will come in such a way and under such circumstances that it will be impossible for the Plaintiff to protect himself against it if relief is denied to him in a *quia timet* action."*Fletcher*, 28 Ch. 688 (1885); *see* FISS & RENDLEMAN, *supra* note 32, at 110-11.

178. 43A C.J.S. INJUNCTIONS § 40 (2004) (citing Ormco Corp. v. Johns, 869 So.2d 1109 (Ala. 2003); Callis, Papa, Jackstadt & Halloran, P.C. v. Norkolk & W. Ry. Co., 748 N. E.2d 153 (Ill. 2001); Frey v. DeCordova Bend Estates Owners Ass'n, 647 S.W.2d 246 (Tex. 1983).

179. 43A C.J.S. INJUNCTIONS § 40 (2004) (citing Kucera v. State Dep't of Transp., 995 P.2d 63 (Wash. 2002)).

180. Venez. Amparo Law, Art. 2

181. Venez. Amparo Law, Art. 8.1.

182. Venez. Amparo Law, Art. 6.2. See Decision nº 203 of the former Supreme Court of Justice, Politico Administrative Chamber of June 9, 1988, in REVISTA DE DERECHO PÚBLICO, nº 35, Editorial Jurídica Venezolana, Caracas, 1988, p. 119, and decision of the same Chamber nº 398 of Aug. 14, 1992, in *Revista de Derecho Público*, nº 51, Editorial Jurídica Venezolana, Caracas, 1992, pp. 158–159. See *also* Decision of the First Court on Judicial Review of Administrative Action, decision of June 30, 1988, *Joao Gomez E.* case in REVISTA DE DERECHO PÚBLICO, nº 35, Editorial Jurídica Venezolana, Caracas, 1988, p. 120. These general conditions have been considered as concurrent ones when referring to the constitutional protection against harms that someone will soon be inflicting on the rights of other. See Decision nº 315 of the former Supreme Court of Justice, Politico Administrative Chamber, of May 24, 1993, in *Revista de Derecho Público*, nº 55–56, Editorial Jurídica Venezolana, Ca-

In the same sense, the former Supreme Court of Justice of Venezuela in 1989 ruled that:

The opening of a disciplinary administrative inquiry is not enough to justify the protection of a party by means of the judicial remedy of amparo, moreover when the said proceeding, in which all needed defenses can be exercised, may conclude in a decision discarding the incriminations against the party with the definitive closing of the disciplinary process, without any sanction to the party.[183]

The criteria of the imminent character of the threat to constitutional rights for the admission of the amparo action has also led the former Supreme Court of Justice of Venezuela to reject the amparo proceeding against statutes, arguing that a statute or a legal norm, in itself, cannot cause a possible, imminent and feasible threat.[184] Nonetheless, the Court has considered that the plaintiff can always file the amparo action against the public officer that applies the statute, and seek a court prohibition directed to said public officer, compelling him not to apply the challenged norm.[185]

---

racas, 1993, p. 289; and decision of Mar. 22, 1995, *La Reintegradora* case, in Rafael CHAVERO, *El nuevo régimen del amparo constitucional en Venezuela*, *supra* note 5, p. 239.

183. See Decision of the Politico Administrative Chamber of Oct. 26, 1989, *Gisela Parra Mejía* case, in Rafael CHAVERO, *El nuevo régimen del amparo constitucional en Venezuela*, *supra* note 5, pp. 191, 241.

184. In a Decision nº 315 of May 24, 1993, the Politico Administrative Chamber of the former Supreme Court ruled: "The same occurs with the third condition set forth in the Law; the threat, that is, the probable and imminent harm, will never be feasible –that is, concreted– by the defendant. If it could be sustained that the amparo could be filed against a disposition the constitutionality of which is challenged, then it would be necessary to accept as defendant the legislative body or the public officer that had sanctioned it, being the latter the one that would act in court defending the act. It can be observed that in case the possible harm would effectively arrive to be materialized, it would not be the legislative body or the state organ which issued it, the one that will execute it, but the public official for whom the application of the norm will be imposing in all the cases in which an individual would be in the factual situation established in the norm. If it is understood that the norm can be the object or an amparo action, the conclusion would be that the defendant (the public entity sanctioning the norm the unconstitutionality of which is alleged) could not be the one entity conducting the threat; but that the harm would be in the end concretized or provoked by a different entity (the one applying to the specific and particular case the unconstitutional provision). In *Revista de Derecho Público*, nº 55-56, Editorial Jurídica Venezolana, Caracas, 1993, pp. 289–290.

185. In the same decision nº 315 of May 24, 1993, the Politico Administrative Chamber of the former Supreme Court ruled as referenced *supra* in footnote 87, the Court ruled as follows: "Nonetheless, this High Court considers necessary to point out that the previous conclusion does not signify the impossibility to prevent the concretion of the harm –objection that could be drawn from the thesis that the amparo can only proceed if the unconstitutional norm is applied–, due to the fact that the imminently aggrieved person must not necessarily wait for the effective execution of the illegal norm, because since he faces the threat having the conditions established in the Law, he could seek for amparo for his constitutional rights. In such case, though, the amparo would not be directed against the norm, but against the public officer that has to apply it. In effect, being imminent the application to an individual of a normative disposition contrary to any of the constitutional rights or guaranties, the potentially affected person could seek from the court a prohibition directed to the said public officer

VII. THE INJURING PARTY IN THE AMPARO PROCEEDING

Because the amparo procedure is governed by the principle of bilateralism, the party that initiates it, that is the plaintiff, whose constitutional rights and guarantees have been injured or threatened, must always file the action against an injuring party whose actions or omissions are those that have caused the harm or threats. This means that the action must always be filed against a person or a public entity that must also be an individual.[186] That is why the amparo proceeding, as well as injunctions in the United States, have the result of a judicial order "addressed to some clearly identified individual, not just the general citizenry."[187]

Thus, since the beginning of the proceeding when the amparo action is filed, or during the procedure, the bilateral character of the amparo suit implies the need to have a procedural relation that must be established between the injured party and the injuring one who must also participate in the process.[188]

This need for the individualization of the defendant also derives from the subjective or personal character of the amparo in the sense that the plaintiff's complaint, as provided in article 18,3 of the Amparo Law, must clearly identify the authority, public officer, person or entity against whom the action is filed. In the case of amparo actions filed against artificial persons, public entities or corporations, the petition must also identify them with precision and if possible, also identify their representatives.

In these cases of harms caused by entities or corporations, the action can be filed directly against the natural person acting on its behalf as representative of the entity or corporation, for instance, the public official or directly against the entity in it-

---

plaintiff, compelling not to apply the challenged norm, once evaluated by the court as being unconstitutional." *Id.* at 290.

186. The only exception to the principle of bilateralism is the case of Chile, where the offender is not considered a defendant party, but is instead considered only a person whose activity is limited to inform the court and give it the documents it has. That is why in the regulation set forth by the Supreme Court (*Auto Acordado*) it is said that the affected state organ, person or public officer "can" just appear as party in the process. See Juan Manuel ERRAZURIZ G. and Jorge Miguel OTERO A., *Aspectos procesales del recurso de protección*, Editorial Jurídica de Chile 1989, p. 27.

187. See FISS, *supra* note 63, at 12.

188. In this regard, the former Supreme Court of Justice of Venezuela in a decision nº 649 of Dec.15, 1992, pointed out that: "The amparo action set forth in the Constitution, and regulated in the Organic Amparo law, has among its fundamental characteristic its basic personal or subjective character, which implies that a direct, specific and undutiful relation must exist between the person claiming for the protection of his rights, and the person purported to have originated the disturbance, who is to be the one with standing to act as defendant or the person against whom the action is filed. In other words, it is necessary, for granting an amparo, that the person signaled as the injurer be in the end, the one originating the harm." Supreme Court of Justice, Politico Administrative Chamber, decision dated Dec. 16, 1992, *Haydée Casanova* Caso, in *Revista de Derecho Público*, nº 52, Editorial Jurídica Venezolana, Caracas, 1992, p. 139.

self.[189] In this latter case, according to the expression used in civil right injunctions in the United States, the action is filed against "the office rather than the person."[190]

Consequently, in cases of amparo actions filed against entities or corporations, the natural person representing them can be changed, as it commonly happens with public entities, [191] a circumstance that does not affect the bilateral relation between aggrieved and aggrieving parties.

As aforementioned, the action can also be personally filed against the representative of the entity or corporation itself, for instance the public officer or the director or manager of the entity, particularly when the harm or threat has been personally provoked by him, independent of the artificial person or entity for which he is acting.[192]

In these cases, when, for instance, the public official responsible for the harm can be identified with precision as the injuring party, it is only him, personally, who must act as defendant in the procedure, in which case no notice is needed to be sent to his superior or to the Attorney General.[193] In such cases, it is the individual natural person or public officer that must personally act as the injuring party.[194]

---

189. This implies that in the filing of the action of amparo in cases of Public Administration activities, "the person acting on behalf of (or representing) the entity who caused the harm or threat to the rights or guaranties must be identified, which is, the signaled person who has the exact and direct knowledge of the facts." Decision of the First Court on Judicial Review of Administrative Actions, dated July 14, 1988, *Aurora Figueredo* case, in *Revista de Derecho Público*, nº 35, Editorial Jurídica Venezolana, Caracas, 1988, pp. 138-39.

190. See FISS, *supra* note 63, at 15.

191. As decided by the Venezuelan First Court on Judicial Review of Administrative Action in a decision of Sept. 28, 1993, *Universidad de Los Andes* case, regarding an amparo action filed against the dean of a law faculty, in which case the person in charge as dean was changed: "The heading of the position does not change its organic unity. If the dean of the Faculty changes, it will always be a subjective figure that substitutes the previous one. That is why in a decision of September 11, 1990, this Court ruled that the circumstance of the head of an organ mentioned as aggrieving being changed does not alter the procedural relation originated with the amparo action. In addition, it must be added that it would have no sense to rule for the procedural relation be continued with the person that doesn't occupy anymore the position, because in case the constitutional amparo is granted, then the ex public official would not be in a position to reestablish the factual infringed situation. As much, the former public officer could be liable for the damages caused, but as it is known, the amparo action has the only purpose of reestablishing the harmed legal situation, and that can only be assured by the current public official."First Court on Judicial Review of Administrative Action in a decision of Sept., 28, 1993, See in *Revista de Derecho Público*, nº 55-56, Editorial Jurídica Venezolana, Caracas, 1993, p. 330.

192. In such cases, when the action is filled against public officers, as it is established in Article 27 of the Venezuelan Amparo Law, the court deciding on the merits must notify its decision to the competent authority "in order for it to decide the disciplinary sanctions against the public official responsible for the violation or the threat against a constitutional right or guaranty." Venez. Amparo Law, Art. 27.

193. See First Court on Judicial Review of Administrative Action, decision of May 12, 1988, in *Revista de Derecho Público*, nº 34, Editorial Jurídica Venezolana, Caracas, 1988, p. 113; Venezuelan Supreme Court of Justice, Politico Administrative Chamber, decision nº 57 of

On the contrary, if the action is filed, for instance, against a ministerial entity as a public administration organ, in this case the Attorney General, as representative of the state, is the entity that must act in the process as its judicial representative.[195] In other cases, when the amparo action is exercised against a perfectly identified and individuated organ of a public administration and not against the state, the Attorney General, as its judicial representative, does not necessarily have a procedural role to play,[196] and cannot act on its behalf.[197]

One of the most important aspects in the Venezuelan amparo proceeding regarding the injuring party is that the action for amparo can be filed not only against public authorities, but also against individuals. In other words, this specific judicial means is conceived for the protection of constitutional rights and guarantees against harms or threats regardless of the actor, which can be public entities, authorities, individuals or private corporations.

The amparo proceeding was originally created to protect individuals against the state and that is why some countries like Mexico remain with that traditional trend; but that initial trend has not prevented the possibility for the admission of the amparo proceeding for the protection of constitutional rights against other individual's actions. The current situation is similar in the majority of Latin American countries, the admission of the amparo action against individuals is accepted, as is the case in Argentina, Bolivia, Chile, the Dominican Republic, Paraguay, Peru, Venezuela and Uruguay, as well as, although in a more restrictive way, in Colombia, Costa Rica, Ecuador, Guatemala and Honduras. In this sense, the writ of amparo is also regulated in the Philippines, which can be filed against acts or omissions "of a public official or employee, or of a private individual or entity."[198] In only a minori-

---

Mar. 16, 1989, in *Revista de Derecho Público*, nº 38, Editorial Jurídica Venezolana, Caracas, 1989, p. 110; Venezuelan First Court on Judicial Review of Administrative Action, decision of Sept. 7, 1989, in *Revista de Derecho Público*, n° 40, Editorial Jurídica Venezolana, Caracas, 1989, p. 107.

194. See former Supreme Court of Justice, Politico Administrative Chamber, decision nº 109 of Mar. 8, 1990, in *Revista de Derecho Público*, nº 42, Editorial Jurídica Venezolana, Caracas, 1990, p. 114; Venezuelan First Court on Judicial Review of Administrative Action, decision of Nov. 21, 1990, *Comisión Nacional de Valores* case, in *Revista de Derecho Público*, nº 44, Editorial Jurídica Venezolana, Caracas, 1990, p. 148.

195. See First Court on Judicial Review of Administrative Action, decision of Sept. 7, 1989, in *Revista de Derecho Público*, n° 40, Editorial Jurídica Venezolana, Caracas, 1989, p. 107.

196. See First Court on Judicial Review of Administrative Action, decision of Nov. 21, 1990, *Comisión Nacional de Valores* case, in *Revista de Derecho Público*, nº 44, Editorial Jurídica Venezolana, Caracas, 1990, p. 148.

197. See former Supreme Court of Justice, Politico Administrative Chamber, decision nº 391 of Aug. 1, 1991, in *Revista de Derecho Público*, nº 47, Editorial Jurídica Venezolana, Caracas, 1991, p. 120; First Court on Judicial Review of Administrative Action, decision of July 30, 1992, in *Revista de Derecho Público*, n° 51, Editorial Jurídica Venezolana, Caracas, 1992, p. 164; Former Venezuelan Supreme Court of Justice, Politico Administrative Chamber decision nº 649 of Dec. 15, 1992, *Haydée M. Casanova* case, in *Revista de Derecho Público*, nº 52, Editorial Jurídica Venezolana, Caracas, 1992, p. 139.

198. Phil. Amparo Law, § 1.

ty of Latin American countries the amparo action remains exclusively as a protective means against authorities, as happens in Brazil, El Salvador, Panama, Mexico and Nicaragua. This is also the case in the United States where the civil rights injunctions, in matters of constitutional or civil rights or guaranties,[199] can only be admitted against public entities.[200]

In Venezuela, the amparo action is admitted against acts of individuals. The 1988 Organic Law of Amparo[201] provides that the amparo action "shall be admitted against any fact, act or omission from citizens, legal entities, private groups or organizations that have violated, violates or threaten to violate any of the constitutional guaranties or rights."[202]

VIII. THE INJURING PUBLIC ACTIONS AND OMISSIONS

Being that the amparo action was originally established to defend constitutional rights from state and authority violations, the most common and important injuring parties in the amparo proceeding are, of course, the public authorities or public officials when their acts or omissions, whether of legislative, executive or judicial nature, cause the harm or threats.

The general principle in this matter in Venezuela, with some exceptions, is that any authority can be questioned through amparo actions, and that any act, fact or omission of any public authority or entity or public official causing an injury to constitutional rights can be challenged by means of such actions. This is the wording used in the Amparo Law of Venezuela, providing that the action can be filed against "any fact, act or omission of any of the National, State, or Municipal branches of government" (*Poderes Públicos*);[203] which means that the constitutional protection

---

199. In other matters, injunctions can be filed against any person such as "higher public officials or private persons." ABERNATHY & PERRY, *supra* note 16, at 8.

200. As explained by M. Glenn Abernathy and Barbara A. Perry: "Limited remedies for private interference with free choice. Another problem in the citizen's search for freedom from restriction lies in the fact that many types of interference stemming from private persons do not constitute actionable wrongs under the law. Private prejudice and private discrimination do not, in the absence of specific statutory provisions, offer grounds for judicial intervention in [sic] behalf of the sufferer. If one is denied admission to membership in a social club, for example, solely on the basis of his race or religion or political affiliation, he may understandably smart under the rejection, but the courts cannot help him (again assuming no statutory provision barring such distinctions). There are, then, many types of restraints on individual freedom of choice which are beyond the authority of courts to remove or ameliorate. "It should also be noted that the guarantees of rights in the United States Constitution only protect against *governmental* action and do not apply to purely private encroachments, except for the Thirteenth Amendment's prohibition of slavery. Remedies for private invasion must be found in statutes, the common law, or administrative agency regulations and adjudications." ABERNATHY & PERRY, *supra* note 16, at 6.

201. See the reference in Rafael CHAVERO G., *El nuevo régimen del amparo constitucional en Venezuela*, *supra* note 5, p. 188, note 178, 214 & 246.

202. Venez. Amparo Law, Art. 2.

203. *Id.*

can be filed against any public action, that is, any formal state act, any substantive or any factual activity (*vía de hecho*);[204] as well as against any omission from public entities. That is also why the courts in Venezuela have decided that "there is no State act that can be excluded from revision by means of amparo, the purpose of which is not to annul State acts but to protect public freedoms and restore its enjoyment when violated or harmed," thereby admitting that the constitutional amparo action can be filed even against legislative acts excluded from judicial review, when a harm or violation of constitutional rights or guarantees has been alleged.[205]

---

204. Venez. Amparo Law, Art. 5.

205. See the former Supreme Court of Justice decision n° 22 dated Jan. 31, 1991, *Anselmo Natale* case, in *Revista de Derecho Público*, n° 45, Editorial Jurídica Venezolana, Caracas, 1991, p. 118. See *also* Decision of the First Court on Judicial Review of Administrative Action of June 18, 1992, in *Revista de Derecho Público*, n° 46, Editorial Jurídica Venezolana, Caracas, 1991, p. 125. The universal character of the amparo regarding public authorities, acts or omissions, according to the Venezuelan courts, implies that: "From what Article 2 of the Amparo law sets forth, it results that no type of conduct, regardless of its nature or character or their authors, can per se be excluded from the amparo judge revision in order to determine if it harms or doesn't harm constitutional rights or guaranties." Decision of the First Court on Judicial Review of Administrative Action of Nov. 11, 1993, *Aura Loreto Rangel* case, in REVISTA DE DERECHO PÚBLICO, n° 55–56, Editorial Jurídica Venezolana, Caracas, 1993, p. 284. The same criterion was adopted by the Political Administrative Chamber of the former Supreme Court of Justice in a Decision n° 315 of May 24, 1993, as follows: "The terms on which the amparo action is regulated in Article 49 of the Constitution (now Article 27) are very extensive. If the extended scope of the rights and guaranties that can be protected and restored through this judicial mean is undoubted; the harm cannot be limited to those produced only by some acts. So, in equal terms it must be permitted that any harming act—whether an act, a fact or an omission—with respect to any constitutional right and guaranty, can be challenged by means of this action, due to the fact that the amparo action is the protection of any norm regulating the so-called subjective rights of constitutional rank, it cannot be sustained that such protection is only available in cases in which the injuring act has some precise characteristics, whether from a material or organic point of view. The jurisprudencia of this Court has been constant regarding both principles. In a decision n° 22, dated January 31, 1991, *Anselmo Natale* case, it was decided that "there is no State act that could not be reviewed by amparo, the latter understood not as a mean for judicial review of constitutionality of State acts in order to annul them, but as a protective remedy regarding public freedoms whose purpose is to reestablish its enjoyment and exercise, when a natural or artificial person, or group or private organization, threatens to harm them or effectively harm them."(See regarding the extended scope of the protected rights, Decision of Dec. 4, 1990, *Mariela Morales de Jimenez* case, n° 661); See in *Revista de Derecho Público*, n° 55-56, Editorial Jurídica Venezolana, Caracas, 1993, pp. 284–85. See on the *Mariela Morales de Jiménez* case in *Revista de Derecho Público*, n° 45, Editorial Jurídica Venezolana, Caracas, 1991, p. 115 In another decision dated February 13, 1992, the First Court ruled: "This Court observes that the essential characteristic of the amparo regime, in its constitutional regulation as well as in its statutory development, is its universality.., [if this is a proper omission, the ellipses should be . . . BB rule 5.3, page 78] so the protection it assures is extended to all subjects (physical or artificial persons), as well as regarding all constitutionally guaranteed rights, including those that without being expressly regulated in the Constitution are inherent to human beings. This is the departing point in order to understand the scope of the constitutional amparo. Regarding Public Administration, the amparo against it is so extended that it can be

In particular, regarding the possibility to file amparo actions against legislative actions or omissions when they cause harms on constitutional rights of individuals, a distinction can be made between when the harm or threats are caused by statutes or by other decisions adopted, for instance, by parliamentary commissions.

Regarding congressional and parliamentary commissions' acts, including regional or municipal legislative councils,[206] when they harm constitutional rights and guarantees, in principle, it is possible to challenge them through amparo actions before the competent courts.[207] In contrast, in the United States, the general rule is that injunctions may not be directed against Congress so injunctions have been rejected, for instance, when seeking to suspend a congressional subpoena, regarding which the plaintiff had an adequate remedy to protect his rights.[208]

Regarding statutes, although in the majority of Latin American countries the amparo action against them is rejected, in Venezuela, it is expressly accepted, but only regarding self-executing statutes that can harm the constitutional rights without the need for any other state act executing or applying them, or only regarding the acts applying the particular statute. In effect, in Venezuela, due to the universal character of the system for constitutional protection, which eventually was consolidated in the 1999 Constitution, one of the most distinguishable innovations of the 1988 Amparo Law was to establish the amparo action against statutes and other normative acts, complementing the general mixed system of judicial review.[209]

---

filed against all acts, omissions and factual actions, without any kind of exclusion regarding some matters that are always related to the public order and social interest. [BB rule 5.1, page 76]"See in *Revista de Derecho Público*, nº 49, Editorial Jurídica Venezolana, Caracas, 1992, pp. 120–21.

206. In the United States, municipal council acts can be challenged through injunctions. Staub v. City of Baxley, 355 U.S. 313, 317 n.3 (1958). See ABERNATHY & PERRY, *supra* note 16, at 12–13.

207. In Venezuela, the Supreme Court, even recognizing the existence of exclusive attributions of legislative bodies, which according to the 1961 Constitution (Article 159) were not subjected to judicial review, admitted the amparo protection against them for the immediate restoration of the plaintiff's harmed constitutional rights. It admitted the amparo action against legislative acts, in a decision nº 22 dated January 31, 1991 in *Anselmo Natale*, ruling as follows: "The exclusion of judicial review regarding certain parliamentary acts—except in cases of extra limitation of powers—set forth in Article 159 of the Constitution, as a way to prevent, due to the rules of separation of powers, that the executive and judicial branches could invade or interfere in the orbit of the legislative body which is the trustee of the popular sovereignty, is restricted to determine the intrinsic regularity of such acts regarding the Constitution, in order to annul them, but it does not apply when it is a matter of obtaining the immediate reestablishment of the enjoyment and exercise of harmed rights and guaranties set forth in the Constitution." *Anselmo Natale* case. See in *Revista de Derecho Público*, nº 45, Editorial Jurídica Venezolana, Caracas, 1991, p. 118.

208. 43A C.J.S. INJUNCTIONS § 202 (2004) (citing Mins v. McCarthy, 209 F.2d 307, 307 (D.C. Cir. 1953) (per curiam)).

209. According to Article 3 of the Amparo Law, two ways are established through which an amparo pretension can be filed before the competent court: (1) in an autonomous way, or (2) exercised together with the popular action of unconstitutionality of statutes. Venez. Amparo Law, Art. 3. In the latter case, the amparo pretension is subordinated to the principal action

When filed directly against statutes, the purpose of the Amparo Law's provision was to secure the inapplicability of the statute to the particular case, with *inter partes* effects.[210] Yet in spite of the Amparo Law provisions, the jurisprudence of the Supreme Tribunal rejected such actions, imposing the need to file them only against the state acts issued to apply the statutes and not directly against the statutes themselves.[211] The Court, in its decisions, even though admitting the distinction between the self-executing and not self-executing statutes,[212] concluded its ruling by declaring the impossibility for a real normative act to directly and by itself harm the constitutional rights of an individual. The Court also considered that a statute cannot be a threat to constitutional rights, because for an amparo to be filed, a threat must be "imminent, possible and realizable," considering that in the case of statutes such conditions are not fulfilled.[213]

---

for judicial review, producing only the possibility for the court to suspend the application of the statute pending the unconstitutionality suit. See BREWER-CARÍAS, *Instituciones Políticas y Constitucionales, Tomo V, El derecho y la acción de amparo*, *supra* note 5, at 227. In this case, the situation is similar to the one of the popular action of unconstitutionality in the Dominican Republic when the amparo pretension is filed together with it. See Eduardo Jorge PRATS, *Derecho Constitucional*, Vol. II, Gaceta Judicial, Santo Domingo, 2005, p. 399.

210. See BREWER-CARÍAS, *Instituciones Políticas y Constitucionales,* Tomo V, *El derecho y la acción de amparo*, *supra* note 5, at 224; CHAVERO, *El nuevo régimen del amparo constitucional en Venezuela*, *supra* note 5, at 553 ff.

211. The Politico Administrative Chamber of the former Supreme Court issued a decision n° 315 dated May 24, 1993, that has been the leading case on the matter, ruling that: "[T]hus, it seem that there is no doubt that Article 3 of the Amparo law does not set forth the possibility of filing an amparo action directly against a normative act, but against the act, fact or omission that has its origin in a normative provision which is considered by the claimant as contrary to the Constitution and for which, due to the presumption of legitimacy and constitutionality of the former, the court must previously resolve its inapplicability to the concrete case argued. It is obvious, thus, that such article of the Amparo law does not allow the possibility of filing this action for constitutional protection against a statute or other normative act, but against the act which applies or executes it, which is definitively the one that in the concrete case can cause a particular harm to the constitutional rights and guaranties of a precise person." *Revista de Derecho Público*, n° 55-56, Editorial Jurídica Venezolana, Caracas, 1993, pp. 287–88.

212. Ruling that the self-executing statutes impose an immediate obligation for the person to whom it is issued, with its promulgation, and, on the contrary, those statutes not self-executing require an act for its execution, in which case its sole promulgation cannot produce a constitutional violation. See decision n° 315 of the Politico Administrative Chamber of the former Supreme Court of Justice, of May 24, 1993, in *Revista de Derecho Público*, n° 55-56, Editorial Jurídica Venezolana, Caracas, 1993, pp. 285-86.

213. The Court, in the same decision n° 315 dated May 24, 1993, rejected the possibility of a threat caused by a statute, with the following argument: "In case of an amparo action against a norm, the concretion of the possible harm would not be 'immediate', because it will always be the need for a competent authority to execute or apply it in order for the statute to effectively harm the claimant. It must be concluded that the probable harm produced by the norm will always be a mediate and indirect one, due to the need for the statute to be applied to the particular case. So that the harm will be caused by mean of the act applying the illegal norm. The same occurs with the third condition, in the sense that the probable and imminent threat

Regarding executive authorities, the general principle is that the action is admitted against acts, facts or omissions from public entities or bodies conforming to the public administration at all its levels (national, state, municipal), including decentralized, autonomous, independent bodies and including acts issued by the Head of the Executive, that is, the President of the Republic. This last aspect, for instance, is contrary to the rule regarding injunctions in the United States where the principle is that such a coercive remedy "may not be directed against the President."[214]

Regarding administrative acts, as mentioned, the Amparo Law admits the filing of amparo actions against them, providing for possibility of exercising the amparo action in two ways: in an autonomous way or conjunctly with nullity recourse for judicial review of the administrative act.[215] The main distinction between both

---

will never be made by the possible defendant. If it would be possible to sustain that the amparo could be admissible against a statute whose constitutionality is challenged, it would be necessary to accept as aggrieved party the legislative body issuing it, being the party to participate in the process as defendant. But it must be highlighted that in the case in which the possible harm could be realized, it would not be the legislative body the one called to execute it, but rather the public officer that must apply the norm in all the cases in which an individual is located in the situation it regulates. If it is understood that the object of the amparo action is the statute, then the conclusion would be that the possible defendant (the public entity enacting the norm whose unconstitutionality is alleged) could not be the one that could make the threat. The concrete harm would be definitively made by a different entity or person (the one applying the unconstitutional norm to a specific and particular case)."REVISTA DE DERECHO PÚBLICO, nº 55-56, Editorial Jurídica Venezolana, Caracas, 1993, pp. 288, 290. From the abovementioned, the Venezuelan Supreme Court's conclusion rejected the amparo action against statutes and normative acts, not only because it considered that the Amparo Laws do not set forth such possibilities –bypassing its text– but because even being possible to bring the extraordinary action against a normative act, it would not comply with the imminent, possible and realizable conditions of the threats set forth in Article 6.2 of the Amparo Law. See the comments in Allan R. Brewer-Carías, *La acción de amparo contra leyes y demás actos normativos en el derecho venezolano*, in LIBER AMICORUM. HÉCTOR FIX-ZAMUDIO, Vol. I, Secretaría de la Corte Interamericana de Derechos Humanos. San José, Costa Rica 1998, pp. 481-501.

214. 43A C.J.S. INJUNCTIONS § 201 (2004) (citing Sloan v. Nixon, 60 F.R.D. 228 (S.D.N.Y. 1973), *aff'd* 493 F.2d 1398 (2d Cir. 1974), *aff'd* 419 U.S. 958 (1974)).

215. Venez. Amparo Law, Art. 5. Regarding the latter, the former Supreme Court of Justice in the decision nº 343 of July 10, 1991, *Tarjetas Banvenez* case, clarified that in such case, the action is not a principal one, but subordinated and ancillary regarding the principal recourse to which it has been attached, and subjected to the final nullifying decision that has to be issued in it. See in *Revista de Derecho Público*, nº 47, Editorial Jurídica Venezolana, Caracas, 1991, pp. 169–74. That is why, in such cases, the amparo pretension that must be founded in a grave presumption of the violation of the constitutional right has a preventive and temporal character, pending the final decision of the nullity suit, consisting of the suspension of the effects of the challenged administrative act. This provisional character of the amparo protection pending the suit is thus subjected to the final decision to be issued in the nullity judicial review procedure against the challenged administrative act. See the same decision nº 343 of July 10, 1991, in *Revista de Derecho Público*, nº 47, Editorial Jurídica Venezolana, Caracas, 1991, pp. 170–71.

means[216] lies, first, in the character of the allegation. In the first case, the alleged and proved constitutional right violation must be a direct, immediate and flagrant one. In the second case, what has to be proved is the existence of a grave presumption of the constitutional right violation. The distinction next lies in the general purpose of the proceeding. In the first case, the judicial decision issued is a definitive constitutional protection of restorative character. In the second case, it has only a preliminary character of suspension of the effects of the challenged act pending the decision of the principal judicial review process.[217]

Contrary to what happens in the majority of Latin American countries, in Venezuela, the amparo action is admitted against judicial acts, except decisions of the Supreme Tribunal of Justice.[218] Article 4 of the Amparo Law provides that in the cases of judicial decisions "the action for amparo shall also be admitted when a court, acting outside its competence, issues a resolution or decision, or orders an action that impairs a constitutional right."[219] Considering that no court has any power to unlawfully cause harm to constitutional rights or guarantees, the amparo against judicial decisions is extensively admitted when a court decision directly harms the constitutional rights of the plaintiff, normally related to the due process of law rights.[220] In a certain way regarding injunctions on judicial matters, it can also

---

216. The main difference between both procedures according to the Supreme Court doctrine is that in the first case of the autonomous amparo action against administrative acts, the plaintiff must allege a direct, immediate and flagrant violation to the constitutional right, which in its own demonstrates the need for the amparo order as a definitive means to restore the harmed juridical situation. In the second case, given the suspensive nature of the amparo order which only tends to provisionally stop the effects of the injuring act until the judicial review of administrative action confirming or nullifying it is decided, the alleged unconstitutional violations of constitutional provisions can be formulated together with violations of legal or statutory provisions developing the constitutional ones, because it is a judicial review action against administrative acts, seeking their nullity, they can also be founded on legal texts. What the court cannot do in cases of filing the actions together, in order to suspend the effects of the challenged administrative act, is to base its decision only in the legal violations alleged, because that would mean to anticipate the final decision on the principal nullity judicial review recourse. See the former Supreme Court of Justice in the decision nº 343 of July 10, 1991, *Tarjetas Banvenez* case, in *Revista de Derecho Público*, nº 47, Editorial Jurídica Venezolana, Caracas, 1991, pp.171–72.

217. *Id.* at 172. See *also*, regarding the nullity of Article 22 of the Organic Amparo Law, the former Supreme Court of Justice decision nº 644 dated May 21, 1996, in REVISTA DE DERECHO PÚBLICO, nº 65-66, Editorial Jurídica Venezolana, Caracas, 1996, pp.332 ff. See the comments in Allan R. BREWER-CARÍAS, *Instituciones Políticas y Constitucionales,* Tomo V, *El derecho y la acción de amparo, supra* note 5, at 392 ff.

218. Venez. Amparo Law, Art. 6.6.

219. Venez.Amparo Law, Art. 4.

220. As was decided by the Cassation Chamber of the former Supreme Court of Justice in a decision from Dec. 5, 1990, the amparo against judicial decisions is admitted, "when the decision in itself injures the juridical conscience, when harming in a flagrant way individual rights that cannot be renounced or when the decision violates the principle of juridical security (judicial stability), deciding against *res judicata*, or when issued in a process where the plaintiff's right to defense has not been guaranteed, or in any way the due process guaranty has

be said that in the United States, injunctions can also be granted when, for instance, it clearly appears that the prosecution of law actions are the result of fraud, gross wrong or oppression, in which cases justice clearly requires equitable interference.[221]

On the other hand, although in many countries the amparo proceedings cannot be the object of another amparo action, in a way similar to the rule established in the United States regarding an injunction against another injunction, sometimes referred to as a "counter injunction," which cannot be admitted,[222] in Venezuela the amparo actions are admitted even against previous amparo judicial decisions.[223] Considering that such decisions can also, by themselves, violate constitutional rights of the plaintiff or of the defendant, different to those claimed in the initial amparo action, such an admission of the amparo action is necessary.

Beside the legislative, executive and judicial branches of government, the amparo action can also be filed against the acts of other independent organs or branches of government like, for instance, the electoral bodies in charge of governing the electoral processes, the People's Defendant Office, the Public Prosecutor Office of the General Comptroller Office, including the judiciary organs in charge of the government and administration of courts and tribunals. Because those entities are state organs, in principle their acts, facts and omissions can also be challenged by means of amparo actions when violating constitutional rights.

Apart from the positive acts or actions from public officers, authorities or from individuals, that amparo action can also be filed against the omissions of authorities when the corresponding entities or public officials fail to comply with their general obligations, thereby causing harm or threat to constitutional rights. In the cases of public officers' omissions, the amparo action is generally filed in order to obtain

---

been violated." Case *José Díaz Aquino*, also referred to in decision dated Dec.14, 1994, of the same Cassation Chamber. See the reference in BREWER-CARÍAS, *Instituciones Políticas y Constitucionales,* Tomo V, *El derecho y la acción de amparo*, *supra* note 5, at 261; and CHAVERO, *El nuevo régimen del amparo constitucional en Venezuela*, *supra* note 5, at 483 ff. See *also* Allan R. Brewer-Carías, *El problema del amparo contra sentencias o de cómo la Sala de Casación Civil remedia arbitrariedades judiciales*, in *Revista de Derecho Público*, n° 34, Editorial Jurídica Venezolana, Caracas 1988, pp. 157-71.

221. As has been decided by the courts: "The power of a court of equity to interfere with the general right of a person to sue and to restrain the person from prosecuting the action will be exercised only where it appears clearly that the prosecution of the law action will result in a fraud, gross wrong, or oppression, and that conscience and justice clearly require equitable interference. Accordingly, an action at law may be restrained under these restrictive rules where a person is attempting to, or would, through the instrumentality of an action at law, obtain an unconscionable advantage of another."43A C.J.S. INJUNCTIONS § 96 (2004) (citing Miles v. Illinois Cent. R.R Co. 315 U.S. 698 (1942)); *see also* Kardy v. Shook, 207 A.2d 83 (Md. 1965); Langenau Mfg. Co. v. City of Cleveland, 112 N.E.2d 658 (Ohio 1953).

222. 43A C.J.S. INJUNCTIONS § 69 (2004) (citing Sellers v. Valenzuela, 32 So.2d 520 (Ala. 1947)).

223. See ALLAN R. BREWER-CARÍAS, *Instituciones Políticas y Constitucionales,* Tomo V, *El derecho y la acción de amparo*, *supra* note 5, at 263; and *El recurso de amparo contra sentencias de amparo dictadas en segunda instancia*, in *Revista de Derecho Público*, N° 36, Editorial Jurídica Venezolana, Caracas 1988, pp. 160-72.

from the court an order directed against the public officer compelling him to act in a matter with respect to which he has the authority or jurisdiction. In these cases, the effect of the amparo decision regarding omissions is similar to the United States mandamus or mandatory injunction,[224] which consists in "a writ commanding a public officer to perform some duty which the laws require him to do but he refuses or neglects to perform."[225]

In any case, for an omission to be the object of an amparo action, it must also inflict a direct harm to the constitutional right of the plaintiff. If the violation is only referring to a right of legal rank, the amparo action is inadmissible and the affected party is obliged to use the ordinary judicial remedies, like the judicial review of administrative omission action to be filed before the special courts of the matter (*contencioso-administrativo*).[226] In order to determine when it is possible to file an amparo action against public officers' omissions, the key element established by the Venezuelan courts refers to the nature of the public officers' duties, because the

---

224. In the United States, "[w]hile as a general rule courts will not compel by injunction the performance by public officers of their official duties, a court may compel public officers or boards to act in a matter with respect to which they have jurisdiction or authority[.]" 43A C.J.S. INJUNCTIONS § 194 (2004) (citing Erie v. State Highway Comm'n, 461 P.2d 207 (Mont. 1969); Bellamy v. Gates, 200 S.E.2d 533, (Va. 1973)).

225. See ABERNATHY & PERRY, *supra* note 16, at 8. The consequence of this rule is that mandamus cannot be used if the public officer has any discretion in the matter; "but if the law is clear in requiring the performance of some ministerial (nondiscretionary) function, then mandamus may properly be sought to nudge the reluctant or negligent official along in the performance of his or her duties." As it was decided by the United States Supreme Court in Wilbur v. U. S. *ex. rel.* Kadrie: "Where the duty in a particular situation is so plainly prescribed as to be free from doubt and equivalent to a positive command, it is regarded as being so far ministerial that its performance may be compelled by mandamus, unless there be provision or implication to the contrary. But where the duty is not thus plainly prescribed, but depends upon a statute or statutes the construction or application of which is not free from doubt, it is regarded as involving the character of judgment or discretion which cannot be controlled by mandamus."281 U.S. 206, 218-19 (1930) (footnote omitted). See the references in ABERNATHY & PERRY, *supra* note 16, at 8.

226. According to the judicial doctrine established by the former Supreme Court of Justice of Venezuela, the amparo action against omissions by the Public Administration, must comply with the following two conditions: "a) That the alleged omissive conduct be absolute, which means that Public Administration has not accomplished in any moment the due function; and b) that the omission be regarding a generic duty, that is, the duty a public officer has to act in compliance with the powers attributed to him, which is different to the specific duty that is the condition for the judicial review of administrative omissive action. Thus, only when it is a matter of a generic duty, of procedure, of providing in a matter which is inherent to the public officer position, he incurs in the omissive conduct regarding which the amparo action is admissible."See the Decision nº 541 of the former Supreme Court of Justice, Politico Administrative Chamber, dated Nov. 5, 1992, *Jorge E. Alvarado* case, in *Revista de Derecho Público*, nº 52, Editorial Jurídica Venezolana, Caracas, 1992, p. 187; and decision nº 766 Nov.18, 1993, in *Revista de Derecho Público*, nº 55-56, Editorial Jurídica Venezolana, Caracas, 1993, p. 295.

amparo action is only admissible when the matters refer to a generic constitutional duty and not to specific legal ones.[227]

Because the judicial order of mandamus in the amparo decision regarding public authorities' omissions is a command directed to the public officer to perform the duty that the constitution requires him to do, which he has refused or neglected to perform,[228] the general rule is that the court order cannot substitute the public officer's power to decide. Only in cases when a specific statute provides what it is called a "positive silence" (the presumption that after the exhaustion of a particular term, it is considered that public administration has tacitly decided accordingly to what has been asked in the particular petition) the judicial order is considered as implicitly giving positive effects to the official abstention or omission.[229]

IX. THE ADMISSIBILITY CONDITIONS OF THE AMPARO ACTION BASED ON ITS EXTRAORDINARY CHARACTER

Since the amparo action is a judicial means specifically established for the protection of constitutional rights, it is conceived in Venezuela as an extraordinary judicial instrument that, consequently, does not substitute for all the other ordinary judicial remedies established for the protection of personal rights and interests. This implies that the amparo action, as a matter of principle, only can be filed when no other adequate judicial mean exists and is available in order to obtain the immediate protection of the violated constitutional rights. This implies the need for the courts

227. As defined by the same former Supreme Court of Justice, Politico Administrative Chamber, in a decision n° 69 dated February 11, 1992: "In cases of Public Administration abstentions or omissions, a distinction can be observed regarding the constitutional provisions violated when they provide for generic or specific duties. In the first case, when a public entity does not comply with its generic obligation to answer [a petition] filed by an individual, it violates the constitutional right to obtain prompt answer [to his petition] as set forth in Article 67 of the Constitution; whereas when the inactivity is produced regarding a specific duty imposed by a statute in a concrete and ineludible way, no direct constitutional violation occurs, in which case the Court has imposed the filing of the judicial review of administrative omissions recourse . . . ..From the aforementioned reasons the Court deems conclusive that the inactivity of Public Administration to accomplish a specific legal duty precisely infringes in a direct and immediate way the legal (statutory) text regulating the matter, in which case the Constitution is only violated in a mediate and indirect way. For the amparo judge, in order to detect if an abstention of the aggrieved entity effectively harms a constitutional right or guaranty, it must first, rely himself on the supposedly unaccomplished statute in order to verify if the abstention is regarding a specific obligation; in which case it must deny the amparo action, having the plaintiff the possibility to file another remedy, like the judicial review action against Public Administration omissions."*Revista de Derecho Público*, n° 53-54, Editorial Jurídica Venezolana, Caracas, 1993, pp. 272–73.

228. For instance, to promptly issue the corresponding decision accordingly to the formal petition filed before the authority. VENEZ. CONST. ART. 51 (1999). See the First Court on Judicial Review of Administrative Actions decision dated Aug. 26, 1993, *Klanki* case, in *Revista de Derecho Público*, n° 55-56, Editorial Jurídica Venezolana, Caracas, 1993, p. 294.

229. See the First Court on Judicial Review of Administrative Actions decision dated Dec. 20, 1991, *BHO, C.A.* case, in *Revista de Derecho Público*, n° 48, Editorial Jurídica Venezolana, Caracas, 1991, pp. 141–43.

to, determine the existence or nonexistence of other adequate judicial means for the immediate protection of the rights, which justifies or not the use of the extraordinary action.

This question of the adjective rules of the admissibility of the amparo action derives from the relation that exists between the amparo action as an extraordinary judicial means, and the other ordinary judicial means. In this context, the general rule of admissibility refers to two aspects: first, that the amparo action can only be admissible when there are no other judicial means for granting the constitutional protection; and second, that when the legal order provides for these other judicial means for protection of the right, they are inadequate in order to obtain the immediate protection of the harmed or threatened constitutional rights. In a contrary sense, the amparo action is inadmissible for the protection of a constitutional right if the legal order provides for other actions or proceedings that are adequate for such purpose, guaranteeing immediate protection to the right.

This rule of admissibility of the amparo action is similar to the general rule existing in the United States regarding injunctions and all other equitable remedies, "like mandamus and prohibitions, is reserved for extraordinary cases",[230] in the sense that they are "available only after the applicant shows that the legal remedies are inadequate."[231] It is a traditional and fundamental principle for granting an injunction that the "inadequacy of the existing legal remedies" must be established.[232] This condition of the "availability" or of the "sufficiency"[233] has also been referred to as the rule of "irreparable injury," meaning that the injunction is only admissible when the "harm cannot be repaired by the remedies available in the common law courts." That is, if the threatened rights are rectified by a legal remedy, then the judge will refuse to grant the injunction.[234]

---

230. 43A C.J.S. Injunctions § 2 (2004) (citing *Ex-parte* Collet, 337 U.S. 55, (1949)). This main characteristic of the injunction as an extraordinary remedy has been established since the nineteenth century in *In re Debs*, 158 U.S. 564 (1895), in which case, in the words of Justice Brewer, who delivered the opinion of the court, it was decided that: "As a rule, injunctions are denied to those who have adequate remedy at law. Where the choice is between the ordinary and the extraordinary processes of law, and the former are sufficient, the rule will not permit the use of the latter." *Debs*, 158 U.S. at 583. See Fiss & Rendleman, *supra* note 32.

231. Fiss & Rendleman, *supra* note 32, at 59.

232. 43A C.J.S. Injunctions § 71 (2004) (citing Beacon Theatres, Inc. v. Westover, 359 U.S. 500 (1958)). The judicial doctrine on the matter has been summarized as follows: "[A]n injunction, like any other equitable remedy, will only issue [sic] where there is no adequate remedy at law. Accordingly, except where the rule is changed by statute, an injunction ordinarily will not be granted where there is an adequate remedy at law for the injury complained of, which is full and complete. Conversely, a court of equitable jurisdiction may grant an injunction where an adequate and complete remedy cannot be had in the courts of law, despite the petitioner's best efforts. Moreover, a court will not deny access to injunctive relief when local procedures cannot effectively, conveniently and directly determine whether the petitioner is entitled to the relief claimed."*Id.*

233. 43A C.J.S. Injunctions § 100 (2004).

234. See Fiss & Rendleman, *supra* note 32, at 59. This situation, as pointed out by Owen M. Fiss, "[M]akes the issuance of an injunction conditional upon a showing that the plaintiff has

This rule always imposes the need for the plaintiff and for the court to determine in each case, not only the existence and availability of ordinary judicial means for obtaining the constitutional protection, but also the adequacy of such existing and available recourses for granting the immediate constitutional protection to the constitutional right. In this sense, in Venezuela, without an express provision in the Amparo Law, the Supreme Court has ruled that "the amparo is admissible even in cases where, although ordinary means exist for the protection of the infringed juridical situation, they would not be suitable, adequate or effective for the immediate restoration of the said situation."[235] Also, the question of the adjective consequences

---

no alternative remedy that will adequately repair his injury. Operationally this means that as general proposition the plaintiff is remitted to some remedy other than an injunction unless he can show that his noninjunctive remedies are inadequate." FISS & RENDLEMAN, *supra* note 32. This term "inadequacy," according to Tabb and Shoben, "has a specific meaning in the law of equity because it is a shorthand expression for the policy that equitable remedies are subordinate to legal ones. They are subordinate in the sense that the damage remedy is preferred in any individual case if it is adequate." TABB & SHOBEN, *supra* note 47, at 15. In particular, regarding constitutional claims involving constitutional rights such as those for school desegregation, it has been considered that their protection precisely requires the extraordinary remedy that can be obtained by equitable intervention, as was decided by the Supreme Court regarding school desegregation in its second opinion in Brown v. Board of Education, 349 U.S. 753 (1955) and regarding the unconstitutional cruel and unusual punishment in the prison system in Hutto v. Finney, 437 U.S. 678 (1978). TABB & SHOBEN, *supra* note 53, at 25–26.

235. Decision nº 109 of the former Supreme Court of Justice of Venezuela of Mar. 8, 1990, in REVISTA DE DERECHO PÚBLICO, nº 42, Editorial Jurídica Venezolana, Caracas, 1990, pp. 107–08. In a similar sense, the Supreme Court in a decision nº 705 dated Dec. 11, 1990, ruled that: "The criteria of this High Court as well as the authors' opinions has been reiterative in the sense that the amparo action is an extraordinary or special judicial remedy that is only admissible when the other procedural means that could repair the harm are exhausted, do not exist or would be inoperative. Additionally, Article 5 of the Amparo Law provides that the amparo action is only admissible when no brief, summary and effective procedural means exist in accordance with the constitutional protection. This objective procedural condition for the admissibility of the action turns the amparo into a judicial mean that can only be admissible by the court once it has verified that the other ordinary means are not effective or adequate in order to restore the infringed juridical situation. If other means exist, the court must not admit the proposed amparo action." *Revista de Derecho Público*, nº 45, Editorial Jurídica Venezolana, Caracas, 1991, p. 112. The Supreme Court, in another decision nº 270 dated June 12, 1990, decided that the amparo action is admissible: "when there are no other means for the adequate and effective reestablishment of the infringed juridical situation. Consequently, one of the conditions for the admissibility of the amparo action is the nonexistence of other more effective means for the reestablishment of the harmed rights. If such means are adequate to resolve the situation, there is no need to file the special amparo action. But even if such means exists, if they are inadequate for the immediate reestablishment of the constitutional guaranty, it is also justifiable to use the constitutional protection mean of amparo." See decision nº 270 of the Politico Administrative Chamber of the Supreme Court of Justice of June 12, 1990, in *Revista de Derecho Público* nº 43, Editorial Jurídica Venezolana, Caracas, 1990, p. 78. See *also* decision nº 656 of the Politico Administrative Chamber of the Supreme Court of Justice of Dec. 2, 1993, in *Revista de Derecho Público*, nº 55-56, Editorial Jurídica Venezolana, Caracas, 1993, pp. 311–13.

resulting from the plaintiff's previous election of other remedies for the claimed protection filed before the amparo action must also be analyzed.

Of course, this question of the availability and of the adequacy of the existing judicial means for the admissibility or inadmissibility of the amparo action eventually is a matter of judicial interpretation and adjudication, which must always be decided in the particular case decision, when evaluating the adequacy question.[236]

In Venezuela, particularly regarding the amparo action against administrative acts, the prevalent doctrine on the matter for many years, established by the former Supreme Court of Justice, was to admit the amparo action in spite of the existence of the specific recourse before the Judicial Review of Administrative Action Jurisdiction. Yet this wide protective doctrine has been unfortunately abandoned in recent years by the Supreme Tribunal of Justice, applying a restrictive interpretation regarding the adequacy of the judicial review action for the annulment of administrative acts, and rejecting the amparo action when filed directly against them.[237]

---

236. For instance, in a decision of the First Court on Judicial Review of Administrative Actions dated May 20, 1994 (*Federación Venezolana de Deportes Equestres* case), it was ruled that the judicial review of administrative acts were not adequate for the protection requested in the case, seeking the participation of the Venezuelan Federation of Equestrian Sports in an international competition, being the opinion of the courts: "[T]hat when the action was brought before it, the only mean that the claimant had in order to obtain the reestablishment of the infringed juridical situation was the amparo action, due to the fact that by means of the judicial review of administrative acts recourse seeking its nullity, they could never be able to obtain the said reestablishment of the infringed juridical situation that was to assist to the 1990 international contest." See in *Revista de Derecho Público*, nº 57-58, Editorial Jurídica Venezolana, Caracas, 1994, pp. 284 ff..; and in CHAVERO, *El nuevo régimen del amparo constitucional en Venezuela*, *supra*, note 5, at 354.

237. This can be realized from the decision taken in a recent and polemic case referring to the expropriation of some premises of a corn agro-industry complex, which developed as follows: in Aug. 2005, officers from the Ministry of Agriculture and Land and military officers and soldiers from the Army and the National Guard surrounded the installation of the company *Refinadora de Maíz Venezolana, C.A. (Remavenca)*, and announcements were publicly made regarding the appointment of an Administrator Commission that would be taking over the industry. These actions were challenged by the company as a *de facto* action alleging the violation of the company's rights to equality, due process and defense, economic freedom, property rights and to the non-confiscation guarantee of property. A few days later, the Governor of the State of Barinas, where the industry was located, issued a decree ordering the expropriation of the premises, and consequently the Supreme Tribunal declared the inadmissibility of the amparo action that was filed, basing its ruling on the following arguments: "The criteria established up to now by this Tribunal, by which it has concluded on the inadmissibility of the autonomous amparo action against administrative acts has been that the judicial review of administrative act actions –among which the recourse for nullity, the actions against the administrative abstentions and recourse filed by public servants– are the adequate means, that is, the brief, prompt and efficient means in order to obtain the reestablishment of the infringed juridical situation, in addition to the wide powers that are attributed to the administrative jurisdiction courts in Article 29 of the Constitution. Accordingly, the recourse for nullity or the expropriation suit are the adequate means to resolve the claims referring to supposed controversies in the expropriation procedure; those are the preexisting judicial means in order to judicially decide conflicts in which previous legality studies are required,

The other question related to the admissibility of the amparo action is related to the question of the existence of a pending action or recourse already filed or brought before a court for the same purpose of protecting a constitutional right. This question regarding the admissibility of the amparo action also has some similarities with the United States' injunction procedure regarding defenses, called the "doctrine of the election of remedies," which is applied when an injured party having two available but inconsistent remedies to redress a harm, chooses one, which is considered a binding election that forecloses the other.[238] In a similar sense, this is the general rule in Venezuela, which is nonetheless only applied when the plaintiff has filed other judicial means for protection; not being applied if only administrative recourses have been filed before the public administration organs.[239]

This condition of inadmissibility of the amparo action when the plaintiff has chosen to file another action has also been regulated, in particular regarding the case of the previous filing of another amparo action that is pending to be decided.[240] In these cases, it is necessary that a previous amparo action had been filed regarding the same violation, the same action and the same persons.

---

and which the constitutional judge cannot consider. Thus, the Chamber considers that the claimants, if they think that the alleged claim persists, can obtain the reestablishment of their allegedly infringed juridical situation, by means of the ordinary actions and to obtain satisfaction to their claims. So because of the existing adequate means for the resolution of the controversy argued by the plaintiff, it is compulsory for the Chamber to declare the inadmissibility of the amparo action, according to what is set forth in Article 6,5 of the Organic Law."Decision of the Constitutional Chamber of the Supreme Tribunal of Justice n° 3375 of Nov. 4, 2005, *Refinadora de Maíz Venezolana, C.A. (Remavenca), y Procesadora Venezolana de Cereales, S.A. (Provencesa) vs. Ministro de Agricultura y Tierras y efectivos de los componentes Ejército y Guardia Nacional de la Fuerza Armada Nacional* See also in *Revista de Derecho Público*, n° 104, Editorial Jurídica Venezolana, Caracas, 2005, pp. 239 ff.

238. See TABB & SHOBEN, *supra* note 53, at 56.

239. In this case, the inadmissible clause is not applied because the administrative recourses are not judicial ordinary means that can prevent the filing of the amparo action. See the Decision of the First Court on Judicial Review of Administrative Actions, which decided on a decision dated Mar. 8, 1993, *Federico Domingo* case, in *Revista de Derecho Público*, n° 53-54, Editorial Jurídica Venezolana, Caracas, 1994, p. 261. See *also* the Decision dated May 6, 1994, *Universidad Occidental Lisandro Alvarado* case, in *Revista de Derecho Público*, n° 57-58, Editorial Jurídica Venezolana, Caracas, 1994. See, pp. 297 ff.; and in CHAVERO, *El nuevo régimen del amparo constitucional en Venezuela*, *supra* note 5, at 250 ff.

240. Article 6.8 of the Amparo Law provides the inadmissibility of the action for amparo when a decision regarding another amparo suit has been brought before the courts regarding the same facts and is pending decision. Venez. Amparo Law, Art. 6.8. See, *e.g.*, Decision of the Politico Administrative Chamber of the Supreme Court of Justice of Oct. 13, 1993, *Escuela Básica Juan Lovera* case, in *Revista de Derecho Público*, n° 55-56, Editorial Jurídica Venezolana, Caracas, 1993, pp. 348–49.

X. THE MAIN PRINCIPLES OF THE PROCEDURE IN THE AMPARO PROCEEDING

The extraordinary character of the amparo proceeding also conditions the general rules governing the procedure, which in general terms are related to its bilateral character; to the brief and preferred character of the procedure; to the role of the courts directing the procedure and to the need for the substantial law to prevail regarding formalities.

In effect, as aforementioned, one of the fundamental principles regarding the amparo proceeding is that although being of an extraordinary nature, the bilateral character of the proceeding must always be guaranteed. This implies that the amparo proceeding must always be initiated by a party or parties (the injured or offended party), so that no *ex officio* amparo proceeding is admissible.[241] Consequently, the amparo proceeding must always be initiated by means of an action or a recourse brought before the competent court by a party against another party (the injurer or offender party) whose actions or omissions have violated or have caused harm to the complaining party's constitutional rights. This defendant must always be brought to the procedure in order to guarantee his rights of defense and due process.

From the amparo proceeding, its final outcome is always a judicial order, as also happens in the United States with the writs of injunction, mandamus or error, which are directed to the injuring party ordering him to do or to abstain from doing something, or to suspend the effects, or in some cases, to annul the damaging act.[242] In Venezuela, as already mentioned, the amparo statutes not only refer to the amparo as a remedy or as the final court written order (writ) commanding the defendant to do or refrain from doing some specific act, but in addition, it is regulated as a complete proceeding that is specifically designed to protect constitutional rights following an adversary procedure according to the "cases or controversy" requirement. All the phases or stages of the procedure are regulated. The procedure ends with a judicial decision or judicial order directed to protect the constitutional rights of the injured party.

Consequently, the general rule in the amparo proceeding is that although it is brief and speedy, the procedural adversary principle or the aforementioned principle

---

241. Only in cases of habeas corpus actions do some amparo laws provide for the power of the courts to initiate the proceeding *ex officio*. GUATEMALA CONSTITUTION, art. 86; HONDURAS CONSTITUTION, art. 20.

242. The amparo suit has similarities with the civil suit for an injunction in the United States that an injured party can bring before a court to seek for the enforcement or restoration of his violated rights or for the prevention of their violation. It also can be identified with a "suit for mandamus," brought by an injured party before a court against a public officer whose omission has caused harm to the plaintiff, in order to seek for a writ ordering the former to perform a duty that the law requires him to do but he refuses or neglects to perform. Also, the suit for amparo has similarities with a "suit for writ of error" brought before the competent superior court by an injured party whose constitutional rights have been violated by a judicial decision, seeking the annulment or the correction of the judicial wrong or error.

of bilateralism must be preserved, assuring the presence of both parties and the respect of the due process constitutional guarantees, particularly the rights to defense.[243] That is why no definitive amparo adjudication can be issued without the participation of the defendant or at least without his knowledge about the filing of the action. The exception to this rule being very rare, as is the case of Colombia, where the *Tutela* Law admits the possibility for the court to grant the constitutional protection (tutela) *in limine litis*, that is, "without any formal consideration and without previous enquiry, if the decision is founded in an evidence that shows the grave and imminent violation of harm to the right."[244]

This Colombian provision undoubtedly was inspired by the 1988 Venezuelan Amparo Law that also provided for the possibility for the amparo judge "to immediately restore the infringed juridical situation, without considerations of mere form and without any kind of brief enquiry," requiring in such cases, that "the amparo protection be founded in evidence constituting a grave presumption of the violation of harm of violation."[245] Nonetheless, in Venezuela this article was annulled by the former Supreme Court, which refused to interpret it in harmony with the constitution, as only providing for preliminary decisions and as not intending to establish the possibility of a definitive amparo decision that could be issued *inaudita parte* because such action would be unconstitutional. In particular, a popular action was filed in 1988 before the former Supreme Court of Justice based on the alleged unconstitutionality of such provision. In it, it was requested from the Supreme Court to interpret it according to the constitution (*secundum constitucione*), in the sense that what was intended with the provision was to establish a legal authorization for the courts to simply adopt, in an immediate way, preliminary protective measures, pending the resolution of the case, but not definitive amparo decisions. Nonetheless, the Supreme Court rejected this interpretation, and in a decision dated May 21, 1996, eventually annulled Article 22 of the Amparo Law considering that it violated in a flagrant way the constitutional right to defense.[246] The adjective consequence was

243. Thus, a judicial guarantee of constitutional rights like the amparo suit can in no way transform itself into a proceeding violating the other constitutional guarantees, such as the right to defense. Except regarding preliminary judicial orders, the principle of *audi alteram partem* ("hear the other party" or "listen to both sides") must then always be respected.

244. Tutela Law of Columbia, Art. 18.

245. Venez. Amparo Law, Art. 22 (referring to the 1988 version).

246. This Article, as mentioned, allowed the courts to adopt final decisions on amparo matters in cases of grave violations of constitutional rights, reestablishing the harmed constitutional right without any formal or summary inquiry and without hearing the plaintiff or potential injurer. Even if the Article could have been constitutionally interpreted as only directed to allow the adoption of *inaudita partem* preliminary decisions or injunctions in the proceeding, the Supreme Court considered its contents as a vulgar and flagrant violation of the constitutional right to self-defense, and annulled it. See decision nº 644 of the Supreme Court of Justice of May 21, 1996, in *Gaceta Oficial* EXTRA. nº 5071 of May 29, 1996, and in REVISTA DE DERECHO PÚBLICO, nº 65-66, Editorial Jurídica Venezolana, Caracas, 1996, pp.332 ff. See the comments in Allan R. BREWER-CARÍAS, *Instituciones Políticas y Constitucionales,* Tomo V, *El derecho y la acción de amparo*, *supra* note 5, at 388-96; and in Chavero, *El nuevo régimen del amparo constitucional en Venezuela*, *supra* note 5, AT 212, 266 FF., 410 FF.

that failing to interpret the norm according to the constitution, no legal support could be identified in the special Amparo Law empowering the courts to adopt provisional or preliminary relief,[247] which were then adopted applying the general provisions of the Procedural Civil Code.

Because the amparo suit is an extraordinary remedy for the immediate protection of constitutional rights, its main feature is the brief and prompt character of the procedure, which is justified because the purpose of the action is to immediately protect persons in cases of irreparable injuries or threats to constitutional rights. This irreparable character of the harm or threat and the immediate need for protection have been the key elements that have molded the procedural rules of the amparo proceeding. Such considerations have also dictated injunctions in the United States, where the judicial doctrine on the matter is also that "an injunction is granted only when required to avoid immediate and irreparable damage to legally recognized rights, such as property rights, constitutional rights or contractual rights."[248]

The same principles also apply to the amparo proceeding, originating with the configuration of a brief and preferred procedure, precisely justified because of the protective purpose of the action and the immediate protection required because of the violations of constitutional rights. For these purposes, Article 27 of the Venezuelan Constitution expressly provides that the procedure of the constitutional amparo action must be oral, public, brief, free and not subject to formality.[249]

---

247. See the comments in BREWER-CARÍAS, *Instituciones Políticas y Constitucionales,* Tomo V, *El derecho y la acción de amparo*, *supra* note 5, at 398.

248. Consequently, "[t]here must be some vital necessity for the injunction so that one of the parties will not be damaged and left without adequate remedy." Treadwell v. Inv. Franchises, Inc., 543 S.E.2d 729, 730 (Ga. 2001). In other words, to warrant an injunction it ordinarily must be clearly shown that some act has been done, or is threatened, which will produce irreparable injury to the party asking for the injunction, U.S. v. Am. Friends Serv. Comm., 419 U.S. 7, (1974). In the same sense it has been established that, "[t]he very function of an injunction is to furnish preventative relief against irreparable mischief or injury, and the remedy will not be awarded where it appears to the satisfaction of the court that the injury complained of is not of such character." State Comm'n on Human Rels. v. Talbot Cnty. Det. Ctr., 803 A.2d 527, 542 (Md. 2002). More specifically, a permanent, mandatory injunction, a preliminary, interlocutory or temporary injunction, a preliminary mandatory injunction, or a preliminary, interlocutory or temporary restraining order, will not, as a general rule, be granted where it is not shown that an irreparable injury is immediately impending and will be inflicted on the petitioner before the case can be brought to a final hearing, "no matter how likely it may be that the moving party will prevail on the merits." Packaging Indus. Group, Inc. v. Cheney, 405 N.E.2d. 106, 114 (Mass. 1980). See *also* 43A C.J.S. *Injunctions* § 192 (2004).

249. VENEZ. CONST. ART. 27. Regarding some of these principles, the Venezuelan First Court on Judicial Review of Administrative Actions, even before the sanctioning of the Amparo Law in 1988, ruled that because of the brief character of the procedure, it must be understood as having "the condition of being urgent, thus it must be followed promptly and decided in the shortest possible time." Additionally, the First Court determined that it must be summary, in the sense that "the procedure must be simple, uncomplicated, without incidences and complex formalities." In this sense, the procedure must not be converted in a complex and confused procedural situation." See Decision of Jan. 17, 1985, in *Revista de Derecho Público,*

One of the consequences of the brief and prompt character of the procedure in the amparo proceeding is its preferred character that imposes, as it is provided in the Venezuelan Constitution, that "any time will be workable time, and the courts will give preference to the amparo regarding any other matter."[250] This preferred character of the procedure also implies that the procedure must be followed with preference, so when an amparo action is filed, the courts must postpone all other matters of different nature.[251]

In the amparo procedure, as a general rule, due to its brief character, the procedural terms cannot be extended, nor suspended, nor interrupted, except in cases expressly set forth in the statute. Any delay in the procedure is the responsibility of the courts. In addition, Article 11 of the Amparo Law restricts motions to recuse judges, establishing specific and prompt procedural rules regarding the cases of impeding situations of the competent judges to resolve the case.

Another principle governing the procedural rules in matters of amparo, in order to guarantee the brief and prompt character of the procedure, is the principle of the prevalence of substantive law over formal provisions, which, for instance, is referred to in the Venezuelan Constitution as a general principle applicable to all proceedings,[252] regarding the prevalence of "substantive justice" over "formal justice."

Another aspect to be analyzed regarding the procedure in the amparo proceeding refers to the specific configuration of the main phases or steps of the procedure, in particular, those related to the filing of the petition, the court decision on the admissibility of the action, the evidence activity, the defendant's pleading, and the hearing of the case.

The first specific trend to be highlighted regarding the judicial procedure of the amparo proceeding refers to the formalities of the petitions that are to be brought before the courts, being the general principle that the petition must be filed in writing, as is the case regarding injunctions in the United States.[253] Nonetheless, the

---

n° 21, Editorial Jurídica Venezolana, Caracas, 1985, p. 140. According to these principles, the 1988 Venezuelan Amparo Law provided for the brief, prompt and summary procedure that governed the amparo proceeding up to the enactment of the 1999 Constitution, when the Constitutional Chamber of the Supreme Tribunal of Justice interpreted the provisions of the Law, according to the new constitution, in some way rewriting its regulations through constitutional interpretation. See the Decision of the Constitutional Chamber of the Supreme Tribunal of Justice n° 7 dated Feb. 1, 2000 (Case *José Amando Mejía*), in *Revista de Derecho Público*, n° 81, Editorial Jurídica Venezolana, Caracas, 2000, pp. 245 ff. See the comments in Allan R. BREWER-CARÍAS, *El sistema de justicia constitucional en la Constitución de 1999. Comentarios sobre su desarrollo jurisprudencial y su explicación, a veces errada, en la Exposición de Motivos*, Editorial Jurídica Venezolana, Caracas, 2000; CHAVERO, *El nuevo régimen del amparo constitucional en Venezuela, supra* note 5, at 203 ff.

250. Venez. Const. Art. 27.

251. Venez. Amparo Law, Art. 13.

252. Venez. Const. Art. 26.

253. See 43A C.J.S. INJUNCTIONS § 310 (2004).

Amparo Law allows the oral presentation of the amparo in cases of urgency,[254] in which the petitions must be subsequently ratified in writing.

In any case, in the written text of the action, the petitioner must always express in a clear and precise manner, all of the necessary elements regarding the alleged right to be protected and the arguments for the admissibility of the action. That is why the Amparo Law establishes, in general terms, the minimal content of the petition or complaint, which in particular must refer to the following aspects.[255] First, the complete identification and information regarding the plaintiff, and if someone is acting on behalf of the plaintiff, his identification is also required. If the plaintiff is an artificial person, the references regarding its registration as well as the representative's complete identification are also required. Second, the petition must establish the individuation of the injured party. Third, the detailed narration of the circumstances in which the harm or the threat has been caused, and the act, action, omission or fact causing the harm or threat must be identified. Fourth, the written text of the petition must indicate the constitutional right or guarantee that has been violated, harmed or threatened, with precise reference to the articles of the constitution or the international treaties containing the rights or guarantees claimed to be violated or harmed. Fifth, the plaintiff must specify the particular protective request asked from the court as well as the judicial order to be issued in protection of his rights that is requested from the court. Finally, the plaintiff must argue about the fulfillment of the conditions for the admissibility of the action, in particular, regarding the inadequacy of other possible judicial remedies and the irreparable injury the plaintiff will suffer without the amparo suit protection.[256]

In order to soften the consequences of not mentioning correctly all the above-mentioned requirements that have to be contained within the written text of the petition, the Amparo Law, in protection of the injured party's right to sue, provides that the courts are obliged to return to the plaintiff the petition that does not conform with those requirements in order for the plaintiff to make the necessary corrections. Consequently, in these cases, the petition will not be considered inadmissible because of formal inadequacies regarding the noncompliance with the petition's requirements set forth in the statutes, and in order to have them corrected or mended the court must return it to the petitioner for him to correct it in a brief amount of time. Only if the petitioner does not make the corrections will the complaint be rejected.[257]

The second important phase of the procedure in the amparo proceeding is the power of the competent courts at the beginning of the procedure to decide upon the admission of the petition when all the admissibility conditions set forth in the Amparo Law are satisfied. Consequently, the courts are empowered to decide *in limine litis* about the inadmissibility of the action when the petition does not accom-

254. Venez. Amparo Law, Arts. 16, 18.

255. Venez. Amparo Law, Art. 18.

256. In a similar way as in the injunction petition in the United States. See 43A C.J.S. INJUNCTIONS § 314 (2004).

257. Venez. Amparo Law, Art. 19.

plish in a manifest way the conditions determined in the statute; for instance, when the term to file the action is evidently exhausted; when the challenged act is one of those excluded from the amparo protection; when there are ordinary means for the protection of the rights that must be previously filed or that give adequate protection; or when ordinary judicial means that can adequately guarantee the claimed rights have already been filed.

The main effect of the admission decision of the action is for the court to notify the interested parties of the initiation of the process, to request from the defendant a report on the violations, and to adopt, if necessary, preliminary amparo decisions for the immediate protection of the harmed or threatened constitutional rights, pending the development of the process.

The third phase in the amparo proceeding refers to the evidence activity and the burden of proof. As has been mentioned, the amparo suit is a specific judicial means regulated in order to obtain the immediate protection of constitutional rights and guarantees when the aggrieved or injured parties have no other adequate judicial means for such purpose. That is why this situation must be alleged and proven by the claimant. This implies that in order to file an amparo action and to obtain immediate judicial protection, the violation of the constitutional right must be a flagrant, vulgar, direct and immediate one, caused by a perfectly determined act or omission. Regarding the harm or injury caused to the constitutional rights, it must be manifestly arbitrary, illegal or illegitimate, a consequence of a violation of the constitution. All these aspects for obtaining the immediate judicial protection must be clear and ostensible, the plaintiff being obliged to argue them in his petition and support it with the needed evidence.

Consequently, as it is also established in the United States regarding injunctions,[258] in the amparo proceeding, the plaintiff has the burden to prove the existence of the right, the alleged violations of threat, and the illegitimate character of the action causing it with clear and convincing evidence. The consequence of the aforementioned is that in matters of amparo, due to the brief and prompt character of the procedure, the immediate protection of constitutional rights that can be granted needs to be based on existing sufficient evidence.

Accordingly, the courts have rejected amparo actions in complex cases where a major debate is needed, and in cases in which proof is difficult to provide, which is considered incompatible with the brief and prompt character of the amparo suit that requires that the alleged violation be "manifestly" illegitimate and harming. Even without clear provisions on the matter, this principle has been applied by the courts in Venezuela.[259]

In this matter of constitutional protection, the courts have *ex officio* powers to obtain evidence, provided that it does not cause an irreparable prejudice to the par-

---

258. See 43A C.J.S. INJUNCTIONS § 310 (2004).

259. See CHAVERO, *El nuevo régimen del amparo constitucional en Venezuela*, *supra* note 5, at 340.

ties.[260] On the other hand, the general principle in the amparo procedure is that all kinds of evidence is admitted, so the court can base its decision to grant the required protection on any type of evidence.

The fifth important phase of the amparo proceeding is the need for the court to notify the aggrieving party in order to request from it a formal written answer or report regarding the alleged violations of constitutional rights of the plaintiff, to which, in addition, the defendant can put forward his counter evidence, before the hearing on it.[261] Due to the bilateral and adversarial character of the procedure, as also happens in the injunctive relief procedure in the United States, an amparo ruling must not be issued until the defendant has been asked to file his plea.[262]

The defendant's answer or plea regarding the harm or threat alleged by the plaintiff, must be sent to the court within a very brief term of forty-eight hours.[263] The omission of the defendant to send his report or plea in answer to the court implies that the plaintiff's alleged facts must be considered as accepted by the defendant.[264]

Finally, one of the most important phases in the procedure is the hearing that the court must convene, also in a very prompt period of time, seeking the participation of the parties before adopting its decision on the case.[265] This hearing which must be oral, public and contradictory, in principle must always take place and must not be suspended.

The absence of the defendant's participation in the hearing, in general terms, does not produce its suspension, in which case, the evidence presented by the plaintiff will be accepted and the court must then proceed to decide. Regarding the plaintiff, his absence from the hearing is understood as his abandonment of the action.

The final decision of the amparo proceeding must be adopted after the hearing has taken place, although the Constitutional Chamber of the Supreme Tribunal has

---

260. Venez. Amparo Law, Art. 17.

261. This is what was established in Article 24 of the Venezuelan Amparo Law, which nonetheless has been eliminated by the Constitutional Chamber in its decision nº 7 of February 1, 2000, *José A. Mejía et al.* (issue interpreting the Amparo Law according to the new 1999 Constitution, and reshaping the amparo suit procedure). See in *Revista de Derecho Público*, nº 81, Editorial Jurídica Venezolana, Caracas, 2000, pp. 349 ff; CHAVERO, *El nuevo régimen del amparo constitucional en Venezuela*, *supra* note 5, at 264 ff.; Allan R. Brewer-Carías, *El juez constitucional como legislador positivo y la inconstitucional reforma de la Ley Orgánica de Amparo mediante sentencias interpretativas*, in Eduardo FERRER MAC-GREGOR y Arturo ZALDÍVAR LELO DE LARREA (COORDINATORS), *La ciencia del derecho procesal constitucional. Estudios en homenaje a Héctor Fix-Zamudio en sus cincuenta años como investigador del derecho*, Instituto de Investigaciones Jurídicas, Universidad Nacional Autónoma de México, México 2008, Tomo V, pp. 63-80.

262. See 43A C.J.S. INJUNCTIONS § 318 (2004).

263. Venez. Amparo Law, Art. 24.

264. *Id.*

265. Venez. Amparo Law , Art. 26.

established that in matters of amparo the court must make its decision in the same hearing or trial.[266]

XI. THE PRELIMINARY PROTECTIVE MEASURES ON MATTERS OF AMPARO

The purpose of the amparo proceeding eventually is for the plaintiff to obtain a judicial adjudication from a competent court, providing for the immediate protection of his harmed or threatened constitutional rights. These judicial decisions, for instance, may restrain some actions, preserve the status quo, or command or prohibit actions.[267]

Amparo and injunctions are both extraordinary remedies having the same purpose, the main difference between them being the rights to be protected. In the United States, injunctions are equitable remedies that can be used for the protection of any kind of personal or property rights. On the other hand, in Latin America, the amparo proceeding is conceived only for the protection of constitutional rights, which explains its regulations in the constitutions, and not for the protection of rights established in statutes.[268]

---

266. In Venezuela, the Amparo Law established that the decision ought to be issued in the following days after the hearing. Venez. Amparo Law, Art. 24. Nonetheless, the Constitutional Chamber in decision nº 7 of February 1, 2000 (*José A. Mejía et al.* case), has modified this provision, providing that the decision must be issued at the end of the hearing. See in *Revista de Derecho Público*, nº 81, Editorial Jurídica Venezolana, Caracas, 2000, pp. 349 ff.

267. In a very similar way, the injunctive decisions that the United States' courts can adopt injunctions for the immediate protection of rights, which can consist of restrain action or interference of some kind. Putnam v. Fortenberry, 589 N.W.2d 838 (Neb. 1999); Anderson v. Granite School Dist., 413 P.2d 597 (Utah 1996). Courts in the United States may also impose injunctions to furnish preventive relief against irreparable mischief or injury; or to preserve the *status quo*. Sndyer v. Sullivan, 705 P.2d 510 Colo 1985); Jenkins v. Pedersen, 212 N.W.2d 415 (Iowa 1973). An injunction is a remedy designed to prevent irreparable injury by prohibiting or commanding certain acts. Nat'l Compressed Steel Corp. v. Unified Gov't of Wyandotte County, 38 P.3d 723 (Kan. 2002). The function of injunctive relief is to restrain motion and to enforce inaction. State ex rel. Great Lakes College, Inc. v Med. Bd., 280 N.E.2d 900 (Ohio 1972). An injunction is designed to prevent harm, not redress harm; it is not compensatory. Klinicki v. Lundgren, 695 P.2d 906 (Or. 1985); Simenstad v. Hagen, 126 N.W.2d 529 (Wis. 1964). The remedy grants prospective, as opposed to retrospective, relief, Jefferson v. Big Horn Cnty., 4 P.3d 26 (Mont. 2000), and it is preventive, protective or restorative. United States v. White Cnty. Bridge Comm'n, 275 F.2d 529 (7th Cir. 1960); Colendrea v. Wilde Lake Cmty. Ass'n, Inc., 761 A.2d 899 (Md. 2003); Stoetzel & Sons, Inc. v. City of Hatings, 658 N.W.2d 636 (Neb. 2003); Hunsaker v. Kersh, 991 P.2d 67 (Utah 1999). However, an injunction is not addressed to past wrongs. *Snyder v. Sullivan*, 705 P.2d 510 (Colo. 1985). See *generally* 43A CJS INJUNCTIONS § 2.

268. In this sense, in Venezuela the courts have ruled that the harm caused must always be the result of a violation of a constitutional right that must be "flagrant, vulgar, direct and immediate, which does not mean that the right or guaranty is not due to be regulated in statutes, but it is not necessary for the court to base its decision in the latter to determine if the violation of the constitutional right has effectively occurred." Supreme Court of Justice, *Tarjetas Banvenez* case, decision nº 343 of July 10, 1991, in REVISTA DE DERECHO PÚBLICO, nº 47,

In this matter of the amparo proceeding, as well as in matters of injunctions, two general sorts of judicial adjudications can be issued by the courts for the protection of constitutional rights: preliminary measures that can be ordered from the beginning of the procedure, with effects subject to the final court ruling; and definitive decisions preventing the violation or restoring the enjoyment of the threatened or harmed rights.

In Venezuela, as in all Latin American countries, according to the general regulations established in the Civil Procedure Codes, all courts are empowered to adopt, during the course of a procedure, what are called "*medidas preventivas*" or "*medidas cautelares*," that is, interlocutory and temporal judicial measures that are also applied to the amparo proceeding. The expression refers to interlocutory or preliminary measures; so in this sense, a "*medida preventiva*" is not equivalent to the English expression "preventive measure," which is used in the sense of preventing or avoiding harm, and can be decided both in a definitive or a preliminary injunction.[269] That is, both the definitive and preliminary judicial amparo decisions can have "preventive" effects in the sense of preventing harms or preserving the status quo, the preliminary ones having only a temporary basis, pending the termination of the pro-

---

Editorial Jurídica Venezolana, Caracas, 1991, pp. 169–170. See *also* Decision of May 20, 1994, First Court on Judicial Review of Administrative Actions, *Federación Venezolana de Deportes Ecuestres* Case, in *Revista de Derecho Público*, nº 57-58, Editorial Jurídica Venezolana, Caracas, 1994, pp. 284 ff.. In other words, only direct and evident constitutional violations can be protected by means of amparo; thus, for instance, as ruled in 1991 by the same First Court, the internal electoral regime of political parties or of professional associations could not be the object of an amparo action founded in the right to vote set forth in the constitution, "which only applies to the national electoral process [not being applied] to the internal electoral process of the political parties," concluding that the amparo "only protects constitutional rights and guaranties and not legal (statutory) ones, and much less the ones contained in association's by laws." Decision of Aug. 23, 1991, in *Revista de Derecho Público*, n° 47, Editorial Jurídica Venezolana, Caracas, 1991, pp. 129 ff. In other decisions, the courts declared inadmissible amparo actions for the protection of rights when the allegations were only founded "in legal (statutory) considerations," as the right to work commonly conditioned by statutes regarding dismissals. Thus, the amparo is not the judicial mean for the protection of such right if the violation is only referring to the labor law provisions. See Decision of the First Court of Oct. 8, 1990, *Rafael Rojas* case, in REVISTA DE DERECHO PÚBLICO, nº 44, Editorial Jurídica Venezolana, Caracas, 1990, pp. 139–40. In a similar sense, the violation of the right to self-defense because a party's right to cross-examine a witness was denied according to Article 349 of the Civil Procedural Code cannot be founded in Article 68 of the Constitution because it implies the need to analyze norms of legal rank and not of constitutional rank. In this regard it was decided by the former Supreme Court of Justice, Politico Administrative Chamber, decision nº 614 of Nov. 8, 1990, in *Revista de Derecho Público*, nº 44, Editorial Jurídica Venezolana, Caracas, 1990, pp. 140–41.

269. In other words, as explained by Tabb and Shoben: "[t]he classic form of injunctions in private litigation is the preventive injunction. By definition, a preventive injunction is a court order designed to avoid future harm to a party by prohibiting or mandating certain behavior by another party. The injunction is 'preventive' in the sense of avoiding harm. The wording may be either prohibitory ("do not trespass") or mandatory ("remove the obstruction")." TABB & SHOBEN, *supra* note 53, at 22.

cedure.[270] Consequently, in order to avoid confusion, I use the expression "preliminary" measures to identify what in the Latin American procedural law are called "*medidas preventivas*" or "*medidas cautelares*," as interlocutory, preliminary and temporal judicial protective measures that can be issued pending the procedure, similar to the United States "preliminary injunctions" also issued as interlocutory and temporal relief pending the trial.[271]

Based on this distinction between preliminary measures ("*cautelares*") and definitive adjudications or decisions, the amparo proceeding in Venezuela is not just of a "*cautelar*" or preliminary nature, and on the contrary, it seeks to protect in a definitive way the constitutional right alleged as harmed or threatened. The precision is important because in some countries a distinction has been made in procedural law between "*cautelar*" measures and "*cautelar*" actions, causing some terminological confusion when giving to the amparo the character of a "*cautelar*" action. In such cases, the expression is used, not in the sense of just having a "preliminary" nature, but in the sense of being confined to decide the immediate protection of a constitutional right without resolving any other matters or merits of the controversy.[272]

---

270. As the same authors Tabb & Shoben have said: "[u]pon a compelling showing by the plaintiff, the court may issue a coercive order even before full trial on the merits. A preliminary injunction gives the plaintiff temporary relief pending trial on the merit. A temporary restraining order affords immediate relief pending the hearing on the preliminary injunction. Both of these types of interlocutory relief are designed to preserve the status quo to prevent irreparable harm before a court can decide the substantive merits of the dispute. Such orders are available only upon a strong showing of the necessity for such relief and may be conditioned upon the claimant posting a bond or sufficient security to protect the interests of the defendant in the event that the injunction is later determined to have been wrongfully issued." TABB & SHOBEN, *supra* note 53, at 4.

271. In both cases, the preliminary measures are different from the final judicial protective (permanent injunction) decisions, which can have preventive or restorative effects. See 43A C.J.S. INJUNCTIONS § 6 (2004).

272. In this sense, in Ecuador and Chile, the amparo proceeding has been considered to have "*cautelar*" nature, but in another sense, not equivalent to a "preliminary" nature. The Constitutional Court of Ecuador, for instance, has decided as follows: "[t]hat the amparo action set forth in Article 95 of the Constitution is in essence *cautelar* regarding the constitutional rights, not allowing [the court] to decide on the merits or to substitute the proceedings set forth in the legal order for the resolution of a controversy, but only to suspend the effects of an authority act which harms those rights; and the decisions issued in the amparo suit do not produce *res judicata*, so the authority, once having corrected the incurred defects, may go back to the matter and issue a new act, providing it is adjusted to the constitutional and legal provisions." Hernán SALGADO PESANTES, *Manual de Justicia Constitucional Ecuatoriana,* Corporación Editora Nacional, Quito, 2004, p. 78. In a similar way, in Chile the action for protection has been considered to have a "*cautelar*" nature, not in the sense of "preliminary" measures, but as tending to obtain a definitive protective adjudication regarding constitutional rights. See Eduardo SOTO KLOSS, *El recurso de protección. Orígenes, doctrina y jurisprudencia*, Editorial Jurídica de Chile, Santiago, 1982, p. 248; *see also* Juan Manuel ERRAZURIZ and Jorge Miguel OTERO A., *Aspectos procesales del recurso de protección*, Editorial Jurídica de Chile, Santiago, 1989, pp. 34–38.

However, putting aside these terminological differences, in the amparo procedure, preliminary measures can be adopted by the courts pending the final adjudication and with effects during the development of the procedure, in order to preserve the status quo, avoiding harms or restoring the plaintiff's situation to the original one it had before the harm was inflicted. These preliminary measures are regulated in the Amparo Law and the Civil Procedure Code in two ways.

First, by establishing a precise and identified measure, called a *medidas cautelares nominada*, as is the case of the suspension of the effects of the challenged act of the amparo action. This is the most common preliminary judicial measure expressly established in the Amparo Law. When the action is filed against state acts, particularly administrative acts, the power is given to the courts to suspend their effects, at the request of the affected party, during the course of the procedure and pending the final decision of the proceeding.[273] Also, in addition to the provision establishing the court's possible decision to suspend the effects of the challenged acts, in the case of the filing of the amparo petition conjunctively with other actions seeking judicial review of statutes or administrative acts, the amparo essentially has suspensive effects.[274]

Second, without any particular enumeration, other measures that can be adopted by the courts in order to protect the injured right are the *medidas cautelares innominadas* according to the provisions of the Civil Procedure Code.

In order to adopt all these preliminary measures, a few conditions must be met as has been established by the jurisprudence of the courts. The courts must consider, first, "the appearance of the existence of a good right" (*fumus boni juris*), that is, the need for the petitioner to prove the existence of his constitutional right or guarantee as being violated or threatened. Second, the "danger because of the delay" (*periculum in mora*), that is, the need to prove that the delay in granting the preliminary protection will make the harm irreparable. Third, the "danger of the harm" (*periculum in dammi*"), that is the need to prove the imminence of the harm that can be caused. Fourth, the balance between the collective and particular interest in-

---

273. Venez. Amparo Law, Art. 5.

274. When the amparo action is filed jointly with the judicial review popular action for nullity against statutes, or with the judicial review of administrative actions recourse, the amparo petition has always had this preliminary (*cautelar*) character, in the sense that the decision granting the amparo pending the principal nullity suit is always of a preliminary character of suspension of the effects of the challenged act. Thus, in the case of statutes, the Constitutional Chamber, the competent court, decides to suspend its effects, in such cases, even with *erga omnes* effects. See CHAVERO, *El nuevo régimen del amparo constitucional en Venezuela*, *supra* note 5, at 468 ff., 327 ff.; BREWER-CARÍAS, *Instituciones Políticas y Constitucionales,* Tomo V, *El derecho y la acción de amparo*, *supra* note 5, at 277. Regarding administrative acts, the courts of the Administrative Jurisdiction are the ones that can decide the matter of the suspension of the effects of the administrative challenged act, pending the judicial review proceeding final decision. BREWER-CARÍAS, *Instituciones Políticas y Constitucionales,* Tomo V, *El derecho y la acción de amparo*, *supra* note 5, at 281.

volved in the case.[275] As ruled by the Politico Administrative Chamber of the Supreme Tribunal of Justice of Venezuela, in a decision nº 488 dated March 16, 2000:

In order for an anticipated protective measure to be granted, due to its preliminary content it is necessary to examine the existence of three essential elements, always balancing the collective or individual interest; such conditions are:

1. *Fumus Boni Iuris*, that is, the reasonable appearance of the existence of a "good right" in the hands of the petitioner alleging its violation, an appearance that must derive from the written evidences (documents) attached to the petition.

2. *Periculum in mora*, that is, the danger that the definitive ruling could be illusory, due to the delay in resolving the incident of the suspension.

3. *Periculum in Damni*, that is, the imminence of the harm caused by the presumptive violation of the fundamental rights of the petitioner and its irreparability. These elements are those that basically allow one to seek the necessary anticipatory protection of the constitutional rights and guaranties.[276]

All these general conditions for the issuance of the preliminary protective measures are very similar to those prerequisites needed to be tested by the United States' courts when issuing preliminary injunctions, which are: (1) a probability of prevailing on the merits; (2) an irreparable injury if the relief is delayed; (3) a balance of hardship favoring the plaintiff; (4) and a showing that the injunction would not be adverse to the public interest; all of which must be proven by the plaintiff.[277]

Due to the extraordinary character of the amparo action, the preliminary protective measures requested by the plaintiff, if the above-mentioned conditions are fulfilled, can be decided and issued by the court in an immediate way, even without a previous hearing of the potential defendants. That is, *inadi alteram parte* or *inaudita pars*, as it is expressly provided in the Civil Procedure Code. In a similar sense, the courts in the United States, in cases of great urgency and when an immediate threat of irreparable injury exists, can issue preliminary injunctions or restraining orders without giving reasonable notice to the defendant, but always balancing the harm sought to be preserved with the rights of notice and hearing.[278]

Finally, the general rule is that in the amparo proceeding, as in the United States,[279] the effects of the preliminary measures are essentially modifiable or revocable by the court, particularly at the request of the defendant or of third parties.

---

275. As for instance has been decided by the Venezuelan First Court on Judicial Review of Administrative Actions, *Video & Juegos Costa Verde, C.A. vs. Prefecto del Municipio Maracaibo del Estado Zulia* case, in *Revista de Derecho Público*, nº 85-98, Editorial Jurídica Venezolana, Caracas, 2001, p. 291.

276. See the Politico Administrative Chamber decision nº 488 of March 16, 2000, *Constructora Pedeca, C.A. vs. Gobernación del Estado Anzoátegui* case, in *Revista de Derecho Público*, nº 81, Editorial Jurídica Venezolana, Caracas, 2000, p. 459.

277 See TABB & SHOBEN, *supra* note 53 at 63.

278. See 43A C.J.S. INJUNCTIONS § 305 (2004).

279. See, *e.g.*, 43A C.J.S. INJUNCTIONS § 368 (2004).

On the other hand, the preliminary measures have effects during the course of the procedure, finishing with the definitive decision granting or rejecting the amparo. Nonetheless, if the final decision grants the amparo, the effects of the preliminary measures will be kept and will be converted if definitive.

XII. THE DEFINITIVE JUDICIAL ADJUDICATION ON MATTERS OF AMPARO

Regarding the definitive judicial decisions in the amparo proceedings, their purpose for the injured party (the plaintiff) is to obtain the requested judicial protection (*amparo*) of his constitutional rights when illegitimately harmed or threatened by an injuring party (the defendant).

Consequently, the final result of the amparo process, characterized by its bilateral nature that imposes the need for the defendants to have the right to participate and to be heard,[280] is a formal judicial decision or order issued by the court. Such order, as is also the case with the injunctions, is for the protection of the threatened rights or to restore the enjoyment of the harmed party, which can consist, for instance, of a decision commanding or preventing an action, or commanding someone to do, not to do or to undo some action.[281] This is to say, the amparo, as the injunction,[282] is a writ framed according to the circumstances of the case commanding an act that the court regards as essential to justice, or restraining an act that it deems contrary to equity and good conscience.

Consequently, the function of the amparo court's decision is, on the one hand, to prevent the defendant from inflicting further injury on the plaintiff that can be of a prohibitory or mandatory character; or on the other hand, to correct the present by undoing the effects of a past wrong.[283]

That is why the amparo judicial order in Venezuela, as in all Latin American countries, even without the distinction between equitable remedies and extraordinary law remedies, is very similar in its purposes and effects not only to the United States' injunction, but also to the other equitable and non-equitable extraordinary

---

280. Similarly, regarding definitive injunctions, they only can be granted if process issues and service is made on the defendant. See, *e.g.*, 43A C.J.S. INJUNCTIONS § 304 (2004).

281. In the United States' injunction, the order can be "commanding or preventing virtually any type of action". 43A C.J.S. INJUNCTIONS § 1 (citing Dawkins v. Walker, 794 So. 2d 333 (Ala. 2001); Levin v. Barish, 481 A.2d 1183 (Pa. 1984). The injunction may also be imposed to command an individual to redress some wrong or other injury." 43A C.J.S. INJUNCTIONS § 1 (citing . State Game & Fish Com'n v. Sledge, 42 S.W.3d 427 (Ark. 2001). "It is a judicial order requiring a person to do or refrain from doing certain acts" 43A C.J.S. INJUNCTIONS § 1 (citing. Skolnick v. Altheimer & Gray, 730 N.E.2d 4 (Ill. 2000). The order requires an individual to refrain "for any period of time, no matter its purpose." 43A C.J.S. INJUNCTIONS § 1 (citing Sheridan County Elec. Coop v. Ferguson, 227 P.2d 597 (Mont. 1951)).

282. 43A C.J.S. INJUNCTIONS § 1 (2004).

283. This is similar to the "preventive injunction" and to the "restorative or reparative injunction," in the United States. See TABB & SHOBEN, *supra* note 53, at 86-89; 43A C.J.S. INJUNCTIONS § 8 (2004).

remedies, like the mandamus, prohibition and declaratory legal remedies. Accordingly, for instance, the amparo order can be first, of a prohibitory character, similar to the prohibitory injunctions issued to restrain an action, to forbid certain acts or to command a person to refrain from doing specific acts. Second, it can also be of a mandatory character, that is, like the mandatory injunction requiring the undoing of an act, or the restoring of the status quo. The amparo may also act like the writ of mandamus, issued to compel an action or the execution of some act, or to command a person to do a specific act. Third, the amparo order can also be similar to the writ of prohibition or to the writ of error when the order is directed to a court,[284] which normally happens in the cases of amparo actions filed against judicial decisions. Fourth, it can also be similar to the declaratory legal remedy through which courts are called to declare the constitutional right of the plaintiff regarding the other parties.

Consequently, in the amparo proceeding, the courts have very extensive powers to provide for remedies in order to effectively protect constitutional rights, issuing final adjudication orders to do, to refrain from doing, to undo or to prohibit,[285] or as the Amparo Law establishes in Article 32,b the decision must "determine the conduct to be accomplished."[286]

The judicial amparo order can be of a restorative or of a preventive nature. In the first case, it may consist of an order seeking for the reestablishment of the juridical situation of the plaintiff to the stage it had before the violation or to the most similar one. In the second case, when of a preventive nature, it can consist in compelling the defendant to do or to refrain from doing certain acts in order to maintain the enjoyment of the plaintiff's rights. Nonetheless, in the case of being of a restorative character, in general terms, when the amparo action is filed against acts, particularly authorities' acts causing the harms or threats to constitutional rights, the immediate effect of the decision is to suspend the effects of the challenged act regarding the plaintiff, the amparo proceeding not having the purposes of annulling those state acts. In principle, it is for the Constitutional Jurisdiction and for the Administrative Jurisdictions' courts and not for the amparo judges to adopt decisions annulling statutes or administrative acts.

In particular, regarding statutes and specifically self-executing ones, when an amparo action is filed directly against them,[287] the amparo judge when granting the amparo has no power to annul them, and in order to protect the harmed or threatened right he can declare their inapplicability to the plaintiff in the particular case. The

284. See TABB & SHOBEN, *supra* note 53, at 86, 246; 43A C.J.S. INJUNCTIONS § 5 (2004).

285. See BREWER-CARÍAS, *Instituciones Políticas y Constitucionales,* Tomo V, *El derecho y la acción de amparo*, *supra* note 5, at 143.

286. CHAVERO, *El nuevo régimen del amparo constitucional en Venezuela*, *supra* note 5, at 185 ff., 327 ff.; BREWER-CARÍAS, *Instituciones Políticas y Constitucionales,* Tomo V, *El derecho y la acción de amparo*, *supra* note 5, at 399.

287. CHAVERO, EL NUEVO RÉGIMEN DEL AMPARO CONSTITUCIONAL EN VENEZUELA, *supra* note 5, at 468 ff.; BREWER-CARÍAS, *Instituciones Políticas y Constitucionales,* Tomo V, *El derecho y la acción de amparo*, *supra* note 5, at 399.

competence to annul statutes is exclusively granted to the Constitutional Chamber of the Supreme Tribunal of Justice.[288]

Regarding administrative acts, the general rule is also that the amparo decision cannot annul the challenged administrative act, being that the amparo judge is only empowered to suspend its effects and application to the plaintiff. The power to annul administrative acts is also exclusively a power attributed to the Administrative Jurisdiction courts.[289]

Conversely, regarding the amparo actions filed against judicial decisions, the effects of the ruling granting the amparo protection consists in the annulment of the challenged judicial act or decision.[290]

Another aspect that must be mentioned regarding amparo decisions in Venezuela is that it has no compensatory character[291] because it is the function of the courts in these proceedings only to protect the plaintiff's rights and not to condemn the defendant to pay the plaintiff any sort of compensation for damages caused by the injury.[292] That is, the amparo proceeding is, in general terms, a preventive and restorative process, but not a compensatory one,[293] the courts being empowered to prevent harms or to restore the enjoyment of a right, for instance by suspending the effects of the injuring act, but not to condemn the defendant to the payment of a compensation. The judicial actions tending to seek compensation from the defendant, because of its liability as a consequence of the injury inflicted to the constitutional right of the plaintiff, must be filed by means of a separate ordinary judicial remedy established for such purpose before the civil or administrative judicial jurisdiction.[294]

---

288. VENEZ. CONST. ART. 336.

289. VENEZ. CONST. ART. 259l. See CHAVERO, *El nuevo régimen del amparo constitucional en Venezuela, supra* note 5, at 358 ff.; Brewer-Carías, *Instituciones Políticas y Constitucionales,* Tomo V, *El derecho y la acción de amparo, supra* note 5, at 144 & 400.

290. See CHAVERO, *El nuevo régimen del amparo constitucional en Venezuela, supra* note 5, at 511; BREWER-CARÍAS, *Instituciones Políticas y Constitucionales,* Tomo V, *El derecho y la acción de amparo, supra* note 5 at 297; BREWER-CARÍAS, *El problema del amparo contra sentencias o de cómo la Sala de Casación Civil remedia arbitrariedades judiciales, supra* note 123, at 157–71.

291. In a similar way to the United States injunctions. See *Simenstad v. Hagen*, 126 N.W.2d 529 (Wis. 1964).

292 For instance in the case of an illegitimate administrative order issued by a municipal authority demolishing a building, if executed, even if it violates the constitutional right to property, the amparo action has not the purpose to compensate, being in this case inadmissible, particularly due to the irreparable character of the harm.

293 See CHAVERO, *El nuevo régimen del amparo constitucional en Venezuela, supra* note 5, at 185, 242, 262, 326, 328; BREWER-CARÍAS, *Instituciones Políticas y Constitucionales*, Tomo V, *El derecho y la acción de amparo, supra* note 5, at 143.

294 Article 27 of the Venezuelan Amparo Law also expressly provides that in cases of granting an amparo, the court must send copy of the decision to the competent authority where the public officer causing the harm works, in order to impose the corresponding disciplinary measures. Venez. Amparo Law, Art. 27.

Finally, regarding the economic consequences of the amparo suit, in Venezuela the order to pay the costs is established in a very restrictive way, only in cases of amparo actions filed against individuals and not against public authorities.[295]

Another important aspect of the amparo definitive decisions is related to their effects. The general rule regarding the amparo judicial decisions is that they only have *inter partes* effects, that is, between the parties that have been involved in the suit (the plaintiff, the defendant and the third parties) and those that have participated in the process. So in a similar way to the injunctive decisions in the United States,[296] the amparo decisions only have binding effects regarding the parties to the suit, and only regarding the controversy; this being the most important consequence of the personal character of the amparo, as an action mainly devoted for the protection of personal constitutional rights or guarantees.[297] The only exception to this principle in the United States refers to the effects of the ruling when constitutional questions are decided by the Supreme Court, in which cases, due to the doctrine of precedent (*stare decisis*), all courts are obliged to apply the same constitutional rule in cases with similar controversies.[298] The same rule exists in Venezuela regarding the Constitutional Chamber rulings[299] that can be issued with binding general character and effects.

Nonetheless, the general principle of the *inter partes* effects also has its exceptions due to the progressive development of the collective nature of some constitutional rights, as for instance, is the case of violation of environmental rights, indigenous people's rights and other diffuse rights,[300] in which cases,[301] the definitive ruling can benefit other persons different to those that have actively participated in the procedure as plaintiff. In these cases, due to the constitutional provision regarding the protection of diffuse or collective interests, the Constitutional Chamber of the Supreme Tribunal has admitted action for amparo seeking the protection and enforcement of those collective interests, including for instance, voting rights. In such cases, the Chamber has even granted *erga omnes* effects to the precautionary measures adopted "for both the individuals and entities that have filed the action for

295. Venez. Amparo Law, Art. 33.

296 See, *e.g.*, ESP Fidelity Corp. v. Dep't of Hous. & Urban Dev., 512 F.2d 887 (9th Cir. 1975).

297. The Venezuelan regulations can be highlighted in this regard. In principle, the court decisions have been constant in granting the action of amparo a personal character where the standing belongs firstly to "the individual directly affected by the infringement of constitutional rights and guaranties." See, *e.g.*, the decision nº 94 of the Constitutional Chamber of Mar. 15, 2000, *Corporación 18.625 C.A.* case, in *Revista de Derecho Público*, nº 81, Editorial Jurídica Venezolana, 2000, pp. 322–23.

298. See ABERNATHY & PERRY, *supra* note 16, at 5.

299. VENEZ. CONST. ART. 336.

300. See CHAVERO, *El nuevo régimen del amparo constitucional en Venezuela*, *supra* note 5, at 333.

301. As also happens regarding the class actions in the United States. See ABERNATHY & PERRY, *supra* note 16, at 6.

constitutional protection and to all the voters as a group."[302] In addition, the Office of the People's Defendant has the authority to promote, defend, and guard constitutional rights and guaranties "as well as the legitimate, collective or diffuse interests of the citizens,"[303] being consequently his standing admitted to file actions for amparo on behalf of the citizens as a whole.[304] In all these cases, the judicial ruling benefits all the persons enjoying the collective rights or interest involved.

On the other hand, as all definitive judicial decisions, the amparo decisions also have *res judicata* effects, providing stability to the ruling. That means that the courts' decisions are binding not only for the parties in the process or its beneficiaries, but also regarding the court itself, which cannot modify its ruling (immutability). *Res judicata* implies then, the impossibility for a new suit to take place regarding the same matter already adopted, or that a decision is issued in a different sense than the one already decided in a previous process.[305] Nonetheless, on this matter, of the *res judicata* effects, the scope of those effects is different when referring to the so-called "substantive" (*material*) or to the "formal" *res judicata* effects. In general terms, the concept of "formal *res judicata*" effects applies to judicial deci-

302. See Decision of the Constitutional Chamber nº 483 of May 29, 2000, *"Queremos Elegir" y otros* case, in *Revista de Derecho Público*, nº 82, Editorial Jurídica Venezolana, 2000, pp. 489–491. In the same sense, decision of the same Chamber nº 714 of July 13, 2000, *APRUM* Case, in REVISTA DE DERECHO PÚBLICO, nº 83, 2000, Editorial Jurídica Venezolana, pp. 319 ff. The Constitutional Chamber has decided that "any individual is entitled to bring suit based on diffuse or collective interests" and has extended "standing to companies, corporations, foundations, chambers, unions and other collective entities, whose object is the defense of society, as long as they act within the boundaries of their corporate objects, aimed at protecting the interests of their members regarding those objects." See Decision of the Constitutional Chamber n° 656 of May 6, 2001, *Defensor del Pueblo vs.Comisión Legislativa Nacional* Case, available at http://www.tsj.gov.ve/decisiones/scon/Junio/656-300600-00-1728%20.htm. See also decision n° 379 of Feb. 26, 2003, *Mireya Ripanti et vs. Presidente de Petróleos de Venezuela S.A. (PDVSA)* case, in *Revista de Derecho Público*, n° 93-96, Editorial Jurídica Venezolana, Caracas, 2003, pp. 152 ff.

303. VENEZ. CONST. ART. 280 & 281,2.

304. In one case the Defender of the People acted against a threat by the 2000 National Legislative Commission to appoint the Electoral National Council members without fulfilling constitutional requirements. In that case, the Constitutional Chamber decided that "the Defender has standing to bring actions aimed at enforcing diffuse and collective rights or interests" without requiring the acquiescence of the society on whose behalf he acts, but this provision does not exclude or prevent citizens' access to the judicial system in defense of diffuse and collective rights and interests. Decision of the Constitutional Chamber n° 656 of May 6, 2001, *Defensor del Pueblo vs. Comisión Legislativa Nacional* case, available at http://www.tsj.gov.ve/decisiones/scon/Junio/656-300600-00-1728%20.htm.

305. In contrast, these *res judicata* effects, as a general rule, are not applicable to the injunction orders in the United States, which can be modified by the court. As it has been summarized regarding the judicial doctrine on the matter: "Injunctions are different from other judgments in the context of *res judicata* because the parties are often subject to the court's continuing jurisdiction, and the court must strike a balance between the policies of *res judicata* and the right of the court to apply modified measures to changed circumstances." Town of Durham v. Cutter, 428 A.2d 904 (N.H. 1981). See *also* FISS & RENDLEMAN, *supra* note 32, at 497–98, 526.

sions that even when enforced do not impede the development of a new process between the same parties, provided that the matter has not been decided in the amparo proceeding on the merits of the case and its defense. On the other hand, the concept of "substantive *res judicata*" effects applies when the judicial decision has been decided on the merits, not allowing for other processes to develop regarding the same matter.

The matter decided in the amparo proceeding, that is the merits of the case, is related to the manifest illegitimate and arbitrary harm or threat caused by an identified injuring party to the constitutional right or guarantees of the plaintiff; a matter that is to be resolved in a brief and prompt procedure. Thus, the merits on the matters in the amparo proceeding are reduced to determining the existence of such illegitimate and manifest violation of the right, regardless of the other possible matters that can or may be resolved by the parties in other processes. In this regard, Article 36 of the Venezuelan Amparo Law, giving a different approach regarding the substantive or formal *res judicata* effects[306] provides that "[t]he definitive amparo decision will produce legal effects regarding the right or guaranty that has been the object of the process, without prejudice of the actions or recourses that legally correspond to the parties."[307]

According to this provision, *res judicata* in the amparo proceeding only refers to what has been argued and decided in the case regarding the violation or injury inflicted to a constitutional right or guarantee.[308] Thus, in general terms, the amparo decision does not resolve all the other possible matters that could be raised, but only the aspect of the violation or injury to the constitutional rights or guarantees; this being the only aspect regarding which the decision can produce *res judicata* effects. For example, if an amparo decision is issued regarding an administrative act because it causes harm to constitutional rights, it only has restorative or reestablishing effects, suspending the application of the challenged act, but it does not have annulling effects.[309] Consequently, the amparo decision in such cases does not have *res judi-*

306. In this regard, the First Court on Judicial Review of Administrative Actions, in a decision dated Oct. 16, 1986, the *Pedro J. Montilva* case, decided that if in a case: "the action of amparo is filed with the same object, denouncing the same violations, based on the same motives and with identical object as the previous one and directed against the same person, then it is evident that in such case, the res judicata force applies in order to avoid the rearguing of the case, due to the fact that the controversy to be resolved has the same subjective and objective identity than the one already decided." See *Revista de Derecho Público,* nº 28, Editorial Jurídica Venezolana, Caracas, 1986, p. 106. See also CHAVERO, *El nuevo régimen del amparo constitucional en Venezuela supra* note 5, at 338 ff.; Gustavo LINARES BENZO, *El proceso de amparo en Venezuela*, Caracas, 1999, p. 121.

307. *Venez. Amparo Law*, Art. 36.

308. See First Court on Judicial Review of Administrative Action, decision of Oct. 16, 1986, *Pedro Montilva* case, in *Revista de Derecho Público,* nº 28, Editorial Jurídica Venezolana, Caracas, 1986, p. 106.

309. Due to this fact, by means of the amparo suit, as it has been ruled by the Supreme Court of Venezuela, "none of the three types of judicial declarative, constitutive or to condemn decision can be obtained, nor, of course, the interpretative decision." Decision nº 211 of the Poli-

cata effects regarding the judicial review action that can be filed against the administrative act before the Administrative Jurisdiction Courts in order to have its nullity declared.[310]

In these cases, after the amparo decision has been issued, other legal questions can remain pending to be resolved in other processes, and that is why the amparo decision in these cases is issued "without prejudice of the actions or recourses that could legally correspond to the parties."[311]

One last aspect that must be highlighted regarding the effects of the amparo decision refers to its obligatory character. As all judicial decisions, the amparo ruling is obligatory not only for the parties to the process but regarding all other persons or public officers that it applies to. The defendant, for instance, is compelled to immediately obey it, as it is expressly set forth in the Amparo Law.[312]

In order to execute the decision, the courts, *ex officio* or at the party's request, can adopt all the measures directed to its accomplishment. Yet the amparo judges in Venezuela do not have direct power to punish by imposing criminal sanctions for disobedience of their rulings. In other words, they do not have criminal contempt power, which in contrast is one of the most important features of the injunctive relief system in the United States.[313] These contempt powers are precisely what gave the injunction in the United States its effectiveness regarding any disobedience, being the same court empowered to vindicate its own power by imposing criminal or economic sanctions by means of imprisonment and fines. In Venezuela, in contrast, the amparo courts do not have such powers, and regarding the application of criminal sanctions to the disobedient party, the amparo courts or the interested party must

---

tico Administrative Chamber of July 15, 1992, *Comité Campesino Provisional Corocito*, in *Revista de Derecho Público,* nº 51, Editorial Jurídica Venezolana, Caracas, 1992, pp. 171 ff.

310 See BREWER-CARÍAS, *Instituciones Políticas y Constitucionales,* Tomo V, *El derecho y la acción de amparo*, *supra* note 5, at 346.

311. Venez. Amparo Law, Art. 36.

312. Venez. Amparo Law, Art. 29-30.

313. This is particularly important regarding criminal contempt, which was established since the *In Re Debs* case, where according to Justice Brewer who delivered the Court's opinion, it was ruled: "But the power of a court to make an order carries with it the equal power to punish for a disobedience of that order, and the inquiry as to the question of disobedience has been, from time immemorial, the special function of the court. And this is no technical rule. In order that a court may compel obedience to its order it must have the right to inquire whether there has been any disobedience thereof. To submit the question of disobedience to another tribunal, be it a jury or another court, would operate to deprive the proceedings of half its efficiency." 158 U.S. 564, 594-95 (1895). In *Watson v. Williams,* it was said: "The power to fine and imprison for contempt, from the earliest history of jurisprudence, has been regarded as the necessary incident and attribute of a court, without which it could no more exist than without a judge. It is a power inherent in all courts of record, and coexisting with them by the wise provisions of the common law. A court without the power effectually to protect itself against the assaults of the lawless, or to enforce its orders, judgments, or decrees against the recusant parties before it, would be a disgrace to the legislation, and a stigma upon the age which invented it."36 Miss. 331, 341 (Hight Ct. of Errors & Appeals 1858). See *also* FISS & RENDLEMAN, *supra* note 32, at 13; TABB & SHOBEN, *supra* note 53, at 72.

seek for the initiation of a judicial criminal procedure against the disobedient to be brought before the competent criminal courts.[314]

Due to the general by-instance procedural principle, the amparo decisions can be appealed before the superior courts according to the general rules established in the procedural codes. This general principle, of course, does not apply when the decision is adopted by the Supreme Tribunal. Consequently, the amparo decisions can only be adopted by the Supreme Tribunal, when having original jurisdiction, when deciding on appellate jurisdiction or when an extraordinary mean for revision is filed, similar to the writ for certiorari in the United States. In effect, particularly when constitutional issues are involved, the United States Supreme Court, when considering a petition for a writ of certiorari, is authorized to review all the decisions of the federal courts of appeals, and of the specialized federal courts, and all the decisions of the supreme courts of the states involving issues of federal law, but on a discretionary basis. In all such cases where there is no right of appeal and no mandatory appellate jurisdiction of the Supreme Court established, the cases can reach the Supreme Court as petitions for certiorari, when a litigant who has lost in a lower court and petitions a review in the Supreme Court, setting out the reasons why review should be granted.[315] This method of seeking review by the Supreme Court is expressly established in the cases set forth in the Title 28 of the United States Code, and according to Rule 10 of the Rules of the Supreme Court adopted in 2005, where it is established as not being "a matter of right, but of judicial discretion," granted only "for compelling reasons," that is, when there are special and important reasons.[316]

According to this rule, to promote uniformity and consistency in federal law, the following factors might prompt the Supreme Court to grant certiorari: (1) Important questions of federal law on which the court has not previously ruled; (2) Conflicting interpretations of federal law by lower courts; (3) Lower courts' decisions that conflict with previous Supreme Court decisions; and (4) Lower courts' departures from the accepted and usual course of judicial proceedings.[317]

Of course, review may be granted on the basis of other factors, or denied even if one or more of the above-mentioned factors is present. The discretion of the Supreme Court is not limited, and it is the importance of the issue and the public interest considered by the Court in a particular case that leads the Court to grant certiorari and to review some cases.

In countries with a mixed system of judicial review, as is the case in Venezuela, the appellate jurisdiction of the Constitutional Chamber of the Supreme Court as Constitutional Jurisdictions, in order to review lower courts' decisions on constitu-

314. Venez. Amparo Law, Art. 31.

315. See Lawrence BAUM, *The Supreme Court* 81 (1st ed. 1981).

316. SUP. CT. R. 10.

317. *Id.* See *also* Ralph. A. ROSSUM & G. Alan TARR, *American Constitutional Law. Cases and Interpretation*, 28 (1st ed. 1983).

tional matters, is also established in a discretionary basis,[318] and by means of an extraordinary recourse for review, regarding lower courts decisions applying the diffuse method and also the decisions issued on amparo proceedings (Article 336,10)..[319]

In this matter, in Venezuela, the Constitutional Chamber of the Supreme Court, as Constitutional Jurisdiction, has developed *ex officio* powers for reviewing lower courts' decisions on constitutional matters, without any constitutional or statutory support. Based on the aforementioned power of the Constitutional Chamber to review in a discretionary way lower courts' decisions on constitutional matters of importance, the Constitutional Chamber distorting its constitutional review powers, has extended it to other decisions different from those issued on judicial review cases or on amparo proceedings, as established in the constitution.[320] Through obligatory judicial doctrine, the Chamber extended its review power regarding any other judicial decision issued in any matters when it considers it contrary to the constitution, a power that the Chamber considered authorized to exercise although without any constitutional provision, even *ex officio*. These review powers have also been developed in cases of particular judicial decisions when considered contrary to a Constitutional Chamber interpretation of the constitution, or when considered a grievous error regarding constitutional interpretation.[321]

On the other hand, since 2004, the Organic Law of the Supreme Tribunal, following such doctrine established by the same Tribunal, gave general powers to all the Chambers of the Tribunal to take away cases (*avocamiento*) from the jurisdiction of lower courts, also *ex officio* or through a party petition, when considered convenient, and to decide them.[322] This power, which has been highly criticized because it breaches due process rights, and particularly, the right to trial in a by-instance basis by the courts, has allowed the Constitutional Chamber to intervene in any kind of process, including cases being trialed by the other Chambers of the Supreme Tribunal, with very negative effects. For instance, the Constitutional Chamber power was used in order to annul a decision issued by the Electoral Chamber of the Supreme

318. This occurs in a similar way to the operation of the writ of certiorari in the United States. See Jesús María CASAL, *Constitución y Justicia Constitucional*, 92 (1st ed. 2002).

319. VENEZ. CONST. ART. 336.10 (1999)..

320. VENEZ. CONST. ART. 336.10 (1999)..

321. See Decision nº 93 of Feb. 6, 2001, *Olimpia Tours and Travel vs. Corporación de Turismo de Venezuela* case, in *Revista de Derecho Público*, N° 85-88, Editorial Jurídica Venezolana, Caracas, 2001, pp. 414–15. See also Allan R. BREWER-CARÍAS, *Quis Custodiet ipsos Custodes: De la interpretación constitucional a la inconstitucionalidad de la interpretación*, in ***VIII Congreso Nacional de Derecho Constitucional, Perú, Sept.*** 2005, Fondo Editorial, Colegio de Abogados de Arequipa, Arequipa, 2005, pp. 463–89.

322. See Article 25.16 of the *Ley Orgánica del Tribunal Supremo de Justicia*, *Gaceta Oficial* N° 5991 Extra. of July 29, 2010. See Allan R. BREWER-CARÍAS, *Crónica de la "In" Justicia Consituticional. La Sala Constitucional y el autoritarismo en Venezuela*, Editorial Jurídica Venezolana 91 (2007).

Tribunal[323] seeking to protect the citizens' right to political participation, in which the latter suspended the effects of a decision of the National Electoral Council (Resolution nº 040302-131 of Mar. 2, 2004), objecting to the presidential repeal referendum petition of 2004. The Constitutional Chamber, in this way, by means of a decision nº 566 of April 12, 2004, interrupted the process that was normally developing before the Electoral Chamber of the Supreme Tribunal, took away the case from such Chamber, and annulling its decision, decided in a contrary sense, according to what was the will of the executive, restricting the people's right to participate through petitioning referendums.[324]

CONCLUSIONS

The two century tradition of Venezuelan constitutions of inserting very extensive declarations on human rights, has proven that in order for human rights to be effectively protected, independently of such formal declarations, the most important and necessary tool is to have not only effective judicial remedies for the immediate protections of rights, but an independent and autonomous judiciary.

Due to the traditional inefficacy of the ordinary and extraordinary judicial remedies that in other countries have proven to be effective for the protection of rights, in Venezuela, since 1961, the constitution has incorporated an express provision regarding the judicial guarantee of constitutional rights, establishing a specific judicial remedy for its protection, called the amparo action or proceeding, having different procedural rules when compared with the general judicial remedies that the legal system provides for the protection of personal or property rights. As it has been analyzed, this constitutional feature is one of the most important of Latin America constitutional law, particularly when contrasted with the constitutional system of the United States or of the United Kingdom, where the protection of human rights is effectively carried on through the general judicial actions and equitable remedies, that are also used to protect any kind of personal or property rights or interests.

This amparo remedy has been a very effective mean for the protection of constitutional rights, particularly in democratic regimes where the Judiciary has been preserved as an independent branch of government. Consequently, even providing in the constitution for this specific remedy of amparo to assure the immediate protection of constitutional rights, the very essence of its effectiveness is the existence of an independent and autonomous judiciary that could effectively protect human

323. See Decisions nº 24 of Mar.15, 2004, (Exp. AA70-E 2004-000021; Exp. x-04-00006); and nº 27 of Mar. 29, (*Julio Borges, César Pérez Vivas, Henry Ramos Allup, Jorge Sucre Castillo, Ramón José Medina y Gerardo Blyde vs. Consejo Nacional Electoral* case (Exp. AA70-E-2004-000021- AA70-V-2004-000006). See *Revista de Derecho Público,* nº 97-98, Editorial Jurídica Venezolana, Caracas, 2004, pp. 373 ff.

324. See in Allan R. BREWER-CARÍAS, *La Sala Constitucional versus el Estado Democrático de Derecho. El secuestro del poder electoral y de la Sala Electoral del Tribunal Supremo y la confiscación del derecho a la participación política*, Los Libros de El Nacional, Colección Ares, Caracas, 2004.

rights. Unfortunately, in the Latin American countries, the judiciary has not always accomplished its fundamental duty, so that in spite of the constitutional declarations and provisions for amparo, many countries have faced, and others are still facing, a rather dismal situation regarding the effectiveness of the Judiciary as a whole, as an efficient and just protector of fundamental rights.

That is why, in spite of the extensive constitutional declarations of rights, in order to achieve the aims of the State of Justice, the most elemental institutional condition needed in any country, is the existence of a really autonomous and independent judiciary, out of the reach and control from the other branches of government, empowered to interpret and apply the law in an impartial way and protect citizens, particularly when referring to the enforcement of rights against the state. Such judiciary has to be built upon the principle of separation of powers. If this principle is not implemented and the government controls the courts and judges, no effective guarantee can exist regarding constitutional rights, particularly when the offending party is a governmental agency. In this case, and in spite of all constitutional declarations, it is impossible to speak of rule of law, as happens in many Latin American countries.

This is important, precisely on matters of amparo, particularly when the petition is filed against a government or authoritative act, in which case, no judicial protection can be given if the government controls the judiciary. Just one example can highlight this situation. In a case developed in Venezuela in 2003, where as a consequence of an amparo decision, the Judicial Review of Administrative Action Jurisdiction (*Jurisdicción contencioso-administrativa*) was intervened by the government, after being for three decades a very important autonomous and independent jurisdiction in order to control the legality of Public Administration activities.

In effect, in 2003 the Mayor of Caracas, the Ministry of Health and the Caracas Metropolitan Board of Doctors (*Colegio de Médicos*) decided to hire Cuban doctors for an important popular governmental health program in the Caracas slums, but without complying with the legal conditions established for foreign doctors to practice the medical profession in the country. Based on the democratic tradition the country had since 1958 in matters of control and review of Public Administration actions, on July 17, 2003, the Venezuelan National Federation of Doctors brought before the aforementioned Judicial Review of Administrative Actions highest Court in Caracas (First Court) a nullity claim against the aforementioned decision The National Federation of Doctors considered that the program was discriminatory and against the rights of Venezuelan doctors to exercise their medical profession, allowing foreign doctors to exercise it without complying with the Medical Profession Statute regulations. The consequence was the filing of an amparo petition against both public authorities, seeking the collective protection of the Venezuelan doctors' constitutional rights.[325]

325. See Claudia NIKKEN, "El caso "Barrio Adentro": La Corte Primera de lo Contencioso Administrativo ante la Sala Constitucional del Tribunal Supremo de Justicia o el avocamiento como medio de amparo de derechos e intereses colectivos y difusos", *Revista de Derecho Público*, nº 93-96, Editorial Jurídica Venezolana, Caracas 2003, pp. 5 ff.

One month later, in August 21, 2003, the First Court issued a preliminary protective amparo measure, considering that there were sufficient elements to deem that the equality before the law constitutional guarantee was violated in the case. The Court ordered in a preliminary way the suspension of the Cuban doctors' hiring program and ordered the Metropolitan Board of doctors to substitute the Cuban doctors already hired, by Venezuelan ones or foreign doctors who had fulfilled the legal regulations in order to exercise the medical profession in the country.[326]

Nonetheless, in response to that preliminary judicial amparo decision, instead of enforcing it, the Minister of Health, the Mayor of Caracas, and even the President of the Republic made public statements to the effect that the decision was not going to be respected or enforced.[327] Following these statements, the government-controlled Constitutional Chamber of the Supreme Tribunal of Justice adopted a decision, without any appeal being filed, assuming jurisdiction over the case and annulling the preliminary amparo ordered by the First Court; a group of Secret Service police officials seized the First Court's premises; and the President of the Republic, among other expressions he used, publicly called the President of the First Court a "bandit."[328] A few weeks later, in response to the First Court's decision in an unrelated case challenging a local registrar's refusal to record a land sale, a Special Commission for the Intervention of the Judiciary, which in spite of being unconstitutional continued to exist, dismissed all five judges of the First Court.[329] In spite of the protests of all the bar associations of the country and also of the International Commission of Jurists;[330] the First Court remained suspended without judges, and its premises remained

326. See Decision of Aug. 21, 2003; *Id.* at 445.

327. The President of the Republic said: "*Váyanse con su decisión no sé para donde, la cumplirán ustedes en su casa si quieren . . .* " ("You can go with your decision, I don't know where; you will enforce it in your house if you want . . . "). See EL UNIVERSAL, Caracas Aug. 25, 2003 and EL UNIVERSAL, Caracas Aug. 28, 2003.

328. See *Apitz-Barbera et al. ("First Court on Judicial Review of Administrative Actions") v. Venezuela*, Inter-Am. Ct. H.R., ser. C N° 182, Aug. 5, 2008, available at http://www.corteidh.or.cr. Excepción Preliminar, Fondo, Reparaciones y Costas, Serie C, N° 182.

329. See *El Nacional*, Nov. 5, 2003, at A2. The dismissed President of the First Court said: "La justicia venezolana vive un momento tenebroso, pues el tribunal que constituye un último resquicio de esperanza ha sido clausurado." ("The Venezuelan judiciary lives a dark moment, because the court that was a last glimmer of hope has been shut down."). *Id.* The Commission for the Intervention of the Judiciary had also massively dismissed almost all judges of the country without due disciplinary process, and had replaced them with provisionally appointed judges beholden to the ruling power.

330. See in *El Nacional*, Caracas Oct. 10, 2003, at A6; *El Nacional*, Caracas Oct. 15, 2003, at A2; *El Nacional*, Caracas Sept. 24, 2003, at A4; *El Nacional*, Caracas Feb. 14, 2004, at A7.

closed for about nine months,[331] a period during which simply no judicial review of administrative action could be sought in the country.[332]

The dismissed judges of the First Court brought a complaint to the Inter-American Commission of Human Rights for the government's unlawful removal of them and for violation of their constitutional rights. The Commission, in turn, brought the case, captioned *Apitz Barbera et al.* (*Corte Primera de lo Contencioso Administrativo vs. Venezuela*) before the Inter-American Court of Human Rights. On August 5, 2008, the Inter-American Court ruled that the Republic of Venezuela had violated the rights of the dismissed judges established in the American Convention of Human Rights, and ordered the state to pay them due compensation, to reinstate them to a similar position in the Judiciary, and to publish part of the decision in Venezuelan newspapers.[333] Nonetheless, on December 12, 2008, the Constitutional Chamber of the Supreme Tribunal issued Decision No. 1.939, declaring that the August 5, 2008 decision of the Inter-American Court of Human Rights was unenforceable (*inejecutable*) in Venezuela. The Constitutional Chamber also accused the Inter-American Court of having usurped powers of the Supreme Tribunal of Justice, and asked the executive branch to denounce the American Convention of Human Rights.[334]

In general terms, this was the global governmental response to an amparo judicial preliminary decision that affected a very sensitive governmental social program; a response that was expressed and executed through the government-controlled judiciary.[335] The result was that the subsequent newly appointed judges replacing those dismissed, began to "understand" how they needed to behave in the future. That same Commission for the Intervention of the Judiciary, as mentioned, was the one that massively dismissed without due disciplinary process almost all judges of the country, substituting them with provisionally appointed judges, thus dependent on

331. See *El Nacional*, Caracas Oct. 24, 2003, A2; and *El Nacional*, Caracas July 16, 2004, at A6.

332. See Allan R. BREWER-CARÍAS, *La justicia sometida al poder (La ausencia de independencia y autonomía de los jueces en Venezuela por la interminable emergencia del Poder Judicial (1999-2006)*, in *Cuestiones Internacionales*. Anuario Jurídico Villanueva, Madrid 2007, 25–57.

333. *Apitz-Barbera et al. ("First Court* on Judicial Review *of* Administrative Actions*") v. Venezuela,* Inter-Am. Ct. H.R., ser. C N° 182, Aug. 5, 2008, available at http://www.corteidh.or.cr. Excepción Preliminar, Fondo, Reparaciones y Costas, Serie C, N° 182.

334. Supreme Tribunal of Justice, Constitutional Chamber, Decision N° 1.939 of Dec. 18, 2008, *Abogados Gustavo Álvarez Arias et al.* case, (Exp. N° 08-1572), in *Revista de Derecho Público,* n° 116, Editorial Jurídica Venezolana, Caracas 2008, pp. 89-96.

335. See Allan R. BREWER-CARÍAS, *La progresiva y sistemática demolición institucional de la autonomía e independencia del Poder Judicial en Venezuela 1999–2004*, XXX *Jornadas J.M Domínguez Escovar, Estado de derecho, Administración de justicia y derechos humanos,* Instituto de Estudios Jurídicos del Estado Lara, Barquisimeto 2005, pp. 33-174.

the ruling power, who in 2006 were granted permanent status without complying with the constitutional provisions.[336]

This emblematic case, contrasted with the very progressive text of the constitution in force in Venezuela (1999), which contains one of the most extensive declaration of constitutional rights in all Latin America, including the provision for the amparo action, even considering it as a constitutional right; shows that the judicial guarantee of constitutional rights always requires an independent and autonomous judiciary, conducted out of the reach of the government. On the contrary, with a judiciary controlled by the executive, as the aforementioned Venezuelan case illustrates, the declaration of constitutional rights is a death letter, and the provision of the action for amparo is no more than an illusion. This has been the tragic institutional result of the deliberated process of dismantling democracy to which Venezuela has been subjected during the past decade, through the imposition of an authoritarian government, defrauding the constitution and democracy itself.[337]

---

336. In this regard, the Venezuelan 1999 Constitution established, in general terms, the regime for entering the judicial career and promotion only "through public competition that assures suitability and excellence," guarantying "citizen's participation in the procedure of selection and appointment of the judges." The consequence is that they may not be removed or suspended from their positions except through a legal proceeding before a disciplinary jurisdiction. *Venez. Const. Art.* 255. This, again, unfortunately is just a theoretical aim, because all contests for judge's appointment have been suspended since 2002. Almost all judges are being provisionally appointed without citizen participation, and there is no disciplinary jurisdiction for their dismissal. Furthermore, the suspension and dismissal of all judges corresponds to a commission for the intervention of the judiciary that is not regulated in the constitution. See Inter-American Commission on Human Rights, *Report on the Situation of Human Rights in Venezuela*, OEA/Ser.L/V/II.118, doc. 4 rev. 2, Dec. 29, 2003, para. 174. See http://www.cidh.oas.org/ country-rep/Venezuela2003eng/toc.htm. See also the *2009 Annual Report*, para.479, available at http://www.cidh.oas.org/annualrep/2009eng/Chap.IV.f.eng.htm

337. See Allan R. BREWER-CARÍAS, *Dismantling Democracy. The Chávez Authoritarian Experiment*, (1st ed. 2010).

VI

THE QUESTION OF LEGITIMACY: HOW TO CHOOSE THE JUDGES OF THE SUPREME COURTS (2005)

This Paper on the "The Question of Legitimacy: How to Choose the Judges of the Supreme Court. The European Doctrine and the Latin American contrast," was written for my participation in the *6th International ECLN–Colloquium/IACL Round Table*, on *The Future of the European Judicial System. The Constitutional Role of European Courts*, held in Berlin, Germany on 2–4 November 2005. Published in Ingolf Pernice, Julianne Kokott and Cheryl Sauders (eds), *The Future of the European Judicial System in Comparative Perspective,* 6th International ECLN Colloquium/IACL Round Table, Berlin, 2–4 November 2005, European Constitutional Law Network Series, Vol. 6, Nomos, Berlin 2006, pp. 153–182

I. THE QUESTION OF LEGITIMACY: PURPOSE OR ORIGIN OF THE JUDGES SELECTION PROCESS

The question of legitimacy as it refers to the selection and designation of Supreme Court Judges is related to the political method established in the Constitution to ensure not only the professional competence of judges, but mainly their independence and autonomy. The question is to guarantee the selection of judges based on objective criteria without outside or political influence, their independence from the State's other branches of government when imparting justice, and their autonomy, so that they will be able to decide solely based on the law, without outside pressure or political influence. Ultimately, the question of legitimacy is a matter of determining how Judges will fulfill their "duty of lack of gratitude" (Louis Favoreu).

This question, of course, can only be raised in democratic systems of government based on the rule of law and on the principle of the separation of powers, in which the independence and autonomy of the judicial branch of government can only be ensured.

The question can also be analyzed from the point of view of the democratic origin of judges as it applies to their popular election by the citizens, or their appointment only by democratically elected State bodies. But this approach, which places emphasis on the elected origin of judges, in my opinion, does not focus on the essence of the judicial function: that judges must be independent of the other branches of government and when deciding cases they must not be subject to pressures so that they can decide only according to law. Citizen election of judges does not ensure such independence and autonomy or the objective criteria for the selection, with the question of "democratic legitimacy" being secondary in this case.

On the other hand, in comparative constitutional law, there are no examples of systems where the Supreme Court justices are elected by citizen vote. Additionally, in those systems in which lower court judges are popularly elected, while it might be said that the election could be more democratic and transparent, such elections have been questioned, precisely because they do not ensure that the most suitable candidates will be elected to guarantee the right of citizens to be tried by an independent and impartial tribunal, as guaranteed by the Constitution.

That is why the *Human Rights Committee of the United Nations on the United States of America*, since 1979, has expressed its concern about the suitability of the candidates popularly elected in some states of the United States; and has welcomed "the efforts of a number of states in the adoption of a merit–selection system," recommending that the system of "appointment of judges through elections be reconsidered with a view to its replacement by systems of appointment on merit by an independent body."[1]

That is why, as mentioned above, regarding the method adopted for the election of Supreme Court judges, the question of legitimacy must focus on what is essential to the judiciary, in order to guarantee the independence and autonomy of judges, something that cannot be achieved solely by popular election of judges, a process which cannot ensure the suitability of the elected candidate. Thus, in the *Explanatory Memorandum to the Charter on the Statute for Judges of the Council of Europe*[2], it is recognized that "many of the Charter's provisions are inapplicable in systems where judges are directly elected by the citizens".

In conclusion, what is required in order to consider the election of judges legitimate is the adoption of a political method that will ensure their independence, autonomy and impartiality. To this end, election methods need to be implemented in order to guarantee, *first*, that judges will be appointed transparently based on merit through objective selection criteria; and *second*, that such designations will be made

---

1 Concluding Observations of the Human Rights Committee on the United States of Ame-rica, UN document CCPR/C/79/Add.50; A/50/40, paragraphs 266–304, paragraphs 288 and 301. See the reference in International Commission of Jurists, *International Principles on the Independence and Accountability of Judges, lawyers and prosecutors. A Practitioners' Guide*, 2004, p. 49

2 See the text in Stefanie Ricarda ROOS and Jan WOISCHNIK, *Códigos de ética judicial. Un estudio de derecho comparado con recomendaciones para los países latinoamericanos*, Konrad Adenauer Stiftung, Programa de Estado de Derecho para Sudamérica, Montevideo 2005.

so as to ensure the independence, autonomy and impartiality of the judge, regardless of the organ or body called upon to make the election.

II. ASPECTS OF THE EUROPEAN DOCTRINE AND PRINCIPLES

The topic of the legitimacy of the selection of judges, which includes the selection of Supreme Court justices, has been addressed in Europe specifically by international entities and bodies specialized in the functioning of the Judicial Branch in a democratic society, which have formulated overall valid principles and recommendations on the matter.

For example, the *Judges' Charter in Europe of the European Association of Judges*, adopted in 1993, established the principle that:

> The selection of judges must be based exclusively on objective criteria designed to ensure professional competence. Selection must be performed by an independent body which represents the judges. No outside influence and, in particular, no political influence must play any part in the appointment of judges[3].

Derived therefrom is the general principle or recommendation that the aim of the election method for judges must be to ensure its application by a government body particularly independent from the executive and legislative branches, which must represent the judges in general, meaning that there should be no political or any other type of influence in the process.

In the same sense, the Committee of Ministers of the Council of Europe, in *Recommendation N° R (94) 12 to the Member States on the Independence, Efficiency and Role of judges*, adopted in 1994, stated in *Principle* I, 2,c, that:

> All decisions concerning the professional career of judges should be based on objective criteria, and the selection and career of judges should be based on merit, having regard to qualifications, integrity, ability and efficiency. The authority taking the decision on the selection and career of judges should be independent of the government and the administration. In order to safeguard its independence, rules should ensure that, for instance, its members are selected by the judiciary and that the authority decides itself on its procedural rules.

The general principle derived from this recommendation with respect to the selection method is, again, that it must be carried out by an authority independent of the government and the administration (Executive Branch), adding that in those cases in which constitutional or legal provisions allow the designation of judges by the government, then:

> [T]here should be guarantees to ensure that the procedures to appoint judges are transparent and independent in practice, and that the decision will not be influenced by any reason other than those related to the objective criteria mentioned above. These guarantees could be, for example, one or more of the following:

3 See the text in Stefanie Ricarda ROOS and Jan WOISCHNIK, *Códigos de ética judicial. Un estudio de derecho comparado con recomendaciones para los países latinoamericanos*, Konrad Adenauer Stiftung, Programa de Estado de Derecho para Sudamérica, Montevideo 2005, p. 77.

I. a special independent and competent body to give the government advice which it follows in practice; or

II. the right for an individual to appeal against a decision to an independent authority; or

III. the authority which makes the decision safeguards against undue or improper influences[4].

The same Committee of Ministers adopted an *Explanatory Memorandum to Recommendation N° R (94) 12*, in which it insisted that "it is essential that the independence of judges should be guaranteed when they are selected and throughout their professional career" and that "in particular, where the decision to appoint judges is taken by organs which are not independent of the government or the administration or, for instance, by parliament or the president of the state, it is important that such decisions are taken only on the basis of objective criteria"; adding the following:

> Although the recommendation proposes an ideal system for judicial appointments, it was recognized (see sub–paragraph 2) that a number of member states of the Council of Europe have adopted other systems, often involving the government, parliament or the head of state. The recommendation does not propose to change these systems which have been in operation for decades or centuries and which in practice work well. But also in states where the judges are formally appointed by the government, there should be some kind of system whereby the appointment procedures of judges are transparent and independent in practice. In some states, this is ensured by special independent and competent bodies which give advice to the government, the parliament or the head of state which in practice is followed or by providing a possibility of appeal by the person concerned. Other states have opted for systems involving wide consultations with the judiciary, although the formal decision is taken by a member of government.
>
> It was not felt appropriate to deal explicitly in the text of the recommendation with systems where appointments are made by the president or the parliament, although the Committee was of the opinion that the general principles on appointments would apply also for such systems.
>
> An important aspect of ensuring that the most suitable persons are appointed as judges is the training of lawyers. Professional judges must have proper legal training. In addition, training contributes to judicial independence. If judges have adequate theoretical and practical knowledge as well as skills, it would mean that they could act more independently against the administration and, if they so wish, could change legal profession without necessarily having to continue to be judges[5].

In the same line of thought, four years later, in 1998, the Council of Europe adopted in Strasbourg the *European Charter on the Statute of Judges,* in which the following principles were set forth:

> 1. *General Principles*. 1.3. In respect of every decision affecting the selection, recruitment, appointment, career progress or termination of office of a judge, the statute envisages the intervention of an authority independent of the executive and legislative powers within

4 *Ibid.,* p. 80

5 *Ibid.,* pgs. 87–88

which at least one half of those who sit are judges elected by their peers following methods guaranteeing the widest representation of the judiciary...

2. *Selection, Recruitment, Initial Training.* 2.1. The rules of the statute relating to the selection and recruitment of judges by an independent body or panel, base the choice of candidates on their ability to assess freely and impartially the legal matters which will be referred to them, and to apply the law to them with respect for individual dignity.

In the *Explanatory Memorandum to the Charter on the Statute for Judges,* as mentioned, the Council recognized that notwithstanding the general applicability of principle 2.1, "many of the Charter's provisions are inapplicable in systems where judges are directly elected by the citizens," empathizing the following:

1.3. The Charter provides for the intervention of a body independent from the executive and the legislative where a decision is required on the selection, recruitment or appointment of judges, the development of their careers or the termination of their office.

The wording of this provision is intended to cover a variety of situations, ranging from the mere provision of advice for an executive or legislative body, to actual decision by the independent body.

Account had to be taken here of certain differences in the national systems. Some countries would find it difficult to accept an independent body replacing the political body responsible for appointments. However, the requirement in such cases to obtain at least the recommendation or the opinion of an independent body is bound to be a great incentive, if not an actual obligation, for the appointment body. In the spirit of the Charter, recommendations and opinions of the independent body do not constitute guarantees that they will in a general way be followed in practice. The political or administrative authority which does not follow such recommendation or opinion should at the very least be obliged to make known its reasons for its refusal so to do.

The wording of this provision of the Charter also enables the independent body to intervene either with a straightforward opinion, an official opinion, a recommendation, a proposal or an actual decision[6].

Of course, the question of legitimacy in the intervention of an independent body to select judges also relates to the selection itself of the members of the independent body. In this respect, the Charter:

[Stipulates] that at least one half of the body's members should be judges elected by their peers, which means that it wants neither to allow judges to be in a minority in the independent body nor to require them to be in the majority. In view of the variety of philosophical conceptions and debates in European States, a reference to a minimum of 50% judges emerged as capable of ensuring a fairly high level of safeguards while respecting any other consideration of principles prevailing in different national systems.

The Charter states that judges who are members of the independent body should be elected by their peers, on the grounds that the requisite independence of this body precludes the election or appointment of its members by political authority belonging to the executive or legislature.

There would be a risk of party–political bias in the appointment and role of judges under such a procedure. Judges sitting on the independent body are expected, precisely, to refrain

---

6 *Ibid.* pgs. 101–102

> from seeking the favour of political parties or bodies that are themselves appointed or elected by or through such parties.
>
> Finally, without insisting on any particular voting system, the Charter indicates that the method of electing judges to this body must guarantee the widest representation of judges[7].

As it is evident, the question of legitimacy as regards the election of judges has been studied extensively in Europe, giving rise to the aforementioned principles and recommendations with respect to all judges, which of course can also be applied to the election of Supreme Court judges.

It is not up to me, as a Latin American jurist, to make recommendations or formulate critiques of the European systems; consequently, for this *6th International ECLN–Colloquium/IADC Round Table on The future of European Judicial Systems/ The Constitutional Role of the Europeans Courts*, I have deemed it more appropriate, from the point of view of comparative constitutional law, to analyze the attempts made in Latin American constitutionalism to ensure the legitimacy of the appointment of judges, not only of the Supreme Courts, but also of Constitutional Courts or Tribunals, which, in general and contrary to what occurs in Europe, are integrated into the judicial branch on the Latin American continent.

In this matter, it can be said that in Latin America everything has been attempted to try to ensure the legitimacy of the election judges of Supreme Courts or Tribunals, in order to ensure the independence and impartiality of justice. This has even been ruled on directly in the Constitutions of all the countries, that is, "in the normative rules at the highest level," as recommended by the *European Charter on the Statute of Judges* of the Council of Europe (1. General Principles. 1.2) and its Explanatory Memorandum (1.2) even if not always with the desired success.

Latin American constitutional systems can then be classified according to whether or not the designation of Supreme Court judges (i) is accomplished with the participation of all State bodies; (ii) is attributed to the President of the Republic, always with the intervention of the parliament or the Senate; (iii) is carried out directly by the full legislative body or by the Senate in certain bicameral systems, even with the intervention of independent bodies; (iv) is attributed to an independent Judiciary Council; or (v) is made by co–opting mechanisms by the Court itself. This variety of election methods has been regulated by the Constitutions, usually to legitimize the election of Supreme Courts judges in order to ensure their independence and autonomy. However, in many cases, whether because of mistaken legislation or political practice, the results pursued by the Constitutions have not always been achieved.

Nonetheless, we will analyze all those systems, both in theory and in practice, to determine to what degree they effectively ensure their independence and autonomy.

---

7 *Idem.*

III. DESIGNATION OF SUPREME COURT JUDGES BY ALL THE BRANCHES OF GOVERNMENT

In the first place, mentioned can be the method of choosing the Supreme Court Justices with the participation of all the branches of government, particularly in order to avoid the predominance of one branch over the others. This is the case of the Dominican Republic where the Supreme Court judges are designated with the participation of all the different branches of government; a method that seeks to guarantee that no one branch of government will have predominance in making the designation. Nevertheless, this method in itself does not guarantee a merit–based selection of the judges to assure their independence and autonomy.

The same occurs in the case of judges of the Constitutional Court of Guatemala, the Constitutional Tribunal of Chile and the Constitutional Tribunal of Ecuador, all conceived as independent jurisdictional bodies not integrated into the judicial branch, where the intervention and participation of all different governmental bodies is a requirement for the designation of their members. In these cases, because of the control they exercise over the constitutionality of state acts the aim here is to protect the balance of powers and to make sure that the necessary autonomy exists to perform their functions.

1. Designation of: the Judges of the Supreme Court of Justice in the Dominican Republic by a Judiciary Council with the participation of all government bodies

According to article 64 of the Constitution of the Dominican Republic, judges of the Supreme Court of Justice are appointed by a National Judiciary Council, created not as a permanent government body, but solely in order to make such designations; therefore, it does not have among its attributions and contrary to other organs with similar names, the government and administration of the judicial power.

This Dominican National Judiciary Council is comprised of the following 7 members:

The President of the Republic, who presides. His absences are covered by the Vice President of the Republic and by the Solicitor General of the Republic in the event of the absence of the first two;

The President of the Senate and a senator elected by the Senate who must belong to a party different from that of the President of the Republic;

The Chairman of the Chamber of Deputies and a deputy elected by the Chamber who must belong to a different party than that of the Chairman of the Chamber of Deputies;

The Chief Justice of the Supreme Court of Justice; and

A magistrate of the Supreme Court of Justice elected by the Court itself, who will act as Secretary.

According to the Organic Law of the National Judiciary Council (Law Nº 169–97), the candidacies can be proposed before the Council in an absolutely free manner, and "the candidates can be nominated by institutions as well as individuals, within the timeframes set and in accordance with the formalities established by the National Judiciary Council" (Art. 12). The members of the National Judiciary Council can also nominate candidates (Art. 13), and they, themselves, can also be nominated as candidates, in which case they must abstain from voting (Art. 14).

As regards the election, Article 15 of the Law states that once candidates for Supreme Court judges have been nominated, the National Judiciary Council may convene them for evaluation of the different aspects it deems advisable and, moreover, may submit candidacies to public examination, as the Council is authorized to inquire into everything it considers pertinent, in order to collect the opinions of institutions and citizens.

Once a preliminary selection has been made from among the candidacies, the Council will proceed with the election, which must be made with at least four (4) assenting votes of the members present (Art. 16) and the judges elect must take their oath before the Council.

In addition to electing the judges of the Supreme Court of Justice, the Judiciary Council must decide who will be the President of the Supreme Court, proceeding to designate a first and second alternate to replace the President in the event of the latter's absence or impediment.

2. Designation of the members of the Constitutional Tribunals of Chile, Guatemala and Ecuador

A. *Exclusive attribution of government authorities for the appointment of the magistrates of the: Constitutional Tribunal of Chile*

In Chile, in accordance with the constitutional amendment of 2005 and as set forth in Article 81 of the Constitution, the 10 magistrates of the Constitutional Court must be appointed for a term of 9 years as follows:

Three (3) magistrates must be elected by the President of the Republic without the interference of any state organs. The election must be made successively and in steps, over time, every three (3) years as follows:

Four (4) judges must be elected by the Senate, in sessions especially convened for this purpose, by a two–thirds majority: two directly elected by the Senate and the other two proposed by the Chamber of Deputies; and,

Three (3) magistrates elected by the Supreme Court of Justice from outside that court and by absolute majority in successive and secret ballots.

B. *Appointment of the members of Constitutional Court of Guatemala by government authorities and by representatives of civil society*

In 1965, a Constitutional Court was established in Guatemala initially as a non–permanent body that was integrated by the judges of the Supreme Court and of other courts of appeals and of administrative judicial review jurisdiction, whenever a case of unconstitutionality was brought.

In 1985, the Constitutional Court was regulated as a permanent jurisdiction for judicial review of constitutionality of statutes, integrated by five magistrates, designated:

One by the Supreme Court of Justice;

One by the Congress of the Republic;

One by the President of the Republic, in a Cabinet meeting;

One by the University Council of the San Carlos University of Guatemala; and

One by the assembly of the Bar Association of Guatemala.

C. *Appointment of the members of the Constitutional Court of Ecuador by the National Congress, subject to proposals by government bodies and representatives of civil society*

According to Article 130 of the Ecuadorian Constitution, it is the National Congress that appoints the 9 members of the Constitutional Court, by majority, as follows:

Two members from a list of three sent by the President of the Republic;

Two members from a list of three sent by the Supreme Court of Justice, and who must not be members of the Court;

One member from a list of three sent by the mayors and provincial authorities (prefects);

One member from a list of three sent by the workers' unions and the legally recognized national organizations of indigenous peoples and farm workers; one from a list of three sent by the legally established Production and Commerce Chambers; and

Two members directly elected by the Congress who must not be legislators.

The 1997 statute on Judicial Review (control of constitutionality) specifically regulated the procedure for the integration of the three–person lists referred to in the lasts sub–paragraphs.

IV. DESIGNATION OF THE SUPREME COURT JUDGES BY THE PRESIDENT OF THE REPUBLIC WITH THE INTERVENTION OF THE LEGISLATIVE BRANCH

The second most common method for the designation of Supreme Court judges established in Latin American Constitutions, following the general trend of the presidential systems of governments, is characterized by attributing the power to designate those Justices to the President of the Republic, always with the intervention in some way of the legislative branch of government. In the case of Panama, this is done with the approval of the unicameral Congress, and in the case of Argentina, Brazil, and Chile, countries that have a bicameral legislative system, only with the approval of the Senate.

1. Designation in Panama of the Supreme Court members by the President of the Republic with the agreement of the Legislative Assembly

In Panama, the Constitution set forth that the judges of the Supreme Court of Justice are to be appointed for a period of 10 years, by agreement passed by the President of the Republic in a Cabinet Council meeting (Arts. 194 y 195,2), subject to approval by the Legislative Assembly (Art. 200). In this case no specific majority is established.

2. Designation of the Supreme Court judges by the President of the Republic in agreement with the Senate

A. *The Federal Supreme Court and the Supreme Court of Justice of Brazil*

The judges of the Federal Supreme Court and also of the Supreme Court of Justice of Brazil, who must be "honorable, renowned citizens with noteworthy legal experience," are all appointed by the President of the Republic, after the approval of the proposal by absolute majority of the Federal Senate (Art. 101).

In the case of the Supreme Court of Justice, it is required that one–third of its members be selected from the ranks of the Regional Federal Courts; one–third from the ranks of the Supreme Court of Justice, according to the list prepared by the Court; and one–third, in equal parts, on rotation from the ranks of public prosecutors, lawyers and members of the federal and states' attorneys offices of the Federal District and the Territories.

B. *The Supreme Court of Argentina and the voluntary restraint of the presidential power*

In Argentina, according to article 99.4 of the Constitution, the President of the Nation has the power to appoint the justices to the Supreme Court "with the agreement of two–thirds of the members of the Senate, at a public meeting called for this purpose." The special quorum and the public character of the meeting of the Senate were introduced in the constitutional reform of 1994[8].

Nonetheless, the President has voluntarily restricted the exercise of his powers[9], for which purpose Decree N° 222/2003 of June 19, 2003 was issued, establishing a procedure for the exercise of power by means of a "Regulatory framework for the pre–selection of candidates to cover vacancies". This procedure was enacted in order to establish rules "to be followed for the best selection of the proposed candidate, so that such designation would in some way contribute to an effective improvement in the service of justice," also establishing "requirements related to moral integrity and technical suitability and commitment to democracy and defense of human rights that the nominee or nominees must fulfill".

For the best fulfillment of these requirements it was considered "appropriate to facilitate, with express agreement from the nominee or nominees, the display of their professional and academic records, their public or private commitments, the accomplishment of requirements stipulated in the Law of Ethics of Civil Service and

---

8 See Carlos María BIDEGAIN, "La provisión de vacantes de jueces de la Corte Suprema de Justicia de la nación", *Anales, Academia Nacional de Derecho y Ciencias Sociales de Buenos Aires*, Anticipo Año XVV, N° 38, la Ley, Buenos Aires, 2000

9 See Julio Rodolfo COMADIRA, "Selección de jueces y control judicial", *Revista de Derecho Público*, Rubinzal–Culzoni–Editores, Buenos Aires, N° 2004–1, pg.22 and following.

the fulfillment of their respective tax obligations." At the same time, the regulation was intended to create a mechanism that would "allow citizens, individually or collectively, professional, academic or scientific organizations or associations, or non–governmental organizations with interests and actions in this matter, to express their points of view or objections they might have with respect to the appointment to be made."

Consequently, the Decree stipulated the procedure for the President to exercise his power of nomination, ultimately for the "pre–selection of candidates to cover vacancies in the Supreme Court of Justice, within a reasonable pre–selection framework of respect for the good name and honor of the nominees, correct assessment of their moral standing, their technical and legal suitability, their record and commitment to the defense of human rights and democratic values that make them worthy of such an important function." (Art. 2).

For those purposes, it was determined that once a vacancy arises in the Supreme Court of Justice, within a maximum term of 30 days, the name and curriculum vitae of the person or persons being considered for the vacancy must be published in an Official Press Release for three days, in at least two newspapers with nationwide circulation, as well as on the official web page of the Ministry of Justice, Safety and Human Rights (Art. 4). The individuals included in the aforementioned publication must submit "an affidavit listing all personal property belonging to them, their spouses and/or common–law spouse, marital property and that of their minor children, under the terms and conditions set forth in Article 6 of the Public Service Law of Ethics N° 25.188 and its Regulations." They must also submit another affidavit "with a list of civil associations or companies they are members of or have been members of during the past eight years, law firms they were or are concurrently members of, a list of clients or contractors for at least eight years, as allowed by the rules of professional ethics in force and, in general, any type of commitment that may affect the impartiality of their opinion due to their own activities, those of their spouse, ascendants and descendants in the first degree, in order to allow an objective evaluation of the existence of incompatibilities or conflicts of interest." (Art. 5).

Article 6 of the Decree allows citizens in general, non–governmental organizations, professional associations, academic and human rights entities, within a period of 15 days as of the latest publication in the Official Bulletin, to submit to the aforementioned Ministry "in writing, well–based and documented, the positions, observations and circumstances they believe must be stated with respect to those included in the pre–selection process, with an affidavit regarding their own objectivity vis–à–vis the nominees." Additionally, within the same period, opinions may be requested of the relevant organizations in the professional, legal, academic, social, political and human rights fields for evaluation (Art 7) and to be submitted to the Federal Administration of Public Income, "preserving the tax secret, [in a] report on fulfillment of tax obligations by the individuals eventually proposed." (Art. 8).

Within a period not to exceed 15 days as of the expiration of the period stipulated for the submission of opinions or observations, on the basis of the reasons provided for the decision, the President will decide on whether or not to submit the respective proposal, and in the event of a positive decision, the respective designation must be sent to the Senate.

C. *The Supreme Court of Justice of Chile and proposals provided by the Judicial Branch*

In accordance with Article 75 of the Constitution of Chile, the 21 ministers of the Supreme Court are designated by the President of the Republic, who must select them from a list of five (5) individuals for each seat to be filled, proposed by the Court in agreement with the Senate, passed by a two–thirds vote of its members, at a special meeting called for this purpose.

If the Senate does not approve the proposal of the President of the Republic, the Supreme Court will complete the list by submitting a new name to replace the one rejected. This process will be repeated until an appointment is approved.

Five members of the Supreme Court must be lawyers, unrelated to the administration of justice, at least fifteen years must have passed since they received their law degree, and they must have been outstanding in professional or academic activity, and in addition they must meet any other requirements stipulated in the respective constitutional organic law.

When a vacancy in the Judicial Branch needs to be filled, the Supreme Court will prepare a list exclusively with members of this Branch, including the most senior member of the Court of Appeals, who appears on the merits list. The other four vacancies will be filled based on the merits of the candidates. In the case of a vacancy pertaining to lawyers unrelated to the administration of justice, with prior public pre–qualification, only the names of lawyers who meet the requirements can be included on the list.

V. DESIGNATION OF THE SUPREME COURT JUDGES BY THE LEGISLATIVE BODY

In the majority of Latin American countries, as a counter balance to the presidential system of government, a never–ending constitutional struggle which has characterized our constitutional history, the power to appoint the Supreme Court Judges has been attributed to the Legislative Branch. In certain cases the power is attributed to the Congress and in other cases to the Senate.

Relative to the first case, when attributed to the entire Legislative body, such power can be exercised with exclusivity as in the case of Costa Rica, Nicaragua and Uruguay, and also of Bolivia and Peru, but in these latter cases, with respect to the Constitutional Court Justices or with the intervention of an independent body. This can be an independent State body, a Council of the Judiciary, as is the case of Bolivia and El Salvador as regards the Supreme Court justices, or it can be an independent body integrated by representatives of the citizens' organizations, as is the case of Guatemala and Honduras, and could have been the case for Venezuela.

Regarding the second case, when the power to appoint the Supreme Court justices is attributed to the Senate, such power is not exercised with exclusivity, but with the intervention of another body; with the intervention of other Judicial jurisdictions, as is the case of Colombia for the Constitutional Court justices, or from a proposal submitted by the President of the Republic, as is the case of Mexico, for the appointment of the Supreme Court justices. This is also the case of Paraguay, where the Senate appoints the Supreme Court justices from a proposal submitted by the Council of the Judiciary and with the agreement of the Executive Branch.

1. Appointment of the Supreme Court justices by the Congress or Legislative Assembly

A. *Exclusive powers of the Legislative Branch of government to appoint the judges*

a. *The appointment of the judges of the Supreme Court of Justice by the Legislative Assembly in Costa Rica*

In accordance with Articles 121,3 and 157 of the Constitution, it is the exclusive responsibility of the Legislative Assembly to appoint the 22 principal and alternate justices of the Supreme Court of Justice. The latter in a number of no less than 25 alternate justices selected from a list of 50 candidates to be submitted by the Supreme Court of Justice (Art. 164).

As regard the principal justices, the procedure for the Assembly to elect them begins before the Special Permanent Committee for Appointments, as stipulated in the Regulations of the Assembly (Arts. 84, 85), which must initially evaluate the candidates for justices.

The Committee must convene through the media all those interested in participating in the election process by requesting that they submit their postulation. The Committee will then hold an oral and public meeting in order to interview the candidates, and will later prepare a recommendation to the Plenary of the Assembly of the five best qualified candidates (at least two of which must be women). This recommendation, however, is not binding and the Assembly may freely appoint anyone meeting the requirements, even if this person did not participate in the previous prequalification.

The Legislative Assembly, through Agreement N° 6209–04–05, adopted at Meeting N° 87, dated October 14, 2004, established the following Procedure for the Election of Justices of the Supreme Court of Justice, comprising two rounds:

> First Round: Three votes will take place: In the first two the candidates the deputies deem advisable will participate. In the third vote of this first round, only the candidates who have obtained five or more votes may participate.
>
> Second Round: There will be five votes. In the first vote the deputies may participate with the names they consider appropriate. In the second, only those candidates who obtained one or more votes in the preceding vote will participate. In the third vote, only candidates who have obtained ten or more votes in the preceding vote will participate. In the fourth vote, only candidates who have obtained fifteen or more votes in the preceding vote will participate, and in the fifth, only the two candidates who obtained the larger number of votes in the preceding vote may participate.

In each vote, if only one candidate obtained the number of votes stipulated in order to participate in the following vote, the voting round will be closed without an election.

The candidate obtaining at least 38 effective votes will be elected justice.

If during this process no candidate obtains the 38 effective votes, or only one candidate obtains the number of votes stipulated in order to participate in the following vote, the voting will be postponed for one week, after which the aforementioned procedure will be performed once again."

Lastly, the Nominations Committee will be responsible for analyzing and submitting a report on the nominations to be sent to the Plenary.

b. *The appointment of the Constitutional Court justices by Congress in Bolivia*

In accordance with Article 119 of the Constitution of Bolivia, the Constitutional Court "is independent and is only subject to the Constitution." The Constitutional Court is comprised of five justices designated by Congress (at a joint session of the Chambers of Deputies and Senators) by two–thirds of the votes of the members attending the meeting.

Law N° 1836 of the Constitutional Court stipulates that the Minister of Justice, as well as the Professional Association of Lawyers and Law Schools, may submit to Congress lists of candidates for Justices for the Constitutional Court (Article 14).

c. *The appointment of Constitutional Court justices by Congress in Peru*

In accordance with Article 201 of the Constitution of Peru, the Constitutional Court is the controlling body of the Constitution. It is autonomous and independent and has seven members elected for five– year terms (Organic Law N° 26.435 of the Constitutional Court).

The members of the Constitutional Court are elected by the Congress of the Republic with the assenting vote of two–thirds of the legal number of its members. Judges or prosecutors who have not left office one year earlier may not be elected.

Each time elections are to be held, Congress approves a regulation that is published by the media to regulate a public competition and provide information on the candidates, and likewise allows for removal of names and public hearings by the respective Committee.

d. *The appointment of the Supreme Court justices by the National Assembly in Nicaragua*

In accordance with Article 163 of the Constitution, the Supreme Court of Justice is comprised of 16 justices elected by the National Assembly for a term of five years. The National Assembly will also appoint an alternate for each justice.

e. *The appointment of the Supreme Court justices by the General Assembly in Uruguay*

In Uruguay, pursuant to Articles 234 and 236 of the Constitution, the five members of the Supreme Court of Justice are designated by the General Assembly with two–thirds of the votes of the total number of its members.

The designation must be made within ninety days of the vacancy, for which purpose the General Assembly will be especially convened. Upon expiration of this term and if no designation has been made, the most senior member of the Court of Appeals, or if there is equivalent seniority in this position, the one with more years in the Judiciary or Office of the Public Prosecutor or State's Attorney, will be automatically designated to the Supreme Court of Justice.

B. *Competence of the Legislative body as proposed by another State body*

a. *The designation of the Supreme Court justices by Congress as proposed by a Council of the Judiciary in Bolivia*

In accordance with Article 117,IV of the Bolivian Constitution, Justices of the Supreme Court are elected by the National Congress (at a meeting of the Senate and Deputies) for a term of 10 years, by two–thirds of the total votes of the members (Arts. 59,20; and 68,12), from lists proposed by the Council of the Judiciary, which is the administrative and disciplinary body of the Judicial Branch (Arts. 116,1; 122,1; 123,I,1)).

Pursuant to Article 122 of the Constitution, the Council of the Judiciary, presided over by the President of the Supreme Court of Justice, has four members designated by the National Congress with the votes of two–thirds of the members present at the meeting. They hold office for a period of 10 years and may not be reelected until a period equal to that of their mandate has expired.

b. *The designation of the Supreme Court judges by the Legislative Assembly as proposed by the National Judiciary Council in El Salvador*

In El Salvador, Article 173 of the Constitution likewise provides that the magistrates of the Supreme Court of Justice must be elected by the Legislative Assembly with the assenting vote of at least two–thirds of the elected Deputies (Art. 186) for a period of nine years. The justices may be reelected. One–third of them will be renewed every three years, and one will be the President of the Court, also considered President of the Judiciary.

The Justices will be elected from a list of candidates compiled by the National Judiciary Council, one–half of which will be furnished by entities representing the lawyers of El Salvador, in all legal specializations.

According to Article 187 of the Constitution, the National Judiciary Council is an independent body "responsible for proposing candidates for the positions of Justices of the Supreme Court of Justice, Justices of the Second Instance Divisions, Trial Judges and Justices of the Peace." It is also responsible for the organization and operation of the School of Judicial Training, the purpose of which is to ensure improvement in the professional training of judges and other judicial officials. Its members are elected and removed by the Legislative Assembly with the qualified vote of two–thirds of the elected Deputies.

C. *Competence of Congress at the proposal of an independent nominations body*

In certain countries, although the Supreme Court justices are designated by the legislative body, the Constitutions have sought to restrict its political and discretionary powers, by requiring that the nomination of the candidates come from an external body independent of the Assembly and include representation from civil society organizations. These are the cases of Guatemala and Honduras, and could have been the case for Venezuela, were because of the constitutional fraud perpetrated by the National Assembly, the Constitution in this matter is not in effective force.

a. *The designation of the justices of the Supreme Court of Justice by Congress based on a proposal by a Nominations Committee in Guatemala*

In accordance with Articles 214 and 215 of the Constitution of Guatemala, the Supreme Court of Justice is comprised of 13 Justices, including its President, elected by the Congress of the Republic for a period of five years from a list of 26 candidates proposed by a Nominations Committee, which is made up as follows:

One representative of the Chancellors of the Universities in the country, who presides over this Committee;

The deans from the Schools of Law or Social Sciences from each university in the country;

An equivalent number of representatives elected by the General Meeting of the Professional Association of Lawyers and Notaries in Guatemala; and

An equal number of representatives elected by principal magistrates of the Courts of Appeals and other courts referred to in Article 217 of the Constitution.

The election of candidates requires the vote of at least two–thirds of the members of the committee.

In the voting either to be on the Nominations Committee or for inclusion in the list of candidates, representation will not be accepted.

b. *The designation by Congress of the justices of the Supreme Court of Justice from a proposal by a Nominations Board in Honduras*

In accordance with Articles 308 and 311 of the Constitution, the 15 justices of the Supreme Court of Justice must be elected by the National Congress with the assenting vote of two–thirds of its members, from a list of candidates of not less than three names per each justice to be elected, which must be submitted by a Nominations Board.

This independent body, regulated by the Organic Law of the Nominations Board for the election of candidates for justices of the Supreme Court of Justice (Decree N° 140–2001), conceived as "a qualified and deliberating body, with absolute independence and autonomy of its decisions," (Art. 1) has as its "only function" to prepare the list of candidates for Justices to be submitted to Congress.

In its composition, "the principles of publicity, transparency, strict adherence to the Law, ethics, suitable selection, independence and respect for democratic principles" must be observed. The statute demands that "the authorities and pertinent social and professional groups must honor the independence of the Board in all of its decisions" (Art. 3).

The Nominations Board is composed as follows:

One representative from the Supreme Court of Justice elected by the favorable vote of two–thirds of the justices at a special plenary session called for this purpose by the President of the Court (Art. 22);

One representative from the Professional Association of Lawyers, elected at a meeting and following the same procedure that is used for the election of its National Board of Directors (Art. 23);

The National Commissioner for Human Rights that propose its alternate (art. 24);

One representative from the Honduran Council for Private Enterprise, elected at a meeting and following the same procedure that is used for the election of its National Board (Art. 25);

One representative from the faculties of professors of the Schools of Juridical Sciences, whose proposal will be made through the National University of Honduras (UNAH). For that purpose, professors from the faculties of the Schools of Juridical Science of the Universities must be convened by the President of the National University of Honduras, in order to elect their members for the Nominations Board (art. 26),

One representative elected by organizations from civil society. It is the responsibility of the Secretariats of State in the offices of the Interior and of Justice to publicly convene the duly registered civil social organizations to a meeting, in which they will elect their representatives (art. 27). And,

One representative from the Confederations of Workers, which must be organized in a special meeting pursuant to their specific rules, in order to proceed with the election of their representative and alternate to the Nominations Board (art. 28).

Each of the organizations represented on the Nominations Board must prepare a list of not more than 20 candidates who are lawyers, according to the same rules followed for the election of its representatives before the Board, to be proposed to the Board. From those lists the Board must in turn prepare its own list to be submitted to Congress.

For this purpose, in accordance with Article 312 of the Constitution, the President of Congress must convene the organizations comprising the Nominations Board no later than October 31st of the year prior to the election of justices, and they must deliver their proposals to the Permanent Committee of Congress on January 23rd, at the latest, so that the election can take place on January 25th.

The election must be held once the proposal for the entire number of justices has been submitted to Congress. If the qualified majority for the election of all of the justices required is not met, a direct and secret ballot must be held as often as necessary to achieve the favorable vote of two–thirds, in order to elect the remaining justices individually.

If the Nominations Board is convened and no proposals are made, Congress must proceed with the election by the qualified majority of all its members.

c. *The designation of the Supreme Court justices by the National Assembly from a proposal by a Judicial Nominations Committee in Venezuela*

One of the main reasons underlying the political crisis in Venezuela during the late nineties, and which led to the convening of a National Constituent Assembly, was the reaction against a merely partisan representative democracy, seeking to improve it with aspects of participatory democracy. The election of Supreme Court Justices was a main issue in that crisis, because the 1961 Constitution granted excessive discretionary power to Congress and its party majorities for that purpose. The complaint referred to the lack of participation by citizens' organizations and the monopoly by the political parties represented in Congress when it came to such designations.

Thus, the principle of participation was imposed over the principle of representation, and while it is true that the National Assembly was authorized to designate the Justices, the most significant reform consisted of eliminating from the Assembly the discretionary power to make such designations,[10] by creating a Judicial Nominations Committee with the *exclusive power* to nominate candidates and present them to the National Assembly. The candidates are presented before the Committee on their own initiative or through propositions by organizations connected with judicial activity.

As a result, nominees may not be presented directly to the National Assembly, and the National Assembly may not designate people other than those nominated by the Nominations Committee. The Committee is conceived of as an intermediate and permanent body comprised of *"representatives from different sectors of the community"* (Art. 270). The Committee is different from the National Assembly and its parliamentary committees and, consequently, the people's representatives (deputies) may not be members of such Committees.

The constitutional procedure stipulated for the designation of the justices of the Supreme Tribunal is the following: The Committee, having received the nominations and "heard the opinion of the community, will carry out a screening to be submitted to the Citizen's Branch of government." This body, made up of the Public Prosecutor, the Ombudsman or Public Defender and the Comptroller General of the Republic (Article 273) must carry out a "second screening to be submitted to the National Assembly, which will make the final selection" (Art. 264).

After the Constitution was approved through a referendum (Dec. 15, 1999), the Constituent National Assembly issued a Decree on the Transitory Regime of Government, which, among other provisions, proceeded to designate the justices of the Supreme Tribunal *without adhering* to the Constitution approved the previous week by the people, indicating that these designations would be "temporary" until the Na-

---

10 See Allan R. BREWER–CARÍAS, *Golpe de Estado y proceso constituyente en Venezuela*, Universidad Nacional Autónoma de México (UNAM), México, 2001

tional Assembly made the final designations or confirmations *pursuant to the Constitution* (Art. 20).

The National Assembly, elected in August 2000, had the Constitutional mandate (by virtue of the text of the Constitution, and by virtue of the Transitory Regime of December 22, 1999, with respect to which the Supreme Tribunal recognized its constitutional ranking) to designate the permanent justices, pursuant to the Constitution and adhering to its rules.

The form of integration of the Nominations Committees was essential in order for the Constitution to be applied; therefore, the National Assembly was *obliged to fill the legal vacuum* by legislation to regulate the Nominations Committees. It was inadmissible for the National Assembly to intend to legislate, in order not to legislate, as occurred with the Special Law for the Confirmation or Designation of Officials for the Citizen's Branch and Justices of the Supreme Tribunal of Justice for the first constitutional period as of November 14, 2000, which violated Articles 264, 270 and 279 of the Constitution and Articles 20 and 33 of the Decree on the Transitional Regime for Government. These rules required that the National Assembly, once elected, make the permanent designations of Supreme Tribunal justices "pursuant to the Constitution."

The previously mentioned Special Law for the designation of senior public officials for the Judicial Branch and the Citizen's Branch violated the Constitution by not having organized the Judicial Nomination Committee as provided for and as required by the Constitution, to include only "representatives of the different sectors of the community." On the contrary, this Special Law created a "Parliamentary Committee" with additional, external members elected by the National Assembly from a list of 12 representatives of the different sectors of the community elaborated by the deputies, members of the Committee (Art. 4).

Nominations for the designation of Supreme Court justices were to be subjected to public consultation so that reasoned support or objections could be submitted to the Committee (Art. 7). As a result of the process, the Committee had to prepare a list of nominees to be submitted to the National Assembly for permanent designation (Art.9).

It suffices to read the Special Law to understand its unconstitutionality. The statute contradicted the Constitution and confiscated the right to political participation as expressly guaranteed in the Constitutional text. Consequently, in 2000, the National Assembly designated the justices of the Supreme Court of Justice without adhering to the provisions of Articles 264, 270 and 279 of the Constitution. This provoked the Public Defender, before his replacement, to file a judicial review nullity action challenging the Special Law before the Constitutional Chamber of the Supreme Tribunal of Justice. To date, the case has not been decided (Oct. 2005).

In May 2004, the National Assembly enacted the long–awaited Organic Law of the Supreme Tribunal of Justice,[11] one of whose objectives was to increase the number of justices for the Chambers of the Supreme Tribunal. Thus, the government, which controlled the Assembly through the government's party, whose directors were the President of the Republic and his Ministers, by designating the Justices by simple majority, would be able to completely control the Supreme Tribunal of Justice.

Regarding the process for the nomination of justices, the statute organizing the Judicial Nominations Committee was approved violating the Constitution and the political right to participate[12]. Following the trend of the previous Special Law of 2000, the Organic Law, the Judicial Nominations Committee instead of solely and exclusively being integrated by *"representatives of different sectors of the community,"* as required by the Constitution (Art. 270), was integrated by "eleven principal members with their respective alternates, five of which will be elected from the national legislative body and the other six members from other sectors of the community, which will be elected through a public procedure" (Art. 13, Second Paragraph). The deputies to the National Assembly, however, cannot be considered representatives of the community, thus the statute again violated the Constitution by actually forming an extended *Parliamentary Committee,* headquartered at the National Assembly.

The essential function of the Judicial Nominations Committee is to select "in a public and transparent process, in accordance with constitutional requirements," the candidates for justices of the Supreme Tribunal of Justice, who must be presented to the Citizen's Branch for a second screening under the terms of Article 264 of the Constitution. Article 13, fourth paragraph, also unduly limited the constitutional power of the Citizen's Branch by stipulating that this Branch "must, to the extent possible, except for a serious cause, respect the selection made by the Judicial Nominations Committee."

It has been pursuant to this Organic Law and a distorted Nominations Committee such as the one described that the justices of the Supreme Tribunal have been designated, in violation of the Constitution.

2. The designation of the Supreme Court justices by the Senate

In numerous countries with a bicameral legislative organization, the power to designate Supreme Court Justices has been attributed to the Senate, as is the case of Colombia for the Constitutional Court, with the intervention of other Jurisdictions, and the Supreme Court of Mexico, from a proposal submitted by the President of the

---

11 See the comments in Allan R. BREWER–CARÍAS, *Ley Orgánica del Tribunal Supremo de Justicia. Procesos y procedimientos constitucionales y contencioso–administrativos,* Editorial Jurídica Venezolana, Caracas 2004

12 See Allan R. BREWER–CARÍAS, "La progresiva y sistemática demolición institucional de la autonomía e independencia del Poder Judicial en Venezuela 1999–2004", in *XXX Jornadas J.M Dominguez Escovar, Estado de derecho, Administración de justicia y derechos humanos,* Instituto de Estudios Jurídicos del Estado Lara, Barquisimeto 2005, pgs. 33–174.

Republic, and Paraguay, from a proposal submitted by the Council of the Judiciary with the agreement of the Executive Branch.

A. *The designation of the Constitutional Court justices by the Senate from a proposal submitted by other jurisdictions in Colombia*

In the case of the Constitutional Court of Colombia, Article 173,6 of the Constitution attributes to the Senate the power to elect the nine justices of the Constitutional Court, as determined by Law N° 5 of 1992 and Law 270, for an eight–year period, from individual lists submitted to the Senate by the President of the Republic, the Supreme Court of Justice and the State Council (Art. 239).

According to Article 44 of the Statutory Law of the Administration of Justice of 1996, for the designation the Senate must select a justice from each of the three lists submitted by the President of the Republic, one from each of the three lists submitted by the Supreme Court of Justice, and one from each of the three lists submitted by the Council of State.

B. *The designation of the Supreme Court of Justice by the Senate from a proposal submitted by the President of the Republic in Mexico*

In Mexico, Article 96 of the Constitution stipulates that for the designation of the 11 ministers of the Supreme Court of Justice, the President of the Republic must submit a list of three candidates to be considered by the Senate, which, upon prior appearance of the nominees, will designate a justice to fill the vacancy.

The appointment must be made with the vote of two–thirds of the members of the Senate present at the meeting, within an inextensible thirty–day period. If the Senate does not decide within this term, the position of justice will be filled by a nominee from the list submitted by the President of the Republic.

If the Senate rejects the entire list of nominees, the President of the Republic will submit a new list, abiding by the terms of the preceding paragraph. If the second list is rejected, the position will be filled by an individual from this new list of nominees designated by the President of the Republic.

Also, pursuant to Article 98 of the Constitution, when the absence of a justice exceeds one month or if a justice has passed away or is permanently absent for any other reason, the President of the Republic must designate an interim justice and submit this appointment for approval by the Senate, thus fulfilling the previously indicated provisions (Art. 96).

C. *The designation of the Supreme Court justices by the Senate from a proposal submitted by the Judiciary Council and with the agreement of the Executive Branch in Paraguay*

In accordance with Article 264,1 of the Constitution of Paraguay, the Senate is responsible for designating the members of the Supreme Court of Justice, with the agreement of the Executive Branch, as per the proposal from the Judiciary Council.

In accordance with Article 262 of the Constitution, the Judiciary Council is made up of:

– One member of the Supreme Court of Justice, designated by this Court;

– One representative of the Executive Branch;

– One Senator and one Deputy, both nominated by the respective Chambers;

– Two registered lawyers designated by their peers in a direct election;

– One professor from the Law School of the *Universidad Nacional*, elected by his or her peers; and

– One professor from the Law Schools of private Universities, with not less than twenty years experience in this field, elected by his or her peers.

The Judiciary Committee has the power to propose three candidates for the Supreme Court of Justice, with prior selection based on suitability and after having considered the candidates' merits and qualifications, for subsequent submittal to the Senate.

VI. DESIGNATION OF THE SUPREME COURT JUSTICES BY AN INDEPENDENT JUDICIARY COUNCIL

The efforts to guarantee the independence and autonomy of the Supreme Court justices, has led some countries to create an independent body to be in charge of the government and administration of the Judiciary, to which, additionally, the power to appoint the Supreme Court judges has been attributed, as in the case of Peru.

Thus, the Peruvian Constitution is the only Latin American Constitution which attributes to the Council of the Judiciary, as a permanent body within the structure of the State, competence to designate the justices of the Supreme Court of Justice and, in general, all of the judges. We have indicated that in the Dominican Republic, while the Justices of the Supreme Court of Justice are also designated by a Council of the Judiciary, this Council is made up only of representatives of other branches of government and its only function is to designate the aforementioned justices.

Article 150 of the Peruvian Constitution establishes that the Council of the Judiciary "is responsible for the selection and appointment of judges and prosecutors, except when these are elected by the people," and article 154,1 establishes among the functions of the Council, the "appointment of the judges and prosecutors *at all levels*, upon prior public pre–qualification of merits and personal evaluation," with the appointments requiring the affirmative vote of two–thirds of the members of the Council.

The Constitution regulates the Council of the Judiciary as an independent body with the following members (Article 155):

One elected by the Supreme Court, in plenary session, by secret vote.

One elected by the Board of Supreme Prosecutors, by secret vote.

One elected by members of the country's Bar Association, by secret vote.

Two elected by the members of the other Professional Associations in the country, as stipulated in the law, by secret vote.

One elected by the presidents of national universities, by secret vote, and,

One elected by the presidents of private universities, by secret vote. The Judiciary may increase to nine the number of its members, with two additional members elected by secret vote by the Judiciary from among individual lists proposed by institutions representing the labor and business sector.

In this case, the election of justices of the Supreme Court of Justice by the Council of the Judiciary also includes a public invitation, through publications in the newspaper, to pre–qualify with written and oral examinations and the possibility of objections from the public.

VII. DESIGNATION OF THE SUPREME COURT JUSTICES BY MEANS OF A COOPTION SYSTEM

Finally, in the constitutional effort to ensure the independence of the judiciary, some countries have established the cooption system to appoint Supreme Court justices. According to a constitutional tradition, this is the case of Colombia, where the justices are nominated by the Supreme Court itself but from a proposal submitted by the Superior Council of the Judiciary, and there is the unique case of Ecuador, where it is an exclusive attribution of the Supreme Court, a perhaps ideal system that has not functioned.

1. The cooption system for the designation of Supreme Court justices as per the proposal of the Superior Council of the Judiciary in Colombia

It could be said that Colombia is the only country in Latin America with a constitutional tradition when it comes to the designation of senior judges through the co–option system.

Even if the constitutional reform of 1991 modified the preceding general system, that tradition has been kept in place with respect to the justices of the Supreme Court of Justice and the State Council, which, as established in Article 231 of the Constitution, "will be designated by the respective body" but "from lists sent by the Superior Council of the Judiciary."

This Superior Council of the Judiciary, according to Article 254 of the Constitution, has two divisions:

The Administrative Division, made up of six justices elected for a period of eight years as follows: two by the Supreme Court of Justice, one by the Constitutional Court and three by the State Council.

The Disciplinary Jurisdictional Division, made up of seven justices elected for a period of eight years by the National Congress from lists of three candidates, each sent by the government.

2. The impracticality of the cooption system in Ecuador and attempts to replace it by the Qualifications Committee system

The Constitution of Ecuador, in Article 202, provides for a system to designate justices of the Supreme Court of Justice by cooption from the same Court, by establishing that "when a vacancy arises the Supreme Court of Justice, in full session, will designate the new justice with the favorable vote of two–thirds of its members, observing the criteria of professionalism and of the legal profession, in accordance with the law. For the designation, professionals who have experience in court, have taught at universities or have practiced their profession independently will be alternatively selected in this same order."

A law was never enacted to regulate the cooption selection procedure, and the designation of the first 31 justices in 1977 was made by Congress after consulting the citizen's body; therefore, this designation was preceded by a selection process in which the candidates were qualified by nominating associations.

In subsequent years of Court operations, vacancies arose due to deaths and resignations and the new justices were designated, in full session, with the favorable vote of 2/3 of its justices. However, when at a specific time vacancies arose in the Criminal Chamber, the remaining justices of the Supreme Court could not reach a decision on the designation of the replacements. The positions were then filled by alternate judges, who are designated by the Court for fixed periods as per the proposal of its own members.

Due to the irregular integration of the Supreme Court, in May 2005, the then President of the Republic, Lucio Gutiérrez, issued a decree, upon prior declaration of a State of Emergency, in which he suspended the justices of the Court, which evidently was inconsistent with the Constitution. Immediately thereafter, Congress determined to annul the resolution of the President of the Republic and, in turn, resolved to suspend the Court, which was also inconsistent with constitutional provisions.

Having suspended the Court, in late May 2005, Congress reformed the Organic Law of the Judiciary, establishing a new system for the designation of the Supreme Court, which was also inconsistent with the provisions of the Constitution, but sought to provide a political way out of the serious institutional situation of the lack of integration of the Court, given its suspension. The Reform Law set forth that "In view of the permanent absence of the entire number of justices of the Supreme Court of Justice, their designation, this time only, will be made by a qualifications committee," comprised of the following five members:

> One designated by the Presidents of the Courts of Professional Honors of the Bar Associations in the country.
>
> One designated by the Deans or Directors of the law schools or academic units legally recognized by the State and which can prove to this entity that they have existed for at least ten years.
>
> One designated by the judges of Superior Courts and Administrative or Tax District Courts.
>
> One designated by the Committee for the Civic Control of Corruption.
>
> One designated by human rights organizations with at least five years of legal experience in Ecuador.

These members must be elected by the respective electoral colleges with at least one–half plus one of the votes of the attendees, which must be secret, and the decisions so made may not be challenged.

The Committee was to issue a regulation, which would have to include requirements, a call for presentation of candidates, selection of the best candidates, and designation and swearing–in of these candidates.

By July 2005, the Committee had not yet been formed and by October 2005, Ecuador was lacking a Supreme Court. Certain members of the Qualifications Committee asked the President of the Republic to convene a consultation with the people, in order to ask Ecuadorians if they agreed with the selection process. The President, in response to this request, sent a petition to the National Congress to declare the urgency of the call to consultation and proposed several questions. The petition was returned so that a mixed Committee (Government–Congress) would be the one to prepare the subject matter of the consultation, all of which occurred in August 2005.

The Ecuadorian general institutional crisis provoked by the absence of a Supreme Court spurred the decision of the United Nations to appoint observers to follow the process.

FINAL REMARKS

As mentioned at the beginning, the question of the legitimacy as it relates to the selection of Supreme Court justices must focus on what the essential trend of the judiciary must be in a democratic society, that is, the selection of judges based solely on objective criteria without outside or political influence, in order to guarantee their independence from other branches of government and their autonomy, in the sense that they will be able to decide solely based on the law, without outside pressure or political influence. To put it succinctly, using the expression of my remembered friend, Louis Favoreu, the question of legitimacy is a matter of determining how Judges will accomplish their "duty of lack of gratitude".

The selection method of judges, above all and in fact must guarantee that the appointees will not remain grateful to the nominator, or simply that the appointed justices must not be burdened with any sense of gratitude toward the State organ that had selected them. Thus, the question of legitimacy in this matter tends to answer the question of how the appointed judges will be devoid of any sense of gratitude toward the nominating body, so that when the time arrives they will be able to rule autonomously and independently against the interest of such body.

To this end, all kind of methods have been implemented to guarantee *first*, that judges will be appointed transparently based on merit through objective selection criteria; and *second*, that such designations will be made so as to ensure the independence, autonomy and impartiality of the judge, regardless of the organ or body called upon to make the election.

One conclusion can be pointed out, which is that there are no examples of systems where the Supreme Court justices are elected by citizens. The popular election of judges does not ensure that the most suitable candidates will be elected to guarantee the right of citizens to be tried by an independent and impartial tribunal.

Regarding the European doctrine, the tendency is to propose the selection of judges based exclusively on objective criteria that is performed by an independent body (mainly from the government and the administration) which represents the judges, in order to avoid outside influence, particularly political influence in the appointment of judges.

In Latin America, by including the regulations in the Constitutions, it can be said that everything has been attempted, in order to ensure the legitimacy of the election of the Supreme Courts justices and to guarantee their independence and impartiality, not always with the desirable success in practice. Nonetheless, five methods can be distinguished for the appointment of Supreme Court justices: first, the appointment of Justices with the participation of all State bodies; second, the appointment by the President of the Republic, always with the intervention of parliament or the Senate; third, appointment by the full legislative body or by the Senate in certain bicameral systems, even with the intervention of independent bodies, a method that is the most widespread; fourth, appointment by an independent Council of the Judiciary; and fifth, appointment made by co–opting mechanisms by the Court itself.

The first method tends to arrange the appointment of Supreme Court justices with the participation of all the branches of government, in order to avoid the predominance of one branch over the others. Such is the case of the Dominican Republic where this is done through a Council of the Judiciary, integrated exclusively by the head of the Branches of government and with the sole purpose of making the appointments. As regards the appointment of the judges of the Constitutional Court or Tribunal of Guatemala, Chile, and Ecuador this is also accomplished with the exclusive participation of all the branches of Government.

The second most common method for the designation of Supreme Court judges, following the general trend of the presidential systems of governments, attributes the power to designate Supreme Court justices to the President of the Republic, always with the intervention in some way of the legislative branch of government, the Congress, as in the case of Panama, or of the Senate, as in the case of Argentina, Brazil, and Chile.

In some cases, as occurred in Argentina, executive decisions have imposed self–restraint regulations on presidential powers, setting conditions to be fulfilled by the nominees relative to moral integrity and technical suitability and commitment to democracy and defense of human rights; allowing citizens, individually or collectively, as well as professional, academic or scientific organizations or associations, or non–governmental organizations to express their points of view or objections with respect to the appointment to be made.

The third method adopted in the majority of the Latin American countries, as a counterbalance in the case of the presidential system of government, is to attribute the power to appoint the Supreme Court Judges to the Legislative Branch, or to Congress and to the Senate.

With respect to the first case, when attributed to the Legislative body such power can be exercised with exclusivity as exemplified by Costa Rica, Nicaragua and Uruguay and also by Bolivia and Peru (regarding the Constitutional Court Justices); or with the intervention of an independent body that can be an independent State body such as a Council of the Judiciary, as is the case of Supreme Court justices in Bolivia and El Salvador; or an independent State body integrated by representatives of the citizens organizations, as is the case of Guatemala and Honduras and as could have been the case in Venezuela.

Regarding the second option, when the power to appoint the Supreme Court justices is attributed to the Senate, such power is always exercised with the intervention of another body: with the intervention of other Judicial jurisdictions as in the case of the Constitutional Court in Colombia; or appointment from a proposal submitted by the President of the Republic as is the case of Mexico for the appointment of the Supreme Court justices. The same is true of Paraguay where the Senate appoints the Supreme Court justices from a proposal submitted by the Council of the Judiciary, with the agreement of the Executive Branch.

The fourth method adopted only in Peru for the appointment of Supreme Court justices in order to guarantee their independence and autonomy, is to attribute such power to an independent body in charge of the government and administration of the Judiciary, the Council of the Judiciary. It is the only case in which the appointment of the Supreme Court justices is attributed to the head of the Judiciary, with the Council being integrated not only by representatives of the Supreme Court and the Board of Supreme Prosecutors, but also by members of the country's Bar Association, members of other Professional Associations in the country, and the chancellors of national as well as private universities.

Finally, the fifth method for the appointment of Supreme Court justices that can be found in Latin America is the cooption system (appointments by the Court itself), a long–standing tradition in Colombia which now is carried out on the basis of a proposal submitted by the Superior Council of the Judiciary. This system has been established in a unique form also in Ecuador, where it is an exclusive attribution of the Supreme Court. It is an ideal method, but one that in practice has proven its virtual inoperability in political crises, to the point that for almost all of 2005, Ecuador simply lacked a Supreme Court.

It is clear that anything can be tried in an attempt to ensure the legitimacy of the method for the appointment of Supreme Court justices and guarantee the Court's independence and autonomy, but from the Latin–American experience, it is likewise clear that the constitutional formulas do not serve to achieve this purpose. What is required, above all, is the political commitment of all of the political parties and organizations of a country to integrally distance the Judiciary from the political struggle. This has been achieved in Continental Europe since the XIX Century; conversely, and unfortunately, it is a commitment not yet adopted in our countries.

www.ingramcontent.com/pod-product-compliance
Lightning Source LLC
Chambersburg PA
CBHW061147240926
51846CB00006B/948
9789803652128